JIM'S G… AUSTRALIA

Down-to-Earth Guide for Independent Travellers

by Jim Rickman

Published by Jim Rickman

JIM'S GUIDE TO AUSTRALIA

**Down-to-Earth Guide for
Independent Travellers**

by Jim Rickman

Copyright © 2003 by Jim Rickman

First Edition : January 2003

Published by Jim Rickman
Blaenwaun, Coedwig Hudol,
Lampeter SA48 8LS,
Wales, U.K.

Tel: +44 (0)7092-271324
Fax: +44 (0)7092-066001

Author's E-mail: travelbook@supanet.com
Author's Homepage: http://www.users.totalise.co.uk/~travelbook/home.htm

Publishing E-mail: travelbook@totalise.co.uk
Publishing Homepage: http://travelbook.bizland.com

ISBN: 0-9539531-1-4

Printed in the U.K.

PREFACE

The objective of this book is simply to be as helpful as possible to the independent traveller.

The author is also a traveller and knows that what one needs most upon arrival in a strange town is a map and an indication of where accommodation of an appropriate price and quality is to be found.

To be sure, there are often tourist offices offering without charge colourful maps of dimensions and quality greatly superior to anything which can be fitted into a book of this size. The problem is that without a map it is very difficult to locate those offices.

Accommodation of all prices has been included in this book, and in almost every case the hotels and hostels are marked on the maps so that they can be located easily. In general, the author has tried to refrain from making recommendations concerning accommodation because these matters change so quickly. Accommodation recommended in a famous guide book (which this is not - yet - of course) quickly becomes overcrowded and often starts to be complacent, so that by the time you - or I - arrive, it may well be the worst place in the town to stay at, rather than the best. Anyway, making your own decisions, or acting on current tips from fellow travellers, is much more fun, just as long as you can locate that accommodation.

The next thing which the author requires from a book is information about transport, so this book has tried to be comprehensive in that respect. Details of virtually every long-distance and medium-distance train and bus service in the country are included, with journey times, frequencies and prices. In the case of the railways, precise timetables are provided, since train times do not generally change very often or very significantly in Australia. Bus times tend to change more often, so the frequency of each service is given, rather than exact times. In many cases details of local short-distance transport are also given, especially to likely destinations.

Prices will change, of course, so be prepared to add an appropriate factor to compensate for inflation. Regard these rates as being accurate for the year 2003 and add about 5% for each year thereafter.

The author has lived in Australia for five years and made many other visits there, especially, of course, immediately prior to the compilation of this book. Here and there in the book will be found short anecdotes of personal experiences. It is hoped that these will be found entertaining and illustrative, rather than irritating, but, just in case, they are placed in their own little boxes to enable the reader who does not enjoy such distractions to pass on without too much annoyance.

This book is for those who want to see a little more and be a little different, so before you purchase your bus pass, please read the suggestions on page 13.

Please heed the author's advice (on page 4) to travel light, but one item not to forget to take with you, despite its weight, is this book.

Happy Travelling!

CONTENTS

MAP OF AUSTRALIA AND STATISTICS 1
RECOMMENDATIONS 2
GREAT RAILWAY JOURNEYS 2

INTRODUCTION

WHY AUSTRALIA? 4
TWO SUGGESTIONS FOR THE TRAVELLER 4
PRICES AND TIMES 5
GETTING TO AUSTRALIA 5
VISAS AND FORMALITIES 6
HEALTH 6
GEOGRAPHY 6
CLIMATE 7
HISTORY 10
TRANSPORT 13
    Railways 13
    Buses 18
    Bus Tours 22
    Air 23
    Private Transport 24
    Bicycling 26
    Hitch-Hiking 26
ACCOMMODATION 27
    (i) Good Quality Accommodation, but on a Budget 27
    (ii) Cheap Accommodation, but without using Backpackers Hostels 28
    (iii) Backpackers Hostels and Alternatives 28
    (iv) General Comments on Hotel Accommodation 29
    (v) General Comments on Backpackers Hostels 30
BACKPACKERS CARDS 31
FOOD 32
DRINK 32
TELEPHONING 33
E-MAIL 34
TIME ZONES 34
BUSINESS HOURS 36
BANKS AND MONEY 36
POSTAL SERVICES 37
TOILETS 37
SPORTS AND GAMES 37
MAP SHOPS AND BOOKSHOPS 38

CONTENTS (iii)

NEW SOUTH WALES

NEW SOUTH WALES	39
SYDNEY	40
NEWCASTLE	96
KATOOMBA AND THE BLUE MOUNTAINS	101
WOLLONGONG	105
YASS	111
BATEMANS BAY	113
COOMA	116
BOMBALA	117
BEGA	119
MERIMBULA	121
EDEN	123
THREDBO	125
WAGGA WAGGA	129
ALBURY	131
GRIFFITH	136
BATHURST	140
ORANGE	142
DUBBO	145
LIGHTNING RIDGE	148
BOURKE	150
GREAT RAILWAY JOURNEYS (1) - INDIAN-PACIFIC, PART 1	154
BROKEN HILL	159
MOREE	163
TAMWORTH	165
INVERELL	171
ARMIDALE	174
GLEN INNES	177
TENTERFIELD	180
PORT MACQUARIE	184
NAMBUCCA HEADS	188
COFFS HARBOUR	190
GRAFTON, MACLEAN, YAMBA AND ILUKA	193
LISMORE	198
BYRON BAY	201
CABARITA BEACH	206
MURWILLUMBAH	208
TWEED HEADS	211
LORD HOWE ISLAND	214

AUSTRALIAN CAPITAL TERRITORY

AUSTRALIAN CAPITAL TERRITORY	219
CANBERRA	219

(iv) CONTENTS

QUEENSLAND

QUEENSLAND	227
BRISBANE	229
COOLANGATTA	240
SURFERS PARADISE	244
NORTH STRADBROKE ISLAND	250
TOOWOOMBA	253
CHARLEVILLE	255
SUNSHINE COAST	257
GYMPIE	267
MARYBOROUGH	271
HERVEY BAY	278
FRASER ISLAND	281
CHILDERS	287
BUNDABERG	290
GLADSTONE	294
ROCKHAMPTON	297
GREAT KEPPEL ISLAND	303
EMERALD	304
GREAT RAILWAY JOURNEYS (2) - SPIRIT OF THE OUTBACK	308
LONGREACH	315
WINTON	318
MACKAY	324
AIRLIE BEACH, PROSERPINE AND THE WHITSUNDAYS	326
BOWEN	331
TOWNSVILLE	334
MAGNETIC ISLAND	339
CHARTERS TOWERS	344
CARDWELL AND HINCHINBROOK ISLAND	346
MISSION BEACH AND DUNK ISLAND	351
CAIRNS	356
GREAT RAILWAY JOURNEYS (3) - KURANDA SCENIC RAILWAY	366
GREAT RAILWAY JOURNEYS (4) - SAVANNAHLANDER	368
ATHERTON TABLELANDS	372
PORT DOUGLAS	376
DAINTREE AND CAPE TRIBULATION	381
COOKTOWN	383
CAPE YORK	386
THURSDAY ISLAND AND HORN ISLAND	389
CLONCURRY	396
MT. ISA	398
GREAT RAILWAY JOURNEYS (5) - GULFLANDER	402
NORMANTON, KARUMBA AND CROYDON	405

CONTENTS (v)

NORTHERN TERRITORY

- NORTHERN TERRITORY 407
- DARWIN 409
- KAKADU NATIONAL PARK 423
- LITCHFIELD NATIONAL PARK 426
- NHULUNBUY (GOVE) 428
- PINE CREEK 430
- KATHERINE 433
- TIMBER CREEK 437
- MATARANKA 439
- TENNANT CREEK 441
- ALICE SPRINGS 445
  - GREAT RAILWAY JOURNEYS (6) - GHAN 461
- AYERS ROCK 464
- KING'S CANYON 470

WESTERN AUSTRALIA

- WESTERN AUSTRALIA 471
- PERTH 473
- FREMANTLE 488
- ROTTNEST ISLAND 493
  - GREAT RAILWAY JOURNEYS (1) - INDIAN-PACIFIC, PART 3 496
- BUNBURY 501
- BUSSELTON 507
- DUNSBOROUGH 509
- MARGARET RIVER 511
- AUGUSTA 514
- PEMBERTON 515
- WALPOLE 518
- DENMARK 521
- ALBANY 522
- ESPERANCE 531
- NORSEMAN AND THE NULLARBOR PLAIN 538
- KALGOORLIE 541
- YORK 555
- LANCELIN, CERVANTES AND THE PINNACLES 557
- GERALDTON 559
- KALBARRI 568
- DENHAM AND MONKEY MIA 571
- CARNARVON 575
- EXMOUTH 577
- KARRATHA AND DAMPIER 581
- ROEBOURNE, POINT SAMSON, WICKHAM AND COSSACK 586
- PORT HEDLAND 589

(vi) CONTENTS

MEEKATHARRA 596
NEWMAN AND TOM PRICE 600
KARIJINI NATIONAL PARK 603
BROOME 605
DERBY 611
FITZROY CROSSING 613
HALLS CREEK 616
KUNUNURRA 619

SOUTH AUSTRALIA

SOUTH AUSTRALIA 623
ADELAIDE 625
KANGAROO ISLAND 644
VICTOR HARBOR AND GOOLWA 649
BAROSSA VALLEY 653
RENMARK 656
YORKE PENINSULA 660
    GREAT RAILWAY JOURNEYS (1) - INDIAN-PACIFIC, PART 2 668
PORT AUGUSTA 674
FLINDERS RANGES 687
    INTERLUDE - THE STORY OF BURKE AND WILLS 700
COOBER PEDY 704
EYRE PENINSULA 708
CEDUNA AND THE NULLARBOR PLAIN 714
MT. GAMBIER 719

VICTORIA

VICTORIA 727
MELBOURNE 729
GEELONG AND THE BELLARINE PENINSULA 756
APOLLO BAY AND THE GREAT OCEAN ROAD 765
WARRNAMBOOL, PORT FAIRY AND PORTLAND 775
BALLARAT 781
HORSHAM AND THE GRAMPIANS 788
BENDIGO 795
ECHUCA 803
SWAN HILL 807
MILDURA 812

CONTENTS (vii)

SHEPPARTON 816
BEECHWORTH, BRIGHT AND MT. HOTHAM 819
WODONGA 827
MANSFIELD AND MT. BULLER 829
PHILLIP ISLAND 831
SOUTH GIPPSLAND 836
LAKES ENTRANCE 840
ORBOST 845
MALLACOOTA 848

TASMANIA

TASMANIA 851
HOBART 853
BRUNY ISLAND 863
DOVER, LUNE RIVER AND COCKLE CREEK 867
MT. FIELD NATIONAL PARK AND SCOTTS PEAK 872
RICHMOND 875
PORT ARTHUR 877
ORFORD, TRIABUNNA AND MARIA ISLAND .882
SWANSEA 886
COLES BAY AND FREYCINET NATIONAL PARK 888
BICHENO 893
ST. HELENS, DERBY, SCOTTSDALE AND BRIDPORT 895
LAUNCESTON 902
DEVONPORT 914
BURNIE 919
CRADLE MOUNTAIN 927
LAKE ST. CLAIR 932
QUEENSTOWN 935
STRAHAN 946
FLINDERS ISLAND AND KING ISLAND 950

TWO BIG SECRETS

TRANSPORT SECRET 13
ACCOMMODATION SECRET 27

THANKS

Thanks to all who have helped with the production of this book, not least to my brother 'Little Rickman', who has coped with all the eccentricities of the computer, and even offered the sound financial advice that I should never publish another book if I want to remain solvent.

Thanks to those who have checked and commented on parts of this book - to John in Melbourne, to Lyn and Len in Perth, and to Tony now escaped from Alice Springs. Tony has also assisted by providing meteorological information which the author has found fascinating, but which the reader may find more resistible.

Thanks, in advance, to readers who may make comments, as they have done in regard to previous books. Those comments are appreciated and noted, and regarded as valuable. Thank you too for making them polite and helpful as you have always done to date.

Thanks to my Little Old Mother for continuing to provide a place where the book can be written, even if she is finding the stairs too hard to ascend for the provision of essential supplies such as coffee.

Thanks most of all to you, the reader, for choosing this book when there is so much competition from better-known names. The author sincerely hopes that you will be satisfied with your purchase and thoroughly enjoy your time in this truly beautiful country.

MAP 1

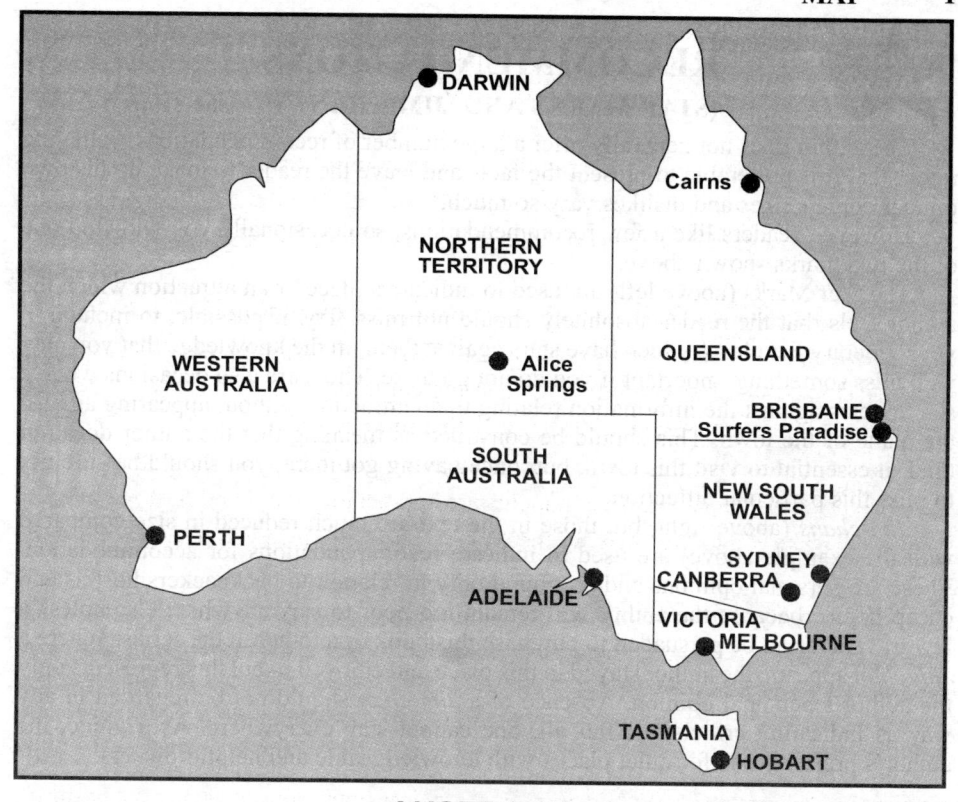

AUSTRALIA

AREA - 7,692,000 square kilometres   Population - 20,000,000 (approx.)

New South Wales	800,640 square kilometres	Population - 6,500,000
Victoria	227,420 square kilometres	Population - 5,000,000
Queensland	1,730,650 square kilometres	Population - 3,600,000
Western Australia	2,529,880 square kilometres	Population - 2,000,000
South Australia	983,480 square kilometres	Population - 1,500,000
Tasmania	68,400 square kilometres	Population - 500,000
Aust. Capital Territory	2,360 square kilometres	Population - 330,000
Northern Territory	1,349,130 square kilometres	Population - 200,000

MAJOR CITIES

Sydney	4,000,000		Newcastle	300,000
Melbourne	3,250,000		Wollongong	250,000
Brisbane	1,600,000		Surfers Paradise	250,000
Perth	1,400,000		Hobart	200,000
Adelaide	1,100,000		Geelong	200,000
Canberra	330,000		Townsville	160,000

 # RECOMMENDATIONS
(STAR MARKS AND 'JIM-CHANS')

JIM-CHAN

The author does not generally offer a large number of recommendations, believing rather that it is preferable to present the facts and leave the reader to make up his own mind. People's likes and dislikes vary so much.

However, readers like a few recommendations, so occasionally you will find one of the two marks shown above.

The Star Marks (above left) are used to indicate a place or an attraction which the author feels that the reader absolutely should not miss. Try, if possible, to include in your itinerary the places which have stars against them, in the knowledge that you may well miss something important if you do not go there. There are also occasions when a star appears against the information relating to an attraction without appearing against the name of the town. This should be construed as meaning that the author does not think it essential to visit this town, but, once having got there, you should be sure not to miss this particular attraction.

Jim-chans (above right, but those in the text are much reduced in size compared with the example above) are used to indicate recommendations for accommodation. These are personal opinions and are found only in relation to backpackers hostels and cheap hotels, because the author will remain too poor to stay anywhere else unless a few travellers can be persuaded to purchase this book or another in the series. Where a *Jim-chan* appears, the author stayed in this place and enjoyed it, but this represents only the author's personal opinion. Absence of a *Jim-chan* should not be regarded in any way as indicating criticism. After all, one cannot stay everywhere. As a guide, the author's preference is for quiet places with knowledgeable and helpful owners.

GREAT RAILWAY JOURNEYS

It should be no secret that the author believes that there is no travel as civilised as rail travel. Hopefully the reader will agree (at least by the time that he or she has finished travelling with this book as a companion).

Herein you will find descriptions of six of Australia's greatest railway journeys, all of which could rank amongst the best in the world for their own unique features. Try as many of these as you can. They will add greatly to your appreciation of this magnificent country.

Here is a summary of the six best journeys.

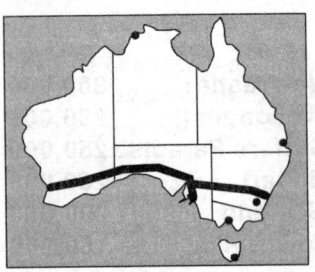

THE INDIAN-PACIFIC
Sydney to Perth
4,352 kilometres
68 hours 35 minutes
Average speed - 63 km/hr
Twice weekly service
Description. Part 1 on pages 154 to 158. Part 2 on pages 668 to 673. Part 3 on pages 496 to 500.
Features the crossing of the desolate Nullarbor Plain.

GREAT RAILWAY JOURNEYS 3

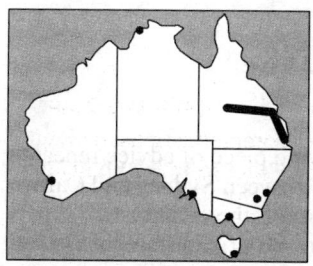

SPIRIT OF THE OUTBACK
Brisbane to Longreach
1,325 kilometres
23 hours 33 minutes
Average speed - 56 km/hr
Twice weekly service
Description on pages 308 to 313
Features the crossing of the Great Divide and magnificent outback scenery.

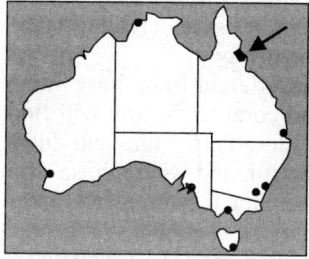

THE KURANDA SCENIC RAILWAY
Cairns to Kuranda
34 kilometres
1 hour 45 minutes
Average speed - 19 km/hr
Twice daily service
Description on pages 366 to 367
Features lush mountain scenery in an antique train. The most popular tourist rail journey in Australia.

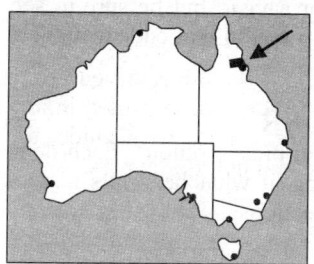

THE SAVANNAHLANDER
Cairns to Forsayth
423 kilometres
35 hours 15 minutes
Average speed - 12 km/hr
Weekly service
Description on pages 368 to 370
Features an outback journey through Gulf country in a 1960s rail motor, with an overnight stop.

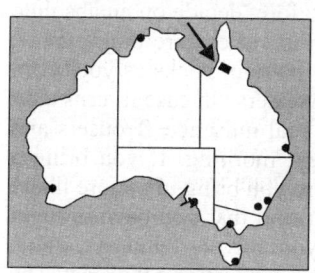

THE GULFLANDER
Normanton to Croydon
151 kilometres
4 hours 30 minutes
Average speed - 34 km/hr
Weekly service
Description on pages 402 to 404
Features a unique journey in a bus on rails along a remote line disconnected from any other rail system.

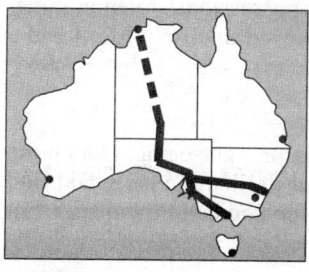

THE GHAN
Sydney or Melbourne to Alice Springs (and Darwin)
Sydney to Alice Springs - 3,270 kilometres
45 hours 20 minutes
Average speed - 72 km/hr
Twice weekly service
Description on pages 461 to 463
Features a modern railway through outback scenery.

INTRODUCTION

WHY AUSTRALIA?

Australia is unique. However, you will find the following piece of advice repeated throughout this book. If you travel only the tourist groove between Sydney and Cairns, you will not really appreciate the uniqueness and the beauty of the country.

All around the eastern coast, and other coastlines too, lie pristine beaches, coral reefs, surf and diving opportunities. Yet Australia is not just a country but almost a whole continent. By all means explore the coastline, but try to get to the interior also, for there you will discover a land as different from the east coast as anything to be found anywhere in the world - and just as beautiful in its own way.

In Australia you will find flora and, particularly, fauna, different from those in the rest of the world. You will find those beautiful beaches and coral reefs. You will find lush rainforests and rugged mountains. You will also find deserts, though, and dusty wide open spaces where nature still remains strongly in control, and where those who do not show sufficient respect for her risk death. To the author these outback areas represent the real Australia and these are the places which make Australia unique and a country which, once visited, infiltrates into one's soul and can never be forgotten.

Beaches and reefs may offer sufficient temptation for a visit, but be sure to see Australia while you are here. This book is designed to help you in that endeavour.

TWO SUGGESTIONS FOR THE TRAVELLER

To tell people how to do their travelling is, of course, presumptuous. Each does best travelling in his own way, at his own speed, looking at what he wants to see. Nevertheless, the author would like to offer just two suggestions.

(i) Bring half of what you consider essential

People always travel with too many possessions. Therefore, decide on an absolute minimum — and then bring only half of that. The things to cut out are bulky items. Basically, you can bring as much underwear and as many pairs of socks as you wish, but do not bring spare pairs of trousers and several thick sweaters "in case it turns a bit chilly". Unnecessary encumbrances will turn out to be a real nuisance. Trousers and similar can be washed overnight and worn again the next morning. If you bring a sweater, you should make it a light one. Moreover, the more you bring, the more likely you are to forget or lose something along the way. If you find that you have brought too much, try to leave the excess somewhere while you travel round Australia. Remember that the happiest travellers are usually those who are carrying the least. The author recalls once meeting a traveller who had had all his possessions stolen in India. "I had only a change of shirt," he said. "I was never so relieved in all my life! I had a really good time from then on."

(ii) Get up and get moving early

This is always the best way, whether you are travelling or sightseeing. Get on the road before the masses do. It always helps to arrive at your destination early and find somewhere to stay before it gets dark. Sometimes one has no choice in the matter, but where there is a choice, early is always best.

INTRODUCTION 5
PRICES AND TIMES

It is one of the disturbing practicalities of life that prices and times do change, and that prices always seem to go up and never down! The reader will naturally want to know how reliable the information contained in this book is. All information contained herein was gathered in the year 2001 and checked for accuracy immediately prior to publication, in October 2002.

In 2000, Australia introduced a Goods and Services Tax (G.S.T.) at the rate of 10%. It is the author's belief that this tax is included in all prices quoted.

As for inflation, that appears to be an unavoidable feature of modern life. It seems reasonable to suggest that the reader should regard the prices given in this book as being accurate for 2003 and should add approximately 5% per year after that.

Regarding transport services, train times do not change much, so are likely to be reasonably accurate for some years to come, except those for the *Ghan*, which will change when the line is extended to Darwin at the end of 2004. The new timetables are not available at the time of writing.

Bus and ferry times, on the other hand, are constantly changing, so in most cases frequencies of services have been stated, rather than exact times. Even so, these too sometimes change, so the reader should regard the information given as a guide, hopefully useful and reasonably accurate, but should check before travelling, especially where services are listed as being infrequent.

GETTING TO AUSTRALIA

Australia is a popular destination, so from most parts of the world discounted tickets are available. However, Australia is a long way from almost everywhere, so why not take a stop on the way? Many of the tickets available permit this. From Europe, a stop may be allowed in India or in Bangkok, Hong Kong or Singapore. Some tickets permit a stop in South Africa as an alternative. From North America, stopping places include Hawaii, Tahiti and New Zealand.

At whichever airport one enters Australia, the cost will be similar, although one will, of course, be limited to the ports served by the airline chosen. Possible entry ports are Sydney, Melbourne, Brisbane, Cairns, Perth and Darwin. With some types of ticket, Qantas permits passengers to continue to the Gold Coast (Coolangatta) without additional charge. In the past, there have also been some services from Indonesia to Port Hedland, and from New Zealand to Hobart, but these have not operated recently.

Here are examples of lowest prices commonly available for return air tickets to Australia.

From London	£600
From Los Angeles	U.S.$1,400
From Tokyo	¥100,000

Many such tickets also permit one stop in each direction. Prices tend to be seasonal, and it should be noted that the above are low-season fares. The cheapest time to start one's journey is usually in the period April until June, with another dip in fares in the northern hemisphere autumn (Australian spring).

Discount tickets available in Australia are almost exclusively return tickets, so, even apart from immigration considerations, it would be unwise to enter Australia without a ticket out of the country.

6   INTRODUCTION
VISAS AND FORMALITIES

Most people need a visa for Australia. Usually it is in the form of an *Electronic Travel Authority* (ETA), of which there is no evidence in the passport. However, by apparent magic, the immigration officer's computer knows that you are coming and processes you accordingly. Just in case anything should go wrong with the system, be sure to take along the slip of paper with which you will be issued at the time of application for the ETA. The ETA is usually free. It permits a stay of up to three months and is valid for multiple entries over a period of twelve months. The period of stay can be extended within Australia. The ETA is available from Australian Embassies, but it can also be obtained over the Internet.

The principal exception to the visa rule is that citizens of New Zealand do not need a visa to enter Australia. Instead they are granted one upon arrival. It used to be the case that they did not need a passport either, as long as they could present some other acceptable form of identification, but this regulation has been tightened, and it is now inadvisable to try to enter without a passport.

Visitors of certain nationalities can obtain Working Holiday visas. Such visas cost A$160. They are usually valid for one year (i.e. you must enter Australia within one year of obtaining the visa) and allow a total period of stay of one year from your first entry into Australia (whether or not you stay there for the whole year). The regulations suggest that the holder of the visa is expected to work for up to half of the total time, but the reality is that it is difficult to know how much time was spent working and how much playing and that, unless there is deep suspicion, nobody is going to waste much time trying to find out. However, the holder of the visa is not permitted to work for more than three months for the same employer. Working Holiday visas are usually granted only to those under the age of thirty, and only once to any person. There is also an annual quota for the number of Working Holiday visas to be issued.

HEALTH

There are no inoculation requirements for visitors to Australia, unless they have come recently from a list of rather unlikely countries. If you have visited somewhere off the beaten track on your way, check with an Australian embassy prior to travelling.

Of course, medical attention, if required, will be expensive in Australia, so some form of health insurance might be a wise investment. Note, though, that some countries have reciprocal arrangements with Australia for health cover. This applies particularly to various nations which are members of the British Commonwealth. If you check this situation when you apply for your ETA, you may find that you are already covered for your time in Australia.

GEOGRAPHY

Australia is huge. The most common mistake made by visitors is to underestimate it. To fly from Perth to Sydney takes four hours. To make the same journey by train or bus takes nearly three days. Perhaps even more important, though, is the distance between towns. The east coast is the only really populated area, and even there towns are often a hundred kilometres apart. Once one moves west, though, the meaning of isolation becomes apparent. Places along Australia's Highway Number One across the Nullarbor Plain can be found marked on globes of the world, but when you reach them, you find that the name is actually that of a roadhouse or sheep station, and that the next similar concentration of population is a further hundred or hundred and fifty kilometres on. Imagine the situation, then, when you move off the main highways.

> *I love a sunburnt country,*
> *A land of sweeping plains,*
> *Of ragged mountain ranges,*
> *Of droughts and flooding rains.*
>   *(Dorothea Mackellar)*

Experiencing the geography of Australia is a major part of the attraction of the country, so make sure that you do see it. There are beautiful and almost deserted beaches all round its shores. There are the mountain ranges which run down the east coast and occupy the north-west. There are the deserts of the interior. There is the fascinating oxidised soil of the 'Red Centre'. There is the tropical north with its lush rainforests. There is the unparalleled bushwalking country of Tasmania. There is so much variety that unless one has visited every state and territory, one cannot really say that one has seen Australia.

CLIMATE

Australia is too extensive to have a single climate. It is not necessarily 'hot and dry', as it tends to be characterised, although such a description can be applied with moderate accuracy to the interior. It is important to realise that the Tropic of Capricorn runs through Rockhampton, towards the south of Queensland, and that approximately one-third of Australia is tropical.

One can, therefore, make a basic separation into two distinct climates - tropical and temperate. Again, very roughly, but for simplicity of explanation, Queensland, the Northern Territory and the northern half of Western Australia may be regarded as tropical, while New South Wales, the Australian Capital Territory, Victoria, Tasmania, South Australia and the southern half of Western Australia are temperate.

In the temperate area, the seasons are similar to, but at the opposite time of the year to, those in the northern hemisphere - in Europe or North America, for example. In an average year, the southern capital cities (Sydney, Canberra, Melbourne, Hobart, Adelaide and Perth) will experience one or two occasions when the temperature rises to 40°C and one or two occasions when the temperature descends to 0°C (except that Perth has recorded 0°C (32°F) only once in its meteorological history - on 15th July 1997 - and Sydney's lowest is 2.1°C (35.8°F) on 22nd June 1932). As one moves further inland, temperatures tend to be more extreme and rainfall tends to decrease. Australia claims to be the driest continent on this planet, and South Australia claims to be the driest state in the driest continent. In general, the rain falls mainly around the coast, so that inland one finds dry, dusty conditions unsuitable for much agriculture and only very sparsely populated. Snow lies only in a small area around the border of New South Wales and Victoria where the nation's highest mountains are to be found, and also in some parts of Tasmania.

The northern parts are quite different in climate, for they have not summer and winter, but tropical Wet and Dry Seasons. Those unfamiliar with such a climate often misunderstand the temperatures which accompany such seasons. The Wet is the hotter of the two, while the Dry is pleasantly warm, but not overpoweringly hot. In between the two is sandwiched a season generally known as the Build-Up, when humidity gradually increases until it reaches almost 100% and temperatures too become higher and higher, reaching the highest levels of the whole year, until one day the heavens open and general relief is felt that the Wet has at long last started. If there is a season to avoid, it is the Build-Up.

The Wet typically lasts from December until March, the Dry from April until August and the Build-Up from September until November. Typical maxima might be 33°C in the Wet, 28°C in the Dry and 36°C in the Build-Up. This type of climate is coastal. As one moves inland rainfall decreases and day temperatures tend to be higher.

Most people believe that the best time to be in the southern half of Australia is during the summer or autumn, that is December until May, and the best time to be in northern Australia is during the Dry, that is April until August. The author, however, rather likes weather and believes these considerations to be minor. The torrential downpours at the start of the tropical Wet Season, for example, are awe-inspiring sights. Just take the weather as it comes and enjoy it.

However, if your main purpose is lying on the beach, it is worth noting that from July until November you would be better off in the northern part of Australia, and also that the tropical Wet Season will limit access to places off the main routes. Also note that the north and north-west are prone to some very fierce cyclones during the Wet.

On the topic of climate, some of the Australian records are interesting and surprising. For example, which capital city has recorded the highest temperature? When asked this question, many people guess Darwin. However, in fact all of the other seven capital cities, even Hobart (40.8°C, 105.4°F), have recorded higher temperatures than Darwin's 40.5°C (104.9°F) on 17th October 1892. The capital city with the highest temperature is actually Adelaide with 47.6°C (117.7°F) on 12th January 1939.

The highest temperature ever recorded anywhere in Australia was 53.1°C (127.6°F) in Cloncurry, Queensland on 16th January 1889. In recent years, the validity of this record has been challenged, since it was a while ago and the equipment used would not satisfy today's standards. However, most people still regard this as the record. The Meteorological Office, however, is prepared to vouch only for the 50.7°C (123.3°F) recorded in Oodnadatta, South Australia on 2nd January 1960.

Marble Bar in Western Australia claims a world record by having recorded 160 consecutive days with a temperature of over 100°F (37.8°C), from 31st October 1923 until 7th April 1924.

The coldest capital city, as one might expect, is Canberra, since it is inland and at an altitude of approximately 550 metres. It recorded -10°C (14°F) on 11th July 1971. The lowest temperature ever recorded in Australia was -23°C (-9.4°F) at Charlotte Pass, New South Wales on 29th June 1994.

The wettest place in Australia is Mt. Bellenden Ker, near Tully in northern Queensland. It holds the record for rainfall in a year - 12,461 millimetres (490.6 inches, or nearly 41 feet) in 2000, and the record for rainfall in a day - 1,140 millimetres (44.9 inches) on 4th January 1979. During the same downpour, it also recorded 2,517 millimetres (99.1 inches) over a period of three days.

The record for wind speed is claimed by Learmonth, near Exmouth in Western Australia, where 267 km/hr (166 m.p.h.) was recorded on 22nd March 1999, during the passing of Cyclone Vance. There may have been higher speeds during Cyclone Tracy in Darwin in 1974, but the wind speed gauge jammed at 217 km/hr (135 m.p.h.).

ANECDOTE

Living in a remote part of the Northern Territory, I volunteered to man one of our four daily weather schedules - that is recording the weather information and sending it as an encrypted telegram to the Meteorological Office to assist in making the weather forecast.

My first duties were assigned when a cyclone threatened and we were asked to make three-hourly reports as an emergency measure. The person in charge briefed me. "Would you mind doing midnight and 3 a.m.? I'll do it with you the first time and you can do it by yourself at 3:00."

I was shown how to read the instruments, with the aid of a flashlight, and how to encrypt the telegram. Then the radio was switched on and I called Darwin. "Shshsh. Sh. Sh," said the voice at the other end. "Well, go ahead. Read it," said my prompter. I read the message. "Sh. Sh. Shshsh," said the voice on the radio. "Say roger and out," said Prompt. I complied. "That's it," said Prompt. "It's as easy as that. Just do the same at 3:00 - and watch out for the snakes." I began to have doubts about having volunteered, but exactly repeated the performance at 3:00, without understanding a single word which Darwin said. "How did it go?" enquired Prompt in the morning. "All right," I replied, rather exaggerating the success of the mission.

As a result of that success, however, I was allocated the 5:15 p.m. schedule as my own regular possession, and came to enjoy this daily reassurance that the outside world was still there. I also came to be able to understand what was being said to me after a while.

One of the duties was recording the type of cloud cover, and for the assistance of amateur meteorologists there was a set of cloud pictures stationed by the door of the radio room. I would look up at the heavens, then go and look at the pictures, go back and study the clouds, have another examination of the pictures, back to the clouds, one more look at the pictures, and give up. Then I would look in the weather book to see what had been recorded at 14:30. Reckoning that the clouds had probably not changed, I would record the same.

After my schedule one day, I walked across to the library to see whether I had any mail, and met there the man who was responsible for the 14:30 schedule. "I'm glad you knew what those clouds were," I said, "Because I had no idea." "Well, actually," he confessed, "I couldn't decide either, so I wrote down what was recorded at 9:00." Whereupon the 9:00 man spoke up. "I didn't know, so I put down the same as 6:00." We looked at the baker, who had responsibility for the 6:00 schedule, since his duties required early rising in any case. "Well, of course," he said, "It's too dark to be able to see much at 6:00, so I put down the same as you recorded yesterday at 5:15 p.m."

As the Build-Up intensified, we all longed for the relief of a downpour. And then one day when I went to the rain gauge I found the first rains in it. I had not actually noticed the shower, but it was a wonderful sign and I duly recorded the first rain of the season. The next day there was more, and the third day even more. The rain was duly recorded and reported. As I went home on the third day, I overheard the Superintendent saying, "You know, it was getting so dry outside my office that I've had to put the sprinkler on the grass for the last few days." A sudden suspicion occurred to me. I went back and checked the location of rain gauge and sprinkler. I said nothing, but waited until I actually saw the rain before I reported any more healthy showers.

And on such well-meaning incompetence is the nation's weather forecast based.

INTRODUCTION
HISTORY

Theoretically, of course, Australia has at least fifty millennia of human history, but the problem is that we do not know much about most of it.

The aborigines migrated to this continent from south-east Asia about 55,000 years ago. Their entry point was probably in the north-west and from there they gradually spread across the whole land. They were nomadic, or semi-nomadic, people, which should not be taken to mean that they moved without pattern. They moved from place to place according to the season of the year and the availability of supplies. Very often they returned to the same places at the same times each year and the territory over which they ranged and the distances covered reflected the amounts of food to be procured. They developed into various tribes, each having its own territory and each speaking its own language, but there was inter-communication and the aborigines were often able to speak and comprehend the languages of their neighbours.

This situation continued unchanged until the relatively very recent arrival of the Europeans, which destroyed the pattern of aboriginal existence due, in many cases, to the European notion that land could be owned rather than simply regarded as an asset for all to enjoy and manage.

The aborigines have survived, and in some remote places still practise their traditional life styles. Recently, and probably too late, court decisions have recognised some of their rights to occupy the land, and vast tracts in unfrequented places have been set aside for their use. However, the most fertile of the land has already been taken from them and most of the territory which they now occupy is relatively inhospitable. More serious, though, has been the threat from western society. The aborigines find western society glamorous and are drawn to the towns, where they succumb to its temptations, especially to that of alcohol.

These are the circumstances in which most visitors find the aborigines, which is a pity, because this is really aboriginal society at its lowest ebb. To see the aborigines at their best it is necessary to visit them in their own communities, and it is not easy to do that, both because their communities are remote and because they are as they are largely through being isolated from the intrusion of outside influences.

Long prior to the arrival of the Europeans, the Macassan traders from the port of Macassar (Ujung Pandang) and the island of Celebes (Sulawesi) in what is now Indonesia visited the northern parts of Australia and traded with the aborigines.

The first European known to have sighted Australia was the Spaniard Luis Vaez de Torres. He sailed through what is now named the Torres Strait, separating Australia from Papua New Guinea, in 1606. Immediately afterwards, the Dutch arrived and investigated parts of northern Australia. However, they found the territory unappealing and were much more interested in establishing their influence in the Dutch East Indies (Indonesia).

In 1616, the first known landing by a European took place. The Dutchman Dirk Hartog landed at Cape Inscription, on the west coast, on an island now known as Dirk Hartog Island, in Shark Bay, near Monkey Mia. He left behind a pewter plate engraved with details of his landing. The plate is now in the *Rijksmuseum* in Holland, having been recovered by another Dutch explorer, Willem de Vlamingh, in 1697.

In 1628, the Dutch ship, the *Batavia,* on her maiden voyage to Batavia (Jakarta), was shipwrecked near Geraldton in Western Australia (see the account on page 563), as a result of which two seamen were abandoned to their fates on the mainland of this new continent, the first two reluctant European settlers.

INTRODUCTION

In 1642, Abel Tasman charted much of the coastline of eastern Australia and Tasmania, which is now named after him, without, however, realising that Tasmania was a separate island.

The first Englishman to venture here was the buccaneer William Dampier, in 1688. He landed in north-western Australia, near the current site of the town named in his honour.

It was nearly a century later that James Cook came to Australia and thought, in 1770, that it might be useful to His Majesty King George III. Having travelled all the way up the east coast, he therefore hoisted the British flag and claimed possession on the aptly named Possession Island off the north-eastern tip of Australia, near Cape York.

In 1788, eleven ships under Captain Arthur Phillip arrived in Botany Bay, near Sydney, bringing 1,373 new settlers to this land, of whom 732 were convicts. They moved to the present site of Sydney and established a new British colony there on 26th January 1788. 26th January is now Australia Day and a national holiday here.

A further penal settlement was established near the present site of Hobart in Tasmania in 1803. The Brisbane River settlement which was to become the new colony of Queensland was established in 1824. In 1826, a settlement was established in Albany, then in 1829 on the Swan River (Perth), both in what is now Western Australia. Portland in Victoria dates from 1834, while Port Phillip (Melbourne) was founded a year later. Adelaide was chosen in 1836 as the capital of South Australia.

Not all settlements were penal, but a total of approximately 100,000 convicts were brought to this country. The last state to accept such prisoners was Western Australia and transportation to there ceased in 1868.

Of all the European influences which have transformed Australia, perhaps none has been greater than the introduction of sheep. Sheep farming has destroyed the traditional lifestyles of the aborigines and it has damaged the land by denudation in places, but it also made Australia prosperous and provided the impetus for further development.

In the nineteenth century, great inland explorations took place, of which the most famous was the Burke and Wills Expedition (see page 700).

In 1851, gold was discovered in Bathurst in New South Wales, then in Ballarat and Bendigo in Victoria. Diggers rushed to the scene and tent cities sprang up. Few made individual fortunes, but the cities prospered and Victoria became the most prestigious of the states. The largest nuggets in the history of the world were discovered here. Later Western Australia experienced its own gold rushes and Kalgoorlie became the most famous gold town in the nation. It is still producing gold more than a century later.

The states gradually achieved a major degree of independence, and then took the most important step in their history when they agreed to federation as the Commonwealth of Australia. The Commonwealth came into being on 1st January 1901 with Melbourne as its temporary capital.

The Australian Capital Territory was proclaimed in 1911 and a competition was held for the design of a new capital, being won by Walter Burley Griffin from Chicago. Canberra was named in 1913 and Parliament moved to its new home in 1927.

Australia found that it had no choice but to be involved in both World Wars and, like the rest of the world, endured hard times during the depression of the late 1920s and 1930s, but it recovered.

During the Second World War some bombing raids were made by the Japanese on

INTRODUCTION

towns in the north, of which the most serious was the raid on Darwin on 19th February 1942 when 243 people were killed and twelve ships destroyed. The incident which caused most concern, however, was the discovery of a Japanese submarine in Sydney Harbour. Australia was not invaded, though, the Japanese advance being halted in Papua New Guinea.

In the post-war years, Australia portrayed itself as the 'lucky country' and invited immigration. There was first a major influx of British, but then the emphasis changed to those from other European countries, especially Italy and Greece. In more recent years, immigrants have been from south Asian countries, as a result of which Australia now offers considerable ethnic diversity.

With fewer and fewer inhabitants of British origin, Australia has felt pressure to cut its remaining links with the U.K. and to replace the monarchy with a presidency. To date this has not occurred, but the general sentiment is that it will happen at some time within the next decade.

ANECDOTE

Recruited as a teacher and flown to Australia, I was allocated to a school in a Melbourne suburb.

"What do you teach?" asked the Deputy Principal.

"English and maths."

"Oh, that's a pity." A pause. "I suppose you couldn't manage geography and music, could you?"

I doubted whether I could, and he thought for a moment.

"Well, how about history and legal studies?"

I said that I would have a go at them and he seemed greatly relieved.

"Right, that's settled then. You'll have Year Three, Australian History."

That was a shock to me. I had been in Australia for only ten days.

"Australian history? I didn't know Australia had any history."

It proved to be the wrong thing to say. He eyed me coldly over the top of his spectacles and handed me a drab book entitled *Landmarks*.

"Go and read it every night," he commanded, "And then at least you'll be one step ahead of everybody else."

And so I discovered that Australia really does have history. It may not have buildings dating from the Middle Ages, as in Europe, but it has plenty of interest once one reconciles oneself to the different time scale. As a result of being entrusted with Year Three, Australian History, I came to appreciate especially the great achievements of the European pioneers of my new host country.

The reader needs to make this adaptation too and appreciate that history is here as well, and fascinating history, if we care to look for it.

TRANSPORT

For the visitor there are four obvious choices for travel within Australia. These are train, bus, aircraft and private vehicle. Each will be detailed in turn and any other possibilities examined.

However, at this point the author will reveal one of the two big secrets regarding visiting Australia. The way to see Australia comfortably and economically is to purchase a rail pass. Few visitors discover this. The majority buy bus passes. This is because of their misunderstanding and because of superior marketing by the long-distance bus companies. Visitors believe that rail passes limit them to trains and they look on the map and see relatively few railways in Australia. However, in fact, rail passes also permit the use of the state bus services in New South Wales, Victoria and Western Australia, plus a limited service in Queensland. You will find that you can go almost anywhere with a rail pass, except the north-west and Tasmania (the latter not covered by the major bus passes either). Unless the journey from Perth to Darwin and on to Alice Springs or Mt. Isa is one of your major objectives, you will be better off with a rail pass. Read on and then make your own decision before being lured into purchasing your bus pass without proper examination of the situation.

Railways

Historically, the problem with Australian railways has been that each state constructed its own and that each chose its own gauge. New South Wales chose a standard 4 feet 8½ inches gauge. Victoria chose a 5 feet 3 inches broad gauge. Queensland, Western Australia and Tasmania chose a 3 feet 6 inches narrow gauge, and South Australia used both the broad and the narrow gauges. Then, when the Commonwealth of Australia was formed, a federally-operated trans-continental line was built to standard gauge. Thus no single train could operate between any two capital cities, except between Melbourne and Adelaide. It has taken more than a century to resolve this situation, and even then only partially.

The states still operate to their own gauges, but there is now a standard gauge line from Perth to Adelaide and on to Melbourne, Sydney and Brisbane, although no single train operates this long route. There are also standard gauge lines connecting Adelaide with Sydney and with Alice Springs, and the latter line will soon continue to Darwin.

To the traveller, these gauge problems will be unimportant, except that he or she will notice that it is still necessary to deal with several different railway companies.

Great Southern Railway has taken over the operation of what used to be the federal (Commonwealth Railways, then Australian National Railways) lines. Three services are operated and these will be the most important three services to the visitor. They are:

The Indian-Pacific	Sydney - Adelaide - Perth
The Ghan	Sydney / Melbourne - Adelaide - Alice Springs (- Darwin)
The Overland	Melbourne - Adelaide

Countrylink operates trains and buses in New South Wales, with its network extending to Melbourne in the south and Brisbane in the north. You can travel to virtually any destination in New South Wales with Countrylink.

V-Line operates trains and buses in Victoria, with its network extending to Adelaide and Mt. Gambier in the west (by train plus bus service), and to Canberra and Batemans Bay in the north (also both by train plus bus service). You can travel to virtually any destination in Victoria with V-Line.

14 INTRODUCTION

Queensland Railways operates trains and a few connecting buses in Queensland. You cannot reach places in the extreme north, such as Port Douglas, Cape Tribulation and Cooktown, and some of the popular beaches entail short bus rides from the railway stations, but otherwise coverage is comprehensive.

Western Australian Government Railways operates a few trains and many buses in Western Australia. These services are limited to the southern part of the state, extending north only to Kalbarri and Meekatharra, but coverage within the area served is comprehensive. Moreover, most of this area cannot be reached at all with the long-distance bus companies.

South Australia no longer has any intra-state rail services. The only services are the interstate trains provided by Great Southern Railway and the V-Line bus plus train services to Melbourne via Bendigo and to Sydney via Albury. However, in fact, these options satisfy most requirements.

The Northern Territory is served by the *Ghan* to Alice Springs, with service soon to be extended to Darwin.

The map below shows passenger rail routes within Australia, and that opposite shows both the rail and the bus services which are available to users of a rail pass. As can be seen, the only area which is not well served is the north-west, although there is also the handicap that there is no connecting route between the centre and the north-east.

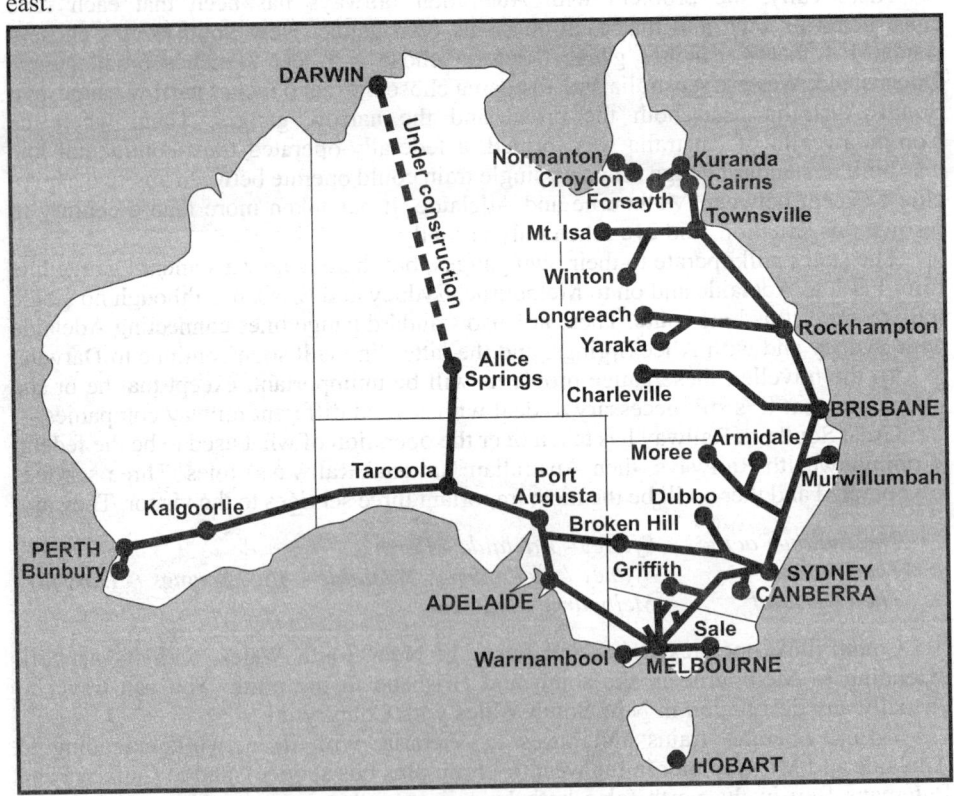

AUSTRALIAN PASSENGER RAILWAY ROUTES

INTRODUCTION 15

Now to the types of rail pass which are available. For most visitors, the type likely to be most useful is the *Austrail Flexipass*. This is valid for fifteen days of economy class travel over a period of six months and costs $800. There are also passes valid for eight days, for 22 days and for 29 days, but the eight-day pass does not permit travel to Perth or Alice Springs. For most visitors the fifteen-day pass will be about right. There are first-class passes too, but do not make the mistake of purchasing one of those, as most trains do not offer first-class sitting accommodation, so you then have to pay enormous supplements for a first-class sleeping berth, plus meals, in order to be able to use the benefit conferred by your first-class pass. Only in New South Wales and Victoria is first-class sitting accommodation offered, and, of course, only on the rail services in those states, not on the connecting buses.

For the purposes of the pass, a day is a period of twenty-four hours from when the journey starts. If you start at 19:00, you can travel until 19:00 the following day by the use of one day on the pass. Go to the ticket office with your pass and state your destination and date of travel, but do not allow the pass to be marked yet, otherwise you cannot change your mind. You will be issued with a ticket for travel, and immediately prior to departure you return to the ticket office and ask for the journey to be recorded on your pass. If there is no ticket office at your point of departure it is usually acceptable to ask the conductor on the train to mark the pass. You will sometimes find, incidentally, that this system, unlike that of the long-distance bus companies, allows a

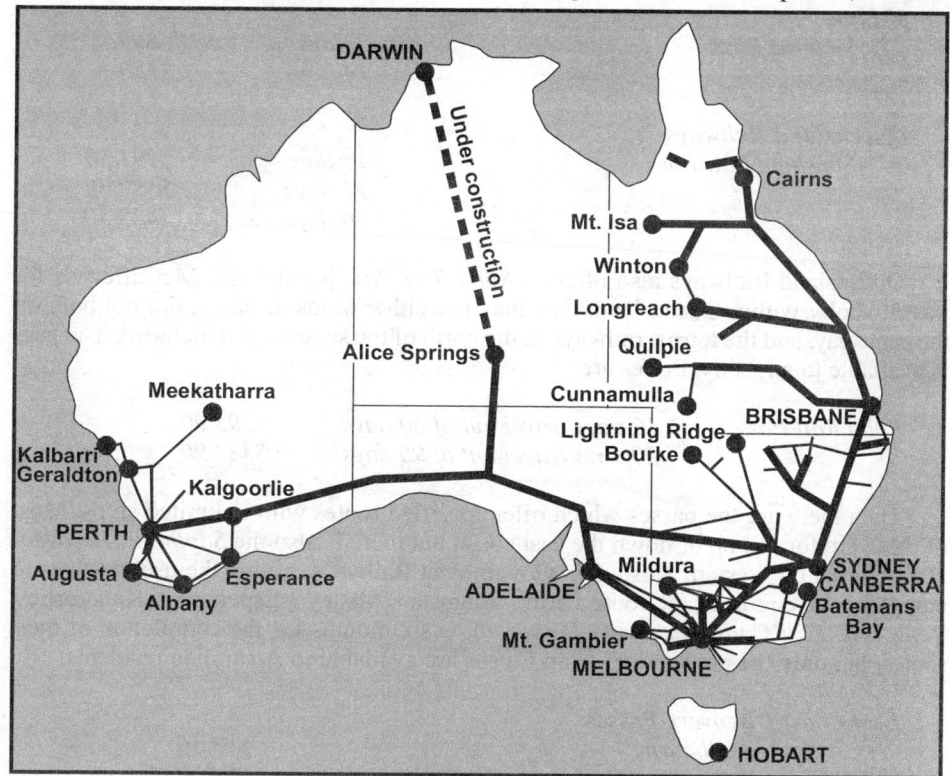

SERVICES AVAILABLE TO RAIL PASS HOLDERS

16 INTRODUCTION

day or two of bonus travel. Bus drivers, in particular, are not keen to spend their time bureaucratically marking days off passes.

There is also an *Austrail Pass* (not *Flexi*), which allows a solid period of travel of between fourteen and ninety days. Unless you intend to be travelling very busily, though, the *Flexipass* will usually be more appealing.

In addition to the *Austrail Passes*, the various railway companies offer rail passes for their own services only. Here is a summary of such passes, with prices correct as at 31st March 2003. Only the 14-day *Victoria Pass* and the *Sunshine Rail Pass* may be used by Australian residents.

Great Southern Railway
Great Southern Railway Pass	6 months	$490
Great Southern Railway Backpackers Pass	6 months	$350

Countrylink
Backtracker Rail Pass	14 days	$165
	1 month	$198
	3 months	$220
	6 months	$330

V-Line
Victoria Pass	7 days	$99
	14 days	$150

Queensland Railways
Sunshine Rail Pass	14 days	$291.50
	21 days	$337.70
	30 days	$423.50

Queensland Railways also offers a *Road Rail Pass* jointly with McCafferty's for travel wholly within Queensland. One may use either trains or buses, but not both on the same day, and the tourist railways in the north of the state are not included. The pass is available to anybody. Prices are:

Road Rail Pass	10 days travel out of 60 days	$295.90
	20 days travel out of 90 days	$383.90

Then there are the passes which offer specified routes with unlimited stops. Most of these are for use up or down the east coast, but there is also the *Southern Discovery Pass* offered by Western Australian Government Railways, giving the user 28 days to complete one circuit of the route Perth - Augusta - Albany - Esperance - Kalgoorlie - Perth. The *East Coast Discovery Passes* allow six months for the completion of their routes, but only the passes to or from Cairns are available to Australian residents.

East Coast Discovery Passes
Sydney - Melbourne	$93.50
Sydney - Brisbane	$93.50
Sydney - Surfers Paradise	$93.50

Sydney - Cairns	*$292.60*
Melbourne - Brisbane	*$176*
Melbourne - Surfers Paradise	*$176*
Melbourne - Cairns	*$374*
Brisbane - Cairns	*$204.60*

Southern Discovery Pass

Perth - Augusta - Esperance - Kalgoorlie - Perth   *$150*

Well, then, out of this multitude of passes, which should we choose? For most travellers, the fifteen-day *Austrail Flexipass* will be the best bet. However, your itinerary will be an important factor. If you do not need to travel far north of Brisbane, the Countrylink *Backtracker Rail Pass* will be very good value. You can go almost anywhere between Melbourne and Brisbane for three months at a cost of $220, for example, travelling as often as you wish.

If an itinerary of Perth - Alice Springs - Adelaide - Melbourne - Sydney and all in between suits you, you can do this as many times as you wish over a period of six months for $350 (with a backpacker card, which costs only a small amount if you do not already own one).

If you just want to travel up or down the east coast, one of the *East Coast Discovery Passes* will be ideal.

You will find most of the trains in Australia spacious and comfortable. The Great Southern Railway trains have plenty of leg room, a lounge available, a restaurant and snack bar (but serving pre-packaged food from the Qantas caterers). There are also showers at the end of each carriage, and towels are provided on overnight services. For those with a weakness, a cramped smoking cubicle is provided, with an atmosphere through which one can barely make out the other side of the room. Unfortunately, though, sleeping berths now involve an impossibly high supplement. The trains are usually reasonably punctual, since the timetables allow margins for delays.

Queensland Railways trains are also comfortable, with ample leg room. Showers are provided, but no towels for sitting passengers. However, the supplement of $44 for a shared sleeping berth is within the realm of possibility. If you invest in this luxury, choose the upper berth, and then you will get the window also. There are three passengers to a compartment. At present, Queensland Railways has not degenerated to the level of pre-packaged food. Meals are still cooked to order by the chef on the train, and prices are not unreasonable. Punctuality is usually quite good. In fact, the author finds the Queensland Railways services the best in Australia and the routes served some of the most fascinating.

Countrylink has a modern fleet of trains with aircraft-type seats. There are no showers for sitting passengers on overnight trains and berths are prohibitively expensive. The food is pre-packaged, but reasonable in price. Punctuality is variable.

V-Line offers only medium-distance trains. The seats are padded bench-type with five across the carriage, half of them facing backwards. There are no overnight trains. Catering is limited, but the journeys are not so long. Punctuality is fair.

Western Australian Government Railways has few trains. The *Australind* is relatively new and aircraft-style with pre-packaged food. The *Prospector* is ageing, but reasonably comfortable. Its disadvantage is that it is not a corridor train. Both trains tend to find it a little difficult to maintain their schedules.

18 INTRODUCTION

The buses operated by W.A.G.R., Countrylink and V-Line are generally of the highest quality, with air-conditioning and toilets, and they are driven well. As long as the connecting rail services arrive on time, the buses are usually punctual.

There is no doubt in the author's mind that this is the way to see Australia. Purchase the most suitable type of rail pass, and then see the country comfortably and surprisingly cheaply. You will be able to travel to places of which you never would have heard if travelling by long-distance bus, and you will meet people too in a way which you would not on the buses.

Most importantly, realise that a rail pass does not restrict you to trains. You can also use bus networks which cover the whole of New South Wales and Victoria and the southern part of Western Australia. Your opportunities are much greater than with the long-distance bus companies and you will find that your costs are lower and your comfort enhanced too.

For maps which show the individual state transport networks better, see the first pages of each state's information in this book. Timetables are given for all long-distance trains in Australia. Look under the section relating to the place where the service originates.

Buses

This is how most independent visitors elect to travel in Australia. There are two principal long-distance companies - McCafferty's and Greyhound. However, since McCafferty's now owns Greyhound, there is less competition than might appear. The advantage for the traveller, though, is that now he or she can use the services of both companies with a single bus pass.

There is still some competition, however. Premier operates services up and down the east coast between Melbourne and Cairns. Unlike its competitors, it travels the coastal route between Melbourne and Sydney. Premier generally offers lower fares than McCafferty's and Greyhound. However, this tends to be nullified by the fact that one can use a section of a *Kilometre Pass* on McCafferty's or Greyhound buses, but nothing similar is currently available for Premier. Premier, though, does offer various unlimited-stops passes on its routes.

Between Sydney and Melbourne and between Melbourne and Adelaide services are operated by Firefly and these are often cheaper even than using a *Kilometre Pass* with McCafferty's and Greyhound. In Western Australia, Integrity offers competition on the Perth to Broome route, including an unlimited-stops ticket for the standard fare of $285. This is appealing, but there is no onward service to Darwin with Integrity, whereas Greyhound can offer a pass right through from Perth to Darwin.

The map opposite shows all the routes operated by McCafferty's and Greyhound.

If one purchases individual tickets, travel with McCafferty's and Greyhound tends to be expensive, even with a 10% backpackers discount. Therefore, most visitors purchase a pass. There are two types of pass - fixed-route passes and distance passes. The former are shown as borders to the following pages, with maps, names and prices. Not all passes are shown, but this is a good selection of the options. If your itinerary fits one of these routes exactly, this will probably be the cheapest way for you to travel. The period of validity varies according to the distance to be travelled. The shortest period is one month and the longest one year. The most common period is six months. You will have flexibility as to time, but no flexibility as to route. Moreover, in some cases, the bus company requires you to list all your stops in advance and you cannot

INTRODUCTION 19

then put in additional stops without a penalty (and sometimes not even with a penalty). Although you do not have to decide your dates of travel in advance, you cannot travel without a reservation (theoretically) and if you ask one of the company's agents to make a reservation for you, you will be charged a fee. Instead, you must either make your reservations in advance, or telephone the company's reservations service (and be kept waiting for ages) every time you wish to travel.

Certain of the passes include Greyhound tours. These are marked on the maps on the following pages by the letter 'T'. Now a tour does not necessarily mean a tour. It may just mean that transport is provided from the main route of the bus to a nearby place of interest. However, even that is a valuable addition to the pass, of course, as getting from main highways to places of interest is often one of the most difficult parts of travelling. Here are the tours offered by Greyhound. A glance at the pertinent map will enable you to tell whether one is included in your chosen route or not.

Ayers Rock, the Olgas and King's Canyon
Kakadu
Exmouth
Monkey Mia
Kalbarri
The Pinnacles

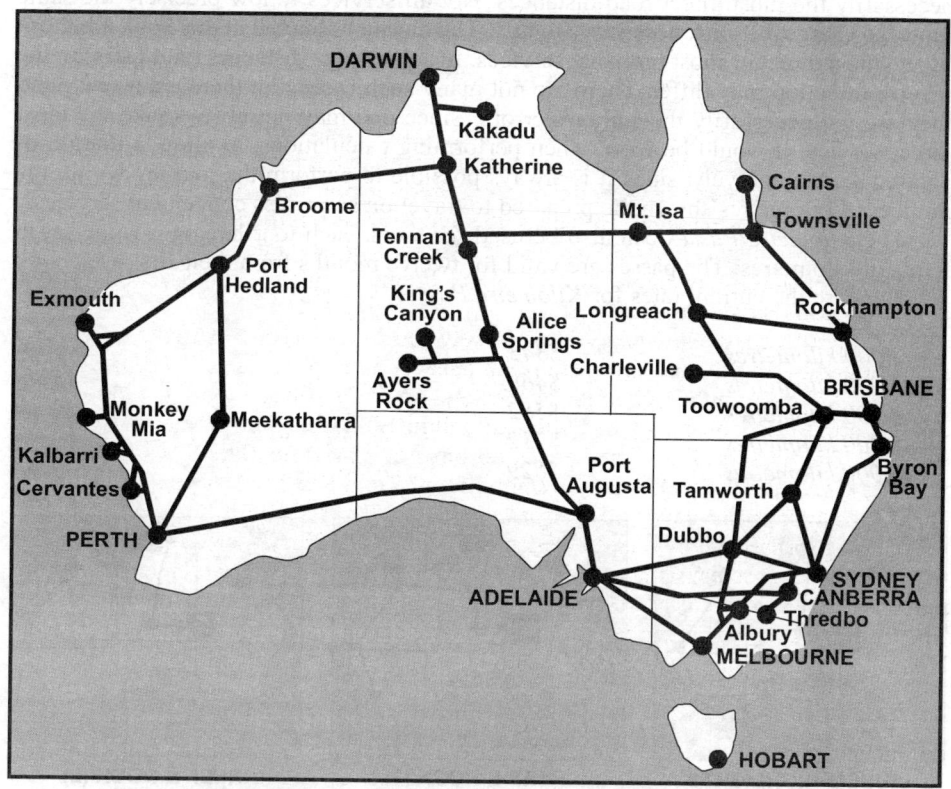

McCAFFERTY'S AND GREYHOUND BUS ROUTES

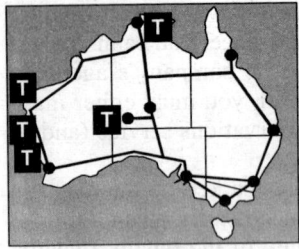
ALL AUSTRALIAN
One circuit
22,000 km $2,566

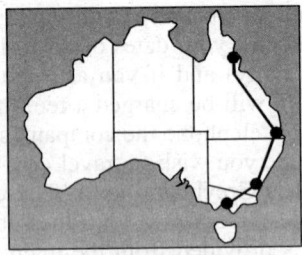
SUNSEEKER
Melbourne to Cairns
4,200 km $502

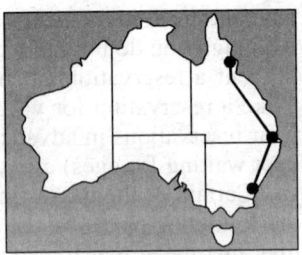
TRAVELLERS' PASS
Sydney to Cairns
3,100 km $340

The second type of bus pass is a distance pass, named by McCafferty's and Greyhound the *Aussie Kilometre Pass*. In this case, one purchases a certain number of kilometres of travel and uses those kilometres just as one thinks fit. Throughout this book, where bus services are shown (and all long-distance services are shown), you can see the number of kilometres involved, which will enable the ascertainment with precision of the exact number of kilometres required for any itinerary.

Note the following points. In the case of McCafferty's and Greyhound services, the distances shown in this book are those charged by the bus company. They are not necessarily the most direct road distances. Not all services follow precisely the same route, so chargeable distances vary slightly. The distances quoted in this book are those by the most direct or most probable services. In some cases distances (and fares) in the reverse direction may differ. There are not many such cases, but there are a few - and they are not necessarily the author's errors. Since one may not always take the most direct service, it would be wise, when performing calculations, to allow a margin of about 5%. Alternatively, since it is always possible to perform the journey within the number of kilometres shown, be prepared to travel on some less convenient services.

The *Kilometre Passes* can also be used for tours, each tour having a value set in terms of kilometres. The passes are valid for twelve months from their first use.

Here are the current rates for *Kilometre Passes*.

2,000 kilometres	*$343*
3,000 kilometres	*$460*
4,000 kilometres	*$582*
5,000 kilometres	*$712*
6,000 kilometres	*$829*

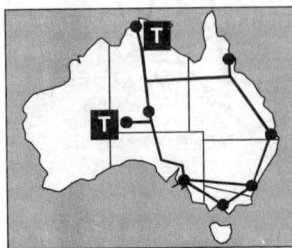
AUSSIE HIGHLIGHTS
One circuit
12,600 km $1,531

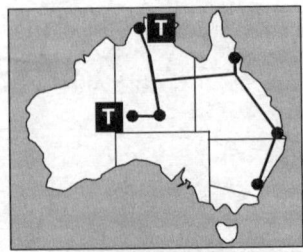
REEF & ROCK (1)
Sydney to Darwin
9,800 km $1,181

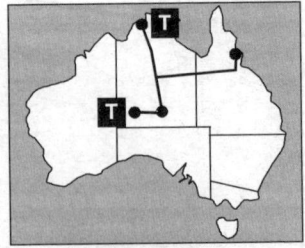
REEF & ROCK (2)
Cairns to Darwin
6,900 km $728

INTRODUCTION

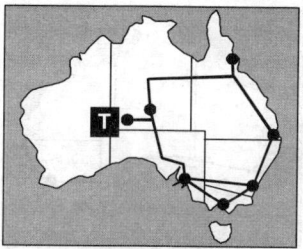

BEST OF THE EAST
One circuit
10,100 km $1,253

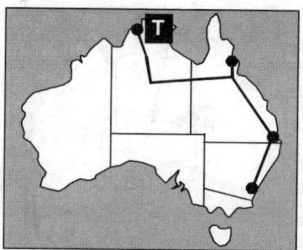

OUTBACK & REEF
Sydney to Darwin
6,900 km $887

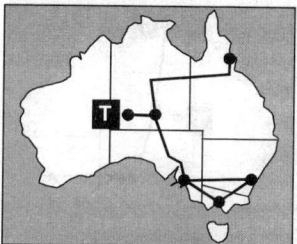

COUNTRY ROAD
Sydney to Cairns
6,800 km $869

Kilometre Passes, continued
7,000 kilometres	$946
8,000 kilometres	$1,063
9,000 kilometres	$1,187
10,000 kilometres	$1,315
11,000 kilometres	$1,431
12,000 kilometres	$1,537
13,000 kilometres	$1,664
14,000 kilometres	$1,773
15,000 kilometres	$1,888
16,000 kilometres	$1,957
17,000 kilometres	$2,067
18,000 kilometres	$2,177
19,000 kilometres	$2,301
20,000 kilometres	$2,411

The *Kilometre Passes* are useful to everybody. Even if you decide to purchase a rail pass, if you are staying in Australia for any length of time, you will probably need to supplement your rail travel with a little bus travel. A 2,000 kilometre pass will enable you to make a number of short journeys which would otherwise be expensive. There is a small discount for producing a backpackers card.

All of the long-distance bus companies operate comfortable vehicles, air-conditioned and with reclining seats and toilets. They make regular meal stops at intervals of three to four hours. However, despite the attempts at comfort, one does tend to feel cramped when confined to these vehicles for long periods - and some of the journeys in Australia can involve very long periods on the same vehicle.

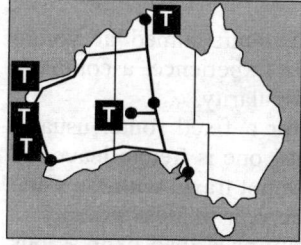

BEST OF THE WEST
One circuit
14,000 km $1,542

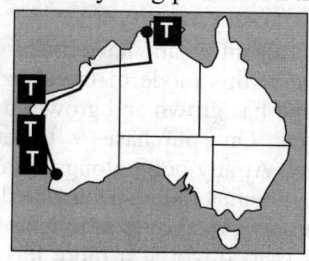

WESTERN EXPLORER
Perth to Darwin
6,900 km $719

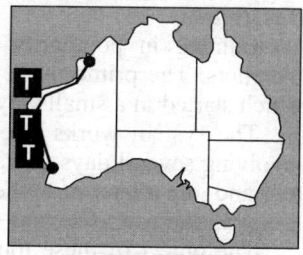

PEARL DIVER
Perth to Broome
4,100 km $463

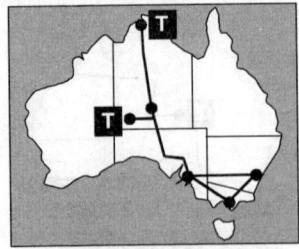
BEST OF THE OUTBACK
Sydney to Darwin
6,800 km $854

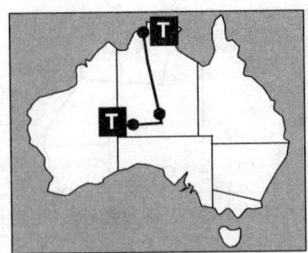
ROCK TRACK
Darwin to Alice Springs
3,800 km $486

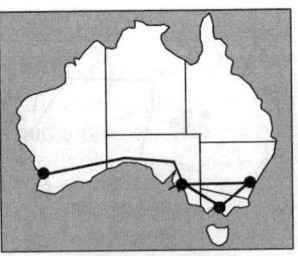
COAST TO COAST
Sydney to Perth
4,600 km $518

Punctuality is variable with the long-distance bus companies, affected mostly by weather and road conditions.

Using a bus pass, one can reach all major places in mainland Australia, but one cannot travel to many of the smaller communities served by the state systems in New South Wales, Victoria and Western Australia. Such communities can, though, be reached with a rail pass. Where the bus pass offers better coverage is in the north-west and in reaching out-of-the-way popular attractions such as Ayers Rock and Kakadu National Park.

It should be noted too that there are restrictions on short-distance travel with the long-distance bus companies. In general, journeys of less than forty kilometres are not permitted, although there are exceptions, and some of the states do not allow competition with their own transport systems. This is particularly so in Victoria and South Australia. Even though a fare and distance is shown in this book for a journey, that does not necessarily mean that one may make that journey in isolation. In some cases, it may be made only as part of a longer journey. As an example, a fare is quoted with McCafferty's from Geelong to Melbourne, but one cannot travel only from Geelong to Melbourne. One may travel from Geelong to Melbourne and there change buses and continue to Albury or Sydney, or any other place outside Victoria. The rules are relaxed somewhat for those with route passes, but still there may be some restrictions imposed, so check before committing yourself.

Tasmania has buses too, of course, but they are operated by different companies. TassieLink offers passes which are good value. See page 853 for details of these. Because of limited demand, some of the services in Tasmania are operated with smaller and less comfortable vehicles, but the routes served are relatively short, so this does not usually create problems.

Bus Tours

Gaining in popularity in recent years have been bus tours aimed at young travellers. The prime purveyor of this mode of travel is Oz Experience, a company which started in a small way and has grown and grown in popularity.

The system works like this. One purchases a ticket for a fixed route, usually involving several days of travel. At any point along the route, one is free to leave the tour and join a later bus when it comes round. Thus one does not travel with the same group all the way. The tour can be spread over as long as one year in most cases.

The object of these tours is to travel at a more leisurely pace than express bus services, to travel less direct and more interesting routes and to allow the passengers to see more of the countryside by stopping at points of interest, or even on request for photographs or replenishing of supplies.

At the end of the day, the driver will usually suggest places to stay, and those places will try to make sure that they have sufficient space available, since they value the regular custom of the bus.

This seems a good way to see in a simple manner places which one would not easily reach otherwise. On the other hand, one is still part of a group, even if that group is constantly changing, and that does tend to limit one's freedom to some extent.

The different routes offered are too numerous to show here, but at present they cover only the eastern half of Australia. That is to say that the western boundary of places served is the road between Adelaide and Darwin, except that there is a tour to Ayers Rock. There are also options which involve flying one way, or flying certain sectors. For full details of all the options offered and current prices, look at www.ozexperience.com.

A similar scheme is operated by the Wayward Bus, which has also proved popular enough to expand its routes and now has several options between Adelaide and Alice Springs, between Alice Springs and Darwin, and between Adelaide and Melbourne. One of these routes is a trip along the Oodnadatta Track, as described on page 695. There is also a tour of Kangaroo Island offered. Look at www.waywardbus.com.au.

Air

The domestic air travel situation has been subject to considerable turmoil over the years. Since the reader will not want to read the history of the rise and fall of Ansett, A.N.A. and various other contenders, it will be sufficient to state that two main players remain. These are Qantas and Virgin Blue.

Virgin Blue offers cheap flights on certain main routes, at least at the time of writing, while Qantas provides a more extensive service, operating some flights under its own name and some under the names of regional subsidiaries using the Qantas logo. There are also some smaller regional airlines serving limited areas and routes, and these airlines are usually rather expensive.

Qantas offers a ticket known as a *Boomerang Pass* to overseas visitors holding an international air ticket to and from Australia, New Zealand or certain Pacific Islands (not necessarily with Qantas). To make good use of this offer, one needs to study the rules carefully and then see how it can fit most advantageously with one's itinerary.

The *Boomerang Pass* covers flights within Australia and to New Zealand and various Pacific Islands with Qantas, Qantas subsidiaries, Air Pacific and Air Vanuatu. These areas are divided into six zones, comprising Western Australia, Central Australia, Eastern Australia major airports, Eastern Australia regional airports, New Zealand, and the Pacific Islands. Flights within a single zone are charged at $250. Flights from one zone to another are charged at $300. A minimum of two flights must be purchased before arrival in any of the countries covered by the *Boomerang Pass*. Other sectors, up to ten in total, may be added later. No transits are allowed on international flights, but within Australia same-day transits are permitted as long as the routing is reasonable. Thus one may, for example, fly from Perth to Adelaide in the morning, spend the day looking at Adelaide, and move on to Melbourne in the evening. This is a useful ticket, especially for those short of time, but it is best used for long hops and to places which are otherwise expensive to reach, such as Darwin and Tasmania.

24 INTRODUCTION

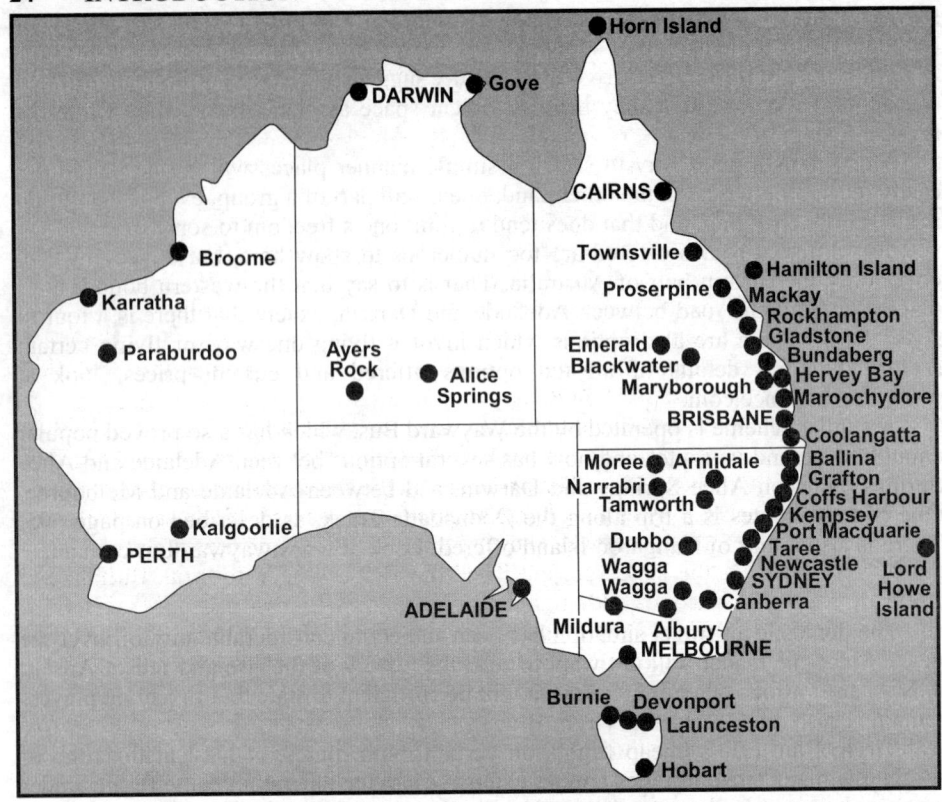

AUSTRALIAN AIRPORTS SERVED BY QANTAS
Capital letters indicate international services

The map above shows all airports in Australia currently served by Qantas or Qantas subsidiaries. Note, though, that there are some places not included in the *Boomerang Pass* scheme, for example Horn Island and Lord Howe Island.

Also note that the *Boomerang Pass* does not necessarily offer the cheapest fares. Even Qantas itself may have cheaper discount fares on some routes, so, apart from the two initial journeys required in order to purchase the pass, it may be better not to commit oneself too far in advance.

Private Transport

Purchasing a car for the duration of a visit, and then reselling it upon departure, is quite a popular way of seeing Australia. The advantage is flexibility. One can go where one wishes when one wishes and one can reach places not easily accessible by public transport.

The disadvantages are the responsibility of having a vehicle, the doubts as to its reliability unless you are an expert in car mechanics and really can judge what you are purchasing, and the fact that travelling in this manner may end up being quite expensive.

Notice boards at backpackers hostels often have vehicles for sale by other

INTRODUCTION 25

travellers who have finished their wanderings, and there are even weekend markets of backpackers vehicles in some places, so it is not difficult to find private transport being sold at moderate prices. The problem is not the purchase so much as the cost of operation of the vehicle. In the end it is almost certainly going to cost more than you expected. Distances are vast in Australia, so fuel is going to be costly. Then the vehicle is likely to break down once or twice, and that might be quite expensive. Pray that it breaks down near a town and not in the middle of the outback.

If you are travelling alone, a vehicle is going to be the most expensive option. If you are a couple, it will be more expensive than well-planned public transport, but you will have more freedom. If you are three or four, this option seems better value.

Amongst the things to remember are that backpackers cars get stolen, especially in popular backpacker locations, so you constantly have risk and responsibility. Try not to leave all your possessions attractively stowed on the back seat, therefore. It is bad enough to lose your transport. You do not want to lose everything else with it.

Then think about the road conditions. Outside the cities, traffic is not too much of a problem, but the roads themselves have hazards with which you may not be familiar, so always expect the unexpected. The passenger in the front seat should always regard himself or herself as on duty as a spotter. Kangaroos are a hazard. If you see a kangaroo anywhere near the road, slow down. They are unpredictable - and big. A collision may not be very good for the kangaroo, but it will be almost as bad for you. Buffalo and cattle are even larger hazards, although their movements are less susceptible to sudden changes of direction. Then there is the question of road surface. Although Australian roads are improving, always be on the lookout for anything which appears odd in the road surface ahead, and slow down. If it looks odd, it probably is.

Once one leaves bitumen roads and starts driving on dirt, there are all sorts of additional hazards. The most obvious are the dust thrown up by other vehicles and the stones which fly off the road surface as another vehicle passes, and which can easily crack or break a windscreen. Then there are the corrugations in the surfaces of well-used roads, which will shake your vehicle to pieces, and also lessen your control over it, since the wheels are touching the road for only part of the time. There may be wash-aways where streams cross the road, so always slow down for dips. Realise in advance that driving on a dirt road is going to reduce your average speed and increase your fuel consumption, so plan for this, rather than feeling pressure to reach a pre-determined destination on time.

Travelling at night is particularly not recommended. At dusk and dawn the kangaroos come out in force. They stand in the road and are mesmerised by the lights of oncoming vehicles. They appear to hop away and then, at the last moment, change their minds and hop back in front of your vehicle. Have a look at the front armour of the long-distance buses and trucks which are obliged to drive through the night. If you have something similar on the front of your vehicle, then drive at night with extreme caution. If not, then do not consider driving at night at all.

The remote areas of Australia are really worth seeing, for they are unique, but bear in mind that they can also be dangerous. Travelling by public transport will allow you to see plenty of remote places. However, if you choose to use private transport, remember that you must be well prepared. You need spare fuel, plenty of water, some common spare parts for your vehicle, a good detailed map and a plan for emergencies. This should involve telling somebody ahead (for example the police) when you will arrive at your destination and being sure that action will be taken if you do not so arrive. Every year people die on remote roads in Australia and you do not want to be included in such statistics.

Hiring a vehicle is expensive, but there are businesses which rent out older vehicles especially to backpackers. However, this is suitable only for a brief tour of a particular location. If you want the vehicle for longer, it would be better to purchase. There are also rental companies wanting vehicles returned to their home bases. If this suits your plan, you might consider moving such a vehicle from one location to another. There is usually a charge, but it is a much reduced one, typically around $10 per day, plus the fuel required for the journey. The disadvantage is that a fairly strict time limit is usually set for the repatriation.

Then there is the question of the environment. Should we really be running round in private vehicles consuming irreplaceable resources and increasing pollution when there is public transport readily available? In the author's opinion, this can be justified only if you are going to reach places which are otherwise inaccessible, and if your vehicle is filled with passengers to its capacity. However, it is the reader's conscience which must be placated if you do otherwise. If such considerations do not weigh with you, at least bear in mind that, in the end, the private vehicle probably will not turn out to be a cheap option.

Bicycling

The author always admires those who try to travel under their own steam like this, recalling meeting, for example, a Dutchman in Indonesia who had cycled there from his homeland (wet sections excluded, of course). In Australia, though, steam may be one of the major factors. Distances are great and temperatures often unpleasantly high. Thus two of the most important requirements are plenty of water and covering from the rays of the merciless sun. Stamina is another vital quality.

The bicycle is an option worth considering for the east coast, where communities are not too far apart. There are some problems, though. Roads are often comparatively narrow and traffic is travelling at speed, making cycling unpleasant. Especially be careful of vehicles crossing each other and having no spare road for the cyclist. Cyclists usually prefer, understandably, to get off main roads, but in Australia that is not always easy. The minor roads are even more narrow, although with much less traffic, of course, and they tend to degenerate into dirt surfaces unpleasant for those on two thin wheels. Nevertheless, cycling up or down the east coast, and across to Adelaide, is certainly perfectly feasible and there have been books published recently recommending to the cyclist less frequented but reasonably surfaced routes.

Going further west, though, is more difficult, although not impossible. You really need to be well prepared for this - and the most important supply will be water. Be prepared to cover a stretch of 200 kilometres without replenishing supplies and then you can probably see Australia by bicycle - and have the great admiration of the author for your achievement.

Hitch-Hiking

Hitch-hiking is not really easy in Australia. Distances are great and those travelling are not usually keen to pick up an unknown quantity with whom they will be stuck for a long period. Nevertheless, it is not impossible and you will probably get there in the end.

Bearing in mind that you may be standing at the roadside for quite a long time, carry plenty of water with you and be sure that you have covering to protect you from the sun, particularly a hat. Also consider, before accepting a ride, the convenience of the place where you are to be left. You do not want a location where traffic will be passing at high speed, and you particularly do not want a place where you cannot, if necessary, find more water and somewhere to sleep when night falls.

ACCOMMODATION

Here we come to the second secret of how to save money. Accommodation lists in this book have been divided into two categories, labelled Hotel Accommodation and Backpackers Hostels. The basic difference is that hotel accommodation is quoted on a per room basis and is thus most suitable for couples, while backpackers hostels quote a per person rate most suitable for those travelling alone. Here, though, we shall divide into three categories. It is assumed that all readers of this book are interested in saving money, so choose the category which is most relevant to your requirements and read on to see how you can get the best value.

(i) Good Quality Accommodation, but on a Budget

Even though you want a good standard of accommodation, you still do not want to waste money. Reduced expenditure means more time in Australia, so how is it to be achieved?

This is the method. Do not book in advance. Plan to arrive at your destination not too late in the day and go straight to the Tourist Office. If you arrive by air, there is usually an office at the major airports. Otherwise there is nearly always one in the centre of the town, marked on the maps in this book in most cases.

The Tourist Office has bargains on offer from good quality hotels which have not filled their rooms for that day. Some of these bargains are very good value indeed. In fact, if your budget can run to a reasonable standard of hotel, you will find that by this means you will get a very good one for the same price, and it is readers in this category who will get the best value of all. The larger the town or city, the better the offers are likely to be, but in most cases you will not get them by approaching the hotels themselves. You need to do it through the Tourist Office. Expect to pay about $100 per couple per night and then you can usually get something in the highest range.

Using this method will create a feeling of uncertainty in some readers, who prefer to have the security of knowing where they are going to stay, but try it once or twice and see how well it works.

What if you are going to arrive late and the Tourist Office will be closed? If you are in the same state, you can visit the local Tourist Office, which will either have information or be able to telephone your destination. You will not be able to examine the offers quite as carefully in this way, but you are still likely to get good value. If you are in a different state, you may have to telephone the Tourist Office at your destination and be prepared to pay using a credit card. You will usually get the best value by leaving this process until the last moment, rather than by booking far ahead, because good offers are often made precisely because the hotel finds that its advance reservations are inadequate.

If this method fails to produce good value, which is rare, try looking on the Internet. You will certainly get a discount by booking in that manner, but usually it is not equal to the bargains available on the day from the Tourist Office.

28 INTRODUCTION
(ii) Cheap Accommodation, but without using Backpackers Hostels

Now here is where Australia is just made for you, for in all the older towns you will find older hotels. If price is your main concern, but you would like a room to yourself, you will find these hotels to be just what you are looking for. Average price is about $25 for one or $40 for two. The most you should ever be obliged to pay is about $35 for one or $50 for two. If you are quoted more than that, look around for better value. Now, of course, this is not luxury accommodation, but it is self-contained and you will have the security of a door which locks.

Typically, these old hotels are constructed of wood and many of the rooms are just as they would have been a century ago. Showers and toilets will be communal - one set for ladies and one for gents. In the room will be an oldish bed and a wardrobe and chest of drawers of uncertain antiquity. There may also be a hand basin with dubious plumbing. The floor will have faded linoleum on it and the walls will be of painted wood. If you are lucky, outside will be a magnificently wide open wood-floored communal balcony, and here you can sit in the evening watching the sunset with a bottle of beer to soothe the nerves. Down below will be a pub, but the author's experience is that, contrary to what one might expect, that causes very little disturbance. There will usually be a lounge with a television and some communal facilities for making a cup of tea. There may also be a kitchen, but it often lacks obvious essentials such as plates and cups and is sometimes quite dirty, so do not depend on it for much more than hot water.

The atmosphere in these hotels is like staying in something out of a wild west film. The hotels are undeniably rough and basic, but they have great character. They tend to be neglected somewhat by travellers, because they look too rough for those wanting a reasonable standard of accommodation, while backpackers believe that the hostels are the cheapest accommodation around and rarely think of staying in these hotels until obliged to do so by circumstance.

These older hotels are rather shy about advertising themselves, so you will not easily find information about them, even in this book, but they are there, in every old town. Just look around the main street. The places where you will not find them are in the centres of big cities and in new towns, but everywhere else they are there giving their own special character to the town centre. It is those balconies which the author really loves. If you want to economise, but still have your own room, these are the places for you.

(iii) Backpackers Hostels and Alternatives

If your object is to do things as cheaply as possible, you will already have decided that you need to stay in backpackers hostels. The secret, though, is that you do not. However much you may think that you fit into this category, first read the section above and then think again.

The average price for a backpackers hostel is about $22 per person. Double rooms are often available, but command a small premium, so a couple may find that the price asked is about $50.

Taking the case of the individual traveller first, would you rather pay $22 for a bed in a crowded dormitory, or $25 for your own room? Then why are you rushing off to a hostel, or even reserving it ahead, instead of asking one or two of the centrally located old-style hotels about their prices first?

In the case of a couple, it is even likely that it will actually be cheaper to stay in the hotel than in a hostel, so why not give it a try?

Now there are some who do actually prefer to stay in the backpackers accommodation, saying that it has advantages, and there is some truth in this. You will meet other travellers more easily and be able to obtain travel information. You may also be able to get special deals on tours or on entrance fees to attractions. If you are lucky you will find a helpful owner and staff who can give you advice about local attractions and how to reach them, familiar with the needs of similar travellers. You will usually find a much better equipped kitchen and a washing machine and dryer, even though they will require feeding with suitable coins.

Therefore, the reader will still want to know which are the better hostels. Many of the hostels in Australia belong to one of four groups. These four are Y.H.A. (the Youth Hostels Association), V.I.P., Nomads, and Black and White. The author finds little to choose among the first three, although there are minor differences in operating technique.

The Y.H.A. is the longest established. It requires membership and, if you are not a resident of Australia, you must join in your own country, before coming to Australia, or obtain a different and rather more expensive type of temporary membership once here. Some Y.H.A. hostels will refuse to accept you if you are not a member.

V.I.P. and Nomads have their own individual membership schemes. You can join in Australia, at the first hostel you visit in the group. Usually hostels do not refuse to take non-members, but they give a small discount to members. However, you need to make sure that you ask for this discount. It is not generally offered without enquiry.

Black and White is different. This is a group of smaller, more homely hostels. There is no membership involved and there are no discounts. Hostels are not automatically accepted for inclusion in the list. They need to meet certain standards. The list is run by Ken and Liz who operate Centaur House on Magnetic Island. The author has found the hostels on this list to be generally (not always, but generally) of good quality and recommends this list to readers. Look at www.bpf.com.au to see which hostels are on the list. They are also marked in this book.

The author has put recommendation marks against certain hostels and cheap hotels in this book. The reader should realise that these are purely personal opinions. The author's preference is for small, quiet hostels with helpful and knowledgeable owners. If this is not what appeals to the reader, then please ignore the recommendations and make your own choices based on your own criteria.

As to the choice of older hotel or backpackers hostel, the author finds it good policy to try some of each, but do not neglect those hotels as many travellers do. It is a great experience to stay in some of them. They deserve some degree of your patronage, and will not be a burden on your budget. They are, in fact, one of the big secrets which you should be let into by reading this book. Enjoy them.

(iv) General Comments on Hotel Accommodation

As explained above, the Hotel Accommodation category includes all accommodation which generally offers rates by the room, expecting two people to share a room. This includes high-class hotels, motels and older pub-style hotels. Bed and breakfast accommodation is sometimes included too where the other options are limited.

This book gives lowest rates for hotels. The problem is that, especially with the hotels at the upper end of the scale, - the 4, 4½ and 5 star hotels - there is no such animal as a lowest rate. There are so many different rates available. There are rates for ordinary rooms, rates for superior rooms, rates for rooms with a better view. Then there are surcharges for peak periods, discounts for slack periods, special rates for businessmen, Internet rates, rates for booking long in advance, Tourist Office rates, and a multitude of others. The rate given in this book is, as far as can be ascertained, the rate for an ordinary room in a non-peak season without any discount. However, you should never have to pay this rate. You should always be able to find a discount for something. As suggested above, the Tourist Office will usually have the best deal, but failing that, unless you look really desperate for somewhere to stay, the hotel is usually able to find some reason for a discount if asked. "Well, sir, I *could* put you down as a business account if you don't mind paying cash," etc. Therefore, the only reality in the prices quoted is that you should always, except at a really peak period, be able to obtain a room at the price stated, which is the official rate, but in practice should expect never to pay that much. It is a strange system.

When we come to the more moderately priced accommodation, often in motels, the situation is different. The rate quoted in this book is usually what you will be asked to pay, but there may be seasonal fluctuations, especially in popular holiday areas. Rates quoted are low-season rates, but in this type of accommodation high-season rates will not be ridiculously high, unless a warning note appears in the text. It is the 'resorts' which tend to be greatly affected by season.

Bed and breakfast establishments are generally not the bargain in Australia that they are in certain European countries. Generally they offer high standards and are expensive. They also tend to be away from town centres. For these reasons, they are generally not included in this book, although where the options are limited they are sometimes mentioned.

At the bottom end of this scale come the older-style hotels offering very reasonable rates. These rates are not subject to much change. These hotels do not indulge in sophisticated theories such as seasonality. Moreover, they are the only type of accommodation in this division which caters specifically for the single guest. Although single prices are not mentioned here, they can be expected to be approximately two-thirds of the double/twin rate. These hotels can be identified simply because their name includes the word 'hotel' and their charges are low. Only the cheapest and the most expensive accommodation, curiously enough, uses this nomenclature. Those in between are all resorts, motels, motor inns or motor lodges.

Listings are generally by price, from the most expensive to the cheapest, but sometimes geography is taken into consideration too and hotels in a particular area are grouped together in the list, if that seems a more logical way of presenting the information.

(v) General Comments on Backpackers Hostels

Backpackers hostels are marked on the maps with white numerals on a black background, but where an establishment offers both hotel accommodation and a backpackers hostel, which is not uncommon, the map may show only the hotel identification (in black on white). The listing, however, will show that it is also a hostel.

Backpackers hostels too do not change their rates much according to season, so expect the prices stated in this book to be reasonably accurate, except for the effects of inflation. The difference which season makes to a backpackers hostel is whether it is likely to be full or not.

INTRODUCTION 31

Facilities and services offered by backpackers hostels vary considerably, but some offer many useful extras. Typical of these extras are pick-up at the railway or bus station, or even the airport, return to the same at the end of your stay, free tea and coffee, discounts on tours and bus tickets, free tours of the neighbourhood, a light breakfast, transport into town and back at certain times, apple pie and ice-cream for supper, a free barbecue once a week, a free night after staying for three or four nights, cheap meals in a local pub, free entry into a nightclub or a free drink in a similar establishment, and free luggage storage. Of course, not all hostels are able to offer all of these, but many offer some of them, so there is much to be said for the best of the hostels. They really do try, in some cases, to think of their guests and make life a little easier for them.

In many cases when one arrives in a new town one will find a line of minibuses and drivers with signboards proclaiming the advantages of particular hostels. The author's opinion is that if hostels go to this trouble, one of them deserves my custom. The only problem is to decide which one.

Hostels are not always safe, so take precautions. One cannot help leaving one's possessions around to some degree, but do not leave tempting valuables, such as a watch, for example, and certainly keep all money, travellers cheques and credit or bank cards either with the management, if the offer is available, or on your person, not just in the day, but particularly at night. Ideally this means that you should have a money belt. It is a pity that this type of security has to be necessary, when 99% of your fellow travellers will be pleasant, decent, honest people, but the other 1% poses too big a risk to be ignored. In general, the more rural your location, the less worried you need to be, and the more urban your surroundings, the more care is needed. The most dangerous places are the trendy backpackers locations and the most dangerous people are Australians. That is not because of inherent dishonesty, but because of their different circumstances. A European, for example, with dishonest intentions does not usually make his way to Australia especially to steal something, but an unscrupulous local may well think that a night or two in a backpackers hostel might be rewarding. There is no need to be paranoid about the possibility of theft, but reasonable precautions should become a matter of routine.

In this book backpackers hostels are generally listed in order of price, from most expensive to cheapest, but sometimes geographical circumstances are taken into consideration where that seems to make the order of listing more logical.

BACKPACKERS CARDS

Here is something which you should most certainly purchase. It matters not at all that you have no intention ever of staying in a backpackers hostel. You will get the value back in all sorts of other ways, if you are an independent traveller.

The most obvious benefit is actually in travel, not accommodation. Every time you buy a long-distance bus ticket or bus pass you will save 10%. One pass will save you far more than the cost of the card. On the railways too you will reap benefits. If you buy the Great Southern Railway Pass, which is a particularly attractive pass to purchase (see page 16), you will save no less than $140 by producing a backpackers card. Various other railway tickets also offer discounts for backpackers. There are discounts on tours and activities. There are even discounts on pizzas and haircuts.

Which card should you purchase then? Well, as far as the discounts are concerned, it does not make any difference. Perhaps you are already a youth hostel member in your own country. Then that will do quite well. If not, maybe you should become one, so that you have the option of staying in Australian youth hostels. Otherwise, just pick the card of whichever group you feel that you are most likely to stay with. V.I.P. and Nomads hostels offer a small discount to members staying at their hostels. Most people find that they stay about the right number of nights to recoup the cost of the card, and then any other discounts are a bonus. Do buy a card, though, because those discounts will mount up and far exceed the cost of the card itself.

V.I.P. cards currently cost $35 for one year or $50 for two years. Nomads cards cost $30 for one year. The price of Y.H.A. membership varies according to the country in which it is purchased.

FOOD

British influence can still be felt in the gastronomic delicacies available in Australia, such as fish and chips, for example, and that which Australia has really made into its own speciality - the meat pie with sauce.

However, such purity of diet has become contaminated in recent years by the influx of immigrants from nations which have not such a refined cuisine, and now it is common to find dishes of Italian, Greek, Chinese and other Asian origin.

In point of fact, one can find almost any type of food in Australia - and one can find it in all price ranges. Some of the restaurants are very good indeed, but if you are on a limited budget you can still find tasty food in a diversity of ethnic styles at reasonable prices.

Mr. MacDonald has established his hamburgers in every corner of the nation, and Colonel Sanders is not far behind with his fried chicken. Almost every corner shop can sell you the ubiquitous meat pie, and usually has some other similar delicacies also. If you have a good appetite, the counter lunch will solve the problem. Most hotels (pubs) serve a hearty lunch at a modest price to anybody willing to sup a beer in the smoky bar. Often these meals are very good value, especially if you look around a little before making your choice.

If you really want to save money, though, you need to cook for yourself, which is easy enough for those staying in backpackers hostels, where kitchen facilities are provided. Visit the supermarket late in the day when some bargains will be available, and then you can live quite cheaply. Life is hard when trying to compete with the big names in travel guide publishing and, faced with the need to limit expenses to the minimum possible level while undertaking research for this book, the author found that he was able to cut expenditure on food to $3 per day by this method. However, a budget of $5 per person per day would offer a better diet.

DRINK

Perhaps it is the Australian climate which creates the Australian thirst. At any rate, Australians have something of a reputation for liking to down a beer or two.

Two of the more unusual alcoholic world records are held by Australia, according to Mr. Guinness. One is that Darwin has the highest per capita consumption of beer in the world, with peak consumption estimated at 236 litres (52 gallons) per person per annum. It is claimed that a society for the prevention of alcoholism in Darwin had to be disbanded in 1966 due to lack of support. Whilst in Darwin, try asking for a *Darwin Stubby*, a size of bottle suited to those with big thirsts.

The second record is that the Men's Working Club in Mildura, Victoria claims the longest permanent bar with beer pumps in the world. It is 90.8 metres (298 feet) long, with 27 pumps.

Fosters Lager is known throughout the world, so it is perhaps something of a surprise to discover that it is a beer not as popular in its homeland as overseas. In Australia, each state has its own brands of beer and only in the last few years have the breweries been successful in expanding their sales into the foreign territory of other states. The most popular brand of beer is probably *V.B. (Victoria Bitter)*, brewed, of course, in Victoria. A superior beer (in taste and price) which is gaining in popularity is *Cooper's*, brewed in South Australia.

Australia has also become the home of some good quality wines. Although the Barossa Valley in South Australia has long been the most famous area for wine production, in recent years a determined challenge has come from Western Australia, and latterly from Victoria and New South Wales too.

TELEPHONING

There are always techniques to learn about each country's telephone system. Australia's system consists of timed long-distance calls, but local calls of unlimited duration. Public telephones exist, although not in abundance, and sometimes they work.

When making calls, look for 1-800... numbers. These calls are free. However, the owner of the number can choose the area from which he is willing to accept such calls. Quite often the 1-800 numbers can be used only within the same state as the party being called, and occasionally the effective area is even more limited.

1-300... numbers and six-digit numbers starting with 13 are charged as local calls, as long as you are calling from within Australia (but are extremely expensive or unusable if you attempt to call them from overseas).

Telephone cards are available and it is desirable to have one because telephones do not necessarily accept both coins and cards. At the time of writing a telephone call costs 40 cents per unit, a local call being always a single unit.

As for international calls, the way to make these is to purchase one of the variety of cards available for the purpose. The author does not recommend one rather than another. In his experience there are always problems of some sort eventually with any of these cards, but they are very much cheaper than using the conventional Telstra system. One first telephones the office of the company issuing the card. Then one taps in the code number on the card. Then one dials the number required. The most important thing with these cards is to ensure that you can telephone the office of the company by making a local telephone call. This means that there must be either a 1-300 number given or a local number for the city from which you are making the call. Check this point before purchasing the card. It will affect the cost of the call very considerably. Provided that you can connect using a local call, your international telephone call will then cost the price charged by the card company per minute, plus a single charge of 40 cents no matter how long you speak. Most cards offer the option of using a free 1-800 number, but you should understand that, although the 1-800 call is free, your international call will be charged at a considerably higher per minute charge

34   INTRODUCTION

than if you pay yourself for the call to the company. All this sounds complex, but the instruction is simple. Always use a local telephone number to contact the card company, so make sure that such a number is available before purchasing the card.

There are also kiosks provided for international telephone calls in some Internet shops. This is not a particularly cheap way of making a call, but it is simple, and still cheaper than using the Telstra system. If you just intend to make a single call, so do not want to purchase a card, this will probably be the best method.

It should be noted that some establishments have private coin-operated telephones for the use of their customers or guests. With these telephones, local calls are usually timed and 1-800 numbers are sometimes unacceptable. These are not good telephones from which to make international card calls. It is better to go out and look for an ordinary public telephone.

E-MAIL

It is not difficult to find e-mail facilities. There are shops devoted to this purpose, and hotels and backpackers hostels often provide facilities for their guests. Where the major differences lie is in the price charged.

In major cities it is usually possible to find facilities for a charge of about $3 per hour. In remote areas, you may be asked to pay $10 per hour. Therefore, use the cheap facilities where they are available and try to limit your use to a very brief session in the more expensive places.

TIME ZONES

This is not a matter as simple as one might suppose, so here are the facts.

Winter

Australia is divided into three zones east to west. From the east:

Queensland, New South Wales (except Broken Hill), the Australian Capital Territory, Victoria and Tasmania are 10 hours ahead of G.M.T.

South Australia, the Northern Territory and Broken Hill are 9½ hours ahead of G.M.T. (30 minutes behind Sydney).

Western Australia is 8 hours ahead of G.M.T. (2 hours behind Sydney).

BUT the area in Western Australia between the South Australian border and Caiguna, or, along the railway, between the border and just east of Kalgoorlie, likes to keep an unofficial local time which is 8¾ hours ahead of G.M.T. (1¼ hours behind Sydney).

Summer

HOWEVER, in summer the southern states and territories of New South Wales, the Australian Capital Territory, Victoria, Tasmania and South Australia keep daylight saving time, which advances them one hour, but the other states and territories do not

INTRODUCTION 35

do so. Therefore, in summer the situation is as follows.

New South Wales (except Broken Hill), the Australian Capital Territory, Victoria and Tasmania are 11 hours ahead of G.M.T.

South Australia and Broken Hill are 10½ hours ahead of G.M.T. (30 minutes behind Sydney).

Queensland is 10 hours ahead of G.M.T. (1 hour behind Sydney).

The Northern Territory is 9½ hours ahead of G.M.T. (1½ hours behind Sydney).

Western Australia is 8 hours ahead of G.M.T. (3 hours behind Sydney).

The area in Western Australia between the South Australian border and Caiguna, or, along the railway, between the border and just east of Kalgoorlie, is 8¾ hours ahead of G.M.T. (2¼ hours behind Sydney).

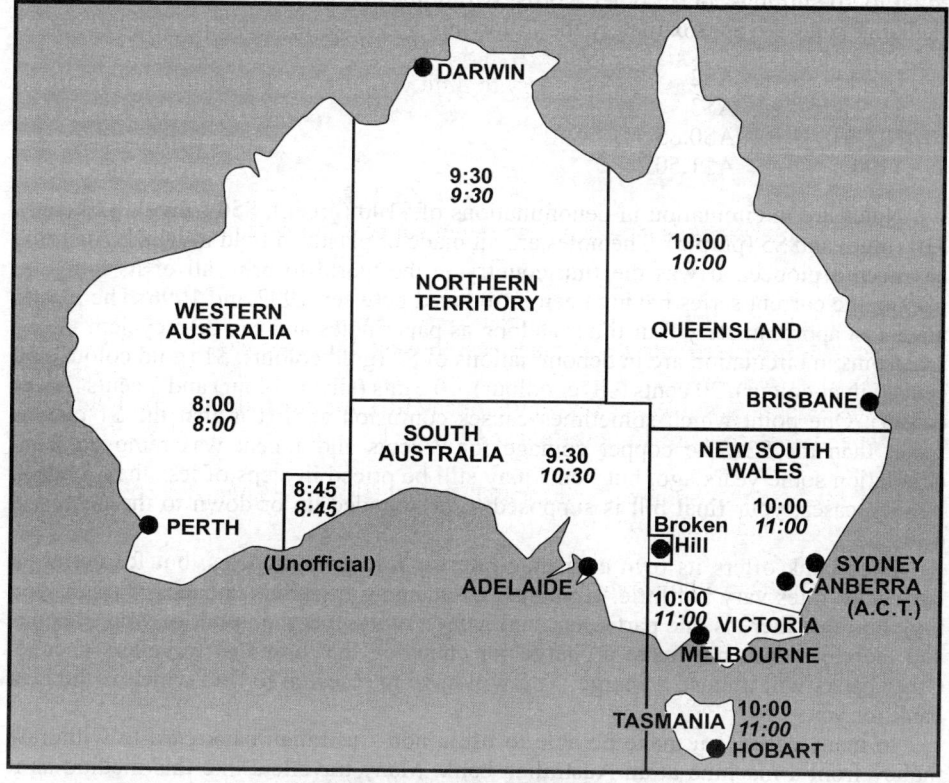

AUSTRALIAN TIME ZONES
Times as at midnight G.M.T.
Top line (bold print) shows winter time
Bottom line (bold italic) shows summer time

INTRODUCTION
BUSINESS HOURS

Business hours are most commonly 9:00 until 17:30, Monday to Friday, with a small variation either side. Places in the north of Australia sometimes open and close a little earlier. If trying to contact a business in another part of Australia, remember about time differences (previous page).

Government offices often close at 17:00, or even 16:30.

Shops may stay open later, particularly on Thursday and Friday evenings, and most will be open on Saturdays, and some on Sundays. The larger the town, the more likely shops are to indulge in extended trading hours.

Corner shops will usually stay open until about 20:00, and some even later. Supermarkets in the big cities are often open 24 hours a day, and even in smaller towns they are likely to remain open until about 22:00 on weekdays.

BANKS AND MONEY

The unit of currency is the Australian dollar, divided into 100 cents. Originally Australia used pounds, as in Britain, but the switch was made in 1966, with the dollar equal to 10 shillings, or, in other words, two dollars equal to one old pound. Current exchange rates are approximately the following.

U.S.$1	=	A$2
£1	=	A$3
N.Z.$1	=	A$0.85
¥100	=	A$1.50

Notes are in circulation in denominations of $100 (green), $50 (olive), $20 (red), $10 (blue) and $5 (purple). The notes are all made of plastic, a field in which Australia has been a pioneer. It was the first country in the world to print all of its notes on plastic, the current series having been introduced between 1992 and 1996. The plastic notes last approximately four times as long as paper notes and can be recycled.

Coins in circulation are in denominations of $2 (gold colour), $1 (gold colour), 50 cents (silver colour), 20 cents (silver colour), 10 cents (silver colour) and 5 cents (silver colour). One point which sometimes causes confusion at first is that the $1 coin is larger than the $2. The copper coinage for 2 cents and 1 cent was removed from circulation some years ago, but items may still be priced in steps of less than 5 cents. In such cases, your final bill is supposed to be rounded up or down to the nearest 5 cents.

Each bank offers its own exchange rate for foreign currencies, but for common currencies rates vary but little. If you are exchanging travellers cheques, though, you may find that there is one particular bank which represents the issuer of your cheques and therefore does not make a charge for changing that brand of travellers cheque. Other banks will impose a charge. You will have to research to find which is the best bank for you.

In many cases you make be able to use a non-Australian bank card to withdraw money from a machine at an Australian bank. Many travellers like this method as it avoids their having to safeguard too much cash or too many travellers cheques. There will be a small fee for this service, but the fee will be determined by your home bank, so ask before you set out.

POSTAL SERVICES

Australia has a postal system which is reasonably efficient. Domestic postage costs 50 cents for a letter. Overseas postage costs $1 for a postcard and $1.65 for a letter to most countries.

One oddity of the system is that G.S.T. (Goods and Services Tax) applies to domestic postage, but not to international postage. As a result, different stamps must be used for the two purposes. When purchasing stamps, therefore, you must make it clear whether you require domestic stamps, with G.S.T. included, or international stamps, on which G.S.T. is not paid. You may not use international stamps on domestic mail. You may use domestic stamps on international mail, but only if you put on 10% extra (to cover the fact that 9.09% of the money paid for the stamps will not go to the Post Office, but will have to be given to the government as tax).

Parcels to overseas destinations may be sent by air mail, by economy air mail (slower and slightly cheaper), or by sea mail to more distant countries only. All methods are relatively expensive. As an example, 5 kilograms sent to the U.K. will cost $98 by air mail, $74 by economy air mail or $44.50 by sea mail.

For items weighing up to 250 grams, a prepaid air mail envelope can be purchased. If you buy a pack of ten such envelopes, the cost of the envelopes themselves is negligible. You pay only for the postage. If your envelope weighs more than 250 grams, you may add the extra postage.

The Poste Restante system allows mail to be held for you for collection at any post office for up to a month. There is no charge. At the larger post offices a computerised system is employed and you can use a computer terminal to check whether you have mail or not. This is reasonably effective until the post office staff mis-spell your name when entering it into the system, after which there is little chance of your ever seeing that item. If your surname is one which might easily be mis-spelt, check the likely mis-spellings as well.

If you leave a location and want mail forwarded, that can be arranged, but there is a healthy charge for the service, and a likelihood, in the author's experience, that not all items will get sent on.

TOILETS

Toilets are an important consideration for the traveller, and in Australia the situation is good. Public toilets do exist and are usually open for most of the day.

Bus stations and larger railway stations usually have toilets, and their use is free. Trains, of course, are equipped with toilets, except for suburban services, and long-distance buses now have toilets too, although they have a habit of not keeping still when you want them to.

Cleanliness varies, but is usually reasonable.

SPORTS AND GAMES

The principal sports in Australia are cricket, rugby and Australian Rules football.

In the summer sport of cricket Australia is generally regarded currently as the world leader, especially in five-day test cricket. The nation has also produced the man usually regarded as the best cricketer ever, or certainly the best batsman - Sir Donald Bradman, who died in Adelaide at the beginning of 2001 at the age of 92. In Australia cricket is popular and draws large crowds, the greatest struggle, of course, being against the old enemy, England, in a battle which takes place twice every four years - once in Australia and once in England - in a series of five five-day test matches, the reward for winning which is the title to the Ashes. The Ashes is a trophy reputedly containing the ashes of the stumps or bails from the first match in which Australia ever defeated England on English soil, on 29th August 1882, although probably it does not actually contain those ashes. The principal arena for cricket is the Melbourne Cricket Ground, built for the 1956 Olympic Games, and in which 97,000 spectators can be accommodated. However, other capital cities also have their famous cricket grounds - the Sydney Cricket Ground, the Gabba in Brisbane, the W.A.C.A. in Perth, and the Adelaide Oval.

In the winter Australia is divided between rugby and Australian Rules football. Rugby is the major sport in New South Wales and Queensland, while Victoria is the stronghold of Australian Rules football, with support from South Australia and Western Australia.

Australian Rules football is a fast and exciting game played on an oval field with an oval shaped ball. Two slightly different codes have teams of fifteen or eighteen players. The ball can be carried by players as long as they bounce it every ten metres (no mean feat) and it can be passed by being kicked or being punched, but not thrown. If another player catches a kicked ball, he may claim a 'mark' and have a free kick, and one of the most exciting moments in the sport is seeing players rise high into the air to take marks. At each end of the field are four goal posts in line. If the ball is kicked between the centre two posts, a goal is scored and six points awarded to the team kicking the goal. If the ball passes between one of the centre posts and an outer post, however, only a 'behind' is scored and just a single point is awarded. A game consists of four quarters of twenty-five minutes of actual playing time each.

Horse racing is popular in Australia, mostly as a sport on which to bet. Greyhound racing serves a similar purpose.

Australia has also produced some fine swimmers and tennis players over the years, as well as one or two famous golfers. As one might expect, surfing too is a sport at which Australians excel.

MAP SHOPS AND BOOKSHOPS

For the traveller, or even the would-be traveller, the map shops which can be found in Australia are fascinating places. There is at least one in every capital city, nearly always managed and staffed by wonderful eccentrics who know absolutely everything there is to know about maps, travel guides and travel in general.

As for general bookstores, in Australia, as in the rest of the world, there is a danger of the book trade being taken over by the large chains. For the reader, and for the small man like the author and publisher of this book, that is likely to mean limitations on choice. Basically, competition ensures the survival of quality and freedom of choice, so it is up to us all to give support to the small bookshops - the places where the owners know their businesses and can give good advice and service.

Mentioned in this book are the map shops and bookshops throughout Australia which have been willing to take the the author's previous publications and thereby help the small man and offer choice to the reader. If you need a book, please consider giving your support to these shops, in order to assist their survival in difficult circumstances.

NEW SOUTH WALES

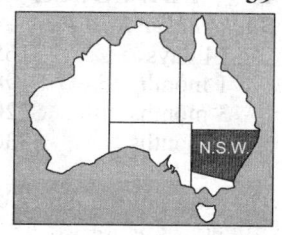

On 13th May 1787, Captain Arthur Phillip left England with eleven ships filled principally with soldiers and convicts. He landed successfully at Botany Bay on 18th January 1788, but found the position too exposed and moved to Port Jackson, a few kilometres further north, and established a new settlement there on 26th January 1788. The new settlement was to become Sydney and the new colony New South Wales, Sydney being named after Lord Sydney, the British Secretary of State for Home Affairs, who had authorised the colonisation scheme. There were 1,373 new settlers, of whom 732 were convicts.

Now New South Wales is the most populous of the Australian states with 6.5 million people, almost exactly one-third of the total population of Australia. Many visitors see only the coastal areas, but inland lies a different type of outback terrain well worth investigating. Your impression of the state, and indeed of Australia, will be totally different depending on whether you have simply followed the tourist groove up the coast or whether you have explored the splendour of the interior.

Transport

Transport in New South Wales is operated under the generic name of Countrylink. The only services not under the control of Countrylink are the city and medium-distance rail services around Sydney, which are operated by CityRail; the city and large town local bus services, the long-distance interstate bus services operated by McCafferty's, Greyhound, Premier, Firefly and Murray's; and just a few intra-state privately operated bus services.

Countrylink operates trains to Brisbane, Murwillumbah, Armidale, Moree, Dubbo, Broken Hill, Canberra, Griffith and Melbourne, and a network of bus connexions from those trains to places all over the state. If you purchase either a national or a state rail pass, you can use all of these services. With the national pass, you can use the CityRail metropolitan and medium-distance services as well. Here again is one of the basic misconceptions of visitors who think that if they purchase a rail pass they are restricted to using trains. That is not the case. Look at the map on page 41 and see just how many places you can reach in New South Wales - far more than are covered by the long-distance bus companies.

When you come to use these buses, you will find that they are not usually marked with the name of Countrylink. Countrylink lets contracts to local bus companies to operate them on its behalf. Nevertheless, they can be used by rail pass holders.

Countrylink offers passes for use for a fixed period, and also various journey passes with unlimited stops. These are well worth considering, since travel by train is more comfortable than travel by long-distance bus and the coverage of the state is far more comprehensive. The *Backtracker Rail Pass* is valid on all Countrylink services (including those which run beyond the state borders to Brisbane, Canberra, Melbourne and other places). It also has four vouchers for single journeys on CityRail services, but is available only to overseas residents, with prices as follows:

40   NEW SOUTH WALES
Backtracker Rail Pass
- 14 days $165
- 1 month $198
- 3 months $220
- 6 months $330

The prices of the *East Coast Discovery Passes* with unlimited stops are as follows.

East Coast Discovery Pass
- Sydney - Melbourne $93.50
- Sydney - Brisbane $93.50
- Sydney - Surfers Paradise $93.50
- Melbourne - Brisbane $176.00
- Melbourne - Surfers Paradise $176.00
- Melbourne - Cairns $374.00
- Sydney - Cairns $292.60
- Brisbane - Cairns $204.60

Only the passes to or from Cairns are available to Australian residents. The others are limited to overseas residents. All passes are valid for six months and can be used in either direction on Countrylink and Queensland Railways services, but without any back-tracking.

The long-distance bus companies offer passes too, but not specifically for New South Wales. There are, however, passes which run up the east coast from Sydney to Cairns. If you look around the travel agents in King's Cross in Sydney, you can often find such passes offered at discounted rates, and also discounted bus tickets to Brisbane and Melbourne.

SYDNEY
Population 4,000,000

10 hrs 30 mins by train from Melbourne
12 hrs by bus from Melbourne
14 hrs 30 mins by train from Brisbane
15 hrs by bus from Brisbane

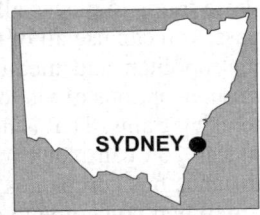

Sydney is the largest city in Australia. It contains four million people, more than one-fifth of the total population of the whole country. For many visitors, Sydney is the point of entry into Australia. Let us start, therefore, at the airport and get into town.

FROM THE AIRPORT

The first point to note is that Australia is very strict on the import of food and other animal and vegetable matter. The reason given for this is that Australia, as an island continent, has evolved in a different manner from the other continents and is free from certain diseases and pests which exist elsewhere. It does not want to introduce such problems now.

Formerly, immediately a flight landed, quarantine officers used to enter the aircraft

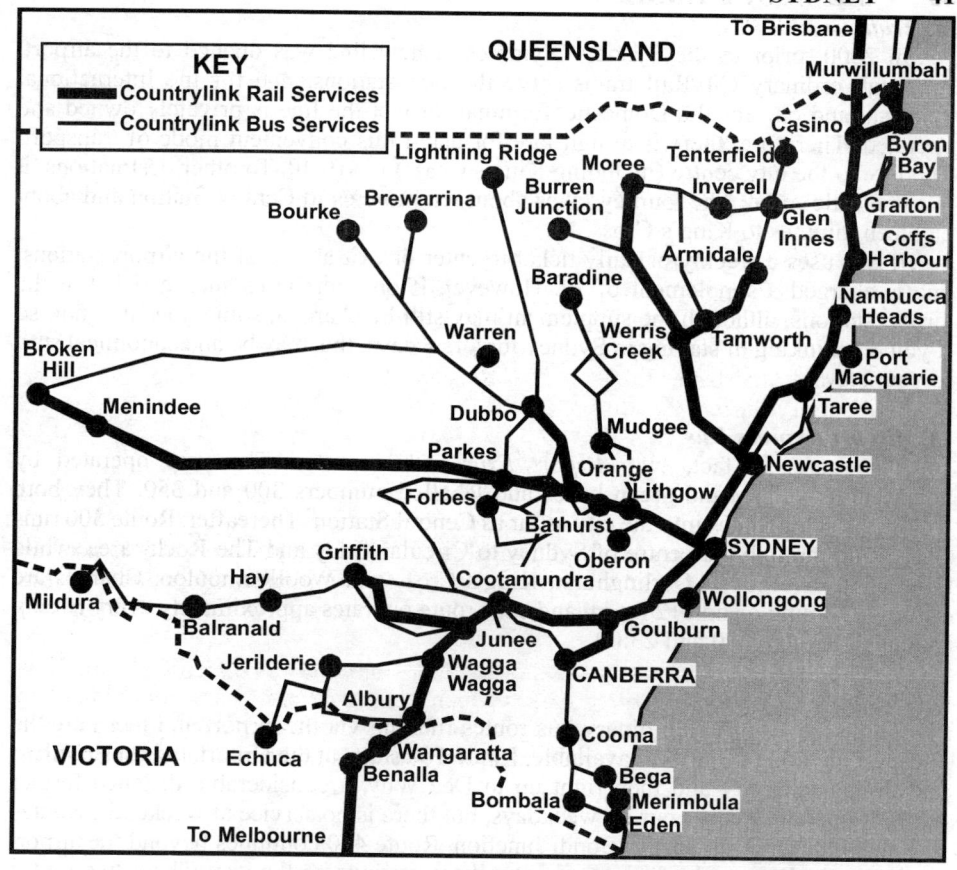

COUNTRYLINK SERVICES

and spray everything and everybody with a copious supply of fly killer. Any passenger who stood up prematurely and obstructed the officers in the execution of their insecticidal duties was dealt generous quantities of the spray as a reward. Spraying is not usually carried out now, although occasionally the can still appears. However, the prohibition on food remains strict. Certain items are permitted, in fact, but it is difficult to know which and the best advice is probably to carry in nothing edible at all.

Once immigration and customs have been negotiated, you will have the opportunity to exchange money. Rates at the airport do not differ significantly from those obtainable in the city, so this is as good a chance as any.

Next you will observe, in two slightly different locations, boards giving details of and advertisements for hotel accommodation and backpackers hostels. Choose whichever suits your budget and use the free telephones available. Many of these establishments will arrange to collect you from the airport, since it is only nine kilometres from the city centre. Others will give you instructions on how to make your own way to your destination. If you have to make your own arrangements, here are the options available.

NEW SOUTH WALES

(a) Train

In 2000, prior to the Sydney Olympics, a new line was opened to the airport. Although ordinary CityRail trains serve the two stations, one for the International Terminal and one for the Domestic Terminal, in fact the line is privately owned and operated. Therefore, there is a high fare for using this convenient mode of transport. The fare to the city centre (including King's Cross) is $10.40. To other destinations, it is just a little more. The journey takes about ten minutes to Central Station and about eighteen minutes to King's Cross.

If one uses a weekly or daily ticket to enter or exit at one of the airport stations, one is charged a supplement of $7. However, if one purchases such a ticket at the airport stations, although the supplement may still be charged, sometimes it is not, so if you are thinking of staying in Sydney for a few days, this may be an economical start to your stay.

(b) Airport Express Bus

There are, in fact, two *Airport Express* bus routes. They are operated by conspicuous yellow and green buses and labelled numbers 300 and 350. They both follow the same routes into the city as far as Central Station. Thereafter, Route 300 runs straight up through the centre of Sydney to Circular Quay and The Rocks area, while Route 350 diverges to Darlinghurst, King's Cross and Woolloomooloo. Charges are currently $7 single and $12 return and each route operates approximately every twenty minutes between 5:00 and 23:00.

(c) Ordinary City Bus

There are also three ordinary bus routes running via the airport and these are the cheapest method of transport available. Route 100 starts at the airport and runs north to and through the city and then right up to Dee Why, a considerable distance further north. It operates every hour on weekdays, but there is no service at weekends. Routes 353 and 400 run north-east to Bondi Junction. Route 400 continues beyond the airport north-west to Burwood, passing several railway stations on the way. These two routes operate every twenty to thirty minutes. The bus fare is determined by distance, but will be $2.60 or $3.40 to most likely destinations.

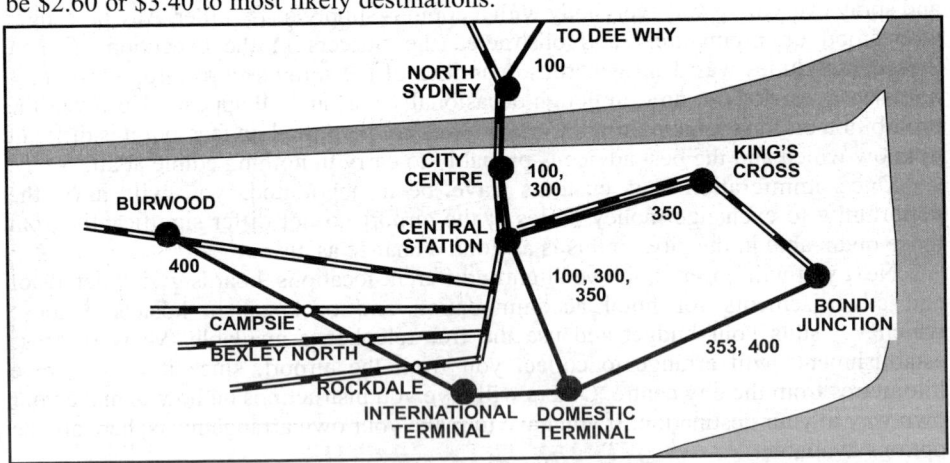

BUS SERVICES FROM AIRPORT, SHOWING RAIL CONNEXIONS

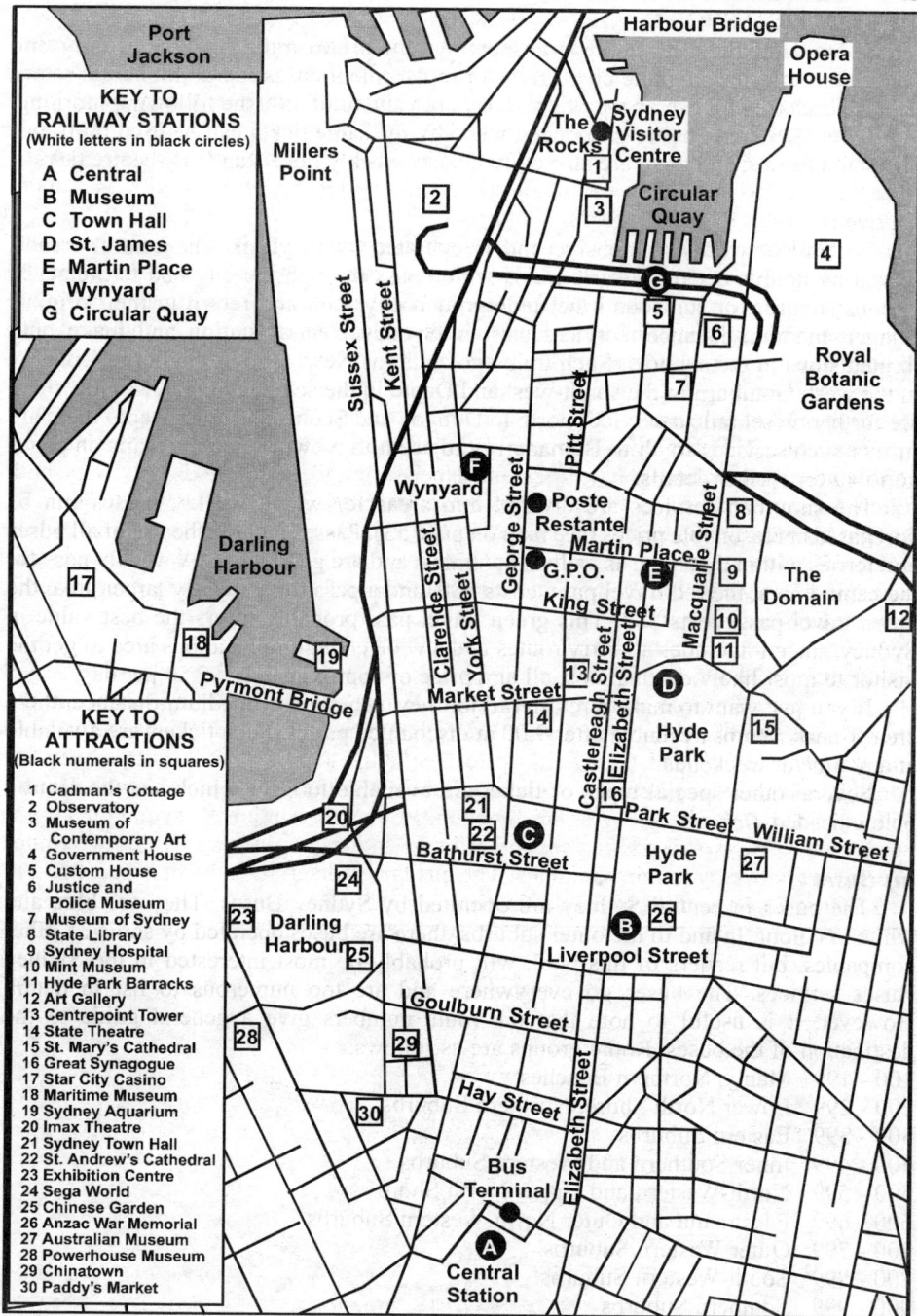

NEW SOUTH WALES
PUBLIC TRANSPORT

Sydney has the best public transport system in Australia, making it easy and convenient to get around the city. Trains or replacement buses run all night and return tickets purchased for use on a particular day are valid until 4:00 the following morning.

A new system is being introduced whereby the same ticket can be used on trains, buses and ferries, and there are also daily tickets, weekly tickets and city centre tickets.

(i) Trains

The rail network is extensive and is operated by CityRail. The central area is served by double-decker electric trains which pass through the city and terminate in various suburbs, or run round the underground city loop and return to their origins. Longer, medium-distance, services start in Sydney Central station and make only limited stops in the suburbs. Such trains go as far as Newcastle in the north, Lithgow in the west, Goulburn in the south-west and Dapto in the south. From Newcastle, there are further diesel railcar services north to Dungog and Scone, and from Dapto there are further such services south to Bomaderry (adjacent to Nowra). See the maps on pages 46 to 49 for further details.

The suburban services are divided into areas for which weekly passes can be purchased at reasonable prices (see map on page 53). Passes include the use of all buses and ferries within that area, as well as the trains, and are good value. A weekly pass for the central area, the red travel pass, costs $30, and a pass for a slightly larger area, the green travel pass, costs $38. This green travel pass probably offers the best value in Sydney, since it includes all ferry routes and a wide enough rail and bus area to get the visitor to most likely destinations, all at a price of approximately $5.50 per day.

If you just want to make a return rail journey, suburban or medium-distance, there are off-peak returns available after 9:00 at discounted prices. Such tickets are available at any time at weekends.

Several other special types of ticket are available too, for which see the section below headed *Tickets*.

(ii) Buses

The buses in central Sydney are operated by Sydney Buses. They are blue and white in colour. In and to the outer suburbs, there are buses operated by some 35 other companies, but readers of this book will probably be most interested in the Sydney Buses services. The buses go everywhere and are too numerous to list in detail. However, it is useful to note that the route numbers give a general guide to the destination of the buses. Route groups are as follows.

100 - 199	Manly, Northern Beaches
200 - 299	Lower North Shore, Northern Suburbs
300 - 399	Eastern Suburbs
400 - 499	Inner Southern and Western Suburbs
500 - 599	North-Western and Upper North Shore
600 - 699	Parramatta and Outer North-Western Suburbs
700 - 799	Outer Western Suburbs
800 - 899	South-Western Suburbs
900 - 999	Southern Suburbs

If you need assistance with buses, the telephone number to call is 131 500.

There are also weekly travel passes for buses and ferries only (without trains). Although these are slightly cheaper, the buses tend to be rather slow and tedious for long journeys. The blue travel pass corresponds to the red area mentioned above in the *Trains* section and costs $27 for a week, while the orange travel pass corresponds to the green area (but, of course without the train services) and costs $34. The third pass is called the *Pittwater Pass* and includes all Sydney Buses services and all ferry services. It costs $47.

In addition to the ordinary bus services, some special buses are operated by Sydney Buses, catering mainly to the requirements of visitors to the city. These services are the airport buses (green and yellow), which are routes 300 and 350, as mentioned at the start of this section, the Sydney Explorer bus (red) and the Bondi Explorer bus (blue). These buses are conspicuously different because of their colouring, and all require special tickets. They cannot be used with ordinary bus tickets or with travel passes. For further details, see the section below on *Tickets*.

(iii) Ferries

Sydney is a city which makes use of its harbour. Various ferry services operate, of which the most famous is the one to Manly. To this destination there are both conventional ferry services and *Jetcat* (fast catamaran) services. A *Rivercat* also operates to Parramatta in the west. To other destinations, only the traditional ferry services operate. The ferries are fun. They provide some beautiful views and they are also quite a quick way to reach the points which they serve. The city terminal is at Circular Quay, easily reached by train. For a diagram of services, see below.

The conventional ferry services can be used with all of the travel passes, except that with the red and blue passes one cannot travel as far as Parramatta or Manly. Conventional ferries to Manly can be used with other passes at any time, but the *Jetcats* are available only after 19:00.

Harbour cruises are also operated by the ferry company. Morning cruises last one hour and cost $15. Afternoon cruises last for two and a half hours and cost $22. Evening cruises last for one and a half hours and cost $19. However, only with the afternoon cruise will you get to places which you cannot reach on an ordinary ferry.

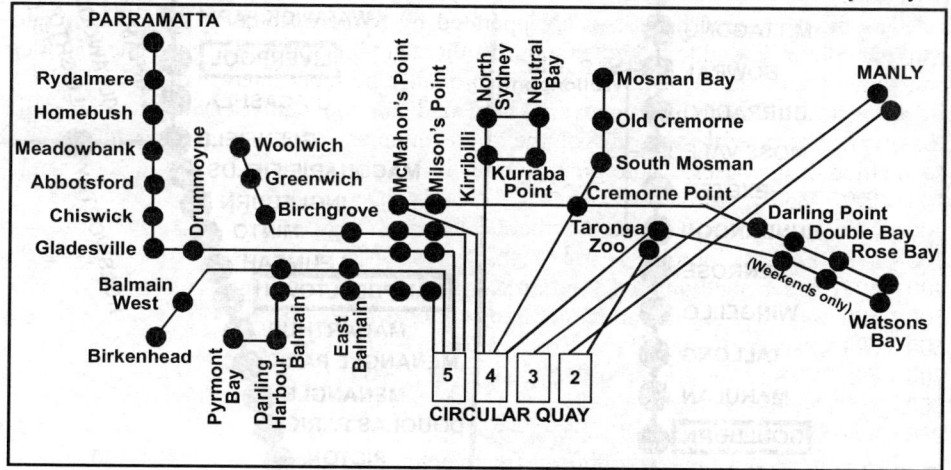

SYDNEY FERRY SERVICES

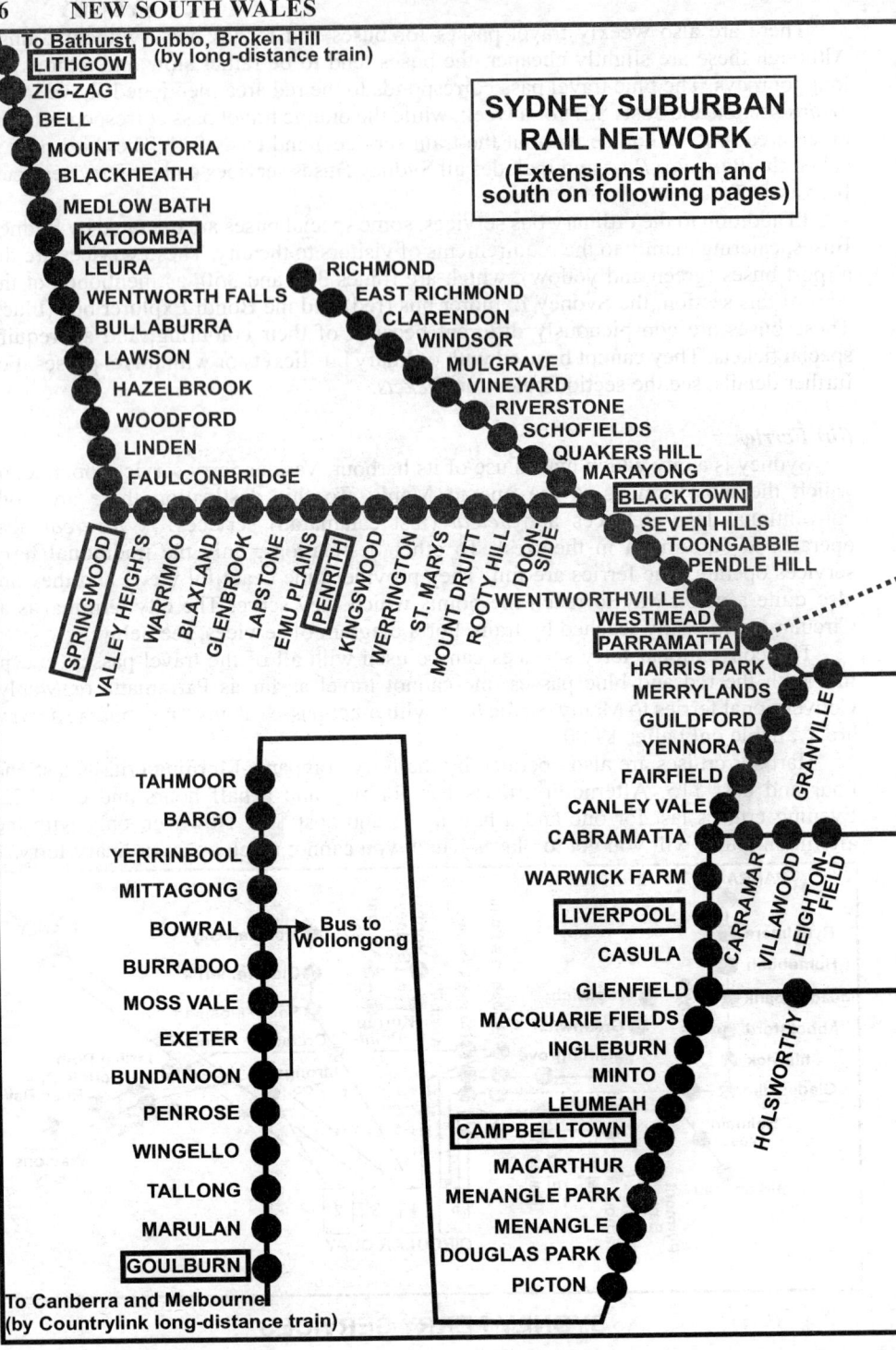

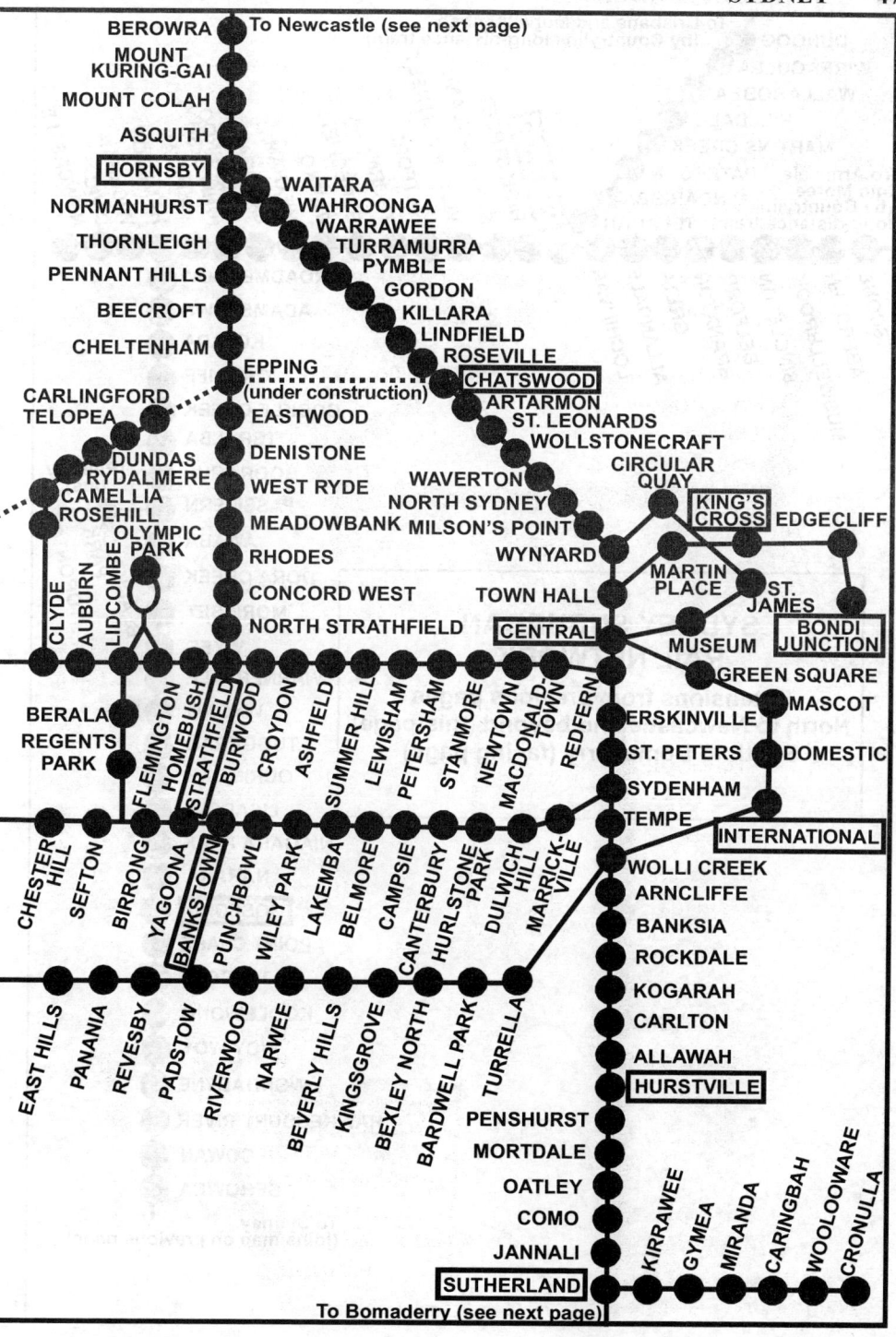

48 NEW SOUTH WALES

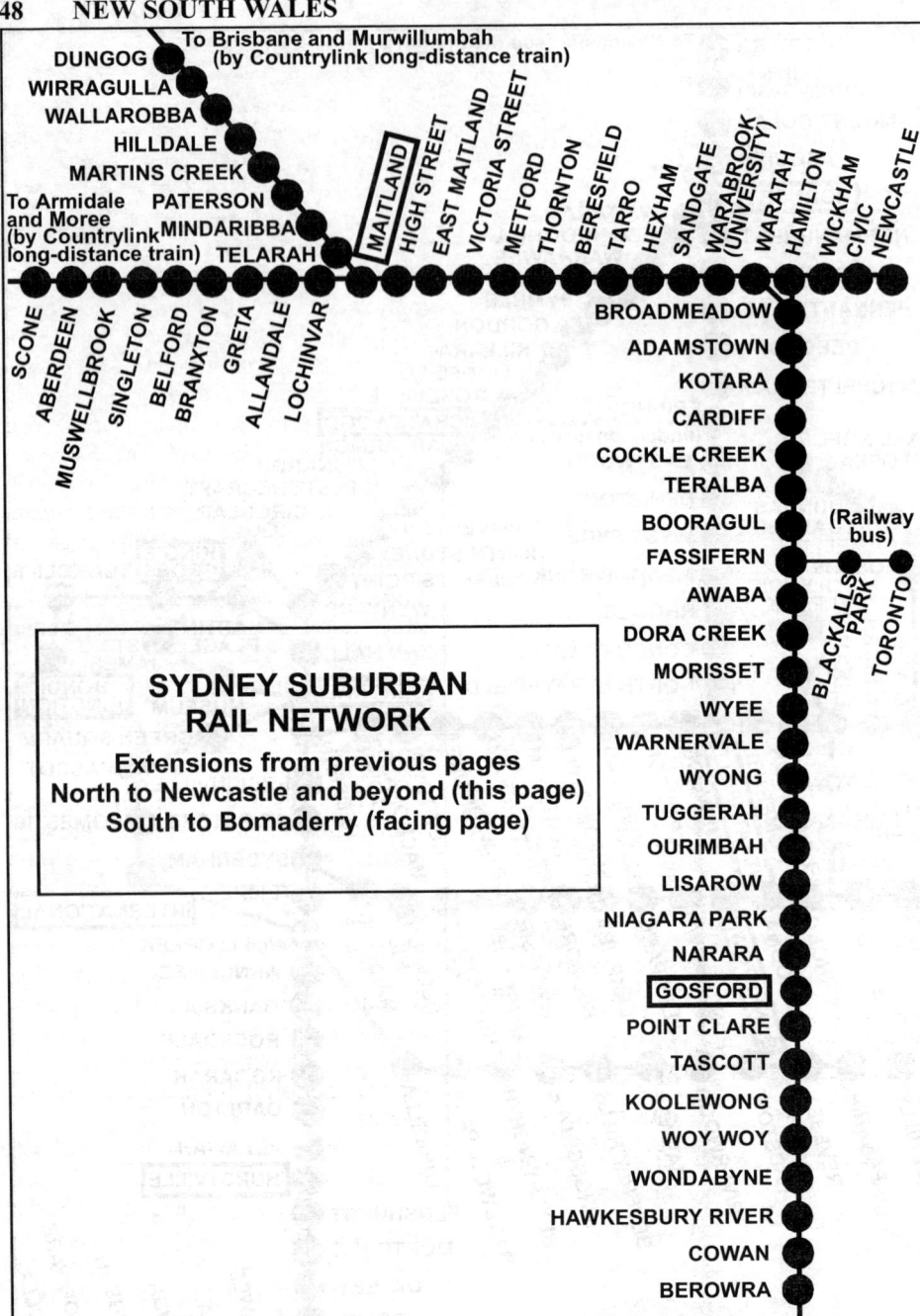

SYDNEY

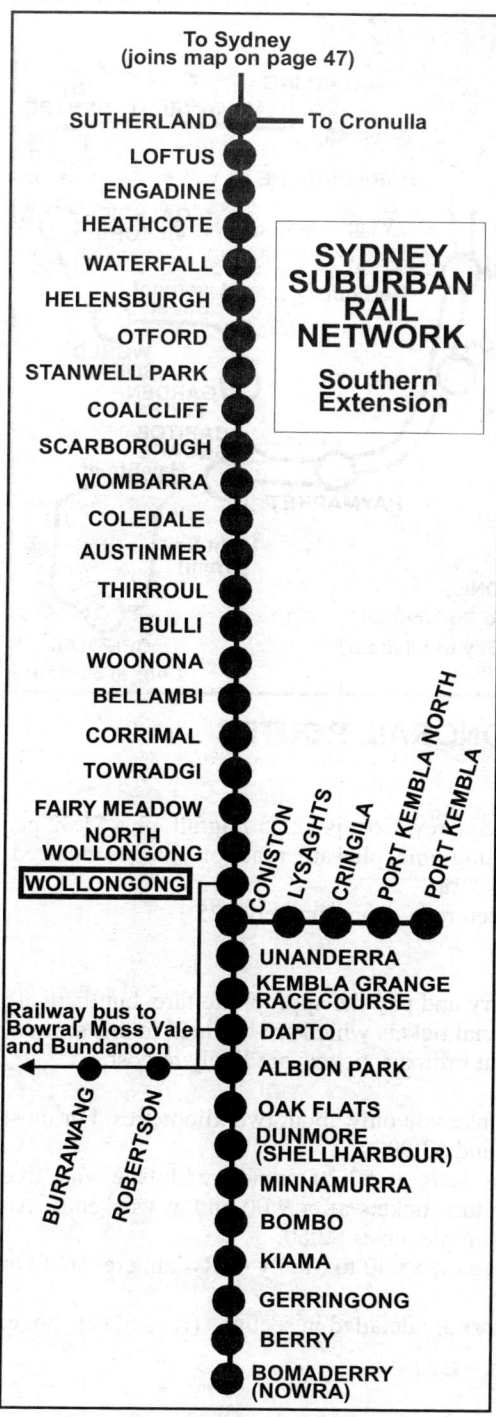

(iv) Light Rail (Tram)

Recently, in August 1997, one tram route was reinstated in Sydney. It runs from Central Station via Darling Harbour to Lilyfield, a distance of 6.7 kilometres (see diagram on page 50). This service operates 24 hours per day every day of the year. However, between 23:00 and 6:00 services go only as far as Star City. Frequency is every ten to fifteen minutes during the day and every thirty minutes at night.

Unfortunately, fares are relatively high. There are two zones, as shown on the diagram on the next page. Fares are $2.60 single or $3.60 return within a single zone. A ride which covers parts of both zones costs $3.60 single or $4.90 return. A day ticket costs $8 and a weekly ticket costs $19. Tickets for other forms of public transport cannot be used on the tram, except for a weekly tram plus monorail ticket, which costs $28.

(v) Monorail

The elevated monorail service which runs round the city centre was opened in July 1988 and is operated by the same company as the tram (*Connex*). It runs every three to five minutes between 7:00 and 22:00 (later on Thursday to Saturday nights). The operator claims that four million people use the service every year, but actually you can walk between any two stations on the monorail route in only a few minutes.

A single trip of up to one complete circuit, which takes twelve minutes, costs $4 and a day ticket costs $8, the latter also offering some discounts on local purchases. A *Metrocard* offers six trips for $18. Tickets for other forms of public transport cannot be used on the monorail, except for the weekly ticket offering the use of both tram and monorail for $28.

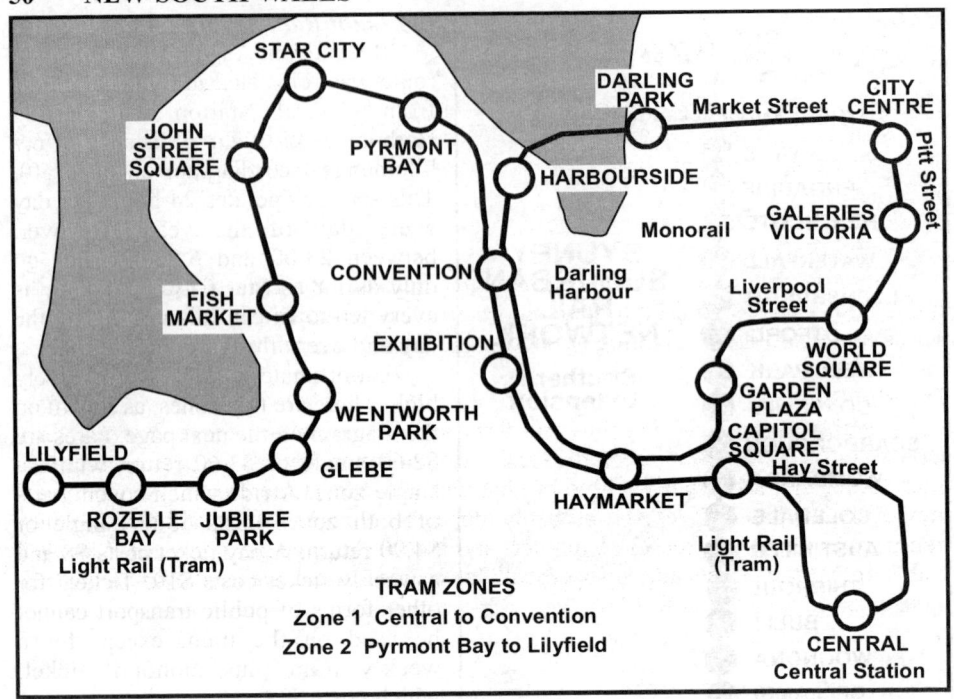

TRAM AND MONORAIL ROUTES

(vi) Taxis

There are plenty of taxis available in Sydney. Cost is $2.35 flagfall, plus $1.32 per kilometre and 62 cents per minute for waiting time, plus any road toll charges incurred. Summoning a taxi by telephone costs $1 extra.

The fare to the airport from the city centre is approximately $25.

(vii) Tickets

You can just get on a bus, train or ferry and pay the appropriate fare, but there are ways of saving money by purchasing special tickets which are outlined in this section. First, though, for comparison, here is what ordinary tickets are likely to cost.

Bus Fares start at $1.50, which will take you only about two kilometres. For most journeys, the fare will be between $2.60 and $3.90.

Train Fares are by distance. Fares start at $2.20, which will take you five kilometres. You can purchase off-peak return tickets after 9:00 and at weekends. An off-peak return for five kilometres, for example, costs $2.60.

Ferry Fares are $4.30 per shorter journey, $5.40 to Manly or Rydalmere, $6.40 to Parramatta and $6.70 to Manly by *Jetcat*.

Light Rail (Tram) and Monorail Fares are detailed in sections (iv) and (v) above.

SYDNEY 51

Special Tickets
The following special tickets are available.

TravelTen and FerryTen Tickets
These are tickets giving ten trips at the same fare on buses or ferries. *TravelTen* (for buses) offers discounts of about 25%. *FerryTen* (for ferries) offers discounts of 20% to 35%.

Seven Day Rail Passes
These passes are weekly tickets for a specified rail journey at about 7.5 times the single fare. There is no limit to the number of journeys which can be made within the period and boarding or alighting at intermediate stations is permitted.

Travel Passes
Travel passes cover train, bus and ferry services, or, alternatively, bus and ferry services only, within the chosen area for a period of seven days. If the pass is purchased after 15:00, the ticket may be used on that day, plus seven more days. As mentioned previously, the green travel pass probably represents the best value available in Sydney transport, as this is a ticket for commuters and it does not have the high rates associated with some of the tickets aimed specifically at visitors. Areas are as shown on the map on page 53. Prices are as follows.

Red Travel Pass	$30
Green Travel Pass	$38
Yellow Travel Pass	$42
Pink Travel Pass	$45
Purple Travel Pass	$52
Blue Travel Pass	$27 (same as red area, but trains not included)
Orange Travel Pass	$34 (same as green area, but trains not included)
Pittwater Travel Pass	$47 (all buses and ferries; no trains)

BusTripper
This is a one-day ticket for use on all Sydney Buses, except special services. It costs $10.

DayTripper
This is a one-day ticket for use on all Sydney Buses, except special services, all ferries except the Manly *Jetcat* before 19:00, and suburban rail services in the area covered by the Purple Travel Pass. The ticket costs $14.

CityHopper
This is a one-day ticket for trains and Sydney Buses within a small central city area, the limits of which are the stations of Redfern, North Sydney and King's Cross. There are two types of ticket: peak and off-peak. The peak ticket costs $6.40, while the off-peak ticket (after 9:00) costs $4.60. It is also possible to purchase the ticket from railway stations outside the area and include return travel to the city. Rates vary according to the length of the journey involved. You cannot break your journey outside the *CityHopper* area.

Sydney Explorer

The *Sydney Explorer* is a special bus service which travels round all the interesting sights of the city and King's Cross, crosses the harbour by the tunnel and returns via the Harbour Bridge. There is a commentary and the buses run every twenty minutes and are a conspicuous red colour. If you complete the whole circuit, it will take approximately one hour and forty-five minutes, but you do not need to go all the way round on one bus. You can get on and off as you please. You can also use any ordinary buses which are operating along the same route, except across the bridge and through the tunnel. *Sydney Explorer* buses operate from 8:40 until 17:30, but you can continue to use the ticket on ordinary buses until midnight.

Unfortunately, the cost is $30 for a one-day ticket. Bear in mind that for the same price you can buy a ticket (Travel Pass, above) for a whole week which will cover bus, train and ferry in a much wider area. All you will be missing is the commentary and something of the convenience of a bus which visits all the sites in turn.

Bondi Explorer

Building on the success of the *Sydney Explorer*, the *Bondi Explorer* offers much the same service for the Bondi area. The *Bondi Explorer* starts from Circular Quay and then goes round the coastline on a 30 kilometre circular route, a journey which takes two hours. Again there is commentary and again you can get on and off as you please. The *Bondi Explorer* buses are blue and operate approximately every thirty minutes from 9:15 until 16:30. You can also use ordinary buses operating along the same route, again up until midnight, and once again the cost is $30 for a one-day ticket. The same comment about the Travel Pass applies.

A two-day Twin Ticket is also available. This costs $50 and allows the use of both *Explorer* services for two days (both services on both days). The two days do not need to be consecutive, but the second day must be within six days of the first.

Sydney Pass

This is a ticket which combines the services comprised in the red Travel Pass with other special services for visitors. Specifically, the *Sydney Pass* covers:

- Trains, buses and ferries within the red Travel Pass area.
- *Airport Express* bus. Unlimited travel during the validity, plus one return trip outside the validity of the *Sydney Pass*.
- *Sydney Explorer* services.
- *Bondi Explorer* services.
- *Jetcat* ferries as well as conventional ferries.
- Sydney harbour cruises.

For a one-week period, this ticket costs $140. It can also be purchased for a period of three days for $90 or five days for $120. For these two periods the days do not need to be consecutive. They can be at any time within a one-week period.

Bearing in mind that this ticket includes a free return trip from the airport, the return to be completed within two months, if you intend to use the *Sydney Pass* and are arriving by air, you should purchase at the airport and use the ticket to travel into town.

ZooPass

This ticket includes the return ferry across the harbour and admission to Taronga Zoo, with the *Sky Safari* ride. It costs $30.

AquariumPass

This ticket includes the return ferry ride to Darling Harbour (which can actually be reached quite easily on foot) and admission to Sydney Aquarium. It costs $29.

ATTRACTIONS

Sydney has a great deal to offer, not only in terms of history, but also in natural beauty. If it were not for all those people, Sydney would be a beautiful rustic estuary and one does not have to go far to experience the attraction of the location. If you have not already done so after reading the section above relating to transport, purchase a Travel Pass and start with a ferry ride. You will immediately begin to appreciate Sydney.

There is so much to see that it is difficult to know where to start, but best to begin in the centre and work our way out.

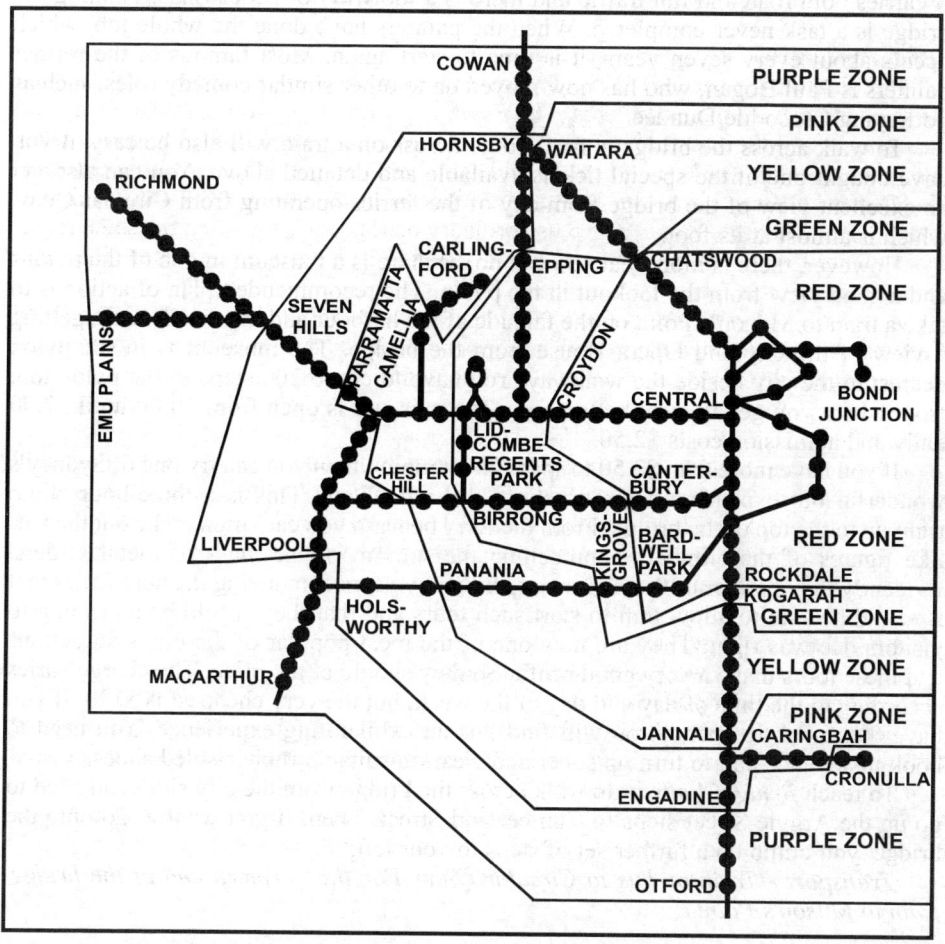

TRAVEL PASS ZONES

The Opera House *(marked on map on page 43)*

This famous landmark was completed in 1973, having taken fourteen years to construct. The architect, Joern Utzon, included in his design the surfacing of the 'sails' with more than a million ceramic tiles, which were imported from Sweden. Tours are available, lasting one hour and departing once or twice every hour. Many concerts are available too - 3,000 per year of all types. They range from small free concerts to lavish operatic performances.

Transport - Train or bus to Circular Quay. Sydney Explorer, Stop 2.

Sydney Harbour Bridge *(marked on map on page 43)*

The other famous landmark of Sydney is the Harbour Bridge, which took nine years to build and was opened in 1932. It is 502 metres long and 48.8 metres wide and it weighs 52,800 tonnes. The top is 134 metres above sea level. It carries both road and rail traffic and there is a footway for pedestrians. Painting the bridge is a task never completed. When the painters have done the whole job, which occurs about every seven years, it is time to start again. Most famous of the former painters is Paul Hogan, who has now moved on to other similar comedy roles, such as portraying Crocodile Dundee.

To walk across the bridge is free. To go across on a train will also be easy, if you have bought one of the special tickets available and detailed above. You can also get an excellent view of the bridge from any of the ferries operating from Circular Quay, which is almost at its foot.

However, there is more that you can do, as there is a museum in one of the pylons and a good view from the lookout in the pylon. The recommended plan of action is to take a train to Milson's Point on the far side of the harbour and then walk back, getting a view of the city and Opera House from the bridge. The museum is in the pylon nearest to the city beside the walkway. You have to climb 200 steps to the pylon top, from where you get an even better view. The museum is open from 10:00 until 17:00 daily and admission costs $2.50.

If you have more than $2.50 to spare - a lot more - then you can try one of Sydney's wonderful but expensive new attractions - *BridgeClimb*. This is a three-hour climb right up to the top of the bridge. From the ferry beneath you can often make out the ant-like figures of the climbers approaching the summit of the mass of metal girders. Evidently the operator of these climbs spent many years convincing the authorities that it would be safe to allow him to start such tours and that they would be appealing to visitors. He was right. They are now one of the most popular of the city's attractions and these tours make a very good profit. So they should at the price. The charge varies according to the time of day and day of the week, but the very cheapest is $120. If you have that much to spend, you will find this an exhilarating experience. You need to book in advance and to turn up sober and wearing suitable rubber-soled shoes.

To reach *BridgeClimb*, or to walk across the bridge from the city side, you need to go up the Argyle Street steps to Cumberland Street. Then, if you want to go onto the bridge, you climb up a further set of steps to your left.

Transport - Train or bus to Circular Quay. For the northern end of the bridge, train to Milson's Point.

▲ Circular Quay, Sydney

Sydney Harbour ▼

▲ *Tin Hare* operating between Canberra and Royalla (p. 223)
Backpacker Luxury in Surfers Paradise (p. 248) ▼

▲ *Tilt Train*, Queensland

Emerald Station, Queensland (p. 304) ▼

▲ From the Footplate of Ravenshoe to Tumoulin Train, Queensland (p. 374)
Lord Howe Island, N.S.W., Mt. Lidgbird (left) and Mt. Gower (right) (p. 214) ▼

SYDNEY

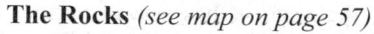

The Rocks *(see map on page 57)*

The Rocks is one of the oldest areas of Sydney. Lying beside the harbour in a central location, it was naturally one of the first places to be settled.

When the first fleet arrived on 26th January 1788, the new arrivals, led by Captain Arthur Phillip, constructed their first wooden shacks along the natural rock ledges near the water's edge. Therefore, the area became known as 'The Rocks' and Sydney's first named street was here - George Street, in honour of the British monarch of the time, King George III.

The first shacks did not survive long, and by the 1840s they had been replaced by sandstone structures. These are the buildings some of which survive now. In 1900, there was an outbreak of bubonic plague and many houses were demolished in the subsequent cleansing. Then, over the years, the older buildings fell into a state of disrepair and at one time it was suggested that total demolition would be the solution. Fortunately, though, the alternative view prevailed and the area has been renovated and turned into a thriving tourist attraction, full of souvenir shops and cafés, galleries and museums.

Every weekend there is a market in George Street. There is street entertainment and a whole range of food available. It is, though, touristic, and it is not an area where you are likely to pick up a lot of bargains. Nevertheless, the little twisting alleys and old courtyards are definitely worth visiting, having an old-world character which is not often found in Australia.

The map on page 57 shows The Rocks area in detail, with some of the more prominent buildings marked. The main Sydney Visitor Centre is here, at 106 George Street (see map) and is a place to visit. It has comprehensive information not only on Sydney but for the whole of New South Wales. Opening hours are 9:00 until 18:00 every day.

There are walking tours of The Rocks available, but they cost $15 for a ninety-minute tour. There is even a night-time ghost tour. Cheaper, though, is to just set out and explore by yourself, perhaps with the assistance of *The Rocks Self-Guided Walking Tour*, obtainable from the abovementioned Sydney Visitor Centre for the sum of $2.50, perhaps just by wandering at random, or perhaps by following the walk suggested on page 73.

The following few attractions lie within The Rocks area but merit their own individual entries.

Transport - *Train or bus to Circular Quay.*

Cadman's Cottage *(see map on page 57)*

This is one of Sydney's oldest surviving buildings, dating from 1816. It was built to house the Government Coxswain, who had the important task of organising all the water transport on the harbour. The cottage was named after the third and longest-serving such coxswain, the ex-convict John Cadman.

Originally the cottage was at the water's edge, but it is now

56 NEW SOUTH WALES

100 metres back from the harbour. Over the years it has served various purposes, including acting as a court and as a sailors' home. It became disused in the 1960s, but has now been taken over by the Sydney Harbour National Park, excavated and restored. It also serves, on its upper level, as the Information Office for the Sydney Harbour National Park. It is open from 9:30 until 16:30 and admission is free.

Transport - Train or bus to Circular Quay. Sydney Explorer, Stop 25.

The Museum of Contemporary Art *(see map opposite)*

This 1930s building used to be the home of the Maritime Services Board, but has served in its present capacity since 1991. Opening hours are 10:00 until 17:00 (16:00 in winter) and admission is free, except to special exhibitions.

Transport - Train or bus to Circular Quay.

The Bounty *(see map opposite)*

The Bounty is a replica of Captain Bligh's ship, recreated to star in the film *Mutiny on the Bounty*. Now it serves as a floating restaurant, sailing out onto the harbour at meal times. It is not cheap to eat here, but admiring from a distance is free. The ship is based in Campbell's Cove.

Transport - Train or bus to Circular Quay. Sydney Explorer, Stop 24.

Sydney Observatory *(see map opposite)*

Perched up on Observatory Hill above The Rocks is the Sydney Observatory. The hill commands a fine view of the harbour. It is the site of a former fortification, with the remnants of a wall constructed in 1804. The observatory can be visited free during the day between 10:00 and 17:00. In the evening, there are tours which include astronomical viewing and which cost $10.

Transport - Train or bus to Circular Quay.

Susannah Place *(see map opposite)*

Susannah Place is a group of terraced houses retaining the traditional atmosphere of The Rocks and now converted into a museum. It is in Gloucester Street, overshadowed by the elevated highway leading to the Harbour Bridge. Nearby you can explore the narrow alleys of this area, passing through such lanes as Suez Canal, for example, at the mouth of which two pedestrians can barely pass. Admission to Susannah Place costs $7. Alternatively, one may purchase the *Ticket Through Time* for $23 and gain admission to this and ten other museums in Sydney.

Transport - Train or bus to Circular Quay.

Customs House *(no. 5 on map on page 43)*

Customs House is right outside Circular Quay Station and dates in part from 1840. It is now used as an exhibition centre and restaurant area and is open from 9:30 until 17:00. Object Galleries on the third floor has Australia's largest exhibition of craft and design and is free. The City Exhibition Space on the fourth floor is also free and has an intricate model of the entire city area. Just to the west of Customs House, in Loftus Street, is the spot where the British flag was first raised by the new settlers on 26th January 1788. A plaque commemorates the precise location.

Transport - Train or bus to Circular Quay.

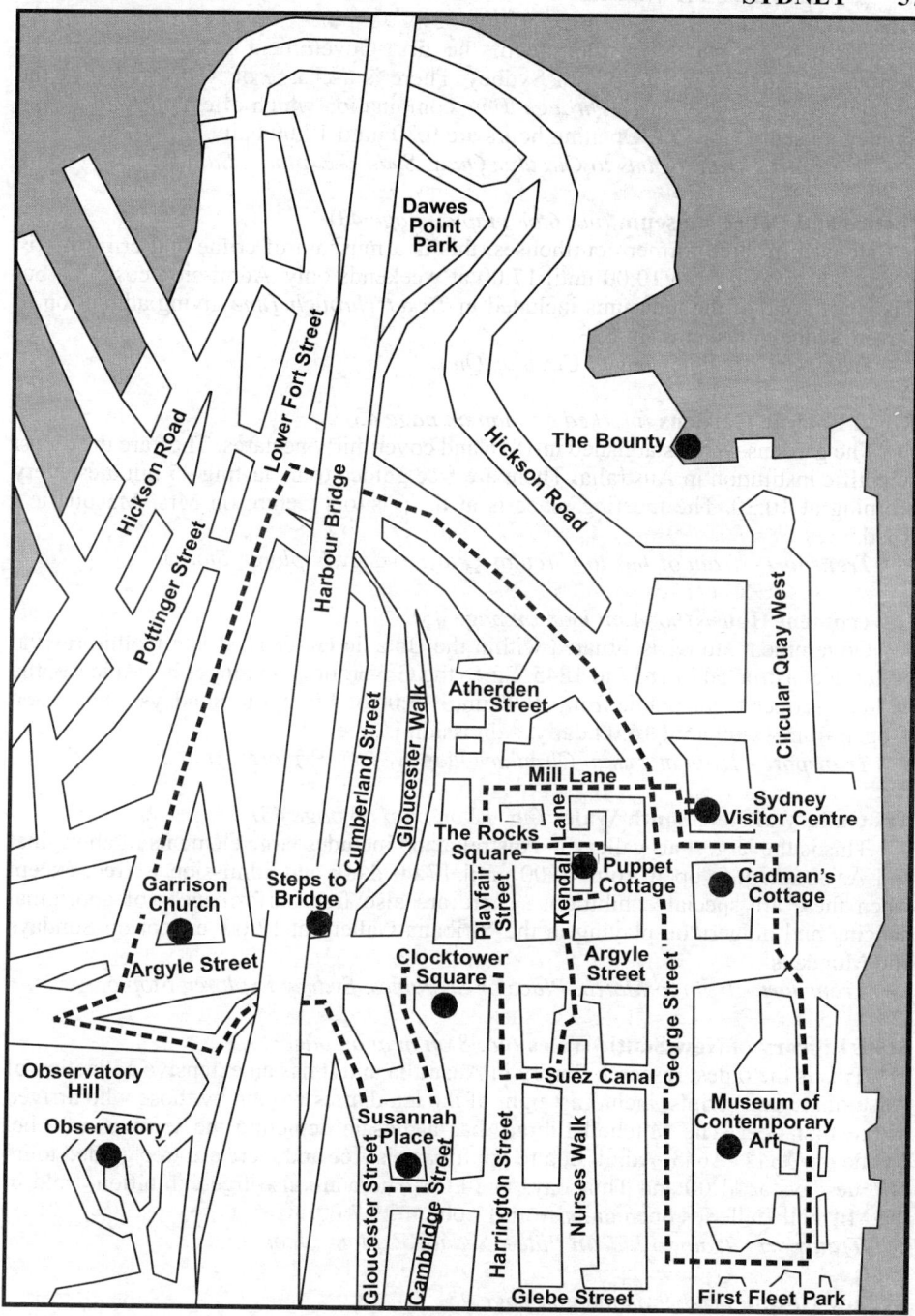

THE ROCKS
Dashed line shows Rocks Walk on page 73

NEW SOUTH WALES

Museum of Sydney *(no. 7 on map on page 43)*

The museum stands on the site of the first Government House and contains exhibitions showing the history of Sydney. There is a charge of $7 for entry, or the museum is part of the *Ticket Through Time* combination which offers entry to eleven Sydney museums for $23. Opening hours are 9:30 until 17:00 daily.

Transport - Train or bus to Circular Quay. Sydney Explorer, Stop 3.

Justice and Police Museum *(no. 6 on map on page 43)*

Housed in three former courthouses, this is a museum of crime and criminals in Sydney. It is open from 10:00 until 17:00 at weekends only. Admission costs $7, but this is also one of the museums included in *Ticket Through Time* giving admission to eleven Sydney museums for $23.

Transport - Train or bus to Circular Quay.

Royal Botanic Gardens *(marked on map on page 43)*

The gardens were established in 1816 and cover thirty hectares. They are the oldest scientific institution in Australia. There are free guided tours lasting 45 minutes every morning at 10:30. The meeting place is at the Visitors Centre on Mrs. Macquarie's Road.

Transport - Train or bus to Circular Quay. Sydney Explorer, Stop 5.

Government House *(no. 4 on map on page 43)*

Government House is situated within the Botanic Gardens. It is a Gothic revival building constructed in 1837 to 1845. Since the Governor is no longer in residence, the building is open to the public from 10:00 until 15:00 on Fridays to Sundays. The garden is open from 10:00 until 16:00 daily. Admission is free.

Transport - Train or bus to Circular Quay. Sydney Explorer, Stop 2.

Art Gallery of New South Wales *(no. 12 on map on page 43)*

This is the largest art gallery in Australia and includes large elements of aboriginal and Asian art. It is open from 10:00 until 17:00 daily and admission is free, except when there are special exhibitions. There are also free performances of aboriginal dancing and didgeridoo playing in the Yiribana Gallery at 12:00, except on Sundays and Mondays.

Transport - Train to Martin Place or St. James. Sydney Explorer, Stop 6.

State Library of New South Wales *(no. 8 on map on page 43)*

This is the oldest research library in Australia and it has an extensive collection of Australian manuscripts, including eight of the ten diaries written by those who arrived in the first fleet. The Mitchell Library has a mosaic depicting the voyages of Abel Tasman in 1642 - 1643. Admission to the library is free and there are free guided tours on Tuesdays at 11:00 and Thursdays at 14:00. There are also free exhibitions held in the Mitchell Galleries open daily from 11:00 until 17:00.

Transport - Train to Martin Place. Sydney Explorer, Stop 4.

Sydney Hospital *(no. 9 on map on page 43)*

Hopefully you will not be needing this landmark, most of which was constructed in 1894, for its principal purpose. Its most interesting feature is the Florence

SYDNEY 59

Nightingale Wing, adjacent to the courtyard, which was built to Florence Nightingale's specifications in order to house the nurses who were sent to Australia in 1868.
Transport - *Train to Martin Place. Sydney Explorer, Stop 4.*

Hyde Park Barracks *(no. 11 on map on page 43)*
This building originally housed convicts. It was designed in 1819 by Governor Macquarie and a convict architect named Francis Greenway. Now it is a museum of Australian history, with particular emphasis on the life of Francis Greenway and the history of this building. Opening hours are 9:30 until 17:00. Admission costs $7, or $23 for this and ten other museums with the *Ticket Through Time*.
Transport - *Train to St. James. Sydney Explorer, Stop 4.*

St. Mary's Cathedral *(no. 15 on map on page 43)*
The first cathedral was burnt down. This, the second, was started in 1868, but the spires were not added until 2000. Entry to the cathedral is free. The most impressive feature is the floor of the crypt, a mosaic undertaken by Melocco Brothers. It depicts the creation and took sixteen years to complete, being finished in 1946. The crypt is open (free) from 10:00 until 16:00. There are free tours of the cathedral on Sundays at 12:00.
Transport - *Train to St. James. Sydney Explorer, Stop 4 or 7.*

Hyde Park *(marked on map on page 43)*
Named after Hyde Park in London, this area was declared a park as early as 1792 and Australia's first recorded cricket match was played here in 1804. The team has improved a great deal since then.
Transport - *Train to St. James or Museum. Sydney Explorer, Stop 7.*

Anzac War Memorial *(no. 26 on map on page 43)*
This sturdy and imposing building is the state's moving tribute to those who have lost their lives fighting for their country, especially those who died with the first Anzac force at Gallipoli and during the remainder of the Great War. The monument was erected in 1934 and is at the south end of Hyde Park. There is a small war museum in the base of the monument. It is open from 9:00 until 16:30 and admission is free. Free guided tours are also available.
Transport - *Train to Museum. Sydney Explorer, Stop 7.*

Australian Museum *(no. 27 on map on page 43)*
This museum deals with Australian natural history and the culture of the aboriginal people. It is open from 9:30 until 17:00 daily. Admission costs $8.
Transport - *Train to St. James or Museum. Sydney Explorer, Stop 7.*

AMP Centrepoint Tower *(no. 13 on map on page 43)*
The AMP Tower has the tallest observation deck in the southern hemisphere. The tower itself stands 305 metres. It took fourteen years to build, the observation deck being opened in August 1981. The turret weighs 2,259 tonnes and is held by 56 cables, each weighing seven tonnes. It includes a tank holding 162,000 litres of water to act as a counterbalance to strong winds. Views from here extend to the Pacific Ocean in the east, Wollongong in the south and the Blue Mountains in the west. There is also a

60   NEW SOUTH WALES

Virtual Reality Skytour and there are two revolving restaurants. Down below, there is a complex of 140 shops. The tower is open from 9:00 until 22:30. Admission to the observation deck and *Skytour* costs $20. Guided tours are included in the price.
   Transport - Train to St. James. Sydney Explorer, Stop 4 or 15.

State Theatre *(no. 14 on map on page 43)*
   The State Theatre is a grand building constructed in 1929. It boasts the second largest glass chandelier in the world. There are self-guided tours, using audio equipment, which last about 45 minutes and cost $12. Unless performances intervene, the theatre is open from 10:00 until 16:30 on Mondays to Fridays and 10:00 until 14:00 on Saturdays.
   Transport - Train to St. James. Sydney Explorer, Stop 4 or 15.

Great Synagogue *(no. 16 on map on page 43)*
   The synagogue dates from 1878. There are free guided tours on Tuesdays and Fridays at 12:00.
   Transport - Train to St. James or Museum. Sydney Explorer, Stop 7 or 15.

Town Hall *(no. 21 on map on page 43)*
   The Town Hall was constructed to celebrate Sydney's centenary in 1888 and is an imposing edifice, both outside and in. It contains an 8,000-pipe organ, one of the largest in the world, and there are free lunchtime organ recitals held frequently. The Town Hall may be viewed inside between 9:00 and 17:00. There is no charge.
   Transport - Train to Town Hall. Sydney Explorer, Stop 15.

St. Andrew's Cathedral *(no. 22 on map on page 43)*
   St. Andrew's Cathedral was commenced in 1819, but not completed until 49 years later. There is a flag within which was carried at the Gallipoli landings. Admission to the cathedral is free.
   Transport - Train to Town Hall. Sydney Explorer, Stop 15.

Darling Harbour *(marked on map on page 43)*
   Darling Harbour is an area of Sydney which has recently been redeveloped. It now has a very appealing appearance and offers a number of attractions, immediately following this entry. On Wednesday to Sunday evenings there is a free display of sound, lasers, film and water projected onto waterscreens in Cockle Bay.
   Transport - Train to Town Hall. Sydney Explorer, Stops 18 to 23. Ferry, tram and monorail.

Sydney Aquarium *(no. 19 on map on page 43)*
   This is one of the largest aquaria in the world. Its most famous residents are sharks, but there are all types of fishes, as well as seals and penguins, and extensive underwater glass tunnels. The aquarium is open from 9:00 until 22:00 and admission costs $25.
   Transport - Train to Town Hall. Sydney Explorer, Stop 21. Ferry to Darling Harbour. Monorail to Darling Park.

SYDNEY

Panasonic Imax *(no. 20 on map on page 43)*
   A screen ten times as large as that in a conventional cinema is housed in an eight-storey high building. Film shows start every hour on the hour from 10:00 until 22:00 and last for 45 minutes to 75 minutes. Admission costs from $15 to $17.50.
   Transport - Train to Town Hall. Sydney Explorer, Stop 22. Ferry to Darling Harbour. Monorail or tram to Convention.

Sega World *(no. 24 on map on page 43)*
   This is a indoor theme park full of various electronic games and open from 11:00 until 20:00.
   Transport - Train to Town Hall. Sydney Explorer, Stop 22. Monorail to Garden Plaza. Tram to Exhibition.

Powerhouse Museum *(no. 28 on map on page 43)*
   This is Australia's largest museum. With 380,000 exhibits, although not all on display at any one time, it covers everything. It is open from 10:00 until 17:00 daily and admission costs $9, but you can often find vouchers in tourist publications or at the Sydney Visitor Centre giving a small discount. The museum is free on the first Saturday of every month.
   Transport - Train to Town Hall. Sydney Explorer, Stop 21. Monorail to Haymarket. Tram to Exhibition.

Australian National Maritime Museum *(no. 18 on map on page 43)*
   Lots of boats and ships here, including *Australia II*, which won the America's Cup, and the huge destroyer *H.M.A.S. Vampire*. You can take sailing lessons and at the weekend you can go for short voyages on historic vessels. The museum is open daily from 9:30 until 17:00. Admission charges vary from $10 to $20, according to just how much you want to see and do.
   Transport - Train to Town Hall. Sydney Explorer, Stop 20. Ferry to Pyrmont Bay. Monorail to Harbourside. Tram to Pyrmont Bay.

Star City *(no. 17 on map on page 43)*
   This is Sydney's casino, open 24 hours a day. There are also two theatres, a nightclub, restaurants, bars, an hotel, apartments, pools, spas, saunas, a gym and a health club.
   Transport - Bus 443 or 888 from Circular Quay. Sydney Explorer, Stop 19. Ferry to Pyrmont Bay. Tram to Star City.

Buran *(no. 17 on map on page 43)*
   Buran is a Russian space ship and it lives just outside Star City. It is open for inspection, with a space simulation and small museum, from 9:00 until 18:00. Admission costs $20, plus an additional $45 if you want a cockpit tour.
   Transport - Bus 443 or 888 from Circular Quay. Sydney Explorer, Stop 19. Ferry to Pyrmont Bay. Tram to Star City.

Sydney Fish Market

This is a place for eating, as well as purchasing fresh fish. There are restaurants, cafés, bakeries and sushi bars. The market is open from 7:00 until 16:00.

Transport - Train to Town Hall. Ferry to Pyrmont Bay. Tram to Fish Market.

Chinatown *(no. 29 on map on page 43)*

Although Chinatown is best known for its restaurants, there are many other types of establishment in this area, and not all are Chinese, despite the Chinese arch at the end of Dixon Street. This is an Asiatown really, and it incorporates various Vietnamese, Korean, Japanese and Thai shops.

Transport - Train to Central. Sydney Explorer, Stop 17. Monorail to Garden Plaza or Haymarket. Tram to Haymarket.

★ King's Cross *(see map opposite)*

This area, east of the city centre, is well known for its restaurants and night clubs. It is alive 24 hours a day and oozes a general impression of sleaze. Here you may encounter a strange mixture of destitute travellers and cajoling peepshow purveyors, which makes it one of the most fascinating locations in Australia. You will probably have strong reactions of endearment or distaste for this place. In recent years it has also become the prime location for backpackers hostels, so popular that at busy times it is difficult to find a bed here at all (although you sometimes have the impression that nobody sleeps in King's Cross anyway).

Transport - Train to King's Cross. Sydney Explorer, Stop 9. Bondi Explorer, Stop 3. Airport Express Bus 350.

Paddy's Market *(no. 30 on map on page 43)*

Lots of things for sale, and even a few bargains occasionally. The market is open from Thursday until Sunday and on Public Holidays.

Transport - Train to Central. Sydney Explorer, Stop 17. Monorail or tram to Haymarket.

Fox Studios

This is the Australian reply to America's *Universal Studios*. *Fox Studios* is a working film production area. It offers a four-hour *Backlot Tour* and also has a 16-screen cinema complex, shops, bars and restaurants. At weekends there is a market selling items used in films. Entry to the studios area is free, but the *Backlot Tour* (self-guided) costs $25. Some discounts are available.

Transport - Bus 339 from Central Station or 355 from Bondi Junction. Bondi Explorer, Stop 16.

Taronga Zoo *(see map on page 65)*

The zoo is just across the harbour on its north side and it commands a beautiful view of the city, although whether the residents appreciate that is uncertain. It is open from 9:00 until 17:00 and admission costs $25, including the *Sky Safari*. A *ZooPass*, which includes the return ferry fare from Circular Quay, costs $30. There is a *Zoolink* ticket which includes the off-peak return rail fare, cost depending on point of origin.

Transport - Ferry from Circular Quay to Taronga Zoo. Bus 247 from Queen Victoria Building (near Town Hall).

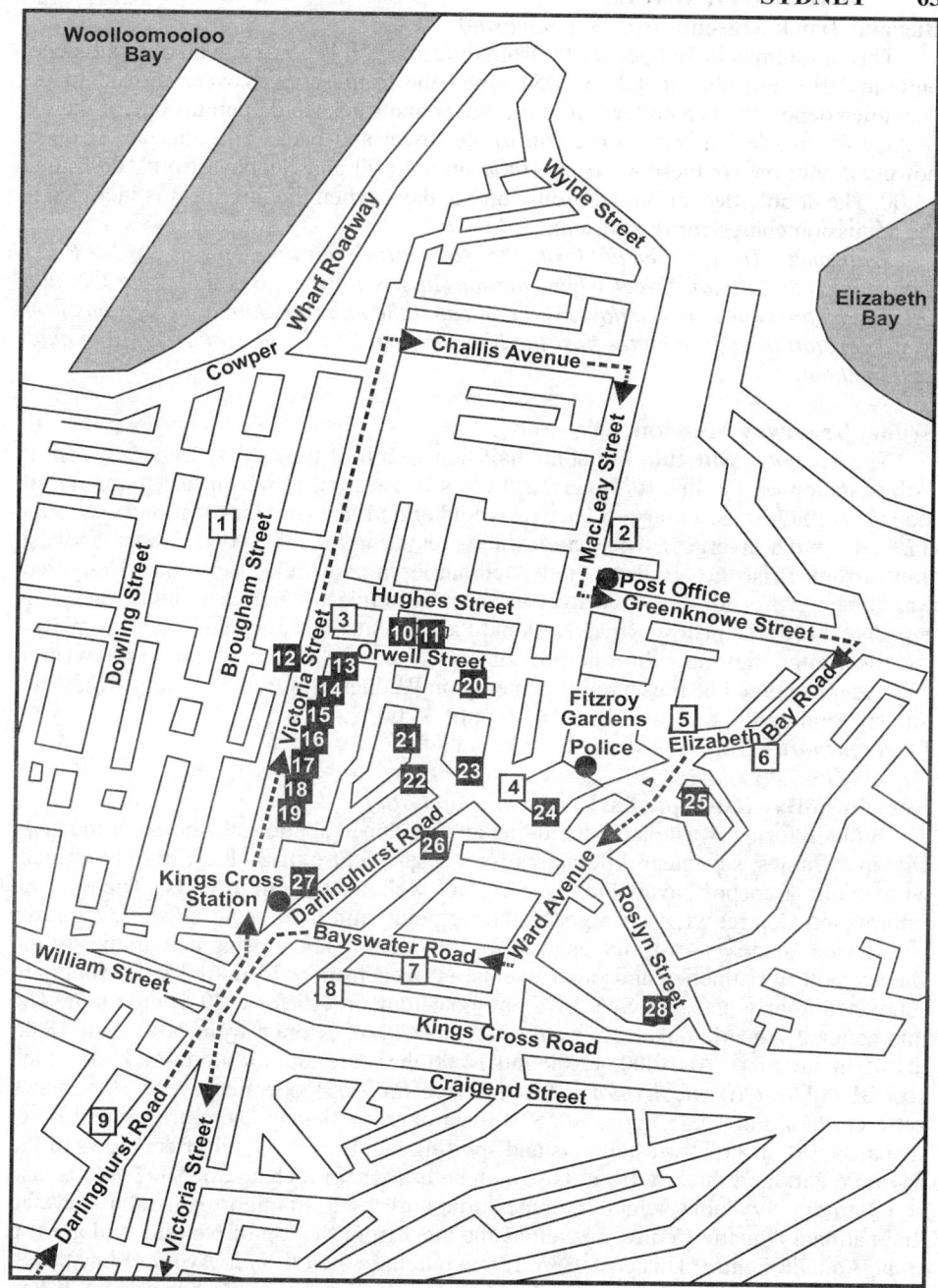

KING'S CROSS

Black numerals in white boxes indicate hotel accommodation (see page 91)
White numerals in black boxes indicate backpackers hostels (see page 91)
Dashed line shows route of Airport Express bus number 350

Bus and Truck Museum *(see map opposite)*

This museum is in Tempe, not far from the airport. It is housed in an old tram depot built in 1912 and abandoned in 1954 when the tram services were moved to the Newtown depot. It has a collection of old buses and trucks and operates one of the old Sydney double-decker buses on a trip to Newtown and back. The museum is open, however, only on Wednesdays from 10:00 until 15:00 and Sundays from 10:00 until 16:00. The double-decker bus runs only on Sundays, when the fare for it is included in the admission charge for the museum.

Transport - Train to Tempe. From the station, turn left into Unwins Bridge Road, then right into Gannon Street where the museum is located. Bus 422 from Circular Quay to its terminus. On Sundays, you can catch the museum double-decker bus from Newtown station at 30 minutes past the hour or from Sydenham station at 40 minutes past the hour.

Sydney Tramway Museum

The Tramway Museum lies some half hour south of the city by train, adjacent to Loftus station on the line to Waterfall. Loftus is a station at which fast trains do not stop, so it may be necessary to change at Sutherland, the previous station (where the line to Cronulla diverges). There are exhibits featuring the old Sydney trams, and also trams from Brisbane, Ballarat and Melbourne in Australia, with San Francisco, Nagasaki, Berlin and Munich as overseas representatives. A tram service is run on the *Parklink* line to the nearby Royal National Park on Sundays only, and rides on this are included in the museum admission fee of $10 (or cost $4 return if you do not wish to visit the museum). The museum is open only on Wednesdays from 9:30 until 15:30 and Sundays and public holidays from 10:00 until 17:00.

Transport - Train to Loftus.

Homebush Bay (Olympic Park) *(see map opposite)*

Built on former waste land, including an abandoned abattoir, the home of the 2000 Olympic Games, seventeen kilometres west of the centre of Sydney, may be visited, with public transport available by ferry as well as by rail or bus. There is an Information Centre, which is a good starting point, and there is an *Olympic Explorer* bus service. Stadium Australia, as used for the opening and closing ceremonies of the Games, and the athletics and other events, is open from 9:30 until 15:30. Tours are conducted hourly and cost $26 for a one-hour tour or $15 for a 20-minute tour. The International Aquatic Centre, with the Olympic Pool, is open from 5:00 until 18:45 (21:45 in summer). At 10:00, 12:00 and 14:00 there are tours lasting one hour which cost $16. The *Olympic Explorer* bus (service no. 405) operates every 30 minutes between 9:15 and 15:45 and costs $10 for a one-day ticket. There are several other stadia, as well as hotels, restaurants and sporting facilities. Novotel offers views of the Olympic Park and the city from its seventeenth floor for a charge of $3. There is also a *Superpass* available which includes tours of both Stadium Australia and the International Aquatic Centre, as well as the view from the top of Novotel and a swim at the Aquatic Centre. This costs $35. If you purchase the *Olympic Explorer* bus ticket, you will get discounts on the individual tour prices (but not on the *Superpass*). If you travel by ferry from Circular Quay, there is a combined return ferry plus *Olympic Explorer* ticket for $20, also offering discounts on the tours.

Transport - Ferry from Circular Quay to Homebush Bay. Train to Olympic Park (usually changing trains at Lidcombe).

SYDNEY 65

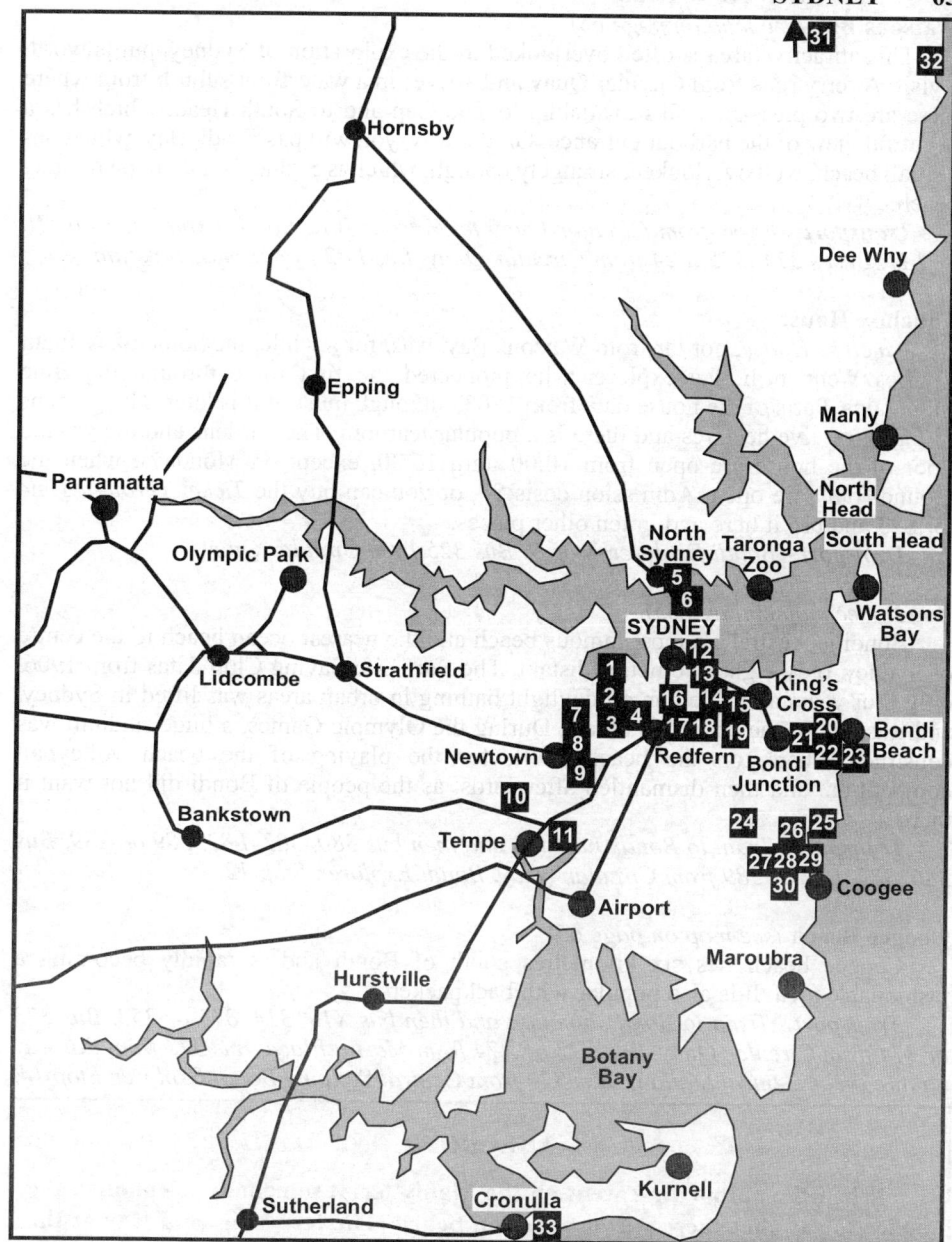

AREA SURROUNDING SYDNEY
Showing railway lines and places of interest
Numerals indicate backpackers hostels. See page 92

NEW SOUTH WALES

Watsons Bay *(see map on page 65)*

This attractive area is often overlooked in the exploration of Sydney, but is worth a visit. A ferry runs from Circular Quay and arrives in a waterfront suburb from where there are two pleasant walks available, to The Gap and to South Head, which has a beautiful view of the harbour entrance. On the way, you will pass Lady Bay, which has a small beach, well overlooked, strangely enough, which is Sydney's only nude bathing beach.

Transport - Ferry from Circular Quay to Watsons Bay. Bondi Explorer, Stops 10 and 11. Buses 324, 325, L24 from Circular Quay. Bus L82 from Bondi Junction.

Vaucluse House

Vaucluse House, not far from Watsons Bay, was, for a while, the home of William Charles Wentworth, the explorer who pioneered the first route through the Blue Mountains. Parts of the house date from 1803, although most of it is later. The gardens extend to twelve hectares and there is a popular tearoom. The gardens and the ground floor of the house are open from 10:00 until 16:30, except on Mondays, when the grounds only are open. Admission costs $7, or you can buy the *Ticket Through Time* for $23 and use it here and in ten other places.

Transport - Bondi Explorer, Stop 9. Bus 325 from Circular Quay.

Bondi *(see map on page 65)*

Bondi is Australia's most famous beach and the nearest ocean beach to the centre of Sydney, only eight kilometres distant. The Surf Life Saving Club dates from 1906, only four years after the ban on daylight bathing in urban areas was lifted in Sydney, and it is one of the country's oldest. During the Olympic Games, a huge stadium was constructed here, on the beach itself, for the playing of the beach volleyball competition, and then dismantled afterwards, as the people of Bondi did not want it there.

Transport - Train to Bondi Junction and then bus 380, 382, L82, 389 or X89. Bus 380, 382, L82 or 389 from Circular Quay. Bondi Explorer, Stop 12.

Coogee Beach *(see map on page 65)*

Coogee beach lies six kilometres south of Bondi and is rapidly becoming a fashionable area. It is also popular with backpackers.

Transport - Train to Bondi Junction and then bus X13, 314, 315 or 353. Bus 373 or 374 from Circular Quay. Bus X73 or X74 from Martin Place. Bus 372 from Railway Square (near Central Station). Bus 374 from Central Station. Bondi Explorer, Stop 14.

ANECDOTE

When the author first went on the Manly ferry, somebody telephoned the police to say that there was a bomb on board. The ferry was mid-way at the time, so nothing could be done but continue. However, when we arrived, police swarmed aboard and rushed everybody ashore, taking the matter very seriously, since a bomb actually had been found at the university the previous day. There turned out to be no bomb on the ferry, however, so I survived my first visit to Sydney.

Manly *(see maps on pages 65 and 74)*

It is worth going to Manly just for the beautiful ferry ride. It is also a popular and fashionable area, famous both for its tree-lined beach and for its food, much of which lies along the short but trendy street known as The Corso, joining the harbour and ocean sides of the peninsula. There is accommodation available from backpackers' up. Manly lies on the North Head of the harbour entrance and there is a pleasant walk up onto the head to the old Quarantine Station, which is interesting in itself, and to the end of North Head. Just to the left of the ferry wharf is *Oceanworld*, open from 10:00 until 17:30, with its displays of Australia's coral and marine life.

Transport - Ferry or Jetcat from Circular Quay. Bus 151 from Queen Victoria Building (Town Hall). Bus 169, E69 or E71 from Wynyard.

Parramatta *(see maps on pages 65 and 81)*

Parramatta lies thirty minutes west of Sydney by fast train, or nearly an hour by ferry. The city was founded as early as November 1788 and there was a brief time when Parramatta was larger than the town of Sydney, but now it is, in practice, merely a suburb of its better known neighbour. However, it has some interesting buildings remaining from its early days of prominence. One is the old Government House in Parramatta Park, built in 1799 and extended in 1815, now home to a fine collection of Australian colonial furniture. It is open from 10:00 (11:00 at weekends) until 16:00, for a fee of $7, and is about 15 minutes walk from Parramatta station. Another old building is *Elizabeth Farm*, parts of which date from 1793. These parts are, therefore, the oldest surviving European construction in Australia. *Elizabeth Farm* is open from 10:00 until 17:00 daily. Admission costs $7, or you can use the *Ticket Through Time* for eleven different museums for $23. The nearest stations to *Elizabeth Farm* are Rosehill or Harris Park. From the ferry wharf it is fifteen minutes on foot. There is also a pleasant riverside walk with aboriginal themes starting at the ferry terminal and leading up one side of the Parramatta River and back on the other, about twenty minutes walk altogether, and at the farthest point of the walk is the Parramatta Heritage and Visitors Information Centre. There is a *Parramatta Explorer* bus service which runs via all of the places mentioned and various other attractions also and which costs $10 for a one-day ticket. There are details of a walking tour of Parramatta on page 81.

Transport - Train to Parramatta (or Rosehill or Harris Park for Elizabeth Farm). Ferry from Circular Quay.

ANECDOTE

Kriskindl was a wonderful hostel in which to stay. John Lizzio, a retired Catholic priest, evidently still feels that it is his vocation to feed the needy. Every evening he would appear with a small vanload of edibles, items which had reached the end of their saleable life and been collected from local retailers.

As I arrived back from a day's exploration, I would be greeted by his voice calling, "Jim, have you had dinner? You haven't, have you? Look, there's a spare dinner here and there's cake and fruit in the fridge. There are some pies over there and there's a box of bananas. Eat up, or you'll waste away."

It was an amazing hostel. After a few days there, I wondered whether I should ever need to eat again.

68 NEW SOUTH WALES

BEACHES

Some of the most famous of the beaches have already been mentioned above, namely Bondi, Coogee and Manly. There are plenty of others, both north and south of the city.

Starting with those to the south, the map on page 65 outlines the locations of the best-known of the various beaches, at Bondi, Coogee and Cronulla, that at Cronulla stretching as far as the eye can see.

To the north, the line also stretches a long way. One of the closest beaches to the city centre is Balmoral, but that is not an ocean beach. It lies on Middle Harbour, sheltered from the sea.

The ocean beaches continue from Manly right up to Palm Beach. Long Reef and Narrabeen are famous for surf, while the prettiest is maybe Avalon. See the adjacent map.

ISLANDS

There are various islands in Sydney Harbour, most of which form part of the Sydney Harbour National Park. In order from the harbour entrance, they are Shark Island, Clark Island, Fort Denison, Goat Island and Rodd Island (see map opposite). It is possible to visit these islands, although not always easy to get to them.

Shark Island *(see map opposite)*

The area of this island is 1.5 hectares, with 500 visitors being permitted at a time. The island was used as an animal quarantine area from 1880 until 1975. It has good views and sandy beaches. However, there are no regular services to Shark Island, so it is usually necessary to arrange to go on a group tour. There is a landing charge of $4.

Clark Island *(see map opposite)*

The area of the island is one hectare, with 150 visitors being permitted at a time. In 1789, Lieutenant Ralph Clark tried to use the island as a vegetable garden, but he eventually abandoned the idea. However, his name has been preserved for posterity. It has natural bushland and grassed areas. Again, there are no regular services to Clark Island. There is a landing charge of $4.

Fort Denison *(see map opposite)*

Fort Denison occupies the entirety of a small island not far from the Opera House. Ferries occasionally stop here and there are tours arranged by the National Park which depart from Cadman's Cottage near Circular Quay station. Breakfast tours (including breakfast) leave at 6:50 on Tuesdays and Thursdays and 6:40 on Sundays and cost $37.

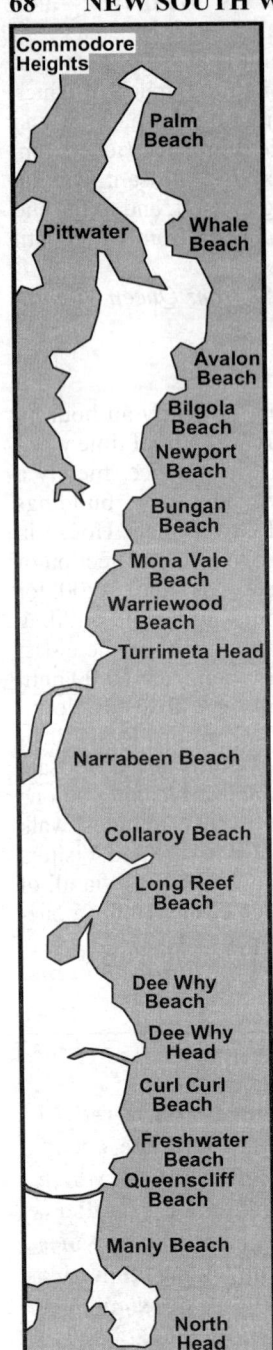

NORTHERN BEACHES

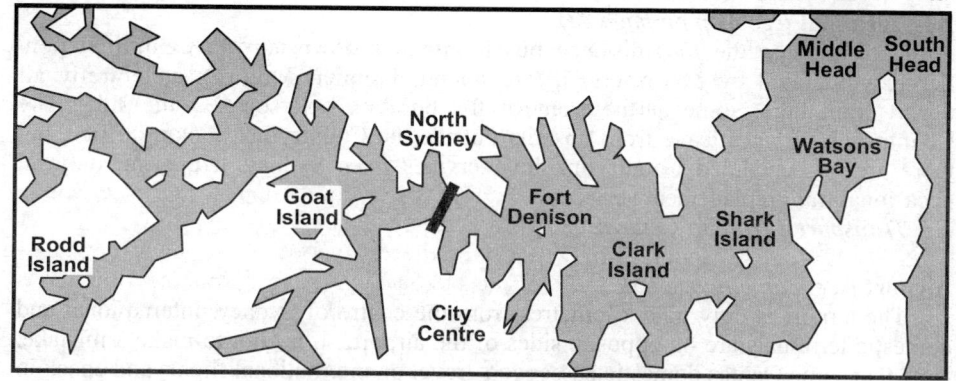

ISLANDS IN SYDNEY HARBOUR

Other tours leave at 9:00, 11:30, 14:00 and 16:15 (slightly different times at weekends) and cost $22.

Goat Island *(see map above)*

Goat Island was first used to dispose of waste from a convict hulk in the harbour. Later, in 1839, a gunpowder magazine was constructed here by convicts and can still be seen. A further magazine was built in the 1850s. In 1900, the Black Death reached Sydney and Goat Island became a quarantine area. In the twentieth century, houses were constructed here and even a shipbuilding yard. The island became part of the National Park only in 1995. There are various tours to Goat Island departing from Cadman's Cottage. The Heritage Tour leaves at 11:45 on Mondays, Fridays, Saturdays and Sundays and costs $20.

Rodd Island *(see map above)*

The area of the island is 0.5 hectares, with 100 visitors being permitted at a time. In 1859, Mr. Brent Rodd paid a deposit for the island, which he later forfeited, but the island kept his name. It became a public reserve, but was also used in the late nineteenth century for biological research under the direction of Dr. Louis Pasteur. It has summer houses from the 1930s and a colonial hall dating from 1889. There are no regular services to Clark Island and there is a landing charge of $4.

OTHER USEFUL PLACES
Railway Station *(see map on page 43)*

Long-distance trains depart from Central Station, platforms 1 to 4. Adjacent to platform 1 there is a Countrylink booking office. Countrylink operates the long-distance services within New South Wales (trains to Murwillumbah, Grafton, Armidale, Moree, Dubbo, Broken Hill and Griffith) and to the cities of Brisbane, Canberra and Melbourne (see pages 93 and 94). There are Countrylink bus connexions from these services to places all over the state. Great Southern Railway operates the trains to Perth and Alice Springs (and to Darwin when the rail line is completed). Countrylink acts as agent for tickets for these services. There is also a Countrylink booking office at Wynyard station.

Transport - Train to Central.

NEW SOUTH WALES

Bus Terminal *(see map on page 43)*

Conveniently, the long-distance bus terminal is downstairs in Central Station. Services operated by McCafferty's, Greyhound, Premier, Murray's and Firefly all depart from here, some at the front of the building and some at the side. Any Countrylink services leave from upstairs outside the Countrylink booking office, but there are no scheduled Countrylink bus services from Sydney at present, only an occasional train replacement service.

Transport - Train to Central.

Airport *(see map on page 65)*

The airport is only nine kilometres from the centre of Sydney. International and domestic terminals are on opposite sides of the airport, so try not to make a mistake. Note that some Qantas domestic passengers travel on international flights and check in at the international terminal. Domestic services are operated by Qantas (and subsidiaries), and by Virgin Blue, from two separate areas.

Transport - Train to International or Domestic. Airport Express bus 300 or 350. Ordinary bus 100, 353 or 400. Taxi costs about $25 from the city centre.

G.P.O. *(see map on page 43)*

There is a magnificent G.P.O. building in Martin Place between George Street and Pitt Street. Sadly, though, only a very small part now operates as a post office. The remainder has been turned into rather high class retail shops. The part which does still function for its original purpose is on the corner of Martin Place and George Street. Note, though, that Poste Restante is not here. It is in a separate office back from the street, but clearly marked, a little further along George Street towards The Rocks (see map on page 43).

Transport - Train to Martin Place or Wynyard.

Shopping

Up-market shopping areas are around Pitt Street Mall, between Market Street and King Street, in The Strand, between George Street and Pitt Street Mall, in the department stores along Market Street, and in Queen Victoria Building, near the Town Hall.

Transport - Train to Town Hall or St. James.

WALKS

There are some very pleasant walks in Sydney. Here are a few of them with accompanying maps.

(i) Harbourfront Walk *(see map on next page)*

This is a walk of approximately eleven kilometres from the Sydney Fish Market to Potts Point. You should allow about five to six hours, although if you just walk without stopping to look at any of the points of interest, four hours will probably suffice. There is, however, plenty to see.

From the Fish Market, most easily reached by taking a tram to Fish Market or Wentworth Park, walk close to the harbour's edge around Blackwattle Bay to Johnston's Bay, and then to Pyrmont Point Park. Past Jones Bay, you reach Pyrmont Bay and the Star City Casino, then Darling Harbour itself and the Australian Maritime

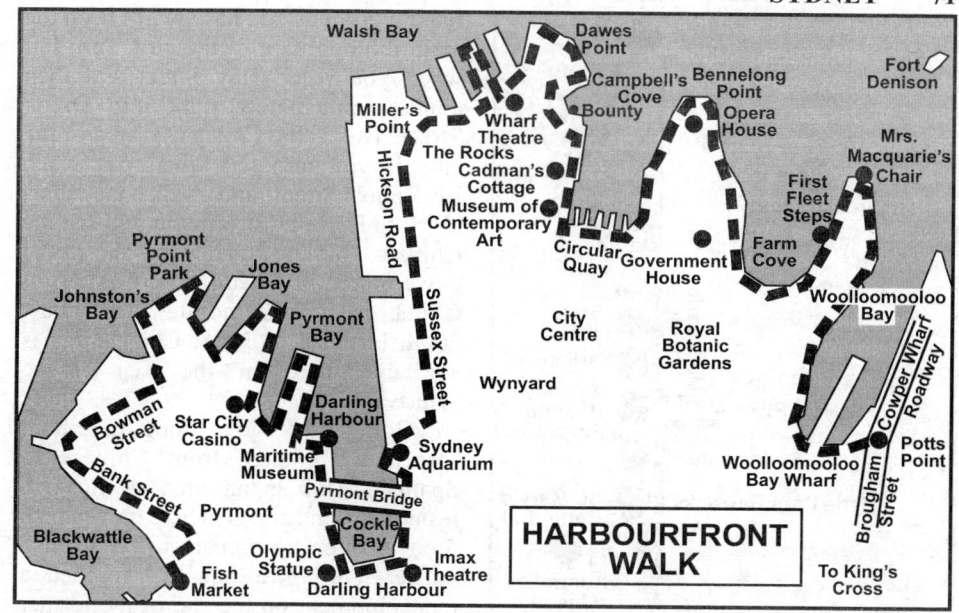

Museum. You can choose to cut across Pyrmont Bridge or to walk round via the Olympic Statue, the Harbourfront Shopping Centre, the Imax Theatre, *Sega World* and the restaurants of Cockle Bay. By either route, you will arrive at Sydney Aquarium.

Next, walk round to Miller's Point and Walsh Bay, followed by Dawes Point, where you pass under the Harbour Bridge. In Campbell's Cove, you will see the replica of the *Bounty*, before reaching the Sydney Visitor Centre, Cadman's Cottage and the Museum of Contemporary Art. If you have time, you can divert to explore The Rocks area from here (see Walk iii). As you approach Circular Quay, look at the plaques embedded in the pavement commemorating famous figures in literature and the arts.

Continue past Circular Quay and out onto the promontory where the Opera House is situated. There is a good view of the Harbour Bridge from here. Following the coastline, you now enter the Royal Botanic Gardens via Farm Cove Gate West and continue round the pretty Farm Cove, feeding the ducks on the way, if you feel so inclined. The First Fleet Steps are encountered on the far side of the bay, and then, at the tip of the next promontory, lies Mrs. Macquarie's Chair, from where, again, there is a good view back, this time with both the Opera House and the Harbour Bridge in the line of vision. Another twenty minutes walk brings one to Woolloomooloo Bay Wharf and then to Potts Point, from where bus no. 311 will take you back to the city. Alternatively, you can turn right and walk into King's Cross in about fifteen minutes.

(ii) City Walk *(see map on next page)*

This stroll through the city from Central Station to Circular Quay covers a distance of approximately five kilometres and lasts about two hours, not allowing for any major stops.

At the rear of Central Station, a tunnel connects Chalmers Street with Railway Square. Notice the artwork in the tunnel and also on the bus shelters in Railway Square. Then turn along George Street, which follows the route of an aboriginal track to the

72 NEW SOUTH WALES

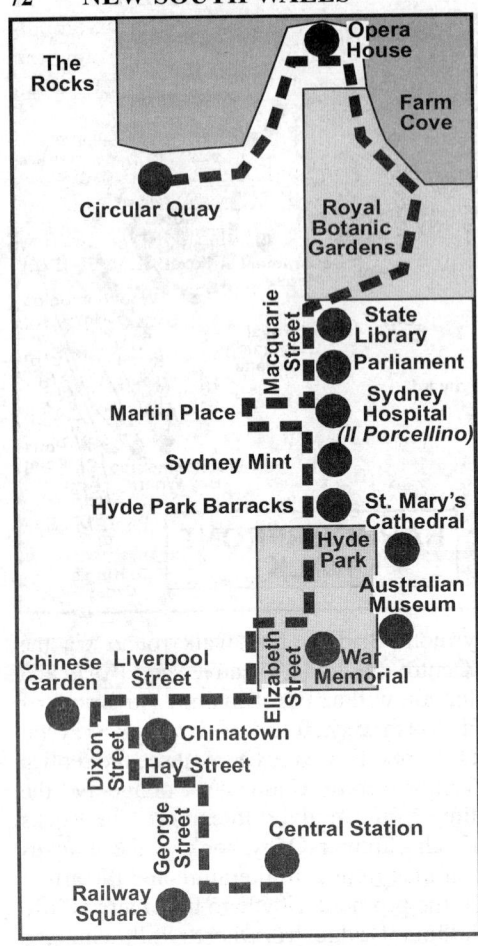

CITY WALK

fishing grounds and has always been the main thoroughfare of the city. Turn left when you reach Hay Street and then almost immediately right into Dixon Street. This is the Chinatown area of the city. If you turn left when you reach Liverpool Street and walk one short block to Harbour Street, you will see the Chinese Garden donated by the Local Government of Guangdong (Canton) in China to commemorate Australia's 200th birthday in 1988. Chinese tea is available here in the Tea House Courtyard.

Going back now along Liverpool Street, we change from Chinese to Spanish. This is an area of Spanish restaurants and shops, where the Spanish food is often accompanied by Spanish music. Soon World Square is reached, a redevelopment on the site of the former Anthony Hordern Department Store, which is why the 45-storey tower is named Hordern Tower.

Turn left into Elizabeth Street and walk one block to the obelisk at the corner of Bathurst Street. What can this impressive Egyptian-style sculpture be? In fact, it is a ventilator for the major sewer running beneath the street. It was erected as long ago as 1857 and nicknamed *Thorton's Scent Bottle*, Mr. Thorton having been the mayor at the time. Now turn right into Hyde Park, in and around which there are several of the attractions which have been mentioned above: the Anzac War Memorial, the Australian Museum, St. Mary's Cathedral, Hyde Park Barracks Museum, and then, continuing along Macquarie Street, Sydney Mint, Sydney Hospital, Parliament House and the State Library of New South Wales. As you pass Sydney Hospital, you will see a statue of a wild boar, *Il Porcellino*, a copy of a statue in a seventeenth-century fountain in Florence. If you rub the shiny snout of the pig, as it is apparent that several others have done before you, and make a wish, good luck is sure to ensue, especially if you donate an appropriate amount of money at the same time. The money goes to the benefit of the hospital, not of the pig. Almost opposite is Martin Place, where you are likely to be asked to contribute to the welfare of Greenpeace or any one of a multitude of other worthy causes. A plan of a house which once stood here is marked by black paving stones and by a misty spray which will catch you unawares as it issues unexpectedly from the ground just as you walk over the spot.

At the State Library, divert right, enter the Royal Botanic Gardens and walk though to the harbour at Farm Cove. Then turn left and continue to the Opera House, round the promontory and to the ferry terminal at Circular Quay.

(iii) The Rocks *(see map on page 57)*

The following walk will take you around the principal sights of The Rocks, covering a distance of about three kilometres. The walk will take about an hour, but allow longer if you want to do more than just glance at the buildings.

Start from the Sydney Visitor Centre, turning left at the door and going down the steps beside the building. Immediately you will see Cadman's Cottage on your right. Turn right and walk to the Museum of Contemporary Art. Next to this building is the First Fleet Park. Turn right into and through the park and then right again into George Street. 135 George Street is the Vault Restaurant, formerly the English, Scottish and Australian Chartered Bank with attractive old leaded windows. Next door at no. 133 is the old Police Station with its impressive stonework. See the lion's jaws holding a truncheon. On the other side of the road, 100 George Street houses the Billich Gallery, but was originally the Seamen's Chapel, notable for its interior design and lofty ceilings. 47 George Street was the Union Bond Store built in 1841. It has seashell fragments visible in the mortar, due to a lack of lime at the time. The next building is the former Australian Steamship Navigation Company office, featuring a turret design. The Rocks Market closes off the road from here on at weekends.

At the end of George Street, turn left into Lower Fort Street. Dawes Point Park has good views of the harbour, and, on the other side of the road, Colonial House Museum is devoted to exhibits related to The Rocks. At the end of the street, on the corner of Argyle Street, is the Garrison Church, with strong military connexions, as may be judged from its name. The eastern window is its most notable feature. Ahead is Observatory Hill, reached by climbing the steps, and the Sydney Observatory.

Turn back under the approach to the Harbour Bridge and then right into Gloucester Street, where Susannah Place is to be found. Now left down the steps, and left again into Cambridge Street. Soon you will come back to Clocktower Square and Argyle Street. Turn right into and down Argyle Street, right into Harrington Street, left into the very narrow Suez Canal and left again into Nurses Walk. Cross Argyle Street into Kendall Lane. Just down a lane on the right is The Coachhouse and behind is the Puppet Cottage. Returning to Kendall Lane, you will find yourself at The Rocks Square, full of restaurants and souvenir shops. When you have finished here, just two minutes' walk down Mill Lane will take you back to the Sydney Visitor Centre.

(iv) Manly to North Head *(see map on next page)*

On the north-east of Manly lies the Pacific Ocean. To the south-west is Sydney Harbour. The two are separated by only a five-minute walk along The Corso. To the south-east of Manly is North Head, the northern portal of the entrance to the harbour. From here there is an excellent view. The walk to the head and back covers about ten kilometres and takes some three hours.

Walk through The Corso and turn right beside the beach. At the end of the beach, continue along the shoreline to Fairy Bower and Shelly Beach and then turn right and right again, up into Bower Street, left into College Street, right into Reddall Street, left into Addison Road and left into Darley Road. It is possible to shorten this route, and you may choose to do so on the return, by proceeding straight along Darley Road, but

NEW SOUTH WALES

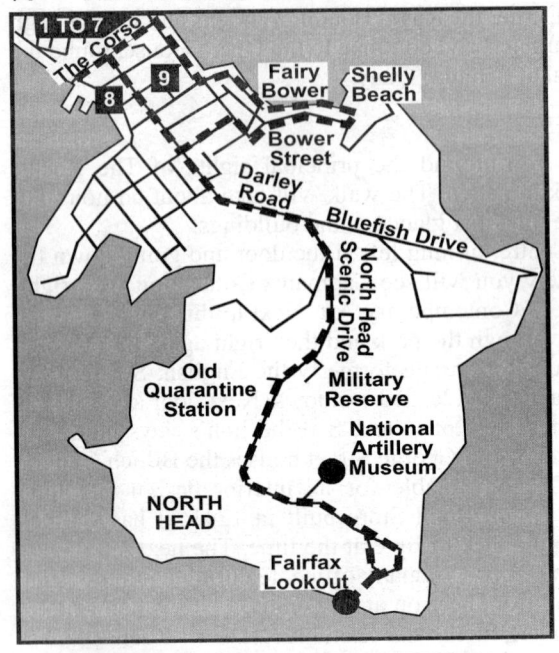

MANLY TO NORTH HEAD
Numerals indicate backpackers hostels. See page 91.

the views on the climb up from the shoreline should not be missed if possible.

There is one fork along the way from here to North Head. You should choose the road on the right, which is named North Head Scenic Drive. On your left, you will pass a military reserve, while on your right is the Old Quarantine Station, a fascinating place to visit, but one which needs a prior reservation. After a bend, the National Artillery Museum is on the left, and then you come to the end of the road and the Fairfax Walking Track. The track is circular and gives fine views of both harbour and ocean sides. It takes about half an hour to go round it. Then return by the same route, but continue along Darley Road straight back to Manly.

(v) Manly to The Spit *(see map on next page)*

This walk, opened in 1988, extends for ten kilometres and takes about three hours. Start from the harbour side of Manly, at the wharf where the ferry arrives, and turn west (left as you leave the wharf). Then simply follow the shoreline past *Oceanworld*, Delwood Beach, Fairlight Beach, North Harbour Reserve and Wellings Reserve. Next you will come to Forty Baskets Beach, connected not with the Sermon on the Mount, but with a good catch sent to feed Sudanese soldiers detained at the Quarantine Station on North Head in 1885.

You now move into an area of National Park as you pass Reef Beach and reach Dobroyd Head, famous for its wild flowers in spring. Via Crater Cove and Washaway Beach to Grotto Point, for a good view of the harbour, then a short backtrack and on to Castle Rock, Clontarf Point and Clontarf Beach. This beach has some history associated with it, for it was here on 12th March 1868 that the Duke of Edinburgh, second son of Queen Victoria, was shot during a picnic by a would-be assassin, the Irishman James O'Farrell. The Duke escaped with a slight wound, but O'Farrell did not. He was executed.

On to Sandy Bay and Fisher Bay before The Spit is reached. The bridge here carries the main highway between Sydney and Manly, but traffic flow is interrupted periodically as the bridge has to be raised to allow boats to pass into the Middle Harbour, Sydney having got its priorities correct in this instance at least. There are good views from this point too.

From here, buses 143, 144, 169, E69 and E71 run back to Manly (the 169 and E69 by a very lengthy and indirect route), while a variety of routes runs into the city.

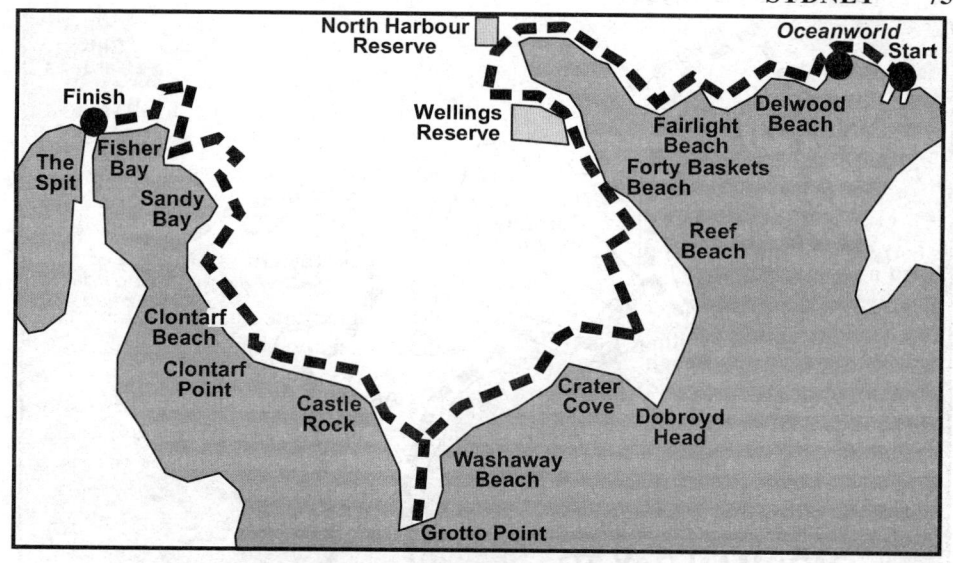

MANLY TO THE SPIT

(vi) Mosman Bay to Taronga Zoo and Clifton Gardens *(see map on nest page)*

Take a ferry to South Mosman (Musgrave Street) to start this walk of about eight kilometres, taking three hours. Climb up the steps to Musgrave Street, then continue up more steps along Herron Walk to Raglan Street. The large stone house there is known as *The Castle*. Turn left along Raglan Street until you reach Illawarra Street on your right. Turn into this street and descend to Sirius Cove Beach. The architecture along the way is an interesting mixture.

Now enter Sirius Cove Reserve and proceed along a bush track through an area which provided the inspiration for the artists of the Heidelberg School a century ago. You will reach Whiting Beach in due course and, soon after, Athol Wharf, where the ferry docks for Taronga Zoo.

If you wish to continue further, keep close to the shore and walk round Athol Bay to Bradley's Head. This is now a National Park, but it was formerly a gun emplacement for the protection of Sydney. In 1839, four American ships entered the harbour unexpectedly, causing the realisation of how badly prepared the city was to deal with any emergency. Cannons were placed here in 1840, but the fortification was not completed until the build-up to Crimea in 1853. (Incidentally, as our walk began in Raglan Street, it is worth remembering that Lord Raglan was the commander of the British troops in the Crimean War, and it was he whose orders were misinterpreted to cause the Charge of the Light Brigade.) There is a fine view from Bradley's Head. There is also a memorial to the four naval vessels which have borne the name *H.M.A.S. Sydney* and the mast from the first of these, a light cruiser which, on 9th November 1914, engaged the German cruiser *Emden* near Cocos Island in the first naval engagement of the Great War involving an Australian ship. Nearby is a stone column from the old Sydney Post Office. This is used to measure a distance of precisely one nautical mile from the tower of Fort Denison.

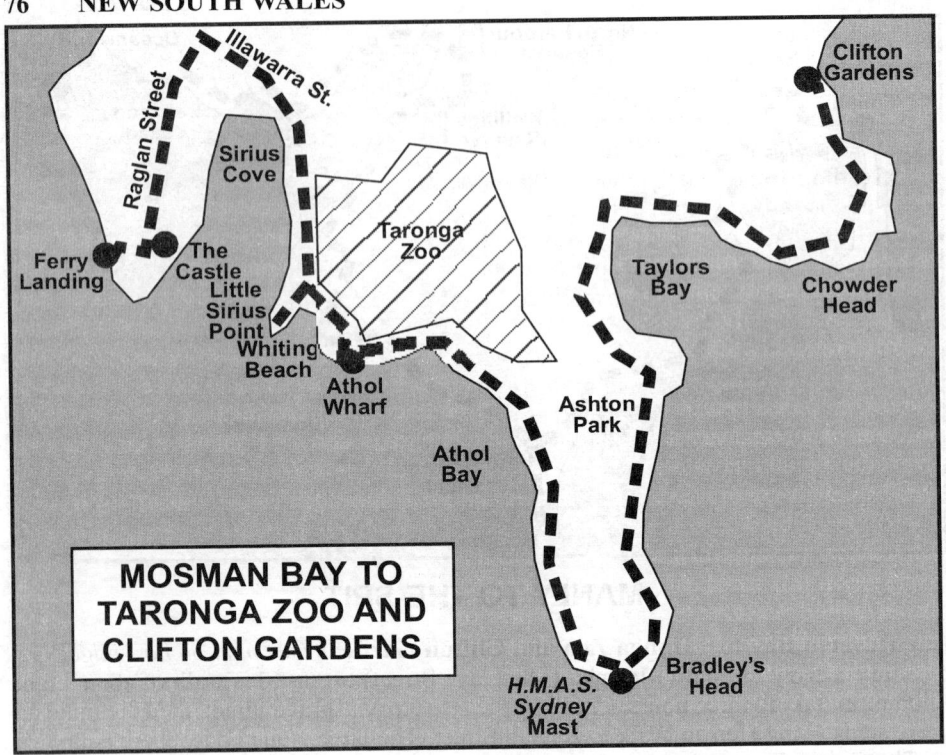

Continue north now on the eastern side of Bradley's Head through Ashton Park to Taylors Bay, then on to Chowder Head and Clifton Gardens. Having reached Clifton Gardens, you can either go back to Taronga Zoo, taking a short cut across the top of Bradley's Head peninsula, or walk up Sarah's Walk to Morella Road, from where bus 228 runs back to Milson's Point at the north end of the Harbour Bridge.

(vii) Double Bay to South Head *(see map opposite)*

This walk covers some twelve kilometres, including the return from South Head to Watsons Bay, and will take about four hours. One can reach Double Bay by ferry, train to Edgecliff and then fifteen minutes walk, or bus no. 323, 324 or 325 from Circular Quay via King's Cross.

Double Bay is an up-market shopping and restaurant area and high class residential suburb, although it was originally intended as the site for the Botanical Garden. To get just a taste of this area, walk ahead down Bay Street after alighting from the ferry until you reach Knox Street, where turn left. If you come by bus or on foot from Edgecliff, you will be travelling along New South Head Road. When you reach Bay Street, alight from the bus, if travelling by that means, and turn left into Bay Street and then right into Knox Street. This will lead you back into New South Head Road once more. Turn left and follow the road as is curves right and passes Seven Shillings Beach, supposedly so named because that was the amount paid to the aborigines as compensation for its surrender. Redleaf Pool, with its landscaped gardens, is off to your left, but requires a short diversion.

The road swings right again and you are in Rose Bay. You can leave the road here and walk along the Esplanade above the beach. Rose Bay used to be a flying boat base and one of the last commercial flights in the world to be operated by flying boat used to take off from here for Lord Howe Island until the late 1970s, a perilous operation as the aircraft had to attain a speed of 150 km/hr in a bay crowded with pleasure boats. This was also the starting point for the first commercial flights from Australia to England in 1938, when the journey took ten days and involved 29 stops, but was no cheaper than it is now. Rose Bay is still used for pleasure trips by small seaplanes. There is a regular service from here to Palm Beach, for example. The seaplane base is at the far end of the beach, just beyond the ferry wharf. You will also see here many expensive yachts and launches, for Sydney's most affluent citizens inhabit this area.

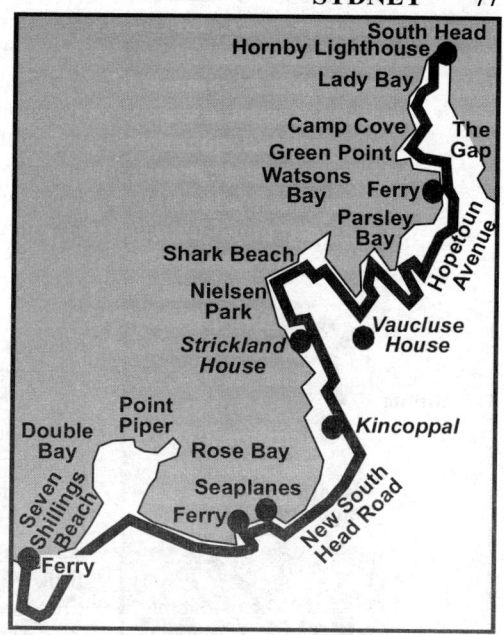

DOUBLE BAY TO SOUTH HEAD

After passing the seaplane base, return to New South Head Road and follow it as it climbs. At the summit is *Kincoppal*, formerly Rose Bay Convent built by French nuns of the Order of the Sacred Heart. There is a very good view from this point. Now bear left into Vaucluse Road. After a while you will come to *Strickland House* which, from the time of the Great War until 1989, was a women's convalescent home. Now it is used for weddings and other functions and as a film location.

The entrance to Nielsen Park is on your left. This is a National Park area, popular for picnics. It also has a netted swimming enclosure in the sea at Shark Beach. The reason for the net is suggested by the name of the location. At the end of the park, turn left into Greycliffe Avenue, then immediately right into Coolong Road. As you meet Wentworth Road, you will see the entrance to *Vaucluse House* opposite. Parts of this house date from 1803 and the extensive gardens are also attractive. Turn left into Wentworth Road and then follow round into Fitzwilliam Road. Left into Parsley Road, and left again into Hopler Avenue, which will lead you into Parsley Bay Reserve. Walk through and exit onto The Crescent. Turn right, then left into Hopetoun Avenue, which follow until you return to the sea and Robertson Park. You are now at Watsons Bay. Originally ships used to anchor here for the inspection of their papers. Now they just slow to take on board the harbour pilot. Walk along by the beach until you can go no further. Then walk up to Pacific Street and turn left along it until it comes to a dead end. From here you can descend and continue along Camp Cove beach, noting as you do so the plaque at Green Point to commemorate the landing of the First Fleet here in 1788.

From the end of Camp Cove, it is a climb up to the point where you can have a fine and interesting view overlooking the Lady Bay nudist beach, Sydney's only such

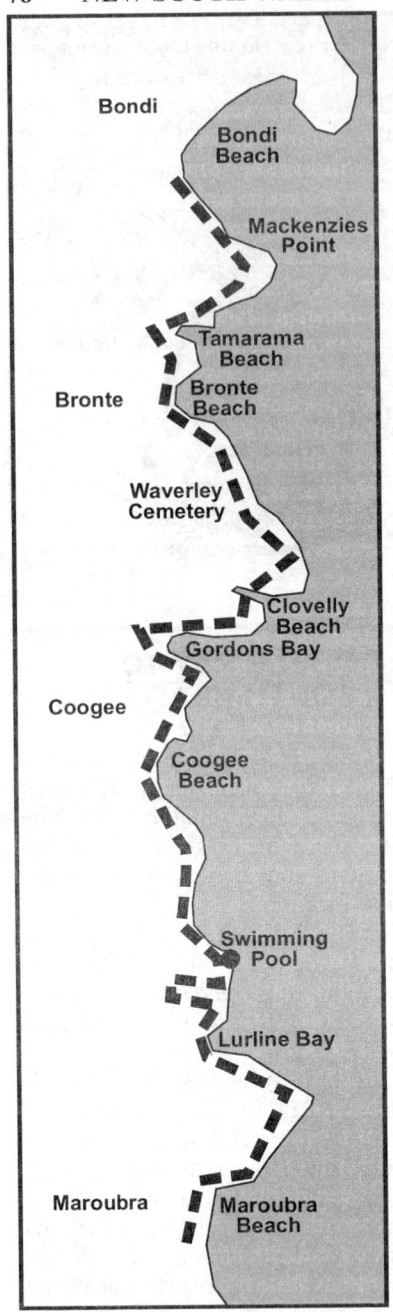

BONDI BEACH TO MAROUBRA BEACH

beach. The track now continues to South Head, where there is another good view of the harbour entrance, and the Hornby Lighthouse. The track goes round in a circle before rejoining itself for the return to Watsons Bay.

If you still have energy, you can walk over to The Gap on the ocean side of this peninsula and get another fine view. It is only a matter of ten minutes from the ferry terminal. This spot has seen several shipwrecks, most notably that of the *Dunbar* on 20th August 1857, when the captain mistook The Gap for the entrance to the harbour, just north of this point at South Head, and ran his ship onto the rocks. 121 lives were lost, there being but a sole survivor. The Dunbar Memorial Lookout now stands at the spot of the disaster.

From Watsons Bay, one may return to the city by ferry or by bus 324 or 325, both of which services run via King's Cross. In fact route 325 follows almost the whole of this walk, so at any time one may give up and return. However, if one does nothing else, the walk from Watsons Bay to South Head is worthwhile and takes only about an hour for a return trip undertaken in leisurely fashion.

(viii) Bondi Beach to Maroubra Beach *(see map adjacent)*

This is a ocean beach-hopping walk of approximately twelve kilometres which could be expected to take about three and a half hours if no major stops are made. It is not difficult to follow. It is a coastal walk, so just stay as close to the coast as you can. For most of the walk there are marker signs *en route*.

Start from Bondi Beach, to reach which see page 66. Note that the twelve kilometres is measured from the south end of the beach. If you want to start from the north end and walk the length of the beach first, add another two kilometres or a little more.

Pass the Bondi Icebergs Club, known for its year-round bathing and walk over Mackenzies Point, from where there are good views. You soon come to Tamarama Beach, a small beach with rough surf. A little further and you are at Bronte Beach, another with rough surf and a strong rip. On now to Waverley Cemetery for more good views, although perhaps rather wasted on the residents. The next beach is Clovelly, This is a sheltered family-type beach, deep but not lengthy. Cut across the beach to avoid the walk round and continue round the next headland to Gordons Bay, popular for scuba diving and snorkelling. A little further and you will reach Coogee, the major beach along this walk. Coogee is becoming increasingly fashionable and starting to rival Bondi in its popularity. There is accommodation of all types here, as well as restaurants and nightclubs.

There is a long stretch next, of three kilometres to Lurline Bay. Most of this part follows the seashore, but just before the bay is reached, and just after you have passed a pool, it is necessary to deviate inland until you reach Malabar Road, where turn left. You can turn left again at the next road to return to the shore, but crossing the bay may not be possible at high tide, in which case continue further along Malabar Road until you reach Mermaid Avenue. There turn left, left again into Lurline Street, and right into Marine Parade, rejoining the coast at that point. Two more kilometres will bring you to the centre of Maroubra Beach.

To return to the city, walk inland about 200 metres to come to Broome Street or Tyrwhitt Street, from where you can take bus no. 397. Just a little further and you will come to Malabar Street, from where no. 377 operates. Alternatively, you can return to the north end of the beach and have a choice of nos. 375, 376, 377, 395 and 396.

(ix) Kurnell to Cronulla *(see maps below and on next page)*

This is a long walk of about fifteen kilometres which will take four to five hours. It can, however, be shortened to ten kilometres by taking one of a choice of two modifications, as noted below. The walk starts at the mouth of Botany Bay, so first it is necessary to get there. Take a train to Cronulla, a journey of about 45 minutes from the city centre. From the station, cross the road and from the bus stop almost opposite, take a bus no. 987 to Kurnell and the Botany Bay National Park.

Walk through the picnic area to the left of the entrance to the National Park for a short distance to the shore and turn right along the Monument Track. You will come first to a very famous site in Australian history - the landing place of one Captain James Cook in 1770. (Actually, he was Lt. James Cook at the time.) The site is at the farthest end of the stretch of beach. A little further along the track is Banks' Memorial. Banks was the botanist who accompanied Captain Cook on his historic voyage and returned with one of the world's greatest botanic collections. Soon after is Cook's Stream, where water was gathered during the first British landing on the Australian continent, and then, on your right, Alpha Farm, one of the first buildings on this peninsula. Nearby, on the left,

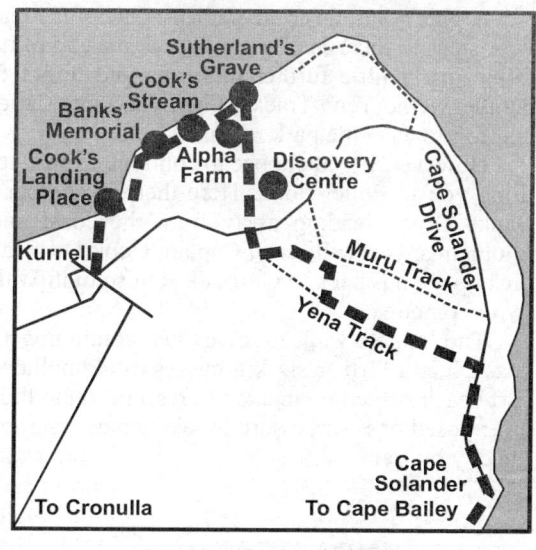

KURNELL AREA

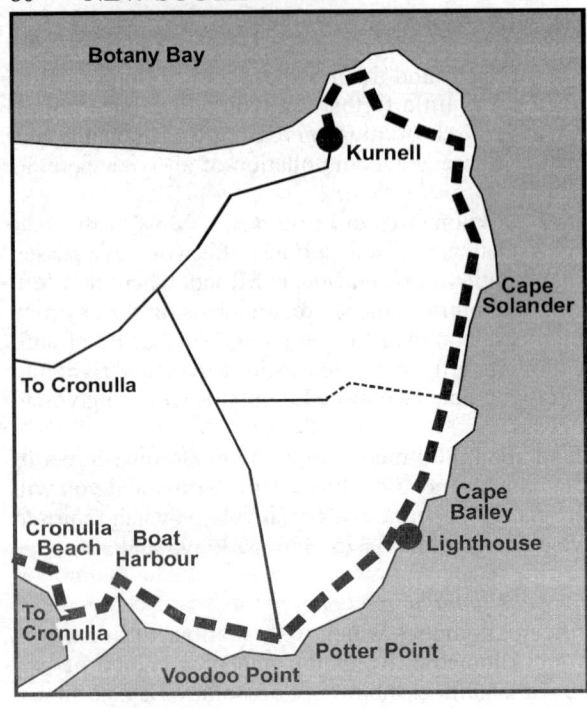

KURNELL TO CRONULLA

is the grave of Forby Sutherland, a seaman on Cook's barque, the *Endeavour*, who died on the journey. The track turns sharply right and inland at this point and leads up to the Environmental Education Field Study Centre on the right and the Discovery Centre on the left. The latter is a museum telling of the history and culture of the area.

Continue across the parking area and main park road (Cape Solander Drive) onto the Yena Track, taking almost immediately the diversion left onto the Banks' Solander Track which leads through coastal woodland for 500 metres before rejoining the Yena Track. Another kilometre and you will come across Cape Solander Drive once more. Turn right for one more kilometre to Cape Solander, where the road ends. The track, however, continues along the coast to Cape Bailey, with some beautiful views.

At this point, there are choices. One of the ten-kilometre options involves retracing your steps to the Yena Picnic Area at the end of the Yena Track. Follow Cape Solander Drive just a little further this time and turn left along the Muru Track which runs parallel to the Yena Track. When you meet Cape Solander Drive once more, turn left and follow it to the park entrance.

However, if you choose to continue from Cape Bailey, another two kilometres will bring you to Potter Point. Here there is another ten-kilometre option. Take the road, Banks Drive, leading away from the coast and if you follow this road for three kilometres, you will reach Captain Cook Drive a little south of Kurnell and be able to pick up the bus back to Cronulla at this point. Walking back into Kurnell will add about two kilometres.

The longest walk involves just continuing from Potter Point pottering round the coast. It is a further six kilometres to Cronulla, much of it beside or along the famed surf beach stretching in a long crescent round the bay. It is a pleasant enough walk, but an exposed one, so be sure to take a hat in summer. From Cronulla, you can return to the city by train.

(x) Around Parramatta *(see map below)*

This walk covers some ten kilometres and needs three hours, or considerably longer if one wishes to visit any of the historical sites *en route*. First get to Parramatta either by ferry or by train. The latter takes half an hour from the city centre by the fastest trains. The ferry takes nearly an hour but is an enjoyable scenic journey. If you arrive by train, exit on the north side of the station, noting, almost opposite, the Lancers Barracks and Linden House Museum. The Barracks were built in 1818 and formerly housed the New South Wales Lancers, the first cavalry regiment in Australia. The history of the regiment is on display inside the Linden House Museum, a building originally constructed in 1828, but moved here from a site in Macquarie Street about 500 metres away. It is open only on Sundays between 11:00 and 16:00 and admission costs $2. Now turn right into Station Street, immediately left into Hassall Street and left into Charles Street, which will lead to the Parramatta River and the ferry terminal.

Turn left, or, for ferry passengers, proceed in the direction in which you were travelling along the river. You can walk on either side of the river, but eventually you will want to be on the other side, so cross over a bridge of your choice on the way. This is Riverside Walk, designed to give an aboriginal interpretation of the river, as you will see from the patterns on the footpaths. Just before Lennox Bridge, built by convict labour in 1836 to 1839 and over which Church Street runs, you will find the Parramatta Heritage Centre and Visitors Information Centre on the northern (far) side. It combines art, craft and history exhibitions with the dispensation of tourist information and has a copy of an 1844 map of the city laid into the floor. Admission is free. After your visit there, come back along Church Street over the sandstone Lennox Bridge, the oldest bridge in Parramatta, and turn right into Phillip Street, then left into Marsden Street. On the next corner is *Brislington*, the oldest residence in central Parramatta, built in 1821

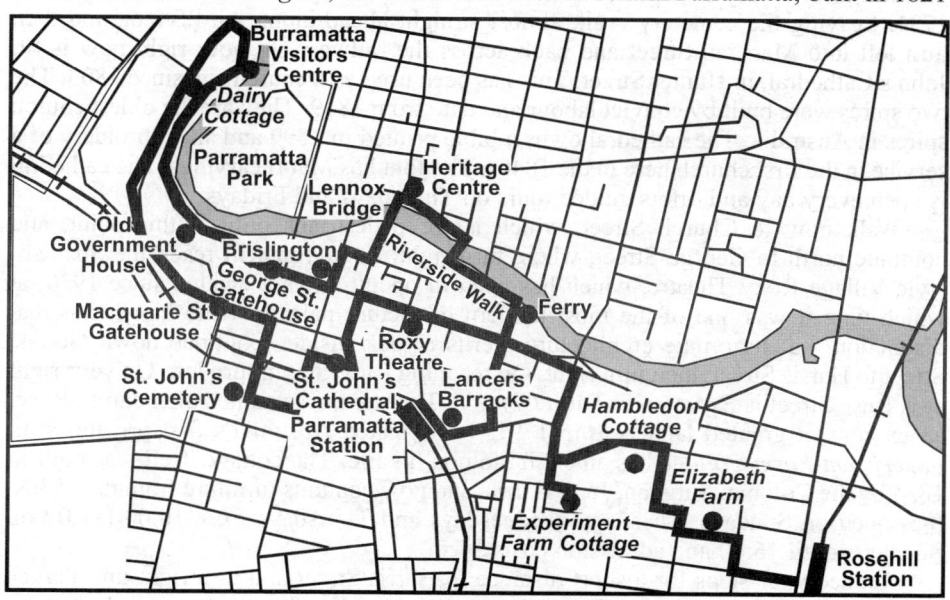

PARRAMATTA WALK

by an ex-convict named John Hodges. It was operated by the members of a single family as a doctor's surgery for almost a century, but now it is a hospital museum, open only on the first and third Sunday in the month and the second and last Thursday, in both cases from 10:30 until 15:30. Admission costs $2.

Turn right into George Street and you will see the George Street Gatehouse at the entrance to Parramatta Park. This has been the principal entrance to the park since 1788, but the gate itself, known because of its design as Tudor Gate, was constructed in 1885. Just inside the park, you will find Old Government House. Governor Phillip built a cottage here in 1790, only two years after the arrival of the first European settlers. The foundations of this building can be seen, but the present edifice was constructed between 1799 and 1818 and inhabited by Governors Hunter and Macquarie. Now it contains an outstanding collection of colonial furniture. It is open from 10:00 (11:00 at weekends) until 16:00 daily. The admission charge is $7.

Continue beside the river through the park, much of which was originally farming land, and, before that, the home of the Burramatta aborigines. You will reach *Dairy Cottage*, built between 1798 and 1806 and one of Australia's oldest buildings. It was converted into a dairy by Governor Macquarie. *Dairy Cottage* is open from 10:00 until 15:00 daily. A little further on is the Burramatta Visitors Centre, also open from 10:00 until 16:00 daily, with free admission. Walk round the park and return this time to the Macquarie Street Gatehouse which dates from 1887 and has the appearance of a rural cottage.

Walk ahead for one block and then turn right into O'Connell Street. Soon after crossing over the railway, you will come to St. John's Cemetery on your right. This is the oldest Christian graveyard in Australia and it contains the country's oldest marked grave, that of Henry Dodd, a servant of Governor Phillip, who was interred here in 1791. Leaving the cemetery, walk almost straight ahead along Aird Street, and then turn left into Marsden Street and back across the railway. On your right now is St. John's Cathedral, in Hunter Street. This has been used as a church site since 1803. The two spires were built by convict labour and date from 1819. They are the oldest church spires in Australia. The cathedral owns a bible printed in 1599 and an embroidery of a service in the first church here in the 1840s. The font has Maori carvings. The cathedral is open every day and offers guided tours on Thursdays and Fridays.

Walk now to Church Street, which is for pedestrians only at this point, and continue north to George Street, where turn right. Soon you will reach the Spanish-style Village Roxy Theatre, which has been in operation as a cinema since 1930, at which time it was one of the most modern of picture palaces. It no longer has that distinction, but its ornate architecture merits a look inside. Continue down George Street to Harris Street, then turn right. On reaching Ruse Street, turn left. On your right at 9, Ruse Street is *Experiment Farm Cottage*. The street was named after James Ruse, an ex-convict granted land here in 1791, who created Australia's first private farm. *Experiment Farm Cottage* has an exhibition on his life. The cottage itself was built in 1834 by the Colonial Surgeon, John Harris, and now contains furniture from the 1830s. It is open on Sundays, Tuesdays, Wednesdays and Thursdays from 10:00 (11:00 on Sundays) until 16:00 and admission costs $5.

Retrace your steps for a short distance to Harris Street and turn right into Parkes Street, which runs into Hassall Street. On your right is *Hambledon Cottage*, the former abode of Penelope Lucas, governess to the daughters of John and Elizabeth Macarthur, the owners of Elizabeth Farm, our next stop. *Hambledon Cottage*, at 63, Hassall Street, was built in 1824 and is open on Wednesdays, Thursdays and weekends from 11:00 until 16:00. Admission costs $3. Continue just a short distance along Hassall Street and then turn right into Gregory Place, at the end of which there is a path connecting to Alfred Street. Turn right and then immediately left into Alice Street, where, at no. 70, you can find *Elizabeth Farm*, as mentioned above, the home of John and Elizabeth Macarthur, Australia's first pastoralists. Parts of the building date from 1793, making these parts the oldest European construction remaining in the country. There is also what is claimed to be the oldest olive tree in Australia, a tree which produced its first fruit in 1805. *Elizabeth Farm* is open from 10:00 until 17:00 and admission costs $7, or the *Ticket Through Time* can be used, covering eleven museums and costing $23. From here, continue to the end of Alice Street, turn right into Arthur Street and left into Weston Street. Ahead is Rosehill Station, with the Rosehill Racecourse on the other side. Trains run from here one station south to Clyde, from where there is a frequent service back to the city.

ONE-DAY TRIPS FROM SYDNEY

There are many locations which can be visited as one-day trips from Sydney. However, most of them really deserve more than the few hours which a day visit offers. Therefore, such places as Newcastle, Wollongong and Katoomba (Blue Mountains) are listed separately in this book. If time presses, however, the best and cheapest method of visiting these locations in a day is to purchase a day return rail ticket (departing after 9:00 on weekdays, any time at weekends). None of the three destinations mentioned above currently costs more than $20 day return, the longest journey being to Newcastle for exactly $20. A day return ticket to Wollongong costs $10.40 and that to Katoomba $13.60.

Here, though, are four suggestions for enjoyable one-day trips which will allow you to see a little of the varied and beautiful countryside which lies close to Sydney.

(i) Zig-Zag Railway

The Zig Zag Railway runs on the original course of the Western Main Railway leading westwards from Sydney to Lithgow and beyond. To cross the Blue Mountains, two switchbacks were constructed here in 1869, involving a climb of 1 in 42 to bring the train up over the summit. It was one of Australia's great nineteenth century railway engineering feats. However, by the turn of the century, the line was becoming so crowded that this developed into a bottleneck for traffic, and, in 1907, it was decided to construct a series of ten tunnels through the mountains to eliminate the switchbacks and stiff climb. The tunnels were completed in 1910 and the old route abandoned until 1975.

To reach the Zig Zag Railway, buy a day return ticket to Zig Zag ($17.80) and take a train for Lithgow. The journey of exactly 150 kilometres takes 2 hours and 40 minutes and trains run only every two hours, so plan in advance. Be sure to tell the driver or conductor (or both, to be safe) that you want to alight at Zig Zag, otherwise the train will not stop there. The platform at Zig Zag is tiny, so only the first or last door of the train will be opened and you will usually be told, therefore, to travel in either the first or the last carriage. As you approach, you will pass through the ten tunnels mentioned above. When the author made a visit, I was told by the driver that I might as well travel in the cab with him as it would be easier for him to open the door in there. This gave an excellent view of the tunnels.

NEW SOUTH WALES

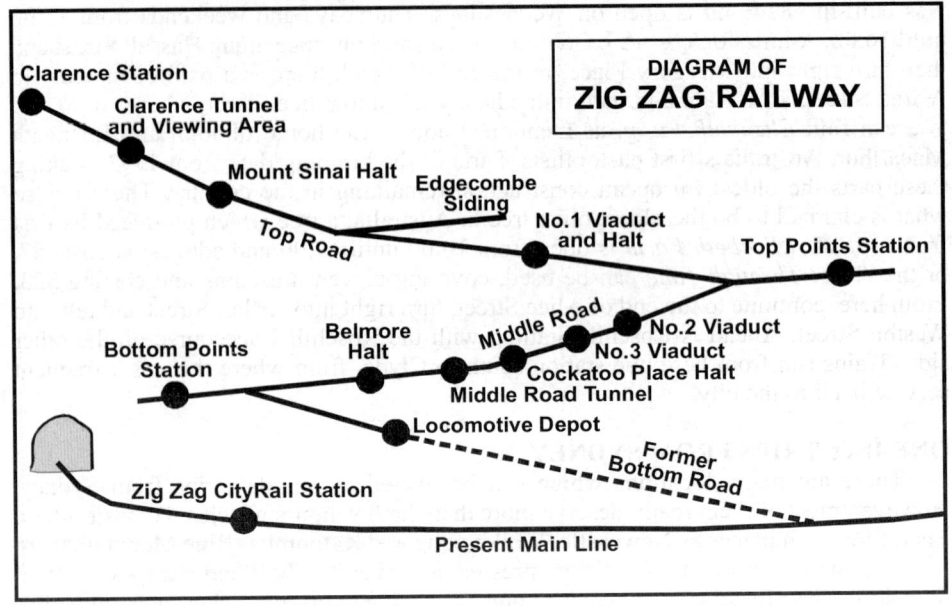

The original Bottom Road of the Zig Zag is mostly still in use as the current main line, with the present locomotive depot located on what used to be the connexion between the Bottom Road and the Zig Zag. Zig Zag services start from the Bottom Points at an altitude of 993 metres, originally the first switchback, and proceed uphill along Middle Road, through a short tunnel and over two viaducts to the Top Points, originally the second switchback. Here the direction of travel reverses and the train goes over another very impressive viaduct, along Top Road, through another tunnel, 493 metres long, and reaches Clarence Station at an altitude of 1,114 metres, near the summit of the original line. The train covers eight kilometres to reach this point and climbs a total of 121 metres, the journey taking twenty to fifty minutes one way. On weekdays, a railcar, which was operating on Queensland Railways until 1994, provides the service. On Saturdays, and throughout the month of January, a steam train runs, and on Sundays both the steam train and the railcar are in operation. If you travel on the railcar, there is a commentary and a tour of the locomotive depot, and photographic halts are made, so, if you have the chance, travel one way on the railcar and the other on the steam train. A round trip will take ninety minutes, or two and a half hours including a tour of the locomotive depot. There is also a walking track between Clarence Station and the Bottom Points.

One of the odd features of the Zig Zag Railway is that although it was originally standard gauge, as the main line is now, it has been rebuilt as a narrow (3 feet 6 inches) gauge line, since available rolling stock was of that gauge. First trains are at 10:10 on weekdays, 9:50 on Saturdays and 8:50 on most Sundays. Last departures from Bottom Points for a round trip are at 16:15 on weekdays, 15:50 on Saturdays and 15:50 on most Sundays. A return journey costs $20.

(ii) Cockatoo Run

The *Cockatoo Run* is a railway journey run by an organisation known as *3801 Limited*. 3801 is a steam engine owned and operated by the organisation, of the last, largest and most powerful type used in New South Wales. It is a magnificent monster. At this point, therefore, lest any misunderstanding arise, it should be made clear that 3801 is not the engine used on this trip. The *Cockatoo Run* is operated by an elderly diesel locomotive.

The train runs every Sunday and Wednesday at present, leaving from Central Station at 9:00 and stopping to pick up passengers at Hurstville at 9:30, Sutherland at 9:50, Thirroul at 10:45, Wollongong at 11:00 and Unanderra at 11:10. The journey thus far is a pretty one, but it can, in fact, be travelled by a double-decker CityRail train offering an even better view. Now, however, the train branches off the main line and runs on a single-track line leading up the Illawarra escarpment to Robertson and Moss Vale. This was originally constructed to take pressure off the main line and to allow heavy trains travelling to the industrial areas around Wollongong and Port Kembla to avoid passing through the Sydney suburbs. The problem with it is that it is very steep. The line rises some 600 metres in sixteen kilometres, a long, long climb at an average gradient of 1 in 27, so it is little used nowadays. CityRail formerly ran one passenger train per week on the line (on Sundays), but now that service has disappeared and the *Cockatoo Run* offers the only passenger train available.

The climb up the escarpment is a scenic one and the views are very good, with the train making one stop for photographs. It is a journey well worth doing, although it is rather expensive. From Sydney, the return trip costs $85, but from Thirroul (or Wollongong or Unanderra) the price is $40 return. Now, as mentioned above, there are CityRail trains to Thirroul which offer a better view and are much cheaper. The day return fare from Sydney to Thirroul is $9.20, so by using CityRail to Thirroul and boarding the *Cockatoo Run* there, the trip can be done for $49.20.

The train reaches Robertson at 13:20, at which point the climb ends and it is a flat run to Moss Vale, reached at 13:55. Passengers have the option of alighting at Robertson and going on a bus tour of the area, including a lavender farm, or continuing

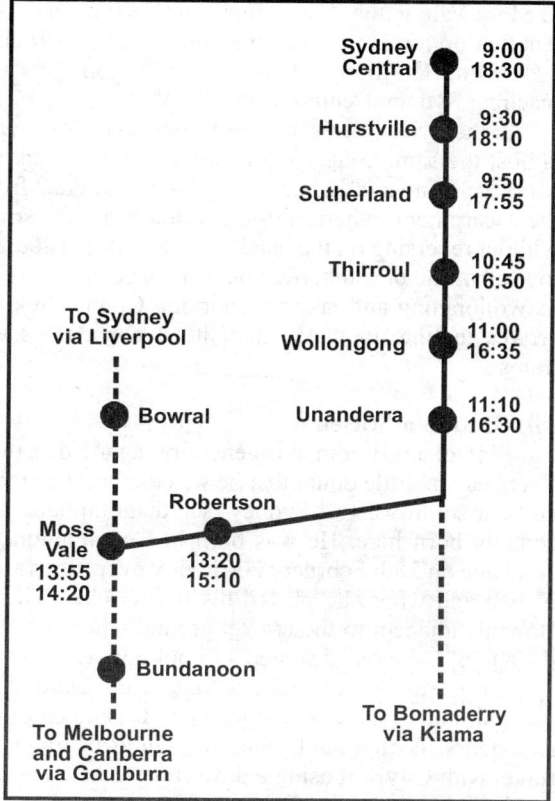

DETAILS OF *COCKATOO RUN*

to Moss Vale without the benefit of the tour. The tour, if taken, is included in the fare. Another option is to have lunch on the train as it climbs the escarpment, but this costs $25 extra. The train returns at 14:20 from Moss Vale and 15:10 from Robertson, reaching Sydney Central at 18:30 (Wollongong 16:35, Thirroul 16:50).

If the price seems too high, one can also undertake a do-it-yourself trip along almost the same route, with similar views, by taking a train to Wollongong, a bus to Moss Vale and a train back to Sydney. The view from the bus is also good as it climbs the escarpment, where, in places, the turns are so tight that it cannot negotiate them without reversing on the bend, a somewhat perilous operation. If you are heading south to Melbourne or Canberra, you can consider this as an alternative route. Stay overnight in Wollongong and take the morning Countrylink bus at 7:20 to Moss Vale, where it arrives in time to make guaranteed connexions with the Canberra and Melbourne trains.

(iii) Bradman Museum

Sir Donald Bradman is generally regarded as the best cricketer there has ever been. There can be little doubt that he was the best batsman. His home town is Bowral, about an hour south-west of Sydney (see diagrammatic map on previous page). He was not actually born here. He was born in Cootamundra on 27th August 1908 and died in Adelaide on 25th February 2001. However, Bowral was where he grew up from the age of two and where he played his first cricket. Therefore, the Bradman Museum is in Bowral, adjacent to the cricket ground where he played his first competitive match at the age of twelve and scored 115 not out, as well as taking eight wickets.

To get to Bowral, take a train from Central. The train will pass through some pleasant countryside on the way and it is an enjoyable journey, which will take about two hours. Both Countrylink and CityRail trains serve Bowral, but it is cheaper to travel with CityRail using a day return ticket. This costs $15.40. Trains are infrequent, so plan your times in advance.

The museum tells the life story of Sir Donald Bradman and contains cricketing trophies, photographs and film of various famous matches, not confined to those in which Sir Donald played. The museum is open from 10:00 until 17:00 daily and admission costs $7.50.

(iv) Royal National Park

The start of the Royal National Park lies only 32 kilometres south of the city of Sydney. This park was established in 1879, making it the oldest national park in Australia and the second oldest in the world. Only Yellowstone National Park in the U.S.A. is older. It offers great natural diversity in a relatively small area, with rivers, surf beaches, and a coastal walk as well as many other inland walks and several cycling tracks

The map opposite gives some idea of the walks available. Most can be completed within half a day, but the coastal walk is 26 kilometres, including some difficult sections, and really needs two days. There is a youth hostel at Garie, about two-thirds of the way along the track from north to south.

To reach the Royal National Park, take a train to Loftus, Engadine, Heathcote, Waterfall, Helensburgh or Otford stations, all of which are adjacent to the park. From Loftus, there is a tram service on Sundays, or you can walk to the Visitor Centre. Trains run from Bondi Junction, King's Cross and Central as far as Waterfall every half hour. The day return fare to Waterfall is $6.20.

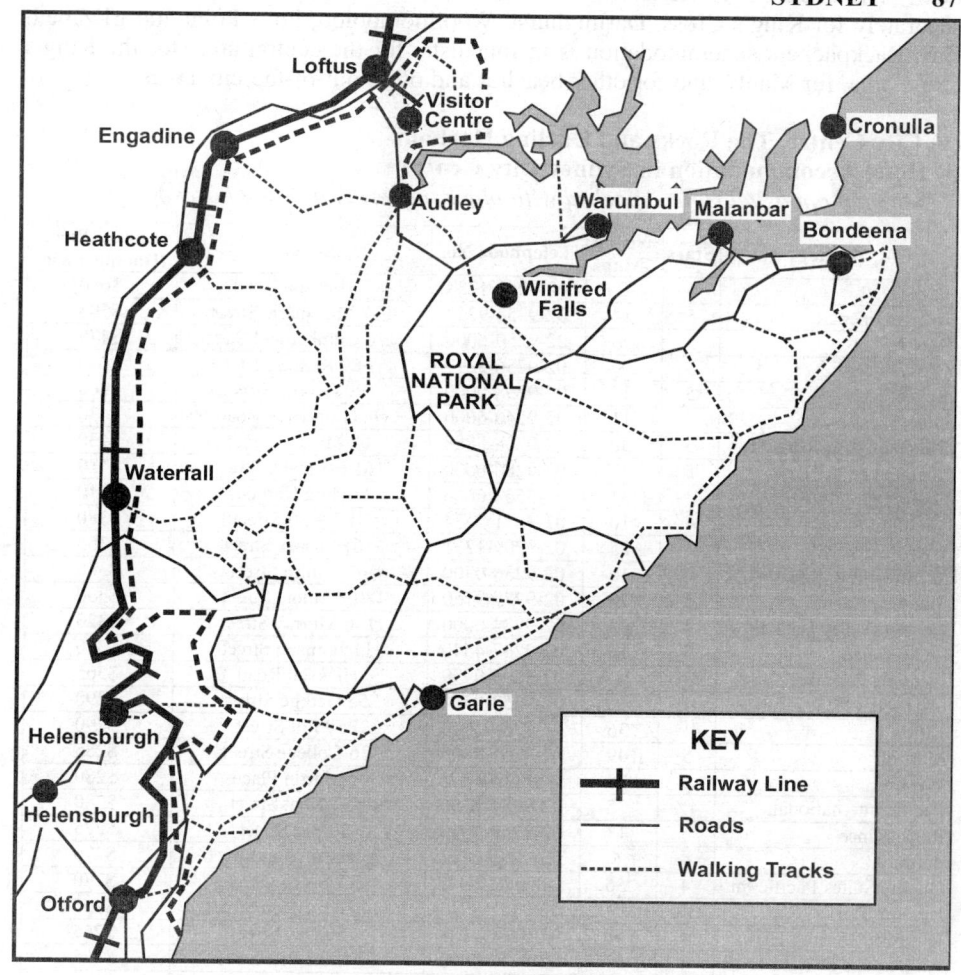

ROYAL NATIONAL PARK

BOOKSHOPS

Collins Booksellers   *Level 2, Broadway Shopping Centre, 1 Bay Street.*

The Broadway Shopping Centre is just off the south of the map on page 43.

ACCOMMODATION

There is, of course, a huge variety of accommodation available in a city as large as Sydney. Generally, it is relatively easy to find higher class hotels, and a little more difficult to locate those lower in price. Therefore, the following information places rather more emphasis on the lower end of the spectrum, although all standards appear in the lists. A division is made, here as elsewhere, into hotels and backpackers (dormitory) accommodation.

Hotels are listed for the central area (City, The Rocks and Darling Harbour) and

88 NEW SOUTH WALES

separately for King's Cross, Darlinghurst, Woolloomooloo, Potts Point and Elizabeth Bay. Backpackers accommodation is in four lists: for the central area, for the King's Cross area, for Manly, and for other beaches and other out-of-the-city areas.

(a) City Centre, The Rocks and Darling Harbour
(i) Hotel Accommodation in Sydney City Centre

(See map opposite. Hotels marked with black numerals in white boxes.)

Name	Stars	No. on Map	Telephone No.	Address	Lowest Price (Double/Twin)
Park Hyatt	5	2	02-9241-1234	7 Hickson Road	$680
Intercontinental	5	14	02-9253-9253	117 Macquarie Street	$505
A.N.A.	5	9	02-9250-6000	176 Cumberland Street	$475
Observatory	5	8	02-9256-2222	89 Kent Street	$470
Regent	5	12	02-9238-0000	199 George Street	$460
Quay West	5	11	02-9240-6000	98 Gloucester Road	$430
Merchant Court Hotel	5	30	02-9238-8888	68 Market Street	$430
Sheraton on the Park	5	37	02-9286-6000	161 Elizabeth Street	$420
Grand Mercure Apts.	4½	31	02-9563-6666	Darling Harbour	$410
Stamford Plaza	4	10	02-9251-7334	187 Kent Street	$380
Four Points Sydney	4½	25	02-9299-1231	161 Sussex Street	$355
Wentworth Rydges	4	19	02-9230-0700	61 Phillip Street	$340
Star City Casino	5	23	02-9777-9150	80 Pyrmont Street	$330
Novotel Darling Harbour	4	33	02-9934-0000	100 Murray Street	$320
Le Meridien	5	16	02-9267-4540	11 Jamison Street	$310
Pier One Parkroyal	4½	1	02-8298-9999	Hickson Road	$305
Old Sydney Holiday Inn	4½	4	02-9252-0524	55 George Street	$290
Hilton	4½	36	02-9266-2000	259 Pitt Street	$290
Marriott	5	49	02-9361-8400	36 College Street	$285
Westin	5	28	1-800-656-535	1 Martin Place	$280
Pacific International	4½	35	02-9284-2306	433 Kent Street	$280
Renaissance	5	13	02-9259-7000	30 Pitt Street	$275
Stafford	4	6	02-9251-6711	75 Harrington Street	$270
Quality Suites Pacific Int.	4	56	1-800-237-442	653 George Street	$270
Harbour Rocks	3½	5	02-9251-8944	34 Harrington Street	$265
Parkroyal Darling Harb.	4	40	02-9261-1188	150 Day Street	$265
All Seasons Darling Harb.	4	53	02-8217-4000	17 Little Pier Street	$265
Southern Cross Harbour	5	54	02-9268-5888	38 Harbour Street	$260
Carrington Apartments.	3½	22	02-9299-6556	57 York Street	$255
Radisson Plaza		18	02-8214-0000	27 O'Connell Street	$245
Saville Park Suites	4	63	02-8268-2500	18 Oxford Street	$245
All Seasons Menzies	4	20	02-9299-1000	14 Carrington Street	$235
Country Comfort	4	71	02-9212-2544	George & Quay Streets	$230
Medina on Crown Hotel		75	02-9360-6666	359 Crown Street	$230
Waldorf Apartments	4	44	02-9261-5355	57 Liverpool Street	$225
Central Park	4	39	02-9283-5000	185 Castlereagh Street	$220
Southern Cross Towers	4½	60	02-9277-3388	Wentworth Av / Goulburn St	$215
Comfort Inn Pacific Int.	3½	69	02-9290-9200	717 George Street	$215
Southern Cross Hotel	4½	59	02-9277-3388	Wentworth Av / Goulburn St	$215
Metro Suites on Sussex	3½	24	1-800-004-321	132 Sussex Street	$205
Avillion	4½	45	02-8268-1888	Liverpool & Pitt Streets	$205
Radisson Hotel	4	43	02-8268-8888	72 Liverpool Street	$200
Hyde Park Plaza	4	50	02-9331-6933	38 College Street	$200
Savoy Apartments	3½	27	02-9267-9211	37 King Street	$195

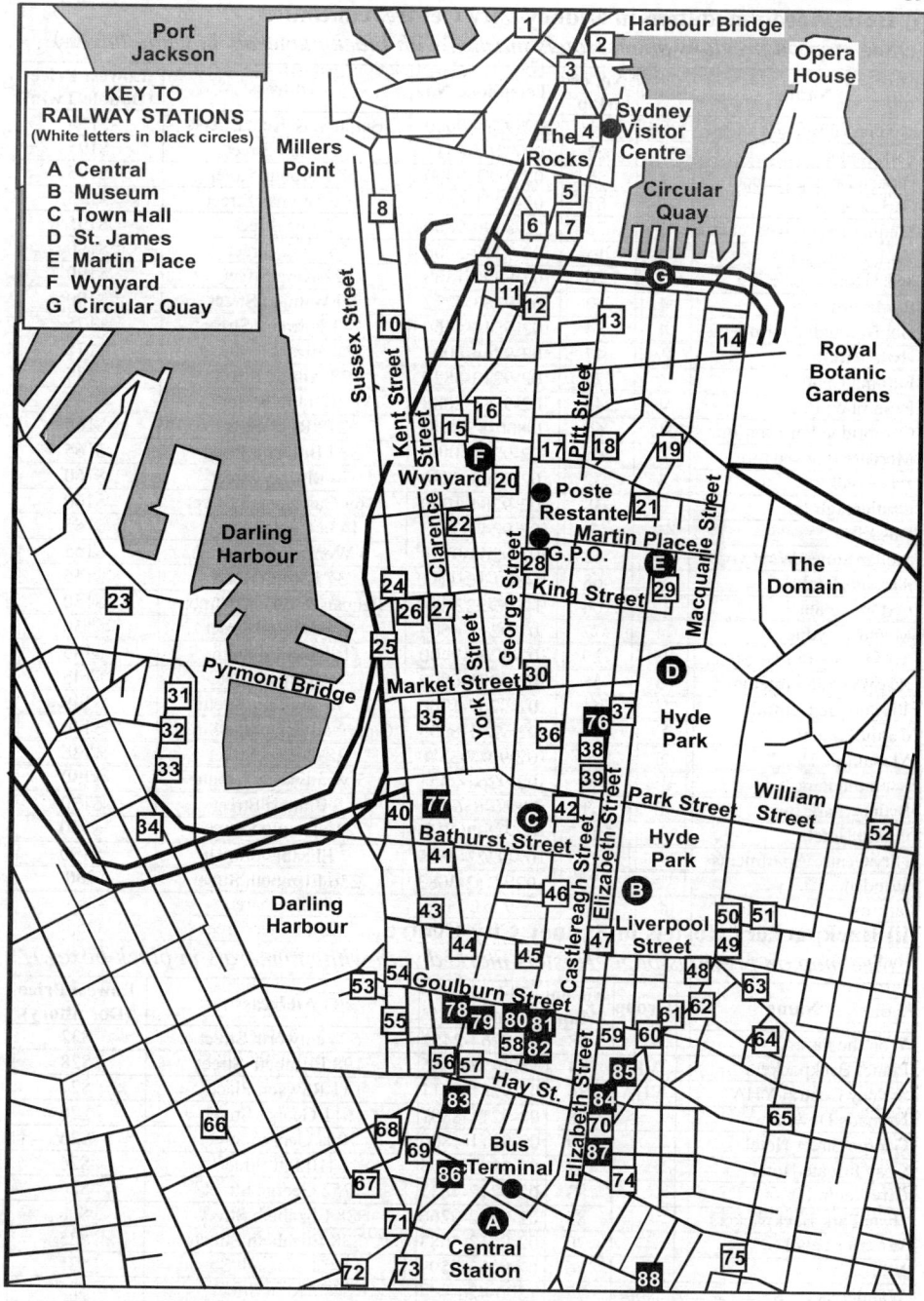

SYDNEY CITY CENTRE ACCOMMODATION
Black numerals in white boxes indicate hotel accommodation
White numerals in black boxes indicate backpackers hostels

90 NEW SOUTH WALES
(i) Hotel Accommodation in Sydney City Centre, continued

(See map on previous page. Hotels marked with black numerals in white boxes.)

Name	Stars	No. on Map	Telephone No.	Address	Lowest Price (Double/Twin)
Medina Grand	5	41	02-9274-0000	Bathurst & Kent Streets	$195
Park Regis	3½	42	02-9267-6511	27 Park Street	$195
Furama Darling Harbour	4	55	02-9281-0400	68 Harbour Street	$195
Carlton Crest	4½	67	02-9281-6888	169 Thomas Street	$195
Medina Executive Central	4½	73	02-8396-9800	2 Lee Street	$195
York Apartments	4½	15	02-9210-5000	5 York Street	$190
Metro Suites on King	3	26	02-9299-1388	27 King Street	$190
Boulevard	4	52	02-9383-7222	90 William Street	$190
Goldsbrough Apartments	4	34	02-9518-5166	243 Pyrmont Street	$175
Hyde Park Inn	3½	47	02-9264-6001	271 Elizabeth Street	$175
Furama Central	4	74	02-9213-3820	28 Albion Street	$175
Pentura on Pitt	4	46	02-9283-8088	300 Pitt Street	$165
Cambridge Park Inn Int.	3½	65	1-800-355-189	212 Riley Street	$165
Mercure Lawson	4	66	02-9211-1499	383 Bulwara Road	$165
Ibis Hotel	3	32	02-9563-0888	70 Murray Street	$160
Castlereagh Inn	3	38	02-9284-1000	169 Castlereagh Street	$160
Russell	4½	7	02-9241-3543	143a George Street	$155
Stellar Suites Wentworth	3½	62	02-9264-9754	4 Wentworth Avenue	$155
Aarons Hotel	3	68	1-800-101-100	37 Ultimo Road	$155
Oxford Koala	3½	64	1-800-222-144	Pelican & Oxford Streets	$150
Mercure Sydney	4	72	02-9217-6666	818 George Street	$150
Travelodge Phillip Street	3½	29	02-8224-9400	165 Phillip Street	$145
Royal Garden Internat'l	3	58	02-9281-6999	431 Pitt Street	$145
Travelodge Central		61	02-8267-1700	27 Wentworth Avenue	$145
Capitol Square	3½	57	02-9211-8633	Campbell & George Streets	$140
Mercantile Hotel	3	3	02-9247-3570	25 George Street	$135
Y on the Park	2½	48	02-9264-2451	5 Wentworth Avenue	$130
Sydney Park Inn	3	51	1-800-656-708	2 Francis Street	$130
Grand Hotel		17	02-9232-3755	30 Hunter Street	$100
City Centre Apartments	2	21	02-9223-3529	7 Elizabeth Street	$100
Windsor		70	02-9212-3083	236 Elizabeth Street	$60

(ii) Backpackers Hostels in Sydney City Centre

(See map on previous page. Hostels marked with white numerals in black boxes.)

Name	Group	No. on Map	Telephone Number	Address	Lowest Price (Dormitory)
Y on the Park		48	02-9264-2451	5 Wentworth Street	$32
Planet Backpackers	VIP	84	1800-774-545	198 Elizabeth Street	$28
Sydney Central YHA	YHA	86	02-9281-9111	11 Rawson Place	$27
Nomads Downtown		78	02-9211-8801	611 George Street	$26
George Street Hotel		79	02-9211-1800	700a George Street	$26
Cosy Private Hotel		82	02-9212-1893	410 Pitt Street	$26
City Central		83	02-9212-4833	752 George Street	$26
Hyde Park Backpackers		85	02-9282-9266	88 Elizabeth Street	$26
Windsor Hotel		70	02-9212-3083	238 Elizabeth Street	$25
Millet's		76	02-9283-6599	161 Castlereagh Street	$25
Wanderers on Kent	Nom	77	1800-424-444	477 Kent Street	$25
Hotel Bakpak C.B.		80	1800-813-522	417 Pitt Street	$25
Hotel Bakpak Westend		81	1800-013-186	412 Pitt Street	$21
Noah's City Central		87	02-9211-9111	240a Elizabeth Street	$20
Excelsior Hotel		88	02-9211-4945	46 Foveaux Street	$26

SYDNEY

(b) King's Cross and Surrounding Area
(i) Hotel Accommodation in King's Cross
(See map on page 63. Hotels marked with black numerals in white boxes.)

Name	Stars	No. on Map	Telephone No.	Address	Lowest Price (Double/Twin)
Kirketon	5	9	02-9332-2011	229 Darlinghurst Road	$255
Crescent on Bayswater	4½	7	1-800-243-481	33 Bayswater Road	$190
17 Elizabeth Bay Road	4	6	02-9358-8999	17 Elizabeth Bay Road	$190
Gazebo	3½	5	1-800-355-187	2 Elizabeth Bay Road	$175
Millennium	4½	8	02-9356-1234	King's Cross Road	$160
Azure MacLeay Apts.	3½	2	1-800-786-370	40 MacLeay Street	$155
Mariners Court Hotel	3½	1	1-800-359-295	44 McElhone Street	$135
Kingsview	3	4	02-9358-5599	30 Darlinghurst Road	$125
Victoria Court Hotel	4	3	02-9357-3200	122 Victoria Street	$95

(ii) Backpackers Hostels in King's Cross
(See map on page 63. Hostels marked with white numerals in black boxes.)

Name	Group	No. on Map	Telephone Number	Address	Lowest Price (Dormitory)
Highfields		18	02-9326-9539	166 Victoria Street	$26
Virgin Backpackers		13	02-9358-6400	144 Victoria Street	$26
Pink House Travellers		25	02-9358-1689	6 Barncleuth Square	$26
Travellers Rest		16	02-9358-4606	156 Victoria Street	$26
Eva's		10	02-9358-2185	6 Orwell Street	$26
Cross Road		19	02-9356-4551	174 Victoria Street	$26
Maksim Lodge		22	02-9356-3399	37 Darlinghurst Road	$26
Springfield Lodge		21	02-9358-3222	9 Springfield Avenue	$26
Globe		26	02-9326-9675	40 Darlinghurst Road	$26
Victoria Lodge		14	02-9358-5085	152 Victoria Street	$25
Backpackers Headquarters	VIP	28	02-9331-6180	79 Bayswater Road	$24
Jolly Swagman	VIP	20	1800-805-870	27 Orwell Street	$23
Funk House	VIP	23	1800-247-600	23 Darlinghurst Road	$22
Lido Apartments		24	02-9358-4844	2 Roslyn Street	$22
Cooee		27	02-9331-0009	107 Darlinghurst Road	$22
Sydney Central	VIP	11	1800-440-202	16 Orwell Street	$21
Original Backpackers	VIP	17	1800-807-130	160 Victoria Street	$21
Potts Point House		15	02-9368-0733	154 Victoria Street	$17
Kanga House		12	02-9357-7897	141a Victoria Street	$16

(c) Manly - Backpackers Hostels
(See map on page 74. Hostels marked with white numerals in black boxes.)

Name	Group	No. on Map	Telephone Number	Address	Lowest Price (Dormitory)
Manly Beach Hut	Nom	5	02-9977-8777	77 Whistler Street	$33
Manly Bunkhouse	VIP	4	1800-657-122	35 Pine Street	$28
Manly Lodge		9	02-9977-8514	22 Victoria Parade	$28
Manly Beachside		7	1800-656-299	28 Raglan Street	$26
Travellers Hostel		6	02-9977-1299	6 Denison Street	$26
Wharf Backpackers		8	02-9977-2800	48 East Esplanade	$26
Manly Astra	VIP	3	02-9977-2092	68 Pittwater Road	$26
Manly Beach Resort		1	02-9977-4188	6 Carlton Street	$24
Manly Cottage Inn	VIP	2	02-9976-0297	25 Pittwater Road	$22

92 NEW SOUTH WALES
(d) Beaches and Out-of-City Areas - Backpackers Hostels
(See map on page 65. Hostels marked with white numerals in black boxes.)

Name	Group	No. on Map	Telephone Number	Address	Lowest Price (Dormitory)
Glebe Village	VIP	1	1800-801-983	256 Glebe Point Road, Glebe	$26
Glebe Point YHA	YHA	2	02-9692-8418	262 Glebe Point Road, Glebe	$25
Forest Lodge	Nom	3	1800-737-378	117 Arundel St., Forest Lodge	$21
Wattle House		4	02-9552-4997	44 Hereford Street, Glebe	$26
Elite Private Hotel		5	02-9929-6365	133 Carabella Street, Kirribilli	$26
A.A. Tremayne		6	02-9955-0341	89 Carabella Street, Kirribilli	$26
Sydney Summer Y.H.A.	YHA	7	02-9557-1133	St Andrews, Carillion Av, Newtown	$26 (Dec - Jan)
Billabong Gardens	VIP	8	1800-806-419	5 Egan Street, Newtown	$22
Australian Sunrise		9	02-9550-4999	485 King Street, Newtown	$26
Dulwich Hill Y.H.A.	YHA	10	02-9550-0054	407 Marrickville Rd., Dulwich	$20
Kriskindl	B&W	11	02-9558-3332	22a Hillcrest Street, Tempe	$25
Harbour City Hotel	VIP	12	02-9380-2922	50 Sir John Young Cr., Wmloo.	$25
City Resort		13	02-9357-3333	Palmer Street, Woolloomooloo	$26
Tokyo Joe's		14	02-9311-4279	132 Bourke Street, W'mooloo	$26
Crown Budget Inn		15	02-9360-9744	199 Crown Street, Darlinghurst	$29
Kangaroo Bak-Pak	B&W	16	02-9319-5915	665 S. Dowling St., Surry Hills	$22
Alfred Park Lodge		17	02-9319-4031	207 Cleveland Street, Redfern	$26
Central Student Accom.		18	02-9698-8839	243 Cleveland Street, Redfern	$26
Captain Cook Hotel		19	1800-737-378	162 Flinders St., Darlinghurst	$21
Bondi View Lodge		20	0412-099-007	41 Bennett Street, Bondi	$25
Lamrock Hostel		21	02-9365-0221	7 Lamrock Avenue, Bondi	$26
Lamrock Lodge		22	02-9130-5063	19 Lamrock Avenue, Bondi	$26
Biltmore Private Hotel		23	02-9130-4660	110 Campbell Parade, Bondi	$30
Kensington Summer YHA	YHA	24	02-9315-0022	Gate 6, High Street, Kensington	$30 (Dec - Jan)
Backpackers Clovelly		25	02-9665-3333	272 Clovelly Road, Clovelly	$26
Coogee Beach		26	02-9315-8000	94 Beach Street	$22
Aegean		27	02-9314-5324	40 Coogee Bay Road, Coogee	$26
Wizard of Oz	VIP	28	1800-013-460	172 Coogee Bay Road	$25
Surfside	VIP	29	02-9315-7888	186 Arden Street, Coogee	$26
Beachside Budget		30	02-9315-8511	178 Coogee Bay Road	$26
Pittwater Y.H.A.		31	02-9999-2196	Kuringai National Park	$21
Beachhouse Y.H.A.	YHA	32	02-9981-1177	4 Collaroy Street, Collaroy	$27
Cronulla Beach Y.H.A.	YHA	33	02-9527-7772	40 Kingsway, Cronulla	$27

MOVING ON
Sydney is a hub for all transport in Australia. From Central Station, trains and buses depart directly or with connexions to all parts of the country.

(i) By Train
Here are current timetables for the interstate services to Adelaide, Perth and Alice Springs operated by Great Southern Railway, for the interstate services operated by Countrylink to Brisbane, Canberra and Melbourne, and for the services within New South Wales operated by Countrylink to Murwillumbah, Grafton, Armidale, Moree, Dubbo, Broken Hill and Griffith.

There are connecting bus services from the trains within New South Wales to many other destinations. The most useful of these are also shown on the timetables.

These are timetables for trains departing from Sydney. For services in the opposite direction, see the entry for the point of departure.

SYDNEY

Sydney to Perth or Alice Springs via Adelaide

Days of Operation	M, Th	Sun
Sydney	1455	1310
Days	Tu, F	M
Broken Hill	0920	0550
Adelaide (arrive)	1555	1215
Adelaide (depart)	1830	1500
Port Augusta	2320	1920
Days	W, Sat	Tu
Cook	0918	
Kalgoorlie (arrive)	1920	
Kalgoorlie (depart)	2230	
Days	Th, Su	
Perth	0930	
Alice Springs		0900

Sydney to Canberra, with connexions to Eden

Days of Operation	Daily	M, W, F (Bus)	Daily	Daily (Bus)	Daily
Sydney	0705		1144		1814
Strathfield	0716		1155		1825
Moss Vale	0854		1331		2002
Goulburn	0941		1418		2049
Queanbeyan	1058		1535		2206
Canberra Jolimont		1155		1550	
Canberra Station	1115	1215	1550	1610	2221
Cooma		1330		1730	
Bombala		1440			
Bega				1925	
Merimbula				1951	
Eden		1610		2020	

Sydney to Melbourne and Griffith, with connexions to Echuca and Mildura

Days of Operation	Sat	Daily	Daily (Bus)	Daily (Bus)	M, W, F, Sun (Bus)	Tu, Th, Sat (Bus)	Daily	Mon, Sat (Bus)	Daily (Bus)
Sydney	0705	0743					2043		
Strathfield	0716	0754					2054		
Moss Vale	0854	0932					2231		
Goulburn	0941	1020					2319		
Yass Junction	1045	1125					0024		
Cootamundra	1200	1245	1405				0142		
Wagga Wagga	1305	1348		1415	1415		0243	0255	
Albury		1502				1520	0355		0425
Echuca					1850	1935			0805
Adelaide									1615
Griffith	1538		1641	1653				0533	
Mildura			2236						
Wangaratta		1543					0436		
Benalla		1614					0500		
Melbourne		1815					0700		

Sydney to Dubbo and Broken Hill, with connexions to Bourke and Lightning Ridge

Days of Operation	Mon	Daily	Tu, Th, Sat, Sun (Bus)	M, W, F (Bus)	Tu, Th, F, Sun (Bus)	Daily (Bus)	Daily (Bus)	Sun	M, Th
Sydney	0620	0710						1310	1455
Strathfield	0631	0721							
Katoomba	0807	0851							
Lithgow	0847	0931						1607	1809
Bathurst	0958	1041						1732	1945
Orange	1117	1156	1205	1205				1926	2135
Parkes	1249		1320	1412				2106	2333
Dubbo		1340			1359	1410	1415		
Bourke					1825				
Lightning Ridge						1830			
Menindee	1822							0425	0627
Broken Hill	1910						2245	0531	0830

NEW SOUTH WALES

Sydney to Tamworth, Armidale and Moree, with connexions to Tenterfield and Inverell

Days of Operation	Daily	Daily (Bus)	Daily (Bus)
Sydney	0935		
Strathfield	0946		
Broadmeadow	1152		
Werris Creek	1509		
Tamworth	1552	1610	
Armidale	1749		1800
Glen Innes			1916
Tenterfield			2031
Narrabri	1716		
Moree	1833		
Warialda		1834	
Inverell		1930	

Sydney to Brisbane and Murwillumbah, with connexions to Gold Coast

Days of Operation	Daily	Daily (Bus)	Daily (Bus)	Daily (Bus)	Daily (Bus)	Daily (Bus)	Daily	Daily (Bus)	Daily	Daily (Bus)	Daily (Bus)
Sydney	0715						1135		1624		
Strathfield	0726						1146		1636		
Broadmeadow	0934						1354		1845		
Taree	1235						1711		2142		
Wauchope	1341						1819	1830	2250		
Port Macquarie								1855			
Nambucca Heads	1515						1952		0021		
Coffs Harbour	1557						2031		0059		
Grafton City	1708		1720				2200		0221		
Casino	1835								0348	0400	0400
Lismore	1910	1925									0425
Ballina		2007	2028								0508
Lennox Head		2025									0516
Byron Bay	2000		2105								0539
Murwillumbah	2100			2115	2115	2120					0637
Bogangar										0549	
Tweed Heads						2136					0707
Palm Beach						2146				0617	
Burleigh Heads						2151				0623	
Robina						2205					
Surfers Paradise				2215						0643	
Southport				2230							
Beenleigh					2220						
Brisbane					2250				0635		

(ii) By Bus

Here is a summary of direct services to all principal destinations from Sydney. Connecting services are not shown, but note that both Firefly services to Melbourne connect with onward services to Adelaide. Firefly offers a through fare from Sydney to Adelaide of $100.

Destination	Operator	Via	Distance (km)	Fare	Journey Time	Frequency
Brisbane via Coast	McCafferty's		1018	$103	14½ - 17½ hrs	2/day
		Surfers Paradise	930	$103	13 - 16 hrs	2/day
		Byron Bay	819	$103	12 - 14 hrs	1/day
		Coffs Harbour	577	$85	8½ - 11 hrs	2/day
		Port Macquarie	413	$76	6 - 8½ hrs	2/day
Brisbane via Coast	Greyhound		1018	$103	17 hrs	3/day
		Surfers Paradise	930	$103	15½ hrs	3/day
		Byron Bay	819	$103	13½ hrs	3/day
		Coffs Harbour	577	$85	8½ - 10 hrs	3/day
		Port Macquarie	426	$76	7¼ hrs	1/day
Brisbane via Coast	Premier		1018	$93	16½ - 17½ hrs	3/day
		Surfers Paradise	930	$93	15 - 17½ hrs	3/day
		Byron Bay	819	$90	13½ - 15½ hrs	3/day
		Coffs Harbour	577	$63	9¼ - 10½ hrs	3/day
		Port Macquarie	413	$58	7 - 8¼ hrs	3/day
Brisbane via Inland	McCafferty's		1066	$103	18¼ hrs	1/day
		Toowoomba	940	$98	16¼ hrs	1/day
		Tamworth	440	$74	8½ hrs	1/day
Melbourne via Inland	McCafferty's		923	$73	12¼ - 14 hrs	2/day
		Albury	640	$54	8 - 10 hrs	2/day
Melbourne via Inland	Greyhound		923	$73	11½ - 14½ hrs	3/day
		Albury	640	$54	7¼ - 9½ hrs	3/day
Melbourne via Inland	Firefly		923	$60	12¼ hrs	2/day
		Albury	640	$60	8 hrs	2/day
Melbourne via Coast	Premier		1225	$76	17½ hrs	1/day
		Lakes Entrance	840	$71	11¾ hrs	1/day
		Eden	591	$63	8¾ - 9¾ hrs	2/day
		Batemans Bay	330	$39	5½ hrs	3/day
Adelaide	McCafferty's		1546	$141	23¾ hrs	1/day
		Nuriootpa	1486	$141	22½ hrs	1/day
		Mildura	1170	$113	17¾ hrs	1/day
Adelaide	Greyhound		1684	$141	24¼ hrs	3/week
		Broken Hill	1125	$147	17 hrs	3/week
		Dubbo	402	$74	7 hrs	3/week
Canberra	McCafferty's		278	$40	4¾ - 5 hrs	3/day
Canberra	Greyhound		278	$40	3½ - 5 hrs	5/day
Canberra	Murray's		214	$39	3½ - 3¾ hrs	3/day
Thredbo (Winter)	Greyhound		337	$101	8¼ hrs	1 - 2/day
		Ski Tube	332	$101	8 hrs	1 - 2/day
Scone	Keans		309	$47	5 hrs	1/day

NEW SOUTH WALES
NEWCASTLE

Population 300,000

2 hrs 30 mins by train from Sydney
3 hrs by bus from Sydney

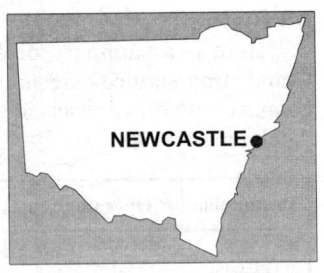

Newcastle lies approximately 160 kilometres north of Sydney, a journey of two and a half hours by CityRail train. It is a city which can be visited as a day trip from Sydney, or more often, unfortunately, not visited at all. In fact, though, it is an old industrial city of some interest.

If you decide to go as a one-day excursion, a day return ticket from Sydney costs $20 and is available after 9:00 on weekdays, or at any time at weekends. Direct trains leave from Central Station every hour during the main part of the day (currently at 17 minutes past each hour). On the way, you will have some beautiful views of mountains and rivers, particularly the area around the **Hawkesbury River**, 50 to 70 minutes into the journey. You can also stay in this attractive area if time permits. All types of accommodation are available here, including backpackers accommodation. This is the main line north from Sydney, so if you are heading for Brisbane or the Gold Coast or Tamworth by train, you will still get these views, but not with the advantage of a double-decker CityRail train. Just before Newcastle, immediately after Broadmeadow station, the main line swings west and electrification ends, while the train to Newcastle swings east and continues for four more short stations, all within the city of Newcastle, to the terminus at the station named Newcastle.

Newcastle is the seventh largest city in Australia and is the largest city which is not a state or federal capital. It has a population of approximately 300,000. Newcastle was founded on 30th March 1804 as a penal settlement, so has a selection of buildings old by Australian standards, as well as beaches, surf, impressive coastal scenery, bushland and a well-known lake. It is also an important port, especially for the export of coal, of which resource some 70 million tonnes passes through the city annually. It is, in fact, the largest coal exporting port in the world.

One of the most famous events in the city's recent history occurred at 10:27 on Thursday, 28th December 1989 when an earthquake registering 5.6 on the Richter Scale shook the city and resulted in the loss of thirteen lives. It was the first time in Australian history that an earthquake was known to have caused fatalities.

Most of the attractions of Newcastle are within walking distance of the station, as can be seen from the map opposite, so let us take a walking tour.

Walking Tour

This tour covers about five kilometres and will last for some two hours, if no lengthy stops are made.

First of all, the **station** itself is relatively old. There has been a station here since the Great Northern Line started to operate, in the late 1850s. The present building dates from 1878.

Customs House is just to the east of the railway station. It has a clock tower with a time ball on top. Since Customs House was constructed in 1876, the ball was dropped every day at 13:00 as a visual time signal. However, since the earthquake it has not worked properly. The building is now used as a pub and restaurant. Next to it is the old **Paymaster's Office** for New South Wales Government Railways, dating from 1879. It also is now a restaurant.

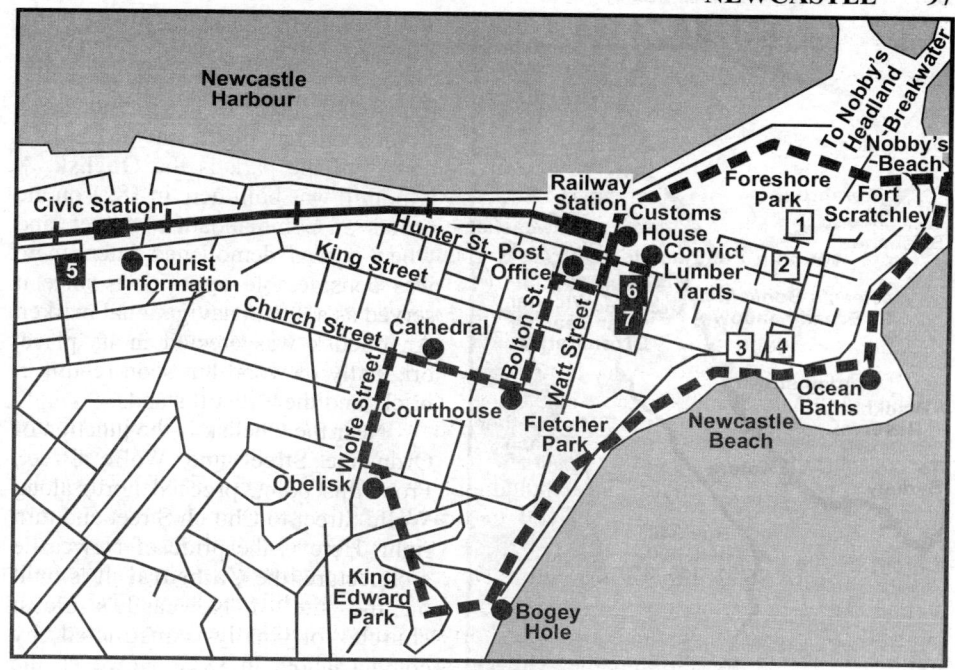

NEWCASTLE

Dashed line shows Walking Tour
Black numerals in white boxes indicate hotel accommodation
White numerals in black boxes indicate backpackers hostels

Beyond these two buildings is the site of the former **Convict Lumber Yards**. This is the oldest surviving example of a convict industrial site. It was in operation between 1814 and 1846. Moreover, beneath it is an **aboriginal site** which dates back several thousands of years.

Further on still is **Foreshore Park**, an area which used to be railway yards, but now has been transformed into a park, with the old warehouses used as shops and restaurants. To its eastern side is **Fort Scratchley**, constructed in 1882, because of fears of a Russian invasion. However, its first and only action occurred on 7th June 1942, when a Japanese submarine arrived and fired 24 shots at Newcastle. Fort Scratchley fired two rounds in reply before the submarine disappeared. The fort is now a Maritime and Military Museum, open from 12:00 until 16:00 every day except Monday.

Beyond the fort is the Breakwater constructed by convict labour to protect the port. At its tip is the conspicuous Nobby's Headland, which was, in fact, originally an island.

Returning next to the eastern foreshore, we come first to **Nobby's Beach**, and then to the **Ocean Baths**, an interesting enclosed swimming area dating from 1922, when mixed bathing was first permitted in the city. Beyond is **Newcastle Beach**, the longest of the beach areas in the city, and then **Fletcher Park** at its end. Continuing south, we reach **Bogey Hole**, a swimming hole cut in the natural rock, at the order of Commandant Morisset in 1819. Originally it was his private swimming place, but it became a public pool in 1863. The term 'Bogey' Hole is evidently derived from the aboriginal word for bathing.

NEW SOUTH WALES

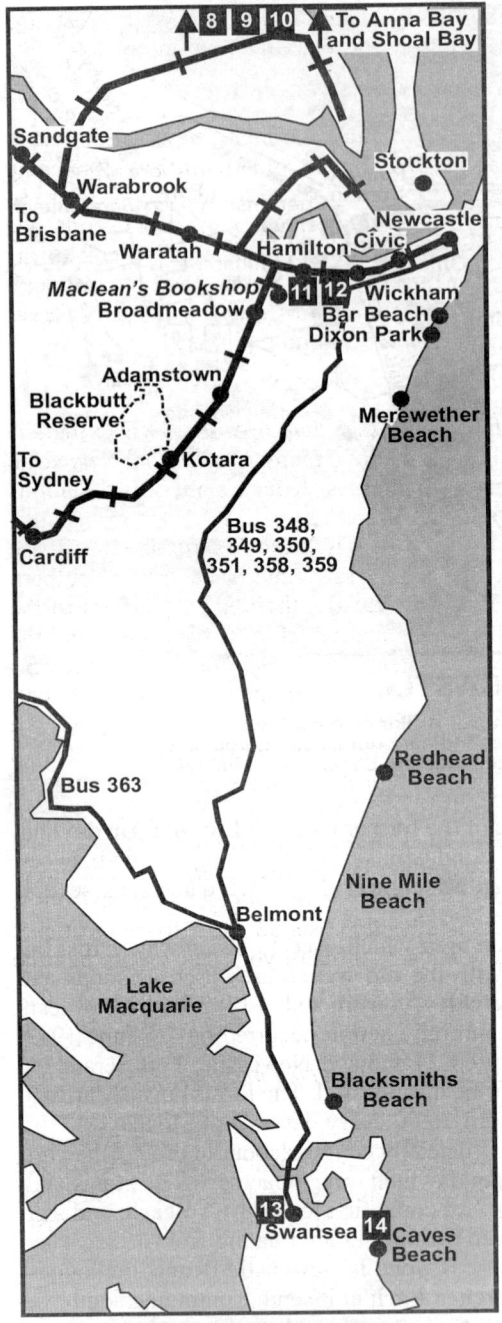

**NEWCASTLE TO
LAKE MACQUARIE**
Numerals indicate backpackers hostels

Back from the Bogey Hole is **King Edward Park**, given to the city in 1865, but renamed later after the monarch of the time. The rotunda dates from Victorian times. In the farthest corner of the park is the **Obelisk**. A windmill was built here in 1821 on the orders of Commandant Morisset, and when it was demolished later, there was considerable opposition, since it served as a useful navigational marker. An obelisk was erected in its place, originally of wood but soon rebuilt in brick, and there it still stands.

Near the Obelisk is the junction of Ordnance Street and Wolfe Street. From this point, proceed north along Wolfe Street to Church Street and turn right. Here is the pride of Newcastle architecture, the **Cathedral**. It is built on the site of Newcastle's oldest church, originally constructed by convict labour in 1817. However, the use of poor workmanship and materials led to the demolition of the original church, and the construction of the present cathedral started in 1884. There were several disputes over its design, so it was not until 1902 that it was completed. The tower was added in 1979, but ten years later the earthquake occurred, resulting in considerable damage to the entire building. Restoration has now taken place.

Continue east along Church Street to reach the Courthouse at the junction with, and looking down, Bolton Street. The **Courthouse** is an imposing piece of Victorian architecture, built in 1890.

Now walk two blocks down the slope of Bolton Street to the **Post Office**, on the corner of, and facing, Hunter Street. This Post Office has survived the fate of many like ornate buildings and is still used for its original purpose. It was constructed in 1902.

NEWCASTLE

Walk past the Post Office along Hunter Street, then turn left into Watt Street, and you will find yourself back at the Railway Station, the Walking Tour complete.

Beaches

As for beaches, known for their surf are **Nobby's Beach, Newcastle Beach**, already mentioned, then, a little further south, **Bar Beach** and **Dixon Park** (see map opposite). Further south still is **Merewether Beach**, a little too far away to walk, so take bus no. 207. The journey takes about fifteen minutes. Still continuing south, one reaches **Redhead Beach**, for which take bus no. 322 for almost an hour; **Blacksmiths Beach**, the scene of the 1994 Australian Surfing Carnival and reached by an hour's journey on bus no. 349 (or 348, 350, 351 or 359, plus a short walk), and finally **Caves Beach**, reached by bus 348, 350, 351 or 358 after a 75-minute journey.

Attractions around Newcastle

The bushland is situated at **Blackbutt Reserve** (see map opposite), where there is an expanse of native countryside with walking tracks and picnic areas. From Newcastle take bus no. 232 or 363. The journey takes 35 minutes. Kotara station, two stations south of Broadmeadow, is also near the reserve.

The well-known lake in the vicinity of Newcastle is **Lake Macquarie** (again see map). This is a salt water lake, in fact the largest salt water lake in the southern hemisphere, and a picturesque one too. From Newcastle, there is easy access to the eastern side of the lake along the narrow strip of land which runs between it and the sea. To get the best view of the lake, however, take bus 363 to **Belmont**. This route runs along the lake shore almost all the way, taking about 90 minutes to reach Belmont. From there, take bus 348, 349, 350, 351, 358 or 359 to **Swansea** to see where the lake empties into the sea. This second journey will take fifteen minutes. All of these buses return directly to Newcastle if you do not wish to repeat the journey round the shore of the lake. The direct return route takes approximately 75 minutes. The western side of Lake Macquarie can be reached from **Fassifern** station. There used to be a branch line from here to Toronto, but now there is a railway bus. The journey takes fifteen minutes.

Newcastle has an efficient bus network, operated, as in Sydney, by State Transit. Tickets are based on time. A one-hour ticket currently costs $2.50. A four-hour ticket costs $5 and an all-day ticket costs $8. As long as you board your bus within the time limit, you may complete your journey on that vehicle.

BOOKSHOPS

Maclean's Booksellers   69 Beaumont Street, Hamilton (see map opposite)

ACCOMMODATION

Here is some of the accommodation available in Newcastle. Hotels included are only those in the city centre. Backpackers accommodation, however, includes all within the Newcastle area, with those in the immediate vicinity of the city listed first.

(i) Hotel Accommodation in Newcastle

Name	Stars	No. on Map	Telephone No.	Address	Lowest Price (Double/Twin)
Holiday Inn, Esplanade	4½	4	02-4929-5576	Shortland Esplanade	$205
Dunvegan House		1	02-4929-4103	4 Shepherds Place	$145
Noah's on the Beach	3½	3	02-4929-5181	Shortland Esplanade	$130
Anne's B&B at Ismebury		2	02-4929-5376	3 Stevenson Place	$108

NEW SOUTH WALES

(ii) Backpackers Hostels in the Newcastle Area

Name	Group	No. on Map	Telephone No.	Address	Lowest Price (Dormitory)
Hunter on Hunter		5	02-4929-3152	417 Hunter Street	$22
Nomads by the Beach	Nom	6	02-4926-3472	34 Hunter Street	$24
Newcastle Beach Y.H.A.	YHA	7	02-4925-3544	30 Pacific Street	$22
Shoal Bay YHA	YHA	8	02-4981-0982	59 Shoal Bay Road, Shoal Bay	$19
Melaleuca Backpackers		9	02-4981-9422	33 Eucalyptus Drive, Anna Bay	$24
Samurai Beach Bungalows		10	02-4982-1921	Frost Road, Anna Bay	$24
Backpackers Newcastle	VIP	11	1800-333-436	42 Denison Street, Hamilton	$18
Accommodation West End		12	02-4961-4446	775 Hunter Street, Newcastle	$28
Swansea Backpackers		13	02-4971-1227	196 High Street, Swansea	$24
Caves Beach Hotel		14	02-4971-1532	Caves Beach Rd, Caves Beach	$24

MOVING ON

(i) By Train

To Sydney, take a CityRail train for the journey of two and a half hours. Trains run hourly during most of the day. The first train is at 2:47 and the last at 23:19. Most trains during the main part of the day depart at 37 minutes past the hour.

To move north, take a local train, or a bus no. 226, 227 or 228, to Broadmeadow station. Then catch a Countrylink train to Moree, Armidale, Grafton, Murwillumbah or Brisbane, for which see the timetables on page 94.

There is also a CityRail service which runs at least hourly all day and night as far as Maitland, and then occasional trains continue along the main lines as far as Dungog on the line to Brisbane and as far as Scone on the line to Tamworth, Armidale and Moree.

(ii) By Bus

As for long-distance buses, here is a summary of the services available.

Destination	Operator	Via	Distance (km)	Fare	Journey Time	Frequency
Sydney	McCafferty's		162	$33	3½ - 4 hrs	2/day
Sydney	Greyhound		177	$33	2¾ - 3¼ hrs	3/day
Sydney	Premier		162	$32	3½ - 3¾ hrs	2/day
Brisbane via Coast	McCafferty's		847	$91	13½ hrs	2/day
		Surfers Paradise	768	$91	12¾ hrs	1/day
		Coffs Harbour	419	$62	7 hrs	1/day
		Port Macquarie	251	$47	4½ hrs	1/day
Brisbane via Coast	Greyhound		843	$91	13½ hrs	2/day
		Surfers Paradise	755	$91	12¼ hrs	2/day
		Byron Bay	644	$90	10 - 10½ hrs	2/day
		Coffs Harbour	402	$62	6¼ - 6¾ hrs	2/day
		Port Macquarie	251	$47	4¼ hrs	1/day
Brisbane via Coast	Premier		843	$74	14¾ hrs	1/day
		Surfers Paradise	768	$74	13¼ hrs	1/day
		Byron Bay	644	$70	11 hrs	1/day
		Coffs Harbour	419	$55	6¼ hrs	1/day
		Port Macquarie	251	$46	4 hrs	1/day

KATOOMBA AND THE BLUE MOUNTAINS
Population 20,000

2 hrs by train from Sydney

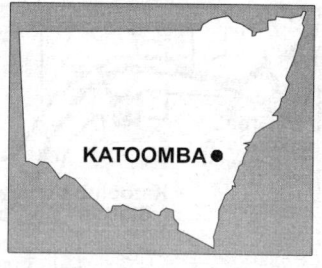

Katoomba is the favourite destination in the area of the Blue Mountains National Park. It is 110 kilometres west of Sydney by CityRail train, a journey which takes two hours. It is, therefore, quite possible to visit Katoomba as a day trip, in which case a day return ticket costs $13.60. However, the area deserves more than a day visit and is, in any case, a pleasant place to stay, so stay if you can.

The railway line runs through the **Blue Mountains National Park** from **Lapstone** onwards and offers some splendid views. This is the main line westwards, so you will also get these views if you are travelling from Sydney to Adelaide, Broken Hill or Dubbo. The reason for the name Blue Mountains soon becomes apparent, for the distant ranges do indeed appear to be covered in a blue haze. One theory is that this is caused by the evaporation of eucalyptus vapour, but it is only a theory.

The Blue Mountains were a great barrier in the way of penetration inland for the first European settlers and it was not until May 1813 that the first route through them was discovered by Blaxland, Wentworth and Lawson, all of whose names you will now find given to stations and communities on the journey up to Katoomba. By 1815, there was a road through the mountains. The railway was built in 1868 and tourism started in the area soon after. The Blue Mountains National Park was declared in 1959 and covers 248,433 hectares. Its most spectacular feature is an escarpment with sheer waterfalls and impressive views. There are also some caves, and in the past the area has been mined for coal.

Katoomba is a medium-sized town, now dependent almost entirely on tourism. Because of its elevation, it is also a town which can get quite chilly in the winter evenings, so bring a sweater if you are staying overnight and it is that time of the year. Accommodation here specialises in offering log fires for the delight of guests during the cooler months.

Walking Tour *(see map on next page)*

This walk covers approximately five kilometres and will take about two hours. It can be extended to some nine kilometres, taking three hours, as noted below.

When you leave the station, you will see the main street (Katoomba Street) straight ahead of you. Walk down this road for about a kilometre until you reach Katoomba Falls Road on your right. Take this road and you will come to **Katoomba Skyway** and **Scenic Railway**. The Skyway is a ropeway suspended across a deep valley. The car attached goes across the valley and then returns.

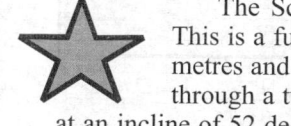

The Scenic Railway is, in the author's opinion, much more exciting. This is a funicular railway which descends at an acceptable angle for a few metres and then plunges off the edge of the 170-metre-high escarpment and through a tunnel. It claims to be the steepest funicular railway in the world, at an incline of 52 degrees, an angle which is terrifyingly steep. This railway was not built as a tourist attraction. It used to be a working line, for at the bottom of the terrifying descent is an abandoned coal mine. The railway used to take the miners down

KATOOMBA

Dashed line shows Walking Tour
Black numerals in white boxes indicate hotel accommodation
White numerals in black boxes indicate backpackers hostels

to the pit entrance and haul the coal back up. To see the entrance to the old mine, with the cliff face at your back turn right and walk just a short distance from the foot of the railway. You can make either a single or a return journey on this railway, but the author recommends a single. From the lower station, which is a horizontal section of rail extending precariously out over the abyss, you can walk east, in the opposite direction to the mine, to the Three Sisters Lookout at Echo Point, a walk of about 45 minutes, or to the Sisters themselves, if you prefer. Although it would seem more practical to walk down from the lookout and then take the railway up again, the author recommends the opposite in this case, as the descent on the railway is the real experience rather than the return trip.

The **Three Sisters** are, as the name implies, a group of three pinnacles standing out and isolated from the escarpment. At the **Echo Point Lookout**, you will have a magnificent view, weather permitting, not only of the Sisters, but of the Jamison Valley continuing into the distance and the great expanse of unspoilt bushland. There is also a **Visitor Information Centre** here with maps available of further walks.

From Echo Point, follow Echo Point Road until it runs into Lurline Street, and so return to the town.

What is described above is just a stroll, although one rewarded by some excellent views. To extend the walk to approximately nine kilometres and include some extra and impressive cliff-top views, continue along the Cliff Walk beyond Echo Point. You will encounter two lookouts, first **Honeymoon Lookout**, then **Kiah Lookout**, and after those, views of **Leura Falls** and **Gordon Falls**. Thence retrace your steps for a short distance and walk north up Leura Mall, either all the way to Leura Station or to Megalong Street, where turn left and, via Clarence Street and Lovel Street, return to Katoomba Station.

If, on the other hand, so much exercise seems too strenuous, there are two bus companies operating services following the route of the longer walk, plus just a little extra, but minus the walk from the foot of the funicular railway up to Echo Point, of course. These two companies are *Trolley Tours* and *Blue Mountains Explorer Bus*. Buses depart hourly from 9:30 until 16:30 on a circular route, making 27 stops, at any of which passengers may alight and reboard later in the day. A one-day ticket costs $25, and offers discounts on admission charges to various attractions including the Katoomba Skyway and Scenic Railway. It is cheaper to walk!

For those who are serious about exploration there are scores of other walks available, too many to be listed here. Obtain information from the Visitor Information Centre if these walks appeal.

Other Attractions Nearby

Another popular destination in the Blue Mountains is **Wentworth Falls**, two stations from Katoomba in the direction of Sydney. It is also possible to walk between Katoomba and Wentworth, part of the walk being along the edge of the escarpment, as described above. The falls are triple-tiered and 180 metres high in total.

The famous caves are the **Jenolan Caves**, just outside the south-western boundary of the Blue Mountains National Park. Nine limestone caverns are open to the public. The easiest way to see these is to take a tour from Katoomba or Lithgow, but it is also possible for the determined walker to get there along the Six Foot Track from Katoomba (referring to the width, no doubt; extra legs are not required). This is a three-day hike of 42 kilometres, first blazed in 1884. Camping facilities are available *en route*.

NEW SOUTH WALES
ACCOMMODATION

Listed here is a sample of the accommodation available in Katoomba only.

(i) Hotel Accommodation in Katoomba

Name	Stars	No. on Map	Telephone No.	Address	Lowest Price (Double/Twin)
Lilianfels Blue Mountains	5	17	02-4780-1200	Lilianfels Avenue	$375
Mountain Heritage	4½	4	02-4782-2155	Apex Street	$350
Palais Royale	5	12	02-4784-6300	228 Katoomba Street	$220
Megalong Lodge		18	02-4782-2036	Acacia Street & Cliff Drive	$190
Carrington Hotel		6	02-4782-1111	15 Katoomba Street	$185
Alpine Motor Inn	4	1	02-4782-2011	Great Western Highway	$155
Kurrara Guest House		14	02-4782-6058	17 Coomonderry Street	$150
Jamison Guest House	4	13	02-4782-1206	48 Merriwa Street	$150
Metropole Guest House		5	02-4782-5544	Gang Gang & Lurline St.	$145
Sirens B&B		8	02-4782-9386	3 Duff Street	$145
Clarendon Guest House	3½	10	02-4782-1322	68 Lurline Street	$145
Balmoral House		3	02-4782-2264	196 Bathurst Road	$135
Three Explorers Motel	3½	15	02-4782-1733	197 Lurline Street	$125
St. Elmo		9	02-4782-1266	218 Katoomba Street	$120
Echo Point Holiday Villas	4	19	02-4782-3275	36 Echo Point Road	$115
Town Centre Motel	3½	11	02-4782-1266	222 Katoomba Street	$98
Echo Point Motor Inn		16	02-4782-2088	18 Echo Point Road	$90
Mountain Lodge	2½	7	02-4782-3933	31 Lurline Street	$88
Sky Rider Motor Inn	3	2	02-4782-1600	Great Western Highway	$86

(ii) Backpackers Hostels in Katoomba

Name	Group	No. on Map	Telephone Number	Address	Lowest Price (Dormitory)
No. 14 Budget Accom.		20	02-4782-7104	14 Lovel Street	$22
Blue Mountains YHA	YHA	22	02-4782-1416	207 Katoomba Street	$19
Katoomba Mountain Lodge	VIP	7	02-4782-3933	31 Lurline Street	$16
Blue Mountains Katoomba	VIP/B&W	21	1800-624-226	190 Bathurst Road	$16

MOVING ON
(i) By Train

To return to Sydney, take the hourly CityRail train. To move further west, see the timetables on page 93 showing Great Southern Railway services to Adelaide, Perth and Alice Springs and Countrylink services to Dubbo and Broken Hill. Note, however, that Great Southern Railway trains do not usually stop at Katoomba, although they may be persuaded to do so for pre-booked passengers.

(ii) By Bus

There is a Greyhound service on three days a week between Sydney and Adelaide via Katoomba.

Destination	Operator	Via	Distance (km)	Fare	Journey Time	Frequency
Sydney	Greyhound		110	$36	3 hrs	3/week
Adelaide	Greyhound		1549	$147	22 hrs	3/week
		Broken Hill	990	$147	15 hrs	3/week
		Dubbo	267	$64	5 hrs	3/week

WOLLONGONG
Population 250,000

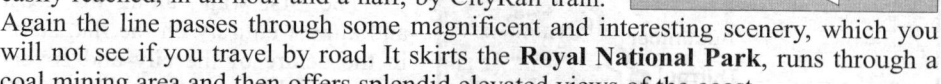

1 hr 30 mins by train from Sydney

Wollongong has found favour in recent years with the surfing fraternity and has become, therefore, much more touristic than it used to be.

The city lies 83 kilometres south of Sydney, and is easily reached, in an hour and a half, by CityRail train. Again the line passes through some magnificent and interesting scenery, which you will not see if you travel by road. It skirts the **Royal National Park**, runs through a coal mining area and then offers splendid elevated views of the coast.

Although it is possible to visit Wollongong as a day trip, the area is extensive and in a single day one can do little more than obtain a glimpse. If you do decide, though, that a day is all that can be made available, CityRail trains start from Central and run approximately every hour, currently leaving at 28 minutes past the hour during the main part of the day. Do not make the mistake of taking a local train to Waterfall, where that service ends, and then waiting there to pick up the fast train, as the fastest services do not stop at Waterfall. From Waterfall to Wollongong, there is only a train every two hours, and that service stops at every station. The day return fare from Sydney to Wollongong is $10.40.

Starting with the beaches, there are seventeen within the area covered by the city of Wollongong, all of them popular for surfing (see map on next page). Of those, the most famous is **Bulli**, ten kilometres to the north of the city of Wollongong. The slower trains from Sydney stop at Bulli. The faster ones stop at the previous station, **Thirroul**, from where there is a connecting service, or it is possible to walk. From Wollongong, there is a bus service. Take bus no. 1 or 4, operated by Dion's Buses. There is also a cycling track leading from Bulli, through the city of Wollongong and on to Lake Illawarra in the south.

One of the reasons why Wollongong has not been more popular in the past is its proximity to heavy industry. Apart from the coal mining in the area and, as a result of locally available fuel, power generation, nearby **Port Kembla** has a thriving steel industry. From Wollongong, you can look out over the peninsula south of the city and view the industrial chimneys smoking away. Wollongong, though, has been concentrating on cleaning up its image.

The main street of the city (Crown Street) is for pedestrians only now, and is the site of various activities. When the author last visited, an Italian Festival was in full swing, to celebrate the ethnic origins of many of the city's residents. At the point where Crown Street accepts motor vehicles once more is the **Wollongong Visitor Centre**, with plenty of useful information available, and only a few metres away, in Kembla Street, is the **Art Gallery**, one of the largest regional galleries in Australia.

Just beyond the Visitor Centre, along Crown Street, one reaches the nearest of the beaches, **Wollongong Beach**. The bus terminal is located here too, although local services can be picked up more conveniently in Keira Street at the city end of the Crown Street Mall (see map on page 107).

Two Walks

There are many walks around Wollongong. If you want information on these, ask

NEW SOUTH WALES

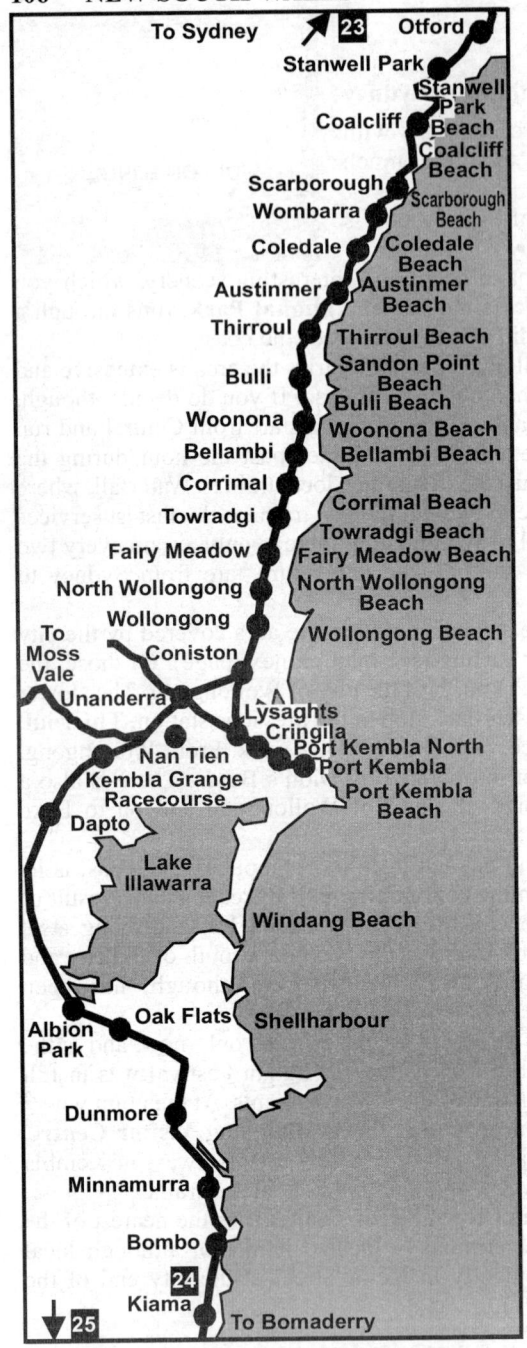

WOLLONGONG AREA
Showing railway lines and beaches
Numerals indicate backpackers hostels

the Visitor Centre, which has details of several available free on photocopied sheets. Here we shall mention just two, neither of them too strenuous, one coastal and one uphill and inland for some views.

(i) Coastal Walk *(see map opposite)*

The first walk, along the coast and almost entirely on the flat, starts in the centre of the city and covers about four kilometres. It will take 90 minutes without any lengthy stops, but allow another 30 minutes for the return journey by bus or train, including some waiting time.

First, walk along Crown Street and turn left at the beach, beside Marine Drive. Soon you will come to **Flagstaff Point**, where you can walk round the bluff before continuing to **Wollongong Harbour**, known for its fishing. A walking and cycling track starts at this point. Follow it north and you will come to the **City Rockpool**, where you can swim in sea water (no charge). Then you reach **North Wollongong Beach**, another for the surfers, and Stuart Park. Here the path swings right and a boardwalk begins, carrying you over water into Brandon Park. When you reach Elliotts Road, turn left to get to Fairy Meadow Station for the return to Wollongong by train or bus. The nearest bus stop is only a short distance along Elliotts Road and is served by buses 3 and 8 operated by John J. Hill. Additional services run along the Princes Highway, just beyond the station. If you still feel like walking, however, the path does not finish at Elliotts Road, but continues northwards up the coast all the way to Bulli. It is paralleled, a little way inland, by bus routes and the railway line, so you can walk as far as you wish and then return by public transport.

WOLLONGONG 107

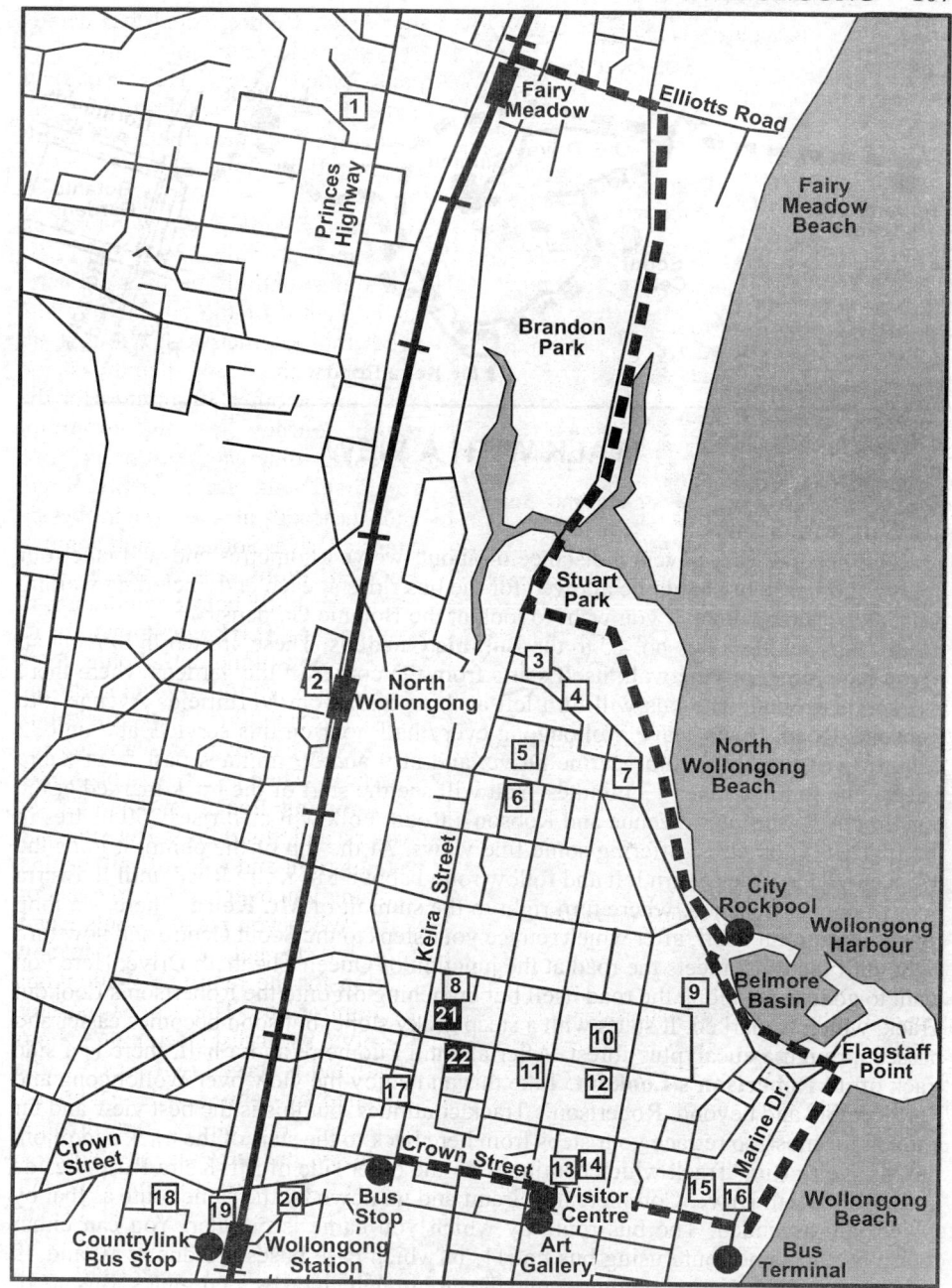

WOLLONGONG
Dashed line shows Coastal Walk
Black numerals in white boxes indicate hotel accommodation
White numerals in black boxes indicate backpackers hostels

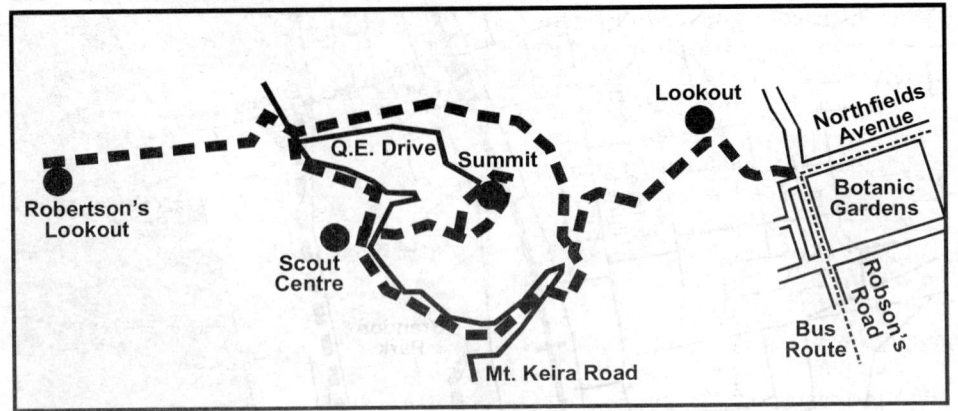

WALK WITH A VIEW

(ii) Walk with a View

This second walk covers a distance of about twelve kilometres and will take four hours. Another hour should be allowed for the bus rides at each end, including waiting time, and a further hour if you want to look at the Botanic Gardens.

Start by taking a bus no. 10 to the **Botanic Gardens**. These are worth looking at, if you have time, but the walk itself starts from the corner of the gardens where there is a sports ground. The bus will turn left at this point, from Northfields Avenue into Robson's Road. Buses leave Wollongong every half hour on this service, at 2 and 32 minutes past the hour from Marine Drive, and at 9 and 39 minutes past from Keira Street. The journey takes 13 minutes. You will see the start of the track marked at the junction of Northfields Avenue and Robson's Road. Follow it as it rises 250 metres in the first 1.6 kilometres, offering some fine views. At the top of the climb, it joins the Mt. Keira Ring Track. Turn left and follow round above Mt. Keira Road until Illawarra Scout Centre is reached, where turn right to the summit of **Mt. Keira**. There is a loop round the summit itself, after which retrace your steps to the Scout Centre and now turn right until the track meets the road at the junction of Queen Elizabeth Drive. Here you want to go left, not along the road itself but branching off onto the Robertson's Lookout Track, which is marked. It starts with a steep rocky slope, but soon becomes easier and passes through a eucalyptus forest. After about a kilometre and a half, there is a side track off to **Robertson's Lookout**. Take this and enjoy the view over Wollongong and Port Kembla and beyond. Robertson's Track continues, but this is the best view and far enough for most, so retrace your steps from here back to the start of the track and rejoin the Mt. Keira Ring Track which continues on the other side of Mt. Keira Road, beside Queen Elizabeth Drive. Complete the circuit and go down by the same route as that by which you ascended. The bus route by which you came is circular. You can either return by the same route using bus no. 11, in which case buses are due at 10 and 40 minutes past the hour, or continue round the circuit, which takes 35 minutes. Bus no.10 is due at 52 minutes past the hour only in this direction.

Other Attractions near Wollongong

The **Nan Tien Temple** in **Berkeley** claims to be the largest Buddhist temple in the southern hemisphere. The author, however, wonders whether it is really bigger than Borobudur in Java. Perhaps it depends upon what one classifies as the temple itself and what as outlying buildings. The temple can be reached by bus no. 34. Bus no. 67 also runs nearby. The journey takes about 35 minutes, Berkeley lying south of Wollongong City adjacent to **Lake Illawarra**, although the temple itself is set back some distance from the lake (see map on page 106).

Further south is **Albion Park**, from where the scenic road route runs inland to **Robertson** and **Moss Vale**. Countrylink buses run on this route from Wollongong three times a day. See pages 85 to 86 for a mention of this journey and a suggestion on how it may be incorporated into an itinerary. Also at Albion Park is the short **Illawarra Light Railway**, which operates only on the second Sunday in each month.

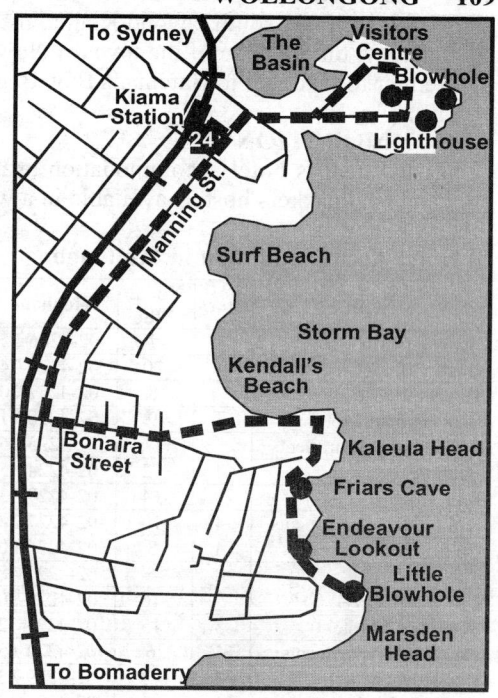

KIAMA

Dashed line shows suggested walk
Numerals indicate backpackers hostels

Albion Park is most easily reached by train. Trains run hourly from Wollongong, but it is usually necessary to change trains at Dapto, the previous station, as electrification ends there and a diesel railcar takes over the service from that point on. The journey is one of twenty kilometres and takes half an hour by train, or an hour by bus no. 51.

Still further south is the pleasant town of **Kiama**, famous for its coastal scenery, and especially for two blowholes. Take a train from Wollongong for the 36 kilometre journey (change at Dapto) which takes 50 minutes and costs $6.20 day return. Trains run hourly. Alternatively, bus no. 50 takes 75 minutes, but runs only five times a day. At other times, Kiama can be reached by taking a bus no. 50 or 53 to Shellharbour and changing there to a no. 71

Assuming arrival by train, exit on the eastern side into Morton Street, which will lead you into Manning Street, where turn left, right into Terralong Street and then immediately left. A short walk will take you to the **Pilot's Cottage Museum**, the **Visitors Centre**, the **lighthouse** and then the **blowhole**. Discovered on 6th December 1797 by George Bass, the blowhole is at its best when the swell is from the south-east. It is floodlit at night until 1:00. There is another blowhole further south, known as the **Little Blowhole**. To reach it, retrace your steps to Manning Street and then follow that street to its conclusion and turn left into Bonaira Street. You will reach Kaleula Head, Friars Cave, Endeavour Lookout and the Little Blowhole. The distance between the two blowholes is approximately two kilometres.

NEW SOUTH WALES

If you continue south beyond Kiama, the railway runs on for another half hour to **Bomaderry**, on the edge of the town of **Nowra**, from where there are buses operated by Premier to take you to Batemans Bay, Bega, Eden and Melbourne.

ACCOMMODATION

Listed here is hotel accommodation available in the central part of Wollongong only and backpackers hostels available in a wider area.

(i) Hotel Accommodation in Wollongong

Name	Stars	No. on Map	Telephone No.	Address	Lowest Price (Double/Twin)
Novotel North Beach	4	7	02-4226-3555	Cliff Road	$220
Quality Hotel City Pacific	4	20	02-4229-7444	112 Burelli Street	$155
Tamada House		8	02-4227-2030	67 Campbell Street	$135
Boat Harbour Motel	3	9	02-4228-9166	Campbell & Wilson Streets	$125
Wollongong Apartments		11	02-4225-2544	54 Kembla Street	$125
Belmore	4	12	02-4224-6500	39 Smith Street	$125
Harp Hotel		14	02-4229-1333	124 Corrimal Street	$125
Smith Street Apartments	4	10	02-4227-2430	36a Smith Street	$110
Golden Pacific Motel	4	3	02-4226-3000	16 Pleasant Avenue	$105
The Normandie		5	02-4229-4833	30 Bourke Street	$105
City Beach B&B		16	02-4228-3088	2 Parkside Avenue	$100
Surfside 22 Motel	3	15	02-4229-7288	Crown & Harbour Streets	$95
Park Street Apartments	3½	6	02-4224-6500	1 Park Street	$85
Downtown Motel	3	13	02-4229-8344	76 Crown Street	$85
Beach Park Motor Inn	3½	4	02-4226-1577	10 Pleasant Avenue	$75
Piccadilly Motor Inn	2	19	02-4226-4555	341 Crown Street	$75
Cabbage Tree Motel		1	02-4284-4000	1a Anama Street	$65
Illawarra Hotel		17	02-4229-5411	Keira & Market Streets	$60
Sky Accommodation	3	18	02-4228-9320	5 Parkinson Street	$55
International House		2	02-4221-5250	Porter St. & Hindmarsh Av.	$49

(ii) Backpackers Hostels in and around Wollongong

Name	Group	No. on Map	Telephone Number	Address	Lowest Price (Dormitory)
Richard Johnson College		22	02-4229-1980	65 Smith Street	$39
International House		2	02-4221-5250	Porter Street & Hindmarsh Av.	$29
Sky Accommodation		18	02-4228-9320	5 Parkinson Street	$28
Cooee Guest House		21	02-4229-1615	77 Keira Street	$18
Garie Beach Y.H.A.	YHA	23	02-9520-5617	Royal National Park	$10
Kiama Backpackers Hostel		24	02-4233-1881	31 Bong Bong Street, Kiama	$25
Nestor House, Gerringong	YHA	25	02-4234-1249	Fern Street, Gerringong	$22

MOVING ON
(i) By Train

To return to Sydney from Wollongong, take the hourly CityRail train. To move south, there are trains only as far as Bomaderry (Nowra). A convenient route to Melbourne is to catch the Countrylink bus which runs three times a day to Moss Vale, and then take a train. The morning bus, at 7:20 from Wollongong, makes guaranteed connexions with both the Canberra and the Melbourne trains. The 11:25 bus from Wollongong also makes a connexion with the train to Canberra. Shown opposite is the timetable of bus plus train connexions from Wollongong to Melbourne and Canberra.

Days of Operation	Daily (Bus)	Daily	Sat	Daily	Daily (Bus)	Daily	Daily (Bus)	Daily	Daily
Wollongong	0720				1125		1720		
Moss Vale	0845	0854	0854	0932	1300	1331	1853	2002	2231
Goulburn		0941	0941	1020		1418		2049	2319
Canberra			1115			1550		2221	
Yass Junction				1045	1125				0024
Cootamundra				1200	1245				0142
Wagga Wagga				1305	1348				0243
Albury					1502				0355
Griffith				1538					
Wangaratta					1543				0436
Benalla					1614				0500
Melbourne					1815				0700

(ii) By Bus

Premier operates bus services from Sydney via Wollongong to Batemans Bay, Bega, Eden and Melbourne. Murray's operates a service from Wollongong to Canberra.

Destination	Operator	Via	Distance (km)	Fare	Journey Time	Frequency
Sydney	Premier		126	$15	2 hrs	3/day
Melbourne	Premier		1100	$76	15½ hrs	1/day
		Lakes Entrance	713	$71	9¾ hrs	1/day
		Eden	466	$61	7¼ - 7¾ hrs	2/day
		Batemans Bay	205	$37	3½ hrs	3/day
Canberra	Murray's		210	$34.80	3½ hrs	1/day
Moss Vale	Countrylink		68	$8.80	1½ hrs	3/day

YASS
Population 5,400

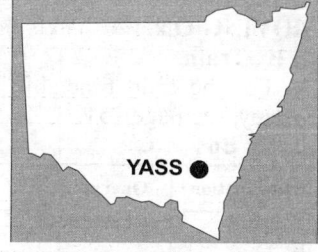

4 hrs by train from Sydney
4 hrs 30 mins by bus from Sydney
45 mins by bus from Canberra

The most likely reason for visiting Yass is that Yass Junction is the station at which to change if travelling from Melbourne to Canberra by train. Yass Junction, however, is not in the town of Yass, but lies several kilometres away from it to the north-west. A tramway used to run from Yass Junction to Yass, but that is long abandoned now, and instead there is a bus, operated by Transborder, which connects with train arrivals and runs from Yass Junction to Canberra via Yass Town.

Yass is actually quite an old and well preserved town. It was first inhabited by Europeans in 1821, following exploration by Hamilton Hume, after whom the main highway between Sydney and Melbourne is now named. Hume later lived here in the property known as *Cooma*, which is now owned by the National Trust, and he is buried in the **cemetery** here.

Yass is an agricultural area well known for its high quality wool production, and its relative prosperity has permitted it to restore many of its older buildings. The town

112 NEW SOUTH WALES

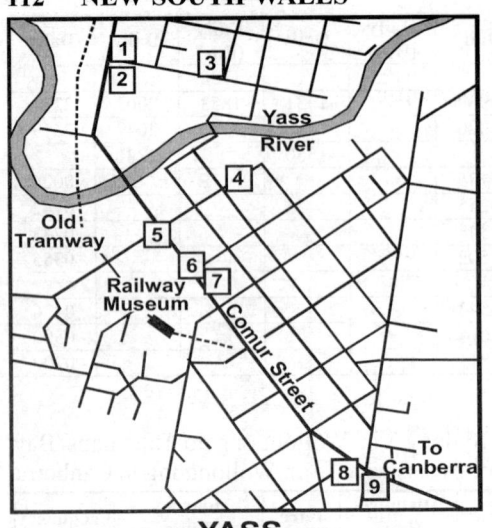

YASS
Numerals indicate accommodation

is worth a look if time permits.

Cooma Cottage still stands, although it is three kilometres east of the town centre. It is open daily except Tuesdays, from 10:00 until 16:00. There is also a small museum in the town, the **Hamilton Hume Museum**, and there is a **Railway Museum** in the old station, although this is open only on Sundays from 12:00 until 16:00.

ACCOMMODATION

There is a range of accommodation available in Yass, but there are no backpackers hostels. Establishments named as hotels are in a price range suitable for backpackers. The Australian Hotel, for example, has single rooms available for $20.

Accommodation in Yass

Name	Stars	No. on Map	Telephone No.	Address	Lowest Price (Double/Twin)
Kerrowgair B & B	4	3	02-6226-4962	24 Grampian Street	$135
Globe B & B	4½	4	02-6226-3680	70 Rossi Street	$125
Colonial Lodge Motor Inn	3½	8	1-800-807-686	McDonald Street	$90
Hamilton Hume Motel		1	02-6226-1722	Grampian and Laidlaw Sts.	$75
Woodhill's Apartments		5	02-6226-3165	Rossi & Comur Streets	$75
Hi-Way Motor Inn		9	02-6226-1300	Yass Valley Way	$65
Yass Caravan Park		2	02-6226-1173	Grampian & Laidlaw Streets	$65
Royal Hotel		6	02-6226-1005	Meehan and Comur Streets	$35
Australian Hotel / Motel		7	02-6226-1744	180 Comur Street	$25

MOVING ON
(i) By Train
For the train timetable to Melbourne, see page 93. For the train timetable to Sydney, see page 751.
(ii) By Bus

Destination	Operator	Via	Distance (km)	Fare	Journey Time	Frequency
Sydney	McCafferty's		307	$41	6 hrs	2/day
		Canberra	60	$28	1 hr	2/day
Sydney	Greyhound		388	$41	6 hrs	1/day
		Canberra	91	$28	45 mins	1/day
Sydney	Fearne's		307	$47	4¾ hrs	1/day
Canberra	Transborder		60	$16	1 hr	4/day
Melbourne	McCafferty's		594	$70	9¼ hrs	1/day
		Albury	290	$31	4 hrs	1/day
Melbourne	Greyhound		594	$70	8¾ hrs	1/day
		Albury	290	$31	3½ hrs	1/day
Melbourne	V-Line		594	$62	8½ - 8¾ hrs	1/day
		Wodonga	295	$39	5 hrs	1/day
Adelaide	McCafferty's		1208	$141	17¾ hrs	1/day
		Nuriootpa	1148	$141	16¼ hrs	1/day
		Mildura	825	$95	11½ hrs	1/day
Wagga Wagga	Fearne's		143	$33	2½ hrs	1/day

BATEMANS BAY
Population 12,000
5 hrs 30 mins by bus from Sydney

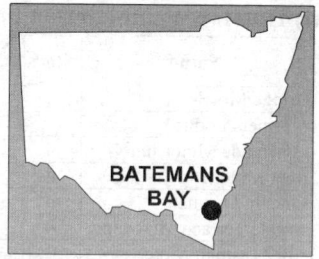

Batemans Bay is a coastal town of moderate size which has become popular in recent years for its pleasant atmosphere and for its good fishing. The bay, at the mouth of the Clyde River, was named by Captain Cook in 1770, but the town with the same name did not appear until a century later. Batemans Bay offers beaches and views across the estuary, and nearby National Parks suitable for trekking. For a map of the town of Batemans Bay, see page 115, while for a strip map of the coastline between Kiama and Batemans Bay, see the right side of this page.

Batemans Bay has daily bus services from Sydney and Melbourne operated by Premier, a daily bus service from Canberra operated by Murray's and a connecting train plus bus service from Melbourne on three days a week (Mondays, Thursdays and Saturdays) operated by V-Line. If time allows, therefore, Batemans Bay can be a convenient stop on the coastal route between Sydney and Melbourne.

One hour south of Batemans Bay is **Narooma**, which was known, until 1972, as Noorooma. It has a population of 3,500 and lies on the Wagonga Inlet. The area became a sheep run in the 1840s, and gold was discovered nearby in 1880. Then timber became the industry of importance at the turn of the century. However, in the end it was tourism which really developed the town, starting in the 1930s. Narooma too has a reputation for good fishing.

Transport services from Narooma are the same as those from Batemans Bay, except that between Melbourne and Narooma a daily train plus bus connecting service is offered by V-Line.

ACCOMMODATION

The hotels listed are all within the town of Batemans Bay. There is other accommodation at the beaches south of the town.

There are two places for backpackers, both in the town of Batemans Bay. Further details are on the next page.

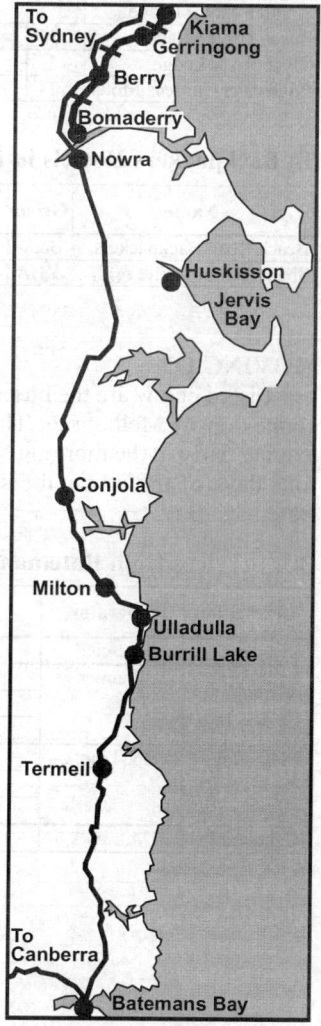

FROM KIAMA TO BATEMANS BAY

114 NEW SOUTH WALES

(i) Hotel Accommodation in Batemans Bay

Name	Stars	No. on Map	Telephone No.	Address	Lowest Price (Double/Twin)
Bridge Motel	4	4	02-4472-6344	29 Clyde Street	$220
Mariners Lodge		5	1-800-355-216	31 Orient Street	$120
Esplanade Motor Inn	4	6	02-4472-0200	23 Beach Road	$105
Reef Motor Inn	4	3	1-800-024-902	27 Clyde Street	$105
Lincoln Downs	4	1	02-4478-9250	Princes Highway	$105
Argyle Terrace Motor Inn	4	8	02-4472-5022	32 Beach Road	$102
Abel Tasman Motel	3½	9	02-4472-6511	222 Beach Road	$75
Araluen Motor Lodge	3½	10	02-4472-6266	226 Beach Road	$75
Beach Drive Motel	3	7	02-4472-4845	24 Beach Road	$65
Clyde River Lodge	3	2	02-4472-6444	3 Clyde Street	$65
Edgewater Gardens Motel	3	11	02-4472-4381	338 Beach Road	$65

(ii) Backpackers Hostels in Batemans Bay

Name	Group	No. on Map	Telephone Number	Address	Lowest Price (Dormitory)
Beach Road Backpackers	B&W	13	02-4472-3644	92 Beach Road	$25
Shady Willows Y.H.A.	YHA	12	02-4472-4972	Old Princes Hwy. & South St.	$20

MOVING ON

Listed below are the buses from Batemans Bay, including the V-Line bus plus train connexion to Melbourne. This service operates on Tuesdays, Fridays and Sundays, leaving early in the morning and reaching Melbourne in the early evening. On the other four days of the week, the service operates only from Narooma, one hour south of Batemans Bay.

Bus Services from Batemans Bay

Destination	Operator	Via	Distance (km)	Fare	Journey Time	Frequency
Sydney	Premier		350	$47	5½ - 5¾ hrs	3/day
Melbourne	Premier		895	$65	12 hrs	1/day
		Lakes Entrance	508	$50	6¼ hrs	1/day
		Eden	261	$33	3¼ - 4 hrs	2/day
Melbourne	V-Line		825	$70	11½ hrs	3/week
		Sale	588	$63.40	8½ hrs	3/week
		Lakes Entrance	483	$63.40	6¾ hrs	3/week
Canberra	Murray's		146	$26.95	2½ hrs	1/day

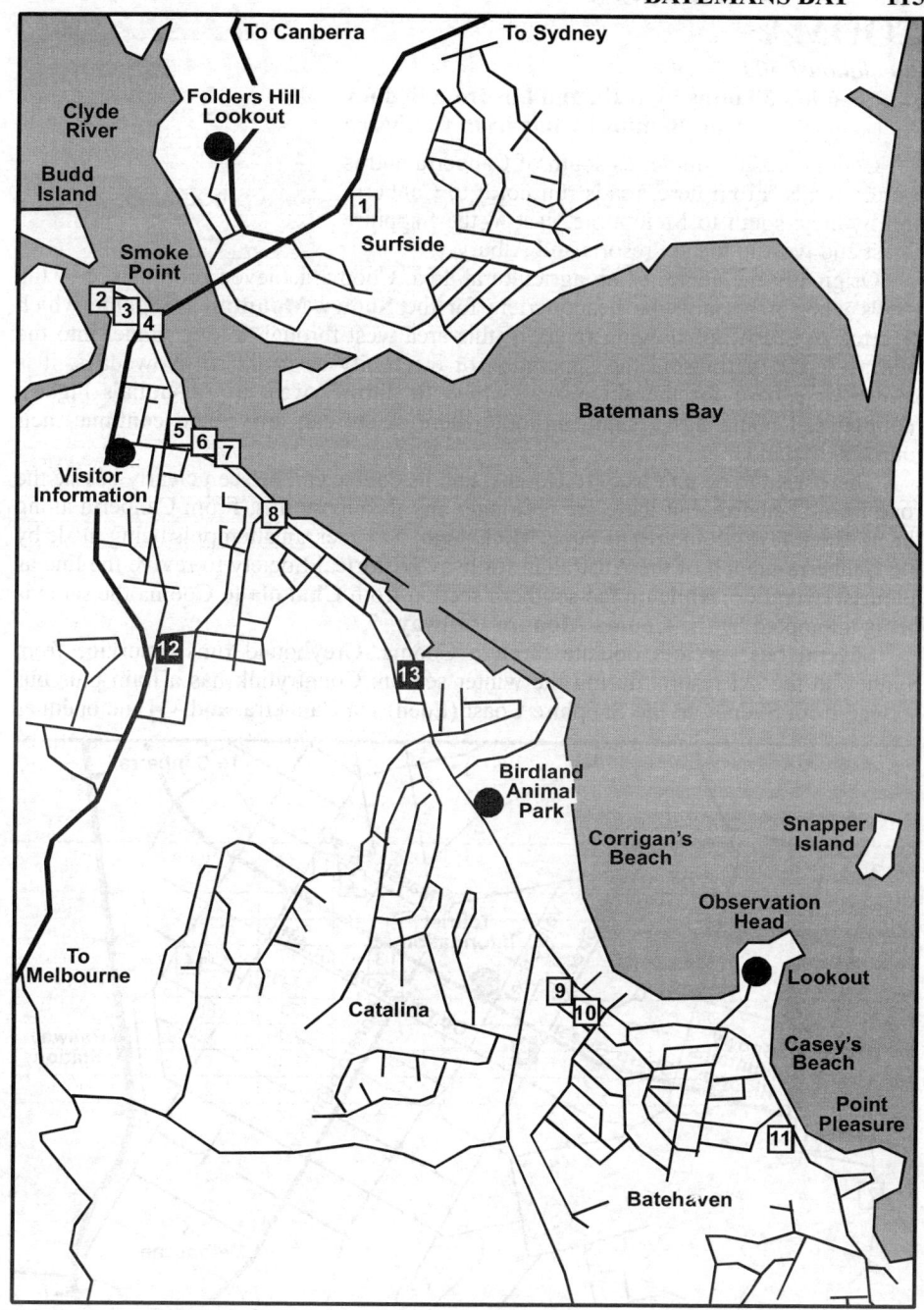

NEW SOUTH WALES
COOMA
Population 7,500

6 hrs 30 mins by train and bus from Sydney
1 hr 30 mins by bus from Canberra

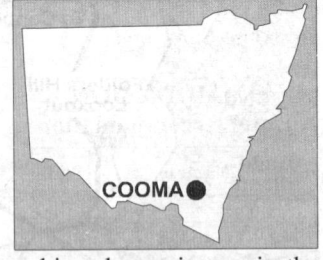

Cooma is 120 kilometres south of Canberra and is a cross-roads. From here, roads run north to Canberra and Sydney, south to Melbourne, east to the Sapphire Coast and west to the ski resorts and Albury.

Originally the centre of an agricultural area, Cooma achieved prominence in the 1950s when it became the headquarters for the **Snowy Mountains Scheme** which diverted the eastward-flowing rivers of this area west through a long tunnel into the Murray River, permitting the generation of electricity as it did so. Nowadays, it is known as a base for the ski resorts which lie further west in Australia's highest mountains. Cooma has a small airport, where skiers can arrive and continue their journeys by land.

There used to be a railway to Cooma, and its course can be seen clearly beside the road from Canberra, but there are no longer any through trains. From Canberra along the northern few kilometres as far as **Michelago**, however, an attempt is being made by the Canberra branch of the Australian Railway Historical Society to revive the line as a tourist operation, while on the southern section from **Chakola** to Cooma the same is being attempted by the **Cooma Monaro Railway**.

Several bus services operate through Cooma. Greyhound runs a service from Sydney to the ski resorts during the winter season. Countrylink has a train plus bus service from Sydney to the Sapphire Coast (Eden) via Canberra, and V-Line operates

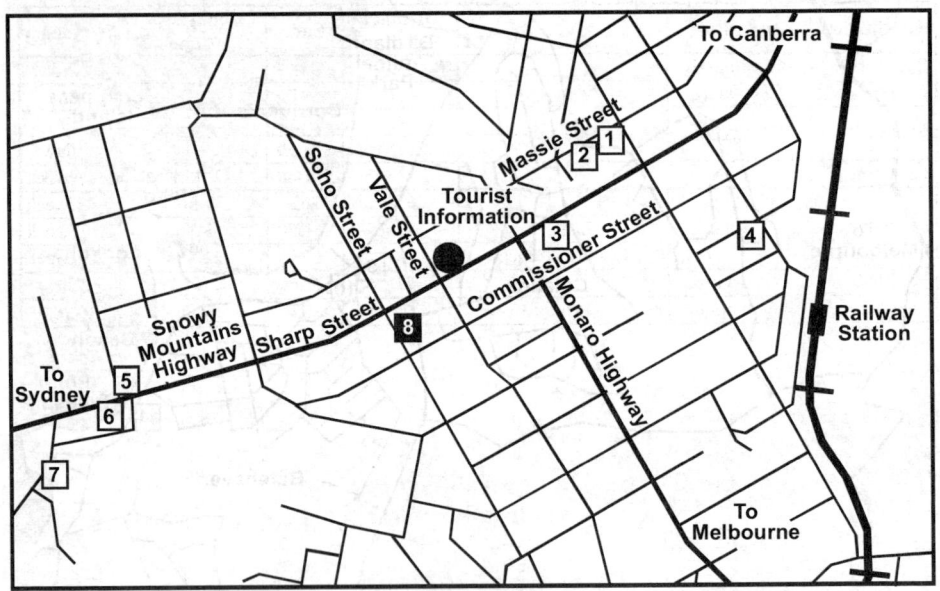

COOMA
Black numerals in white boxes indicate hotel accommodation
White numerals in black boxes indicate backpackers hostels

a train plus bus service from Melbourne to Canberra via Sale on Mondays, Thursdays and some Saturdays.

ACCOMMODATION
(i) Hotel Accommodation in Cooma

Name	Stars	No. on Map	Telephone No.	Address	Lowest Price (Double/Twin)
Flag Cooma Motor Lodge	4	3	1-800-686-559	6 Sharp Street	$90
White Manor Motel		6	02-6452-1152	252 Sharp Street	$75
High Country Motel	2½	7	1-800-630-303	12 Chapman Street	$70
Alkira Motel	3½	5	02-6452-3633	213 Sharp Street	$65
Swiss Motel	2	2	02-6452-1950	34 Massie Street	$55
Coffey's Hotel		4	02-6452-2064	6 Short Street	$45
Alpine Country Guest Hse	2	1	02-6452-1414	32 Massie Street	$45

(ii) Backpackers Hostel in Cooma

Name	Group	No. on Map	Telephone Number	Address	Lowest Price (Dormitory)
Bunkhouse Backpackers	VIP	8	02-6452-2983	28 Soho Street	$25

MOVING ON

The bus services to the ski fields and direct to Sydney with Greyhound are seasonal and operate in winter and early spring only. The connecting train and bus service to Melbourne with V-Line operates only on Tuesdays, Fridays and some Sundays.

Bus Services from Cooma

Destination	Operator	Via	Distance (km)	Fare	Journey Time	Frequency
Sydney	Greyhound (seasonal)		388	$85	6 - 6¾ hrs	1 - 2/day
		Canberra	120	$41	1¾ - 2 hrs	1 - 2/day
Sydney	Countrylink		425	$73	6¼ hrs	1/day
		Canberra	118	$18.50	1¾ hrs	1/day
Canberra	V-Line		118	$17.60	1¾ hrs	2 - 3/week
Melbourne	V-Line		653	$62	9 hrs	2 - 3/week
		Sale	416	$61.60	6¼ hrs	2 - 3/week
		Lakes Entrance	311	$55	4½ hrs	2 - 3/week
Eden	Countrylink		171	$31.60	2¾ - 3 hrs	2/day
Thredbo	Greyhound	(seasonal)	90	$33	1¾ hrs	1 - 2/day

BOMBALA
Population 1,500

7 hrs 30 mins by train and bus from Sydney
3 hrs by bus from Canberra
8 hrs by train and bus from Melbourne

Bombala's claim to fame is **platypus**. This small town claims to have the highest concentration in the state of New South Wales of these very Australian creatures.

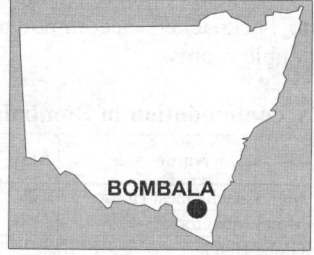

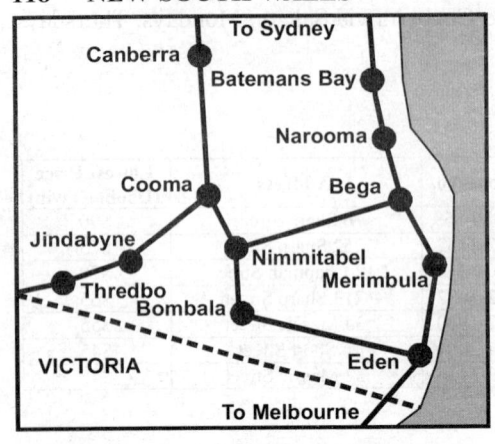

TOWNS AROUND BOMBALA

The platypus is such an unusual and such a shy creature that when it was first discovered scientists refused to believe in its existence. If you want to prove those scientists wrong, Bombala is a good place to visit. The platypus looks like an otter, but with the beak of a duck, webbed feet and a fat tail used to store fat for lean times. It is a monotreme, that is a mammal which lays eggs. The only other such mammal is the echidna, also Australian. Platypus grow to about fifty centimetres in length and can live to the age of fourteen years, although in the wild they rarely achieve such longevity. The males have a venomous spur on their hind legs. Platypus live on worms, beetles, shrimps and yabbies, which they find at the bottom of gently-flowing streams. They can stay under water for fifteen minutes, but usually dive for between one and two minutes at a time. Although shy, they will not usually be frightened by immobile humans, so the way to observe them is to sit quietly and watch for rising bubbles. If you want to get nearer, move quietly only while they are submerged.

Platypus can be seen in fine weather even within the township of Bombala along the Bombala River, and especially behind the swimming pool in Therry Street near the bridge. They can also be found in the **Coolumbooka River** where it crosses the road to the coast three kilometres east of Bombala, and in the Bombala River at **Bibbenluke**, twelve kilometres north of Bombala, on the road to Cooma.

This used to be the end of a railway line from Sydney via Queanbeyan and Cooma, and you can still see remnants of that line. Indeed there has even been talk in recent years of reopening it for forestry purposes, but that is unlikely ever to happen. Instead there are now two bus services passing through Bombala. One is the Countrylink train plus connecting bus service from Sydney, for a timetable of which see page 93. The other is the V-Line train plus connecting bus service from Melbourne to Canberra, for a timetable of which see page 754. Note that this service operates only on Mondays, Thursdays and some Saturdays, and returns from Canberra on the following days.

ACCOMMODATION

There is limited accommodation in Bombala, as shown below. Although there is no backpackers accommodation, the hotels can offer reasonably priced single and double rooms.

Accommodation in Bombala

Name	Stars	Telephone No.	Address	Lowest Price (Double/Twin)
Mail Coach Guest House	2½	02-6458-3721	160 Maybe Street	$70
Motel Maneroo	3	02-6458-3500	129 Maybe Street	$65
Globe Hotel		02-6458-3077	101 Maybe Street	$45
Imperial Hotel		02-6458-3211	77 Maybe Street	$45

MOVING ON

A service is offered daily to Sydney via Canberra with Countrylink. The timetable appears on page 225. To Melbourne there is a service with V-Line on Tuesdays, Fridays and some Sundays. The timetable appears on page 226. The Countrylink bus continues beyond Bombala to Eden at 14:40 every day, but note that there is no service in the reverse direction, from Eden to Bombala. A summary of bus services from Bombala appears below.

Bus Services from Bombala

Destination	Operator	Via	Distance (km)	Fare	Journey Time	Frequency
Sydney	Countrylink		514	$82.80	8 hrs	1/day
		Canberra	204	$34.80	2¾ hrs	1/day
Canberra	V-Line		204	$34.40	2¾ hrs	2 - 3/week
Melbourne	V-Line		567	$62	8 hrs	2 - 3/week
		Sale	330	$59	5¼ hrs	2 - 3/week
		Lakes Entrance	225	$42.70	3½ hrs	2 - 3/week
Eden	Countrylink		82	$14.10	1½ hrs	1/day

BEGA

Population 4,200

8 hrs by train and bus from Sydney
8 hrs by bus from Sydney

Bega is reached just before the sea on the inland route down from Canberra towards the Sapphire Coast. Alternatively, it is a slight deviation inland from the coastal route. The Princes Highway makes this

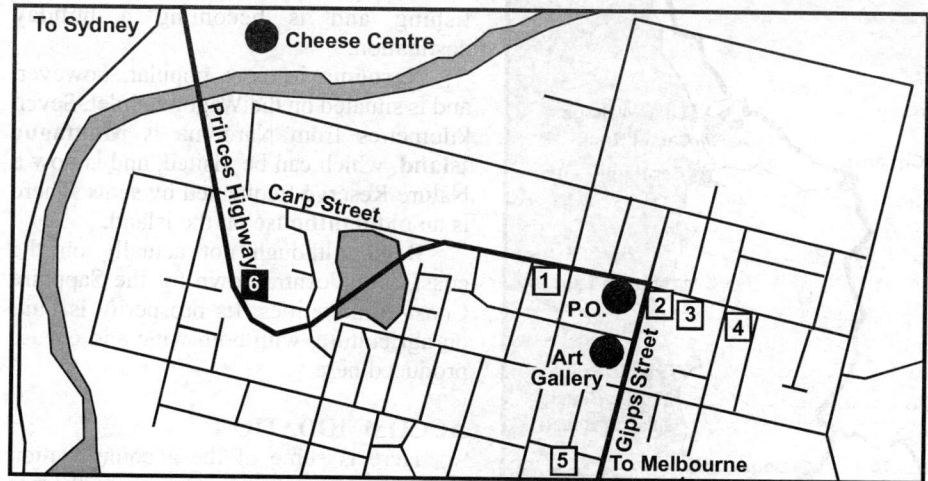

BEGA

Black numerals in white boxes indicate hotel accommodation
White numerals in black boxes indicate backpackers hostels

NEW SOUTH WALES

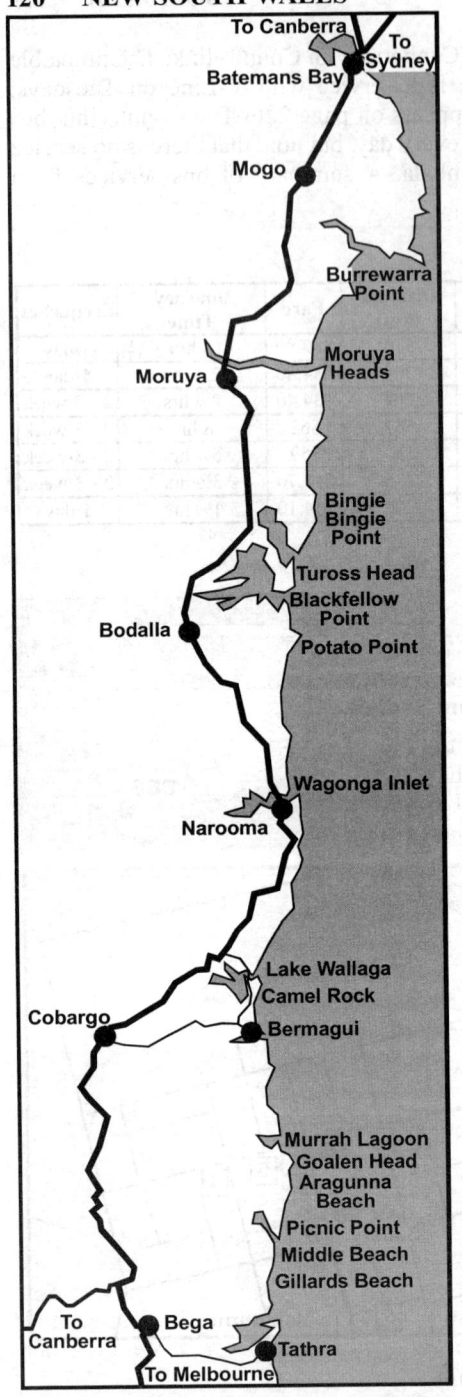

FROM BATEMANS BAY TO BEGA

deviation, so Bega is where the inland route meets the coastal route.

The more spectacular route is that from Canberra via Cooma. This is a real mountain road and as one descends the Great Dividing Range one is offered some fine views along the coast, making the journey worthwhile just for the scenery. This service is operated daily by the Countrylink train plus bus service from Sydney via Canberra.

The town of Bega may also be reached by Premier bus following the coastal route between Sydney and Melbourne.

This route is less spectacular, but still pretty. From Batemans Bay it travels south through Mogo, Moruya and Narooma, but, as can be seen from the map on the left, it does not follow the coast closely and most of the views are of pleasant agricultural landscapes.

Mogo is an old goldrush town, but now very small. However, it has a recreation of a nineteenth-century goldfields community, with a **working gold mine** and restored traction engine operating a stamper. There is also a **zoo** here, with its emphasis on rare and endangered animals.

Moruya is another town known for its fishing and is becoming a holiday destination.

Narooma is more popular, however, and is situated on the Wagonga Inlet. Seven kilometres from Narooma is **Montague Island**, which can be visited, and is now a Nature Reserve frequented by **seals**. There is an old **lighthouse** on the island.

Bega, although not actually on the coast, is the central town for the Sapphire Coast communities. Its prosperity is built on agriculture, with both wine and cheese produced here.

ACCOMMODATION

Here is some of the accommodation available in Bega. For backpackers, there is a small modern youth hostel.

BEGA 121

(i) Hotel Accommodation in Bega

Name	Stars	No. on Map	Telephone No.	Address	Lowest Price (Double/Twin)
Pickled Pear B&B	4	4	02-6492-1393	60 Carp Street	$105
Bega Downs Motor Inn	3½	5	02-6492-2944	Princes Highway & High St.	$104
Central Hotel		2	02-6492-1263	90 Gipps Street	$65
Grand Hotel		1	02-6492-1122	236 Carp Street	$55
Browny's Bega Hotel		3	02-6492-1120	98 Carp Street	$50

(ii) Backpackers Hostel in Bega

Name	Group	No. on Map	Telephone Number	Address	Lowest Price (Dormitory)
Bega Valley Y.H.A.	YHA	6	02-6492-2335	Kirkland Crescent	$16

MOVING ON

Buses run to Sydney and to Melbourne, to which two cities there are also bus plus train connecting services, operated by Countrylink to Sydney via Canberra, and by V-Line to Melbourne via Sale.

Bus Services from Bega

Destination	Operator	Via	Distance (km)	Fare	Journey Time	Frequency
Sydney	Premier		516	$55	8 - 9 hrs	3/day
		Batemans Bay	166	$36	2¼ - 3½ hrs	3/day
Sydney	Countrylink		535	$82.80	7½ hrs	1/day
		Canberra	225	$37	3¾ hrs	1/day
Melbourne	Premier		704	$51	9½ hrs	1/day
		Lakes Entrance	319	$26	4 hrs	1/day
		Eden	70	$13	1 hr	2/day
Melbourne	V-Line		674	$68	9½ hrs	1/day
		Sale	437	$63.40	6½ hrs	1/day
		Lakes Entrance	332	$55	5 hrs	1/day

MERIMBULA
Population 4,000

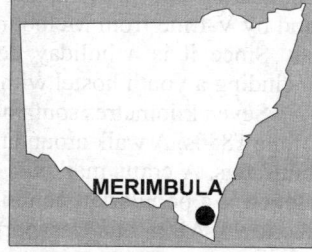

9 hrs by train and bus from Sydney
8 hrs by bus from Sydney
9 hrs by train and bus from Melbourne
9 hrs by bus from Melbourne

Twenty kilometres east of Bega is the seaside town of **Tathra**. It is known for its beaches, but also for fishing, diving and snorkelling. There are **shipwrecks** here to be dived upon and **underwater caves**, as well as a display of **coral**. However, public transport does not reach the small town of Tathra.

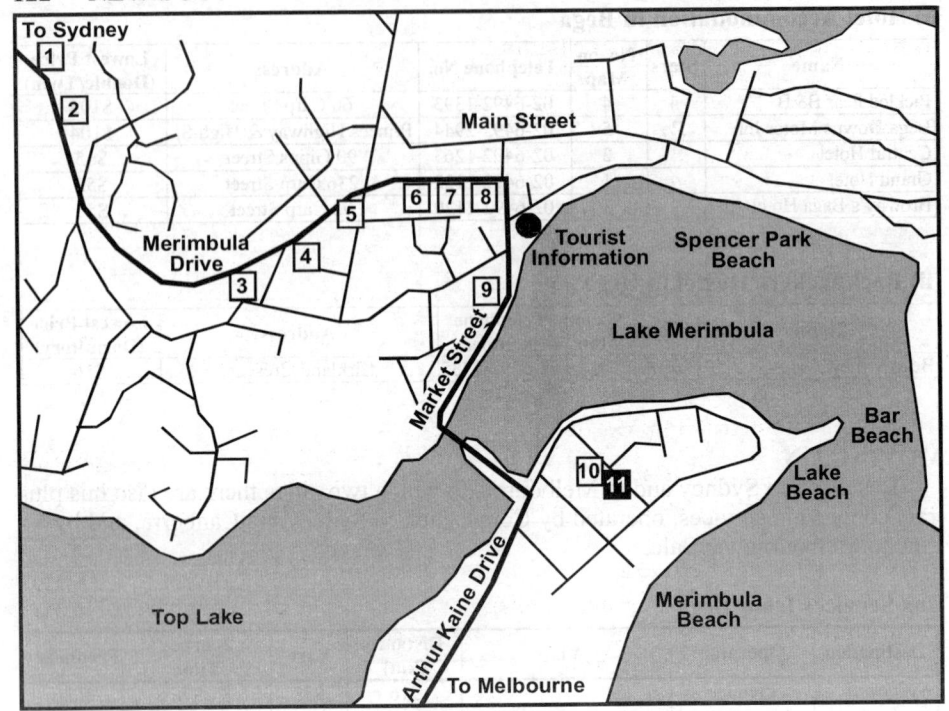

MERIMBULA

**Black numerals in white boxes indicate hotel accommodation
White numerals in black boxes indicate backpackers hostels**

Merimbula is one of the larger towns in the area known as the Sapphire Coast. It is especially famous for **whale watching** during the September to November season, and for attractive beaches. There are coastal walks available and in the town there is a small **museum** and an **aquarium**. Beaches are both on the ocean and on sheltered Lake Merimbula.

Merimbula can be reached by bus from Sydney or Melbourne, and there are also connecting train and bus services offered by Countrylink from Sydney via Canberra and by V-Line from Melbourne via Sale.

Since it is a holiday destination, there is plenty of accommodation available, including a youth hostel with a good reputation.

Seven kilometres south of Merimbula lies **Pambula**, dating from the goldrush days of the 1850s. A walk around this town is of some interest, since it has a number of older buildings. A crafts market is held on the second Sunday in each month, and **Pambula Beach** is a popular attraction. Note, though, that the beach lies four kilometres east of the town. All public transport passes through Pambula.

MERIMBULA

ACCOMMODATION
(i) Hotel Accommodation in Merimbula

Name	Stars	No. on Map	Telephone No.	Address	Lowest Price (Double/Twin)
Merimbula Motor Inn		5	02-6495-3077	Reid St. & Merimbula Dr.	$110
Summerhill Motor Inn	3½	6	1-800-024-946	24 Merimbula Drive	$95
Sea Spray Motel	4	4	02-6495-3299	38 Merimbula Drive	$85
South Seas Motel	3	7	02-6495-1911	12 Merimbula Drive	$75
Tuscany Apartments	3½	10	02-6495-2030	10 Marine Parade	$75
Merimbula Motor Lodge		1	02-6495-1748	131 Merimbula Drive	$70
Ocean View	3	3	02-6495-2300	View St. & Merimbula Dr.	$70
Lakeview Hotel		9	02-6495-1202	1 Market Street	$65
Town Centre Motor Inn	3	8	02-6495-1163	8 Merimbula Drive	$65
Kingfisher Motel	3	2	02-6495-1595	105 Merimbula Drive	$50

(ii) Backpackers Hostel in Merimbula

Name	Group	No. on Map	Telephone Number	Address	Lowest Price (Dormitory)
Wandarrah Lodge	YHA	11	02-6495-3503	8 Marine Parade	$20

MOVING ON

There are buses to Sydney and Melbourne, as well as the connecting bus plus train services offered by Countrylink to Sydney with a change at Canberra, and by V-Line to Melbourne with a change at Sale.

Bus Services from Merimbula

Destination	Operator	Via	Distance (km)	Fare	Journey Time	Frequency
Sydney	Premier		541	$61	8½ - 9¾ hrs	2/day
		Batemans Bay	191	$28	4½ hrs	2/day
Sydney	Countrylink		571	$87.20	8¾ hrs	1/day
		Canberra	261	$43.60	4¼ hrs	1/day
Melbourne	Premier		679	$51	9 hrs	1/day
		Lakes Entrance	292	$26	3½ hrs	1/day
		Eden	45	$7	30 mins	2/day
Melbourne	V-Line		634	$63.40	9 hrs	1/day
		Sale	397	$61.60	6 hrs	1/day
		Lakes Entrance	292	$54.10	4¼ hrs	1/day
Eden	Countrylink		27	$6.50	30 mins	1/day

EDEN

Population 3,100

9 hrs 30 mins by train and bus from Sydney
8 hrs 30 mins by bus from Sydney
8 hrs 30 mins by train and bus from Melbourne
8 hrs 30 mins by bus from Melbourne

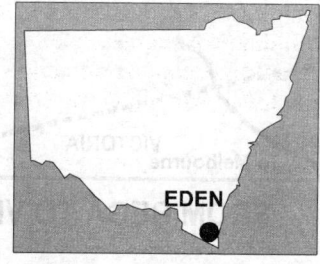

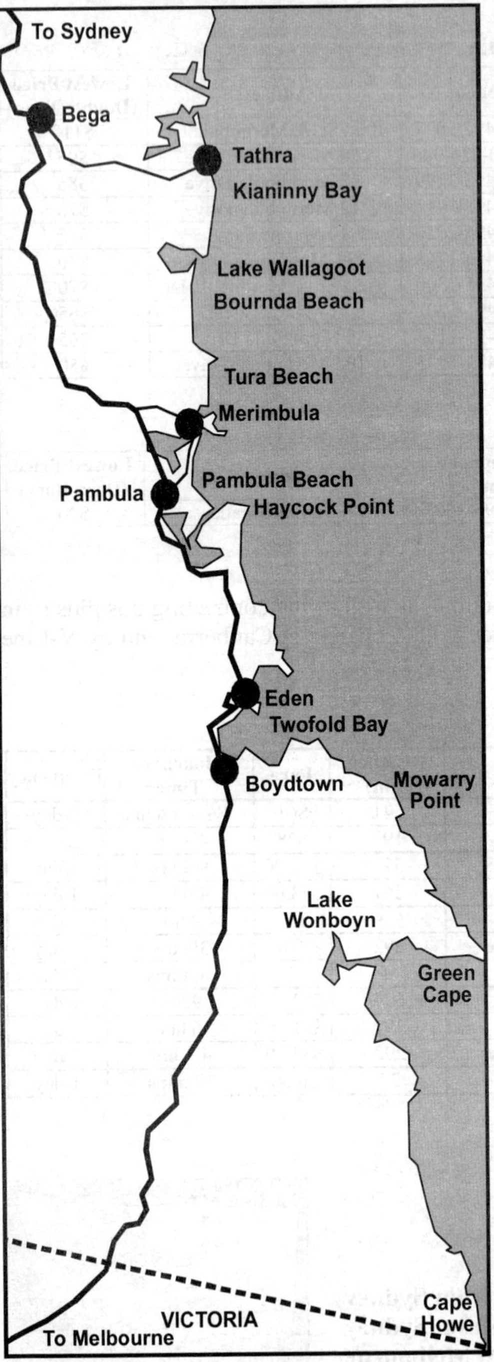

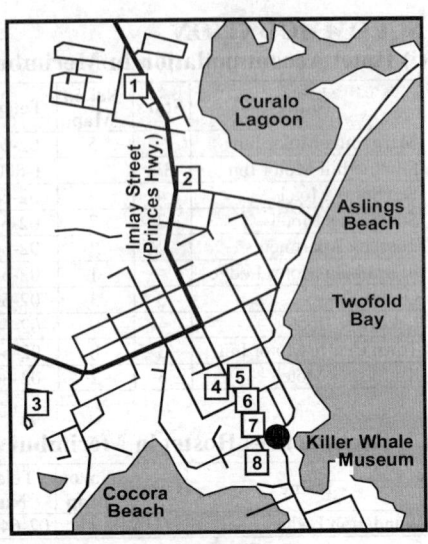

EDEN
Numerals indicate accommodation

On the Sapphire Coast just half an hour beyond Merimbula is Eden, also known for **whale watching** and for **beaches**. **Twofold Bay** is a haven for humpback whales and for various other species, even including the occasional rare blue whale. The whales migrate south each year and are to be found here from September until November. There is an old whaling station at **Kiah Inlet**, ten kilometres south of Eden. The **Eden Killer Whale Museum**, in the town, has exhibits from the time when whalers utilised the services of killer whalers (which are not really whales at all) to help them to herd the whales into the bay. The skeleton of Old Tom, the last killer whale to be used in this way, is on display.

35 kilometres south of Eden, but twelve kilometres off the main road, is attractive Lake Wonboyn.

Eden can be reached by the same services as Merimbula, above, but is half an hour further from Sydney and half an hour nearer to Melbourne, placing it almost equidistant from the two.

FROM BEGA TO VICTORIA

EDEN 125

ACCOMMODATION

Here is a small selection of accommodation available in Eden. There is no accommodation specifically for backpackers, but the caravan park has cabins at $32 for two people, while the Great Southern Hotel offers single rooms for $25 or double rooms for $40.

Accommodation in Eden

Name	Stars	No. on Map	Telephone No.	Address	Lowest Price (Double/Twin)
Bellevue Lodge B&B	3½	3	02-6496-1575	13 Bellevue Place	$105
Crown and Anchor	4	8	02-6496-1017	239 Imlay Street	$100
Twofold Bay Motor Inn	3½	6	02-6496-3111	164 Imlay Street	$80
Whale Fisher Motel	3	7	02-6496-1266	170 Imlay Street	$65
Blue Marlin Motor Inn	3	1	02-6496-1601	87 Princes Highway	$60
Centretown Motel	2	4	02-6496-3155	167 Imlay Street	$55
Great Southern Hotel		5	02-6496-1515	158 Imlay Street	$40
Garden of Eden C'van Pk.		2	1-800-224-460	Princes Hwy. & Barclay St.	$32

MOVING ON

As for Merimbula, there are bus services to Sydney and Melbourne, and bus plus train services to Sydney via Canberra and to Melbourne via Sale.

Bus Services from Eden

Destination	Operator	Via	Distance (km)	Fare	Journey Time	Frequency
Sydney	Premier		586	$63	9 - 10 hrs	2/day
		Batemans Bay	261	$33	3¼ - 4½ hrs	2/day
Sydney	Countrylink		596	$87.20	9¼ hrs	1/day
		Canberra	286	$46.80	4¾ hrs	1/day
Melbourne	Premier		634	$51	8¾ hrs	1/day
		Lakes Entrance	249	$26	3 hrs	1/day
Melbourne	V-Line		607	$63.40	8½ hrs	1/day
		Sale	354	$59	5¼ hrs	1/day
		Lakes Entrance	249	$46.30	3¾ hrs	1/day

THREDBO

Population 300

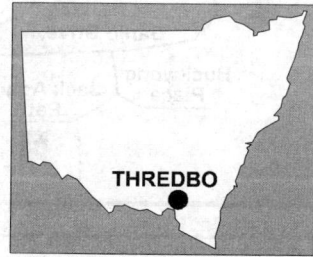

8 hrs by bus from Sydney
3 hrs 30 mins by bus from Canberra

Thredbo lies within the **Kosciuszko National Park** and, together with the neighbouring town of **Jindabyne**, is the centre of the New South Wales ski resort area, the type of place which visitors to Australia do not always expect to find - an Alpine village. The popularity of skiing has increased greatly in recent years and Australia is no exception. Since only this region on the

126   NEW SOUTH WALES

border of New South Wales and Victoria, and a small area in Tasmania also, has mountains which receive snow in winter and are suitable for skiing, people often travel quite surprising distances for the pleasure of a few days here. The laws of supply and demand dictate that, during the season, this is not a cheap place to visit. Note that the rates given below in the accommodation section are low season rates. At peak skiing time, prices will be very much higher, and still accommodation may be difficult to find.

Outside the winter ski season, however, there is still plenty of reason to come here and admire the mountain scenery. The highest mountain in Australia, **Mt. Kosciuszko**, 2,228 metres high, is near Thredbo and in summer a hiking trail can be followed to its summit. The mountain was first climbed in 1840 by the Polish explorer, Paul de Strzelecki (you will find his name given to a famous track in central Australia, to a mountain on Flinders Island and to a whole range in Victoria), and was named by him after a famous Polish patriotic hero, General Tadeusz Kosciuszko. It used to be possible to go by vehicle to the top of the mountain, but the road was closed a few years ago because of the damage being caused by the traffic to the local environment. Now it is necessary to walk the last eight kilometres from **Charlotte Pass**. Alternatively, you can take the **Crackenback chairlift** from Thredbo and travel over alpine moorland past the headwaters of the **Snowy River** and the granite boulders of the **Ramshead Range**. In this case, the walk is about 6½ kilometres each way. There are excellent views from the summit of the mountain. There are also many other walking trails available.

The **Kosciuszko Alpine Way** runs from Cooma to Albury and is a scenic route to take if travelling between Canberra and Melbourne. Although bus services have been operated by this route in recent years, and the author has travelled it by Greyhound bus, unfortunately no regular scheduled service uses the road at the time of writing. One can, however, reach Thredbo by this route with Greyhound's seasonal service from Sydney.

On leaving Cooma, you will enter the treeless **Monaro Plains**, immediately recognised by the first European settlers as ideal grazing pastures, for which purpose they have been used profitably ever since. After passing **Berridale**, the road climbs to

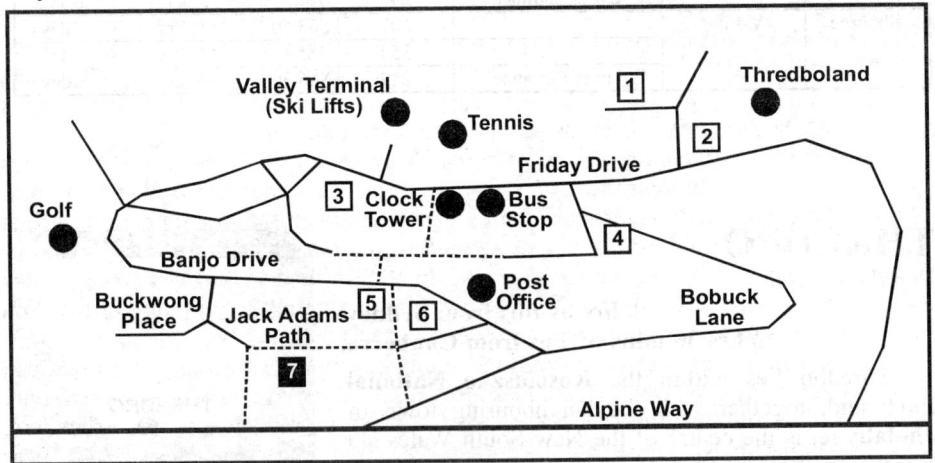

THREDBO
Black numerals in white boxes indicate hotel accommodation
White numerals in black boxes indicate backpackers hostels

1,000 metres and presents some fine views over **Lake Jindabyne**, the second largest of the artificial lakes created by the Snowy Mountains Scheme. Jindabyne itself has the **Snowy Region Visitor Centre**, displaying the history of the region and of the Snowy Mountains Scheme.

The road climbs over **Penderlea Gap**, and then, twelve kilometres before Thredbo, we reach the **Ski Tube**, one of Australia's few rack railways. It was constructed in 1987 and its purpose is evident from its name. It takes skiers up to commence their own perilous descents. The Ski Tube claims to be Australia's highest railway and the longest rack railway in the southern hemisphere. It runs in two sections, from **Bullocks Flat** via **Perisher** to **Mt. Blue Cow**, a journey which takes nineteen minutes, with the latter section in a tunnel bored through the mountain, in one place as deep as 550 metres below the surface. Top speed uphill is 40 km/hr, while downhill the limit is 21 km/hr. The line is electrified and is 8.5 kilometres in length, of which 6.3 kilometres is in tunnel. The fare is $31 day return, or $25 uphill and $21 downhill. From Mt. Blue Cow there is an excellent view which includes five of the highest peaks in Australia, one of which is Mt. Kosciuszko.

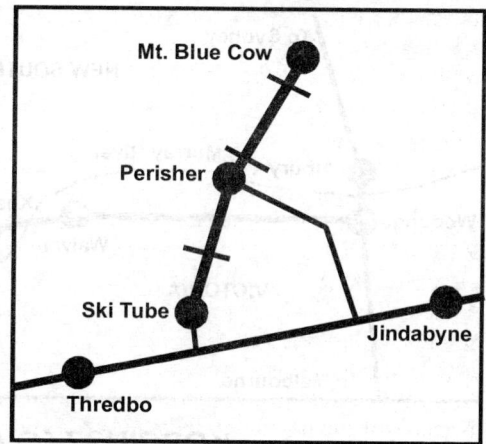

THE SKI TUBE

This area was at the heart of the **Snowy Mountains Scheme**, a determined effort to alter the geography of Australia by diverting the waters flowing east off the Great Divide through a series of lakes, dams and tunnels into the Murray River flowing west. Achieved in the 1950s, it was one of the great engineering feats of the twentieth century. It required the construction of sixteen large dams in this area, as well as many smaller dams, and also resulted in the building of seven hydro-electric power stations. Lake Jindabyne is the southernmost of the lakes formed or extended by this damming. Another of the lakes, **Lake Blowering**, achieved fame in 1978 when Ken Warby set a world water speed record of 511.11 km/hr (317.57 m.p.h.) on it.

If you are able to continue west to Wodonga and Albury, and public transport does sometimes operate through this route, you will find it a beautiful mountain journey. West of Thredbo, you pass through **Dead Horse Gap**, the highest point on the road, at 1,580 metres. This point is also a watershed. East of here water flows into the Snowy River, and it is this water which has been diverted into the Murray by the Snowy Mountains Scheme. West of this point, the water flows naturally into the Murray. You may also see wild horses (brumbies) wandering in this area.

The vegetation now changes from the stunted snow gums, which are all that can grow at the altitude of Dead Horse Gap, to tall forests of alpine ash. Looking south (left), you will see **Mt. Pilot** at 1,828 metres. Soon the Murray River is met. From here, near its source, it has some 2,500 kilometres to flow until it reaches the sea near **Goolwa** in South Australia.

Eight kilometres before Khancoban is reached, you will see the huge pipes of the Snowy Mountains Scheme bringing the water to the **Murray No. 1 Power Station**.

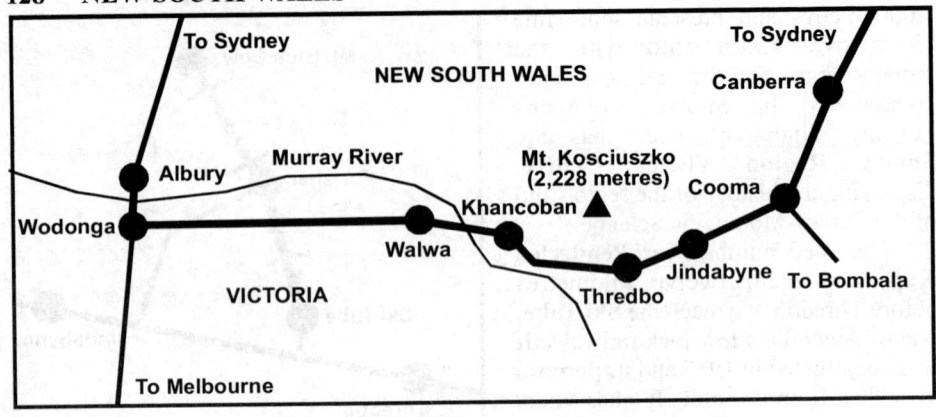

KOSCIUSZKO ALPINE WAY

Khancoban is a pretty little town, originally built to house the construction workers. It has trees, parks and a lake known for its trout fishing.

Beyond Khancoban, the Murray is crossed and we pass into Victoria and reach the small towns of **Towong** and **Tintaldra**, following beside the river. Tintaldra was established in 1846, and has a store dating from that year.

Next is **Walwa**, a quiet and attractive small town, again on the banks of the Murray. Before Wodonga is reached, **Bethanga Bridge** leads the road across pretty **Lake Hume**. The end of the Alpine Way is in the Victorian town of **Wodonga**, just across the river from its big brother **Albury** on the New South Wales side.

ACCOMMODATION
(i) Hotel Accommodation in Thredbo

Name	Stars	No. on Map	Telephone No.	Address	Lowest Price (Double/Twin)
House of Ullr		4	02-6457-6210	Mowamba Place	$275
Woodridge Chalets		1	02-6457-6123	Mountain Drive	$165
Thredbo Alpine Hotel	3	3	1-800-026-333	Friday Drive	$160
River Inn	3	2	02-6457-6505	1 Friday Drive	$135
Snowgoose Lodge	3	6	02-6457-6415	Banjo Drive	$120
Bursills Lodge		5	02-6457-6222	Banjo Drive	$70

(ii) Backpackers Hostel in Thredbo

Name	Group	No. on Map	Telephone Number	Address	Lowest Price (Dormitory)
Thredbo Y.H.A.	YHA	7	02-6457-6376	8 Jack Adams Pathway	$20 summer, $49 winter

MOVING ON

Greyhound operates a seasonal bus service to Sydney via Canberra, as summarised on the next page.

Bus Service from Thredbo

Destination	Operator	Via	Distance (km)	Fare	Journey Time	Frequency
Sydney	Greyhound		488	$101	7¾ - 8½ hrs	1 - 2/day
		Canberra	210	$60	3½ - 4¾ hrs	1 - 2/day

WAGGA WAGGA
Population 57,000

6 hrs by train from Sydney
8 hrs 30 mins by bus from Sydney
4 hrs 30 mins by train from Melbourne
6 hrs by bus from Melbourne

Wagga Wagga is, of course, an aboriginal name. It means "the place of many crows." Captain Charles Sturt passed through here in 1829 by sailing down the **Murrumbidgee River** which runs through the city. Within three years, cattle stations lined the banks of the river and Wagga Wagga had been transformed into a European settlement, although retaining the aboriginal name. It became a town in 1849, a municipality in 1870 and a city in 1946. Now it is the largest inland city in New South Wales. Its prosperity depended originally on the steamers which used to ply the long distance from the sea to here and provide transport needed by the cattle stations and other settlers.

The current attractions of the city include the **National Art Glass Gallery** opened in 1999 as part of the **Wagga Wagga Civic Centre**. There are also a **museum**, a **botanic garden**, the **Victory Memorial Gardens** created at the end of the Great War, and the **R.A.A.F. museum**.

Wagga Wagga has produced three famous sporting figures: in golf Steve Elkington, in tennis Tony Roche and in cricket Australian test captain Mark Taylor.

The most convenient and comfortable way to reach Wagga Wagga is by train. From the timetable on page 93, it will be seen that from Sydney there is one train by day and one by night. Since the night train arrives at 2:43, the day service seems preferable. Similarly, there is one train by day and one by night from Melbourne with the night train arriving, rather inconveniently, at six minutes after midnight. The timetable for trains in this direction is to be found on page 751. Bus travel from Sydney takes considerably longer than rail travel, but, if it is preferred, there are services operated by both McCafferty's and Fearne's.

ACCOMMODATION

Unfortunately, accommodation in Wagga Wagga tends to be costly, but, at the lower end of the scale, Romano's offers single rooms for $39 and doubles for $51.

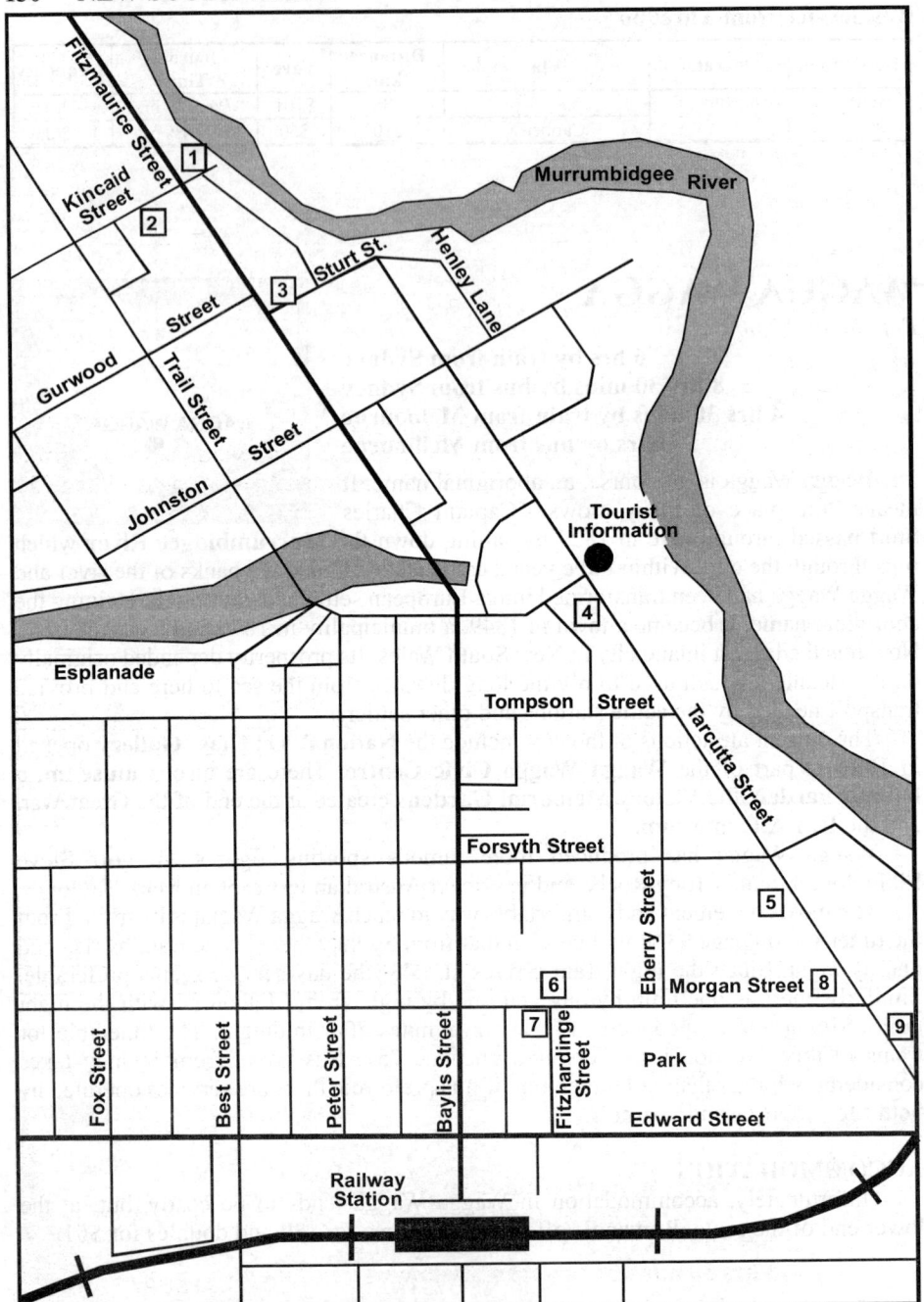

Accommodation in Wagga Wagga

Name	Stars	No. on Map	Telephone No.	Address	Lowest Price (Double/Twin)
Flag Pavilion Motor Inn	4	2	1-800-633-453	22 Kincaid Street	$145
Country Comfort	4	8	02-6921-6444	Morgan & Tarcutta Streets	$115
Townhouse Motor Inn	3½	7	02-6921-4337	70 Morgan Street	$109
Charles Sturt Motor Inn	3½	5	02-6921-8088	82 Tarcutta Street	$104
Flag Prince of Wales Inn	3½	1	1-800-355-195	142 Fitzmaurice Street	$99
Central Point Motel	3½	4	02-6921-7272	164 Tarcutta Street	$85
City Park Motel		9	02-6921-4301	1 Tarcutta Street	$75
Club Motel	3	6	02-6921-6966	73 Morgan Street	$75
Romano's		3	02-6921-2013	Sturt Street	$51

MOVING ON
(i) By Train
The same rail services continue to Melbourne via Albury, or to Sydney with a bus connexion from Yass Junction to Canberra. There are also Countrylink buses to Griffith and Echuca (Victoria). For all of these services, see the timetables on pages 93 and 751.

(ii) By Bus
McCafferty's operates buses to Sydney via Canberra and to Melbourne, and also has a service to Adelaide. Fearne's too operates a daily service to Sydney with a Transborder connecting bus from Yass to Canberra. Here is a summary of the bus services available.

Destination	Operator	Via	Distance (km)	Fare	Journey Time	Frequency
Sydney	McCafferty's		450	$54	8½ hrs	2/day
		Canberra	236	$38	3¼ hrs	2/day
Sydney	Fearne's		450	$53	7¼ hrs	1/day
Melbourne	McCafferty's		393	$54	5¾ hrs	1/day
		Albury	110	$30	1¾ hrs	1/day
Adelaide	McCafferty's		1020	$138	15½ hrs	1/day
		Nuriootpa	960	$138	14 hrs	1/day
		Mildura	637	$95	9½ hrs	1/day
Griffith	Countrylink		130	$25	2¾ hrs	2/day
Echuca	Countrylink		379	$65.40	4¾ hrs	4/week

ALBURY
Population 41,500

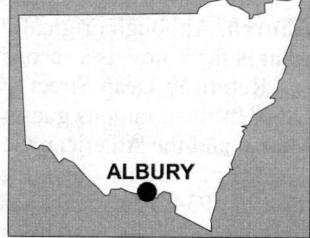

       7 hrs 30 mins by train from Sydney
           8 hrs by bus from Sydney
   3 hrs 30 mins by train from Melbourne
    3 hrs 30 mins by bus from Melbourne

The twin cities of Albury and Wodonga lie on the Murray River, Albury to the north and Wodonga to the south. The only problem with this pairing is that Albury is in New South Wales and Wodonga is in Victoria, the river being the border.

132 NEW SOUTH WALES

If you arrive by train, as you should, you will be impressed first by the grand architecture of the station, especially its exterior. In fact, there are several interesting and imposing buildings to see in Albury, so let us start here at the station for a walking tour of the city.

Walking Tour

This tour covers approximately four kilometres and will take about ninety minutes if no lengthy stops are made.

The **Railway Station** was designed by John Whitton, who also designed Sydney Central station, and built in 1882. It was restored to its former grandeur in 1992 - 1995. The station is interesting in another way too, for this is the meeting point of the New South Wales railway system, built to a standard 4 feet 8½ inches gauge, and the Victorian railway system, built to a 5 feet 3 inches broad gauge. The main platform is used by Countrylink for its services between Sydney and Melbourne, while the shorter platform to the side is used by V-Line and is the terminus for its services from Melbourne. These two tracks are, therefore, of different gauge.

Walk away from the station and turn right at the main road (Young Street) for one block, then left into Dean Street. At the second main corner you will find David Street and on your right is the Cinema Centre, originally the **Regent Theatre**. It was built in 1925 to 1927 and was completed just in time to be the venue for one of Dame Nellie Melba's farewell concerts in July 1927.

Continue north for two blocks along David Street until Wilson Street, where turn left. Then one block to Olive Street, and turn right. Here is **Charles Sturt University**. Although it was established only in 1989, it is unusual in consisting mostly of old cottages.

Retrace your steps along Olive Street and turn right into Dean Street once more. Dean Street is the main street of Albury and here is a cluster of imposing buildings, some of them with a little history. On your right is the **Murray Conservatorium**, which was originally the Albury Telegraph Office. It was constructed in 1886 and used as the first telephone exchange in the area. Next to it is the **Albury Regional Art Centre**, originally the Town Hall, opened in 1908. This building also has a small **Visitor Information Centre** in it now, which is useful, as the **Gateway Visitor Information Centre**, the principal office, is some distance from the town centre on the Lincoln Causeway between Albury and Wodonga along the main Hume Highway. At least this small office kindly recognises that not all visitors arrive by car.

Opposite the Art Centre is **Mate's Building**, on the corner of Kiewa Street, where, in 1944, Robert Menzies founded the present-day Liberal Party, one of the two major forces in Australian politics.

Turn right into Kiewa Street and walk just a few metres to see **St. Matthew's Church**. Although originally constructed in 1859, it was destroyed by fire in 1991, so what is there now is a reconstruction which has cost $3 million.

Return to Dean Street and turn right to see the **Globe Hotel**, which was built in 1860. Its most famous guests have been the great Australian opera singer, Dame Nellie Melba, and the American General MacArthur.

A little further down the street on the left is the **Ambulance Station** which was built in 1934. Previously a station had not been thought necessary, as the town's first ambulance service was by converted bicycle. Presumably if one survived that ordeal

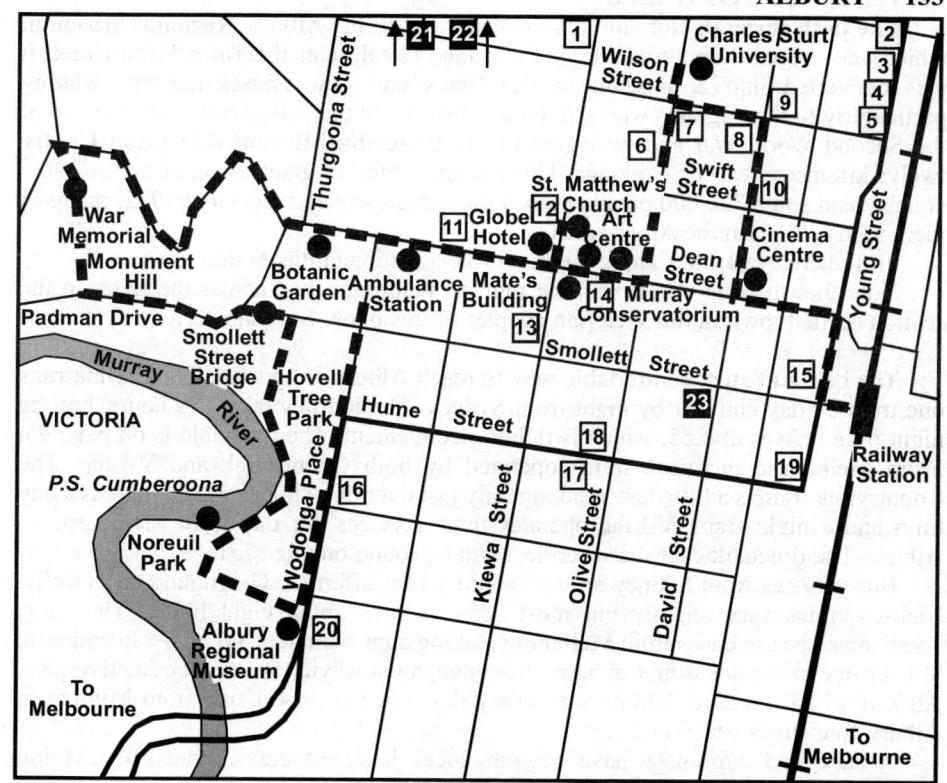

ALBURY
Dashed line shows Walking Tour
Black numerals in white boxes indicate hotel accommodation
White numerals in black boxes indicate backpackers hostels

one deserved the hospital treatment. The first motorised ambulance came in 1927, with this building following seven years later.

Next on the left is the **Botanic Garden**, founded in 1878. The **rotunda** was built in 1890. Just beyond Thurgoona Street, turn right and go up to **Monument Hill** with the **War Memorial** at its top. This memorial was built in 1925, is 30 metres high and was the first such memorial in Australia to be floodlit.

Walk back through the park to Padman Drive and turn left. When you reach Smollett Street, turn right and cross the **Smollett Street Bridge**. This is one of only two metal arched road bridges in New South Wales, the other being a somewhat larger construction known as the Sydney Harbour Bridge.

Turn right and walk through Hovell Tree Park following the course of the **Murray River**. On the other bank is Victoria. Just after the bend you will come to the paddle steamer **Cumberoona**, a reconstruction built for Australia's bi-centenary and launched in 1986. The *Cumberoona* cruises on the Murray at 10:00, 12:00 and 14:00 on Wednesdays, Saturdays and Sundays during the summer. It has a wood-fired boiler and uses steam engines dating from 1906.

134 NEW SOUTH WALES

The path through Noreuil Park will take you to the **Albury Regional Museum**, which was originally built as the Union Bridge Hotel, later the Turks Head Hotel. It was converted into a museum in the 1950s and now houses exhibits relating particularly to the migrants who arrived in Australia in the period following the end of the Second World War and were sent to the **Bonegilla Migrant Reception Centre** twelve kilometres east of Wodonga. This was the largest migrant reception centre in the country and some 320,000 people passed through it between 1949 and 1972, many of them then settling in the Albury area.

From here, walk back along the main road (Wodonga Place) into town.

Note that there is also a walking tour of **Wodonga**, just across the river, in the section on that town in the Victorian chapter of this book. See page 827.

The best and most comfortable way to reach Albury is by train. Countrylink runs one train by day and one by night from Sydney. The journey takes 7½ hours, but the night train arrives at 3:55, which is rather inconvenient. The timetable is on page 93. From Melbourne there are trains operated by both Countrylink and V-Line. The Countrylink train is a little faster, taking only just over three hours. Again there is a day train and a night train. V-Line operates three services per day from Melbourne to Albury. The timetables for these services can be found on page 751.

Bus services from Sydney are operated by McCafferty's, Greyhound and Firefly. Journey times vary slightly but most services take about eight hours. The same companies operate buses from Melbourne, taking approximately 3½ hours. In addition, V-Line operates a bus from Canberra to Wodonga via Albury once every day (see page 226), from Adelaide to Albury once every day (see page 643), and from Mildura to Albury four times per week.

Albury and Wodonga have regular local bus services operated by Mylon Motorways. An all-day ticket is offered for $10, but it is unlikely that one would want to undertake sufficient travelling to make this worth while.

There are other attractions in the Albury-Wodonga area, most of them in towns included in the Victoria section of this book. One unusual and notable attraction on the New South Wales side of the border, though, is the **Ettamogah Pub**. This resulted from a series of cartoons by Ken Maynard depicting a typical, but exaggeratedly dilapidated, Australian drinking establishment. The cartoons achieved great popularity and eventually it was decided to build the Ettamogah Pub. Ettamogah is on the Hume Highway, which is the principal route between Sydney and Melbourne, about forty kilometres north of Albury. There is also a **wildlife sanctuary** at Ettamogah, where kangaroos, wallabies, wombats, dingoes and other native Australian animals can be found.

Finally, one of the most unusual incidents in the history of Albury occurred in 1934, during the London to Melbourne Centenary Air Race. A Dutch aircraft became lost in thunderstorms and started circling over Albury at about midnight on 23rd October. A local radio station appealed to all owners of motor vehicles to go to the racecourse and guide the plane in with their headlights. The aircraft made a perfect landing in pouring rain with only about two hundred metres on which to operate. However, it was bogged in the soft ground, so in the morning 300 residents assembled with ropes to pull it out. The aeroplane abandoned all non-essential items and managed to take off and continue to Melbourne, winning the handicap section of the race and coming second overall. The journey from London had taken less than four days, a remarkable achievement at the time. The Dutch subscribed to a memorial to be erected in Albury and now a similar aircraft is on view at Albury Airport with the story of the rescue.

ACCOMMODATION

Albury offers all types of accommodation, including three choices for backpackers. However, two of the three are well to the north of the city centre. Albury Central Tourist Park is only a short distance off the map shown on page 133, but the youth hostel is some four kilometres from the town centre. Long-distance bus services will stop at the youth hostel on request, but there is no local bus running that far.

(i) Hotel Accommodation in Albury

Name	Stars	No. on Map	Telephone No.	Address	Lowest Price (Double/Twin)
Manor House Motel	4	5	1-800-641-774	593 Young Street	$120
Country Comfort Albury	4½	11	1-800-065-064	Dean & Elizabeth Streets	$120
Hovell Tree Inn	4½	16	02-6041-2666	Hume Highway & Hovell St	$120
Greentree Inn	4	6	1-800-226-466	579 Olive Street	$105
Seaton Arms Motor Inn	3	7	1-800-152-552	Olive & Wilson Streets	$104
Paddlesteamer Lodge	4	20	1-800-654-576	324 Wodonga Place	$102
Matador Motor Inn	3½	3	1-800-501-571	617 Young Street	$97
Meramie Motor Inn		1	02-6021-8100	595 Kiewa Street	$90
Astor Hotel / Motel		2	02-6021-1922	Hume Hwy. & Guinea St.	$90
Town House Motel	3½	8	02-6021-3000	David & Wilson Streets	$90
Fountain Court Motor Inn	3½	10	02-6021-8411	568 David Street	$90
Commodore Motel	3½	12	1-800-674-555	515 Kiewa Street	$90
Winsor Park Motor Inn	3½	15	02-6021-8800	471 Young Street	$90
Allawa Motor Inn		18	02-6021-6133	Hume Highway & Olive St.	$90
Georgian Motor Inn	3½	4	1-300-135-744	599 Young Street	$85
Cottage Motor Inn		17	02-6021-3899	523 Hume Street	$75
New Albury Hotel		13	02-6021-3599	491 Kiewa Street	$65
Viscount Motor Inn		19	02-6021-2444	437 Young Street	$65
Albion Hotel		14	02-6021-3377	593 Dean Street	$50
Soden's Australia Hotel	1½	9	02-6021-2400	David & Wilson Streets	$39

(ii) Backpackers Hostels in Albury

Name	Group	No. on Map	Telephone Number	Address	Lowest Price (Dormitory)
Albury Motor Village YHA	YHA	21	02-6040-2999	372 Wagga Road	$18
Albury Central Tourist Park		22	02-6041-1844	286 North Street	$16
Albury Backpackers	VIP	23	02-6041-1822	452 David Street	$16

MOVING ON
(i) By Train

There are two trains to Sydney and five to Melbourne every day. For the timetable to Sydney, see page 751 and for the timetable to Melbourne see the next page.

NEW SOUTH WALES

Albury to Melbourne

Days of Operation	Daily	M-Sat	Sun	F (Bus)	M - F	Sun	Daily	M - F	Sat	Sun
Albury	0357	0635	0755	0900	1225	1445	1504	1610	1615	1640
Wodonga		0643	0803	0910	1233	1453		1618	1623	1648
Wangaratta	0436	0726	0846	1005	1314	1533	1543	1702	1708	1732
Benalla	0500	0755	0911	1045	1339	1558	1614	1725	1734	1756
Melbourne	0700	1010	1131	1325	1551	1810	1815	1939	1950	2014

(ii) By Bus

There are buses to Sydney operated by McCafferty's, Greyhound and Firefly, and to Melbourne with the same companies. Most of the McCafferty's and Greyhound buses to Sydney travel via Canberra. V-Line operates buses from Albury to Canberra, Adelaide and Mildura. Here is a summary of bus departures from Albury.

Destination	Operator	Via	Distance (km)	Fare	Journey Time	Frequency
Sydney	McCafferty's		640	$54	8¾ - 9¼ hrs	2/day
		Canberra	343	$38	4¼ - 4¾ hrs	2/day
Sydney	Greyhound		640	$54	7½ - 9½ hrs	3/day
		Canberra	343	$38	4½ hrs	2/day
Sydney	Firefly		640	$60	7¾ - 8 hrs	2/day
Melbourne	McCafferty's		283	$47	3¼ - 3½ hrs	2/day
Melbourne	Greyhound		283	$47	3½ - 4½ hrs	3/day
Melbourne	Firefly		283	$60	3¾ hrs	2/day
Canberra	V-Line		347	$39	4¾ hrs	1/day
Adelaide	V-Line		907	$69	12½ hrs	1/day
Mildura	V-Line		610	$69	10 hrs	4/week
Falls Creek	Pyle's		125	$41	3¼ hrs	1/day
		Mt. Beauty	93	$20	2¼ hrs	1/day
Beechworth	Wangaratta		47	$8.10	1 hr	2/day

GRIFFITH

Population 23,000

9 hrs by train, or train and bus from Sydney
6 hrs by train and bus from Melbourne

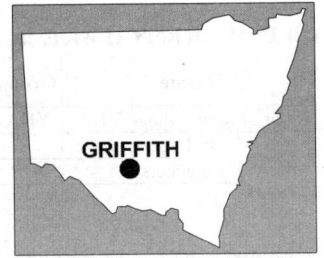

Griffith is a town which has been growing rapidly in recent years, to a large extent because of the increasing popularity of wine in Australia and the extension of the wine-growing belt. So successful has Griffith and the surrounding area become in this enterprise that now 70% of New South Wales wine is produced here, and 15% of Australian wine. There are more than 10,000 hectares of vines in the area, producing 150,000 tonnes of grapes, enough for 150 million bottles of wine. Griffith has thus established itself as the centre of Riverina wine production.

Griffith and area is also responsible for 90% of Australia's rice production and 70% of New South Wales citrus fruit production.

GRIFFITH

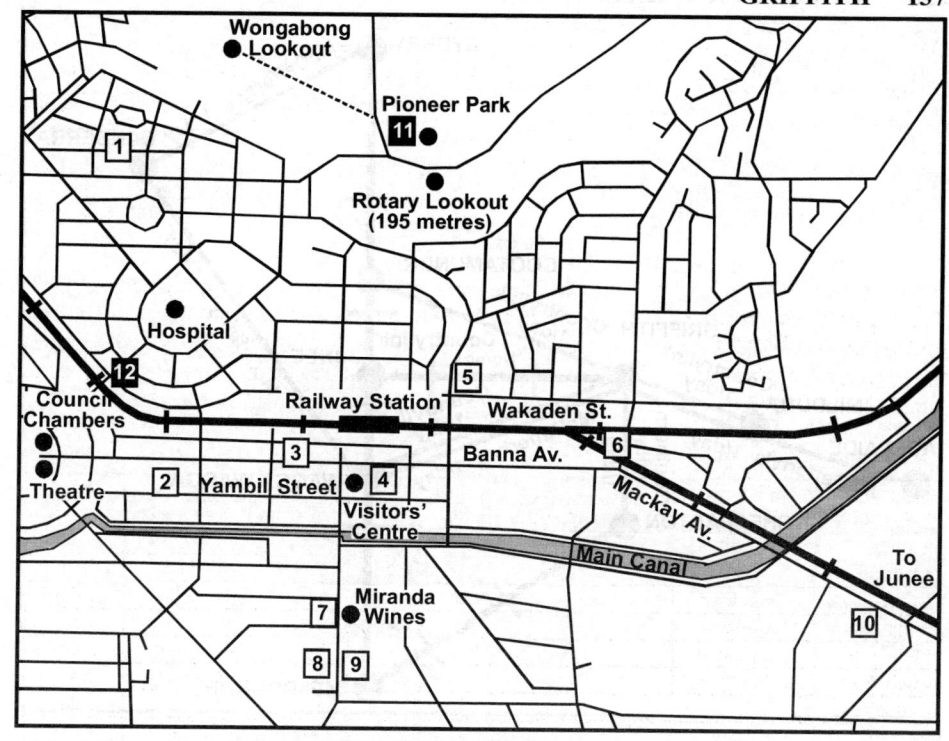

GRIFFITH
Black numerals in white boxes indicate hotel accommodation
White numerals in black boxes indicate backpackers hostels

Another token of the town's recent prominence is that its rail service has been restored. When the author first lived in Australia, Griffith used to have a daily train to and from Sydney, which I took once from Narrandera to Sydney. Soon after that, the service was withdrawn and the line used only for goods traffic for a long while. Now a passenger service has been reinstated. It is true that the train runs only once a week, but it is a start, and I was recently able to travel the section of line between **Narrandera** and Griffith for the first time.

If you want to take this infrequent train, you need to travel to Griffith on a Saturday (timetable on page 93), or travel back to Sydney on a Sunday (timetable on page 815). From Sydney the train runs attached to the Canberra train as far as Goulburn, where the two are separated. The Griffith section then runs on to **Junee**, where there is a pause while it is fuelled and watered before reversing its direction to continue at limited speed on the rather uneven branch line to Griffith. On other days there are bus connexions to Griffith from the Sydney - Melbourne and Melbourne - Sydney trains at **Cootamundra** or **Wagga Wagga**, as can be found on the timetables mentioned above. There is also a McCafferty's bus service between Sydney and Adelaide, via Canberra. This passes through Griffith during the night in both directions. In addition, there is a service from Melbourne by train to Shepparton and by connecting bus from there. This is operated by the Goulburn Valley Railway, but can be used with V-Line tickets and Rail Passes.

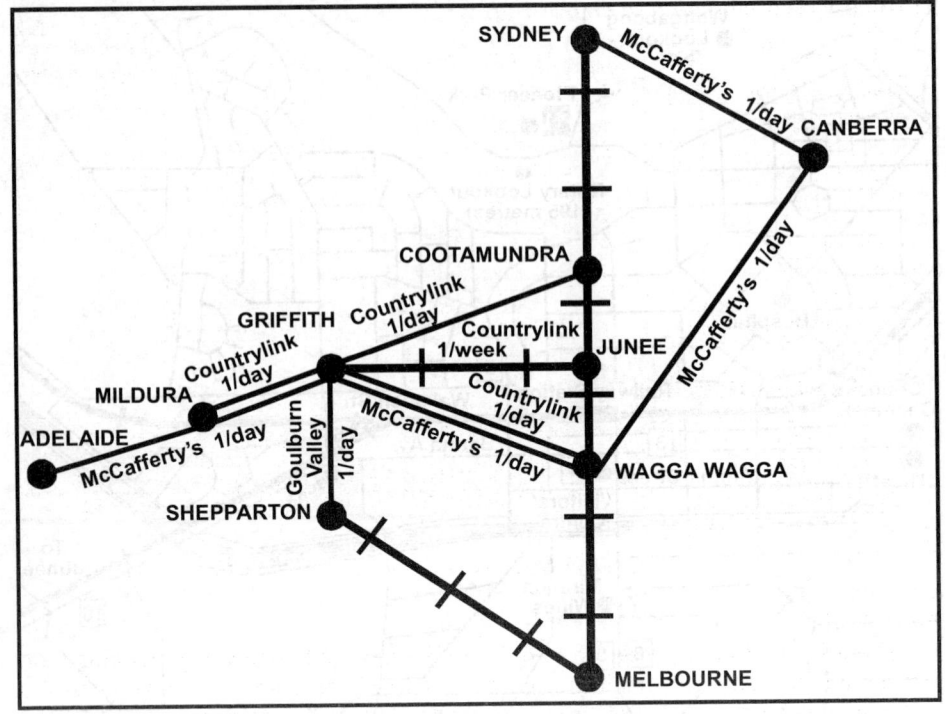

TRANSPORT AROUND GRIFFITH

Griffith was originally a barren, dry area lacking sufficient rainfall for successful farming. That changed in 1913 when the **Murrumbidgee Irrigation Scheme** commenced. A canal runs through the town, bringing the water needed for its prosperity. The town itself was designed by Burley Griffin, the man who provided the plan for Canberra. It now has a population of 23,000.

The principal attractions are the **wineries** and the local **restaurants**, which have a high reputation. Tours to the wineries are available locally. There are fifteen wineries within twenty kilometres of the town, of which eleven welcome visitors, in the hope, of course, that you will be tempted to purchase some of their products. Within the town, there is the open-air **Pioneer Park Museum**, which deals especially with the history of the Murrumbidgee Irrigation Scheme, and there is also a prominent **art gallery**.

ACCOMMODATION

There is a variety of accommodation in Griffith, although somewhat limited at the lower end of the scale. The Shearers' Quarters are part of the Pioneer Park Museum, so best contacted during working hours. The museum is open from 9:00 until 16:30.

GRIFFITH

(i) Hotel Accommodation in Griffith

Name	Stars	No. on Map	Telephone No.	Address	Lowest Price (Double/Twin)
Kidman Wayside Inn	4	7	02-6964-5666	58 Jondaryan Avenue	$125
Yambil Inn Motel	4	2	02-6964-1233	155 Yambil Street	$120
Gemini Motel	3½	3	02-6962-3833	201 Banna Avenue	$103
Bagtown Inn Motel	3½	6	02-6962-7166	2 Blumer Avenue	$100
A-Line Motel	3	5	02-6962-1922	187 Wakaden Street	$90
Acacia Motel	3	8	02-6962-4422	Jondaryan Avenue	$90
Citrus Motel	3	9	02-6962-6233	71 Jondaryan Avenue	$90
Griffith Motor Inn	3	4	02-6962-1800	96 Banna Avenue	$90
M.I.A. Motel	3	10	02-6962-1866	144 Mackay Avenue	$80
Griffith Northside Apts.		1	02-6964-5416	31 Edmondson Avenue	$60

(ii) Backpackers Hostels in Griffith

Name	Group	No. on Map	Telephone Number	Address	Lowest Price (Dormitory)
Shearers' Quarters		11	02-6962-4196	Pioneer Park Museum	$25
Griffith International Hostel		12	02-6964-4236	112 Binya Street	$25

MOVING ON

(i) By Train

There is one train a week, on Sunday, to Sydney, and connecting bus plus train services on other days (timetable on page 815). These buses also connect with trains to Melbourne, but there is a more direct bus plus train service to Melbourne operated by the Goulburn Valley Railway via Shepparton, the timetable for which appears on page 818.

(ii) By Bus

McCafferty's has one bus to Sydney via Canberra and one to Adelaide every day, both departures being during the night. There is also one bus a day to Mildura, operated by Countrylink.

Destination	Operator	Via	Distance (km)	Fare	Journey Time	Frequency
Sydney	McCafferty's		640	$72	11¾ hrs	1/day
		Canberra	426	$54	6½ hrs	1/day
Sydney	Countrylink		641	$94.80	9½ hrs	1/day
		Cootamundra	217	$37	2¾ hrs	1/day
		Wagga Wagga	130	$25	2¾ hrs	1/day
Melbourne	Goulburn V Rly		474	$61.60	5¾ hrs	1/day
		Shepparton	296	$45.30	1¾ hrs	1/day
Adelaide	McCafferty's		830	$138	12 hrs	1/day
		Nuriootpa	770	$138	10½ hrs	1/day
		Mildura	447	$61	5¾ hrs	1/day
Mildura	Countrylink		447	$79.50	6 hrs	1/day

NEW SOUTH WALES
BATHURST
Population 30,000

3 hrs 30 mins by train from Sydney
4 hrs 30 mins by bus from Sydney

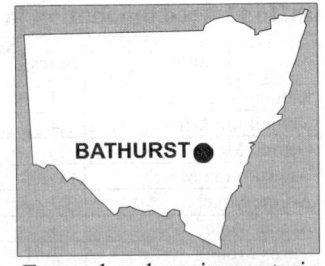

We move now to the central part of New South Wales and proceed west from Sydney along the course of the trans-continental railway line (about which more on page 154). The edge of the Sydney suburban system is reached at **Lithgow**. Bathurst lies an hour further west. Every day there is one train operated by Countrylink which runs to Dubbo via Bathurst, and this is the most convenient method of travel. The timetable appears on page 93. In addition, there are six bus connexions every day to Bathurst from CityRail services which terminate at Lithgow. On Mondays there is an additional Countrylink train running through Bathurst on its way to Broken Hill, while on Sundays, Mondays and Thursdays, there is a service on the *Indian-Pacific* or the *Ghan*, operated by Great Southern Railway. Greyhound operates a thrice-weekly service between Sydney and Adelaide which passes through Bathurst.

Bathurst (pronounced with a short 'a') was Australia's first inland settlement. It was named after the British Secretary of State for War and the Colonies (an interesting combination of duties) of the time, Lord Bathurst, and founded on 7th May 1815, at a time when the Lord was probably quite busy with the other part of his portfolio.

In February 1823, traces of gold were first discovered in the river, but it was not until 1851 that Australia's first gold rush began here in earnest, causing the Bathurst population to swell to 5,000 by 1862. There were, at that time, fifty hotels in the town to support thirsty diggers.

In 1862, Bathurst became the headquarters of the famous Cobb and Co. stagecoach company, and a restored coach is now on display at the Visitor Information Centre. Then, in 1863, bushrangers, led by Ben Hall, successfully ransomed the Gold Commissioner of the time. In 1876, the transport system improved considerably when the railway reached here.

Bathurst is proud of having reared a well respected Prime Minister of Australia, **Ben Chifley**. A former train driver, he took up the post of Prime Minister just before the end of the war, in July 1945, and held it until December 1949. He died on 13th June 1951 at the age of 66. His modest home is open for viewing from 14:00 until 16:00 on Tuesdays to Saturdays, and on Sunday mornings.

However, what Bathurst is best known for is a car race. Formerly known as the *Bathurst 500* and raced over a distance of 500 miles, it has now become the ***Bathurst 1000***, raced over a distance of 1000 kilometres. Motor-cycle racing started in Bathurst as early as 1911, but the *500* arrived only in 1963, when it was transferred from Phillip Island in Victoria. The circuit is at the top of **Mt. Panorama** which is 874 metres above sea level. The track is 6.213 kilometres in length and has a height variation of 174 metres, with slopes as steep as 1 in 6. It is reckoned to be one of the world's most demanding circuits. When not in use for racing, the circuit is a public road, although the speed limit out of race times is 60 km/hr. The **National Racing Museum** is near the start and finish line of the circuit and is open daily from 9:00 until 16:30.

ACCOMMODATION

Here is a selection of accommodation available. There is nothing specifically for backpackers, but there are several older hotels offering basic rooms at reasonable rates.

Accommodation in Bathurst

Name	Stars	No. on Map	Telephone No.	Address	Lowest Price (Double/Twin)
Ben Chifley Motor Inn	3½	3	1-800-021-028	272 Stewart Street	$115
Country Lodge Motor Inn	3½	4	02-6331-4888	145 William Street	$105
Sundowner Motor Inn	4	9	1-800-654-576	19 Charlotte Street	$93
Abercrombie Motor Inn	3	2	02-6331-1077	362 Stewart Street	$90
Bathurst Explorers Motel	2½	1	02-6331-2966	357 Stewart Street	$90
Knickerbocker Hotel		7	02-6332-4500	110 William Street	$90
Panorama City Lodge	2½	10	02-6331-2666	51 Durham Street	$85
Park Hotel / Motel		6	02-6331-3399	201 George Street	$75
Bathurst Motor Inn	2½	8	1-800-047-907	87 Durham Street	$70
Edinboro Castle Hotel	2	5	02-6331-5020	134 William Street	$70

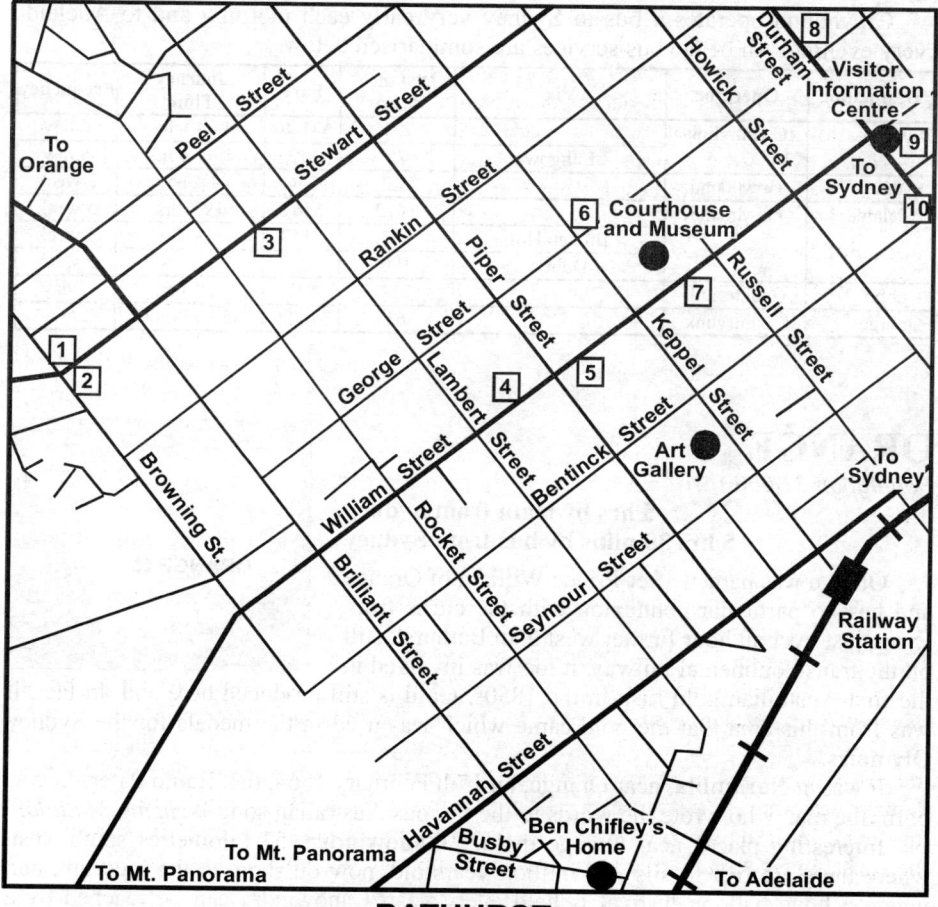

BATHURST
Numerals indicate accommodation

NEW SOUTH WALES
MOVING ON
(i) By Train

There is a daily train from Bathurst to Sydney operated by Countrylink, as well as six buses connecting at Lithgow with CityRail services to the city. There is an additional Countrylink train on Tuesdays and there are the *Indian-Pacific* and *Ghan* services operated by Great Southern Railway running in to Sydney very early on Sunday, Monday and Thursday mornings. In the opposite direction, these services run to Adelaide and Perth on Monday and Thursday evenings, and to Adelaide and Alice Springs on Sunday evening. The timetable for these trains appears on page 93. Going west, there is a daily Countrylink service by train to Dubbo and then by connecting bus on to Broken Hill, or to Lightning Ridge, or, on Sundays, Tuesdays, Thursdays and Fridays, to Bourke. There is a Countrylink train to Broken Hill on Mondays. The timetable for all of these services also appears on page 93. There are Countrylink buses to Orange five times a day, and one of those continues to Dubbo.

(ii) By Bus

Greyhound operates a bus to Sydney very early each morning and to Adelaide every evening. All of the bus services are summarised below.

Destination	Operator	Via	Distance (km)	Fare	Journey Time	Frequency
Sydney	Countrylink		231	$41.40	4 - 4¾ hrs	6/day
		Lithgow	75	$13	1 - 1½ hrs	6/day
Sydney	Greyhound		212	$36	4¾ hrs	3/week
Adelaide	Greyhound		1472	$147	19¾ hrs	3/week
		Broken Hill	913	$147	12¾ hrs	3/week
		Dubbo	190	$57	2¾ hrs	3/week
Dubbo	Countrylink		214	$37	2¾ hrs	1/day
Orange	Countrylink		65	$10.90	45 - 75 mins	5/day

ORANGE
Population 31,000

5 hrs by train from Sydney
5 hrs 30 mins by bus from Sydney

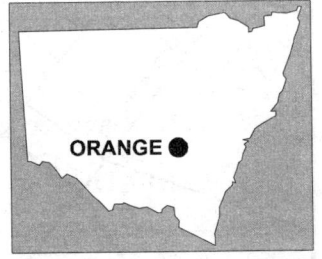

Orange was named after Prince William of Orange and has no particular connexion with the citrus fruit. Lying just over an hour further west than Bathurst, still on the trans-continental railway, it too was involved in the first Australian gold rush in the 1850s. Gold is still produced here and, in fact, it was from this area that the gold came which was used in the medals for the Sydney Olympics.

It was at **Narambla**, near Orange, on 17th February 1864, that Banjo Paterson was born, the man who wrote the words to the famous Australian song *Waltzing Matilda*.

Interesting places near Orange include **Canowindra**, 53 kilometres south-west, where there are fish fossils 365 million years old, now on show in the museum, and where a huge balloon festival is held every year. Canowindra can be reached by a Countrylink bus which runs to Cootamundra twice a day.

There is also **Carcoar**, a similar distance south, listed by the National Trust because of its many **fine old buildings**. Carcoar can be reached by a Countrylink bus which operates from Bathurst (but not Orange) to Grenfell, twice a day.

North of Orange is **Ophir**, twenty kilometres away, and there you will find, not, as you might anticipate, a quinquireme of Ninevar, but gold. This is the spot where Australia's very **first commercial find of gold** was made, but now the cash comes from the tourists, rather than from the gold deposits, and the panning is just for fun. Tours operate to Ophir, but there is no public transport.

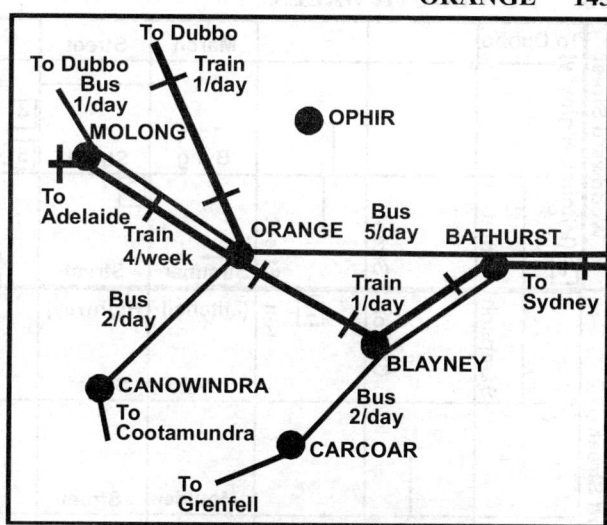

COUNTRYLINK SERVICES AROUND ORANGE

Molong is 32 kilometres north-west of Orange and is another small town of **historic buildings** in a pretty setting. The Countrylink bus between Lithgow and Dubbo passes through Molong, operating once every day. The railway line to Adelaide and beyond also travels this way, but trains do not stop at Molong.

To reach Orange from Sydney, the Countrylink train from Sydney to Dubbo stops here every day, and there is a train to Broken Hill on Mondays. There are also five daily Countrylink bus services connecting from CityRail suburban trains which terminate at Lithgow. Great Southern Railway operates the *Indian-Pacific* and the *Ghan* from Sydney on Sundays, Mondays and Thursdays. It is at Orange that the line to Dubbo diverges from the trans-continental line, so the *Indian-Pacific*, the *Ghan* and the Broken Hill train use a different station from the trains to Dubbo. This station is right on the triangular junction and is known as Orange East Fork (see map). There is also a Greyhound bus once a day which runs between Sydney and Adelaide via Orange.

ACCOMMODATION
Accommodation in Orange

Name	Stars	No. on Map	Telephone No.	Address	Lowest Price (Double/Twin)
Central Caleula Motor Inn	4½	2	1-800-024-845	60 Summer Street	$125
Town Square Motel	4	4	02-6369-1444	246 Anson Street	$120
Templer's Mill Motel	3½	3	02-6362-5611	94 Byng Street	$105
Mid-City Motor Lodge	3	6	1-800-047-906	243 Lords Place	$100
Royal Hotel		8	02-6362-1855	Summer St. & Lords Place	$85
Oriana Motor Inn	3½	1	02-6362-3066	178 Woodward Street	$84
Hotel Conobolas		9	02-6362-2444	Summer St. & Lords Place	$80
Down Town Motel	2½	7	02-6362-2877	243 Summer Street	$70
Metropolitan Hotel	1½	5	02-6362-4833	107 Byng Street	$65
Occidental Hotel / Motel	1	10	02-6362-4833	Lords Place & Kite Street	$65

144 NEW SOUTH WALES

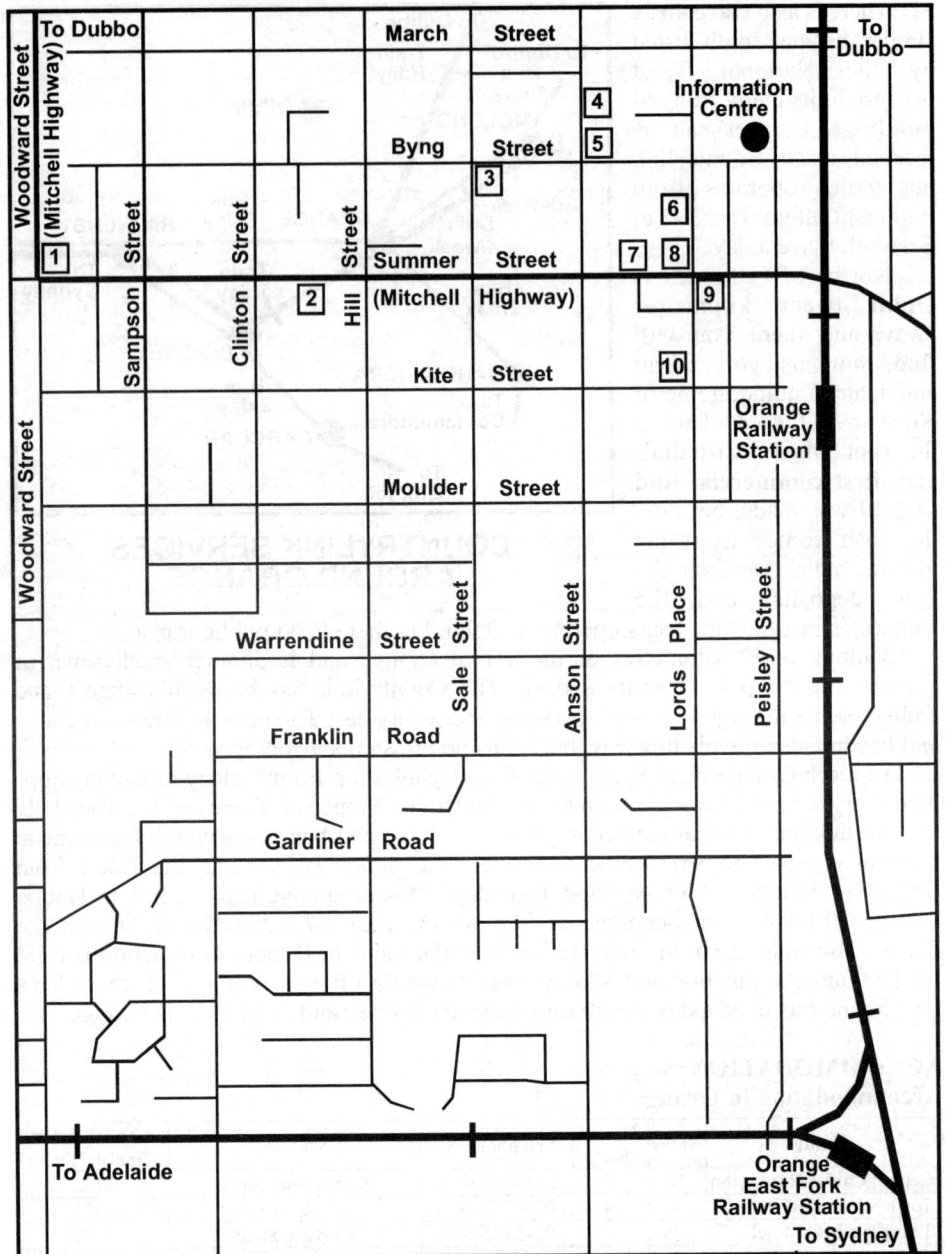

ORANGE
Numerals indicate accommodation

MOVING ON

(i) By Train

Countrylink operates a daily train to Sydney, as well as five buses connecting at Lithgow with CityRail services to the city. There is an additional Countrylink train on Tuesdays, and there are the *Indian-Pacific* and *Ghan* services operated by Great Southern Railway very early on Sunday, Monday and Thursday mornings. The timetable for these trains appears on page 162. The same services run to Adelaide and Perth on Monday and Thursday evenings, and to Adelaide and Alice Springs on Sunday evening. There is a daily Countrylink train service to Dubbo and then connecting buses to Broken Hill, Lightning Ridge, and, on Sundays, Tuesdays, Thursdays and Fridays, Bourke. There is a Countrylink train to Broken Hill on Mondays and a bus to Dubbo once every day. The timetable for these westbound services is on page 93.

(ii) By Bus

Greyhound has a bus to Sydney very early in the morning and to Adelaide in the evening, each on three days a week. The bus services are summarised below.

Destination	Operator	Via	Distance (km)	Fare	Journey Time	Frequency
Sydney	Countrylink		296	$50.10	4¾ - 5¼ hrs	5/day
		Lithgow	140	$25	1¾ - 2 hrs	5/day
Sydney	Greyhound		250	$50	5½ hrs	3/week
Adelaide	Greyhound		1434	$147	19 hrs	3/week
		Broken Hill	475	$147	12 hrs	3/week
		Dubbo	152	$50	2 hrs	3/week
Dubbo	Countrylink		149	$25	2 hrs	1/day

DUBBO
Population 30,000

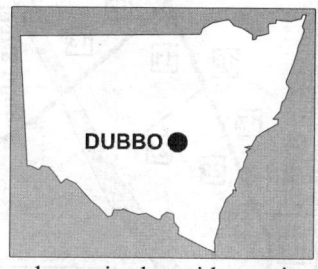

6 hrs 30 mins by train from Sydney
7 hrs by bus from Sydney

Dubbo claims to be the fastest growing city in the state of New South Wales. It is most famous for its zoo, known as the **Western Plains Zoo**. The zoo is on the outskirts of the city and can be reached by a long walk or by a city bus ride costing $2.10. It is an open range zoo, started in 1977 and covering 300 hectares. Just to walk round it takes some time. The main route is six kilometres long and the total length of paths is fifteen kilometres. Nor is it cheap. Admission costs $25 and a bicycle may be hired for a further $11 for four hours (plus a deposit). Private vehicles are admitted free of charge. The zoo is open daily from 9:00 until 17:00, but the latest time for admission is 15:30. Although it is expensive, it is an interesting zoo and one which has won several awards for its lay-out and presentation. It just needs energy and stamina.

Other attractions of Dubbo include the **Old Gaol**, in the heart of the city, with an interesting history. It was in service from the 1880s until 1966 and eight men were hanged here during that time. The Old Gaol is open from 9:00 until 16:30 and admission costs $7.

146 NEW SOUTH WALES

Dundullimal Homestead, near the zoo, has performing farm animals at 15:30, at a cost of $6. Then there are **cruises on the river**, some operating from Dundullimal and some from Bligh Street in the heart of the city. There is an **Observatory** with shows nightly for $13.50 and there is a **Museum** open from 12:00 until 16:30 and costing $6.

Countrylink operates one train per day from Sydney to Dubbo, and also one bus connecting with a CityRail suburban train service at Lithgow. For Greyhound, this is a cross-roads, where the Sydney - Adelaide service meets the Melbourne - Brisbane service, and transfer is possible, although in the middle of the night.

Dubbo has its own city bus service, with fares ranging from $1.40 to $3.80, but actually the only destination for which the visitor is likely to require a bus is the zoo.

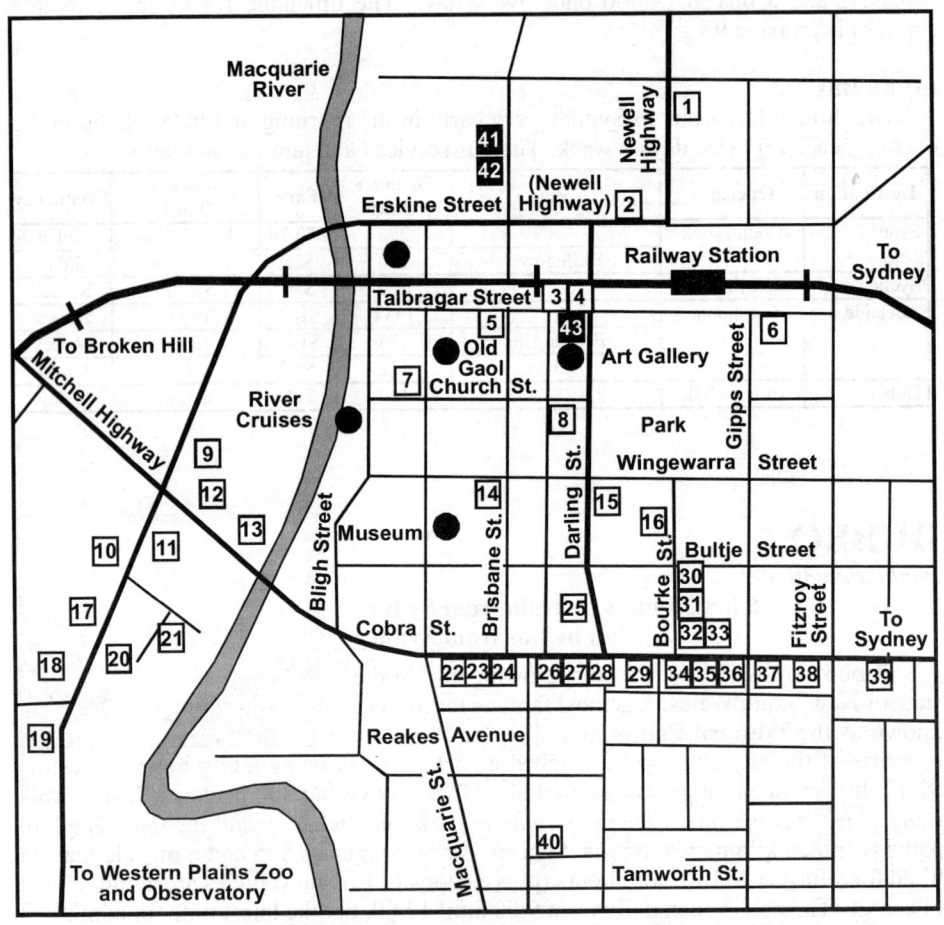

DUBBO

Black numerals in white boxes indicate hotel accommodation
White numerals in black boxes indicate backpackers hostels

DUBBO 147

ACCOMMODATION

Because it is a popular destination, Dubbo has a considerable amount of accommodation - over 3,000 beds available in all price ranges.

For backpackers, there are two hostels in Brisbane Street. Then just near the station and Countrylink bus terminus, is Imperial Backpackers, offering single rooms at $28. Opposite is the Civic Hotel with single rooms at $30 and just a little further down the street is the Pastoral Hotel at $28 for a single and $44 for a double. The Garden Hotel, in the opposite direction from the station, has single rooms at $25, including breakfast, so there is plenty of choice in this city for those on a budget.

(i) Hotel Accommodation in Dubbo

Name	Stars	No. on Map	Telephone No.	Address	Lowest Price (Double/Twin)
Country Apartments	4	40	02-6885-1141	226 Brisbane Street	$120
Australian Heritage Inn	4	26	02-6884-1188	Cobra & Brisbane Streets	$115
Dubbo RSL Club Resort	4	14	02-6884-9099	Brisbane & Wingewarra Sts.	$109
Abel Tasman Motor Inn	3½	18	02-6885-2555	135 Whylandra Street	$109
Country Comfort Inn	3½	19	02-6882-4777	Newell Highway	$108
Aberdeen Motor Inn	3½	22	1-800-044-552	25 Cobra Street	$106
Endeavour Court Inn	4	1	1-800-081-100	94 Bourke Street	$105
Countryman Motor Inn	3½	27	1-800-022-773	47 Cobra Street	$104
Palms Motor Inn	3½	24	1-800-688-686	35 Cobra Street	$103
Blue Diamond Motor Inn	4	15	1-800-027-236	113 Wingewarra Street	$96
Blue Lagoon Motor Inn	3½	29	02-6882-4444	79 Cobra Street	$95
Golden West Motor Inn	3½	34	02-6882-2822	87 Cobra Street	$95
Dubbo City Motor Inn	3½	28	02-6882-7033	57 Cobra Street	$93
Cascades Motor Inn	3½	39	02-6882-3888	147 Cobra Street	$90
Ashwood Country Club	4	17	02-6881-8700	Whylandra & Easts Streets	$88
Amaroo Hotel	2	7	02-6882-3533	81 Macquarie Street	$87
Blue Gum Motor Inn	3½	37	1-800-027-247	109 Cobra Street	$85
All Seasons Motor Lodge	3½	20	02-6882-6377	78 Whylandra Street	$80
Shearing Shed Motor Inn	3½	23	02-6884-2977	31 Cobra Street	$80
Mayfair Cottage	3½	21	02-6882-5226	10 Baird Street	$75
Castlereagh Hotel	1	5	02-6882-4877	Talbragar & Brisbane Sts.	$75
Cattleman's Country Inn	4½	9	02-6884-5222	10 Whylandra Street	$75
Matilda Motor Inn	2½	25	02-6882-3944	231 Darling Street	$75
Fountain View Motel	3½	38	02-6882-9777	113 Cobra Street	$75
Atlas Motel	3½	31	1-800-024-972	140 Bourke Street	$74
Across Country Motor Inn	2½	10	02-6882-0877	Newell Hwy. & Baird Street	$70
Tallarook Motor Inn	3	13	02-6882-7066	Victoria St & Stonehaven Av	$70
Green Gables Motel	3	30	02-6882-5588	134 Bourke Street	$70
Gallop Inn Motel	3½	35	02-6882-7888	95 Cobra Street	$70
Homestead Motel	3½	36	02-6882-4944	101 Cobra Street	$70
Westside Hotel / Motel	1½	11	02-6882-3500	Newell & Mitchell Hwys.	$65
Merino Motel	1½	8	02-6882-4133	65 Church Street	$65
Centrepoint Motel	3	32	02-6882-7644	146 Bourke Street	$65
Country Leisure Inn	3	33	02-6882-3988	86 Cobra Street	$65
Park Vue Motel	2	16	02-6882-4253	131 Bourke Street	$60
Western Star Hotel		2	02-6882-4644	62 Erskine Street	$55
Motel Formule I	2	12	02-6882-9211	14 Victoria Street	$50
Civic Hotel		4	02-6882-3688	Talbragar & Darling Streets	$49
Garden Hotel		6	02-6882-3371	Talbragar & Gipps Streets	$49
Pastoral Hotel		3	02-6882-4219	110 Talbragar Street	$44

148 NEW SOUTH WALES

(ii) Backpackers Hostels in Dubbo

Name	Group	No. on Map	Telephone Number	Address	Lowest Price (Dormitory)
Imperial Backpackers	VIP	43	02-6882-4455	163 Talbragar Street	$28
Dubbo Y.H.A. Backpackers	YHA	42	02-6882-0922	87 Brisbane Street	$19
Hub of the West		41	02-6882-5004	79 Brisbane Street	$19

MOVING ON
(i) By Train

There is an afternoon train back to Sydney, for which the timetable appears on page 162. Then there is a morning Countrylink bus to Lithgow, from where there is a train connexion with CityRail to Sydney. In the opposite direction, Countrylink has services to Broken Hill and Lightning Ridge every day and to Bourke on Sundays, Tuesdays, Thursdays and Fridays. These services are scheduled to co-incide with the arrival of the train from Sydney and all leave at approximately 14:00.

(ii) By Bus

Greyhound has buses to Sydney, Adelaide and Brisbane and McCafferty's has a bus to Melbourne, all leaving Dubbo in the middle of the night and permitting connexions from one to the other. Additionally, McCafferty's has a service to Brisbane leaving in the evening.

Destination	Operator	Via	Distance (km)	Fare	Journey Time	Frequency
Sydney	Countrylink		445	$82.80	7½ hrs	1/day
		Lithgow	289	$46.80	4¼ hrs	1/day
Sydney	Greyhound		402	$74	7¼ hrs	3/week
Melbourne	McCafferty's		691	$131	11 hrs	1/day
Adelaide	Greyhound		1282	$131	16 hrs	3/week
		Broken Hill	723	$131	9 hrs	3/week
Brisbane	McCafferty's		854	$125	12¼ hrs	1/day
		Toowoomba	724	$125	9¾ hrs	1/day
Brisbane	Greyhound		961	$125	14½ hrs	4/week
		Toowoomba	828	$125	12¼ hrs	4/week
Broken Hill	Countrylink		723	$94.80	9 hrs	1/day
Bourke	Countrylink		373	$62.10	4½ hrs	4/week
L'ning Ridge	Countrylink		360	$62.10	4½ hrs	1/day

LIGHTNING RIDGE

Population 2,000
11 hrs 30 mins by train and bus from Sydney

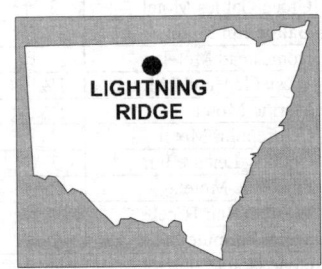

Lightning Ridge is really in the outback of New South Wales, just 65 kilometres south of the Queensland border, the type of small town reached by only a few of the visitors to Australia, but an endearing place well worth a visit.

Why is it there at all? The reason for its existence is **opals**, the semi-precious stone which is a symbol of Australia. Opals are found in few places, and the location known to visitors and stopped at by many of them is Coober Pedy in South Australia, which, as a result, has become rather touristic. Now, for those willing to go further off the beaten track, here is Australia's second opal mining town, Lightning Ridge, famous particularly for its rare black opals.

Many of the people here are engaged in mining, either full time or as a hobby. Few of them get rich, but they seem to enjoy it. When the author was here, the owners of the accommodation where I stayed also operated a back yard mine and were willing to take me down to see what went on underground. Much of the mining here is on such a scale - a one-man tunnelling operation. The miners usually find enough opal to be able to survive, but it is hard and rather unhealthy work and really valuable finds are infrequent, although always dreamed of and providing the impetus to continue. However, it all makes Lightning Ridge a fascinating place to visit.

Some of the larger mines offer **tours**, as do independent operators, and there are plenty of shops making and selling opal products. There are free **hot artesian baths** and there is a **cactus nursery**.

Be careful when walking round this area. There are unexpected holes in the ground, so watch where you are treading. Falling down an abandoned mine shaft is not good for the health.

Countrylink runs a daily service to Lightning Ridge, by train from Sydney to Dubbo and then by connecting bus. There is also a bus from the Queensland side of the border, operated by Kynoch Coaches. It runs from Toowoomba on Mondays and Thursdays, leaving at 10:30 and reaching Lightning Ridge at 19:00. There are connexions from Brisbane to Toowoomba.

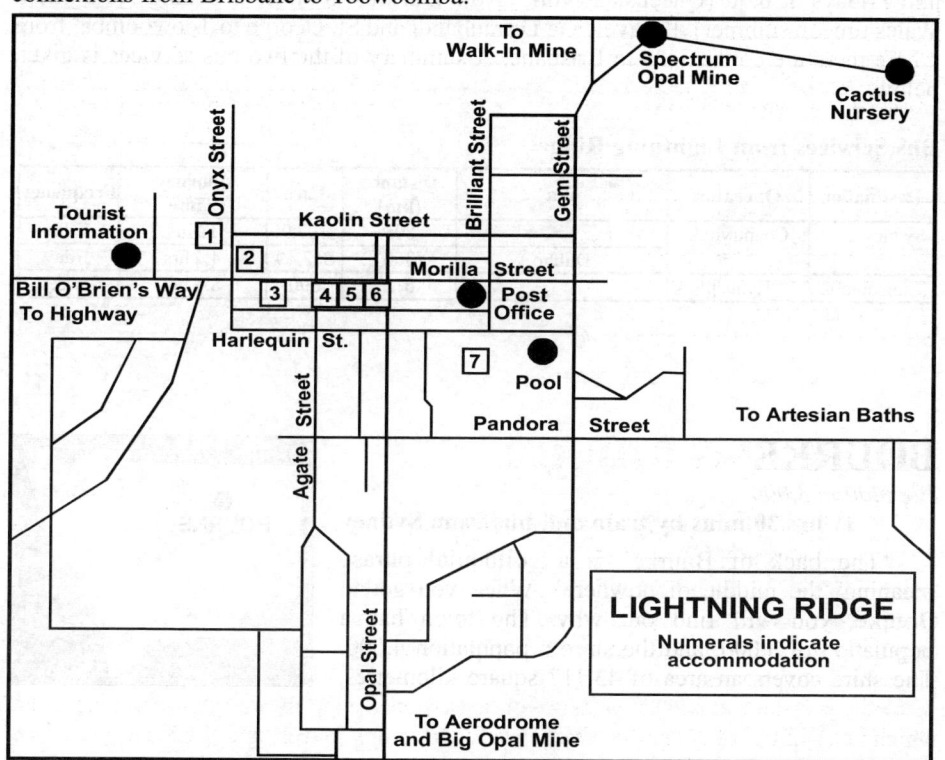

150 NEW SOUTH WALES
ACCOMMODATION

There are several motels in Lightning Ridge. For backpackers there are choices too. The caravan parks have cabins, the Lightning Ridge Hotel has rooms, and there is the Tram-O-Tel, which really is made from disused trams and offers unusual and reasonably priced accommodation.

Accommodation in Lightning Ridge

Name	Stars	No. on Map	Telephone No.	Address	Lowest Price (Double/Twin)
Black Opal Motel	2½	6	02-6829-0518	Opal Street	$90
Bluey Motel		5	02-6829-0380	Morilla Street	$85
Wallangulla Motel	2½	4	02-6829-0542	Morilla Street	$80
Lightning Ridge Hotel	2½	1	02-6829-0304	Onyx Street	$65
Tram-O-Tel		3	02-6829-0448	Morilla Street	$50
Lightning Ridge C'van Pk		7	02-6829-0532	Harlequin Street	$45
Crocodile Caravan Park		2	02-6829-0437	Morilla Street	$45

MOVING ON

Although Lightning Ridge is only 65 kilometres from the Queensland border, the regular bus service is with Countrylink back to Dubbo, with a connecting train to Sydney. The timetable for this service is on page 162. There is a service to Queensland, though. This is operated by Kynoch Coaches and leaves Lightning Ridge on Tuesdays and Fridays at 6:30 (Queensland time. Note that this is an hour behind New South Wales time in summer). It travels via Dirranbandi and St. George to Toowoomba, from where there are connexions to Brisbane. A summary of the two bus services is given below.

Bus Services from Lightning Ridge

Destination	Operator	Via	Distance (km)	Fare	Journey Time	Frequency
Sydney	Countrylink		805	$107.90	12 hrs	1/day
		Dubbo	360	$62.10	4¾ hrs	1/day
Toowoomba	Kynoch		612	$90	8½ hrs	2/week

BOURKE

Population 3,000

11 hrs 30 mins by train and bus from Sydney

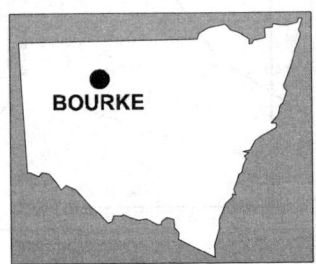

'The back of Bourke' is a colloquial phrase meaning 'the middle of nowhere'. When you get to Bourke, you will find out why. The town has a population of 3,000, and the shire a population 4,000. The shire covers an area of 43,117 square kilometres, approximately the size of Denmark. Bourke is in the farthest corner of New South Wales from Sydney, its capital, and yet it has a long history and has been a prosperous town in the past. It is certainly a place which should be visited, because it is such an essentially Australian place, whereas the cities, one feels, are not. They are just like cities the world over. Moreover, Bourke is a place which everybody with a knowledge of Australia has heard of, but which few have visited. Visiting Bourke is, in a sense, a pilgrimage, an acknowledgment that one has got to the geographical and metaphorical heart of the land. Australia's most famous author, Henry Lawson, lived here for eight months in 1892, and wrote that, "If you know Bourke, you know Australia."

It was in 1829 that Sturt discovered the **Darling River** and in 1835 Major Mitchell built the wooden **Fort Bourke Stockade**. Soon the first paddle steamers were finding their way here and Fort Bourke pastoral station was established. A bridge was built across the Darling, allowing the camels and their Afghan drivers to cross and provide transport north, but it was the presence of the river which ensured the survival and success of Bourke, for the paddle steamers could come all the way up to Bourke, a journey of 1,500 kilometres from the sea, bringing supplies and taking back agricultural produce, mainly wool and processed meat.

When the railway reached Bourke, however, the river traffic started to decline. A change of emphasis occurred when the cotton industry was established here in 1966. Later peanut farming started too. Then in the 1960s a sealed road reached Bourke and the railway started to fall into decline. A passenger service continued, though, until a huge flood came to Dubbo and the surrounding area in the 1990s. The railway suffered considerable, but not irreparable, damage, and it was decided not to bother to reinstate it. All rail services to Bourke stopped and the station is now the **Tourist Centre**.

Countrylink operates a bus service to Bourke from Dubbo, connecting with the train from Sydney. This service runs on Sundays, Tuesdays, Thursdays and Fridays.

In the town of Bourke, there are several buildings worth a look. There is also the old **bridge** across the Darling and a replica of the **stockade** which started the history of Bourke. This last, however, is several kilometres from the town and beyond comfortable walking distance. Here is a short walking tour of the town of Bourke.

Walking Tour

This walk is short in terms of distance, less than three kilometres. It will take an hour if no lengthy stops are made.

Start near the Tourist Centre and walk down Richard Street. At the first corner on the left you will see *Ardsilla*, which was built in the 1890s. Proceed to the next corner and turn left into Mertin Street, where you will find, on your left, a handsome wooden house which was formerly the **Police Inspector's Quarters**, built in 1901. It now belongs to the Historical Society and is used as a womens' refuge. Next to it is Bourke's oldest building, although its age is not quite certain. It was originally the **Methodist Church**.

BOURKE COURTHOUSE

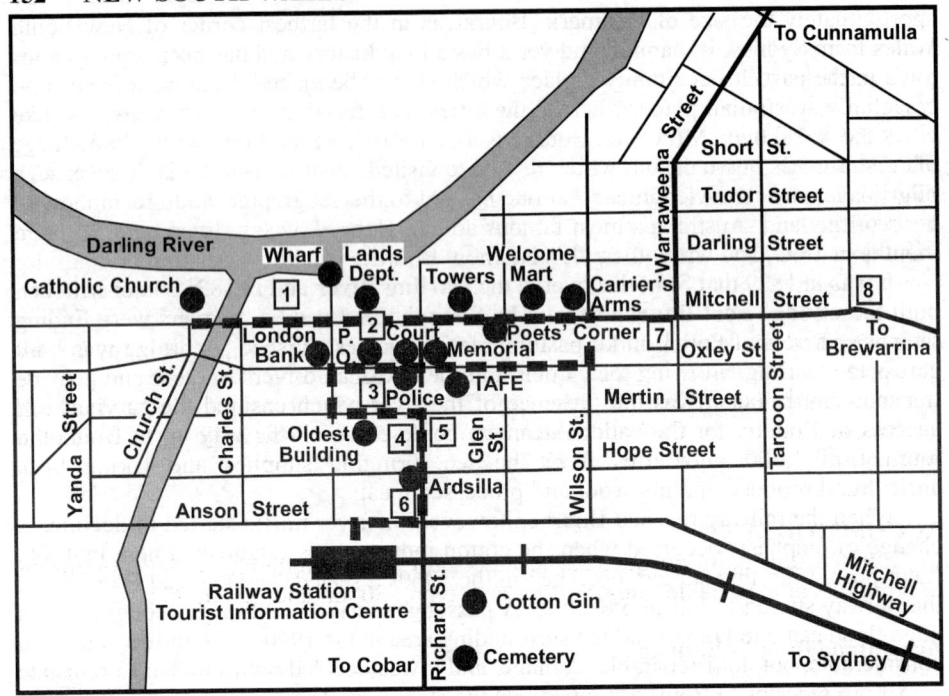

BOURKE
Dashed line shows Walking Tour
Numerals indicate accommodation

Turn right into Sturt Street and at the next corner you will see the former **London Bank**, built in 1888. It did not survive long as a bank, however, as it closed in the 1890s. Turn right into Oxley Street and you will encounter several interesting buildings. On the left of the street is the **Post Office**, built in 1880. It has a marker on it to show the height of the **1890 floods**. Opposite is the **Post Office Hotel**, built in 1888 and operated by one family until 1957. A little further on the right is the **Police Station**, dating from 1889, and on the left the **Courthouse**, built in 1900. The crown on the spire denotes its function as a maritime court. It is the farthest inland such court in Australia. It can be visited when the court is not in session.

Across Richard Street on the left is the **Bourke Soldiers Memorial**, and then on the right the **Bourke TAFE College**, built in 1876 as the Primary School. It has a **mural** of Bourke inside and a **Bush Poets Exhibition**, photographs taken at the time when Henry Lawson and other poets lived here. Next door is Outback Radio Station 2WEB.

Continue along Oxley Street to Wilson Street and then turn left. Turn left again into Mitchell Street and on the corner notice the **Carrier's Arms Hotel**, dating, in part, from 1876. Henry Lawson stayed here briefly and then lived nearby and mentioned the hotel in some of his short stories, calling it the Shearer's Arms. Continuing along the street, you will find on the right the Welcome Mart. This was originally the **Shakespeare Hotel**. In 1887, the second branch of the Amalgamated Shearers' Union was established here. A little further, at the corner of Glen Street, **Poet's Corner** is on the left, commemorating those who have lived in or near, and written about, this town.

Keep going along Mitchell Street and you will find all the remainder of the places of interest on the right side. Muda is the Aboriginal Language Centre and Radio 2CUZ. The old **Towers Drug Company** building was constructed in 1889 and was a medical centre. The Anglican Church is not so old, built in 1939. The previous church here burnt down in 1895. The **Lands Department building** is a good example of naturally cool architecture in a hot place. It was built in 1898. The **Bourke Wharf**, just down Sturt Street, is a reconstruction of the 1898 wharf which was so important to the town as it permitted the loading of wool and processed meat onto the paddle steamers for transport down the river. Bourke was the farthest place along the Darling which the steamers could reach. Next, the **Telegraph Hotel**, now the Riverside Motel, was built in 1876, and finally the **Catholic Church** is the oldest surviving building of which the date is firmly established. It was built in 1874.

ACCOMMODATION

Limited, but quite adequate. The hotels can offer single and double rooms to backpackers at reasonable rates. Singles are about $30, doubles about $50.

Accommodation in Bourke

Name	Stars	No. on Map	Telephone No.	Address	Lowest Price (Double/Twin)
Darling River Motel		7	02-6872-2288	Mitchell & Warraweena Sts.	$90
Riverside Motel		1	02-6872-2539	Mitchell Street	$85
Major Mitchell Motel		5	02-6872-2311	Richard Street	$85
Outback Motel		3	02-6872-2716	Mertin Street	$80
The Gables		4	02-6872-2136	Richard & Mertin Streets	$65
Port of Bourke Hotel		2	02-6872-2544	32 Mitchell Street	$60
Central Australian Hotel		6	02-6872-2151	Richard & Anson Streets	$50
Mitchell Caravan Park		8	02-6872-2791	Mitchell Street	$45

MOVING ON

It would be wonderful to travel back by steamer along the Darling, but sadly those days are long gone and now the only scheduled public transport is the Countrylink bus to Dubbo which connects with the train to Sydney. This service operates on Mondays, Wednesdays, Fridays and Saturdays.

Bus Service from Bourke

Destination	Operator	Via	Distance (km)	Fare	Journey Time	Frequency
Sydney	Countrylink		818	$107.90	11½ hrs	4/week
		Dubbo	373	$62.10	4½ hrs	4/week

GREAT RAILWAY JOURNEYS

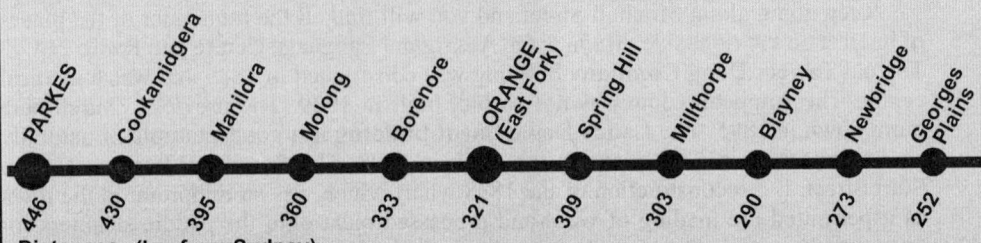

Distances (km from Sydney)

One of the world's great railway journeys, the *Indian-Pacific*, travels 4,352 kilometres between Sydney and Perth, including a 200-kilometre backtrack between Crystal Brook and Adelaide. It spans the continent from the Indian Ocean on the west to the Pacific Ocean on the east, hence its name.

It is a surprise to many to learn that the first train on this route did not run until 1970, departing from Sydney on 23rd February and arriving in Perth on 27th February, such a journey on a single train having been impossible prior to that date due to variations in track gauge. Indeed, even in 1970, Adelaide was not on the route because the line to that city was still a broad gauge one, so a connecting service operated to and from Port Pirie.

The *Indian-Pacific* still uses the original 1970s rolling stock with a standard consist comprising sixteen carriages plus the locomotive, forming a train 498 metres long, weighing 733 tonnes, with accommodation for 88 first-class (*gold kangaroo*) sleeper passengers, 64 standard-class (*red kangaroo*) sleeper passengers and 124 standard-class (*red kangaroo*) sitting passengers, a total complement of 276. Top speed is generally 115 km/hr.

The *Indian-Pacific* leaves from Sydney Central Station on Monday and Thursday afternoons and starts its long journey west by rolling through the Sydney suburbs. Penrith is reached after an hour, 56 kilometres out, and shortly afterwards the Nepean River is crossed, marking the boundary of Australia's most populous city. From here a steady climb of 1,000 metres begins, up into the Blue Mountains, as majestic views unfold, especially to the left of the train. The mountains are composed largely of sandstone and shale, with coal found in the region, and the blue-tinged haze which gives them their name is thought to be caused either by moisture in the valleys or by evaporating eucalyptus from the trees.

Three stations beyond Penrith is Glenbrook, near where, early on the morning of 2nd December 1999, a CityRail train ran into the rear of the stationary *Indian-Pacific*, resulting in the deaths of seven passengers in the front carriage of the local train.

The first explorers of this region in the early nineteenth century are commemorated in the names of the stations through which we pass now - Blaxland, Lawson and Wentworth.

Katoomba is the most famous of the towns in the Blue Mountains, the site of what claims to be the world's steepest funicular railway, with a gradient of 52°, and the well known Three Sisters landmark resembling a ruined castle.

GREAT RAILWAY JOURNEYS 155

1. THE INDIAN - PACIFIC
PART 1   SYDNEY TO ADELAIDE

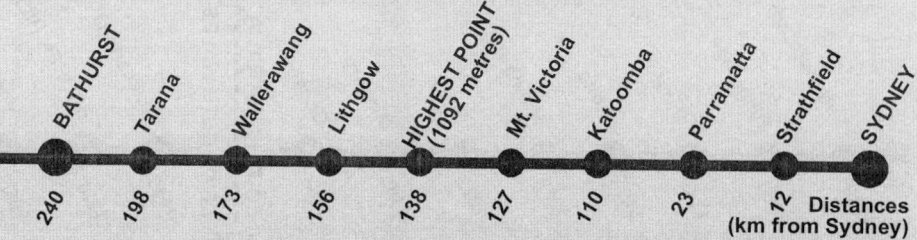

We travel on, passing through Medlow Bath, Blackheath and Mt. Victoria stations. Mt. Victoria, only 127 kilometres from Sydney, is the highest station on the journey to Perth, at an altitude of 1,047 metres. Soon after, by the 138-kilometre post, we reach the highest point on the entire route of the *Indian-Pacific*, at 1,092 metres above sea level.

Near Lithgow, named after the Colonial Surveyor of the day, we pass through a series of ten tunnels built in 1910 to eliminate the previous Zig-Zag switchback route over the summit of the Blue Mountains via Clarence, formerly the toughest stretch of railway in New South Wales. In 1975, the Zig-Zag was restored by a group of enthusiasts and now operates a daily narrow-gauge steam or diesel railcar service up the slopes to Clarence. As we pass, the three splendid viaducts can be seen on the left of the train. Lithgow is reached three hours and 156 kilometres after leaving Sydney.

The next main station is Bathurst, on the Macquarie River, the first inland settlement in Australia and the scene of the country's first gold rush in 1851. The railway reached here in 1876. We are now five hours into the journey and 240 kilometres from Sydney and, according to the current timetable, this is the last place of which we shall see much for a while, as darkness is descending. Bathurst is best known for its 1,000-kilometre motor race on the difficult track at the summit of nearby Mt. Panorama.

Another hour takes us to Orange, near where Banjo Paterson, the author of *Waltzing Matilda* and one of Australia's greatest literary figures, was born in 1864. On our left is Mt. Canobolas, rising to 1,397 metres. This is the last mountain that we shall approach until nearing Perth, over two days' travel away. From here the track is almost flat for more than 3,000 kilometres.

Through Borenore, Molong, Manildra and Cookamidgera to Parkes, named after the great politician, Sir Henry Parkes, who was premier of New South Wales five times and a driving force behind the creation of the Commonwealth of Australia in 1901. This too was originally a gold town, but it is best known now for its radio telescope. It is also famous for its connexion with the bushranger Ben Hall, for it was here that he was shot to death on 5th May 1865 at the age of 27. Here the landscape starts to change and to become much more arid.

Wake early, so as not to miss anything, and you will probably be near Menindee, where the Menindee Lakes mark the edge of arable land. This is a great haven for wildlife - birds, animals and fishes. All can be found in and

NEW SOUTH WALES

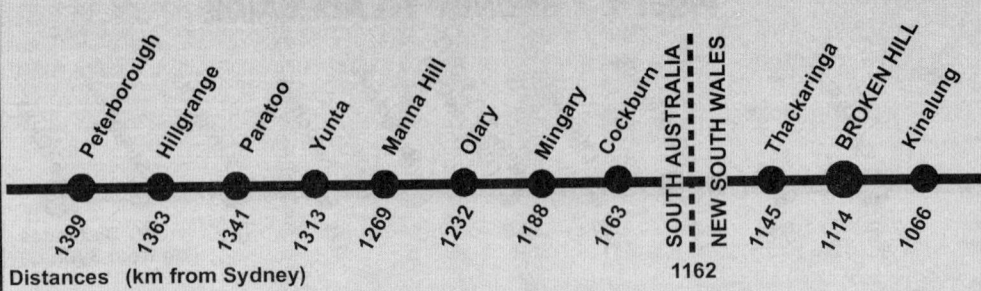

GREAT RAILWAY JOURNEYS

Distances (km from Sydney)

Peterborough 1399 — Hillgrange 1363 — Paratoo 1341 — Yunta 1313 — Manna Hill 1269 — Olary 1232 — Mingary 1188 — Cockburn 1163 — SOUTH AUSTRALIA / NEW SOUTH WALES 1162 — Thackaringa 1145 — BROKEN HILL 1114 — Kinalung 1066

around the lakes. Here the famous Burke and Wills Expedition made a long stop. Burke's room can be seen at the local hotel, almost unchanged from that time, and it was here that Wills was promoted to second-in-command of the expedition. Here too their camel-driver Dost Mahomet later died and his grave can be seen in the local cemetery. The bridge on which we cross the lakes bears a notice reading 'Warning. Trains cross this bridge in thirty seconds - whether you are on it or not'. We are here crossing the Darling River, the basin of which is home to two million people. This area was formerly served by the steamers which plied the 3,750-kilometre long Murray-Darling system, the longest river system in Australia. The water in the lakes results from a 1950s irrigation project which utilised these usually dry reservoirs as natural storage tanks for the water required for agriculture.

Sturt passed this way on his explorations and those following in his steps soon discovered minerals. Boundary rider Charles Rasp was the man who made the discovery which led to the foundation of Broken Hill. He thought that he had found tin, but it turned out to be the richest seam of lead, zinc and silver ever discovered in the world, sufficient to sustain the mines here for over a century of continuous production. The find led also to the formation of Australia's most famous company - B.H.P. (Broken Hill Proprietary). The story of Broken Hill has not always been a happy one. The miners here suffered from disease and harsh working conditions, and Broken Hill was the scene of one of Australia's most prolonged and bitter industrial disputes. As you approach, you will be shocked by the wastelands through which the train passes, the residue of the century of mining, but it is an interesting place to visit, and if the train is on time you will have an hour and a half to do so. The city is a Royal Flying Doctor Service base and it has now transformed itself into something of a city of culture, too, particularly a city of art. Pro Hart, probably the most famous living Australian artist, has his studio here, as do several other top artists. A quick stroll will enable you to see a few of the grand old buildings in the main street (Argent Street). Interestingly, the first find of uranium ore in Australia was also made here, at the appropriately named Radium Hill.

For the railway, Broken Hill was the last stumbling block in the creation of the through trans-continental line, for here the Silverton Tramway continued to operate until 1970 (and still carries out shunting operations), using a

1. THE INDIAN - PACIFIC
PART 1   SYDNEY TO ADELAIDE
(continued)

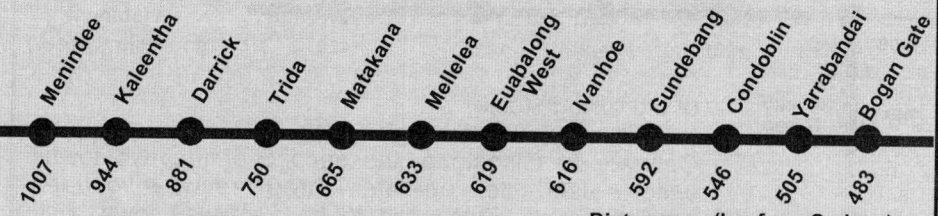

Distances   (km from Sydney)

narrow gauge 3 feet 6 inches track as far as the South Australian border, from where South Australian Railways continued as far as Port Pirie. Until 1970, passengers had to alight from the New South Wales standard gauge train here and make their way across the city to the Silverton Tramways station in Sulphide Street in order to continue to Peterborough or Port Pirie, where another change would be necessitated. Only in 1970 were such parochial disputes finally resolved so that a through standard gauge track could be opened. Here at Broken Hill we are eighteen hours and 1,114 kilometres into our journey. Here too we change to South Australian time, half an hour behind New South Wales time, for it is another of Broken Hill's idiosyncrasies that so closely does it associate itself with South Australia that it keeps the time of that state rather than that of the state within which it falls geographically.

The border comes just before the small South Australian town of Cockburn, developed as a railway border post, but still existing, with a current population of 38. We move on through Mingary and Olary to Manna Hill, which received its name because this was the place where local shearers used to congregate to be fed. Yunta, the next small settlement, was another gold rush town, which survived, however, when others disappeared, because of its proximity to the route of this railway.

At Peterborough, we are 22 hours and 1,399 kilometres from Sydney and another change of scenery takes place, as we cross 'Goyder's Line', marking the edge of the area with rainfall adequate for agriculture. Farming starts again from here, especially wheat-growing and sheep farming. Peterborough, founded in 1880, was originally named Petersburg, but German names were unpopular at the time of the Great War, so, in 1917, it was changed to Peterborough. Here, at Peterborough, three different railway gauges once used to meet, one of two such towns along this line, and passengers formerly had to change trains again at Peterborough and take the narrow gauge line which ran to Quorn, and on to Port Augusta, where another change back to standard gauge would be made for the train across the Nullarbor. However, the narrow gauge line to Quorn has been closed since 1969 and is now being used by a preservation group operating trains to Orroroo and Eurelia, hoping one day to extend their run all the way to Quorn. The line can be seen on the right of the train. There is also a museum

GREAT RAILWAY JOURNEYS
1. THE INDIAN - PACIFIC   PART 1   SYDNEY TO ADELAIDE
(continued)

Distance (km from Sydney)	Station
1486	Crystal Brook
1465	Gladstone
1449	Caltowie
1425	Jamestown
1410	Yongala
1491	Rocky River
1511	Redhill
1540	Snowtown
1565	Nantawarra
1584	Bowmans
1609	Long Plains
1624	Mallala
1641	Two Wells
1654	Bolivar
1670	Dry Creek
1686	ADELAIDE

of old rolling stock.

We continue through Yongala, Jamestown and Caltowie to Gladstone, the second of the two towns which used to operate three railway gauges simultaneously. This used to be a railway town, with constant trans-shipment from one gauge to another necessary. It was also a major locomotive depot. When the change from steam to diesel occurred and the narrow gauge line was closed, then later the broad gauge too, the town went into decline, as can be seen, although the hotel used by passengers waiting for onward connexions still stands next to the station.

Another 21 kilometres takes us to Crystal Brook, where you will see a triangle on the right as the train curves left. This is where the trans-continental line to Perth meets the branch south to Adelaide, and we turn south to visit the latter. It is exactly 200 kilometres to Adelaide from here.

We pass through a series of small towns, usually without stopping, and our first sign of the proximity of Adelaide is Edinburgh Airfield, on the left of the train. Then we come to Dry Creek Goods Yard, an extensive area dealing only with standard gauge trains now, although the suburban railway on our left is still broad gauge. A few more minutes and we can see the fine city of Adelaide on our left and even glimpse the stately railway station. We do not approach it, however, but sidle past and crawl into Keswick Terminal, inconveniently located some three kilometres from the city centre. If you look at the track here, you will find that this station remains of dual gauge, as until recently the *Overland* from Melbourne, which terminates here, used to be a broad gauge train.

We have travelled 1,686 kilometres from Sydney to Adelaide, a journey taking 25½ hours. Now the train will take a break of two and a half hours before continuing to Perth, enough time to allow passengers a visit to the city. For the continuation of the story of the journey to Perth, see page 668.

BROKEN HILL
Population 21,000

13 hrs 30 mins by train from Sydney
17 hrs by bus from Sydney
9 hrs by train from Adelaide
7 hrs by bus from Adelaide

Broken Hill is an unusual city. Although in New South Wales, it is so far from Sydney that it thinks itself to be in South Australia and keeps South Australian time. It is thus half an hour behind the rest of the state.

Broken Hill is a mining town, and one which has endured mixed fortunes since a boundary rider named Charles Rasp first noticed in 1883 the outcrops of what he believed to be tin ore and staked his claim here. The tin turned out to be an amalgam of lead, zinc and silver, and not just that, but it proved to be the richest such seam ever discovered in the world, with 800 ounces of silver per ton of ore. The mining here started in 1885 when a syndicate of seven men established the Broken Hill Proprietary Company and it has continued for over a century, and indeed still continues. By the early 1890s, Broken Hill was producing one-third of the world's supply of silver. Broken Hill Proprietary soon became known simply as B.H.P. and became Australia's largest and most powerful company. It is still powerful, but it no longer operates in Broken Hill.

As you arrive in Broken Hill, especially if by train, you may imagine that you have left this planet and are perhaps on its moon instead. Towering mullock heaps almost surround the city. Their size is awe-inspiring (ore-inspiring, perhaps) from the railway, since the rail system is used to carry away much of the ore and therefore runs adjacent to the workings. These enormous piles of tailings seem about to engulf the city and nothing grows on or near them. Such is the legacy of a century of mining.

Broken Hill has produced great prosperity, but you will not see so much evidence of that prosperity around the town. Most of the profit went to the company, not the miners, whose working and living conditions were harsh and primitive.

At first, it was not known how long the ore would last, so the miners lived in temporary tin shacks where little thought was given to hygiene. They worked in dusty conditions and suffered from various diseases. Plagues spread through the community on occasions. As it became evident that mining here would be long-term and that there was a disproportionate distribution of the wealth derived from it, a campaign began to improve the conditions of the miners, reduce their hours and increase their wages. It proved to be a long and fierce battle, but one which was won in the end by the unions. It is from this point in Australian history that the rights of workers came to be acknowledged, but it was a struggle which was to leave Broken Hill embittered.

Broken Hill is far from anywhere and transport has always been a problem. At first transport was provided by the river steamers, which reached this area as early as 1859. They were supplemented by bullock teams for local haulage, and camels were also introduced in the 1880s. The railway from Adelaide was extended to the South Australian border in 1888, but it was not permitted to come to Broken Hill, because Broken Hill is in New South Wales, and there was already in existence the Silverton Tramway Company which had commenced operations in 1886. This company, which, being privately operated, was not allowed to call itself a 'railway', built a line from

Broken Hill, and the other nearby mining community of Silverton, to the border to meet the South Australian Railways line. These lines were built to a narrow 3 feet 6 inches gauge, and they continued to operate until 1970. The ore from Broken Hill was thus transported to Port Pirie in South Australia, where it was smelted and then mostly exported. It was not until 1927 that the railway line from Sydney reached Broken Hill, and, since it was a standard gauge line, it could not be joined to the line westwards to South Australia, so here until 1970 it finished.

As time went on, the ore became depleted and Broken Hill started to face hard times once more, with fears that it would disappear completely. However, new lodes have always been discovered and the mining has continued, albeit at reduced capacity. The latest forecasts are that the ore will be completely worked out by 2010, and that mining will cease then, but Broken Hill has become accustomed to such predictions, and subsequent reprieves.

Realising, though, that mining cannot last for ever, the city has tried to avert extinction by inventing an alternative *raison d'être* and has found that, rather unexpectedly, in art. Certainly the landscapes here, the open spaces and glowing sunsets, the typically Australian buildings and the wildlife give plenty of scope to the artist, and in particular the painter, but it still comes as something of a surprise that an apparently rough mining community could transform itself so successfully into a thriving cultural centre. Here you will find a multitude of **art galleries** featuring the work of the nation's greatest living painters. They all seem to gravitate to Broken Hill. Pro Hart, internationally acclaimed for his uniquely Australian themes and style, makes this his home and has here a gallery. This art boom seems to have ensured the survival of Broken Hill, and it has also brought a degree of unexpected affluence which the city has wisely invested in restoring its old and imposing buildings, promoting its interesting history and attracting tourists to this distant corner of the state. Regeneration schemes have also been implemented to deal with the surrounding barren landscape.

As you walk round the town, you will find plaques giving information on the interesting old buildings and showing photographs of them as they were in former times. You will also note the names of the streets, indicating the most important aspect of life for this community. Most of them are named after minerals.

Argent Street is the centre of the city and here the most interesting of the old buildings are to be found. The **Courthouse** and **Police Station** both date from1890. The **Town Hall** was built in 1891 and the **Post Office** dates from 1892. There is a comprehensive **Visitors Information Centre** in Blende Street, and this is also where buses arrive and depart, except the Countrylink bus, which uses the railway station some distance away. Behind the Visitors Information Centre, there is also a youth hostel.

In Sulphide Street, at the junction with Blende Street, is the **Railway Museum**. This is the old Silverton Tramway station. Until 1970, anybody wishing to travel from Sydney to Adelaide or beyond had to change from the standard gauge New South Wales Government line to the Silverton Tramway and South Australian Railways narrow gauge line by crossing the town to this station and proceeding from here to Peterborough or Port Pirie, where a further change would be necessary. The museum has Silverton Tramway and other rolling stock on display.

The Silverton Tramway used to run to **Cockburn**, the first town across the border into South Australia, a distance of approximately 50 kilometres. It did not follow the current course of the line, but ran further north through the town of Silverton, named after the find of silver which had been made there prior to the discovery of the same metal in Broken Hill. The abandoned track of this old line can still be followed, and if you go along it for about three kilometres you will find an interesting marker, for here occurred the only **enemy action** to take place on Australian soil during the Great War. On New Year's Day 1915, two misguided Turks living here hid behind a mound beside the track and ambushed an excursion train taking Broken Hill residents for a picnic. Two people were killed on the train and two more were killed later in the pursuit of the Turks. Seven people were injured on the train and a policeman was injured later. The Turks died in the pursuit.

As usual, the author believes that the best way to travel to Broken Hill is by train. Here you have a choice. You can use the Great Southern Railway *Indian-Pacific* or *Ghan* services, or take the newly reinstated Countrylink train which runs here from Sydney on Mondays only. Another possibility is the daily Countrylink train to Dubbo and connecting bus from there. The *Indian-Pacific* and *Ghan* leave from Sydney in the early afternoon on Sundays, Mondays and Thursdays, and arrive in Broken Hill early the next morning. The Dubbo train leaves every morning, with the connecting bus reaching Broken Hill late in the evening. The Countrylink direct train on Mondays leaves Sydney very early in the morning and reaches Broken Hill, therefore, at a better time, in the early evening. The timetable for all these services appears on page 93.

If you prefer a bus all the way, however, a Greyhound bus passes through Broken Hill on three days a week on its route between Sydney and Adelaide. There is also a bus from Mildura to Broken Hill on Mondays, Wednesdays and Fridays.

162   NEW SOUTH WALES
ACCOMMODATION
There is a good range of accommodation in Broken Hill and the budget traveller is well taken care of. The youth hostel, right outside the bus terminal, but one kilometre from the railway station, has dormitory beds for $18, but it is also a guest house with single rooms for $25 and doubles for $40 in the hostel, or singles for $33 and doubles for $47 in the guest house. The hotels are economical too. The Black Lion has singles for $22 and doubles for $35. Mario's Palace and the West Darling Hotel have single rooms for $31. The latter is only a short walk from the railway station.

(i) Hotel Accommodation in Broken Hill

Name	Stars	No. on Map	Telephone No.	Address	Lowest Price (Double/Twin)
The Imperial	4½	13	02-8087-7444	88 Oxide Street	$150
Crystal Motel	3½	16	02-8088-2344	326 Crystal Street	$104
Charles Rasp Motor Inn	4	10	02-8087-1988	158 Oxide Street	$103
Old Willyama Motor Inn	4	15	1-800-100-777	30 Iodide Street	$99
Mine Host Motel	3½	4	02-8088-4044	120 Argent Street	$92
Miners Lamp	3	12	1-800-355-174	357 Cobalt Street	$92
Overlander Motor Inn	4	11	02-8088-2566	142 Iodide Street	$90
Silver Spade Motel	3½	5	02-8087-7021	151 Argent Street	$75
Daydream Motel	3½	1	02-8088-3033	77 Argent Street	$70
Grand Guest House	4	8	02-8087-5305	317 Argent Street	$70
Lodge Motel	3½	9	02-8088-2722	252 Mica Street	$70
Annexe Motel	3	2	02-8087-8495	76 Argent Street	$60
West Darling Hotel		14	02-8087-2691	Argent & Oxide Streets	$59
Mario's Palace		7	02-8088-1699	Argent & Sulphide Streets	$49
Tourist Lodge	2½	3	02-8088-2086	100 Argent Street	$47
Black Lion Inn		6	02-8087-4801	Blende & Bromide Streets	$35

(ii) Backpackers Hostel in Broken Hill

Name	Group	No. on Map	Telephone Number	Address	Lowest Price (Dormitory)
Tourist Lodge	YHA	3	02-8088-2086	100 Argent Street	$18

MOVING ON
(i) By Train
Broken Hill, Lightning Ridge, Bourke and Dubbo to Sydney

Days of Operation	Daily (Bus)	Daily (Bus)	M, W, F, Sat (Bus)	M, W, F (Bus)	Tu, Th, Sat, Sun (Bus)	Daily	Tu	Sun, W	Sat
Broken Hill	0400						0730	1630	1725
Menindee							0924	1818	1916
Lightning Ridge		0850							
Bourke			0915						
Dubbo	1325	1325	1339			1410			
Parkes				1422	1340		1454	0027	0125
Orange				1547	1547	1555	1643	0315	0333
Bathurst						1714	1759	0452	0459
Lithgow						1825	1913	0625	0625
Katoomba						1906	1955		
Strathfield						2034	2134		
Sydney						2048	2148	0915	0915

Trains leave for Sydney on Sunday, Wednesday and Saturday evenings, reaching Sydney the next morning, and on Tuesday morning, arriving the same evening. The Countrylink bus leaves every morning at 4:00 (South Australian time) and connects at Dubbo with the train to Sydney. The early departure time may not appeal, but the journey is a beautiful one as the sun rises slowly above the horizon and fills the sky with a glorious crimson. Sunsets are often written about, but sunrises are beautiful too. You will enjoy this one. Do not slumber and miss it. The timetable for these services is given on the previous page.

(ii) By Bus

Greyhound operates a service on three days a week to Sydney and Adelaide, in addition to which there is a bus to Mildura at 15:45 on Mondays, Wednesdays and Fridays, operated by Junction Tours, the fare being $54. It connects with the overnight V-Line bus service from Mildura to Melbourne. Here is a summary of those services.

Destination	Operator	Via	Distance (km)	Fare	Journey Time	Frequency
Sydney	Greyhound		1125	$147	17¼ hrs	3/week
		Dubbo	723	$131	9 hrs	3/week
Sydney	Countrylink		1100	$128.60	16½ hrs	1/day
		Dubbo	655	$94.80	9 hrs	1/day
Adelaide	Greyhound		559	$93	7 hrs	3/week
Mildura	Junction Tours		296	$54	4 hrs	3/week

MOREE
Population 10,000

9 hrs by train from Sydney

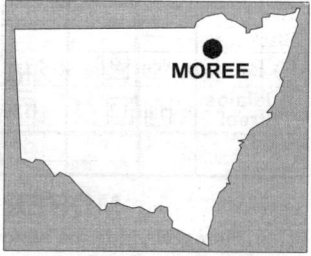

Moree is famous as an **artesian spa** town. The waters were discovered by chance when, in 1895, a search was made for water for irrigation purposes and a shaft sunk into the Great Artesian Basin. The water duly appeared, but at a temperature of 41°C. Since then, it has been regarded as a cure for everything from rheumatism to paralysis. Baths were built and they are now visited by 300,000 people per year. The baths are open from 6:00 until 19:00 every day. There is also a naturally heated swimming pool.

Most of Moree's current prosperity comes from farming, especially the production of **cotton**. Two-thirds of Australia's cotton is grown here. The cotton is harvested in March and April and taken to the cotton gins which can be seen around, especially adjacent to the railway. Another unexpected crop is **pecan nuts**. 95% of Australia's pecans are grown on *Trawalla Farm*, 35 kilometres from Moree, where there are 70,000 trees. This claims to be the largest orchard in the southern hemisphere. One more unusual crop is **olives**, while more conventional ones are oats, barley, sorghum and wheat. Sunflower, safflower and canola are also grown for their oil.

The success of modern-day farming has resulted in a rejuvenation of Moree. Its older buildings have been restored and some of them have been put to fresh uses. A museum of indigenous art is housed in the **Moree Plains Gallery**, for example, formerly a magnificent old bank building. Also in Frome Street is the restored **Lands Office**. After being damaged by fire in 1982, it won a prize for the best restored

NEW SOUTH WALES

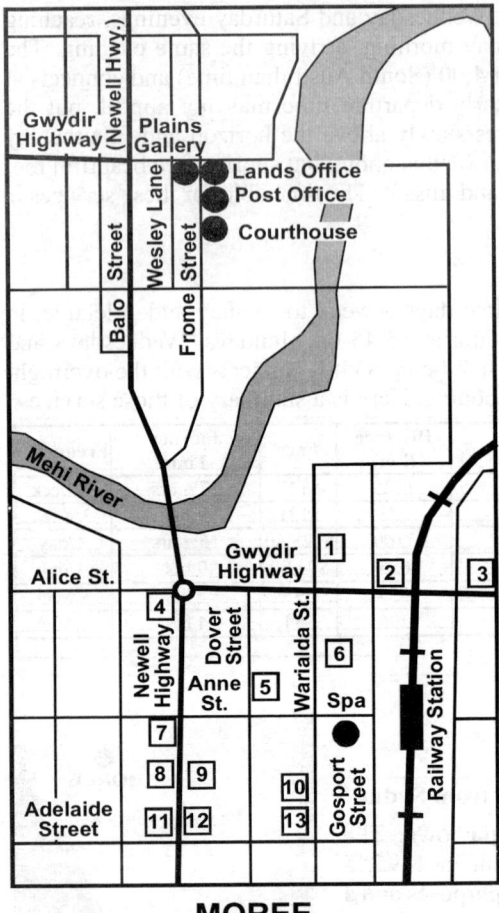

MOREE
Numerals indicate accommodation

building in Australia. Then there is the **Courthouse**, which is worth a look.

Another positive effect of the success of modern agriculture in the Moree area is the restoration of the passenger rail service which had previously been withdrawn. Now a six-carriage train leaves Sydney every morning and travels up the coast to Broadmeadow, near Newcastle, before turning inland and then diverging from the main line north to travel north-west to Werris Creek. **Werris Creek** is the site of a railway workshop and extensive yard, where you may see the bodies of old locomotives gradually rusting into oblivion. Werris Creek is also a junction. The train will be halted just outside the station while the front three carriages are uncoupled from the rear three, and then the two sections will be brought onto opposite sides of the curved platform. The section on the right of the platform heads off to Tamworth and Armidale, while that on the left goes to Moree. From Werris Creek it is a flat run of three and a half hours, a pleasant but not really scenic trip. The station is about fifteen minutes walk from the town centre, but most of the accommodation is in the vicinity of the station. The artesian spa is also adjacent to the station.

ACCOMMODATION
Accommodation in Moree

Name	Stars	No. on Map	Telephone No.	Address	Lowest Price (Double/Twin)
Spa Village Travel Inn	4	6	1-800-023-554	300 Warialda Street	$94
Dragon & Phoenix Motel	3½	11	02-6752-5555	Newell Hwy. & Adelaide St.	$93
Winchester Motel	3½	7	02-6752-4666	54 Anne Street	$84
Billabong Motel	3	8	1-800-636-683	353 Frome Street	$80
Alexander Motor Inn	3½	4	02-6752-4222	Newell & Gwydir Highways	$75
Golden Harvest Motor Inn	3	9	02-6752-2200	366 Newell Highway	$74
Jacaroo Motor Inn	2	12	02-6752-3233	378 Newell Highway	$65
Moree Lodge Motel	2½	1	02-6752-4504	296 Warialda Street	$55
Moree Spa Motor Inn	2	2	02-6752-3455	Alice & Gosport Streets	$55
Baths Motel	2	13	02-6752-5155	339 Warialda Street	$55
Dover Motel		5	02-6752-2880	20 Dover Street	$55
Mehi River Van Park	3½	3	02-6752-7188	28 Oak Street	$50
Odessa Guest House		10	02-6752-2063	337 Warialda Street	$44

MOVING ON
(i) By Rail

The train runs back to Sydney every morning, but another option is to take the Countrylink bus which runs on Mondays, Wednesdays and Fridays via Inverell and Glen Innes to Grafton. There it connects with the train to Murwillumbah and a further bus connexion to Surfers Paradise and Brisbane. The timetable for the train to Sydney is shown here.

Moree to Sydney

Days of Operation	Daily
Moree	0820
Narrabri	0933
Werris Creek	1138
Broadmeadow	1441
Strathfield	1645
Sydney	1700

(ii) By Bus

McCafferty's operates a bus between Brisbane and Melbourne via Moree and Crisps Coaches has a daily service to Brisbane. A summary of the bus services available from Moree follows.

Destination	Operator	Via	Distance (km)	Fare	Journey Time	Frequency
Melbourne	McCafferty's		1067	$161	16¼ hrs	1/day
		Dubbo	376	$79	5 hrs	1/day
Brisbane	McCafferty's		478	$79	7¼ hrs	1/day
Brisbane	Crisps		478	$63	6¾ hrs	1/day
Grafton	Countrylink		366	$62.10	5¾ hrs	3/week
		Glen Innes	207	$34.80	3 hrs	3/week
		Inverell	142	$25	2 hrs	3/week

TAMWORTH
Population 32,000

6 hrs 30 mins by train from Sydney
8 hrs 30 mins by bus from Sydney

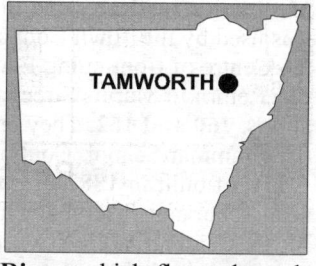

Tamworth's claim to fame is as the centre of **country music** in Australia. A Country Music Festival is held here every year, attracting thousands of visitors and many of the famous names in such music.

In 1818, the explorer John Oxley reached the **Peel River**, which flows through Tamworth, and wrote that, "No place in the world can afford more advantages to the industrious settler than this extensive vale." However, it was not until 1834 that the area was actually settled, beginning with the part now designated as West Tamworth.

In 1851, gold was discovered at **Nundle**, 60 kilometres south of here, and Tamworth developed as a commercial centre supplying the goldfields. The railway reached West Tamworth in 1878, but the river presented an obstacle and it was not until 1881 that a viaduct was constructed and the line extended to the present Tamworth station.

Nowadays Tamworth is a thriving centre, the largest city in this part of the state and one with many handsome buildings which we shall look at later on our walking tour. It is, however, as the country music centre that it is known by most Australians, and that theme is constantly evident as one walks around the small city.

NEW SOUTH WALES

The way to reach Tamworth is by the daily train from Sydney, which divides at Werris Creek, with half going to Moree and half to Tamworth and on to Armidale. This journey takes around 6½ hours and is comfortable and pleasant. The timetable appears on page 94. If you prefer bus, McCafferty's has a service from Sydney to Brisbane via Tamworth, while Greyhound has a bus from Dubbo. The McCafferty's bus leaves Sydney in the afternoon and reaches Tamworth in the late evening, after a journey lasting 8½ hours. There is also a bus service from Port Macquarie to Tamworth on Sundays, Tuesdays and Thursdays. There is a town bus service which can be used to reach outlying attractions, and Perrett's operates a service to Werris Creek and Quirindi, but it cannot be used to make a return trip to either of those places within a single day. There is a bus service to Tamworth from Scone via Quirindi and Werris Creek on Mondays, Wednesdays and Fridays.

Now let us have a walk round the city and look at some of the places of interest.

Walking Tour

This tour begins and ends at the railway station. It covers about five kilometres and will take an hour and a half, not allowing for any detours or lengthy stops.

The attractive **Railway Station** was constructed in 1882, after the viaduct had been built to cross the river from West Tamworth. It was this railway which really ensured the prosperity of Tamworth by linking it with Sydney so that produce could be shipped cheaply. 6,000 people came to see the opening of the line by the Governor of New South Wales. Outside the station is the **Boer War Memorial** constructed in 1901.

With your back to the station, turn left and walk along Marius Street to the first junction. Here you will find **St. Andrew's Church**, an imposing Presbyterian church dating from 1909. Now turn right into Brisbane Street and on your left is the **Mechanics Institute**, one of the oldest buildings in Tamworth, dating from 1866. It was used by the Town Council for a while until its own premises were built. Now it is the Centre of Continuing Education, part of the University of New England.

Return to Marius Street and turn right. Soon you will come to two quaint cottages at **nos. 160 and 162**. They date from the nineteenth century and were formerly part of the Grammar School. Continue for a further block and you will reach the **Dominican Convent** built in 1882. It housed the Dominican Sisters and boarders at the Catholic school, but now it serves an an office for community organisations and for the Regional Music Centre. On the next corner is **St. Nicholas' Church**, the third Catholic church to be built here. It was started in 1877 and completed in 1886.

Turn right into White Street. On your left is **Tamworth Club**, established in 1905 for gentlemen of the district and one of the oldest such facilities in Australia. It claims to have been the first club in Australia to gain a liquor licence.

Turn right again at the next corner into Peel Street and note the **A.N.Z. Bank** on your left. It was built in 1892 of local bricks and has always been a bank, originally the Bank of New South Wales, then the Bank of Australasia, now the A.N.Z. At the next corner on the right is the imposing **Post Office**, opened on 31st May 1886 and, fortunately, still used as the Post Office. The **clock** is a landmark from anywhere in the city centre. Postal services started in Tamworth in 1840 and this site has been used for the Post Office since 1865. The entrance is in Fitzroy Street, and if you go just a little further up that street you will reach the **District Office**, constructed in 1900. It has high ceilings and colonnaded verandahs to keep the building cool but light.

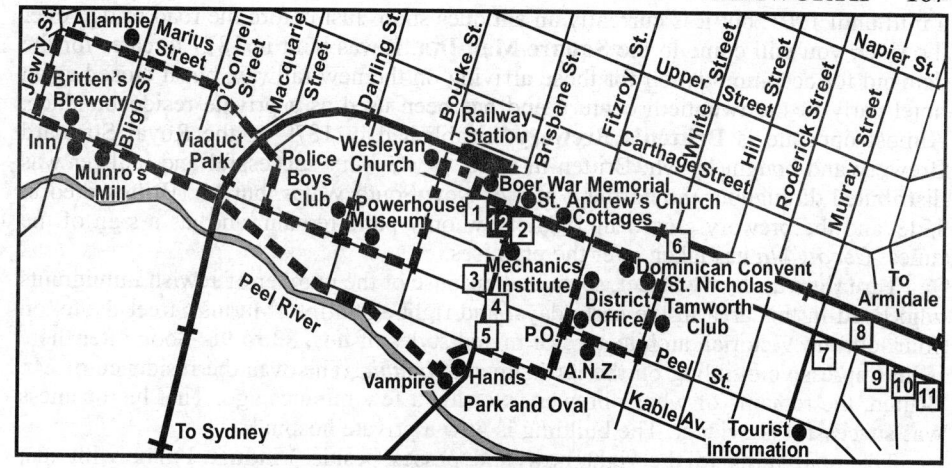

TAMWORTH

Dashed line shows Walking Tour
Black numerals in white boxes indicate hotel accommodation
White numerals in black boxes indicate backpackers hostels

Turn round and walk back down Fitzroy Street towards the river. You will find a park and oval. This area was once used for watering travelling livestock, water being supplied at a cost of one penny per 250 gallons. Then it became a showground, but a great flood in 1910 washed away all buildings here except the **grandstand** which survives today. Turn right and walk to Brisbane Street where the bridge crosses the river.

On the other side of Brisbane Street you will see an interesting little park. It contains the **Hands of Fame memorial**. Singers at the annual Country Music Festival provide imprints of their hands in concrete here. This custom started in 1986 and there is now quite a collection of famous hands. There is also an aeroplane here, a **Vampire** used in the Second World War. This is a memorial to the Australian Flying Corps and the Royal Australian Air Force and was erected in 1970.

Walk up now onto the **river bank** and notice how it has been raised in an effort to prevent future floods from inundating the city. Turn right and keep walking for some distance until you reach the impressive **railway viaduct** originally constructed in 1881. This viaduct took more than two years to plan and build. It is 815 metres long and consists of 88 spans which are between 4 and 5.2 metres high. The central span over the river itself is 47.7 metres long and was built in Britain and then shipped here to be assembled. It was a popular type of bridge at that time, but now only one other remains on this railway. The supports for the viaduct were originally of wood, but they were weakened by the great flood of 1910 and gradually replaced, until, by 1929, all were of steel. The viaduct is still very impressive, viewed either from the train or, as now, from the riverside. In its day, it was considered a great feat of engineering.

Continue along Peel Street beside the river and, at the junction with Bligh Street, you will find **Munro's Mill**, dating from 1863. Cereal crops were the essence of Tamworth's early prosperity and a mill was a necessity for the town's success. This was the first major one, built, as the name suggests, for one Donald Munro. It was used as a mill until 1901, but it is currently an antiques shop. Just before the road bridge over the river, you will come to the **Square Man Inn**. It was built in 1877 to cater for the demand for accommodation for those arriving on the new railway, but it closed as an hotel early in the twentieth century and has been used as a private residence since. Almost opposite is **Britten's Brewery**, established in 1879 as the Royal Standard Brewery and bought by Mr. Britten in 1885. It was very successful and its beer was distributed throughout the northern part of New South Wales, but Mr. Britten died in 1919 and the brewery closed in 1921. Now only parts remain, and, as a sign of the times, *Coca-Cola* has taken over the premises.

Turn right up Jewry Street, so named because of the number of Jewish immigrants who lived in this area in the early days, and right again into Marius Street. Note, on your left, the Victorian architecture of mixed styles of **nos. 82 to 96**. Soon after there is an impressive building on the left named *Allambie*. This was the residence of Mr. Britten, the remains of whose brewery we saw a few minutes ago. That his business was successful is evident. The building is now a private hospital.

The road turns to the right now and passes beside **Viaduct Park**, with that impressive structure curving its way through the park. The park has always been here and was dedicated to public use in 1897. The farther part is laid out as formal gardens.

Turn right into Macquarie Street, then left into Peel Street. On the left is the site of the former hospital, erected in 1854, but long gone. The hospital was originally thought too grand for a small town such as Tamworth, but by the 1870s it had become too small. The move to the new hospital was made in 1884.

Turn left upon reaching Darling Street and see, on your left, the **Police Boys Club**. Although it looks modern, this was the original Courthouse, dating from 1860, and parts still survive. In particular, the section to the right of the entrance is original. It was used as a court until 1938. Opposite are the **Army Barracks**, originally the Town Hall, built in 1906, but used for a long period until 1984 by the local Army Reserve. The first government school in Tamworth was originally here. It opened in 1855, without any luxuries such as desks, books or pens.

Turn round and return to Peel Street, where turn left. On your left is one of the most interesting of Tamworth's buildings. It is now the **Powerhouse Museum**, but it was originally the power station supplying electricity to Tamworth and later to an area including the whole of north-western New South Wales and parts of southern Queensland. History was made here, for Tamworth was the first place in Australia to have electric street lights. The first street light in the town was installed in 1876 and was powered by oil. It was outside the Post Office. By 1888, there were 52 street lights, mostly gas lights. Tamworth Council made a contract with *Crompton and Company* of Chelmsford in England to install two steam-driven electric generators to produce a total of 36kW of electricity in order to operate three 3,000 candlepower arc lamps and 85 sixteen candlepower street lamps. The lights were first switched on by the mayoress on Friday, 9th November 1888. Power was generated here until 1958, when Tamworth was connected to the main New South Wales power system by a 300,000 volt line built from Muswellbrook. The power station itself has gone, but the general office remains and forms today's museum. It is open on Tuesdays to Fridays from 9:00 until 13:00 and admission costs $3.

Continue along Peel Street and turn left into Bourke Street. At the end of the street is the **Wesleyan Church**. It was built in 1871 and is the oldest church in Tamworth still in use. It has attractive stained glass windows and the original pipe organ.

And here we are back at the Railway Station, our walking tour complete.

There are some other places of more recent origin which we have not yet seen in Tamworth, however. In the city centre there is the **Australian Country Music Foundation Museum** at 93 Brisbane Street, a museum mainly of the festival which takes place annually in this city. Admission costs $6 and hours are 10:00 until 14:00, except on Sundays.

On the south side of the river is *Calala Cottage* at 142 Denison Street. This is the city's museum, contained in a house built for the mayor in 1875. It is open from 14:00 until 16:00 on weekdays and 10:00 until 16:00 at weekends, but closed on Mondays. Admission costs $5.

Further out to the south is the **Golden Guitar**, a replica of the award given at the annual Country Music Festival, but rather bigger. This one stands twelve metres high beside the New England Highway. On the opposite side of the highway is the **Roll of Renown**, honouring those who have made major contributions to Australian country music and been awarded Golden Guitars. In the *Golden Guitar Complex* is a **wax museum** of country music stars. Nearby, in Greg Norman Drive, within the T.R.E.C. Building, is a display called *Walk a Country Mile*, an exhibition of the evolution of country music in Australia. These attractions are indeed a country mile from the city centre and too far for comfortable walking - about four kilometres. The author could not find a city bus which went there, although there may be one. Bus no. 435 goes within about one kilometre and runs approximately every hour, usually on the hour, from the city bus terminal in Kable Avenue. It is operated by Tamworth Coaches.

ACCOMMODATION

There is a range of accommodation, although the motels are nearly all out of the main part of the city. The hotels are in the centre and moderately priced. There is a friendly, pleasant and clean youth hostel right outside the station.

(i) Hotel Accommodation in Tamworth

Name	Stars	No. on Map	Telephone No.	Address	Lowest Price (Double/Twin)
Powerhouse Boutique	4½	8	1-800-355-193	Armidale Road	$130
Quest Tamworth		9	02-6761-2366	327 Armidale Road	$120
Golf Links Motel	4	16	02-6762-0505	Bridge Street & Mahony Av	$120
Country Comfort	3½	7	02-6766-2903	293 Marius Street	$110
Tamworth Flag Inn	3½	21	02-6765-7022	236 Goonoo Goonoo Road	$110

170 NEW SOUTH WALES
(i) Hotel Accommodation in Tamworth, continued

Name	Stars	No. on Map	Telephone No.	Address	Lowest Price (Double/Twin)
All Settlers Motor Inn	4½	18	02-6762-1566	191 Goonoo Goonoo Road	$109
Ashby on Ebsworth	3½	14	02-6762-0033	83 Ebsworth Street	$100
Tamworth Motor Inn	3½	19	1-800-022-107	212 Goonoo Goonoo Road	$92
Tamworth Towers Inn	3½	13	02-6765-8361	Oxley Hwy. & Ebsworth St.	$90
Abraham Lincoln	3½	10	1-800-028-225	343 Armidale Road	$85
Town and Country Inn	3½	20	1-800-028-506	217 Goonoo Goonoo Road	$80
Citysider	3½	6	02-6766-4777	237 Marius Street	$75
Cadman	3½	15	02-6765-3333	103 Ebsworth Street	$70
Motabelle Motel		22	02-6765-7274	303 Goonoo Goonoo Road	$70
Almond Inn	2½	11	02-6766-1088	389 Armidale Road	$65
Marion	2	17	02-6765-5585	159 Goonoo Goonoo Road	$55
Tamworth Hotel		1	02-6766-2923	Marius Street	$50
Central Hotel		3	02-6766-2160	Peel & Brisbane Streets	$50
Tudor Hotel		4	02-6766-2930	Peel Street	$50
Good Companions		5	02-6766-2850	Brisbane Street	$50
Imperial Hotel		2	02-6766-2613	Brisbane & Marius Streets	$45

(ii) Backpackers Hostel in Tamworth

Name	Group	No. on Map	Telephone Number	Address	Lowest Price (Dormitory)
Country Backpackers	YHA/B&W	12	02-6761-2600	169 Marius Street	$20

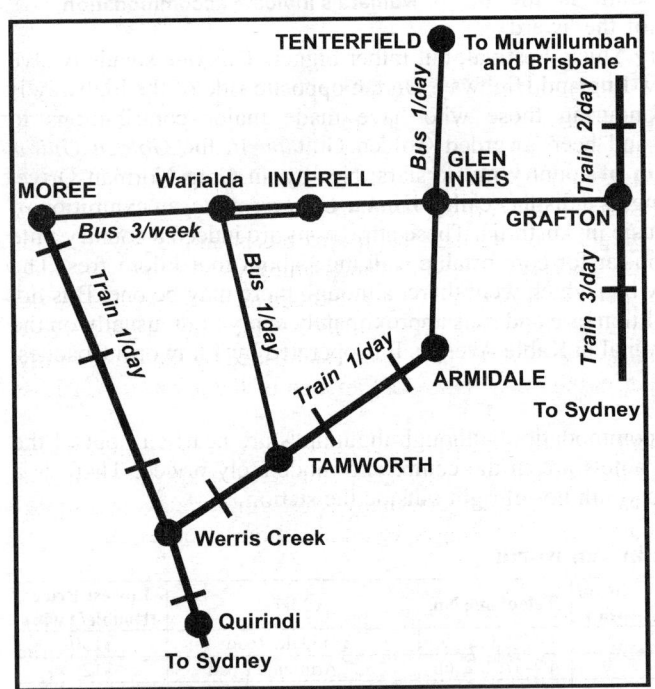

COUNTRYLINK SERVICES IN NORTH-WESTERN NEW SOUTH WALES

MOVING ON
(i) By Train

The train goes back to Sydney every morning. To go in the opposite direction, there is a train to Armidale every afternoon with a connecting Countrylink bus as far as Tenterfield. There is also a Countrylink bus north to Inverell. The Countrylink timetables appear on page 176 towards Sydney and on page 94 for services heading north. A diagram of Countrylink services in this area appears on the left.

(ii) By Bus

There is a McCafferty's bus to Sydney which leaves

very early in the morning. Then there are McCafferty's and Greyhound bus services to Brisbane. Greyhound leaves early in the morning, while McCafferty's leaves late in the evening and travels overnight. On Mondays, Wednesdays and Fridays, there is a bus service to Armidale, Coffs Harbour and Port Macquarie operated by Keans.

Bus Services from Tamworth

Destination	Operator	Via	Distance (km)	Fare	Journey Time	Frequency
Sydney	McCafferty's		440	$74	8 hrs	1/day
Dubbo	Greyhound		343	$86	4¼ hrs	4/week
Brisbane	McCafferty's		626	$76	10 hrs	1/day
		Toowoomba	500	$75	8 hrs	1/day
Brisbane	Greyhound		618	$76	10 hrs	4/week
		Toowoomba	485	$75	8 hrs	4/week
Tenterfield	Countrylink		277	$52.30	4¾ hrs	1/day
		Glen Innes	186	$37	3½ hrs	1/day
Inverell	Countrylink		226	$43.60	3½ hrs	1/day
Pt Macquarie	Keans		462	$71.50	8¼ hrs	3/week
		Coffs Harbour	289	$57	6 hrs	3/week
		Armidale	90	$25	2½ hrs	3/week
Scone	Keans		136	$19	2¼ hrs	3/week

INVERELL
Population 10,000

10 hrs by train and bus from Sydney

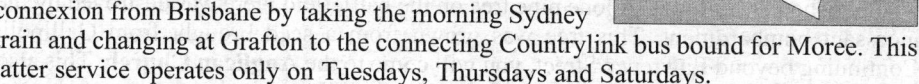

Inverell is reached by taking a train from Sydney to Tamworth and then the connecting Countrylink bus for a journey of a further 3½ hours north. There is also a connexion from Brisbane by taking the morning Sydney train and changing at Grafton to the connecting Countrylink bus bound for Moree. This latter service operates only on Tuesdays, Thursdays and Saturdays.

As you may surmise, Inverell was named by a Scotsman, one Mr. Alexander Campbell, who came here in 1835 and established a farm which he called Inverell Station. There was already a store in Inverell, however, established by the Ross family, so there is now a Ross Street in the town centre and an area of the town named Ross Hill.

Inverell is a very pleasant town of moderate size, known as one of the best inland fishing areas in the state and for fossicking for precious stones, especially sapphires. It is proud of its Scottish origins and of the fact that many Scottish migrants came to this area in its pioneer days. Let us begin by taking a walk around the town centre.

Walking Tour

This is a brief tour of some three kilometres. It will take about an hour to complete. Start at the **Tourist Information Centre** which is in Campbell Street next to the Macintyre River. This building was formerly the water towers, but the Copeton Dam has eliminated the need for storage facilities and the constructions have been put to a new use. They also house the **Mining Museum**.

INVERELL

Dashed line shows Walking Tour
Numerals indicate accommodation

Come out of the Tourist Information Centre and turn right. On the corner of Evans Street is the **Inverell Club**, built in 1909, a Federation style building. Proceed along Evans Street and you will come next to the **Inverell Arts Society Gallery** in Butler Hall, which was also built in 1909. The hall may be visited and the exhibitions viewed. Next is the **Town Hall**, built in 1905. It was designed to have two storeys, but there was a shortage of funds, so just the ground floor was built.

Turn right into Otho Street and you will find the **Post Office**. Postal services in Inverell started in 1885, but the Post Office was not constructed until 1904. A little further on is the **Courthouse**, a grand-looking building constructed in 1886 and restored in 1986 to mark its centenary.

Continue along Otho Street until it bears left. On your left now is the **Bicentennial Memorial** located in Sinclair Park. It celebrates the community spirit of the Inverell District. At night, this memorial is floodlit. Walk to the end of the park and turn sharp left into Vivian Street. On your right now is the **Presbyterian Church** built in 1878. It is a typically British Gothic-type buttressed building made of brick.

Walk along Vivian Street as far as Rivers Street and then turn right. You will pass **Victoria Park** on your left. This was Inverell's first park land and was so proclaimed in 1877. In the park is a lone pine tree, planted as a memorial to those Anzac forces who perished at Gallipoli. A lone pine tree on the battlefield there was destroyed by the incessant bombardment. This tree was grown from a seed brought from Gallipoli. Continuing beyond Lawrence Street, you will come to the **Anglican Church**. This also was built in 1878 and is also a Gothic-style brick building, this time on a stone base.

Now turn left into Mansfield Street and walk until the roundabout is reached at Byron Street. Turn left into Byron Street for one block, then right into Lawrence Street to see the **Suspension Bridge** across the river. A bridge was built here in 1911, but it was washed away by floods in 1991. A new bridge was immediately constructed and that is the one which is in use now. It is one metre higher than the old one used to be. Continue by the river and reach Campbell Park. The **weir** in the river dates from 1916. It provided a reservoir of water for fire fighting and for watering grass, but it also served as a swimming pool until the construction of a proper pool in 1958.

Now turn left into Byron Street, an area which was formerly swamp land. **Ross's Store**, mentioned above, was on the site currently occupied by Coles. On the left are the **old Council Chambers**, in a building which was originally the Bank of New South Wales when built in 1890. It was used by the council from 1962 until 1983.

Turn right into Otho Street, which is the town's main street. Towards the end of the first block, you will find on the right the **C.B.C. Bank**, built in 1890 and typical of bank buildings of the time. There was originally a verandah upstairs, but it has been enclosed. Now turn right into Evans Street and you are back at the Tourist Information Centre where you started.

Further from the town centre, **Lake Inverell Reserve** covers 100 hectares and is the home of many species of birds, as well as wallabies and platypus. For 45 years, prior to the construction of the Copeton Dam, this was Inverell's source of water. Black swans are here in abundance, and it is also a good area for fishing. It is, however, quite a long walk, of about four kilometres, to the east of the town.

To the south of the town is the *Pioneer Village*, a collection of 21 buildings, all local, showing how life used to be in the early days of Inverell and district. The *Pioneer Village* is open from 10:00 until 17:00, except on Mondays.

To the north is the **Transport Museum**, containing a surprisingly large collection of more than 200 cars, trucks, fire engines, motorcycles, tractors, bicycles, pedal cars, scooters, aircraft and models, including some rare ones. The museum is open from 10:00 until 16:00 daily and admission costs $6.

Since Inverell is known for its **sapphires**, there are several places where one may fossick for stones. The nearest is the *Pioneer Village*. There are several other and more authentic places, but they are not within walking distance of the town. The Tourist Information Centre incorporates the Mining Museum (free) and can readily offer advice on mining locations if you can find transport there. There are also shops in the town selling precious stones.

Copeton Waters State Park is 40 kilometres south-west of Inverell and is an artificial lake formed by the construction of Copeton Dam. The dam itself is huge, 113 metres high and 1.5 kilometres across. At its maximum, the dam wall is 427 metres thick. The dam took eight years to construct. The volume (not area) of the lake is three times that of Sydney Harbour and it is most famous for its fishing. There are also walking and cycling trails. Admission costs $2 including the use of barbecues, nine-hole golf course and tennis courts, with extra charges if vehicles are brought in. There is a bunkhouse available for overnight accommodation at $14 per night including the park entry fee. However, there is no public transport available to and from the park.

ACCOMMODATION
Accommodation in Inverell

Name	Stars	No. on Map	Telephone No.	Address	Lowest Price (Double/Twin)
Cousins Motor Inn	3½	6	1-800-023-118	9 Glen Innes Road	$85
Sapphire City Motel	3	7	02-6722-2500	34 Glen Innes Road	$80
Inverell Motel	2½	5	02-6722-2077	49 Otho Street	$65
Royal Hotel / Motel		1	02-6722-2811	260 Byron Street	$60
Australian Hotel		2	02-6722-1611	81 Byron Street	$50
Empire Hotel		4	02-6722-1411	1 Byron Street	$50
Imperial Hotel		3	02-6722-1511	Otho & Byron Streets	$40

MOVING ON

Going south, there is a morning bus to Tamworth which connects with the train to Sydney. The timetable for this is on page 176. Going west, there is a bus on Tuesday, Thursday and Saturday afternoons to Moree, from where there is a train to Sydney every morning. Travelling east and north, there is a Countrylink bus on Monday,

174   NEW SOUTH WALES

Wednesday and Friday afternoons which connects at Grafton with the train to Murwillumbah, and there are further connexions from there to Surfers Paradise and Brisbane. There is also a bus at 8:35 on Mondays to Fridays operated by Black and White Bus Services to Glen Innes, one hour east of Inverell, where it connects with the Greyhound bus to Brisbane.

Bus Services from Inverell

Destination	Operator	Via	Distance (km)	Fare	Journey Time	Frequency
Tamworth	Countrylink		226	$43.60	3¾ hrs	1/day
Moree	Countrylink		142	$25	2 hrs	3/week
Grafton	Countrylink		224	$37	3¾ hrs	3/week
		Glen Innes	65	$13	1 hr	3/week
Glen Innes	Black & White		65	$13	1 hr	2/day

ARMIDALE
Population 22,000
8 hrs 30 mins by train from Sydney
10 hrs 30 mins by bus from Sydney

Armidale is a **university city** of some 22,000 inhabitants. It claims to be the highest city in Australia, located at an elevation of 980 metres.

Armidale is most easily reached by the direct train service from Sydney which takes 8½ hours. The train divides at Werris Creek, so make sure that you are in the correct section, as indeed you should be since all seats are reserved on this service. This used to be the main line between Sydney and Brisbane, but, following the construction of a standard gauge coastal route all the way between the two cities, this line lost its popularity and no passenger services ran beyond Tamworth. More recently, however, passenger trains have been restored as far as Armidale. If you wish to go further, there is a connecting Countrylink bus running on to Tenterfield via Glen Innes (see diagram on page 170).

There is also a McCafferty's bus service from Sydney, but that takes 10½ hours and arrives, inconveniently, after midnight. On Sundays, Tuesdays and Thursdays, there is a bus service from Port Macquarie and Coffs Harbour operated by Keans which runs via the *Waterfall Way* up the slopes of the Great Dividing Range. This is reckoned to be one of the most scenic routes in New South Wales, so this is a bus worth taking if it proves convenient. At the time of writing, departure from Port Macquarie is at 9:00 (13:00 on Sundays), from Nambucca Heads at 10:40 (14:40 on Sundays) and from Coffs Harbour at 11:40 (15:40 on Sundays). Arrival at Armidale is at 15:15 (19:15 on Sundays).

Armidale offers many fine **tree-lined streets** and **English-style buildings**, including schools and cathedrals. A free two-hour **Heritage Trolley Tour** is offered, departing from the **Visitor Information Centre** every morning. There is also the **New England Regional Art Museum**, containing 3,500 works of art, some famous. The Art Museum is open from 10:30 until 16:00, with free admission. There is a **Railway Museum**, next to the railway station, with many exhibits outside. Those that are

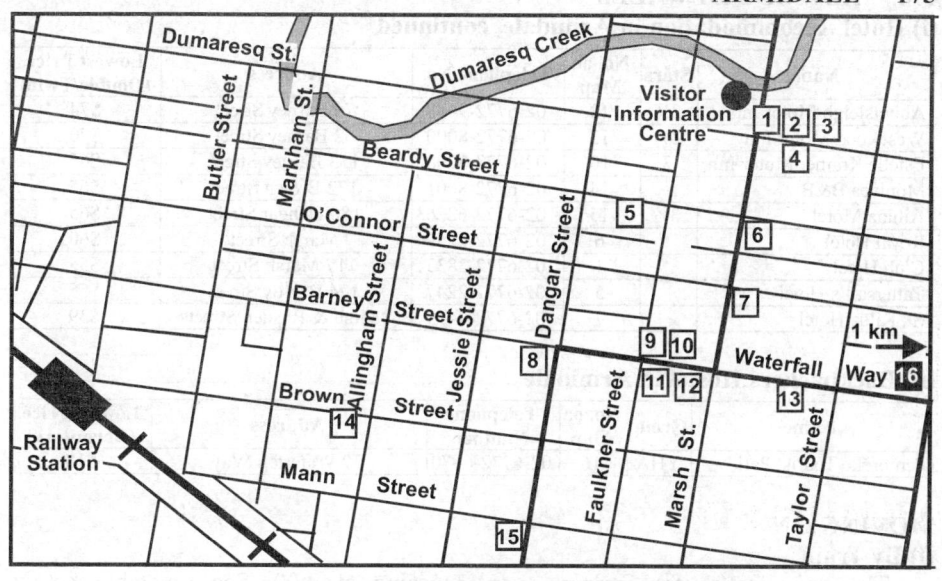

ARMIDALE

Black numerals in white boxes indicate hotel accommodation
White numerals in black boxes indicate backpackers hostels

housed within, however, can be inspected only between 11:00 and 11:30 every morning. Admission is free. The **Saumarez Homestead**, owned by the National Trust, is an impressive building with typically English gardens. It is open during the summer.

The bushranger Thunderbolt is associated with this part of the state and a **cave** which he is reputed to have used is located some twenty kilometres north of the city of Armidale. It is close to the main New England Highway.

ACCOMMODATION

Plenty of accommodation is available, as one might expect in a university town. For backpackers, there is a youth hostel in the Pembroke Tourist Park, about 1.5 kilometres from the town centre. It also offers on-site caravans at $38 for a double. There are several old-style hotels nearer to the town centre. The St. Kilda, for example, offers single rooms for $28 and doubles for $39. There are also the the Club Hotel, the Royal Hotel and Tattersall's Hotel which are only slightly more expensive. Here is a sample of the accommodation in Armidale.

(i) Hotel Accommodation in Armidale

Name	Stars	No. on Map	Telephone No.	Address	Lowest Price (Double/Twin)
Country Comfort	3½	11	02-6772-8511	86 Barney Street	$105
New England Motor Inn	4	4	02-6771-1011	100 Durmaresq Street	$92
Cedar Lodge Motel	3½	9	1-800-067-829	119 Barney Street	$90
Cameron Lodge	3½	8	02-6772-2351	Barney & Dangar Streets	$80
Sandstock Motor Inn	3½	2	1-800-658-277	101 Durmaresq Street	$75
Club Motel	3½	3	02-6772-8777	105 Durmaresq Street	$75

176 NEW SOUTH WALES
(i) Hotel Accommodation in Armidale, continued

Name	Stars	No. on Map	Telephone No.	Address	Lowest Price (Double/Twin)
Abbotsleigh Motor Inn	3½	12	02-6772-9488	76 Barney Street	$74
Westwood Motor Inn	3½	13	02-6772-8000	62 Barney Street	$70
Estelle Kramer Motor Inn	3	10	02-6772-5200	113 Barney Street	$65
Monivea B&B		14	02-6772-8001	172 Brown Street	$65
Alluna Motel	3½	15	02-6772-6226	180 Dangar Street	$65
Royal Hotel		6	02-6772-2259	Marsh Street	$60
Club Hotel		1	02-6772-3833	117 Marsh Street	$55
Tattersall's Hotel		5	02-6772-2247	174 Beardy Street	$55
St. Kilda Hotel		7	02-6772-4459	Marsh & Rusden Streets	$39

(ii) Backpackers Hostel in Armidale

Name	Group	No. on Map	Telephone Number	Address	Lowest Price (Dormitory)
Pembroke Tourist Park	YHA	16	02-6772-6470	39 Waterfall Way	$18

MOVING ON
(i) By Train
The train leaves for Sydney every morning at 9:00. See timetable below. Countrylink also runs a bus as far north as Tenterfield via Glen Innes. This service connects at Armidale with the arrival of the train from Sydney.

Tenterfield, Armidale, Inverell and Tamworth to Sydney

Days of Operation	Daily (Bus)	Daily (Bus)	Daily
Inverell	0710		
Warialda	0800		
Moree			0820
Narrabri			0933
Tenterfield		0600	
Glen Innes		0720	
Armidale		**0840**	**0900**
Tamworth	1046		1055
Werris Creek			1138
Broadmeadow			1441
Strathfield			1645
Sydney			1700

(ii) By Bus
There is a McCafferty's bus to Sydney, but that passes through Armidale at 2:30, which is less than convenient. There is a Greyhound bus to Dubbo every evening. There connexions can be made in the middle of the night to Melbourne, Adelaide and Sydney.

To go north, there is a McCafferty's bus just after midnight which reaches Brisbane next morning. More comfortably, there is a Greyhound bus leaving Armidale in the morning and reaching Brisbane in the afternoon. Then there is the Keans bus which runs east through the pretty *Waterfall Way* to Coffs Harbour, then on to Port Macquarie. This service operates on Mondays, Wednesdays and Fridays. On Sundays, Tuesdays and Thursdays, it runs in the opposite direction to Tamworth and Scone.

Bus Services from Armidale

Destination	Operator	Via	Distance (km)	Fare	Journey Time	Frequency
Sydney	McCafferty's		550	$82	10¼ hrs	1/day
		Tamworth	110	$32	2 hrs	1/day
Dubbo	Greyhound		438	$101	6½ hrs	4/week
		Tamworth	95	$32	2 hrs	4/week
Brisbane	McCafferty's		516	$76	7¾ hrs	1/day
		Toowoomba	390	$75	5¾ hrs	1/day
Brisbane	Greyhound		523	$76	8 hrs	4/week
		Toowoomba	390	$75	6 hrs	4/week
Tenterfield	Countrylink		187	$34.80	2¾ hrs	1/day
		Glen Innes	96	$15.20	1½ hrs	1/day
Pt Macquarie	Keans		372	$50.50	6 hrs	3/week
		Coffs Harbour	199	$29.50	4¾ hrs	3/week
Scone	Keans		226	$32	4¼ hrs	3/week
		Tamworth	90	$25	2 hrs	3/week

GLEN INNES
Population 6,500

10 hrs by train and bus from Sydney
12 hrs by bus from Sydney

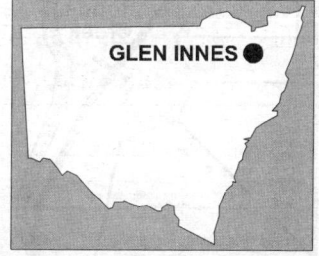

Glen Innes seems to be so strongly conscious of its Celtic roots that it almost thinks that it is a part of Scotland. Many Celts migrated to this area, not only Scots, but Irish, Welsh, Cornish and Manx too, and these Celtic roots have prompted the citizens of Glen Innes to erect the first circle of **Standing Stones** to be set up in more than 3,000 years.

Although they used the famous circles such as the Ring of Brodgar as an example, one could not mistake this location for the wilds of Orkney. It is not just the absence of the howling gale. These stones are shaped differently and bear the marks of the materials used to mine them. They have some new features too. The stones are laid out in the form of a Celtic cross, a cross superimposed on a circle, and include a representation of the Southern Cross. It is these modern Standing Stones which are the reason why the name of Glen Innes is known to many Australians.

Glen Innes is a crossroads. It is where the New England Highway, running north and south, crosses the Gwydir Highway, running east and west. It is also a town in which one feels that one wants to stay. In the main street there are some thirty listed buildings, for nobody has bothered much to change most of this town. Why not lodge in one of the pubs here? It will not be expensive and it will have character.

The first settler to arrive in Glen Innes was a man named Archibald Boyd in 1838. Although the district originally thrived on agriculture, tin was soon discovered nearby, as well as sapphires and some other precious stones, so Glen Innes became a rural centre supplying the various industries. The town is at an elevation of 1,062 metres, so it gets cold here in winter and snow falls occasionally. Be warned, if you stay in winter,

178 NEW SOUTH WALES

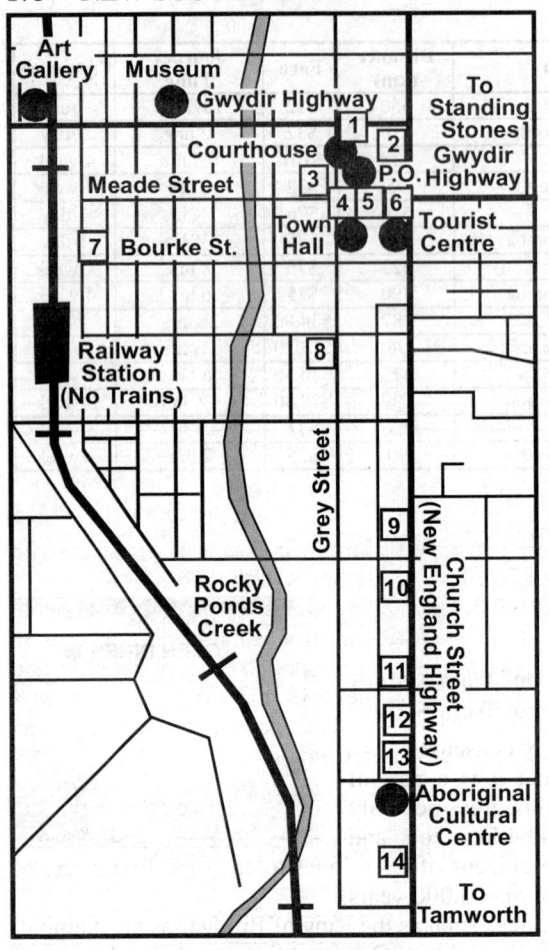

GLEN INNES

Numerals indicate accommodation

that it is not easy to get up early in the mornings. However, the town has the blessing of four seasons and a delight in nature that not all of Australia experiences. Autumn, with its falling leaves, is, as always in temperate climates, a particularly beautiful time here.

Glen Innes is most easily reached from Sydney by taking the train to Armidale and then the connecting Countrylink bus for a little less than a further hour and a quarter to here. In fact, though, Glen Innes is nearer to Brisbane than to Sydney, and a McCafferty's or Greyhound bus will bring you here from that city in about 6½ hours. It is also possible to take the Sydney-bound train from Brisbane as far as Grafton and then the Countrylink bus bound for Moree as far as Glen Innes. This service operates only on Tuesdays, Thursdays and Saturdays. There is a Countrylink service from Moree to Glen Innes on Mondays, Wednesdays and Fridays.

Attractions within the town include the buildings in the town centre, particularly those in Grey Street. The **Courthouse** dates from 1874 and the **Royal Hotel** was built in 1860. The *Land of the Beardies Museum* in Ferguson Street is a sizeable display of pioneer history filling twenty-four different rooms. It is so called because two bearded stockmen, John Duval and William Chandler, directed Archibald Boyd to this place back in 1838. Every year in early May the Australian Celtic Festival is held here, and in November there is the *Land of the Beardies Festival*. It is an interesting and unusual town.

ACCOMMODATION

There is a reasonable choice here, with a number of modern motels. Much more interesting, though (and cheaper), are the old hotels which still trade in the town centre. The Royal Hotel, for example, mentioned above, built in 1860, is still in business and will offer a single room for $31, or a double for $42, and other hotels are similar prices.

Accommodation in Glen Innes

Name	Stars	No. on Map	Telephone No.	Address	Lowest Price (Double/Twin)
Rest Point Motel	3½	9	02-6732-2255	New England Highway	$101
New Eng. Motor Lodge	4	2	02-6732-2922	160 Church Street	$90
Clansman Motel	3½	14	1-800-077-647	522 Armidale Road	$84
Central Motel	3½	5	1-800-639-144	Meade Street	$75
Glen Masterton Motel	3½	12	02-6732-1211	New England Highway	$75
Alpha Motel	3	10	02-6732-2688	New England Highway	$70
Jillaroo Motel	3	13	02-6732-3388	8 Church Street	$70
Glen Haven Motor Inn	3	11	02-6732-3266	Church & Heron Streets	$65
New Tattersalls Hotel	2½	8	02-6732-3011	Grey Street	$60
Amber Motel	2½	6	02-6732-2300	135 Meade Street	$55
Railway Tavern		7	02-6732-1504	Lambeth & Bourke Streets	$45
Imperial Hotel		3	02-6732-3103	Grey & Meade Streets	$43
Royal Hotel		1	02-6732-3179	Grey & Ferguson Streets	$42
Great Central Hotel		4	02-6732-3107	Grey & Meade Streets	$39

MOVING ON

To return to Sydney, the Countrylink bus every morning connects at Armidale with the train. There is also a McCafferty's bus in the early hours of the morning.

To go to Brisbane, there are bus services operated by McCafferty's and Greyhound. There is also a Countrylink bus to Grafton where a connexion is made with the train to Murwillumbah and then onward bus connexions are provided to Surfers Paradise and Brisbane. This service operates on Mondays, Wednesdays and Fridays. There is a Countrylink bus to Moree via Inverell on Tuesdays, Thursdays and Saturdays, and there is a Black and White bus service to Inverell twice a day.

Bus Services from Glen Innes

Destination	Operator	Via	Distance (km)	Fare	Journey Time	Frequency
Sydney	McCafferty's		648	$82	11½ hrs	1/day
		Tamworth	208	$50	3¾ hrs	1/day
Dubbo	Greyhound		536	$104	7¾ hrs	4/week
		Tamworth	193	$50	3½ hrs	4/week
Brisbane	McCafferty's		418	$76	6½ hrs	1/day
		Toowoomba	292	$65	4½ hrs	1/day
Brisbane	Greyhound		425	$76	6¾ hrs	4/week
		Toowoomba	292	$65	4½ hrs	4/week
Tenterfield	Countrylink		91	$15.20	1¼ hrs	1/day
Grafton	Countrylink		159	$28.30	2¾ hrs	3/week
Armidale	Countrylink		96	$15.20	1½ hrs	1/day
Moree	Countrylink		207	$34.80	3½ hrs	3/week
		Inverell	65	$13	1 hr	3/week
Inverell	Black & White		65	$13	1 hr	2/day

180 NEW SOUTH WALES
TENTERFIELD
Population 3,200

11 hrs by train and bus from Sydney
13 hrs by bus from Sydney
5 hrs 30 mins by bus from Brisbane

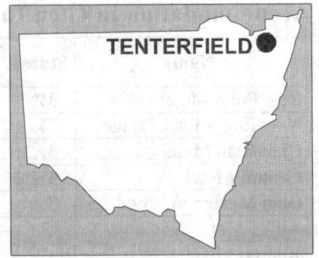

Tenterfield is a small town close to the Queensland border which likes to refer to itself, perhaps a little self-flatteringly, as the "Birthplace of our Nation." The history behind this title is that on 24th October 1889, Sir Henry Parkes, a very well respected politician, five times premier of New South Wales, gave a speech in the School of Arts in Tenterfield urging the various colonies which existed in Australia at the time to join together to form a single Commonwealth of Australia, a vision which was eventually realised on 1st January 1901. The School of Arts, where this famous speech was given, is now owned by the National Trust and contains a collection of historical documents relating to Sir Henry Parkes.

Walking Tour

There are several interesting buildings in Tenterfield, so let us have a short walking tour. This walk will cover about 3.5 kilometres and will take just over an hour.

Start at the **Visitors Information Centre** at the corner of Rouse Street (the main street of the town, through which runs the New England Highway) and Miles Street and proceed north along Rouse Street. At the first corner, you will come to the **School of Arts** just mentioned above. The **Parkes Collection** can be viewed here on weekdays. The **Post Office** is on the opposite corner, an impressive building constructed in 1881.

Proceed one more block to High Street and then turn right. Soon you will see on your right **The Saddler's Shop** made of blue granite. Peter Allen was a famous performer born in Tenterfield and one of his songs was entitled the *Tenterfield Saddler*. It told the story of his grandfather, George Woolnough, who worked as a saddler in this shop for more than half a century. The shop is open daily from 10:00 until 16:00.

Turn left into Logan Street and come to the **Centenary Cottage Complex**, which is a group of old cottages dating back to 1860 and now used to house a collection of historical materials relating to Tenterfield. The cottages are open from 10:00 until 16:00 on Wednesdays to Sundays and admission costs $3.

Turn left into Molesworth Street. After crossing Rouse Street, you will see on your right the **Tenterfield Courthouse**, which was built in 1885 and has been restored recently. The court room features a glass ceiling. Next door is the **Police Station** and **Gaol**, constructed in 1874 and still in use.

Continue down Molesworth Street for some distance and cross the railway line. Just after this on your left is **Ghost Gully**, where erosion has created some unusual and interesting formations.

Return across the railway and turn right into Railway Avenue. On your right is the **Railway Station**, another handsome building, opened with great ceremony in 1886 and closed as a station in 1989. It is now a Railway Museum, giving the appearance of just waiting for the next train to arrive. That will be a long wait, however, as part of the track south of Tenterfield has already been lifted. For many years, this was the main line between Sydney and Brisbane, and Tenterfield was the last major station in New South Wales. A little further up at Wallangarra, the line reached the Queensland border

TENTERFIELD 181

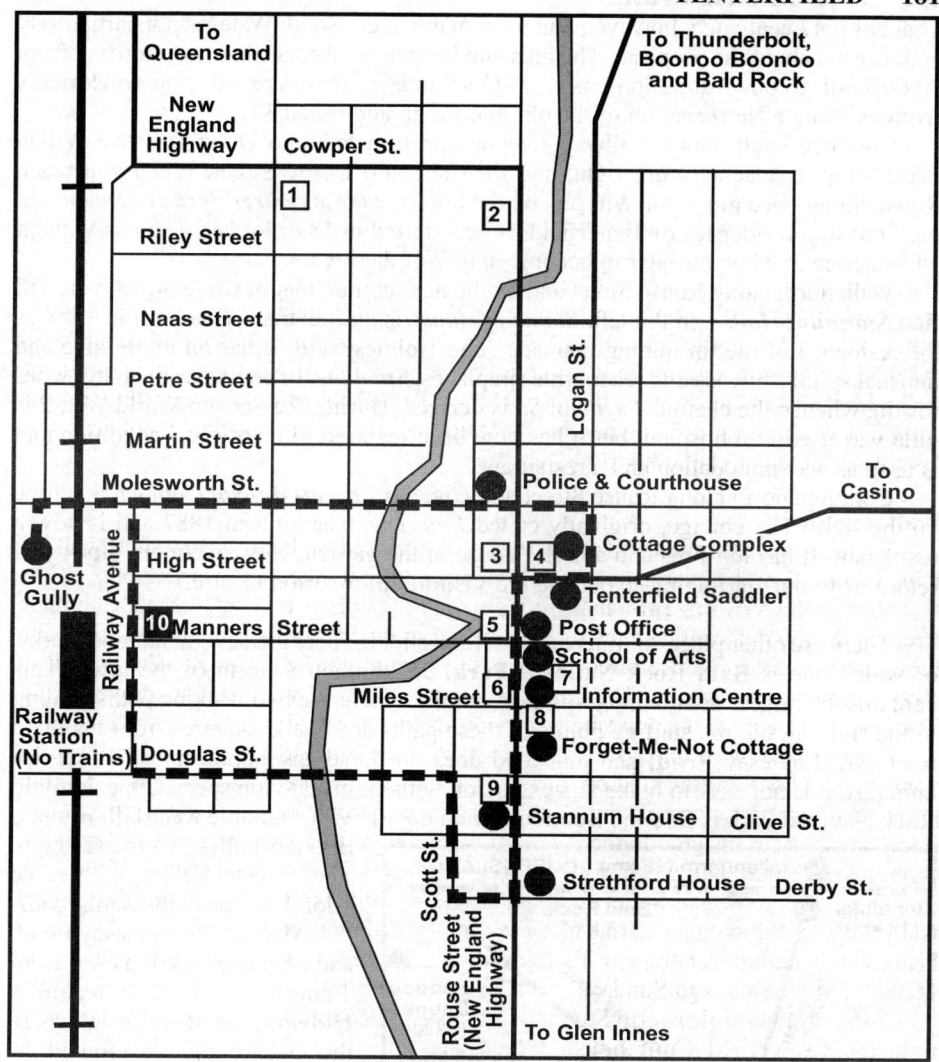

TENTERFIELD

Dashed line shows Walking Tour
Black numerals in white boxes indicate hotel accommodation
White numerals in black boxes indicate backpackers hostels

and passengers had to transfer to a Queensland Railways narrow-gauge train. More recently, a direct standard-gauge line was completed via the coastal route and this inland service lost popularity, so that now no trains at all run on it in New South Wales north of Armidale. Queensland Railways still operates narrow-gauge goods trains as far south as the border and was reported to be interested in taking over this northern section of the New South Wales line and converting it to narrow gauge, so that agricultural products could be shipped to Brisbane, which is much closer than Sydney.

182 NEW SOUTH WALES

That has not eventuated, however, and presumably New South Wales is not particularly enthusiastic about the proposal. The museum is open on Wednesdays to Saturdays from 10:00 until 16:00. Admission costs $3. On Sundays, there are rides on **workmen's trolleys** along a short section of the old line for an additional $3.

Continue south along Railway Avenue and turn left into Douglas Street. When Scott Street is reached, turn right, and then left into Derby Street. When you reach Rouse Street once more you will see, on the opposite corner, **Strethford House**, one of the imposing residences of Tenterfield. It was started in 1896 for Mr. Thomas Walker, a businessman who was later to become mayor of the town.

Walk north along Rouse Street and on the next corner, that of Clive Street, you will find **Stannum House** on the left. *Stannum House* is an Italianate villa built in 1888 as the residence of the tin mining magnate John Holmes Reid. It has an impressive and unusual spiral staircase and ten marble fireplaces. *Stannum*, of course, is the Latin word for tin, whence the chemical symbol *Sn* is derived. During the Second World War, this villa was used as a hospital, but it has now been restored to its original condition and is used as accommodation and a restaurant.

Continue north along Rouse Street and come to **Forget-Me-Not Cottage**, this time on the right. The cottage, originally called *Fairview*, was built in 1887 and is now a restaurant. It has log fires and a dolls' house in the garden. Now one more block will return us to our starting place outside the Visitors Information Centre.

There are other places of interest near Tenterfield. There are several national parks, of which one is **Bald Rock National Park**, 35 kilometres north of the town. This contains the largest granite monolith in Australia. There are two walking paths leading to the summit, but the starting points of these paths are five kilometres from the main road (Mt. Lindesay Road) and that road does not have any public transport service either, so it is not easy to make this excursion without private transport. Opposite Bald Rock National Park is **Boonoo Boonoo** National Park with a notable waterfall, Boonoo Boonoo Falls, 210 metres high. The waterfall is twelve kilometres from the main road.

Also on Mt. Lindesay Road, and only twelve kilometres from Tenterfield, is **Thunderbolt's Hideout**, another place where the bushranger is reputed to have sheltered. There are two caves formed by granite boulders. One cave was evidently used for stabling a horse, while the other was used as a camp site. There is a good view of the road, which used to be the main route north, from the top of the boulders. One kilometre further north are some **tank traps** constructed during the Second World War.

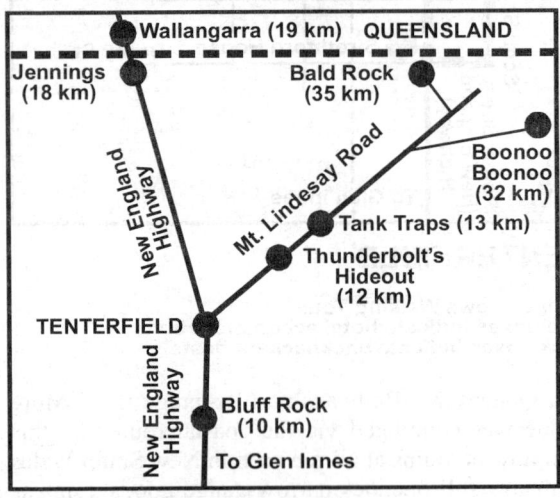

AROUND TENTERFIELD

Distances are from Tenterfield

TENTERFIELD 183

Ten kilometres south of Tenterfield on the New England Highway is **Bluff Rock**, an unusual granite outcrop right beside the road. It can be seen quite well from the bus if there is daylight when you pass and there is also a viewing area provided along the highway.

Tenterfield is reached by train plus bus connexion from Sydney, changing at Armidale. There are buses from Sydney and Brisbane operated by McCafferty's and Greyhound, and there is also a Crisps Coaches service daily to and from Brisbane. Note, if it is summer, that this last-mentioned bus operates on Queensland time.

At **Wallangarra**, nineteen kilometres north of Tenterfield, New South Wales ends and Queensland starts. When the rail link was completed in 1888, New South Wales rejected Queensland's offer of a sum of twelve thousand pounds per annum in lieu of Customs Duties and a border station check-point was constructed here. Wallangarra **Customs House** still exists, although no longer collecting duties, at this border settlement which sprang up only because of the work associated with a change of rail gauge and movement of goods from one colony to another. The larger township, on the Queensland side of the border, is Wallangarra. The smaller settlement, on the New South Wales side, is **Jennings**.

ACCOMMODATION

There are several motels in Tenterfield, but the older hotels are more interesting, as well as being more economical. For backpackers, there is a youth hostel near the railway station. The owners, who run a caravan park also, are willing to pick up from either of the bus stops used. However, the hotels in town cost little more than the hostel, in fact.

(i) Hotel Accommodation in Tenterfield

Name	Stars	No. on Map	Telephone No.	Address	Lowest Price (Double/Twin)
Henry Parkes Motor Inn	4	6	02-6736-1066	144 Rouse Street	$100
Settlers Motor Inn	3½	9	02-6736-2333	Rouse & Douglas Streets	$85
Jumbuck Motor Inn	3	8	02-6736-2055	141 Rouse Street	$80
Peter Allen Motor Inn	3	7	1-800-803-559	177 Rouse Street	$80
Tally-Ho Motor Inn		2	02-6736-1577	New England Highway	$65
Commercial Hotel		1	02-6736-1027	288 Rouse Street	$50
Telegraph Hotel / Motel	2½	5	02-6736-1015	139 Manners Street	$45
Golfers Inn	3	3	02-6736-3898	189 Pelham Street	$40
Royal Hotel / Motel		4	02-6736-1833	130 High Street	$40

(ii) Backpackers Hostel in Tenterfield

Name	Group	No. on Map	Telephone Number	Address	Lowest Price (Dormitory)
Tenterfield Lodge	YHA	10	02-6736-1477	2 Manners Street	$20

MOVING ON

The Countrylink bus every morning connects at Armidale with the train to Sydney. See page 176 for the timetable. McCafferty's runs a bus to Sydney leaving Tenterfield at midnight and arriving in Sydney at lunch-time the next day.

Heading north, there are buses to Brisbane operated by McCafferty's, Greyhound and Crisps Coaches. Here is a summary.

NEW SOUTH WALES
Bus Services from Tenterfield

Destination	Operator	Via	Distance (km)	Fare	Journey Time	Frequency
Sydney	McCafferty's		742	$82	12¾ hrs	1/day
		Tamworth	302	$53	4¾ hrs	1/day
Dubbo	Greyhound		630	$106	9 hrs	4/week
		Tamworth	287	$53	4¾ hrs	4/week
Brisbane	McCafferty's		324	$61	5½ hrs	1/day
		Toowoomba	198	$55	3½ hrs	1/day
Brisbane	Greyhound		331	$61	5½ hrs	4/week
		Toowoomba	198	$55	3½ hrs	4/week
Brisbane	Crisps		275	$51.50	4 hrs	1/day
Armidale	Countrylink		96	$34.80	2¾ hrs	1/day

PORT MACQUARIE
Population 28,000

    7 hrs 30 mins by train and bus from Sydney
    6 hrs 30 mins by bus from Sydney

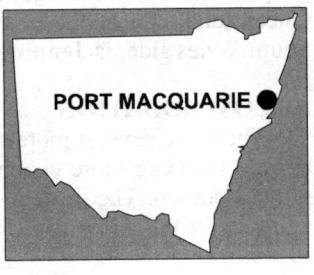

Port Macquarie was established as a penal settlement and has turned into a popular holiday resort. Its history has almost been lost sight of in the wealth of publicity about its excellent beaches and wonderful surfing opportunities.

Captain Cook noted the location of Port Macquarie and the Hastings River during his voyage of 1770, but it was not until Oxley was sent to explore the region in detail in 1818 that the town and the river received their European names. Macquarie was the Governor of New South Wales at the time and Warren Hastings had been a famous

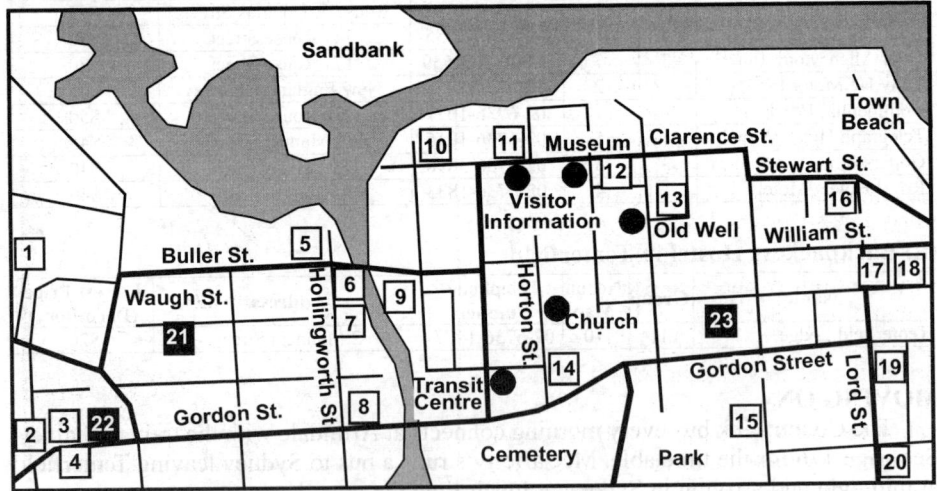

PORT MACQUARIE
Black numerals in white boxes indicate hotel accommodation
White numerals in black boxes indicate backpackers hostels

Governor-General of India. As a result of Oxley's report, the penal settlement was established in 1821, led by Captain Francis Allman, who landed at what is now called **Town Green**, at the end of Clarence Street, with a contingent of sixty convicts. It was here in Port Macquarie that the first planting of sugar in Australia was carried out, and it was so successful that by 1824 a sugar mill had been established.

In 1830, the area was opened to free settlers and by 1847 all convict labour had been withdrawn. This led to a temporary decline in the settlement's prosperity, but it recovered as more pastoralists began to arrive.

The North Coast Railway was built nearby in 1910, and this made transport easier and helped the settlement to prosper, but it is since the 1960s that it has really grown, as it was discovered as a holiday resort. Now it is a popular destination with all types of holidaymaker, domestic or international, rich or poor. Port Macquarie seems to be on everybody's itinerary.

In fact, there is no direct passenger rail service to Port Macquarie. The train goes to Wauchope, from where it is a journey of 25 minutes by bus. If you take the 11:35 train from Sydney, reaching Wauchope at 18:19, there is a connecting Countrylink bus to Port Macquarie. That is the only connexion which is guaranteed, but, if you catch the morning train from Sydney at 7:15, you will reach Wauchope at 13:41, if the train happens to run to time, and at 14:05 (13:55 at weekends) there is a bus no. 334 operated by Port Macquarie Bus Service from Wauchope station to Port Macquarie. Similarly, if you are approaching from the north, the train from Brisbane reaches Wauchope at 15:25, and at 16:05 there is a bus no. 334 from the station to Port Macquarie (weekdays only).

From Sydney, there are six buses per day to Port Macquarie, two operated by McCafferty's, one operated by Greyhound and three operated by Premier.

PORT MACQUARIE

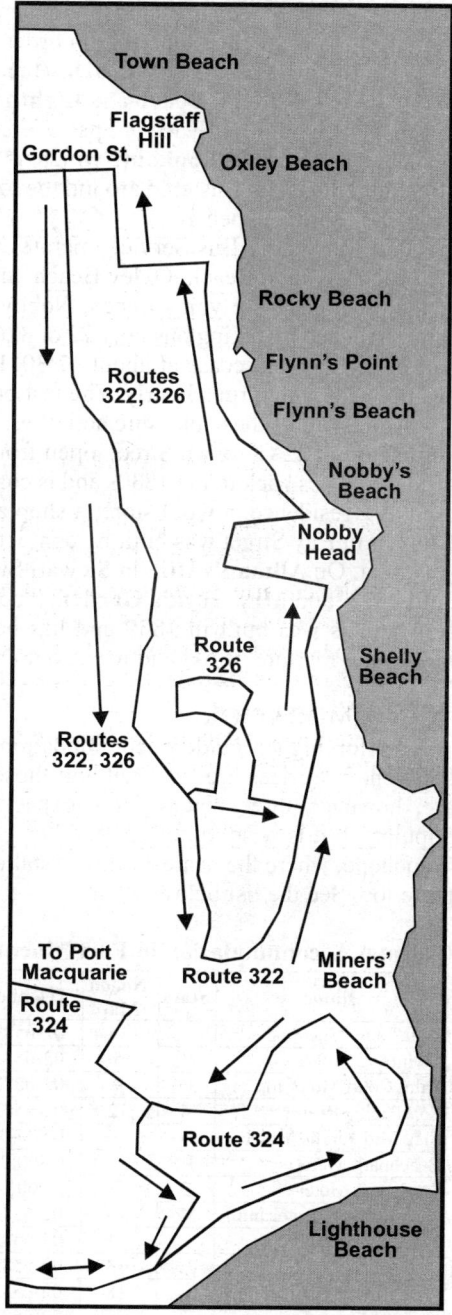

PORT MACQUARIE BEACHES
Showing local bus routes

186 NEW SOUTH WALES

One of Port Macquarie's most popular activities is sitting on the beach. Proceeding from north to south, and therefore in order of decreasing proximity to the town centre, we have **Town Beach, Oxley Beach, Rocky Beach, Flynn's Beach, Nobby's Beach, Shelly Beach, Miners' Beach** and **Lighthouse Beach**. Of these, Town Beach, Flynn's Beach and Lighthouse Beach are patrolled. Windsurfing is popular and hang-gliding is available at **Harry's Lookout**, which is above Shelly Beach. Various **cruises** are offered by the boats clustered around the top of Clarence Street, although most seem to the author a little expensive.

Port Macquarie Bus Service operates various local bus routes, including those to the beaches. Town Beach, Oxley Beach and Rocky Beach are within walking distance of the town centre. Flynn's Beach, Nobby's Beach, Shelly Beach and Miners' Beach can be reached by taking bus no. 322 or 326. Buses run every half hour during the main part of the day, but cease at about 17:30. Lighthouse Beach can be reached by taking bus no. 324, which runs hourly. The last bus back from Lighthouse Beach is at 18:00.

Amidst all of these pleasure activities, do not forget to look at the history. There is a **museum** at 22 Clarence Street, open from 9:30 until 16:30. The building in which it is housed dates back to the 1830s and is constructed of convict-made bricks. It has been used as a residence, a wool store, a shop and now a museum. **St. Thomas' Anglican Church** in Hay Street was built by convicts in 1828. It is one of the oldest churches in Australia. On **Allman's Hill**, in Stewart Street, is the settlement's first **cemetery**, used until 1823, and **Mrs. York's Garden**. The **Courthouse** on the corner of Clarence and Hay Streets was built in 1859 and has been restored recently. Port Macquarie is an interesting mixture of old and new, so do not forget the old while pursuing the new.

ACCOMMODATION

As for higher grade accommodation, there is plenty in such a holiday resort location, but prices are seasonal and those quoted below are low season rates. There are, however, three places for backpackers, as detailed below. Port Macquarie is popular, so it is wise to book ahead here. If you find that you need or wish to stay in Wauchope, where the nearest railway station is located, there is one backpackers hostel there too. See the list below.

(i) Hotel Accommodation in Port Macquarie

Name	Stars	No. on Map	Telephone No.	Address	Lowest Price (Double/Twin)
Four Points Sheraton		14	02-6584-7070	2 Hay Street	$160
Country Comfort	3½	5	02-6583-2955	Buller & Hollingworth Sts.	$135
Palm Court Motor Inn	3½	9	02-6583-5155	138 William Street	$120
Port Pacific Resort	4	12	02-6583-8099	6 Clarence Street	$120
Flag Mid Pacific Motel	3½	10	1-800-024-894	Short & Clarence Streets	$109
Beachpark Motel	3½	17	1-800-224-438	44 William Street	$95
Le George Motel	3	7	1-800-648-835	4 Hollingworth Street	$87
Historic Well Motor Inn	3½	16	02-6583-1200	1 Stewart Street	$80
Macquarie Hotel		11	02-6583-1011	Horton & Clarence Streets	$75
Port Aloha	3½	13	02-6583-1455	3 School Street	$75
Beachfront Regency Inn	3½	18	02-6583-2244	40 William Street	$75
Horizon Motor Lodge	3	6	02-6583-2888	William & Hollingworth Sts	$70
Shangri La	3	8	02-6583-2500	119 Gordon Street	$70
Golden Beaches Inn	3	19	02-6583-8899	Lord & Gordon Streets	$70
Bayview Motor Inn	3	1	02-6583-3266	22 Mort Street	$65
Koala Tree Motel		3	02-6583-2177	179 Gordon Street	$65

(i) Hotel Accommodation in Port Macquarie, continued

Name	Stars	No. on Map	Telephone No.	Address	Lowest Price (Double/Twin)
Arrowyn Motel	3½	4	02-6583-1633	170 Gordon Street	$65
John Oxley	2½	2	02-6583-1677	171 Gordon Street	$55
East Port Motor Inn	3	20	02-6583-5850	Lord & Burrawan Streets	$55
Macquarie Motel	1½	15	02-6583-1533	21 Grant Street	$50

(ii) Backpackers Hostels in Port Macquarie and Wauchope

Name	Group	No. on Map	Telephone Number	Address	Lowest Price (Dormitory)
Lindel Backpackers	VIP	22	1800-688-882	2 Hastings River Drive	$25
Ozzie Pozzie	Nom/B&W	21	1800-620-020	36 Waugh Street	$22
Beachside Backpackers	YHA	23	02-6583-5512	40 Church Street	$20
Auntie Ann's			02-6586-4420	19 Bruxner Av., Wauchope	$22

MOVING ON

The guaranteed bus plus train connexion to Sydney leaves Port Macquarie at 9:00. There is no bus connexion for other services travelling south. To travel north, catch Port Macquarie Bus Service bus no. 334 at 13:00. This bus will travel via Wauchope Railway Station on request, so be sure to request it. It arrives at 13:25 and the train departs at 13:41 for Murwillumbah with bus connexions to Surfers Paradise and Brisbane. See page 94 for this timetable. When leaving Wauchope to travel north, look for the big cow to the right of the railway soon after departure.

McCafferty's operates two buses per day to Sydney. Greyhound operates one and Premier operates two. To Brisbane, there are two McCafferty's buses, one Greyhound and three Premier. Additionally, there is a Keans bus to Scone via Coffs Harbour and Tamworth. This operates on Sundays, Tuesdays and Thursdays.

Bus Services from Port Macquarie

Destination	Operator	Via	Distance (km)	Fare	Journey Time	Frequency
Sydney	McCafferty's		398	$76	6 - 8¾ hrs	2/day
Sydney	Greyhound		428	$76	7 hrs	2/day
Sydney	Premier		428	$58	6¾ - 7¼ hrs	2/day
Brisbane	McCafferty's		596	$76	9¼ - 10 hrs	2/day
		Surfers Paradise	517	$76	7¾ - 8¼ hrs	2/day
		Byron Bay	406	$76	6½ hrs	1/day
		Coffs Harbour	164	$40	2¼ - 3 hrs	2/day
Brisbane	Greyhound		592	$76	9¾ hrs	1/day
		Surfers Paradise	504	$76	8 hrs	1/day
		Byron Bay	393	$76	6 hrs	1/day
		Coffs Harbour	151	$40	2½ hrs	1/day
Brisbane	Premier		596	$65	9¼ - 11 hrs	3/day
		Surfers Paradise	517	$65	8¼ - 9½ hrs	3/day
		Byron Bay	406	$63	6½ - 7¼ hrs	3/day
		Coffs Harbour	164	$46	2¼ - 2½ hrs	3/day
Scone	Keans		598	$83	10½ hrs	3/week
		Tamworth	462	$71.50	9 hrs	3/week
		Coffs Harbour	173	$26	2¾ hrs	3/week

188   NEW SOUTH WALES
NAMBUCCA HEADS
Population 6,500

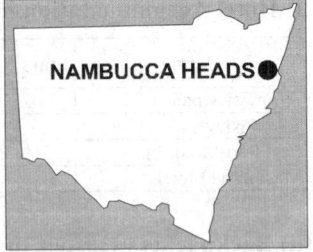

8 hrs by train from Sydney
8 hrs by bus from Sydney

Nambucca Heads is a quiet little beach resort in a very attractive location. It offers beaches, yachting, surfing, windsurfing, swimming, fishing, birdwatching and walking, but without the busy atmosphere of many resort areas. One of the town's unusual features is the **Vee Wall**, beside the sea and the river mouth, where it has become a custom over the years for visitors to inscribe a record of their visit. You may too if you happen to have some paint handy.

Some forty kilometres from Nambucca Heads lies **'The Pub with No Beer'**, made famous in a song recorded some years ago by Australia's most celebrated country music singer, Slim Dusty. The poem on which the song was based first appeared in 1944, but it was revised and put to music, with verses added alluding to the patrons of the Commercial Hotel in Taylors Arm. The **Commercial Hotel** still functions there, its success Fostered no doubt by the Slim Dusty ballad, and accommodation is offered too at reasonable rates. A single room costs $28 and a double $50.

Nambucca Heads is 47 kilometres south of Coffs Harbour, about 45 minutes by train or bus. From Sydney, it takes eight hours by train to here, or from Brisbane just over six hours. Timetables for these services can be found on pages 94 and 238.

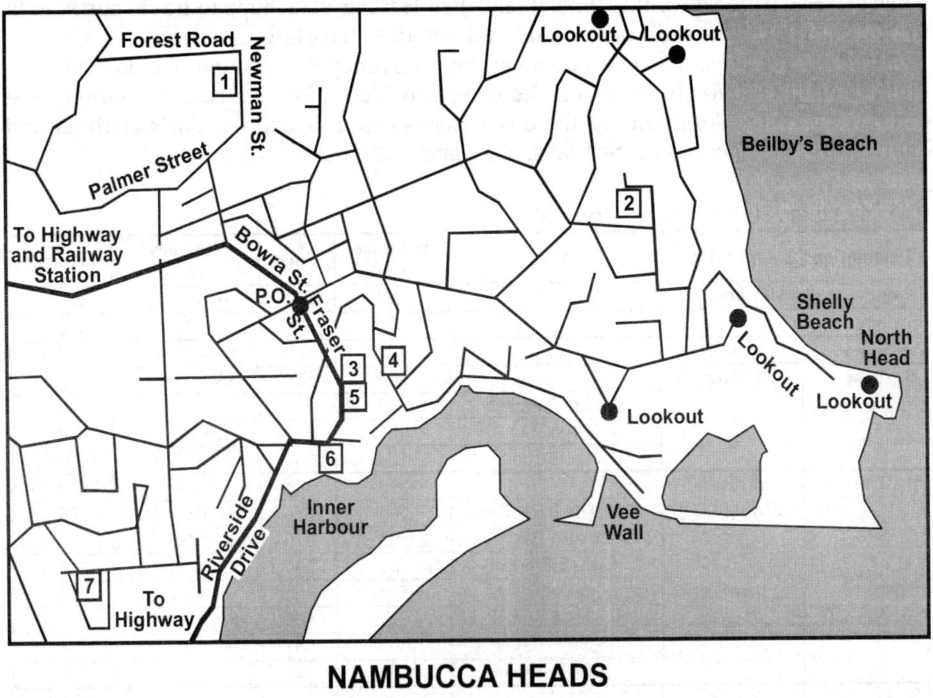

NAMBUCCA HEADS
Numerals indicate accommodation

NAMBUCCA HEADS

McCafferty's operates two buses a day from Sydney, Greyhound has three and Premier has three also. The journey takes approximately eight hours on the fastest services, and an hour or so longer on the slower ones. From Brisbane, there is one McCafferty's bus daily, two Greyhound services and three Premier buses. Travelling time is 7½ to 8½ hours.

There are some local bus services around Nambucca Heads, for example to Bellingen and Urunga. These are operated by Joyce's Valley Link Bus (Tel. 02-6655-6330).

ACCOMMODATION

The motels here nearly all have good views from at least some of the rooms. Backpackers are spoilt by two excellent choices in such a small town. Whatever budget you are on, Beilby's offers very good value indeed. It is like living at home. You will be picked up and returned to the station or bus stop upon request, given a free drink on arrival and provided with a fine breakfast. It is worth the price, but if that is beyond your budget, Nambucca Backpackers, a little further inland but nearer to the town centre, is also a good place to stay. Like Beilby's, it takes guests on all budgets and provides for them accordingly.

(i) Hotel Accommodation in Nambucca Heads

Name	Stars	No. on Map	Telephone No.	Address	Lowest Price (Double/Twin)
Dunaber House		7	02-6568-9434	35 Piggott Street	$85
Scott's Boutique B & B	4	4	02-6568-6386	4 Wellington Drive	$80
Max Motel		5	02-6568-6138	4 Fraser Street	$65
Motel Miramar		6	02-6568-7899	1 Nelson Street	$65
Blue Dolphin Motel		3	1-800-501-879	Fraser Street	$60
Forest Lodge Units	3½	1	1-800-630-663	3 Newman Street	$55
Beilby's Beach House	4	2	02-6568-6466	1 Ocean Street	$47

(ii) Backpackers Hostels in Nambucca Heads

Name	Group	No. on Map	Telephone Number	Address	Lowest Price (Dormitory)
Beilby's Beach House	B&W	2	02-6568-6466	1 Ocean Street	$33
Nambucca Backpackers	VIP	1	1800-630-663	3 Newman Street	$21

MOVING ON
(i) By Train

There are three trains every day to Sydney, although one of them is in the middle of the night. The timetable is on page 238. Heading north, there is a train to Brisbane during the night. In the afternoon, there is a train to Murwillumbah with bus connexions to Surfers Paradise and Brisbane, and then in the evening there is a train which runs only as far as Grafton. The timetable is on page 94.

(ii) By Bus

A summary of the bus services is overleaf. Note that McCafferty's, Greyhound and Premier do not come into the town of Nambucca Heads, but merely stop at the turn-off on the main Pacific Highway. It is a good idea to ask your accommodation to pick you up, if possible. Keans comes into the town and stops near the Police Station.

190 NEW SOUTH WALES
Bus Services from Nambucca Heads

Destination	Operator	Via	Distance (km)	Fare	Journey Time	Frequency
Sydney	McCafferty's		549	$79	10¼ hrs	1/day
		Port Macquarie	121	$32	1¾ hrs	1/day
Sydney	Greyhound		549	$79	8¾ - 9 hrs	2/day
		Port Macquarie	121	$32	2¼ hrs	2/day
Sydney	Premier		549	$61	7½ - 9¼ hrs	3/day
		Port Macquarie	121	$36	1¾ - 2 hrs	2/day
Pt Macquarie	Keans		123	$19	1¾ hrs	3/week
Brisbane	McCafferty's		475	$71	7¾ - 8 hrs	2/day
		Surfers Paradise	400	$71	6¼ hrs	2/day
		Byron Bay	289	$70	4½ hrs	1/day
		Coffs Harbour	47	$32	45 mins	2/day
Brisbane	Greyhound		488	$71	7¾ - 9¼ hrs	3/day
		Surfers Paradise	400	$71	6¼ - 7½ hrs	3/day
		Byron Bay	289	$70	4½ - 5½ hrs	3/day
		Coffs Harbour	47	$32	45 mins	3/day
Brisbane	Premier		488	$61	7¾ - 9¼ hrs	3/day
		Surfers Paradise	400	$61	6¾ - 7¾ hrs	3/day
		Byron Bay	289	$55	5 - 5¾ hrs	3/day
		Coffs Harbour	47	$32	45 mins	3/day
Scone	Keans		475	$66	8¾ hrs	3/week
		Tamworth	339	$60.50	7½ hrs	3/week
		Coffs Harbour	50	$19	1 hr	3/week

COFFS HARBOUR
Population 25,000

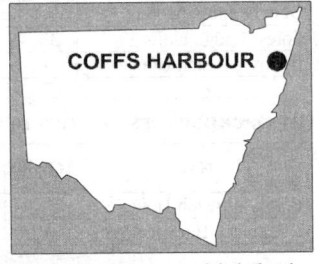

9 hrs by train from Sydney
9 hrs by bus from Sydney

Coffs Harbour is a comparatively large, but likeable, seaside city lying between Sydney and Brisbane. It is shaped in a triangle. At one point of the triangle lie the **Railway Station** and the **Marina**, at another is the **old town centre**, and at the third is the **Park Beach Plaza**, which is the new shopping centre (where the author managed to get locked in at closing time).

The principal attraction is the **beaches**, for which reason Hoey Moey Backpackers is popular with budget travellers, being right by Park Beach. Another feature of the city is the **Big Banana**, on the Pacific Highway about ten minutes walk from the Park Beach Plaza. Have a look at it. It really is a big banana and it is the symbol of Coffs Harbour. Behind the Big Banana is an **horticultural theme park** open from 9:00 until 16:00.

Also near Park Beach Plaza, but this time in the direction of the old city centre, is the **Clog Barn** and **Holland Downunder**. At the former, there are free clog-making demonstrations and you may purchase a pair should the desire seize you. The latter is a meticulously constructed model Dutch village, with an admission charge of $5.

Along the same road, the Pacific Highway, lies the **Visitor Information Centre**, in an inconspicuous building set back from the road.

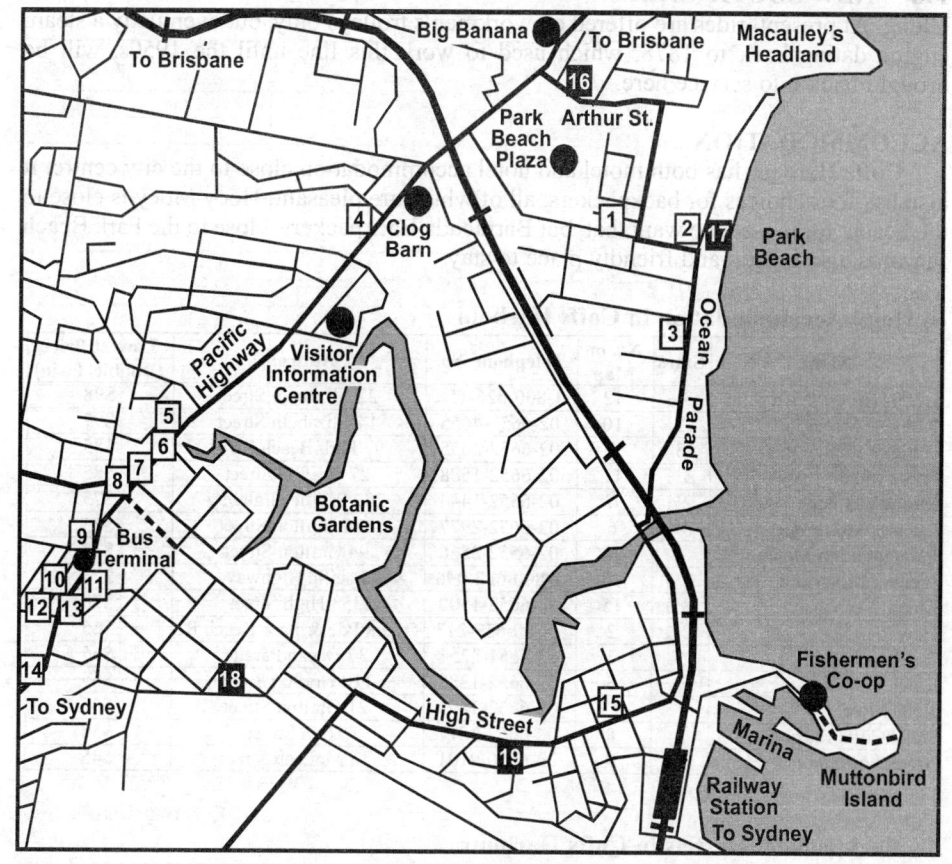

COFFS HARBOUR

**Black numerals in white boxes indicate hotel accommodation
White numerals in black boxes indicate backpackers hostels**

The **Botanic Gardens** are worth visiting, and can be reached from the older part of the city, as shown on the map above.

The **Marina** too should be visited. It is walking distance from the station and includes the **Fishermen's Co-op**, offering such delicacies as fish and chips, as well as fresh fish, and there are several other stores also. From here a causeway leads to **Muttonbird Island**, where there is a walking track.

One of the most attractive drives in New South Wales is along the *Waterfall Way* up the Great Dividing Range to Armidale, a route followed by a Keans bus on Sundays, Tuesdays and Thursdays. On the way, the bus stops at **Dorrigo** for a lunch break. Here in Dorrigo, at the **Dorrigo Steam Railway and Museum**, you will find what is claimed to be the largest collection of steam engines in the southern hemisphere. This is one end of a spectacular branch railway opened in 1924 and closed in 1972. At the other end of the line, 35 kilometres of track is being reclaimed from the bush for the operation of the **Glenreagh Mountain Railway** which will run from Glenreagh to

192 NEW SOUTH WALES

Ulong. At present, rides are offered on workmen's trolleys only, but eventually a steam engine dating back to 1878, which used to work this line until the 1950s, will be brought back into service here.

ACCOMMODATION

Coffs Harbour has both motel and hotel accommodation close to the city centre. It also has four choices for backpackers, all of which are pleasant. Hoey Moey is close to the beach, for those who want that, but Barracuda Backpackers, close to the Park Beach Plaza, is also a good and friendly place to stay.

(i) Hotel Accommodation in Coffs Harbour

Name	Stars	No. on Map	Telephone No.	Address	Lowest Price (Double/Twin)
Coffs Harbour Motor Inn	3½	12	1-800-626-158	22 Elizabeth Street	$98
Parkside Motor Inn	3	10	02-6652-4655	14 Elizabeth Street	$97
Holiday Village Inn	3	1	02-6652-2055	97 Park Beach Road	$85
Zebra Motel	3½	11	02-6652-1588	27 Grafton Street	$85
Midway Motel	2½	4	02-6652-1444	209 Pacific Highway	$75
Chelsea Motor Inn	3½	6	02-6652-2977	106 Grafton Street	$75
Plantation Inn Motel	3	7	02-6552-2566	94 Grafton Street	$75
Premier Motor Inn	3½	14	1-800-622-096	Pacific Highway	$70
Motel Caribbean	3½	15	02-6652-1500	353 High Street	$70
Hawaiian Sands Inn	2½	2	1-800-637-213	Ocean Pde & Park Beach Rd	$65
Bo'Suns Inn	3	3	02-6651-2251	37 Ocean Parade	$65
Town Lodge	3	5	02-6652-1288	110 Grafton Street	$65
Bells Motel		13	02-6652-1493	21 Grafton Street	$65
Hotel Coffs Harbour		8	02-6652-3817	High Street	$50
Motel Formule I		9	02-6650-9101	1a McLean Street	$45

(ii) Backpackers Hostels in Coffs Harbour

Name	Group	No. on Map	Telephone Number	Address	Lowest Price (Dormitory)
Aussietel Backpackers	VIP	19	1800-330-335	312 High Street	$25
Hoey Moey Backpackers	VIP	17	1800-683-322	Ocean Parade	$25
Barracuda Backpackers	Nom/B&W	16	1800-111-514	19 Arthur Street	$22
YHA Backpackers Resort	YHA	18	02-6652-6462	110 Albany Street	$20

MOVING ON
(i) By Train

There are three trains back to Sydney. See the timetable on page 238. There is a train to Brisbane during the night, and at 15:57 there is one to Murwillumbah, with bus connexions to Surfers Paradise and Brisbane.

(ii) By Bus

Buses are as summarised on the next page. There are plenty, as may be seen, including the Keans service to Scone via Armidale and Tamworth. This is a pretty ride up the Great Divide along the *Waterfall Way*, as mentioned above.

Destination	Operator	Via	Distance (km)	Fare	Journey Time	Frequency
Sydney	McCafferty's		596	$86	8½ - 11 hrs	2/day
		Port Macquarie	168	$40	2½ - 2¾ hrs	2/day
Sydney	Greyhound		596	$86	8¾ - 9¾ hrs	3/day
		Port Macquarie	168	$40	3 hrs	1/day
Sydney	Premier		596	$63	8 - 9¾ hrs	3/day
		Port Macquarie	168	$46	2½ hrs	2/day
Pt Macquarie	Keans		173	$26	2¼ hrs	3/week
Brisbane	McCafferty's		428	$62	7 - 7¼ hrs	2/day
		Surfers Paradise	349	$62	5½ - 5¾ hrs	2/day
		Byron Bay	242	$59	3¾ hrs	1/day
Brisbane	Greyhound		441	$62	7 - 8½ hrs	3/day
		Surfers Paradise	353	$62	5½ - 7 hrs	3/day
		Byron Bay	242	$59	3¾ - 5 hrs	3/day
Brisbane	Premier		441	$58	7 - 8¾ hrs	3/day
		Surfers Paradise	353	$58	6 - 7¼ hrs	3/day
		Byron Bay	242	$49	4¼ - 5 hrs	3/day
Scone	Keans		425	$62.50	7¾ hrs	3/week
		Tamworth	289	$57	5½ hrs	3/week

GRAFTON, MACLEAN, YAMBA AND ILUKA

Population 18,500 (Grafton)

10 hrs by train from Sydney (Grafton)
9 hrs 30 mins by bus from Sydney (Grafton)

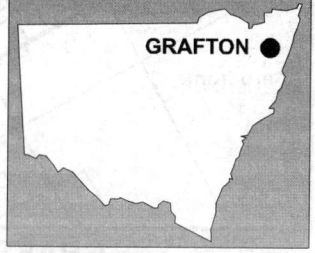

Grafton is a little more than an hour north of Coffs Harbour. It lies on the beautiful **Clarence River** and is, therefore, sometimes subject to flooding. As you approach by train, you will find that the track is elevated to overcome such problems. Until recently, the track rode on a magnificent wooden viaduct as it approached the station, but it has now been moved to something which, although more modern, is less aesthetically delightful. However, parts of the old viaduct remain and can be seen from the train window, or from down below, near the Tourist Centre.

Grafton and the Clarence Valley were discovered by an escaped convict named Richard Craig in 1831. Astutely, he managed to use the information to his advantage by obtaining a pardon and a sum of money for leading others to this site plentiful in good cedar wood. Governor Fitzroy named the place after his grandfather, the Duke of Grafton. By 1885, it had been proclaimed a city.

The present city of 18,500 inhabitants is in two parts, either side of the Clarence River which runs through it. The north, and main, part is Grafton. The south part is, reasonably enough, South Grafton. The railway station is on the south side but, notwithstanding its location, is called Grafton. Between the two parts of the city, there is only a single bridge, shared by rail and road traffic.

As early as 1866, Grafton was starting to pass by-laws to protect its trees, so that there are now 6,500 trees within the city area. **Jacarandas** flower in purple profusion

194 NEW SOUTH WALES

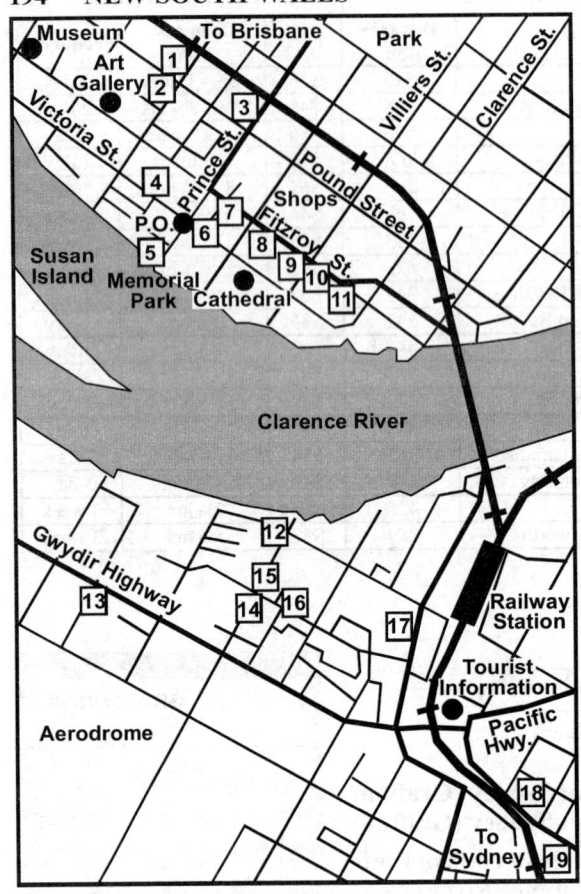

GRAFTON
Numerals indicate accommodation

here every year in November and have provided since 1935 an excuse for an annual festival. This claims to be Australia's longest-running floral festival.

The **Clarence River Tourist Centre** lies just south of the railway station and offers advice, information and even a short video presentation about the area. There is an **Art Gallery** located in Prentice House, a building constructed in 1880 and recently restored. It is open from 10:00 until 16:00, except on Mondays. **Christ Church Cathedral** was built in 1884 and is an impressive building worth visiting.

In the middle of the Clarence River in Grafton lies **Susan Island**. It is the home of what is believed to be the largest **bat colony** in the southern hemisphere. At dusk the bats depart *en masse* to search for dinner. The island can be visited, but there is no regular ferry service. However, the bats' departure can be seen quite well from **Memorial Park** at the southern end of Prince Street.

Grafton can be reached from Sydney by train in ten hours, or a little less. There are three trains each day, but one of them reaches Grafton in the middle of the night. See the timetable on page 94. Grafton is a refuelling and crew-change location for the train, so trains continuing beyond this city stop here for a few minutes. It is also a place for Countrylink bus connexions. There is a connexion from Moree, Inverell and Glen Innes to the day train north on Mondays, Wednesdays and Fridays, and there is a connexion to Byron Bay off the train heading north. The train itself goes to Byron Bay, but the routes followed by bus and train between Grafton and Byron Bay are different. The bus route is the more scenic and interesting. From Brisbane there is only one rail service. It leaves Brisbane at 7:30 (6:30 when New South Wales is operating to daylight saving time) and reaches Grafton at 11:44. See timetable on page 238.

McCafferty's, Greyhound and Premier all run buses between Sydney and Brisbane via Grafton. The journey takes an average of approximately 9½ hours from Sydney and seven hours from Brisbane. Countrylink operates morning bus plus train connexions from Surfers Paradise and Murwillumbah to Grafton, changing at Casino, and a direct bus from Byron Bay to Grafton. There is also a Countrylink bus to Grafton from Moree, via Inverell and Glen Innes, on Mondays, Wednesdays and Fridays.

The bus route between Grafton and Byron Bay is an attractive one and there are several pretty places on the way at which to stay if you prefer somewhere smaller than Grafton and less touristic than Byron Bay. The Countrylink bus passes through Ulmarra, Cowper, Tyndale, Maclean, Palmers Island, Yamba, Chatsworth Island, Woombah, Iluka, Woodburn, Evans Head, Broadwater, Wardell, Ballina and Bangalow, before arriving at Byron Bay, this journey taking nearly four hours. Of these small towns, Maclean, Yamba, Iluka and Ballina are particularly attractive, and all have accommodation, including basic hotels suitable for backpackers (except in Iluka). There are additional local buses operating along this route, or sections of it, run by King Bros.

Maclean thinks that it is a part of Scotland. Even the telegraph poles are decorated with tartans, a different clan on each pole. Rocks from Scotland, as well as Australia, have been used to construct a **cairn** in the town and street signs are in Gaelic as

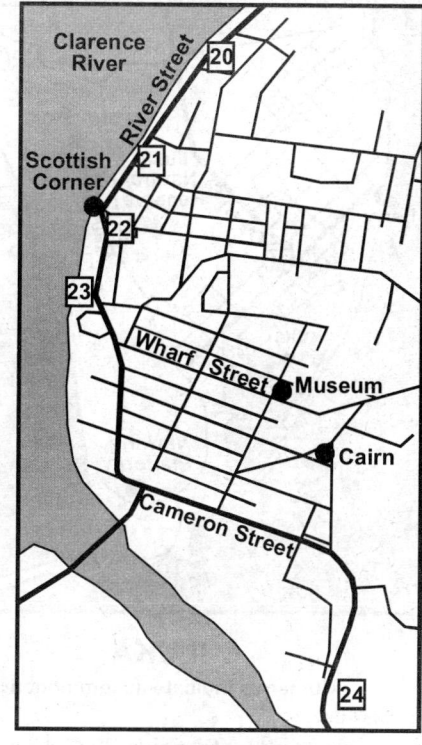

MACLEAN
Numerals indicate accommodation

YAMBA
Numerals indicate accommodation

NEW SOUTH WALES

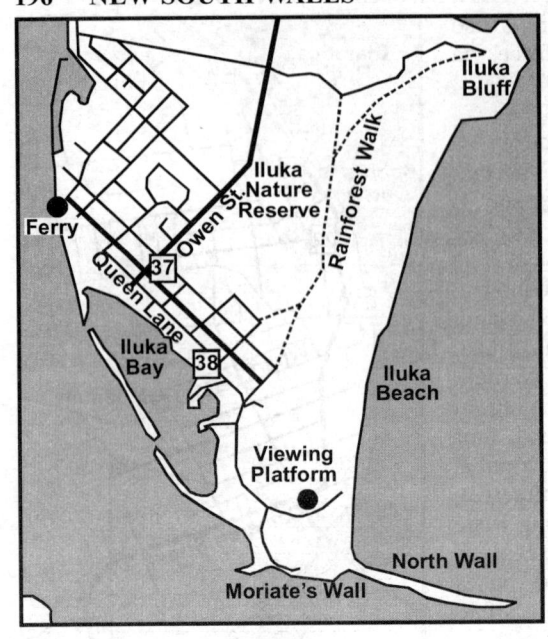

ILUKA
Numerals indicate accommodation

well as English. Maclean is a fishing town. It is the home port for a fleet of ninety prawning boats working in the river estuary, and fishing is a popular and rewarding pastime here.

Yamba is on the south side of the mouth of the Clarence, with Iluka on the north side. A ferry service operates between the two towns four times a day. Both are well known for good fishing and near Iluka there is a large area of rainforest. It is listed as the largest remnant of **littoral rainforest** in the state, surviving by drawing its water from the sea after filtration through the sand, and supporting a great variety of wild life.

Ballina is reached about forty minutes before Byron Bay and is a good alternative to the latter if you want somewhere quieter to stay. There is a regular bus service of ten buses per day between the two towns operated by Blanch's Bus Company. However, the last bus leaves at about 17:00 from each town.

ACCOMMODATION
(i) Hotel Accommodation in Grafton *(see map on page 194)*

Name	Stars	No. on Map	Telephone No.	Address	Lowest Price (Double/Twin)
Clarence Motor Inn	4	9	1-800-245-344	51 Fitzroy Street	$109
Bent Street Motor Inn	4	17	02-6643-4500	62 Bent Street, Sth. Grafton	$95
Fitzroy Grafton Motor Inn	3½	11	02-6642-4477	27 Fitzroy Street	$89
Espana Hotel	3½	19	1-800-668-357	Pacific Highway (South)	$85
Civic Motel	3½	2	02-6642-4922	153 Pound Street	$85
Hi-Way Motel		18	02-6642-1588	Pacific Highway (South)	$65
Abbey Motor Inn	3½	10	02-6642-6122	59 Fitzroy Street	$65
Key Lodge	4	8	02-6642-1944	37 Fitzroy Street	$65
Jacaranda Hotel		1	02-6642-2579	154 Pound Street	$50
Parkview Hotel / Motel		3	02-6642-2375	93 Prince Street	$50
Post Office Hotel		6	02-6642-2199	Victoria Street	$50
Australian		12	02-6642-1566	Thorough St., Sth. Grafton	$50
Great Northern Hotel		16	02-6643-2242	Spring Street, South Grafton	$50
Post Office Hotel		14	02-6642-2032	Skinner Street, Sth. Grafton	$50
Royal Hotel		13	02-6642-3223	Ryan Street, South Grafton	$50
Walkers Marina		15	02-6642-1898	Skinner Street, Sth. Grafton	$50
Roches Family Hotel		4	02-6642-2866	85 Victoria Street	$45
Grafton Hotel		7	02-6642-2000	97 Fitzroy Street	$43
Crown Hotel		5	02-6642-4000	1 Prince Street	$40

GRAFTON, MACLEAN, YAMBA, ILUKA

(ii) Backpackers Hostels in Grafton *(see map on page 194)*

Name	Group	No. on Map	Telephone Number	Address	Lowest Price (Dormitory)
Roches Family Hotel		4	02-6642-2866	85 Victoria Street	$27
Crown Hotel		5	02-6642-4000	1 Prince Street	$20

(iii) Accommodation in Maclean *(see map on page 195)*

Name	Stars	No. on Map	Telephone No.	Address	Lowest Price (Double/Twin)
Waterview Motel		20	02-6645-2494	121 River Street	$75
Maclean Motel		24	02-6645-2473	65 Cameron Street	$75
Clarence Hotel		21	02-6645-2088	173 River Street	$50
Argyle Hotel		22	02-6645-2015	205 River Street	$50
Maclean Hotel		23	02-6645-2412	28 River Street	$50

(iv) Hotel Accommodation in Yamba *(see map on page 195)*

Name	Stars	No. on Map	Telephone No.	Address	Lowest Price (Double/Twin)
Yamba Twin Pines	3	30	1-800-813-033	49 Wooli Street	$105
Moby Dick Resort	4	27	02-6646-2196	27 Yamba Road	$95
Aston Villa	3½	31	1-800-025-690	3 Mulgi Street	$85
Surf		34	02-6646-2200	2 Queen Street	$85
Oyster Shores	3½	25	02-6646-1122	81 Yamba Road	$75
Pegasus	2½	28	02-6646-2314	Angouri & Yamba Roads	$75
Inca Sun		29	02-6646-2144	Wooli & Claude Streets	$75
Blue Dolphin Resort	3½	26	02-6646-2194	Yamba Road	$70
Seaspray	2	33	02-6646-2306	Beach & Clarence Streets	$70
Ocean View Beachfront	3½	35	02-6646-9411	4 Queen Street	$65
Yamba Beach Motel	3	36	02-6646-9411	4 Queen Street	$55
Pacific Hotel		32	02-6646-2466	18 Pilot Street	$50

(v) Backpackers Hostel in Yamba *(see map on page 195)*

Name	Group	No. on Map	Telephone Number	Address	Lowest Price (Dormitory)
Pacific Hotel	VIP	32	02-6646-2466	18 Pilot Street	$20

(vi) Accommodation in Iluka *(see map on page 196)*

Name	Stars	No. on Map	Telephone No.	Address	Lowest Price (Double/Twin)
Iluka Motel	3	37	02-6646-6288	47 Charles Street	$75
Sedgers Reef Hotel		38	02-6646-6122	5 Queen Street	$50

MOVING ON
(i) By Train

Three trains run to Sydney from Grafton every day, although one of them is during the night. The timetable is on page 238. In the opposite direction, the most useful train is that to Murwillumbah at 17:08, with connexions by Countrylink bus to Surfers Paradise and Brisbane. See the timetable on page 94.

198 NEW SOUTH WALES

(ii) By Bus

McCafferty's, Greyhound and Premier all run buses between Sydney and Brisbane via Grafton. Countrylink runs the one service described above connecting off the train from Sydney to places *en route* for Byron Bay. Other services along a similar route are operated during the day by King Bros. There is also a Countrylink bus service to Moree via Glen Innes and Inverell on Tuesdays, Thursdays and Saturdays.

Destination	Operator	Via	Distance (km)	Fare	Journey Time	Frequency
Sydney	McCafferty's		648	$86	9½ - 12 hrs	2/day
		Port Macquarie	250	$41	3½ - 3¾ hrs	2/day
		Coffs Harbour	82	$32	1 hr	2/day
Sydney	Greyhound		678	$86	9¾ - 11 hrs	3/day
		Port Macquarie	250	$41	4 hrs	2/day
		Coffs Harbour	82	$32	1 - 1¼ hrs	3/day
Sydney	Premier		678	$65	9 - 11 hrs	3/day
		Port Macquarie	250	$46	3½ - 3¾ hrs	2/day
		Coffs Harbour	82	$32	1¼ hrs	3/day
Brisbane	McCafferty's		344	$54	6 - 6¼ hrs	2/day
		Surfers Paradise	265	$54	4¾ - 5½ hrs	2/day
		Byron Bay	158	$54	2¾ hrs	1/day
Brisbane	Greyhound		357	$54	6 - 7¼ hrs	3/day
		Surfers Paradise	269	$54	4½ - 5¾ hrs	3/day
		Byron Bay	158	$54	2¾ - 3¾ hrs	3/day
Brisbane	Premier		357	$52	6 - 7¾ hrs	3/day
		Surfers Paradise	269	$52	4¾ - 6¼ hrs	3/day
		Byron Bay	158	$46	3 - 4 hrs	3/day
Byron Bay	Countrylink		190	$34.80	3¾ hrs	1/day
Moree	Countrylink		366	$62.10	5¾ hrs	3/week
		Inverell	224	$37	3¾ hrs	3/week
		Glen Innes	159	$28.30	2¼ hrs	3/week

LISMORE
Population 30,000

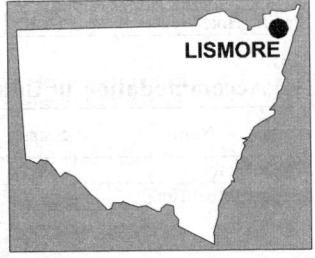

12 hrs by train from Sydney
12 hrs by bus from Sydney
4 hrs 30 mins by bus from Brisbane

Lismore is a city of medium size in an attractive inland setting on the railway line to Murwillumbah. As the main line proceeds north from Sydney, it reaches **Casino** (but no casino there), where it divides. The original line turns east and runs via Byron Bay to Murwillumbah, while the newer spur continues north to Brisbane. Lismore is the first station after Casino on the Murwillumbah line. The day train from Sydney comes this way and the evening train from Murwillumbah (same train) returns via the same route. The night train from Sydney runs on the other line from Casino and goes direct to Brisbane. There is a Countrylink bus connexion from Casino to Lismore at 3:55, arriving here at the rather early hour of 4:20.

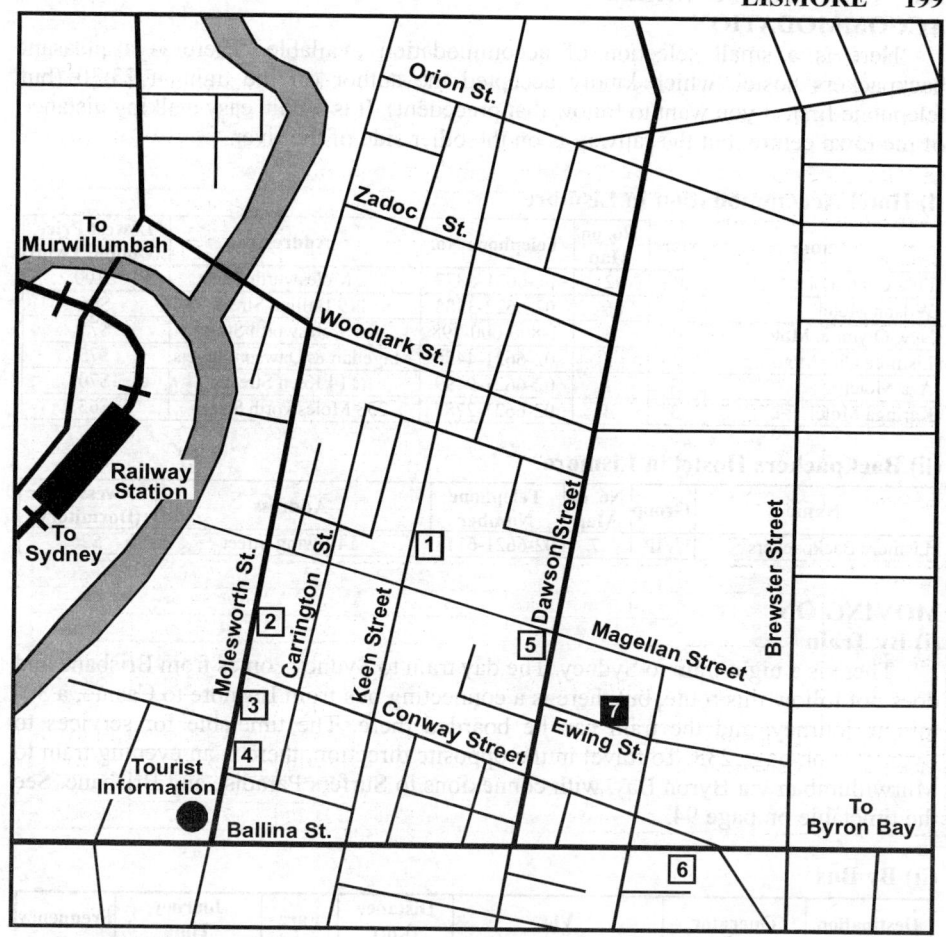

LISMORE

**Black numerals in white boxes indicate hotel accommodation
White numerals in black boxes indicate backpackers hostels**

One Greyhound service between Sydney and Brisbane passes through Lismore, as does one Premier service. The journey from Sydney takes approximately twelve hours. There is no service with McCafferty's. Kirklands operates a bus service between Lismore and Brisbane, a journey of 4½ hours. There are four buses a day, plus one which runs only to Byron Bay. The first part of the journey from here to Brisbane is very pretty.

Lismore is known for its alternative living style. Nearby **Nimbin** was the scene of the *Aquarius Festival* in 1973, promoting options other than city living, and Lismore has become a minor centre for those interested in getting away from big cities. Those people have certainly picked a beautiful spot in the midst of particularly attractive countryside.

NEW SOUTH WALES
ACCOMMODATION

Here is a small selection of accommodation available. There is a pleasant backpackers hostel, which kindly accepted the author off the train at 23:30 (but telephone first, if you want to follow that precedent). It is within easy walking distance of the town centre, but the railway is on the other side of the river.

(i) Hotel Accommodation in Lismore

Name	Stars	No. on Map	Telephone No.	Address	Lowest Price (Double/Twin)
Flag Centrepoint Motel	3½	2	02-6621-8877	202 Molesworth Street	$100
Wilson Motel	3½	6	02-6622-3383	119 Ballina Street	$85
New Olympic Motel	3½	3	1-800-000-298	244 Molesworth Street	$75
Lismore City Motor Inn	2½	5	02-6621-4455	Magellan & Dawson Streets	$75
Aza Motel	3	1	02-6621-9499	114 Keen Street	$70
Karinga Motel	3	4	02-6621-2787	258 Molesworth Street	$65

(ii) Backpackers Hostel in Lismore

Name	Group	No. on Map	Telephone Number	Address	Lowest Price (Dormitory)
Lismore Backpackers	VIP	7	02-6621-6118	14 Ewing Street	$25

MOVING ON
(i) By Train

There is a night train to Sydney. The day train to Sydney comes from Brisbane and does not follow this route, but there is a connecting bus from Lismore to Casino, a 30-minute journey, and the train can be boarded there. The timetable for services to Sydney is on page 238. To travel in the opposite direction, there is an evening train to Murwillumbah via Byron Bay, with connexions to Surfers Paradise and Brisbane. See the timetable on page 94.

(ii) By Bus

Destination	Operator	Via	Distance (km)	Fare	Journey Time	Frequency
Sydney	Greyhound		776	$102	11½ hrs	1/day
		Port Macquarie	250	$71	5½ hrs	1/day
		Coffs Harbour	180	$53	3 hrs	1/day
Sydney	Premier		776	$90	12 hrs	1/day
		Port Macquarie	250	$63	5¼ hrs	1/day
		Coffs Harbour	180	$46	3 hrs	1/day
Sydney	Countrylink		826	$107.90	12½ hrs	1/day
		Casino	33	$6.50	30 mins	1/day
Brisbane	Greyhound		233	$43	5½ hrs	1/day
		Surfers Paradise	145	$33	4 hrs	1/day
		Byron Bay	34	$27	2 hrs	1/day
Brisbane	Premier		233	$38	5¼ hrs	1/day
		Surfers Paradise	145	$36	3¾ hrs	1/day
		Byron Bay	34	$15	1½ hrs	1/day
Brisbane	Kirklands		233	$37	4½ hrs	4/day
		Surfers Paradise	145	$35	3 hrs	2/day
		Byron Bay	34	$14.70	1 - 1¼ hrs	5/day
Byron Bay	Countrylink		34	$8.70	1¼ hrs	1/day

BYRON BAY
Population 6,000

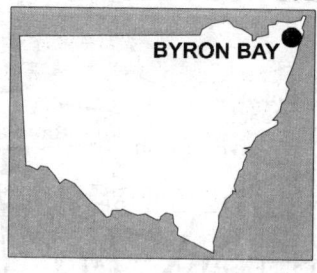

13 hrs by train from Sydney
12 hrs by bus from Sydney
3 hrs 30 mins by bus from Brisbane

Byron Bay is a beach resort in a beautiful setting and one which is extremely popular with young visitors. It is one of the 'in' places, an attribute which has caused it to grow and prosper in the last few years.

Captain Cook noticed Cape Byron as he passed by in 1770, and it was he who named the location. However, it was not settled by Europeans until nearly a century later. The area where the town now stands was originally a swamp, a little of which remains on the eastern side. A jetty was built at the end of the nineteenth century and a steamer service provided to Sydney. Then Byron Bay became a whaling town and a whaling station was built at Belongil Beach.

In 1921, the *S.S. Wollongbar*, a passenger liner which could accommodate 300 passengers, was wrecked here just off Belongil Beach. It remains buried in the sands, causing a surf break by its presence, but all that can be seen are the boilers, visible at low tide.

Byron Bay is small and compact, so finding one's way around is easy. The railway station and bus stop are adjacent to the **Byron Visitor Centre**. Backpackers hostel vans are usually waiting nearby to invite and convey potential guests. There are two shops offering Internet facilities just nearby, and both also sell bus tickets and local tours. On the railway platform is the Rails Bar and just down the road is the Great Northern Hotel which usually has a band, often a well-known one, on duty in the evenings.

As one might anticipate, Byron Bay is a town replete with accommodation, but it is not necessarily cheap, since demand keeps up well with, and sometimes even outstrips, supply. Even backpackers accommodation tends to be rather more expensive than one might expect.

This small town caters very much to the backpacker market, so there are pubs, and a multitude of different and mostly moderately priced food establishments.

As for the beaches, which are one of the main attractions here, **Main Beach** stretches a long way to the east of the town, and **Belongil Beach** a long way to the west and both of them are populated only near the town centre. Main Beach, in particular, is a beautiful stretch of curved sand with cliffs behind, which is very appealing. It is the start of a good walk to the lighthouse, which you should not omit from your itinerary.

Lighthouse Walk

Start from the car park outside the Beach Hotel, at the end of Jonson Street. The walk covers about eight kilometres and takes 2½ hours.

First, walk along **Main Beach** and then **Clark's Beach** as far as you can go. This is a distance of nearly two kilometres. At the end, you will find **The Pass**, and you can walk up to a car park and viewpoint. Take the time to divert the few metres necessary to obtain the views from both of the **lookout points**. They are worth sampling. Then continue on to **Watego's Beach** and beyond. At the end of the beach, you start to climb once more, and then come to a point of decision: up or down. It seems a shame to waste the energy already expended in climbing up some way, but we shall go down, passing

202 NEW SOUTH WALES

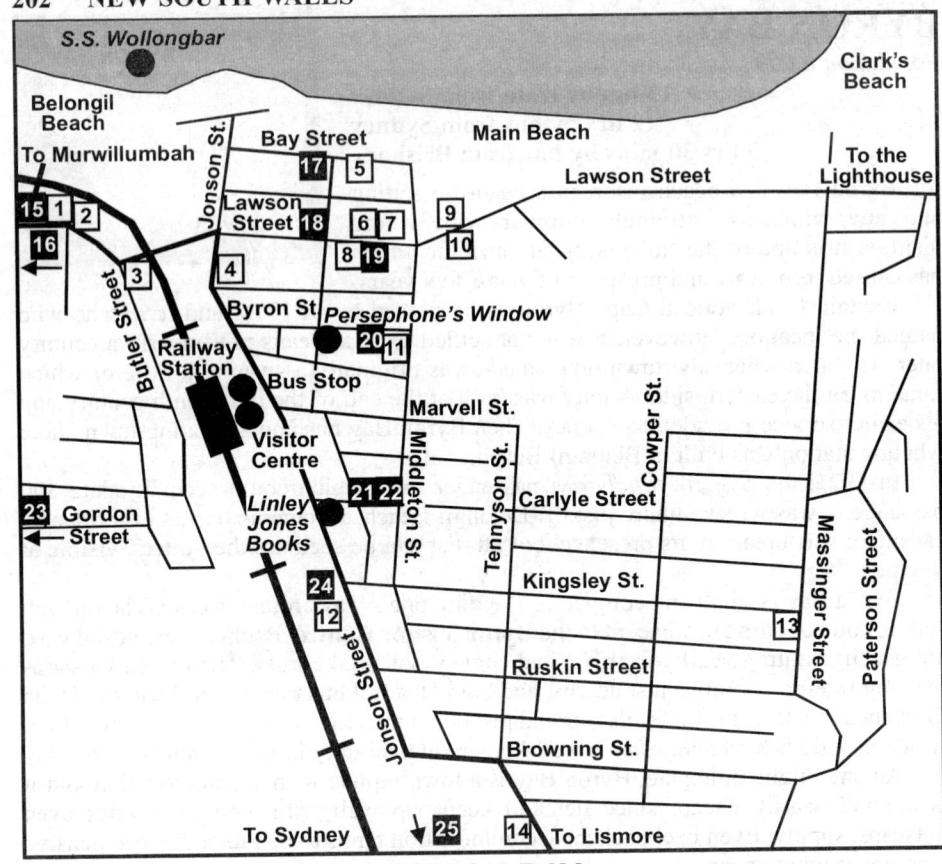

BYRON BAY
**Black numerals in white boxes indicate hotel accommodation
White numerals in black boxes indicate backpackers hostels**

a track on the left which leads to **Little Watego's Beach**, and trek out to the end of the peninsula, where there is another good view. The author's impression when here was that this was the **most easterly point** in mainland Australia, and I therefore hopped from rock to rock out to sea, trying to get as far east as possible. Please do the same, if you feel sufficiently energetic. Having done so, however, and returned to look at the map, I was not so sure whether this peninsula or the next headland was really the most easterly point. However, the next is inaccessible, so I was content to believe that I had stood on the most easterly point in this huge country (or nearly). Please join me.

Return from the easterly peninsula, and now we have a good stiff climb up the cliff. We reach another **lookout** after a while with perhaps the best view yet, which is a good excuse for a short rest. Then more climbing, soon rewarded by yet another **lookout**, this time over what might be a point even further east. If you look carefully and spend a little time on this grassy slope, you are likely to see dolphins frolicking in the ocean far below. There is no doubt that dolphins have extrovert characters and enjoy displaying their gymnastics to the humans who can never rival them in agility, grace or beauty. If it is winter, you may also be able to see whales from this point.

The **lighthouse** is already clearly in view at the top of the slope and a little more exertion brings us up to it. It has been shining its warnings out across these waters for a century now, and is still in use. The headland here is 94 metres above sea level, and the lighthouse is a further 22 metres high. It was built in 1901, made of concrete blocks. It uses a 1000-watt tungsten halogen lamp of 2.2 million candle-power, one of the most powerful lights in the southern hemisphere. It flashes every fifteen seconds and has a range of 27 nautical miles. The mirror is two metres in diameter and it continues to revolve even during the day to minimise the fire hazard.

If we proceed past the lighthouse, we shall come to buildings housing a tea room and souvenir shop and the office of the National Parks and Wildlife Service, and another good view from the car parking area outside. A road comes up this far and we now follow it as we commence our return by a different route. From here we can see out over **Tallow Beach** stretching away down the coast.

The path soon diverges from the road and passes through a shaded forest area, up a knoll and then back down to the road by **Captain Cook's Lookout**, not that he ever did look out here, but we can, and get our last good view of the walk. From here, we can stroll back to town along the cliff top as an alternative to the beach.

This is a very rewarding walk, not requiring unreasonable exertion. If you visit Byron Bay, as most do, you should certainly try it. It will probably improve your impression of the locality.

South of Byron Bay are some quieter beaches. **King's Beach**, which is beyond walking distance, and secluded, is a nudist beach. Beyond that is **Seven Mile Beach**, and then, eventually, we come to **Lennox Head**, where there is Lennox Head Backpackers Hostel.

Local buses here are operated by Blanch's Bus Company and run from Byron Bay to **Mullumbimby** in the north and to **Ballina** in the south. There are ten services per day to and from Ballina. There is also a Byron Bay town service which runs as far north as Sunrise Beach and as far south as Suffolk Park and operates every hour. In addition, Kirklands runs five buses a day to Lismore, and Premier and Greyhound have one each.

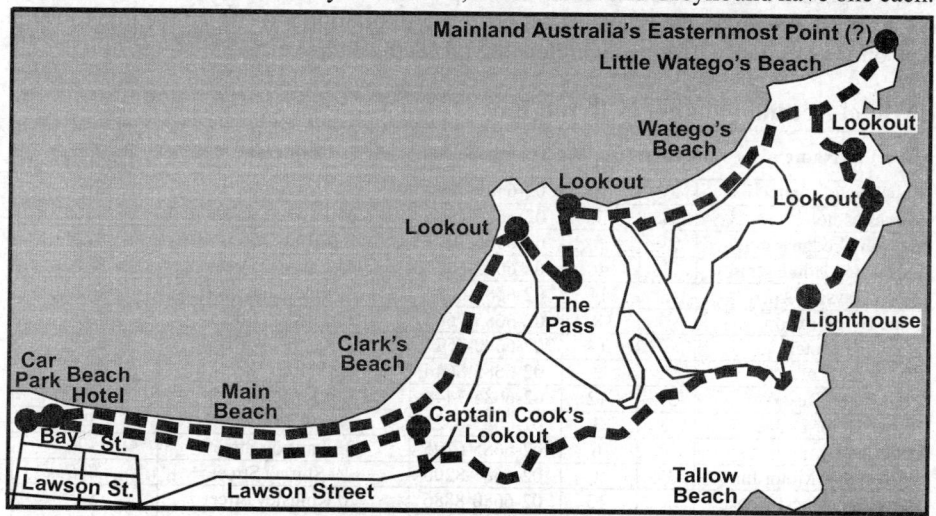

LIGHTHOUSE WALK

204 NEW SOUTH WALES

To reach Byron Bay, there is a daily train from Sydney. There is also a night train which runs to Brisbane with a connexion provided by Countrylink bus from Casino to Byron Bay. The timetable for these services is on page 94. From Brisbane and Surfers Paradise, there are evening bus connexions to Murwillumbah, from where it is an hour by train to Byron Bay.

McCafferty's, Greyhound and Premier all have services between Sydney and Brisbane which pass through Surfers Paradise and Byron Bay. In addition, Kirklands and Suncoast Pacific operate buses between Surfers Paradise and Byron Bay. The Kirklands buses start from Brisbane. The Suncoast Pacific bus (only one) starts from the Sunshine Coast (Noosa Heads) and does not go through the centre of Brisbane, although it stops at the airport.

BOOKSHOPS

Persephone's Window   *Byron and Fletcher Streets*
Linley Jones   *Shop 2, Carlyle Street*

As one might, perhaps, anticipate, in a town where nearly all the street names are literary in origin, there are two fine independent bookshops of character here. *Linley Jones*, at the meeting place of Thomas Carlyle and Ben Jonson, is a well stocked shop, and *Persephone's Window* has a wonderful atmosphere for browsing and, moreover, the two Persephones promise to give 10% discount to anybody producing this book and showing this paragraph. Both of these bookshops are marked on the map on page 202.

ACCOMMODATION

Byron Bay can be a difficult place for accommodation. The author arrived here at 21:00 on a Friday evening and had a real struggle to locate what appeared to be the last backpackers bed left in the town. Telephoning ahead is obviously a good idea here.

Rates given below for higher class accommodation should not be regarded as fixed. More than in other locations, prices vary greatly in Byron Bay. At slack times it may be possible to find considerably lower prices, but at peak periods rates shoot up. By contrast, however, the backpackers hostels will be found to charge the rates stated. It is only availability of space which is the problem in this case.

(i) Hotel Accommodation in Byron Bay

Name	Stars	No. on Map	Telephone No.	Address	Lowest Price (Double/Twin)
Bay Beach Motel	3½	10	02-6685-6090	32 Lawson Street	$180
Waves Motel	4	7	02-6685-5966	35 Lawson Street	$165
Bayview Lodge Units	2½	5	02-6685-7073	22 Bay Street	$125
Byron Bay Holiday Inn	3½	9	02-6685-6373	45 Lawson Street	$120
Byron Bayside Apts.	3	11	02-6685-6004	14 Middleton Street	$120
Cape Byron Resort		8	02-6685-7663	16 Lawson Street	$110
Dolphins Motel		14	02-6680-9577	32 Bangalow Road	$110
Outrigger Bay		2	02-6685-8646	9 Shirley Steet	$105
Lord Byron Resort	3½	12	02-6685-7444	120 Jonson Street	$105
Byron Motor Lodge	3	3	02-6685-6522	Lawson & Butler Streets	$95
Hibiscus	2	6	02-6685-6195	33 Lawson Street	$90
Wollongbar Motor Inn	3½	1	02-6685-8200	19 Shirley Street	$85
Byron Bay Guest House		13	02-6680-8886	70 Kingsley Street	$85
Great Northern Hotel		4	02-6685-6454	Jonson Street	$55

BYRON BAY

(ii) Backpackers Hostels in Byron Bay

Name	Group	No. on Map	Telephone Number	Address	Lowest Price (Dormitory)
Blue Iguana Beachhouse	B&W	17	02-6685-5298	14 Bay Street	$28
Backpackers Inn on Beach	VIP	15	02-6685-8231	29 Shirley Street	$25
Belongil Beachhouse	VIP	16	02-6685-7868	Childe Street	$25
Aquarius Backpackers		19	1-800-028-909	16 Lawson Street	$25
B'packers Holiday Village	VIP	24	1-800-350-388	116 Jonson Street	$25
Cape Byron Lodge		25	02-6685-6445	78 Bangalow Road	$25
Main Beach Backpackers	Nom	18	1-800-150-233	19 Lawson Street	$24
The Bunkhouse		21	02-6685-8311	1 Carlyle Street	$24
Arts Factory Lodge	VIP	23	02-6685-7709	Skinners Shoot Road	$22
J's Bay Y.H.A.	YHA	22	1-800-678-195	7 Carlyle Street	$20
Cape Byron Y.H.A.	YHA	20	1-800-652-627	Byron & Middleton Streets	$19
Lennox Head Beachhouse	YHA		02-6687-7636	3 Ross Street, Lennox Head	$19

MOVING ON
(i) By Train

There is an evening train to Sydney, arriving the following morning. The day train does not pass this way, so there is a Countrylink connecting bus which runs to Grafton, where one transfers to the train. See the timetable on page 238. In the opposite direction, the train runs to Murwillumbah, from where there are connecting buses to Surfers Paradise and Brisbane. The timetable for this service is on page 94.

(ii) By Bus

There are plenty of buses from Byron Bay. McCafferty's, Greyhound and Premier all operate services to Sydney. The same companies have buses to Surfers Paradise and Brisbane, and are joined by Kirklands. Suncoast Pacific operates one bus per day to the Sunshine Coast (Noosa Heads) via Surfers Paradise and Brisbane Airport.

Destination	Operator	Via	Distance (km)	Fare	Journey Time	Frequency
Sydney	McCafferty's		806	$103	12¼ - 14¾ hrs	2/day
		Port Macquarie	400	$76	6 - 6¼ hrs	2/day
		Coffs Harbour	232	$59	3¾ hrs	2/day
Sydney	Greyhound		828	$103	13¼ - 13¾ hrs	3/day
		Port Macquarie	400	$76	7 hrs	2/day
		Coffs Harbour	232	$59	4 - 4½ hrs	3/day
Sydney	Premier		828	$90	12 - 14 hrs	3/day
		Port Macquarie	400	$63	7 - 7¼ hrs	2/day
		Coffs Harbour	232	$49	4¼ - 5 hrs	3/day
Sydney	Countrylink		874	$107.90	14¼ hrs	1/day
		Grafton	190	$34.80	3¾ hrs	1/day
Brisbane	McCafferty's		189	$39	3¼ - 3½ hrs	2/day
		Surfers Paradise	110	$33	1¾ hrs	2/day
Brisbane	Greyhound		192	$39	3¼ - 3¾ hrs	4/day
		Surfers Paradise	111	$33	1¾ - 2 hrs	4/day
Brisbane	Premier		192	$35	3 - 3¾ hrs	3/day
		Surfers Paradise	111	$29	1¾ - 2¼ hrs	3/day
Brisbane	Kirklands		192	$33	3¼ - 3½ hrs	4/day
		Surfers Paradise	111	$30	2¼ hrs	2/day
Sunshine Cst	S'coast Pacific		347	$47.50	6½ hrs	1/day
		Surfers Paradise	111	$25.50	2½ hrs	1/day
Lismore	Kirklands		34	$14.70	1 - 1¼ hrs	5/day

NEW SOUTH WALES
CABARITA BEACH
Population 2,500
13 hrs 30 mins by train and bus from Sydney

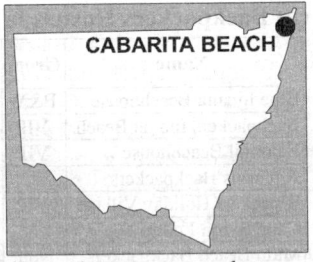

"Tell me a great place that nobody else knows about." It is one of the frequent requests from travellers. Well, Cabarita Beach is not exactly unknown, but it is just far enough off the beaten track to make it a rewarding place to visit if you do not always wish to be in the company of the masses. Better still, there is an excellent place to stay, whatever your budget. This place is the Emu Park Motel, which caters for backpackers by putting them three or four at a time into motel rooms, and caters for motel guests by giving them their own rooms at very reasonable rates. The owner built the premises with the idea of providing backpackers with something superior and took motel guests as rather an afterthought, but his motel has won several awards for offering good value. Unfortunately, his backpacker business has been damaged by the fact that the long-distance buses no longer pass this way, so Cabarita Beach has become something of a backwater. That, of course, is to our advantage, and if you stay here, it will be to the advantage of Emu Park too, which will be well-merited reward. If you stay for three nights, the third is free, and Cabarita Beach is worth three nights.

As one might anticipate, the **beach** is the main attraction here. It stretches for several kilometres and is always sparsely populated. When the author strolled onto this beach, I was hailed by an eccentric Englishman requesting me to hold his kite while he attempted to launch a second, and was trapped indefinitely. **Norries Head** defines the southern extremity of Cabarita Beach and gives a good view of the coastline, a view out to sea, and a view of those surfing on either side. There is also, nearby, a very short walk of about five minutes through the last remaining patch of dense **littoral forest**.

There are only two long-distance bus services which pass through Cabarita Beach now. One is operated by Countrylink and is a connexion off the night train from Sydney. Change at Casino and take the bus at 3:50. It takes nearly two hours to reach here. Note that the stop is called **Bogangar** by Countrylink, not Cabarita Beach. After alighting from the bus, walk back a short distance to find Emu Park Motel.

The other service is operated between Byron Bay and the Sunshine Coast by Suncoast Pacific. It travels south from Noosa Heads in the morning via Brisbane Airport and Surfers Paradise, and travels back in the afternoon, leaving Byron Bay at 13:30 (Queensland time. In summer this is 14:30 in New South Wales).

Because of the shortage of public transport, the owner of Emu Park Motel will pick up guests from Murwillumbah or Coolangatta until 19:00.

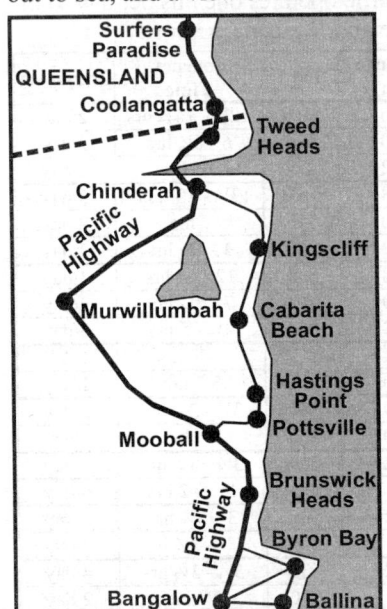

AREA AROUND CABARITA BEACH

CABARITA BEACH 207

There is a local bus service provided by Surfside Buses, which is the company operating all the way up the coast to Surfers Paradise and beyond. To reach Surfers Paradise from here, take a bus no. 603 to Tweed Heads, or just as far as Kingscliff, if you prefer, and then a no. 1 from either of those two changing points. There are more buses from Tweed Heads than from Kingscliff. You can purchase a one-day ticket for Surfside buses for $10. Three days, though, is better value at $25. Five days costs $35, seven days $43, ten days $50 and fourteen days $60.

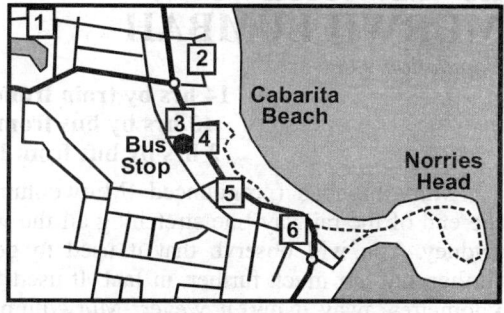

CABARITA BEACH
Numerals indicate accommodation

ACCOMMODATION
(i) Hotel Accommodation in Cabarita Beach

Name	Stars	No. on Map	Telephone No.	Address	Lowest Price (Double/Twin)
International Hotel	3½	4	02-6676-1555	Coast Rd. & Pandanus Pde.	$145
Cabarita Gardens Resort	3½	1	02-6676-2000	Tamarind Avenue	$109
Diamond Beach Resort	3½	6	02-6676-3232	105 Coast Road	$105
Beachfront Hideaway	3	2	02-6676-1444	21 Cypress Crescent	$95
Emu Park Motel		5	02-6676-1190	77 Coast Road	$50
Cabarita Beach House	2½	3	02-6676-1633	39 Coast Road	$45

(ii) Backpackers Hostel in Cabarita Beach

Name	Group	No. on Map	Telephone Number	Address	Lowest Price (Dormitory)
Emu Park Motel	VIP/B&W	5	02-6676-1190	77 Coast Road	$21

MOVING ON

Countrylink operates a popular bus plus train connexion via Casino to Sydney, allowing passengers to leave early in the morning and be in Sydney in the late evening. The timetable is on page 238. There is also a Countrylink bus in the opposite direction very early in the morning (5:49) offering a cheap way of reaching Surfers Paradise.

Suncoast Pacific operates to Byron Bay and to the Sunshine Coast via Surfers Paradise and Brisbane Airport. This service is quite expensive for short distances, however. To Byron Bay, even with a backpackers' discount, will cost $18.

Bus Services from Cabarita Beach

Destination	Operator	Via	Distance (km)	Fare	Journey Time	Frequency
Sydney	Countrylink		938	$115.50	14 hrs	1/day
		Casino	145	$25	2 hrs	1/day
Sunshine Cst	S'coast Pacific		283	$41.50	5¾ hrs	1/day
		Surfers Paradise	47	$20	1½ hrs	1/day
Surfers P'dse	Countrylink		44	$6.50	1 hr	1/day
Byron Bay	S'coast Pacific		64	$20	45 mins	1/day

NEW SOUTH WALES
MURWILLUMBAH
Population 9,000

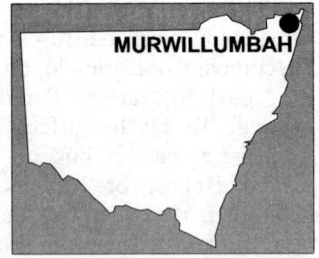

14 hrs by train from Sydney
13 hrs by bus from Sydney
2 hrs by bus from Brisbane

Murwillumbah (pronounced 'Murwoolumbah') is the end of the railway line stretching all the way from Sydney. You will observe that it used to go a little further, but not much further, in fact. It used to continue to some timber mills a few kilometres away. Now, however, Murwillumbah is the single-platformed terminus which never sees a Countrylink passenger train during daylight hours. The daily train from Sydney arrives at 21:00 and departs again for its long journey back at 21:50. Bus connexions convey passengers onward from here to Surfers Paradise and Brisbane.

Actually, however, Murwillumbah is a pleasant place to stay and there is no need to hurry on to more famous locations. For backpackers, there is an attractive youth hostel here, a former sea captain's cottage perched right on the bank of the beautiful Tweed River. Of course, location is not the only standard by which to judge hostels. In the author's opinion, the owner or manager is the most important factor. If you agree, you will not be disappointed here. If conditions are suitable, there will be a campfire in the evening and instructions will be given on how to toast marshmallows (supplied). Ice-cream will follow. However, if the youth hostel does not appeal, there are both motels and economical hotels in the town. The Imperial Hotel, in particular, has an impressive look to it.

The railway station sits on the eastern side of the river, with the **Visitor Centre** just across the road. The town itself is on the western bank, so walk across the bridge. If your destination is the youth hostel, you will be able to see it to your right from the bridge.

One of the attractions of Murwillumbah is **Mt. Warning**, which is only a short distance away. It was named by Captain Cook in 1770, as he sailed past. When mariners saw this mountain, they would be warned of the dangerous reefs all the way along the coast. Of course, the mountain already had a name. To the aborigines of the area, it was known as Wollumbin, and it was, and still is, a sacred place.

Mt. Warning is an extinct volcano, and the Tweed Valley is its caldera, which is to say the depression left behind after erosion of the deposits from the eruptions. The central cone remains, as do the outside walls of the deposits. The diameter of this caldera is some forty kilometres, making it one of the largest in the world. Some claim that it is the largest, but Mt. Aso in Japan makes the same claim and, to the author at least, the Mt. Aso crater seems bigger. One claim which cannot be contested, though, is that the summit is the first place in mainland Australia to see the sun rising on a new day.

Mt. Warning was formed about 23 million years ago, the author is reliably informed, not having been around at the time to check, and was active for some three million years. It rose to about 2,000 metres high and the deposits of volcanic ash reached as far as Lismore. However, twenty million years of erosion have taken their toll, so now Mt. Warning stands 1,157 metres and most of the ash has disappeared.

The mountain can be climbed, but first you have to get to it. If you are staying at the youth hostel, you are lucky again. The owner will provide transport, upon request,

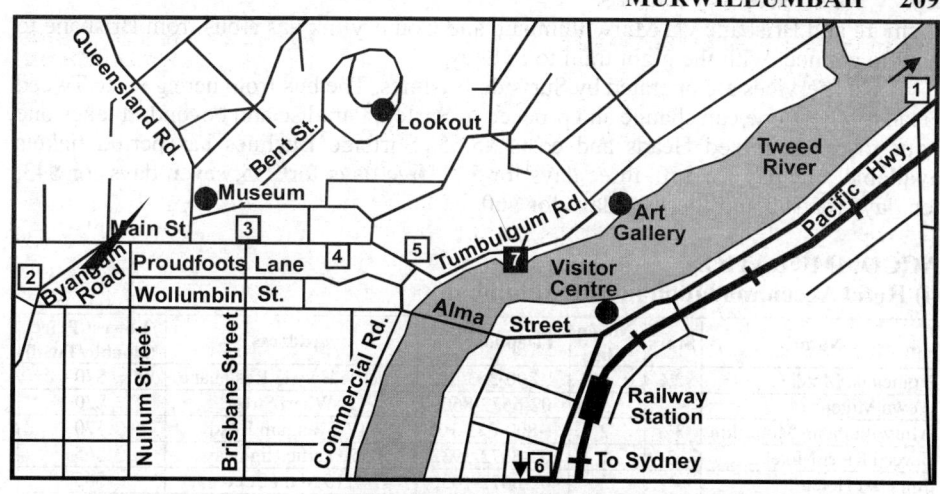

MURWILLUMBAH

Black numerals in white boxes indicate hotel accommodation
White numerals in black boxes indicate backpackers hostels

to **Breakfast Creek**, from where the track starts. If not, there is a bus, but it is a school bus, so arrangements must be made in advance, and it does not go all the way to the start of the track, but near enough. Also you must be sure to complete the walk in time to catch the bus back in the afternoon, which is quite possible for those in reasonable physical condition.

The walk from Breakfast Creek to the summit and back is nine kilometres, and strenuous because of the steep slopes near the top. It requires about five hours.

Although it was mentioned above that no Countrylink train uses Murwillumbah station during daylight hours, there is a private service, known as *V-Ritz Rail*, which utilises the tracks with its restored 1930s style train. This is not a steam train. It is hauled by an old diesel engine. And, as you might have anticipated, it is not cheap.

There are various options. A single trip to Byron Bay costs $30 and a return costs $40. To Bangalow costs $35 single and $45 return, including morning tea. The train, though, goes as far as Lismore. If you go that far, you will get lunch on the train included, but will pay $90 return. The train departs from Murwillumbah at 9:30, reaching Lismore at 12:15. It returns from Lismore at 12:45 and arrives back at Murwillumbah at 15:15, but it operates according to Queensland time, so an hour later in the summer by New South Wales time. If you want to start from and return to the Gold Coast, a bus is provided at a cost of $10 return.

Another of Murwillumbah's claims to fame is that it offers the richest portrait prize in the world. There is a small, but good, art gallery just down the road from the youth hostel. The **Tweed River Art Gallery** is an old house in a beautiful setting beside the river. Admission to the gallery is free and it contains some of the prize-winning portraits from previous annual competitions.

There are plenty of long-distance bus services between Sydney and Brisbane passing through Murwillumbah, operated by McCafferty's, Greyhound and Premier. In addition to the day train from Sydney, Countrylink has a bus connexion at Casino with the night train from Sydney to Brisbane. Kirklands operates four buses a day between

210 NEW SOUTH WALES

Lismore and Brisbane via Murwillumbah, and Countrylink has a bus from Brisbane to here to connect with the night train to Sydney.

Local services are operated by Surfside Buslines. The bus from here goes to Tweed Heads, where one can change and proceed to Surfers Paradise and beyond. It takes one hour to reach Tweed Heads and costs $5.65. Surfside Buslines has period tickets available: one day for $10, three days for $25, five days for $35, seven days for $43, ten days for $50 and fourteen days for $60.

ACCOMMODATION
(i) Hotel Accommodation in Murwillumbah

Name	Stars	No. on Map	Telephone No.	Address	Lowest Price (Double/Twin)
Poinciana Motel	3½	6	1-800-353-987	Pacific Hwy & Rose Lane	$70
Town Motel		5	02-6672-8600	3 Wharf Street	$70
Murwillumbah Motor Inn	3½	2	1-800-023-105	17 Byangum Road	$70
Tweed River Motel	3	1	02-6672-3933	55 Pacific Highway	$65
Imperial Hotel		3	02-6672-1036	115 Main Street	$55
Courthouse Hotel		4	02-6672-1044	60 Main Street	$55

(ii) Backpackers Hostel in Murwillumbah

Name	Group	No. on Map	Telephone Number	Address	Lowest Price (Dormitory)
Riverside Backpackers	YHA	7	02-6672-3763	1 Tumbulgum Road	$21

MOVING ON
(i) By Train

The train back to Sydney leaves in the evening. In the morning, there is a Countrylink bus connexion to Casino, from where one joins the day train to Sydney. The timetable is on page 238. To go north, there are Countrylink buses to Brisbane and Surfers Paradise (separate buses), connecting with the arrival of the train from Sydney. The timetable for these services is on page 94.

(ii) By Bus

Bus, or bus plus train, services are operated to Sydney by three companies and to Brisbane by four.

Destination	Operator	Via	Distance (km)	Fare	Journey Time	Frequency
Sydney	Greyhound		887	$103	14¼ - 14¾ hrs	2/day
		Port Macquarie	459	$76	7¾ hrs	2/day
		Coffs Harbour	291	$59	5 hrs	2/day
		Byron Bay	47	$29	1 hr	3/day
Sydney	Premier		887	$90	13 – 15 hrs	3/day
		Port Macquarie	459	$63	7¾ - 8¼ hrs	2/day
		Coffs Harbour	291	$52	5¼ - 6 hrs	3/day
		Byron Bay	59	$15	1 hr	3/day
Sydney	Countrylink		928	$115.50	14¼ hrs	1/day
		Casino	135	$25	2¼ hrs	1/day

Destination	Operator	Via	Distance (km)	Fare	Journey Time	Frequency
Brisbane	Greyhound		148	$30	2½ - 2¾ hrs	3/day
		Surfers Paradise	60	$19	1 hr	3/day
Brisbane	Premier		148	$28	2¼ – 2¾ hrs	3/day
		Surfers Paradise	60	$17	1 - 1½ hrs	3/day
Brisbane	Kirklands		148	$26	2¼ - 2¾ hrs	4/day
		Surfers Paradise	60	$18.20	1¼ hrs	2/day
Brisbane	Countrylink		135	$20.70	1¾ hrs	1/day
		Surfers Paradise	56	$8.70	1 hr	1/day
Lismore	Kirklands		81	$19.70	2 - 2¼ hrs	4/day
		Byron Bay	47	$15.60	1 hr	4/day

TWEED HEADS
Population 37,000

14 hrs 30 mins by train and bus from Sydney
13 hrs 30 mins by bus from Sydney
2 hrs by bus from Brisbane

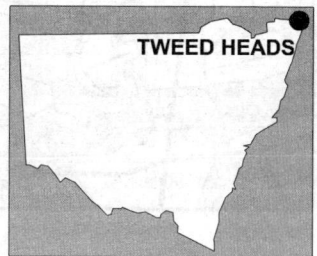

Tweed Heads is the end of New South Wales. This city is almost indivisible from its Queensland neighbour, Coolangatta. Man has, however, contrived to divide the two. First of all, you will find, in the middle of the road, a huge **obelisk** announcing the border. It is, of course, not entirely convenient to have such an administrative division in the middle of a main street, and it is especially inconvenient when, during the summer, the two towns keep different times. Thus the author sold some books to *Collins Bookshop* in Tweed Heads, then walked down the street and found that there was an hour to wait before the bookshop in Coolangatta opened. The locals, though, say that it is handy to be able to stagger across the border and get an extra hour of drinking time.

Coolangatta is the larger of the two neighbours, and is the better place to look for accommodation, but the long-distance bus stop is in Tweed Heads. The airport is called Coolangatta, but has the border between the two states cutting across the runway. This airport, incidentally, is accepted by Qantas as an international gateway. In other words, although there are no international flights to or from here, you may arrive from overseas at another airport and catch a flight to here without additional charge. This ruling does not apply to all types of ticket, but it does apply to some.

This is a beach area, and **beaches** stretch all the way up the 'Gold Coast' from here to Surfers Paradise and beyond. None of them is very crowded, especially in the southern part.

Countrylink runs a connecting bus to Tweed Heads from Murwillumbah upon arrival of the day train from Sydney. There are three buses waiting there and the one for Tweed Heads is that labelled Robina. There is also a connexion from the night train, for which you have to alight at Casino at a very early hour.

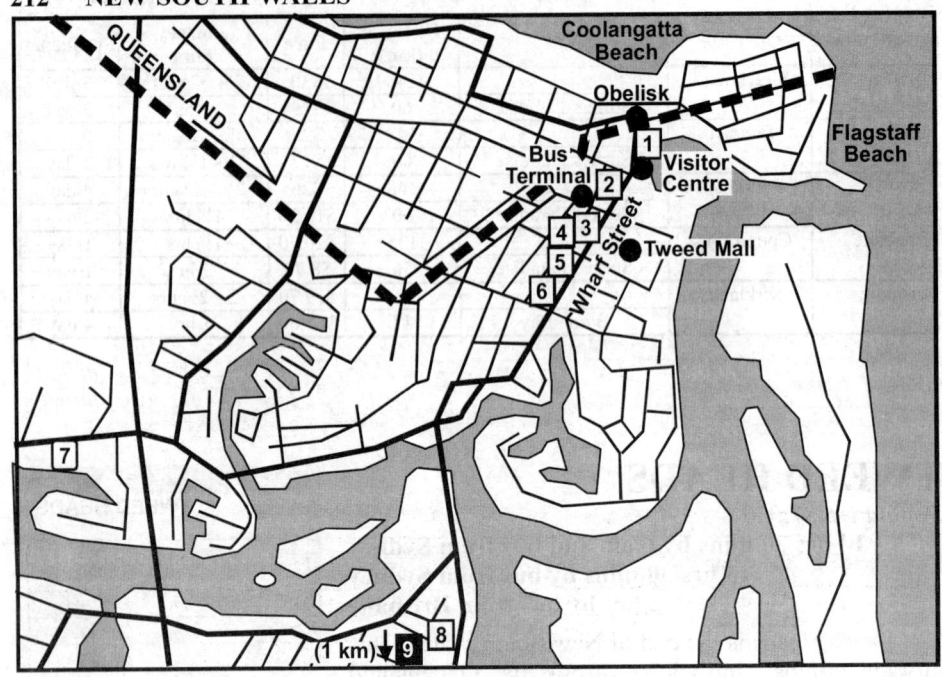

TWEED HEADS

Black numerals in white boxes indicate hotel accommodation
White numerals in black boxes indicate backpackers hostels

There are buses from Sydney and Brisbane operated by McCafferty's, Greyhound and Premier, and there are additional services between Lismore and Brisbane via Tweed Heads operated by Kirklands, between the Sunshine Coast and Byron Bay via Tweed Heads operated by Suncoast Pacific, and between Brisbane and Tweed Heads operated by Coachtrans.

Local bus services are provided by Surfside Buslines, including service no. 1, which operates twenty-four hours a day between Tweed Heads and Surfers Paradise (and further). During the day this bus runs every ten minutes. At night it runs every hour. The fare to Surfers Paradise is $5.25. Period tickets are also available for use on any Surfside bus. A one-day ticket costs $10, three days $25, five days $35, seven days $43, ten days $50 and fourteen days $60.

BOOKSHOPS
Collins Booksellers   *Shop 24, Tweed Mall*

Tweed Mall is just beside all the Surfside bus stops in Wharf Street (see map above). *Collins* is at Shop 24, on the left side of the Mall.

ACCOMMODATION
See also accommodation in Coolangatta, on page 243.

TWEED HEADS

(i) Hotel Accommodation in Tweed Heads

Name	Stars	No. on Map	Telephone No.	Address	Lowest Price (Double/Twin)
Twin Towns	4½	1	1-800-192-020	Griffith Street	$150
Bayswater Motor Inn	4½	6	1-800-501-572	129 Wharf Street	$95
Las Vegas Motor Inn	4	5	1-800-807-351	123 Wharf Street	$85
Blue Pelican Motel	3½	3	07-5536-1777	115 Wharf Street	$70
Cook's Endeavour Inn	3	4	07-5536-5399	26 Frances Street	$70
City Lights Motel	3	8	1-800-659-833	35 Old Pacific Highway	$65
Matilda Motel	3	7	07-5536-7211	108 Kennedy Drive	$50
Dolphin Hotel	3	2	07-5599-1909	23 Wharf Street	$50

(ii) Backpackers Hostel in Tweed Heads

Name	Group	No. on Map	Telephone Number	Address	Lowest Price (Dormitory)
Tweed Coast Backpackers		9	1800-074-328	Pacific Hwy. & Soorley Street	$28

MOVING ON
Bus Services from Tweed Heads

Destination	Operator	Via	Distance (km)	Fare	Journey Time	Frequency
Sydney	McCafferty's		883	$103	13½ hrs	2/day
		Port Macquarie	485	$76	7¾ hrs	2/day
		Coffs Harbour	317	$62	5 hrs	2/day
		Byron Bay	77	$33	1½ hrs	3/day
Sydney	Greyhound		917	$103	14¼ - 14¾ hrs	3/day
		Port Macquarie	489	$76	8½ hrs	2/day
		Coffs Harbour	321	$62	5½ - 5¾ hrs	3/day
		Byron Bay	77	$33	1 - 1½ hrs	4/day
Sydney	Premier		917	$93	13½ – 15½ hrs	3/day
		Port Macquarie	489	$65	8¼ - 8¾ hrs	2/day
		Coffs Harbour	321	$58	5½ - 6½ hrs	3/day
		Byron Bay	77	$21	1½ hrs	3/day
Sydney	Countrylink		957	$115.50	14½ - 15½ hrs	2/day
		Casino	164	$28.30	2¾ - 3¾ hrs	2/day
		Murwillumbah	29	$6.50	30 mins	2/day
Brisbane	McCafferty's		104	$19	2 - 2½ hrs	3/day
		Surfers Paradise	25	$10	30 - 35 mins	3/day
Brisbane	Greyhound		113	$19	2 - 2¼ hrs	4/day
		Surfers Paradise	26	$10	35 mins	4/day
Brisbane	Premier		113	$16	1¾ - 2½ hrs	3/day
		Surfers Paradise	26	$16	30 - 50 mins	3/day
Brisbane	Kirklands		113	$17	1¾ - 2 hrs	4/day
		Surfers Paradise	26	$10.50	40 mins	2/day
Brisbane	Coachtrans		113	$18	2 - 3 hrs	6/day
		Surfers Paradise	26	$5.40	40 - 45 mins	6/day
Sunshine Cst	S'coast Pacific		262	$39	5 hrs	1/day
		Surfers Paradise	26	$20	1 hr	1/day
Lismore	Kirklands		110	$24	2½ - 2¾ hrs	4/day
		Byron Bay	76	$19.50	1½ - 1¾ hrs	4/day
Byron Bay	S'coast Pacific		85	$25.50	1¼ hrs	1/day

Countrylink operates a bus from Tweed Heads in the morning to connect at Casino with the day train to Sydney. In the evening, there is a bus to Murwillumbah to connect with the night train to Sydney. There are no Countrylink services from Tweed Heads to Brisbane or Surfers Paradise.

McCafferty's, Greyhound and Premier all have buses to Sydney. In the opposite direction, the same companies run to Brisbane and Surfers Paradise, as do Kirklands and Coachtrans. Suncoast Pacific runs to the Sunshine Coast.

LORD HOWE ISLAND
Population 300
1 hr 45 mins by air from Sydney
1 hr 35 mins by air from Brisbane

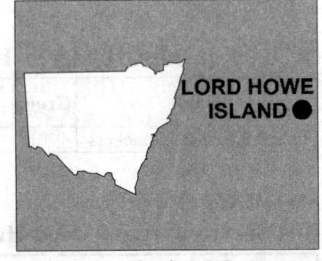

Now here is a real get-away-from-it-all destination. The problem is that, although part of New South Wales, it is an island located far out to sea, 700 kilometres north-east of Sydney and 700 kilometres south-east of Brisbane, and it requires a long and expensive flight to reach it. Moreover, accommodation must be booked in advance and none of it is cheap. It is, however, a beautiful place to visit if you can afford it.

Lord Howe Island was one of the last destinations in the world to be served by a regular scheduled flight operated by flying boat. However, in 1974 an airport was finally constructed and the aircraft no longer had to take off from Sydney Harbour and land in the sea off the island.

Lord Howe Island is crescent shaped, eleven kilometres long and only two to three kilometres wide. At the southern end are two substantial mountains, with a smaller one at the northern end. The island was discovered in 1788, by Lt. Ball, on board the *H.M.S. Supply* whilst *en route* for Norfolk Island, further east, which was a penal colony. However, Lord Howe Island was not settled until 1833. It is the remains of a volcano which was last active about six million years ago, and has gradually been worn away by tides and time ever since. It is now a World Heritage site, the first island in Australia to be so recognised. There are four species of palm which are unique to Lord Howe Island. It is also the home of the almost extinct woodhen, which will probably be encountered somewhere along the walks outlined below.

On 7th July 2002, Lord Howe Island made the news when the British destroyer *H.M.S. Nottingham* was badly holed on Wolf Rocks here whilst evacuating a sailor.

The number of visitors here is limited to 400 at any time and there is a 25km/hr speed limit. There are beautiful beaches and there is a reef for divers. You may swim, fish or sunbathe, but it was the walks which the author enjoyed, so here are two suggested routes. The central area of the island is the inhabited part, so one walk goes from there to the north, and one goes to the south.

(i) Northern Walk
This walk covers about twelve kilometres and will take around four hours, allowing for one short break. Although no extreme heights are reached, there is a lot of up and down hill work and progress will be slower than you might expect by looking at the map.

Start at the **Visitor Centre** - by visiting it if you have not already done so. It has some interesting exhibits, including a video on the history of the island. When you have finished, turn right out of the door and walk past the Post Office and up the hill. The Post Office here, incidentally, does not deliver mail. It has to be collected by residents, so a small local company started a delivery and collection service for mail and issued its own stamps for the performance of the service. The stamps were of interest to collectors and rose greatly in value. Surprisingly, the company was threatened with legal action by Australia Post, which claimed to have the exclusive right to issue stamps. The dispute is an interesting one, but Australia Post does not appear to have won its battle and new issues by the *Lord Howe Island Courier Post* are appearing.

Follow Ned's Beach Road, which branches to the left. At the end is **Ned's Beach**, reasonably enough, where fish feeding takes place at an advertised time each day, the time depending on the tides. You need some bread if you want to hand-feed the fishes. Return a short distance along the road, beyond the bend, and turn right where you see a footpath signposted. This leads first in a curve round sloping pasture land and then up a gradually increasing gradient to Malabar Spur and, by forking right, on to **Malabar Hill**, which is 209 metres high, and which will be the highest point on today's walk. On the way see the notice telling that **Malabar Ridge** is the point which was brushed by an R.A.A.F. Catalina in 1948, causing it to crash near the town down below. We shall see the crash site later. The views from up here are most impressive, especially that over the sheer cliff on the northern side. One false step here and you are doomed.

Return a short distance, to the point where the track forked, and go right. The track descends first, and then climbs once more, to a new cliff-top lookout, which is **Kim's Lookout**, at 182 metres, named after a talented local who died unexpectedly and sadly young. The view from here is perhaps even better, even though the altitude is slightly less than at Malabar Hill.

From here, the track descends steadily, almost all of the way back down to sea level, before you reach a junction with the Max Nicholls Track. Turn right onto this track and begin another steady ascent through damp and slippery forest to **Dawson's Ridge**. Wooden steps have been put in place here to make the walk easier and safer. After the ridge, there is the descent, equally steep, on the western side, where you will be rewarded by a beach, probably deserted, at **North Bay**. Have a rest here, either now, as this is about half way and one of the most pleasant spots on the journey, or on the way back if you prefer.

There is more climbing to be done yet, though. First you can walk to the **Old Gulch** on the opposite side of the island. This, at least, is on the flat, but there is not a lot to see here except a great number of stones. If the tide is out, though, it is possible to hop over the rocks to the **Herring Pools**, where there are corals and tropical fishes. Then proceed from the picnic area up the **Mt. Eliza** Track, which leads to the summit of the northern end of the island at 147 metres. Start through thick palm forest, then watch as the trees thin out and become stunted because of the salt spray from the sea. Near the top, you find that you are invading the territory of the sea birds. When the author went, the ground was so covered with nests that one had to exercise great care in order not to tread on the single egg in each of them, and the attentions of the birds, despite my assurances to them that I was indeed being very careful, did not make the task easier. If you walk to the end of the peninsula, you will have some of the best views of the day, because from here you can look back over the whole length of the island to the dominating mountains at its southern extremity.

Now it is time to return. First back down Mt. Eliza, then up and over Dawson's Ridge. This time, when you emerge from the forest, take the path which leads down through the meadow to **Old Settlement Beach**. A walk along here brings you to the point where habitation commences. Now turn sharp left, beside Milky Way Apartments, and you will just be able to distinguish, in the field ahead, the wreckage of the **Catalina aircraft** which clipped the Malabar Ridge and crashed here in 1948. You can walk right up to it and see what remains.

Return to the main road and from here it is only a short distance back to the town.

(ii) Southern Walk

This walk covers approximately fifteen kilometres and involves one very steep climb. Allow six hours.

Start from the Visitor Centre again, but this time walk along Lagoon Road beside the sea, passing, after a while, the hospital and the **war memorial**, which is interesting enough to stop and have a look at. Turn left when you reach Bowker Avenue, by the Administration Centre. This soon becomes only a track and then **Transit Hill** Track runs off to the right. Take this and follow it through a wooded area, and, inevitably, up. You come to a clearing and a field, which offers a view, but then back into the trees and up to the summit at 121 metres. Because even the summit is tree-covered, a viewing platform has been built. Climb up the metal steps and you have a view all round. Then continue downhill until you reach **Blinky Beach**. There is a path through the dunes which will lead you back to the main road by the end of the airstrip.

Turn left onto the main road for a short distance and where the road leads off to the right to the terminal building, take the track opposite it on the left. After a short distance, the track divides into two paths. Take the left path, marked Muttonbird Point Track. This path climbs up to and then continues along the cliff top, not so high here, and after a while there is a path off to the left in the direction of Muttonbird Point. Although attached at the base, **Muttonbird Point** seems like a separate island and is not accessible from the cliff top. However, there is a viewing platform and you can see that the point is covered with nesting mutton birds in summer.

Continue along the track and you will have the chance of two detours, both on your left, one to **Rocky Run**, where you can follow a creek down to the sea, and one to the **Boat Harbour**, a pleasant secluded spot. However, neither of these detours takes you to any sights which cannot be missed, and there is a stiff climb coming, so decide whether to take the detours or not based on your energy level and the time available. Where the track runs off to your left to the Boat Harbour, if you decide to omit that detour, turn right instead and start climbing. After a while, there is a junction and you want to turn left onto **Goathouse Track**.

From here, everything is uphill, and it gradually gets steeper and steeper, for you are starting to climb Mt. Lidgbird, one of the two mountains which dominate the southern tip of the island. **Mt. Lidgbird** rises to 777 metres, but there is no way to the top. After clambering up ropes and walking along a ridge of rock, you will eventually get to **Goathouse Cave**, sheltered by overhanging rock, at about 430 metres. From here there is a magnificent view back over the island. If you cautiously work your way round the cliff face, you will also be able to see, far away to sea, **Ball's Pyramid**, named after the same man as that who discovered Lord Howe Island. Ball's Pyramid is claimed to be the tallest monolith in the world. It is twenty kilometres from here, so is only a speck in the distance. When the author climbed up here, it started, at this stage,

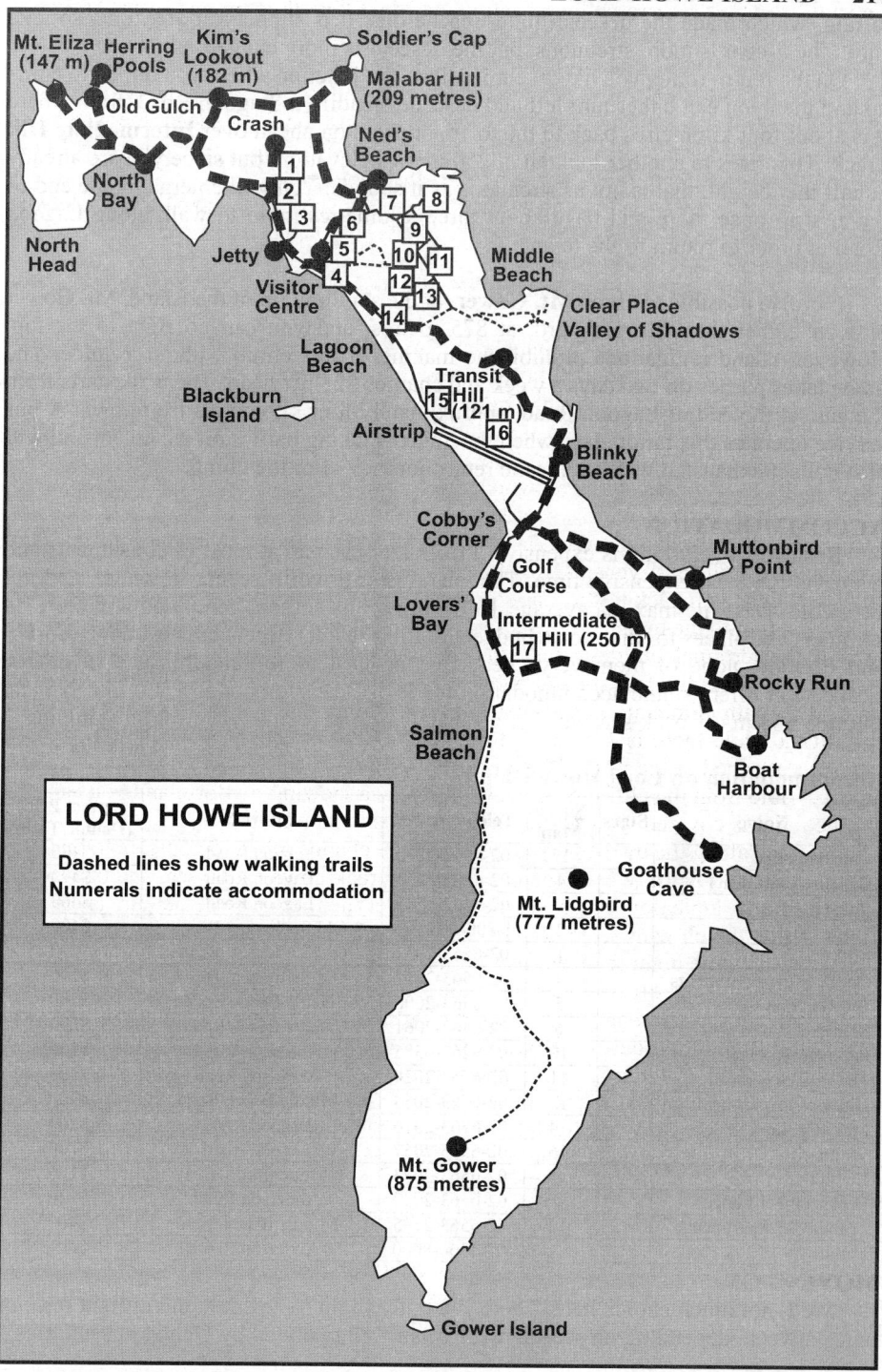

to rain, which made the descent quite treacherous. It is slippery at any time, so take care. The ascent is more strenuous, but the descent is more dangerous.

On the return route, you have a choice. Pass the junction where you turned to come up and then you can either turn left and descend steadily to Lagoon Road, from where it is about four kilometres back to the town, or press on ahead over **Intermediate Hill Track**. This rises to another lookout at 250 metres elevation, but since you are already at half that height, that is not as strenuous as it sounds. You will emerge by the end of the airstrip once more and have about three kilometres more to walk along Lagoon Road in order to return to the town.

It is also possible to climb **Mt. Gower**, at the southern tip of the island. Mt. Gower is even higher than Mt. Lidgbird, at 875 metres, and you can go right to the top. However, island regulations prohibit the making of this climb without a guide. The guide takes parties on two days a week and charges $25 per head. The walk starts from the gate at the end of Lagoon Road, approximately four kilometres from town. A bus service operates this far on days when the guide is taking parties on the ascent and will also collect exhausted walkers for the return journey after the climb.

ACCOMMODATION

Basically, everything is expensive. Prices are seasonal at most establishments and winter is the least expensive time. The island is still worth seeing in winter, and not very cold. Daytime maxima average 16°C during this season, compared with 26°C in summer. The places for those on a budget are Leanda Lei, Beachcomber Lodge, Lorhiti and Ebbtide, none of them very cheap, but at least more economical than others. Leanda Lei offers single accommodation for $55, Beachcomber $75, Lorhiti $75 and Ebbtide $85 in off-peak seasons. Unfortunately, island regulations prohibit camping.

Accommodation on Lord Howe Island

Name	Stars	No. on Map	Telephone No.	Address	Lowest Price (Double/Twin)
Capella Lodge		17	02-6563-2273	Lagoon Road	$480
Capella Apartments		4	02-6563-2273	Lagoon Road	$470
Pinetrees		15	02-9262-6585	Lagoon Road	$460
Trader Nick's		2	1-800-063-928	Old Settlement Beach	$400
Milky Way		1	02-6563-2012	Old Settlement Beach	$200
Ocean View Apartments		3	02-6563-2041	Old Settlement Beach	$200
Blue Lagoon		5	02-6563-2006	Ned's Beach Road	$200
Somerset		6	02-6563-2061	Ned's Beach Road	$200
Palm Haven Flats		10	02-9262-6585	Anderson Road	$200
The Broken Banyan		11	02-6563-2024	Anderson Road	$200
Hideaway Apartments		13	02-6563-2054	Middle Beach Road	$200
Mary Challis Cottages		14	02-6563-2076	Lagoon Road	$200
Waimarie		16	02-6563-2057	Lagoon Road	$200
Ebbtide		8	02-6563-2023	Muttonbird Drive	$150
Beachcomber Lodge		9	02-6563-2032	Anderson Road	$120
Leanda Lei Apartments		12	02-6563-2195	Middle Beach Road	$100
Lorhiti		7	07-3366-8000	Anderson Road	$95

MOVING ON

Well, not much choice here. There is a daily flight to Sydney, and a flight once or twice a week, depending on season, to Brisbane, all operated by Qantas subsidiaries.

AUSTRALIAN CAPITAL TERRITORY

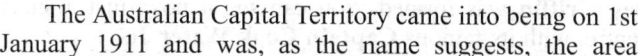

The Australian Capital Territory came into being on 1st January 1911 and was, as the name suggests, the area reserved for the new national capital. The Commonwealth of Australia had been formed on 1st January 1901 and since then Melbourne had played the role of temporary capital. Now a new capital was to be built on this land given by New South Wales for that purpose.

The Australian Capital Territory comes under the direct jurisdiction of the Commonwealth (Federal) Government of Australia. Administratively, therefore, it is independent. Geographically, though, it is completely surrounded by New South Wales, on which state it tends to rely for some of its services. The rail service, for example, is provided by Countrylink.

The Australian Capital Territory occupies an area of 2,360 square kilometres and consists of Canberra and its suburbs, together with some surrounding countryside. That is all. It has, therefore, the distinction of being both the smallest and the most densely populated of the Australian states and territories. It even spills over into New South Wales, for Queanbeyan is in New South Wales, but the majority of that town's working population is employed in Canberra.

CANBERRA
Population 330,000
4 hrs 30 mins by train from Sydney
4 hrs by bus from Sydney

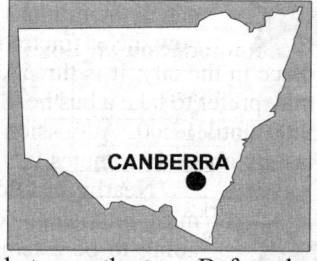

Canberra has been the capital of Australia since parliament moved here in 1927. It is essentially an artificial city, created because both Sydney and Melbourne aspired to the position of national capital, so the logical compromise was to build somewhere new between the two. Before the decision was taken in 1908 to create the capital here, Canberra hardly existed. Some people love the feeling of a newly created and purpose-built city, while others wonder why it is here at all.

The Australian Capital Territory came into being on 1st January 1911, and an international competition was held for the design of the capital itself.

Finally, an American from Chicago, Walter Burley Griffin was declared the winner. Canberra was named on 12th March 1913 and construction began soon after.

You will soon find that Mr. Burley Griffin was not much of a straight lines man. Many of the roads in Canberra are parts of circles, so remember to take your compass with you when walking on an overcast day. He also believed in grand sweeping avenues and using plenty of space, since it was readily available. This means that it is not easy to walk from one place to another in Canberra. Be prepared to use buses, or expend a lot of energy.

Burley Griffin's basic plan remains at the heart of Canberra. He designed a triangle of avenues linking three circles, Vernon Circle in the commercial heart of the city, Capital Hill, which is the centre of the nation's government, and Russell, lying to the east. In the centre of these was to be a lake, with important public buildings to its south, so that the sun, shining from the north, would strike them and cause them to be reflected in the lake. The damming of the Molonglo River in 1964 brought this dream to fruition and **Lake Burley Griffin** was formed. You can see it now, just a short distance south of the city centre, with its famous **Captain Cook Water Jet**.

Burley Griffin's Canberra was designed for a population of 25,000. Now the city accommodates 330,000 and it has spread out from its main centre to include four other major conurbations. These are Woden to the south, Tuggeranong even further south, Belconnen to the north and Queanbeyan to the east. Queanbeyan, however, does not lie within the Australian Capital Territory, but is a part of New South Wales.

Canberra can be reached in a little over four hours by train from Sydney. From Melbourne, there are three different connecting routes, changing from train to bus at Yass (Countrylink to Yass and Transborder bus from there), Wodonga (V-Line) or Sale (V-Line). The last of these operates only on Mondays, Thursdays and some Saturdays.

By bus, services from Sydney are operated by McCafferty's, Greyhound and Murray's. The last is quickest and cheapest. Average journey time is four hours. There are also services from Melbourne, Adelaide, Wollongong, Batemans Bay and beyond, and the ski fields around Thredbo.

There is so much to see in Canberra - and a lot of it free. This book details the major attractions, but if you have time you will discover more to suit your own particular interests.

Of course, the most important sight is **Parliament House**, sitting atop Capital Hill and ruling the nation. This is a spectacularly new construction, which the hill had been awaiting for a long time. It was opened in 1988 and now the 81-metre flagpole which surmounts it can be seen from almost any place in the city. It is three kilometres from the city centre, quite a long walk, so you may prefer to take a bus no. 34 or 39. Parliament House is always open to visitors from 9:00 until 17:00. Admission is free and there are free guided tours every half hour lasting about 45 minutes.

Nearby is **Old Parliament House**, a much more traditional, but still most imposing, construction. Burley Griffin imagined that this was just going to be a temporary building, but, in fact, Parliament sat here for 61 years, from 1927 until 1988. There are guided tours lasting about an hour for the sum of $2, and there is also a sound and light presentation entitled *Order! Order!* The **National Portrait Gallery** is housed here too. Old Parliament House is open daily from 9:00 until 17:00.

In front of Old Parliament House, the **Aboriginal Embassy** may still be standing, although threatened with demolition. It is (or was) a temporary structure erected some years ago, in this most conspicuous of positions, by the aboriginal communities of Australia to emphasise and publicise their complaint that they had no say in the government of their own country.

Walking a little further towards the lake, you will come to a string of important national buildings. On your left is the **National Library**, open daily (free) from 9:00 until 21:00 (17:00 at weekends). There are free guided tours. Outside the library is a Henry Moore statue.

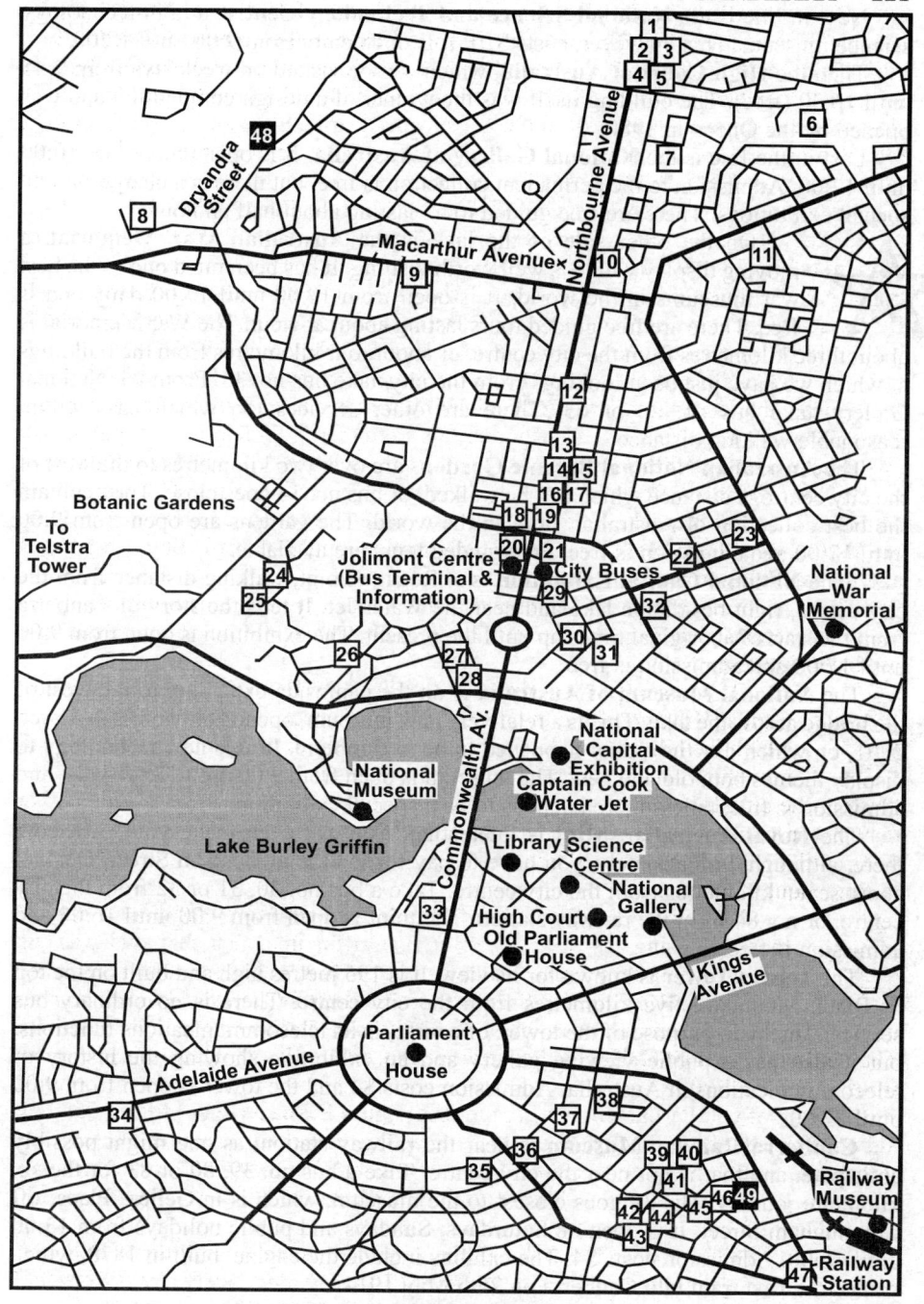

CANBERRA

Black numerals in white boxes indicate hotel accommodation
White numerals in black boxes indicate backpackers hostels

222 AUSTRALIAN CAPITAL TERRITORY

Next in line is the **National Science and Technology Centre**, a high-technology science museum. This, however, costs $10. It is open daily from 9:00 until 17:00.

Then the **High Court of Australia**, which can be visited on weekdays from 9:45 until 16:30 (free). The building itself was the winner of a design competition and was opened by the Queen in 1980.

Last in the line is the **National Gallery of Australia**. It is open daily from 10:00 until 17:00. Admission to the permanent collection is free, but there is a charge for any special exhibitions. There are free guided tours lasting about half an hour.

On the other side of the lake is the **Australian War Memorial**, a moving display which is well worth visiting. It has been rated one of the best war museums in the world. It is open from 10:00 until 17:00 daily and is free. There are free guided tours lasting about an hour. The War Memorial is about three kilometres from the city centre, or about four kilometres from the buildings at which we have just been looking. From the city, take bus no. 33. From the National Gallery, take bus no. 28 or 63. There are other services too which pass within reasonable walking distance.

The **Australian National Botanic Gardens** are over two kilometres to the west of the city centre, a distance which can be walked, or bus no. 34 goes close. They contain the best collection of Australian flora in the world. The gardens are open from 9:00 until 17:00 and admission is free. Free guided tours are available.

The **National Capital Exhibition** is at Regatta Point, walking distance from the city centre, right beside the lake and near the Water Jet. It tells the story of Canberra from the start of aboriginal times up until the present. The exhibition is open from 9:00 until 17:00 and admission is free.

The **National Museum of Australia** is on the peninsula extending to the west of the bridge across the lake. This is a relatively new museum, opened only on 11th March 2001, on which day the author happened to be in Canberra. It uses new technology to display themes both old and new. The museum is open from 9:00 until 17:00 daily, and admission is free, unless there happens to be a special exhibition.

The **Royal Australian Mint** is interesting. You can even make your own coin there, although, unfortunately, you have to pay for it. It is in Denison Street, Deakin, about seven kilometres from the city centre. Take a bus no. 30, 31 or 32 from the city centre, or no. 84 from the railway station. The mint is open from 9:00 until 16:00 and admission is free.

The **Telstra Tower** is known for its view. It is 195 metres high and built on the top of Black Mountain, five kilometres from the city centre. There is no ordinary bus service. The main purpose of the tower, of course, is its telecommunications functions, but it also has a public viewing gallery and an exhibition showing the history of telecommunications in Australia. Admission costs $4 and the tower is open from 9:00 until 22:00.

Canberra Railway Museum is near the railway station, as one might possibly anticipate, and that is not near the city centre. Take a bus no. 39, 80 or 83 for the six kilometre journey. The 39 goes closest to the museum, which is in Geijera Place, off Cunningham Street. It is open on Saturdays, Sundays and public holidays from 13:00 until 16:00. Admission costs $4. The exhibits include the engine, built in 1878, which hauled the first train into Canberra on 25th May 1914.

Although the railway did not come to Canberra until 1914, because Canberra was not even named until the previous year, it reached nearby Queanbeyan in 1887 and was

CANBERRA

continued to Michelago in the same year. Now the Canberra Branch of the Australian Railway Historical Society runs trains on this line between Canberra and Royalla via Queanbeyan on Sundays only. On the first and third Sundays, there is a steam service costing $20, and on the other Sundays a *Tin Hare* 1920s rail motor operates at a cost of $16. It is hoped that services will be extended to Michelago when a dispute with a local farmer can be resolved.

Local bus services within the Australian Capital Territory are operated by a company known as Action. The routes are divided into three zones, but almost all journeys which visitors are likely to make will be within the central zone. The fare for a single journey within one zone is $2.30 and this permits any transfers within the same zone made within one hour of boarding the first bus. Better value is an off-peak day ticket. This costs $4.40 and allows unlimited travel in all zones between 9:00 and 16:30, and again after 19:00.

If you arrive by bus, you will find yourself at the Jolimont Centre in the middle of the city. If you arrive by railway bus (Countrylink or V-Line), you will find that the bus visits the station, except for the V-Line bus from Wodonga, and then continues to the Jolimont Centre. If you arrive by train from Sydney, you will be at the railway station some six kilometres from the city centre. Take bus no. 39 or 80 to reach the city centre.

If you want to go to Queanbeyan, which is in New South Wales, there is a regular service from the city centre, and also from Woden, operated by Deane's Buses.

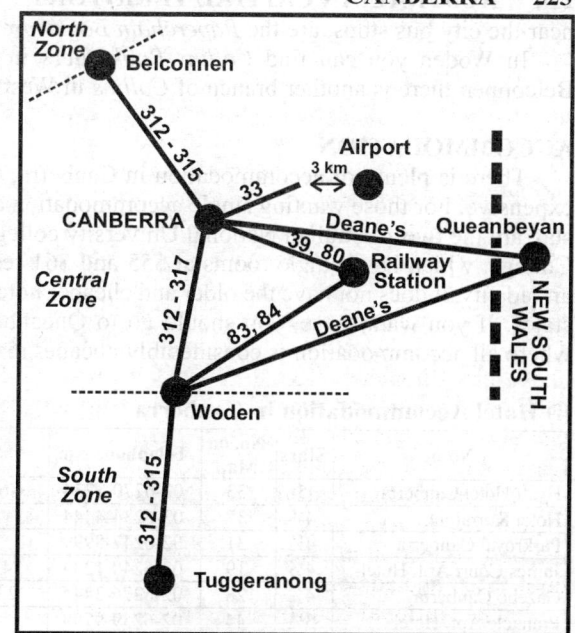

CANBERRA SUBURBS
Showing principal bus routes and bus zones

MAP SHOPS AND BOOKSHOPS

Map World	*Jolimont Centre, 65 - 67 Northbourne Avenue*
Dymocks	*177 - 179 City Walk*
Smith's Alternative Bookstore	*76 Alinga Street*
Paperchain Bookstore	*City Walk*
Collins Booksellers	*Shops G33 - G34, Woden Plaza, Woden*
Collins Booksellers	*Shop 32, Westfield Shopping Town, Belconnen*

Canberra is a city with plenty of good bookshops, and also a specialist map and travel guide shop. This is *Map World*, located within the Jolimont Centre where all long-distance buses arrive and depart. Just round the corner, opposite the post office, at 76 Alinga Street, is *Smith's Alternative Bookshop*. In City Walk, the pedestrian area near the city bus stops, are the *Paperchain Bookstore* and *Dymocks*.

In Woden you can find *Collins Booksellers* in the shopping precinct, while in Belconnen there is another branch of *Collins* in Westfield Shopping Town.

ACCOMMODATION

There is plenty of accommodation in Canberra, but, unfortunately, it is relatively expensive. For those wanting single accommodation at reasonable prices, the places to stay are the two Australian National University colleges, Burgmann House and Ursula College, which have single rooms at $55 and $61 respectively. Since Canberra is not an old city, it does not have the older and cheaper hotels found in most towns in eastern states. If you want those, you should go to Queanbeyan, half an hour away by bus, where all accommodation is considerably cheaper than in Canberra.

(i) Hotel Accommodation in Canberra

Name	Stars	No. on Map	Telephone No.	Address	Lowest Price (Double/Twin)
Hyatt Hotel Canberra	5	33	02-6270-1234	Commonwealth Avenue	$220
Hotel Kurrajong	4½	37	02-6234-4444	8 National Circuit	$211
Parkroyal Canberra	4½	31	02-6247-8999	1 Binara Street	$208
James Court Apt. Hotel.	4½	19	02-6240-1234	74 Northbourne Avenue	$205
Gazebo Canberra	4½	28	02-6276-3444	2 Marcus Clarke Street	$200
Pinnacle Apt. Hotel	3½	44	02-6239-9799	11 Ovens Street	$200
York Canberra	4½	39	02-6295-2333	31 Giles Street	$200
Capital Hotel	4	13	1-800-026-129	108 Northbourne Avenue	$195
Olims Canberra Hotel	4	23	1-800-020-016	Ainslie & Limestone Avs.	$185
Rydges Canberra	4½	27	02-6247-6244	London Circuit	$185
Rydges Capital Hill	4	36	02-6295-3144	Canberra Av & National Cct	$185
Argyle Executive Apts.	4	32	02-6275-0800	Currong & Boolee Streets	$170
Brassey of Canberra	2½	38	02-6273-3766	Belmore Gs & Macquarie St	$170
Novotel		21	02-6245-5000	65 Nortbourne Avenue	$170
Chifley on Northbourne	4½	14	02-6249-1411	102 Northbourne Avenue	$165
Medina Classic Canberra	4½	40	02-6239-8100	11 Giles Street	$165
Quest Canberra	4	20	02-6243-2222	28 West Row	$158
Saville Park Suites	4½	16	02-6243-2500	84 Northbourne Avenue	$158
Waldorf Apt. Hotel	4½	30	02-6229-1234	2 Akuna Street	$155
Kingston Court Apts.		41	02-6295-2244	4 Tench Street	$150
Kingston Terrace Apts.	3½	45	02-6239-9411	16 Eyre Street	$150
Oxley Court Apartments	3½	43	02-6295-6216	Oxley & Dawes Streets	$149
Diplomat Boutique Hotel	4	47	1-800-355-169	Canberra Avenue & Hely St.	$145
Kythera Motel	2½	15	02-6248-7611	98 Northbourne Avenue	$145
Manuka Park Apartments	3½	42	02-6239-0000	Manuka Circle & Oxley St.	$140
Pavilion on Northbourne	3½	12	02-6247-6888	242 Northbourne Avenue	$140
Embassy Motel	3½	34	1-800-659-950	Adelaide Av & Hopetoun C	$135
Parklands Apt. Hotel	4	6	02-6262-7000	Hawdon Place	$135
Tall Trees Motel	3½	11	02-6247-9200	21 Stephen Street	$135
Blue and White Lodge	3½	4	02-6248-0498	524 Northbourne Avenue	$125
Canberran Lodge		2	02-6247-1600	528 Northbourne Avenue	$125
Forrest Inn	3½	35	1-800-355-170	30 National Circuit	$125
Northbourne Lodge	3	5	02-6257-2599	522 Northbourne Avenue	$125
Quality Inn Downtown	3½	17	1-800-026-150	82 Northbourne Avenue	$125
University House	3½	26	02-6249-5211	1 Balmain Crescent	$120
Dickson Premier Inn	4	7	1-800-100-215	Badham & Cape Streets	$110
Motel Monaro	3	46	1-800-241-721	27 Dawes Street	$110

CANBERRA 225

(i) Hotel Accommodation in Canberra, continued

Name	Stars	No. on Map	Telephone No.	Address	Lowest Price (Double/Twin)
Burgmann College		24	02-6267-5222	Daley Road	$107
Canberra Motor Village	3½	8	1-800-026-199	Kunzea Street	$105
Pasmore Cottage B&B	3½	9	02-6247-4528	3 Lilley Street	$105
Canberra Rex Hotel	3½	10	02-6248-5311	150 Northbourne Avenue	$101
Miranda Lodge	4	1	02-6249-8038	534 Northbourne Avenue	$99
Parkview		3	02-6248-0655	526 Northbourne Avenue	$99
Acacia Motor Lodge	2½	22	02-6249-6955	65 Ainslie Avenue	$95
Ursula House		25	02-6279-4300	Daley & Dickson Roads	$92
City Walk Hotel		29	02-6257-0124	2 Mort Street	$80
Canberra Central Apts.	2	18	02-6230-4781	Northbourne Av & Barry Dr	$75

(ii) Backpackers Hostels in Canberra

For backpackers, there are three choices. There is a youth hostel, which is cheapest, but rather a long walk from anywhere. Take bus no. 35 from the city centre. There is Victor Lodge, near the railway station and a very pleasant place to stay. And there is City Walk Hotel, right in the centre of the city, which offers some backpackers' rooms.

Name	Group	No. on Map	Telephone Number	Address	Lowest Price (Dormitory)
City Walk Hotel		29	02-6257-0124	2 Mort Street	$28
Victor Lodge	VIP	49	02-6295-7777	29 Dawes Street	$25
Canberra Y.H.A.	YHA	48	02-6248-9155	191 Dryandra Street	$20

MOVING ON
(i) By Train

There are three trains a day back to Sydney. For the timetable see below.

Eden, Bombala and Canberra to Sydney

Days of Operation	Daily	Daily (Bus)	M, W, F (Bus)	Daily	Daily
Eden		0720			
Merimbula		0750			
Bega		0824			
Bombala			0830		
Cooma		1019	0940		
Canberra Station	0645	1140	1100	1215	1715
Canberra Jolimont		1205	1115		
Queanbeyan	0653			1223	1723
Goulbourn	0811			1342	1844
Moss Vale	0901			1432	1934
Strathfield	1042			1610	2112
Sydney	1055			1624	2126

Then there are three different bus plus train routes to Melbourne (following page). The most comfortable is by Transborder bus to Yass, where the day train to Melbourne may be boarded. The bus leaves Canberra Jolimont, Bay 8, at 10:05. The second route is by V-Line bus to Wodonga and then train to Melbourne. The longest but prettiest route is by V-Line bus to Sale and then train to Melbourne. This service operates only on Tuesdays, Fridays and some Sundays. There are also Countrylink buses to Cooma, Bega and Eden. These buses start from Jolimont and call at the railway station on their way, awaiting rail connexions if necessary. The timetable for these is on page 93.

AUSTRALIAN CAPITAL TERRITORY

Canberra to Melbourne via Yass, Wodonga or Sale

Days of Operation	M – F (Bus)	M – F	Tu, F, Sun* (Bus)	M – F	Sun	Daily (Bus)	Daily	Sat (Bus)	Sat	Sun (Bus)	Sun
Canberra Jolimont	0730		0850			1005		1115		1140	
Canberra Station			0905								
Yass	0815					1057	1125	1200		1225	
Albury	1210	1225				1502	1555	1615	1620	1640	
Wodonga	1220	1233					1605	1623	1630	1648	
Cooma			1025								
Bombala			1130								
Orbost			1405								
Lakes Entrance			1455								
Bairnsdale			1535								
Sale			1635	1650	1655						
Melbourne		1551		1930	1943		1815		1950		2014

* Operates only on certain Sundays.

(ii) By Bus

There are bus services to Sydney operated by McCafferty's, Greyhound and Murray's. Murray's is cheapest, quickest and most comfortable. McCafferty's and Greyhound also operate to Melbourne, and McCafferty's has a daily service to Adelaide. Murray's operates to Wollongong, and to Batemans Bay and Narooma. Transborder runs four times a day to Yass. A summary follows.

Destination	Operator	Via	Distance (km)	Fare	Journey Time	Frequency
Sydney	McCafferty's		214	$40	4 – 4½ hrs	3/day
Sydney	Greyhound		262	$40	3¾ - 4½ hrs	6/day
Sydney	Murray's		214	$39	3¾ - 4 hrs	3/day
Melbourne	McCafferty's		626	$70	8¼ - 8¾ hrs	2/day
		Albury	343	$38	4¾ – 5 hrs	2/day
Melbourne	Greyhound		626	$70	8 – 10 hrs	2/day
		Albury	343	$38	4 - 5¾ hrs	2/day
Melbourne	V-Line		651	$62	8½ hrs	1/day
		Wodonga	352	$39	5 hrs	1/day
Melbourne	V-Line		771	$62	10¾ hrs	2 - 3/week
		Sale	534	$62	7¾ hrs	2 - 3/week
		Lakes Entrance	429	$61.60	6¼ hrs	2 - 3/week
Adelaide	McCafferty's		1268	$141	19 hrs	1/day
		Nuriootpa	1208	$141	17¼ hrs	1/day
		Mildura	885	$95	12¾ hrs	1/day
Wollongong	Murray's		210	$34.80	3½ hrs	1/day
Narooma	Murray's		195	$40.25	4½ hrs	1/day
		Batemans Bay	146	$26.95	3 hrs	1/day
Yass	Transborder		57	$16	1 hr	4/day
Eden	Countrylink		280	$46.80	4¼ - 4½ hrs	1 - 2/day
Thredbo (Winter)	Greyhound		123	$60	2¾ hrs	2/day
		Ski Tube	118	$59	2¼ hrs	2/day

QUEENSLAND

The first European exploration of Moreton Bay, where Brisbane lies, was carried out in 1797 by Matthew Flinders, who landed where today Redcliffe is situated. In 1799, Flinders, in the *Norfolk*, charted the east coast of Queensland. In 1823, John Oxley in the *Mermaid* named the Brisbane River after the Governor of New South Wales at the time and travelled 100 kilometres up the river.

A convict settlement was established at Redcliffe in 1824 and moved to Brisbane in the following year. At the time, this territory was still part of New South Wales. The first free settlers arrived in 1837 and by 1840 all convicts had been withdrawn from Brisbane.

By 1851, the residents of Queensland had started to think of independence from New South Wales. Queen Victoria was petitioned and agreed, understandably preferring the name Queensland to the alternative suggestion of Cooksland. Queensland was proclaimed on 6th June 1859.

Queensland is the second largest state in Australia, covering an area of 1,730,650 square kilometres and with a coastline stretching for 7,400 kilometres. It is seven times the size of the United Kingdom, or five times the size of Japan, or twice the size of Texas. The population is 3.5 million, of whom nearly half live in Brisbane. It can claim to be both the wettest and the hottest state in Australia. Mt. Bellenden Ker, near Tully, once recorded 1.14 metres of rain in a single day, while Cloncurry claims Australia's record temperature of 53.1°C (127.6°F) on 16th January 1889.

One of the great wonders of the world is the Great Barrier Reef stretching up the coast of Queensland, and it is this which makes Queensland the most popular state for visitors to Australia. The Great Barrier Reef extends for over 2,000 kilometres and actually consists of some 2,500 individual reefs and 700 small islands, covering a total area of 345,000 square kilometres.

Transport

Queensland Railways provides the state-wide transport system, almost entirely by rail, but with a few bus connexions (see map on next page). More than any other state, Queensland has kept its branch railways and continued to operate passenger services on them. However, in recent years this state too has bowed to economic pressures and the branch lines have been discontinuing passenger service one by one, so that what is left now is a route all the way up the coast from Brisbane to Cairns, plus three lines leading inland - from Brisbane to Charleville with bus connexions to Cunnamulla and Quilpie, from Rockhampton to Longreach with a bus connexion to Winton, and from Townsville to Mt. Isa. These are supplemented by three tourist train routes in the north of the state and a good electric suburban service around Brisbane. The *Tilt Train* operated by Queensland Railways between Brisbane and Rockhampton is the fastest service in Australia.

Long-distance bus services are operated by McCafferty's, Greyhound and Premier. McCafferty's is a Queensland company, based in Toowoomba, and serves the state well, travelling to some destinations in remote parts which cannot be reached by any other means. Some other companies operate more local routes, particularly Coral

QUEENSLAND

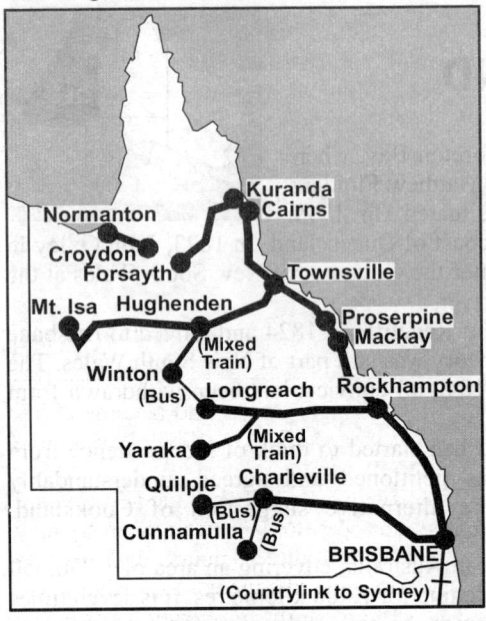

QUEENSLAND RAILWAYS SERVICES

Coaches in the area north and west of Cairns.

Queensland Railways offers the *Sunshine Rail Pass* for unlimited use on its services, including Brisbane suburban trains. Sleeping berths can be used on payment of the usual supplement. However, the pass is relatively expensive and most visitors find that the national rail passes are better value. Here are the prices for the *Sunshine Rail Pass*.

Sunshine Rail Pass
14 days	$291.50
21 days	$337.70
30 days	$423.50

The *East Coast Discovery Pass* is also available, offering journeys up or down the east coast, as its name suggests, with unlimited stops. Six months is allowed for the completion of the journey, but sleeping berths cannot be used, nor can Brisbane suburban trains. Travel is restricted to Queensland Railways trains and Countrylink trains and connecting buses. The passes are available only to overseas residents, except for the ones to or from Cairns, which are available to Australians too. Prices are as follows.

East Coast Discovery Pass
Cairns - Brisbane	$204.60
Cairns - Sydney	$292.60
Cairns - Melbourne	$374.00
Brisbane - Sydney	$93.50
Brisbane - Melbourne	$176.00
Surfers Paradise - Sydney	$93.50
Surfers Paradise - Melbourne	$176.00

A *Road Rail Pass* is available for travel within Queensland, allowing use of Queensland Railways services and McCafferty's bus services, but not both on the same day. The pass costs $295.90 for ten days of travel within two months or $383.90 for twenty days of travel within three months.

The long-distance bus companies offer passes from Sydney, Melbourne or Adelaide up to Cairns with unlimited stops. There are also sometimes discounted bus tickets available for travel between Brisbane and Cairns and between Brisbane and Sydney or Melbourne.

Oz Experience offers a tour running between Byron Bay and Cairns with two detours *en route*. Current price is $250 one way.

BRISBANE
Population 1,600,000

14 hrs 30 mins by train from Sydney
15 hrs by bus from Sydney

Brisbane, although with a population of a million and a half, has quite a different atmosphere from the larger capital cities, Sydney and Melbourne. It seems more parochial in its ways, and also a warmer place, both literally and metaphorically.

Brisbane was founded in July 1825 as a penal settlement, on the orders of the Governor of New South Wales, Sir Thomas Brisbane, and it soon gained a reputation as one of the harshest of such settlements. By 1840, however, all the convicts had been withdrawn and Brisbane had become a city for free settlers. In 1859, Queensland was separated from New South Wales and became a colony in its own right, with Brisbane as its capital.

Brisbane is connected with Sydney by a standard gauge rail line and services are operated by Countrylink, the New South Wales train operator. The train from Sydney to Brisbane runs overnight, taking rather more than fourteen hours, and reaches Brisbane early in the morning, early enough to make onward connexions further north should you so wish. The timetable is on page 94. It then returns to Sydney by day. The train arrives at Roma Street Station these days, in the heart of the city, not at South Brisbane, as it used to do when the author first took it. The day train from Sydney runs to Murwillumbah, in the north-eastern corner of New South Wales, from where there are connecting buses to Surfers Paradise and Brisbane.

There are bus services from Sydney to Brisbane operated by McCafferty's, Greyhound and Premier. Average journey time is fifteen hours. There is also a direct service from Melbourne via the inland route by-passing Sydney. This route, operated by McCafferty's, takes almost one day.

Brisbane receives international flights from all over the world. The airport is ten kilometres from the city centre and there is now a rail link, newly opened, which takes 22 minutes and costs $9. There is also a bus service to the city centre, or to your accommodation, for $10, and other buses operate directly from the airport to the Gold Coast and the Sunshine Coast. Some trains from the airport also run directly to the Gold Coast.

If you are arriving by bus or train, your service will terminate at the Roma Street Transit Centre, which is in the heart of the city, and a useful place. Here you will find, on the top floor, where buses arrive and depart, an information desk which will, on request, arrange accommodation for you if you arrive at a reasonable hour, and often arrange for you to be picked up by your accommodation too. It is worth mentioning, though, that this service operates on commissions received from the establishments which it is serving, so the advice which you receive will not be completely impartial. If accommodation is not willing to provide such a commission, it will not usually be mentioned to you. On the middle floor of the building are places to eat and free showers. On the ground floor is the railway station.

Brisbane has a suburban rail service, which is narrow gauge (3 feet 6 inches), as are all railways in Queensland except the line from Sydney (and, to be absolutely accurate, also a short private line near the top of Cape York used for moving bauxite). The electric suburban trains run as far as the Gold Coast in the south, Ipswich in the west and Caboolture in the north. There are occasional trains which run further north and further west, including an infrequent service as far north as Gympie (see map opposite). Day return tickets, available after 9:00, give a saving of approximately 30%.

Queensland also has a good long-distance train network, with trains from Brisbane all the way up to Cairns, inland to Charleville and Longreach and, with a change of train, to Mt. Isa. In recent years other trains of considerable character have disappeared, but still Queensland has placed more faith in the future of its rail network than other states have done. The line as far north as Rockhampton is electrified and the *Tilt Train* which operates on it is Australia's fastest train service, despite its narrow gauge handicap. Electrification is continuing and will soon extend to Townsville, and then all the way to Cairns. This is the only non-suburban electric passenger train service in Australia.

Brisbane also has a comprehensive local bus network and various ferry services across and along the Brisbane River which lies at its heart (see map of ferry services below). The city is divided into circular zones, with a minimum fare of $2 for a one-zone single ticket. An all-zones single ticket costs $4. There are also two-hour transfer tickets available for $4, and a 20% discount for purchasing ten tickets in advance. Better value are the all-day tickets. With an *Off-Peak Saver*, you can travel anywhere by Brisbane Transport buses between 9:00 and 15:30 and after 19:00 on weekdays, and at any time at weekends. This costs only $5. If you want longer weekday hours, the *Day Rover* gives unlimited travel all day on buses, ferries and *CityCat* services for $9.

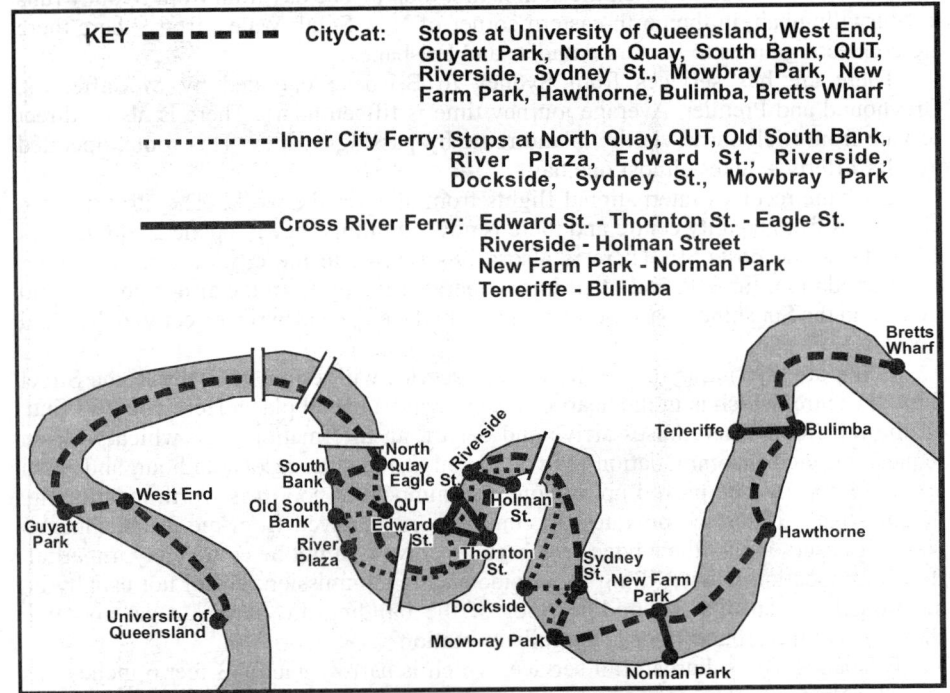

BRISBANE FERRIES

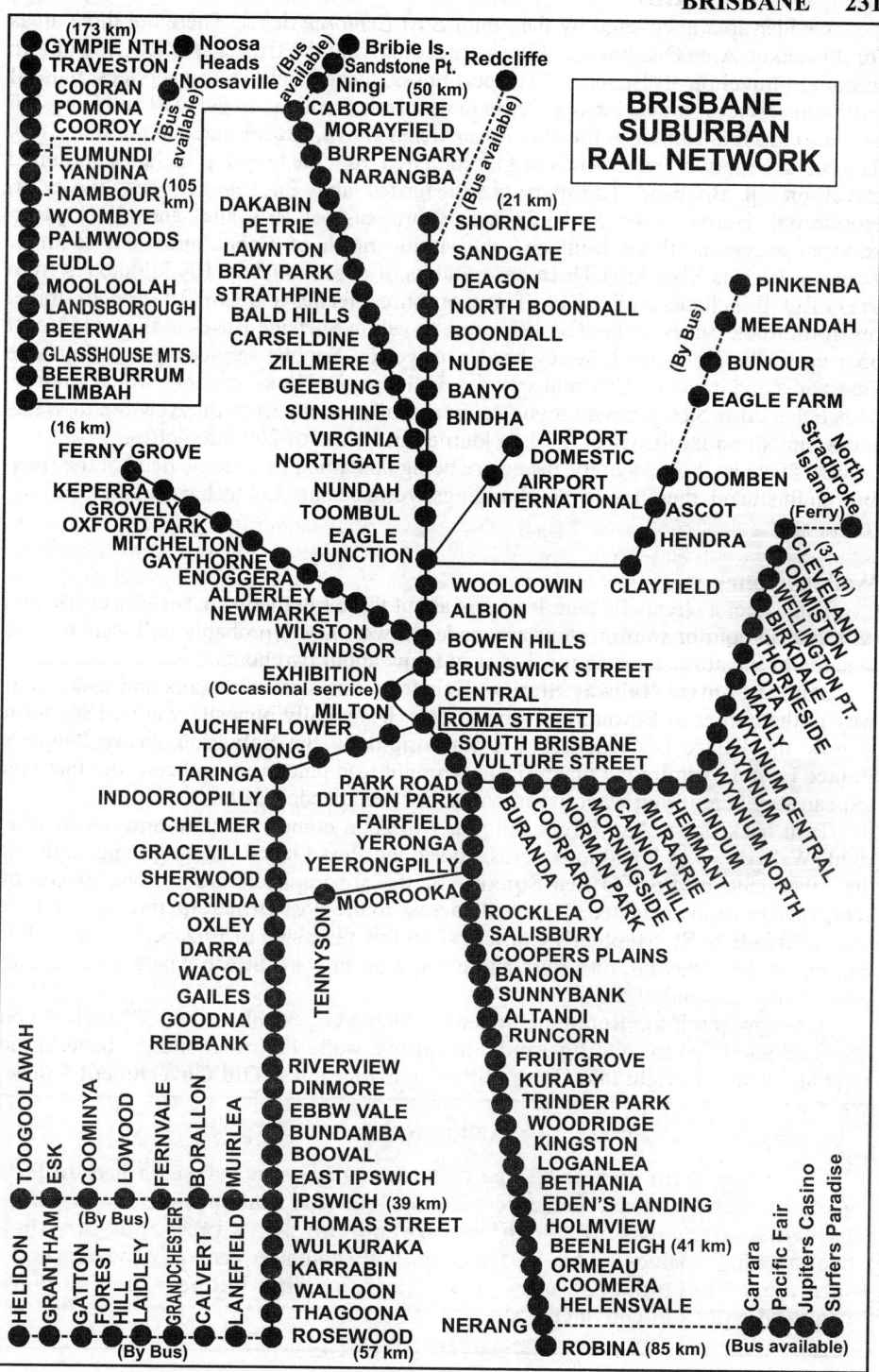

A wider area is covered by the *South-East Explorer* ticket. There are three areas for this ticket. Area One has a 25 kilometre radius from the Brisbane G.P.O. and allows unlimited travel on all Brisbane Transport buses, ferries and *CityCat* services, plus all Citytrain services, except beyond Petrie in the north, Redbank in the west and Kingston in the south. It is similar to the *Day Rover* ticket above, except that you get trains too. The cost is $9. Area Two extends to 45 kilometres from the G.P.O. It includes unlimited travel on all Brisbane Transport buses, ferries and *CityCat* services, travel on Hornibrook Buses in the Redcliffe area (north-east of Brisbane) and all Citytrain services except north of Elimbah (one station north of Caboolture) and south of Ormeau. It costs $16. Area Three has a radius of approximately 100 kilometres from the G.P.O. It includes all Brisbane Transport buses, ferries and *CityCat* services, travel on Hornibrook Buses in the Redcliffe area, travel on Surfside Buses in the Gold Coast area up to the New South Wales border, travel on Sunbus services in the Sunshine Coast area and travel on Citytrain services, including bus links, except north of Cooroy. This ticket costs $23 and with it you can travel all the way from the New South Wales border to Noosa Heads if you wish, a journey in excess of 200 kilometres.

Brisbane is a compact city, the centre being contained by a single bend of the river. Within this bend, there are several buildings worth seeing. Let us have a short walking tour.

Walking Tour

This is not a strenuous tour. It covers about three kilometres in the city centre and will take an hour or so if no stops are made. However, you probably will want to look at some of the attractions, so it is better to allow about two hours.

Start at **Central Railway Station**. Exit from this station upstairs and make your way to the corner of Edward and Ann Streets. Diagonally opposite you will see what is now the Palace Backpackers, but was originally the **Salvation Army People's Palace** Hostel. Admire the magnificent wrought iron balconies, and consider that you too can stay here if you want to (probably, but see anecdote below).

Turn back down Ann Street and you will soon come to **Anzac Square** on your right. Walk down to it and look across to see the **Post Office** standing imposingly on the other side of **Post Office Square**. In the square itself are various **pieces of sculpture** to be investigated. Then walk across to the Post Office and through the Post Office Arcade to **St. Stephen's Cathedral** on the other side of Elizabeth Street. After looking at the cathedral, turn right and emerge on Edward Street, where turn left and walk to the very end of the street.

You now reach the **Botanic Gardens**, which were established in 1855. Here you can find elderly palms and figs, and a mangrove walk. Follow round the bend in the river and then turn right into George Street. On your left is **Old Government House**,

---

ANECDOTE

Arriving at the *Palace Backpackers,* the author was refused a bed on the grounds that, "You are not a genuine backpacker. Your pack is too small." Evidently standards of which we are not always aware apply to the backpacking business. This hostel is popular, being so centrally located and such a beautiful building, so try your luck if you wish, but bear in mind that you need a pack of convincing size.

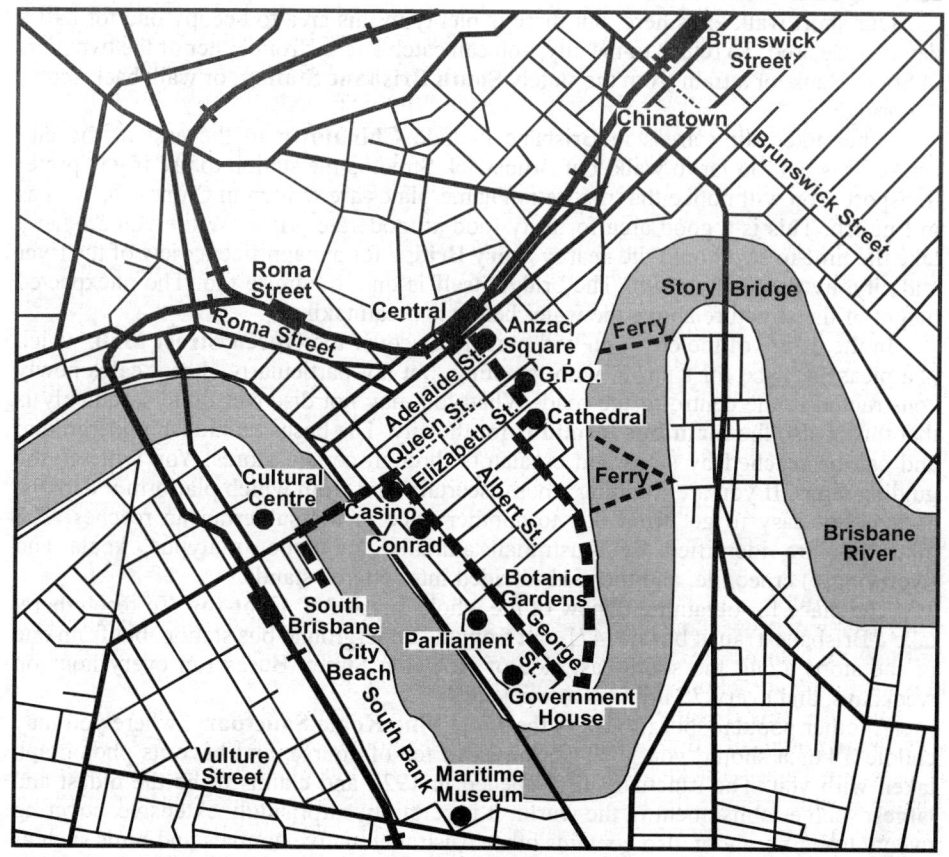

BRISBANE

Dashed line shows Walking Tour

now used by the National Trust. Then comes **Parliament House**, where free guided tours are available. Follow along George Street and you will find, on your left, the **Conrad International Hotel** in a fine building which used to be the Lands Building. Beyond Elizabeth Street is the **Casino** in another imposing building, the former Treasury Building. Turn left now and walk across **Victoria Bridge** to **South Bank** to your left on the other side.

This development has been made on the site of *World Expo '88*. When the exhibition was finished, there was uncertainty as to what to do with the site, but the result, as you will see, has been very successful and this is now one of Brisbane's favourite playgrounds. It offers parklands, gardens, lagoons, restaurants, an Imax theatre and even a man-made beach. You will also find nearby the **Queensland Cultural Centre** containing the **Art Gallery** and the **Museum** and, beyond, the **Queensland State Library**. The **Convention and Exhibition Centre** is a little further back from the river and the **Maritime Museum** is at the southern end of the South Bank.

QUEENSLAND

Our short walk ends here, but there is plenty in this area to occupy one for half a day if so desired. To return to the city, you can catch a ferry from either of the two piers in South Bank, or a train from the stately **South Brisbane Station**, or walk back across the bridge.

Other interesting areas in Brisbane include **Chinatown** to the east of the city centre. It is not too far to walk, but Brunswick Street is the station to use if you prefer transport. You will notice that the station name-plates are written in Chinese as well as in English. This is a good area for tasty food at moderate prices. While you are here, take the time to stroll onto the nearby **Story Bridge** for a magnificent view of the river and city, by day or by night. The bridge itself is one to admire too. The unexpected height of the structure above the water below is breathtaking.

In the centre of the city, you will quickly discover the **Queen Street Mall**, which is a pleasant place for a stroll, with tempting, but not particularly cheap, cafés newly constructed in the centre of the road. What you may not discover quite so quickly is that this is also the **main bus terminus** for the city. The buses lie hidden underground and can be reached by steps and escalators through certain stores. You will see the guiding signs. If you are catching a bus, ascertain first from which platform it departs, as it is not easy to get from one to another once in the subterranean reaches. The platforms are identified by Australian animals: kangaroo, platypus, koala and (worryingly) crocodile, and then sub-divided into lettered stands.

The place for obtaining a view of the whole city is **Mt. Coot-tha**. To reach there, take a Brisbane Transit bus no. 471, not from the underground bus station, but from one of the stops along the south-east side of Adelaide Street. Buses run every hour on weekdays, and every 75 minutes at weekends.

Another popular spot to visit is the **Lone Pine Koala Sanctuary**, where you may cuddle a koala should you wish, for an extra fee of course, and have its photograph taken with you. The sanctuary first opened in 1927 and claims to be the oldest and largest such establishment in the world. It is certainly surprisingly extensive, covering twenty hectares, and it also contains other Australian native animals and birds such as kangaroos, emus, wombats, Tasmanian devils, dingoes and various reptiles. There are 130 koalas housed here, and a similar number of kangaroos. Admission costs $15 and a koala photograph is $10. Hours are 7:30 until 17:00. To get to the sanctuary, take bus no. 430 or 445. No. 430 is an express which runs every hour and leaves from the Koala platform (reasonably enough), stand N, of the subterranean bus station. Bus. no 445 leaves hourly from the same bus stops in Adelaide Street as the Mt. Coot-tha bus mentioned above.

MAP SHOPS AND BOOKSHOPS

World Wide Maps and Guides   187 George Street
Coaldrake's Bookshop   32 Park Road, Milton

World Wide Maps and Guides is a fine shop in the heart of the city, its specialty obvious from its name, while a small but good independent bookstore is *Coaldrake's Bookshop* at 32 Park Road in Milton, about two kilometres to the west of the city centre. The nearest station is Milton, on the suburban line to Ipswich.

ACCOMMODATION

Brisbane has a good range of accommodation within walking distance of the city centre, including some at quite reasonable prices, especially in the Spring Hill area just

BRISBANE 235

to the north of the city. There are three concentrations of backpackers accommodation. One is just to the west of the Roma Street Transit Centre, within easy walking distance. The second is to the east of the city near Chinatown and Brunswick Street station. The third is to the south in South Brisbane. The nearest station is South Brisbane, but that is not really close. Most hostels will collect their guests from the Transit Centre.

(i) Hotel Accommodation in Brisbane *(see map on page 237)*

Name	Stars	No. on Map	Telephone No.	Address	Lowest Price (Double/Twin)
Stamford Heritage Hotel	5	44	07-3221-1999	1 Edward Street	$450
Quality Suites Pacific Int.	4	24	07-3234-8888	570 Queen Street	$300
Holiday Inn	3½	30	07-3238-2222	Transit Centre, Roma Street	$265
Carlton Crest	5	34	07-3229-9111	Ann & Roma Streets	$250
Hilton Brisbane	4½	37	07-3234-2000	190 Elizabeth Street	$235
Rydges Hotel and Resort	4	50	07-3255-0822	9 Glenelg Street	$235
Novotel Brisbane	4	18	07-3309-3309	200 Creek Street	$230
Conrad International	5	40	07-3306-8888	130 William Street	$215
Marriot Hotel	4½	25	07-3303-8000	505 Queen Street	$210
Royal Albert Apartments	5	38	07-3291-8888	Albert & Elizabeth Streets	$200
Quay West	5	42	07-3853-6000	132 Alice Street	$200
Country Comfort Lennons	4½	36	07-3222-3222	66 Queen Street	$190
Chifley on George	4½	41	07-3221-6044	103 George Street	$185
Sheraton Brisbane	5	22	07-3835-3535	249 Turbot Street	$180
Rothbury on Ann	4½	23	07-3239-8888	301 Ann Street	$175
Central Brunswick Apts.	4	27	1-800-622-686	455 Brunswick Street	$175
Quest on North Quay	4½	28	07-3236-1440	293 North Quay	$175
Sebel of Brisbane	4½	39	07-3224-3500	Albert & Charlotte Streets	$175
Royal on the Park	4½	43	07-3221-3411	Alice & Albert Streets	$175
Dockside Apt. Hotel	4½	57	07-3891-6644	44 Ferry Street	$175
Bridgwater Quest Apts.	4½	60	07-3391-5300	55 Baildon Street	$175
Manor Apartment Motel	3½	35	07-3229-2700	289 Queen Street	$165
Sedgebrook on Leichhardt	5	12	07-3831-6338	83 Leichhardt Street	$150
Gazebo Brisbane	4½	13	07-3831-6177	345 Wickham Terrace	$150
Medina Executive	4½	26	07-3218-5800	45 Kemp Place	$150
Riverside Hotel	4	45	07-3846-0577	20 Montague Road	$150
Flag Heritage Inchcolm	4½	20	07-3226-8888	73 Wickham Terrace	$145
Centrepoint Central Hotel	4½	11	07-3832-3000	69 Leichhardt Street	$140
Astor Apartments	4½	16	07-3839-9022	35 Astor Terrace	$135
Summit Apartment Hotel	4½	7	07-3839-7000	32 Leichhardt Street	$125
Metro Inn	4	14	1-800-022-523	239 Wickham Terrace	$125
Belvedere Motor Inn	3½	55	1-800-355-199	Shafston Av. & Thorn Street	$125
Oakford Kangaroo Point	4	59	1-800-642-188	85 Deakin Street	$120
Wickham Terrace Hotel	3½	6	1-800-773-069	491 Wickham Terrace	$115
South Bank Heritage	3½	47	07-3846-5555	23 Edmonstone Street	$115
Albert Park Inn	3	5	1-800-355-132	551 Wickham Terrace	$110
Hotel Grand Chancellor	4½	10	07-3831-4055	23 Leichhardt Street	$110
Camelot Inn	3½	17	1-800-501-573	40 Astor Terrace	$110
Abbey Hotel		29	1-800-777-911	160 Roma Street	$110
Ibis Hotel	3	31	07-3237-2333	27 Turbot Street	$110
Hotel George William	3	33	1-800-064-858	325 George Street	$110
Park View Motel	3	49	1-800-642-511	41 Russell Street	$110
Point on Shaftson	4	56	1-800-088-388	21 Lambert Street	$110
Ryan's on the River	4	58	07-3391-1011	269 Main Street	$110
Flag Gregory Terrace Inn	3½	3	1-800-801-722	397 Gregory Terrace	$105

236 QUEENSLAND
(i) Hotel Accommodation in Brisbane, continued *(see map opposite)*

Name	Stars	No. on Map	Telephone No.	Address	Lowest Price (Double/Twin)
City Park Apartments	5	4	1-800-700-038	251 Gregory Terrace	$105
Metropolitan Motor Inn	3	9	1-800-453-000	106 Leichhardt Street	$105
Comfort Inn South Bank	4	46	1-800-805-318	55 Boundary Street	$99
SDK Central Apartments	3	8	1-800-077-777	28 Fortesque Street	$89
Explorers Inn	3	32	1-800-623-288	63 Turbot Street	$85
Dorchester	3	15	07-3831-2967	484 Upper Edward Street	$80
Edmonstone	3	48	07-3255-0777	24 Edmonstone Street	$80
Kangaroo Point Apts.	3½	51	1-800-676-855	819 Main Street	$80
A1 Motel		53	07-3391-0720	Main & Sinclair Streets	$75
Paramount Motel	3	54	1-800-636-772	649 Main Street	$75
Acacia Hotel	2	19	07-3832-1663	413 Upper Edward Street	$65
Annies Shandon Inn	3	21	07-3831-8684	405 Upper Edward Street	$65
Southern Cross Motel		52	07-3391-2881	721 Main Street	$65
Spring Hill Terraces	4	2	07-3854-1048	260 Water Street	$55
Balmoral House		1	07-3252-1397	33 Amelia Street	$36

(ii) Backpackers Hostels in Brisbane *(see map opposite)*

Name	Group	No. on Map	Telephone No.	Address	Lowest Price (Dormitory)
Irish Murphy's		67	07-3221-4377	George & Elizabeth Streets	$25
Balmoral House Best Inn	VIP	1	1800-066-202	33 Amelia Street	$20
Aussie Way	VIP	61	1800-242-997	34 Cricket Street	$20
Banana Bender	VIP	62	1800-241-157	118 Petrie Terrace	$20
Y.H.A. Brisbane City	YHA	63	07-3236-1004	392 Upper Roma Street	$20
City Backpackers		64	1800-062-572	380 Upper Roma Street	$20
Yellow Submarine	B&W	65	07-3211-3424	66 Quay Street	$20
Palace Backpackers	VIP	66	1800-676-340	Ann & Edward Streets	$20
Backpackers Resort	VIP	68	1800-626-452	110 Vulture Street	$20
Swagman's Backpackers		69	07-3844-9454	145 Vulture Street	$20
Pete's Place		71	07-3254-1984	515 Brunswick Street	$20
Globe Trekkers	B&W	72	07-3358-1251	35 Balfour Street	$20
Somewhere To Stay	Nom	70	07-3846-2858	45 Brighton Road	$17
Homestead	VIP	73	1800-658-344	57 Annie Street	$17
Moreton Bay Lodge	VIP		1800-800-157	45 Cambridge Parade, Manly	$18

MOVING ON
(i) By Train

There is a morning train to Sydney. The timetable appears on page 238. Note that this train leaves an hour earlier in the summer, since it operates by New South Wales time, and New South Wales observes daylight saving time in the summer. The night train to Sydney leaves from Murwillumbah and there is a connecting Countrylink bus from Brisbane. Again see the timetable on page 238.

Heading north, the excellent *Tilt Train* runs to Rockhampton every day except Saturday. This, Australia's fastest train, covers the 639 kilometres in just seven hours at a top speed of 160 km/hr. On Saturday, there is still a service, but it is known as the *Spirit of Capricorn* and is operated by the predecessor of this train, the *ICE* train (Inter-City Express). This is also a comfortable train, but it takes nine hours over the journey. There is also a service to Bundaberg by *Tilt Train* most evenings, extended to

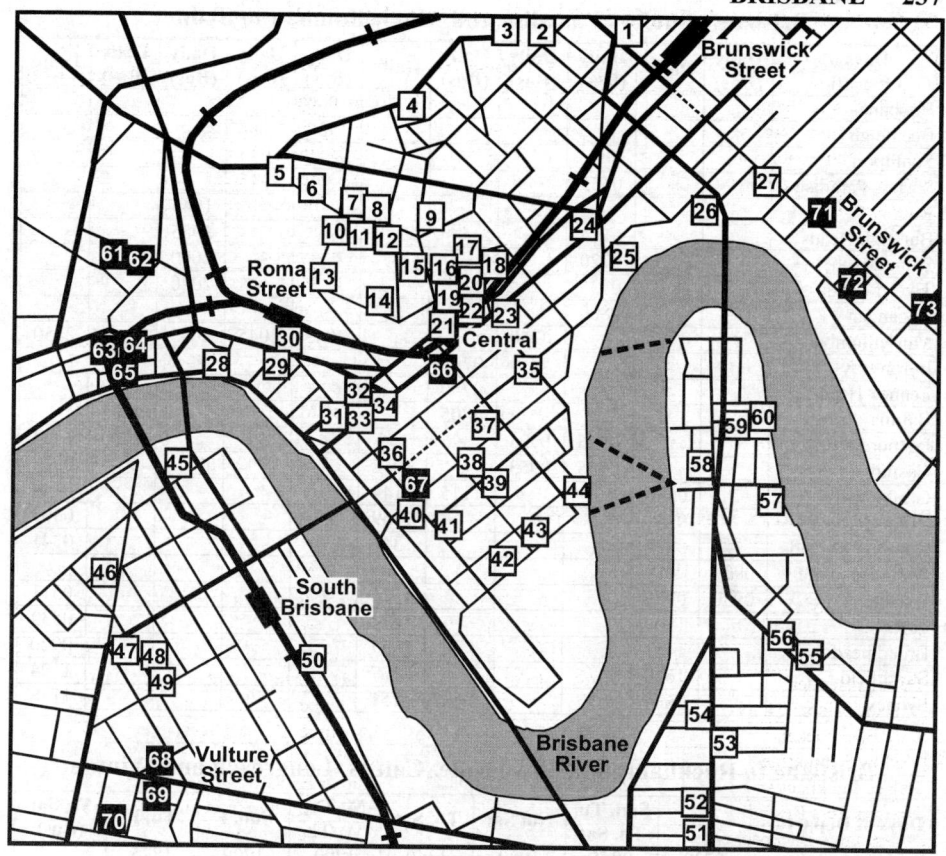

ACCOMMODATION IN BRISBANE

Black numerals in white boxes indicate hotel accommodation
White numerals in black boxes indicate backpackers hostels

Rockhampton on Fridays and Sundays. Then there are longer-distance services, of which the most popular is the route all the way up the coast to Cairns, a scenic treat, although it should be mentioned that one glimpses the sea only twice during the whole 1,681 kilometres. This journey is operated by the *Sunlander* on Tuesdays, Thursdays and Saturdays, and by the *Queenslander* on Sundays. The two trains run to the same schedule. The difference is in their composition. The *Sunlander* has first class sleeping berths, economy class sleeping berths and economy class seats. The *Queenslander* has first class sleeping berths and economy class seats, but no economy berths. The author recommends a berth. Queensland Railways alone in Australia now offers berths at an acceptable price. A supplement of $44, at the time of writing, will obtain for you an air-conditioned berth in a shared compartment (three occupants) for the whole journey and you will enjoy it very much more. Ask for the top berth, because then you will also be allocated the window seat. However, this train is popular and becoming ever more so, so berths are not easy to obtain. If you cannot get a bed on this train, there is another

238 QUEENSLAND
Brisbane, Surfers Paradise and Murwillumbah to Sydney

Days of Operation	Daily (Bus)	Daily	Daily (Bus)	Daily (Bus)	Daily (Bus)	Daily	Daily (Bus)	Daily (Bus)	Daily (Bus)	Daily (Bus)	Daily
Brisbane						0730	1900				
Beenleigh							1930				
Southport								1930			
Surfers Paradise			0655					1945			
Robina								1945			
Burleigh Heads			0714					1955			
Palm Beach			0720					2000			
Tweed Heads			0735					2020			
Bogangar			0800								
Murwillumbah				0750			2045	2045	2045		2150
Byron Bay					0735						
Lennox Head					0750					2150	
Ballina					0805					2205	
Lismore				0926	0925					2255	2334
Casino				0956	0953		1012				0008
Grafton City		0630				1115	1144				0144
Coffs Harbour		0741					1259				0303
Nambucca Heads		0822					1341				0341
Port Macquarie	0900										
Wauchope	0930	0959					1525				0511
Taree		1109					1632				0532
Broadmeadow		1421					1937				0920
Strathfield		1620					2137				1124
Sydney		1634					2151				1138

Brisbane to Rockhampton, Townsville, Cairns, Longreach and Winton

Days of Departure	Sat	Sun, Tu, Th, Sat	Not Sat	Tu, Sat	M, Tu, W, Th	Sun, F	Tu, F	W, Sat (Bus)
Brisbane	0730	0855	1030	1340	1700	1700	1825	
Gympie North	1039	1337	1257	1709	1928	1928	2139	
Maryborough West	1202	1510	1356	1836	2027	2027	2306	
Bundaberg	1303	1615	1449	1941	2115	2125	0011	
Gladstone	1508	1844	1624	2219		2301	0249	
Rockhampton	1630	2040	1730	0010		0005	0435	
Emerald							0918	
Alpha							1257	
Barcaldine							1546	
Longreach							1758	1805
Winton								2005
Mackay		0229		0526				
Proserpine		0424		0746				
Bowen		0532		0841				
Townsville		0843		1150				
Tully		1249						
Innisfail		1359						
Cairns		1625						
Days of Arrival		Sun, M, W, F		W, Sun		M, Sat	W, Sat	

on which you usually can. That is the *Spirit of the Tropics*, which runs on Tuesday and Saturday afternoons, but only as far as Townsville.

On Tuesday and Friday evenings, the *Spirit of the Outback* follows the same coastal route as far as Rockhampton and then turns inland to Longreach, with a bus connexion on to Winton. This is the best of the long-distance routes in Queensland, and one of the most beautiful in Australia. The climb up the Great Dividing Range is followed by some real outback scenery, a good introduction to the true Australia if you have not seen it before.

Travelling inland from Brisbane, the *Westlander* runs to Charleville. When the author last took this train, it used to divide at Charleville and continue to Cunnamulla and Quilpie, but now those towns are served by connecting buses from Charleville.

Brisbane to Charleville, Cunnamulla and Quilpie

Days of Departure	Tu, Th	W, F (Bus)	W, F (Bus)
Brisbane	1920		
Toowoomba	2310		
Roma	0620		
Charleville	1150	1205	1205
Cunnamulla		1435	
Quilpie			1440
Days of Arrival	W, F		

(ii) By Bus

Bus services to Sydney are operated by McCafferty's, Greyhound and Premier, including one inland route operated by McCafferty's via Tamworth. There are additional services to Lismore, via Surfers Paradise and Byron Bay, run by Kirklands, and to Surfers Paradise and Tweed Heads, run by Coachtrans. McCafferty's has a service to Melbourne via Moree and Dubbo. Greyhound has a service to Dubbo via Tamworth, with connexions to Adelaide.

Heading north, there are services by McCafferty's, Greyhound and Premier, all by similar coastal routes, to Cairns. McCafferty's operates a service to Mt. Isa, via Longreach, Winton and Cloncurry. There are services to the Sunshine Coast (Noosa Heads) with Suncoast Pacific, and the morning bus continues to Hervey Bay. Brisbane Bus Lines also runs three buses a week to the Sunshine Coast (Maroochydore) and on to Gympie and beyond.

Services west are sparser, but McCafferty's has seven buses a day as far as Toowoomba, and Greyhound one. Crisps operates two services per day to Warwick, the morning one continuing to Moree, and the afternoon one to Tenterfield.

Destination	Operator	Via	Distance (km)	Fare	Journey Time	Frequency
Sydney via Coast	McCafferty's		988	$103	15½ - 17¾ hrs	2/day
		Port Macquarie	590	$76	9¼ - 10 hrs	2/day
		Coffs Harbour	422	$62	5¼ - 6¾ hrs	2/day
		Byron Bay	182	$39	3¼ - 3¾ hrs	3/day
		Surfers Paradise	79	$19	1¼ - 1½ hrs	3/day
Sydney via Coast	Greyhound		1022	$103	16½ - 17½ hrs	3/day
		Port Macquarie	594	$76	10¾ hrs	2/day
		Coffs Harbour	426	$62	7¾ - 8 hrs	3/day
		Byron Bay	182	$39	3½ - 4 hrs	4/day
		Surfers Paradise	79	$19	1½ - 1¾ hrs	4/day
Sydney via Coast	Premier		1018	$93	15½ - 17¾ hrs	3/day
		Port Macquarie	594	$65	10 - 11 hrs	2/day
		Coffs Harbour	426	$58	7½ - 8½ hrs	3/day
		Byron Bay	182	$35	3¼ - 3¾ hrs	3/day
		Surfers Paradise	79	$16	1½ hrs	3/day

QUEENSLAND
Bus Services from Brisbane, continued

Destination	Operator	Via	Distance (km)	Fare	Journey Time	Frequency
Lismore	Kirklands		233	$37	4½ - 5½ hrs	4/day
		Byron Bay	182	$33	3¼ - 3½ hrs	4/day
		Surfers Paradise	79	$17	1¼ – 1½ hrs	4/day
Tweed Heads	Coachtrans		113	$18	2¼ - 3 hrs	6/day
		Surfers Paradise	79	$16	1¾ hrs	6/day
Sydney via Inland	McCafferty's		1066	$108	18¼ hrs	1/day
		Tamworth	626	$76	10½ hrs	1/day
Dubbo	Greyhound		961	$125	14¼ hrs	4/week
		Tamworth	618	$76	10 hrs	4/week
Toowoomba	McCafferty's		126	$25	2 - 2¼ hrs	5/day
Toowoomba	Greyhound		133	$25	2¼ hrs	1/day
Melbourne via Inland	McCafferty's		1800	$202	23¼ hrs	1/day
		Dubbo	852	$125	12¼ hrs	1/day
		Moree	476	$79	7¼ hrs	1/day
Cairns	McCafferty's		1933	$212	27½ - 28¾ hrs	4/day
		Townsville	1562	$184	22½ - 23 hrs	4/day
		Rockhampton	796	$93	11½ - 12¾ hrs	4/day
		Hervey Bay	344	$49	4½ - 6¼ hrs	7/day
Cairns	Greyhound		1933	$212	28¼ hrs	2/day
		Townsville	1562	$184	22 - 22½ hrs	2/day
		Rockhampton	796	$93	10¾ - 11 hrs	2/day
		Hervey Bay	344	$49	4¾ - 5½ hrs	1/day
Cairns	Premier		1933	$193	28½ hrs	1/day
		Townsville	1562	$173	23 hrs	1/day
		Rockhampton	796	$84	12¼ hrs	1/day
		Hervey Bay	344	$36	6 hrs	1/day
Mt. Isa	McCafferty's		1893	$167	25¼ hrs	1/day
		Longreach	1259	$124	17¼ hrs	1/day
Charleville	McCafferty's		743	$79	11½ hrs	1/day
Hervey Bay	S'coast Pacific		344	$39.50	6½ hrs	1/day
		Sunshine Coast (Noosa)	139	$29	2¾ - 3¼ hrs	7/day
Tenterfield	Crisps		275	$51.50	4¼ hrs	1/day
Moree	Crisps		478	$63	6¾ hrs	1/day
Warwick	Crisps		161	$32	2¼ hrs	2/day

COOLANGATTA
Population 4,000

2 hrs by bus from Brisbane

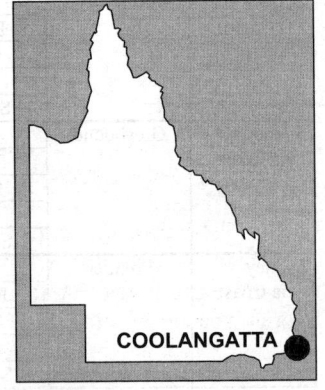

One is never quite sure whether Coolangatta is the other half of Tweed Heads, or whether Tweed Heads is the other half of Coolangatta. It is one of the less satisfactory divisions in Australian geography, especially with New South Wales's observance of daylight saving time and Queensland's disdain of the same. It is not every town which has a monument in its centre to show that one half is in a different state from the other, or which has a political division cutting through the runway of its airport. However, Coolangatta - Tweed Heads does not seem to allow this bureaucratic absurdity to bother it too much, perhaps regarding honours as about even. Coolangatta is the larger and has more of the accommodation. Tweed Heads has the bus stop, though, for the long-distance buses, and the shopping mall opposite. Coolangatta has the airport, and at least the terminal is in Queensland, and the majority of the runway too. Both have beautiful beaches. It is that time difference in the summer, between two states which are at the same longitude, which is really inconvenient.

Coolangatta is reached in two hours by bus from Brisbane. Long-distance buses stop only in Tweed Heads, just across the border, but the Coachtrans services stop at various points along the route. The bus stops at these points bear an indication to the effect that Coachtrans services stop there. Within Coolangatta, they stop almost outside the Tourist Bureau, by Douglas Street in Kirra, and by Surf Street near the airport. Countrylink services do not stop in Coolangatta, only at Palm Beach and Tweed Heads.

The railway from Brisbane runs only to Robina, with some services direct from Brisbane Airport. From Robina, however, it is necessary to take two buses to reach Coolangatta. You can also alight from the train at Helensvale, from where there are some local buses no. 1A to Coolangatta. However, most of these terminate at Coolangatta Airport, which is not really convenient.

Coolangatta (Gold Coast) is recognised by Qantas as an 'international gateway'. This means that, although there are no international flights to Coolangatta, with some types of ticket, but not all, it is permitted to make a same-day change of aircraft and proceed to Coolangatta without additional charge. Coolangatta has domestic Qantas or Qantas subsidiary services from Brisbane, Melbourne and Sydney, as well as Coffs Harbour and Newcastle.

Local bus services are operated by Surfside Buslines. Bus no. 1 starts in Kingscliff in the south and runs north through Tweed Heads, Coolangatta, Surfers Paradise and Southport, terminating at Paradise Point. This route runs twenty-four hours a day between Tweed Heads and Southport. During the day it runs every ten minutes according to the timetable, although in practice services are rather unpredictable. During the night it runs every hour. Route 1A runs from Coolangatta Airport north through Surfers Paradise and Southport, then to Helensvale, *Wet 'n' Wild Water Park*, *Movieworld* and *Dreamworld*. There are many other Surfside bus routes, but these two are the most useful.

Coolangatta is most famous for its beaches and surf. From here, golden sands stretch all the way up to Surfers Paradise and beyond. Here is a short walk around Coolangatta.

Walking Tour

This is a walk of about three kilometres. Allow an hour. However, it can be extended up the coast as long as you have energy.

Start in the heart of Coolangatta at the eastern end of **Coolangatta Beach**. If you follow the path at the end of the beach past the public toilets (useful) and up the hill, you will come to the **Cliff Hargraves Waterfall** and then arrive at the top of **Greenmount Point**. Now follow the path down to and along beside **Rainbow Bay Beach**, shaded by pine trees. This is a popular swimming beach, at the end of which you will arrive at **Snapper Rocks**.

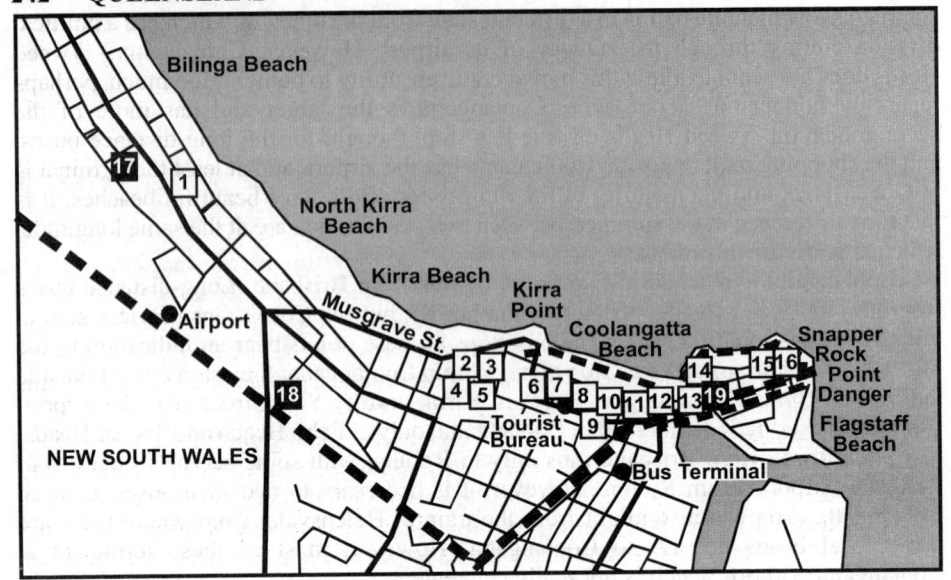

COOLANGATTA
Thinner dashed line shows Walking Tour
Black numerals in white boxes indicate hotel accommodation
White numerals in black boxes indicate backpackers hostels

Following the boardwalk, you reach the path leading up to the top of **Point Danger**. The point was named by Captain Cook in 1770, as he passed by, and this is Australia's second most easterly point, after Cape Byron. The reason for its name is evident, but the Captain must have been feeling in sombre mood, with Mt. Warning and Point Danger in close proximity. He certainly would never have guessed that this was to become the prime holiday destination of the new southern continent. The view from here is especially good. Looking north, you can see the coastline stretching all the way up to the towers of Surfers Paradise. Looking south, you can see first one of the world's most famous surf beaches, **Duranbah Beach**, then the long sandy spur of **Fingal Head**, and, further away, **Cook Island**. On this point is a modern **memorial** to Captain Cook. The border between Queensland and New South Wales runs through Point Danger, so now we venture into New South Wales, and lose an hour if it be summer.

Walk along Boundary Street and see on your left the pretty **Jack Evans Boat Harbour**, with parkland adjoining. Now walk up to the junction of Wharf Street and Boundary Road and admire the impressive **obelisk** which notifies you that you are about to cross back into Queensland, and regain your hour, if necessary. Continue along Wharf Street and you will come back to Coolangatta Beach near your starting point. This time turn left and walk along or beside the beach for five minutes until you come to **Kirra Point**. Climb up the steps to the top of the point, where there is another good view. When the wind is in a suitable direction, this is one of the best and most popular places along the coast for surfing.

This is the end of our walk. From here it is just five minutes into the centre of Coolangatta, as you can see, or you can continue heading north as far as you like to go along the beach or the path beside. If you have enough energy, you can walk all the way to Surfers Paradise, about twenty-five kilometres. There is beach for most of the journey. When you get tired, bus no. 1 runs parallel and close to the beaches all the way.

ACCOMMODATION

There is plenty of accommodation in Coolangatta, but it tends to be holiday accommodation aimed at those staying for a week or so. In some cases, those wishing to stay for a single night may not be accepted at peak periods. Also rates fluctuate very considerably here with season, so prices below may prove to be quite inaccurate if you go at the wrong time. If you cannot find anything suitable in Coolangatta, just move a little further north. Between here and Surfers Paradise, motels line the road, so many of them that you can find some very good deals, even at busy periods. It is always possible to find a motel along the highway for $50 for two people. Watch for the signs outside the various establishments until you find one to your taste.

For backpackers there are three places to stay in Coolangatta. In the heart of the town, right on the state border, is Sunset Strip Budget Resort, which offers shared rooms at $25. On the edge of the town, by the airport, is the youth hostel. This distance is too far to walk comfortably, so a pick-up and drop-off service is offered for long-distance bus arrivals. The best value in Coolangatta, though, is offered by the Kirra Beach Tourist Park, which has 'lodgings' at $25 for a single room or $37 for a double. These are really quite comfortable, although linen is not provided. The state border runs a few metres away from here too, at the edge of the park. This distance is just within walking range of the town with a pack, or you can take the bus to the end of Kirra Beach.

(i) Hotel Accommodation in Coolangatta

Name	Stars	No. on Map	Telephone No.	Address	Lowest Price (Double/Twin)
Calypso Plaza Suites		11	1-800-062-189	87 Griffith Street	$215
Outrigger Beach Resort		10	1-800-688-774	88 Marine Parade	$200
Beach House Seaside		6	07-5536-7466	12 Marine Parade	$150
Pacific Place Apartments		1	1-800-358-778	Golden 4 Dr. & Graham St.	$145
Beachcomber International.	4½	9	07-5536-9555	122 Griffith Street	$130
Bella Mare Apartments	4½	13	07-5599-2755	Hill & Boundary Streets	$125
Rainbow Commodore	4	15	07-5536-7758	255 Boundary Street	$125
Ocean Plaza Resort	4½	8	07-5536-9999	Marine Parade & Warner St.	$120
Columbia Beach Front	3½	16	07-5599-0666	184 Marine Parade	$120
Kirra on the Beach Apts.		5	1-800-677-181	92 Musgrave Street	$110
Kirra Palms Holiday Apts.		4	07-5599-2888	112 Musgrave Street	$95
Points North Apartments	4½	7	07-5536-0000	Marine Parade & Dutton St.	$95
Kirra Vista Holiday Units		3	07-5536-7375	12 Musgrave Street	$90
Greenmount Beach Resort	3½	14	1-800-073-211	Hill Street & Eden Avenue	$75
On The Beach	2	12	07-5536-3624	118 Marine Parade	$55
Kirra Beach Hotel		2	07-5536-3311	Miles St. & Marine Parade	$50

(ii) Backpackers Hostels in Coolangatta

Name	Group	No. on Map	Telephone No.	Address	Lowest Price (Dormitory)
Sunset Strip Budget Resort	VIP	19	07-5599-5517	199 Boundary Road	$25
Kirra Beach Tourist Park		18	07-5581-7744	Charlotte Street	$25
Coolangatta Y.H.A.	YHA	17	07-5536-7644	230 Coolangatta Road	$22

QUEENSLAND
MOVING ON

Only local buses operated by Surfside Buslines and services to Brisbane operated by Coachtrans stop in Coolangatta. For other long-distance services refer to the section on Tweed Heads on page 213.

SURFERS PARADISE
Population 250,000
1 hr 30 mins by bus from Brisbane

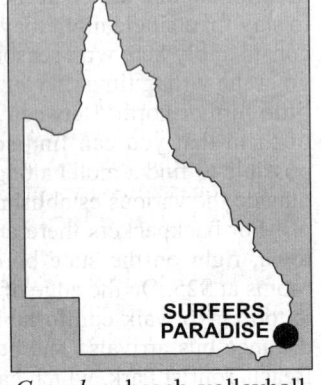

The author likes to think that Surfers Paradise is the most un-Australian place in Australia. It is a holiday city throbbing with life, but with something of a feeling of superficiality about it.

However, it is certainly an interesting place and one where a number of bargains can be discovered, since there is plenty of competition in all fields. Food, in particular, can be found cheaply. Attractions in the heart of Surfers Paradise include Cavill Mall, *Ripley's Believe it or Not Museum*, the *Hard Rock Café*, *Hoyt's Cinema Complex*, beach volleyball, many shops, restaurants, hotels and nightclubs, and, of course, the beach itself.

Surfers Paradise lies an hour and a half south of Brisbane by bus. There used to be a railway to the Gold Coast, but it was abandoned as unprofitable. The popularity of the area then increased considerably and it was realised that there should be a railway. However, unfortunately, the original right of way had disappeared, so it was decided to build a new railway at great expense. That has now been done and the line was opened in 1998. It is a good fast route, with a train every half hour, and a pleasant way to reach this area. The problem is that it does not go to where it is really needed. One can take the train from Brisbane, or from Brisbane Airport, to Helensvale, Nerang or Robina, but from any of those stations one has then to change to a bus to reach Surfers Paradise. Nerang is the most popular choice, and buses meet arriving trains, then proceed directly to the centre of the city. From Brisbane to Nerang takes 70 minutes by train, and the bus ride from Nerang to Surfers Paradise takes a further 25 minutes.

From the south, many long-distance buses pass through here. McCafferty's, Greyhound and Premier all run services from Sydney. Kirklands operates from Lismore via Byron Bay, and Suncoast Pacific operates from Byron Bay. The day train from Sydney runs to Murwillumbah and then there is a bus connexion to Surfers Paradise, continuing to Southport. From the night train from Sydney, there is a bus connexion at Casino which takes three more hours to reach Surfers Paradise, where it terminates.

Local services are operated by Surfside Buslines (see map opposite). To the south, buses run as far as Kingscliff directly, and, with changes, on to Cabarita Beach, Pottsville and Murwillumbah. To the north, they run to Paradise Point, Helensvale and, during opening hours, to the attractions of *Wet 'n' Wild Water Park*, *Movieworld* and *Dreamworld*. The last is a slightly lengthy walk from Coomera Station, on the Gold Coast Railway line from Brisbane. Surfside Buslines offers a one-day ticket for $10, or three days for $25, five days for $35, seven days for $43, ten days for $50 or fourteen days for $60.

The names of the attractions to the north of Surfers Paradise explain their themes. They are popular with day-trippers from Brisbane and also with families spending their holidays here. Visitors from overseas tend to be less interested, but if you wish to visit them, it is easy to do so. Bus no. 1A runs to all three of the places mentioned in the paragraph above. If you purchase your ticket in advance, the bus fare is included. There is also *Seaworld*, a huge aquarium north of Surfers Paradise, which is served by buses 2 and 2A.

Surfers Paradise is Australia's response to Miami. Indeed, there is even a beach named Miami here. As in the American city, you will find here sunshine, beaches and canals. Like Miami, it is a long and thin city. Like Miami, the railway station is inconveniently located. It is smaller than Miami, but it is alive all night, and full of lights and sound. Most people who pass through Surfers Paradise say that it is an experience which they would not have wanted to miss, as there is really nowhere else quite like this in Australia.

Although Surfers Paradise is the centre, and the well known name, the Gold Coast area stretches from Tweed Heads and Coolangatta in the south to Southport in the north. Southport is distinct from the other beaches in lying on an inland stretch of calm water. The map on the next page shows the geographical relationship of these other beaches to Surfers Paradise itself. All are popular places, but all are a little quieter than Surfers Paradise, if that is what you prefer.

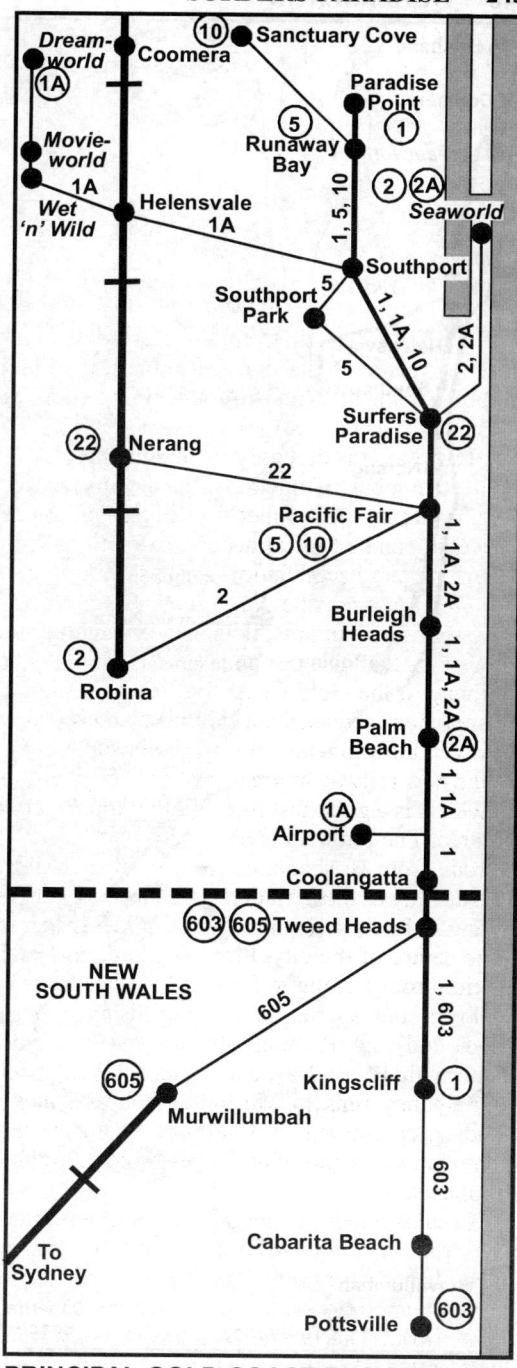

PRINCIPAL GOLD COAST BUS SERVICES
Numerals in circles indicate termini

QUEENSLAND

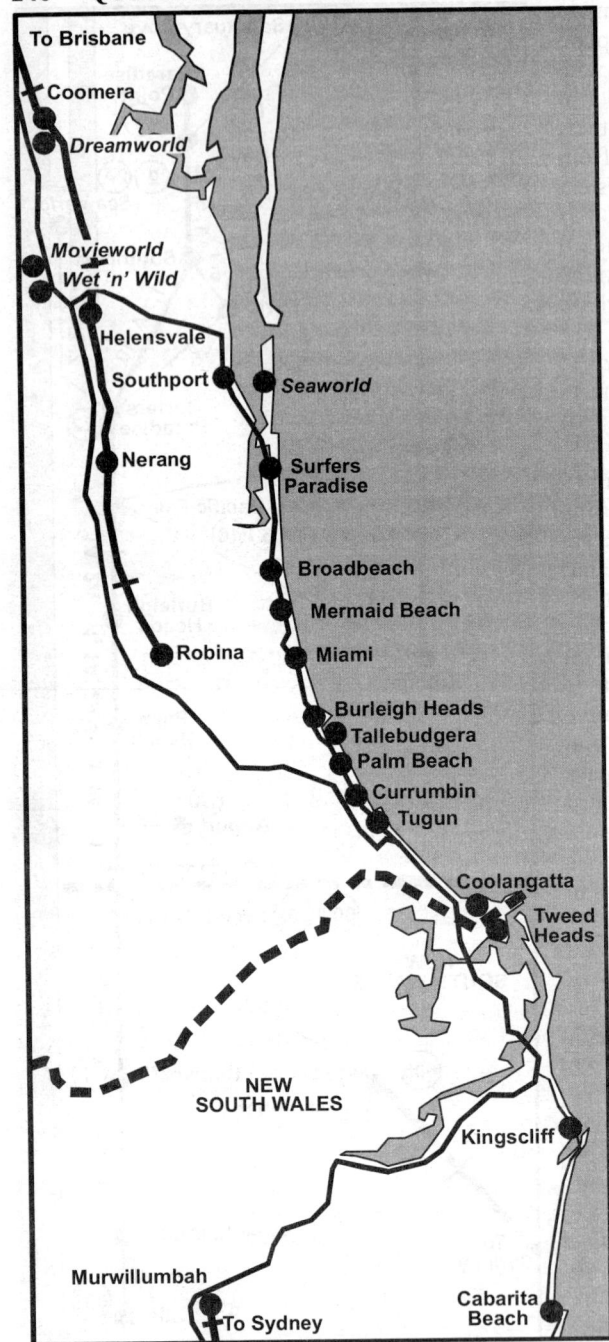

THE GOLD COAST

Even around Surfers Paradise, though, there are quiet places. The following walk will allow the discovery of some of them.

Walking Tour

This is an easy walk without any hills or difficult terrain. It covers five kilometres and will take no more than an hour and a half, even at a leisurely stroll.

Start at **Eileen Peters Park**, which lies on the beach front just south of the Cavill Mall centre of Surfers Paradise, and start walking north. You will soon come to the **Peter Lacey Monument** and to other monuments at the end of the **Cavill Mall**, celebrating the fame of this city and the reason why it has its name. Cavill Mall is really the heart of Surfers Paradise. Here you will find a shopping centre, *Ripley's Believe It or Not Museum* (a sort of *Guinness Book of Records* in visual form), restaurants and pubs offering some good value, a police box and the overworked **Tourist Information Centre**.

Continue northwards along or beside the beach and when you reach View Avenue, you will be at the start of the straight of the circuit used for the **Indy Car Race** held here annually. Continue along the straight for about a further kilometre, albeit at a slower pace than the Indy racers, enjoying the sands more than they have the opportunity to do, until you reach **Narrowneck**, which is indeed a narrow neck, barely a hundred metres wide at this point. Leave the beach here, cross the road, and cross the **Nerang River** on the wooden **suspension bridge** provided. You are now entering **Macintosh Island Park**, which is a bird sanctuary. One wonders what the birds think of the noisy cars which race along both sides of the park every year. Turn left and walk through the park.

At the end of Macintosh Island Park, pass under both carriageways of the Gold Coast Highway and then cross back over the Nerang River. You will find the **Marriott Resort Hotel** on your right. Turn right immediately and walk round the edge of the attractive resort gardens. After passing along Paradise Place, you will come to **Budd's Beach** on the Nerang River. Follow River Drive round and then turn left into Cypress Avenue. On your left you will find the *Bungee Rocket*, *Banzai Bungey* and *Flycoaster* attractions, just in case you feel that this has been too sedate a walk and you need some excitement. Continue for a short distance until you meet the Gold Coast Highway travelling south and then turn right into it. Another two or three minutes and you are back in the centre of Surfers Paradise, where our walk ends.

BOOKSHOPS

Try the following, although neither is in the centre of Surfers Paradise.

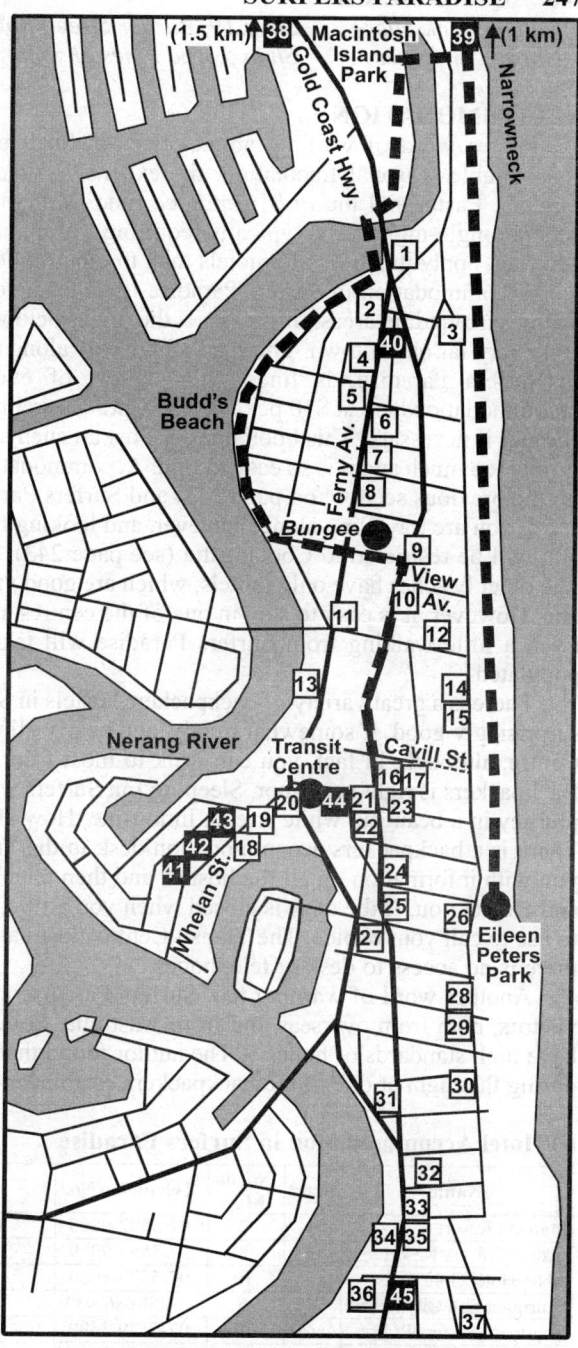

SURFERS PARADISE
Dashed line shows Walking Tour
Black numerals indicate hotel accommodation
White numerals indicate backpackers hostels

248 QUEENSLAND

Collins Booksellers   Shop 19, Bazaar Street, Robina Town Centre
Hooked on Books   Shop 5, The Pines Shopping Centre, Leonora

ACCOMMODATION

First a word of warning about prices in Surfers Paradise. They are subject to considerable seasonal fluctuation, the expensive times being the school holidays in summer, Easter and the *Indy Car Race* time. Moreover, many of the establishments decline single-night stays, typically requiring a minimum of three nights. Such caveats, however, apply much less to motels than to other holiday-oriented accommodation.

Accommodation in Surfers Paradise itself tends to be rather more expensive than that in surrounding areas, of course. If the prices below seem too high, you do not need to go very far out of town. The road all the way along the coast, especially to the south of Surfers Paradise, is lined with motels of every grade. It is easy to find accommodation here at $50 per couple. A little searching will discover something even cheaper if necessary. This book does not list all such accommodation, because there is simply too much and it is so easy to find. Accommodation listed here is for Coolangatta (in the previous section, on page 243) and Surfers Paradise city centre only.

If you are travelling alone, however, and looking for backpackers accommodation, you will be restricted to Coolangatta (see page 243), Surfers Paradise and Southport. The other beaches have only motels, which are good value for two but a little costly for one. However, it is easy to stay in one of the centres and take a bus to a quieter beach. Even a little walking from Surfers Paradise will take you to somewhere much less populated.

There is a great variety of backpackers hostels in Surfers Paradise. They are mostly surprisingly good, if somewhat trendy, and nearly all will collect you from the Transit Centre, although, in fact, you can walk to most from there. Indeed, Nomads Islander Backpackers is right next door. Sleeping Inn Surfers will even pick you up for the short journey in a beautiful white stretch limousine. How about that for backpacker luxury? There is a backpackers accommodation desk in the Transit Centre which will provide you with information on all the hostels and then telephone to ask your choice to come and collect you. If the desk is closed when you arrive, there is a free telephone for you to use to call your choice. The Transit Centre closes at 21:00, though, so after that time there is no access to desk or telephones.

Another word of warning too. Surfers Paradise attracts a lot of different types of visitors, both from overseas and from Australia. Some of these types may not always have high standards of honesty. The author found that his wallet had been "borrowed" during the night at one of the backpackers establishments here. Be careful!

(i) Hotel Accommodation in Surfers Paradise

Name	Stars	No. on Map	Telephone No.	Address	Lowest Price (Double/Twin)
Marriott Resort	5	2	07-5592-9800	158 Ferny Avenue	$290
Crown Towers Resort	5	8	07-5555-9999	5 Palm Avenue	$195
ANA Hotel Gold Coast	5	10	07-5579-1000	22 View Avenue	$190
Outrigger Sun City Resort	4½	6	1-800-686-939	Ocean Avenue	$185
Courtyard Surfers P'dise	4	16	07-5579-3499	Paradise Centre	$165
Paradise Centre Apts.	4	17	07-5579-3399	Hanlan Street	$165
Gold Coast International	4½	7	07-5584-1200	Gold Cst Hy & Staghorn Rd	$160
Peninsula Apartments	4	26	07-5570-2777	Clifford St & Esplanade	$160
Moroccan Apartments	5	12	07-5526-9500	14 View Avenue	$150

(i) Hotel Accommodation in Surfers Paradise, continued

Name	Stars	No. on Map	Telephone No.	Address	Lowest Price (Double/Twin)
Zenith		15	07-5538-0788	20 The Esplanade	$150
Novotel	4	23	07-5570-1000	18 Hanlan Street	$150
Watermark Hotel	4	27	1-800-808-877	3032 Gold Coast Highway	$150
Surfers Plaza Resort		20	07-5592-3888	4 Ferny Avenue	$145
Grosvenor Beach Front	3½	14	07-5570-3111	26 The Esplanade	$140
Aegean Resort Apts	4	25	07-5570-2388	30 Laycock Street	$140
Australis Sovereign	4½	4	07-5579-3888	138 Ferny Avenue	$120
Mercure Resort	3½	5	07-5579-4444	122 Ferny Avenue	$120
Biarritz Apartments	3½	37	07-5570-1377	85 Old Burleigh Road	$120
Legends Hotel	4	24	07-5588-7888	Gold Cst Hwy & Laycock St	$115
Shangri-La		28	07-5570-2366	28 Northcliffe Terrace	$115
Centrepoint Resort	3½	11	07-5538-9955	67 Ferny Avenue	$110
Concorde	3	13	07-5539-0444	42 Ferny Avenue	$110
K Resort	4½	19	07-5531-6655	55 Whelan Street	$110
Surfers Hawaiian Apts.	4½	34	07-5592-2380	2890 Gold Coast Highway	$110
Hi-Surf	4½	3	07-5538-8011	150 The Esplanade	$105
Surfers Beachside Apts.	3½	31	07-5570-3000	Garfield Terrace & Vista St.	$105
Cannes Court		36	07-5538-1288	17 Genoa Street	$105
Cosmopolitan Apartments	3	21	07-5570-2311	Gold Cst Hwy. & Beach Rd.	$98
Pacific Towers	3	29	07-5539-9611	3 Northcliffe Terrace	$95
Quarterdeck	3½	9	07-5592-2200	3263 Gold Coast Highway	$85
Surfers Del Ray Apts.	3½	18	07-5592-0877	37 Whelan Street	$85
Le Chelsea		32	07-5538-3366	11 Frederick Street	$85
D'Arcy Arms Motel		33	07-5592-0882	2923 Gold Coast Highway	$85
Pink Poodle Motel	3½	35	07-5539-9211	2903 Gold Coast Highway	$85
Beach Lodge		1	07-5539-8077	3343 Gold Coast Hwy. S.	$79
Islander Resort Hotel	3	22	07-5538-8000	6 Beach Road	$75
Thornton Tower		30	07-5592-0043	33 Thornton Street	$75

(ii) Backpackers Hostels in Surfers Paradise

Name	Group	No. on Map	Telephone No.	Address	Lowest Price (Dormitory)
Surf n Sun Beachside B/P	VIP	40	1800-678-194	3323 Gold Coast Highway	$24
Backpackers in Paradise		43	1800-268-621	40 Whelan Street	$24
Couple o' Days B/P		41	07-5592-4200	18 Whelan Street	$24
Backpackers Resort	VIP	45	1800-282-800	2837 Gold Coast Highway	$22
British Arms	YHA	39	1800-680-269	70 Seaworld Drive	$22
Trekkers Backpackers	VIP	38	1800-100-004	22 White Street, Southport	$22
Sleeping Inn Surfers	B&W	42	1800-817-832	26 Whelan Street	$21
Nomads Islander B/P	Nom	44	1800-074-393	6 Beach Road	$20

MOVING ON

Countrylink bus connexions operate from here to connect with both day and night trains to Sydney. The day connexion is at Casino, the night one at Murwillumbah. The timetable is on page 238. There is no Countrylink service between Surfers Paradise and Brisbane, but there is the Gold Coast Railway operated by Queensland Railways. To catch this, first take a Surfside bus no. 1A to Helensvale Station or a no. 22 to Nerang Station. There are special train plus bus fares via Nerang, or, if you are going to do enough travelling in the day, you can buy a *South-East Explorer* ticket, which will give you unlimited travel on Surfside Buslines down to the New South Wales border, Citytrain services except north of Cooroy, Brisbane Transport buses, ferries and

250 QUEENSLAND

CityCat services, Hornibrook Buses in the Redcliffe area (north-east of Brisbane), and Sunbus services in the Sunshine Coast area. This ticket costs $23. Another point worth noting is that if you are travelling on by a Queensland Railways long-distance train the same day, your journey to the city by suburban train will be free. Just show the long-distance ticket when asked. A similar rule applies upon arrival in Brisbane. One journey by suburban train is free to complete your journey on the same day.

From Surfers Paradise, there are bus services to Brisbane, Sydney, Lismore, Byron Bay and the Sunshine Coast. There are also buses to Brisbane Airport.

Bus Services from Surfers Paradise

Destination	Operator	Via	Distance (km)	Fare	Journey Time	Frequency
Sydney	McCafferty's		909	$103	14¼ - 16½ hrs	2/day
		Port Macquarie	511	$76	7¾ - 8¼ hrs	2/day
		Coffs Harbour	343	$62	5½ - 5¾ hrs	2/day
		Byron Bay	103	$33	1¾ - 2¼ hrs	3/day
Sydney	Greyhound		943	$103	15 - 16 hrs	3/day
		Port Macquarie	515	$76	9¼ hrs	2/day
		Coffs Harbour	347	$62	6 - 6½ hrs	3/day
		Byron Bay	103	$33	2 - 2¼ hrs	4/day
Sydney	Premier		943	$93	14 - 16¼ hrs	3/day
		Port Macquarie	515	$65	8¾ - 9½ hrs	2/day
		Coffs Harbour	347	$58	6¼ - 7 hrs	3/day
		Byron Bay	103	$29	2 - 2¼ hrs	3/day
Sydney	Countrylink		982	$115.50	15 - 16 hrs	2/day
		Casino	189	$31.60	3 - 4 hrs	2/day
		Murwillumbah	54	$8.70	1 hr	1/day
Brisbane	McCafferty's		79	$19	1½ - 2 hrs	3/day
Brisbane	Greyhound		80	$19	1½ - 1¾ hrs	4/day
Brisbane	Premier		79	$16	1¼ - 1½ hrs	3/day
Brisbane	Kirklands		79	$17	1¼ - 1½ hrs	2/day
Brisbane	Coachtrans		79	$16	1¼ - 2¼ hrs	7/day
Sunshine Cst	S'coast Pacific		236	$39	4 hrs	1/day
Lismore	Kirklands		145	$35	3¼ - 3¾ hrs	4/day
		Byron Bay	111	$30	2¼ hrs	4/day
Byron Bay	S'coast Pacific		111	$25.50	2¾ hrs	1/day

NORTH STRADBROKE ISLAND

Population 3,000

2 hrs by train and ferry from Brisbane

North Stradbroke Island is a miniature version of the more famous Fraser Island further north. Fraser Island is composed totally of sand and North Stradbroke is almost completely sand. These two are amongst the largest such islands in the world. North Stradbroke Island has the advantages of being easily accessible from Brisbane and being more developed in terms of transport.

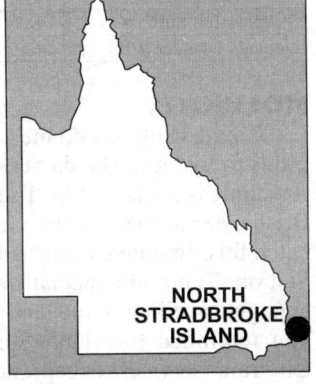

First take a suburban train from Brisbane to Cleveland, which will take a little less than an hour. Trains run every thirty minutes. There are also buses from Brisbane (Elizabeth Street), operated by the National Bus Company, but the train is faster and more comfortable. From Cleveland Station, walk down to the harbour, a walk of about fifteen minutes. There is a bus available if you prefer, but the distance is quite walkable and the route signposted. From Toondah Harbour in Middle Street, a ferry runs across to the island, taking about twenty minutes. Although passenger ferries run regularly, the time of two hours mentioned above from Brisbane assumes a good connexion at Cleveland. It would be wise to allow rather longer for the journey unless you plan carefully. If you wish to plan, telephone 07-3286-2666 for ferry times. At the time of writing, there are eleven departures per day, the last at 18:15.

When you arrive, it will be in the small town of **Dunwich** on the west side of the island. There is a **Tourist Information Centre**, a **museum**, open only on Wednesdays and Saturdays from 10:00 until 14:00, an **art gallery**, and an old **cemetery** with, surprisingly, as many as 10,000 graves. Moreover, evidence of aboriginal occupation in this town goes back 21,000 years. Dunwich has been, in its time, a convict settlement, a Catholic mission, a quarantine station and a

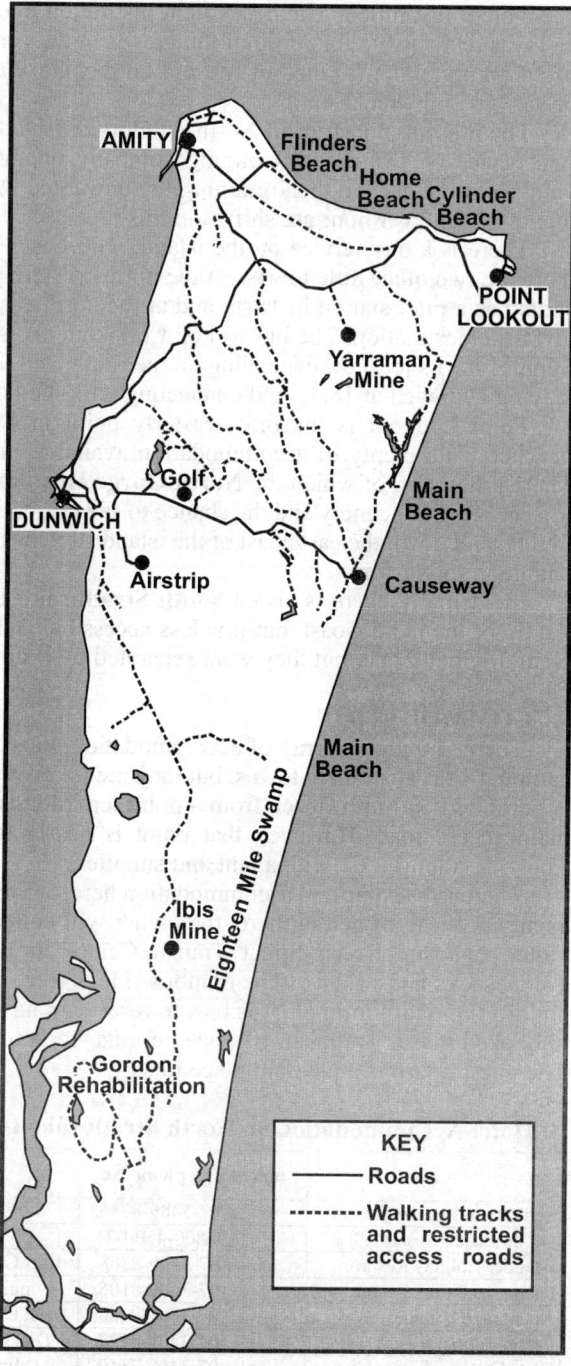

benevolent institution. The benevolent institution operated here from 1866 until 1947 and was responsible for 8,000 of the graves in the cemetery. There are also the graves of 26 immigrants who died of typhoid on the ship *Emigrant* in 1850, and the victims of various shipwrecks.

The present industries of North Stradbroke Island are tourism and sand mining. In two places on the island a mining company operates, mining the sand, extracting valuable minerals and then returning the unwanted 99% to its original location. 3,000 tonnes of sand per hour are shifted in this process.

There is a bus service on the island, with buses meeting most ferry arrivals, and there are two other little towns. At the north-western point of the island is **Amity**, first settled as a pilot station in 1825, and at the north-eastern point is **Point Lookout**, the favourite destination. The bus to Point Lookout takes between twenty minutes and 45 minutes for its journey, depending on the route, and there are nine buses a day, the last leaving Dunwich at 18:45 and connecting with the last ferry arrival from Cleveland.

Point Lookout is the most easterly point in Queensland. There is a series of beaches, with plenty of accommodation available, for this is a popular holiday spot. There are walks, of which the **North Gorge Headlands** walk is the most spectacular, offering coastal scenery and the chance to see turtles and dolphins. There are places for diving, and down the east coast of the island stretches **Main Beach**, 32 kilometres long and good for surfing.

Incidentally, there is also a **South Stradbroke Island**, stretching down nearly to the tip of the Gold Coast, but it is less accessible and less developed. The two islands were originally one, but they were separated by a storm in 1896.

ACCOMMODATION

There is quite an array of accommodation, most of it at Point Lookout. There are camping sites at all three towns, but they are relatively expensive at $13. Free camping is permitted on Main Beach from a point ten kilometres south of the causeway on the main access road. However, that point is nearly twenty kilometres south of Point Lookout, a long walk with a tent and supplies.

There is backpackers accommodation here, at Stradbroke Island Guest House, and, as an easy way of getting here, the owner will collect guests from outside the Abbey Hotel, opposite Roma Street Transit Centre in Brisbane, at 14:20 on Mondays, Wednesdays and Fridays. The minibus ride is free, but you pay for the ferry crossing and for the return journey. It is best to reserve in advance for this minibus service, but unbooked guests are taken if space permits, so you can make a last-minute decision. The guest house is a pleasant place to stay.

(i) Hotel Accommodation on North Stradbroke Island

Name	Stars	Telephone No.	Address	Lowest Price (Double/Twin)
Samarinda Holiday Resort	4	07-3409-8785	Point Lookout	$140
Ocean Beach Resort		1-800-450-004	Point Lookout	$135
Islander Holiday Resort		07-3409-8388	East Coast Road, Pt Lookout	$110
Pandanus Palms Resort		07-3409-8106	Cummings Pde, Pt Lookout	$110
Anchorage Village		07-3409-8266	East Coast Road, Pt Lookout	$110
Island Tourist Resort		07-3409-8127	Dickson Way, Pt. Lookout	$105
Cosy Cottages		07-3409-7119	Mirimar Street, Amity	$79
Amity Holiday Village		07-3409-7161	Cook Street, Amity	$75
Stradbroke Beach Hotel	3	07-3409-8188	East Coast Road, Pt Lookout	$75

NORTH STRADBROKE ISLAND 253

(ii) Backpackers Hostel on North Stradbroke Island

Name	Group	Telephone No.	Address	Lowest Price (Dormitory)
Strradbroke Island Guest Hse		07-3409-8888	1 East Coast Road, Point Lookout	$22

MOVING ON

Moving on is by bus to Dunwich, ferry across to Cleveland and then train to Brisbane, as you came. If you stay at Stradbroke Island Guest House minibus transport is available to Brisbane on Mondays, Wednesdays and Fridays.

TOOWOOMBA
Population 90,000

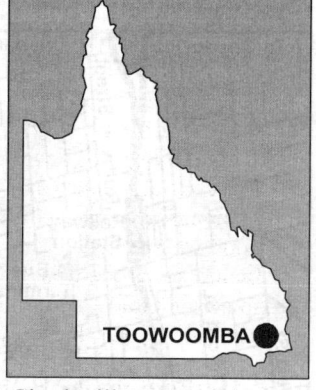

2 hrs by bus from Brisbane

Toowoomba is the largest inland city in Queensland and is known for its gardens. It hosts the Carnival of Flowers at the end of September each year. Perched high on the Great Dividing Range, it has good views over the Lockyer Valley and just the journey up to the city from Brisbane, or back down again, is worth experiencing.

Queensland Railways has long given up operating trains to Toowoomba, claiming that the service was too slow to be able to compete with buses. The only train which does pass this way now is the *Westlander*, bound for Charleville, on Tuesday and Thursday evenings. It takes almost four hours to make the journey of 161 kilometres from Brisbane to Toowoomba, compared with the two hours, or just over, taken by buses operated by McCafferty's and Greyhound for their journey of only 126 to 133 kilometres. Even though the rail route is a scenic one, the train departure is in the evening, so one does not see it in any case. What is recommended, if it should prove convenient, is the return rail trip on Thursdays and Saturdays. The train leaves Toowoomba at 7:00 and reaches Brisbane at 11:05. It is a pretty journey. On the way, the train will pass through **Spring Bluff Station**, and stop there on request. This is a particularly attractive station in a beautiful hillside setting. In 1914, Queensland Railways staged a competition for railway station gardens, a challenge which the stationmaster here really took to heart. The garden has been kept up in later years by volunteers, since the station is no longer staffed, and has a fine display of flowers.

However, the bus ride is also scenic. McCafferty's operates five services per day between Brisbane and Toowoomba, while Greyhound has one.

Toowoomba has a university and several well known schools, and also has some interesting old buildings. The **Cobb and Co. Museum** of horse-drawn vehicles is at 27 Lindsay Street, open daily from 10:00 until 16:00 and costing $5. It includes the vehicle used on the last Cobb and Co. stagecoach journey operated in Australia, from Yuleba to Surat, both towns in Queensland, in 1924.

There is a **Waterbird Sanctuary** in Mackenzie Street, open from 6:00 until 18:30 every day. Admission is free. There is a **Japanese Garden** in the University grounds, and there is in the city the oldest regional **art gallery** in Queensland, established in 1938, but now housed in a new building in Ruthven Street. The gallery is open from 10:00 (13:00 on Sundays) until 16:00, except on Mondays. Admission is free.

254 QUEENSLAND
ACCOMMODATION
Accommodation in Toowoomba

Name	Stars	No. on Map	Telephone No.	Address	Lowest Price (Double/Twin)
Burke and Wills	4	4	1-800-633-679	554 Ruthven Street	$125
Grammar View	4	7	1-800-192-122	39 Margaret Street	$107
Applegum Inn	4	6	1-800-659-142	41 Margaret Street	$101
Park Motor Inn	4	5	1-800-244-800	88 Margaret Street	$100
Highlander Motor Inn	4½	1	07-4638-4955	226 James Street	$80
Blue Violet Motor Inn	3½	8	07-4638-1488	31 Margaret Street	$75
Shamrock Hotel	4	3	07-4632-2666	604 Ruthven Street	$75
Whiteoaks Motel	3	10	07-4639-2999	12 Margaret Street	$75
Apollo Lodge	3	2	07-4632-1222	210 James Street	$75
Motel Glenworth	3½	9	07-4638-1799	1 Margaret Street	$70

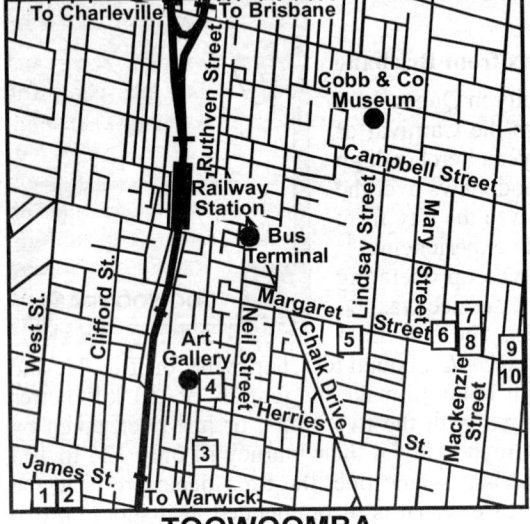

TOOWOOMBA
Numerals indicate accommodation

MOVING ON
(i) By Rail

To Brisbane there are only the two trains mentioned above. The timetable for this service is on page 257. The timetable to Charleville, and on by bus to Cunnamulla or Quilpie, appears on page 239.

(ii) By Bus

There are five bus services per day with McCafferty's to Brisbane, and one with Greyhound. Travelling west and north, there is one McCafferty's bus a day to Charleville, and one to Mt. Isa. To the south, there is a McCafferty's service to Sydney via Tamworth, a Greyhound service to Dubbo via Tamworth, and a McCafferty's service to Melbourne via Moree and Dubbo. Crisps operates two services a day to Warwick. The morning bus connects with an onward service to Moree and also one south a short distance to Stanthorpe. The afternoon bus connects with an onward service to Tenterfield.

Destination	Operator	Via	Distance (km)	Fare	Journey Time	Frequency
Brisbane	McCafferty's		126	$25	2 - 2¼ hrs	5/day
Brisbane	Greyhound		133	$25	2¼ hrs	1/day
Mt. Isa	McCafferty's		1760	$167	22¼ hrs	1/day
		Longreach	1126	$113	14¾ hrs	1/day
Charleville	McCafferty's		610	$71	9¼ hrs	1/day
Melbourne	McCafferty's		1670	$202	22 hrs	1/day
		Dubbo	719	$125	11 hrs	1/day
		Moree	343	$79	6 hrs	1/day
Dubbo	Greyhound		828	$125	13 hrs	4/week
		Tamworth	485	$75	8¾ hrs	4/week
Sydney	McCafferty's		940	$98	17 hrs	1/day
		Tamworth	500	$75	9 hrs	1/day
Warwick	Crisps		84	$18	1¼ hrs	2/day

CHARLEVILLE
Population 3,500
16 hrs 30 mins by train from Brisbane
11 hrs by bus from Brisbane

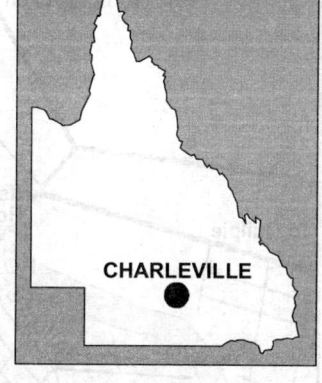

Charleville is not a place which many visitors get to, but McCafferty's operates a bus to here every day, and it is only just off the same company's route to Mt. Isa. Charleville is also the town at the end of a long rail journey west, so it is quite a convenient stopping point for those who are trying to see a little more than the well trodden route up and down the east coast.

Charleville is a typical outback town, small, a long way from anywhere else, rough, friendly and with no immediately apparent reason for its existence. It is, in fact, a centre for the sheep and cattle farming industries and a town through which several road routes pass, and it is in this location, rather than another, because of the **Warrego River** which runs through its heart.

Queensland Railways still runs a train here twice a week, the *Westlander*, departing from Brisbane on Tuesdays and Thursdays. It is not the best of the journeys in the state because it leaves Brisbane in the evening, just as it is getting dark, so one sees nothing until the next morning, by which time one is already at **Roma**, a former exploration area for natural oil and gas, and onto the endless flat western plains. However, even the few hours of daylight between Roma and Charleville give one a chance to appreciate the desolation and harshness of the Australian outback. Moreover, who knows how long this train will continue to run, so take it while you can. The other delightful train which used to head west from Brisbane, the *Dirranbandi Mail*, one of Queensland's few remaining 'mixed' trains (i.e. goods trains with a couple of passenger carriages attached to the rear) has already disappeared. When the author last took the *Westlander*, it used to divide at Charleville and continue part to Cunnamulla and part to Quilpie, but now there are only bus connexions to those two towns.

The journey to Charleville by bus is a faster one than by train. McCafferty's has a service every morning, the journey being completed in just under eleven hours.

In the early days, several explorers passed near here. Kennedy passed within about ten kilometres in 1847. Gregory came in 1858, and Landsborough also, while searching for Burke and Wills in 1862. A tree marked by Landsborough is visible some twenty kilometres from Charleville. The first settlers arrived in 1863 and the first hotel was erected in 1865. The town was surveyed and named, after the Irish hometown of the surveyor, in 1868. Cobb and Co. established a coach works here in 1886, and the railway arrived in 1888. The first Qantas scheduled flight was between Charleville and Cloncurry, starting on 2nd November 1922 and taking two days.

There is a **Visitor Information Centre** in Charleville, a short walk south of the railway station, and some places of interest around the town. There is an **aboriginal workshop**, open on weekdays from 8:00 until 16:00 at a cost of $2. The **Royal Flying Doctor Service Visitor Centre** is open daily from 9:00 until 17:00, with admission costing $3. The **National Parks and Wildlife Visitor Centre** is open on weekdays from 9:00 until 16:00, with donations solicited. The **School of the Air** costs $2 and is open on schooldays from 10:00 until 14:00. **Stargazing** at the airport every evening

256 QUEENSLAND

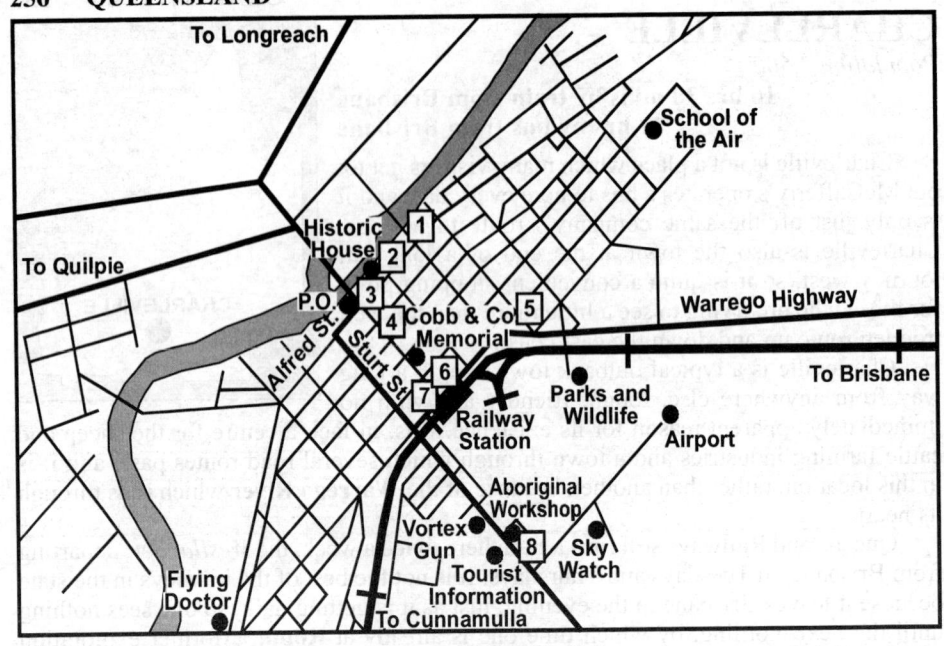

CHARLEVILLE
Numerals indicate accommodation

costs $10. There are also tours of **Gowrie** Cattle Station, the first settlement established in the area, 24 kilometres from the town. These cost $20, including refreshments. Then there is a stone marking the site of the **Cobb and Co. factory** which was the last in Australia to produce the company's coaches, closing down in 1920. The factory itself was burnt down on Christmas Eve 1980. You will also find around the town photographs of the **amazing hailstorm** which hit in 1947, killing hundreds of chickens and other birds and leaving indentations on canopies which can still be seen today.

ACCOMMODATION
Accommodation in Charleville

Name	Stars	No. on Map	Telephone No.	Address	Lowest Price (Double/Twin)
Mulga Country Motor Inn		8	07-4654-3255	Sturt Street	$97
Charleville Motel		5	07-4654-1566	148 King Street	$75
Warrego Motel	3½	6	07-4654-1299	73 Wills Street	$75
Waltzing Matilda Inn	2½	2	07-4654-1720	125 Alfred Street	$50
Cattle Camp Hotel		1	07-4654-3473	Alfred Street	$45
Charleville Hotel		3	07-4654-1076	Wills Street	$45
Corones Hotel / Motel		4	07-4654-1022	Wills Street	$45
Railway Hotel		7	07-4654-1091	Wills Street	$45

MOVING ON
(i) By Train
The train timetable for the return journey to Brisbane, including bus connexions from Cunnamaulla and Quilpie, is given to the right.

(ii) By Bus
Buses operate once a day to Brisbane. By going back to the next town of Morven, it is then possible to continue north to Mt. Isa. On Wednesdays and Fridays there are Queensland Railways buses to Cunnamulla and Quilpie, connecting with the arrival of the *Westlander*.

Quilpie, Cunnamulla and Charleville to Brisbane

Days of Departure	W, F (Bus)	W, F (Bus)	W, F
Quilpie	1505		
Cunnamulla		1505	
Charleville	1740	1735	1815
Roma			2337
Toowoomba			0700
Brisbane			1105
Days of Arrival			Th, Sat

Destination	Operator	Via	Distance (km)	Fare	Journey Time	Frequency
Brisbane	McCafferty's		743	$79	9½ hrs	1/day
Cunnamulla	QR		208	$19.60	2½ hrs	2/week
Quilpie	QR		216	$19.60	2¾ hrs	2/week

SUNSHINE COAST
Populations - Bribie Island 15,000
Caloundra 25,000
Maroochydore 18,000
Noosa Heads 10,000
3 hrs by bus from Brisbane (Noosa Heads)

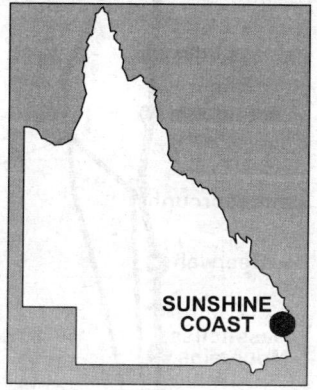

Less famous than its southern neighbour the Gold Coast, the Sunshine Coast perhaps benefits from its lack of fame. It lies to the north-east of Brisbane, and has two well known centres: Maroochydore, where there is an airport, and Noosa Heads, which is a popular destination with visitors. In fact, though, a series of beaches stretches up the coast here, as can be seen from the map on the following page. All offer accommodation of various standards, including backpackers hostels in several places.

Buses are operated by both Brisbane Bus Lines and Suncoast Pacific to Maroochydore, and by Suncoast Pacific to Noosa Heads. In addition, some of the long-distance services operated by McCafferty's and Greyhound (but not all) pass through the Sunshine Coast, and Premier runs its service by this route too.

To travel by rail, one takes a suburban train to Nambour and then a connecting bus to Noosa Heads. However, Nambour is outside the area of frequent services, so there are only eight such connexions per day. There are also buses from Nambour to Maroochydore and Caloundra. These do not connect with trains, but run hourly - at present at 20 minutes past most hours. The journey takes half an hour to Maroochydore and an hour and a half to Caloundra.

Local services on the Sunshine Coast are provided by Sunbus. Buses run along the coast, serving all the beaches, at approximately half-hourly intervals.

QUEENSLAND

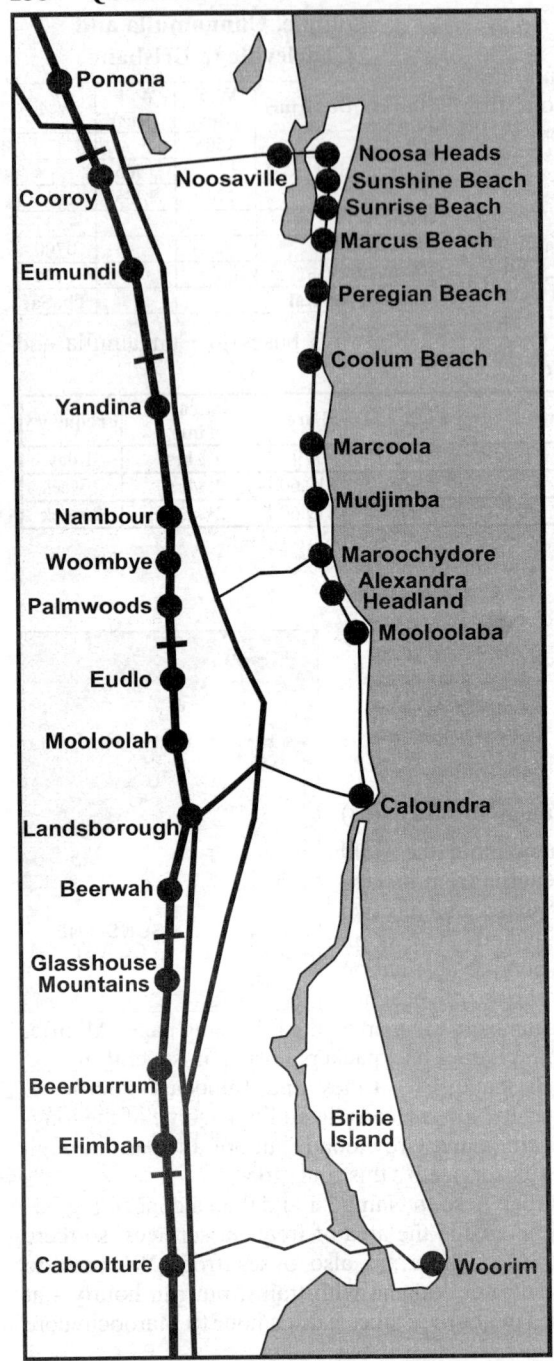

THE SUNSHINE COAST

At the southern extremity of the Sunshine Coast area, **Bribie Island** is becoming a popular destination. The island is reached via the short connecting **Pumicestone Passage Bridge**. Buses run from **Caboolture**, which is the last station on the frequent-service suburban rail network. The train takes approximately 65 minutes from Brisbane to Caboolture and the connecting bus takes 30 minutes. There are fourteen buses a day.

Bribie Island (see map opposite) is 31 kilometres long and has a population of 15,000. Most of the island is a National Park. It offers long white sandy beaches and chances to view marine life. The main towns, both quite small, are **Bongaree** and **Woorim**. Most buses from Caboolture run through to Woorim, but there are also local bus services on the island, operated by Bribie Island Coaches, and connexions to these services are made at the **Bribie Centre** in Bongaree. Route 1 runs north to **Bellara** and **Banksia Beach**, while route 2 runs between Bongaree and Woorim, travelling via the suburbs of Bongaree on the return journey.

Bribie Island has a number of **canals** surrounded by desirable housing in the south-western part of the island. North of Woorim are some **Second World War relics**. There are three **talking monuments**. There is an **Arts Centre** in Bellara, and near Woorim there is a good lookout with a **statue of Matthew Flinders**. The nearby point was named **Skirmish Point** by Flinders because of an altercation which he had there with the aborigines.

SUNSHINE COAST

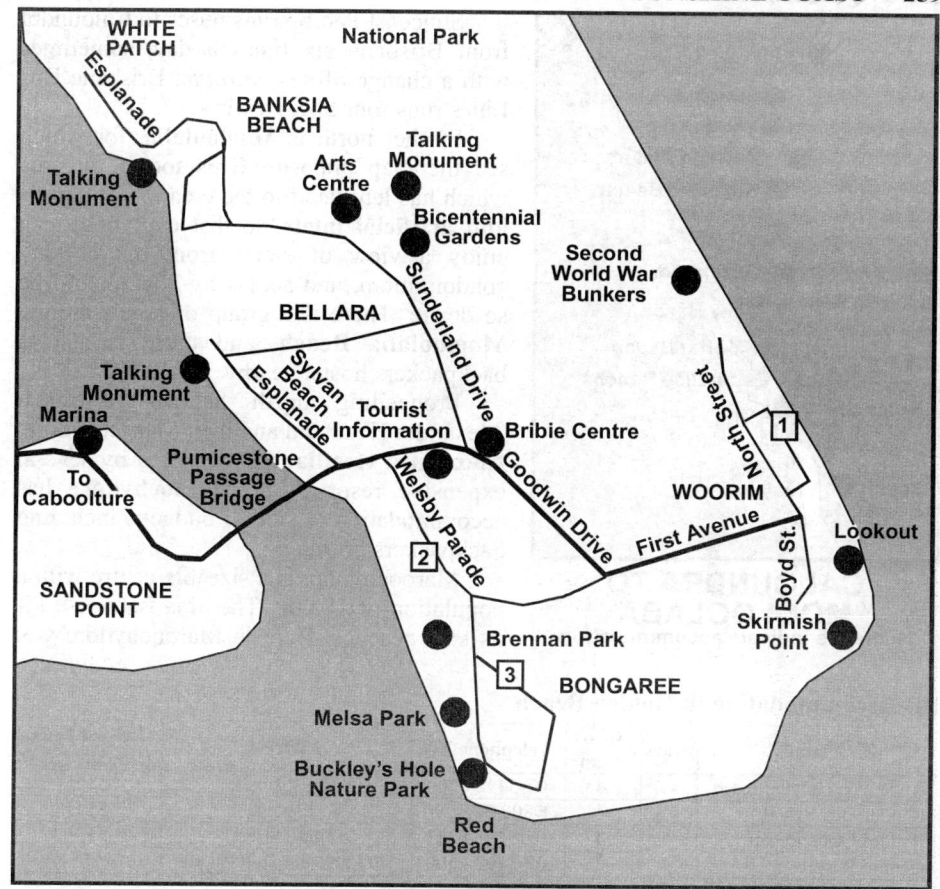

BRIBIE ISLAND
Numerals indicate accommodation

ACCOMMODATION
(i) Accommodation on Bribie Island

Name	Stars	No. on Map	Telephone No.	Address	Lowest Price (Double/Twin)
Placid Waters Apartments		3	07-3408-2122	Toorbul Street, Bongaree	$105
Bribie Waterways Resort		2	1-800-072-080	155 Welsby Pde., Bongaree	$65
Surf Side Oceanfront		1	07-3408-1077	Rickman Parade, Woorim	$45

Limited accommodation is available on Bribie Island, of which a sample is above.

The largest place on the Sunshine Coast is one of the less known - **Caloundra**, with a population of 25,000. Again beaches are its attraction. Starting in the south, one finds **Golden Beach** and **Bulcock Beach**, both sheltered from the open sea by Bribie Island. Near the centre of Caloundra are **Kings Beach** and **Shelley Beach**, both popular. Further north lie **Moffat Beach** and **Dicky Beach** (see map on next page). The area is known for its good fishing as well as for its beaches.

260 QUEENSLAND

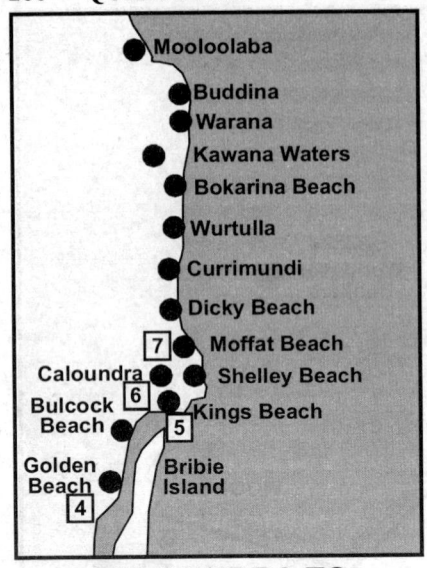

CALOUNDRA TO MOOLOOLABA
Numerals indicate accommodation

Suncoast Pacific runs buses to Caloundra from Brisbane six times a day, sometimes with a change of bus *en route*. Brisbane Bus Lines runs four buses a week.

Further north is **Mooloolaba**, for which see the map opposite. This too is an area which has lent itself to the creation of **canals and artificial inlets**, so that everybody can enjoy a view of water from his holiday condominium, and access by boat should he so desire. There is a group of hotels around **Mooloolaba Beach**, and there is also a backpackers hostel nearby.

Proceeding north again, we reach Alexandra Headland and then Maroochydore. **Alexandra Headland** is occupied by several expensive resorts, but **Maroochydore** has accommodation to suit all budgets, including backpackers hostels.

Maroochydore is a sizeable centre with a population of 18,000. The area is known for its surf beaches. Here in Maroochydore you

(ii) Accommodation in Golden Beach

Name	Stars	No. on Map	Telephone No.	Address	Lowest Price (Double/Twin)
Riviere on Golden Beach	4½	4	07-5492-3200	72 Esplanade	$145
Rendezvous Resort	4½	4	1-800-222-290	75 Esplanade	$135
Rydges Oasis Resort	4	4	07-5491-0333	North Street	$135
Gemini Resort	4	4	07-5492-2200	49 Landsborough Parade	$85

(iii) Accommodation in Kings Beach

Name	Stars	No. on Map	Telephone No.	Address	Lowest Price (Double/Twin)
Cape View Apartments		5	07-5491-6436	26 Orvieto Terrace	$145
Casablanca Apartments	3½	5	07-5491-4323	Edmund Street	$125
Seapoint Ocean Apts.		5	07-5491-2433	32 Victoria Terrace	$125
Rolling Surf Resort		5	07-5491-9777	100 Levuka Avenue	$90
Pandanus Shores Apts.	4½	5	07-5492-8922	1 The Esplanade	$75
Pacific View Resort		5	07-5491-1200	34 Victoria Terrace	$75
Lindomare Apartments	3½	5	07-5492-5922	11 Orvieto Terrace	$70

(iv) Accommodation in Central Caloundra

Name	Stars	No. on Map	Telephone No.	Address	Lowest Price (Double/Twin)
Portobello by the Sea	4½	6	07-5491-9038	6 Beerburrum Street	$110
Belaire Place		6	07-5491-8688	34 Minchinton Street	$105
Anchorage Motor Inn	3½	6	07-5491-1499	18 Bowman Road	$85
Caloundra Motel	2½	6	07-5491-1411	30 Bowman Road	$55
Hotel Caloundra		6	07-5491-1388	12 Bulcock Street	$55

SUNSHINE COAST

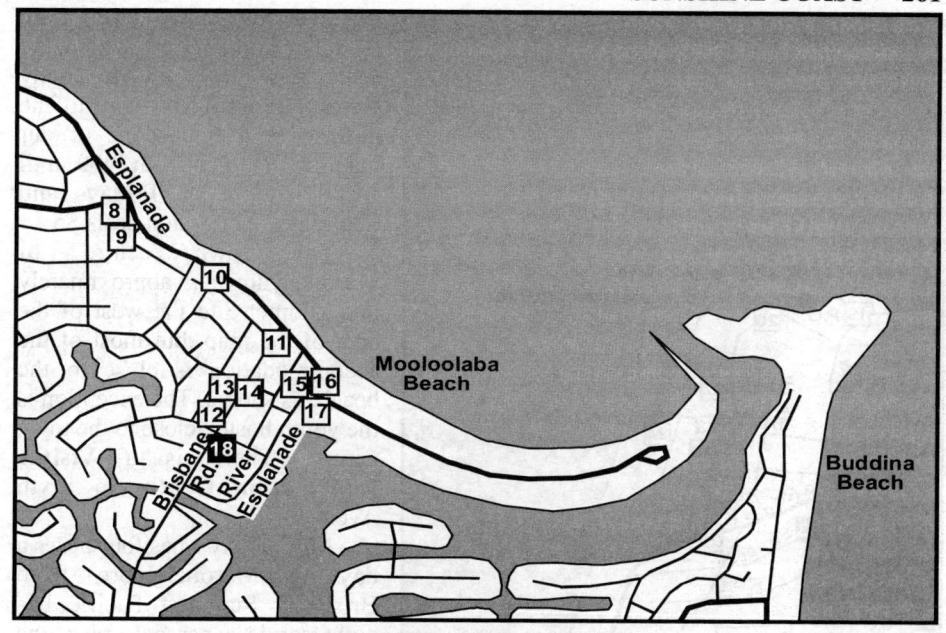

MOOLOOLABA
Black numerals in white boxes indicate hotel accommodation
White numerals in black boxes indicate backpackers hostels

(v) Accommodation in Moffat Beach

Name	Stars	No. on Map	Telephone No.	Address	Lowest Price (Double/Twin)
The Norfolks	3½	7	07-5492-6666	32 Queen of Colonies Pde.	$135
Raintrees Resort	3½	7	07-5491-5555	1 Bryce Street	$90
Wandalua Motel	3½	7	07-5491-2122	Roderick & Buccleugh Sts.	$70
Estoril on Moffat	3	7	07-5491-5799	38 McIlwraith Street	$70

(vi) Hotel Accommodation in Mooloolaba

Name	Stars	No. on Map	Telephone No.	Address	Lowest Price (Double/Twin)
Osprey Apartments	4	8	07-5444-6966	Buderim Av. & Esplanade	$155
Sandcastles on the Beach	3½	17	07-5478-0666	Parkyn Parade & River Esp.	$155
Pacific Beach Resort	3½	10	07-5444-4733	95 Esplanade	$150
Beach Club Resort	4	9	1-800-682-181	Meta Street & First Avenue	$110
Peninsular		11	07-5444-4477	Esplanade & Brisbane Road	$100
Nautilus Resort	4	15	07-5444-3877	30 River Esplanade	$100
Beachside Mooloolaba	4	14	07-5478-3911	35 Brisbane Road	$98
Flag Mooloolaba Motel	3½	12	07-5444-2988	46 Brisbane Road	$90
Newport Motel	3½	16	1-800-645-410	Parkyn Parade & River Esp.	$90
Twin Pines	3	13	07-5444-2522	36 Brisbane Road	$65

(vii) Backpackers Hostel in Mooloolaba

Name	Group	No. on Map	Telephone No.	Address	Lowest Price (Dormitory)
Mooloolaba Beach B/P	VIP	18	1800-020-120	75 Brisbane Road	$24

QUEENSLAND

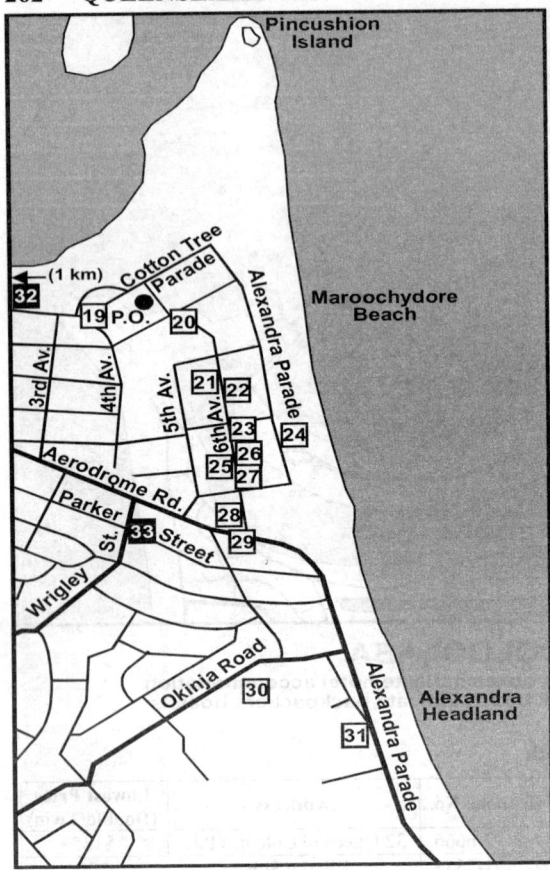

MAROOCHYDORE BEACH
Black numerals indicate hotel accommodation
White numerals indicate backpackers hostels

can also find a two-thirds scale model of Captain Cook's ship, the *Endeavour*. It is at **Maroochy River Resort**, some way to the north-west of the scope of our map, and is open from 9:00 until 14:00, except on Fridays and Saturdays. Admission costs $5.

The town centre of Maroochydore is approximately one kilometre to the west of the area of the map, but most of the accommodation is close to the beach, as shown. The exception is the youth hostel, close to the town centre. There is a **Visitor Information Centre** in Sixth Avenue.

McCafferty's has four buses a day to Maroochydore from Brisbane. Suncoast Pacific has eight services per day, plus one from Byron Bay and Surfers Paradise. Brisbane Bus Lines operates four times a week.

Again moving north, we come to **Coolum Beach**, favoured by surfers. See the map on the next page. Accommodation here is clustered around the south of the beach, but the backpackers hostel is near the northern

(viii) Hotel Accommodation in Maroochydore

Name	Stars	No. on Map	Telephone No.	Address	Lowest Price (Double/Twin)
Ocean Boulevard	4	31	07-5443-4933	136 Alexandra Parade	$155
Argyle on the Park	4½	19	07-5443-3022	31 Cotton Tree Parade	$130
Catalina Resort	4	22	07-5443-8666	47 Sixth Avenue	$110
Chateau Royale	4	20	07-5443-0300	Sixth & Memorial Avenues	$105
Coachman's Courte	3½	25	07-5443-5876	94 Sixth Avenue	$99
Beach Motor Inn	3	23	1-800-817-593	61 Sixth Avenue	$98
Sundeck Gardens Apts.	3½	24	07-5443-2797	70 Alexandra Parade	$90
Heritage Motor Inn	3½	26	07-5443-7355	69 Sixth Avenue	$90
Maroochy Sands Units		28	07-5443-1637	Sixth Av. & Aerodrome Rd.	$85
Blue Waters Motel	3	21	07-5443-6700	64 Sixth Avenue	$75
Beachfront Towers	3½	29	07-5443-3443	4 Aerodrome Road	$75
Elouera Tower	3½	27	07-5443-5988	81 Sixth Avenue	$70
Alexandra Gardens		30	07-5443-2356	Okinja Road	$55

(ix) Backpackers Hostels in Maroochydore

Name	Group	No. on Map	Telephone No.	Address	Lowest Price (Dormitory)
Suncoast Backpackers	VIP	33	07-5443-7544	50 Parker Street	$24
Maroochydore Y.H.A.	YHA	32	07-5443-3151	24 Schirrmann Drive	$22

extremity at the corner of Ann Street.

Still proceeding north, **Sunrise Beach**, and then **Sunshine Beach**, lie adjacent to Noosa Heads, but while the two beaches are on the eastern sea coast, Noosa Heads is on the sheltered estuary of the Noosa River. See the maps on the following two pages.

There is accommodation at both Sunrise and Sunshine Beach, including a backpackers hostel at the latter.

Noosa Heads, though the smallest of the main towns, with a population of 10,000, is the most popular and fashionable of the Sunshine Coast destinations, and is filled with restaurants and accommodation of all types. **Hastings Street** is its heart and there you can find not only the most expensive resorts, but also one of the three backpackers hostels.

A **National Park** includes the area immediately to the east of the town, and is a good place for walking. The National Park can also be reached from the north of Sunshine Beach.

First Point and **Alexandria Bay** are the spots for surfers.

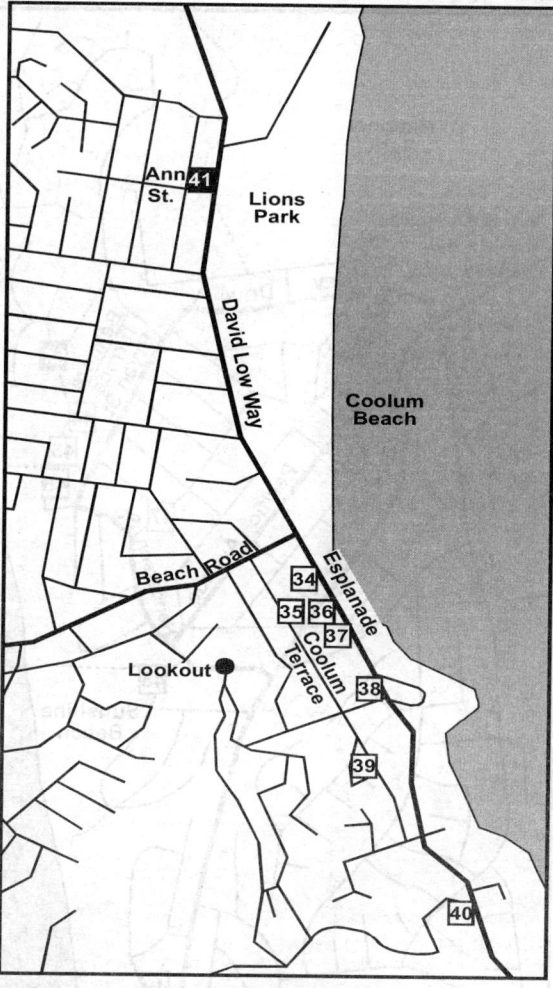

COOLUM BEACH

Black numerals indicate hotel accommodation
White numerals indicate backpackers hostels

(x) Hotel Accommodation in Coolum Beach

Name	Stars	No. on Map	Telephone No.	Address	Lowest Price (Double/Twin)
Pandanus Coolum Beach	3½	38	07-5446-3905	1 Coolum Esplanade	$200
Coolum Baywatch	4½	36	07-5446-5500	1766 David Low Way	$165
Coolum Caprice	4	37	07-5446-2177	1770 David Low Way	$165
The Point	4½	40	07-5440-9888	1 Bay Terrace	$135
Beach Retreat	4½	34	1-800-068-648	1750 David Low Way	$100
Villa Coolum		39	07-5446-1286	102 Coolum Terrace	$90
Surf Dance Coolum		35	07-5446-1039	29 Coolum Terrace	$85

(xi) Backpackers Hostel in Coolum Beach

Name	Group	No. on Map	Telephone No.	Address	Lowest Price (Dormitory)
Coolum Beach Budget		41	07-5471-6666	Ann Street	$25

QUEENSLAND

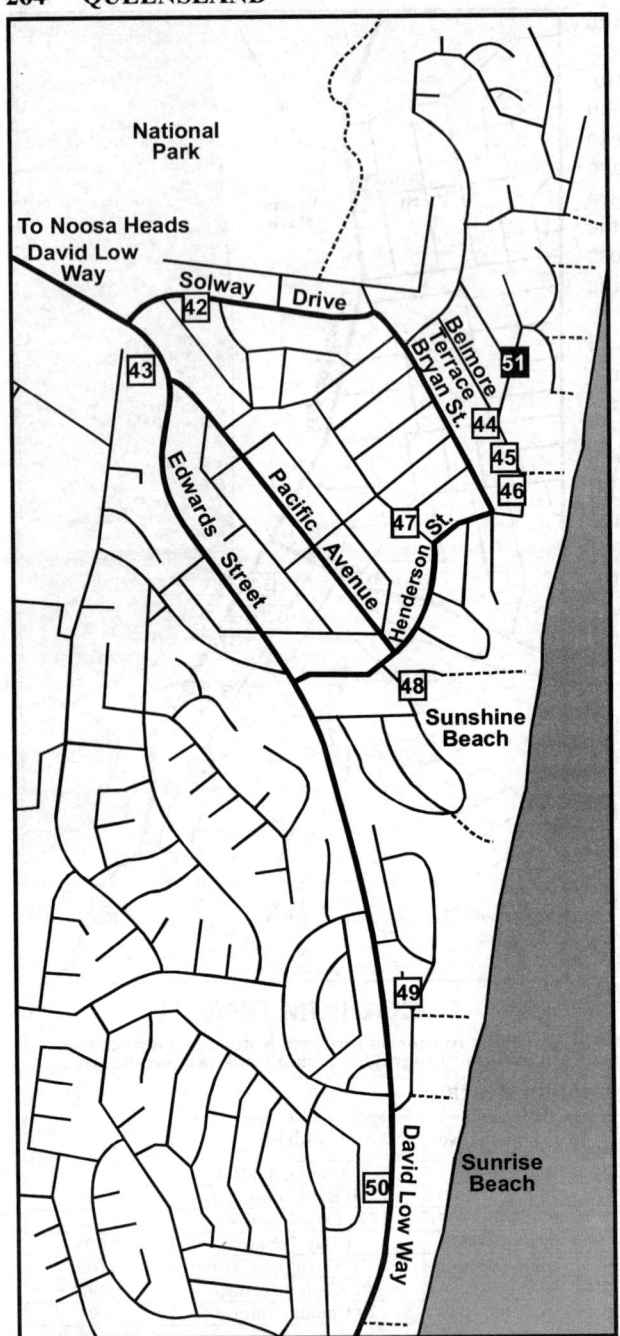

SUNSHINE BEACH AND SUNRISE BEACH
Black numerals indicate hotel accommodation
White numerals indicate backpackers hostels

Noosa Heads is served by Suncoast Pacific buses seven times a day from Brisbane and once from Byron Bay and Surfers Paradise. McCafferty's runs five services from Brisbane. There are also services from Brisbane Airport. By train, there are eight connecting buses per day from Nambour.

ACCOMMODATION

There is a great deal of accommodation in this region, but again, since it is a holiday area, there may be problems at busy times of the year with substantial increases in rates compared with those stated here, and also with establishments requiring minimum lengths of stay. In general, the lower priced accommodation tends to increase rates less and to accommodate one-night stays more readily.

For backpackers, there is plenty of choice in this area, with Maroochydore and Noosa the favoured locations, but there are also hostels in Mooloolaba, Coolum Beach and Sunshine Beach. A further hostel is located in **Tewantin**, on the banks of the Noosa River. Gagaju Bush Camp specialises in environmentally acceptable methods of backpack travel.

Prices of backpackers accommodation do not vary seasonally, but availability does, of course.

SUNSHINE COAST

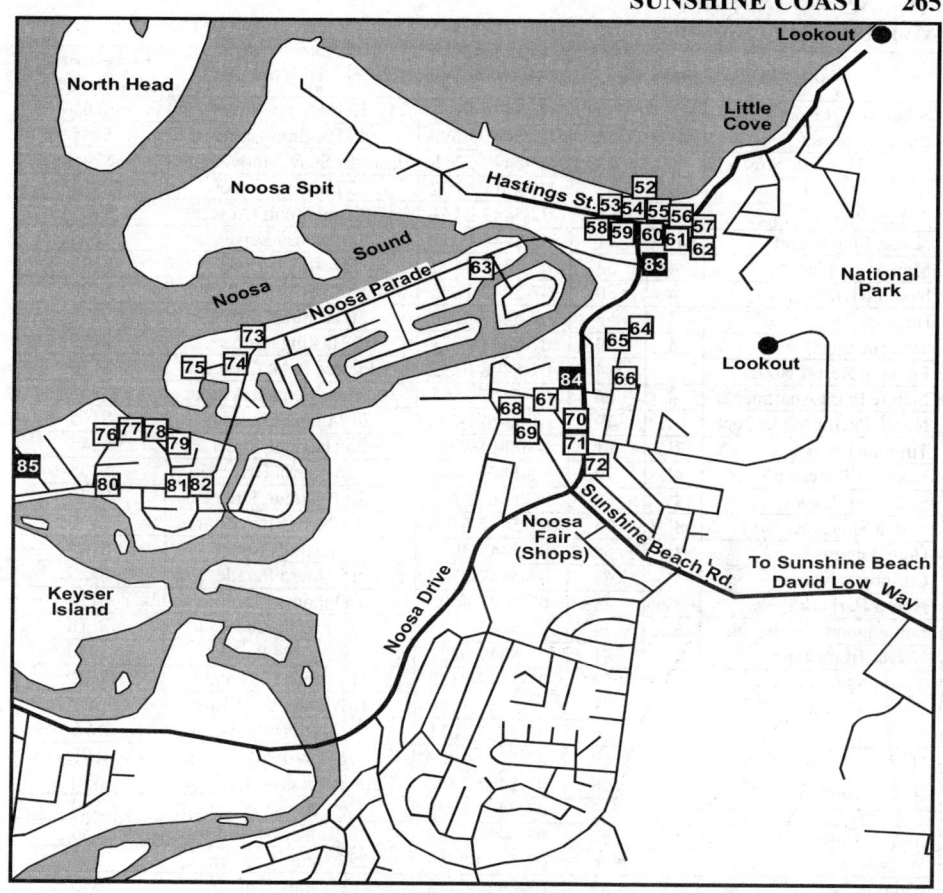

NOOSA HEADS

Black numerals in white boxes indicate hotel accommodation
White numerals in black boxes indicate backpackers hostels

(xii) Hotel Accommodation in Sunshine Beach and Sunrise Beach

Name	Stars	No. on Map	Telephone No.	Address	Lowest Price (Double/Twin)
Costa Nova	4½	46	07-5447-2709	1 Belmore Terrace	$210
Sunseeker Lodge	3½	48	07-5447-5344	Ross Cres. & Pilchers Gap	$155
Sunshine Vista	4½	47	07-5447-2487	45 Duke Street	$150
La Mer Sunshine	4½	45	07-5447-4200	5 Belmore Terrace	$140
Aqua Promenade	4½	49	07-5474-5788	1 Selene Street	$125
Beach Breakers	3½	50	07-5447-2829	75 David Low Way	$120
Andari Units	4½	44	07-5474-9996	19 Belmore Terrace	$110
Northgate Holiday Apts.	2½	42	07-5449-2009	4 Solway Drive	$90
Chez Noosa Resort Motel		43	07-5447-2027	263 David Low Way	$80

(xiii) Backpackers Hostel in Sunshine Beach

Name	Group	No. on Map	Telephone No.	Address	Lowest Price (Dormitory)
Backpackers on the Beach	VIP	51	1800-240-344	26 Stevens Street	$24

266 QUEENSLAND

(xiv) Hotel Accommodation in Noosa Heads

Name	Stars	No. on Map	Telephone No.	Address	Lowest Price (Double/Twin)
Sebel Resort Noosa		52	07-5474-6400	32 Hastings Street	$265
Emerald Noosa	4½	54	1-800-803-899	42 Hastings Street	$245
No.1 in Hastings Street	4½	62	07-5449-2211	Hastings St. & Morwong Dr	$245
Netanya Noosa	4½	57	1-800-072-072	75 Hastings Street	$215
Picture Point Terraces	4½	65	07-5449-2433	47 Picture Point Crescent	$205
Noosa Blue Resort	4½	71	07-5447-5699	16 Noosa Drive	$205
Maison La Plage	4	53	07-5447-4400	5 Hastings Street	$195
Noosa Riviera	4	80	07-5474-1800	Munna Cres. & Noosa Pde.	$190
Hastings	3½	55	07-5447-5100	30 Hastings Street	$175
Two Hastings	4	59	07-5448-0777	2 Hastings Street	$175
Lookout Resort Noosa		64	07-5448-0533	1 Picture Point Crescent	$170
Picture Point Apartments	4	66	07-5447-5255	30 Edgar Bennett Avenue	$165
Noosa Pacific Waterfront	4½	79	1-800-671-544	24 Munna Crescent	$165
Tingirana Noosa	2½	61	1-800-089-642	25 Hastings Street	$145
Noosa Hill Resort	4½	70	1-800-631-050	26 Noosa Drive	$135
Seahaven Resort	3½	60	1-800-072-013	13 Hastings Street	$130
Noosa Shores Resort	3½	73	07-5447-5766	86 Noosa Parade	$130
Hotel Laguna	3½	58	07-5447-3077	6 Hastings Street	$125
Caribbean Noosa	3½	63	07-5447-2247	15 Noosa Parade	$125
Noosa Harbour Resort	3½	75	07-5447-4500	Quamby Place	$115
Sun Lagoon Apartments	3½	74	07-5447-4833	1 Quamby Place	$110
Noosa Tropicana	4½	81	07-5449-0222	140 Noosa Parade	$110
Noosa Sound Resort	3	77	07-5449-8122	11 Munna Crescent	$100
Skippers' Cove		78	07-5449-8946	16 Munna Crescent	$98
Jacaranda Units	3	56	07-5447-4011	12 Hastings Street	$95
Grantlea Holiday Lodges	4	69	07-5447-4467	34 Grant Street	$95
Killara Apartments	4	68	07-5447-2800	Grant Street & Banksia Av.	$90
Bottlebrush Townhouses	3½	72	07-5447-3188	1 Bottlebrush Avenue	$90
Myuna Units	3½	67	07-5447-5588	19 Katharina Street	$80
Wolngarin	3½	76	07-5449-8755	27 Munna Crescent	$80
Nautilus Noosa	3½	82	07-5449-9188	124 Noosa Parade	$75

(xv) Backpackers Hostels in Noosa Heads

Name	Group	No. on Map	Telephone No.	Address	Lowest Price (Dormitory)
Koala Beach Resort	VIP	84	1800-357-457	44 Noosa Drive	$24
Noosa Backpackers Resort	VIP	85	1800-626-673	9 William Street	$24
Halse Lodge Guesthouse	YHA	83	1800-242-567	2 Halse Lane	$21
Gagaju Bush Camp	B&W		07-5474-3522	118 John's Drive, Tewantin	$22

MOVING ON

Suncoast Pacific has plenty of services back to Brisbane, some via Brisbane Airport, and one to Surfers Paradise and Byron Bay. McCafferty's and Premier offer services further north. Not all services north go through here, but there are several services a day to Hervey Bay and, beyond that, two services by McCafferty's and one by Premier. Suncoast Pacific also operates one bus per day to Hervey Bay.

To catch any rail services, it is necessary to take a bus first to Nambour, from where there are occasional trains in both directions.

Bus Services from Noosa Heads

Destination	Operator	Via	Distance (km)	Fare	Journey Time	Frequency
Brisbane	McCafferty's		139	$25	2¼ - 2¾ hrs	4/day
Brisbane	Greyhound		137	$25	2¾ hrs	1/day
Brisbane	Premier		139	$20	2¼ hrs	1/day
Brisbane	S'coast Pacific		139	$29	2¾ - 3½ hrs	7/day
Cairns	McCafferty's		1773	$206	26 - 26¼ hrs	2/day
		Townsville	1502	$174	20¼ - 20¾ hrs	2/day
		Rockhampton	636	$87	9¼ - 9½ hrs	2/day
		Hervey Bay	184	$29	2½ - 3¾ hrs	5/day
Cairns	Premier		1773	$192	26¼ hrs	1/day
		Townsville	1502	$161	20¾ hrs	1/day
		Rockhampton	636	$70	10 hrs	1/day
		Hervey Bay	184	$21	3¾ hrs	1/day
Hervey Bay	S'coast Pacific		184	$26.50	3½ hrs	1/day
Byron Bay	S'coast Pacific		347	$47.50	6 hrs	1/day

GYMPIE
Population 16,000

2 hrs 30 mins by train from Brisbane
3 hrs 30 mins by bus from Brisbane

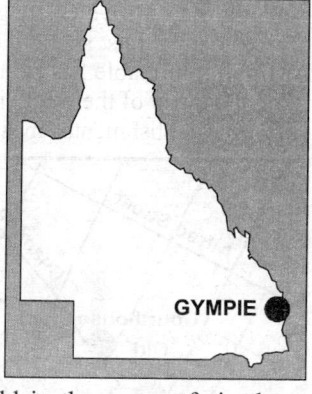

Those more interested in beaches than in history will by-pass Gympie, which is a shame, because it is a town which played an important part in Queensland's history. In fact, it was known as the town which saved Queensland, because, in 1867, with the state facing a drought coupled with an unexpected drop in the price of wool, bankruptcy loomed. At such a vital moment, one James Nash arrived in the district and, on the site where the Town Hall now stands, discovered 72 ounces of gold in the space of six days, triggering a huge gold rush and bringing to Queensland sudden and urgently needed revenue.

Mary Street is the centre of the town and buildings from that time of affluence are to be found there, including several old hotels where one may stay cheaply, yet with a feeling of history (see map overleaf and accommodation section for details). The **Courthouse** and the former **Post Office** in Channon Street are also worth a look. Jacaranda trees dot the town and are in purple profusion at the end of October.

The quickest and most convenient way to reach Gympie is by train. The *Tilt Train* covers the 174 kilometres to Gympie North station from Brisbane in 2½ hours. See the timetable on page 238. Gympie North is on the outskirts of the town, and from the station there is a free connecting bus service into town. Gympie is, unfortunately, one of the victims of the modern theory that a good way to encourage people to use public transport is to put the railway station outside the town. There is, of course, a fine station near the centre of the town, the use of which was abandoned when the line was

268 QUEENSLAND

electrified a few years ago. We shall see the current use of that building in a couple of paragraphs.

If you prefer bus travel, McCafferty's operates five services a day to here from Brisbane, while Greyhound has two, Premier one, Suncoast Pacific one and Brisbane Bus Lines six a week.

Now what of that fine **railway station** near the town centre? Well, it has been taken over by the **Mary Valley Heritage Railway** and is used for the operation of occasional trains on the branch line to **Imbil**. This line runs along the Mary Valley and was used by Queensland Railways until recently to provide a goods service, but passenger trains had not been run for many years. The line is in good condition, but it became uneconomical and Queensland Railways eventually decided to cease operations on it. Now it has been adopted by a private group and the line has passenger services once more. On Sundays the *Valley Rattler* runs the 40 kilometres to Imbil, using a 1923 steam locomotive and taking two hours over the journey. This has caused great delight among the residents along the way. As the train starts off along what was originally the main line to Brisbane, people come out to wave and a banner wishes the passengers a good journey. The line then meets the current main line and runs right beside it for a little distance (which, of course, can also be seen from main line trains south of Gympie) before diverging into the Mary Valley. A stop is made at **Kandanga** where a little market has been set up selling various produce, but predominantly the **macadamia nuts** which are grown in the district. The author purchased here 500 grams of macadamia nuts, shelled, but with shells included in the weight, for the sum of $2. At Imbil a turntable has been installed and the town comes to life upon arrival of the train, the event of the week, it seems. Again there is a market, and lunch is available at various establishments, most conspicuously, but rather expensively, at the Railway

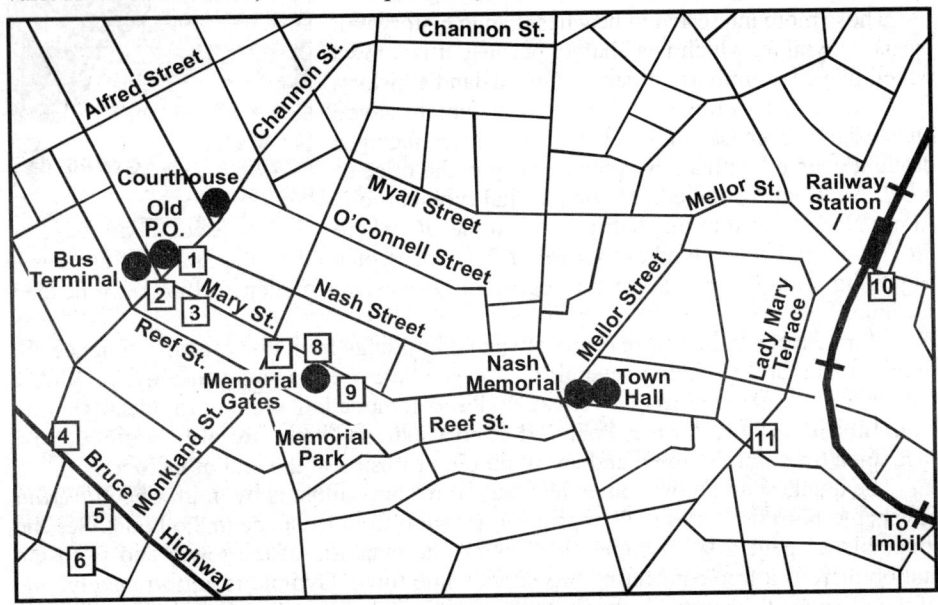

GYMPIE
Numerals indicate accommodation

Hotel next to the station. The line used to continue further, but beyond here it is not in such good condition, so there are no plans for extension. On the return journey, the stop is made at **Dagun** where there is **wine and cheese tasting**. 50 cents buys a tiny plastic glass into which unlimited samples of wine are poured, the limitation, however, being the time available for the stop. Locally manufactured wines and cheeses, both of which are good, are available for purchase. This day out costs $30. On Wednesdays, a similar service is operated by a 1960s ex-QR Rolls-Royce railcar at the same price.

Gympie Railway Station houses a small **railway museum** open for an hour prior to the departure of trains and for a short while following their return. There is no charge for admission. There is also a tea room on the platform with refreshments and vocal entertainment on days when trains run.

Also in Gympie is a **Gold Mining Museum** open every day from 9:00 until 16:30. Admission costs $7. Local transport is provided by a 1931 Leyland bus. Gympie still has a mine in operation producing gold, and this is the eighth largest such mine in Australia, producing 27,000 ounces of gold per year.

57 kilometres east of Gympie is **Tin Can Bay** (see map above). This unusual name is derived not from the accumulation of rubbish there, but from the aboriginal name, Tuncanbar, meaning 'the place of the dugong (sea cows)'. It has a population of 2,000 and is the home base for a small fleet of prawn trawlers. However, it is best known for its **dolphins**, which have been visiting since 1974. They seem to like humans and come to play, and be fed, early in the mornings. The humans also seem to like dolphins and are always ready to wade out a few metres to reciprocate the playfulness. This is one of three places in Australia famed for its friendly dolphins, the others being Monkey Mia and Bunbury, both in Western Australia.

A little further east still is **Rainbow Beach**, with many kilometres of unspoilt white beaches, as well as some distinctively coloured sands. To the east there is the wreck of the *Cherry Venture*, stuck in the sands. This was a former sand-mining area and the remains of an **old mining works** can be seen on the beach. From **Inskip Point**, north of Rainbow Beach, a ferry runs to Fraser Island and this crossing, taking only ten minutes, is the shortest and cheapest ferry journey to the popular island.

A regular local bus service operates from Gympie to Tin Can Bay and Rainbow Beach. Suncoast Pacific also operates its daily Brisbane to Hervey Bay service via Tin Can Bay.

AROUND GYMPIE

Black numerals indicate hotel accommodation
White numerals indicate backpackers hostels

270 QUEENSLAND
ACCOMMODATION

(i) Accommodation in Gympie

Name	Stars	No. on Map	Telephone No.	Address	Lowest Price (Double/Twin)
Great Eastern Motor Inn	4	6	1-800-072-093	27 Geordie Road	$95
Flag Gympie Muster Inn	4	4	1-800-359-925	21 Wickham Street	$90
Gympie Motel		5	07-5482-2722	Bruce Highway	$60
Northumberland Hotel		1	07-5482-2477	29 Channon Street	$55
Empire Hotel		3	07-5482-8444	196 Mary Street	$50
Railway Hotel		10	07-5483-7600	1 Station Road	$50
Commercial Hotel		2	07-5482-1007	250 Mary Street	$50
Royal Hotel		7	07-5482-1611	Mary & Monkland Streets	$45
Australian Hotel		11	07-5482-1070	1 Lady Mary Terrace	$40
Golden Age Hotel		8	07-5482-2411	135 Mary Street	$40
Imperial Hotel		9	07-5482-1506	170 Mary Street	$35

(ii) Accommodation in Tin Can Bay

Name	Stars	No. on Map	Telephone No.	Address	Lowest Price (Double/Twin)
Seychelle Luxury Apts.	4	12	07-5486-2056	23 Bream Street	$105
Dolphin Waters Apts.		12	07-5486-2600	40 Esplanade	$100
Sandcastle Motel	3	12	07-5486-4555	Tin Can Bay Road	$70
Tin Can Bay Motel	3	12	07-5486-4269	11 Mitchell Street	$55
Bayview Holiday Units	2½	12	07-5486-4141	148 Toolara Road	$55
Toolara Holiday Units		12	07-5486-4237	152 Toolara Road	$55
Sleepy Lagoon Hotel		12	07-5486-4124	Bream Street	$50

(iii) Hotel Accommodation in Rainbow Beach

Name	Stars	No. on Map	Telephone No.	Address	Lowest Price (Double/Twin)
Rainbow Shores Resort		13	1-800-801-789	Rainbow Shores Drive	$95
Mikado Motor Inn	3	13	1-800-243-211	105 Cooloola Drive	$70
Rainbow Getaway Apts.	4	13	07-5486-3500	Double Island Drive	$70
Rainbow Beach Inn		13	07-5486-3255	Spectrum Avenue	$65
Rainbow Sands Units		13	1-800-633-516	42 Rainbow Beach Road	$65

(iv) Backpackers Hostels in Rainbow Beach

Name	Group	No. on Map	Telephone No.	Address	Lowest Price (Dormitory)
Rainbow Beach B/P		14	07-5486-3288	66 Rainbow Beach Road	$22
Rocks Backpacker Resort	YHA	14	1800-646-867	Lot 3, Spectrum Avenue	$20

MOVING ON
(i) By Train

The *Tilt Train* runs from Gympie to Brisbane twice a day, and longer-distance trains also pass through and can be used if space is available. The timetable for these services is on page 302. In the opposite direction, there are trains to Rockhampton, Townsville, Cairns and Longreach. The timetables for these appear on page 238.

GYMPIE

(ii) By Bus

Buses from Gympie are as summarised below.

Destination	Operator	Via	Distance (km)	Fare	Journey Time	Frequency
Brisbane	McCafferty's		200	$35	3¾ - 4½ hrs	5/day
Brisbane	Greyhound		200	$35	3¼ - 4½ hrs	2/day
Brisbane	Premier		200	$25	4 hrs	1/day
Brisbane	S'coast Pacific		200	$32.50	4 hrs	1/day
Brisbane	Brisbane Bus		200	$35.50	3¼ - 5¾ hrs	6/week
Cairns	McCafferty's		1712	$206	24¼ - 25½ hrs	4/day
		Townsville	1341	$174	18¼ - 19¼ hrs	4/day
		Rockhampton	575	$83	7½ - 8½ hrs	4/day
		Hervey Bay	123	$16	1¾ - 2 hrs	5/day
Cairns	Greyhound		1712	$206	25 hrs	2/day
		Townsville	1341	$174	18¾ hrs	1/day
		Rockhampton	575	$83	7¾ hrs	1/day
		Hervey Bay	123	$16	1¾ hrs	1/day
Cairns	Premier		1712	$190	24½ hrs	1/day
		Townsville	1341	$151	19 hrs	1/day
		Rockhampton	575	$60	8¼ hrs	1/day
		Hervey Bay	123	$13	2 hrs	1/day
Hervey Bay	S'coast Pacific		123	$18	2¼ hrs	1/day

MARYBOROUGH
Population 21,500

3 hrs 30 mins by train from Brisbane
4 hrs 30 mins by bus from Brisbane

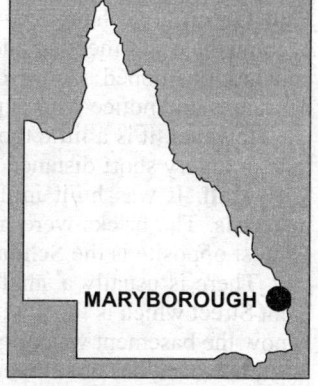

Nearby Hervey Bay is one of the east coast's fashionable destinations, but Maryborough has a much more interesting history than its popular neighbour.

Maryborough West can be reached on the *Tilt Train* in 3½ hours from Brisbane. Maryborough is another of those unfortunate places by-passed by main line. Formerly trains used to take a short branch line into Maryborough, which is a terminal station, and then return to the main route after their stop here. Now, however, a free bus connects with the train at the new Maryborough West station and brings passengers to the old station in the town centre. This journey takes about ten minutes. Only specially-operated occasional steam services now use Maryborough station.

Bus services from Brisbane are operated by McCafferty's seven times a day and by Greyhound once. Premier and Suncoast Pacific also each operate one service every day. Average time taken is 4½ hours. The services all stop at Maryborough Railway Station.

Although the coastline in this region was charted at an early date, it was not until 1842 that the Mary River was explored. A woolstore was established on its banks in 1847 and in 1850 the site of the present city was surveyed and laid out. When Queensland became an independent state in 1859, this was a major port of entry. 21,000 new immigrants entered Australia through Maryborough. There is a walk designed by the Maryborough Heritage Centre, so let us follow it.

Walking Tour

This tour covers approximately three kilometres and will take about an hour if no stops are made.

Let us begin at the **Railway Station**, since that will be the arrival point of most visitors. It seems a shame that such a handsome station cannot be used for its true purpose, but that is the price of progress. The building of the railway from here to Gympie was commenced in 1878 and completed three years later. Railways have always been important to Maryborough. The local company of Walkers has built most of the engines used by Queensland Railways throughout more than a century and is still building them. Inside the station building is now housed a Railway Museum, and stationary at one of the platforms you will probably find the steam engine used for special trains. Just outside the station is an interesting, although not aesthetic, concrete **air-raid shelter** "for the use of passengers only".

Opposite the station is **St. Paul's Anglican Church**. The first church was built in 1852 and moved to this site in 1856, but this construction dates from 1879, with the bell tower and nine bells added in 1887. Walk down Ellena Street away from the station and turn left into Adelaide Street. You will reach the pleasant open space of the **Town Hall Green**. Two hangings were carried out here in 1877, but more recently it has become the city's meeting and resting place. The local citizens insist that they want the benches positioned facing outwards, so that they can see the parades on special occasions and notice who is passing by at other times.

However, it is a little too early in our walk for a rest, so let us proceed by turning left for a very short distance into Kent Street and observing on our left the impressive **City Hall**. It was built in 1908 in American Colonial style and uses mostly local materials. The bricks were made here and the red cedar timber was obtained locally. Almost opposite is the **School of Arts** constructed in 1887 as the cultural centre of the city. There is usually a small historical exhibition in the foyer. Now walk east along Kent Street which is lined with shops of various types. Notice the **Queens Hotel**. What is now the basement was originally the ground floor, but the road level has been raised. That, however, has not prevented periodic floods. One of the worst, in Australia's great year of floods, 1974, reached the ground floor windows of the School of Arts.

Continue to Bazaar Street, where you can find the **Royal Hotel**. The Bush Inn was originally here, from 1857. The inn was rebuilt and became the Royal Hotel. It has an impressive foyer and staircase. These days it also offers an eat-as-much-as-you-want lunch for $6. Further along Kent Street, at the junction with Richmond Street, is the former Hotel Francis on your right, with attractive verandahs. Diagonally opposite is the former **Union Bank Building**, built in 1882 as the Australian Joint Stock Bank Building and used by the Union Bank from 1906. **Mary Poppins** was born here! To be more accurate, it was the birthplace of P. L. Travers, who wrote Mary Poppins. Before making your visit here, would you ever have imagined that this small Queensland city had such a claim to literary fame?

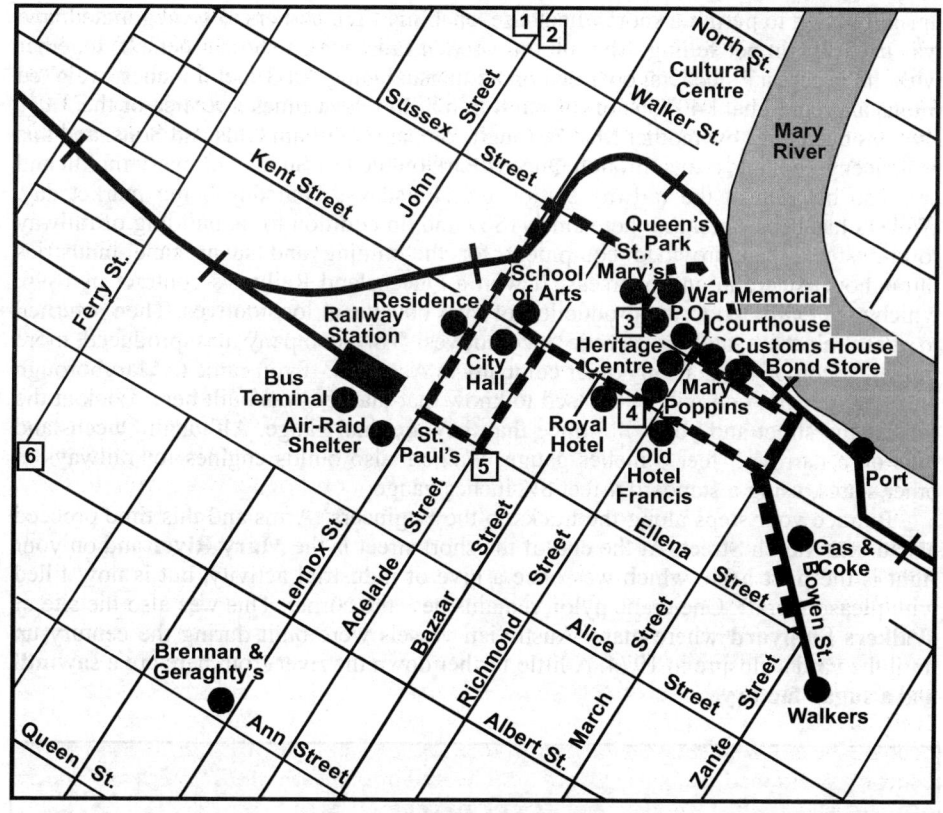

MARYBOROUGH
Dashed line shows Walking Tour
Numerals indicate accommodation

Still continue along Kent Street and on your left is **Gataker's Building**, built in 1868, but used from 1885 by the wine merchants Graham and Gataker. The present **Winehouse Gallery** at the back is in the old bonded liquor store. A little further along is the former **Royal Bank of Queensland**, built in 1888. Opposite, at **no. 264**, was the business of one J. H. Bliss, who supplied and repaired marine chronometers, barometers, sextants and navigational instruments, and made false teeth! The building was constructed in 1875. Also on the right is the former **Maryborough Co-Operative Dairy Association**, which opened its first factory in 1902 and later had six butter factories and two creameries in the district.

You now reach the corner of March Street and can see to your right the former **Engineers' Arms Hotel**, with its unusual wedge shape. You will also notice railway tracks in the street. Follow these and you will find, on your left, the **Maryborough Gas and Coke Company**. Gas street lighting started in Maryborough in 1879. Further along the street, you will find **Walkers Limited**, the builders of railway rolling stock mentioned earlier. This company constructed, in 1873, the first steam locomotive to be built in the southern hemisphere. The unusual engine, named the *Mary Ann*, had an upright boiler, to permit a short wheelbase, enabling tight corners to be negotiated, and was used for timber felling. She ran on wooden rails, which she cut herself, together with the necessary sleepers, operated on an unusual gauge of 3 feet 3 inches, weighed 6 tons and could haul 40 tons of logs at 8 m.p.h. In recent times a replica of the *Mary Ann* has been built by another Maryborough company, William Olds and Sons, and this replica engine hauls trains through Queens Park on the last Sunday of every month and can also be seen at the railway station on Thursdays, Thursday being market day. Walkers has been operating here since 1869 and, in addition to its building of railway rolling stock, has provided equipment for the mining and sugar cane industries throughout Australia and overseas. It won a Queensland Railways contract in 1896, which eventually led to the production of over 600 steam locomotives. Then it turned to diesel-electrics and to electric locomotives. This company has produced more railway locomotives than any other company in Australia. If you came to Maryborough on the *Tilt Train*, you will be pleased to know that that too was built here. Look at the rails in the street and you will notice that they are dual gauge. Although Queensland runs on a narrow 3 feet 6 inches gauge, Walkers also builds engines for railways in other states, using a standard 4 feet 8½ inches gauge.

Retrace your steps along the tracks to the Engineers' Arms and this time proceed ahead into March Street. At the end of the short street is the **Mary River** and on your right is the **port area**, which was once a hive of industrial activity, but is now filled with pleasure craft. One crane pylon remains near the corner. This was also the site of **Walkers Shipyard** where many Australian vessels were built during the century up until the yard's closure in 1974. A little further down the river from here are a **sawmill** and a **sugar factory**.

ANECDOTE

When the author arranged a frequent flyers award itinerary, 28 kilometres remained out of the 11,000 kilometres permitted. I noticed that the flight distance between Maryborough and Hervey Bay was 27 kilometres, so, since this appeared to be the shortest commercial flight operated in Australia, I felt that I must travel it and added the journey to my itinerary.

The flight operates in a triangle Brisbane - Maryborough - Hervey Bay - Brisbane, and when I boarded I was regarded as something of a curiosity by the crew, who said that they had never before had a passenger travelling only the sector between Maryborough and Hervey Bay. All others always travel to or from Brisbane. I was even introduced specially to the captain.

I am now pleased to be able to claim that I have travelled the shortest commercial air route in this vast continent, but getting to Maryborough Airport and from Hervey Bay Airport into the town took about three times as long as if I had gone by local bus.

Now turn the corner into Wharf Street. On your left is the **J. E. Brown Warehouse** constructed in 1879 and used also for dances and boxing tournaments in its time. It is now a restaurant. On the right of Wharf Street, next to the river, is the **Bond Store**, now a museum, open every day, from 9:00 until 16:00 on weekdays and from 10:00 until 13:00 at weekends. Admission costs $3. Since bonded goods, especially liquor, were originally kept here, it has a strong and impenetrable appearance. On the corner of Richmond Street stand four interesting buildings. **Customs House**, suitably close to the Bond Store, was built in 1901, replacing an earlier wooden building. It has an impressive exterior. The **Customs House Hotel**, opposite, was built in 1868. It therefore reflects the time of affluence following the discovery of gold in Gympie in 1867 and the rapid increase in importance of the port of Maryborough as a result. The former Bank of New South Wales building, on the third angle of the corner, is now the **Maryborough Heritage Centre**, dispensing helpful information to all those who ask, as well as operating a family history and genealogical centre. During the gold rush days, four million ounces of gold passed through Maryborough's three banks, of which this was one. On the fourth angle of the corner is the **Courthouse**, an imposing Italianate building, with courts still held on the upper floor.

From the end of Richmond Street, one can enter **Queens Park**. The first trees were planted here in 1864. The large banyan tree dates from 1900. The cannons came as decorations in 1879 to 1885. The fountain was imported from Scotland in 1890 and was originally situated beneath the roof visible a little distance away. It was later moved to allow the covered area to be used as a band rotunda. You will also find here circles of tiny railway tracks used for running miniature trains periodically, generally on the days when the *Mary Ann* is operating. It is a pleasant park with an elevated view over the river valley. Down below, bordering the Mary River, wider railway tracks run and it is here that the replica *Mary Ann* steam locomotive hauls its trains on the last Sunday in each month. The new engine weighs 9 tonnes and is built to a 3 feet 6 inches gauge, so that it can use the Queensland Railways tracks. Rides cost $3.

ANECDOTE

Waiting at Maryborough Airport proved quite interesting. First I learnt that this had been a major base for the R.A.A.F. during the Second World War. Then, being the only passenger boarding that morning, I was regaled with aviation tales by the officer in attendance.

"We had a problem with an undercarriage which was not coming down properly," he said. "The mechanic fixed it, but we thought that we had better take it for a test run before using it for passengers and I went up too for the test flight. When we put the wheels down, the warning alarm went off and we could not tell whether the alarm was faulty or whether the wheels really were not down properly. We got people out with binoculars. It looked all right, but they could not really be sure either. Somebody suggested that we ought to go to Bundaberg because they have a fire engine there, but the pilot thought it was probably all right to land. I kept muttering, "Let's go to Bundy," but nobody took any notice of me, and in the end we landed with no problems at all. I didn't go up on any more test flights after that."

Now leave the park by the gate into Bazaar Street and turn left. Immediately on your left is the **Post Office**, a classical building constructed in 1866, again reflecting the prosperity of the times, and still in use. Opposite is **St. Mary's Catholic Church**, consecrated in 1871. Turn back along Bazaar Street, and on the corner with Sussex Street is the **War Memorial**, an impressive granite obelisk with Italian marble statues. Now walk down Sussex Street, observing the **Fernery** on your right. Turn left into Lennox Street, noticing that here you rejoin the railway tracks running beside the road. The line is still in use, with occasional goods trains passing through here. Cross Kent Street and on your right is the former residence of the District Railway Superintendent, constructed in 1882 and a typical Queensland home of the time, with high ceilings to keep the building cool. And now here we are back at the Railway Station where we started.

If you have more time, you can continue to walk south on Lennox Street and after about ten minutes you will come to **Brennan and Geraghty's Museum** at 64 Lennox Street. It was originally a general store. At one time, this business, opened in 1871, included orchards, a brickworks, a preserves factory and a winery. It was passed on as a family business, but went gradually into decline. The last owner continued to operate the shop into his eighties, but eventually gave up the business in 1972. Investigation showed that some of the stock remaining in the store dated back decades, with curry

---

ANECDOTE

Continuing his stories designed for the reassurance of nervous intending passengers, the officer at Maryborough Airport went on, "We used to have an old pilot here who ran the supplies out to Lady Elliot Island. He was an ex-wartime pilot and he could really fly. He always overloaded the plane, but nothing really seemed to bother him. I went up with him one day and we had got about half way when there was a big bang from one of the engines and oil flew all over the windshield. He turned the plane round and said, "We'll get back all right on the other engine, but we're going to be losing height all the way." He knew what he was doing, of course, but we were losing height a lot too quickly for me. "How about throwing some of this milk and stuff out?" I suggested. "Oh, you don't want to do that," he replied. "It would get into all the papers, you know." We got back all right, but I was pretty nervous.

"Another time we went out to the island and the engine went wrong when we were going to take off again. There was no airstrip there at the time, so we used to land on the beach and you had to get down and up while it was low tide. He got out his bag of tools and started fiddling around with the engine while I watched the tide getting higher and higher. "Are we going to make it?" I said. "Maybe," was all he would commit himself to. Finally he said, "Right. Hop in," and the water had already reached one wheel. "Will we get off?" I asked. "Oh, yes," he said. "This plane is light as a feather now that we've unloaded everything." We had to run through water, but we got off all right. I doubt whether any other pilot would even have tried it, but he had a pretty good relationship with that plane. They were probably about the same age."

MARYBOROUGH

powder, for example, from the 1890s, so the business was left as it was and turned into a little museum. Original account books and correspondence show the difficulties of operating a shop here when many of the suppliers were on the other side of the world. Admission costs $4.

The replica *Mary Ann* steam engine is housed at the foundry of William Old, a business which has been operating here since 1918. Walk north along Lennox Street and then turn west (left) along North Street for ten minutes. The foundry is at 78 North Street, on the corner of Ferry Street. There are tours of the foundry on Thursdays between 9:30 and 16:00, costing $5.

There is a local bus service from Maryborough to Hervey Bay provided by Wide Bay Transit. Route 5 operates nine times per day, and there is also a *Trainlink* service which connects with *Tilt Train* services and operates a further four times a day. It is not necessary to be travelling on the train in order to use this bus, but its only stop in Maryborough is at the Railway Station. Route 5 services stop at all bus stops and take 40 minutes for the journey and then continue all the way along the foreshore in Hervey Bay. The *Trainlink* service takes 30 minutes and terminates at Hervey Bay Bus Terminal (Bay Central).

ACCOMMODATION

There are several motels in Maryborough, but why not stay in one of those beautiful old nineteenth century hotels and be right in the centre of the city and paying very modest rates?

For backpackers, there are no hostels, but who needs hostels when the Post Office Hotel offers a single room for $20, and the Central Hotel for $17, and even the Royal Centrepoint Motel will accommodate backpackers for $24?

Accommodation in Maryborough

Name	Stars	No. on Map	Telephone No.	Address	Lowest Price (Double/Twin)
Kimba Lodge Motel	4	2	1-800-337-980	177 John Street	$90
Mineral Sands Motel	3	6	07-4121-2366	Ferry & Albert Streets	$85
Royal Centrepoint Motel		4	07-4121-2241	326 Kent Street	$75
McNevins Parkway Motel	4	1	1-800-072-000	188 John Street	$65
Post Office Hotel		3	07-4121-3289	Wharf Street	$35
Central Hotel		5	07-4121-3105	Adelaide & Ellena Streets	$33

MOVING ON
(i) By Train

Trains run south to Brisbane and north to Rockhampton, Townsville, Cairns and Longreach, all from Maryborough West station. The connecting bus leaves Maryborough station approximately half an hour before the times shown in the timetables on pages 238 and 302 for Maryborough West departures.

(ii) By Bus

Bus departures are summarised on the next page. From Maryborough to Hervey Bay, there is a local bus service. The last departure of service no. 5 is at 17:25, but there is also a *Trainlink* bus at 20:45.

278 QUEENSLAND
Bus Services from Maryborough

Destination	Operator	Via	Distance (km)	Fare	Journey Time	Frequency
Brisbane	McCafferty's		289	$43	4¾ - 5¾ hrs	5/day
Brisbane	Greyhound		289	$43	3½ - 5½ hrs	3/day
Brisbane	Premier		289	$33	5 hrs	1/day
Brisbane	S'coast Pacific		289	$40.50	5¾ hrs	1/day
Cairns	McCafferty's		1623	$195	23¼ - 24½ hrs	4/day
		Townsville	1252	$163	17¼ - 18¼ hrs	4/day
		Rockhampton	486	$80	6½ - 7¼ hrs	4/day
		Hervey Bay	34	$16	30 - 50 mins	7/day
Cairns	Greyhound		1623	$195	23 - 24 hrs	2/day
		Townsville	1252	$163	17¾ - 18 hrs	2/day
		Rockhampton	486	$80	6¼ - 6¾ hrs	2/day
		Hervey Bay	34	$16	30 - 40 mins	1/day
Cairns	Premier		1623	$187	23½ hrs	1/day
		Townsville	1252	$140	18 hrs	1/day
		Rockhampton	486	$50	7¼ hrs	1/day
		Hervey Bay	34	$13	50 mins	1/day
Hervey Bay	S'coast Pacific		34	$18	45 mins	1/day

HERVEY BAY
Population 40,000
4 hrs 30 mins by train and bus from Brisbane
5 hrs 30 mins by bus from Brisbane

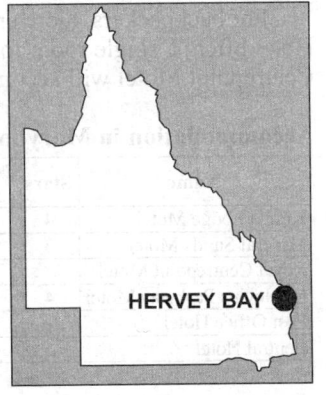

Hervey Bay (pronounced 'Harvey Bay') has become a fashionable place to visit in recent years, partly because of its proximity to Fraser Island. However, it is itself a pleasant town, or rather a series of conjoined small towns strung out all the way along the bay. Hervey Bay is relatively undeveloped, offering sparsely populated beaches and whale watching in season, but what most of the visitors here are doing is trying to find a good way to look at Fraser Island.

To reach Hervey Bay from Brisbane by rail, take the *Tilt Train* to Maryborough West, from where there is a connecting *Trainlink* bus to Hervey Bay Bus Terminal (Bay Central), stopping only at Maryborough on the way. The journey by train to Maryborough West takes 3½ hours and the bus ride from Maryborough West station to Bay Central takes 45 minutes. The fare for the bus is $5.

Buses from Brisbane to Hervey Bay are operated by McCafferty's (7 per day), Greyhound (1 per day), Premier (1 per day) and Suncoast Pacific (1 per day).

All services, both long-distance buses and *Trainlink*, arrive at the Bay Central Bus Terminal. This is quite a long walk from the centre of Hervey Bay, which is in the area known as Torquay. Suncoast Pacific alone continues its service to Urangan Harbour. Outside the terminal, awaiting most bus arrivals, will be found a row of backpackers' minibuses silently soliciting custom (those are the rules). You may pick whichever

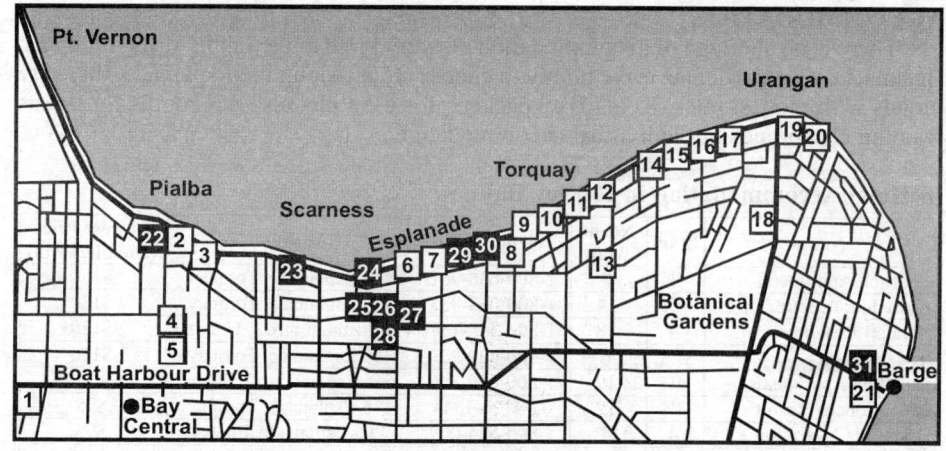

HERVEY BAY

Black numerals in white boxes indicate hotel accommodation
White numerals in black boxes indicate backpackers hostels

appeals to your taste. For those not on such a strict budget, your accommodation will probably be willing to come and pick you up here if telephoned in advance. If not, there is a local bus service operated by Wide Bay Transit. Buses to Torquay and Urangan operate approximately hourly, but follow three different routes. The driver will help you to find the right stop if you know your destination.

Whales come here to be viewed for three months of the year - August to October. They are returning from their annual migration north during the antipodean winter and have already covered 5,000 kilometres by the time they arrive in Hervey Bay for a rest. Some will be mothers travelling with calves. Although there used to be whaling stations in this area, the whales have learnt quickly that humans here no longer mean them any harm. Various boats take visitors out for a look at the whales and rules have been laid down to preserve the safety of these huge mammals. No boat may approach within a hundred metres of a whale, for instance, and no boat may come between a mother and her calf. However, nobody has bothered to tell these rules to the whales, who seem to enjoy the pastime of human-watching, so often they come right up to the boats to assuage their curiosity. Moreover, every year they seem to be staying longer and longer to enjoy looking at the humans. This is one of the best places in the world for human-watching (and whale-watching too). The weather is clement, and agreeable even for the 5:00 sailings. The prices are reasonable, especially towards the end of the season (free for the whales). The water is placid, and both the whales and the humans are getting curiouser and curiouser. Expect to pay about $75 for the cheapest whale watching voyages.

The **Botanic Gardens**, in Urangan, are worth a visit. They are unusual in being built on former sand dunes.

As for Fraser Island, see the next section, but here in Hervey Bay you will find all the choices you could want for visiting the island. Just pick whatever appeals to your taste.

QUEENSLAND
ACCOMMODATION

There is no shortage of accommodation of every price range in this string of towns. Backpackers, in particular, have plenty to choose from. Along the Esplanade, there are motels with modest rates. Koala Backpackers, for example, also has rooms for guests wanting cheap rates but individual accommodation.

(i) Hotel Accommodation in Hervey Bay

Name	Stars	No. on Map	Telephone No.	Address	Lowest Price (Double/Twin)
Charlton Apartments	4½	9	1-800-636-901	451 Esplanade, Torquay	$130
Alexander Apartments	4½	14	1-800-068-833	496 Esplanade, Torquay	$130
Kondari Resort	4	18	1-800-355-137	49 Elizabeth Street, Urangan	$120
Riviera Resort	4½	6	1-800-629-929	385 Esplanade, Torquay	$110
Santalina Apartments	4½	19	1-800-646-346	566 Esplanade, Urangan	$100
Playa Concha Resort	3½	12	07-4125-1544	475 Esplanade, Torquay	$98
Beachside Motor Inn	4	3	1-800-654-009	298 Esplanade, Pialba	$95
Fraser Gateway Motor Inn	4	5	07-4128-3666	68 Main Street, Pialba	$95
Shelly Bay Resort		11	1-800-240-797	466 Esplanade, Torquay	$95
Boatharbour Resort		21	07-4125-1771	650 Esplanade, Urangan	$95
Ambassador Motor Lodge	4	2	07-4124-0044	296, Esplanade, Pialba	$93
White Crest Apartments	4½	7	1-800-100-808	397 Esplanade, Torquay	$90
Wanderer Villas	4½	13	1-800-444-040	105 Truro Street, Torquay	$84
Golden Sands Motor Inn	3	4	07-4128-3977	44 Main Street, Pialba	$75
Arches Apartments	3½	15	07-4124-9498	507 Esplanade, Urangan	$75
Fairway Motel	3	1	07-4128-1911	29 Boat Harbour Dr., Pialba	$68
Atlantis on the Bay		10	1-800-241-322	458 Esplanade, Torquay	$65
Shelly Beach Motel	3½	16	07-4128-9888	510 Esplanade, Urangan	$65
Hervey Bay Motel	3½	17	07-4128-9277	518 Esplanade, Urangan	$65
Urangan Motor Inn		20	07-4128-9699	573 Esplanade, Urangan	$60
Fraser Lodge	4½	8	1-800-641-444	Fraser Street, Torquay	$50

(ii) Backpackers Hostels in Hervey Bay

Name	Group	No. on Map	Telephone No.	Address	Lowest Price (Dormitory)
Koala Backpackers		29	1800-354-535	408 Esplanade, Torquay	$24
Friendly Hostel	B&W	25	07-4124-4107	182 Torquay Road, Scarness	$20
Beaches Backpackers	VIP	27	1800-655-501	195 Torquay Terrace	$20
Palace Backpackers		26	1800-063-168	184 Torquay Road, Scarness	$20
Boomerang Backpackers		23	1800-243-970	335 Esplanade, Scarness	$20
Fraser Escape		28	07-4124-6237	Torquay & Denman Camp Rds.	$20
Fraser Roving		30	1800-989-811	412 Esplanade, Torquay	$20
Nomads Smugglers Rest	Nom	24	1800-502-115	369 Esplanade, Scarness	$17
Colonial Log Cabin Resort	YHA	31	1800-818-280	820 Boat Harbour Dr., Urangan	$16
Fraser Lakes Beachside		22	07-4124-5588	264 Charles Street, Pialba	$15

HERVEY BAY

MOVING ON
(i) By Train

There are *Trainlink* connecting buses for all *Tilt Train* services. The buses leave Hervey Bay at 4:35 and 10:05 to connect with trains south to Brisbane, and at 12:50 (10:55 on Saturdays) and 19:25 for trains north to Bundaberg and Rockhampton. Check the timetables on pages 238 and 302 for details of times, destinations and days of operation of trains. There are no buses to connect with trains running north beyond Rockhampton.

(ii) By Bus

McCafferty's has five buses a day back to Brisbane, while Greyhound has three, Premier one and Suncoast Pacific one. The Suncoast Pacific bus operates via Brisbane Airport. In the opposite direction, McCafferty's runs four services a day to Cairns, via Rockhampton and Townsville, while Greyhound and Premier have one each.

Destination	Operator	Via	Distance (km)	Fare	Journey Time	Frequency
Brisbane	McCafferty's		323	$49	4¾ - 6¼ hrs	5/day
Brisbane	Greyhound		323	$49	4 - 6 hrs	3/day
Brisbane	Premier		323	$36	5¾ hrs	1/day
Brisbane	S'coast Pacific		323	$42.50	6¼ hrs	1/day
Cairns	McCafferty's		1589	$195	22½ - 23¾ hrs	4/day
		Townsville	1218	$163	16½ - 17½ hrs	4/day
		Rockhampton	452	$80	5¾ - 6½ hrs	4/day
Cairns	Greyhound		1589	$195	23½ hrs	1/day
		Townsville	1218	$163	17¼ hrs	1/day
		Rockhampton	452	$80	6¼ hrs	1/day
Cairns	Premier		1589	$184	22½ hrs	1/day
		Townsville	1218	$149	17 hrs	1/day
		Rockhampton	452	$50	6¼ hrs	1/day

FRASER ISLAND
Population 200
45 mins by ferry from Hervey Bay

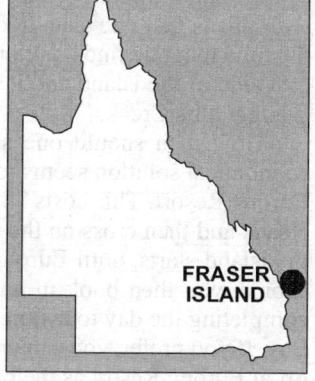

Fraser Island claims to be the largest sand spit in the world. Seeing the island on the map, one does not always appreciate its extent. It is approximately 125 kilometres from north to south, and it is composed entirely of sand. Since sand contains no nutrients, it is a matter of wonder that it is, in many parts, lushly vegetated. Airborne nutrients and seeds have accumulated until vegetation could gain a hold, and then the decaying vegetable matter has allowed other plants and trees to grow, and forests have sprung up. There are even lakes where rotting vegetable matter has accumulated in depressions and created a lining of impervious material. However, not all of the island is covered with vegetation. Some is still composed of shifting dunes. Fraser Island is a World Heritage Site, and a fascinating place to visit.

282 QUEENSLAND

Access is by ferry ('barge'), or by a short flight which lands on the beach of the island at low tide. The water services operate from three points. The most accessible from Hervey Bay is Urangan, the harbour at the eastern point of the bay. A local bus can be taken to this point for $2, or it is possible to walk in about 45 minutes from Torquay. There are two services from here. There is a barge to Moon Point for $16.50 return. This service departs twice a day, at present at 8:30 and 15:30, and takes an hour to cross. It is operated with an old landing craft which simply noses its way as far up the beach as possible. Then vehicular traffic drives off and passengers take off their shoes and socks, roll up their trousers, and wade ashore. There is nothing on the shore. There is just a beach and a track leading inland, so unless you have transport, you are now stuck there until the next barge service comes along.

The other service from Urangan goes to Kingfisher Bay, where there is a resort built. This has more purpose, for there are facilities available, including meals, and walks which can be undertaken. The service is operated by a smart passenger vessel, but the disadvantage is that the return fare is $35. The ferry operates four times a day, at 8:30, 12:00, 16:00 and 18:30. On Fridays and Saturdays, there is an additional service at 22:30. The crossing takes 45 minutes.

There are further ferry services from River Heads, but the problem here is that River Heads is fourteen kilometres south of Hervey Bay and there is no public transport available. If you can find a way to get there, however, there are barges to Kingfisher Bay three times a day, at 7:15, 11:00 and 14:30, and to Wanggoolba Creek three times a day, at 9:00, 10:15 and 15:30. To Kingfisher Bay takes 50 minutes. To Wanggoolba Creek takes only 30 minutes. Fares are again $16.50 return.

The third departure point is not useful to those who are already in Hervey Bay, but it is the cheapest. A barge runs between Inskip Point, near Rainbow Beach, and Hook Point at the southern tip of Fraser Island. This crossing takes only fifteen minutes and costs $2 each way. It operates frequently from 7:00 until 16:30, according to demand.

Accommodation is available on Fraser Island, but it is nearly all expensive. It is mostly owned by one person, who also runs the ferries and tours, so competition is somewhat limited. There is, however, one cheap option. Eurong Resort, on the east side of the island, offers beds in cabins at $19 per night on a stand-by basis. The problem with this is that one cannot know in advance whether a bed is available or not, and by the time that one finds out, one is already on the island. Moreover, one has to reach the east side of the island and it is twenty kilometres from the arrival point of the ferry at Wanggoolba Creek.

How then should one set about seeing the island at minimum cost? The most economical solution seems to be to book on the Day Tour from Hervey Bay offered by Eurong Resort. This costs $85 at the time of writing. You will be taken by bus to River Heads and then cross on the ferry to Wanggoolba Creek. On the other side, the tour of the island starts, until Eurong Resort is reached for lunch. If space is available in the cabins, you then book in and spend as much time on the island as you wish before completing the day tour itinerary on the day of your departure and returning to Hervey Bay. If you prefer, you can undertake the tour on the day of your arrival and be dropped off at Eurong Resort as the bus passes on its return journey. However you arrange your itinerary, you are allowed to take part of the day tour on one day and part on another, space permitting, and spend time on the island for the intervening period. If the worst happens and there is no space available at Eurong Resort, you complete your day tour and return to Hervey Bay on the same day.

What is there to see, then, on the island? First, and most obviously, there is a large amount of sand, including pristine beaches and impressive dunes. Not so obviously, there are dingoes in large numbers. Although this is an opportunity to see these animals in the wild more easily and more closely than in any other place, one should exercise caution. They are unpredictable, not very frightened of man, and sometimes aggressive. In 2001, a child was mauled to death on the island by dingoes. They should be treated with respect. Do not leave anything outside at night, as it may be destroyed by dingoes, just for the pleasure of destruction, it seems.

You will see shifting sand dunes, unusual rock formations, coloured sands, lakes, amazingly lush rainforest, the wreck of the *Maheno*, washed ashore in a cyclone in 1935, and beautifully clear streams, and probably wonder how all this could come about on what is just a patch of sand.

In the middle of the island is an **Information Centre** at Central Station, mid-way between Wanggoolba Creek and Eurong Resort. Near here is also the best walk on the island, through dense rainforest. There are some other walks too, but the fact that one is walking through sand all the time makes all of the walks rather tiring.

There are no surfaced roads on Fraser Island. The beach acts as the main north-south highway, while the tracks which cross the island are merely that - sand tracks. Visitors are advised that it is impossible to use a two-wheel-drive vehicle on the island. A four-wheel-drive is a necessity. In fact, though, the main difficulty is not the sand itself, but the problem that the heavy four-wheel-drive buses used by the tour companies have created deep indentations on the tracks, leaving a raised central portion, almost certain to foul the differential of a conventional vehicle. Thus low-slung four-wheel-drives would also have difficulties. One needs a vehicle which has good clearance.

Camping on Fraser Island is permitted, but there are some restrictions. In the interior of the island, camping is allowed only at established camp grounds, of which there are several. There is a fee of $4 per person per night. On the beaches, camping is permitted, but not within 50 metres of a waterway, not where there are 'no camping' signs, and not where it would disturb dune vegetation, and you must still pay the fee.

Now here is a suggested walk. It is long and strenuous, involving constant walking in sand, and takes a recommended three days. It covers 56 kilometres in total and a tent is required for camping for two nights. Tents can be hired in Hervey Bay. It is possible to shorten the walk to two even harder days if preferred, and it is also possible to stay in Eurong and still undertake the walk, using the two-day plan, if only you can arrange a ride either to or from Central Station on each day.

Day 1

Today's walk covers eighteen kilometres and is fairly strenuous. Start from Eurong Resort by walking 4.3 kilometres north along the beach. Then turn inland at the second track (not the first. The second is about 500 metres beyond the first). There are not many trees in this area. Mostly midyim grows, a plant with small, pointed, pinkish leaves. After three kilometres, you will come out into the open on Hammerstone Sandblow. Not much can survive here, but there are a few plants which fix nitrogen from the air in order to overcome the lack of nutrients in the soil. The sand has its pale yellow colour because it is a mixture of wind-blown surface sand and exposed layers of coloured sands. The sandblow is moving west and gradually inundating Lake Wabby. It has already created a dam which prevents water from escaping from the lake.

Now continue south along the track, climbing through stunted eucalyptus trees. You will get a good view of the lake from this vantage point. Along the track you will notice animal holes. These are the marks of bandicoots, slinks and echidnas. The trees gradually become taller and closer together as the dunes become older and more established. After a long walk of more than two hours (eight kilometres) from Lake Wabby, you will reach a vehicular track. Follow it for three more kilometres to **Lake McKenzie**.

The track follows round the north of Lake McKenzie and there is a camp site here. This is the end of our first day's walk. Note that this camp site is frequently full by lunch time, being the most popular place on the island for camping, so make sure that you arrive early. If you are unlucky, you will have no choice but to continue to Central Station (another six kilometres) according to the plan for covering the walk in two days instead of three.

Day 2

Today's walk covers a distance of fourteen kilometres and, although the country to be covered is still difficult, the distance is less than yesterday's.

The walking path now diverges from the vehicular route, continuing beside the lake along the ridge of a dune. There are tall eucalyptus trees here. Proceeding south, you can notice the differences in vegetation between swamp areas, which harbour sedges, and periodically wet areas, which typically grow paperbark trees. You will also find areas which were logged in the 1950s and bear evidence thereof. There is a log across the track at one point and there are tree stumps evident. You will pass into more open woodland, a sign that older dunes have been exposed beneath the layer of nutrients, so that growth is more limited. Broom grows in these areas.

Then you come to Basin Lake, smaller than the two lakes passed yesterday. However, the slightly acidic waters in this lake support seven species of frog and some freshwater turtles, as well as being the home of the Australian grebe, a common small waterbird. Sometimes sea eagles can be found here, searching for their lunch.

Now the track rises through tall forest. Then, as it descends, it passes through grey myrtle, also known as carrol, and then through kauri pine with vines beneath. You come to a clearing, which was once horse paddocks, later planted with eucalyptus.

Finally, there is a log bridge, then a boardwalk, and you have arrived at **Central Station**, where there are camping facilities, for use if you wish to complete the walk in two days instead of three. There is an Information Centre here with useful and informative details on the terrain, so plan to take a short break before continuing.

Resuming from Central Station, head south through tall eucalyptus forests and high dunes, where there is plenty of bird life. Again you will see signs of logging in the past. After a while, you will cross a vehicular track.

As the track rises, the forest becomes more open. To your right, you can glimpse Lake Jennings, while ahead you can see Lake Birrabeen. The track soon skirts the shores of Lake Birrabeen and curves to the right round the southern end of the lake, where it crosses another vehicular track. Now the trees become sparser, their roots unable to reach down through a hardened layer to the nutrients below, and various heath plants thrive. The path passes Barga Lagoon, a small body of water on your left. Here you will find birds including doves and ducks.

The path turns to the right and follows the shore of **Lake Benaroon**, fringed by melaleucas. There is a path off to the right to a camp site, our destination for today.

FRASER ISLAND

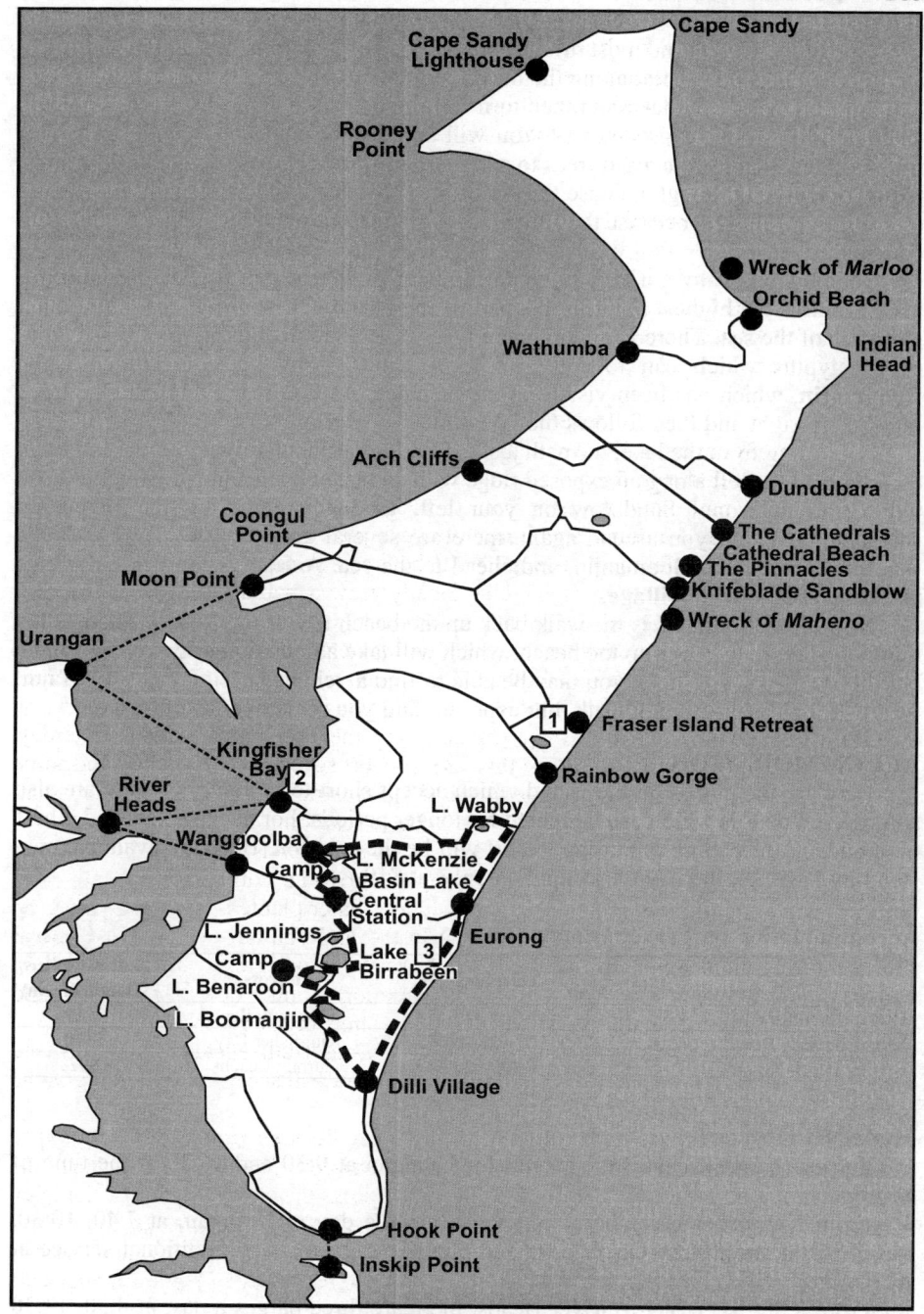

FRASER ISLAND
Dashed line shows Walking Tour
Numerals indicate accommodation

Day 3

This is the longest and most tiring day, a journey of 24 kilometres, although the last ten kilometres is on the flat along the beach.

Start off beside the lake and then turn right to cross the vehicular track. The path leads uphill, through closed forest. You will see further evidence of logging and of forest fires which have caused trees to sprout again from the base of damaged trunks. Now you descend though a dense thicket of grey myrtle, with surprisingly few leaves on the ground. That is because they are all dragged underground for supper by the giant cockroach.

You now walk along a high ridge. Off to your right, you can see **Mt. Boomanjin**, at 211 metres the highest point in this part of the island. On your left, you can obtain glimpses of the sea. There is a more open type of vegetation consisting of those types of eucalyptus which can tolerate salt-laden winds. Now you descend to **Lake Boomanjin**, which has been visible in the distance. As you reach the lake, the track turns sharp right and then follows the lake shore.

Ascending from the lake, the path just touches the vehicular track for one last time, then turns to the left along an exposed ridge with an open canopy and grass below. You will come to Wongi Sandblow on your left, gradually engulfing the vegetation surrounding it.. As you ascend again, there are several good views - back over the sandblow, over Lake Boomanjin, and ahead to the sea. A fairly steep descent brings you to the sea at **Dilli Village**.

Now all that remains is the walk back up the beach to Eurong Resort. There is ten kilometres more to cover up the beach, which will take about another two to two and a half hours. If you are lucky you may be able to find a vehicle passing that way. If not, well it is a pleasant enough walk, but exposed. Did you remember to bring a hat?

ACCOMMODATION

Here are the places on the island which accept short term visitors. There are also some beach houses which can be rented for longer periods. For backpackers and others on a budget, the cabins at Eurong Resort will be the solution. Beds are available on a stand-by basis, on the day of occupation only, at $19.

Accommodation on Fraser Island

Name	Stars	No. on Map	Telephone No.	Address	Lowest Price (Double/Twin)
Fraser Island Retreat		1	1-800-627-583	Happy Valley	$110
Kingfisher Bay Resort	4	2	07-4124-9685	Kingfisher Bay	$110
Eurong Beach Resort		3	1-800-627-583	Eurong Beach	$97

MOVING ON

Ferries (barges) leave Moon Point for Urangan at 9:30 and 16:30 at the time of writing.

From Kingfisher Bay, there are five services a day to Urangan, at 7:40, 10:30, 14:00, 17:00 and 20:00. On Fridays and Saturdays, there is an additional service at 23:30.

From Kingfisher Bay to River Heads, there are three barges a day, at 8:30, 13:30 and 16:00.

From Wanggoolba Creek to River Heads, there are three crossings, at 9:30, 14:30 and 16:00.

From Hook Point to Inskip Point, the ferry runs frequently from 7:15, according to demand, with the last crossing at approximately 16:45.

CHILDERS
Population 4,300

6 hrs by bus from Brisbane

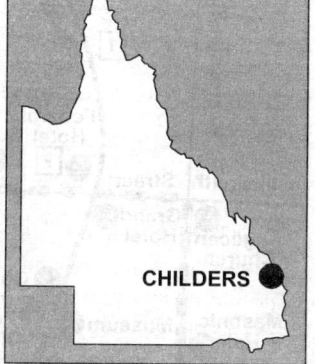

Childers is famous for two sensational fires. The first occurred in 1902 and destroyed much of the central part of the town. Rebuilding, however, was rapid and in the town centre little has changed since that time, so Childers presents the façade of a century-old Australia and is interesting in that respect.

The second disastrous fire occurred almost a hundred years later, in 2000, when the Palace Backpackers, formerly the fine old Palace Hotel, was engulfed in flames late one June night and fifteen of its guests died, although a further 69 escaped. It soon became apparent that this was an act of arson, and this recent fire has damaged not only Childers but the whole backpacking business in Australia.

Despite the damage caused, Childers is still a small town worth looking at, if you have the time. It is also the centre of a fruit-growing area where casual work can be found at various times of the year.

There is a station at Childers, but it is not really in the town and, more serious, trains do not usually stop here. Therefore, it is easier to reach Childers by bus. McCafferty's operates four services a day from Brisbane, while Greyhound has two and Premier one. Six hours is an average journey time.

A walk around the town centre takes only about an hour, so one can actually look around and move on in the same day if one is short of time and so wishes. Here is a walking tour of Childers.

Walking Tour

This tour covers about two and a half kilometres and will take an hour.

Start at the Tourist Information Centre, which is also the **Pharmaceutical Museum** and Art Gallery, at 90 Churchill Street. This was originally Gaydon's Building, constructed in 1894. The ground floor was used by Thomas Gaydon as a chemist's shop, and is preserved in that form, claiming to be the only pharmaceutical museum in Australia. It is open from 9:00 until 16:00 on weekdays and from 9:00 until 11:30 on Saturdays. Admission costs $4. Mr. Gaydon was also the local dentist, optician and anaesthetist, and he used the first floor of this building as his dentist's surgery. It is now the **Art Gallery**, opened in 1988 and containing examples of local and national art work, including a fine display of pottery. It is open for the same hours as the museum downstairs, and admission is free.

Almost opposite Gaydon's Building is the **Courthouse**, just to the left of Crescent Street. This was built in 1896 and extended in 1900. On the other side of Crescent Street is the Post Office, built in 1887 and almost unchanged since then. Walk south along Churchill Street and you will see opposite the remains of the Palace Backpackers, where the fifteen unfortunate victims lost their lives. Nearby are several

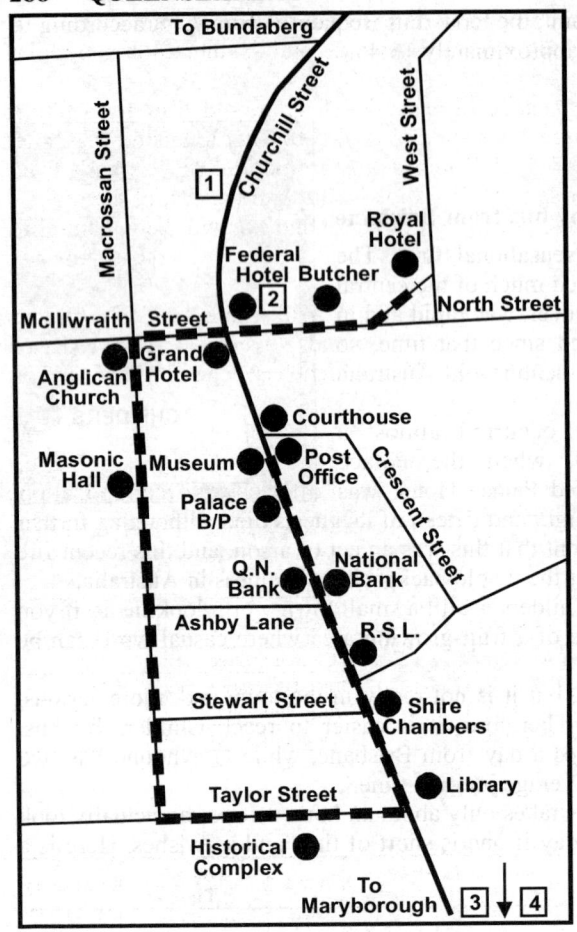

CHILDERS

Numerals indicate accommodation

buildings with their interesting original façades, and on the corner of Ashby Lane is Ye Olde Boutique, which was originally the Q.N. Bank. Opposite is the current National Bank, built in 1895 as the Bank of North Queensland.

Continue south along Churchill Street and you will reach the R.S.L. Club, in a building which was originally the C.B.C. Bank, built in 1901. A little further on are the Isis Shire Chambers and within is the **Isis Hall of Memories**. This memorial to the 59 Childers men who died in the Great War is constructed in the shape of a Maltese Cross. There is a bronze plaque to commemorate each man, and plaques were added later for the 21 who died in the Second World War. The memorial was opened on Anzac Day 1926. Outside is a Howitzer captured on the Western Front by Childers soldiers. It was made in 1916 by Krupps of Essen. The new Library a little further along the street houses a Bicentennial Quilt depicting the historic buildings of Childers.

Turn right upon reaching Taylor Street and you will find on the left an **historical complex**, consisting primarily of a cottage and school moved here from Isis Central Mill. The cottage dates from 1890 and houses various period furniture and exhibits. The school contains a collection of aboriginal artefacts and other local items. There is also a locomotive imported from Britain in 1916 to work on the local sugar cane railways. These exhibits are open from 9:00 until 12:00 on weekdays, and on Sunday from 9:00 until 15:00.

Turn right again into Macrossan Street. After a little walk, you will find the Masonic Hall and, beyond, the Anglican Church built in 1901. It is known for its stained glass windows. Turn right once more, into McIllwraith Street, and return to Churchill Street. On the corner is the **Grand Hotel**, in a grand building which was moved here in the 1880s. Diagonally opposite is the **Federal Hotel**, built in 1907. It has its original swinging doors and iron latticework, and is therefore a popular photographic subject.

Proceed along North Street (ahead) and on your left is the old **Butcher's Shop**, built in 1896. It claims to have been the state's first tiled butcher's outside Brisbane. Set back a little on the left is the **Royal Hotel**, dating from 1894. It was built from timber cut to accommodate the passage of the railway a little to the east of the town.

Our tour finishes here. Walk back down North Street and you will be in Churchill Street near our point of origin.

A few kilometres north of Childers is the **Isis Sugar Mill** where the Central Sugar Mill Company conducts popular tours between July and November. To the east of Childers is **Woodgate**, with a population of 700, which has a good beach and is adjacent to the Woodgate National Park.

ACCOMMODATION

For those on a budget, the older hotels in the town offer cheap accommodation. The motels, although offering a higher standard, are a little way out of the town centre.

Accommodation in Childers

Name	Stars	No. on Map	Telephone No.	Address	Lowest Price (Double/Twin)
Motel Childers		1	07-4126-1177	136 Churchill Street	$75
Gateway Motor Inn	3½	3	07-4126-1288	Bruce Highway	$65
Panda Motel		4	07-4126-1773	Bruce Highway	$60
Federal Hotel		2	07-4126-1438	71 Churchill Street	$50

MOVING ON
Bus Services from Childers

Destination	Operator	Via	Distance (km)	Fare	Journey Time	Frequency
Brisbane	McCafferty's		391	$59	6 - 7 hrs	4/day
		Hervey Bay	68	$15	1 hr	3/day
Brisbane	Greyhound		391	$59	5¼ - 7 hrs	2/day
		Hervey Bay	68	$15	1 hr	2/day
Brisbane	Premier		391	$43	6¾ hrs	1/day
		Hervey Bay	68	$10	1 hr	1/day
Cairns	McCafferty's		1521	$191	21¼ - 22¾ hrs	4/day
		Townsville	1150	$154	15½ - 16½ hrs	4/day
		Rockhampton	384	$72	4¾ - 5½ hrs	4/day
Cairns	Greyhound		1521	$191	22¼ - 22½ hrs	2/day
		Townsville	1150	$154	16 - 17¼ hrs	2/day
		Rockhampton	384	$72	5¼ - 5½ hrs	2/day
Cairns	Premier		1521	$169	21½ hrs	1/day
		Townsville	1150	$123	16 hrs	1/day
		Rockhampton	384	$41	5¼ hrs	1/day

BUNDABERG
Population 55,000

4 hrs 30 mins by train from Brisbane
6 hrs 30 mins by bus from Brisbane

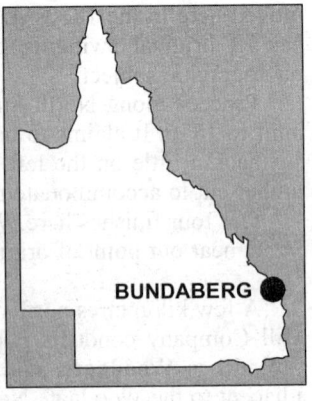

Bundaberg's greatest claim to fame is its rum, a commodity for which it is known all over Australia. That is reasonable enough when one considers the city's location in the midst of a sugar cane production area. When one walks into a pub here, one asks not for a "glass" or a "schooner", but for a "dark and stormy" (rum and ginger beer) or for a "moonbeam" (rum and lemonade). Naturally, only Bundaberg rum will be served.

The city also made the news headlines in April 2002 when an English girl on holiday here was thrown off a bridge and killed.

The advent of the *Tilt Train* has meant that Bundaberg can be reached in a mere 4½ hours from Brisbane. There are two services per day, the second terminating here on weekdays and returning to Brisbane early the next morning.

If you prefer, however, it is possible to spend an average of 6½ hours on a bus from Brisbane to Bundaberg. McCafferty's operates two services per day, while Greyhound also has two and Premier one.

The first European inhabitants of Bundaberg did not arrive until as late as 1867. A sawmill was erected in 1868 and timber became the first industry of the locality. Bundaberg was surveyed, laid out and named in 1870. Corn production was established in the 1870s, followed by experimental sugar cane growing. This industry proved particularly successful and gradually became firmly established, with complete sugar mills following, manufacturing raw sugar.

Local government arrived in 1873. In 1881, Bundaberg became a municipality. In 1902, it was a town, and by 1913 it had become a city. A port was established in the city, which is now used by pleasure craft, the commercial port having been shifted in the 1950s to Burnett Heads at the mouth of the river.

Whilst in Bundaberg, you should visit the **Rum Distillery**. It is a long way from the centre of the city and will take about 45 minutes to reach on foot (not twenty minutes, as various tourist information will suggest). Duffy's operates buses along the main road nearby, but services are not frequent. However, there is a service no. 4 at 10:25 from the city centre which will connect well with the 11:00 tour. There is still some 800 metres to walk from the bus stop (in Princess Street) to the distillery.

Tours are operated at the distillery every hour from 10:00 until 15:00 and cost $6, including a drink at the end. You will see the stages of the process of rum manufacture. One of the by-products of sugar production is molasses, a rich, black, heavy liquid, which is piped into the distillery, where it is clarified and then mixed with water and a yeast solution and allowed to stand and ferment for 36 hours. It is distilled by being put through a wash column with high pressure steam which hisses out from various joints around the factory, giving a general air of excitement. The process is repeated and, behold, rum emerges - not just ordinary rum, but rum at around 80% alcohol. It is stored for at least two years in huge old vats of oak imported from North America, some seeping out from the cracks between the timbers, if your fingers are quick

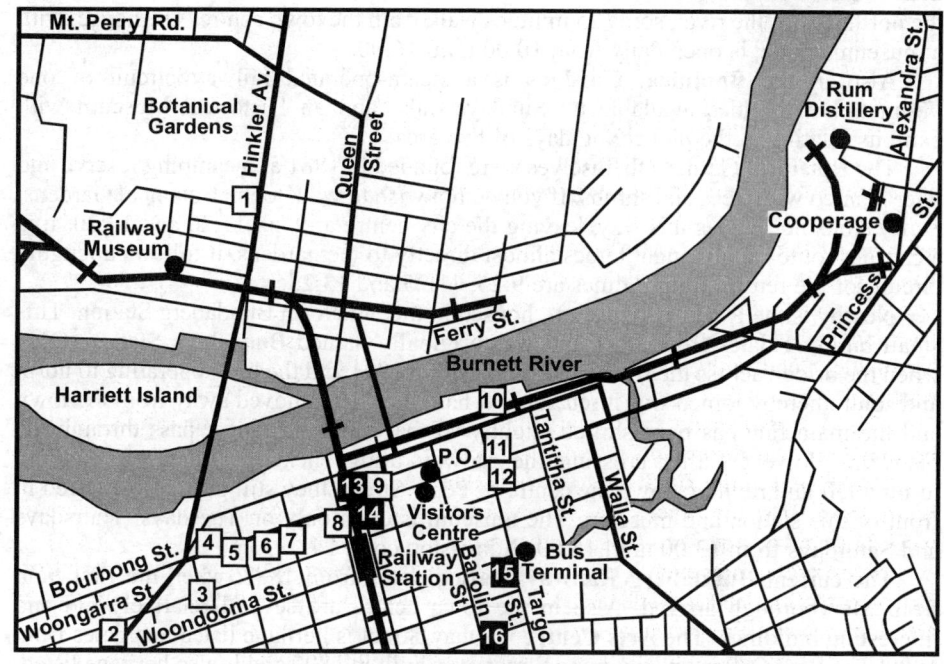

BUNDABERG
Black numerals in white boxes indicate hotel accommodation
White numerals in black boxes indicate backpackers hostels

enough. Sadly, in the author's opinion, at the last stage, it is both watered down to the required level of alcohol and mixed with caramel to give it the colour which customers like. The distillery suffered a disastrous fire in the 1920s, when almost the whole plant was destroyed, but has recovered and succeeded in making its product a popular one in this part of Australia at least.

As you walk back, you will find **Schmeider's Cooperage** just before you reach the main road. Mr. Schmeider was the last man to be apprenticed by Bundaberg Distillery to learn the art of making wooden barrels. With his skills no longer required up the road, he has set up a workshop making mostly miniature barrels, which are for sale. There is a video showing the entire process and Mr. Schmeider and his own apprentices can be seen at work. There is no charge, unless you wish to purchase an item. This venture has gradually expanded, and other craftsmen have joined the little group of workshops, their skills on display making jewellery, furniture, leatherwork, ceramics, paintings, and various other art and craft forms. Tour buses arrive periodically and refreshments are available here, so it is quite a busy place at certain times.

Another of Bundaberg's claims to fame is that the pioneer aviator **Bert Hinkler** lived here. Hinkler built a glider in 1912 and conducted experimental flights by launching himself from the sand dunes at Mon Repos Beach, near Bundaberg. There is a Hinkler Glider Museum on the corner of Bourbong and Mulgrave Streets, to the west of the city, open daily from 9:00 until 17:00. Hinkler's original home was also brought from Southampton, in Britain, and reassembled in the Botanical Gardens, which are on the north side of the river, some 25 minutes walk from the town centre. The house, with a museum inside, is open daily from 10:00 until 16:00.

Also in the **Botanical Gardens** is a steam-operated railway circuit of one kilometre, with rides available on Sundays only, and an Historical Museum with exhibits relating to the pioneering days of this area.

The Botanical Gardens themselves were founded in 1881 as a camping reserve and later planted with trees and shrubs. If you do not wish to walk to the Botanical Gardens, Duffy's bus no. 3 goes this way, leaving the city centre at 9:20, 11:20 and 13:20. It is a circular route, so although it goes almost directly to the gardens, it follows a lengthy circuit for the return. Return times are 9:25, 11:25 and 13:25.

Nearby is the **Railway Museum**, housed in the old North Bundaberg Station. This small building dates from 1881 and was originally named Bundaberg Station. Only when the bridge across the river was completed in 1891 and the lines operating to north and south thereby joined was it renamed. It has since been moved away from the town and the main line has been shifted slightly so that trains no longer pass through the platform. However, after crossing the railway bridge next to Bundaberg Station, turning left and running down the centre of Perry Street, they still pass at low speed in front of this station and museum. The museum is open only on Tuesdays, Thursdays and Saturdays from 13:00 until 15:00. Admission costs $4.

The current **Bundaberg Railway Station** dates from 1888, when the first train from Maryborough arrived. Also in the town centre are several relatively old and interesting buildings. The **Arts Centre** in Quay Street is heritage listed and dates from 1889. The **Post Office**, in Bourbong Street, was built in 1890 and is also heritage listed, as is the nearby **National Australia Bank Building**, constructed in 1890 for the Commercial Banking Company of Sydney. The **Grand Hotel**, further down Bourbong Street, dates from 1885 and is still being used. A single room here costs only $19.

Bundaberg is not beside the sea, but there are several beaches nearby (see map opposite). All require a bus ride, however, so here are details. There is backpackers accommodation at Innes Park and Bargara (see accommodation listings below).

Innes Park Beach is 14 kilometres south-east of Bundaberg, **Coral Cove** is 19 kilometres south-east and **Elliott Heads** is 21 kilometres south-east. Buses are operated by Stewart and Sons and, at the time of writing, depart from Bundaberg at 7:05 on schooldays and 8:30, 12:20 and 15:15 on all weekdays. They return at 9:00 and 13:00 on weekdays and 16:00 on schooldays only from Elliott Heads, and a few minutes later from Coral Cove and Innes Park.

Bargara Beach, Nielsen Park Beach and Kelly's Beach are 13 to 14 kilometres east of Bundaberg. Buses are operated by Duffy's. Services 4 and 4A go this way, leaving the city at 10:25 and 12:25 and returning from the beaches at 11:07 and 13:07. Services operate on weekdays only.

Mon Repos Beach is 16 kilometres north-east of the city, about two kilometres north of the nearest stop on the route of the 4 and 4A buses (Nielsen Park Caravan Park).

Moore Park Beach is 24 kilometres north of Bundaberg. Services are operated by Stewart and Sons and depart from the city centre at 7:00 on schooldays and 9:30 and 14:00 on weekdays, returning from Moore Park at 10:00 and 14:30 on weekdays, and 16:20 on schooldays only.

In November each year, a **Turtle Festival** is held at the various beaches to celebrate the arrival of the turtles to lay their eggs, particularly at Mon Repos Beach.

The egg-laying continues from November until March.

Two other places to visit are **Burnett Heads**, at the mouth of the Burnett River flowing through the centre of Bundaberg, and **Sloping Hummock** which is the site of a dormant volcano, from which a good view of the city can be obtained. This volcano, dormant, but not extinct, was named in 1799 by Matthew Flinders. It is 96 metres high and eight kilometres east of Bundaberg.

Burnett Heads can be reached by Duffy's bus service no. 5. Buses leave the city centre at 11:45 and 14:15 and return from Burnett Heads at 12:12, 14:42 and 15:55. They operate on weekdays only.

Sloping Hummock can be reached by Duffy's services nos. 4 and 4A. Buses leave the city at 10:25 and 12:25 and return from Bargara Road, close to Sloping Hummock, at 11:21 and 13:21, again on weekdays only.

ACCOMMODATION

Higher class accommodation mentioned is all in the city area, but the backpackers accommodation includes the two hostels near the beaches.

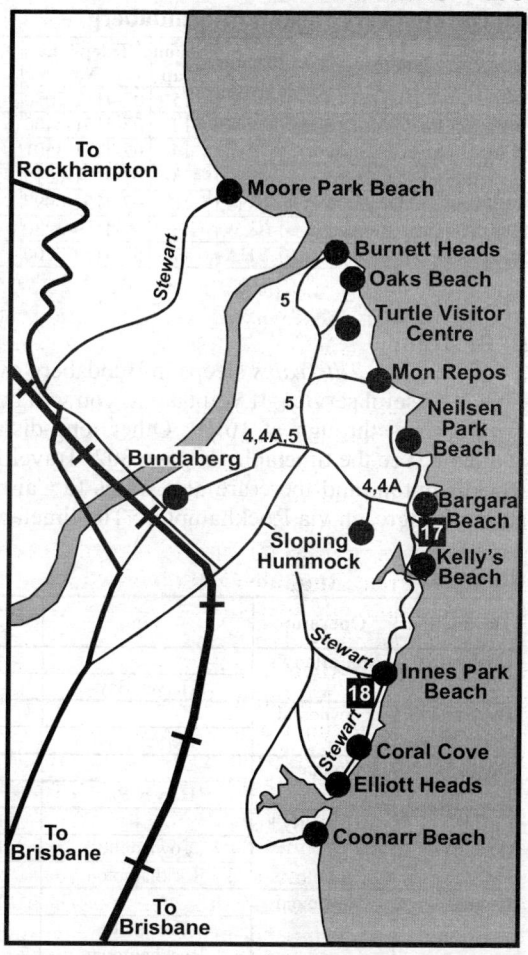

BEACHES AROUND BUNDABERG
Numbers and names on roads show bus routes
Numerals in boxes indicate backpackers hostels

(i) Hotel Accommodation in Bundaberg

Name	Stars	No. on Map	Telephone No.	Address	Lowest Price (Double/Twin)
Quality Burnett Riverside	4½	10	07-4155-8777	7 Quay Street	$125
Reef Gateway Motor Inn	4	2	07-4153-2255	11 Takalvan Street	$110
Sugar Country Motor Inn	4	8	07-4153-1166	220 Bourbong Street	$98
Bundaburg City Inn	3½	6	1-800-814-930	246 Bourbong Street	$95
Chalet Motor Inn		7	07-4152-9922	242 Bourbong Street	$75
Spanish Motor Inn		3	1-800-807-479	Mulgrave & Woongarra Sts.	$70
Sun City Motel	3½	1	07-4152-1099	11a Hinkler Avenue	$65
Matilda Motel		9	07-4151-4717	209 Bourbong Street	$65
Bourbong Street Motel	2½	4	07-4151-3089	265 Bourbong Street	$55
Oscar Motel	4	5	07-4152-3666	252 Bourbong Street	$55
Grand Hotel		11	07-4151-2441	Targo & Bourbong Streets	$35
Central Hotel		12	07-4151-3159	18 Targo Street	$35

QUEENSLAND

(ii) Backpackers Hostels in Bundaberg

Name	Group	No. on Map	Telephone No.	Address	Lowest Price (Dormitory)
Bundaberg Backpackers	VIP	15	07-4152-2080	2 Crofton Street	$20
Central Hotel Backpackers		12	07-4151-2400	18 Targo Street	$20
City Centre Backpackers		14	07-4151-3501	216 Bourbong Street	$20
Federal Backpackers		13	07-4151-6010	221 Bourbong Street	$20
Workers and Divers Hostel	Nom	16	07-4151-6097	64 Barolin Street	$19
Iluka Gardens Retreat	B&W	18	07-4159-3230	127 Logan Road, Innes Park	$22
Kelly's Beach Resort	YHA	17	07-4154-7200	6 Trevors Road, Bargara	$21

MOVING ON
(i) By Train

One of the *Tilt Trains* sleeps in Bundaberg overnight, leaving for Brisbane at 5:00. This is a useful service. If you take it, you will be in Brisbane by 9:20. The second *Tilt Train* comes through at 10:19. Other long-distance trains may be used if space is available. See the timetable on page 302. Travelling north, there is a daily *Tilt Train* to Rockhampton, and there are also trains to Cairns via Rockhampton and Townsville, and to Longreach via Rockhampton. The timetable is on page 238.

(ii) By Bus

Destination	Operator	Via	Distance (km)	Fare	Journey Time	Frequency
Brisbane	McCafferty's		444	$64	7 - 7¼ hrs	2/day
		Hervey Bay	121	$30	1¾ hrs	2/day
Brisbane	Greyhound		444	$64	6 - 7¾ hrs	2/day
		Hervey Bay	121	$30	1¾ hrs	2/day
Brisbane	Premier		444	$48	7¼ hrs	1/day
		Hervey Bay	121	$14	1¾ hrs	1/day
Cairns	McCafferty's		1468	$171	20¾ - 21½ hrs	2/day
		Townsville	1097	$142	14 - 15¼ hrs	2/day
		Rockhampton	331	$62	4 - 4¼ hrs	2/day
Cairns	Greyhound		1468	$171	21¼ - 21¾ hrs	2/day
		Townsville	1097	$142	15 - 16½ hrs	2/day
		Rockhampton	331	$62	4 - 4¾ hrs	2/day
Cairns	Premier		1468	$158	21 hrs	1/day
		Townsville	1097	$117	15½ hrs	1/day
		Rockhampton	331	$36	4¾ hrs	1/day

GLADSTONE
Population 43,000

6 hrs by train from Brisbane
10 hrs by bus from Brisbane

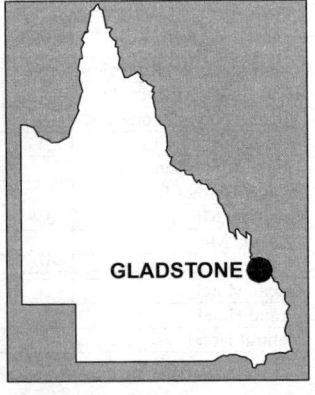

Gladstone is basically an industrial city, 550 kilometres north of Brisbane. The excellent deep water harbour here was discovered and charted by Matthew Flinders in 1802, and now the city's greatest claim to fame is that it has the largest alumina refinery in the world. It also has the largest aluminium smelter in

Australia. In case these two claims do not appear to make Gladstone the ideal holiday location, it should be added that it also has nearby beaches, that at Tannum being well known, safe and suitable for swimming at any time of year. Tannum is joined to Boyne Island by a bridge and the latter is famous for its foreshore parks. The southernmost tip of the Great Barrier Reef stretches down to Gladstone, and Heron Island, lying 73 kilometres off Gladstone, is popular for diving.

Gladstone is six hours from Brisbane by *Tilt Train*, or approximately ten hours by bus. McCafferty's runs four services a day to here, while Greyhound has two. Premier does not currently serve Gladstone.

There is an attractive **marina** in the city, another of Gladstone's claims being that it has a higher rate of boat ownership than any other place in Australia. On the marina, the Visitor Information Centre is to be found. There are also the **Tondoon Botanic Gardens**, in Glenlyon Road, to the south of the city. These gardens are devoted entirely to Australian native plants, mostly local, and are free. There is an **Art Gallery** and **Museum** in the old Town Hall on the corner of Goondoon and Bramston Streets. These are also both free.

An interesting location 125 kilometres south of Gladstone is the **Town of Seventeen Seventy**, where Captain Cook anchored his ship the *Endeavour* in Bustard

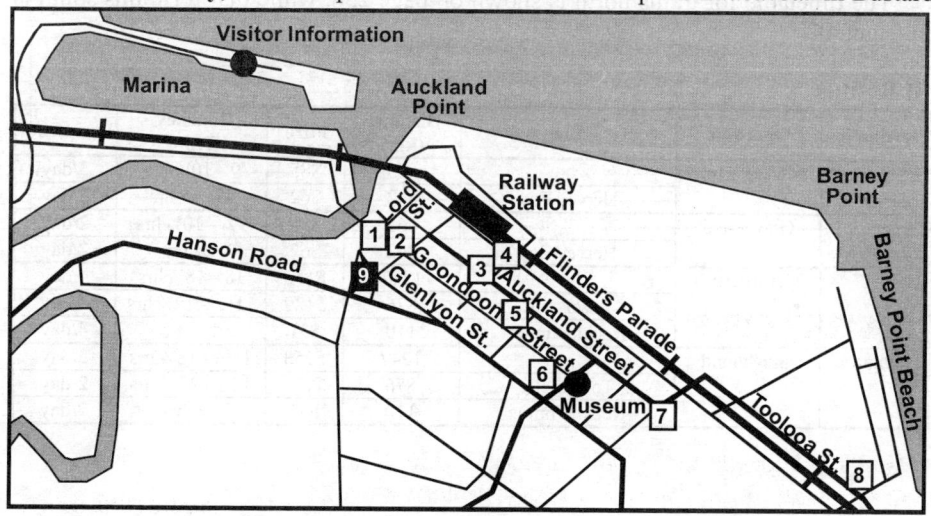

AROUND GLADSTONE

GLADSTONE

Black numerals in white boxes indicate hotel accommodation
White numerals in black boxes indicate backpackers hostels

296 QUEENSLAND

Bay and made his second landing on the continent of Australia, this being in 1770, as the name of the town suggests. The *Tilt Train* stops at Miriam Vale on request, but that is 63 kilometres away from the Town of Seventeen Seventy, and buses run only twice a week (originating in Bundaberg). Long-distance buses will also stop on request at Miriam Vale. Six kilometres south of the Town of Seventeen Seventy is **Agnes Water**, the most northerly of the surf beaches on the eastern coast of Australia, for, just north of this point, the Great Barrier Reef begins.

ACCOMMODATION
(i) Hotel Accommodation in Gladstone

Name	Stars	No. on Map	Telephone No.	Address	Lowest Price (Double/Twin)
Flag Metro Hotel & Suites	4½	3	1-800-004-321	22 Roseberry Street	$140
Country Plaza Internat'l	4½	5	1-800-355-136	100 Goondoon Street	$130
A1 Motel		8	07-4972-1655	84 Toolooa Street	$95
Gladstone Reef Hotel	3	2	07-4972-1000	38 Goondoon Street	$85
Mid City Motor Inn	4	1	07-4972-3000	26 Goondoon Street	$80
Why Not Motor Inn		7	07-4972-4222	23 Coon Street	$65
Harbour Lodge Motel	3	4	07-4972-6463	16 Roseberry Street	$65
Rusty Anchor Motor Inn	3½	6	07-4972-2099	167 Goondoon Street	$65

(ii) Backpackers Hostel in Gladstone

Name	Group	No. on Map	Telephone No.	Address	Lowest Price (Dormitory)
Gladstone Backpackers	VIP	9	07-4972-5744	12 Rollo Street	$22

MOVING ON
(i) By Train
The timetable for trains north is shown on page 238, while that for trains south is on page 302.

(ii) By Bus

Destination	Operator	Via	Distance (km)	Fare	Journey Time	Frequency
Brisbane	McCafferty's		665	$85	9 - 10½ hrs	3/day
		Hervey Bay	342	$62	4¼ - 5 hrs	2/day
Brisbane	Greyhound		665	$85	9¼ - 10¾ hrs	2/day
		Hervey Bay	342	$62	4¾ hrs	2/day
Cairns	McCafferty's		1247	$158	18 - 18¾ hrs	4/day
		Townsville	876	$129	11¼ - 12¾ hrs	4/day
		Rockhampton	110	$31	1½ hrs	4/day
Cairns	Greyhound		1247	$158	18¼ - 18¾ hrs	2/day
		Townsville	876	$129	12½ - 13¼ hrs	2/day
		Rockhampton	110	$31	1½ hrs	2/day

ROCKHAMPTON
Population 60,000

7 hrs by train from Brisbane
11 hrs 30 mins by bus from Brisbane

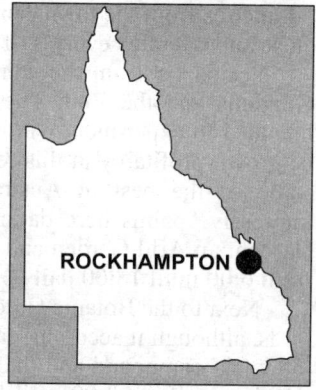

Rockhampton is a city through which most visitors to Australia pass without giving it much attention. It is, in fact, quite an interesting place and well worth a stop. Since it is a reasonable day's journey from Brisbane, it is a convenient location at which to break one's journey if travelling further north, particularly if one is travelling by train.

It takes seven hours by *Tilt Train* to travel the 639 kilometres from Brisbane to Rockhampton. If you prefer a bus, average travelling time is 11½ hours. Note that McCafferty's and Greyhound arrive at a terminal in North Rockhampton, across the river from the city centre. The youth hostel is near this point, but it is not really central. On request, these services will also stop at the Railway Station, although the distance of about one kilometre from there to the city centre is similar. Premier stops at the Mobil Roadhouse on the south side of the river and a little closer to the centre.

One of the odd features of this city is that the railway line passes down the centre of one of the main streets. If you are travelling further north by train, you can watch as you clatter slowly past the pubs and shops before turning sharp right to cross the Fitzroy River. If you are alighting from a train and looking for the town centre, just follow the railway line north and you will soon get there. However, if you stay in the town centre, you will know in the morning just how many trains pass through during the night and at what times, and the number is greater than you might have expected (this from experience).

This area was first settled in 1853, when the Archer family arrived. Trading commenced when the *Ellida* arrived with supplies, at a point marked by a monument on the bank of the river in the southern part of the city. In 1858, gold was discovered in Canonona, sixty kilometres north of Rockhampton and, as the miners were dependent upon supplies shipped through here, the prosperity of Rockhampton increased accordingly. Further goldfields were later discovered at Bouldercombe and Mount Morgan (see map on page 300). Finally, in 1903, the railway reached Rockhampton.

At first, sheep farming was practised here, but gradually the emphasis changed to cattle. Now Rockhampton claims that it is 'the beef capital of Australia'. 2.5 million head of cattle are kept within a radius of 250 kilometres of Rockhampton.

A stroll along the banks of the Fitzroy River will give a good impression of Rockhampton. The river is attractive and some of the buildings facing it are stately. The Tourist Information Centre is housed in one of the most impressive, the former Customs House. The Criterion Hotel, next to the bridge, also has the grandeur of a past age.

Rockhampton is a tropical city - just. The **Tropic of Capricorn** runs through the southern edge of the city and is marked by the **Capricorn Spire** beside the main highway. If you look to the left from either bus or train just as you enter Rockhampton, you will see it. If you miss it and want to go back to see it, it is a walk of about three kilometres from the town centre. If you prefer to take a bus, Sunbus service no. 1 goes close and operates every half hour.

Not so far from the spire, still in the southern part of the city are the **Botanic Gardens** and the **Zoo**. The Botanic Gardens date from 1869 and were originally intended to experiment with the cultivation of various plants, to establish what could be grown profitably in this region. These gardens are worth seeing, being regarded as some of the best in Australia outside capital cities. There are some especially impressive palms here dating back a century or longer. There are also a Japanese Garden, an Arid Garden and a Tropical Fruits Garden. The Botanic Gardens are open from 6:00 until 18:00 daily. Admission is free.

Next to the Botanic Gardens is the Zoo. Its emphasis is on Australian animals and birds, although it accommodates foreigners also. There are elevated walkways through the koala compound and the aviary, to permit better observation of the residents. The Zoo is open from 8:00 until 17:00 daily, with feeding time at 15:00 (for the permanent residents, not the visitors). Admission to the Zoo also is free.

The Botanic Gardens and the Zoo are about three kilometres from the city centre. If that is too far to walk, Sunbus no. 4A will take you there. It operates every hour.

In North Rockhampton there are some more gardens. The **Kershaw Gardens** were started in 1976 on a land fill area, and opened to the public in 1988. They aim at a bush environment and stretch for a kilometre beside the main highway north. The Kershaw Gardens are free and open day and night. They are within walking distance of the town centre - about 1.5 kilometres, but if a bus is needed, services 1, 3, 3A, 4A, 6 and 10 all pass nearby. Alight at Charles Street and walk down to the end of that street where there is a bridge across to the gardens.

On the northern outskirts of the city is the **Heritage Village**. This is a collection of old dwellings from pioneer times, and includes an exhibition of vintage vehicles and one of various types of clocks. The Heritage Village is open from 9:00 until 16:00 daily and admission costs $10. To reach the village, take bus no. 10, which operates every hour on Mondays to Fridays only.

In the centre of the city is **Archer Park Station**. This was the original Rockhampton Station. It opened in 1899, at which time there were only local services along the line to Emu Park. The railway from Brisbane reached here in 1903 and then this station found itself handling up to 25 trains per day. However, there were problems with the station, principally because the platform was too short, so it gradually declined in importance. By 1957, it was used only by local trains and in 1970 it was closed for passenger service and used only for goods. Then the weight of heavy goods vehicles using the area caused the platform to start to subside, while local residents complained about the constant noise associated with the goods operations, and eventually, in 1990, use of the station was given up completely and it was presented to the local council. Now it is a Railway Museum.

It is a handsome station, both from the front (entrance) side and from the Denison Street side where an arched roof covers platform and tracks. The main line still runs down the middle of Denison Street, so you can see this station from your train window, on the right of the street as you head north. It is not just a museum. A steam locomotive has been restored and hauls a set of old carriages on occasional trips, usually to the seaside at Yeppoon.

In addition, Rockhampton used to operate, from 1909 until 1939, a city tram system, consisting of nine trams, plus six trailers. Over their thirty years of service, the

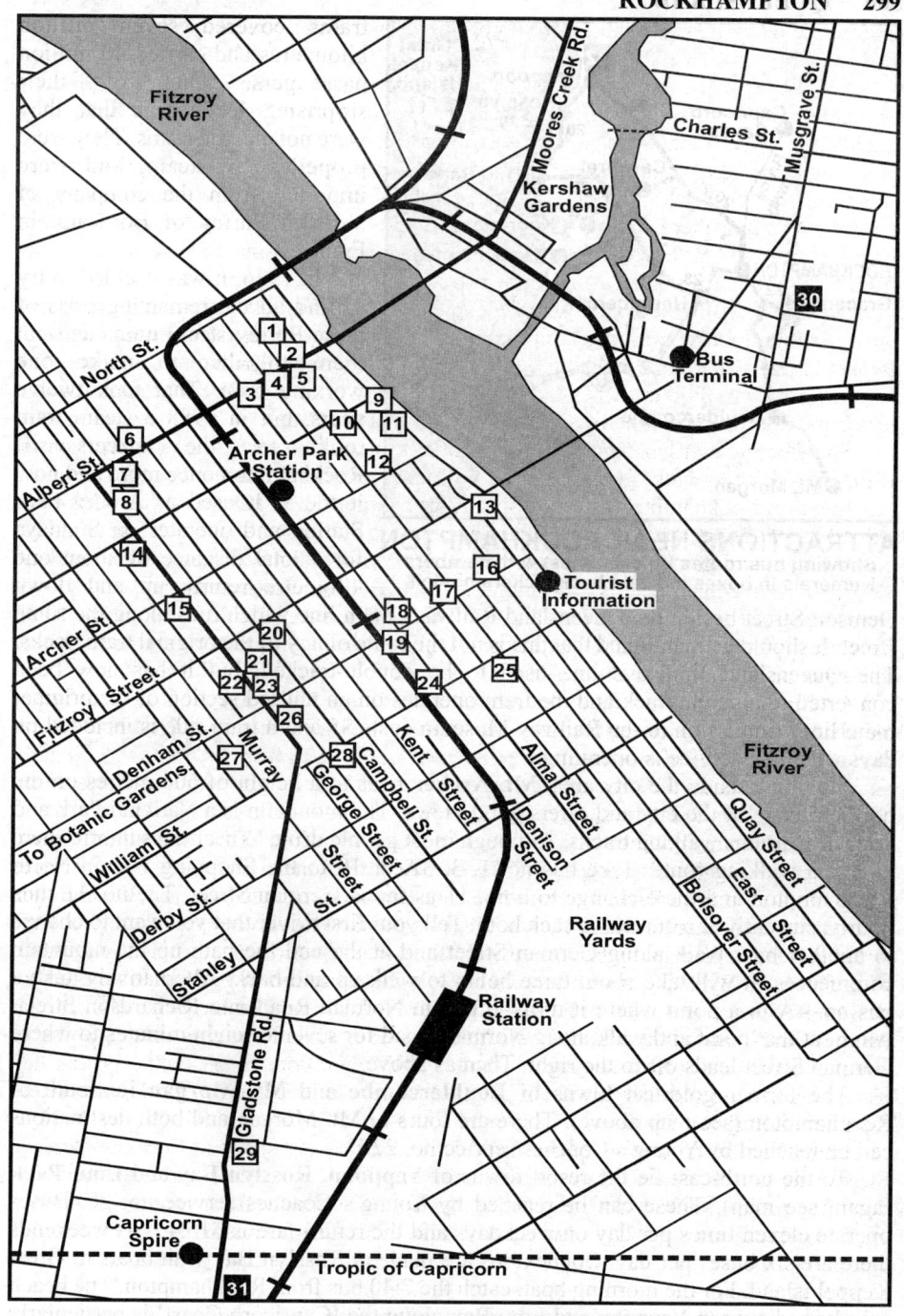

ROCKHAMPTON
Black numerals in white boxes indicate hotel accommodation
White numerals in black boxes indicate backpackers hostels

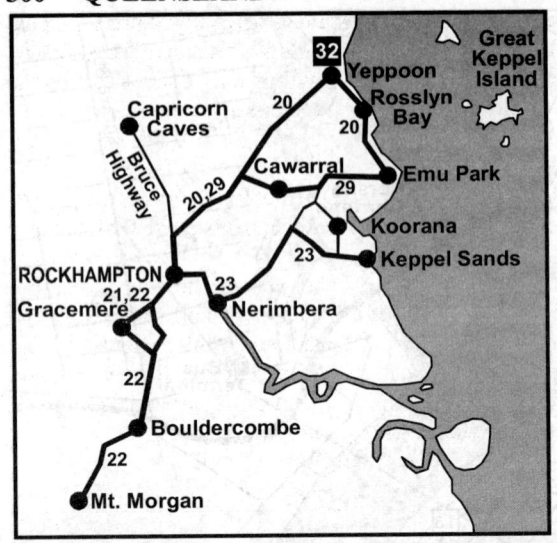

ATTRACTIONS NEAR ROCKHAMPTON
Showing bus routes (thicker lines) with numbers
Numerals in boxes indicate backpackers hostels

trams covered seven million kilometres and carried 40 million passengers. One of their surprising features is that they were not electric trams. They were propelled by steam, and were imported from the company of Valentin Purrey of Bordeaux in France.

In 1976, it was decided to try to find all the remaining parts of these Purrey steam trams and put them together to make one working tram. That took twelve years, but in 1988 a steam tram took to the streets of Rockhampton once more and now it too is housed at Archer Park Station and operates on Sundays for a total distance of about one kilometre return, up and down Denison Street beside the Queensland Railways main line which runs along the same street. It should be mentioned that this is not the route of any of the original tram tracks. The Queensland Railways line used to be double-tracked, but it has now been converted to a single track and the tram operates on an unused section of the original main line. Admission to the Railway Museum costs $5 and a tram ride is included on days when the service is operating.

Moving outside the city area, **Mt. Archer** rises to a height of 604 metres on the northern edge of the city and offers good views. The mountain is a National Park and there are various walking tracks. Although most people drive to near the summit, there is also a walking route. Take bus no. 1, 3, 3A or 10 to the Shopping Fair in North Rockhampton and there change to a no. 11 as far as German Street. The no. 11 runs hourly, currently at a quarter to each hour. Tell your first driver that you want to change to another bus. Walk along German Street and at the end the path up the mountain commences. It will take about three hours to walk up and back. Alternatively, take a bus no. 4A to a point where it turns left from Norman Road into Richardson Street. Alight at that point and walk along Norman Road for seven or eight minutes to where German Street leads off to the right. Then as above.

The former goldrush towns of **Bouldercombe** and **Mt. Morgan** lie south of Rockhampton (see map above). There are tours to Mt. Morgan and both destinations can be reached by Young's Coaches service no. 22.

To the north-east lie the resort towns of **Yeppoon, Rosslyn Bay** and **Emu Park** (again see map). These can be reached by Young's Coaches service no. 20. Buses operate eleven times per day on weekdays and the return fare is $15.40. At weekends there are six buses per day. Connexions are made at Rosslyn Bay with boats to Great Keppel Island. For the morning boat, catch the 7:40 bus from Rockhampton. The beach area lying between Yeppoon and Emu Bay along the 'Capricorn Coast' is particularly pretty and has led to the seventeen-kilometre road between the two being named the Scenic Highway.

ROCKHAMPTON 301

Other attractions nearby include the **Capricorn Caves**, formerly called Olsens' Caves, and a **Crocodile Farm** at Koorana, near Keppel Sands, south of Emu Park. Young's service no. 23 runs to Keppel Sands twice a day, but not really close to the crocodile farm. A walk of about five kilometres each way would be necessary.

ACCOMMODATION

Rockhampton is a favoured stopping place, so there is no shortage of accommodation here, especially along the main highway, which runs close to the centre of the city.

For backpackers, too, there is plenty of choice. The official hostels are rather inconveniently located, one a long walk to the south of the town and one across the river to the north, but in the town centre there are at least four hotels where one can have a single room at a very reasonable price. The author stayed at the Swan Hotel and was actually asked to pay only $10 for a slightly inferior, but quite adequate, room. It was my cheapest accommodation in Australia in the twenty-first century.

(i) Hotel Accommodation in Rockhampton

Name	Stars	No. on Map	Telephone No.	Address	Lowest Price (Double/Twin)
Mercure Leichhardt Hotel	4½	17	07-4927-6733	Bolsover Street	$130
Country Comfort Inn	4½	11	07-4927-9933	86 Victoria Parade	$125
Club Crocodile Motor Inn	3½	3	07-4927-7433	Albert & Alma Streets	$110
Centre Point Motel	4½	21	07-4927-8844	131 George Street	$110
Coffee House Apartments		25	07-4927-5722	William & Bolsover Streets	$105
Cattle City Motor Inn	4½	29	1-800-812-961	139 Gladstone Road	$105
City-Ville Luxury Apts.	4	1	07-4922-8322	21 Bolsover Street	$95
Regency on Albert	4	6	07-4922-6222	28 Albert Street	$95
Fitzroy Motor Inn	3½	20	1-800-066-136	Fitzroy & Campbell Streets	$95
Archer Park Motel	3½	7	1-800-220-444	39 Albert Street	$89
Cosmopolitan Apartments		5	07-4931-0222	Bolsover Street	$88
O'Dowds Motel		24	07-4927-0344	William & Denison Streets	$88
Rockhampton City Inn		4	07-4922-6800	11 Albert Street	$85
Rockhampton Palms Inn		8	07-4922-6577	55 George Street	$85
Motel 98	2½	9	07-4927-5322	98 Victoria Parade	$80
Cambridge Hotel / Motel	3	10	07-4922-3006	Cambridge Street	$80
Rockhampton Court Inn	3	14	07-4927-8277	82 George Street	$75
Travellers Motor Inn	3½	15	1-800-355-141	110 George Street	$75
Central Park Motel		27	07-4927-2333	224 Murray Street	$75
Bridge Motor Inn	3	2	07-4927-7488	31 Bolsover Street	$65
City Walk Motor Inn	3	28	07-4922-6009	129 William Street	$65
Simpson's Motel	3	22	07-4927-7800	156 George Street	$60
Porkey's Motel	2	23	07-4927-8100	141 George Street	$60
Ambassador on the Park		26	1-800-027-855	161 George Street	$55
Criterion Hotel / Motel	3	13	07-4922-1225	Quay Street	$45
O'Dowds Hotel		24	07-4927-0344	William & Denison Streets	$45
Grand Hotel		12	07-4922-1833	16 Archer Street	$35
Oxford Hotel		16	07-4922-1837	East Street	$35
Savoy Hotel		18	07-4927-2005	William & Alma Streets	$35
Swan Hotel		19	07-4922-1865	Denham & Denison Streets	$30

302 QUEENSLAND
(ii) Backpackers Hostels in Rockhampton

Name	Group	No. on Map	Telephone No.	Address	Lowest Price (Dormitory)
Southside Holiday Village	VIP	31	1800-075-911	Lower Dawson Road	$19
Rockhampton Y.H.A.	YHA	30	07-4927-5288	60 MacFarlane Street	$19
Downtown Backpackers		16	07-4922-1837	East Street	$17
Swan Hotel		19	07-4922-1865	Denison & Denham Streets	$15
Yeppoon Backpackers	VIP	32	1800-636-828	Queen Street, Yeppoon	$20

MOVING ON
(i) By Train

The *Tilt Train* runs back to Brisbane every morning. Then there are trains north to Townsville and Cairns. To Longreach, moving inland, the *Spirit of the Outback* runs twice a week and this is a beautiful route, thoroughly recommended for the traveller who wants to see something of the real Australia - that is something other than the beaches of the east coast. Try it. You will not be disappointed. Timetables are shown below and more detail about this journey is given on page 308.

Rockhampton to Longreach, Winton, Townsville and Cairns

Days of Departure	W, Sun	W, Sat	W, Sat (Bus)	Sun,Tu, Th, Sat
Rockhampton	0010	0435		2040
Emerald		0918		
Alpha		1257		
Barcaldine		1546		
Longreach		1758	1805	
Winton			2005	
Mackay	0526			0229
Proserpine	0746			0424
Bowen	0841			0532
Townsville	1150			0843
Tully				1249
Innisfail				1359
Cairns				1625
Days of Arrival				Sun, M, W, F

Rockhampton to Brisbane

Days of Departure	M - F	Not Sat	Daily	Sun, Th
Rockhampton		0500	0740	1945
Gladstone		0643	0842	2141
Bundaberg	0500	0925	1019	0037
Maryborough W	0549	1035	1109	0147
Gympie North	0646	1224	1207	0321
Brisbane	0910	1555	1440	0620
Days of Arrival				M, F

(ii) By Bus

Buses operate south to Brisbane, north to Townsville and Cairns and west to Emerald, as shown below.

Destination	Operator	Via	Distance (km)	Fare	Journey Time	Frequency
Brisbane	McCafferty's		775	$93	10½ - 11½ hrs	4/day
		Hervey Bay	452	$80	5¾ - 6¾ hrs	3/day
Brisbane	Greyhound		775	$93	10¾ - 12 hrs	2/day
		Hervey Bay	452	$80	6 hrs	2/day
Brisbane	Premier		775	$84	11¾ hrs	1/day
		Hervey Bay	452	$48	6¼ hrs	1/day
Cairns	McCafferty's		1137	$142	16 - 16¾ hrs	4/day
		Townsville	766	$115	9½ - 10¾ hrs	4/day
Cairns	Greyhound		1137	$142	16¼ - 16¾ hrs	2/day
		Townsville	766	$115	10½ - 11 hrs	2/day
Cairns	Premier		1137	$130	16¼ hrs	1/day
		Townsville	766	$81	10¾ hrs	1/day
Longreach	McCafferty's		668	$79	10½ hrs	2/week
		Emerald	265	$43	3½ hrs	1/day

GREAT KEPPEL ISLAND
Population 100

45 mins by boat from Rosslyn Bay

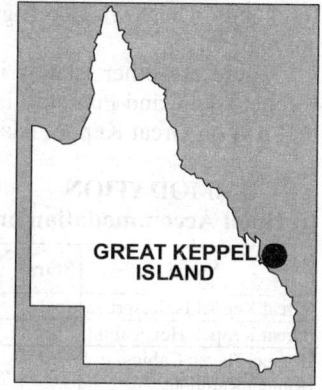

Gaining in popularity as a place to visit is Great Keppel Island, only fifteen kilometres off the 'Capricorn Coast'. Originally known as Wapparaburra by the local aborigines, whose history here dates back 4,500 years, the island was given its European name by Captain Cook as he sailed by in 1770.

It is an island for relaxing on the beautiful beaches, diving, or enjoying various types of water sports. The fact that it now has reasonably priced backpackers accommodation has increased its popularity greatly.

To reach the island, take a launch from Rosslyn Bay, south of Yeppoon. Launches are frequent and now take only 45 minutes to reach the island. To reach Rosslyn Bay, there are bus services operated by Young's from Yeppoon and from Rockhampton. These buses operate eleven times a day during the week and six times a day at the

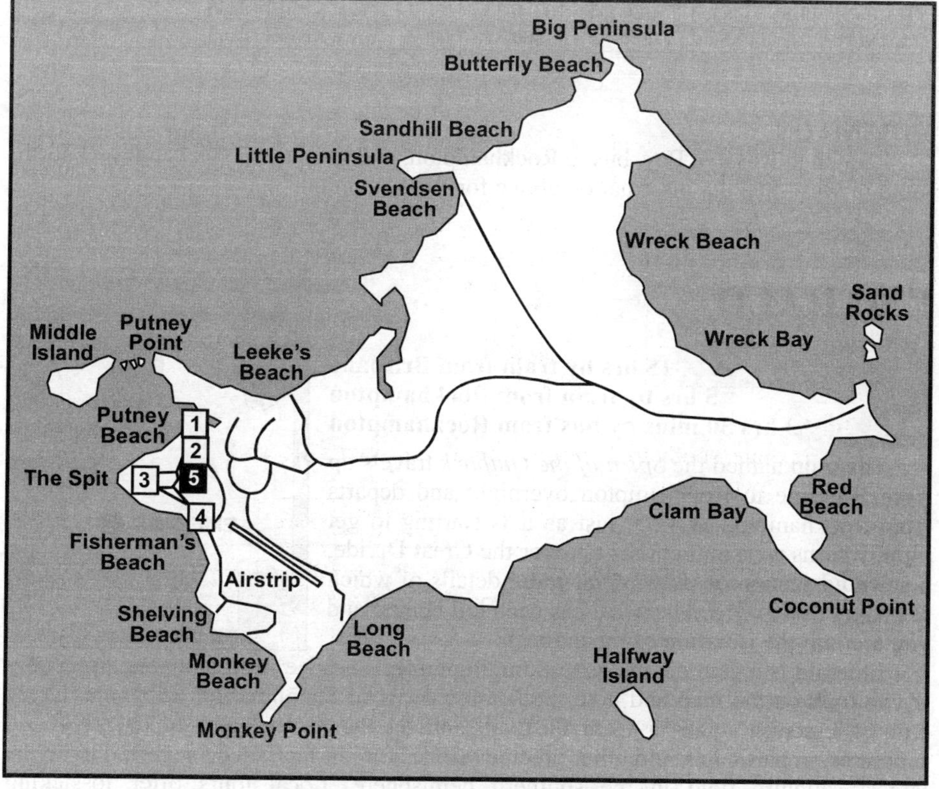

GREAT KEPPEL ISLAND

Black numerals in white boxes indicate hotel accommodation
White numerals in black boxes indicate backpackers hostels

weekends. There are also flights from Rockhampton to Great Keppel Island, but they are expensive.

There are other islands in the Keppel Group which can be visited. Both North Keppel Island and Pumpkin Island offer accommodation, but it is not quite the bargain that it is on Great Keppel Island, so Great Keppel remains the firm favourite.

ACCOMMODATION
(i) Hotel Accommodation on Great Keppel Island

Name	Stars	No. on Map	Telephone No.	Address	Lowest Price (Double/Twin)
Great Keppel Is. Resort		4	1-800-245-658	Great Keppel Island	$170
Great Keppel Hol. Cabins		1	07-4939-8655	Great Keppel Island	$100
Keppel Haven Cabins		3	07-4933-6744	Great Keppel Island	$85
Keppel Kampout		2	07-4933-6744	Great Keppel Island	$75

(ii) Backpackers Hostels on Great Keppel Island

Name	Group	No. on Map	Telephone No.	Address	Lowest Price (Dormitory)
YHA Backpackers Village	YHA	5	07-4933-6416	Great Keppel Island	$22
Great Keppel Island Cabins	VIP	2	1800-356-744	Great Keppel Island	$22

MOVING ON
Launch to Rosslyn Bay, bus to Rockhampton, and from there you can travel north, south or west. See the information above for Rockhampton.

EMERALD
Population 9,500

15 hrs by train from Brisbane
5 hrs by train from Rockhampton
3 hrs 30 mins by bus from Rockhampton

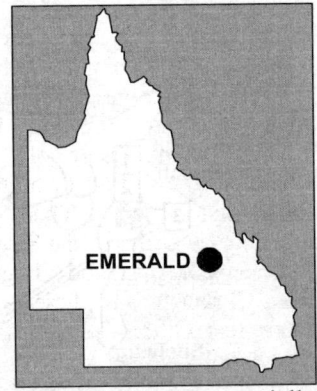

The train named the *Spirit of the Outback* travels up from Brisbane to Rockhampton overnight and departs from Rockhampton at 4:35, just as it is starting to get light. It turns west and climbs up over the Great Divide, a splendid section of railway, for more details of which see pages 308 to 313. The coast has been left behind and you are into the isolation of the outback.

Emerald is a gem centre, as you might perhaps surmise from its name, especially if you look on the map and note the nearby towns of Sapphire and Rubyvale. Every August Emerald stages a Gem Festival, and on the nearby gem fields are found sapphires, in particular, and other precious stones too. In fact, this is reported to be the largest sapphire field in the southern hemisphere. Local tours offer fossicking opportunities if one has the time. The main gem fields are located about thirty to sixty kilometres from the town of Emerald.

One of the attractions of Emerald is its **railway station**, built in 1900 and restored in 1986. If you have time to spend in this town, there are other things to see too. There is an **Art Gallery**, and there are attractive **Botanic Gardens**. **Lake Maraboon** is nearby. Free **mine tours** are available, but on Thursdays only. There is also one of the largest citrus orchards in the southern hemisphere. In the Town Hall is a piece of a fossilised tree, found only 45 centimetres beneath the surface while a new railway bridge was being constructed nearby. When carbon dated, it was found to be 250 million years old.

Nearby (relatively) are other places to visit. **Capella**, 51 kilometres to the north, has a Pioneer Village, open from 9:00 until noon on Tuesdays, Wednesdays and Thursdays, and from 10:00 until 15:00 on Sundays, at a cost of $3. The Cultural Centre has displays of arts and crafts. Accommodation is available both in Capella and in **Tieri**, 37 kilometres to its east. Although a railway line runs to Capella, it is used for coal only.

A further 55 kilometres north of Capella, along the same railway line, is the historic town of **Clermont**. It claims to have been the first inland settlement in Australia within the tropics. In 1861, there was a gold rush there and visitors can still be found searching for gold. The town was almost destroyed by a flood in 1916, after which it was shifted to higher ground. The traction engine which did most of the shifting is on display. There is also a piano in a tree. **Mother Mary MacKillop**, who founded the Order of the Sisters of St. Joseph, lived in Clermont in 1877, and there is a shrine to her at Hood's Lagoon. Copper was found at **Copperfield**, eight kilometres from Clermont, and there is an old smelter chimney there, and the old Copperfield Store. Just a little further north is **Blair Athol**, the whole reason for the existence of the branch railway line, for here is the richest seam of steaming coal yet found in the world. Tours are available on Tuesdays only.

If one travels 75 kilometres south from Emerald, one reaches the pretty town of **Springsure**. The notorious **Wills Massacre** occurred 30 kilometres north-west of here, when, on 17th October 1861, aborigines retaliated for the killing of some of their own members by storming Cullin-la-Ringo station and massacring nineteen white settlers. It was the worst incident of its kind in Australian history. In Springsure, there is a large rock known as **Big St. Peter**, with the *Virgin in the Rock*, a formation supposed to resemble the Virgin Mary, although it is gradually being eroded by the elements. There

AROUND EMERALD
Distances shown are from Emerald

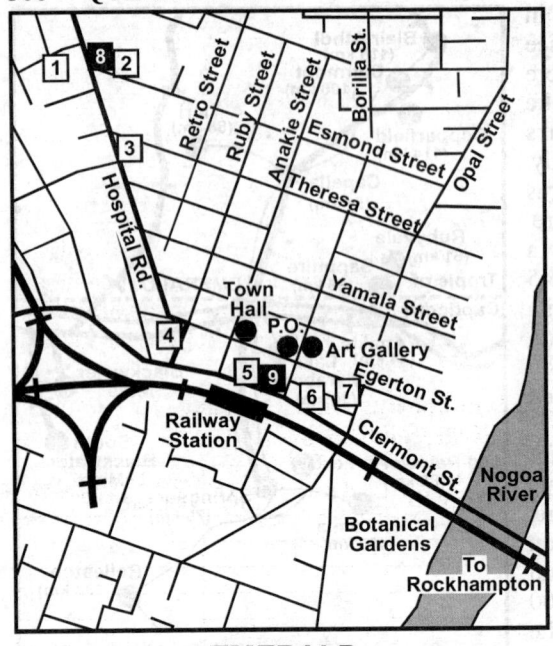

EMERALD
Black numerals in white boxes indicate hotel accommodation
White numerals in black boxes indicate backpackers hostels

is a **railway station**, built in 1887, but, unfortunately, no passenger trains. **Mt. Zamia Environmental Park** is 25 kilometres to the west, offering good views. Ten kilometres from Springsure is **Old Rainworth Fort**, a food store erected in 1862, together with **Cairdbeign Homestead**, built in the late 1870s, and **Cairdbeign School**, dating from 1896. These are open from 9:00 until 14:00, except on Thursdays. Admission costs $7.

Continuing south-east, one comes to **Rolleston**, and, then, eighty kilometres south of that, **Carnarvon Gorge**, a total distance of 213 kilometres from Emerald. This attractive sandstone gorge is popular with walkers. It has aboriginal paintings, cliffs, moss gardens and wildlife, and is one of the most popular National Parks in Queensland. The problem is that, like all of the places mentioned in this section, it is difficult to reach. There is no public transport available, so one must either get a ride, which is by no means impossible, or join a local tour, which is generally expensive. What a pity it is that these branch railways do not have any passenger trains.

Emerald itself can be reached by bus as well as by train. McCafferty's runs a service every morning from Rockhampton, taking only 3½ hours. On two days a week, Sundays and Thursdays, there is a connecting service from Emerald on to Longreach.

Emerald has another little claim to fame, and that is that it has, or had, one of the last two 'mixed' train services in Australia. The train runs west to Jericho and then turns south-west to the small settlement of Yaraka, with a population of 27. Although the train still operates, it is rumoured that, from mid-2001, it stopped accepting passengers. For more information about this interesting service, see page 311 and the anecdote on page 314.

ACCOMMODATION
(i) Hotel Accommodation in Emerald

Name	Stars	No. on Map	Telephone No.	Address	Lowest Price (Double/Twin)
Maraboon Tavern	4	2	07-4982-0777	Hospital Road & Esmond St	$110
Meteor Motel	3½	7	07-4982-1166	Opal & Egerton Streets	$100
Western Gateway Motel		3	1-800-638-801	Hospital Road & Theresa St.	$95
A & A Lodge	3	6	07-4982-2355	Clermont Street	$75
Highlanders Motel	3½	1	07-4982-1922	5 Cypress Drive	$75
Motel 707		4	07-4982-1707	17 Ruby Street	$65
Central Inn	3	5	07-4982-0800	90 Clermont Street	$55

(ii) Backpackers Hostels in Emerald

Name	Group	No. on Map	Telephone No.	Address	Lowest Price (Dormitory)
Leichhardt Hotel		9	07-4982-1146	Clermont Street	$25
Emerald Hostel		8	07-4982-4188	Hospital Road	$20

MOVING ON
(i) By Rail

There are two trains a week west to Longreach and two a week east to Rockhampton, plus, of course, the mixed train to Yaraka mentioned above. A summary of all trains from Emerald is given on the timetable below, including connexions from Longreach to Winton and connexions north from Rockhampton to Townsville and Cairns.

Emerald to Longreach, Winton, Hughenden, Yaraka, Brisbane, Townsville and Cairns

Days of Departure	F	F	W, Sat	W, Sat (Bus)	Th	Sun, Th	Sun, Tu, Th, Sat	Sun, W
Yaraka		1845						
Blackall		2355						
Jericho		0320						
Alpha		0530						
Emerald	0050	0940	0918			1530		
Alpha	0600		1257					
Jericho	0715		1400					
Blackall	1145							
Yaraka	1625							
Barcaldine			1546					
Longreach			1758	1805				
Winton				2005	2030			
Hughenden					0345			
Rockhampton						1945	2040	0010
Brisbane						0620		
Mackay							0229	0526
Proserpine							0424	0746
Bowen							0532	0841
Townsville							0843	1150
Tully							1249	
Innisfail							1359	
Cairns							1625	
Days of Arrival		Sat			F	M, F	Sun, M, W, F	

(ii) By Bus

Buses run from Emerald to Rockhampton every afternoon, and to Longreach on Sundays and Thursdays.

Destination	Operator	Via	Distance (km)	Fare	Journey Time	Frequency
Rockhampton	McCafferty's		260	$43	3½ hrs	1/day
Longreach	McCafferty's		405	$59	5½ hrs	2/week

GREAT RAILWAY JOURNEYS

The most popular of the long-distance routes offered by Queensland Railways is the journey by the *Sunlander* or the *Queenslander* up the coast from Brisbane to Cairns, but the most diverse and scenic long-distance route is that of the *Spirit of the Outback* travelling between Brisbane and Longreach, with a bus connexion on to Winton.

The *Spirit of the Outback* leaves Brisbane every Tuesday and Friday evening, usually from platform 10 of Roma Street Station, for its journey of 1,325 kilometres, following the coastal route as far north as Rockhampton and then turning inland. Since Queensland Railways offers the only sleeping berths in Australia available at an appealing price, currently requiring a supplement of $44 per night, why not take one and enjoy this journey in comfort, with a place to sleep at night and the choice of a compartment for three or a lounge car during the day?

The train usually sets off via the Showgrounds, on a line not used by suburban trains except when an event is being held at the Showgrounds, and then travels through the Brisbane suburbs to its first halt at Caboolture. By now darkness is descending and little more will be seen until tomorrow morning, so here retire to either restaurant or bar. In Queensland, meals are still cooked on the train, as at the time of writing, rather than brought on board pre-packaged, and are not unreasonable in price. If you do want to see the scenery between Brisbane and Rockhampton, however, you can travel up on the *Tilt Train* and then join the *Spirit of the Outback* there for the second half of its journey.

We travel on from Caboolture, weaving our way through the scenic Glasshouse Mountains, a series of unusual rounded green hummocks, and pass through Nambour, from where bus connexions are made to the Sunshine Coast.

Gympie North is 174 kilometres from Brisbane, Gympie being one of those places now by-passed by the main line. As we approach the city, we run parallel to the line to Imbil, now operated by the Mary Valley Heritage Railway's *Valley Rattler* service, for details of which see page 268.

Maryborough is another unfortunately by-passed city, Maryborough West station being a further hundred kilometres into our journey. Maryborough has been an important railway location, with most of Queensland's railway locomotives, and many of those used in other states too over the last century, manufactured here by Walkers Limited. Queensland's record-breaking *Tilt Train* is the latest of the company's achievements. Here too was born P.L. Travers, the creator of *Mary Poppins*.

As we approach Bundaberg, we enter the realm of sugar cane, which extends from here for 1,500 kilometres up the coast. Bundaberg has

2. SPIRIT OF THE OUTBACK
BRISBANE TO LONGREACH

discovered one of the most popular applications of this crop, for here is found the Bundaberg Rum Distillery. Bundaberg was also the home of the pioneer aviator Bert Hinkler. We cross the Burnett River on a grand steel bridge constructed in 1891, turn left and proceed at very limited speed down the middle of the street for a short distance before passing the former North Bundaberg Station, now a Railway Museum, on our right and continuing on our journey north.

Gladstone is a modern industrial city, an excellent deep water port and the site of the largest alumina refinery in the world and the largest aluminium smelter in Australia, but also a port greatly favoured by boat owners. Gladstone has the highest rate of boat ownership in Australia.

We arrive in Rockhampton, approximately the half-way point of our journey, just as dawn is breaking. Rockhampton lies exactly on the Tropic of Capricorn and, if you are alert. you will see the Capricorn Spire marking the precise location of the tropic on the left of the train as we approach the city. If you are still sleeping, however, you will get a second chance as we leave again. Rockhampton is the largest place on our route and the train stops here for twenty minutes before changing direction to continue its journey.

For the first few kilometres we travel in reverse formation back down the line towards Brisbane, then turn on a triangle south of Rockhampton and head west. Soon you begin to understand why this train is named the *Spirit of the Outback*. As we move inland we start to experience the real flavour of the outback. The highlight of this journey occurs as the train struggles over the Great Divide, a really beautiful piece of line. By the time Emerald is reached in the mid-morning, we are beginning to understand the isolation of this country as soon as the coast is left behind. It is five hours and 265

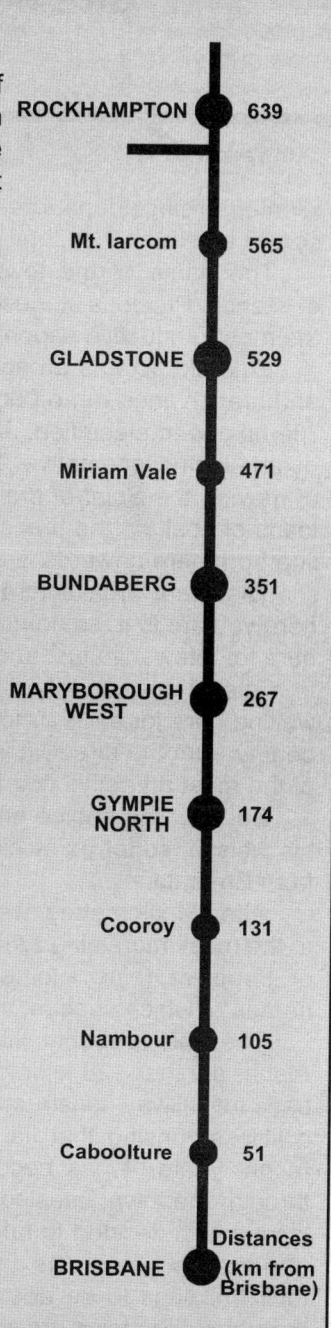

Station	Distances (km from Brisbane)
ROCKHAMPTON	639
Mt. larcom	565
GLADSTONE	529
Miriam Vale	471
BUNDABERG	351
MARYBOROUGH WEST	267
GYMPIE NORTH	174
Cooroy	131
Nambour	105
Caboolture	51
BRISBANE	

GREAT RAILWAY JOURNEYS

Jericho	Alpha	Bogantungan	Anakie
To Yaraka 1132	1076	998	948

kilometres since departure from Rockhampton, yet this is the first town of any size to be seen since then - and even Emerald is not very big.

The name of the town gives us a hint as to one of its reasons for existence. Precious stones are found in this area, and, indeed, it claims to be the most productive sapphire field in the southern hemisphere.

Emerald acts as an agricultural centre too, but it is also known for coal, and branch lines run off both north and south to coal mines. Up to here the line has been electrified, although our train has not necessarily been hauled by an electric locomotive. The electrification is not, however, for the purpose of moving the *Spirit of the Outback* twice a week. It is for shifting the heavy loads of coal, so the branch lines continue the electrification, while the main line from here onwards is diesel operated.

The great architectural attraction of Emerald is its railway station, and here you are in it, so do not just stay in your railway carriage. The train stops here for a few minutes, and sometimes the electric engine has to be changed to a diesel one, so take the opportunity (carefully, as otherwise you will be waiting here for three or four days) to step outside the station and admire its beauty from the street. It was built in 1900 and restored in 1986, and is one of the most attractive country stations in Australia.

But now the engine has been changed and the stationmaster is blowing his whistle, so let us quickly get back on board the train and continue west from Emerald.

After 44 kilometres, we come to the small town of Anakie. Anakie is close to the most interesting area of the gemfields. Just north of here are the towns of Sapphire (nine kilometres) and Rubyvale (seventeen kilometres), the names of which suggest their specialities.

The train probably will not even stop at Anakie, but will continue on to Alpha, another 128 kilometres beyond. Alpha was established in 1884 as a base for railway construction workers. With such a background, it is perhaps a little surprising that its streets should be named after English poets. In recent years, it has become the town of murals. In 1990, a flood swept through the town, causing considerable hardship. When it had receded, two local artists decided to brighten up the community by painting the first mural (the nearest one on the right of the train). Gradually other premises asked for their buildings to be decorated similarly. Now painted on various buildings throughout the town are scenes of past and present life in Alpha. These have

2. SPIRIT OF THE OUTBACK
BRISBANE TO LONGREACH
(continued)

EMERALD	Blackwater	Bluff	Distances (km from Brisbane)	ROCKHAMPTON
904	831	812		639

all been created on a voluntary basis, with the owners of the properties providing only the materials. The train will stop here for a few minutes, permitting the nearest paintings to be viewed - the ones on the railway goods shed and the public toilets, at least, and those opposite on the walls in Shakespeare Street. Alpha has now become a bush art centre and the Jane Neville Rolfe Gallery in Dryden Street has local art works on display and for sale.

Back on the train, it is another 56 kilometres to Jericho. Right beside the railway here is the modern sculpture of the *Crystal Trumpeters*, a rocky depiction of the battle wot Joshua fit.

As the train leaves the station, you will see on your left a branch line going off to Yaraka, to where, surprisingly, a train still runs once a week. It is, or was, one of the last two 'mixed' train services in Australia. The train still operates at the time of writing, but it is rumoured that, from mid-2001, it stopped accepting passengers. It is a goods train with a guard's van on the rear with some passenger accommodation. If the van is still attached, the chances are that passengers would be accepted, and, if so, it is a fascinating ride. The train starts from Emerald at 00:50 on Fridays and first heads west along the main line for 228 kilometres to Jericho, which it reaches at 7:15. There it turns onto the branch line and heads south-west for another nine hours. It travels through the small town of Blackall, and stops there for over an hour, giving passengers the chance to explore. Blackall's claim to fame is that the record for shearing the most sheep in one day was established nearby. The terminus for the train, reached at 16:25, after a journey of 499 kilometres, completed in a mere 15½ hours, is Yaraka, a railhead and opal mining town with a population of 27. The train stays for two hours and then leaves again at 18:45, reaching Jericho at 3:00 and Emerald at 9:40 on Saturdays. A connexion can be made at Jericho or Alpha with the *Spirit of the Outback* heading west. Ask whether this little adventure is still possible, but do not necessarily take no for a final answer. It is only no when the crew of the train refuses you.

Officially, Jericho is where the outback begins. Here the western plains commence and the landscape becomes interminably flat.

The last pause for the train is at Barcaldine, which has a population of 2,000. The name comes from Barcaldine Castle in Argyllshire, Scotland, the ancestral home of an uncle of Donald Cameron, one of the first settlers along the nearby Alice River in 1863. He called his holding Barcaldine Downs, and

GREAT RAILWAY JOURNEYS

LONGREACH	Ilfracombe
To Winton 1325	1298

the town of Barcaldine was later constructed on land from that holding. Barcaldine is an historic spot and there will be an opportunity to alight from the train and view the *Tree of Knowledge*, which is right outside the station.

Barcaldine is another railway town, formed in 1886 as the railway passed here and continued west. The principal residents of Barcaldine were railway construction workers, and later railway maintenance gangs. In 1891, however, Barcaldine was to achieve unexpected fame, for in that year the Great Shearers' Strike occurred, when sheep shearers struck to improve their working conditions and wages. Barcaldine became the headquarters for this, the greatest upheaval in Australian social history. The workers' meetings took place under the ghost gum tree outside the station, which eventually became known as the *Tree of Knowledge*. In the end, the leaders were arrested and imprisoned, and the strike failed, but the result was the formation of the Australian Labour Party and the pursuit of workers' rights by political means.

It is also said that soldiers drafted here to oversee the strike meetings first used emu feathers to decorate their slouch hats in a manner which was later to become a symbol of Australia.

The first free-flowing bore on the Great Artesian Basin was sunk just outside Barcaldine in 1886. The windmill next to the Tourist Information Centre dates from 1917 and was originally used at this same bore.

There are two National Trust buildings in the town, St. Peters Church, dating from 1899, and the Masonic Hall, built in 1901. The Masonic Hall is particularly interesting, as its board exterior is painted to make it appear as though constructed of stone.

Now there is in Barcaldine the Australian Workers Heritage Centre, opened on the centenary of the Great Strike and depicting the events of that time and of subsequent years. There is also the Outback Zoo, one kilometre west of the town, while Mad Mick's Funny Farm has a variety of hand-reared Australian wildlife.

From Barcaldine to Longreach is another 107 kilometres. As the train approaches the end of its long journey, almost exactly a day after leaving Brisbane, you may be able to observe a glorious outback sunset, particularly if the service is a little late, which is not unknown.

27 kilometres before Longreach, the line passes through Ilfracombe. Rail services to here started in 1891 and for a year it was the terminus. It has two claims to fame. First, it is believed that the first motorised mail service in

2. SPIRIT OF THE OUTBACK
BRISBANE TO LONGREACH
(continued)

Barcaldine

1218　　　　　　　　　Distances　(km from Brisbane)

Australia operated from here to Isisford in 1910, and secondly, it is recognised in the *Guinness Book of Records* as having had the sheep station with the greatest head of sheep at any one time. This was Wellshot Station, which boasted 460,000 sheep in 1892.

On the outskirts of Longreach, in the gathering gloom, you may just be able to make out the Qantas Hangar. This was the first operational base of Qantas, from 1922 until 1934, and in this hangar several of its early aircraft were not just housed, but actually built. It is an unimpressive looking building, but best to see it from the train, because it is rather a long walk from the town.

Longreach, like other towns through which we have passed, owes its existence to the railway. Longreach was established in 1887, named after a pastoral outstation, on the land of which it was developed. When the railway arrived in 1892, with Longreach as its terminus, the town began to prosper. Now it has a population of 4,300 and is the largest settlement for four hundred kilometres in any direction.

The most famous of the attractions of Longreach is the Stockman's Hall of Fame, opened in 1988, which attracts over 60,000 visitors every year.

The railway does not finish at Longreach, but continues to Winton, from where a loop leads up to Hughenden on the line from Townsville to Mt. Isa. The passenger train used to continue beyond Longreach to Winton, but it was a slow journey, with the track limited to 40 km/hr in many places, and few passengers used this section of the line, so now the train has been replaced by a bus, which takes only two hours over the 173-kilometre journey.

Winton is famous as the town where *Waltzing Matilda* was first performed, having been written by Banjo Paterson while he was staying on nearby Dagworth Station in 1895. It was also the town where Qantas was born. The company was registered here on 16th November 1920, and the first board meeting was held in the Winton Club on 21st February 1921. These two historic events are celebrated in the *Waltzing Matilda Centre* in the town.

There is also a weekly train between Winton and Hughenden which, like that on the Yaraka branch line, might convey passengers.

For most, however, the journey will finish in Longreach. The 1,325 kilometres has taken 23 hours and 33 minutes at an average speed of 56 km/hr. We have travelled from the sprawling city of Brisbane along the populated coastal fringe before turning inland and experiencing the real outback desolation which represents the truly unique spirit of Australia.

ANECDOTE

Taking the train on the branch line to Yaraka meant changing at Emerald in the middle of the night, but it was well worth while. To my surprise, I was not the only passenger. There was also an elderly couple who muttered something about the travel agent having told them that this train was "basically the same standard" as the one on the main line, as we got into our hot and dusty half of the brake van, but who proved to be very good company as far as Blackall, which was their destination.

In the middle of the morning we stopped at a tiny wayside halt with no habitation in sight. Upon my enquiring of the crew what we would do here, I was informed, "Morning smoko."

An hour's shunting in Blackall gave an opportunity for a look at the town where Jack Howe established a world record in 1892 by shearing 321 sheep in 7 hours 40 minutes, using only hand shears, and then we rumbled on to the railhead in Yaraka, the climax of a journey of nearly sixteen hours.

I disembarked and was soon located by one of the residents. "I was told that there was a passenger," he said. "We don't often get passengers, so I've come to show you round." And he took me all round the town and introduced me to every one of the 27 inhabitants - man, woman, child, baby and dog. He showed me the local industry, which was polishing opals, and the tour concluded, reasonably enough, in the local pub, where we just had time for a quickie before the train blew its weekly whistle as a warning of the imminent resumption of operations.

On board again, I was approached by the guard, who wanted to know where I was hoping to go next. "Longreach," I replied. "Well," he said. "There's no train for three days [the timetable was different then], but I know that there's a ballast train coming through, so I'll see whether I can get you a ride from Jericho. Get a good night's sleep [impossible] and I'll wake you up in the morning."

We arrived back at Jericho as dawn was breaking and I was informed that, "This ballast train has two engines on it and the crew say that you can ride in the cab of the second engine, but whatever you do, don't touch anything in there. Oh, and they have to do a bit of ballast-spreading on the way too, so it may be a bit slow."

Gratefully I climbed up into the second cab, the warning about not touching any controls being reiterated, and we set off. After ninety seconds of motion, there was a piercing screech from the controls which drowned even the throaty rumble of the engine. I soon realised that it must be the 'dead man's handle' alarm, which needs to be cancelled by the driver at regular intervals to prove that he is still *compos mentis* and avoid the application of the emergency brakes. But the brakes did not go on and the ear-shattering screech did. Remembering my warning, I hesitated for a moment or two, but no longer. I could not endure that noise incessantly for the next six hours or longer. A quick search led me to a likely-looking knob and I pressed it. The noise ceased - for ninety seconds - and then started again. I pressed the knob once more. And so I learnt that Queensland Railways has developed an infallible method of keeping sleepy passengers awake to enjoy the scenery of the Western Plains and marvel at the wonders of modern ballast-spreading techniques. I pressed that knob every minute or so for the next seven hours and thoroughly enjoyed my ride. Rail travel is always more fun than any other method!

LONGREACH
Population 4,300

23 hrs 30 mins by train from Brisbane
17 hrs 30 mins by bus from Brisbane

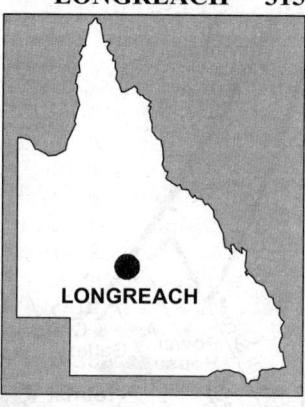

In recent years, the continuing prosperity of Longreach can be attributed to one surprising factor - the construction of the Stockman's Hall of Fame. Opened by the Queen in 1988, in the first dozen years of its existence it attracted over three-quarters of a million visitors, most of them people who would not otherwise have thought of visiting this remote part of Australia. One suspects that, but for the Hall of Fame, the passenger train service to here would no longer exist.

The **Stockman's Hall of Fame** was the inspiration of the outback artist Hugh Sawrey, who wanted to collect and preserve the tales of the pioneers of rural Australia before it became too late. The story starts with the arrival of the aborigines here some 40,000 years ago, but concentrates mainly on the exploration, settlement and development of this huge area of inland Australia. It is an exhibition which needs time, so allow at least half a day. The Hall of Fame is open every day from 9:00 until 17:00. Admission costs $20, but if you cannot complete your tour on the day of entry, you are permitted to obtain a pass and return the following day.

The second attraction of Longreach is the **Qantas hangar** which we saw at the airport on our way into town on the train. Until recently, this was just a slightly shabby hangar, a reminder of where Qantas had its roots, but now it has been developed into a museum displaying the interesting history of the world's second-oldest international airline. The Qantas Founders Outback Museum has here a replica of the Avro 504K which was the first type of passenger aircraft used by the airline. Six such aircraft were built in this hangar between 1926 and 1930. The Museum is open daily from 9:00 until 17:00 and admission costs $8. It seems a pity, really, that Qantas no longer flies to here.

There is another museum in the town, and that is the **Powerhouse Museum** in what was originally the electricity generation station. The old generating equipment is on display, but there are also displays of local social history, and agricultural and building machinery. The Museum is open daily from 14:00 until 17:00 in the winter (April until October). In March and November it is open only on Sundays, Thursdays and Saturdays. In January it is open every evening from 16:30 until 19:30, and in December and February it is closed completely. Admission costs $5.

There is an **Arts and Crafts Gallery** adjacent to the Powerhouse Museum. At the other end of town, near the Stockman's Hall of Fame, is the **School of the Air**, which can be visited between 9:00 and 10:00 on schooldays.

One of the interesting local stories of this area is the tale of **'Captain Starlight'**, one Harry Readford, who is believed to have stolen 1,000 head of cattle from the nearby Bowen Downs station in 1870 and, with a few helpers, herded them through unexplored country for 1,300 kilometres along the Barcoo River and Cooper Creek, then down the Strzelecki Track into South Australia, an amazing journey. The cattle were sold in South Australia, but the law caught up with Starlight and he was tried in Roma for cattle stealing. Surprisingly, he was found not guilty, as a result of which verdict the District Court of Roma lost its criminal jurisdiction for two years. There is

QUEENSLAND

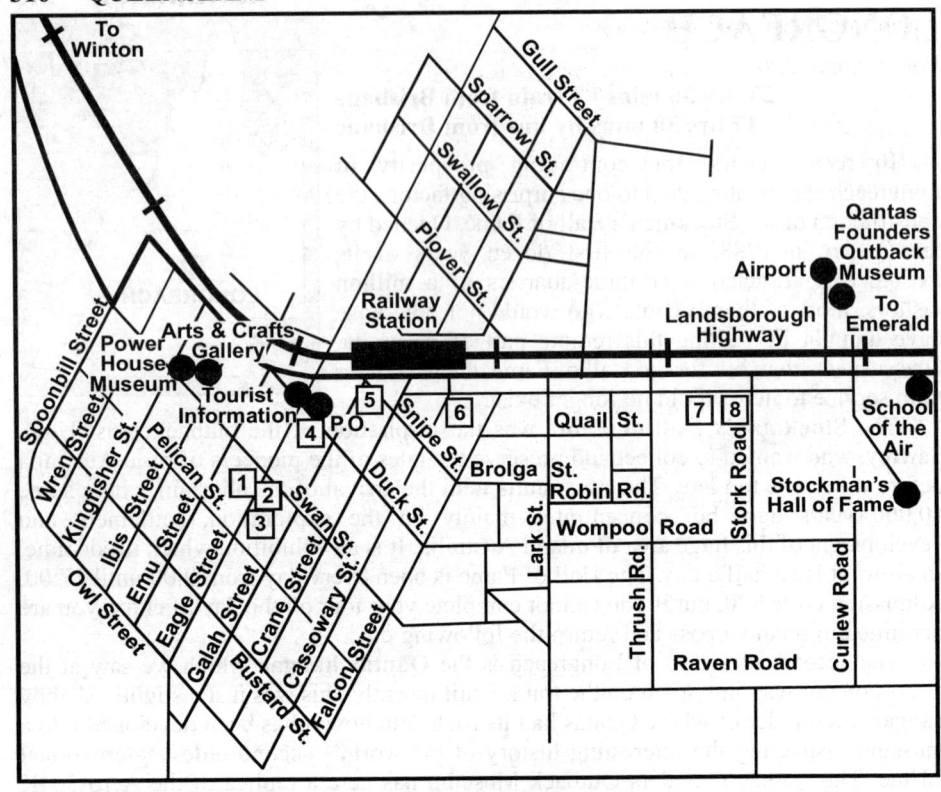

LONGREACH
Numerals indicate accommodation

a Captain Starlight Lookout, where, reputedly, a member of the gang kept watch while the cattle were being rounded up on Bowen Downs to start the journey. However, this is 56 kilometres from Longreach and not easily accessible.

It is possible to travel to Longreach by bus, as well as by train, of course. McCafferty's operates a service from Brisbane every day. This is the quickest route, taking 17½ hours. There is also a connecting service from Rockhampton, with a change of bus at Emerald, on Sundays and Thursdays only. This takes 10½ hours from Rockhampton to Longreach.

ACCOMMODATION

Longreach has a good range of accommodation. It used to have a very pleasant backpackers hostel near the Stockman's Hall of Fame, but sadly that has gone. However, in the town centre there are several older hotels offering cheap rooms. These include the Central Hotel, the Commercial Hotel and the Welcome Home Hotel, all of which have single rooms at $28.

Accommodation in Longreach

Name	Stars	No. on Map	Telephone No.	Address	Lowest Price (Double/Twin)
Abajaz Motor Inn	3½	6	1-800-081-288	11 Wonga Street	$85
Albert Park Motel	4	8	1-800-812-811	Sir Hudson Fysh Drive	$85
Jumbuck Motel	3½	7	1-800-061-573	Sir Hudson Fysh Drive	$85
Longreach Motor Inn	3½	5	1-800-076-020	84 Galah Street	$85
Longreach Motel	3	1	1-800-499-854	127 Eagle Street	$75
Commercial Hotel / Motel		4	07-4658-1677	102 Eagle Street	$70
Central Hotel		2	07-4658-2263	126 Eagle Street	$45
Welcome Home Hotel		3	07-4658-3086	128 Eagle Street	$40

MOVING ON
(i) By Train

The train to Brisbane departs on Sunday and Thursday mornings. There is a Queensland Railways bus on to Winton, connecting with the arrival of the *Spirit of the Outback* on Wednesday and Saturday evenings. These services, together with onward connexions from Rockhampton to Townsville and Cairns, are shown on the timetable below.

Days of Departure	W, Sat (Bus)	Th	Sun, Th (Bus)	Sun, Th	Sun, Tu, Th, Sat	Sun, W
Winton			0400			
Longreach	1805		0600	0700		
Winton	2005	2030				
Hughenden		0345				
Barcaldine				0911		
Alpha				1143		
Emerald				1530		
Rockhampton				1945	2040	0010
Brisbane				0620		
Mackay					0229	0526
Proserpine					0424	0746
Bowen					0532	0841
Townsville					0843	1150
Tully					1249	
Innisfail					1359	
Cairns					1625	
Days of Arrival		F		M, F	Sun, M, W, F	

(ii) By Bus

McCafferty's operates daily buses to Brisbane and Mt. Isa, and a twice-weekly service, on Mondays and Fridays, to Rockhampton via Emerald.

Destination	Operator	Via	Distance (km)	Fare	Journey Time	Frequency
Brisbane	McCafferty's		1259	$124	17 hrs	1/day
Mt. Isa	McCafferty's		634	$91	8 hrs	1/day
Rockhampton	McCafferty's		668	$79	10¼ hrs	2/week
		Emerald	405	$59	5¾ hrs	2/week
Winton	QR		173	$20.70	2 hrs	2/week

WINTON

Population 1,200

26 hrs by train and bus from Brisbane
19 hrs 30 mins by bus from Brisbane

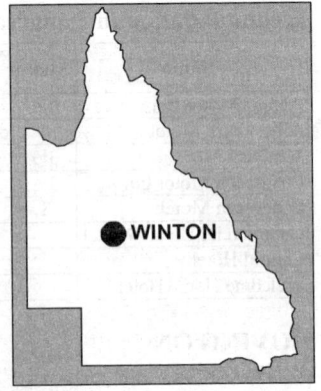

When the *Spirit of the Outback* arrives in Longreach, there will be a small bus waiting to convey any passengers on to Winton. Until a few years ago, the rail service used to commence in Rockhampton, with only a connexion from Brisbane, and then continued all the way to Winton. However, it was poorly patronised on this last section, and, because the tracks were not in good condition, with speed limited for much of the journey to 40 km/hr, the journey from Longreach to Winton used to take four hours. Now the bus covers those 173 kilometres in just two hours, there being nothing between the two towns except some kangaroos.

Winton is another very interesting little town. It has made its main claim to a place in history the legend of *Waltzing Matilda*. The song was written by Banjo Paterson while he was staying at nearby Dagworth Station in 1895 and it seems probable that it was based on events which had occurred locally at that time.

The area around Winton was first settled in 1873, and the town itself had its first inhabitant, a Mr. Robert Allen, in 1876. It was originally called Pelican Waterhole, but Mr. Allen thought that the name was too long and changed it to the name of the suburb of Bournemouth in England where he was born. During the Great Shearers' Strike in 1891, and again in 1894, the town was under martial law. During the strike of 1891, a group of 500 shearers was forced to set up camp outside the town. During the second strike, the body of a 'swagman', a Bavarian named Hoffmeister, was discovered in a billabong. There was also an incident in which a local shearing shed was burnt down, and there was general ill-feeling between the property owners and the itinerant workers on whom they depended. With this as a background, Banjo Paterson visited Dagworth Station and wrote the verses for *Waltzing Matilda*. A friend there, Christina MacPherson, set the words to an old Scottish tune which she had evidently heard at the Warrnambool races in Victoria, and Australia's most famous song had come into being. It was given its first public performance at a dinner held at the North Gregory Hotel in Winton on 6th April 1895 to celebrate the approach of the railway. The North Gregory Hotel is still there, but not the same one. It has been burnt down three times since then.

Proud of this piece of cultural heritage, Winton has been staging the Bronze Swagman Bush Poetry Competition since 1972, and has had a competition for performed poetry since 1995. In 1998, the town opened the **Waltzing Matilda Centre**, a museum based on the history of the town, with *Waltzing Matilda*, of course, as its central theme. Having cost $3.3 million to set up, the museum is an enormously expensive project in all senses, but not least because it costs $15 to get in. If you think that rather costly, you can at least collect tourist information there, and sit on some fine old ex-railway leather seats to watch the free video about the area.

Winton, though, has another claim to be mentioned in the history books. At the end of the Great War, two men named Hudson Fysh and Paul McGuiness returned home having experienced the thrills of flying in early aircraft. They appreciated the potential for outback areas of this form of transport, and decided, despite the difficulties of long distances, harsh terrain and sparse population, to try to start an outback airline. On 16th November 1920, **Queensland and Northern Territory Aerial Service** was registered in Winton as a company. A ground survey was carried out of a possible route from Cloncurry to Darwin, and on 21st February 1921 the company's first board meeting was held in the **Winton Club**. The club is still there, on the corner of Vindex and Oondooroo Streets, proud of its place in history and pleased to invite visitors to view its interior. One of the reasons for the choosing of Winton as a base for the new airline was that the local council supported the idea and was willing to provide a landing site as a contribution to the project. If you walk a short distance along the Hughenden Road, and then turn into the first dirt road on the left, you will find a memorial cairn showing where this landing strip was. Nowadays it looks improbable that an aircraft could ever have landed there in safety, but Qantas has a good record in that respect.

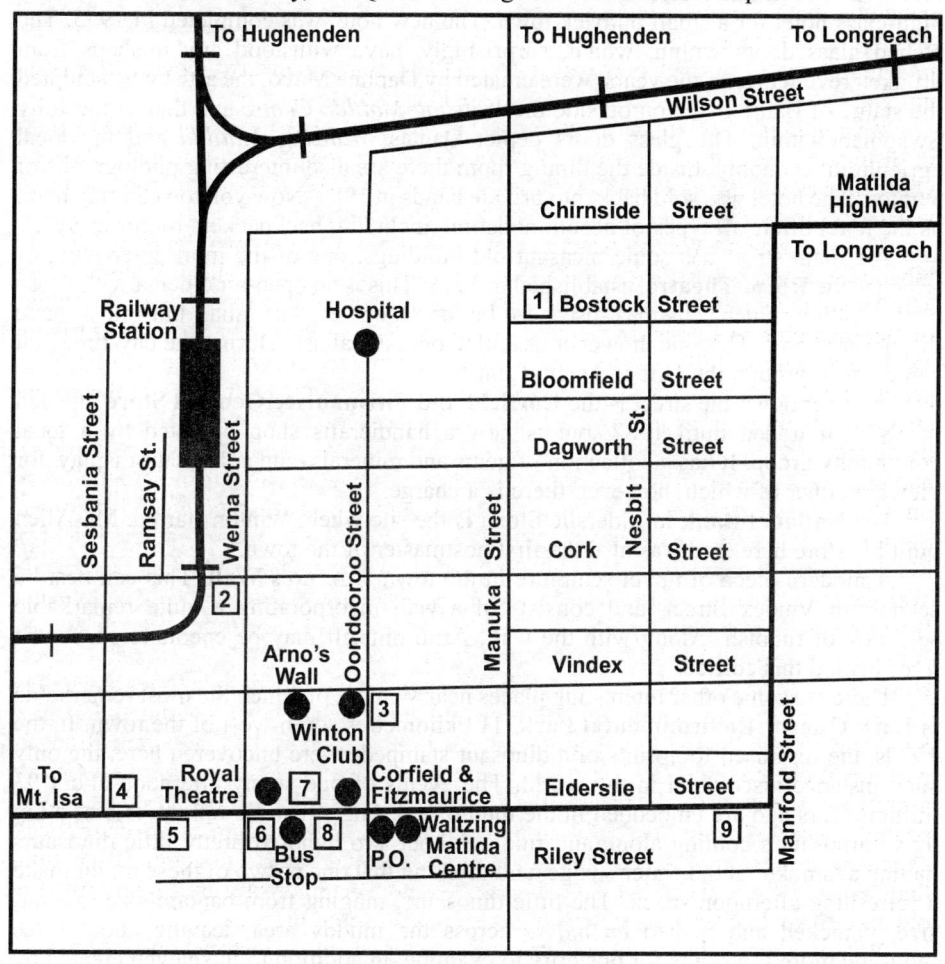

WINTON
Numerals indicate accommodation

The most interesting accommodation that Winton has to offer is the **North Gregory Hotel**. The first North Gregory was built in 1878 by Corfield and Fitzmaurice, whose store you can see just down the road. It was in this hotel that *Waltzing Matilda* was first publicly performed in 1895. That hotel was burnt down in 1900, and a new one was constructed. That too was burnt down in 1915. A third North Gregory Hotel was built, and was standing here during the Second World War when an American military B-42 aircraft was forced to land on the strip at Carisbrooke Station, 85 kilometres south-west of Winton. On board the aeroplane was a man who was to become president of the United States, one Lyndon B. Johnson. He was brought to Winton, where he stayed at the North Gregory Hotel. That hotel was burnt down in 1946, and, in the depressed post-war years, nobody wanted to rebuild it. The council took over the site and raised money for the construction of what was, at the time, a very high-class hotel for a small outback town. The new hotel was completed in 1955. The etched glass doors within, which, surprisingly, have withstood any mishaps from drunken revellers over the years, were created by Daphne Mayo, the artist who sculpted the statue of Banjo Paterson outside the *Waltzing Matilda Centre* and that of the Jolly Swagman within. The glass doors depict Qantas, *Waltzing Matilda* and the local agricultural economy. Inside the dining room there are also interesting photographs of Winton. The hotel was sold back into private hands in 1987. Now you too can stay here, as the hotel offers all types of accommodation, including backpackers rooms at $17.

The main street has some pleasant old buildings, one of the more interesting of which is the **Royal Theatre**, established in 1918. This is an open-air cinema with deck-chair seating. Such cinemas used to be common in Australia, but most have disappeared now. This one, however, is still in occasional use. During the day-time you can enter it through the Gift and Gem Centre.

Further down the street is the **Corfield and Fitzmaurice General Store**, opened in 1878. It traded until 1987, but is now a handicrafts shop operated by a local community group. It has a collection of gems and minerals, and a dinosaur display, for viewing either of which, however, there is a charge.

The **National Bank** in Elderslie Street is the site where Winton started. Mr. Allen built his store here, and was also the first postmaster of the town.

A modern piece of novel sculpture in the town is **Arno's Wall**. This can best be seen from Vindex Street, and consists of a wall incorporating a quite remarkable selection of rubbish. Along with the wall, Arno himself may be encountered, for he lives behind this edifice.

There are some other interesting places near Winton, of which the most remarkable is **Lark Quarry Environmental Park**, 113 kilometres south-west of the town. In the 1970s, the fossilised footprints of a dinosaur stampede were uncovered here, the only such instance discovered in the world. The events of one sunny afternoon about 93 million years ago are embedded in the mud of a drying stream to tell the tale of a big ugly carnosaur's coming along and finding about two hundred pretty little dinosaurs having a 'smoko' at the water's edge, and thinking that one or two of these might make a refreshing afternoon snack. The little dinosaurs, ranging from bantam-size to emu-size, panicked and rushed *en masse* across the muddy area, leaving about three thousand more footprints for posterity to examine, in addition to the eleven created by the big carnosaur.

In the same general direction, but on a different road, is **Opalton**, 170 kilometres from Winton. The name gives the clue as to the main livelihood of the fifteen inhabitants. The area has been mined continuously since 1893 and at one time there were 600 miners here, but numbers have become somewhat depleted in recent years. Much of the opal is brought to Winton to be cut and polished and you can see shops in the town working on these semi-precious stones.

Carisbrooke Station, mentioned above as the forced landing place of President-to-be Johnson, now offers accommodation ($31 per person per night) and beautiful scenery, but day tours of the station cost $125 per person, so are not within the range of every visitor.

Returning to the town of Winton, the centre of Elderslie Street, the main street, has been made into a Matilda-scape with various sculptures depicting the ballad. These are illuminated at night. Another feature of the town which you will not have failed to observe is the quaint dinosaur-foot rubbish bins. Whoever produced these must have found them a good stock item, for they line the streets in Hughenden too, another town with dinosaur ancestors. Winton also has cow-benches placed at strategic intervals along the streets, for those feeling weary, this reflecting the agricultural dependence of the region. Do not just sit, but read the amusing artwork on them too.

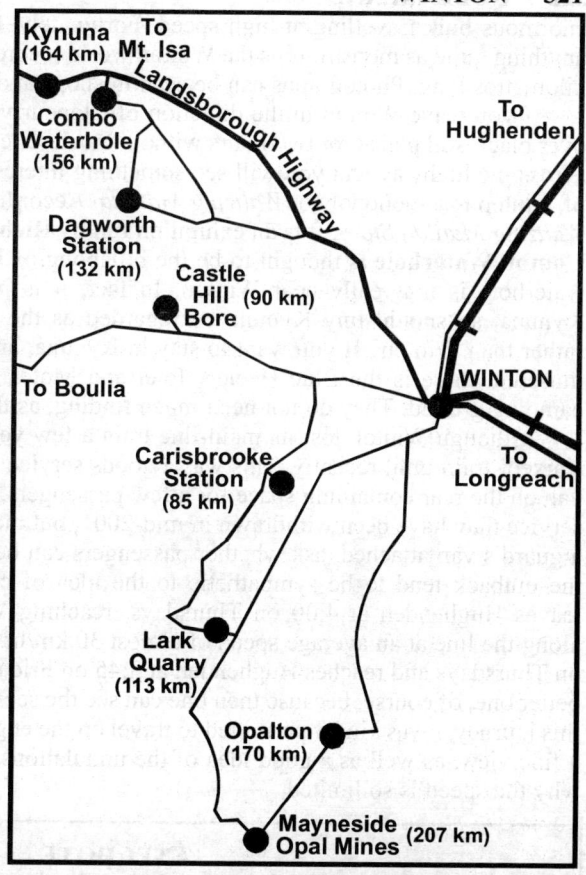

ATTRACTIONS AROUND WINTON
Distances shown are from Winton

The water used in Winton is from artesian bores, the deepest of them stretching down 1,222 metres. Water comes up at 83°C, so, when you take a shower, the hot water is coming straight from the ground, and that is why it sometimes takes a while to arrive. The cold water is from the same supply, but stored in tanks for a while to allow it to cool down. The water straight from the bore has a smell and taste of sulphur, but when it is allowed to stand for a while the gases in it evaporate and the water becomes clear and pleasant to drink. The bore at **Castle Hill Station**, ninety kilometres west of Winton, goes down 1,379 metres and produces water at 99°C.

Yet another record held by Winton, at least at the time of writing, is the longest road train in the world. Travelling along the roads in these outback areas, one will meet these huge monsters and, even in a sturdy bus, feel the air displacement created by their enormous bulk travelling at high speed. Fortunately, though, one is unlikely to meet anything quite as monstrous as the Winton world record road train, which was over two kilometres long. Photographs can be seen in shops and on post-cards.

If you leave Winton in the direction of Cloncurry and Mount Isa, you will travel over black-soil plains for two hours without much relief until you reach **Kynuna**. Look across the highway and you will see something interesting, and relevant to the claims of Winton to a monopoly of *Waltzing Matilda*. According to the banner, this is the *True Waltzing Matilda Story*. It is an exhibition run by **Richard Magoffin**. The point is that **Combo Waterhole** is thought to be the billabong of *Waltzing Matilda* fame, and that waterhole is not really near Winton. In fact, it is just eighteen kilometres east of Kynuna, so should tiny Kynuna be regarded as the birthplace of *Waltzing Matilda* rather than Winton? If you want to stay in Kynuna, and view this rather unusual little museum, there is the Blue Heeler Hotel and Motel, and also a caravan park and a camping ground. They do not need much finding, as there is nothing else here.

Although Winton lost its main-line train a few years ago, it managed to retain its 'mixed' train until recently. This was a goods service from Hughenden with a guard's van on the rear containing space for a few passengers. It is believed that the passenger service may have been withdrawn in mid-2001, but the train still operates, and if it has a guard's van attached, ask whether passengers can be accommodated. Train crews in the outback tend to be sympathetic to the idea of conveying passengers. The train leaves Hughenden at 4:00 on Thursdays, reaching Winton at 11:30, having rushed along the line at an average speed of almost 30 km/hr. It returns from Winton at 20:30 on Thursdays and reaches Hughenden at 3:45 on Fridays. The journey to Winton is the better one, of course, because then one can see the scenery. When the author undertook this journey, I was kindly permitted to travel on the engine most of the way, which gave a fine view, as well as a good idea of the undulations of the track and a realisation of why the speed is so limited.

ANECDOTE

Once off the bitumen, one can have a lot of problems in the Wet in the black soil plains of western Queensland. The unofficial motto here is, "Stick to the black soil plains, and they'll stick to you."

So it was that, struggling through, rather than over, the road from Winton to Kynuna in the days before bitumen had been invented in this part of the state, we came across an R.A.C.Q. rescue truck well and truly bogged at the side of the highway.

We stopped and performed our Samaritan duties and were kindly rewarded with two stubbies of beer, which we put in the vehicle for consumption at a more appropriate juncture, and then continued on our slipping, sliding, bumping, crashing way. The bottles withstood this treatment for about half an hour, and then there was a loud explosion and beer flew all over the vehicle. The smell of breweries lasted for some three days, but one lesson of outback motoring had been learnt. Never take beer on a dirt road unless you have some very good padding and insulation.

ACCOMMODATION

Although there are motels in Winton, the old hotels are the places with character. The North Gregory is still the most élite, and has history on its side, but the others are cheaper. For backpackers, single rooms are available at all of the hotels, including the North Gregory, for $20 or less.

Accommodation in Winton

Name	Stars	No. on Map	Telephone No.	Address	Lowest Price (Double/Twin)
Pelican Waters Motel		9	07-4657-1211	16 Elderslie Street	$95
Matilda Motel		3	07-4657-1433	20 Oondooroo Street	$70
Banjo's Motel	3	1	07-4657-1213	64 Manuka Street	$65
Outback Motel		4	07-4657-1422	95 Elderslie Street	$65
North Gregory Hotel		7	07-4657-1375	67 Elderslie Street	$50
Pelican Caravan Park		5	07-4657-1478	92 Elderslie Street	$45
Tatt's Hotel		6	07-4657-1309	78 Elderslie Street	$35
Winton Hotel		2	07-4657-1519	43 Werna Street	$35
Australian Hotel		8	07-4657-1214	70 Elderslie Street	$25

MOVING ON
(i) By Train

To return to Brisbane by train, one must be up to catch the connecting bus at 4:00. The driver stays at the North Gregory Hotel, so best to stay there too and ask him to make sure that you are up in the morning. The mixed train mentioned above leaves for Hughenden at 20:30 on Thursday evenings, which still gives you time to find accommodation if you are refused conveyance on the train. A summary of train and connecting bus times from Winton is shown on page 317.

(ii) By Bus

McCafferty's runs daily bus services north to Mt. Isa and south to Brisbane. There is also the *Town-Win Bus* which leaves on Mondays and Thursdays at about 10:00 for Townsville. Although more officially known as the *Winton Express*, this service is generally called by the name mentioned above. It carries mostly freight, but will squeeze a passenger in on request. Arrival time in Townsville is not specified, but usually the trip takes about nine hours. However, due to condition of the roads on which this service travels, it is subject to the vagaries of the weather, and is especially susceptible to heavy rains. If you are interested in travelling on this vehicle, telephone 07-4773-4191 or 0427-002-030.

Destination	Operator	Via	Distance (km)	Fare	Journey Time	Frequency
Brisbane	McCafferty's		1432	$141	19 hrs	1/day
		Longreach	173	$33	2¼ hrs	1/day
Mt. Isa	McCafferty's		461	$79	6 hrs	1/day
Longreach	QR		173	$20.70	2 hrs	2/week
Townsville	Winton Express		588	$100	9 hrs	2/week

MACKAY

Population 59,000

17 hrs 30 mins by train from Brisbane
16 hrs by bus from Brisbane

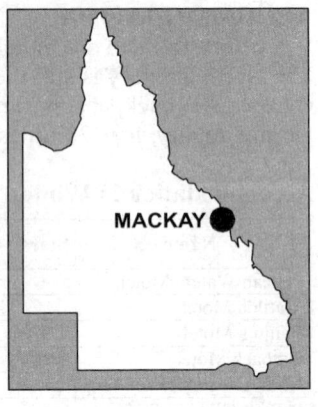

Mackay is principally a port for the export of coal and sugar. However, it also has beaches and offers access to various islands on the Great Barrier Reef, of which the best known is Brampton Island.

The first settler here was John Mackay in 1862, and it was he who gave the city its name. He developed a pastoral property, but, in fact, it was sugar which soon became the dominant industry, as it has remained ever since.

The city of Mackay has several attractive buildings, particularly the Courthouse and the Commonwealth Bank, both built in 1880. In recent years, the city has been the subject of a beautification project which has greatly improved its appearance. A marina is still under development and will have 500 berths available.

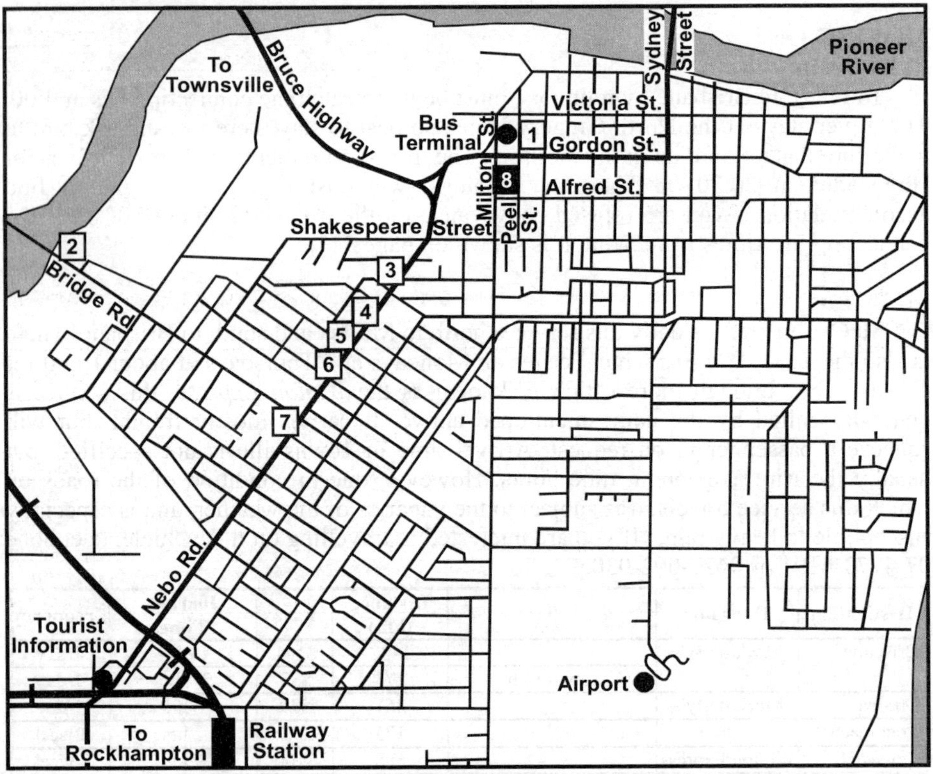

MACKAY
Black numerals in white boxes indicate hotel accommodation
White numerals in black boxes indicate backpackers hostels

MACKAY 325

There is a local bus service which includes most of the beaches, but it operates on weekdays only.

Although there are boat services to various islands, most of them are relatively distant from Mackay and so such services are less popular with visitors than those from Airlie Beach, further north.

ACCOMMODATION
(i) Hotel Accommodation in Mackay

Name	Stars	No. on Map	Telephone No.	Address	Lowest Price (Double/Twin)
Marco Polo Motel	4	4	1-800-152-666	46 Nebo Road	$110
Rose Motel	4	7	1-800-676-572	164 Nebo Road	$105
Miners Lodge Motor Inn	3½	5	1-800-650-195	60 Nebo Road	$95
Sugar City Motel	3½	6	1-800-645-525	66 Nebo Road	$95
El Toro Motel	4	3	1-800-687-186	14 Nebo Road	$75
Paradise Lodge Motel		1	07-4951-3644	17 Peel Street	$70
Riverside Holiday Units		2	07-4957-2501	480 Bridge Road	$70

(ii) Backpackers Hostel in Mackay

Name	Group	No. on Map	Telephone No.	Address	Lowest Price (Dormitory)
Larrikin Lodge	YHA	8	07-4951-3728	32 Peel Street	$19

MOVING ON
(i) By Train

The rail timetable north is shown on page 238 and that south on page 338.

(ii) By Bus

Buses run up the coast north to Townsville and Cairns, and south to Rockhampton, Hervey Bay and Brisbane.

Destination	Operator	Via	Distance (km)	Fare	Journey Time	Frequency
Brisbane	McCafferty's		1121	$141	14¾ - 16¼ hrs	4/day
		Hervey Bay	798	$125	9¾ - 11 hrs	3/day
		Rockhampton	346	$58	3¾ - 4 hrs	4/day
Brisbane	Greyhound		1121	$141	15¾ - 16¼ hrs	2/day
		Hervey Bay	798	$125	10¼ hrs	2/day
		Rockhampton	346	$58	3¾ - 4¼ hrs	2/day
Brisbane	Premier		1121	$120	15¾ hrs	1/day
		Hervey Bay	798	$85	10¼ hrs	1/day
		Rockhampton	346	$37	3¾ hrs	1/day
Cairns	McCafferty's		791	$114	11½ - 12½ hrs	4/day
		Townsville	420	$75	4¾ - 6¼ hrs	4/day
Cairns	Greyhound		791	$114	11½ - 12½ hrs	2/day
		Townsville	420	$75	6¼ hrs	2/day
Cairns	Premier		791	$103	11¾ hrs	1/day
		Townsville	420	$65	6¼ hrs	1/day

AIRLIE BEACH, PROSERPINE AND THE WHITSUNDAYS

Population 4,000 (Airlie Beach)

19 hrs 30 mins by train from Brisbane
18 hrs 30 mins by bus from Brisbane

Airlie Beach owes its popularity, gradually increasing over the years, to its proximity to the Whitsunday Islands. Although it is possible to stay on some of the islands, it is generally expensive to do so, so many visitors stay at Airlie Beach and travel by ferry to one of the islands for the day, or take a cruise around the various islands. None of the islands is more than an hour away by boat.

This destination consists of three distinct areas, to be dealt with in turn. First there is the old town of Proserpine. Secondly there is the modern beach resort of Airlie Beach. Thirdly there are the Whitsunday Islands themselves.

Proserpine (see map on page 328) is where the railway station is. It is a typical North Queensland medium-sized town dependent on agriculture, and sugar cane farming in particular. It has a sugar mill on the northern edge of the town, and a Tourist Information Office to the east. There is an **Historical Museum** here, but it is open only on Tuesdays and Thursdays. Out of the town there is **Dittmer Gold Mine**, closed in the 1930s, and the attractive **Faust Dam**, some twenty kilometres to the west of the town centre. Accommodation is available in Proserpine.

Most people, however, stay at **Airlie Beach** (see map on page 329), which is packed with accommodation covering every price range. It is an 'in' place, with plenty of restaurants, partying and entertainment. Airlie Beach is 26 kilometres from Proserpine. Most of the long-distance bus services divert to here and if this is your destination, it is best to take such a service, although local buses, operated by Whitsunday Transit, run regularly from Proserpine if needed. If you arrive by train, even early in the morning, a bus will be waiting at the station to take passengers to Airlie Beach, and also to **Shute Harbour**, from where the ferries leave.

As for the **Whitsundays**, there are 74 islands, most of them uninhabited. The name Whitsunday was ascribed by Captain Cook, but not actually to the islands themselves. He named the Whitsunday Passage, which runs between the shore and the larger islands. The reason for the name is, as one might perhaps guess, that he passed through on Whitsunday, according to G.M.T., although actually it was already the following day in Australia. The date was 3rd/4th June 1770. Most of the islands are now part of a National Park, the prominent exceptions being Hamilton Island and Hayman Island, which are privately owned. Hamilton Island even has an airport and is served by Qantas subsidiary flights. There are nine resort locations on various islands, but they will be too expensive for most visitors. However, plenty of day trips to islands are available at moderate prices, or you can just get on one of the many ferries and spend the day where you wish. Boats leave from Shute Harbour, nine kilometres east of Airlie Beach. There are regular local buses available to the harbour. Here are brief descriptions of some of the main islands, starting in the north and moving south.

Hayman Island is a small island at the northern tip of the group, and is privately owned. The expensive Hayman Island Resort is here. It is reached by a similarly

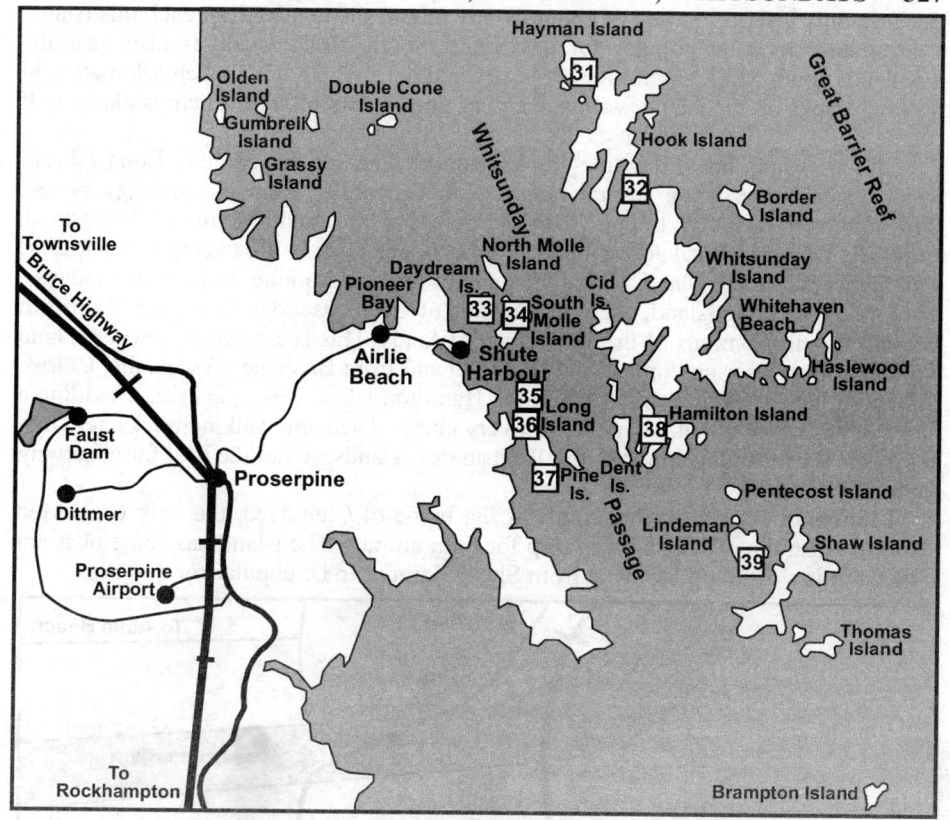

WHITSUNDAY ISLANDS
Numerals indicate accommodation

luxurious launch. Just south of Hayman Island is the much larger **Hook Island**, the site of a budget resort named Hook Island Wilderness Lodge. This is one of the few islands upon which camping is permitted. There are walking trails and two substantial peaks, of which the higher is Hook Peak at 459 metres. At Nara Inlet, at the south of the island, there are **aboriginal cave paintings**. There is also an **underwater observatory** nine metres beneath the surface of the sea off the island. This is a popular island for day visits.

Next south is the largest island of all, **Whitsunday Island**. It is sometimes said that this island has the best beach in the world. The six-kilometre **Whitehaven Beach** is on the eastern side of the island and is the most popular destination for day trips. The island is uninhabited, though, and camping is not permitted.

Inland from Whitsunday Island, on the inside of the Whitsunday Passage, are three small islands: **North Molle Island, Daydream Island** and **South Molle Island**. North Molle is not much visited. Daydream Island is not part of the National Park and is the site of Novotel Daydream Island Resort. On the central hill of this small island is dense tropical vegetation which provides a home for colourful tropical birds, especially parrots and sunbirds. It is also one of the best islands for swimming and for snorkelling.

328 QUEENSLAND

Because only a short journey of about twenty minutes is involved to reach this island, it is another location popular for day visits. South Molle Island is also near the mainland. South Molle Island Resort is situated here. There are sixteen kilometres of walking tracks on the island, with some very good views offered. There is also a golf course.

Moving south, but still inside the Whitsunday Passage, we come to **Long Island**, which has three separate resorts on it: Club Crocodile, Palm Bay Hideaway and Whitsunday Wilderness Lodge, the last being at the southern tip of the island, extremely expensive, and accessible only by helicopter. There are twenty kilometres of walking tracks on the island, including some of the best walking in the Whitsundays.

Level with Long Island, but on the outside of the Whitsunday Passage is **Hamilton Island**, the most famous of the Whitsunday Islands. This is a privately owned island with an airport offering commercial flights to and from Brisbane, Townsville, Cairns, Brampton Island, Sydney and Melbourne. Hamilton Island Resort is here, providing a range of accommodation, but none of it very cheap. There are walking tracks here too, but this is the most developed of the Whitsunday Islands, so not the best for observing nature.

Lindeman Island, further south, is the home of Club Med, the only Club Med resort in Australia. There is an airstrip for light aircraft. The island has some pleasant walks, but is a little too far away from Shute Harbour to be popular for day trips.

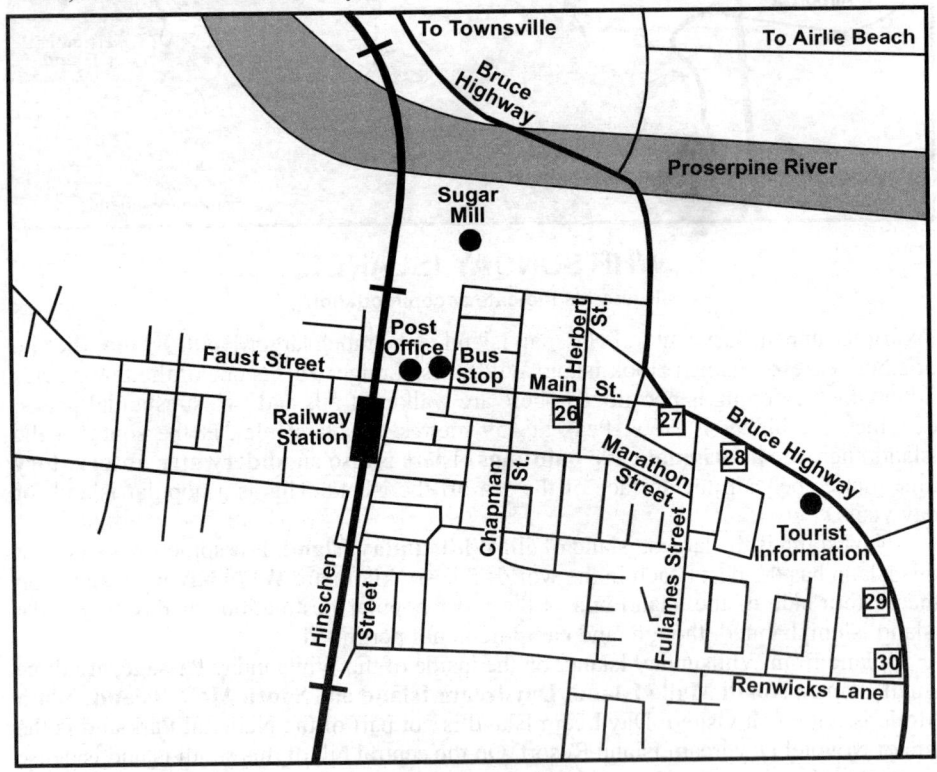

PROSERPINE
Numerals indicate accommodation

AIRLIE BEACH, PROSERPINE, WHITSUNDAYS

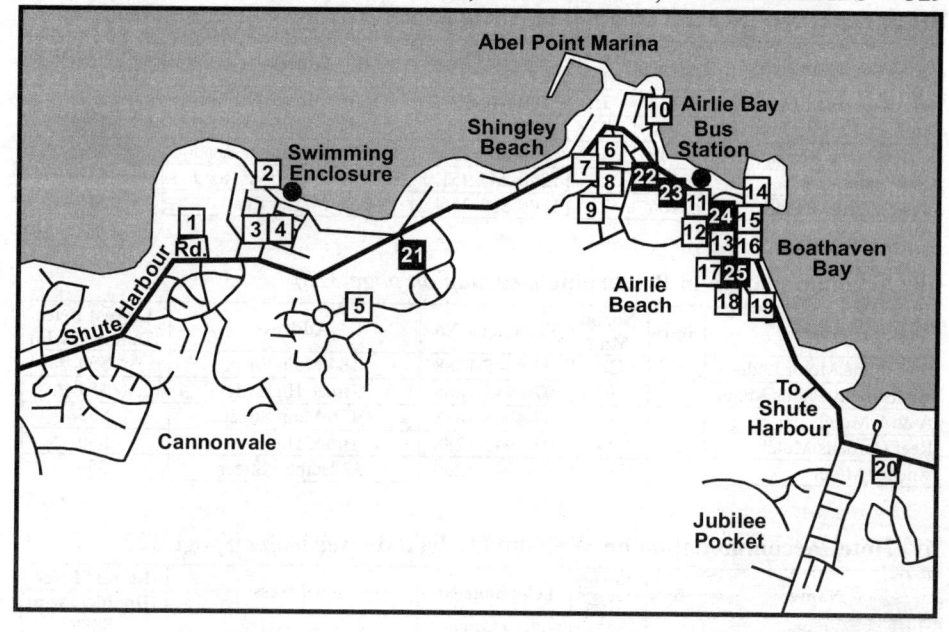

AIRLIE BEACH

Black numerals in white boxes indicate hotel accommodation
White numerals in black boxes indicate backpackers hostels

ACCOMMODATION
(i) Hotel Accommodation in Airlie Beach *(see map above)*

Name	Stars	No. on Map	Telephone No.	Address	Lowest Price (Double/Twin)
Toscana Village		13	07-4946-4455	10 Golden Orchid Drive	$155
Martinique Whitsunday		18	07-4948-0401	18 Golden Orchid Drive	$155
Sea Star Luxury Apts.		9	1-800-300-088	6a Orana Street	$150
Mediterranean Resorts	4½	17	1-800-802-089	14 Golden Orchid Drive	$150
S.A.I.L.Z. Holiday Villas		1	1-800-806-688	Pandanus Drive	$125
Reefside Villas		5	1-800-062-779	12 Eshelby Drive	$120
Airlie Beach Hotel	3½	14	07-4946-6233	Esplanade & Coconut Grove	$110
Colonial Palms Motor Inn	3½	19	1-800-075-114	Hermitage Drive	$105
Mango House Resort	4	20	1-800-673-835	Erromango Drive	$105
Airlie Apartments	3	7	07-4946-6222	22 Airlie Crescent	$85
Seaview Apartments		15	07-4946-6911	404 Shute Harbour Road	$85
Boathaven Lodge		16	07-4946-6421	440 Shute Harbour Road	$85
Airlie Beach Motor Lodge		8	1-800-810-925	6 Lamond Street	$76
Whitsunday Apartments	3	2	07-4946-6778	48 Coral Esplanade	$70
Sunlit Waters Studio Apts		6	07-4946-6352	20 Airlie Crescent	$65
Colonial Court		10	07-4946-6180	Broadwater Avenue	$65
Airlie Court Hol. Units	3	11	07-4946-6218	382 Shute Harbour Road	$65
Elanora Holiday Units		12	07-4946-6482	1 Harper Street	$65
Orana Lodge		3	07-4946-7124	13 Beach Road	$55
Palm Tree Lodge	2½	4	07-4946-6461	14 Beach Road	$55

330 QUEENSLAND

(ii) Backpackers Accommodation in Airlie Beach *(see map on page 329)*

Name	Group	No. on Map	Telephone No.	Address	Lowest Price (Dormitory)
Backpackers by the Bay	VIP	25	1800-646-994	12 Hermitage Drive	$22
Beaches Backpackers	VIP	23	1800-636-630	356 Shute Harbour Road	$22
Koala Beach Resort	VIP	22	1800-800-421	336 Shute Harbour Road	$22
Club Habitat	YHA	24	1800-247-251	394 Shute Harbour Road	$19
Bush Village Resort	Nom	21	1800-809-256	2 St. Martin Road	$18

(iii) Accommodation in Proserpine *(see map on page 328)*

Name	Stars	No. on Map	Telephone No.	Address	Lowest Price (Double/Twin)
Proserpine Motor Lodge		28	07-4945-1788	184 Main Street	$70
Whitsunday Palms Motel		30	07-4945-1868	Bruce Highway	$55
A & A Motel		27	07-4945-1888	156 Main Street	$55
Reef Gardens Motel	2½	29	07-4945-1288	Bruce Highway	$50
Anchor Motel		26	07-4945-1200	32 Herbert Street	$50

(iv) Hotel Accommodation on Whitsunday Islands *(see map on page 327)*

Name	Stars	No. on Map	Telephone No.	Address	Lowest Price (Double/Twin)
Wilderness Lodge		37	07-4946-9777	Long Island	$880
Hayman Island Resort		31	07-4940-1234	Hayman Island	$495
Hamilton Island Villas		38	1-800-075-110	Hamilton Island	$465
Hamilton Island Beach Cl.	5	38	1-800-075-110	Hamilton Island	$465
Palm Bay Hideaway		36	07-4946-9233	Long Island	$420
Club Med		39	1-800-801-823	Lindeman Island	$375
Reef View Hotel		38	1-800-075-110	Hamilton Island	$335
Whitsunday Holiday Apts	3½	38	1-800-075-110	Hamilton Island	$315
Club Crocodile Resort	3½	35	1-800-075-125	Long Island	$310
South Molle Resort	3	34	07-4946-9433	South Molle Island	$270
Palm Bungalows	3	38	1-800-075-110	Hamilton Island	$265
Palm Terrace		38	1-800-075-110	Hamilton Island	$235
Novotel Daydream Island		33	1-800-075-040	Daydream Island	$200
Hook Island Resort		32	07-4946-9380	Hook Island	$85

(v) Backpackers Hostel on Whitsunday Islands *(see map on page 327)*

Name	Group	No. on Map	Telephone No.	Address	Lowest Price (Dormitory)
Hook Island Resort		32	07-4946-9380	Hook Island	$25

MOVING ON

(i) By Train
The rail timetable north is shown on page 238 and that south on page 338.

(ii) By Bus
McCafferty's, Greyhound and Premier all operate buses north up the coast to Cairns, and south to Brisbane.

AIRLIE BEACH, PROSERPINE, WHITSUNDAYS

Bus Services from Airlie Beach

Destination	Operator	Via	Distance (km)	Fare	Journey Time	Frequency
Brisbane	McCafferty's		1269	$160	18 - 19¼ hrs	4/day
		Hervey Bay	946	$143	13 - 14 hrs	3/day
		Rockhampton	494	$81	6¾ - 7¼ hrs	4/day
Brisbane	Greyhound		1269	$160	19 - 19¼ hrs	2/day
		Hervey Bay	946	$143	13¼ hrs	2/day
		Rockhampton	494	$81	6¾ - 7½ hrs	2/day
Brisbane	Premier		1269	$136	18¼ hrs	1/day
		Hervey Bay	946	$101	12¾ hrs	1/day
		Rockhampton	494	$53	6½ hrs	1/day
Cairns	McCafferty's		643	$93	9¼ - 10¼ hrs	3/day
		Townsville	272	$55	3¾ - 4¼ hrs	3/day
Cairns	Greyhound		643	$93	9 - 10 hrs	2/day
		Townsville	272	$55	3¾ hrs	2/day
Cairns	Premier		643	$84	10 hrs	1/day
		Townsville	272	$48	4½ hrs	1/day

BOWEN

Population 8,500

21 hrs by train from Brisbane
19 hrs 30 mins by bus from Brisbane

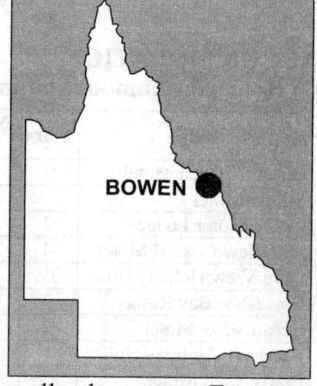

On his way up the coast in 1770, Captain Cook sighted and named Cape Gloucester, just off the present site of Bowen. Unfortunately, the cape turned out to be an island, not a cape at all, but it still bears the name of Gloucester. Bowen, however, was not founded until nearly a century later, in 1861. Nevertheless, it claims to be the oldest town in North Queensland, pre-dating Townsville and Charters Towers, for example. It was named after the first Governor of Queensland. Rather unusually, there was a European living here even prior to the founding of the town. James Morrill was shipwrecked in 1846 just north of the site of Bowen and managed to survive with the assistance of the local aborigines until a town was founded for him. When it was, he moved here in 1863, and spent the rest of his life in Bowen. He is buried in the cemetery here.

It takes 21 hours to reach Bowen by train from Brisbane, and just a little less by bus. This town had, until recently, a really impressive railway station, to reach which the train performed a complete circuit of a loop off the main line. The author used to enjoy this novelty greatly, but, alas, in the name of progress it has disappeared, despite the fact that the extra couple of kilometres wasted little time. Now the train stops at a characterless halt on the main line and passengers are taken into the town by bus. Although this is another example of putting a station out of the reach of those who need it most, it must be conceded, in fact, that the old station was not very near the town centre either.

Bowen offers some pretty views. The town slopes down to the sea and looks attractive from the top of the hill as one arrives. It has a good museum, and some interesting history to display. In 1875, the *Gothenburg* was wrecked off the shore here, with the loss of more than a hundred lives. Then, during the Second World War, it was a base for the Catalina Flying Boats. There is a monument on the foreshore to show the site of the base. Going further back into history, charcoal from a campsite discovered here was found to date back 2,500 years, and a skeleton found locally is thought to be as much as 6,000 years old, so evidently there have been aborigines here for a while.

A few years ago, Bowen was described as "Queensland's best-kept secret", but then it is fashionable to describe everywhere as a best-kept secret, and it certainly is a secret no longer. As a result, it seems to have lost some of its attraction. Only five years ago, it was difficult to find anywhere at all to sleep here, but now a bed can be located without undue hardship, so once more it has become a good place to visit, for it is surrounded by attractive beaches. The best-known beach is at **Horseshoe Bay**, a small sandy beach with elevated viewpoints at the sides. However, there are other beaches too, and all within walking distance of the town. On one side of Horseshoe Bay is **Coral Bay**, which is the town's nudist beach. Then there are also **Queen's Beach** and **Gray's Bay** to the north, and **Murray Bay, Rose Bay** and **King's Beach** to the east.

Bowen has also made itself into a town of **murals**. 22 pictures are painted on the sides of buildings, mostly in the main area of town. They tell the history of Bowen.

There is a local bus service, operated by just a single bus, which goes around the suburbs three times every day.

ACCOMMODATION
(i) Hotel Accommodation in Bowen

Name	Stars	No. on Map	Telephone No.	Address	Lowest Price (Double/Twin)
Queen's Beach Motel	3	2	07-4785-1555	101 Golf Links Road	$80
Milton Motel		6	07-4786-1433	Richmond Road	$75
Castle Motor Lodge	3	7	07-4786-1322	6 Don Street	$75
Sky View Coastal Motel	4	5	07-4786-2232	49 Horseshoe Bay Road	$70
Palm View Holiday Units	3½	3	07-4785-1415	Soldiers Road & Howard St.	$68
Horseshoe Bay Resort	3	1	07-4786-2564	Horseshoe Bay	$65
Ocean View Motel	3	12	07-4786-1377	Bruce Highway	$65
Beachside Holiday Units		4	07-4786-2561	38 Horseshoe Bay Road	$60
Pearly Shell Motel	2½	8	07-4786-1788	2 Don Street	$55
Big Mango Motel	2½	13	07-4786-2499	Bruce Highway	$55
Denison Hotel		9	07-4786-1238	55 Powell Street	$50
Central Hotel		10	07-4786-1812	29 Herbert Street	$50
Grand View Hotel		11	07-4786-4122	5 Herbert Street	$50

(ii) Backpackers Hostels in Bowen

Name	Group	No. on Map	Telephone No.	Address	Lowest Price (Dormitory)
North Australian Hotel		16	07-4786-1277	55 Herbert Street	$25
Barnacles Backpackers		15	07-4786-4400	16 Gordon Street	$22
Harbour Lights Caravan Pk		17	07-4786-1565	40 Santa Barbara Parade	$22
Trinity's at the Beach		14	07-4786-4199	93 Horseshoe Bay Road	$22

MOVING ON
(i) By Train

The rail timetables north and south are shown on pages 238 and 338.

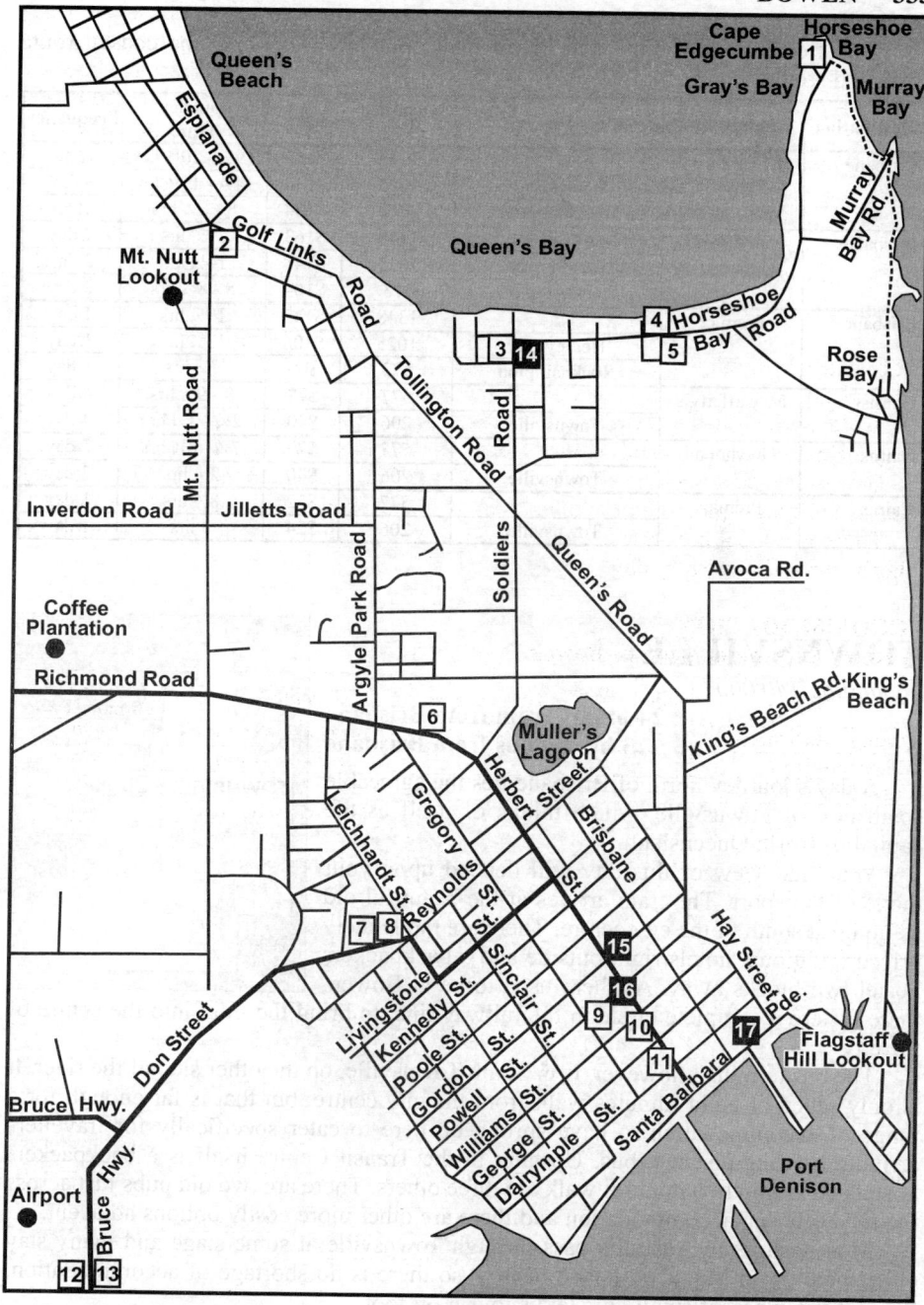

BOWEN

Black numerals in white boxes indicate hotel accommodation
White numerals in black boxes indicate backpackers hostels

(ii) By Bus

McCafferty's, Greyhound and Premier all operate buses along the coastal route north and south, as summarised below.

Destination	Operator	Via	Distance (km)	Fare	Journey Time	Frequency
Brisbane	McCafferty's		1348	$163	19¼ - 20½ hrs	4/day
		Hervey Bay	1025	$146	14¼ - 15¼ hrs	3/day
		Rockhampton	573	$104	8 - 8¼ hrs	4/day
Brisbane	Greyhound		1348	$163	20¼ hrs	2/day
		Hervey Bay	1025	$146	14¼ hrs	2/day
		Rockhampton	573	$104	8 - 8¾ hrs	2/day
Brisbane	Premier		1348	$142	19¼ hrs	1/day
		Hervey Bay	1025	$106	13¾ hrs	1/day
		Rockhampton	573	$60	7½ hrs	1/day
Cairns	McCafferty's		577	$79	8 - 9½ hrs	4/day
		Townsville	206	$40	2½ - 3¼ hrs	4/day
Cairns	Greyhound		577	$79	7¾ - 8¾ hrs	2/day
		Townsville	206	$40	2½ hrs	2/day
Cairns	Premier		577	$72	8½ hrs	1/day
		Townsville	206	$24	3 hrs	1/day

TOWNSVILLE

Population 140,000

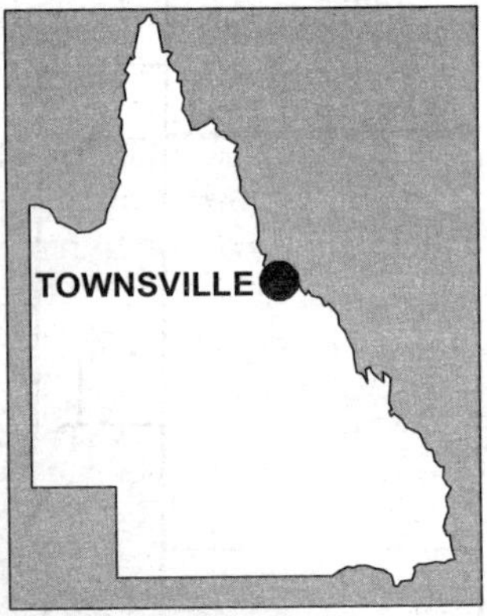

24 hrs by train from Brisbane
23 hrs by bus from Brisbane

A day's journey north of Brisbane lies the agreeable small city of Townsville, which thinks of itself as the capital of North Queensland.

Your first view of this city will depend upon your mode of transport. The train arrives at the beautiful old station just south of the city centre. There are moderately priced traditional hotels right outside and a backpackers hostel two blocks away. As there used to be at Bowen, there is here a complete circle in the railway line, to bring the train into the centre of the city.

The bus terminal, however, is in South Townsville, on the other side of the river. It is only seven or eight minutes walk from the city centre, but that is far enough for a range of accommodation to have sprung up here to cater specifically for travellers arriving by long-distance bus. Upstairs in the Transit Centre itself is a backpackers hostel and within two minutes walk are three others. There are two old pubs just across the road offering accommodation and there are other more costly options adjacent.

Most visitors to Australia pass through Townsville at some stage and many stay either here or on Magnetic Island nearby, so there is no shortage of accommodation. Since it is a pleasant small city, let us tour it on foot.

TOWNSVILLE 335

Walking Tour *(see map on page 336)*

The following tour starts at the Railway Station and finishes at the beginning of the Flinders Mall. It covers about eight kilometres and will take approximately two and a half hours.

The centre of the city is Flinders Street, running from the Railway Station almost to the Strand. Walk along it and you will see some fine old buildings, starting with the **station** itself, then the **hotels** on the corner, and the **old newspaper office**. You will soon come to **Flinders Mall**, the central section of the street, which has become much more pleasant since being converted into a pedestrian-only area. Here is the **Tourist Information Centre**, manned by volunteers and very helpful, as volunteers usually are. On your right at the end is a grand old Post Office, with ancient post box outside. If you continue, you will come to an area of restaurants and nightclubs on your left, with the terminal for the passenger ferry to Magnetic Island on your right. Then, where Wickham Street goes off to the left, is more budget accommodation, including the Downtown Motel, which offers a bed in a large air-conditioned dormitory for $17. Next to the river is the Imax theatre and the new **Museum of Tropical Queensland**. If you continue beside the river, you can walk out to **Jupiters Casino**, and even stay there if you feel sufficiently wealthy.

Returning from the Casino, turn right into **Anzac Park**, lined with tropical palm trees. In the park are some talking trees. Try them out. A little further along is an interesting **War Memorial** commemorating the Battle of the Coral Sea fought near here, which was, perhaps, the turning point in the Pacific War. It is not generally known that Townsville was one of the few places in Australia to be bombed during the Second World War. There is also here a memorial to the Australian holders of the V.C.

If you look left beyond the fountain, you will see another splendid old building currently occupied by a television company. Continue along the Strand and you will reach the **Marina** on your right and a small waterfall tumbling from the high cliff on your left. Ahead is the **Tobruk Pool** and beyond the newly developed **Strand** area. A few years ago this was just a very ordinary beach, but now it is one of the delights of the city, with a promenade, grass, playgrounds for children, and, of course, the beach, now extended and looking much more appealing. It is quite a long walk to the end of this development, over two kilometres. Motels and other rental accommodation overlook the bay, their values no doubt increased considerably by the work which has been carried out here. Half way along is a restaurant, and in the sea there is a swimming area with netting to guard against jellyfish. At the end of the Strand, at **Kissing Point**, is a rock pool (free), another swimming enclosure, and a lookout at the top of the headland there. Just beyond is Jezzine Barracks, now the **Army Museum**, open from 8:30 until 12:30 on Mondays, Wednesdays and Fridays.

We now retrace our steps a little way along the Strand until we reach Landsborough Street, where we turn right and follow the street right to the end, crossing the main Warburton Street about half way along. At the end, turn left into Stanley Street, and then right into Castle Hill Road. After a short distance, you will see on the right the 'Goat Track' leading steeply up to the top of the hill. Follow this and you will arrive at the **hill-top lookout**, with a fine view of the whole city.

To return to the city centre, go back down the Goat Track and Castle Hill Road to Stanley Street once more. Turn right into Stanley Street and simply follow this road back to the city centre.

336 QUEENSLAND

At the end of Flinders Street we passed the Museum of Tropical Queensland. One of the main exhibits here is items salvaged from the wreck of **H.M.S. Pandora**. This wreck is not near Townsville. The ship foundered after striking the northern edge of the Great Barrier Reef in 1791. It is famous as the vessel which had pursued the *Bounty* mutineers and captured fourteen of them in Tahiti. Four of the mutineers died in the shipwreck of the *Pandora*, as did 31 crew members. The remainder were rescued eventually and tried in England, where six were sentenced to death and four acquitted. Of the six convicted, three were actually hanged. The wreck of the *Pandora* was discovered in 1977, lying in 33 metres of water 120 kilometres east of Cape York, and

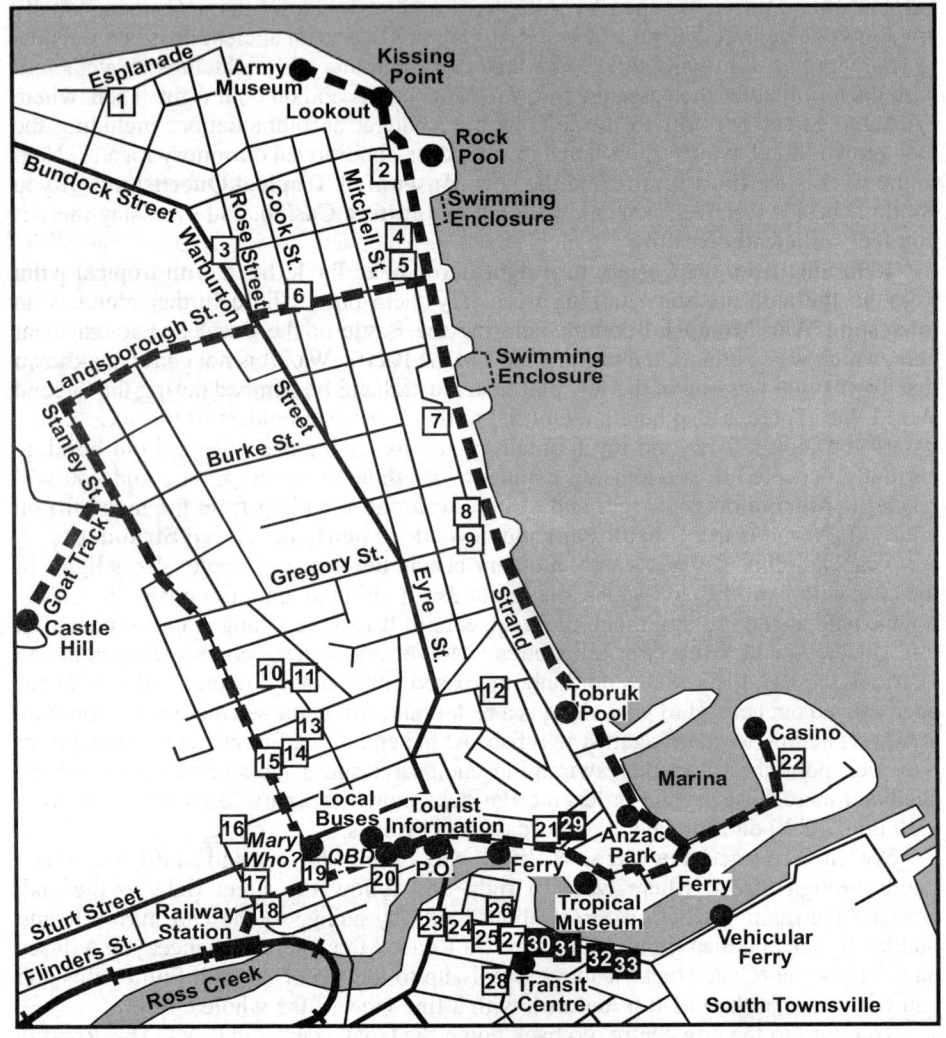

TOWNSVILLE

Dashed line shows Walking Tour
Black numerals in white boxes indicate hotel accommodation
White numerals in black boxes indicate backpackers hostels

provides an insight into the great age of maritime exploration. The museum is open daily from 9:00 until 17:00 and admission costs $10.

Next door are the Imax theatre, with the largest screen in Australia, and **Reef HQ**, which has the largest land-based living coral reef system in the world.

Local bus services around Townsville are provided by Sunbus and include a bus every half hour at holiday times along the Strand. In fact, though, it is usually quicker to walk to most places likely to be visited by non-residents. There is a service to the airport (almost) by bus no. 5 or 5A. No. 4 also goes near. A one-day ticket is available for the Sunbus services for $10, but again it is not likely to be sufficiently useful for most visitors. Sunbus services leave from the northern side of Flinders Street Mall.

Many people will be wanting to go to Magnetic Island (see next entry), so note that there are two different ferry services. The passenger ferry is well publicised. It costs $18 return and operates from two points on the city side of the river. The terminal is in Flinders Street, just beyond the end of Flinders Street Mall. There is a second pick-up point closer to the mouth of the river, on the breakwater along the road to the Casino, but most passengers find the terminal more convenient. This passenger ferry sails to Picnic Bay on Magnetic Island. The last sailing is at 21:45 (20:15 on Sundays).

Not so well known is the vehicular ferry which operates from the other side of the river, a little further along than the Transit Centre. For those arriving by bus and wishing to proceed immediately to the island, this might prove more convenient. It is also slightly cheaper, at $15 return. Moreover this ferry sails to Geoffrey Bay, adjacent to Arcadia, which may be a more convenient location for those whose accommodation is not already booked. The last ferry sails at 17:15 (15:15 on Saturdays).

BOOKSHOPS

QBD's Bumble Bee Bookshop   305 Flinders Mall
Mary Who? Bookshop   155 Stanley Street

Both of these bookshops are marked on the map opposite.

ACCOMMODATION

Many people choose either Townsville or Magnetic Island for a stopping point, so there is plenty of accommodation available here. Some of the backpackers hostels get crowded at times, but it is always possible to find a bed somewhere. The author likes the Downtown Motel, where a dormitory bed in a large air-conditioned room costs only $17, and, because the accommodation is not well known, that room is often almost empty.

(i) Hotel Accommodation in Townsville

Name	Stars	No. on Map	Telephone No.	Address	Lowest Price (Double/Twin)
Centra Holiday Inn		20	07-4772-2477	334 Flinders Mall	$245
City Oasis Inn		14	1-800-809-515	143 Wills Street	$175
Jupiters Casino		22	07-4722-2333	Sir Leslie Thiess Drive	$165
Aquarius on the Beach	4	7	1-800-622-474	75 The Strand	$150
Reef International Hotel	4½	8	1-800-804-812	63 The Strand	$145
Flag Townsville Plaza	3½	19	1-800-355-225	Flinders Mall & Stanley St.	$135
Quality Hotel Southbank	4½	24	1-800-355-143	17 Palmer Street	$135
Quest Townsville		26	07-4772-6477	30 Palmer Street	$135
Southbank Hotel		25	07-4721-1474	23 Palmer Street	$125

338 QUEENSLAND
(i) Hotel Accommodation in Townsville, continued

Name	Stars	No. on Map	Telephone No.	Address	Lowest Price (Double/Twin)
Robert Towns Motel	4½	15	1-800-150-641	261 Stanley Street	$115
Seagulls Resort		1	07-4721-3111	74 The Esplanade	$110
Strand Park Hotel		9	07-4750-7888	59 The Strand	$110
Castle Lodge Motel	3½	3	1-800-777-745	Warburton & McKinley Sts.	$105
Ridgemont Executive	4	10	1-800-804-168	15 Victoria Street	$105
Summit Motel	3½	11	1-800-645-138	6 Victoria Street	$92
Shoredrive Motel	3½	2	07-4771-6851	117 The Strand	$88
Bayside Holiday Apts.	3½	5	07-4721-1688	102 The Strand	$85
Coral Lodge		13	1-800-614-613	32 Hale Street	$85
Palm Waters		6	1-800-804-812	36 Landsborough Street	$70
Downtown Motel		21	07-4771-5000	121 Flinders Street East	$70
Seaside Apartments		4	07-4721-3155	105 The Strand	$65
Historic Yongala Lodge	3½	12	07-4772-4633	11 Fryer Street	$65
Great Northern Hotel		18	07-4771-6191	500 Flinders Street	$50
Shamrock Hotel		27	07-4771-4351	31 Palmer Street	$50
Republic Hotel		28	07-4771-4316	31 McIlwraith Street	$50
Newmarket Hotel		17	07-4721-1377	499 Flinders Street	$45
Australia Hotel		23	07-4771-4339	11 Palmer Street	$45
Civic Guest House		16	1-800-646-619	262 Walker Street	$44

(ii) Backpackers Hostels in Townsville

Name	Group	No. on Map	Telephone No.	Address	Lowest Price (Dormitory)
Shamrock Hotel		27	07-4771-4351	31 Palmer Street	$25
Southbank Village		32	07-4771-5849	35 McIlwraith Street	$20
Adventurers Resort		33	07-4721-1522	79 Palmer Street	$20
Civic Guest House	VIP	16	1800-646-619	262 Walker Street	$19
Downtown Motel		21	07-4771-5000	121 Flinders Street East	$17
Globetrotters	VIP	31	07-4771-3242	45 Palmer Street	$17
Reef Lodge		29	07-4721-1112	4 Wickham Street	$16
Transit Centre Backpackers	VIP	30	1800-628-836	Palmer & Plume Streets	$15

MOVING ON
(i) By Train

Trains run north to Cairns, south to Brisbane, and also west to Mt. Isa. The Mt. Isa service operates on Sunday and Wednesday nights. A summary timetable of all rail services from Townsville is shown to the right.

(ii) By Bus

McCafferty's, Greyhound and Premier all operate bus services both north to Cairns and south to Brisbane. In addition, Greyhound has a service to Mt.

Days of Departure	Sun, M, W, F	Not F	Sun, W	Th
Townsville	0843	1610	1800	
Tully	1249			
Innisfail	1359			
Cairns	1625			
Bowen		1930		
Proserpine		2022		
Mackay		2242		
Rockhampton		0500		
Gladstone		0643		
Bundaberg		0925		
Maryborough West		1035		
Gympie North		1224		
Brisbane		1555		
Charters Towers			2103	
Hughenden			0149	0400
Winton				1130
Cloncurry			0950	
Mt. Isa			1335	
Days of Arrival		Not Sat	M, Th	

TOWNSVILLE 339

Isa, and McCafferty's has a service via Mt. Isa to Tennant Creek in the Northern Territory. From Tennant Creek there are connecting buses to Darwin and Alice Springs. There is also the Winton Express bus to Winton on Sundays and Wednesdays.

Destination	Operator	Via	Distance (km)	Fare	Journey Time	Frequency
Brisbane	McCafferty's		1554	$184	21¾ - 23 hrs	4/day
		Hervey Bay	1231	$163	16¾ - 17½ hrs	3/day
		Rockhampton	779	$115	10½ - 10¾ hrs	4/day
Brisbane	Greyhound		1554	$184	22¾ hrs	2/day
		Hervey Bay	1231	$163	16¾ hrs	2/day
		Rockhampton	779	$115	10½ - 11¼ hrs	2/day
Brisbane	Premier		1554	$173	22½ hrs	1/day
		Hervey Bay	1231	$149	17 hrs	1/day
		Rockhampton	779	$81	10½ hrs	1/day
Cairns	McCafferty's		371	$57	4¾ - 5¾ hrs	4/day
Cairns	Greyhound		371	$57	4½ - 5¾ hrs	2/day
Cairns	Premier		371	$51	5½ hrs	1/day
Tennant Ck.	McCafferty's		1547	$236	20½ hrs	1/day
		Mt. Isa	886	$131	11¾ hrs	1/day
Mt. Isa	Greyhound		886	$131	12 hrs	3/week
Winton	Winton Express		588	$100	9 hrs	2/week

MAGNETIC ISLAND
Population 2,000
20 mins by ferry from Townsville

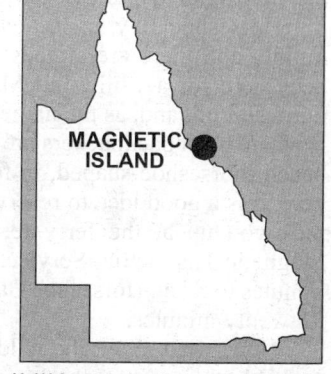

When Captain Cook sailed past here on 6th June 1770, he reported that his compass would not work well, apparently attracted by a magnetic force in the rocks of the nearby island. Accordingly, he named the island Magnetic Island. He may have been mistaken, however, as to the cause of the malfunction, because nothing has been found in the rocks here to cause a magnetic effect.

Magnetic Island is a beautiful haven, only eight kilometres from Townsville, featuring beaches and wildlife. It had no European occupation until a century after Captain Cook's voyage, being first settled in 1870. Its tourist potential was realised, but only in the last thirty years or so has the island really been developed for that purpose. However, more than half of Magnetic Island is a National Park, so there is a limit to the development possible. At present it is still a pleasantly rural community.

There are two different ferry services to Magnetic Island. The more popular is the Sunferries passenger ferry which operates fifteen times a day. This ferry leaves from the city side of the river in Townsville, just beyond the end of Flinders Mall, and makes a further stop at the breakwater along the road to the Casino. It arrives in Magnetic Island at Picnic Bay. It takes twenty minutes and costs $18 return. Tea and coffee are available free on board. The last ferry is at 21:45 (20:15 on Sundays).

The second ferry is a vehicular service operated by Magnetic Island Car Ferry. It sails six times a day, leaving from the South Townsville side of the river beyond the Transit Centre, so those arriving by bus and wishing to continue immediately to Magnetic Island will find this service convenient. It takes 35 minutes and costs $15 return. This ferry arrives at Geoffrey Bay, near Arcadia. The last ferry is at 17:15 (15:15 on Saturdays).

It used to be possible to obtain some discounted packages for backpackers accommodation on the island, plus ferry fares, but these seem to have gone out of fashion now. Typically, one could purchase one, two or three nights' accommodation, plus ferry, plus return bus fare, for just a little more than the cost of the accommodation alone. It is worth asking about this at the Tourist Information Centre in Townsville. Sometimes such deals are still available.

Magnetic Island is roughly triangular and has five main settlements. The passenger ferry arrives at Picnic Bay, which is the southern tip of the island. It has shops and caters well for day trippers, but, although accommodation is available, most visitors do not stay here.

On the north-western tip of the island is West Point. There used to be an occasional bus service along the unmade road to here, but it no longer operates, so few visitors get to West Point.

Along the eastern side of the island, one passes through Nelly Bay and Arcadia before reaching Horseshoe Bay on the northern shore. The vehicular ferry arrives at Geoffrey Bay, adjacent to Arcadia, and there is accommodation here, including the Arcadia Resort, and also Centaur House Backpackers, from where Ken and Liz operate the Black and White List of hostels.

Horseshoe Bay, at the end of the road, is still small, but it is being developed rapidly and there are already two large backpackers hostels here. Geoff's Place has been here for a while, but Maggie's Beach House is relatively new and is popular, purpose-built and, as the name suggests, right on the beach. At present, Horseshoe Bay is where most backpackers are choosing to stay. It certainly has a beautiful long curving beach (horseshoe-shaped, in fact), offering sheltered swimming. If you intend to stay here, it is a good idea to reserve in advance, so that your accommodation will know to pick you up at the ferry terminal. Otherwise, there is a bus service operated by Magnetic Island Bus Service. It runs approximately every 45 minutes and takes 30 minutes to reach Horseshoe Bay. The hostel minibuses, running direct, take only fifteen to twenty minutes.

Now, what about the wildlife on the island? Most famous are the **koalas**. This is probably the most northerly colony of free-range koalas and there are plenty here. One is almost certain to meet some if one goes to the forested areas. One of the favourite locations for koalas is the walking track to *The Forts* (see under), so try to complete at least part of this walk and your efforts will probably be rewarded. The best time is late afternoon, but you are quite likely to find koalas at any time of day on that particular walk.

Koalas are not the only wildlife here. Go to Geoffrey Bay and walk out to the ferry terminal jetty at 17:00 and you will find a group of **rock wallabies** there waiting for their afternoon tea. They prefer fruit and vegetables, if you are thinking of contributing to the Rock Wallaby Benevolent Scheme. Some of these creatures are willing to accept donations direct from the hand. Remember to bring your camera. There are also large numbers of fishes around the jetty, they obviously having been informed that fishing is not permitted in this area.

MAGNETIC ISLAND

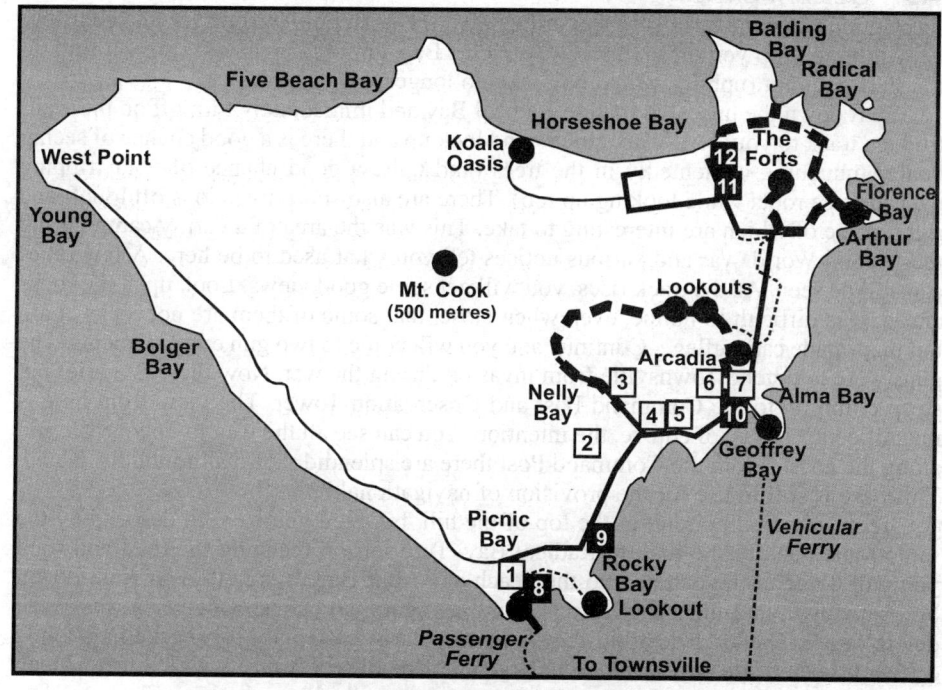

MAGNETIC ISLAND
Dashed lines show Walking Tours
Thicker solid lines denote bus routes
Black numerals in white boxes indicate hotel accommodation
White numerals in black boxes indicate backpackers hostels

At the hostel where the author stayed, a possum appeared on the top of the wall one evening, stretching his hand down and remarking, "Excuse me, I'm hungry." When offered part of a banana, he agilely clung to the top of the wall by his tail and swung down to accept the donation. He had not been seen before, I was told, and did not appear again.

There was a kookaburra in the bar of the pub, known to the staff by name. In the public toilet, there was a snake asleep on top of the cistern, and while the author was writing postcards a gecko fell off the ceiling and landed on my head. You are almost sure to meet some wildlife here on Magnetic Island.

Magnetic Island is surprisingly hilly in the centre and in between the various beaches, with Mount Cook, the highest point, although still somewhat less towering than its New Zealand namesake, rising to 500 metres. There are some good walks here, of which two are suggested below.

Walk 1 (*The Forts* and Beyond)

This walk starts about three kilometres outside Horseshoe Bay and finishes in Horseshoe Bay. It covers ten kilometres and will take some three and a half hours.

It is easy to catch a bus from your accommodation to the start of *The Forts* walk, where the road to Radical Bay diverges from the main road. The bus driver will, of course, be familiar with the spot, if told that you want to walk to *The Forts*. If you are staying in one of the hostels in Horseshoe Bay, the hostel minibus driver will probably be willing to drop you off on his way to Picnic Bay. Or, of course, you can just walk to the starting point (uphill), which will take no longer than 45 minutes.

Start down the unsealed road to Radical Bay and immediately turn off on the well-trodden track to your left. Walk quietly and look up and there is a good chance of seeing koalas munching contentedly in the trees (and quite a good chance of your tripping over the tree roots while looking up too). There are also short diversions off to left and right, some of which are interesting to take. This was the area of an army camp during the Second World War and various notices tell you what used to be here. A few relics can still be seen. As the track rises, you will get some good views. Look up at the rocks ahead. It is difficult to notice, even when close, that some of them are not rocks at all, but man-made camouflage. Continue and you will come to two gun emplacements. The guns were to defend Townsville from invasion during the war. Now there is a brief but steep climb up to the Command Post and Observation Tower. The view from here is magnificent, as was, of course, the intention. You can see all the way to Townsville and along the coast. From the Command Post there are splendid views all round the island. This base is still in use for the provision of navigational lights.

There is a small circuit at the top of the hill, but then you have to descend by the same route back to the road to Radical Bay. Turn left on reaching the road and soon you will come to the entrance to the beach at Arthur Bay. It is not far to walk down, but it is down, and then you have to come up again, so choose whether to make the detour or not. The left side of this bay is a particularly good place for snorkelling, while on the right there are caves sheltering large numbers of reef fishes. A little further along the road and there is a path off to the right to the headland overlooking Florence Bay. This is worth taking, as the view is good, but if you feel tired, you will save about a kilometre by omitting it. Continuing along the road, you come to the entrance to the beach at Florence Bay, again only a very short diversion. This bay is one of the prettiest on the island and you can find coral along the rocks to the right of the bay.

Continue along the road again and about another kilometre will bring you to Radical Bay with its pleasant sheltered beach. Just at the top of the slope down to the beach. a path leads off inland, which follow, climbing up again through eucalyptus trees to a ridge. At the top of the ridge, there is a fork. Take the track on the right and descend to Balding Bay, a pleasant secluded little cove and beach. Now, for the last stage, climb back up to the ridge and turn right, taking the other track, which leads back to Horseshoe Bay. As you approach you will get a different view of the area, as this is the slightly swampy end at which the fishing boats moor. Horseshoe Bay is the largest bay on the island, about four kilometres from end to end. It is popular for aquatic sports, as well as for swimming. The Koala Oasis is at the far end, just in case you did not manage to see any of these creatures along your walk. Buses run back from here to all the other settlements, leaving irregularly, but, on average, approximately every 45 minutes.

Walk 2 (Arcadia to Nelly Bay)

This is a walk of approximately six kilometres, which should take about two hours. It offers some good views of the island.

Perhaps the most difficult aspect of this walk is to find the correct starting point. The bus service goes past here, however, so ask the driver if arriving by bus. Otherwise walk round to the back of Arcadia along Hayles Avenue and look for Endeavour Road, which take. The start of the walking trail is signposted here. It starts as a steep paved road which soon comes to a locked gate. Proceed along the road which continues beyond the gate up the hill. The walking track diverges to the left, but first climb to the top of the hill at the end of the paved road for the good view over Alma Bay. There are storage tanks up here, you will find, which is the purpose of the road.

Now return the short distance down the hill to where the track leads off, now on your right, and start climbing again. Where the track divides, turn right and go to the Sphinx Lookout. Then again return and proceed to one more fork. Do not make a mistake here. You want the left track. The right one leads back down to the main road. As you continue along the crest of the ridge amidst the eucalyptus trees, you will reach three more fine viewpoints, two looking out north to Horseshoe Bay and one looking south over Arcadia.

As you start to descend, the forest thickens, and this is the best area to see a variety of birds and other wildlife. You reach Gustav Creek as the track levels out and eventually emerges in, not Mandalay itself, as you might have supposed from the lush tropical vegetation, but Mandalay Road. If you walk down the road a little way, you will come to Nelly Bay Store, at which point you join the bus route, if you need transport home. If not, continue down to the end of Mandalay Road, from where turn left and it is only about two kilometres back to your starting point in Arcadia, or turn right and it is about four kilometres, much of it along the beach, to Picnic Bay.

If you wish to explore Magnetic Island by bus, a day ticket is available for $11, but, since there is only one route, one has to work hard to get good value from such a ticket. Notice that all the buses on the island have names. There are bicycles for hire, and there are also rather un-environmental mokes available, the last being popular for those who can make up a group of four.

ACCOMMODATION

Although there is accommodation to suit all pockets here, many of the visitors are backpackers. Fashions change, and the fashionable location for the next few years seems likely to be Horseshoe Bay. The hostels there are fine, indeed good, and the staff of both are polite and helpful, but they are crowded and somewhat trendy, which is not what appeals to the author. Many of the readers of this will enjoy the beachside locations, the in-house bars and the camaraderie of the residents. However, if you want somewhere quieter, try Centaur House in Arcadia. You can still have the beach right outside, the use of the resort's swimming pool five minutes away, e-mail facilities and the interesting company of Ken and Liz (and maybe the possum will turn up for you).

For those who are not backpackers, Marshall's Bed and Breakfast is pleasantly located and offers a third night free at off-peak times; or, for a higher standard still, how about the Arcadia Resort, at the end of the road to the jetty used by the vehicular ferry?

(i) Hotel Accommodation on Magnetic Island

Name	Stars	No. on Map	Telephone No.	Address	Lowest Price (Double/Twin)
Magnetic International		3	1-800-079-902	Mandalay Av., Nelly Bay	$130
Arcadia Resort		7	07-4778-5177	7 Marine Parade, Arcadia	$80
Tropical Palms Inn		1	07-4778-5076	34 Picnic Street, Picnic Bay	$75
Camlachie Holiday Units		5	07-4778-5995	122 Sooning St., Nelly Bay	$75
Marshall's B & B		6	07-4778-5112	3 Endeavour Road, Arcadia	$70
Anchorage Apartments	3	4	07-4778-5596	110 Sooning St., Nelly Bay	$65
Magnetic Tropical Resort		2	07-4778-5955	56 Yates Street, Nelly Bay	$55

344 QUEENSLAND
(ii) Backpackers Hostels on Magnetic Island

Name	Group	No. on Map	Telephone No.	Address	Lowest Price (Dormitory)
Maggie's Beach House	VIP	12	1800-001-544	1 Pacific Drive, Horseshoe Bay	$22
Centaur House	B&W	10	1800-655-680	27 Marine Parade, Arcadia	$20
Geoff's Place	YHA	11	1800-285-577	40 Horseshoe Bay Road	$20
Magnetic Tropical Resort	Nom	2	1800-069-122	56 Yates Street, Nelly Bay	$20
Coconuts		9	07-4778-5777	1 Nelly Bay Road, Nelly Bay	$20
Travellers Backpackers	VIP	8	1800-000-290	1 The Esplanade, Picnic Bay	$18

MOVING ON

The first Sunferries service from Picnic Bay is at 6:25 and runs to the Breakwater in Townsville (not to the Flinders Street terminal). There is a connecting bus at 5:40 from Horseshoe Bay and at 5:50 from Arcadia. The ferry reaches Townsville at 6:45. The last ferry to Townsville is at 22:20, except Sundays (20:50) and Tuesdays (23:05).

The first vehicular ferry is at 7:00 (9:00 at weekends), and the last at 18:15 (16:15 on Saturdays).

CHARTERS TOWERS
Population 10,000

3 hrs by train from Townsville
2 hrs by bus from Townsville

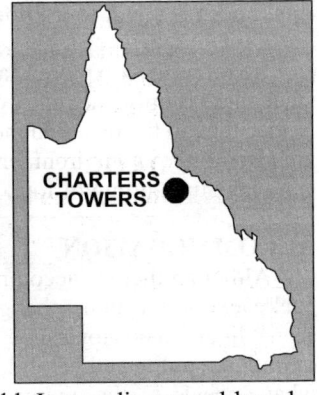

Charters Towers lies 135 kilometres west of Townsville and is a fascinating town with a long (comparatively) and interesting history. It is most easily reached by bus. McCafferty's operates a service every morning from Townsville, and Greyhound has one rather inconveniently late in the evening. There is a train too, but it runs only on Sundays and Wednesdays, again in the evening.

The prosperity of Charters Towers was based on gold. It was discovered here by an aboriginal boy, Jupiter Mosman, in 1871 and a gold rush began. The town was founded in 1872, named after the Mining Warden of the area. It became a municipality in 1877 and a city in 1909. Its population grew to around 30,000 and it became the second city of Queensland. There was a stock exchange located here and the city at one time had seven newspapers and 54 hotels. To local residents, it was known as *The World*.

In the 1920s, the crash came. The gold ran out and there was a worldwide recession. Although Charters Towers suffered from the adverse economic conditions, it survived the hard times, partly because of the local beef industry and partly because of its reputation for high quality education. Even now, there are four highly regarded schools in Charters Towers, and a fifth of the city's population is made up of boarders at these schools.

To everybody's surprise, there has now been a revival, in the form of a second gold boom. The tailings from the old and less sophisticated mines are being reworked and modern processes are extracting the minute particles which were missed before. So far, a further two million ounces of gold have been recovered from these workings. This new prosperity has been invested in reviving the heritage aspects of the city, which, in turn, has attracted tourists to the area. There are several fine buildings in Charters Towers and it is a town in which it is well worth spending a day.

Less accessible than Charters Towers is Ravenswood, 91 kilometres south-east of its better-known neighbour, or 42 kilometres south of Mingela, the nearest point on the highway. This is a ghost gold town which pre-dates Charters Towers. It was established in 1868, but when gold was found at Charters Towers, this town gradually declined. At one time, it had 48 hotels, but by soon after the turn of the century it had fewer than a hundred inhabitants. It is also interesting, but not easily reached, there being no public transport.

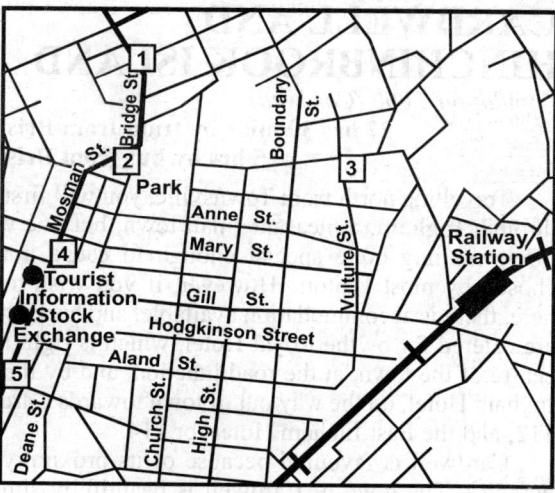

CHARTERS TOWERS
Numerals indicate accommodation

ACCOMMODATION
Accommodation in Charters Towers

Name	Stars	No. on Map	Telephone No.	Address	Lowest Price (Double/Twin)
Park Motel	3	2	1-800-816-754	1 Mosman Street	$80
Cattleman's Rest		1	07-4787-3555	Bridge & Plant Streets	$80
Rix Hotel / Motel		4	07-4787-1605	69 Mosman Street	$75
Crown Hotel		5	07-4787-2471	119 Mosman Street	$50
St. Patrick's Hotel		3	07-4787-2447	Mill & Vulture Streets	$45

MOVING ON
(i) By Train
The train runs to Mt. Isa on Sunday and Wednesday evenings, and to Townsville on Tuesday and Saturday mornings.

(ii) By Bus
McCafferty's offers a daily bus service to Mt. Isa and on to Tennant Creek, from where there are connexions to Darwin and Alice Springs. Greyhound offers an additional service to Mt. Isa. Both companies also run daily buses to Townsville.

Destination	Operator	Via	Distance (km)	Fare	Journey Time	Frequency
Townsville	McCafferty's		135	$31	1¾ hrs	1/day
Townsville	Greyhound		135	$31	1¾ hrs	1/day
Tennant Ck.	McCafferty's		1412	$217	18¼ hrs	1/day
		Mt. Isa	751	$124	10 hrs	1/day
Mt. Isa	Greyhound		751	$124	10¼ hrs	3/week
Winton	Winton Express		453	$100	7 hrs	2/week

CARDWELL AND HINCHINBROOK ISLAND

Population 2,000 (Cardwell)

27 hrs 30 mins by train from Brisbane
25 hrs by bus from Brisbane

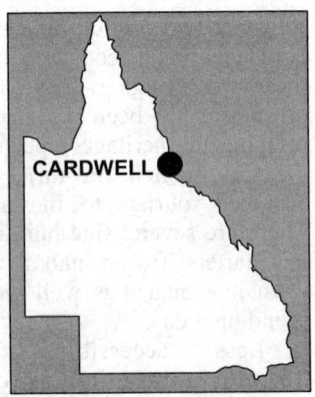

Travelling north from Townsville, you will first pass through **Ingham**, a pleasant small town, but one which offers nothing quite special enough to cause it to be chosen by most visitors. However, if you wish to stay here, there is accommodation available, and backpackers are catered for by the Royal Hotel, which is right in the centre of the town, at the road junction, and by the East Ingham Hotel, on the way out of town towards Cardwell. The Royal Hotel has beds for $12, and the East Ingham Hotel for $14.

Cardwell is favoured because of its proximity to Hinchinbrook Island, a hiker's paradise. The town of Cardwell is beautifully situated, sheltered by the surprisingly large Hinchinbrook Island, and with a fine view across to it. If you are travelling by train, this is one of only two places between Brisbane and Cairns where you actually get a view of the sea, so make the most of this little glimpse. (The other place is 800 kilometres south of here, and passed at night by the *Sunlander* and the *Queenslander*.)

To the south of the town is a controversial development at **Port Hinchinbrook**, which, some say, is spoiling the natural beauty of the area. There is also, at **Lucinda**, further south still, one of the longest single trestle jetties in the world. It extends for 5.6 kilometres and dips a total of 1.2 metres over its length due to the curvature of the earth.

The marine area here is a **Dugong** Protection Area. These endangered herbivorous sea mammals, sometimes known as sea cows, graze on the sea grasses on the ocean floor here and can often be seen on the journey across to Hinchinbrook Island.

There are actually fifteen islands off the coast at this point, but Hinchinbrook is by far the largest. It is Australia's largest island National Park, covering 393 square kilometres. The island probably became separated from the mainland about 100,000 years ago and has remained uninhabited, at least by Europeans, except for a resort built recently in a small area on the far side at Cape Richards. The resort has treetop huts and is nature-oriented, expecting guests to enjoy the beauty of the surroundings rather than be entertained. It is also very expensive.

If you have sufficient time, there is a walking trail along the farther coast of the island, known as the Thorsborne Trail (or East Coast Trail). It is 32 kilometres long and usually takes four days to complete, although it can be walked in three, if preferred. Walkers need to take everything with them, except water, which is available along the way. Alternatively, full-day and half-day cruises to the island are available, allowing time for shorter walks while there, or for snorkelling in the area, for which equipment can be provided at an extra charge. Cruises cost $85. The island is dominated by **Mt. Bowen**, in the centre, which is 1,142 metres high. It is popular with climbers (permit required), but not an easy climb at all. There is no trail to the summit. Also on the island, at the south, is **Mt. Straloch**, where an American bomber crashed on 18th December 1942, with the loss of twelve lives. The wreckage still lies there.

There are walking tracks on some of the other islands too, but they are not as easily accessible, nor as popular.

CARDWELL

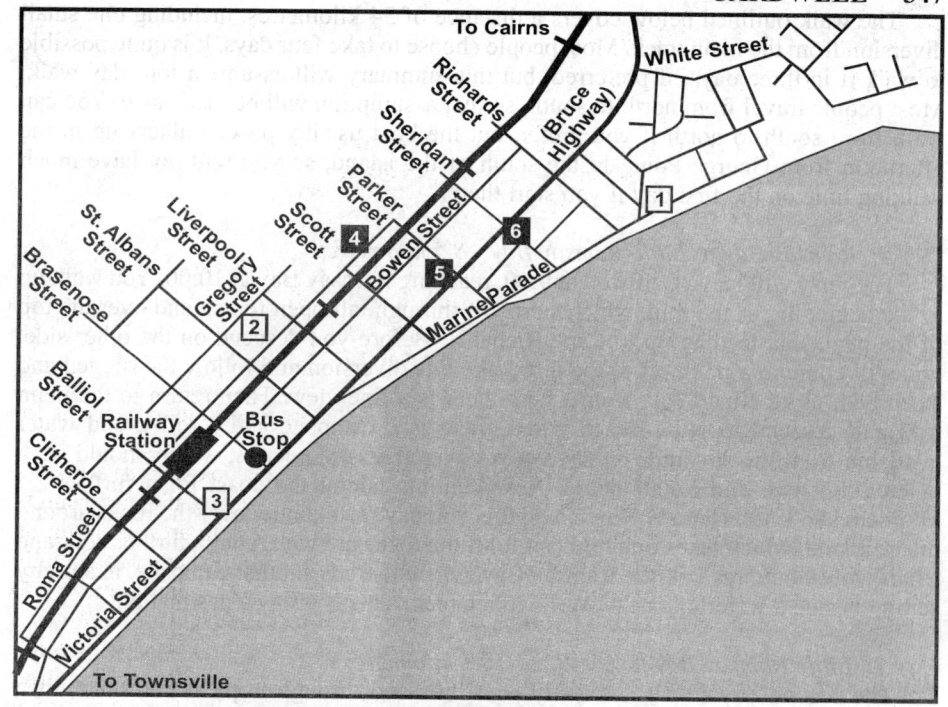

CARDWELL
Black numerals in white boxes indicate hotel accommodation
White numerals in black boxes indicate backpackers hostels

For those who want to attempt to walk the length of Hinchinbrook Island, thought by some to be one of the best hikes in the world, here is a summary of the route.

Hinchinbrook Walk (Thorsborne Trail)

First it is necessary to note that, although the walk itself is not overly strenuous, one needs to be properly equipped, with tent, fuel stove, enough food for at least five days, water container, sufficient clothing and good footwear. Hinchinbrook has one of the highest annual rainfalls in Australia, so be prepared to get damp. Also bear in mind that rain will slow the rate of progress, as the rocks are slippery when wet.

Unfortunately, this is not a cheap walk, because it is expensive to get to the island and back. Just to get to the north end of the trail you will be charged $59 for the ferry. The price to come back is negotiable, depending on how many people are to be picked up from the south end of the island. However, the time for the pick-up must be fixed in advance, and if you are not there, emergency services will be notified. If you prefer to walk back again to the north end of the trail, the return fare to the island will be $85.

A permit is required from the Queensland Department of the Environment (telephone 07-4066-8601), and only forty walkers are allowed on the island at a time, so you should book in advance, although you can pay on arrival in Cardwell. The fee is $4 per person per night. You must also arrange the boat transfers to and from the island in advance, because the service does not operate every day. For this, telephone 07-4066-8270.

QUEENSLAND

The walk outlined below covers a distance of 34 kilometres, including one small diversion from the main track. Most people choose to take four days. It is quite possible to walk it in three days, if preferred, but this summary will assume a four-day walk. Most people travel from north to south, so that assumption will be made also. You can walk from south to north if you prefer, but the boat usually picks walkers up in the afternoon from George Point, in the south of the island, so you will not have much walking time on the first day if you start there.

Day 1. Ramsay Bay to Little Ramsay Bay - 8.5 kilometres

The ferry will leave Cardwell at 9:00, reaching Ramsay Bay at 10:00. You walk up to the beginning of the trail, which starts off through tall open forest, and over the top of the peninsula leading up to Cape Richards. Before you descend on the other side, you will come to a track off to the left. Take this diversion and follow the rugged and steep path up to Nina Peak, from where there is a fine view. Then return to the main trail and descend to Nina Beach where there is a campsite and a toilet, and water available from the stream. You have now covered six kilometres, which should have taken about two and a half hours. Now continue along the coast for a further 2.5 kilometres to Little Ramsay Bay. To do this you have to clamber over the rocks around the headland, which takes time. Be careful if the rocks are wet. After a further hour and a half, you should reach Little Ramsay Bay, where there is another campsite, in a pretty setting beside a waterhole near Warrawilla Creek. This is today's destination.

Day 2. Little Ramsay Bay to Zoe Bay - 10.5 kilometres

The second day's walk is mostly over hills and through tropical rainforest, then around the edge of a mangrove swamp, and finally out onto the beach at Zoe Bay. Although the walk is a beautiful one, there may be a shock waiting when the beach is reached, for this is a very popular stop-off point for yachts. **Zoe Falls** is nearby, where you can swim in the beautiful and famous pool. This is the destination for the second day.

Day 3. Zoe Bay to Mulligan Falls - 7.5 kilometres

The trail today follows what will hopefully be the dry bed of a creek. If it is not dry, or if the rocks are slippery, it will become difficult. In any case, it involves quite a lot of hopping or clambering over boulders. You will reach Mulligan Falls after about four hours, and that is the end of today's walk. Here there is an attractive swimming hole, with plenty of friendly fish for company.

Day 4. Mulligan Falls to George Point - 7.5 kilometres

Today's walk is in two sections. The first part is again through tropical rainforest for about an hour and a half. Progress is slowed by the fact that five creeks have to be crossed in only 2.5 kilometres. Then you emerge onto the beach, and have five kilometres more to walk to George Point where the boat will pick you up for the return to Cardwell. The only difficulty here is the crossing of Mulligan Creek. This should be done near the low-tide point, and it is therefore necessary to wait for low tide to occur. When the pick-up time was arranged, this would have been taken into consideration.

The pick-up boat usually takes walkers back to Lucinda, which is only a short distance away on the mainland, not to Cardwell. A minibus then completes the return journey.

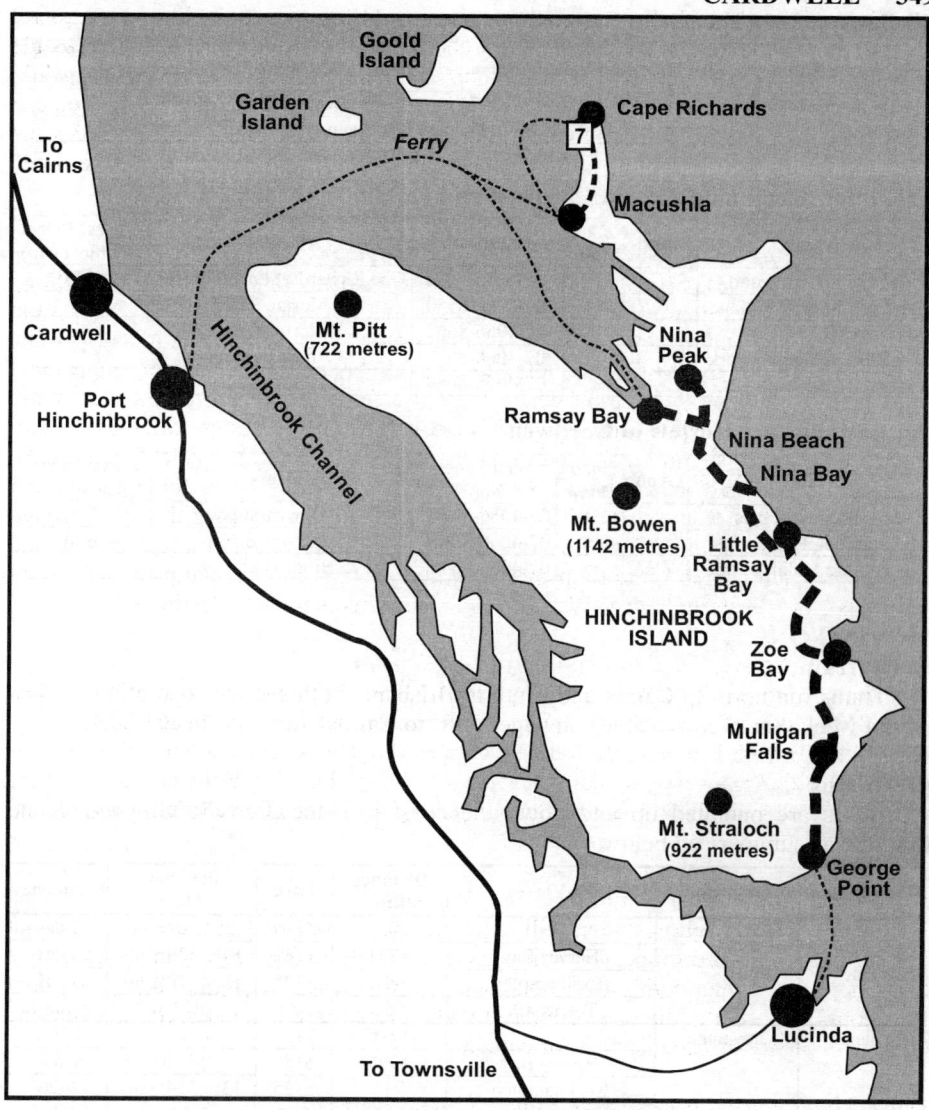

HINCHINBROOK ISLAND
Dashed lines show walking trails
Numerals indicate accommodation

ACCOMMODATION
(i) Hotel Accommodation in Ingham

Name	Stars	Telephone No.	Address	Lowest Price (Double/Twin)
Herbert Valley Motel		07-4776-1777	Bruce Highway, South Ingham	$60
East Ingham Hotel		07-4776-2377	49 Herbert Street	$40
Royal Hotel		07-4776-2024	46 Lannercost Street	$35

350 QUEENSLAND

(ii) Backpackers Hostels in Ingham

Name	Group	Telephone No.	Address	Lowest Price (Dormitory)
East Ingham Hotel		07-4776-2377	49 Herbert Street	$14
Royal Hotel		07-4776-2024	46 Lannercost Street	$12

(iii) Hotel Accommodation in Cardwell and on Hinchinbrook Island

Name	Stars	No. on Map	Telephone No.	Address	Lowest Price (Double/Twin)
Hitchinbrook Is. Resort		7	1-800-777-021	Cpe.Richards, Hinchinbrook	$545
Cardwell Sunrise Village		1	07-4066-8550	43a Marine Parade	$55
Marine Hotel		3	07-4066-8662	Victoria Street	$49
Kookaburra Holiday Park		5	07-4066-8648	175 Bruce Highway	$45
Cardwell Van Park		2	07-4066-8689	107 Roma Street	$40

(iv) Backpackers Hostels in Cardwell

Name	Group	No. on Map	Telephone No.	Address	Lowest Price (Dormitory)
Cardwell Backpackers		4	07-4066-8014	178 Bowen Street	$20
Hitchinbrook Hop		6	07-4066-8671	186 Victoria Street	$20
Kookaburra Holiday Park	YHA	5	07-4066-8648	175 Bruce Highway	$19

MOVING ON
(i) By Train

Trains run north to Cairns and south to Brisbane, both services operating on four days a week. See the timetables on pages 338 (to Cairns) and 364 (to Brisbane).

(ii) By Bus

Buses are operated up and down the coast by McCafferty's, Greyhound and Premier, as summarised below.

Destination	Operator	Via	Distance (km)	Fare	Journey Time	Frequency
Brisbane	McCafferty's		1716	$195	25 - 25¾ hrs	3/day
		Hervey Bay	1393	$180	19½ - 20¼ hrs	3/day
		Rockhampton	941	$125	13¼ - 13½ hrs	3/day
		Townsville	162	$37	2¼ hrs	4/day
Brisbane	Greyhound		1716	$195	25¾ - 26¼ hrs	2/day
		Hervey Bay	1393	$180	19¾ hrs	2/day
		Rockhampton	941	$125	13½ - 14½ hrs	2/day
		Townsville	162	$37	2¼ hrs	2/day
Brisbane	Premier		1716	$180	24¾ hrs	1/day
		Hervey Bay	1393	$164	19¼ hrs	1/day
		Rockhampton	941	$96	13 hrs	1/day
		Townsville	162	$21	2½ hrs	1/day
Cairns	McCafferty's		209	$31	2¾ - 3¼ hrs	4/day
Cairns	Greyhound		209	$31	2½ - 3 hrs	2/day
Cairns	Premier		209	$28	3½ hrs	1/day

MISSION BEACH AND DUNK ISLAND
Population 1,500

26 hrs 30 mins by bus from Brisbane

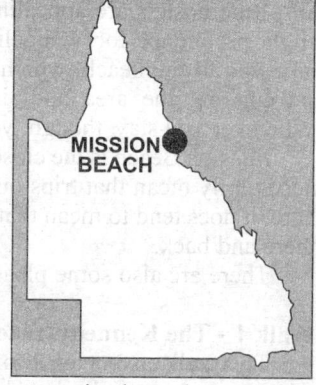

36 kilometres north of Cardwell, we reach **Tully**. Tully has the highest average annual rainfall of any town in Australia (4,252 millimetres). Recently, though, this record has not been given so much publicity, perhaps because it is felt that it does not improve the image of the locality for tourist purposes. Nearby **Mt. Bellenden Ker** (1,555 metres), however, is even wetter and hold the Australian records for the highest rainfall in a period of 24 hours - 1,140 millimetres, in two days - 1,947 millimetres, in three days - 2,517 millimetres, and in one year - 12,461 millimetres (in 2000).

Tully is another pleasant place, built around the sugar industry, with a large mill on the edge of town and narrow gauge sugar trains bringing their wares in season, which is June until November, but again it does not have quite enough to offer to entice most visitors to stay here. If you do, though, there are tours of the sugar mill every day at 10:00 during the crushing season.

However, most people continue to the quiet beachside attractions of Mission Beach, half an hour further on the bus. If you are travelling by train, Tully is as near as you will get to Mission Beach and here you will have to change to a bus. In addition to the services operated by long-distance bus companies, Mission Beach Bus and Coach runs buses from Tully to Mission Beach at 8:35, 14:55 and 16:10 on weekdays.

This area likes to be known as the **Cassowary Coast**, since this is the principal habitat of the third largest bird in the world. At Wongaling Beach you will see a cassowary standing beside the road and wonder just how big the largest (ostrich) and second largest (emu) must be if this is only third on the list.

Mission Beach is unusual in that not only is it in two parts, but the two parts are in different shires. Basically, there is Mission Beach and there is South Mission Beach, but then, to confuse matters, in between has been placed Wongaling Beach, while to the north of Mission Beach lies Bingil Bay. All of these places have accommodation and none of them is very large. As one might expect, the main town is at Mission Beach, named after an aboriginal mission formerly situated here (actually in South Mission Beach). McCafferty's and Greyhound buses call here and a boat service leaves from here for Dunk Island. There are three backpackers hostels.

Wongaling Beach has two more backpackers hostels, and this is the stopping point for the Premier bus. There is also a boat service from here to Dunk Island. It is, of course, a good idea to know where you are going when you arrive in this slightly confusing location, but if your destination is one of the backpackers hostels, you will find that most of the hostels meet most of the buses. If you are unlucky and need to get to another location, there is a bus service operated by Mission Beach Bus and Coach which runs almost every hour (i.e. hourly, but with two gaps during the day). The fare is $1.50 per section, and most rides would be two sections. There is also a $10 all-day ticket, but one is not likely to use it sufficiently for it to be good value.

Mission Beach is a beautiful little quiet place, well known amongst travellers, yet still with a feeling of being off the beaten track. There is no bad place to stay here, and all of the hostels are appealing, but if asked to recommend, the author would have a slight preference for Wongaling Beach. Just a five minute walk from anywhere will take you to the beach, which will be almost deserted, and there is tropical rainforest surrounding the area and, indeed, threatening to take over some of the hostels. Wherever you stay, though, you cannot really go wrong here.

Mission Beach is the closest town to the Great Barrier Reef. Although that does not necessarily mean that trips out to the reef for diving and snorkelling are cheaper from here, it does tend to mean that one spends more time at the reef and less time travelling there and back.

There are also some pleasant walks. Here are two, just to keep the reader busy.

Walk 1 - The Kennedy Track

This walk covers ten kilometres return, the return being by the same route, and will take about three and a half hours. It starts from the southern point of South Mission Beach, to get to which take the local bus to its southern terminal ($3 from Wongaling Beach, or $4.50 from Mission Beach).

This is a coastal walk along a well defined track, mostly in good condition. It is named after Edmund Kennedy, who began his expedition to Cape York from here in 1848. Walking south, you pass along Lovers' Beach and then round Lugger Bay. Here there is a lookout with good views. The path continues round Tam o'Shanter Point and on to Kennedy Bay. As you walk you will be able to distinguish the various islands lying out to sea, stretching right down to Hinchinbrook Island ahead to the south. There is a picnic area here and water is available. Continue along the path and you will come to mangroves growing in the salt water. Finally you will come to Hull Heads, where the track ends and you must return by the same route.

Walk 2 - Licuala Walking Trail

This walk is also approximately ten kilometres of undemanding terrain, which will take three to four hours. The problem is to get to and from the ends of the trail. If you have to walk, it will be necessary to add three to five more kilometres at each end, plus a one-way bus ride. However, if you are staying in a backpackers hostel, you can probably persuade the management to give you a ride to one end of the track when going to meet one of the morning buses.

The walk can be done in either direction, but let us travel from south to north. From the main road to Tully, there is a short unsealed road off to the right, which take. The nearest point on the local bus route is at the junction of South Mission Beach Road and Wheatley Road. From there it is about three kilometres to the start of the walk.

The walk starts at the end of the abovementioned unsealed road with the Rainforest Circuit. There is 536 metres of boardwalk through the Fan Palm Forest, with a complete canopy of licuala fan palms some ten to fifteen metres high. The forests at Mission Beach comprise almost half of the total remaining area of such forests in Australia. Notices give information about the trees and wildlife. The orange fruits of these palm trees are favourites of the cassowaries, which is one of the reasons why the birds are found in this particular area. The total length of this circuit is a little over one kilometre, but there is also a children's circuit of 350 metres. When these circuits have been completed, strike out northwards along the main track through lowland forest. It is 4.6 kilometres of easy walking from here to the El Arish Road (Mission Beach to Innisfail), but just a hundred metres before that road is reached, there is another track off to the left, which you should take. This track follows a disused road for part of the way, and leads back to the El Arish Road after 3.2 kilometres. It travels through similar forest.

Cross the El Arish Road and the path opposite is the Lacey Creek Circuit. This is a rainforest walk with informative notices along the way, covering a little over a kilometre. There is also a picnic area. When you have finished this, you will be back on the El Arish Road. Turn left and you have about five kilometres to walk to the nearest point for a local bus, at the junction of El Arish Road and Cassowary Drive (the main road to Tully), or about seven kilometres to the centre of Mission Beach.

You can, of course, curtail this walk, by taking the El Arish Road back to town when you first meet it after the 4.6 kilometres stretch from the Fan Palm Forest Circuit.

If you meet any cassowaries along the course of your walk, which is not at all impossible, the Visitor Centre would like to have details of the bird (name, address, telephone number, mother's maiden name, etc., but especially the place and time of the rendezvous).

Another reason for coming to Mission Beach is to visit **Dunk Island**, only five kilometres offshore. It can be reached by one of the regular boat services in about thirty minutes. Whether you start from Mission Beach or from Wongaling Beach, the return fare will be $30, as at the time of writing. Currently boats leave from Mission Beach at 8:45 and 10:30, and from Wongaling Beach

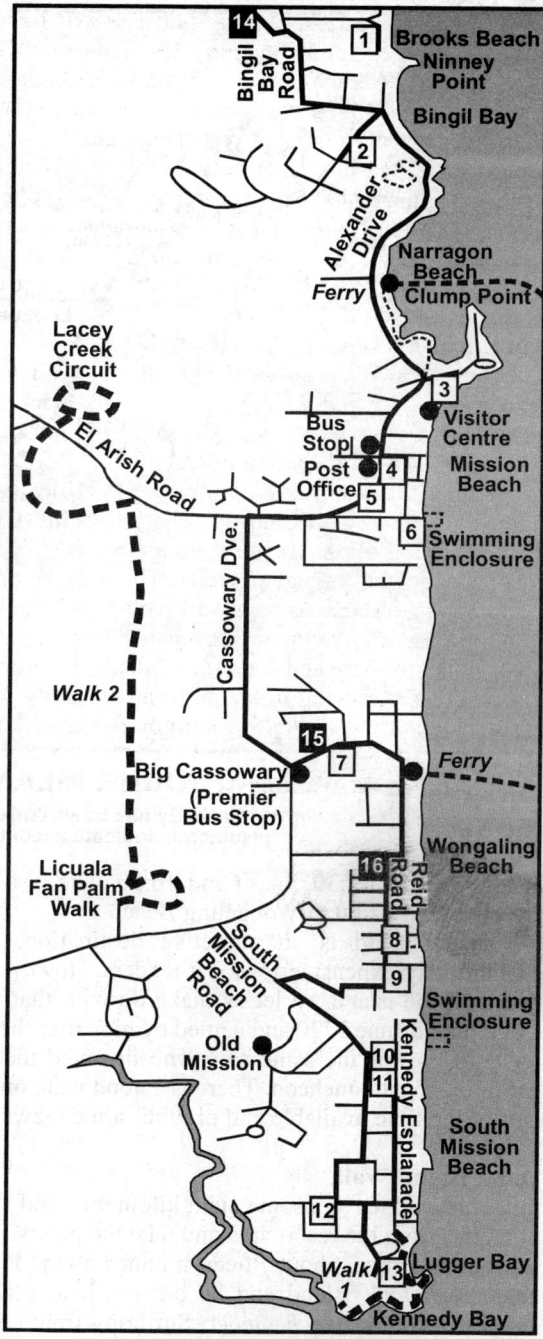

MISSION BEACH
Thicker line denotes local bus route
Dashed lines show walking tracks
Black numerals in white boxes indicate hotel accommodation
White numerals in black boxes indicate backpackers hostels

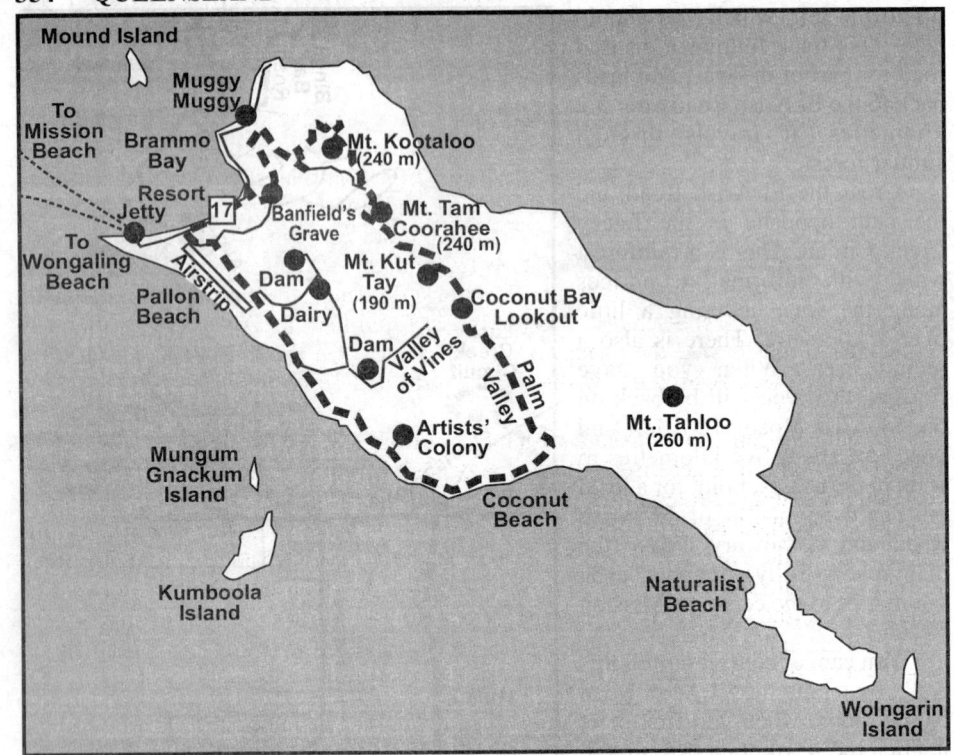

DUNK ISLAND
Dashed line shows Walking Tour
Numerals indicate accommodation

at 9:30, 11:00, 12:30, 14:30 and 16:30. The last boats back are at 16:00 to Mission Beach and at 17:00 to Wongaling Beach.

Dunk Island is an attractive destination, with a resort which is probably prohibitively expensive for most readers. However, a day trip will allow about seven hours on the island, so let us make do with that. The island was sighted by Captain Cook on 8th June 1770 and named by him after the Earl of Sandwich, George Montagu Dunk. This was the same man who invented the sandwich, by not wishing to cease gambling to eat luncheon. There is a good walk on the island, which will occupy about half of the time available and provide some views.

Dunk Island Walk

This walk covers some eight kilometres and should take three hours.

Start from the resort area and take the path signposted to the Swinging Bridge and Banfield's Grave, about fifteen minutes away. **E.J. Banfield** was the first European settler on Dunk Island and he did much to make the island famous by his book, *Confessions of a Beachcomber*. Suffering from consumption, he came to the island in 1897 to die, but so well did he recover in this climate that he lived here with his wife for another 25 years before succumbing in 1923 to a perforated ulcer at the age of seventy. By that time he had already become famous for his writings and for his

MISSION BEACH, DUNK ISLAND

activities as an amateur naturalist. He was buried here, in the grave which you see, by the crew of a passing ship to which his wife was able to signal. Her own ashes were added to the grave a decade later.

From this poignant spot, press on along the track which now climbs steeply up the hill to what is almost the highest point on the island, at the summit of Mt. Kootaloo. This vantage point is at 240 metres. In fact, in the south of the island, Mt. Tahloo reaches 260 metres, but that summit is not easily accessible.

From here it is mostly downhill, as you pass beside Mt. Tam Coorahee on your left, also at 240 metres, and Mt. Kut Tay on your right, at 190 metres, and then reach the viewpoint at Coconut Bay Lookout. The track descends through Palm Valley and eventually you reach the sea at Coconut Beach. From here it takes almost an hour to return on the flat beside the beach to the resort area. On the way you will pass the airstrip, which receives regular flights from Cairns and Townsville.

If you have come to the island with the boat from Mission Beach, you will be able to borrow snorkelling gear free, although a deposit is required, and will be able to use it at Muggy Muggy, fifteen minutes walk north of the resort. The vessel on which you will have travelled has an interesting history too. When the *Lake Illawarra* hit the bridge across the Derwent River in Hobart, Tasmania in 1975 (see page 856), three ferries were built hastily to provide a service across the river until the bridge could be rebuilt. This, the *Lawrence Kavanagh*, is one of those three. It was named after a famous Tasmanian bushranger. He was eventually hanged in 1846 for his part in the Norfolk Island Mutiny.

ACCOMMODATION
(i) Hotel Accommodation in Mission Beach and on Dunk Island

Name	Stars	No. on Map	Telephone No.	Address	Lowest Price (Double/Twin)
Horizon	4	13	07-4068-8154	Explorers Drive	$250
Dunk Island Resort		17	07-4058-8199	Dunk Island	$245
Eco Village		3	07-4068-7534	Clump Point Road	$160
Wongalinga Beach Apts.	4½	8	07-4068-8221	64 Reid Road	$160
Castaways on the Beach		6	07-4068-7444	Pacific Drive & Seaview St.	$150
Coral Trout		9	07-4068-9222	32 Reid Road	$150
Bingil Bay Resort		2	07-4068-7208	Cutten Street	$110
Mission Beach Resort		7	1-800-079-024	Wongaling Beach Road	$110
Montage Beach Apts.		12	07-4066-9251	42 Mitchell Street	$110
Mackays	3½	5	1-800-177-122	7 Porter Promenade	$85
Golden Sands Units		10	07-4068-9088	106 Kennedy Esplanade	$85
Del Rio Apartments		11	07-4068-8270	150 Kennedy Esplanade	$85
Ceud Mille Failte		4	07-4068-7144	23 Porter Promenade	$75
Sanctuary Retreat		1	1-800-777-012	Holt Street	$55

(ii) Backpackers Hostels in Mission Beach

Name	Group	No. on Map	Telephone No.	Address	Lowest Price (Dormitory)
Sanctuary Retreat	B&W	1	1800-777-012	Holt Street	$26
Treehouse Y.H.A.	YHA	14	07-4068-7137	Bingil Bay Road	$21
Scotty's Beach House	VIP	16	07-4068-8676	167 Reid Road	$20
Bingil Bay Resort	Nom	2	07-4068-7208	Cutten Street	$20
Backpackers Lodge	VIP/B&W	15	07-4068-8317	28 Wongaling Beach Road	$19

QUEENSLAND
MOVING ON

There are bus services to Brisbane, via Townsville and Rockhampton, operated by McCafferty's, Greyhound and Premier. The same companies operate to Cairns. Remember that McCafferty's and Greyhound stop in Mission Beach, while Premier stops in Wongaling Beach. There are also services to Cairns with Mission Beach Bus and Coach at 7:30, 11:00 and 17:30. Although these services are more expensive, the buses will pick you up from your accommodation in Mission Beach and deliver you to your accommodation in Cairns, pick up time being up to half an hour earlier than the times stated above. They also run to Cairns Airport ($33) and to the northern beaches of Cairns ($38).

If you want to catch a train south, departures from Tully are at 11:53 on Mondays, Tuesdays, Thursdays and Saturdays (see timetable on page 364). The best connexion for this is offered by the Premier bus service at 10:15.

Bus Services from Mission Beach

Destination	Operator	Via	Distance (km)	Fare	Journey Time	Frequency
Brisbane	McCafferty's		1785	$207	26¾ - 27 hrs	2/day
		Hervey Bay	1462	$191	21 - 21¼ hrs	2/day
		Rockhampton	1010	$142	15 - 15¼ hrs	2/day
		Townsville	231	$53	3¾ - 4 hrs	3/day
Brisbane	Greyhound		1785	$207	27½ hrs	1/day
		Hervey Bay	1462	$191	21½ hrs	1/day
		Rockhampton	1010	$142	15 hrs	1/day
		Townsville	231	$53	3¾ hrs	1/day
Brisbane	Premier		1785	$185	25½ hrs	1/day
		Hervey Bay	1462	$163	20 hrs	1/day
		Rockhampton	1010	$103	13¾ hrs	1/day
		Townsville	231	$43	3¼ hrs	1/day
Cairns	McCafferty's		140	$18	2¼ hrs	3/day
Cairns	Greyhound		140	$18	2¼ hrs	1/day
Cairns	Premier		140	$16	2 hrs	1/day
Cairns	Mission Beach		140	$30.50	2¼ hrs	3/day

CAIRNS
Population 120,000

31 hrs 30 mins by train from Brisbane
28 hrs 30 mins by bus from Brisbane

One of the most popular of all Australian destinations is Cairns. What used to be a quiet seaside town a few years ago has now grown into a major tourist destination. Such growth brings both advantages and disadvantages. It is nostalgic to think of Cairns as it used to be, a quiet backwater basking in the sun and sustaining a leisurely pace of life. However, the development has come, and there is no denying that it has merits. The city has become affluent almost beyond recognition. It now

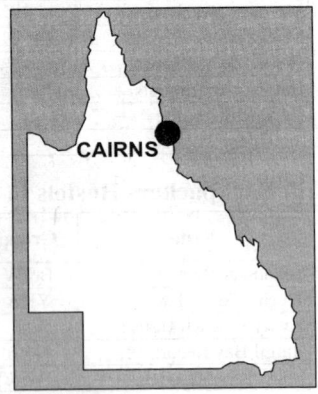

has a reliable and efficient bus service. It has an international airport receiving regular flights from all over the world, the only non-capital city in Australia with that honour. It has a surfeit of accommodation, and it has developed its beaches and even decided to build a new one in the heart of the city. Yet it is still a city of manageable size, one that you can walk around and soon get to know intimately.

There are three points at which you might arrive in Cairns. Let us start with the airport, since those arriving there are most likely to be new to Australia and to need assistance. You will not need much help, however. There is a board in the airport terminal with advertisements for all types of accommodation on it. Select what appeals to you, pick up the free telephone and dial. Most of the backpackers hostels, of which there are an impressive number, will come and collect you from the airport. It is not very far from the city. If not, there is an airport bus for $8. If you really want to save money, you can walk the three kilometres to the airport entrance and take a public bus from there into the city centre for $2.50. Buses are frequent. You can also purchase a 24-hour ticket for the buses. One which covers you from the city centre as far as the airport entrance costs $6.50, and one which covers a wider area, including the beaches, costs $10. If you do not want to go into Cairns at all, there are direct buses from the airport to Mission Beach in the south and to Port Douglas in the north.

Just outside the airport terminal, you will see a nostalgic Bush Pilots DC-3 on a plinth. This particular aircraft is one which once had King George VI as a passenger. The author lived for a while at a settlement served by Bush Pilots with DC-3 aircraft at busy times and with Cessnas at slacker periods and cannot resist going to admire this beautiful piece of machinery whenever at Cairns Airport. Alas, "Bushies" is no more, and DC-3s are no longer in regular service here, but this aircraft evokes memories of outback aviation and pioneering spirits.

If you are arriving by train, you will find the railway station in the heart of the town in the midst of a shopping centre. Actually, the shopping centre is on the site of the old station, while the station is newly built to the west of its original location. The opening of an exit to the west has had a surprising effect on trade there and you will now find a little colony of backpackers hostels in converted old houses just across the road. These are all good places to stay, and they can be reached in just two or three minutes by crossing the bridge over the tracks. They are popular, however, so it would be wise to book in advance if these are your choice, although there is plenty of accommodation in Cairns, so you will find a bed somewhere, even if not here.

In the last part of your journey north, you will have passed some charming North Queensland railway stations, some resembling tropical gardens with their impressive platform foliage. Today you will have come through Tully, recently renovated, and **Innisfail**, another of those towns in which one wants to stay, but feels that it is not quite high enough on the list of priorities. There is accommodation there, though, including backpackers hostels, if you do have time, and it is close to some good walks. The highest peak in Queensland, **Mt. Bartle Frere** (1,622 metres), was to your left as you continued north of Innisfail through **Babinda**. Then, on your approach to Cairns, you will have noted the **Sikh Temple** resplendent against the mountain backdrop and realised that Cairns really is a cosmopolitan city. A little time here will reinforce that impression.

At first, maybe, you will think that Cairns is the end of this pretty railway line, but it is not, and a further treat is in store if you venture north on one of the daily trains to Kuranda, of which more on page 366.

The other arrival possibility is, of course, by bus. Buses arrive at Trinity Wharf, also conveniently located and walking distance from the centre of the city. However, if you are intending to stay at a backpackers hostel, you will find a row of minibuses waiting for you and no walking will be necessary. There will always be a bed available somewhere in Cairns, as there is so much accommodation, but if you want to stay at a particular hostel, it is a good idea to telephone ahead. Many of the hostels have free telephone numbers.

Cairns tends to be popular as a base for exploration as well as for the merits of the city itself. There are trips to the Great Barrier Reef, to the Atherton Tablelands and to the Daintree Rainforest area. The reader will readily find out about these on arrival and decide in which he wishes to participate. Backpackers hostels have plenty of information, operate some excursions themselves, and can obtain discount prices for their guests. The Visitor Information Centre also has many choices, and the city is packed with travel agents. This section, therefore, will concentrate on information concerning Cairns itself and shorter trips from here.

The most interesting street in Cairns is the **Esplanade**, with the sea on one side and a row of restaurants, hotels and backpackers lodges on the other. This area comes to life in the evenings, especially with the **Night Market** now held here. The only aspect which was not quite as it should have been was that there was no beach. The Esplanade ended with a wall and mud flats below, not quite the romantic image which the city wished to propagate. The solution, it seemed, was evident and simple - construct a beach. And so it has been done. A grassy area has been created as an extension to the Esplanade and the beach put in place right in the middle of the city. One wonders now what is to prevent nature from washing that beach away, but such a possibility must have been considered, so presumably all will be well. When you next have $27 million to spare, you will know what to do with it.

Next to the New Esplanade Project is the **Pier Marketplace**, a combination of marina and shopping area which was one of the past wonders of Cairns. It includes **Undersea World**, a living reef aquarium. Just round the corner is the **Casino**, with the Tour Boat Terminals behind, and then the Cruise Liners Terminal, behind the Transit Centre. A little further along Wharf Street, you will come to the new Convention Centre and Concert Hall.

Shields Street is also a busy and popular place. The central area is for pedestrians only, and this effectively blocks off the centre of Lake Street too, so that the section to the south is used as the local bus terminal and that to the north as a taxi rank. At night there are pubs and clubs thriving here and the area is lively, attracting crowds of young visitors.

There is a day market off Sheridan Street between Spence Street and Shields Street, also accessible from Grafton Street.

The main city shopping centre has become **Cairns Central**, next to the railway station, where there are all types of shops including supermarkets and a department store. There are other shopping complexes further out of the city.

There are certain areas of the city where accommodation lies thickest. For example, there are clusters of backpackers hostels around the station, along the Esplanade and to the north of the city, but there is no need to be unduly concerned about location. Wherever you stay here, you will be within walking distance of the city centre.

Other places outside the central area, but well worth a visit, include the following.

CAIRNS 359

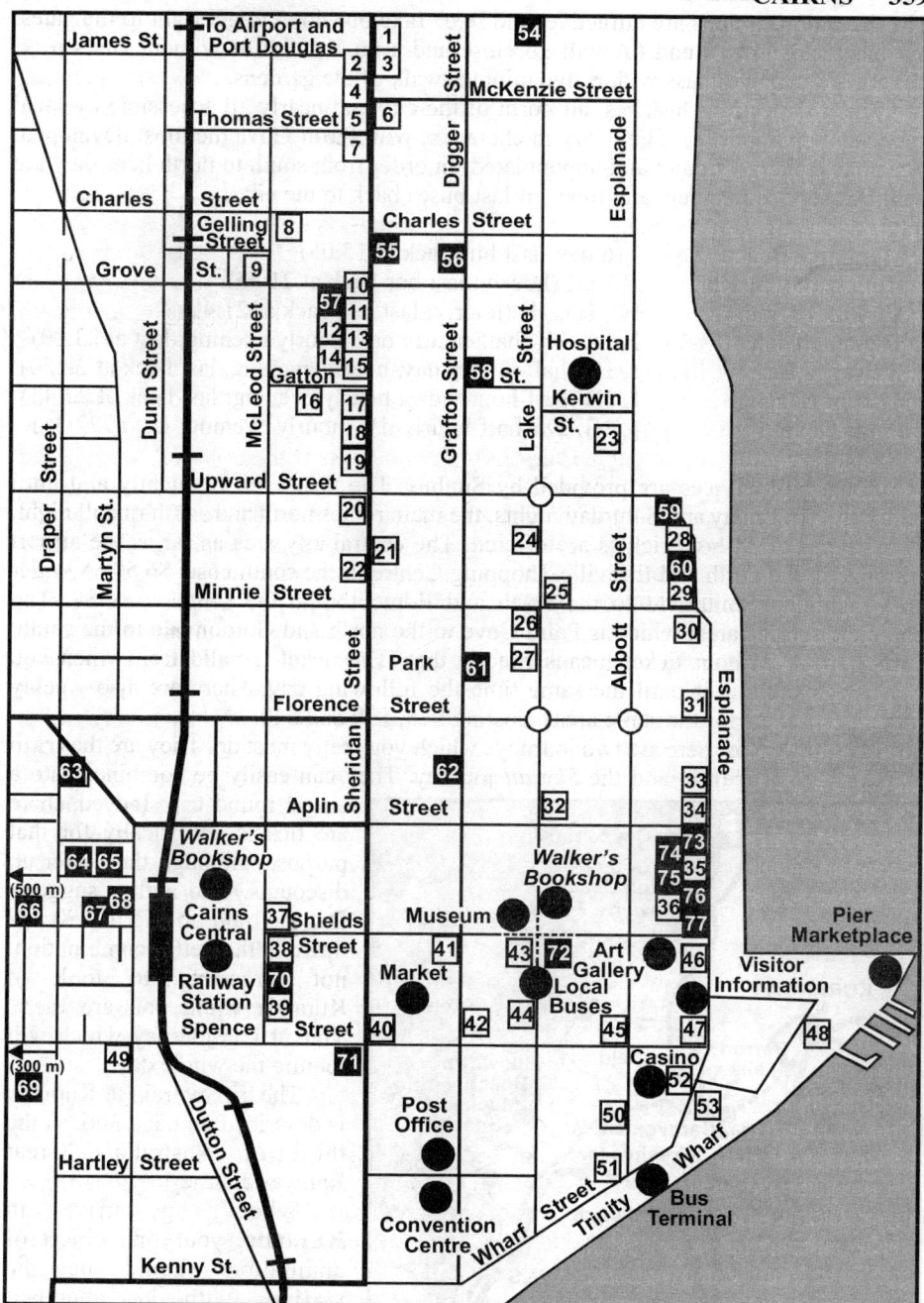

CAIRNS
Black numerals in white boxes indicate hotel accommodation
White numerals in black boxes indicate backpackers hostels

360 QUEENSLAND

The **Botanic Gardens** are attractive, and free. Take bus no. 7 to get right to the gates, but buses nos. 5A, 6 and 6A will go close and a no. 1, with or without any suffix, travelling north will pass within five minutes walk of the gardens.

There are various beaches, all north of the city and nearly all accessible by local bus (see map opposite). They vary in character, with **Palm Cove** the most developed, but all are relatively quiet and unpopulated. In order from south to north here they are with bus service numbers and times of last buses back to the city:

Machan's Beach	7 (6/day; last bus back at 15:05)
Holloway's Beach	1C, 1H (hourly; last bus back at 21:55)
Yorkey's Knob	1C, 1D, 1H (hourly; last bus back at 21:40)
Trinity Beach	1, 1A, 2X (half-hourly day, hourly evening; last at 23:00)
Kewarra Beach	1, 1A (half-hourly day, hourly evening; last back at 22:50)
Clifton Beach	1, 1B (half-hourly day, hourly evening; last back at 22:43)
Palm Cove	1, 1B, 2X (half-hourly day, hourly evening; last at 22:38)

Local bus services are provided by Sunbus. The buses run frequently and until quite late. On Friday and Saturday nights, the main routes north and south run all night. Three types of 24-hour tickets are offered. The central city area as far as the airport entrance in the north and Earlville Shopping Centre in the south costs $6.50. A wider area including Smithfield to the north and Edmonton to the south costs $8. The complete service area, which is Palm Cove to the north and Gordonvale to the south, costs $10. A 24-hour ticket means exactly that. The ticket is valid from when you purchase it until the same time the following day. There are also weekly tickets for the same areas, costing $25, $30 and $40.

Now here are two journeys which you really must do. They are the **train to Kuranda** and the *Skyrail* journey. They can easily be combined into a single round trip. Indeed, there are tickets specifically for that purpose, although they offer no discounts. The author suggests that the train up and the *Skyrail* down is the better combination, not forgetting to look at Kuranda while you are there. Thus it is a journey which will require the whole day.

The trip by train to Kuranda is described on page 366, as the third of Australia's Great Railway Journeys.

When you arrive in **Kuranda**, your first object of admiration should be the **station**, with its abundant foliage almost obscuring its reason for existence. Your old-fashioned train parked there

CAIRNS VICINITY
Dashed line represents *Skyrail*

completes an harmonious picture. You should look around this town. Its difference in altitude, together with its much smaller size, gives it a completely different feeling from its city neighbour. Take a free bus up to the markets (since it is uphill) and walk back later. In the market area you can also find **Birdworld** with many exotic species of Australian and overseas birds, including the cassowary, in case you failed to meet one at Mission Beach. You can also find there a **Butterfly Sanctuary**, the largest in Australia, with some 2,000 butterflies. To return to the station, you have a choice of three routes (see map on page 362): the river route, the rainforest route, or the walk through town. If you have sufficient time, you can try all three. Follow the river route back to Arara Street, turn left into Meeroo Street. Left into Thongon Street and you will come, after a while, to the rainforest route ('jungle walk') on your right. Follow this to Coondoo Street, where turn right and walk back down through the town to the railway station, or to the *Skyrail* station.

Having gone up by train, you should return by *Skyrail*. As mentioned above, there are special tickets for this purpose, but since they offer no discount, there is little point in purchasing one and curtailing your options. Just buy a single ticket for each service. The *Skyrail* costs the same as the train: $35 one way. The return fare is $50. The journey is much shorter than the railway trip. It is 7.5 kilometres and, although expensive, it is a

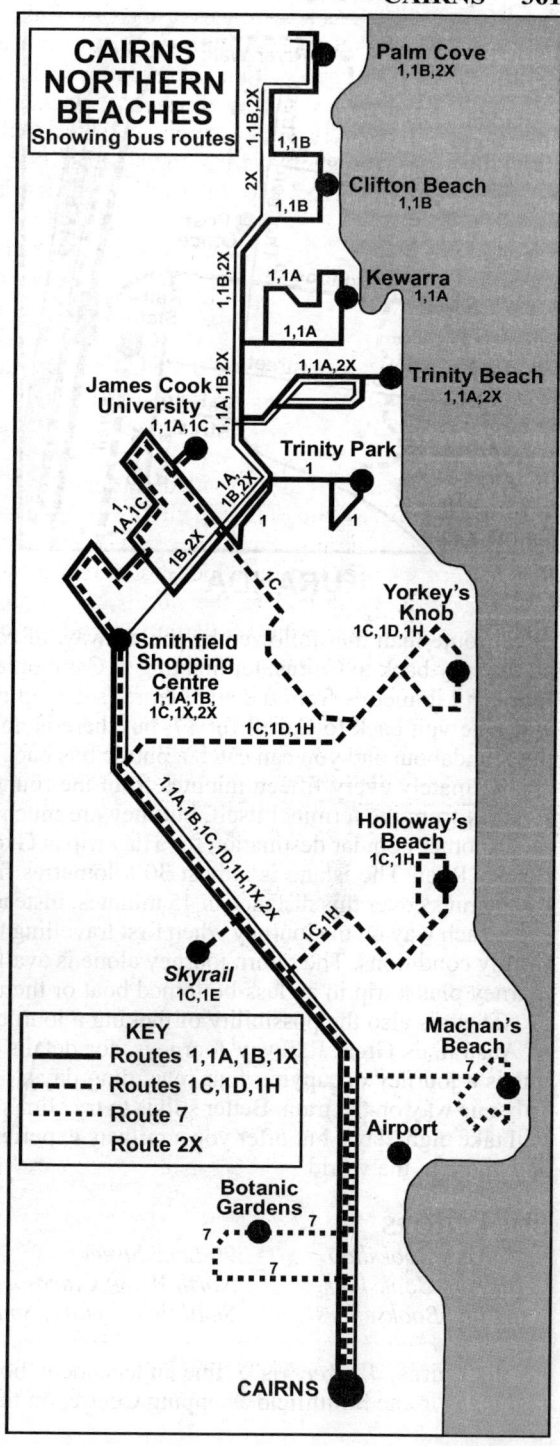

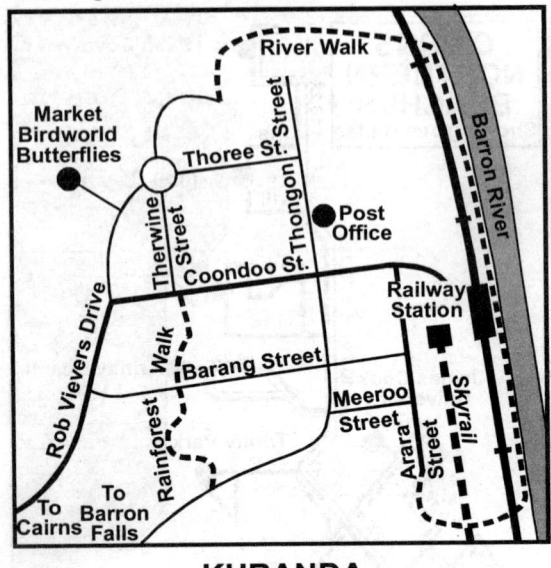

KURANDA

great experience. The recently constructed ropeway carries you above the treetops of the dense rainforest here, causing no disturbance to it. The journey itself takes about 45 minutes, but there are two places on the way at which to stop. The first is **Barron Falls Station**, where walkways lead to three lookouts over the Barron River, the Barron Gorge and Barron Falls. Located there is also the **Rainforest Interpretive Centre**. Since you have already paid plenty for this journey, there is no extra charge for this museum. The route then continues to **Red Peak Station**, where a twenty-minute guided tour of the rainforest environment is available. This is a much more direct route than that followed by the railway, of course, and the *Skyrail* does not run all the way back to Cairns, terminating at Caravonica, at the foot of the hills still some fourteen kilometres from the city centre (see map on page 360). There is a bus which will take you back to Cairns for $7, but there is no need for that. Walk 200 metres to the roundabout and you can catch a public bus back for half the price. Services operate approximately every fifteen minutes from the roundabout. There are some public bus services from the terminal itself, but they are much less frequent.

Another popular destination for a day trip is **Green Island**, a coral cay on the Great Barrier Reef. The island is almost 30 kilometres from Cairns, but nowadays modern catamarans cover this distance in 45 minutes, instead of the two hours which the author spent each way on the journey when first travelling there many years ago in particularly stormy conditions. The return journey alone is available for $45, but better value is the journey plus a trip in a glass-bottomed boat or the use of snorkelling gear for $50.

There is also the possibility of making a journey on the *Savannahlander*, another of Australia's Great Railway Journeys, for details of which, see page 368. However, this is a journey occupying four rewarding days, or three days if you decide to travel only one way on the train. Better still is to try 'Jim's Tour', outlined on page 370, which will take eight days, but offer you a railway experience for which you will find no rival anywhere in the world.

BOOKSHOPS

Walkers Bookshop   96 Lake Street
Walkers Bookshop   North Wing, Cairns Central
Collins Booksellers   Smithfield Centre, Smithfield

In Cairns, *Walkers* is a fine independent bookstore with two branches, while *Collins* is in the Smithfield Shopping Centre, on the way to the Northern Beaches.

CAIRNS 363

ACCOMMODATION
(i) Hotel Accommodation in Cairns

Name	Stars	No. on Map	Telephone No.	Address	Lowest Price (Double/Twin)
Radisson Plaza	5	48	07-4031-1411	Pier Point Road	$385
Reef Hotel Casino Sofitel	5	52	07-4030-8888	35 Wharf Street	$310
Hilton	5	53	07-4050-2000	Wharf Street	$260
Pacific International Hotel	4	47	1-800-079-001	Esplanade & Spence Streets	$245
Cairns International	5	50	07-4031-1300	17 Abbott Street	$225
Outrigger Cairns Resort		46	07-4046-4144	53 Esplanade	$170
Matson Resort	4½	23	07-4031-2211	Esplanade & Kerwin Street	$165
Oasis Resort	5	32	07-4080-1888	122 Lake Street	$165
Tradewinds Esplanade	4	30	07-4053-0331	137 Esplanade	$160
Holiday Inn	4	31	07-4050-6030	Esplanade & Florence Street	$160
Rydges Plaza Cairns	4	42	07-4041-1022	Grafton & Spence Streets	$160
Inn Cairns	4½	44	07-4041-2350	71 Lake Street	$160
Koala Court	4	9	1-800-633-261	147 McLeod Street	$155
Tuna Towers	3½	29	1-800-117-787	145 Esplanade	$150
Cairns Aquarius		33	07-4051-8444	107 Esplanade	$150
All Seasons Esplanade	3½	34	07-4051-2311	Esplanade & Aplin Street	$150
Sunshine Tower	3½	21	1-800-079-074	136 Sheridan Street	$140
Mid City Suites	4½	39	07-4051-5050	6 McLeod Street	$140
Hide's Hotel / Motel	3	43	1-800-079-266	Shields & Lake Streets	$135
Royal Harb. Tradewinds	4	36	07-4080-8888	73 Esplanade	$125
Club Crocodile	3½	24	07-4051-4988	183 Lake Street	$110
Flying Horseshoe Motel	3½	2	1-800-814-171	281 Sheridan Street	$105
Fig Tree Lodge	4	7	07-4041-0000	253 Sheridan Street	$99
Cairns Holiday Lodge	3	5	07-4051-4611	259 Sheridan Street	$95
Grosvenor	4½	8	1-800-629-179	Grove & McLeod Streets	$95
Queen's Court	3	19	1-800-240-052	167 Sheridan Street	$95
Rainbow Palms		20	07-4051-3555	157 Sheridan Street	$90
Cascade Gardens	3½	26	07-4051-8000	175 Lake Street	$90
Great Northern Hotel		45	07-4051-5966	69 Abbott Street	$90
Villa Shangri-La		3	07-4052-1333	288 Sheridan Street	$85
All Round Motel	3½	4	1-800-818-626	263 Sheridan Street	$85
Oasis Inn	3	6	07-4051-8111	276 Sheridan Street	$85
Silver Palm Guest House		28	07-4031-6099	153 Esplanade	$85
Sunray Guest House		25	07-4051-3370	4 Minnie Street	$80
Tropic Towers	4½	1	07-4031-3955	294 Sheridan Street	$75
A-1 Motel		10	07-4051-4499	211 Sheridan Street	$75
Concord		17	07-4031-4522	183 Sheridan Street	$75
High Chaparral	3	11	07-4051-7155	195 Sheridan Street	$70
Rainbow Inn		18	07-4051-1022	179 Sheridan Street	$70
Cairns Motor Inn		15	07-4051-5166	187 Sheridan Street	$65
Pacific Cay		12	07-4051-0151	193 Sheridan Street	$60
Poinsettia Motel	2	27	07-4051-2144	169 Lake Street	$60
Crown Hotel		41	07-4051-1488	35 Shields Street	$60
Arcadia	3	14	07-4051-0908	189 Sheridan Street	$55
Adobe Motel		13	07-4051-5511	191 Sheridan Street	$50
Inn the Tropics		22	07-4031-1088	141 Sheridan Street	$50
Bellview		35	07-4031-4377	85 Esplanade	$50
Railway Hotel		37	07-4051-1700	McLeod Street	$50
Grand Hotel		38	07-4051-1007	34 McLeod Street	$50
Barrier Reef Hotel		51	07-4051-4245	33 Wharf Street	$50
Grey Whale Anchor Inn		16	07-4051-9249	19 Gatton Street	$45
Underdog Hotel	2	40	07-4051-2490	Spence & Sheridan Streets	$40
Cape York Hotel		49	07-4051-2008	147 Bunda Street	$40

QUEENSLAND
(ii) Backpackers Hostels in Cairns

Name	Group	No. on Map	Telephone No.	Address	Lowest Price (Dormitory)
Central Y.H.A.	YHA	70	07-4051-0772	20 McLeod Street	$25
Jimmy's		75	07-4031-4411	83 Esplanade	$25
Cairns Backpackers Inn	VIP	58	1800-681-889	242 Grafton Street	$24
Tropic Days	B&W	66	07-4041-1521	26 Bunting Street	$24
Global Palace		72	07-4031-7921	86 Lake Street	$24
Bel-Air Backpackers		59	07-4031-4790	155 Esplanade	$22
Caravella 149 Backpackers	VIP	60	1800-814-019	149 Esplanade	$22
Traveller's Oasis		67	1800-621-353	8 Scott Street	$22
Gecko		68	07-4031-1344	187 Bunda Street	$22
Hostel 89		74	07-4031-7477	89 Esplanade	$22
Caravella 77 Backpackers	VIP	76	1800-112-159	77 Esplanade	$22
Underdog Hotel		40	07-4051-2490	Spence & Sheridan Streets	$21
Serpent Hostel	Nom	54	1800-737-536	341 Lake Street	$21
Ryan's Rest	B&W	64	07-4051-4734	18 Terminus Street	$21
Y.H.A. Esplanade	YHA	73	07-4031-1919	93 Esplanade	$21
Cairns International Hostel	VIP	77	07-4031-1545	67 Esplanade	$21
Calypso Inn	VIP	56	1800-815-628	5 Digger Street	$20
Dreamtime	B&W	65	07-4031-6753	4 Terminus Street	$20
Up Top Down Under		69	07-4051-3636	164 Spence Street	$20
Bellview Guest House		35	07-4031-4377	85 Esplanade	$19
Captain Cook Backpackers	VIP	55	1800-243-512	204 Sheridan Street	$19
Parkview Backpackers	VIP	61	1800-652-215	174 Grafton Street	$19
Tracks Backpackers		62	07-4031-1474	149 Grafton Street	$19
Billabong Backpackers		71	07-4051-6946	69 Spence Street	$19
Castaways Backpackers	VIP	57	1800-351-115	207 Sheridan Street	$18
Gone Walkabout	B&W	63	07-4051-6160	274 Draper Street	$18
Utopia Backpackers	Nom		1800-354-599	702 Bruce Highway	$22
Palm Cove Retreat			07-4055-3630	Captain Cook Hwy, Palm Cove	$14

MOVING ON
(i) By Train

Trains run back to Brisbane on Mondays, Tuesdays, Thursdays and Saturdays. The Tuesday train is the *Queenslander*, which carries no economy sleeping accommodation - just first class sleepers and economy seats. On Mondays, Thursdays and Saturdays, the *Sunlander* operates, with economy seats and sleepers plus first class sleepers. The timetable is shown to the right.

As mentioned above, the train north to Kuranda runs at least once every day, and usually twice, while the *Savannahlander* leaves Cairns on Wednesday mornings. Timetables are shown on the next page.

Forsayth, Kuranda and Cairns to Brisbane

Days of Departure	Not Sat	Daily	F	Sat	M, Tu, Th, Sat
Forsayth			0745		
Einasleigh			1115		
Mt. Surprise			1300	0815	
Almaden				1210	
Mareeba				1600	
Kuranda	1400	1530		1702	
Cairns	**1545**	**1715**		**1840**	**0835**
Innisfail					1040
Tully					1153
Townsville					1610
Bowen					1930
Proserpine					2022
Mackay					2242
Rockhampton					0500
Gladstone					0643
Bundaberg					0925
Maryborough W					1035
Gympie North					1224
Brisbane					1555
Days of Arrival					Sun,Tu, W, F

(ii) By Bus

McCafferty's, Greyhound and Premier all run bus services down to Brisbane, taking approximately 29 hours. In addition, there are services to Mission Beach operated by Mission Beach Bus and Coach. These will collect passengers from their accommodation if booked in advance. Services north to Port Douglas, Cape Tribulation and Cooktown are operated by Coral Coaches. There are two routes to Cooktown. The more interesting one is along the coast, but the quicker is the inland route. A round trip, up by one route and back by the other, is offered for $120 with one stop in each direction. Coral Coaches also operates a bus three days a week west to Karumba, on the Gulf of Carpentaria, via Mt. Surprise, Georgetown, Croydon and Normanton. This service is useful for making connexions with one-way trips on the *Savannahlander* and *Gulflander* trains. To the Atherton Tablelands, Whitecar Coaches operates services to Kuranda, Mareeba, Atherton, Herberton and Ravenshoe.

Trains from Cairns to Kuranda and Forsayth

Days of Departure	W	Th	Daily	Not Sat
Cairns	0630		0830	0930
Kuranda	0805		1015	1115
Mareeba	0925			
Almaden	1300	0800		
Mt. Surprise		1215		
Einasleigh		1445		
Forsayth		1745		

Destination	Operator	Via	Distance (km)	Fare	Journey Time	Frequency
Brisbane	McCafferty's		1923	$212	28¼ - 29 hrs	3/day
		Hervey Bay	1600	$195	23 - 23½ hrs	3/day
		Rockhampton	1148	$142	15¾ - 17¼ hrs	3/day
		Townsville	369	$57	4¾ - 6¼ hrs	4/day
Brisbane	Greyhound		1923	$212	28¾ - 29¼ hrs	2/day
		Hervey Bay	1600	$195	23¼ hrs	2/day
		Rockhampton	1148	$142	17 - 17¼ hrs	2/day
		Townsville	369	$57	4¾ - 5¾ hrs	2/day
Brisbane	Premier		1923	$193	28¾ hrs	1/day
		Hervey Bay	1600	$184	22¾ hrs	1/day
		Rockhampton	1148	$130	6 hrs	1/day
		Townsville	369	$51	3¼ hrs	1/day
Mission Bch.	Mission Beach		140	$30.50	2¼ hrs	3/day
Cooktown	Coral Coaches		297	$71	5½ - 8 hrs	5/week
		Cape Tribulation	159	$41	4 - 4¼ hrs	2/day
		Port Douglas	70	$25	1½ hrs	8/day
Karumba	Coral Coaches		717	$170.50	11½ hrs	3/week
		Normanton	648	$157	10½ hrs	3/week
Ravenshoe	Whitecar		117	$34.40	2½ - 2¾ hrs	2/day
		Atherton	87	$25	1¾ hrs	3/day

ANECDOTE

Departing from Cairns for Papua New Guinea some years ago, I enquired at the railway station as to whether I could travel to the airport by train. "Well, we don't usually stop at the airport," I was told, "But ask the driver and if he says all right, you can go." The driver agreed, so I bought my ticket and got on the train. To my surprise, we passed through the Airport Station without stopping, and then pulled up right across the entrance road, at the closest possible point to the buildings, halting all traffic. I stepped down and felt majestic as I strode with my backpack the short distance to the terminal watched by the surprised eyes of many stationary motorists.

GREAT RAILWAY JOURNEYS

If you enjoyed travelling up from Brisbane to Cairns by train, you will be in a mood of anticipation upon hearing that there is better to come. If you did not enjoy the journey up by train, that means either that you did not take the train, which was your mistake, or that you omitted to break the journey once or twice along the way, and therefore grew too tired of the long ride. In either case, take the train for this short trip to prove that beautiful traditional railway journeys still exist.

Queensland Railways likes to describe the journey from Cairns to Kuranda as a 34-kilometre-long picture postcard. It is an exaggeration, of course, but the fact is that many visitors to Australia travel this one rail journey and no other, so it has obviously achieved something of a reputation. It is a route which must rank amongst the world's best short journeys and is a ride which you will always remember.

Construction of this route was commenced in 1882, but Kuranda Station was not opened until 1891. The builders had to surmount the tremendous challenge of rising from sea level to an elevation of 328 metres through rugged, inhospitable and thickly forested terrain. It was a great engineering achievement, necessitating the construction of fifteen tunnels and 37 bridges and viaducts. It is a total contrast to all that has gone before on the railway up from Brisbane. Just think, in those 1,681 kilometres, when did you last see a tunnel? (Answer: between Mooloolah and Eudlo, approximately 1,600 kilometres south of Cairns.)

The train starts out from Cairns on the flat through the residential parts of the city, stopping at Freshwater, if required, and Redlynch. This part of the journey, although pretty, gives little hint of what is to follow. Now we start to climb, and this is no ordinary climb, for there was nowhere to put a railway here. It follows the creek bed, twisting and turning with its host, but even here ledges have had to be carved to support the track. Where such engineering works proved impossible, tunnels were constructed, and soon we start to negotiate them. The original plan incorporated nineteen tunnels, but in the end it was decided to convert four of them into deep cuttings, through which we shall pass. Fifteen tunnels remain. They vary in length between 60 metres and 430 metres and all have a gradient of approximately one in sixty. They were all opened to traffic on 15th June 1891.

Particularly in the Wet Season, between December and April, this area receives heavy rainfall, which not only hampered construction of the line, but caused landslides, destroying work already completed and causing several fatal accidents. The difficulties of working in such conditions can be imagined as we crawl up the forested slopes and thread our way through the tunnels. Several times we obtain panoramic views back over the foothills to the

3. THE KURANDA SCENIC RAILWAY
CAIRNS TO KURANDA

coastal plain and the Coral Sea glistening beyond.

Stoney Creek station comes at approximately the mid-point of the climb. If one had to pick a single highlight of this journey, it would be the lofty curving viaduct which carries the railway in front of Stoney Creek Falls. It is the scene most often displayed on leaflets advertising this service and, during the construction of the railway, it was the spot chosen for a banquet held in celebration of the visit of the Governor in April 1890. It is said that the location chosen also eliminated the need for speeches, since nothing could be heard above the noise of the waterfall.

On the section of line between Stoney Creek and Barron Falls we pass through the last two tunnels, the second of which is by far the longest on the line, at 430 metres. If precedent is followed, the train will be stopped at Barron Falls Station, a signal passed and water allowed to escape from the dam on the Barron River in order to permit Barron Falls to flow for the benefit of railway passengers, a charming custom.

Kuranda Station, at the end of our journey, is, in itself, something of a tourist attraction. Constructed in 1915, it has somehow managed to transform itself into a railway botanical garden. Much as stationmasters were once famed for their horticultural instincts, you will never have seen anything on a railway platform quite like this verdant and luxuriant growth.

The train used for this journey consists of refurbished 1920s carriages hauled by a modern diesel locomotive. Trains leave Cairns at 8:30 every day and 9:30 on most days and return at 14:00 on most days and 15:30 every day. The journey takes an hour and 45 minutes and costs $30 single or $48 return.

However, neither is Kuranda the end of this line. Although it was originally constructed to serve Herberton, because of the discovery of gold in the area, that branch is now closed, but the main line continues to Forsayth, with a passenger train once every week. For details of that interesting and unique journey, see the description following on page 368.

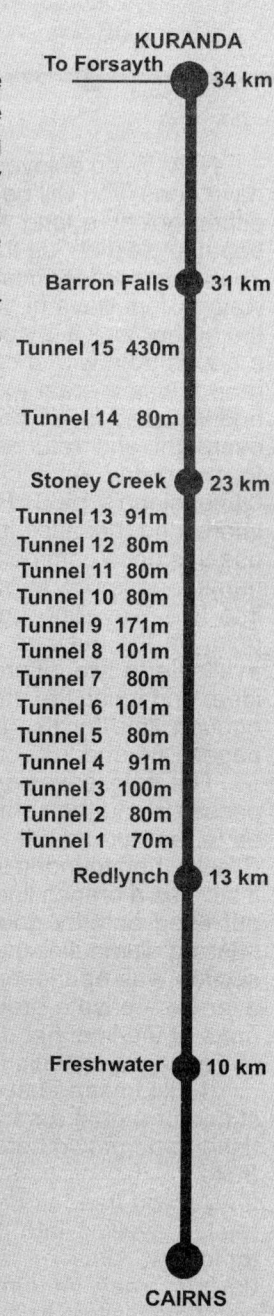

GREAT RAILWAY JOURNEYS

```
           Almaden                              Lappa
              ●                                   ●
━━━━━━━━━━━━━━━━━━━━━━━━━━━━━━━━━━━━━━━━━━━━━━━━━━━━━━━━━━
             194                                 164
```

Now, if you enjoyed the railway journey up to Kuranda, as you surely must have done, you will be pleased to learn that Kuranda is not the end of the line either, not by a long way, and that, although Cairns to Kuranda is the most beautiful section, as this railway continues it becomes even more interesting. You need time for this, though. It is a four-day return trip, costing $110 each way, or four days of your rail pass. This service used to be operated, when the author took it, by one of Quensland's last 'mixed' trains, which is to say by a goods train with a couple of very old passenger carriages tagged onto the rear. It was a great experience. The train started from Cairns in the evening and travelled for 23 hours to reach its destination of Forsayth. There it stayed overnight and returned the next morning, reaching Cairns very early the following day. All is changed now. The mixed train is gone. Instead, one of Queensland's 1960s Rolls-Royce rail motors operates this service. This is still interesting, because it is the only remaining Queensland Railways service to use this once common form of conveyance. The train has even been given a name, and is now known as the *Savannahlander*. The route has been divided into two, travelling only in daylight and with a different overnight stopping point on the outward and return journeys, so that excursions can be made available to two different attractions off the railway line. All of this is a good idea, and it has the effect of sustaining an interesting rail journey. If you have enough time for this adventure, you will enjoy it. The timetables appear on pages 364 and 365.

The train leaves on its 423-kilometre journey on Wednesdays at 6:30 and passes along the same railway line as that described on pages 366 and 367 as far as Kuranda. It then continues to Mareeba, originally known as Granite Creek when founded in 1877. This was once an important railway centre, and it still has a branch line running off to Atherton. The Atherton line is in service, but used only by goods traffic. The line formerly continued to Ravenshoe, passing Tumoulin, the highest station in Queensland, on the way, but that section was abandoned by Queensland Railways, and has now been taken over by a private group which is operating two separate steam services on parts of the line. For details, see page 374. There is a museum in the town of Mareeba which includes an interesting and unusual rail ambulance.

43 kilometres beyond Mareeba is Dimbulah, first settled in 1876 and the scene of a gold rush at that time. Following the Second World War, tobacco used to be grown here, but more recently the main crop has become tropical fruits.

As you head further west, the scenery changes and you feel that you are really travelling into the outback, a feeling which will be greatly reinforced tomorrow. Almaden is reached at lunch time, and that is the end of the first day's journey. At Almaden, a cow, or sometimes more than one, likes to welcome visitors from the train.

4. THE SAVANNAHLANDER
CAIRNS TO FORSAYTH

Dimbulah	Mareeba	KURANDA	To Cairns
117	74	34	

Distances (km from Cairns)

The main line from here used to continue north to Chillagoe, but that line is disused now. Instead you can join a bus trip to Chillagoe and see the old copper smelters there. They were built in the early 1900s and continued to operate until 1943, during which period this was a very busy line, the railway having reached Chillagoe and Mungana, just beyond, in 1901. It was a private railway when built, and was once the busiest private rail network in Australia. Chillagoe also has some spectacular limestone caves and a well known balancing rock. On page 371, there is a list of accommodation available in Chillagoe and Almaden, and at other stops on this route. The bus ride to Chillagoe, and back next morning, is offered by Chillagoe Bus Service for $20. If a tour of Chillagoe is included, the price is $48.50.

The train starts again on Thursday morning at 8:00, reaching Mt. Surprise at lunch time. When the author travelled, we stopped along the way to look at a bower bird's nest in the undergrowth. Mt. Surprise is the point at which the railway meets and crosses the main road to the Gulf country. It is a centre for gem fossicking, especially for topaz.

The next main stop is Einasleigh, where there will be afternoon tea available at a modest price. The railway crosses the Copperfield River on a rustic bridge here and the train will usually stop on it for photographs either now or on the return journey. Here at Einasleigh Gorge there is a swimming hole which there should be enough time to use if you feel so inclined. When the author travelled here, a guided trip to the cemetery was also arranged, which was interesting. Einasleigh was once a copper mining town, but it now depends mostly on local cattle farming. Often more cows can be found wandering the street here than the total human population of the settlement.

From here to Forsayth is another 66 kilometres of unusual scenery with flat-topped mesas punctuating the landscape. Forsayth is reached at 17:45. It is an old gold mining town with a current population of 82. Gold and other gems are still found here, but this weekly train is also a major event in the economy of the town. Accommodation is available at the hotel right next to the railway station. In the morning you can decide whether to return with the train, or whether to take a tour to Cobbold Gorge, 49 kilometres further west, then travel north by bus to Georgetown, and catch the Karumba - Cairns bus back to Cairns. You can also take this bus only as far as Mt. Surprise and rejoin the train there. Another possibility is to take the train to Mt. Surprise and catch the bus from there back to Cairns, thus saving a day's travel.

If you stay with the train for the return journey, you will be issued with bread rations by the hotel. These rations are not for you but for the rock wallabies which will be waiting for the train along the way. One imagines all the mother wallabies saying to their offspring, "And don't forget, dear, today is Friday, so you have to visit the train." There they will all be, as you come along, sitting on the rocks, paws outstretched, waiting for donations. The

GREAT RAILWAY JOURNEYS
4. THE SAVANNAHLANDER   CAIRNS TO FORSAYTH
(continued)

```
FORSAYTH           Einasleigh                        Mt. Surprise
●──────────────────────●──────────────────────────────────●
  423                357    Distances (km from Cairns)  302
```

weekly train is obviously a big event in everybody's life round here. Morning tea for you has to wait, though, until you reach Einasleigh once more.

On the way back, the train stops for the day at Mt. Surprise and tours are available in the afternoon to the Undara Lava Tubes. This is the newest volcanic system in Australia, only 190,000 years old. Lava tube caves are quite different from the more familiar limestone caves caused by the dissolving of the lime by water passing through. Lava tubes are caused by air pockets in the lava flow from a volcano. When the lava cools, the empty tube remains within. These are some of the largest such tubes in the world and, moreover, they have become the home of some species of wildlife found nowhere else on the globe. The return journey to Undara, 50 kilometres each way, is offered for $44. If a tour of the lava tubes is included, the price is $77. There is some interesting accommodation available in Undara, in old railway carriages.

The final day of the journey is from Mt. Surprise back to Cairns, a distance of 302 kilometres. Cairns is reached at 18:40.

It is possible to travel only one way from Cairns to Forsayth, by taking a bus from Forsayth to Georgetown at 10:30 on Friday morning, and then a connecting bus from Georgetown to Cairns at 12:15, arriving in Cairns at 18:00. In the opposite direction, it is possible to take the bus from Cairns to Georgetown at 6:45 on Thursday, with a connexion from there to Forsayth, arriving at 14:00, and then to take the train on Friday and Saturday for the two-day journey back to Cairns.

The most interesting option, though, is the following fascinating tour which will take eight days and include two of the world's most unusual railway lines, some unique remote towns, and stretches of magnificent outback scenery. Details of the *Gulflander* train are given on page 402. If you can afford the time, this will be a week's travelling which you will never forget.

Timetable for Jim's Tour

Day	From	Time	To	Time	Service
Saturday	Cairns	8:35	Townsville	15:45	*The Sunlander*
Sunday	Townsville	18:00	Mt. Isa	13:35 (Mon.)	*The Inlander*
Tuesday	Mt. Isa	9:00	Normanton	16:20	Bus (Coral Coaches)
Wednesday	Normanton	8:30	Croydon	13:00	*The Gulflander*
Thursday	Croydon	10:00	Georgetown	12:15	Bus (Coral Coaches)
	Georgetown	13:30	Forsayth	14:00	Bus
Friday	Forsayth	7:45	Mt. Surprise	13:00	*The Savannahlander*
Saturday	Mt. Surprise	8:15	Cairns	18:40	*The Savannahlander*

ACCOMMODATION ON ROUTE OF *SAVANNAHLANDER*

(i) Accommodation in Almaden

Name	Telephone No.	Address	Lowest Price (Double/Twin)
Railway Hotel	07-4094-8307	Main Street	$110

(ii) Hotel Accommodation in Chillagoe

Name	Telephone No.	Address	Lowest Price (Double/Twin)
Chillagoe Hotel / Motel	07-4094-7168	Tower Street	$110
Chillagoe Bush Camp	07-4094-7155	P.O. Box 35	$110
Chillagoe Cabins	07-4094-7206	Queen Street	$110
Chillagoe Creek Homestead	07-4094-7160	Airport Road	$110
Chillagoe Caves Lodge	07-4094-7106	King Street	$80
Chillagoe Tourist Village	07-4094-7177	Queen Street	$80

(iii) Backpackers Hostel in Chillagoe

Name	Telephone No.	Address	Lowest Price (Dormitory)
Chillagoe Caves Lodge	07-4094-7106	King Street	$14

(iv) Accommodation in Forsayth

Name	Telephone No.	Address	Lowest Price (Double/Twin)
Goldfields Hotel	07-4062-5374	First Street	$121
Forsayth Van Park	07-4062-5386	Fourth Street	$115

(v) Accommodation in Mt. Surprise

Name	Telephone No.	Address	Lowest Price (Double/Twin)
Mt. Surprise Tourist Park	07-4062-3153	Garland Street	$50
Bedrock Village Van Park	07-4062-3193	Garnet Street	$40

(vi) Hotel Accommodation in Undara

Name	Telephone No.	Address	Lowest Price (Double/Twin)
Undara Lava Tube Lodge	1-800-990-992	Gulf Development Road	$37

(vii) Backpackers Hostel in Undara

Name	Group	Telephone No.	Address	Lowest Price (Dormitory)
Undara Experience	YHA	1800-990-992	Gulf Development Road	$19

ANECDOTE

On the day when the author travelled on the *Savannahlander*, the cow at Almaden brought along her friend, a horse, and they both seemed pleased to greet the week's guests. On the return journey, however, the cow was nowhere to be seen, so I enquired of the stationmaster regarding her whereabouts. "I think I've offended her," he admitted. "I found her in the waiting room this afternoon and told her that she couldn't stay there. She looked quite upset and hasn't come back since." There was a silence, and the stationmaster evidently seemed to feel the need to justify his actions. "You just can't have cows in waiting rooms," he continued. "It's against railway regulations."

372 QUEENSLAND
ATHERTON TABLELANDS
Population 6,000 (Atherton)

2 hrs by bus from Cairns

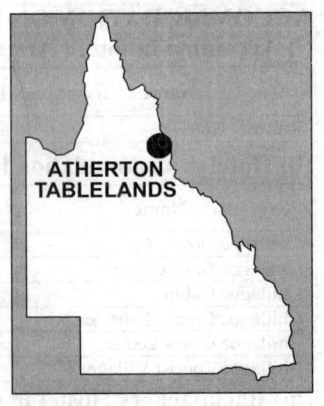

ATHERTON TABLELANDS

The Atherton Tablelands are a beautiful elevated area overlooking the coast between Cairns and Innisfail. They are not a single location, but they have taken the name of the central town, which is Atherton.

There used to be a rail service to the area, passing, rather circuitously, through Kuranda and Mareeba before turning south to Atherton, Herberton and Ravenshoe. Because of the hard climb up to Kuranda, the train was slow, and eventually Queensland Railways decided that it was uneconomical to continue its operation. However, goods trains still run to Atherton. The passenger service is now operated by Whitecar Coaches which has three buses a day from Cairns to Atherton via Kuranda and Mareeba, and two services a day on to Ravenshoe via Herberton. There is also a service between Atherton and Malanda via Yungaburra.

However, if you are thinking of staying at the backpackers hostel in Yungaburra or Atherton, you can usually be collected in Cairns and see a considerable amount of the beautiful scenery on the way. On the Wallaby Lodge in Yungaburra specialises in tours and offers a day tour of the Atherton Tablelands for $70. It is not necessary to stay in the hostel for this, as the tour returns to Cairns in the evening. Here are some of the main attractions around the various towns.

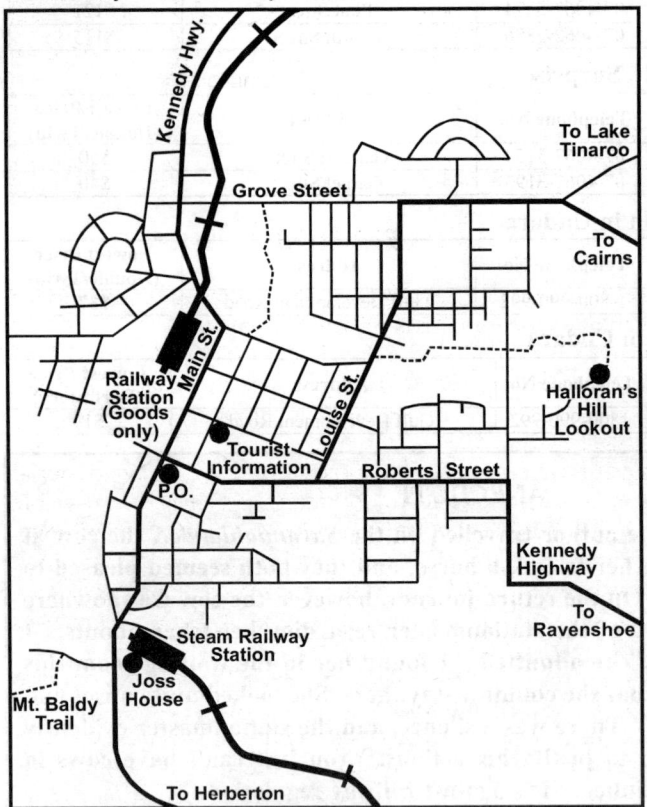

ATHERTON

Atherton is of a moderate size, with shops, accommodation and pretty parks and gardens. There is a lookout at **Halloran's Hill** giving a view over Lake Tinaroo, formed by a modern dam. To the west of the town is **Mt. Baldy**, which can be climbed by a steep path. There used to be a Chinese community in Atherton. Although it has

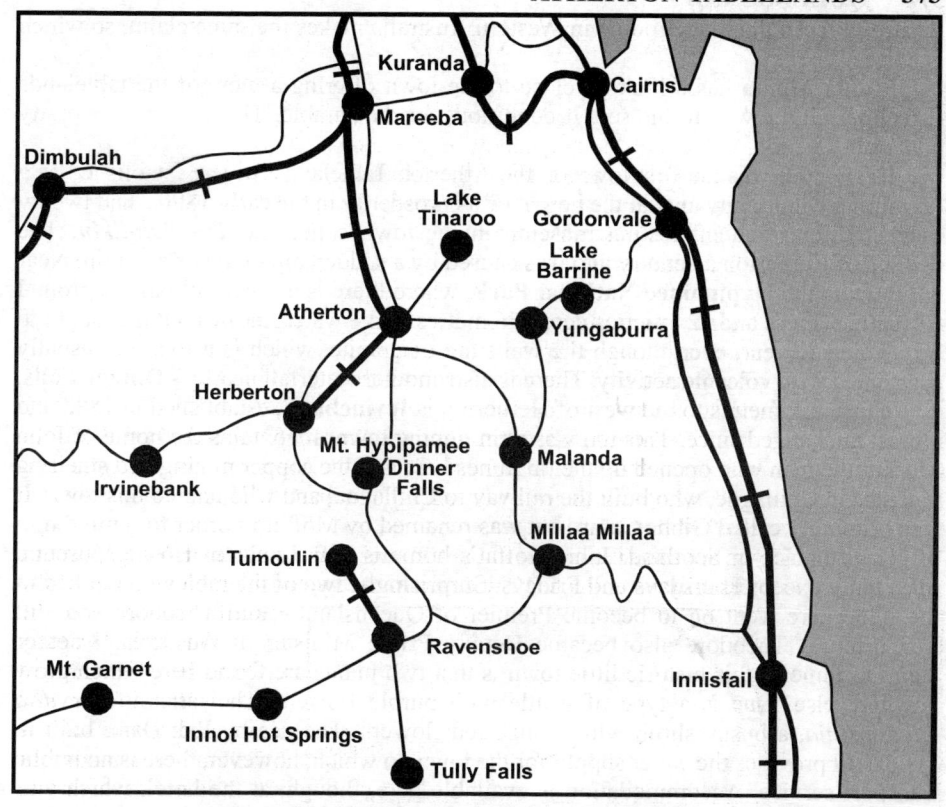

ATHERTON TABLELANDS

disappeared, the '**Joss House**' (Chinese temple) remains. There is a steam train service from here to Herberton on certain days, for details of which see under.

Lake Tinaroo was formed by the building of a dam in the 1950s. It has more than 200 kilometres of coastline and is known for its fishing. It is also a place for water sports, and attracts many types of birds. There is a small town with accommodation, including cheap dormitory-style beds.

Yungaburra is best known for the nearby huge **curtain fig tree**, a mass of aerial roots belonging to this parasitic tree which has unkindly strangled its host. It is possible to walk to the tree from the town. Yungaburra itself is a pleasant old-fashioned town, not much changed since the early 1900s, so retaining a pioneering charm. It is a good place to stay. On the direct road up to Yungaburra from Cairns, if you come that way, you will pass the volcanic crater lake at **Barrine**, a very pretty spot popular for swimming. It is right beside the main road.

Malanda has a background of rolling green hills and offers cool evenings because of its 800-metre elevation. It houses the **Malanda Environmental Centre**, giving a geological history of the Atherton Tablelands. **Malanda Falls** is famous, and you will also get the impression that nearly all milk in Queensland comes from here, since it is the site of a large dairy company. Malanda claims to have the oldest operating picture theatre in Australia, but Broome in Western Australia makes the same claim, so which is correct?

Millaa Millaa has a lookout close to the town offering a view of the tablelands extending all the way to the sea, if conditions are favourable. There is another pretty waterfall here too.

Herberton was the first town on the Atherton Tablelands. It was established as a tin mining community and, at the height of its prosperity in the early 1890s, had twenty hotels. There is an interesting museum in the town called the *Tin Pannikin*. The decline of Herberton a century ago was caused by a sudden dip in the price of tin. Near the town is the **Hypipamee National Park**, where there is a sheer hole in the ground 61 metres across and 124 metres deep (56 metres to the water line) which is thought to be a volcanic vent, even though the walls are of granite, which is a rock not usually associated with volcanic activity. There is also another waterfall nearby - **Dinner Falls**.

Thirty kilometres to the west of Herberton is **Irvinebank**, established in 1882 and almost unchanged since. This too was a tin mining town. It contains the home of John Moffat, the man who opened up the tin mines here and the copper mining and smelting industry in Chillagoe, who built the railway to Chillagoe, and who named this town. It was originally called Gibbs Camp, but was renamed by Moffat in order to remind him of his birthplace in Scotland. John Moffat's home is now Loudoun House Museum, open daily except Thursdays and Fridays. Surprisingly, two of the men who worked in the mine here went on to become Premier of Queensland - Red Theodore and Bill McCormack. Theodore also became Deputy Prime Minister of Australia. Another claim to fame of this historic little town is that two plants are found here which grow nowhere else. One is a type of wattle with purple flowers. The other is *Grevillia Glossanenia*, a bushy shrub with orange-red flowers. The nearby Ibis Dam, built in 1906, still provides the water supply for the town, to which, however, there is no public transport service. Accommodation is available here, though, at the hotel, which also offers a free camp site.

Ravenshoe is the highest town in Queensland, situated at an elevation of 930 metres. Five kilometres away is the Windy Hill Wind Farm, consisting of twenty windmill generators, each 46 metres high, providing electricity to the local community. 25 kilometres south of the town is **Tully Falls** in Tully Gorge. This impressive waterfall is 293 metres high, and is worth seeing, although not easily accessible without transport.

The railway used to come to Ravenshoe, and when you see the station in the town centre, you will be pleased to know that it is still being used. Even though Queensland Railways has given up serving this community, a volunteer group has taken over the track, obtained the steam engine from the park and renovated it, and started to run a **train service** on Saturday and Sunday afternoons from Ravenshoe to Tumoulin and back, a distance of seven kilometres each way, for the price of $12 return. **Tumoulin** has the distinction of being the highest station in Queensland, at an altitude of 980 metres. The return trip takes an hour and a half, including the stop at Tumoulin, and beautiful old leather-upholstered carriages are used for the journey, hauled by a 1925 locomotive. The author was told that I could come back on the footplate of the locomotive as long as I volunteered to go and collect wood afterwards, the wood to be used as the next weekend's afternoon snack for the locomotive. That was fun, but a lot hotter and dirtier than sitting in the comfortable leather seats behind.

The same company has now started **a second service**, that being the 22-kilometre

ATHERTON TABLELANDS

stretch of the same line, but at the other end, from Atherton to Herberton. This service operates on Wednesdays and Sundays, leaving Atherton at 10:30 and returning at 15:00, with an hour and a half allowed for looking round Herberton. A 1927-vintage steam locomotive is used for this service, hauling open-sided carriages along what is claimed to be Queensland's steepest railway climb. The return journey costs $30. Of course, it is hoped to link these two services one day, but the absence of a bridge in the middle of the line makes that impossible for the moment.

ACCOMMODATION
(i) Hotel Accommodation in Atherton

Name	Telephone No.	Address	Lowest Price (Double/Twin)
Blue Gum B & B	07-4091-5149	36 Twelfth Avenue	$80
Wrights Village Motor Inn	07-4095-4141	Sims Road	$65
Hotel Hinterland	07-4091-3311	44 Cook Street	$60

(ii) Backpackers Hostel in Atherton

Name	Group	Telephone No.	Address	Lowest Price (Dormitory)
Travellers Lodge		07-4091-3552	37 Alice Street	$21

(iii) Accommodation in Malanda

Name	Telephone No.	Address	Lowest Price (Double/Twin)
Malanda Lodge	1-800-222-420	Millaa Millaa Road	$95

(iv) Hotel Accommodation in Yungaburra

Name	Telephone No.	Address	Lowest Price (Double/Twin)
Eden House Garden Cottage	07-4095-3355	20 Gillies Highway	$110
Kookaburra Lodge	07-4095-3222	Eacham Road & Oak Street	$110
Banchory B & B	07-4095-3147	8 Bunya Street	$90
Gables B & B	07-4095-2373	5 Eacham Road	$90
Curtain Fig Motel	07-4095-3168	16 Gillies Highway	$75
Yungaburra Park Motel	07-4095-3211	29 Gillies Highway	$75
Lake Eacham Hotel	07-4095-3515	Cedar Street	$60

(v) Backpackers Hostel in Yungaburra

Name	Group	Telephone No.	Address	Lowest Price (Dormitory)
On the Wallaby	B&W	07-4095-2031	34 Eacham Road	$20

(vi) Accommodation in Ravenshoe

Name	Telephone No.	Address	Lowest Price (Double/Twin)
Club Hotel / Motel	07-4097-6109	47 Grigg Street	$50

MOVING ON
Bus services to the Atherton Tablelands are operated by Whitecar Coaches. The current timetables to and from Cairns are given overleaf.

376 QUEENSLAND

Bus Services from Cairns to the Atherton Tablelands

Days of Operation	M – F	M – F	Daily	Sat,Sun	M – F	Sun	M – F	School	M – F	M – F
Cairns		0830	0930	1300	1330	1450			1515	1730
Kuranda		0905	1010	1340	1410	1530			1555	1805
Mareeba		0940	1040*	1415					1630	1840
Atherton	0750	1015	1115*	1445			1500	1515	1700	1915
Yungaburra				1505			1515		1730	
Malanda	0810			1515			1530		1745	
Herberton		1030		1515				1535	1730	
Ravenshoe		1100						1600	1800	

* Saturdays only

Bus Services from the Atherton Tablelands to Cairns

Days of Operation	M – Sat	Sun	Daily	M – F	Sun – F	M – F	School
Ravenshoe			0800*			1415	1600
Herberton			0835†			1440	1630
Malanda			0815†				
Yungaburra			0830†				
Atherton	0630		0915			1530	1650
Mareeba	0700		0945			1600	
Kuranda	0730	0830	1020	1245	1410	1630	
Cairns	0815	0915	1115	1330	1450	1715	

* Mondays to Fridays only   † Pre-booked passengers only

PORT DOUGLAS

Population 3,000

1 hr 30 mins by bus from Cairns

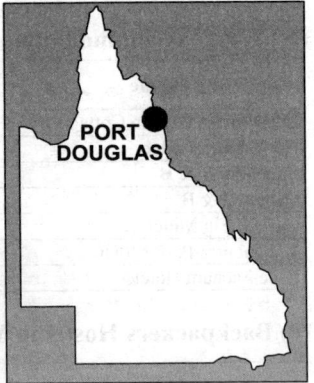

With Cairns such a popular destination nowadays, it is natural that some visitors wish to head to somewhere rather smaller and quieter. That somewhere has become Port Douglas, 70 kilometres of very attractive coastal highway north of Cairns.

The author will mention that he sees little reason for the present existence of Port Douglas other than as a tourist town, which limits its appeal to him. Most visitors, however, think it a wonderful place, with a long, long stretch of beach, restaurants of every type and price range imaginable and, for those on a budget, backpackers hostels with bars and pool tables and yet in the rainforest. Indeed, one of the merits of the town is that it has something for everybody. Accommodation ranges from high-class resorts, through moderately priced motels to good-value backpackers hostels. There are even golf courses here.

To reach Port Douglas from Cairns, take the bus service provided by Coral Coaches. It operates eight times a day from the city and fourteen times a day from the airport, taking an hour and a half and costing $25 ($30 from the airport, rather curiously). If, however, you intend to stay at one of the backpackers hostels, Dougies and Port o'Call will pick you up in Cairns and bring you here free. The route is a scenic one, with the sea immediately on one side and often high hills on the other.

PORT DOUGLAS

Port Douglas started as a fishing port and then became a busy centre providing supplies for gold miners. When the gold ran out, the sugar industry arrived and Port Douglas was a major port for the shipment of that commodity. Then the sugar started to go elsewhere and Port Douglas returned to being a sleepy fishing village once more. It is only in the last two decades that it has found a new purpose in its existence by serving the thousands of visitors who now throng here.

To the east is **Four Mile Beach** where most people want to spend at least a little part of their time. Then there is a **marina** from which **cruises** operate, usually up the river amongst the mangroves to look for crocodiles. **Diving trips** go out to the Great Barrier Reef from here, and are generally cheaper than those from Cairns. There are also day excursions to the rainforest area around the **Daintree River**.

Port Douglas is a remarkable place for food. The central area has restaurant after restaurant, with all varieties of taste-bud catered for. Although the author did not think to make a count, he was reliably informed that there are in excess of seventy eating houses here. Just find one that suits your tastes, and, if possible, your pocket.

At the edge of Port Douglas, where the road into the town leaves the main highway, is the **Rainforest Habitat**. Here you can view all types of local wildlife in a natural environment. There are 1,600 creatures resident, of 180 different species, including crocodiles, frogs, snakes, kangaroos, koalas, cassowaries and tropical birds. The Rainforest Habitat is open from 8:00 until 17:30 and admission costs $20.

Also in Port Douglas is the *Bally Hooley Railway*. This is one of the few narrow gauge sugar cane railways on which a passenger train operates. These

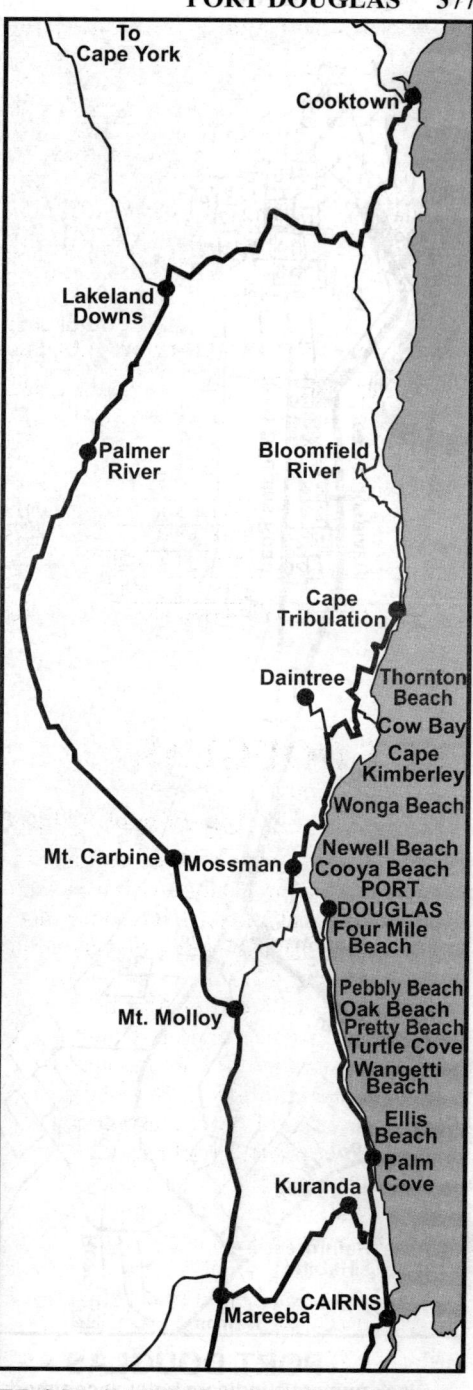

FROM CAIRNS TO COOKTOWN

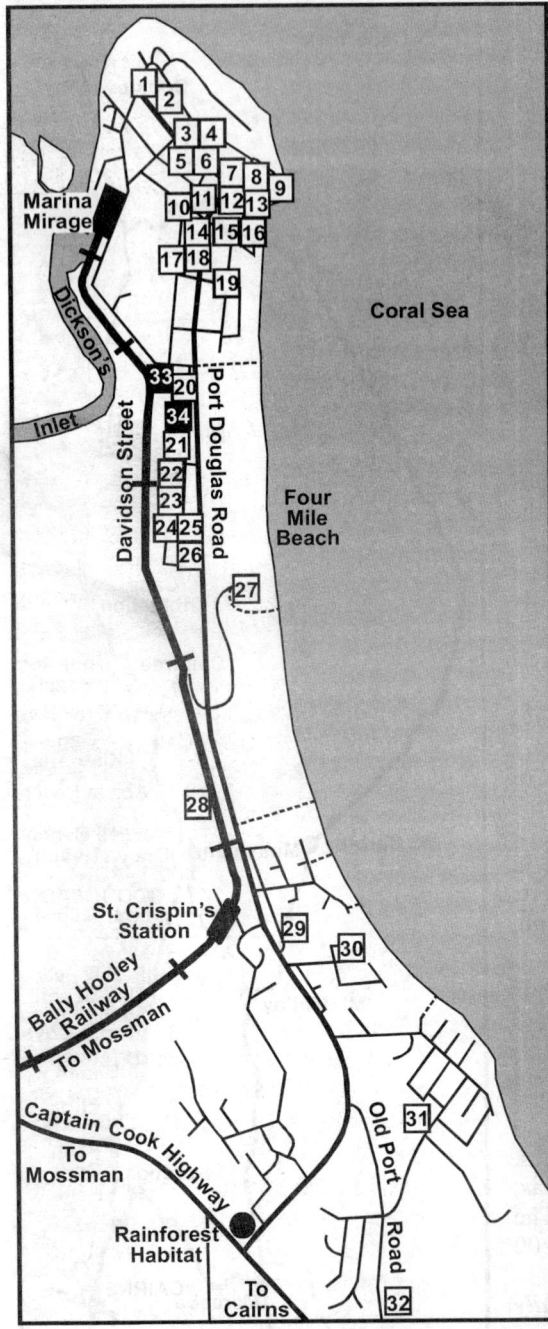

PORT DOUGLAS
Black numerals indicate hotel accommodation
White numerals indicate backpackers hostels

little railways have long been the lifeblood of the sugar cane industry, operating over nearly 2,000 kilometres of the Queensland coast, and yet, when trains are made available for passenger use, the response is insufficient to sustain the service. Thus the *Mulgrave Rambler*, which formerly operated south of Cairns is now kept in a siding, the service abandoned, and even the *Bally Hooley* does not operate the full route which it was formerly intended to serve. Port Douglas used to be a busy sugar port, so when the traffic started to go elsewhere, the tracks remained here with few or no trains using them. It was decided to offer a passenger service designed to appeal to visitors. Originally, the little trains went all the way to the next town of Mossman and included tours of the sugar mill there. Now, however, the train runs only from the Marina to St. Crispin's Station, a distance of approximately five kilometres. This journey takes fifteen minutes and costs $4 one way, or $8 return. The little train is hauled by a little diesel engine, except at the weekends, when a little steam engine comes out to operate five of the day's eight return trips.

Twenty kilometres from Port Douglas is the town of **Mossman**. This is a completely different type of town, in fact just an ordinary North Queensland small town. Few visitors stay here, although if you do, O'Malley's Irish Pub offers good value, but there are two reasons for making an expedition to Mossman. One is the **sugar mill tours** which are offered during the crushing season, June to November; and the other is **Mossman Gorge**, an attractive area for a walk. However, before walking, one must first get to the gorge and it is five kilometres from the town, without public transport available. That means that one must add to the five-kilometre walk in the gorge another ten kilometres to get there and back. The author did, in fact, walk this, but would advise that, considering the distance, and the lack of interest for most of the way there and back, it is worthwhile only if you can find transport in at least one direction. Once you are there, the walk is a pretty one indeed, through dense forest and with pleasant views of the river, but one does not actually get a view into the gorge, since one is already at the foot of it. A self-guided tour of the gorge is free except for a charge of 20 cents for a map. A tour conducted with an aboriginal guide and including tea and damper costs $16.50. There is also a swimming place in the Mossman River here, but a sign advises caution as there have been fatalities at this spot in the past.

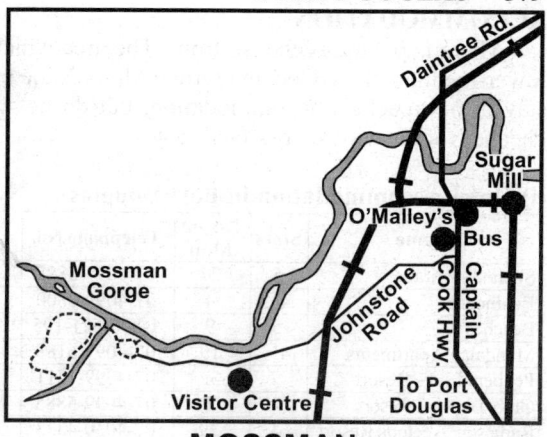

MOSSMAN

There is a local bus service operated by Coral Coaches from Port Douglas to Mossman, but it is quite expensive at $8 one way. Coral Coaches also operates a town bus service around Port Douglas. If you are leaving Australia from Cairns, there are buses from Mossman and Port Douglas to connect with all flights, the first bus to Cairns Airport being at 2:45 from Mossman and 3:15 from Port Douglas. The last is at 18:30 from Mossman and 19:00 from Port Douglas. These buses will pick passengers up from their accommodation if booked in advance.

ANECDOTE

Starting to walk from Mossman to Cooya Beach without appreciating quite how far it was, I was fortunate enough to be given a lift by an ancient farmer in a vehicle which appeared to be of almost equal antiquity. Wisely, he restricted his maximum speed on the journey to 40 km/hr, which also provided him with the opportunity for some talking time.

"These crocs are becoming a real nuisance," he said, "Since they brought in this protection business. A friend of mine was out for a walk the other day along by the river, and he stepped over a log which was in his way. He heard his wife scream out, but he couldn't make out what all the fuss was about. It wasn't till the log moved a bit that he realised. Next day, he went straight to the optician and got his eyes tested for a new pair of glasses."

380 QUEENSLAND
ACCOMMODATION

There is plenty to choose from. The area which is in short supply, however, is the lower-medium class. Coconut Grove Motel is the best bet for those who do not want to stay in backpackers accommodation, but do not wish to pay too much. It has some cheaper rooms with shared facilities.

(i) Hotel Accommodation in Port Douglas

Name	Stars	No. on Map	Telephone No.	Address	Lowest Price (Double/Twin)
Sheraton Mirage	5	27	07-4099-5888	Davidson Street	$600
Boathouse	4½	4	07-4099-8800	41 Murphy Street	$325
Beaches	5	9	1-800-621-195	19 Esplanade	$325
Mandalay Apartments	4½	19	07-4099-6188	Garrick & Beryl Streets	$295
Peppers Links Resort		32	07-4099-1511	Old Port Road	$255
Club Tropical Resort	4	1	07-4099-5885	Wharf & Macrossan Streets	$245
Radisson Treetops Resort	4	29	07-4030-4533	Port Douglas Road	$220
Radisson Reef Resort	4	28	07-4099-5577	Port Douglas Road	$180
Sunseeker Holiday Apts.	4½	13	07-4099-5055	7 Garrick Street	$175
Le Cher du Monde	4	3	07-4099-6400	34 Macrossan Street	$160
Beach Terraces	4	15	07-4099-5998	15 Garrick Street	$160
Quest Resort	4	26	07-4099-4500	Mahogany/Port Douglas Rd	$160
Martinique on Macrossan	4	7	07-4099-6222	66 Macrossan Street	$150
Metro Suites	4½	25	1-800-004-321	9 Port Douglas Road	$145
Port Douglas Apartments	4½	12	1-800-060-843	63 Macrossan Street	$140
Whispering Palms Resort	3½	30	07-4098-5128	20 Langley Road	$140
Garrick House	4	16	07-4099-5322	11 Garrick Street	$135
Lychee Tree Units	3½	20	07-4099-5811	95 Davidson Street	$130
NewPort	4½	2	07-4099-5700	16 Macrossan Street	$125
Port Douglas Palm Villas	3½	5	07-4099-4822	40 Warner Street	$125
Outrigger	3½	18	07-4099-5662	16 Mudlo Street	$125
Driftwood Mantaray	4	8	07-4099-5119	65 Macrossan Street	$120
Tropic Sands	4	14	07-4099-4533	21 Davidson Street	$120
Tropical Nites	3½	22	07-4099-5666	119 Davidson Street	$120
Flag Pelican Inn	4	24	07-4099-5266	123 Davidson Street	$110
Nimrod Resort Apts.	4	31	07-4099-3399	31 Nautilus Street	$110
Port Douglas Retreat	3½	10	07-4099-5053	31 Mowbray Street	$105
Queenslander	3½	17	07-4099-5199	8 Mudlo Street	$105
Lazy Lizard Motor Inn	4	23	1-800-995-950	121 Davidson Street	$105
Hibiscus Gardens	4	11	07-4099-5315	Mowbray & Owen Streets	$100
Talofa Holiday Units		21	07-4099-5416	115 Davidson Street	$95
Coconut Grove Motel		6	07-4099-5124	58 Macrossan Street	$65

(ii) Backpackers Hostels in Port Douglas

Name	Group	No. on Map	Telephone No.	Address	Lowest Price (Dormitory)
Dougies Backpackers	Nom	34	1800-996-200	111 Davidson Street	$25
Coconut Grove Motel		6	07-4099-5124	58 Macrossan Street	$25
Port o'Call Lodge	YHA	33	1800-892-800	Port Street	$22

MOVING ON

There are plenty of buses to Cairns. There are also buses north to Mossman, Cape Tribulation and, twice a week, Cooktown. However, if you stay at either of the two main backpackers hostels for two nights, you can usually be taken back to Cairns free.

Bus Services from Port Douglas

Destination	Operator	Via	Distance (km)	Fare	Journey Time	Frequency
Cairns	Coral Coaches		70	$25	1½ hrs	8/day
Cooktown	Coral Coaches		227	$58	6½ hrs	2/week
		Cape Tribulation	89	$31	2½ - 2¾ hrs	2/day

DAINTREE AND CAPE TRIBULATION
Total Population 600

4 hrs by bus from Cairns

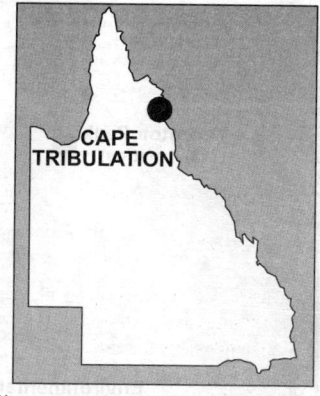

Port Douglas is not the end of the road and many travellers want to venture further. This can be done as a day trip, but there are also places to stay. It is easy to be beguiled into the feeling that travelling gets hard from here on, so it is best and cheapest to join an organised tour. However, that is not really the case. You just have to get on a bus in Port Douglas and get off in Daintree an hour later, or in Cape Tribulation two and a half hours later. From Mossman, mentioned above, to Daintree is a distance of only 35 kilometres. However, you should tell the driver if you want to go into Daintree Village, off the main highway, as otherwise the bus will omit that diversion.

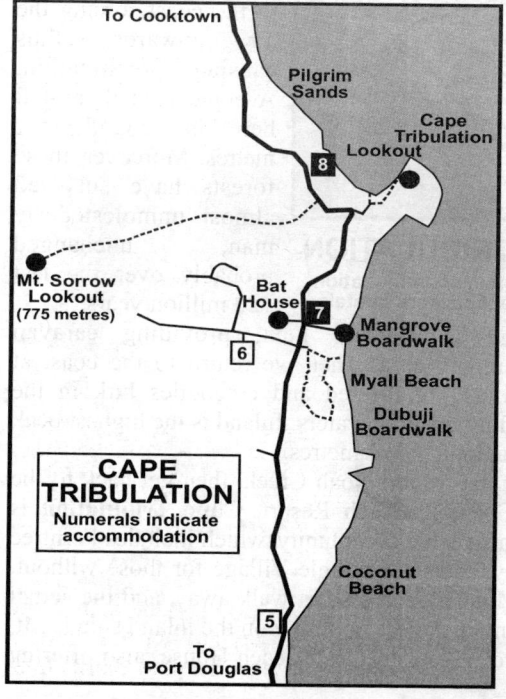

Daintree used to be a timber town, but these days it relies mostly on tourism. The ***Daintree River Train*** operates here - just like a train in appearance but travelling on the river. This is a good place for spotting wildlife, but not the best choice for a swim, as one of the creatures commonly observed in the local waters is the estuarine crocodile. There are cabins here where one can stay fairly economically, and there is also a camp ground. However, most people choose to press on a little further for their accommodation.

Daintree River is crossed by a cable ferry, the only one of its type in Northern Queensland. On the other side, the road rises and one comes to a lookout at the top of the **Alexandra Range** before descending into **Cow**

QUEENSLAND

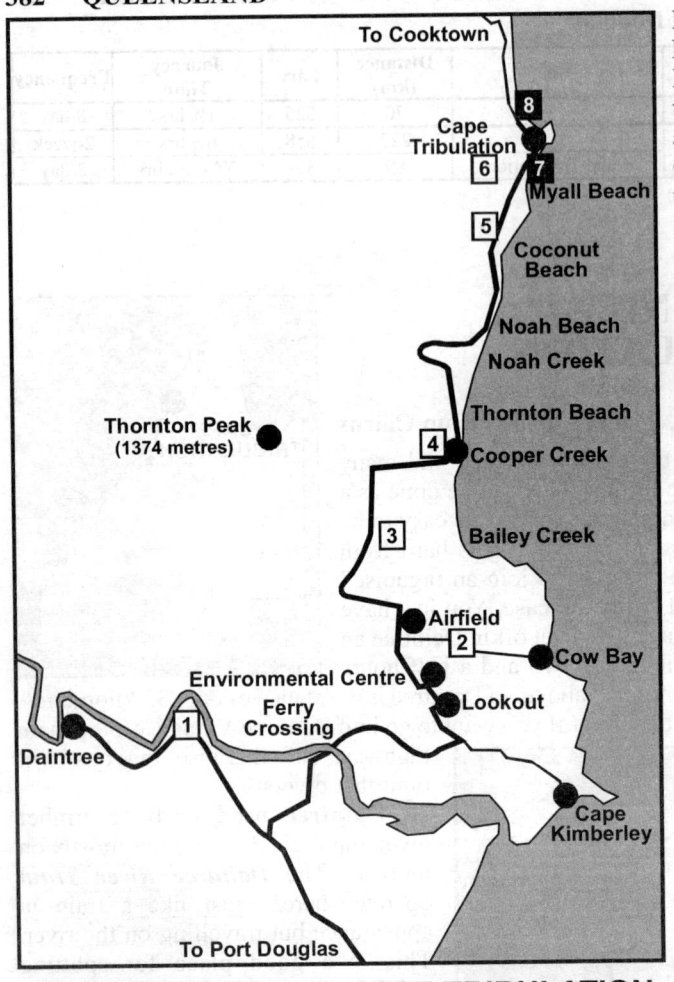

FROM DAINTREE TO CAPE TRIBULATION
Black numerals in white boxes indicate hotel accommodation
White numerals in black boxes indicate backpackers hostels

Bay. On the right is the **Daintree Rainforest Environmental Centre** to tell you all about this area. In Cow Bay is Crocodylus Village, which includes a youth hostel, and also a motel and camping ground. Although this is off the main road, Coral Coaches will bring passengers here. There is an airfield at Cow Bay, although there is really no excuse for anybody to fly here and miss such a beautiful land route.

The area from here on is unique in Australia, consisting of dense tropical rainforest, the result of the mountains adjacent to the coast forcing the air upwards, thus causing precipitation. Average annual rainfall here is around four metres. Moreover, these forests have survived almost unmolested by man, unchanged probably over the last 120 million years.

Rum Runner Rainforest Village is reached next, providing caravan accommodation, as well as another camping area. Then we return to the coast at **Cooper Creek**, another area where tours are offered and crocodiles lurk in the mangrove swamps, so do not be tempted by the cool waters. Inland is the highest peak in the immediate vicinity - **Thornton Peak**, at 1,374 metres.

We continue along Thornton Beach and round Noah Creek, then get back to the coast at Noah Head, before passing Coconut Beach Resort. **Cape Tribulation** is reached an hour after Cow Bay. This is a sizeable community, which includes Ferntree Rainforest Resort, for those with money, and PK's Jungle Village for those without. There is a mangrove boardwalk here, Myall Beach a short walk away, and the actual cape a little further on, but within walking distance. Looming on the inland side is Mt. Sorrow at 775 metres. Just beyond the cape is Cape Trib Beach House, also offering accommodation at modest rates.

DAINTREE, CAPE TRIBULATION

Cape Tribulation was named by Captain Cook, who had a hard time here in 1770. Unable to see the reef at high tide, he ran his barque, the *Endeavour*, aground on it. This must have depressed him somewhat, as he named the cape Cape Tribulation, the nearby mountain Mt. Sorrow, and other prominent features Mt. Despair, Mt. Misery and Weary Bay. The *Endeavour* was refloated, however, and repaired at Cooktown, where the wood of the ship's hull was found to be only half an inch thick in places, so severe was the abrasive effect of the coral.

ACCOMMODATION
(i) Hotel Accommodation from Daintree to Cape Tribulation

Name	Stars	No. on Map	Telephone No.	Address	Lowest Price (Double/Twin)
Daintree Eco Lodge	4½	1	07-4098-6100	20 Daintree Road, Daintree	$475
Crocodylus Village		2	07-4098-9166	Buchanan Creek Road	$60
Rum Runner Village	3	3	0500-509-249	329 Bailey Creek Road	$40
Heritage Lodge		4	07-4098-9138	Turpentine Rd., Cooper Ck.	$195
Coconut Beach Resort	3½	5	07-4098-0033	Cape Tribulation Road	$255
Ferntree Rainforest Resort	3	6	07-4098-0000	Camalot Close	$255

(ii) Backpackers Hostels from Daintree to Cape Tribulation

Name	Group	No. on Map	Telephone No.	Address	Lowest Price (Dormitory)
Crocodylus Village	YHA	2	07-4098-9166	Buchanan Creek Rd., Cow Bay	$20
PK's Jungle Village	VIP	7	07-4098-0040	Cape Tribulation Road	$15
Cape Trib Beach House		8	07-4098-0030	Cape Tribulation Road	$25

MOVING ON
Bus Services from Cape Tribulation

Destination	Operator	Via	Distance (km)	Fare	Journey Time	Frequency
Cairns.	Coral Coaches		159	$41	4½ hrs	2/day
		Port Douglas	89	$31	3 hrs	2/day
Cooktown	Coral Coaches		138	$37	4 hrs	2/week

COOKTOWN
Population 1,500

5 hrs 30 mins by bus from Cooktown

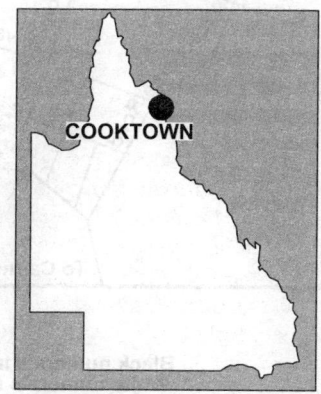

Cape Tribulation is not the end of the road either, for from here we can continue north to Cooktown. This road, the Bloomfield Track, was built only in the 1980s, and that despite protests from conservation groups that this would destroy the last vestiges of the lowland rainforests which once stretched from Mission Beach all the way up to Cooktown. The road is recommended for use only by four-wheel drive vehicles and includes the crossing of the Bloomfield River. However, there is a bus service along here on two days a week (three days a week at some times of the year), so it is not difficult to move on to Cooktown.

From Cairns, the inland route to Cooktown is longer, but it is sealed nearly all of the way, so much faster. Coral Coaches operates a bus by this route three days a week, taking only 5½ hours.

Cooktown is where Captain Cook was compelled by necessity, and by unwelcome close fraternisation with the Great Barrier Reef, to put in to effect repairs to his ship. He stayed here for 48 days, which delay allowed the botanists Joseph Banks and David Solander to discover a great deal about Australian flora and fauna. It was here that the kangaroo was first discovered, for example, kangaroo being a local aboriginal word.

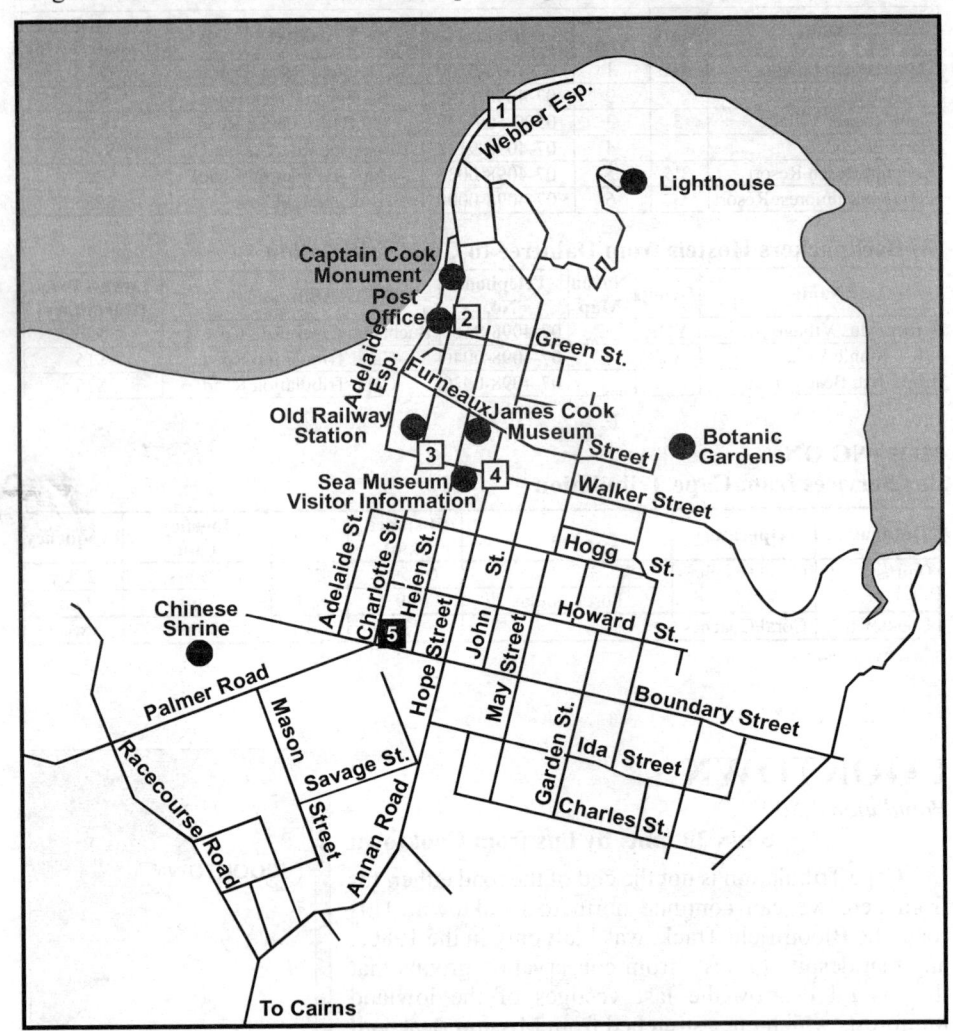

COOKTOWN
**Black numerals in white boxes indicate hotel accommodation
White numerals in black boxes indicate backpackers hostels**

The story is that the aborigines were asked the name of this curious animal and replied "kangaroo", it being realised only much later that "kangaroo" actually meant, "I don't understand." The author does not vouch for the veracity of this tale, though.

After the visit of Captain Cook, it was another century before Europeans ventured here again. Then a gold rush started at Palmer River and a base named Cook's Town was established to serve as a port for the mining community. It quickly developed into a sizeable community, and was, at one time, the second-largest town in Queensland. It has many interesting buildings. One of these is the **Lighthouse** on **Grassy Hill**. This hill was climbed by Captain Cook several times as he searched for a safe passage out through the Great Barrier Reef, a passage which he found eventually. The lighthouse was built in England in 1885, shipped out and assembled here. It was automated in 1927 and served the community for a century, but is now retired.

Other buildings which should be viewed include the **Post Office** in Charlotte Street, built in 1887. Nearby is the **Cook Monument**, commemorating the landing in 1770. There is a **cannon** there too. In 1885, the local council, concerned about the international situation, sent a telegram to the Premier of Queensland requesting some defence against the possibility of a Russian invasion. In response, the government of the colony dispatched a cannon, three cannonballs, two rifles and one soldier. This is the cannon, made in Scotland in 1803. It is fired once every year, to celebrate the Queen's official birthday.

Surprisingly, there used to be a railway in Cooktown. It ran from here to Laura, a distance of 105 kilometres, and operated from 1885 until 1961. The old railway station is now the Cooktown Kindergarten. The **Old Cooktown Hospital** is in May Street and a beautiful example of Queensland colonial architecture. It is now used by the Jehovah's Witnesses. The **James Cook Museum** at the corner of Furneaux and Helen Streets was

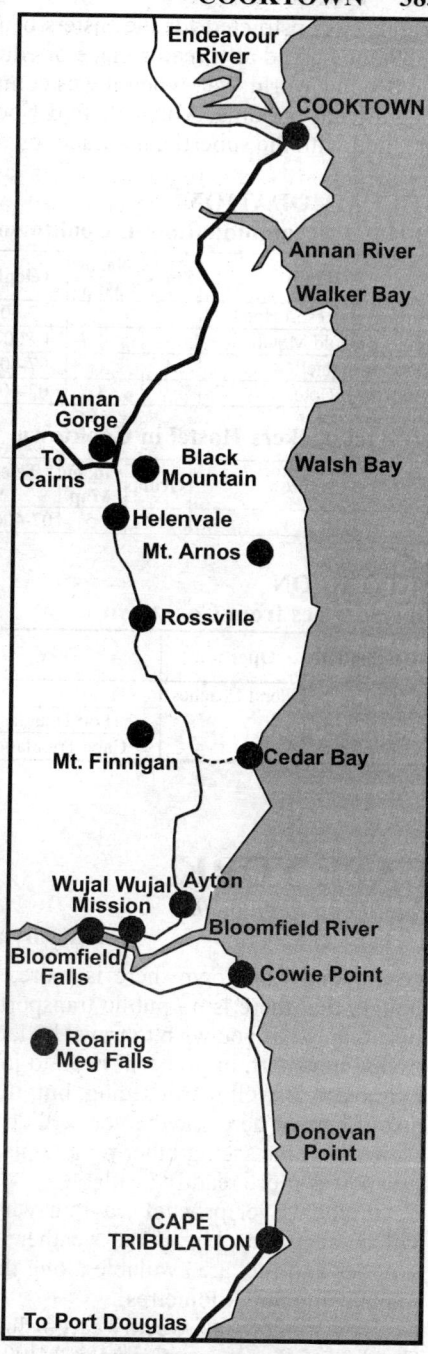

FROM CAPE TRIBULATION TO COOKTOWN

386 QUEENSLAND

originally constructed for the Sisters of Mercy at St. Mary's Convent. It was built in 1889 and served as a major place of education for women in North Queensland until the Second World War, when it was commandeered as a naval radio unit. This too is a magnificent building. You will find Cooktown an interesting town, so try not to be satisfied with the superficial attractions of Cairns and to get this far north at least.

ACCOMMODATION
(i) Hotel Accommodation in Cooktown

Name	Stars	No. on Map	Telephone No.	Address	Lowest Price (Double/Twin)
Sovereign Resort Hotel	4	2	07-4069-5400	Charlotte Street	$110
River of Gold Motel	3	4	1-800-800-993	Hope & Walker Streets	$80
Seaview Motel	3	1	07-4069-5377	Webber Esplanade	$65
Cooktown Hotel		3	07-4069-5308	Charlotte & Walker Streets	$45

(ii) Backpackers Hostel in Cooktown

Name	Group	No. on Map	Telephone No.	Address	Lowest Price (Dormitory)
Pam's Place	YHA	5	07-4069-5166	Boundary & Charlotte Streets	$19

MOVING ON
Bus Services from Cooktown

Destination	Operator	Via	Distance (km)	Fare	Journey Time	Frequency
Cairns.	Coral Coaches		297	$71	5¼ - 7½ hrs	5/week
		Port Douglas	227	$58	6½ hrs	2/week
		Cape Tribulation	138	$37	4¼ hrs	2/week

CAPE YORK
Total Population 6,000

2 hrs by air from Cairns

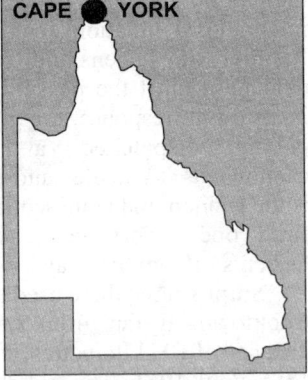

Beyond Cooktown there is more. The problem is, though, that there is no public transport by land beyond this point, so, if you wish to travel by land, you will need private transport, or you will need to join a tour. This is a remote area well worth seeing, but, if you consider the cost of getting here, maybe you will decide that you can get better value seeing other remote places where public transport is more readily available.

If you travel privately, a four-wheel-drive vehicle will be necessary, but, if the weather is clement, there will be no major difficulties. Supplies and fuel are available along the way, the longest stretch between fuel supply points being 360 kilometres.

By sea, there is a weekly cargo ship which carries passengers, but it is expensive. The *Trinity Bay* leaves Cairns at 14:00 on Fridays, reaching Thursday Island (off the tip of Cape York) at 9:00 on Sundays, and Bamaga (on Cape York, near the tip) at 11:00 on Mondays. It arrives back in Cairns at 15:00 on Wednesdays. The fare for a single

CAPE YORK

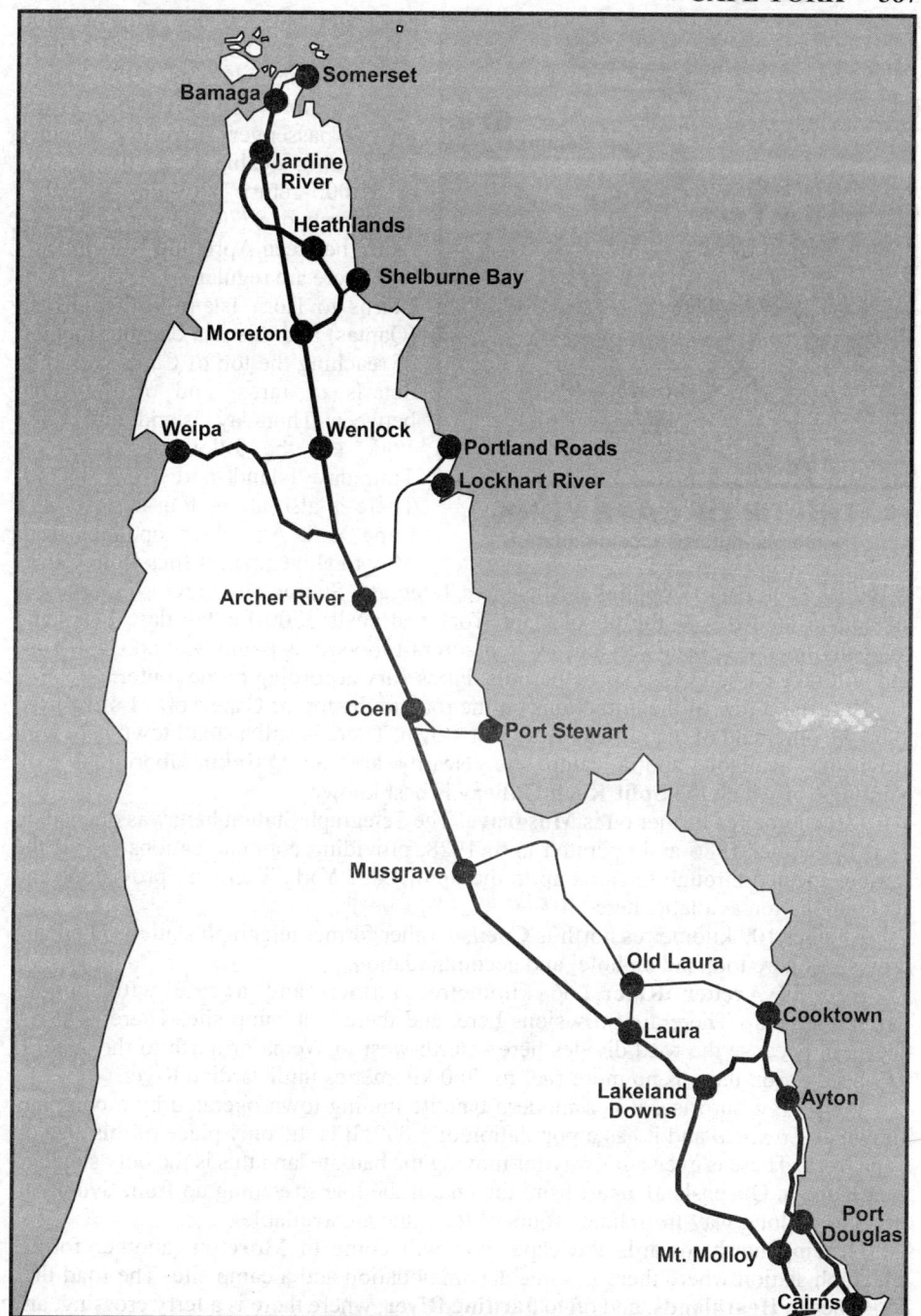

CAPE YORK

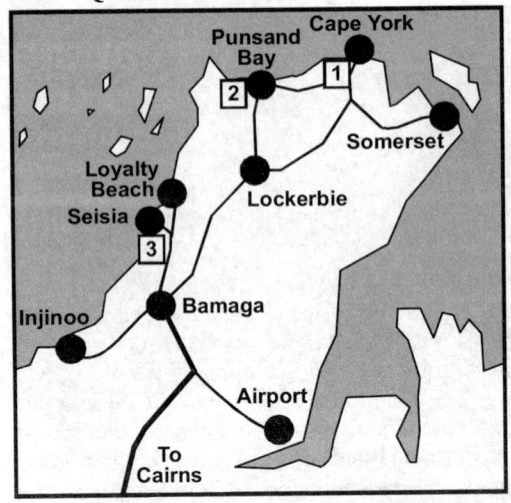

THE TIP OF CAPE YORK
Numerals indicate accommodation

passenger is $380 one way or $700 return between December and March, or $540 one way or $950 return between April and November. Prices for two passengers travelling together and sharing a cabin are $540 one way or $1,000 return between December and March, or $770 one way or $1,385 return between April and November.

There are regular air services from Cairns to Horn Island with Sunstate (Qantas) and this is a cheaper method of reaching the top of Cape York. For details of fares, and of the ferry between Thursday Island and Cape York, see the following section on Thursday Island and Horn Island. There is also an air tour service with Cape York Air which operates from May to November. It flies from Cairns to Bamaga and back, stopping at Musgrave Telegraph Station on the return journey. It includes a land trip to the tip of Cape York and costs $700 for the day. The same company operates postal services by light aircraft to various points around Cape York and will take passengers if space permits. Fares vary according to the route.

Here are a few of the attractions on the road to the top of Cape York. **Laura** used to be the other end of the railway from Cooktown. There is still a small town here with provisions available and a camp site. Nearby are the **Quinkin** aboriginal rock paintings, of which the **Split Rock Gallery** is best known.

136 kilometres further on is **Musgrave**. The Telegraph Station here was opened on 23rd December 1886 and operated until 1928, providing communications for all the stations located through the area up to the tip of Cape York. There are provisions and accommodation available here.

Another 109 kilometres north is **Coen**, another former telegraph station. There are provisions here too, and an hotel and accommodation.

Next is **Archer River**, 66 kilometres further, and a café with famous 'Archerburgers'. There are provisions here, and there is a camp site. There is also a decision, because the road divides here - north-west to Weipa or north to the cape. If you head north, there is no more fuel for 360 kilometres until Jardine River.

Weipa is a surprise. It is a modern bauxite mining town operated by a company known as *Comalco* and it has a population of 3,000. It is the only place of this size on Cape York. There is even a railway for moving the bauxite, and this is the only standard gauge line in Queensland, apart from the end of the line stretching up from Sydney to Brisbane, a long way from here. Tours of the mine are available.

Heading north towards the cape, you will come to **Moreton**, another former telegraph station where there is some accommodation and a camp site. The road then continues to **Heathlands**, and on to **Jardine River**, where there is a ferry crossing, and Bamaga.

Surprisingly, when you get to **Bamaga**, you will find this area relatively populated.

CAPE YORK

Apart from the town of Bamaga (population 800), which is a little way inland, there are coastal settlements with accommodation and camping grounds at Seisia, Loyalty Beach, Punsand Bay and the tip of Cape York (Pajinka).

Seisia is six kilometres north-west of Bamaga and was founded in 1948 by a small group of people from Saibai Island. It has a population of 180. There is a good camping ground here and there is also some accommodation. There is a ferry to Thursday Island, and Seisia is only 32 kilometres from the tip of Cape York.

Loyalty Beach is three kilometres north-east of Seisia. Camping is available here, but there is no other accommodation.

Punsand Bay, much closer to the cape, also has accommodation and a camping ground, a seasonal ferry service to Thursday Island and trips to the cape.

Pajinka Wilderness Lodge is only 400 metres from the northernmost point in mainland Australia. Again there is both accommodation and camping available.

A few kilometres east of here lies the abandoned settlement of **Somerset**, established by John Jardine in 1864 and intended by him to become the future "Singapore of Australia". As you will see, it has not succeeded in achieving that goal, although Jardine was right about the potential of Singapore. Somerset was the administrative centre of Cape York and the Torres Strait until 1877, when power was transferred to Thursday Island. Frank Jardine, the son of John Jardine, famous for an epic cattle-droving exercise in 1864 - 1865 which brought the first livestock to this area, lived here with his Samoan princess wife until his death from leprosy in 1919. The homestead was destroyed by fire in 1960, but the graves of the Jardines remain in this lonely and beautiful spot.

ACCOMMODATION
Accommodation in Cape York

Name	Stars	No. on Map	Telephone No.	Address	Lowest Price (Double/Twin)
Pajinka Wilderness Lodge		1	1-800-802-968	Cape York	$165
Seisia Resort	3	3	1-800-653-243	Seisia, Cape York	$110
Punsand Bay		2	07-4069-1722	Punsand Bay, Cape York	$45

THURSDAY ISLAND AND HORN ISLAND
Population 3,500

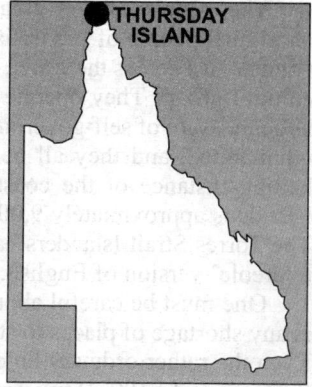

2 hrs by air from Cairns

Thursday Island is the most northerly easily accessible point in Australia. It lies in the Torres Strait which separates Australia from Papua New Guinea and it is approximately 30 kilometres north-west of the tip of Cape York. All you need to get to Thursday Island is a moderate amount of money, but, even though it is not a cheap place to reach, it is not as expensive as Cape York, which we have just mentioned, and from Thursday Island you can take one of the two daily ferries to Cape York if you wish to visit that part of the continent.

Sunstate Airlines, a Qantas subsidiary, runs a twice-daily air service to Horn Island with a launch connexion to Thursday Island. Strangely, Thursday Island is quite well known, but Horn Island, where the aircraft actually lands, is unfamiliar to most people, so most buy an air ticket to Thursday Island. It is, however, much cheaper to travel to Horn Island and then make one's own way to Thursday Island. The full fare to Thursday Island at the time of writing is $835 return, including taxes, whereas to Horn Island it is $772, a saving of $63. However, it is not necessary to pay such a high fare. Book a month in advance and it will cost $469 return to Thursday Island, but only $406 to Horn Island, still a saving of $63. You will need to take a ferry across to Thursday Island, which costs $6 each way, and you will also need to take a taxi for the five kilometres from the airport to the ferry jetty, and later back again, but still your saving is going to be in the region of $40. You might even like to spend your first night on Horn Island, in which case your accommodation will probably collect you from the airport. The settlement is adjacent to the ferry jetty, as it is on Thursday Island.

There are also services by ship to Thursday Island. For details of the *Trinity Bay*, see the section above relating to Cape York, which is also served by the ship. Fares are the same to either destination. There is also the *Gulf Express* operated by Jardine Shipping (tel: 07-4035-1900) which is a cargo vessel permitted to carry a maximum of twelve passengers. It leaves from Cairns on Mondays at 16:00 and reaches Horn Island at 9:00 on Wednesdays. It sails again for Cairns at noon on Wednesdays. This vessel offers a somewhat cheaper service.

Thursday Island and Horn Island are both interesting places. The first European in this region was a Spaniard, Luis Vaez de Torres, after whom has been named the Torres Strait, in which these islands lie. Later came Captain Cook, who claimed possession of the east coast of Australia for Britain by hoisting the British flag on what is now called Possession Island, just off the western side of the tip of Cape York, almost within sight of Thursday Island. The strategic position of this group of islands, named the Prince of Wales Group, was soon recognised, and Thursday Island was chosen as the administrative centre because of its sheltered position almost entirely surrounded by other islands. By 1870, it had developed into a sizeable port serving the local pearling industry, as well as the Pacific traders and various missions which had been established in the Torres Strait. In 1877, Thursday Island officially replaced Somerset as the administrative centre of the Torres Strait.

The people of this area, the Torres Strait Islanders, are not the same as the aboriginal people of Australia. They are closer ethnically to the people of Papua New Guinea, just across the water, but different even from them and recognised as a separate cultural group. They operate Community Councils on the various islands and have a large measure of self-government. There are 133 islands in the Torres Strait, 38 of them uninhabited, and they all belong to Australia, even though some are almost within hailing distance of the coast of Papua New Guinea. The total population of these islands is approximately 9,000 people, of whom over a third live on Thursday Island. The Torres Strait Islanders have their own languages, three main ones, but also speak a 'creole' version of English.

One must be careful about accommodation on Thursday Island. It is not that there is any shortage of places to stay. The problem is that most of them are quite expensive. Even the rather ordinary hotels, which one would expect to be modest in price, are in the region of $100. However, there are three hostels on the island, mostly for the use of Torres Strait Islanders visiting the administrative centre. If you want to stay here cheaply, it might be a good idea to try to book one of these in advance. Mura Mudh Hostel is probably the best bet. Camping is not permitted on the island.

Thursday Island is not so large, and it is quite possible to walk all the way round, so let us do so.

Walking Tour

This tour starts at the end of the jetty and finishes at Green Hill Fort overlooking the town. It covers about ten kilometres and, at a leisurely pace, this will take about four hours, including some sightseeing time.

All traffic arrives at the jetty and here you will find the office of Peddell's, a family enterprise which operates the ferries and a bus tour. Start out east for a very short distance and then turn sharp left and steeply up the minor road leading past the **Grand Hotel**. Not only is the hotel itself imposing, but there is also a good view from here across to nearby Horn Island. Descending again, you come to Victoria Parade, beside the beach and sea. On your right is the office of Torres Strait Travel, where you check in if you have an air ticket from Thursday Island (rather than the cheaper one from Horn Island). A short distance brings you to the Federal Hotel, looking just as an outback hotel should look, but, as mentioned, much more expensive than one might expect, which is a pity, as it would otherwise be a pleasant place to stay.

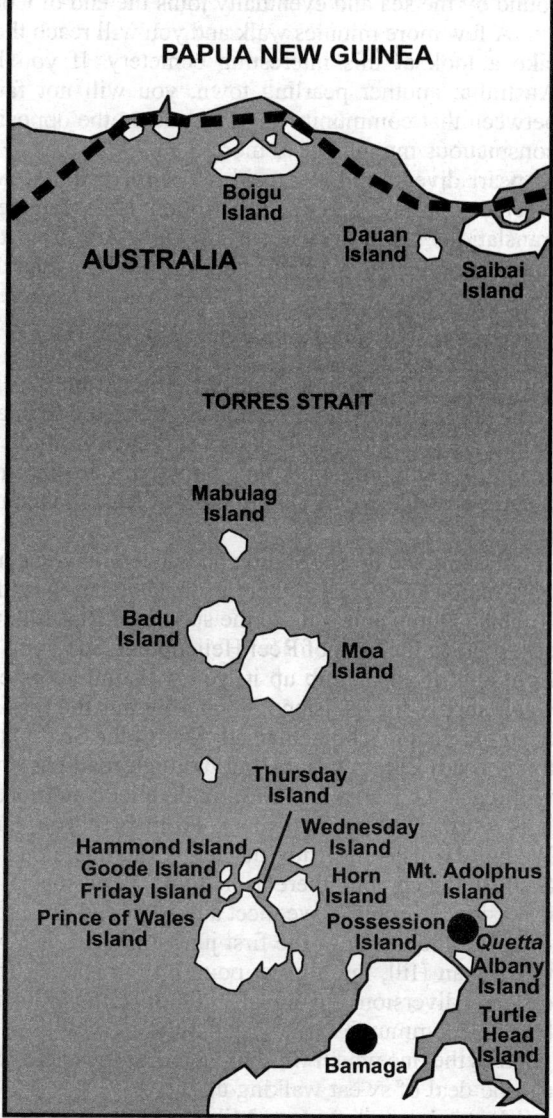

TORRES STRAIT ISLANDS
(Not all islands included)

Continuing, you pass the oval and then take the minor road on your right just beyond the public toilets, leading up past the Courthouse to Douglas Street at the point where the Police Station is located. Turn left and, where there is a public telephone on the corner, you will see the hospital to your left, while the road swings right. Keep following the road until Clark Street leads off uphill on your right and a track goes off to the left. Take the track, which leads round by the sea and eventually joins the end of Cook Esplanade.

A few more minutes walk and you will reach the **cemetery** on your right. Stop and take a look at this interesting cemetery. If you have visited Broome, in Western Australia, another pearling town, you will not fail to be struck by the similarities between that community and this one on the opposite side of the continent. There is a conspicuous monument to more than 700 Japanese who are interred here. They came as pearl divers, and most did not survive to see old age. The monument itself was erected recently, and the inscription is in Japanese, although there is an English translation. The graves nearby, though, date from the nineteenth century up until the time of the Second World War. Some are later than that, but many of the Japanese were interned at that time, as it was felt that they could not be permitted to remain in the Australian front line at this sensitive location. They did not all return later. Looking around the graves in this cemetery, which stretches a long way up the hill, one notices that many of the people here died young, and still continue to do so apparently. The cemetery is divided into sections by religion, with a sizeable Islamic section too, with names from Indonesia, Malaysia and even from distant Arab countries. This is a truly cosmopolitan community and cemeteries are fascinating places to walk around. One obtains a real sense of history here, at least in the author's opinion. However, we must press on.

Passing the Power Station on your right, you come to a major junction, actually the only major junction that there is on Thursday Island. Turn left, past the exotic Council Rubbish Dump and walk to the suburb of Rosehill, where you follow round beside the sea, passing the base of Reef Helicopters. Soon you will reach an embankment on your right and, if you climb up it, you will find an extensive reservoir, which is the main water supply for the island. Soon after this the road peters out in the suburb of Waiben at an old people's home named 'Star of the Sea'. At this point, there is a high road and a low road. Either will do, but the high road has a view, so let us take that. Soon you will reach the **Lions Lookout**, in derelict condition, but still offering a view for which it is worth pausing a moment. From here you can see Horn Island again, but also Wednesday Island off to your left. Continue along the track. There is a path down to Sadie's Beach, but there is nothing very special there, so we shall not take that diversion. Eventually we meet a proper road once more, and we are back at the eastern fringe of the town. At the first junction, there is a road off to the right which leads up to Milman Hill, the highest point on the island. You can take this if you wish, as an optional diversion, but actually, although the hill is the highest, the summit is occupied by a telecommunications installation, as well as a lot of trees, and the view is not as good as the one which we shall obtain at the end of our walk. Besides which, it expends a good deal of sweat walking up there.

Instead, turn left along Milman Street (or proceed straight ahead upon descending the hill, if you take that optional detour), and at the end turn left and immediately right (almost straight across really) into Douglas Street, which is the main street of the town. At this junction you will see the office of the *Torres News*, the newspaper of this area, and above you in the hill to the east are the oil storage tanks built during the war. When they were no longer required, they were sold, with the oil which they contained, to the shipping company serving the area at the time. This was of particular interest to the author, because that ship, the *John Burke*, was the same one as that which used to serve the community where I was living. It would turn up every six weeks to the kind of enthusiastic reception which, one imagines, it was also given here.

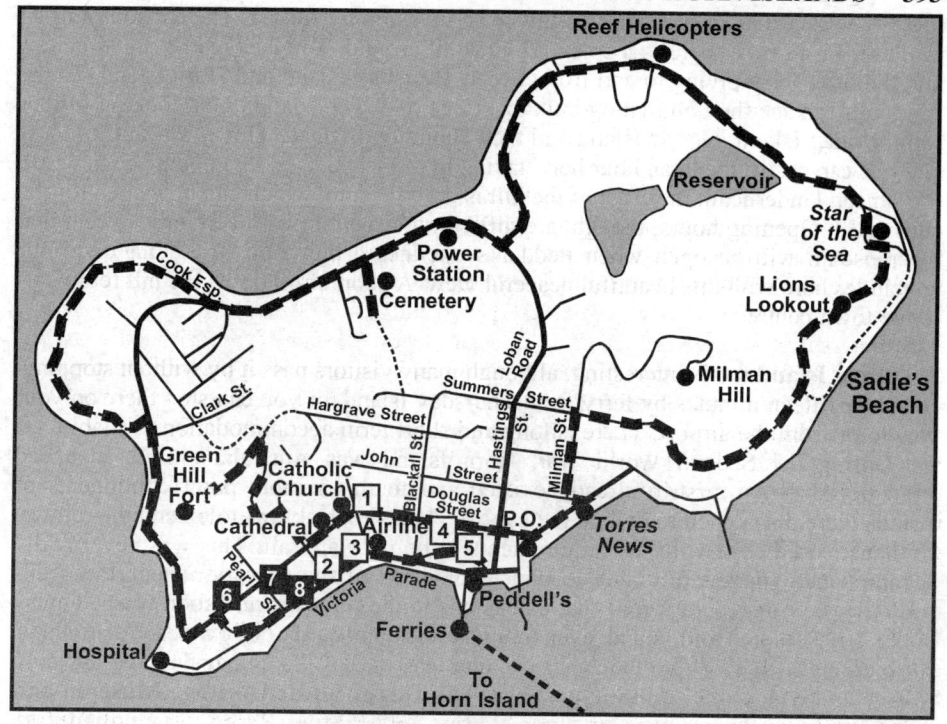

THURSDAY ISLAND
Dashed line shows Walking Tour
Black numerals in white boxes indicate hotel accommodation
White numerals in black boxes indicate backpackers hostels

Walk west along Douglas Street and you will soon pass the Post Office, still operating in its original building with typical tropical verandah. Keep walking along this, the main street, and see what keeps the community functioning. On the corner of Normanby Street is the **Torres Hotel**. This is, by a narrow margin, the most northerly pub in Australia, so better go in and have one quick drink to refresh you before the last section of the walk. Continuing down Douglas Street, you come to two beautiful churches. The first and more beautiful of the two is the **Catholic church**, a white wooden structure with steps leading down to the street. The more poignant, however, is the **Anglican Quetta Cathedral**, completed in 1893. It is named after the ship which foundered near here on 28th February 1890 whilst on a voyage from Brisbane to London. This was Australia's worst peacetime maritime disaster. On a clear moonlit night in calm conditions and with a pilot on board, the ship hit an uncharted rock and sank within an amazing three minutes. 133 lives were lost, out of the 293 passengers and crew on board, several being people from Thursday Island, which was the next stop on the voyage. The bell of the *Quetta* now hangs outside the cathedral. To visit here is a moving experience and one feels as though this disaster happened but last night.

At the next corner, turn right into Jardine Street, then left into Chester Street, and right again into Moa Lane, which leads steadily upwards. Ten minutes walk will bring you out on top of the hill at **Green Hill Fort**. This was indeed once a fort. It was built in 1891 to guard against the possibility of an invasion by Russia. The cannons still sit in place. From here there is a splendid view all around. You can see the town below, and the little ferry plying to and fro between Thursday Island and Horn Island. To the right you can see the dominating bulk of Prince of Wales Island, then, looking further right, Friday Island, Goode Island and then Hammond Island. This is a beautiful view and one can easily spend an hour here, taking in the scenery. It is a good place to watch the sunset. Underneath the crust of the hill is the Museum, which can be visited for the sum of $3. Opening hours, though, are difficult to ascertain with certainty, except that the museum will be open when Peddell's operates a bus tour there. Our own tour concludes here with this beautiful peaceful view. A short stroll down the hill returns us to the town centre.

Horn Island too is interesting, although many visitors pass it by without stopping. It is only fifteen minutes by ferry from Thursday Island, or you can stop there on your way to or from the airport. There is long and short term accommodation available.

During the Second World War, Horn Island was Australia's most advanced strategic base. An airstrip already existed and to this remote point contingents of airmen were dispatched to defend the nation. Their first task was to extend the runway so that it could cope with the requirements of bomber aircraft. This was never really accomplished successfully, due to underestimation of the powers of nature. Creeks could not be bridged easily, so that extensions to the runway were soon washed away in the Wet Season. Horn Island, even though almost unheard of by modern Australians, suffered eight air raids by the Japanese, and was one of the country's most difficult, remote and dangerous domestic postings. The **Torres Strait Heritage Museum and Art Gallery** is located here, in the Gateway Torres Strait Resort, and provides an excellent history of the role of Horn Island during the war, as well as a history of pearl diving here, and an art gallery giving prominence to Torres Strait Islander legends and artists. It was the wartime history which the author found most fascinating. Expecting to spend an hour there, I was enticed to stay all day, since free biscuits and coffee were provided for lunch. Admission costs $6, and is worth such a sum.

The Gateway Torres Strait Resort offers guests a package which includes one night's stay, three meals, free collection from the airport, free entry to the museum, a tour of the remains of the bases set up on Horn Island during the war, a tour of Thursday Island, entry into the Thursday Island museum and return to the airport. This costs $165 per person, with additional nights at $80 per person, not particularly cheap, but interesting.

Tours of Thursday Island are operated by Peddell's, but offer little that cannot be seen on the walk above. The same company provides ferries to the mainland. To Seisia costs $40 one way. A round-trip ticket is offered for $44 provided that one stays on board for the whole voyage, and returns on the same service. A day return (go across on the morning ferry, return on the afternoon boat) costs $72. A tour to the tip of Cape York, including the ferry ride across and back, a vehicle to the tip and back, and lunch, costs $180, which seems to the author a lot of money. To other islands water taxis operate as required, but Hammond Island has a regular morning and afternoon service to bring schoolchildren across and take them back. For a modest sum, it is possible to negotiate a passage on this boat on its reverse trips and spend the day on Hammond Island. Be at the ferry jetty at approximately 8:00.

ACCOMMODATION

(i) Hotel Accommodation on Thursday Island and Horn Island

Name	Stars	No. on Map	Telephone No.	Address	Lowest Price (Double/Twin)
Jardine Motel		3	07-4069-2555	Victoria Parade	$180
Grand Hotel	3½	5	07-4069-1557	1 Victoria Parade	$140
Federal Hotel		2	07-4069-1569	Victoria Parade	$105
Rainbow Motel		4	07-4069-2460	Douglas Street	$85
Torres Hotel		1	07-4069-1141	68 Douglas Street	$80
Gateway Torres Strait			07-4069-2222	24 Outie Street, Horn Island	$80
Elikiam Holiday Park			07-4069-2222	1 Miskin Street, Horn Island	$80
Wongai Hotel / Motel			07-4069-1683	2 Wees Street, Horn Island	$75

(ii) Backpackers Hostels on Thursday Island

Name	Group	No. on Map	Telephone No.	Address	Lowest Price (Dormitory)
Jumula Dubbins Hostel		8	07-4069-2122	60 Victoria Parade	$25
Mura Mudh Hostel		6	07-4069-1678	Douglas Street	$25
Cannon Boggo Pilot Hostel		7	07-4069-3246	145 Douglas Street	$25

MOVING ON

Sunstate (Qantas) operates flights twice a day to Cairns. Otherwise, there are sea services with the *Trinity Bay* and the *Gulf Express*, or overland tours which will return you to Cairns. In fact, though, the air route is likely to prove the most economical.

ANECDOTE

When I took the flight from Horn Island back to Cairns, there was a sudden bang, the aircraft started vibrating and there was a hammering on the fuselage which sounded like a herd of elephants trying to get in. General consternation ensued. We all peered out of the windows, but no elephants were visible. The pilot came out of the cockpit and looked too. "Did anybody see anything?" he asked. "Did anything drop off the engine?" These questions being answered in the negative, he pronounced a reassuring assessment of the situation. "Well, anyway, we still seem to be flying, so it will probably be all right. I'll try slowing down a bit and see whether it stops the vibration." And it did.

We landed safely in Cairns and half of the passengers rushed off as quickly as possible, whilst the other half of us went round to see what had caused the problem. It was a small part of the emergency escape equipment which had inflated by accident and then hammered on the exterior of the fuselage. "I thought that that was what it must be," said the pilot, "but they don't give me a rear-vision mirror, and, Christ, didn't it make a noise!" He was evidently as thankful as we were to have landed safely. Hopefully, the reader's voyages to and from Horn Island will be less eventful than that of the author.

CLONCURRY
Population 4,000

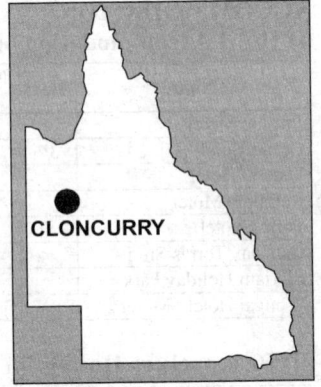

23 hrs 30 mins by bus from Brisbane
16 hrs by train from Townsville
10 hrs 30 mins by bus from Townsville

Returning now from our jaunt up to the northernmost point of Australia, it is time to head west on the only route leading in that direction from Queensland. From Townsville, this can be done by train or by bus. The bus is much quicker, yet, as the reader should know by now, the author's preference is always the train. The *Inlander* operates from Townsville on Sunday and Wednesday evenings. This train is not usually well patronised, unfortunately, so one wonders whether it will survive the modern-day test of economic viability. Sleeping berths are available and usually easy to obtain. The supplement of $44 makes for a very comfortable journey.

After Charters Towers, already mentioned on page 344, the most interesting town on this journey is **Hughenden**. If you travel by train, though, you will not see much of it as you pass through at 1:49. It is dinosaur country once more, the town featuring those novel dinosaur-foot rubbish bins which we saw in Winton. The fossilised remains of some 2,700 dinosaurs and marine reptiles have been found near Hughenden. Skeletons and recreated dinosaurs dot the town, *Hughie*, for example, being on display in the Visitor Information Centre. 63 kilometres north of Hughenden is **Porcupine Gorge**, offering some excellent views. Day tours can be found which run to the gorge. From Hughenden, there is also one of the last possibilities of taking a 'mixed' train (goods plus some passenger accommodation). The train leaves here at 4:00 on Thursdays, making a connexion in the middle of the night off the *Inlander*, and runs to Winton. Whether it will still accept passengers is uncertain, but it might.

You pass through **Julia Creek**, and then come to Cloncurry. Now, Cloncurry deserves a section to itself because it holds a special record, that of the highest temperature ever recorded in Australia - 53.1°C (127.6°F) on 16th January 1889. There is some uncertainty as to whether the record is currently recognised, as the recording facilities may not have satisfied modern standards, but most people regard this as the hottest ever on this continent.

The history of Cloncurry has been based on copper and that mineral is still mined at various places nearby, the best-known being Mt. Isa. Because of this mineral wealth, Cloncurry has been a prosperous town for much of its history, as can be seen from some of the buildings here.

Cloncurry was also the destination of the first Qantas service, from Charleville. The hangar at the airport still bears the legend *Queensland and Northern Territory Aerial Service*, but Qantas comes here no more.

Another claim of the town is that it was the first base of the Royal Flying Doctor Service, the inspiration of the Rev. John Flynn. The modern **John Flynn Place** in the town is a museum and an art gallery combined with a working base. It is open from 7:00 until 16:00 on weekdays and from 9:00 until 15:00 at weekends.

The **Mary Kathleen Museum and Park** is to the east of the main town and tells the story of the failed uranium mining community along the road to Mt. Isa. Some

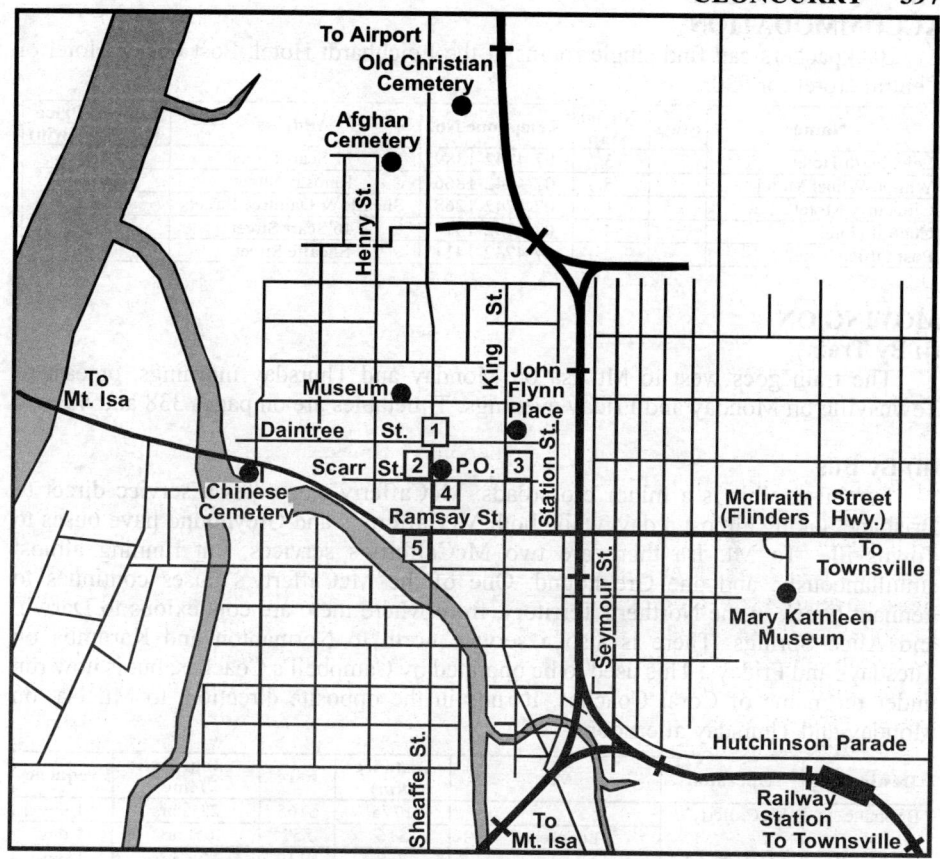

CLONCURRY
Black numerals in white boxes indicate hotel accommodation
White numerals in black boxes indicate backpackers hostels

years ago, the author visited the site of Mary Kathleen, where contaminated water trickled through wasteland on which nothing grew, and thought afterwards that maybe the visit had not been a good idea. Notices there still warn travellers not to call in because of the radiation hazards nearby. Some of the buildings from the town have now been moved to this site in Cloncurry, and there is a fine Rock and Mineral Display. There is also an interesting rail ambulance, a converted 1941 Ford van, which was used to serve mining communities during the Wet Season, when the roads became impassable. The park is open from 7:00 until 16:00 on weekdays and from 9:00 until 15:00 at weekends.

Other places of interest include an old **Chinese cemetery**, containing the remains of hundreds of Chinese gold miners, as well as an **Afghan cemetery**, the Afghans having come here to operate the transport system in the late nineteenth century. The two cemeteries are in different parts of the town, but the Afghan one is close to the old **Christian cemetery**, which is also interesting. There is a lookout with good views over the town, but it is requires a little walking to reach it from the town centre. It is adjacent to the Cloncurry River.

398 QUEENSLAND
ACCOMMODATION

Backpackers can find single rooms at the Leichhardt Hotel, Post Office Hotel or Central Hotel for $30.

Name	Stars	No. on Map	Telephone No.	Address	Lowest Price (Double/Twin)
Leichhardt Hotel	3½	3	07-4742-1389	11 Scarr Street	$70
Wagon Wheel Motel		5	07-4742-1866	Ramsay Street	$70
Cloncurry Motel		1	07-4742-1268	Sheaffe & Daintree Streets	$50
Central Hotel		4	07-4742-1418	46 Scarr Street	$45
Post Office Hotel		2	07-4742-1411	Sheaffe Street	$40

MOVING ON
(i) By Train

The train goes west to Mt. Isa on Monday and Thursday mornings, or east to Townsville on Monday and Friday evenings. Timetables are on pages 338 and 401.

(ii) By Bus

For buses, this is a minor crossroads. McCafferty's operates a service direct to Brisbane, taking almost a day, while both McCafferty's and Greyhound have buses to Townsville. To Mt. Isa there are two McCafferty's services, but running almost simultaneously, and one Greyhound. One of the McCafferty's buses continues to Tennant Creek in the Northern Territory, from where there are connexions to Darwin and Alice Springs. There is also a service north to Normanton and Karumba on Tuesdays and Fridays. This used to be operated by Campbell's Coaches, but is now run under the name of Coral Coaches. It runs in the opposite direction, to Mt. Isa, on Monday and Thursday afternoons.

Destination	Operator	Via	Distance (km)	Fare	Journey Time	Frequency
Brisbane	McCafferty's		1775	$165	23½ hrs	1/day
		Longreach	516	$57	6¾ hrs	1/day
Townsville	McCafferty's		768	$119	10¼ hrs	1/day
Townsville	Greyhound		768	$119	10 hrs	3/week
Tennant Ck.	McCafferty's		779	$135	9¾ hrs	1/day
		Mt. Isa	118	$19	1½ hrs	2/day
Mt. Isa	Greyhound		117	$19	1½ hrs	1/day
Mt. Isa	Coral Coaches		117	$36	1½ hrs	2/week
Karumba	Coral Coaches		445	$102.50	6½ hrs	2/week
		Normanton	376	$87.50	5½ hrs	2/week

MT. ISA
Population 25,000

**25 hrs by bus from Brisbane
19 hrs 30 mins by train from Townsville
12 hrs by bus from Townsville**

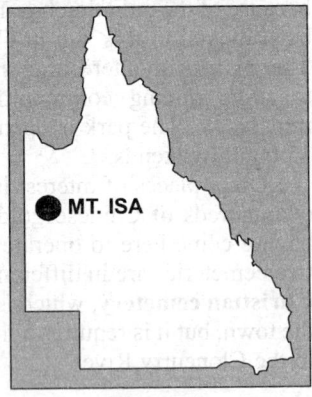

Mt. Isa is a prosperous modern city built on mining. The mine is ever present, looming over the landscape, a constant reminder of why we are all here. By day it appears as a huge black mass of machinery surmounted by smoking chimneys. By night the lights sparkle and glow and make it appear almost attractive.

The presence of copper in the area had been known for a long time, but in 1923 a gold prospector named John Campbell Miles noticed by the Leichhardt River rocky outcrops similar to those in Broken Hill. He took a piece of rock with him and it was later confirmed that it contained both silver and lead. Others rushed to stake their claims here and soon there was a city of tents and makeshift buildings. A mining company was established in 1924, but it took many years before it was successful. In the end, the factor which ensured that Mt. Isa could survive the hard times was the discovery that here not only silver and lead, but also copper and zinc, were present, one of the very few places in the world where the four elements are found in close proximity.

The statistics of this mine are impressive. The daily output of ore is 35,000 tonnes. There is an amazing 600 kilometres of underground tunnels, up to 1.6 kilometres deep. 3,500 people are employed here by the mine, of whom 1,000 work underground. The largest lift can carry 180 workers at a time down to 1,000 metres below ground level. This is one of the most extensive underground mines in the world and it is the world's largest producer of both silver and lead. It is in the world's top ten for copper and zinc.

Mt. Isa can be reached by either bus or train. The train runs from Townsville, taking 19½ hours to cover the 977 kilometres to here in a leisurely fashion. If you can afford a supplement of $44 for a sleeping berth on this train, you will have a comfortable and enjoyable journey. From Cloncurry, the railway follows a circuitous route necessitated by the demands of various mines. For passengers, this half-circle, via Duchess, is interesting, leading through country which one would not otherwise see, but perhaps a little tedious for some. The rail distance between Cloncurry and Mt. Isa is 197 kilometres, compared with 117 kilometres by road.

Buses operate from both Townsville and Brisbane. It takes 25 hours from Brisbane, which is a long time to spend on a bus. From Townsville, the journey is one of a mere twelve hours, comparing well with the time taken by the train.

Accommodation is available in Mt. Isa, and there used to be a youth hostel, almost in the bed of the river. That has gone, but there is still a private hostel, which will willingly collect guests from, and deliver them to, the bus or railway station.

Mt. Isa seems to be making a conscious effort to efface the image of itself as just a mining town, and to show that it has more to offer. The Tourist Information Centre is located in the new **Riversleigh Fossils Museum**. Riversleigh, however, is 250 kilometres north of Mt. Isa. It is a location where a great number of fossilised remains have been found, showing how the ancestors of today's Australian wildlife must have appeared. More are being unearthed every year, but this is the repository of knowledge so far. The Riversleigh Fossils Museum is open from 8:30 until 16:30 daily.

Mt. Isa also has a **Royal Flying Doctor base**, which can be visited between 9:00 and 17:00 on weekdays, and a **School of the Air**, open for inspection between 9:00 and 10:00 on schooldays. Various tours of the town are available and Campbell's offers a surface tour of the mine lasting two hours and costing $20. Underground tours are also available at the mine, but cost $60.

South of Mt. Isa lies **Boulia**, which has a fossil museum with the remains of more dinosaurs. It is also the area of the strange and unexplained **Min Min Light** which has appeared mysteriously at various times over the last century as a hovering luminescent ball seeming to follow travellers.

400 QUEENSLAND

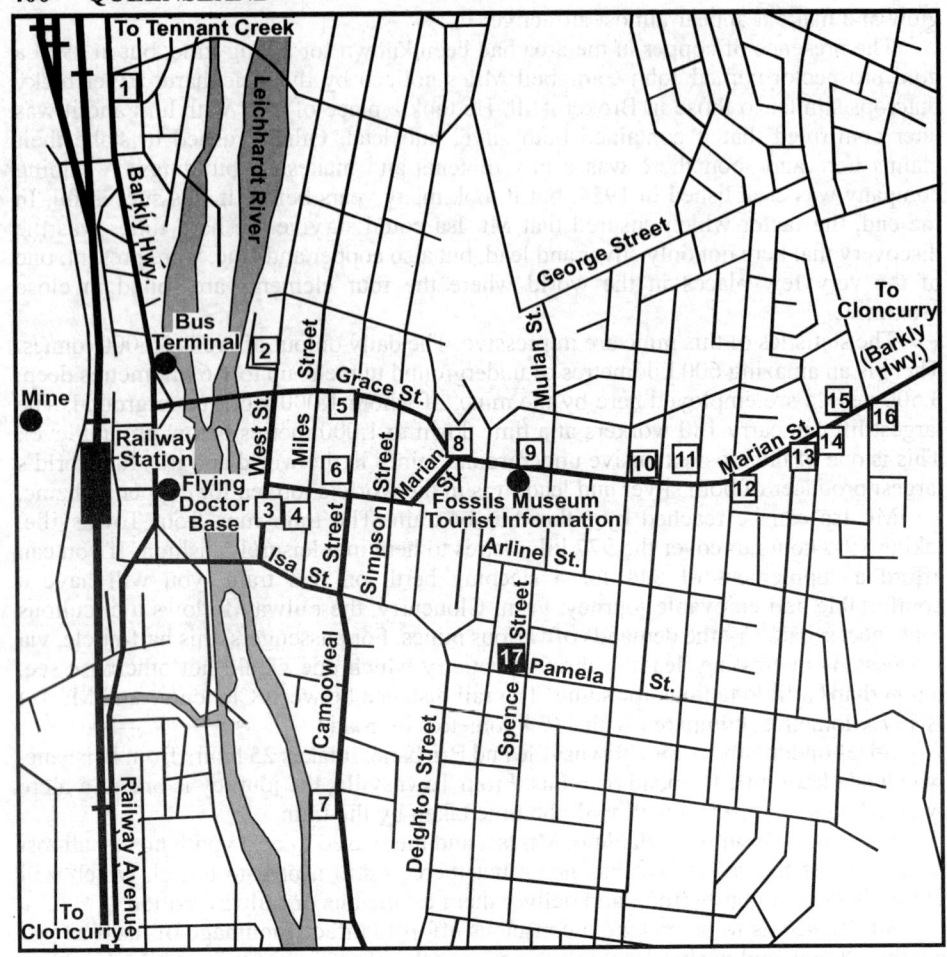

MT. ISA
Black numerals in white boxes indicate hotel accommodation
White numerals in black boxes indicate backpackers hostels

ACCOMMODATION
(i) Hotel Accommodation in Mt. Isa

Name	Stars	No. on Map	Telephone No.	Address	Lowest Price (Double/Twin)
Mercure Hotel	4½	6	07-4743-3024	Marian & Camooweal Sts.	$155
Mt. Isa Outback Inn	4	2	07-4743-2311	45 West Street	$145
Burke and Wills Resort	3½	5	07-4743-8000	Grace & Camooweal Streets	$130
Townview Motel	3½	13	07-4743-3328	112 Kookaburra Street	$105
Overlander Hotel	3½	16	07-4743-5011	119 Marian Street	$95
Barkly Hotel	3½	1	07-4743-2988	Barkly Highway	$85
Mount Isa Hotel	3	4	07-4743-2611	Miles & Marian Streets	$85
Motel Central Point	3	8	07-4743-0666	6 Marian Street	$85
Walton's Motor Court	2½	7	07-4743-2377	23 Camooweal Street	$80
Copper City Motel	3	11	07-4743-2033	105 Butler Strreet	$80

(i) Hotel Accommodation in Mt. Isa, continued

Name	Stars	No. on Map	Telephone No.	Address	Lowest Price (Double/Twin)
Copper Gate Motel	3	12	07-4743-3233	97 Marian Street	$80
Silver Star Motel	3½	14	07-4743-3466	Marian & Doughan Streets	$80
Boyd Hotel		3	07-4743-3000	West Street	$65
Artisans' Block		10	0412-962-069	62 Marian Street	$65
Mt. Isa Caravan Park	3½	15	07-4743-3252	112 Marian Street	$65
Pancake Coffee Lounge		9	07-4743-4004	28 Marian Street	$33

(ii) Backpackers Hostels in Mt. Isa

Name	Group	No. on Map	Telephone No.	Address	Lowest Price (Dormitory)
Artisans' Block		10	0412-962-069	62 Marian Street	$22
Travellers' Haven	VIP	17	07-4743-0313	Spence & Pamela Streets	$19
Pancake Coffee Lounge		9	07-4743-4004	28 Marian Street	$15

MOVING ON
(i) By Train

The train leaves for Townsville on Monday and Friday evenings, arriving at lunch time the following day. The timetable to the right shows connexions to Brisbane and Cairns.

In addition, there is the possibility of travelling to Cairns via Normanton, Croydon and Forsayth and seeing two of the most unusual railways in Australia, together with scenery and small towns which most visitors never approach. This is a truly memorable journey, if you can afford the time required. The timetable for this is on page 370. The journey can be made only at these times, as the trains concerned run only once a week.

Mt. Isa to Townsville
with connexions to Brisbane and Cairns

Days of Departure	M, F	Sun, M, W, F	Not F
Mt. Isa	1800		
Cloncurry	2143		
Hughenden	0539		
Charters Towers	1002		
Townsville	1245	0843	1610
Tully		1249	
Innisfail		1359	
Cairns		1625	
Bowen			1930
Proserpine			2022
Mackay			2242
Rockhampton			0500
Gladstone			0643
Bundaberg			0925
Maryborough West			1035
Gympie North			1224
Brisbane			1555
Days of Arrival	Tu, Sat		Not Sat

(ii) By Bus

Buses operate south-east to Brisbane, east to Townsville, west to Tennant Creek with connexions to Darwin and Alice Springs, and north to Normanton and Karumba. A summary is given below.

Destination	Operator	Via	Distance (km)	Fare	Journey Time	Frequency
Brisbane	McCafferty's		1893	$167	25 hrs	1/day
		Longreach	634	$91	8¼ hrs	1/day
Townsville	McCafferty's		886	$131	11¾ hrs	1/day
Townsville	Greyhound		886	$131	11½ hrs	1/day
Tennant Ck.	McCafferty's		661	$119	7¾ hrs	1/day
Karumba	Coral Coaches		562	$126.50	8½ hrs	2/week
		Normanton	493	$112	7½ hrs	2/week

GREAT RAILWAY JOURNEYS

NORMANTON	Clarina	Glenore	Critters Camp
Distances (km from Normanton)	18	22	26

This is a railway such as you have never seen before. It runs from Normanton to Croydon and is completely disconnected from any other part of the Queensland Railways system. It operates with a staff of two, the officer in charge being also the driver of the train and the stationmaster of both Normanton and Croydon stations. There is one train a week in each direction, out from Normanton on Wednesdays and back on Thursdays. It recent years, this train has even acquired a name, and is now known as the *Gulflander*.

The railway was originally intended to operate between Normanton and Cloncurry when work on it began in 1887. However, in 1886, Croydon, 151 kilometres east of Normanton, was proclaimed a goldfield and, as the population grew, it suddenly seemed a more desirable destination. The first 22 kilometres of the line, therefore, heads south towards Cloncurry, and then the line changes its mind and turns east to Croydon. The first trains ran on the line in 1888, with the first service to Croydon arriving in 1891. By the time that it had arrived, there were already signs that the gold supply there was limited and that it might have been a mistake to choose Croydon as the destination. However, the railway was successful for a while, and at one time it had a staff of 53 employees.

By 1907, it was running at a loss, but, amazingly, it managed to survive the decades until it achieved fame for its uniqueness and started to make a profit again in the 1990s. Right from the start, this was conceived as a low-cost railway. The engineer in charge of the construction, George Phillips, invented and patented the steel sleepers used, which were packed with mud and then put directly into the ground. Most of these sleepers have never been replaced. The track too is made of rails marked *West Cumberland Steel 1886* which have mostly never been replaced. The railway has had only minimal maintenance and yet still functions reasonably efficiently after more than a century of use, a great testimony to its builder. In the twentieth century further efforts were made to economise. Steam locomotives were too expensive to operate on this line, so rail motors were introduced as early as 1922. Basically, these were buses on rails. The vehicle currently used is similar. It was made in 1950 and is a bus with railway bogies attached. The driver has a gear lever (but no steering wheel) and changes gear as he would with a bus. Because of the increase in demand, it now operates with one or two trailers. One of the trailers was originally a suburban carriage, and the other is a converted rail motor. The last steam train ran on this line on 26th May 1929.

Normanton Station was built in 1889 to 1890 and includes a wide arched

5. THE GULFLANDER
NORMANTON TO CROYDON

Crosswater	Haydon	Rail Motor Stop No.1	Blackbull
51	64	78	90

dome over the platform. If you walk around here, you will also find the remains of old rolling stock, including a rebuilt former rail motor, now fit for service once more and used on request for special trips.

The first station along the line was Clarina, eighteen kilometres from Normanton. The water holes here were used to supply the steam locomotives. There was once an hotel here and the Chinese Market Gardens which supplied fresh produce to Normanton.

Glenore was the point at which a decision had to be made. Thus far the line runs south. Now was it to continue south to Cloncurry, or was it to turn east, cross the Norman River and head for Croydon? The decision to divert to Croydon was the one which gave us this unique line, sometimes referred to, somewhat unkindly, as the "railway from nowhere to nowhere". The original timber bridge over the river was washed away in 1902 and the bridge which now spans the Norman is a replacement built at that time. The piles of the original bridge can be seen to the north of the present one. The train will usually pause on the bridge on the return journey from Croydon to Normanton to permit its photograph to be taken. There used to be a station here, with a siding, serving the settlement of Glenore, which included an hotel.

Four kilometres beyond Glenore is Critters Camp, which is a modern name. A triangle has been installed at this point to turn the *Gulflander* on occasions when it is chartered for short trips. The triangle was put in place in 1987 and the gang carrying out the work complained about the level of wildlife found here, particularly the snakes, spiders, centipedes and scorpions. They referred to their base here as 'Critters Camp', and so it is still known. There was a turning triangle here in the early days of the railway too, but not in exactly the same location as the present one.

Crosswater, 51 kilometres out from Normanton, is used as a mail delivery point for Haydon Cattle Station.

Haydon was the terminus of the line for a brief period. There used to be a station here and another turning triangle, as well as a post office, but all of the buildings are gone. The train still stops, though, to deliver mail and freight to Timora Cattle Station.

Rail Motor Stop No. 1 has not managed to acquire a better name in its period of use. The *Gulflander* stops here to deliver mail and goods to Hereford and Gum Creek Cattle Stations. It also sometimes picks up passengers on coach tours at this point and conveys them for a short ride to the next stop at Blackbull.

GREAT RAILWAY JOURNEYS
5. THE GULFLANDER   NORMANTON TO CROYDON
(continued)

Creen Creek	Ellavale	Golden Gate	Croydon
121	129	144	151

Distances (km from Normanton)

At Blackbull, we have completed 60% of the journey, so here the train will stop for morning tea. This repast used to be provided by children from the local cattle station as a way of earning a little pocket money, but the service is now on a more commercial basis. Blackbull was originally the largest station along the line, and is the only one which has survived from the early days, although the station building itself has gone. Recently it was leased out by Queensland Railways and the lessee now provides the morning tea and has established a small museum here in the fettlers' quarters.

We continue through the morning, traversing flat country subject to periodic flooding during the Wet Season from December until April. We pass through Creen Creek and Ellavale, stopping briefly if required.

Our final halt is at Golden Gate, once a suburb of Croydon. The Golden Gate Goldfield was one of the most productive in the area and at one time 2,500 people lived here. The railway used to run commuter services between Croydon and Golden Gate. Now there is nobody at all here. However, the ramp of the railway station can still be seen and there is a variety of abandoned mining and railway equipment in the vicinity. If time permits (i.e. if the driver is not in too much of a hurry for his lunch), the train may stop here to allow a brief examination of the remains visible.

It is only another seven kilometres to Croydon. The station building here has suffered over the years. It was built in 1891, but most of it was destroyed by two storms in 1969, and then another storm took the roof off the fettlers' quarters in 1997, so not much is left now of what was once quite an impressive building. The *Gulflander* will turn on a triangle here and prepare itself for its further exertions tomorrow. Here in Croydon, one of the old steam locomotives which once worked this line has been rebuilt, and parts of two others can be seen near the station. Maybe the rebuilt locomotive will even be in operation if there is some special occasion.

Croydon too is a fascinating former gold mining town, one which seemed to be facing extinction until interest grew in this unique little railway and visitors started coming here again. Walk around the town and see the stately grandeur of the public buildings constructed in a time of affluence when nobody realised how soon the gold would run out.

The Normanton to Croydon Railway may be only 151 kilometres (94 miles) long, but a ride on the *Gulflander* is one which no passenger ever forgets. Try to make it a part of your travels too, perhaps by using the suggested itinerary ('Jim's Tour') on page 370.

NORMANTON, KARUMBA AND CROYDON

Population 1,500 (Normanton)
10 hrs 30 mins by bus from Cairns (Normanton)
7 hrs 30 mins by bus from Mt. Isa (Normanton)

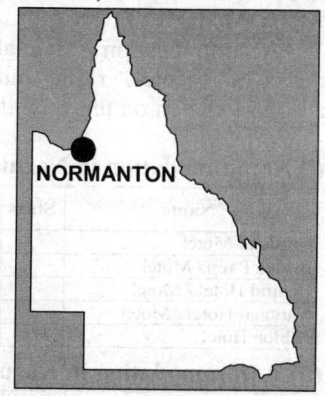

Normanton is a real outback town, formerly an inland river port, but now best known for its Purple Pub and its very unusual railway (see previous section on pages 402 to 404). Normanton is there because of the Norman River, which originally made this the site of an inland port. Now the river is better known as a good fishing ground, and the port has moved to Karumba, on the Gulf of Carpentaria. Architectural features of the town are the fine Victorian **railway station** and the **Purple Pub** (officially the National Hotel), standing out from all else because it is indeed purple. You need not just stand and be amazed by it. You can drink in it and sleep in it too. In fact, you may think that it looks a good deal better from such an interior aspect.

Seventy kilometres north of Normanton is **Karumba**, to which there is a bus service every weekday. Karumba is now the port for this wide area and has a fleet of prawning vessels stationed in it. The population is 700, but, during the southern winter months, that number is augmented by the holidaymakers, with whom this is a popular destination. In past times, Karumba was a staging point on the Sydney to London air route. The Empire Flying Boats used to land on the river here to refuel. It is now another good area for fishing, for birdwatching, for searching out crocodiles and for looking at the wrecks of several unfortunate vessels.

Croydon, at the other end of that railway, reached its zenith in the 1890s. At the height of the gold rush, the area may have had a population as large as 30,000, and this was, for a short while, the fourth largest town in Queensland. 311 gold-bearing reefs were discovered, yielding 1.3 million ounces of gold, which now would be worth in the region of $600 million. The town had twenty hotels and could afford to build wide paved streets and grand municipal buildings. A little of the grandeur still remains, but the principal industry now is tourism, creating a minor revival in the town which almost disappeared completely in the 1950s. Cattle farming is also reviving in the area, and some of the tailings from the old gold mines are being reworked on a minor scale, using modern methods to extract more gold from what was previously discarded. Croydon Shire covers an area of 29,000 square kilometres and has a total population of 500.

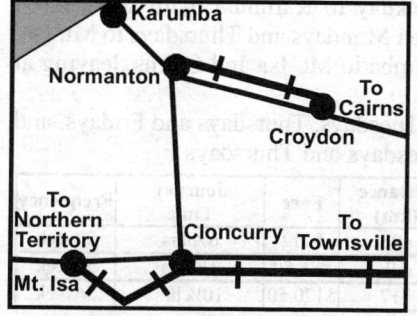

NORMANTON, KARUMBA, CROYDON

Of course, you should come here on the *Gulflander*. It will be one of your most fascinating experiences in Australia. A timetable for a round trip from Cairns including both the *Gulflander* and the *Savannahlander*, another unique train, is given on page 370. This journey takes eight days and can be performed only in the direction shown and only on the days shown if it is to be completed within that period of time. For a really memorable experience, get away from the populated coastal area and try this fascinating trip.

ACCOMMODATION

Accommodation is available in Normanton, Karumba and Croydon. In Croydon, the Club Hotel, right outside the Railway Station, provides backpackers accommodation on the verandah (with fairly mosquito-proof netting) at $12.

(i) Accommodation in Normanton

Name	Stars	Telephone No.	Address	Lowest Price (Double/Twin)
Gulfland Motel		07-4745-1290	Landsborough Street	$85
Brolga Palms Motel		07-4745-1009	Landsborough Street	$75
Central Hotel / Motel		07-4745-1215	Landsborough Street	$65
National Hotel / Motel		07-4745-1324	Landsborough & Brown Sts.	$45
Albion Hotel		07-4745-1218	Haig Street	$40

(ii) Accommodation in Karumba

Name	Stars	Telephone No.	Address	Lowest Price (Double/Twin)
Savannah Shores		07-4745-9126	The Esplanade	$85
Karumba Lodge Hotel		07-4745-9143	Yappar Street	$85
Ash's Holiday Units		07-4745-9132	Ward & Palmer Street	$80
Gee-Dee's Family Cabins		07-4745-9433	27 Palmer Street	$80
Frontier Units		07-4745-9461	Entrance Ln., off Gilbert St.	$80
Matilda's End Units		07-4745-9368	Yappar Street	$80
Gone Fishin Units		07-4745-9502	Ward & Palmer Streets	$75
Jay Seas Holiday Units		07-4745-9414	30 Palmer Street	$75
Sunset Tavern		07-4745-9183	The Esplanade	$55

(iii) Accommodation in Croydon

Name	Stars	Telephone No.	Address	Lowest Price (Double/Twin)
Croydon Gold Caravan Pk		07-4745-6238	Aldridge Street	$65
Club Hotel / Motel	2	07-4745-6184	Brown & Sircom Streets	$42

MOVING ON

(i) By Train

The train runs from Normanton to Croydon on Wednesdays, for which see the timetable at the right. It returns on Thursdays. From Croydon, one can take the bus to Cairns on Thursday, or can take the same bus to Georgetown, then a connecting bus to Forsayth, and on Friday and Saturday can return to Cairns via the *Savannahlander* train, a journey greatly recommended.

Normanton to Croydon

Days of Departure	W
Normanton	0830
Croydon	1300

Days of Departure	Th
Croydon	0830
Normanton	1300

(ii) By Bus

From Normanton, there is a bus every weekday to Karumba, with services on Tuesdays, Thursdays and Fridays to Cairns, and on Mondays and Thursdays to Mt. Isa.

The same buses as above operate from Karumba to Mt. Isa and Cairns, leaving at 6:45 to Cairns, and at 7:30 to Mt. Isa.

From Croydon, there are buses to Cairns on Tuesdays, Thursdays and Fridays, and to Normanton and Karumba on Mondays, Wednesdays and Thursdays.

Destination	Operator	Via	Distance (km)	Fare	Journey Time	Frequency
Mt. Isa	Coral Coaches		493	$112	6¼ hrs	2/week
Karumba	Coral Coaches		69	$26.50	1¼ hrs	5/week
Cairns	Coral Coaches		717	$170.50	10¼ hrs	3/week

▲ Ayers Rock Climb, Looking Up (p. 464)   Ayers Rock Climb, Looking Down ▲
▼ Approaching The Olgas (p. 468)

▲ Todd River, Alice Springs. Who says it never flows? (p. 452)

Camels in Todd River, Alice Springs (p. 455) ▼

▲ Bally Hooley Railway, Port Douglas, Queensland (p. 377)

Afternoon Siesta ▼

Queensland Rail Motor at Dusk
Dig Tree, Queensland (p. 701)

'Matchbox size piece' fallen from Woomera Rocket. Manners Creek, Northern Territory (p. 447)

Author's Students at Local Cinema, Northern Territory

NORTHERN TERRITORY

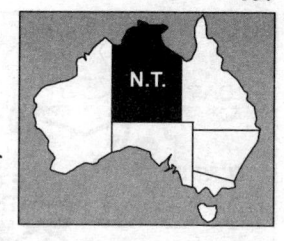

The Northern Territory is the most isolated area of Australia, and one of the most isolated places in the world. The Territory covers an area of 1,349,000 square kilometres, making it the third largest of the Australian states and territories, after Western Australia and Queensland, but it supports a population of only 200,000, even less than the population of the tiny Australian Capital Territory, and is by far the most sparsely populated part of this vast continent. There are but two main centres - Darwin in the north and Alice Springs in the south - and there is a road distance of 1,500 kilometres between these two.

The Territory is an area of majestic grandeur, where nature is strong and those who trifle with her put themselves in peril. It is not an area of a single climate, though, for Darwin, in the north, is a tropical city, with Wet and Dry seasons, the Wet bringing torrential tropical rain and the Dry converting the landscape to parched red earth. Alice Springs, near the south, by contrast, has an arid semi-desert climate, with annual rainfall of only about 350 millimetres and night temperatures falling below freezing in the winter months.

The Northern Territory is the last refuge of the Australian aborigine. Approximately 25% of the population is of aboriginal descent and more than 10,000 full-blooded aborigines survive here. Large tracts of land are Aboriginal Reserves, which cannot be entered without a permit, although where roads pass through it is sometimes permissible to travel those roads without formality.

It is either time-consuming or expensive, or sometimes both, to reach the Territory, so many visitors place it low on their list of priorities. Indeed, a substantial number see nothing but the east coast and leave thinking that they have seen Australia. However, in recent years an increasing number have made the effort to get here and have been well rewarded for doing so. In fact, the new National Parks, Kakadu in particular, have become so popular that they are beginning to suffer some of the minor symptoms of over-tourism.

Throughout Australia, the people have a feeling of state superiority. Somebody from Sydney has a natural suspicion of somebody from Melbourne and *vice versa*, but a Territorian is nobody's enemy and is respected and welcomed everywhere. A Territorian is the nearest that Australia has to a real-life Crocodile Dundee. The Northern Territory is indeed a great little place.

Whilst on the topic of size, and to put matters into perspective, the Northern Territory is about six times the size of Great Britain, and has a total population similar to that of, as an example, Hobart. The total population of the Northern Territory would fit into Sydney twenty times, and nearly half of those live in Darwin, which does not leave many people for the rest of the Territory.

The author used to live in the Northern Territory, which is perhaps why I have such a love for it. The settlement where I was residing was the sixth largest place in the Territory. It had a population of 600, of whom 550 were aborigines. Most people who have lived in this area either love it or hate it, but most have learnt to love the Territory, as you probably will, if you can summon up sufficient energy to get this far.

NORTHERN TERRITORY

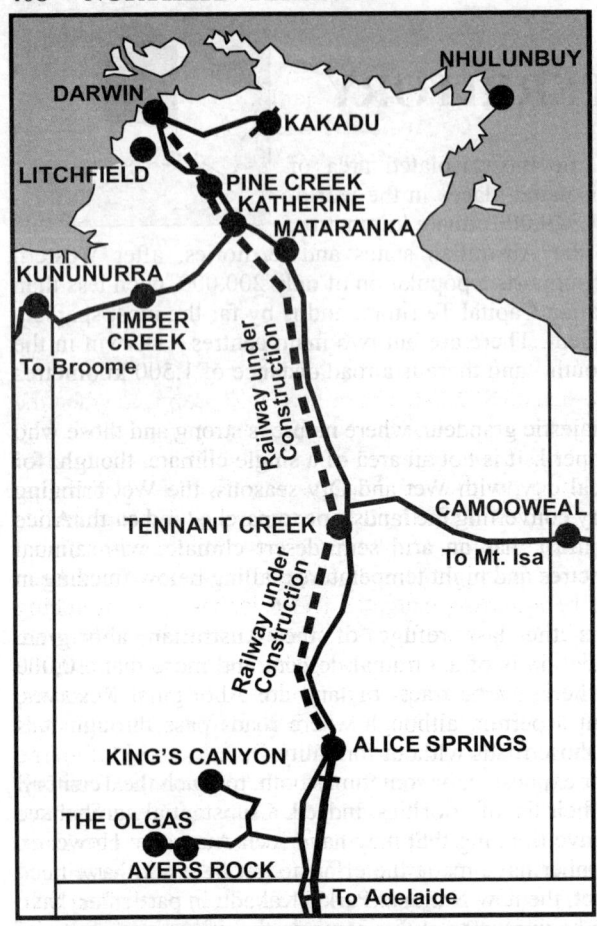

RAILWAY AND BUS ROUTES IN THE NORTHERN TERRITORY

Until 1911, the Northern Territory was a part of South Australia, but then the Commonwealth Government assumed responsibility. In 1978, the Northern Territory was granted a large measure of self-government and given its own parliament, and in 1994 the impressive new Parliament House in Darwin was opened.

The Northern Territory has no transport services of its own, except for the local buses which operate in Darwin and Alice Springs. Passenger rail service is provided by Great Southern Railway, at present from Sydney, Melbourne and Adelaide as far as Alice Springs, but by the end of 2004 the service should be extended along a newly-built line all the way to Darwin. Long-distance bus services are provided by McCafferty's and Greyhound. There is a direct service from Adelaide to Alice Springs, and connecting services link Darwin with Adelaide via Alice Springs, Perth via Broome, and Brisbane via Tennant Creek and Mt. Isa. The bus companies offer various passes aimed specifically at those who wish to visit the Northern Territory, usually including visits to Kakadu National Park and Ayers Rock. If you intend to come here by bus, one of these passes will offer the best value (see pages 20 to 22). The map above shows public transport routes in the Northern Territory.

There are flights to Darwin and Alice Springs with Qantas or Qantas subsidiaries from all major places in Australia. If you use a sector of a *Boomerang Pass* air ticket to get here, it will be good value and a comfortable method of making the journey, but you will miss the experience of seeing the Territory from ground level and the gaining of a true sense of size and distance.

In the author's opinion, the Northern Territory is the best part of Australia and those who do not get here are missing the best and making do with the second-best. Here is where you can really experience why Australia is like no other place on earth, so try to make the effort and see the real Australia.

DARWIN
Population 90,000

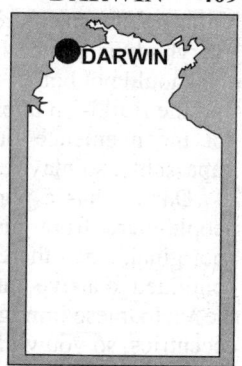

45 hrs by bus from Adelaide
47 hrs 30 mins by bus from Brisbane
59 hrs by bus from Perth

Darwin is a long way from everywhere, as can be seen from the statistics above. Moreover, the bus routes shown are by connecting buses. The Adelaide service involves a connexion at Alice Springs, while the Brisbane service involves connexions at Mt. Isa and Tennant Creek.

During the validity of this book, it should be possible to reach Darwin by train, for a railway is currently under construction and may be open by the end of 2004. The railway was promised when the Commonwealth Government took over control of the Northern Territory in 1911, but, like many things in the Territory, it has been subject to some delay. During the Second World War, the Americans offered to build a standard gauge railway free of charge from Adelaide to Darwin, but the Commonwealth Government refused that generous offer. In 1961, the South Australian Government took the Commonwealth Government to court for its failure to fulfil its promise, but lost because no time limit had been stipulated. In fact, there used to be a narrow gauge (3 feet 6 inches) line stretching down from Darwin to Katherine, and beyond to Larrimah, where goods were transferred to and from road trains. Two mixed trains a week used to operate and the author was fortunate enough to travel on this line prior to its closure in 1976. The same route will be followed, in general, for the new line, which will, however, be standard gauge. The *Ghan* will then provide a service all the way from Sydney and Melbourne to Darwin, via Adelaide and Alice Springs. Traces of the old narrow gauge line can still be seen in Darwin, if you search. For the present, however, the *Ghan* runs from Sydney, Melbourne and Adelaide twice a week to Alice Springs, and from there it is necessary to use a McCafferty's or Greyhound bus for the twenty-hour journey on to Darwin.

The road south is known locally as *The Track* and used to be little more than that. It was constructed during the war to facilitate the deployment of allied troops north. Its critics pointed out that it would also facilitate the deployment of invading troops south.

Because of its isolation, Darwin is a city frequently omitted from the itineraries of visitors, but, in the opinion of the author, the 'Top End', as the northern half of the Territory is known, is the best part of Australia, and should on no account be missed.

The Top End has a tropical climate, and therefore no summer and winter, but instead a Wet Season and a Dry Season. Sometimes visitors unfamiliar with the climate misunderstand this. The Wet is the hotter of the two. The Dry is still pleasantly hot, but without the overpowering combination of heat and humidity. As a guide, the Wet lasts from mid-December until April, with daily maxima of around 33°C. The humidity can be unpleasant but the rain itself usually consists of one hour-long torrential downpour, exhilarating to watch, and does not restrict activities too much. The Dry lasts from May until September and is beautiful. Humidity is low and every day has a maximum temperature of around 28°C. Often it does not rain at all for three months. Sometimes it can be quite cool at night at this time. In between the Dry and the Wet is sandwiched the most unpleasant season of the year, generally known here as the Build-Up, which occurs in October to mid-December. Clouds start to appear in the sky and humidity builds up. Temperatures soar higher and higher, getting up to around 38°C at the peak. Everybody is bathed in sweat, but still it does not rain. The author always thinks that one should not bother too much about season, but most visitors will prefer the Dry, and find the Build-Up unpleasantly sticky. The Wet offers impressive cloudbursts and does not inconvenience one too much in the city, but it soon makes outback roads impassable, so may restrict visits to the nearby National Parks, for example.

Darwin has a pleasant relaxed atmosphere. It is a European city, but there are people here from many different ethnic backgrounds. 23% of the population is aboriginal. Then there are the Chinese who first came for the gold at Pine Creek, but continued to arrive until well into the twentieth century. More recently, there have been the Vietnamese immigrants. In addition to this, Darwin is a place which tends to attract eccentrics, so you will find many 'characters' around. The Smith Street Mall is a good place to start to get the atmosphere of the city. There are also several kerb-side cafés where one can sit and watch life go by. A cheaper place to observe life is from under the attractive Banyan Tree in Harry Chan Avenue. This particular tree has long been a landmark in Darwin and was evidently well established when the city was founded. Plans for recent buildings have been amended in order to go round it, so here it still sits.

Darwin has changed since Cyclone Tracy struck on Christmas Eve 1974, but it still retains something of the atmosphere of a pioneering city, and, of course, it is still proud of its extreme isolation. The population of Darwin is only 90,000, but look on the map and try to find the nearest city of an equivalent size. When you have done that, you will have a better appreciation of just how remote this place is.

There is, of course, the option of flying. You will miss a lot if you do that, but it may be possible to use Darwin as your entry or exit point for Australia. Qantas, for example, has international flights to and from Singapore and Denpasar (Bali). If you arrive by air, there is an information desk at the airport which can arrange accommodation. From the airport, there is an airport bus costing $8 single or $14 return. There is a discount of $2 for backpackers. If you want to take a public bus, you must walk two kilometres to the airport entrance, where, on weekdays, you can take a no. 5. Take the bus in either direction, as it will not make much difference to time or fare. In one direction the bus goes to Darwin by a circuitous route. In the other direction it goes to Casuarina, and you can ask the driver where to change to a no. 10 (Trower Road, where the bus turns right). At weekends, you can take a bus no. 3 and change when you reach Trower Road. Of these buses, only no. 10 runs frequently. No. 5 runs irregularly, but approximately hourly on average on weekdays. Bus no. 3 runs hourly at weekends. The public bus fare to Darwin will be approximately $2.50, with slight variation according to the route followed.

If you arrive in Darwin by long-distance bus, you will find yourself right in the centre of the city.

The modern history of Darwin dates from 1839, when John Lort Stokes, commander of the *Beagle*, entered and named Port Darwin. Interestingly, the port was named after Charles Darwin at a time when he had not become famous. It was not until some twenty years later that he published his *Origin of Species*, but Darwin had been with Stokes on a previous voyage to South America and had impressed him, and the two had become friends. The first Europeans to settle here did not arrive until 1864, at which time this area was part of South Australia. The settlement was originally named Palmerston, but the name was changed later to Darwin.

In 1872, the Overland Telegraph Line was completed, and Darwin was a vital

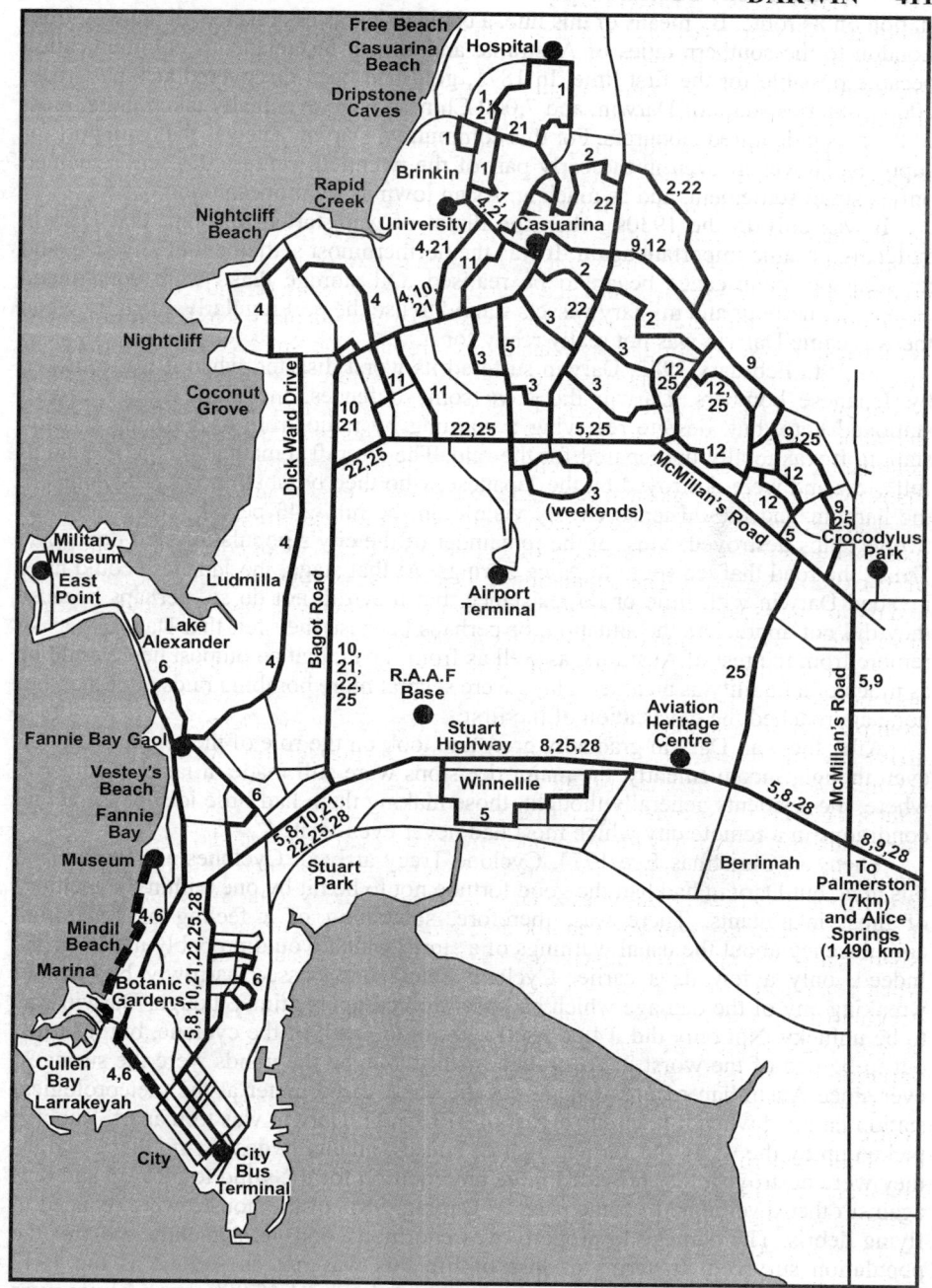

station on its route. By means of this line, a cable link was established all the way from London to the southern cities of Australia, and almost instantaneous communication became possible for the first time. In 1871, gold had been discovered at Pine Creek, 200 kilometres south of Darwin, and 7,000 Chinese were eventually taken there, most of them as indentured labourers. For this community, Darwin acted as the main port for supplies. However, even in the early part of the twentieth century, Darwin remained only a small settlement, and as much an Asian town as a European one.

It was only in the 1930s, when the threat of war started to loom, that Darwin suddenly became important again. It was the northernmost settlement of any size, and its strategic significance began to be realised. Oil storage tanks were constructed around the harbour and military vessels started to use the port regularly. Even so, when the war came Darwin was not really ready for it.

On 19th February 1942, Darwin suffered its worst disaster, when it was attacked by Japanese bombers. Darwin did have some defences, including fighter aircraft stationed here, but, despite receiving a warning by radio from an outlying mission station, it was totally unprepared for the raid. The aircraft remained on the ground in full view and were destroyed by the Japanese, who then bombed the city, the ships in the harbour and the oil tanks clearly visible on the hill. 243 people were killed and twelve ships destroyed. Most of the remainder of the city's population fled down *The Track*, the road that led south to Alice Springs. At that stage, the Japanese could have invaded Darwin with little or no resistance, but they did not do so, perhaps because they did not appreciate the situation, or perhaps because they felt that Darwin was so remote from the rest of Australia, as well as from Japan, that an outpost here would be as much of a liability as an asset. There were several more bombing raids after that, but none approached the devastation of the first.

After the war, Darwin gradually grew and took on the role of the regional capital, even though, inconveniently, the major decisions were still made in far-off Canberra, where, the residents generally thought, those making them had little idea of the actual conditions in a remote city which most had never even visited.

Then, on Christmas Eve 1974, Cyclone Tracy arrived. Cyclones are common in this area, but Darwin had had the good fortune not to be hit by one within the memory of most inhabitants. There was, therefore, something of a feeling of Territorian complacency about the usual warnings of a storm which would probably never arrive. Indeed, only a few days earlier Cyclone Selma had passed narrowly by without wreaking any of the damage which had been forecast. This time, though, Darwin was to be unlucky. Not only did it find itself right in the path of the cyclone, but it turned out to be one of the worst in Australian history. Maybe the winds were the strongest ever since Australian records began, but the wind speed meter at the meteorological station jammed when it recorded a gust of 217 km/hr. Darwin was torn apart. Rubbish picked up by the wind was thrown against houses, gradually destroying them, and, as they were destroyed, that provided more ammunition for the wind to pick up and hurl against other dwellings. In some parts of Darwin, 98% of the houses were reduced to flying debris. The damage to property was enormous, and yet somehow most of the population survived. In terms of loss of life this was not as serious as the 1942 bombing. In a city which had then grown to a population of 45,000, just 64 lives were lost. However, there was now a danger of disease with all amenities destroyed, and so more than 30,000 survivors were air-lifted to southern states, the largest evacuation in Australian history.

Looking around now, you will find little evidence of that calamity. All of the residential areas have been rebuilt and have expanded further, while the central area of the city actually suffered the least, due to its more solid construction. There are some reminders in the city, deliberately left, but now it just seems another episode in the history of a city which is used to being unprepared but surviving.

There are plenty of sights to see in Darwin, but, in addition, the city is a base for tours to other attractions in the Top End. Let us start, though, with a walking tour of the central part of Darwin, plus some coastal scenery.

Walking Tour

This walking tour will cover about nine kilometres and take around four hours, including some time for viewing points of interest, of which there are many. It starts at the beginning of Smith Street Mall and finishes at the Museum, where you will want additional time to look around.

If you prefer, the walk can be divided into two, with Part One a city walk as far as Doctor's Gully, about four kilometres, plus one kilometre back to the city, and Part Two a mostly coastal walk from Doctor's Gully to the Museum, about five kilometres, plus one kilometre from the city to rejoin the route.

Part One

Start at the northern end of **Smith Street Mall**. This is the main shopping street of Darwin, greatly improved since traffic was eliminated from it some years ago. As you walk along, you will see brass plates set in the pavement telling something of the history of Darwin. These make interesting reading. Just over half-way along, you will find the **Victoria Hotel** ('The Vic') on your right, one of the oldest buildings here. Built in 1894 as the North Australian Hotel, it has survived two major cyclones and the war bombings. If you are staying in a backpackers hostel, you will probably be given a voucher for a cheap meal here, and so will get an opportunity to inspect the interior as well. The aviator Kingsford Smith stayed here, and his signature is on the stonework in the arcade. Almost opposite, on the left of this pedestrian area, is an arcade leading off to **Star Village**. This used to be the Star Theatre (cinema), built in the 1930s and destroyed by Cyclone Tracy. The arch to the arcade was the original entrance to the cinema, with the projection bridge surmounting it. The projector used now stands just inside on the left. The old cinema had a half tin roof at the back, but most of the deckchair seating was uncovered, and a white screen was erected at the far end of the cinema. The author watched *The Wizard of Oz* here in the last year of the cinema's existence. It rained during the performance, which gave an interesting effect. At the end of the Smith Street Mall, on the right, is the **Commercial Bank**. Although rebuilt in recent times, it retains the stone colonnade from the original 1893 building.

Turn left at the end of the Smith Street Mall and walk down Bennett Street to the **Chinese Temple** which is near the end of Woods Street. The original 1887 temple was a victim of Tracy, but a new one has been built. There is also a museum devoted to the history of the Chinese in Darwin. The temple is open daily from 8:00 until 16:00 (15:00 at weekends). Admission is free. The museum is open only on Fridays, Saturdays and Sundays from 10:00 until 14:00. Continue along Bennett Street for a short way and then turn right into McMinn Street. Then follow round to Stokes Hill. On your left are the **Australian Pearling Exhibition** and the **Indo Pacific Marine**, both interesting exhibitions. The former, of course, tells the story of the pearling for which this region has been famous since the aborigines first traded pearls with the Macassan sailors who arrived from Celebes (Sulawesi) in Indonesia. The latter displays living coral reefs. Continue on to **Stokes Hill Wharf**. On the way, you will pass an artificial reef and fishing platform. This is a working wharf, but the area contains much else besides. There are restaurants, cafés, shops and entertainment here too.

We have to retrace our steps from here, of course. On the way back, keep left and you will pass **Travellers' Walk**, a path up the hillside constructed as a walkway to the town when Stokes Hill Wharf was being built in 1895. The path which is there now, however, was reconstructed in 1999. There is a Chinese water fountain half-way up and there are various information notices along the path. A little further and you will come to the **Oil Storage Tunnels**. After the Japanese had bombed the oil tanks on the hills here several times, it was decided that it might be a good idea to put the tanks underground where they would be less vulnerable (actually this idea had been mooted before the war started, but it was rejected as being too expensive). Therefore tunnels were constructed and underground storage areas built. This was all done by hand and it took a while. The underground storage areas were ready just as the war finished, and so were never used. Recently one of these tunnels has been opened to the public. It contains a collection of photographs depicting Darwin during the war years. Admission costs $5.

Next to the tunnel is a path up the cliff. Climb up, and you will find yourself at **Survivors' Lookout**. This viewpoint over the harbour tells the story of the bombing of Darwin in 1942 and shows photographs taken at that time, some looking out over the burning ships from roughly this point. If this story interests you, there is more detail in the display in the Harry Chan Arcade which runs between Smith Street and Cavenagh Street in the city (beside 60 Smith Street) and there is a memorial in the new Post Office to those who died in the Post Office of that time. The first bomb of the raid landed on the Post Office and all nine employees there were killed.

Now, if you turn your back to the sea and look inland, you will see, slightly to your right, the **Old Courthouse** and **Police Station** which were built for the South Australian Government in 1884. They suffered greatly from Cyclone Tracy, but have been restored, and are now used as the offices of the Northern Territory Administrator. On the other side of the corner, just a little further along the Esplanade, is **Christ Church Cathedral**. The original was built in 1902, and in 1944 a porch was added, built by the armed forces using the stones of the old Post Office nearby, in memory of those who had lost their lives in the Territory during the war. Cyclone Tracy completely destroyed the Cathedral, except for this porch, which is incorporated in the new cathedral built in 1975. Walk up Smith Street and see **Brown's Mart** on your right, just by the bus station. This building dates from 1885 and was originally a mining exchange. It has had the distinction of having its roof removed by two different cyclones, in both 1897 and 1974, but it has survived both. It is now a community theatre. Opposite, in what is now a park, are the ruins of the Old Town Hall. It was built in 1883 and survived until the cyclone. Now it has been left as a ruinous reminder of the forces of nature. Who could image that a sturdy stone building could be almost totally destroyed by the winds of a single night? The Territory is indeed a place where one learns to respect nature.

Now walk up to Bennett Street at the end of Smith Street Mall once more, and this time turn left to see the Northern Territory **Parliament House**. This modern building, completed in 1994, is most imposing, especially considering that there are only 25

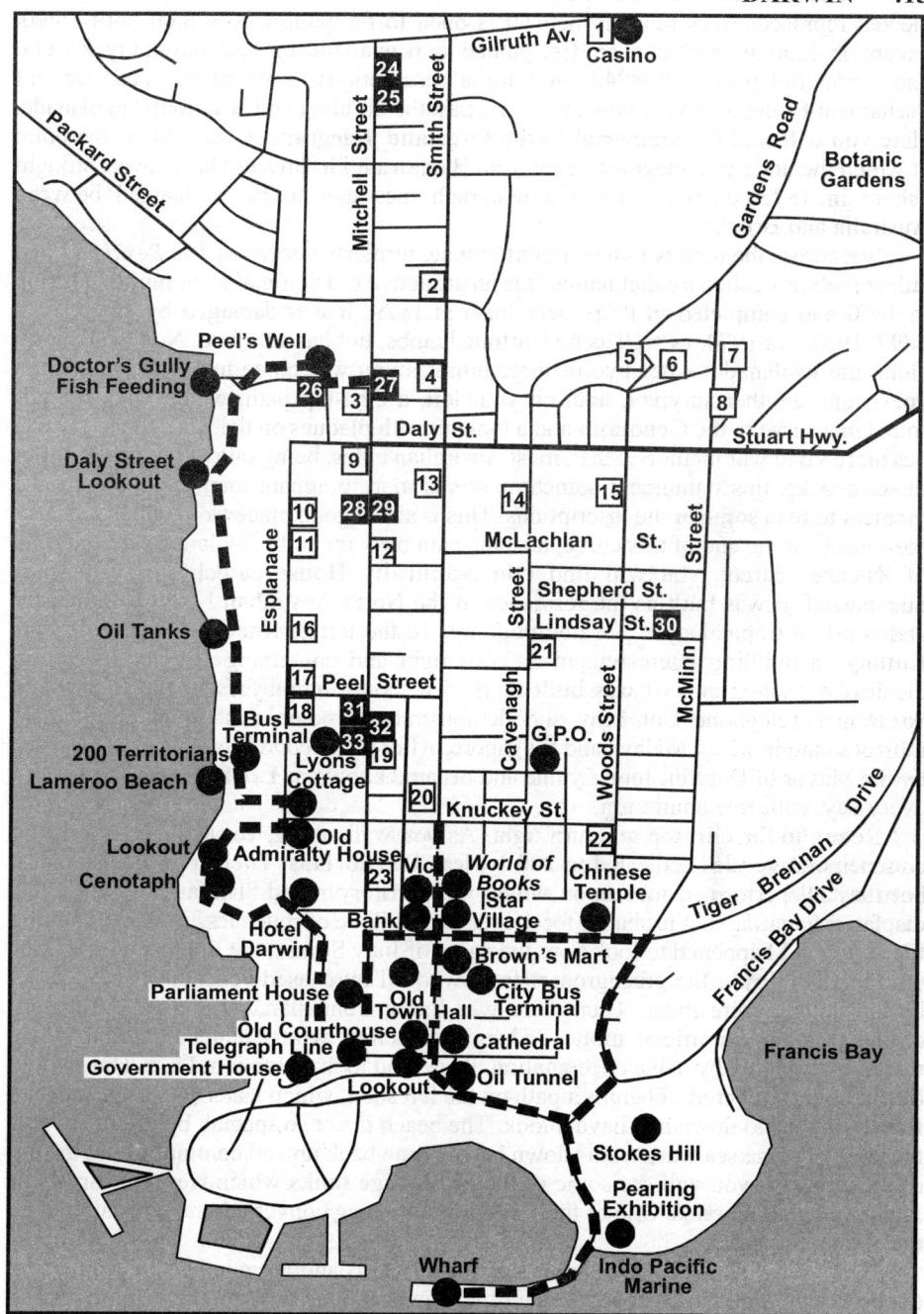

DARWIN CITY CENTRE
Dashed line shows Walking Tour, Part 1
Black numerals in white boxes indicate hotel accommodation
White numerals in black boxes indicate backpackers hostels

elected representatives meeting here. It is open to the public from 8:00 until 18:00, except on Sundays, and there are free guided tours available on Saturdays only at 10:00 and 12:00 (telephone 08-8946-1509 for a reservation). Stay on the near side of Parliament House and walk down the grass past the building and back to the Esplanade. Here you will find the **memorial to the Overland Telegraph Line**. This is the point at which the undersea telegraph cable from Banjawangi in Java to Darwin was brought ashore in 1872, enabling the first telegraph messages to be exchanged between Australia and Britain.

Just across the road is **Government House**, formerly known as *The Residency* and still sometimes called by that name. It is an attractive old colonial style building begun in 1870 and completed in its present form in 1879. It was damaged by cyclones in 1897, 1937 and 1974, as well as by wartime bombs, but has survived. Now walk north along the Esplanade. After two or three minutes you will come to **Hotel Darwin** on your right, another survivor, and, on your left, a cliff-top path, which take. It leads round in a curve to the **Cenotaph** and a lookout with plaques on the wall. Since Darwin has more vivid war memories than most Australian cities, being one of the few to suffer direct attacks, this monument somehow seems more poignant than most, so pause a moment to read some of the inscriptions. This is also a good place from which to watch the sunset. At the end of this curve, take the path back up to the Esplanade. To the right of Knuckey Street, you will find **Old Admiralty House**, which survived Tracy undamaged. It was built as the residence of the North Australian Naval Commander and is a fine tropical-style elevated building. To the left of Knuckey Street is **Lyons Cottage**, a building interesting in its own right and containing also an interesting display of photographs. It was built in 1925 to house employees of the British and Australian Telephone Company and demonstrates a colonial style of architecture mostly found in India, Malaya and Singapore. After the Second World War, it was used by the Mayor of Darwin, John Lyons, and became known as Lyons Cottage. It is open every day, with free admission.

Return to the cliff top and turn right. As you walk along, you will see a series of commemorative tiles dedicated to **200 typical Territorians**. They are not all famous, but they all performed jobs upon which the Territory relied. The author found this display fascinating, but probably for the reader it will be of much less interest. The first tile at which I happened to look bore the name of Judy Stokes, the linguist where I was working. Ah Toy's, the greengrocers from whom I purchased vegetables shipped out by air freight, were there. Then there was Eddie Connellan, who ran the Territory airline Connair (unofficial motto, 'There's no tellin' with Connellan'), and others whom I knew only by name or reputation. Pause and look at a few, at least. They would like to be remembered. There is a path on the left soon, which leads down to **Lameroo Beach**. Let us go down and have a look. The beach is not so special, but there are also the ruins of some sea water baths down here. Climb back up and continue along the top of the cliff, and you will see some of the **oil storage tanks** which were the targets of Japanese bombing raids. One of these is currently being converted into a restaurant, an interesting project.

Now you will reach **Daly Street Lookout**. Here is another good place from which to observe the sunset. If it is not sunset time, however, look down at the mangroves and wonder at their existence so far into the sea. There are big tides here, however. The main path leads off here to the right, but a smaller path descends to **Doctor's Gully**. Follow this one. The area on your right was originally market gardens, and then the site of the first hospital. Soon you will reach Doctor's Gully **Fish Feeding Place** (*Aquascene*). The fish are fed only at particular times, which depend upon the tides, so enquire in advance if you are interested in this activity. Admission costs $5.

From the foot of Doctor's Gully, turn right and follow the path (not the road; the path is to the left of the road) up through lush tropical vegetation, which must be almost unchanged from the time when the first settlers appeared here and dug **Peel's Well**, of which you will see remnants on your ascent. At the top you will find yourself at the back of the Y.M.C.A. (not a bad place to stay if your sojourn is long enough to qualify for a weekly rate). Now you have a choice. Have you had enough for today, or do you want to go on? If you are tired, join the road there and return to Darwin city centre along Mitchell Street. The walk from here will take only about ten minutes. If you have plenty of stamina left, take the path on your left, which cuts through to Mitchell Street, and then turn left.

Part Two

If you are rejoining the walk at this point, all you have to do is walk from the city straight along Mitchell Street. Proceed right to the end of the street and turn right into Lambell Terrace, then soon left into Kahlin Avenue. Turn right into Burnett Place and you will find four pre-war houses which are the headquarters of the National Trust. This, the **Myilly Point Precinct**, was originally housing for high-ranking government employees. It is now open for inspection between 10:00 and 15:00 on weekdays. Admission is free. Walk back along Burnett Place and, just beyond the roundabout, you will find a path off to the right, followed by steps descending to the beach. Follow these and walk along **Mindil Beach**. In the Dry Season, from May until October, this is the scene of a market every Thursday evening, specialising in food from many countries, reflecting the diverse ethnic origins of the residents of Darwin, but including many other wares and entertainments also. The market takes place from 17:00 until 22:00, and there is also a smaller Sunday market from 16:00 until 21:00 in the same season. At the end of Mindil Beach, walk up from the beach to the coastal path, which has been named the **Fairweather Walk**. This is not an indication that it will never rain here, but a memorial to the remarkable artist and adventurer, Ian Fairweather. Read more about him in the panels as you pass along.

Eventually, you will come to the **Museum and Art Gallery** of the Northern Territory, which is our destination. It is built next to the site of the former Vestey's Meatworks. However, this path actually continues further, all the way to East Point, another six kilometres, if you need more exercise. (Note, though, that there is no public bus service from East Point.) The Museum and Art Gallery, however, are worth a good deal of time. They are both free and both interesting. You will probably find that you need three hours here. Opening hours are 9:00 until 17:00 daily.

Here our walk ends. To return to Darwin city centre, you can choose between walking to East Point Road, about a kilometre, from where a regular bus service is available, or walking back again through the **Botanic Gardens**, which date from 1886. The latter is recommended if you have sufficient energy. It is about three kilometres to the city centre via this direct route.

There are other attractions, of course, not on this walking tour. **Mitchell Street** is increasingly popular with young people, with places to eat and drink, as well as a **Night Market** near Peel Street. Nearly all of the backpackers accommodation is in Mitchell Street too.

ANECDOTE

My flight with Connair, the Territory airline, was due out of Darwin at 6:30, so I turned up at the airport at 6:00. Connair was always in need of saving money, as probably airlines serving remote areas always will be, so pilots whose hours in the cockpit were used up were assigned to clerical duties to eke out the airline's existence. Such was the officer on duty at this time. I approached the desk and was greeted with, "Well, and what's your problem then, mate?" Public relations was evidently not part of pilot training for Connair. I presented my ticket and was told, "Right. Gate One. 6:25." At 6:25, I went to the gate. It was locked, with nobody in sight. At 6:35, the same man turned up, unlocked the door and let me out onto the tarmac. Bewildered, I said, "Excuse me, where is it?" "Over there," he replied, pointing to a distant speck in the farthest corner of the tarmac. It proved to be nearly ten minutes walk away, and I felt as though I had travelled all the way to my destination by the time I reached the proudly erect DC-3.

Entering a DC-3 is not like boarding a modern aircraft, because of the angle at which it sits on the ground. Having climbed the metal steps, one still has more mountaineering to accomplish to reach one's assigned seat (or not assigned, in the case of Connair, since there were only seven passengers). Connair's policy was to remove half of the 28 seats to make room for more freight, but to carry the seats along too, just in case, so the interior of the aircraft looked as though the removal men had been in, but had not quite had time to finish.

"Right, safety drill," announced the flight attendant (yes, there was one). "Anybody not been in one of these before? Well, I'd better tell you anyway. Look, there's a door at the back, and there's another one up the front." And that was it. The formalities over, the pilot attempted to start the engines. First attempt - nothing. Second attempt - a loud backfire and quantities of smoke. Third attempt - repeated backfiring. Loads more smoke. Fourth attempt - the engine gradually coaxed into action, as a result of which the whole aeroplane started to bounce up and down, a situation which was stabilised by repeating the whole backfiring process with the port engine. We were ready. Out to the runway. Never mind about going to the end, because in a just a few moments we were airborne, so magnificently built were these old aircraft. DC-3s are not pressurised, of course, so their altitude is limited to 10,000 feet, enabling passengers to enjoy the panorama from an interesting height, cooled by the fresh breeze whistling in round the edges of the single-paned real glass windows, and contemplate the romantic image of this superb flying machine while watching the oil trickle out of the engine, make its way back across the wing and slowly drip off into space. Ah. the nostalgic days of true flying!

An unusual and interesting shop to visit is National Flags, at Shop 8 in Harry Chan Arcade, which runs between Smith Street and Cavenagh Street. Talk to Ron Strachan, who knows just about everything about flags. It does not matter that you are not actually thinking of purchasing a set of world flags today. He will still be pleased to see you.

At the north-western edge of the city is **Cullen Bay Marina**, protected by recently reclaimed land. It is an area becoming known for its restaurants, and it is also the terminal for the Mandorah Ferry. **Mandorah** is on the other side of the harbour and offers beaches and fishing. It is only eight kilometres by ferry, but 130 kilometres by road, and some of it not very good road either. The ferry runs every two hours, at odd hours during the week and at even hours at the weekend. The crossing takes only fifteen minutes, but costs $18 return. The last ferry back is at 18:20 on Mondays and Tuesdays, 22:20 on Sundays, Wednesdays and Thursdays, and 0:20 on Fridays and Saturdays. Cullen Bay is three kilometres from Darwin city centre. There is no bus service which goes there, but you can take no. 4 or no. 6 and walk the last kilometre.

Beyond the Museum, where our walk ended, a path continues to Fannie Bay, and on to East Point. **Fannie Bay Gaol** lies just back from the shore and is famous. It opened in September 1883 and saw service for 96 years, housing some of the Northern Territory's most notorious criminals. During the war it was bombed, and the inmates had to be released. The gallows there were not constructed until after the war and were used for the Territory's last executions, on 7th August 1952. The Gaol is open daily from 10:00 until 17:00 and admission is free. To reach here by bus, take no. 4 or no. 6.

If you continue along the foreshore path, you will reach **East Point**, which is a recreational area with the remains of several military installations. In order, you will pass a searchlight complex, the boom net tower and end anchors, a lookout tower, a defence and command post with a six inch gun emplacement, and then, just inland, a 9.2 inch gun emplacement. Next to the latter gun emplacement is the **East Point Military Museum**. The area also offers good sunset views, wallaby viewing (best at sunset), a monsoon vine forest walk and a mangrove boardwalk (best at low tide). At the southern end of East Point is Lake Alexander, named after a former Lord Mayor of Darwin, which provides all-year salt water swimming, and nearby is a former 'ack ack' battery. There is no bus service to East Point, so you must walk from Fannie Bay, nearly three kilometres away. To Fannie Bay take bus no. 4 or no. 6. The no. 6 goes a little closer, but operates irregularly and infrequently and on weekdays only. The *Tour Tub* operates to East Point every hour, but is rather expensive (see under, page 420).

The main suburban shopping centre is at **Casuarina**, to reach which take a bus no. 4 or no. 10 (also 5, but by a circuitous route).

The **Australian Aviation Heritage Centre** is located on the south side of the airport, to reach which take a bus no. 5 or no. 8.

Crocodylus Park is on the edge of the residential area and has, as one might anticipate, crocodiles. To reach it, take bus no. 5.

Palmerston is the other major residential area, lying east of Darwin. It is not an area especially interesting to visitors, but, if you wish to go there, take bus no. 8.

For those who want to lie on the beach, there are several choices. Right in the city is **Lameroo Beach**, but it is rather small and unappealing. A little further out is **Mindil Beach**, within walking distance, or you can take a bus no. 4 or 6. Slightly further on is **Vestey's Beach**, which can be reached by the same bus routes. **Nightcliff Beach** is pleasant, but further away again. It can be reached by bus no. 4. Then there is the long

NORTHERN TERRITORY

Casuarina Beach, with the Dripstone Caves in the centre of it. To reach this beach, take a bus no. 4 or 10 to Casuarina, and then a no. 1 to the nearest point to the beach, which is a stop in Trower Road (ask the driver). From there you will have to walk one more kilometre. Two kilometres further on along Casuarina Beach, which is usually almost deserted, lies the **Free Beach**, where nude bathing is permitted, but you will have to walk this additional two kilometres in each direction if you wish to use the beach.

Bus services in Darwin are variable, but steadily improving. The triangle Darwin - Casuarina - Palmerston is well served, but local services are irregular and often operate on weekdays only. If you intend to change buses on your journey, ask for a ticket to your destination when boarding. That will be regarded as one extra zone (unless you cross an additional zone boundary), and charged at only an additional 50 cents. An all-day ticket, called a *Tourcard*, is available for $5. Since the shortest journey costs $1.50 (one zone), and most trips cost $2 (two zones), it is usually worth purchasing the all-day ticket if you intend to make more than one return journey during the day. The *Tourcard* must be purchased from the bus company office, however (in Harry Chan Avenue in Darwin). It cannot be bought on the bus.

A tourist bus service is operated by the *Tour Tub*, which makes an hourly circuit of likely destinations and allows passengers to alight and reboard as they wish throughout the day. However, with the exception of East Point, all of these attractions are within walking distance of the city or accessible by more frequent public buses. The *Tour Tub* costs $25 for a day ticket. It operates from 9:00 until 16:00.

Just outside Darwin is **Berry Springs**, a popular and attractive swimming and picnic place. Beyond is the **Crocodile Farm**, forty kilometres south of the city. Feeding time is at 14:00.

Then there are **cruises on the Adelaide River**, 64 kilometres from Darwin. The attraction here is not just the scenic beauty of the river, but the **crocodiles** which have been trained to leap from the water for the tasty morsels suspended temptingly above them.

There is no public transport to the attractions out of Darwin, but tours operate to these places.

There are also **cruises** available on **Darwin Harbour**. Several operators vie for patronage, but none of them offers economy as its virtue. The cruises cost about $50 and last for 90 minutes.

Finally, as mentioned above, Darwin is also a base for tours. Especially popular are the Kakadu and Litchfield National Parks. These can be visited on one-day tours, although if you stay a night there, naturally you see more. Even Katherine Gorge can be seen on a day-tour, although it seems more logical to visit on the way to somewhere else. Some visitors will be using a bus pass which includes or permits a tour of Kakadu, and that will be the cheapest and best way to see the park. For other places, some of the tour operators, for example AAT Kings, offer discounted seats 24 hours before departure to those who are willing to go on a stand-by basis. Even so, expect to pay $100 for a day tour to one of the National Parks. For more information on Kakadu and Litchfield, see under.

BOOKSHOPS

World of Books   *30 Smith Street Mall*
A fine independent bookshop near the southern end of Smith Street Mall.

ANECDOTE

It was during the months just after Cyclone Tracy had hit and Darwin was a mess, with piles of rubble everywhere amidst the leafless trees, the type of devastation which one might expect to see after a series of bomb attacks rather than as the result of one night of nature's fury.

I was in the city to catch a flight to Bacau in Portuguese Timor, as it was then. The flight was officially operated by the Timorese airline, but that airline had no aircraft large enough for the job, so the flight was chartered to the Australian domestic airline T.A.A. (Trans Australian Airlines) which used a 40-seater Fokker Friendship.

I arrived at the roofless airport terminal on time and was checked in for my flight, but nothing more occurred. After a while all the passengers were summoned to the desk and informed, "What has happened is this. There is a problem with the engine of the aircraft which was supposed to go to Bacau and we haven't got a spare engine in Darwin, so we are bringing one from Brisbane. We are bringing it in another Fokker Friendship, but to get the engine in we have had to take half of the seats out. When the plane gets here, we are going to take the engine out and then put some seats from the aircraft with the broken engine into the good one and take you in that. However, it will take a couple of hours for the plane to get here and another hour or so to change the seats over, so please exercise patience."

We exercised patience in the roofless, air-conditionless terminal, and after another three hours were summoned again. "Well, it's like this. We have now discovered that the seats on the two aircraft are not interchangeable, so now we have one plane with only one engine and another with only half the seats. We have decided to take half of you in the plane with twenty seats. These are the names of the passengers who have been selected to go."

I was in the lucky half, or so I thought at the time. We got on board. The front part of the cabin had not only no seats, but also no inner walls - only the ribs and the outer steel shell. The cockpit had no door and one could see out of the front of the aircraft. We made our way to the runway and set off. Half way down, at speed, the plane suddenly lurched to one side. The pilot slammed on the brakes and we came to a nervous halt, just on the edge of the runway. One of the braver voices enquired what was wrong. "Steering's broken," replied the pilot. "Actually, I could probably take off all right using the flaps, but I'm not too sure whether I could land again, especially if there were a wind, so I thought it safer to stop." We concurred with his decision and returned to the hot and sticky terminal for a further two hours, to watch a large jack being dragged across the tarmac and a mechanic peering despondently into the inner mysteries of the steering mechanism.

When the plane was pronounced fit for another attempt, we reboarded with rather more trepidation, but the only further slightly disconcerting event was when the pilot pointed out the Timor coast to us and then added, "Don't all crowd over to one side like that. You're tipping the plane up." Several bodies retreated hastily and, without further mishap, our morning flight landed in Bacau just as dusk was beginning to fall.

422 NORTHERN TERRITORY
ACCOMMODATION
(i) Hotel Accommodation in Darwin

Name	Stars	No. on Map	Telephone No.	Address	Lowest Price (Double/Twin)
Carlton Hotel	5	11	1-800-891-119	The Esplanade	$240
Marrakai Luxury Suites	4	13	1-800-653-532	93 Smith Street	$230
Mirambeena Resort	4	21	08-8946-0111	64 Cavenagh Street	$205
All Seasons Premier Cent.	4½	20	08-8944-9000	Smith & Knuckey Streets	$185
Top End Hotel	3	9	1-800-626-151	Daly & Mitchell Streets	$170
Saville Park Suites	4	18	1-800-681-686	88 The Esplanade	$165
Novotel Atrium	4	17	08-8941-0755	100 The Esplanade	$155
Rydges Plaza	5	23	08-8982-0000	32 Mitchell Street	$155
Emerald Hotel	4	14	1-800-357-760	81 Cavenagh Street	$150
Metro Inn Darwin	3	5	08-8981-1544	38 Gardens Road	$140
Alatai Holiday Apts.		8	1-800-628-833	McMinn & Finniss Streets	$135
Centra Darwin	4	10	08-8981-5388	122 The Esplanade	$135
M.G.M. Grand Casino	5	1	1-800-891-118	Gilruth Avenue	$125
Peninsular Apartments	2½	4	1-800-808-564	115 Smith Street	$125
All Seasons Frontier	3½	6	08-8981-5333	3 Buffalo Court	$125
City Gardens Apartments	3	15	1-800-891-138	93 Woods Street	$110
Asti Motel	3	2	1-800-063-335	Smith Street & Packard Pl.	$105
Poinciana Inn	3½	12	1-800-355-114	Mitchell & McLachlan Sts.	$105
Luma Luma Apartments	3	22	1-800-656-988	Woods & Knuckey Streets	$105
Cherry Blossom Motel	3½	16	08-8981-6734	108 The Esplanade	$95
Palms Motel	2½	7	08-8981-4188	100 McMinn Street	$80
Value Inn		19	08-8981-4733	50 Mitchell Street	$80
Banyan View Y.W.C.A.		3	08-8981-8644	119 Mitchell Street	$50

(ii) Backpackers Hostels in Darwin

Name	Group	No. on Map	Telephone No.	Address	Lowest Price (Dormitory)
Y.M.C.A.		26	08-8981-8377	Doctor's Gully Road	$25
Melaleuca Backpackers	Nom	32	1800-623-543	50 Mitchell Street	$22
Wilderness Lodge		29	1800-068-886	88 Mitchell Street	$21
Banyan View Y.W.C.A.		3	08-8981-8644	119 Mitchell Street	$20
Elke's Inner City Lodge	VIP	27	1800-808-365	112 Mitchell Street	$20
Globetrotters Lodge	VIP	28	1800-800-798	97 Mitchell Street	$20
Frogshollow Backpackers		30	1800-068-686	27 Lindsay Street	$20
Chilli's Backpackers		31	08-8941-9722	69a Mitchell Street	$20
Darwin City Y.H.A.	YHA	33	08-8981-3995	69 Mitchell Street	$20
Gecko Lodge		24	08-8981-5569	146 Mitchell Street	$19
Whoop Whoop B'packers	B&W	25	08-8941-1295	144 Mitchell Street	$17

MOVING ON

Hopefully by the time that this is read, you will be able to get on a train in Darwin and alight eighteen hours later in Alice Springs, or, if you prefer, continue all the way to Adelaide, Sydney or Melbourne.

Until that eventuates, however, both McCafferty's and Greyhound operate bus services down *The Track* to Alice Springs via Katherine and Tennant Creek. There is a connexion on to Adelaide. At Tennant Creek, you can make a connexion east to Mt. Isa and Townsville, changing again at Mt. Isa if you wish to go to Brisbane. To the west,

Greyhound runs to Broome, with an onward service (sometimes the same bus) to Perth. There is also a Greyhound service to Kakadu National Park.

Bus Services from Darwin

Destination	Operator	Via	Distance (km)	Fare	Journey Time	Frequency
Alice Springs	McCafferty's		1515	$214	20¼ hrs	1/day
		Tennant Creek	1012	$151	13¾ hrs	1/day
		Katherine	316	$58	4¼ hrs	1/day
Alice Springs	Greyhound		1515	$214	20¾ hrs	1/day
		Tennant Creek	1012	$151	14 hrs	1/day
		Katherine	316	$58	4¼ - 4¾ hrs	2/day
Broome	Greyhound		1970	$281	25½ hrs	1/day
Kakadu	Greyhound		327	$50	5¾ hrs	1/day

KAKADU NATIONAL PARK
6 hrs by bus from Darwin

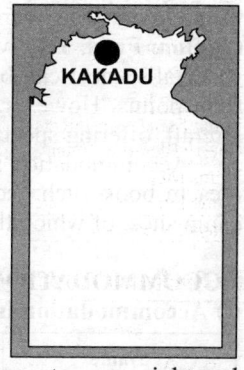

The Kakadu National Park lies some 300 kilometres east of Darwin, and is said by some visitors to be the most beautiful place that they have ever seen. Certainly the escarpment forming the eastern boundary of the park is impressive, and some of the waterfalls, when flowing in the Wet, are awe-inspiring. Unfortunately, the rangers, at such times, often feel it their responsibility to close the roads and prevent visitors from reaching these magnificent sights.

One can travel to Kakadu on a Greyhound bus, or one can go on a tour. Some tours show you the sights in a day, while others stay overnight and let you spend two days here, or three, or even four. Of course, the longer you stay, the more you see, but expect to pay $100 per day for a tour. With the Greyhound bus, you will see some of the sights on the way in, including the aboriginal rock paintings at Nourlangie Rock, and there is also a Greyhound tour available which goes to Ubirr Rock on the eastern edge of the park. Those using bus passes will find these routes either included or available with the pass, and this is likely to prove the most economical method of viewing the park. However you travel, you will be subjected to payment of a considerable fee for entry to the National Park. This fee is currently $16.25, which covers you for a week within its boundaries.

The route to Kakadu first follows the main road south from Darwin, and then, after forty kilometres, turns off east, and soon reaches **Humpty Doo**. Here you can find Graeme Gow's Reptile World, a display of snakes and reptiles, including 25 of the world's most venomous snakes. The Humpty Doo Hotel here offers accommodation, but not at budget prices. The road crosses the Adelaide River after a further few kilometres. This is the place at which there are **cruises** on the river to see the **jumping crocodiles** mentioned in the section on Darwin. It should not be confused, however, with the town of Adelaide River, which is on the main highway south from Darwin to Alice Springs. Continuing, the **Djukbinj National Park** (free admission) is on your left, and then you will come to the **Mary River Crossing**, with Mary River Park and,

424   NORTHERN TERRITORY

three kilometres on, Bark Hut. A little further on is the entrance to the **Mary River Wetlands**, less famous than Kakadu, but offering plenty of wildlife observation, bushwalking and fishing. There are tours operating from here, especially birdwatching tours, for several rare species are found in the area, attracted by the year-round water supply. There are also crocodile cruises every two hours. The scenery is less spectacular than that of Kakadu, but the area has a less touristic feel to it. Everybody knows about Kakadu, but few know how beautiful the Mary River Wetlands can be too. Budget accommodation and camping are both available here.

Travelling on eastwards, you will soon come to the entrance to Kakadu. It is a vast area, so there are several places to stay and many more which one ought to visit. It will be another three hours before the Greyhound bus reaches its terminus, for example.

The aborigines may have lived in this area for some 50,000 years and there are 5,000 sites throughout the park bearing witness to their culture, of which Nourlangie and Ubirr are two of the best known examples. The park covers 19,804 square kilometres and also offers a huge range of wildlife to be observed.

Highlights of Kakadu are the art sites of **Nourlangie** and **Ubirr**, Bowali Visitor Centre at **Jabiru**, Warradjan Cultural Centre at **Cooinda**, **Jim Jim Falls**, **Twin Falls**, **Gunlom Falls**, **Yellow Waters** and **Mamukala** (see the map opposite). Except for the waterfalls, most can be reached just by getting on and off the Greyhound bus at the right points. However, tours are available within the park, as are joy rides on small aircraft, offering spectacular views. These cost about $80 for half an hour.

Accommodation is available in Kakadu, including two youth hostels. It is a good idea to book such accommodation in advance. Camping is permitted at designated camp sites, of which there are about a dozen.

ACCOMMODATION
(i) Accommodation in Humpty Doo

Name	Stars	No. on Map	Telephone No.	Address	Lowest Price (Double/Twin)
Humpty Doo Hotel		1	08-8988-1372	Arnhem Highway	$145

(ii) Hotel Accommodation in Mary River Area

Name	Stars	No. on Map	Telephone No.	Address	Lowest Price (Double/Twin)
Mary River Park	3	2	08-8978-8877	Mary River Crossing	$40
Bark Hut Inn		3	08-8978-8988	Arnhem Highway	$80
Wildman River Lodge		4	08-8978-8912	Off Point Stuart Road	$105
Point Stuart Lodge		5	08-8981-7263	Point Stuart Road	$105

(iii) Backpackers Hostels in Mary River Area

Name	Group	No. on Map	Telephone No.	Address	Lowest Price (Dormitory)
Mary River Park	YHA	2	08-8978-8877	Mary River Crossing	$18
Point Stuart Lodge	VIP	5	08-8936-1311	Point Stuart Road	$25

(iv) Hotel Accommodation in Kakadu National Park

Name	Stars	No. on Map	Telephone No.	Address	Lowest Price (Double/Twin)
Kakadu Resort	3½	6	1-800-818-845	South Alligator	$155
Gagudju Crocodile Hotel	3½	7	08-8979-2800	Flinders Street, Jabiru	$185
Kakadu Lodge	3	8	08-8979-2422	Jabiru Drive, Jabiru	$130
Gagudju Cooinda Lodge	3	9	08-8979-0145	Cooinda	$150

(v) Backpackers Hostels in Kakadu National Park

Name	Group	No. on Map	Telephone No.	Address	Lowest Price (Dormitory)
Gagudju Cooinda Lodge	YHA	9	08-8979-0145	Cooinda	$30
Kakadu Ubirr Road Y.H.A.	YHA	10	08-8979-2232	Oenpelli Road, Ubirr	$25

MOVING ON
Bus Services from Kakadu National Park (Cooinda)

Destination	Operator	Via	Distance (km)	Fare	Journey Time	Frequency
Darwin	Greyhound		311	$50	4½ hrs	1/day
Ubirr	Greyhound		93	$20	1¼ hrs	1/day

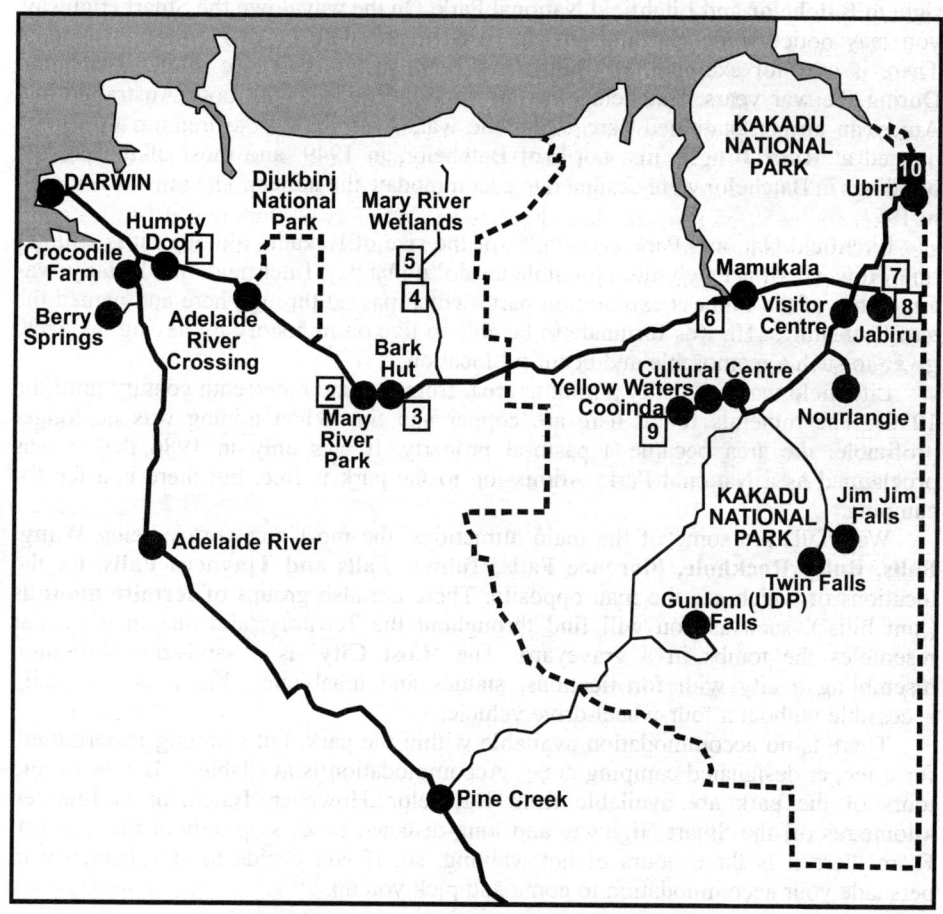

KAKADU NATIONAL PARK
Black numerals in white boxes indicate hotel accommodation
White numerals in black boxes indicate backpackers hostels

LITCHFIELD NATIONAL PARK
No public transport available

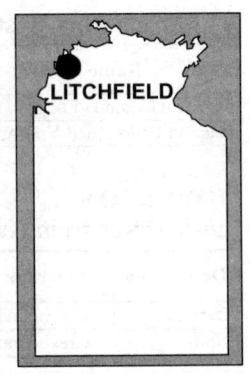

On the other hand, some visitors believe that Litchfield is even more beautiful than Kakadu. Litchfield is closer to Darwin, but has no public transport to it, so, unless you have a private vehicle, you must go on a tour. As with Kakadu, expect this to cost $100 per day and, as with Kakadu, if you want to economise, look for tour operators offering discounted stand-by places on tours.

To reach Litchfield, one travels south on the Stuart Highway beyond the point at which the Arnhem Highway goes off to the east. You will see a turn-off on the left to **Lake Bennett**, where backpackers accommodation is available, and soon afterwards there is a turning on the right to **Batchelor** and Litchfield National Park. On the way down the Stuart Highway, you may notice some wartime airstrips used in the defence of Northern Australia. There is one, for example, at **Coomalie Creek**, just as you turn off for Batchelor. During the war years, Batchelor was an important place, with both Australian and American airmen stationed here. After the war, Australia's first uranium mine was opened at **Rum Jungle**, just north of Batchelor, in 1949, and most of the present buildings in Batchelor were designed to accommodate the miners. The mine was closed in 1971.

Litchfield National Park is only 7% of the size of Kakadu, although it is still not tiny. However, it is much more possible to 'do' it in a day. Litchfield, incidentally, was a member of the Finniss exploration party which passed through here and named the various features. He was fortunate to be able to live on in history by having his name given to such a memorable and beautiful location.

Litchfield was originally a mining area, from the late nineteenth century until the 1950s. The minerals found here are copper and tin. When mining was no longer profitable, the area became a pastoral property. It was only in 1986 that it was proclaimed as a National Park. Admission to the park is free, but there is a fee for camping.

Waterfalls are some of the main attractions, the most noteworthy being **Wangi Falls, Buley Rockhole, Florence Falls, Tolmer Falls and Tjaynera Falls**, for the locations of which see the map opposite. There are also groups of **termite mounds** ('ant hills'), such as you will find throughout the Territory, and one in particular resembles the tombs in a graveyard. The **'Lost City'** is a sandstone formation resembling a city with fortifications, statues and inhabitants, but it is not easily accessible without a four-wheel-drive vehicle.

There is no accommodation available within the park, but camping is permitted, for a fee, at designated camping areas. Accommodation is available at Batchelor and tours of the park are available from Batchelor. However, Batchelor is fourteen kilometres off the Stuart Highway and long-distance buses stop only at the turn off. From there it is three hours of hot walking, so, if you decide to stay here, try to persuade your accommodation to come and pick you up.

LITCHFIELD 427

ACCOMMODATION
(i) Hotel Accommodation in Batchelor Area

Name	Stars	No. on Map	Telephone No.	Address	Lowest Price (Double/Twin)
Lake Bennett Resort	3½	1	1-800-999-089	Chinner Road, Lake Bennett	$155
Rum Jungle Motor Inn		2	08-8976-0123	220 Rum Jungle Road	$110
Jungle Drum Bungalows	3	3	08-8976-0555	334 Meneling Road	$90

(ii) Backpackers Hostels in Batchelor Area

Name	Group	No. on Map	Telephone No.	Address	Lowest Price (Dormitory)
Lake Bennett Resort	Nom	1	1800-999-089	Chinner Road, Lake Bennett	$26

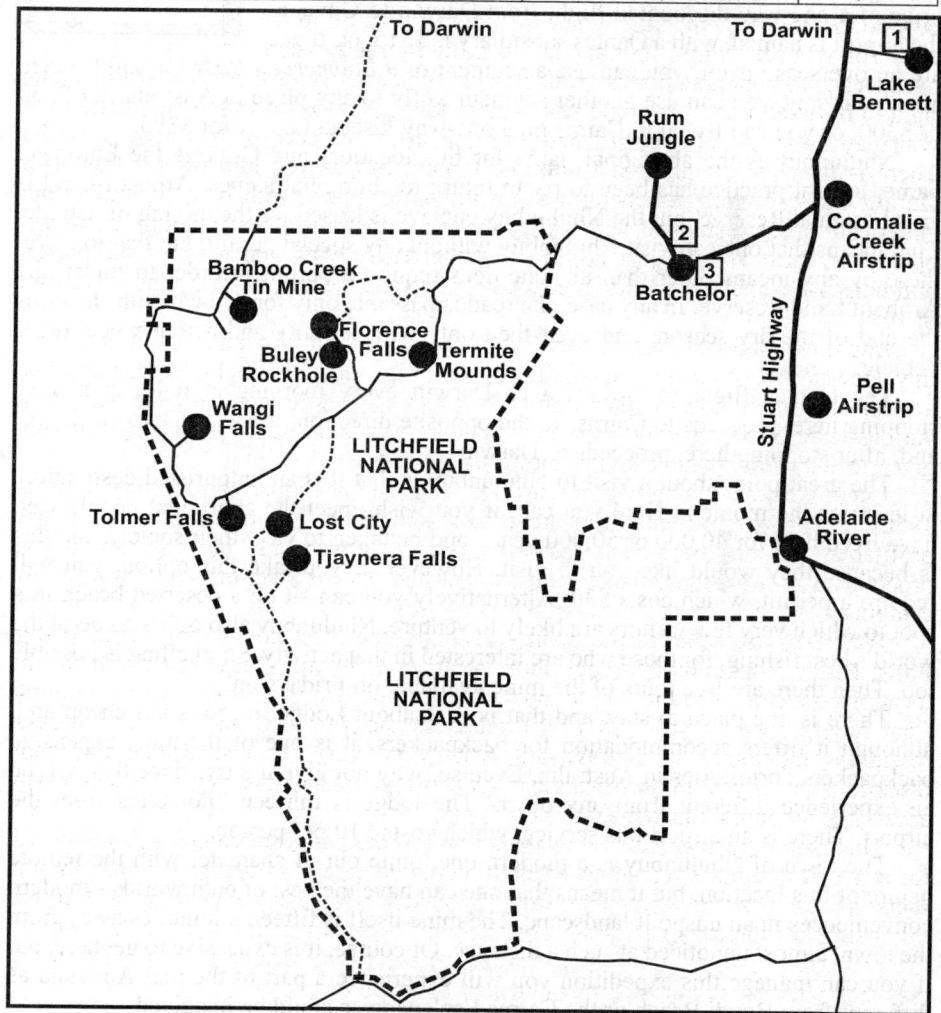

LITCHFIELD NATIONAL PARK
Thin dashed line indicates road suitable for four-wheel-drive vehicle only
Numerals indicate accommodation

NHULUNBUY (GOVE)
Population 4,000

1 hr 15 mins by air from Darwin

In reality, without private transport it is difficult to visit any of the truly remote places in the Northern Territory. Here is one opportunity to visit a place which visitors very rarely get to, and yet where moderately priced accommodation is available. The sting, of course, is the price of getting to Nhulunbuy. However, if you are already in Darwin, it is going to be relatively expensive to get to anywhere else, however you travel. The price of a one-way discounted flight from Darwin to Gove, as the airport is named, with a Qantas subsidiary is $315, or, if you are an overseas visitor, you can use a segment of a *Boomerang Pass* for $300. Then, after your stay, you can use another segment to fly to any place in Australia for $250 or $300, or you can fly on to Cairns on a one-way discount ticket for $395.

Nhulunbuy is the aboriginal name for this location, and Gove is the European name. Recent practice has been to try to return to aboriginal names. Arnhem Land is an Aboriginal Reserve, but the Nhulunbuy enclave is leased for the mining of bauxite. That means that one can visit Nhulunbuy without any special permit, but that to travel there by any means other than air, one does require a permit in order to transit the Arnhem Land Reserve. In any case, the road is passable only for a few months towards the end of the dry season, and even then only with tenacity and a four-wheel-drive vehicle.

The Qantas flight to Gove leaves Darwin every morning at 6:40, and, after stopping here, proceeds to Cairns. In the opposite direction, it leaves Cairns at 17:50, and, after stopping here, proceeds to Darwin.

The great point about a visit to Nhulunbuy is that it is an untouristed destination, at least for the moment. Here you can, if you wish, meet the aboriginal people who have lived here for 40,000 or 50,000 years, and be taken to view their society, and this is because they would like you to visit. However, if you take this option, you will require a permit, which costs $30. Alternatively you can sit on a deserted beach in a spot to which very few visitors are likely to venture. Nhulunbuy also offers some of the world's best fishing, for those who are interested in that activity. Snorkelling is possible too. Then there are free tours of the mine available on Fridays only.

There is one place to stay, and that is Walkabout Lodge. It too is not cheap and, although it offers accommodation for backpackers, it is one of the most expensive backpackers dormitories in Australia. Even so, why not give it a try, since this will be an experience different from any other? The lodge is thirteen kilometres from the airport. There is an airport bus service, which costs $10 per person.

The town of Nhulunbuy is a modern one, quite out of character with the remote nature of this location, but it means that one can have the best of both worlds - modern conveniences in an unspoilt landscape. The mine itself is fifteen kilometres away from the town, almost unnoticed at such a distance. Of course, it is expensive to get here, but if you can manage this expedition you will experience a part of the real Australia as different from Bondi Beach or the Cairns Esplanade as could be imagined.

Although Nhulunbuy is the only location in Arnhem Land which can be visited at a moderate cost, it is also possible to go to the **Cobourg Peninsula**, much further west, which is even more renowned for its fishing. There are two locations available. One is Cobourg Beach Huts and the other is **Cape Don**. The author has fond memories of Cape Don (from a distance) because the lighthouse there used to be on the same radio schedule as the one which I used to man, and *Five Charlie Uniform, Cape Don* was the only station which had precedence (through length of service) over our station. The cheapest accommodation available here, however, is at $165 per night for two guests, in addition to which access is expensive.

ACCOMMODATION
(i) Hotel Accommodation in Nhulunbuy

Name	Stars	No. on Map	Telephone No.	Address	Lowest Price (Double/Twin)
Walkabout Lodge	3	2	08-8987-1777	12 Westal Street	$190
Gove Peninsula Motel		1	08-8987-0700	1 Matthew Flinders Way	$140

(ii) Backpackers Hostels in Nhulunbuy

Name	Group	No. on Map	Telephone No.	Address	Lowest Price (Dormitory)
Walkabout Lodge		2	08-8987-1777	12 Westal Street	$39

(iii) Accommodation on the Cobourg Peninsula

Name	Stars	No. on Map	Telephone No.	Address	Lowest Price (Double/Twin)
Cape Don		3	1-800-000-871	P.O. Box 650, Parap	$935
Cobourg Beach Huts		4	1-800-000-871	P.O. Box 650, Parap	$165

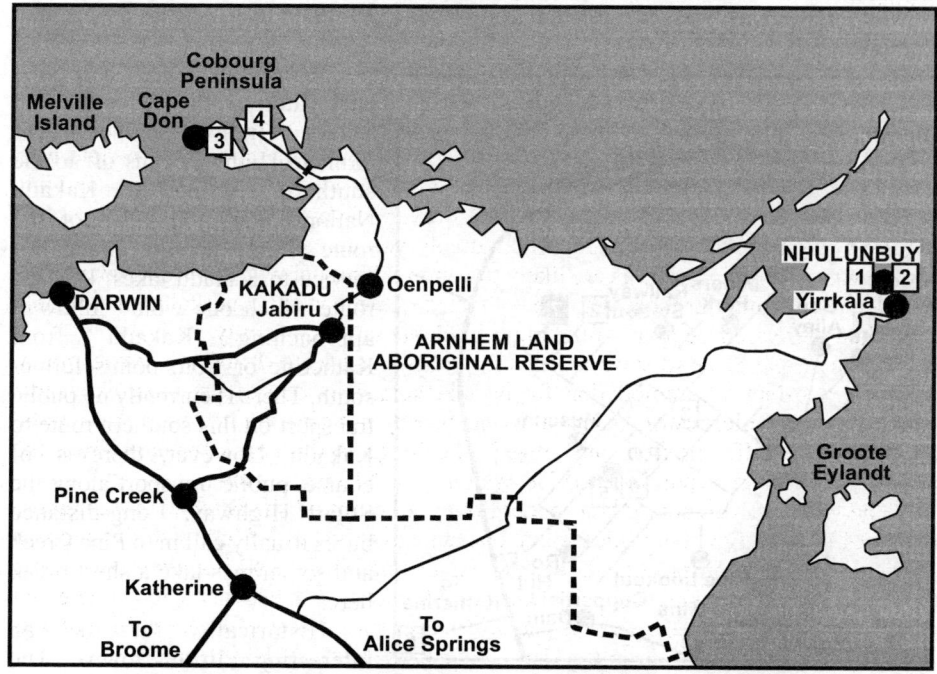

NHULUNBUY (GOVE) AND ARNHEM LAND
Numerals indicate accommodation

430 NORTHERN TERRITORY
PINE CREEK
Population 600

3 hrs 30 mins by bus from Darwin

The journey south from Darwin to Alice Springs is remarkable for the lack of any extensive habitation in the whole 1,500 kilometres. There are only two towns of any size - Katherine and Tennant Creek - and they are not huge. Other settlements are tiny, and yet it is an interesting ride, interesting both because of the isolation, despite being along a major highway, and because of the way in which the scenery gradually changes as the average annual rainfall decreases inland.

After Batchelor, **Adelaide River** is reached. Adelaide River is another small settlement which was important during the war. Just north of the township is the old **Pell Airstrip**, and in the town is the principal **cemetery** for those killed in the various air raids on Darwin during the war. There are 434 servicemen buried here, together with 54 civilians, including the nine post office workers hit by the first bomb dropped on Darwin. Accommodation is available in Adelaide River, including a backpackers hostel three kilometres from the town (pick-up available).

In 1871, while the Overland Telegraph Line was being constructed, gold was discovered at Pine Creek by the men digging post holes. Several thousand Chinese were brought to the location, not all of them voluntarily, as indentured labourers, and Pine Creek became one of the most important places in northern Australia. The North Australian Railway was constructed from Darwin, with Pine Creek as its original terminus.

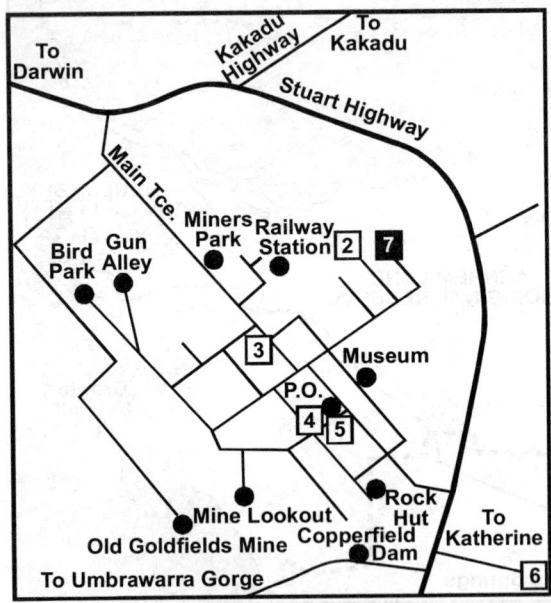

PINE CREEK
Black numerals in white boxes indicate hotel accommodation
White numerals in black boxes indicate backpackers hostels

Today, Pine Creek is a quiet backwater at the place on the Stuart Highway where the Arnhem Highway runs off to the southern entrance to Kakadu National Park. This is not the route which the Greyhound bus service to Kakadu takes. It is the route which one would follow if approaching Kakadu from Katherine or from points further south. There is currently no public transport on this southern route to Kakadu. However, there is, of course, public transport along the Stuart Highway. Long-distance buses usually call in to Pine Creek and sometimes take a short break here.

Historically, it is an interesting little town. The **Miners Park** contains a display of old mining machinery and of the history of mining here, while **Gun Alley Gold Mining** offers a restored steam crusher and stamp battery, as well as gold panning. Admission to *Gun Alley* costs $6.

The **Railway Station** was built in 1888, and continued in use until the North Australian Railway was abandoned in 1976. It is now a small railway museum and outside is one of the locomotives which used to work on the line, an 1877 Beyer Peacock engine made in Manchester. It hauled trains on this line until 1943. There is also a railway carriage on display, appearing considerably more modern than the one in which the author rode when travelling on this line. Perhaps by the time that this is read Pine Creek will once again have a railway service and will be a stopping point for the *Ghan*.

There is a **Museum** in an old building which has served as the mining warden's house, the doctor's residence, a surgery, a clinic, a chemist's shop, an army field hospital, a post office and a telephone exchange. It is now both library and museum, with its emphasis on the history of the Overland Telegraph Line. Admission costs $3.

The **Mine Lookout** offers a view of Enterprise Pit. The first mining here was in 1906, when a shaft was dug, with only mediocre results. Other shafts were sunk by Chinese miners, and some are visible on the hill, but none was really successful. Then, in 1985, Pine Creek Goldfields decided to undertake open-cut mining here, and, in ten years, extracted 764,000 ounces of gold. The pit is now abandoned and filled with water to a depth of 135 metres.

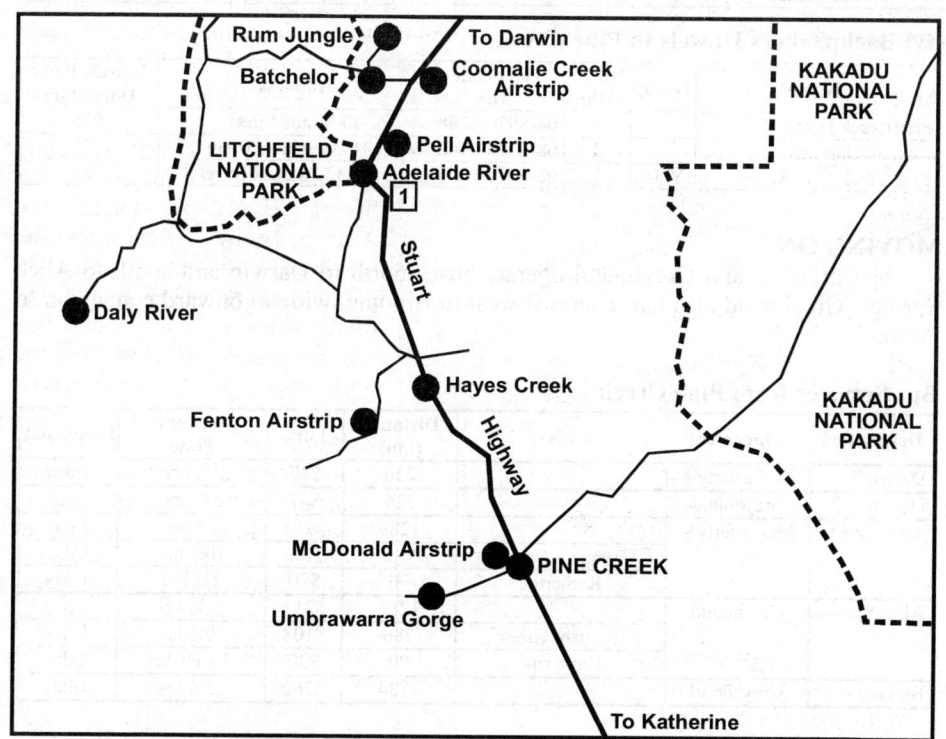

THE TRACK - FROM BATCHELOR TO PINE CREEK
Numerals indicate accommodation

432 NORTHERN TERRITORY

Six kilometres south-west of the town lies **Copperfield Dam**, with picnic facilities, while 22 kilometres south-west is **Umbrawarra Gorge** with attractive pools, wildlife, aboriginal rock paintings and camping facilities.

ACCOMMODATION
(i) Hotel Accommodation in Adelaide River

Name	Stars	No. on Map	Telephone No.	Address	Lowest Price (Double/Twin)
Mount Bundy Station		1	08-8976-7009	Haynes Road	$60

(ii) Backpackers Hostel in Adelaide River

Name	Group	No. on Map	Telephone No.	Address	Lowest Price (Dormitory)
Mount Bundy Station		1	08-8976-7009	Haynes Road	$20

(iii) Hotel Accommodation in Pine Creek

Name	Stars	No. on Map	Telephone No.	Address	Lowest Price (Double/Twin)
Bonrook Lodge		6	08-8976-1232	Bonrook Resort Road	$95
Diggers Rest Motel	3	3	08-8976-1442	32 Main Terrace	$95
Pine Creek Hotel		4	08-8976-1288	40 Moule Street	$85
Kakadu Gateway		2	08-8976-1166	Lot 181, Buchanan Street	$60
B.P. Service Station		5	08-8976-1217	44 Moule Street	$60

(iv) Backpackers Hostels in Pine Creek

Name	Group	No. on Map	Telephone No.	Address	Lowest Price (Dormitory)
Pine Creek Hotel		4	08-8976-1288	40 Moule Street	$25
Kakadu Gateway		2	08-8976-1166	181 Buchanan Street	$25
Pine Creek Y.H.A.	YHA	7	08-8976-1078	Lot 242, Wilcox Street	$15

MOVING ON

McCafferty's and Greyhound operate buses north to Darwin and south to Alice Springs. Greyhound also has a service west to Broome, with an onward connexion to Perth.

Bus Services from Pine Creek

Destination	Operator	Via	Distance (km)	Fare	Journey Time	Frequency
Darwin	McCafferty's		226	$47	3¼ hrs	1/day
Darwin	Greyhound		226	$47	3¼ hrs	2/day
Alice Springs	McCafferty's		1289	$212	17 hrs	1/day
		Tennant Creek	786	$108	10½ hrs	1/day
		Katherine	90	$20	1¼ hrs	1/day
Alice Springs	Greyhound		1289	$212	17½ hrs	1/day
		Tennant Creek	786	$108	10½ hrs	1/day
		Katherine	90	$20	1 - 1¼ hrs	2/day
Broome	Greyhound		1734	$262	22½ hrs	1/day

KATHERINE
Population 10,000

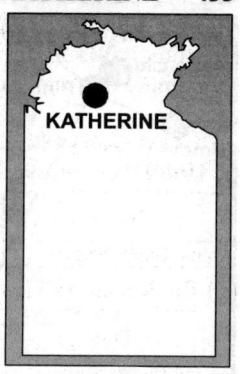

4 hrs 30 mins by bus from Darwin

Katherine is one of only two towns of any size between Darwin and Alice Springs. Leichhardt was the first European to reach here, in 1844, on his exploratory journey to Port Essington, but it was the explorer Stuart who gave the town its name in 1862. He called the river here the Catherine, after the second daughter of his benefactor, James Chambers. However, it seems that spelling was not the strong point of the residents, as the town was first known as Kathryn and then later as Katherine, as at present.

As throughout the Territory, it was the building of the Overland Telegraph Line which breathed life into the town. In 1878, Alfred Giles arrived with 12,000 sheep and 2,000 cattle and set up Springvale Station, eight kilometres outside Katherine. The station is now available as moderately-priced accommodation (see under) and for refreshments, with short free tours of its sandstone homestead provided. It was the cattle which prospered here, as the conditions were too hot for sheep, and this was the start of the cattle industry in the Northern Territory.

The railway from Darwin arrived in 1917, but stayed on the northern side of the river. It was not until 1926 that a bridge was built and a station constructed on the south side, where the present town centre lies.

During the war, Katherine was regarded as sufficiently important to suffer a bombing raid in 1942. The present airport at Tindal, south of the main town, was built at that time, and is still in use as a military air base, the runway being shared with civilian flights. Tindal was the name of the first pilot lost in action in the defence of Darwin.

Katherine is the place where the road west to Broome, and eventually to Perth, diverges from *The Track* (Stuart Highway) south to Alice Springs. *The Track*, until recent years, was just that - a narrow strip of bitumen laid down by the American forces during the war as a tenuous link with the south. Only in the last twenty-five years has it become a highway of ample width for two vehicles for its entire length to Alice Springs. The road west to Perth and Broome, however, was far worse, being sealed only as far as the Western Australian border, from where it became impassable during the Wet Season and all links between the two states were severed, sometimes for months at a time. Now, though, that road is sealed and of a good standard all the way to Perth.

In the last few years, Katherine has expanded rapidly. In 1963, *Northmeat Export Abattoirs* started operations in Katherine. Although the works has changed ownership more than once, it has been a consistent and major source of employment in the area. Then in 1987 the Tindal Air Base increased in importance and 650 military personnel were stationed here, many bringing their families.

Most important of all, though, has been the effect of the steadily developing tourist industry. Katherine's great attraction is the **Katherine Gorge**, 29 kilometres from the town. Nearly a thousand people a day go to see Katherine Gorge. When the author visited some years ago, by contrast, a small boat with a capacity of some twenty-five passengers, but only half full on my trip, made the voyage twice a day.

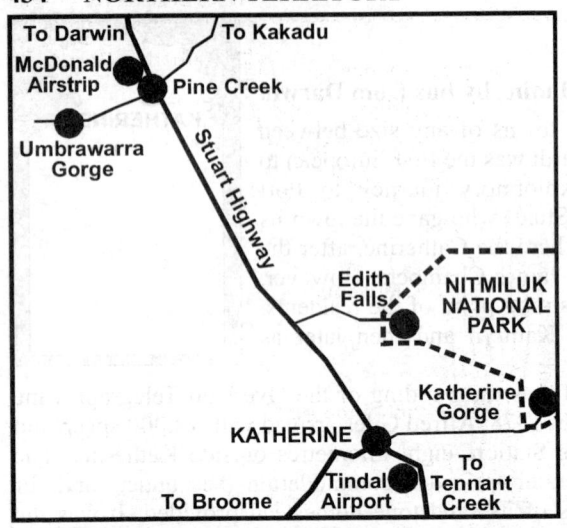

THE TRACK
FROM PINE CREEK TO KATHERINE

If you get to Katherine, a visit to this beautiful gorge is the first priority. There are even day tours here from Darwin, although a 700-kilometre round trip is involved and it seems more logical to stop in Katherine on the way to or from somewhere else. Actually, there is not just a single gorge, but a string of thirteen of them, and they are now a part of the **Nitmiluk National Park**. In 1989, the aborigines of the area lodged a land claim, in which they were successful, and the title to the land was vested in them on condition that they allowed its use as a National Park and shared management responsibilities with the Parks and Wildlife Commission and the local council. The gorges are filled with water and cruises operate regularly on the river which flows through, although occasionally, at the height of the Wet Season, water levels become too high to permit cruises. The cruises usually travel through at least two of the gorges, with a walk involved in between. Cruise prices start at $32 for a two-hour voyage. In addition, there is a Visitor Centre and there are walking tracks totalling 100 kilometres in length. Transport is available from the town to the National Park, but costs $18 return. The last bus back leaves the National Park at 17:00.

There are also aerial tours of the gorge, by light aircraft or by helicopter. Minimum price is $65 for a 15-minute flight.

Within the town, there are a few things to see. There is a **Museum** near the Hospital, but that is some four kilometres from the town centre. The building which houses the Museum was originally the terminal building at the Katherine airfield in 1944. The most interesting exhibit is the Gypsy Moth aeroplane used by the first flying doctor, Dr. Clyde Fenton, in 1934. Between March and October, the Museum is open from 10:00 until 16:00 on weekdays, and from 14:00 until 17:00 at weekends. Between November and February, it is open from 10:00 until 13:00 on Mondays to Saturdays, and from 14:00 until 17:00 on Sundays. There is a walking and cycling path which leads beside the river to a point near the Museum. On the way there, you will pass the **School of the Air**, which can be visited. A little further along the river beyond the Museum is the site of the former **Telegraph Station**. The **Telegraph Pylons** remain and can be seen at Knott's Crossing, which is the original crossing point of the river and the location of the first town.

In the centre of Katherine is the **Railway Museum**, in the old station. It would be pleasant to think that this would soon be put to its proper use again when the new standard gauge railway is completed to Darwin, maybe in late 2004. Unfortunately, however, the plan for the new line by-passes the town centre and involves the building of a new station a long way from anywhere useful. The old station building was

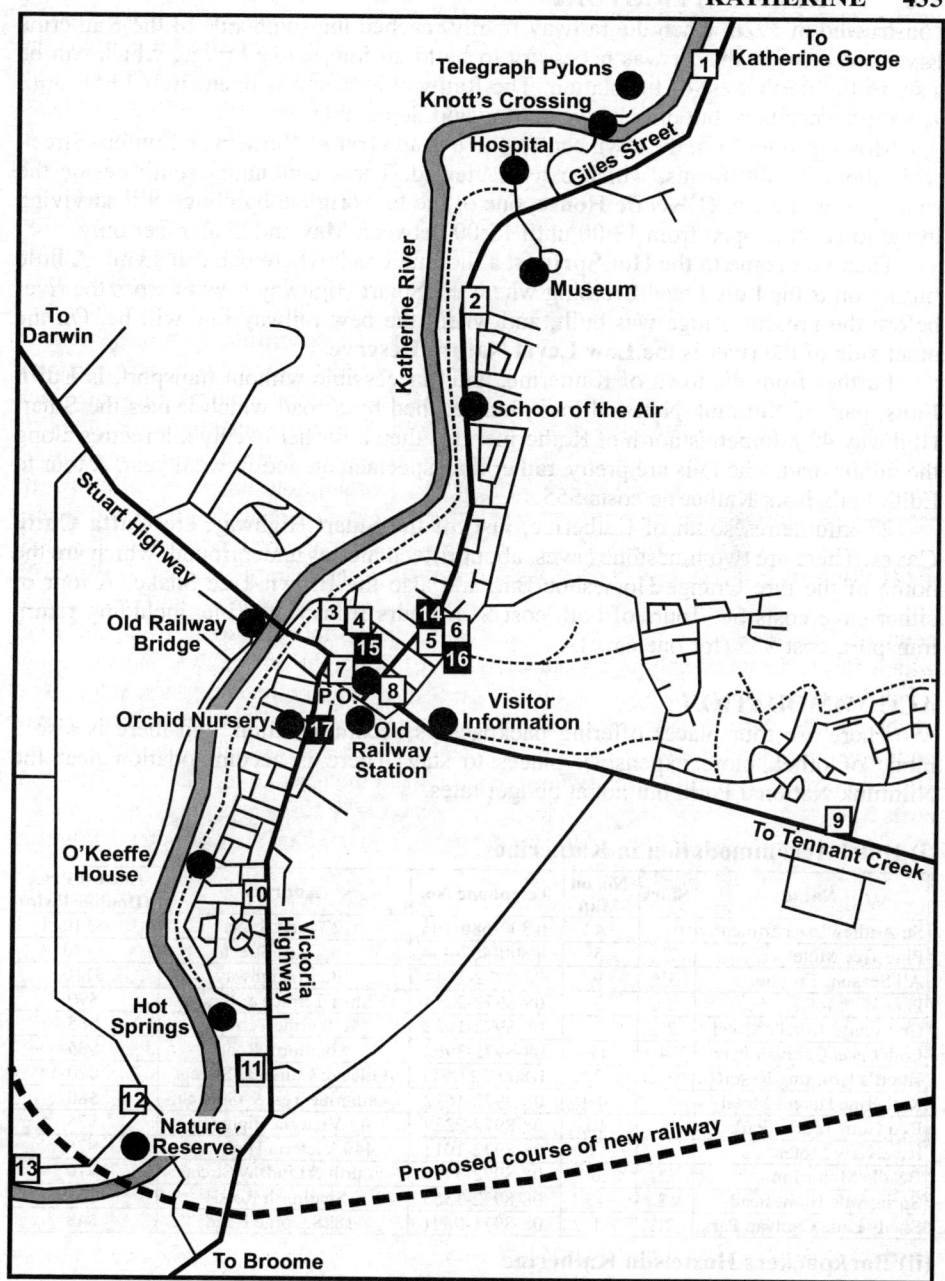

KATHERINE
Black numerals in white boxes indicate hotel accommodation
White numerals in black boxes indicate backpackers hostels

436 NORTHERN TERRITORY

constructed in 1926, when the railway finally reached the south side of the Katherine River. To achieve this, it was necessary to build an impressive bridge, which can be seen to the north-west of the station. The Railway Museum is open from 13:00 until 15:00 on weekdays, but only between May and September.

Moving south from the town centre, there is an **Orchid Nursery** in Stutterd Street, with about 25,000 plants, which can be viewed. Then, continuing south beside the river, you will reach **O'Keeffe House**, one of the few original buildings still surviving in the town. It is open from 13:00 until 15:00 between May and September only.

Then you come to the **Hot Springs**, a thermal creek where one can swim. A little further on is the Low Level Crossing where the Stuart Highway used to cross the river before the present bridge was built, and where the new railway line will be. On the other side of the river is the **Low Level Nature Reserve**.

Further from the town of Katherine, and inaccessible without transport, is **Edith Falls**, part of Nitmiluk National Park, but reached by a road which leaves the Stuart Highway 42 kilometres north of Katherine. It is then a further twenty kilometres along the minor road. The falls are pretty, rather than spectacular, and flow all year. A tour to Edith Falls from Katherine costs $55.

27 kilometres south of Katherine, just off the Stuart Highway, are **Cutta Cutta Caves**. There are two limestone caves, about fifteen metres underground, which are the home of the rare Orange Horseshoe Bat, and also the Brown Tree Snake. A tour of either cave costs $8. Tours of both cost $14. Tours from Katherine, including return transport, cost $35 (for one cave).

ACCOMMODATION

There are four places offering backpackers accommodation, and there is also a range of other, more expensive, places to stay. There is accommodation near the Nitmiluk National Park, but not at budget rates.

(i) Hotel Accommodation in Katherine

Name	Stars	No. on Map	Telephone No.	Address	Lowest Price (Double/Twin)
St. Andrew's Apartments		4	1-800-686-106	27 First Street	$140
Pine Tree Motel	2½	5	1-800-467-434	3 Third Street	$110
All Seasons Frontier	3½	9	08-8972-1744	Stuart Highway	$110
Paraway Motel	2½	3	08-8972-2644	O'Shea Terrace & First St.	$90
Crossways Hotel / Motel	2½	7	08-8972-1022	Katherine Terrace	$85
Low Level Caravan Park	4	12	08-8972-3962	Shadforth Road	$85
Knott's Crossing Resort	3½	2	1-800-222-511	Giles & Cameron Streets	$80
Katherine Hotel / Motel		8	08-8972-1622	Katherine Ter. & Giles St.	$80
Red Gum Tourist Park	3	10	08-8972-2239	42 Victoria Highway	$75
Riverview Motel	3	11	08-8972-1011	440 Victoria Highway	$75
Beagle Motor Inn	2	6	08-8972-3998	Fourth & Lindsay Streets	$70
Springvale Homestead	2	13	08-8972-1355	Shadforth Road	$55
Shady Lane Caravan Park	2½	1	08-8971-0491	1828 Gorge Road	$48

(ii) Backpackers Hostels in Katherine

Name	Group	No. on Map	Telephone No.	Address	Lowest Price (Dormitory)
Victoria Lodge		17	1800-808-875	21 Victoria Highway	$18
Coco's Backpackers		15	08-8971-2889	21 First Street	$18
Kookaburra Lodge	VIP	16	1800-808-211	Lindsay & Third Streets	$17
Palm Court Backpackers	YHA	14	1800-626-722	Third & Giles Streets	$16

MOVING ON

There are three buses per day to Darwin and two to Alice Springs. There is also one service per day west to Broome, with a connexion on to Perth.

Bus Services from Katherine

Destination	Operator	Via	Distance (km)	Fare	Journey Time	Frequency
Darwin	McCafferty's		316	$58	4¼ hrs	1/day
Darwin	Greyhound		316	$58	4 - 4¼ hrs	2/day
Alice Springs	McCafferty's		1199	$197	15¼ hrs	1/day
		Tennant Creek	696	$97	8¾ hrs	1/day
Alice Springs	Greyhound		1199	$197	15½ hrs	1/day
		Tennant Creek	696	$97	8½ hrs	1/day
Broome	Greyhound		1644	$250	20¾ hrs	1/day

TIMBER CREEK
Population 600

8 hrs by bus from Darwin

If one travels west from Katherine on the Victoria Highway, one finds pleasant scenery but almost no habitation before the border with Western Australia. Note, incidentally, that one cannot take fruit or vegetables across this border. A Greyhound bus plies this route once every day.

The two stopping places on the Northern Territory side of the border are Victoria River and Timber Creek. Victoria River, 200 kilometres from Katherine, is just a roadhouse, but Timber Creek, another 90 kilometres further on, has a little history.

It was the explorer Augustus Gregory who named Timber Creek, when, in 1855, he used timber from the trees growing here to repair his boat. He also established a camp site nearby and carved on a boab tree there the dates of his arrival in October 1855 and departure in July 1856. The tree still stands and can be found fifteen kilometres west of Timber Creek.

As the pastoral industry developed in this area, Victoria River Downs station was established, and claimed, at one time, to be the largest cattle station in the world. Supplies were brought to the station along the Victoria River, which is not easily navigated, and unloaded at *The Depot*, which became Timber Creek. The first store opened here in 1904, and in 1908 the Police Station was established and a small township was slowly built up. It remains small, but accommodation is available here.

The **Old Police Station** is now a museum. There are walks available, and there are tours and **cruises** on the beautiful **Victoria River**. The river is inhabited by **crocodiles**, which can usually be viewed, and is also one of the last breeding grounds for a bird known as the Gouldian Finch. Cruises cost $65 for four hours.

438 NORTHERN TERRITORY

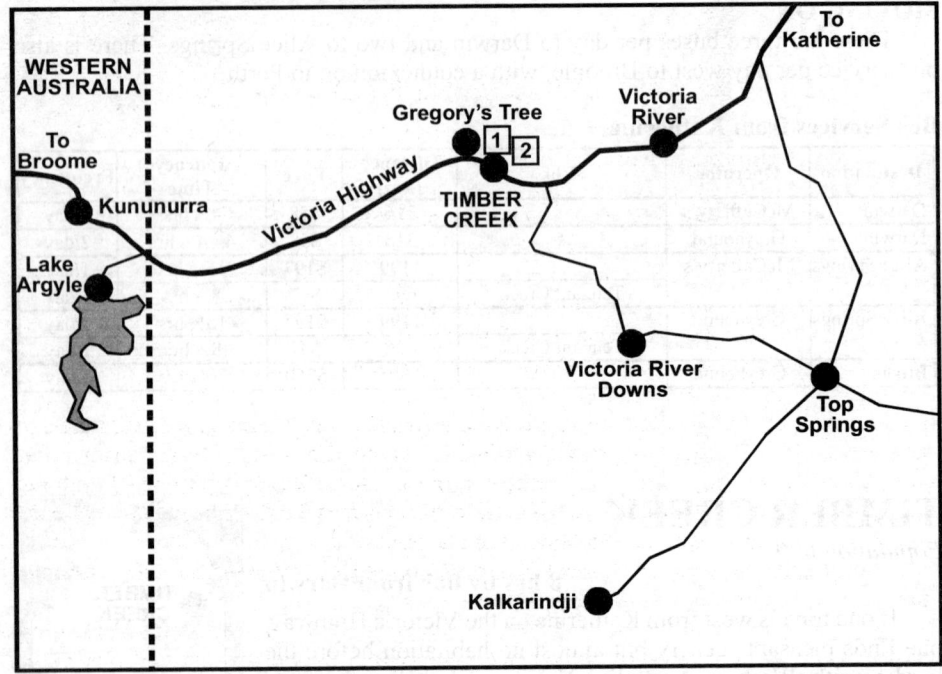

VICTORIA HIGHWAY - TIMBER CREEK VICINITY
Numerals indicate accommodation

ACCOMMODATION
Hotel Accommodation in Timber Creek

Name	Stars	No. on Map	Telephone No.	Address	Lowest Price (Double/Twin)
Wayside Inn		1	08-8975-0732	Victoria Highway	$70
Timber Creek Hotel		2	08-8975-0722	94 Victoria Highway	$43

MOVING ON
Greyhound operates one bus per day to Darwin and one to Broome, with an onward connexion to Perth.

Bus Services from Timber Creek

Destination	Operator	Via	Distance (km)	Fare	Journey Time	Frequency
Darwin	Greyhound		610	$116	7¾ hrs	1/day
		Katherine	285	$50	3¼ hrs	1/day
Broome	Greyhound		1360	$229	17¾ hrs	1/day

MATARANKA
Population 400

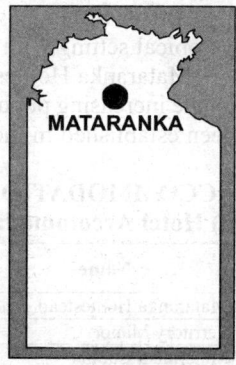

6 hrs 30 mins by bus from Darwin

At a point 106 kilometres south of Katherine, your bus may divert ten kilometres from the highway to Mataranka Homestead, where some services take a meal break. This shady spot is adjacent to **Elsey Station**, where an authoress named **Jeannie Gunn** lived and wrote her famous book, *We of the Never Never*, about life in this area in pioneering days. She came here at the turn of the century and found this spot awe-inspiring in its remoteness. "This tiny homestead of a million and a quarter acres," she wrote, "With the Katherine settlement a hundred miles to the north of it, one neighbour ninety miles to the east, another a hundred and five to the south, and others about two hundred to the west." Her husband, Aeneas Gunn, died of malarial dysentery in 1903 at the age of 41, only a year after their arrival here, and is buried in Elsey cemetery, but Jeannie Gunn lived to be 91 and died only on 9th June 1961. Mataranka thrives in the memory of this famous book, and a film later made of it, and has become a popular tourist destination.

Next to the Mataranka Homestead are **thermal pools**. Water emerges from the ground here at a constant 34°C and at a remarkable volume of 30 million litres per day. It is a major breeding place for the Little Red Flying Fox, to see which animal there are guided walks at certain times of the year. There are also other unguided bushwalks available. The Mataranka Homestead purchased the replica of Elsey Homestead created for the filming of *We of the Never Never*, and this is on display, together with aboriginal shelters also constructed for the film.

Mataranka Homestead was built in 1916 as an experimental horse and sheep station. It later became the residence of the former Administrator of the Northern Territory, Dr. Gilruth, so it also has a history. Now it offers both accommodation and refreshments.

Elsey National Park has its entrance mid-way along the side road leading from the Stuart Highway to Mataranka Homestead. It has some attractive walks. Within the National Park is **Mataranka Falls**, which runs all year.

In the township of Mataranka is the *Never Never Museum*. It has displays related to aboriginal history, the Overland Telegraph Line, the North Australian Railway, and the Second World War airstrips. The key to the museum is available from the Council Offices. In the centre of the town is a **huge termite mound**, typical of those found in this area. At the Territory Manor (hotel), enormous **Barramundi** fish, the speciality of the Northern Territory, are hand fed at 9:30 and 13:00 every day, a performance which may be viewed.

ANECDOTE

In the Wet, some of the low-level road bridges became impassable and signs would direct traffic to cross using the high-level railway bridge. There a further notice would remind motorists that trains had right of way over the bridge. This clarification of the legal situation, however, did little to deal with the practicalities of meeting a train when half way across. Hopefully somebody had also advised the train driver that he might meet a vehicle bumping across the sleepers towards him.

440 NORTHERN TERRITORY

Bitter Springs is two kilometres from Mataranka, and is another thermal pool in a tropical setting with swimming and picnic facilities available.

Mataranka Homestead is not the only place where one can stay here, for, building on the increasing popularity of the area, a little cluster of other accommodation has now been established in the small settlement of Mataranka on the Stuart Highway itself.

ACCOMMODATION
(i) Hotel Accommodation in Mataranka

Name	Stars	Telephone No.	Address	Lowest Price (Double/Twin)
Mataranka Homestead	2	08-8975-4544	Homestead Road	$98
Territory Manor	2½	08-8975-4516	Stuart Hwy. & Martin Road	$95
Mataranka Cabins		08-8975-4838	Martin Road, Bitter Springs	$80
Mataranka Roadhouse		08-8975-4571	118 Roper Terrace	$80
Mataranka Tourist Resort	2	08-8975-4544	Homestead Road	$75

(ii) Backpackers Hostel in Mataranka

Name	Group	Telephone No.	Address	Lowest Price (Dormitory)
Mataranka Tourist Resort		08-8975-4544	Homestead Road	$18

MOVING ON
Bus Services from Mataranka

Destination	Operator	Via	Distance (km)	Fare	Journey Time	Frequency
Darwin	McCafferty's		422	$80	6 hrs	1/day
		Katherine	106	$37	1¼ hrs	1/day
Darwin	Greyhound		422	$80	6½ hrs	1/day
		Katherine	106	$37	1¼ hrs	1/day
Alice Springs	McCafferty's		1093	$186	14 hrs	1/day
		Tennant Creek	590	$92	7½ hrs	1/day
Alice Springs	Greyhound		1093	$186	14¼ hrs	1/day
		Tennant Creek	590	$92	7¼ hrs	1/day

ANECDOTE

Wishing to travel on the North Australian Railway, I sent a letter to the railway company in Darwin asking for a timetable and received in reply a typewritten note saying that trains left at "about 10:00 on Wednesdays and Saturdays", so I arrived at the railway yards accordingly.

"About 10:00" turned out to mean noon and I was the only passenger on the mixed train for the whole journey. There were no signals on this line, so the guard had to telephone the controller from every siding to receive further instructions. However, there were also no telephone boxes, so the guard carried a pole with a telephone connected and placed the cross member at the top of the pole onto the overhead telegraph wires in order to make contact. This was a fascinating process, so I went across to hear how these important control instructions were given.

"Hello, hello," said the guard. "This is no. 2 down and we're at Adelaide River now. Can you tell me who won the 4:30 at Caulfield?"

TENNANT CREEK
Population 4,000

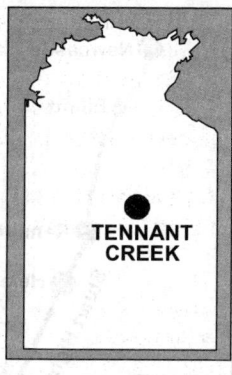

14 hrs by bus from Darwin

Journeying south by bus from Katherine, it is a drive of 700 kilometres to Tennant Creek, with no town of any size along the way. Mataranka is not the sole point of interest on this long 8½-hour journey, however, and here are a few others which deserve mention.

Seven kilometres south of Mataranka, a road turns off east to **Roper Bar**, 177 kilometres away. Leichhardt named the Roper River after one of the party on his 1845 expedition. Roper Bar is now famous for its good fishing. There is a camping ground there, and accommodation is available, but there is no public transport to Roper Bar.

75 kilometres south of Mataranka is **Larrimah**. The North Australian Railway managed to get this far south from Darwin, and, in fact, reached **Birdum**, eight kilometres further on, in 1929. Larrimah was established only during the war, but was found to be a more convenient terminus for the railway because it is adjacent to the highway and less susceptible to waterlogging in the Wet Season, so in 1951 the entire town of Birdum was shifted here and the last eight kilometres of track abandoned. As you will observe as you pass through Larrimah, the entire town of Birdum could not have consisted of very much. Even when the author travelled here on the train at a time

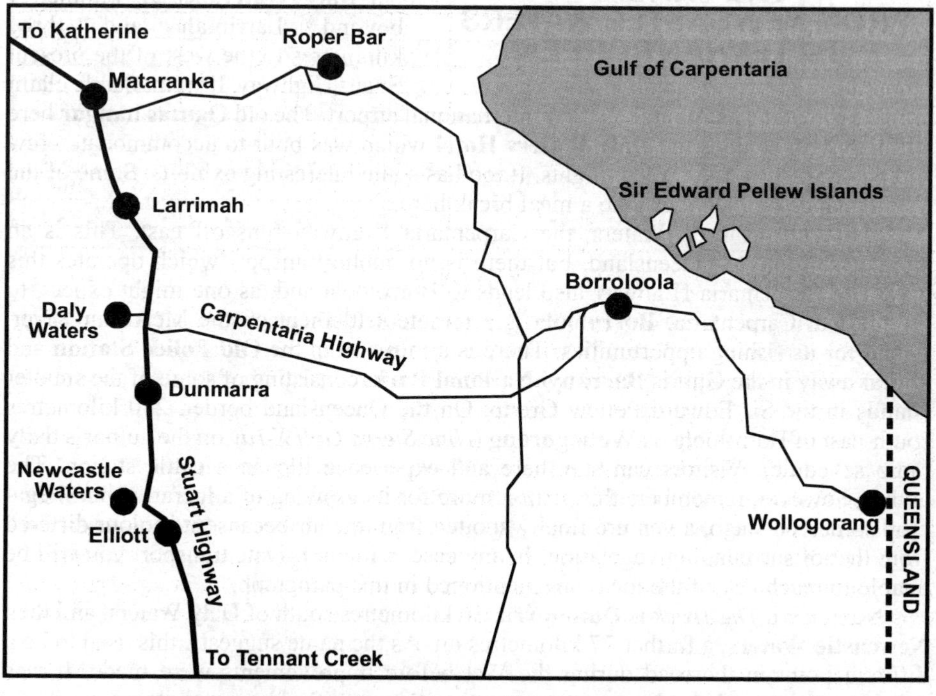

THE TRACK - FROM MATARANKA TO ELLIOTT

442 NORTHERN TERRITORY

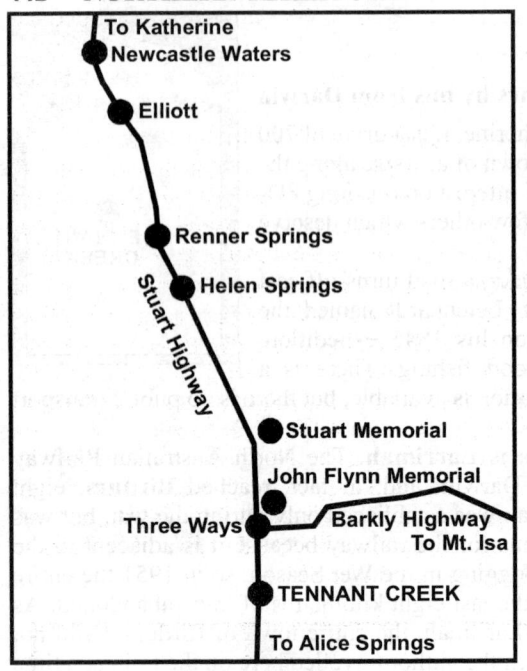

THE TRACK - FROM NEWCASTLE WATERS TO TENNANT CREEK

when the railway was still in operation, there was little at Larrimah except a pub and the railway station, at which all the goods were transferred from road train to rail train, or *vice versa*, whilst the crews of both refreshed themselves in preparation for their long journeys. The pub is still there, in case you feel like following their example. It was originally an officers' mess from the Second World War base, with parts later added from the Birdum Hotel when it was moved here. It has some interesting exhibits within. There is also a little museum in the little township. It is housed in the **Old Telegraph Station** and has exhibits relating to the Overland Telegraph Line, the North Australian Railway and the war. It is open from 7:00 until 21:00.

Daly Waters is 92 kilometres beyond Larrimah and three kilometres to the west of the present Stuart Highway. Its remarkable claim to fame is that it was Australia's first international airport. The old **Qantas hangar** here still survives, as does the **Daly Waters Hotel** which was built to accommodate crew and passengers on the Qantas flights. It too has some interesting exhibits. Some of the long-distance bus services take a meal break here.

Just south of Daly Waters, the Carpentaria Highway runs off east. This is an alternative route to Queensland, but there is no public transport which operates this way. The Carpentaria Highway also leads to Borroloola and, as one might expect, to the Gulf of Carpentaria. **Borroloola** is a remote settlement on the McArthur River, famed for its fishing opportunities. There is a museum in the **Old Police Station** and not far away in the Gulf is **Barranyi National Park**, consisting of some of the smaller islands in the Sir Edward Pellew Group. On the Queensland border, 250 kilometres south-east of Borroloola, is **Wollogorang** (*Nine Sierra Golf X-ray* on the author's daily radio schedule). Visitors can stay here and experience life on a cattle station. The author, however, remembers this station more for its growing of a lucrative but illegal crop some years ago, a venture finally spotted from the air because its colour differed from that of surrounding vegetation. In any case, without private transport you will be unable to reach any of the locations mentioned in this paragraph.

Next down *The Track* is **Dunmarra**, 36 kilometres south of Daly Waters, and then **Newcastle Waters**, a further 77 kilometres on. As the name suggests, this used to be a difficult point in the road during the Wet before improvements were made. It was necessary to negotiate a narrow causeway with water flowing strongly across for a distance of more than two kilometres. Now, however, the highway is raised above the flood plain. There is a sculpture here commemorating the drovers of former days.

24 more kilometres brings us to **Elliott**, a wartime settlement named after the officer in charge of the camp here, and then a further 67 kilometres to **Renner Springs**. Renner was the doctor who attended the men working on the Overland Telegraph Line. Next there is a long stretch of 169 kilometres to Three Ways, which is the name of the roadhouse at the junction of the Barkly Highway leading to Queensland. You will see here the memorial to the **Rev. John Flynn**, the founder of the Royal Flying Doctor Service, so vital to these outback areas. This used to be the changing point for those wishing to travel by bus to Mt. Isa and beyond, but now the bus continues the extra 23 kilometres into Tennant Creek, and the change is made there.

It was the explorer John McDouall Stuart who named Tennant Creek as he passed through on his third, and successful, attempt to cross Australia from south to north. Tennant was a South Australian farmer from Port Lincoln who had provided financial assistance for the expedition. The creek itself runs just north of the town.

Yet again, the settlement here was created as a result of the building of the Overland Telegraph Line, completed in 1872. A temporary repeater station was erected at that time, with the permanent stone building completed in 1874. This building is one of four original **Telegraph Stations** still standing. It can be found twelve kilometres to the north of the town on the far side of and beside the creek.

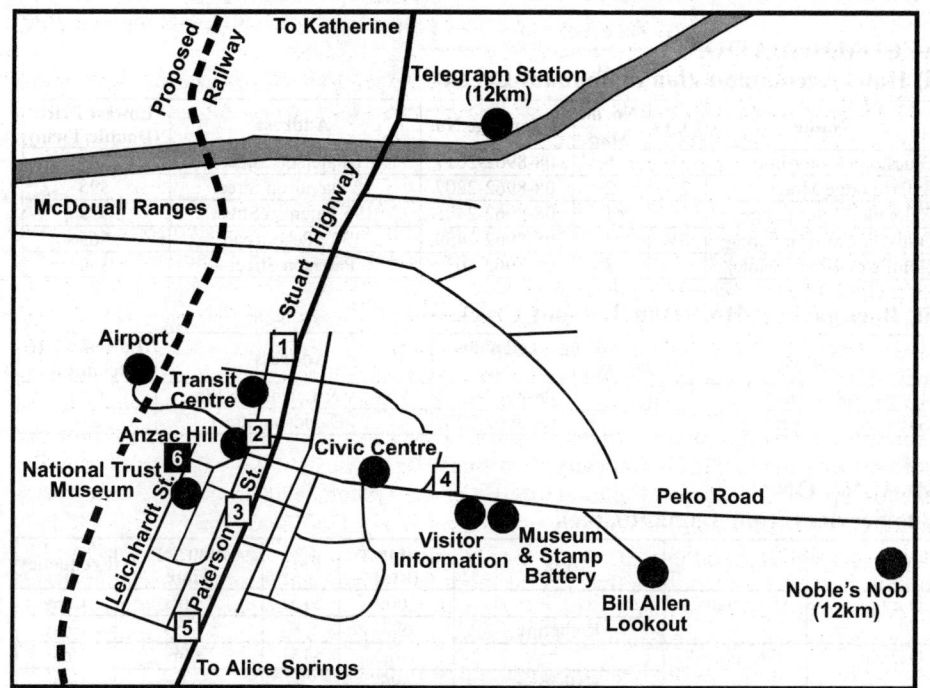

TENNANT CREEK
Black numerals in white boxes indicate hotel accommodation
White numerals in black boxes indicate backpackers hostels

NORTHERN TERRITORY

It is rumoured that the site of the modern Tennant Creek was established because a beer truck became bogged here during the Wet, and the local folks kindly volunteered to assist in lightening its load. However, Tennant Creek would still be just another tiny settlement along *The Track*, were it not for the discovery of gold here in the 1930s. Blind William Weaber and one-eyed Jack Noble found what proved to be four of the richest claims here and Australia's last great gold rush had started. New gold-bearing lodes are still being discovered and this remains a gold-mining community.

Peko Road runs to the east of the town and here is to be found the **Battery Hill Mining Centre**, with a museum (free), an operating stamp battery and an underground mine. There are tours of the stamp battery at 9:30 and 17:00, and of the underground mine at 11:00. Here is also the **Visitor Information Centre**. A little further along the same road is the **Bill Allen Lookout**, with good views of the important sites in Tennant Creek. **Noble's Nob** is further east still, but too far to walk, being twelve kilometres from the town centre. This is where one of the richest mines was located, on a site discovered by Jack Noble in 1933. It was worked as an underground mine until the tunnels collapsed in 1967, whereafter it became a huge open-cut mine until 1985.

Other features of Tennant Creek include an unusual pyramid-shaped **Civic Centre** and, just opposite it, an Art Gallery. There is more art here too, for around the town you will find a series of **murals** depicting the history of Tennant Creek. There is a **Museum** housed in a former army field hospital and there is the **Anzac Hill Lookout** and the **Celebrity Walk**, with the handprints of famous people who have passed through.

ACCOMMODATION
(i) Hotel Accommodation in Tennant Creek

Name	Stars	No. on Map	Telephone No.	Address	Lowest Price (Double/Twin)
Bluestone Motor Inn	3	5	08-8962-2617	1 Paterson Street	$95
Safari Lodge Motel	2½	2	08-8962-2207	12 Davidson Street	$95
Eldorado Motor Lodge	2½	1	08-8962-2402	195 Paterson Street	$75
Outback Caravan Park	3½	4	08-8962-2459	1382 Peko Road	$65
Goldfields Hotel / Motel		3	08-8962-2030	Paterson Street	$50

(ii) Backpackers Hostels in Tennant Creek

Name	Group	No. on Map	Telephone No.	Address	Lowest Price (Dormitory)
Tourist's Rest Hostel	VIP	6	08-8962-2719	Windley & Leichhardt Streets	$19
Safari Backpackers	YHA	2	08-8962-2207	12 Davidson Street	$16

MOVING ON
Bus Services from Tennant Creek

Destination	Operator	Via	Distance (km)	Fare	Journey Time	Frequency
Darwin	McCafferty's		1009	$151	13 hrs	1/day
		Katherine	693	$97	8¼ hrs	1/day
Darwin	Greyhound		1012	$151	14 hrs	1/day
		Katherine	696	$97	8¾ hrs	1/day
Alice Springs	McCafferty's		503	$118	6 hrs	1/day
Alice Springs	Greyhound		503	$118	6¼ hrs	1/day
Townsville	McCafferty's		1547	$236	19¾ hrs	1/day
		Mt. Isa	661	$119	8¼ hrs	1/day

ALICE SPRINGS
Population 27,500

20 hrs by bus from Darwin
19 hrs by train from Adelaide
19 hrs 30 mins by bus from Adelaide

Alice Springs is one of the most famous towns of its size in the world, famous because of its isolation and its romantic pioneering image, and also because of Nevil Shute. It is a day's continuous travel from anywhere else of equivalent size.

Now why, it is natural to ask, is it called Alice Springs? Who was Alice? The answer, like so much in the Northern Territory, depends upon the Overland Telegraph Line. The man in charge of the construction of this line was the Superintendent of Telegraphs for South Australia, Charles Todd. His wife was named Alice. This was the midway point of the Overland Telegraph Line from Adelaide to Darwin, and so one of the most important telegraph stations. It was decided to locate it beside a semi-permanent waterhole in the river, which is otherwise dry for long periods of the year. The river was named the Todd, and the waterhole was named Alice Springs. By association, the Telegraph Station took the same name. At this stage, however, there was no town, but soon there was a ruby rush (actually the stones turned out to be garnets), and then gold was discovered at nearby Arltunga. Both gold diggers and pastoralists started to arrive, and a base was needed for them. Gradually, starting in 1888, a town grew up about three kilometres south of the Telegraph Station and was named Stuart, after the explorer who had opened up this part of the country when he successfully crossed from south to north in 1862. In 1889, an auction of 96 lots of land in the town was held, but only five were sold. In 1926, work started on the extension of the railway line from Oodnadatta to Stuart. At this time the European population of Stuart was about forty, but by the time the railway arrived in 1929 and put the cameleers out of business, it had grown to 200. There was always confusion about the name of the settlement because the Telegraph Station continued to be called Alice Springs, but the town area was known as Stuart. This confusion was exacerbated by the fact that there was another town in South Australia known as Sturt. In 1933, therefore, the name was changed and the town too became Alice Springs. The population had reached nearly 1,000 when the war started. Troops were stationed here and Alice Springs became an important supply depot, resulting in the construction of a high-quality airfield, a water reticulation scheme, a new power generator and other basic infrastructure. In recent years the growth has continued, with tourism becoming ever more important to the town.

ANECDOTE

At the time when I was living in the Territory, there was a two-tier postal system offering domestic air mail or surface mail. However, where I lived there was no surface route available, so air mail items were delivered on the first available flight, while surface mail was delivered by air when there was space.

One day in late March, a large delivery of surface-paid items arrived and my neighbours received an interesting-looking parcel. It was unwrapped amidst general excitement and found to contain a bouquet of flowers in lamentable condition together with a Christmas card.

NORTHERN TERRITORY

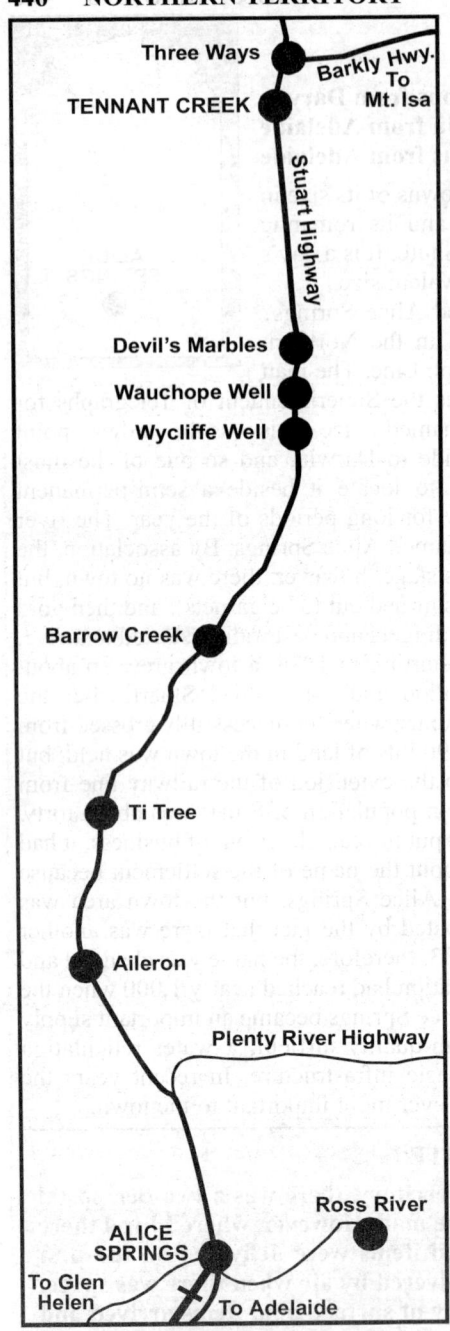

**THE TRACK -
FROM TENNANT CREEK
TO ALICE SPRINGS**

We were coming down *The Track* (Stuart Highway) to Alice Springs, so let us complete that journey now. It is a further six hours, or 556 kilometres, from Tennant Creek to Alice Springs. **Wauchope Well** is 114 kilometres south of Tennant Creek. Just before the small township is reached, though, one comes to the **Devil's Marbles**, a landscape of scattered boulders, some of considerable size, rounded by erosion and balanced in precarious positions. The largest of the Marbles exceed six metres in diameter and these are, perhaps, the most impressive sight on the whole 1,500-kilometre journey from Darwin to Alice Springs.

Wycliffe Well is eighteen kilometres south of Wauchope and is known for its sightings of **U.F.Os.**, not just a single sighting, but several of them. The roadhouse has a display of newspaper articles relating to these phenomena.

Another 88 kilometres brings us to **Barrow Creek**, which has had an eventful history. It was founded, like so many other places on this route, as one of the Overland Telegraph Stations. The original building, erected in 1872, has recently been restored. This was the scene of a conflict in the nineteenth century between aborigines and Europeans which resulted in the death of the staff of the Telegraph Station. There is a memorial here to those who died. More recently, in 2001, it was near here that an English girl on holiday reported that she and her boyfriend had been persuaded to stop for a motorist apparently in trouble, with the result that the boyfriend disappeared, while she apparently managed to escape and was brought here to the Barrow Creek Hotel to recuperate. The Barrow Creek Hotel was constructed in 1929 and is a building of some character.

There are further small settlements at **Ti Tree**, another 91 kilometres south, and at **Aileron**, 60 kilometres further on. 63 kilometres more takes us to the turn-off for the **Plenty River Highway** which leads east into Queensland. Although there is no public transport, there are tours which take this route. It has improved considerably since the author ventured here and found plenty river all right, but not much highway (see anecdote below). On one day, in a four-wheel-drive vehicle, we managed to progress seventeen kilometres in ten hours, digging the vehicle out of the mud four times. However, now part of this road is even sealed.

A final stretch of 48 kilometres takes us through the hills into Alice Springs itself, no doubt with relief that such a long journey has finally reached its conclusion.

If you are approaching from the south, rather than the north, you will have a choice of train or bus. Both of these journeys have become much easier in recent years. The *South Road* (Stuart Highway) used to be sealed only between Alice Springs and the South Australian border, leaving 800 kilometres of pot-holed dirt to be negotiated before the next bitumen was encountered. Now it is sealed highway all the way, with the journey from Adelaide taking 19½ hours, which still seems a long time if you undertake it without a break.

ANECDOTE

The Plenty River Highway turned out to be hard going, akin to driving through the river itself for several hundred kilometres. After eight days, we arrived at Tobermory Cattle Station, where we found that we were expected by the one man left on duty there over Christmas. "Somebody saw your wheel tracks in the road," he explained, "And let me know that you must be coming."

Told that the Georgina River was running high and that, even if it stopped raining, which seemed highly unlikely, it would be three weeks before we could cross, we decided that discretion should subdue valour and that we had better retreat before that too became impossible. Before returning, however, we paid a visit to Manners Creek Station, on the Queensland border, to see the collection there. The owner explained to us.

"When they started launching rockets from Woomera, they told me that I was right in the flight path and that some bits might drop off onto my property, so they built me an air-raid shelter and sent me a message every time they were going to launch. But the shelter was miles away and three-quarters of the time they postponed the launch, so I couldn't afford the time and gave up using the shelter after a while. In any case, they said that from the height of those rockets nothing of any size could ever reach the earth. It would all burn up on the way down, and the biggest bit that could ever arrive here would be about the size of a matchbox. Still, even a matchbox-size piece could kill you. Now here's the collection of matchbox-size pieces which I've picked up over the last twenty years."

And he showed us the amazing collection of rocket parts, the largest being some four or five metres high (see photograph facing page 407). They bore conspicuous markings such as *U.S. Government Property Top Secret*, and one had the impression that certain administrations might be quite willing to pay good money to get hold of some of the items. "Does anybody know that you've got all these?" we asked. "Nope," he replied. "I figured that if they wanted them, they wouldn't go leaving them lying around my station like that."

The rail journey has changed even more. The railway first reached Alice Springs (Stuart) in 1929, replacing the camel services operated by Afghans which had provided the only link up until then. The passenger train came to be known as the *Ghan* in honour of those who had provided the service previously. However, the railway to here was a low-cost one and the *Ghan* was not a rapid service. Even into the 1970s, there was a problem with gauge. To reach Alice Springs from Adelaide, one first had to take a broad gauge train from Adelaide to Port Pirie. It was at Port Pirie that the *Ghan* itself started. The *Ghan* operated on a standard gauge track as far as Marree, from where it was a narrow-gauge service. From Marree, the journey to Alice Springs took 39 hours at an average speed of just over 20 km/hr along a track which was limited to 60 km/hr throughout, and even to 10 km/hr in parts. There was only one bridge on the entire line, and rumour said that that was there only because it had been found to be too short for its intended purpose on a different line. The *Ghan* operated once a week, but, in addition, there were three mixed trains every week taking 42 hours from Marree to Alice Springs, and those were fun on which to travel.

The train runs now on a completely different line, branching off from the main Trans-Australian Railway at Tarcoola, instead of Port Augusta. It is standard gauge all the way on a new and well constructed line. The entire journey from Adelaide takes nineteen hours. Moreover, the line is now finally being extended to Darwin, and by late 2004 it should be possible to travel from Sydney or Melbourne to Darwin without changing trains.

There is also the possibility of arriving in Alice Springs by air, of course. The airport is fifteen kilometres south of the town. There is an airport bus, which costs $10 single, or $17 return.

Like Darwin, Alice Springs is a town visited both for its own attractions and as a base for exploring the surrounding area. In particular, of course, many people take tours from here to King's Canyon and Ayers Rock. Alice Springs has expanded surprisingly in recent years, and is now geared very much to the tourist industry. Although that has changed the character of the town, it is convenient for the visitor, and there is plenty of accommodation available now to suit all budgets.

ANECDOTE

On our return from Manners Creek to Alice Springs along the Plenty River Highway, we rounded a corner to find a truck piled high with an amazing collection of assorted bric-a-brac and the driver sitting disconsolately beside it. We stopped and asked what the problem was.

"Well," he said. "It's like this. I stopped here for the night and unpacked the fridge and got the beer nice and cold, but in the morning I found that the fridge had run the battery flat and I couldn't start the truck."

"How long have you been here?" we asked.

"Two days," he replied mournfully.

"Two days?"

"Yes, you are the first people to come along. And the worst thing is that the beer is all warm now."

In Australia one needs to get one's priorities right. Cold beer first.

ALICE SPRINGS 449

Alice Springs has published a series of leaflets detailing themed trails. Each trail has a Theme Shelter at its commencement and each site on the trail has information displayed. The six themes are *Aboriginal Culture; A River Through Time; Communications; Transportation; Heritage, Culture and the Arts;* and *the Landscape of Alice Springs.* Not all of the sites are within easy walking distance of the town centre, but most are. These leaflets can be obtained from the Visitor Information Centre. Here, though, we shall content ourselves with a general walking tour incorporating some of the most interesting features of the town, plus a look at the Old Telegraph Station which is the reason for the existence of Alice Springs. The tour can be divided into two parts, as shown, if preferred.

Walking Tour
Part 1

Starting from the Visitor Information Centre in Gregory Terrace and finishing at the northern edge of the town, the whole walk will cover about eleven kilometres and take three and a half hours, plus at least another hour for viewing the Old Telegraph Station. If it is divided into two parts, this part, the town section, will cover four kilometres and take about ninety minutes.

At the door of the Visitor Information Centre, turn left and walk the few metres to the corner of Todd Mall, noticing the **Civic Centre** on your left surrounded by a grassy area popular with the local aborigines. At **Todd Mall**, turn right. This is the heart of Alice Springs, where souvenir shops mingle with cafés and where the greatest concentration of visitors to the town is to be found. On your left is the **Flynn Memorial Church**. The Rev. John Flynn ('Flynn of the Inland') was the man who conceived and put into effect the idea of the Royal Flying Doctor Service, and of the Australian Inland Mission, and who did so much to try to promote the welfare of those living in the outback. This church was built as a memorial to the Rev. Flynn. Just beyond is *Adelaide House*, constructed between 1920 and 1926. This building was designed by the Rev. Flynn and features an ingenious ventilation system. Until 1939, it was the only medical centre in the region. Now it is a museum of Alice Springs history, with emphasis on the contribution of the Rev. Flynn. It includes the hut from which Flynn made his first experimental pedal radio transmissions, using the invention of Alf Traeger. *Adelaide House* is open from 10:00 until 16:00 on weekdays and from 10:00 until 12:00 on Saturdays, except that from December until March it is open only from 10:00 until 12:00, Mondays to Saturdays. Admission costs $4.

Continue along Todd Mall and at Parsons Street, where you find the entrance to the indoor shopping centre, turn left. On your right is the **National Pioneer Women's Hall of Fame**. This building was constructed in 1928 and was originally government offices. Then, from 1936, it was used as a courthouse, until it became too small in the 1970s. It was restored and used by the Department of Law. In 1990, it became the temporary site of the National Pioneer Women's Hall of Fame, which is open daily from 10:00 until 17:00. Admission costs $3.

Opposite, on the corner of Parsons Street and Hartley Street, is **The Residency**, an attractive building, refreshingly cool within, which was built in 1927 to house the Government Resident, the Northern Territory having been divided in 1926 into Northern Australia and Central Australia. In 1931, that experiment was ended and the building was used as the home of the senior public servant. It was improved in 1946 for a visit of the Governor-General, and again in 1963 when the Queen and Prince

Philip stayed here. Now the building is open daily from 10:00 until 17:00, and contains some interesting photographs, as well as the toilet used by Her Majesty during her stay! Admission is free.

A little further along Parsons Street on the left is the **Old Stuart Town Gaol**. It was constructed in 1908, receiving its first prisoner in 1909, and is the oldest surviving building in the town area. It is made of local stone and remained in use until 1938, after which the building was used by the police. The Old Gaol is open from 10:00 until 12:30, but closed on Sundays and from December until February. Admission costs $3.

Return to the corner of Parsons and Hartley Streets and turn right (south). You will pass the Post Office on your left, a relatively new building, and come to the **Hartley Street School**. This was the first purpose-built government school in the town. The first section of the building was opened in 1930, with one teacher, Miss Pearl Burton, appointed. It was used, with extensions, until 1965, and is now the office of the National Trust. It is open on weekdays from 10:30 until 14:30. Admission is free. This location is the start of the *Heritage, Culture and the Arts Theme Trail*, and the Trail Shelter is outside the school, giving further details of the route and places of interest.

Walk one more block along Hartley Street until you reach Stott Terrace. On your left here is **Panorama Guth**, a 360-degree panoramic painting of the surroundings of Alice Springs. There are other art works here too, as well as aboriginal artefacts and photographs.

Continue along Hartley Street and you will pass through what is now known as the **Heritage Precinct**. There are no really old buildings here, but these houses and former shops date from the time when Alice Springs was starting to expand in the 1930s and 1940s, following the arrival of the railway. You will now come to a grassed area where the **Stuart Memorial** stands. Lest there be any confusion, it should be made clear that Stuart never came here, although he did pass through the MacDonnell Ranges to the west of where Alice Springs now stands during his successful crossing of the continent from south to north in 1862. The Memorial was erected in 1939.

Cross the grass and, a little to your right on the far (south) side, you will find the **Royal Flying Doctor Service Base**. It is open daily from 9:00 (13:00 on Sundays) until 16:00. The base was built in 1939, and has been extended since. Just a little further on the left is the **Old Alice Springs Gaol**, which came into use in 1938, when the Old Stuart Gaol was found inadequate, and remained in service until 1996. Facing the Gaol is **Billy Goat Hill**, so called because goats were kept here in the early days of the town. Proceed round the hill, back to Stott Terrace, and cross the railway line.

Immediately after crossing, there is a street on the right to which vehicular access is blocked. Turn up this street and at its end, on your left, you will find the **Old Stuart Town Cemetery**. It came into use in 1890 and it is believed that at least 54 people are buried here, but only seven headstones remain now. Unfortunately, it is not possible to cross the railway without returning to the crossing point just used, so go back and recross. Cross the Stuart Highway also, and turn left along Railway Terrace. Notice on your right the former **Post Office**, opened in 1932 and in use until 1977, and, just south of it, the former **Postmaster's Residence**, built at the same time and now an office. Beyond Parsons Street, on the left, you will see some old **Railway Cottages**. Nos. 14 and 16 were constructed for the opening of the railway line in 1929, while nos. 10 and 12 were built later, during the war. The railway station used to be near here, on this side of the tracks, until the standard gauge line was opened in 1980. At the end of Railway Terrace, you will find the **Central Australia Pioneers Memorial**.

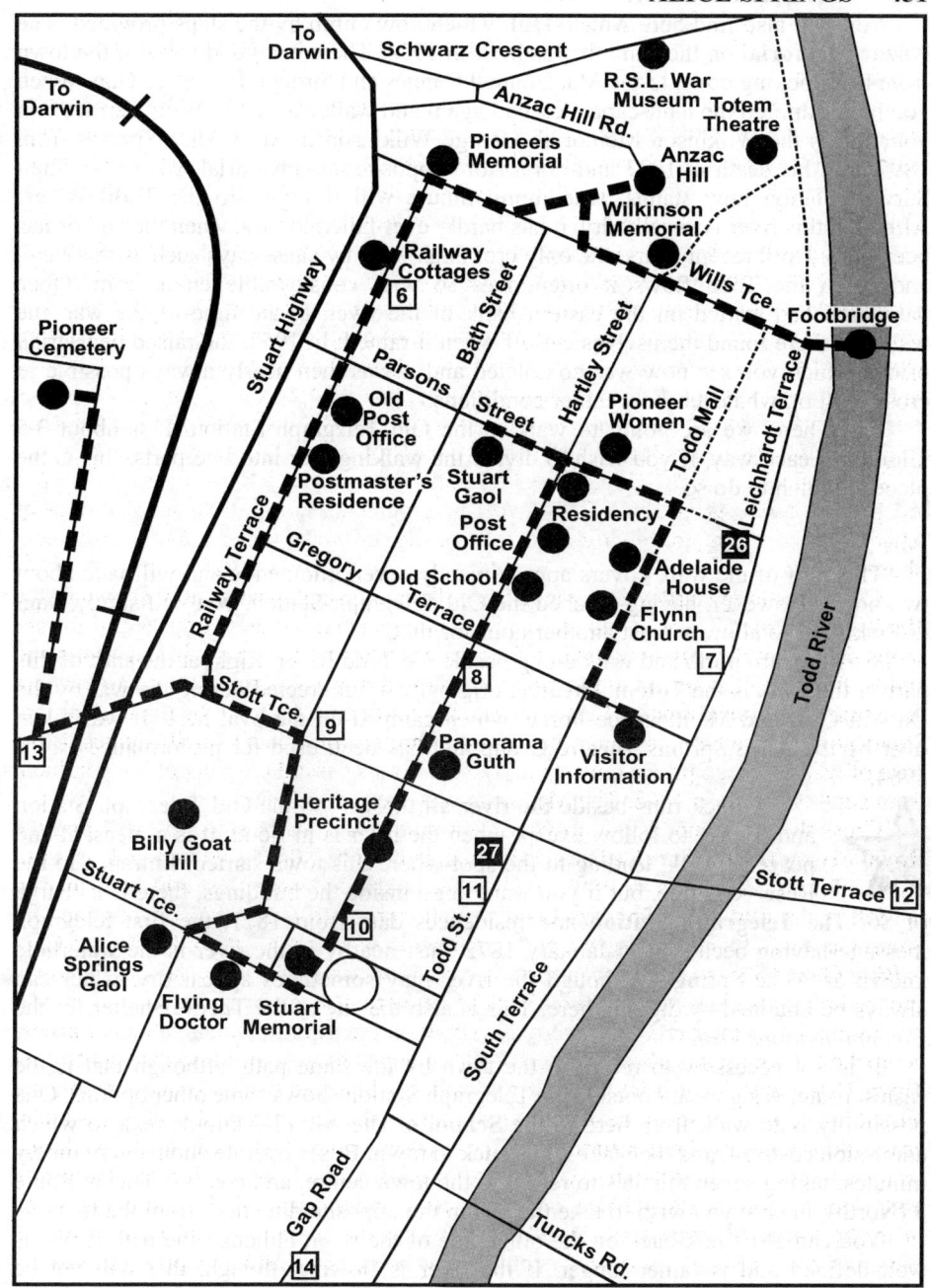

CENTRAL ALICE SPRINGS
Dashed line shows Walking Tour, Part 1
Black numerals in white boxes indicate hotel accommodation
White numerals in black boxes indicate backpackers hostels

You will also find here **Anzac Hill**, which now climb by the steps provided. The **Anzac Memorial** on the summit was built in 1934. There is a good view of the town from here looking down to the MacDonnell Ranges and through Heavitree Gap. When you have admired the landscape, descend again and walk east along Wills Terrace. On your left is the Wilkinson Memorial. George Wilkinson lived in Alice Springs from 1897 until his death in 1933 and ran a store opposite this memorial, where the Shell Service Station now stands. One more minute will bring us to the **Todd River**. Although this river is usually dry, it has hardly ever failed to flow when the author has been here. Until recent years, the only crossings were by causeways such as that here, and when the Todd flows it often does so with considerable enthusiasm. Once habitation had started on the eastern bank of the river, at the time of the war, the residents there found themselves cut off when it rained. In 1957, the raised pedestrian bridge which you see now was completed and it was then nearly always possible to cross on foot, whatever the weather conditions.

From here, we are going to walk to the Old Telegraph Station. It is about 3.5 kilometres each way. If you wish to divide the walking tour into two parts, this is the place at which to do so.

Part 2

This part of the walk covers approximately seven kilometres and will take about two hours. However, having reached the Old Telegraph Station, you will surely want to look at it, so allow at least another hour for that.

We now turn north and walk along beside the Todd River. Right at the start of this part of the walk is the **Totem Theatre**, originally a hut erected during the war by the Darwin Overland Maintenance Force, which camped on the oval here. It was taken over by the Alice Springs Theatre Group and has been used for performances since 1964.

A track runs beside the river all the way to the Old Telegraph Station and is easy to follow except when the river is in flood. It is a pleasant and peaceful walk, leading to the spot where this town started. Entrance to the Reserve is free, but if you want to go inside the buildings, there is a charge of $6. The **Telegraph Station** and residences date from 1871, the first telegraph message having been sent in January 1872. Just nearby in the river is the waterhole known as Alice Springs. Although the river may sometimes appear dry, water can always be obtained by digging here. This is also the site of the Theme Shelter for the *Communications Trail*.

It is not necessary to return to the town by the same path, although that is the easiest route. A signboard outside the Telegraph Station shows some other options. One possibility is to walk from here to the **School of the Air** (2.7 kilometres), to which admission costs $4, and then take a bus back to town. Buses operate about every ninety minutes, taking seven minutes to return to the town centre, and cost $2. This is Route 3 (North), in case you wish to take the bus in the opposite direction, from the town.

You can also walk back on the other side of the river, although the path is not as well defined and is rather longer. If the river is flowing, though, that will not be possible as you will not be able to cross here.

There are other points of interest which have not been covered by our walk, of course, so let us look at a few of those.

ALICE SPRINGS 453

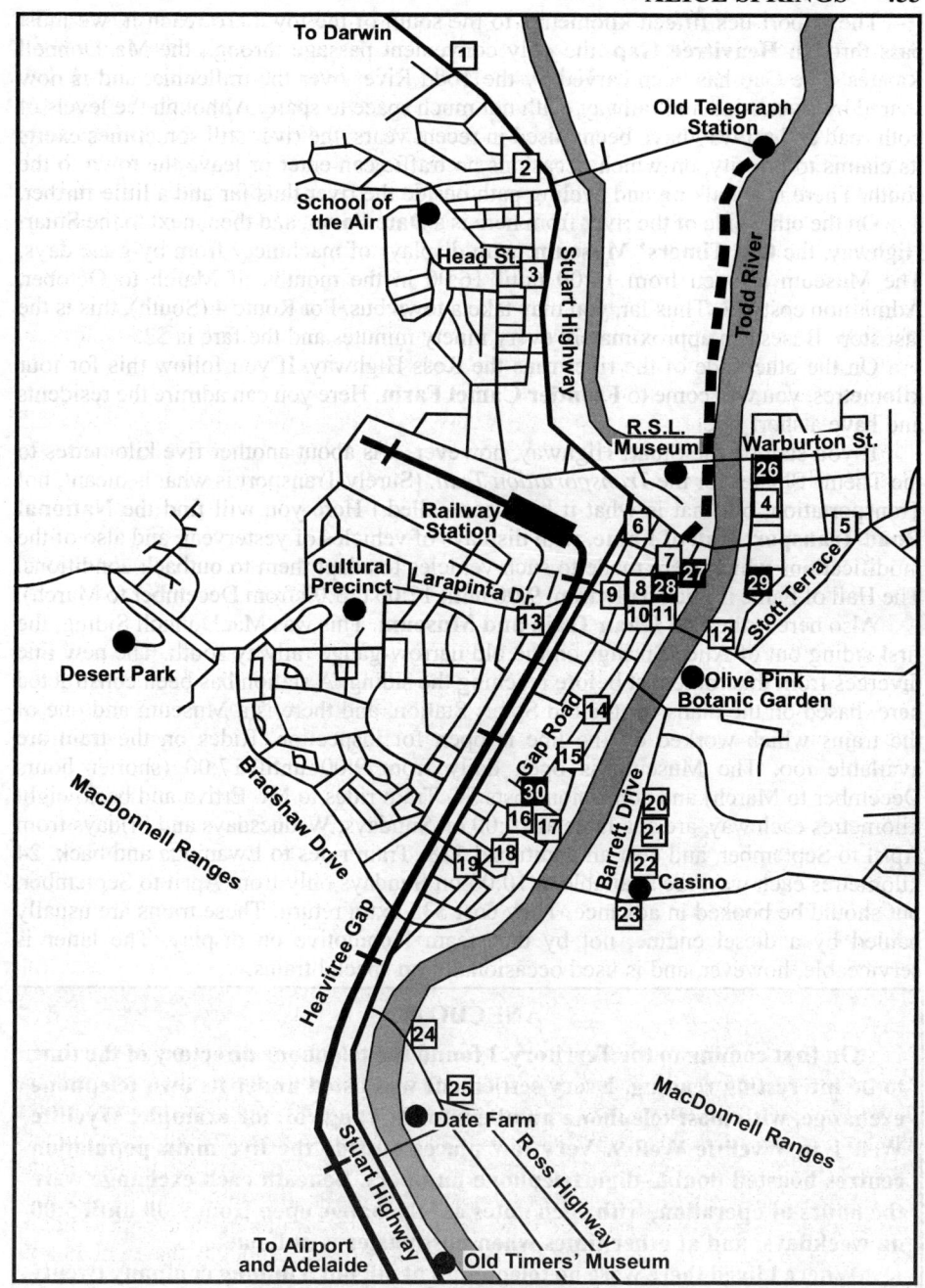

ALICE SPRINGS
Dashed line shows Walking Tour, Part 2
Black numerals in white boxes indicate hotel accommodation
White numerals in black boxes indicate backpackers hostels

The airport lies fifteen kilometres to the south of the town. To reach it, we must pass through **Heavitree Gap**, the only convenient passage through the MacDonnell Ranges. The Gap has been carved by the Todd River over the millennia, and is now shared by river, road and railway, with not much space to spare. Although the levels of both road and railway have been raised in recent years, the river still sometimes exerts its claims to priority, on which occasions no traffic can enter or leave the town to the south. There is a walking and cycling path beside the river thus far and a little further.

On the other side of the river from here is a **Date Farm**, and then, next to the Stuart Highway, the **Old Timers' Museum**, with displays of machinery from by-gone days. The Museum is open from 14:00 until 16:00 in the months of March to October. Admission costs $3. Thus far, you may take a town bus. For Route 4 (South), this is the last stop. Buses run approximately every ninety minutes and the fare is $2.

On the other side of the river runs the Ross Highway. If you follow this for four kilometres, you will come to **Frontier Camel Farm**. Here you can admire the residents and have a short ride.

If you stay on the Stuart Highway, however, it is about another five kilometres to the Theme Shelter for the *Transportation Trail*. (Surely Transport is what is meant, not Transportation, but that is what it has been called.) Here you will find the **National Road Transport Hall of Fame**, with displays of vehicles of yesteryear, and also of the modifications which were made to such vehicles to adapt them to outback conditions. The Hall of Fame is open daily from 9:00 until 17:00 (13:00 from December to March).

Also here is the **Old Ghan Train and Museum**. This was MacDonnell Siding, the first siding out of Alice Springs on the old narrow-gauge railway south. The new line diverges from this route just before reaching the siding. A station has been constructed here, based on the plans for the old Stuart Station, and there is a Museum and one of the trains which worked on the line is open for inspection. Rides on the train are available too. The Museum is open daily from 9:00 until 17:00 (shorter hours December to March) and admission costs $6. Train rides to Mt. Ertiva and back, eight kilometres each way, are available at 10:00 on Sundays, Wednesdays and Fridays from April to September, and cost an additional $18. Train rides to Ewaninga and back, 24 kilometres each way, are available at 10:00 on Sundays only from April to September, but should be booked in advance. They cost $35 extra return. These trains are usually hauled by a diesel engine, not by the steam locomotive on display. The latter is serviceable, however, and is used occasionally on special trains.

ANECDOTE

On first coming to the Territory, I found the telephone directory of the time to be interesting reading. Every settlement was listed under its own telephone exchange, with most telephone numbers in the range of, for example, Wycliffe Well 1 to Wycliffe Well 9. Very few places outside the five main population centres boasted double-digit telephone numbers. Beneath each exchange were the hours of operation, with such notes as 'Exchange open from 9:00 until 5:00 on weekdays, and at other times when postmaster is at home'.

Where I lived there were no telephones at all, but a mining company twenty kilometres away had one which could be used in emergencies. It was connected to the Darwin exchange and I was told that it was the longest local call in the world, approximately 700 kilometres.

The problem with these two attractions, of course, is how to get to them, as they are ten kilometres from the town centre. The only transport service available is the *Alice Wanderer*, a bus which performs a circuit of likely sites for visitors seven times a day, every 70 minutes. You may get on and off as you please, but the price for a day ticket is $25, which is not cheap. Alternatively, you can take the Route 4 public bus to the Old Timers' Museum for $2 each way, and then walk five kilometres in each direction, but it is a long, hot and mostly unshaded walk. Try walking one way, by the river and then attempt to befriend another visitor in order to get a ride back.

Back in town, there is the **R.S.L. War Museum** in Schwarz Crescent, behind Anzac Hill. Then, adjacent to the town centre, but on the other side of the river, is the **Olive Pink Botanic Garden**. Olive Pink arrived in Central Australia in 1930 and lived first with the aborigines in the Tanami Desert, trying to promote aboriginal rights. She later moved to Alice Springs and lived here, creating an arid zone Botanic Garden from 1956 until her death in 1975 at the age of 91. The garden is now owned by the Northern Territory Government and operated mainly by volunteers. There is no fixed charge for admission, but donations are solicited.

South of the Olive Pink Garden is the **Casino**, for those who fancy a flutter. Pyndan Camel Tracks offers more camel rides close to the town centre. These rides depart from the Todd River bank near the Visitor Information Centre four times each afternoon, except on Tuesdays, and cost $30 for a one hour ride down the river and back.

To the west of the town is the **Alice Springs Cultural Precinct**. It takes about twenty minutes to walk to here from the town centre along Larapinta Drive and there is so much to see that it really needs half a day. This was originally the Araluen property of the Territory's great aviator, Eddie Connellan, together with the first aerodrome and the Memorial Cemetery. The Precinct is open from 10:00 until 17:00 daily and admission to the entire complex costs $8.

The **Araluen Centre** was built in 1984 and houses local art works, including those by the famous aboriginal painter, **Albert Namatjira**, and others of the *Hermannsburg School*. There are also a theatre and a craft workshop with artisans at work.

The **Museum of Central Australia** here deals mostly with natural history. It includes the remains of a huge prehistoric freshwater crocodile and of the largest bird which ever lived, dated to about eight million years ago.

The remains of the *Kookaburra* are on display in the **Kookaburra Memorial**. When Kingsford Smith went missing in 1929 at the start of a planned round-the-world flight in the *Southern Cross*, a search was launched. The *Kookaburra*, part of this search, had the misfortune to crash in the Tanami Desert north-west of Alice Springs and the pilot Anderson and engineer Hitchcock could not be rescued.

The **Aviation Museum** is here too. This site was cleared in 1920 by police and prisoners, for use as the first aerodrome. The first aircraft landed here in 1921. In 1939, Eddie Connellan established Connellan Airways (later Connair) and changed the thinking of the Territory. Real isolation became a thing of the past. Here in the museum, you can find one of the typical DC-3 aircraft operated by Connair right into the 1980s and which were so well suited to this terrain, being able to land on anything and endure uncomplainingly all the punishment which could be meted out to them over a lifespan of forty years or more. Unfortunately, though, the story of Connair does not have a happy ending. As Eddie Connellan grew older, he looked to his son Roger to take over the operation of the airline. On 7th January 1977, an ex-pilot, incensed at being dismissed from the airline, took one of the aircraft and flew it round and round Alice

Springs Airport threatening to crash it into the control tower unless Roger Connellan were summoned and succumbed to his demands. Roger Connellan went to the control tower and talked to the pilot by radio for several hours. Eventually, the plane ran short of fuel and the pilot fulfilled his threat to fly it into the control tower, killing himself, Roger Connellan and those in the tower. Eddie Connellan was devastated and died himself a few years later, after which Connair too soon became just a piece of Territory history. The author flew on Connair flights, perhaps even on the aircraft here, and will always remember Connair with a feeling of affection and nostalgia. It represented part of the great pioneering spirit of the Territory.

The **Memorial Cemetery** here includes the graves of Eddie Connellan, Roger Connellan and other members of the Connellan family. Also here is the most famous of aboriginal artists, Albert Namatjira, originally of Hermannsburg Mission. Lasseter's grave too is in this cemetery. He claimed to have discovered a reef of gold in the desert and went out to pinpoint its exact location. Not only did he perish in the attempt, but Lasseter's Reef has never been found and remains one of the most famous stories in Australian history. Many have searched for it over the years, but without success. Olive Pink, mentioned above, is another famous character interred in this cemetery and there is also a section for the Afghan cameleers who made Alice Springs accessible in the early days.

Finally, you will see the **Araluen Homestead**, the home of the Connellan family. It is privately owned, but you can see the site of the swimming pool, the first ever built in Alice Springs, at the summit of the terraced area, and the lawn used as a tennis court.

Further west from the Alice Springs Cultural Precinct is the **Alice Springs Desert Park**, displaying the flora and fauna of Central Australia. There are 350 species of plants here and 120 animals, several of them endangered species. There are three separate habitats: desert rivers, sand country and woodland, and there are sections on bush tucker and bush medicines. The Desert Park is open daily from 7:30 until 18:00. A visit needs half a day. Admission, though, is an expensive $20. The Desert Park provides transport from and to accommodation in Alice Springs, or, if you prefer, take a town bus on Route 1 (West) to its terminus, from where you have to walk for about fifteen minutes. The fare is $2 and the journey takes 25 minutes. Buses operate approximately every ninety minutes, but note that the last bus back is at 16:30.

Beyond the Desert Park is **Flynn's Grave**, perched on the hillside looking out over the landscape which he loved. He died in 1951. The grave is two kilometres from the point on Larapinta Drive where you take the road up to the Desert Park. From the end of the Route 1 bus terminus, it is about 25 minutes walk.

ANECDOTE

My first experience of Connair, the Territory airline, was when, in Darwin, I telephoned the company's office and asked the times of flights to my destination. "Wednesdays and Saturdays," said the voice at the other end. "Yes, and what time?" I persisted. "I just told you," said the voice, "Wednesdays and Saturdays."

I soon learnt about Territory time and about Connair in particular. If the aircraft arrived on Wednesdays and Saturdays, it was on time. If it was Thursday or Sunday, it was late. Scheduling was simple.

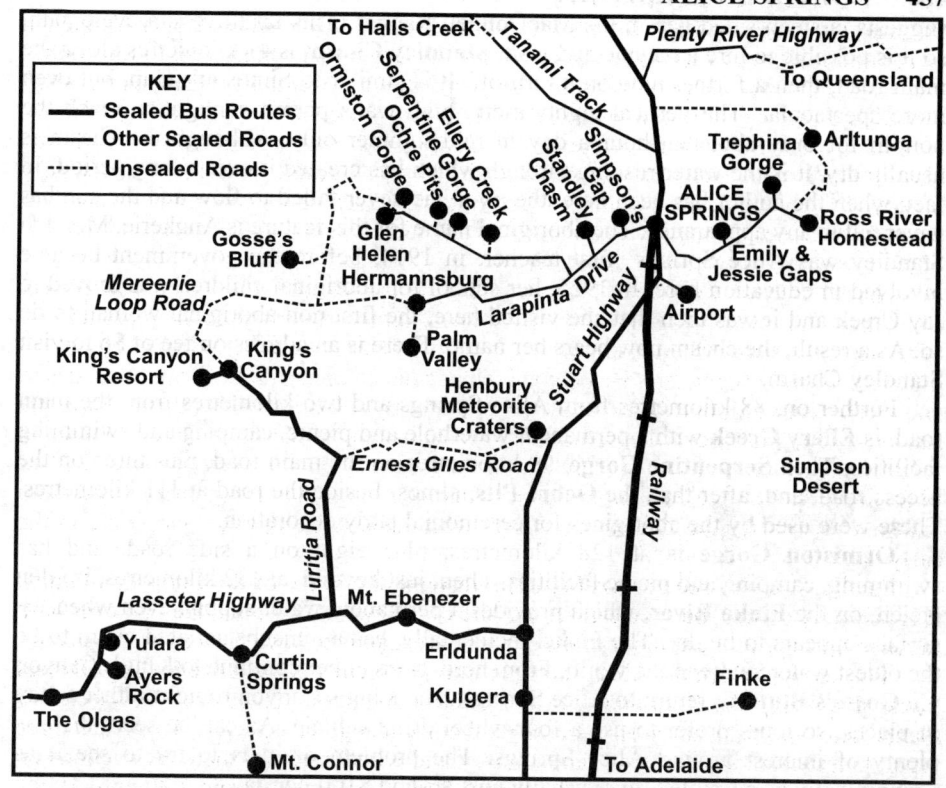

ATTRACTIONS IN THE VICINITY OF ALICE SPRINGS

As mentioned previously, as well as having a great deal of interest in itself, Alice Springs is also a base for tours to the surrounding area. Almost everybody who comes here wishes to travel on to Ayers Rock, and most visit King's Canyon too now. The Greyhound bus service permits this quite conveniently. From Alice Springs, one travels on the first day to Ayers Rock, where there is the opportunity to view the Rock at sunset. The next day one climbs the Rock in the morning, then visits the Olgas and travels to King's Canyon. On the third day one climbs to the top of King's Canyon and then returns to Alice Springs. There are plenty of other similar tours available too, some following the Mereenie Loop Road between King's Canyon and Alice Springs to see more and avoid backtracking.

Of the sights closer to Alice Springs which can be reached by tour, to the east are **Emily Gap, Jessie Gap, Trephina Gorge, the Ross River Homestead**, where accommodation is available, and the **Arltunga Goldfields**, again with accommodation available. Arltunga is 110 kilometres from Alice Springs, so a tour to here can easily be managed in a single day, or you can stay overnight if preferred.

To the south-east is the **Simpson Desert**. Tours run here too, and usually take about three days in special vehicles.

To the west lies a series of attractions. First is **Simpson's Gap**, sixteen kilometres along the main road and then a further seven on a minor road. This is, as the name suggests, a steep-sided gap in the MacDonnell Ranges. This far there is a cycle path, so it is possible to hire a bicycle and visit. **Standley Chasm** is 41 kilometres along the main road, then a further nine on a turn-off. It is similar to Simpson's Gap, but even more spectacular. The vertical eighty-metre-high walls permit sunlight to reach the bottom for only about an hour a day in mid-summer only. Although the chasm is usually dry, it is the water rushing through which has created it over a long period. In fact, when the author has been here, the river has never failed to flow and the sun has never put in any appearance. The aboriginal name for this feature is Angkerie. Mrs. Ida Standley was Alice Springs' first teacher, in 1914, before the government became involved in education here. In 1925, her school for aboriginal children was moved to Jay Creek and it was then that she visited here, the first non-aboriginal woman to do so. As a result, the chasm now bears her name. There is an admission fee of $6 to visit Standley Chasm.

Further on, 88 kilometres from Alice Springs and two kilometres from the main road, is **Ellery Creek** with a permanent waterhole and picnic, camping and swimming facilities. Then **Serpentine Gorge**, 99 kilometres on the main road, plus three on the access road, and, after that, the **Ochre Pits**, almost beside the road at 111 kilometres. These were used by the aborigines for ceremonial body decoration.

Ormiston Gorge is at 128 kilometres, plus eight on a side road, and has swimming, camping and picnic facilities. Then, just beyond, at 132 kilometres, is Glen Helen, on the **Finke River**, which provides a permanent water supply, even when the surface appears to be dry. The Finke, incidentally, has an unsubstantiated claim to be the oldest watercourse in the world. From here, tours either continue to King's Canyon via **Gosse's Bluff**, or return to Alice Springs. The King's Canyon route is rather sandy in places, so tours prefer to use a four-wheel-drive vehicle. As can be seen, there is plenty of interest around Alice Springs. The problem often is to try to see it as economically as possible. Tours usually cost around $100 per day.

Desert Wanderer Tours offers a pass for $350 giving unlimited travel for seven days on its Alice Springs, Glen Helen, King's Canyon, Ayers Rock, Olgas, Lasseter Highway and Stuart Highway Routes. Accommodation is not included in this price.

Alice Springs is a unique town, and displays this in its festivals. The events which the town hosts include the annual **camel races**, and the **Henley-on-Todd Regatta**, a parody of the famous English Henley Regatta. The Regatta is held in (rather than on) the Todd River. Since the river is usually dry, holes are cut in the bottoms of the boats, through which the legs of the participants protrude. They then race along the dry sand of the river bed. A few years ago, the Regatta had to be cancelled, because the river was flowing! On another occasion, the river was ingeniously diverted so that the Regatta could take place.

Around Alice Springs, local bus services are provided by Asbus, with four routes, running north, east, south and west. Services are divided into two zones and cost $1.50 for a single zone and $2 for two zones. Most journeys will involve two zones. All services operate at intervals of approximately ninety minutes.

ACCOMMODATION

There is plenty of accommodation in Alice Springs, now that the town has established itself as a prime tourist destination. For backpackers, there is quite a range. If you arrive at the airport, Melanka Lodge and Elke's will pick you up and bring you into town free of charge, a big bonus, as the airport bus fare is $10. For the journey back to the airport, you have to pay, but Melanka will offer you a ticket on certain services only for $8 instead of $10.

Melanka Lodge is a huge hostel, formerly accommodating government employees in Alice Springs. It has air-conditioning, at night only, a swimming pool and a bar with discounted drinks, but it is somewhat lacking in maintenance. When the author was here, rain poured through the ceiling, accumulated on the floor, inundated guests' packs, overflowed into the corridor and generally made one think that the swimming pool was an unnecessary luxury. The Pioneer Youth Hostel is on the site of the former Pioneer Theatre (cinema) - the so-called 'Walk-In' (to distinguish it from the 'Drive-In' on the edge of the town). Alas, the 'Walk-In' is gone now. Such is progress.

(i) Hotel Accommodation in Alice Springs

Name	Stars	No. on Map	Telephone No.	Address	Lowest Price (Double/Twin)
Rydges Plaza	4	21	1-800-675-212	Barrett Drive	$235
Alice Springs Resort	4½	12	1-800-805-055	34 Stott Terrace	$215
Lasseters Hotel Casino	4	22	1-800-808-975	93 Barrett Drive	$215
Orangewood B & B	4½	4	08-8952-4114	9 McMinn Street	$170
Frontier Oasis	3½	14	1-800-815-658	10 Gap Road	$155
Alice Springs Vista Hotel	3½	23	1-800-810-664	46 Stephens Road	$155
Territory Inn	3½	7	1-800-089-644	11 Leichhardt Terrace	$145
Red Centre Resort	3½	1	1-800-089-616	Stuart Highway North	$125
Diplomat Hotel	4½	8	1-800-804-885	City Central, Gregory Ter.	$110
Elkira Court Motel	3	9	1-800-809-252	65 Bath Street	$105
Desert Palms Resort	3	20	1-800-678-037	74 Barrett Drive	$105
Alice Motor Inn	3	5	1-800-022-801	27 Undoolya Road	$95
Melanka Lodge Motel	3	11	1-800-896-110	94 Todd Street	$95
Outback Motor Lodge	3	17	1-800-896-133	13 South Terrace	$95
Swagman's Rest	3	18	1-800-089-612	67 Gap Road	$95
Alice Tourist Apartments	3	19	1-800-806-142	Gap Road & Gnoilya Ter.	$85
Mt. Nancy Motel		2	1-800-626-213	Stuart Highway North	$80
Larapinta Lodge	3	13	1-800-687-124	3 Larapinta Drive	$80
White Gum Holiday Inn	3	15	08-8952-5144	17 Gap Road	$70
Heavitree Gap Resort	3	24	1-800-896-119	Palm Circuit	$70
Desert Rose Inn	3½	6	1-800-896-116	15 Railway Terrace	$65
Wintersun Caravan Park		3	08-8952-4080	Stuart Highway North	$50
MacDonnell Range Park	4½	25	1-800-808-373	Palm Place	$50
Toddy's		16	1-800-806-240	41 Gap Road	$45
Stuart Lodge Y.W.C.A.		10	08-8952-1894	Stuart Terrace	$40

(ii) Backpackers Hostels in Alice Springs

Name	Group	No. on Map	Telephone No.	Address	Lowest Price (Dormitory)
Elke's Backpacker Resort	VIP	30	1800-633-354	39 Gap Road	$20
Pioneer Y.H.A.	YHA	27	08-8952-8855	Parsons St. & Leichhardt Ter.	$20
Alice Lodge Backpackers	VIP/B&W	29	1800-351-925	4 Mueller Street	$20
Melanka Resort	VIP	28	1800-815-066	94 Todd Street	$18
Toddy's Backpackers	Nom	16	1800-806-240	41 Gap Road	$17
Ossie's Y.H.A.	YHA	26	08-8952-2308	Lindsay Av. & Warburton St.	$15

NORTHERN TERRITORY
MOVING ON
(i) By Train

The *Ghan* runs south to Adelaide on Tuesday and Friday afternoons. On Tuesdays, it continues to Melbourne, arriving on Wednesday evenings, and on Fridays it continues to Sydney, arriving on Sunday mornings. Regrettably, rail pass holders can no longer use a berth for a reasonable supplement, but are obliged to sit up for the entire journey. The timetable for these services is shown to the right.

Alice Springs to Adelaide, Sydney and Melbourne

Days of Operation	Tu	F
Alice Springs	1300	1300
Days	W	Sat
Port Augusta	0300	0300
Adelaide (arrive)	0900	0900
Adelaide (depart)	1015	1010
Broken Hill		1725
Days		Sun
Sydney		0915
Melbourne	2100	

(ii) By Bus

Both McCafferty's and Greyhound operate buses north to Darwin and Greyhound runs south to Adelaide. Each company has one departure every day for Darwin and Greyhound also operates daily to Adelaide. In addition, Greyhound has a daily service to Ayers Rock, with a connexion to King's Canyon.

Destination	Operator	Via	Distance (km)	Fare	Journey Time	Frequency
Darwin	McCafferty's		1515	$214	20¼ hrs	1/day
		Katherine	1199	$197	15½ hrs	1/day
		Tennant Creek	506	$118	6¾ hrs	1/day
Darwin	Greyhound		1515	$214	20¼ hrs	1/day
		Katherine	1199	$197	15 hrs	1/day
		Tennant Creek	503	$118	6 hrs	1/day
Adelaide	Greyhound		1570	$195	19¾ hrs	1/day
		Port Augusta	1224	$184	15½ hrs	1/day
		Coober Pedy	687	$103	8¼ hrs	1/day
Ayers Rock	Greyhound		540	$82	5¼ hrs	1/day

ANECDOTE

Flying with Connair was never dull. The Wet Season was a particularly exciting time, as, with a ceiling of 10,000 feet, the DC-3s were unable to climb above the weather and obliged, therefore, to travel through it. These sturdy workhorses endured the buffets and bangs uncomplainingly - and generously passed them on to all of the passengers. At each stop, the aircraft would "buzz" the settlement, the deep throaty rumble of its engines alerting the residents to the arrival of their supplies and mail for the week. It was also hoped that, if there had been any rain, somebody would run out, arms flailing, to warn that, whilst a landing might be successful, take-off could be delayed for several days.

At each stop, the pilot was obliged to calculate the weight of the aircraft before attempting a take-off, and it was not uncommon to overhear reassuring comments such as, "Well, it's a bit over, but I expect it'll be all right." And all right it always was with the DC-3s, which seemed to have been designed specifically to cope with mistreatment, probably a wise standard in the Territory.

Of all the measures designed to reassure passengers, though, the most ostentatious occurred when Connair accepted a delivery of new Heron aircraft and felt obliged to station the flight attendant in front of the aeroplane with a fire extinguisher each time the engines were started because of their propensity for external, as well as internal, combustion at that vital moment.

GREAT RAILWAY JOURNEYS
6. THE GHAN
SYDNEY OR MELBOURNE TO ALICE SPRINGS

ADELAIDE	Belair	Mt. Lofty	Balhannah	Mt. Barker Jct.	Petwood	Monarto South	MURRAY BRIDGE	Tailem Bend	Coomandook	Coonalpyn	Tintinara	Coombe	Keith	Wirrega	BORDERTOWN	Wolseley	Serviceton	Kaniva	Nhill	Salisbury	DIMBOOLA	HORSHAM	Murtoa	Stawell	Great Western	ARARAT	Maroona	Tatyoon	Vite Vite	Berrybank	Wingeel	Gherringhap	NORTH SHORE GEELONG	MELBOURNE
828	808	799	784	780	768	748	733	709	676	646	618	601	581	557	536	523	515	492	453	442	415	381	350	295	287	265	244	232	188	151	119	83	61	

SOUTH AUSTRALIA | VICTORIA | Distances (km from Melbourne)

The two most famous trains in Australia are the *Indian-Pacific* and the *Ghan*, and yet the author places the *Ghan* only sixth in this list of Great Railway Journeys. Why is that?

Basically, the *Ghan* is famous because of its history, but that is the story of a different train, which ran on a different line from the present service. Also the current service travels mainly by night, so that one sees comparatively little. When the line is extended to Darwin, though, scheduled for the end of 2004, the journey on the *Ghan* will become a trans-continental passage and will rank as one of the world's truly great trips once more.

The old line left the current route at Port Augusta and that former narrow gauge line is currently operated as far as Quorn by the Pichi Richi Railway. Quorn was reached in 1879 and soon became a major railway junction. The railway builders pressed on north to Marree and then to Oodnadatta, arriving there in 1884. Oodnadatta became the railhead for the next 45 years, with goods and passengers for Alice Springs being moved on by teams of camels operated by the famous Afghan cameleers. This journey used to take about three weeks. Only in 1929 was the narrow gauge line finally extended to Alice Springs (known as Stuart at the time). Budgeting problems meant that it was built as a low-cost line and that was to cause problems later. There was but a single bridge between Marree and Alice Springs, for example. When the railway met other rivers, it ran down the bank, across the river on a concrete causeway raised a couple of metres above the bed, and up the bank at the other side. The system worked satisfactorily until it rained. Then the trains had to wait, sometimes for several weeks. The train service to Alice Springs was, at first humourously and unofficially, referred to as the *Afghan Express*, later shortened to the *Ghan*, as recognition of the half century of transport operations provided by the Afghan cameleers prior to its inauguration.

The next major change occurred in 1956, when the line between Port Augusta and Marree was converted to standard gauge, and rerouted slightly, in order to deal with heavy coal traffic from Leigh Creek. The *Ghan* was at this time essentially a service between Adelaide and Alice Springs, but the problem for passengers was that the journey involved a broad gauge track between Adelaide and Port Pirie, a standard gauge track between Port Pirie and Marree and a deteriorating narrow gauge track between Marree and Alice Springs. The train from Adelaide as far as Port Pirie was a daylight connecting service. The *Ghan* itself started from Port Pirie and then passengers had to change trains at Marree the following day before continuing to Alice Springs. It must have been one of the world's slowest 'express' services, taking 39 hours just on the narrow gauge section from Marree to Alice Springs. From Adelaide, the service took three days, if the

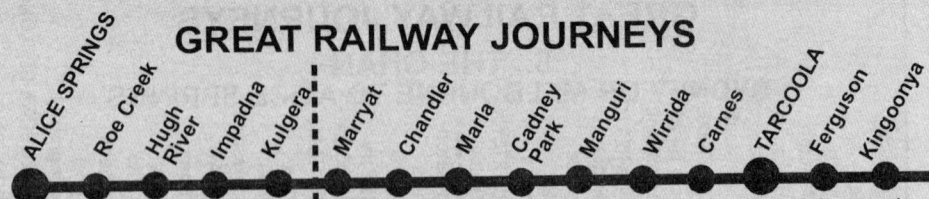

train was on time. Moreover, it was expensive, since only first class passengers were offered sleeping accommodation and the prices charged to them included sumptuous meals. However, it was reckoned to be one of the world's great train experiences, the lounge even being equipped with a grand piano, and the weekly service survived until 1980.

Long before that, though, it was realised that the future lay not in patching up a poorly constructed line which consumed unnecessary man-hours on every journey and provided at best an erratic service, but in investing in a new and efficient standard gauge route. This was finally accomplished in the late 1970s, when the line on which you will travel now was built. It provides a fast, efficient and comfortable service, but, of course, the train does lack the character of the *Old Ghan*, about which you will still hear nostalgic reminiscences, mostly from those who never travelled on it.

The author too never travelled on the *Old Ghan*. It was too expensive. However, I did travel the old route on one of the three mixed trains which ran on it every week and that was a great experience too, different from, but as rewarding as, and much cheaper than, the *Old Ghan* itself.

Traditionally, the *Ghan* has provided a service between Adelaide and Alice Springs, but the recent conversion of the track between Adelaide and Melbourne to standard gauge has prompted the logical decision to extend the route. There is now one train every week between Sydney and Alice Springs via Adelaide and one service every week between Melbourne and Alice Springs via Adelaide. The map for the Melbourne route is shown here.

The *Ghan* leaves Sydney on Sunday afternoons for its journey of 3,270 kilometres to Alice Springs. It follows the same route, of course, as that outlined for the *Indian-Pacific* on pages 154 to 158. It leaves Sydney approximately two hours earlier than the *Indian-Pacific* does, so one sees a little more of eastern New South Wales, and it arrives in Adelaide two and a half hours earlier.

The *Ghan* leaves Melbourne on Wednesday evenings for its journey of 2,383 kilometres to Alice Springs and travels overnight to Adelaide. You will not see much of this journey, therefore (and, indeed, there is no day train in this direction between Melbourne and Adelaide). The route passes mostly through flat agricultural terrain, pleasant but not of exceptional interest. The highlight comes at the end of the journey, as the train travels through the Adelaide Hills, offering some splendid views of the city below and the seashore in the distance. The train arrives at Keswick Station, on the outskirts of Adelaide city, in mid-morning and stays there for five hours, according to the current timetable, perhaps in an effort to emulate the feats of the *Old Ghan*. Although this provides an opportunity to see the sights of Adelaide, it means that most of the journey from Adelaide to Alice Springs is going to be in the dark also.

Both services from Adelaide leave at 15:00 on their journey of 1,555 kilometres to Alice Springs, enabling the scenery to be seen as far as Port

6. THE GHAN
SYDNEY OR MELBOURNE TO ALICE SPRINGS

Augusta, for which see the summary on page 668. Here the train turns west and continues to follow the route of the *Indian-Pacific* as far as Tarcoola, reached just after midnight.

At Tarcoola, the *Ghan* swings north on the newly constructed section of line to Alice Springs. In contrast with the old line, this one is straight and flat, enabling the train to maintain its steady 110 km/hr. Even if it were daylight, there would not be a lot to see. We pass through Manguri during the night. This is the nearest station to Coober Pedy, famous for its opals. Coober Pedy, however, is some forty kilometres east of the railway line, so both timing and location mean that the train is not the ideal method of reaching the town.

When daylight comes, we shall be near Kulgera and already across the border into the Northern Territory. Dawn reveals a barren landscape with the rich red soil supporting only spinifex, with occasional stunted trees in the generally dry watercourses.

We cross the Finke River, usually dry, although when it flows it may be transformed beyond recognition into a raging torrent, a metamorphosis difficult to believe from looking at this dry sandy bed. The Finke has claims to being the oldest watercourse in the world, but the claims have yet to be substantiated beyond doubt.

When we cross the Stuart Highway once more (we crossed once during the night) we know that we are nearing Alice Springs. The MacDonnell Ranges come into sight and we pass through the narrow Heavitree Gap beside the road and the Todd River and are in Alice Springs, the heart of the Centre. From Sydney, the 3,270 kilometres has been completed in 45 hours 20 minutes at an average speed of 72 km/hr. From Melbourne, the 2,383 kilometres has been completed in 36 hours at an average speed of 66 km/hr. From Adelaide we have covered the 1,555 kilometres in 19 hours at an average speed of 82 km/hr.

Within the currency of this book, the line will continue north a further 1,410 kilometres to Darwin and the promise made by the Commonwealth Government in 1911 will have been fulfilled. One becomes accustomed to things running late in the Territory, but this extension must be something of a record, being approximately 95 years behind schedule.

NORTHERN TERRITORY
AYERS ROCK
Population 1,100 (Yulara)
5 hrs 30 mins by bus from Alice Springs

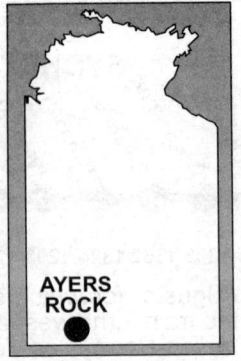

AYERS ROCK

Ayers Rock is the most famous symbol of the Australian outback. Known to the local aborigines as Uluru, it is thought to date back 550 million years to a time when huge ranges were thrust up and then eroded away. Moreover, it is thought that only the tip of the rock is actually visible above ground level, and that it may well stretch down to six kilometres below the surface.

Ayers Rock is 348 metres high. That is to say that it rises 348 metres above the entirely flat surrounding terrain. The summit is actually 862 metres above sea level. It covers an area of 3.3 square kilometres. It is 3.1 kilometres long and 2.0 kilometres wide at its maxima. The distance round the base is 9.4 kilometres. It has a surface weathered into smooth and fascinating curves and a red colour which is famous particularly when it reflects the light of the setting sun. The cause of the red colour is, in fact, rust. Iron in the arkose of which it is composed gradually oxidises and turns red.

Why, then, is it called Ayers Rock (not, incidentally, 'Ayer's Rock', as one sometimes sees)? Who was Ayers? The Rock was discovered, climbed and named by the explorer William Gosse in 1873. He named it after Sir Henry Ayers, who was, at the time, Chief Secretary, but later became Premier of South Australia. He is now remembered mainly because of the name of the Rock. As for the aboriginal name, Uluru, that does not appear to have any meaning, but is just a name. When Gosse found Ayers Rock, he referred to it as "the world's biggest pebble". He appears to have been wrong, however, for there is actually a bigger pebble, Mt. Augustus, in the northern part of Western Australia.

The first misconception of visitors concerning Ayers Rock is that it is near Alice Springs. In fact, it is 441 kilometres by the shortest route from that town, a journey of 5½ hours by bus. A visit to the Rock requires a minimum of two days, one to go and one to come back. In fact, though, most people now spend three days and include King's Canyon on their itinerary, and the Greyhound tour specifically caters for this three-day visit.

The second misconception will occur about four hours into the bus ride to Ayers Rock, when you think that you see the Rock on your left. However, it is not Ayers Rock but Mt. Connor, also rising from the flat plain. Mt. Connor is 90 kilometres from Ayers Rock, and can be seen from the summit of the latter in clear weather.

If there is a third misconception, it is that you will be able to stay at the base of the Rock. In fact, when the author first visited, that was the case. One was free to camp wherever one wished. Now, however, you must stay at Yulara Resort, which is seventeen kilometres from the Rock. The Rock itself is just a speck in the distance.

Yulara Resort is where public transport will bring you. Your options are to come with the Greyhound bus service, to come with one of the many tours, or to fly. Eddie Connellan, of Territory aviation fame, made history by being the first man to land an aircraft at the base of the Rock. At the time, the requirement for a licensed airstrip was that it must be possible to drive a vehicle for the entire length at 50 m.p.h. The undergrowth was cleared and that was achieved and air services had started to this remote location. The original Connellan airstrip was right at the base of the Rock, but

AYERS ROCK 465

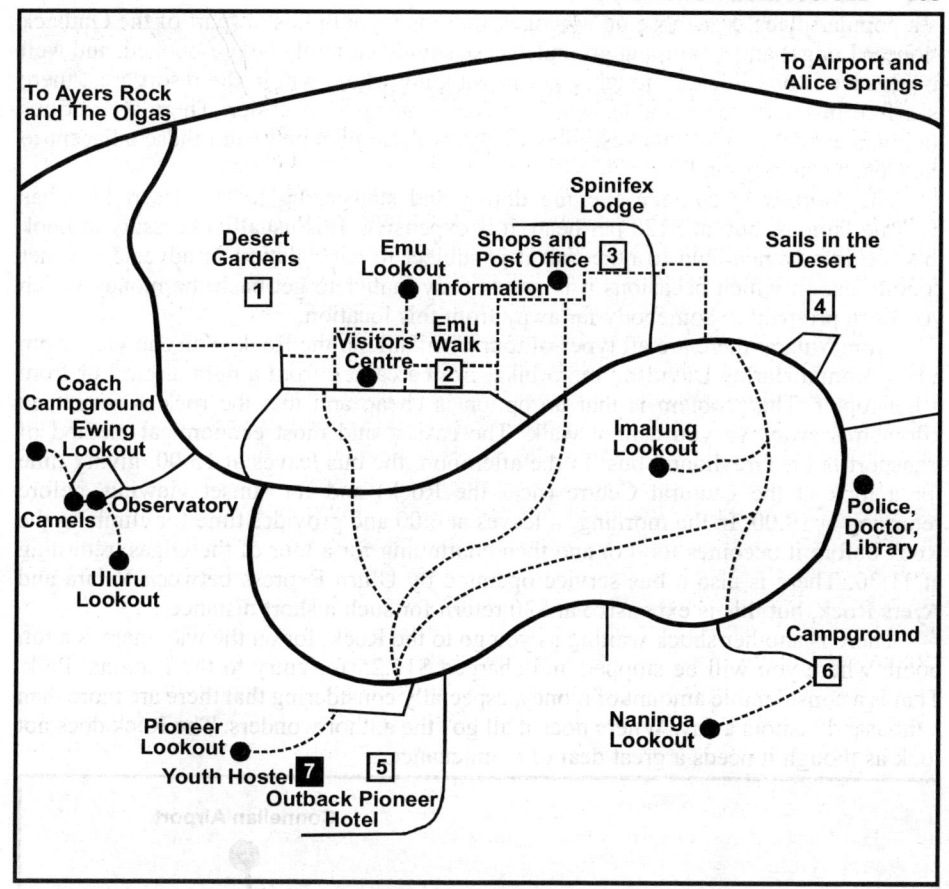

YULARA

Black numerals in white boxes indicate hotel accommodation
White numerals in black boxes indicate backpackers hostels

the current airport is close to Yulara Resort. However, the Connellan name is still preserved. If you arrive by air, you will get a view of the Rock before you land (as you will also in good weather if you fly between Alice Springs and Perth). On arrival, you will find that there is a free bus to take you the five kilometres to Yulara Resort, and to bring you back on departure.

Yulara Resort has been well designed. Its low buildings are scarcely visible in the sand hills of the area and efforts have been taken to minimise its impact on the surrounding environment. The permanent population here is 1,100, and the maximum population, including visitors, is 4,000, which is sizeable by Territory standards. There are more facilities than one would expect. There are a Post Office, a bank, a newsagency, a hairdresser, a photographic shop, a Medical Centre, a Police Station, a Visitors' Centre, an Information Centre and a supermarket with quite reasonable prices. Also, of course, there is a variety of accommodation and of restaurants. The accommodation is not cheap, and it is definitely advisable to book it in advance, as this is a popular place. For those on a budget, there is a youth hostel (part of the Outback Pioneer Lodge) and a camping ground. These should certainly be pre-booked, and well in advance if possible. Although you can walk anywhere within the resort area, there is a free bus service available, which makes matters even easier. There are various lookouts available, with the best view of Ayers Rock obtained from those adjacent to the Coach Campground.

The *Sounds of Silence* evening dining and star-gazing in the desert here has become famous, but, at $120 per head, it is expensive. It is usually necessary to book this too in advance, and to note that it is subject to cancellation in adverse weather conditions, on which occasions it is not an easy matter to get back the money which you have pre-paid to somebody far away from this location.

From Yulara, there are all types of tours available to the Rock. You can view from a bus, from a Harley Davidson motorbike, from a camel, from a light aircraft or from a helicopter. The problem is that no option is cheap and that the rock is seventeen kilometres away, so you cannot walk. The easiest and most economical method of transport is the Greyhound bus. In the afternoon, the bus leaves at 15:00, giving time for a look at the Cultural Centre (near the Rock) and for sunset viewing, before returning at 19:00. In the morning, it leaves at 6:00 and provides time for climbing the Rock before it becomes too hot and then continuing for a tour of the Olgas, returning at 11:30. There is also a bus service operated by Uluru Express between Yulara and Ayers Rock, but this is expensive at $30 return for such a short distance.

There is another shock waiting as you go to the Rock, for on the way there is a toll booth where you will be stopped and charged $16.25 for entry to the National Park. That is a considerable amount of money, especially considering that there are more than a thousand visitors a day. Where does it all go? the author wonders. The Rock does not look as though it needs a great deal of maintenance.

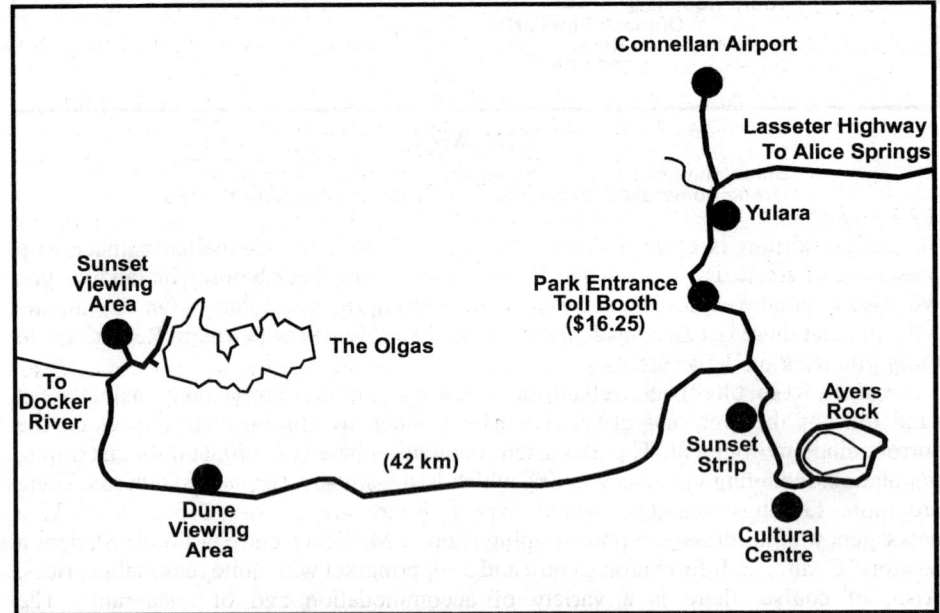

AROUND AYERS ROCK

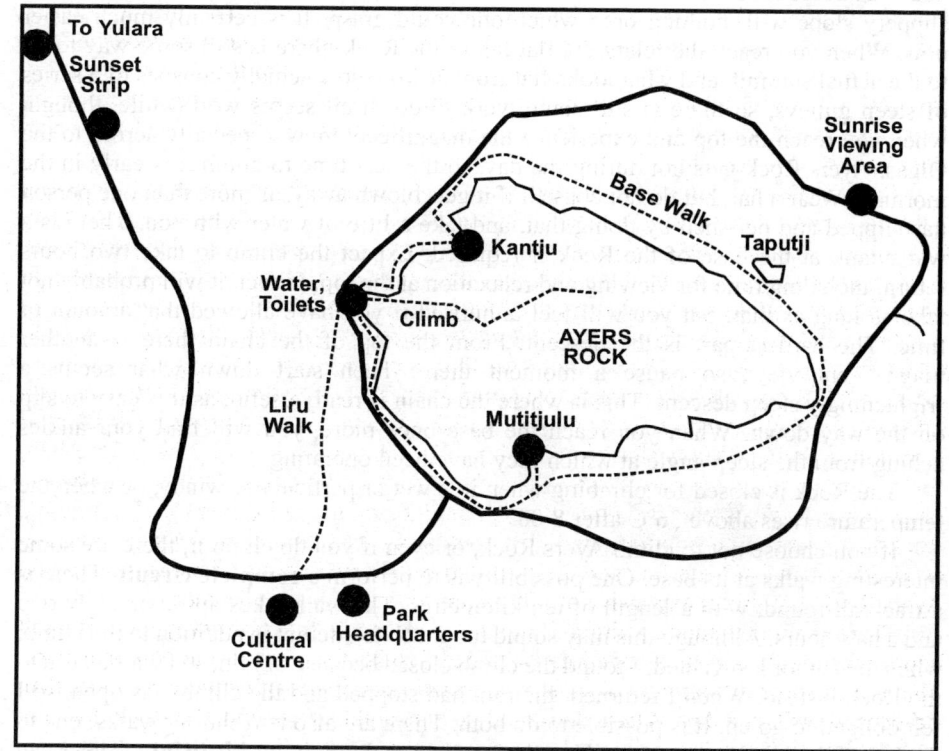

AYERS ROCK
Showing walks available

The current situation of Ayers Rock is a little ambiguous. The local aborigines lodged a claim to the land and were told that, as it was a National Park, they could not succeed. In the end, it was agreed that ownership of the land would be vested in the aborigines provided that they leased it back to the Government and allowed it to continue to be used as a National Park, and that they would be involved in the management of the Park. To date this arrangement seems to be working well, but there is the problem that the aborigines oppose the climbing of the Rock. They say that according to their traditions only the elders are permitted to venture to the summit and even then only on certain ceremonial occasions. On the other hand, it is feared that, if climbing the Rock is prohibited, people will stop coming and revenue will decrease. Moreover, it was a condition of the leasing arrangement that visitors would be allowed to climb. The situation at present is that the aborigines ask visitors to respect their wishes and not climb, but that there is no actual prohibition. Therefore most people climb, as that is what they came here to do. However, it does seem possible that a ban on climbing may be enforced in the future.

The climb is not an easy one, as parts of the Rock are very steep, but it should not be beyond the capabilities of those in reasonable health and fitness. There is now a chain all the way up the side of the Rock, which assists considerably. When the author first made the climb, this chain was incomplete and the steepest section was just a slippery slope with nothing onto which one could grasp. It is certainly much easier now. When you reach the relatively flat top of the Rock, there is still some way to go to the actual summit, and what looks flat from down below actually consists of a series of steep gulleys, so there is still some work to do. It all seems worthwhile, though, when you reach the top and experience the magnificent view, especially across to the Olgas. Ayers Rock gets hot during the day, so the best time to climb it is early in the morning. Wear a hat, but do not chase it if it gets blown away, as more than one person has slipped and perished by doing that, and take a litre of water with you. There is a water tank at the base of the Rock if required. Expect the climb to take two hours return, including time for viewing and relaxation at the top. In fact, it will probably not take as long as that, but you will feel unhurried if you have allowed that amount of time. The hardest part is the descent. From the top of the chain there is another magnificent view, so pause a moment there. Then start down what seems a frighteningly steep descent. This is where the chain is really useful, as it is easy to slip on the way down. When you reach the base once more, you will find your ankles aching from the steep angle at which they have been operating.

The Rock is closed for climbing when it is wet or particularly windy, or when the temperature rises above 36°C after 8:00.

If you choose not to climb Ayers Rock, or even if you do climb it, there are some interesting walks at its base. One possibility is to perform a **complete circuit**. There is a track all round, with a length of ten kilometres. The walk takes approximately two and a half hours. Although this may sound too much to attempt in addition to the climb, when the author last visited, I found the climb closed because of rain, so I walked round the Rock instead. When I returned, the rain had stopped and the climb was open, so I felt obliged to go up. It is possible to do both. There are also two shorter walks, one to the left of the climbing point, to **Kantju**, and one to the right, to **Mutitjulu**. These can easily be incorporated in the circumambulation and add about a kilometre, and half an hour. Both of the short walks lead to waterholes and that to the left of the climb, the Kantju Waterhole, is a particularly delightful and peaceful spot. These walks are closely associated with aboriginal mythology, to explain which there are notices along the way. There are also free conducted walks at certain times with aboriginal guides. In addition, there are guided walks to various other destinations starting from the Cultural Centre, but these are very expensive at $50 per head.

The **Olgas (Kata Tjuta)** lie fifty kilometres west of Ayers Rock and, although rather overshadowed by the fame and magnificence of the Rock, they too are well worth a visit. Indeed, it would seem a pity to have come all this way and not see the Olgas. There are 36 unusual domed peaks, the highest rising some 200 metres above Ayers Rock. Greyhound offers a morning tour which gives the opportunity to climb Ayers Rock and then continue to the Olgas. However, time there is limited, so if you really want to explore the Olgas, you will need to find another means of transport. Uluru Express offers transport from Yulara to the Olgas and back, with sunset viewing of Ayers Rock on the return journey, for $50.

There are two recommended walks at the Olgas. The more famous is the **Valley of the Winds Track**, a circuit of eight kilometres which will take about two hours. The walk is closed after 11:00 on days when the temperature is expected to rise above 36°C. Take at least a litre of water with you on this walk. A shorter walk is the **Olga Gorge Track**. The return journey is three kilometres and it takes about an hour.

AYERS ROCK

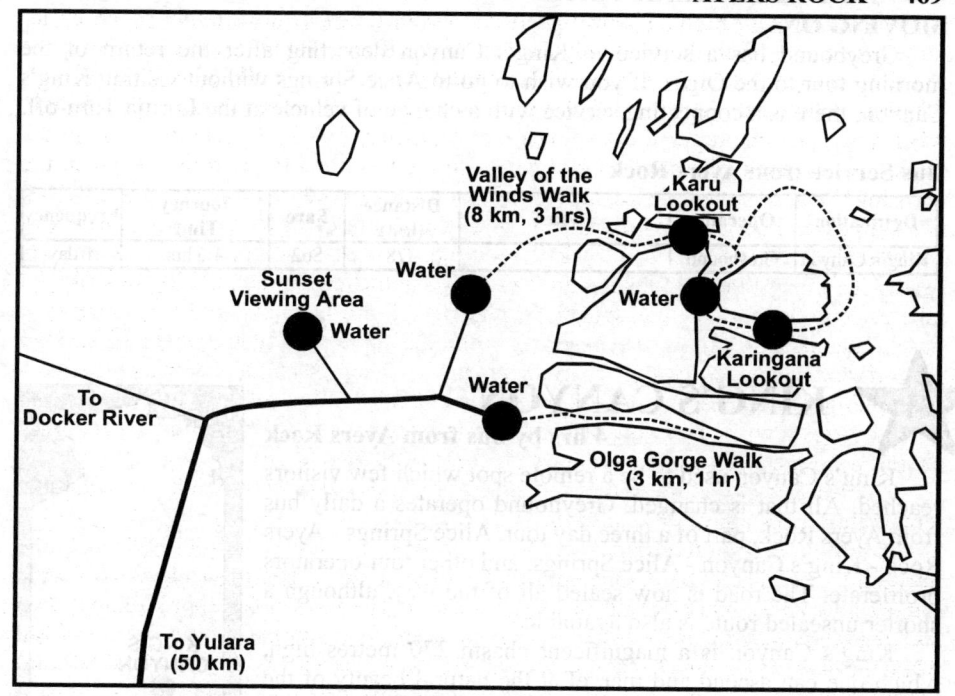

THE OLGAS
Showing Walking Tracks

ACCOMMODATION

Choice is limited to one of the Yulara Resort Hotels, the youth hostel and the camping ground. If you come with a tour, accommodation will usually be arranged. Many of the tours bring tents and use the special Coach Campground.

(i) Hotel Accommodation at Yulara

Name	Stars	No. on Map	Telephone No.	Address	Lowest Price (Double/Twin)
Sails in the Desert Hotel	5	4	08-8957-7888	Yulara Drive	$470
Desert Gardens Hotel	4	1	08-8957-7888	Yulara Drive	$425
Emu Walk Apartments	3½	2	08-8957-7888	Yulara Drive	$365
Outback Pioneer Hotel	3	5	08-8957-7888	Yulara Drive	$160
Spinifex Lodge		3	08-8957-7888	Yulara Drive	$150
Ayers Rock Campground		6	08-8957-7888	Yulara Drive	$135

(ii) Backpackers Hostel at Yulara

Name	Group	No. on Map	Telephone No.	Address	Lowest Price (Dormitory)
Outback Pioneer Lodge	YHA	7	08-8957-7888	Yulara Drive	$30

470 NORTHERN TERRITORY

MOVING ON

Greyhound has a service to King's Canyon departing after the return of the morning tour to the Olgas. If you wish to go to Alice Springs without visiting King's Canyon, there is a connecting service with a change of vehicle at the Luritja Turn-off.

Bus Service from Ayers Rock

Destination	Operator	Via	Distance (km)	Fare	Journey Time	Frequency
King's Canyon	Greyhound		378	$62	4½ hrs	1/day

 # KING'S CANYON

4 hrs by bus from Ayers Rock

King's Canyon used to be a remote spot which few visitors reached. All that is changed. Greyhound operates a daily bus from Ayers Rock, part of a three day tour, Alice Springs - Ayers Rock - King's Canyon - Alice Springs, and other tour operators proliferate. The road is now sealed all of the way, although a shorter unsealed route is also available.

King's Canyon is a magnificent chasm 270 metres high, which one can ascend and marvel at the natural beauty of the outback. On the floor of the chasm are palm trees which seem quite incongruous in this arid landscape, but which thrive on the constant water supply provided by the canyon.

ACCOMMODATION

King's Canyon Resort offers both high-class accommodation and backpackers rooms, although the latter are not at usual backpacker prices.

(i) Hotel Accommodation at King's Canyon

Name	Stars	Telephone No.	Address	Lowest Price (Double/Twin)
King's Canyon Resort	3½	1-800-817-622	Luritja Road	$255

(ii) Backpackers Hostel at King's Canyon

Name	Group	Telephone No.	Address	Lowest Price (Dormitory)
King's Canyon Y.H.A.	YHA	08-8956-7442	Luritja Road	$41

MOVING ON

Greyhound operates a daily service back to Alice Springs.

Bus Service from King's Canyon

Destination	Operator	Via	Distance (km)	Fare	Journey Time	Frequency
Alice Springs	Greyhound		486	$53	5¾ hrs	1/day

▲ *The Gulflander* posing on bridge at Glenore, Queensland (p. 403)
Purple Pub, Normanton, Queensland (p. 405) ▼

▲ Pemberton Tramway, W.A. (p. 517)

Dog Rock, Albany, Western Australia (p. 528) ▼

▲ Gloucester Tree, Pemberton, W.A. (p. 516)

Queensland Outback Railway Station, between Hughenden and Winton ▲

▲ Queensland Architecture, Einasleigh (p. 369)

Qantas Hangar, Longreach, Queensland (p. 315) ▼

▲ Sunset over Darwin, Northern Territory (p. 416)
Driver's-Eye View of Long Straight - 477.14 km. with no bend (p. 672) ▼

WESTERN AUSTRALIA

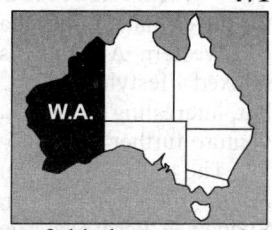

Western Australia covers 2,529,880 square kilometres and is the largest state in Australia. However, although it occupies nearly one third of the total land mass, its population of two million represents only one tenth of the nation's total. Moreover, of the two million in the entire area of this huge state, 1.4 million live in Perth, so the rest of the state is sparsely populated indeed. Even so, if it is compared with its neighbour, the Northern Territory, Western Australia has ten times the population in only twice the area, so even sparseness is relative. What cannot be denied is the remoteness of this state. It is separated from any other centres of population by the Nullarbor Plain in the south, by deserts in the centre and by rugged terrain in the north. Only in recent years has there been a sealed road from Western Australia to anywhere at all. Prior to that, hundreds of kilometres of pot-holed dirt had to be negotiated to enter or leave the state by road, although the railway has provided a link for nearly a century now.

Probably Western Australia was the first part of this continent to be inhabited by humans. The aborigines seem to have arrived in the north-west about 55,000 years ago and moved gradually across the continent from there. The first Europeans to come here were the Dutch. They discovered that the best route to Batavia (Jakarta) was to sail east from the southern tip of Africa and then turn north. In 1616, Dirk Hartog sailed too far east before turning north and found the northern part of what is now Western Australia. He landed near Shark Bay at Cape Inscription and left a pewter plate nailed to a tree with an inscription recording his visit. 81 years later, in 1697, Willem de Vlamingh was skillful enough to be able to navigate to exactly the same place and retrieve the plate, which is now in the *Rijksmuseum* in Holland, leaving another in its place, which is now in the Maritime Museum in Fremantle.

The first Englishman to pass this way was William Dampier in 1688, but it was not until 1791 that Britain claimed this part of the continent, when Commander George Vancouver hoisted the British flag at Possession Point, near Albany.

The British were concerned that the French might attempt to found a colony in this area, so in 1826, Darling, the Governor of New South Wales, dispatched Major Lockyer to Albany in the brig *Amity* with a total of 44 men, including 23 convicts, to establish a settlement and pre-empt any similar French move.

In 1827, the Swan River was explored by Captain James Stirling and there was discussion as to whether to establish the major settlement at Albany or on the Swan River. Eventually the decision went in favour of the Swan River and on 2nd May 1829 Captain Charles Fremantle established the new Swan River Colony.

It was intended that this should be a state for free settlers, but the temptation to import convicts to ease the burden of clearing land proved too great and transportation to Western Australia started in 1850 and continued until 1868. 9,718 convicts were brought to the colony, out of a total population in 1869 of 23,000.

It was the discovery of gold in the 1880s which changed the fortunes of Western Australia. The first find was in Halls Creek in the far north, but soon further discoveries were made in the south of the state, culminating in the gold rush in Kalgoorlie in 1893. Kalgoorlie has been producing gold ever since. Other minerals are produced in Western Australia too and the state is also famous for its wheat, but most visitors will be coming

472   WESTERN AUSTRALIA

for the climate, rather than for the minerals or agricultural produce.

Western Australia is famous for sunshine and for beaches, and for a modern relaxed lifestyle. In fact, many visitors see only the relatively populated south-west, but, interesting though that area is, there is far more to the state than that and those who venture further north are rewarded for their efforts.

The trans-continental railway offers one of the world's great journeys. The *Indian-Pacific* train is now operated by Great Southern Railway and runs twice a week from Sydney to Perth via Adelaide. The description of this journey has been divided into three parts and these can be found starting on pages 154, 668 and 496.

By road, Greyhound operates services to Perth from Adelaide and from Broome, the latter connecting from Darwin. They are both very long journeys, emphasising the isolation of this capital city.

By air, there are services from other mainland capitals and from other towns including Cairns and Alice Springs. Since Perth is so far away from any other major city, this is an opportunity to use a *Boomerang Pass* sector to good effect. However, travel by land in one direction at least, so that you can appreciate the distance involved and see some of the real Australia.

Intra-state services are provided by Western Australian Government Railways to areas which used to have railway service. Now, however, most of these services are provided by bus. The map adjacent shows the routes served by W.A.G.R. These routes do not extend to the northern half of the state, however.

W.A.G.R. offers the *Southern Discovery Pass* which is good value (see map opposite). It permits a circuit of the south-west in either direction, with back-tracking permitted only between Bunbury and Augusta and on the minor branches to Bremer Bay and Hopetoun. The *Southern Discovery Pass* costs $150 and allows 28 days for the circuit to be completed.

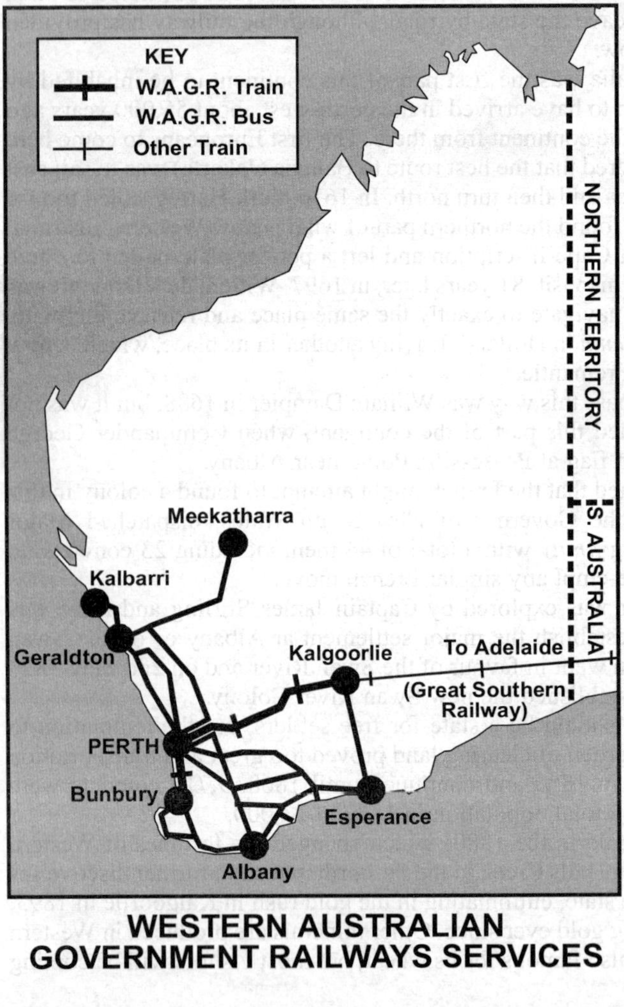

KEY
- ┼ W.A.G.R. Train
- ━ W.A.G.R. Bus
- ┼ Other Train

Meekatharra, Kalbarri, Geraldton, Kalgoorlie, To Adelaide (Great Southern Railway), PERTH, Bunbury, Esperance, Albany

NORTHERN TERRITORY / S. AUSTRALIA

WESTERN AUSTRALIAN GOVERNMENT RAILWAYS SERVICES

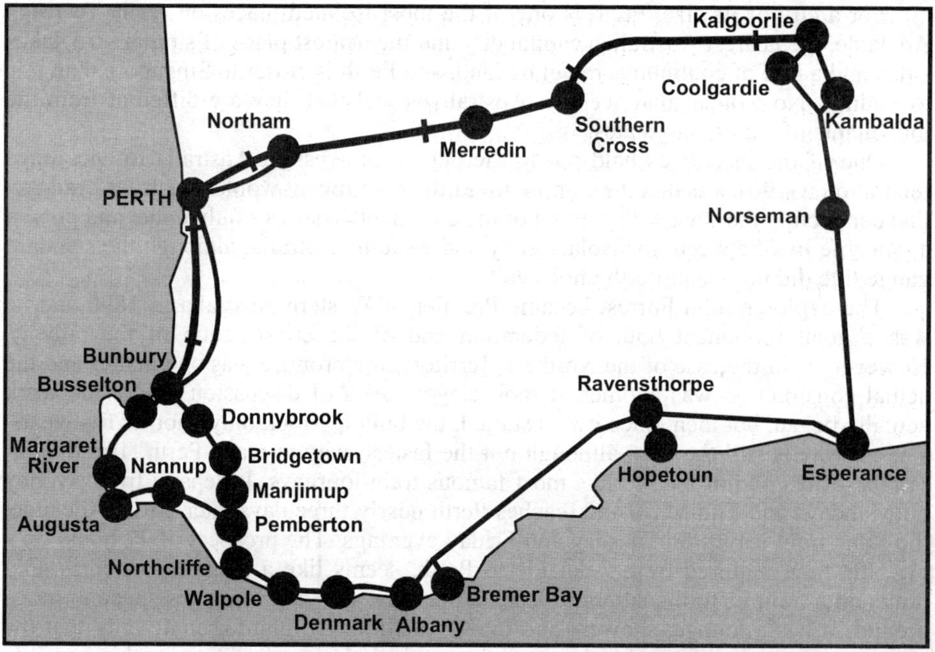

SOUTHERN DISCOVERY PASS AREA

There are also some medium- and long-distance bus services offered by private operators. South West Coach Lines runs to Bunbury, Busselton, Margaret River, Augusta and Manjimup. Goldfields Express runs to Kalgoorlie and Laverton. Integrity runs to Geraldton, Exmouth, Port Hedland and Broome.

PERTH

Population 1,400,000

69 hrs 30 mins by train from Sydney
40 hrs 30 mins by train from Adelaide
37 hrs by bus from Adelaide

Perth was not the first place in Western Australia to be settled. That honour fell to Albany in 1826. Perth was second, the Swan River Colony here being established in 1829. The city was so named because the Secretary of State for the Colonies in Britain at the time, Sir George Murray, was the member for the Scottish city of Perth.

The *West Australian* newspaper was established in 1833 and has been published continuously since, an impressive record.

Although this is not generally thought of as having been a penal settlement, in fact convicts were brought here from 1850 until 1868, and it was the last place in Australia to accept prisoners.

WESTERN AUSTRALIA

For a city of its size, Perth is one of the most isolated places on earth. To reach Adelaide, the nearest Australian capital city and the nearest place of similar size, takes a day and a half of continuous travel by land, and Perth is closer to Singapore than it is to Sydney. No wonder that Western Australians feel that they are different from the inhabitants of the eastern states.

One of the incentives held out to the people of Western Australia to encourage federation in 1901 was that the Commonwealth Government would construct a railway line connecting the state with the rest of the continent. That was duly done, and proved a valuable link between this isolated city and eastern Australia, although the standard gauge line did not reach Perth until 1969.

The explorer John Forrest became Premier of Western Australia in 1890 and he was a great proponent both of federation and of the construction of the railway. However, as in the case of the Northern Territory, the promise was one matter and the actual construction was another. It took eleven years of discussion before the work actually began, but then, once it was started, the building took only another five years. The railway is still the best, although not the fastest, way to reach Perth. The *Indian-Pacific* offers one of the world's most famous train journeys. It departs from Sydney on Mondays and Thursdays and reaches Perth nearly three days later. From Adelaide, the same train leaves on Tuesday and Friday evenings. The prospect of 37 hours on a bus, the time required from Adelaide to Perth, seems like a penance, whereas 40½ hours on a train is, to the author at least, a pleasure, for the train gives space to move around. It has a lounge, showers and dining facilities. It is unfortunate only that the supplement required for a sleeping berth has recently been raised to a level impossible for most travellers. Another great merit of the train is that it crosses the true Nullarbor Plain. The road merely skirts the edge of the plain a hundred kilometres south of the railway line, but the railway heads straight across it and gives passengers an experience of what inland Australia is really like. Straight is the appropriate word here too, for this is the longest stretch of straight railway in the world - 477.14 kilometres with a few gentle ups and downs but nary a deviation to left or right for six hours. The description of this epic journey from Sydney to Perth is given in three parts in this book. Refer to pages 154 to 158 for the section from Sydney to Adelaide, to pages 668 to 673 for the section from Adelaide to Cook, and to pages 496 to 500 for the Western Australian section from Cook to Perth.

Nullarbor is a word manufactured from Latin roots and meaning 'no (null) tree (arbor)'. It lives up to its name, for, except for a few specimens planted in the township of Cook, you will not see a single tree from the 676 kilometres of track which crosses this plain. A few hardy scrubland plants manage to eke out a stunted existence, but trees cannot survive. The Nullarbor Plain, straddling the border of South Australia and Western Australia, covers 250,000 square kilometres, which is the size of the state of Victoria, or twice the size of England. It is ten million years old, but is underlain by a layer of limestone forty to fifty million years old, which was formerly submerged beneath the sea. The plain is littered with limestone caves and there are places even a hundred kilometres from the present coastline where one can reputedly smell and feel the cool salt air of the sea being swept through the underground chasms.

If you travel by train, you will arrive at East Perth Station, where the standard gauge line ends. From there, it is three stations on the narrow gauge suburban railway system to Perth Station, in the heart of the city. East Perth Station is used as the terminus for almost all long-distance Western Australian Government Railways

PERTH 475

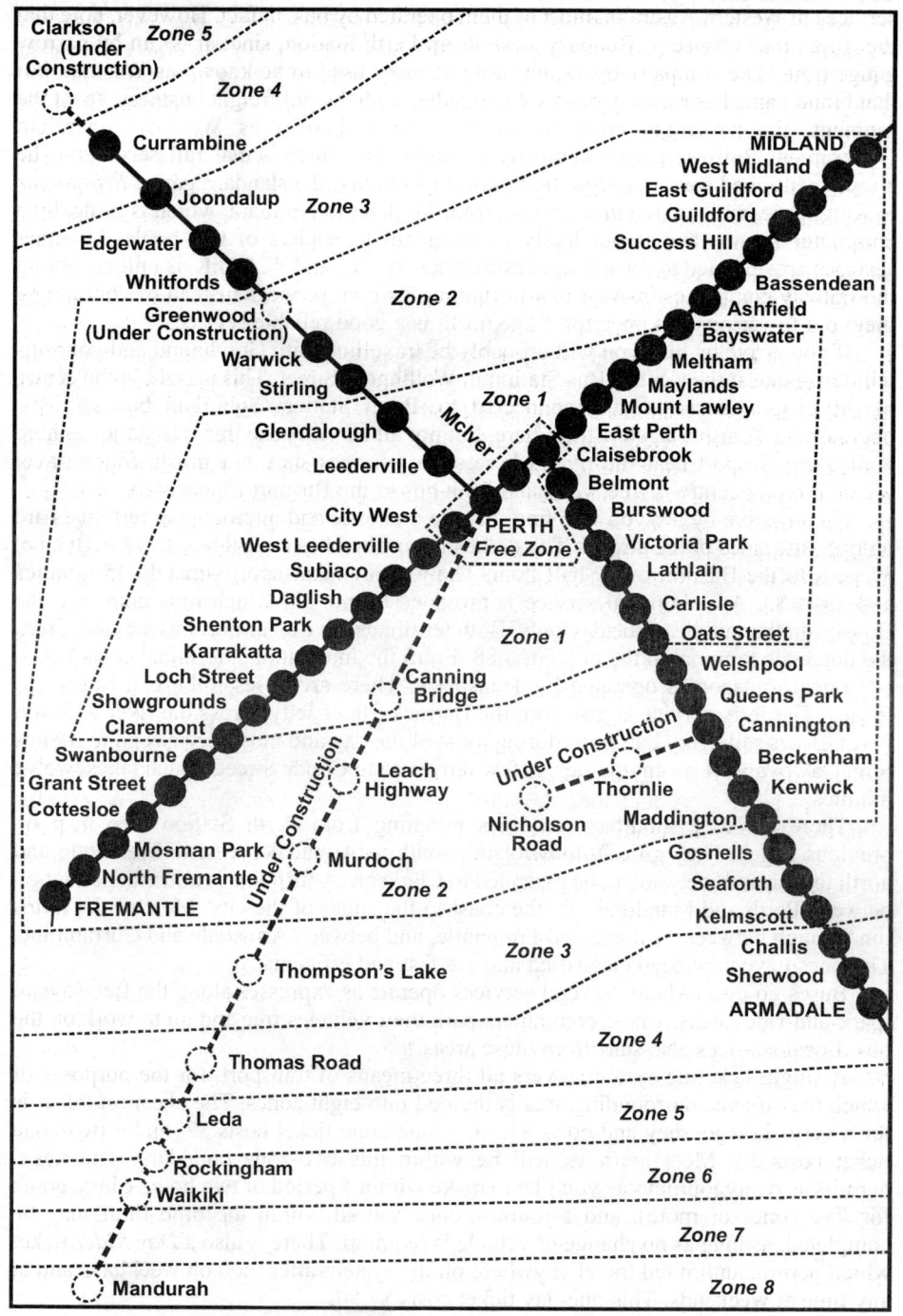

SUBURBAN RAILWAY NETWORK

services in Western Australia, most of them operated by bus, in fact. However, note that the *Australind* service to Bunbury starts from Perth Station, since it is run by narrow gauge train. The company operating these services used to be known as Westrail, but that brand name has recently been sold, together with the rail freight business, so, at the moment, the passenger company is once again known as Western Australian Government Railways. This company operates only three actual rail services - the above-mentioned narrow gauge *Australind* to Bunbury, the standard gauge *Prospector* to Kalgoorlie, and the *Avonlink* service from Midland to Northam, which is basically a commuter service and is not likely to be useful to readers of this book. All other services are operated to former rail destinations by bus, and W.A.G.R. is unique among the railway companies in Australia in running its own services instead of contracting them out to various bus operators. The result is a good reliable service.

If you arrive by bus, you will probably be travelling with Greyhound and your bus will terminate at the Central Bus Station in Wellington Street. This is right in the centre of the city, adjacent to, and connected to, Perth Station. Suburban bus services, operated by Transperth, start from here, but not all services use this bus station. There is also the Busport near the river where some services start and finish. Since travel within the city centre is free, you can take a bus to the Busport if necessary.

If you arrive by air, you will find that the domestic and international terminals are on opposite sides of the airport. The domestic terminal has a local bus service. Bus no. 37 goes to the Busport every half hour. The journey takes approximately 45 minutes and costs $3. An additional service is provided by no. 39, which runs hourly to the Busport in the middle of the day only. Both terminals have an airport bus service. From the domestic terminal to the city costs $8. From the international terminal costs $10.

Local transport is operated by Transperth. There are buses, suburban trains and ferries. The ferry service is just from the Barrack Street Jetty across the river to South Perth. Boats sail every half hour during most of the day and most services go to Mends Street, a voyage of seven minutes. A few ferries go to Coode Street, which takes twelve minutes.

There are four suburban rail lines radiating from Perth Station (see map on previous page). They go east to Midland, south to Armadale, west to Fremantle and north to Currambine, soon to be extended to Clarkson. A fifth line is under construction between Perth and Mandurah, on the coast to the south of the city. Most of the trains run through between Midland and Fremantle, and between Armadale and Currambine. The lines have now been electrified and are fast and efficient.

Buses go everywhere. Several services operate as expresses along the freeways to 'park-and-ride' areas, where commuters park their vehicles free and go to work on the bus. Local services also start from these areas.

A single ticketing system covers all three means of transport, for the purposes of which the city and surrounding area is divided into eight zones. The cheapest ticket is for a very short journey and costs $1.30. A one-zone ticket costs $2, and a two-zone ticket costs $3. Most journeys will be within this two-zone boundary. The ticket permits as many journeys as you like to make within a period of two hours (three hours for five zones or more), and a journey once started within the time limit may be completed, as long as no change of vehicle is required. There is also a *Day Rider* ticket which permits unlimited travel anywhere on the system after 9:00 on weekdays and at any time at weekends. This one-day ticket costs $7.50.

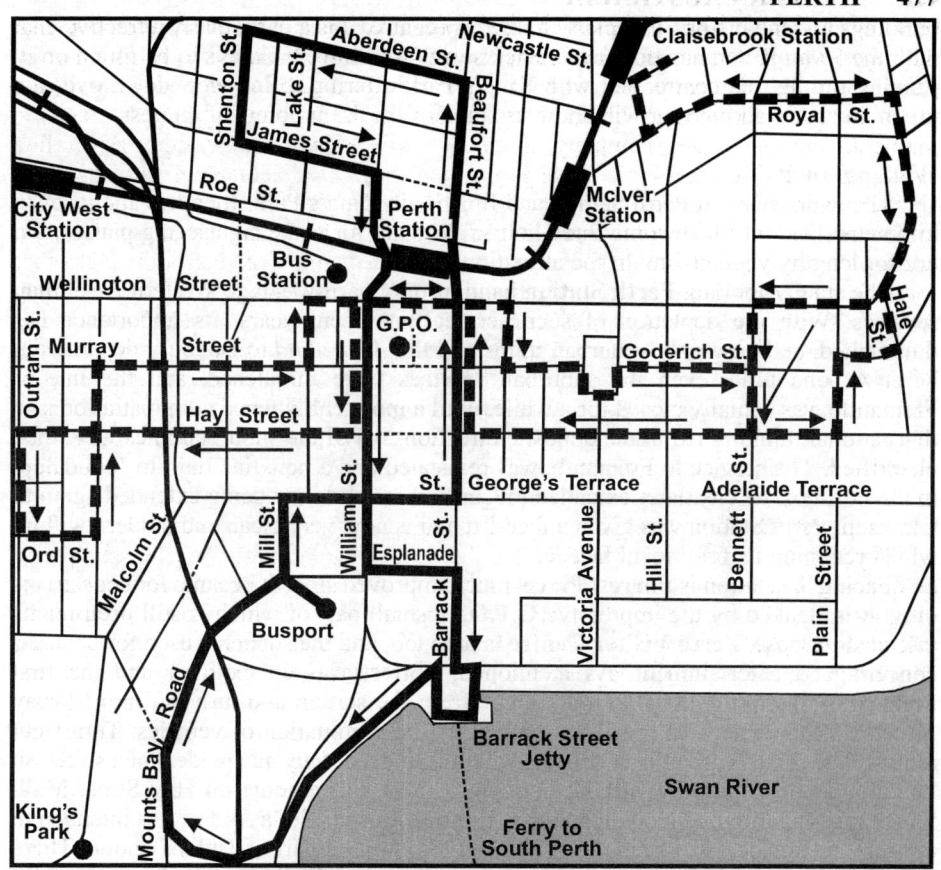

PERTH FREE BUS SERVICES

━━━━━ Blue CAT Route

■ ■ ■ ■ ■ Red CAT Route

Area shown on map represents Free Transit Zone

In the city centre, there are special buses known as CATs (Central Area Transit buses). They are a distinctive silver colour and have a panther emblem on them. These buses are free. There are two routes - the Red CAT and the Blue CAT. Buses operate around the routes in one direction only (see the map above). The Red CAT operates every five minutes on weekdays from 6:50 until 18:20, and infrequently at weekends. The Blue CAT operates every eight minutes on weekdays from 6:50 until 18:20. It also operates on Saturdays from 8:30 and on Sundays from 10:00 running every fifteen minutes. On Friday and Saturday evenings, it operates a service every fifteen minutes until 1:00. That is not all, however. Within the city centre, all buses and trains are free. The free transit zone corresponds with the area covered by the map above.

Despite its fairly long history, by Australian standards, Perth gives the impression of being a thoroughly modern city. Yet, if one looks around, one can still find the older buildings and the history, especially in the city centre. It is a particularly attractive city, with the Swan River, named for the black swans which were always to be found on it, running through its centre, and with King's Park offering a fine view down over the urban area. A walking tour will show us some of the main points of interest.

Walking Tour

This walk starts at Perth Station and finishes in King's Park. It covers about seven kilometres and will take some three hours, allowing for some sightseeing pauses, but not for lengthy visits to any of the attractions.

The stately-looking **Perth Station** handles only narrow-gauge Western Australian services. With the depletion of such services in recent years, its importance has diminished, and now only suburban trains and the *Australind* to Bunbury depart from here. At one time, even the suburban services were threatened, and the line to Fremantle was actually closed for a while, until a more enlightened administration saw that rational thinking led in the opposite direction. All of the suburban lines were then electrified. The service to Fremantle was reinstated and a new line built to Joondalup, in the north of the city, later extended to Currambine and now being extended again to Clarkson. Perth Station was given a face-lift and is now very clean and modern within, whilst retaining its traditional façade.

Facing the station is **Forrest Place**, much improved since it became for pedestrians only. It is flanked by the impressive **G.P.O.**, a small part of which is still used for its intended purpose. **Perth Visitor Centre** is here too, and the square is used for open-air concerts and entertainment. As mentioned, Forrest was an explorer and the first Premier of Western Australia. Walk away from the station and turn left into Murray Street Mall, another area greatly improved by the elimination of vehicles. Turn right almost immediately into Plaza Arcade, which is, indeed, only an arcade, not a street, so be careful not to pass by without noticing it. You will emerge on Hay Street Mall, which cross and immediately opposite is **London Court**. Not as old as it is intended to appear, this arcade dates from the 1930s, but resembles a part of Tudor London. There are clocks at each end with hourly jousting tournaments. Walk through the Court to St. George's Terrace and turn left, and then left again up Barrack Street. On your right at the next corner, you will come to **Perth Town Hall** dating from the 1880s and built by convict labour, but again appearing older, copying a traditional English Jacobean style.

Turn right into Hay Street, and then immediately right again through a passageway into Cathedral Avenue. On your left is **St. George's Anglican Cathedral**, in Gothic style, started in 1880 and completed in 1888. Now turn left into St. George's Terrace once more, and at the corner of Pier Street you will find the **Deanery**, one of the few buildings in Perth dating from the 1850s. It was originally the residence of the first Dean of Perth, but now it is used as Church offices. It still has its original timber shingles on the roof. Turn into Pier Street and then first right into Hay Street. On your left is all that remains of **St. George's Hall**. The building has been demolished, but the portico was allowed to remain as a reminder of the grandeur of Perth's first purpose-built theatre, constructed in 1879.

LONDON COURT

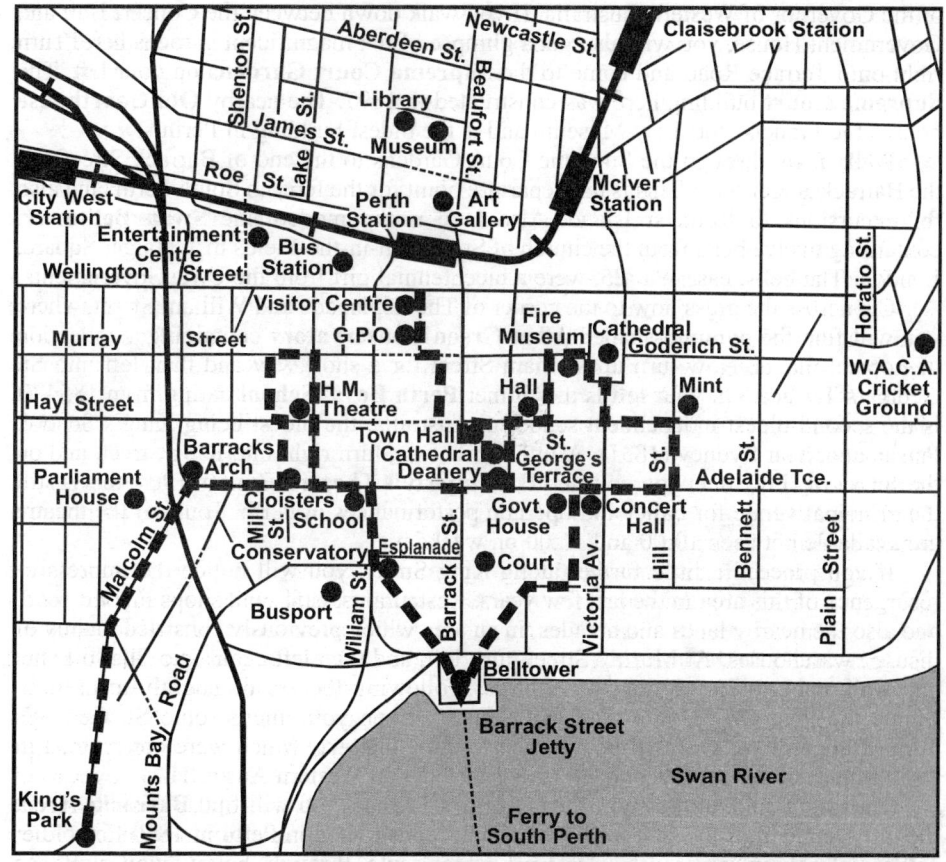

PERTH CITY CENTRE
Dashed line shows Walking Tour

Turn left into Irwin Street and right into Murray Street. On your right is **Perth Fire Station Museum** with a display of fire-fighting equipment, including a 1927 Dennis fire engine. It is open from 10:00 until 15:00 on weekdays. Ahead now is Victoria Square and the splendid **St. Mary's Catholic Cathedral**. The western part of this cathedral was built in 1865. It stands on the highest point in the central part of Perth.

Turn south (right) into Victoria Avenue, and immediately left into Hay Street. One block will take you to the **Perth Mint**. Established in 1899, this is Australia's oldest operating mint. It now specialises in the production of silver, gold and platinum commemorative coins and medals. There is a museum, and you can see a demonstration of gold pouring here. You can hold an ingot worth $200,000 (borrowing not permitted) and see the world's largest collection of natural gold nuggets. The museum is open daily from 9:00 until 16:00 (13:00 at weekends).

Next we go right, down Hill Street, and then turn right into Adelaide Terrace. After passing Victoria Avenue, we reach the modern **Concert Hall** on the left, and then, also on the left, **Government House**, completed in 1864. This is still the official residence of the Governor of Western Australia. If you walk down between the Concert Hall and Government House, you will also get a glimpse of the magnificent gardens here. Turn right onto Terrace Road and come to the **Supreme Court Gardens** on your left. The **Supreme Court** building here was constructed in 1897. The nearby **Old Courthouse** houses the Francis Burt Law Museum and is the oldest building in Perth.

Walk down through the Supreme Court Gardens to the end of Barrack Street and the Barrack Street Jetty. This is the departure point for the ferry to South Perth, and also for excursions to Rottnest Island. Also here is the modernistic **Swan Belltower**, containing twelve bells from the church of St. Martin-in-the-Fields in Trafalgar Square, London. The bells, cast in 1725, were a bicentennial gift from the U.K. Government.

Cut across the grass now to the corner of The Esplanade and William Street, where you will find the pyramid-shaped **Allen Green Conservatory** containing a collection of tropical plants. Now turn up William Street for a short way and then left into St. George's Terrace. On your left is the former **Perth Boys' School** dating from 1854. It is the second oldest independent school in Australia, the oldest being King's School, Parramatta, near Sydney (1831). A little further on, turn right into King Street, and on the corner of Hay Street you will find **His Majesty's Theatre**. Built in 1904, this is still the principal venue for ballet and operatic performances in Perth. Tours of the theatre are available between 10:00 and 16:00 on weekdays.

If you proceed a little further along King Street, you will notice the impressive resurgence of this area in the last few years. Restaurants, cafés and shops line the road, and also the nearby lanes and arcades, in an area which previously consisted mainly of disused warehouses. At Murray Street, turn left, and then left again into Shafto Lane, and walk back to Hay Street, which cross, following the arcade slightly to the left, beside the Post Office, into Cloisters Square. When you emerge onto St. George's Terrace once more, you will be adjacent to the **Cloisters**, which were constructed in 1859 as part of the first secondary school for boys in Western Australia.

Turn right, and, at the end of St. George's Terrace, you will find **Barracks Arch**, the only remnant of the first military barracks constructed in Perth in 1860 for soldier settlers. Looking across the freeway which cuts through below, you will see **Parliament House** ahead. Follow Malcolm Street beside this citadel of power and reach the corner of **King's Park** at the end of the street. Turn left and walk for five minutes along the tree-lined Fraser Avenue to the heart of this 400-hectare area, where the **War Memorial** stands. The trees beside the road are karri, of which you will see more as you travel round the south-eastern part of this state. The War Memorial is impressive in itself, but it also stands at the point where there is a magnificent view down over the whole of the city centre.

If you have energy left, the **Botanic Gardens** are just behind the War Memorial. Otherwise, you can be well satisfied with having seen so much of the city centre in half a day and take a bus back down the hill. Bus no. 33 runs from here every 45 minutes, travelling along St. George's Terrace. Since this is the extreme limit of the free transit zone, the ride back from here will be free.

Another area to explore is **Northbridge**. As you might possibly imagine, Northbridge lies to the north of the horseshoe bridge which crosses the railway line in William Street, between Perth Station and the Wellington Street Bus Station. It is easy walking distance from the city centre, but it is also within the free transit zone and the Blue CAT Bus goes here. **James Street**, the second street after the bridge, has become famous for food, but the surrounding streets too are competing hard. Here you will find every type of cuisine imaginable, a microcosm of the ethnic diversity of Perth. There are also pubs and nightclubs. Immediately to the north of Perth Station, and still in Northbridge, is the **Cultural Precinct**, where one can find the **Museum of Western Australia, the Art Gallery** and the **State Library**. These are open from 9:00 until 17:00 daily, and admission is free, except when there is a special exhibition.

As one walks a little further north, one finds that the Asian community has taken over this area. Shops here are selling Vietnamese, Chinese and Korean products, especially food, and some items are surprisingly cheap. Also here are several backpackers hostels (see map on page 485), creating an unusual mixture of cultures.

To the east of the city, on the other bank of the river, is the impressive **Burswood Casino**, which also contains a high class hotel and conference facilities. It can be reached by taking a train to Burswood Station, on the Armadale Line. Next to the casino is Burswood Park.

Perth Zoo is in South Perth and has more than 2,000 creatures of 280 different species. It tries to present its residents in their natural environment as far as possible. There is an Australian Walkabout section featuring native wildlife, through some parts of which one can wander with the animals. This, the only zoo in Western Australia, is open daily from 9:00 until 17:00, with hours extended until 21:00 in January. Admission costs $15 and the zoo can be reached by bus no. 34 or 35, or, more scenically, by taking the ferry across the river to Mends Street, followed by a short walk.

There is a **Railway Museum** adjacent to Bassendean Station on the Midland Line, but it is open only at weekends from 13:00 until 17:00.

There are plenty of beaches around Perth, along what has become known as the **Sunset Coast**. The most famous of them is **Scarborough**, where there are four backpackers hostels available. Scarborough can be reached by taking bus no. 15, 400 or 402 from the Wellington Street Bus Station. One of the nearest ocean beaches to the city is **Cottesloe**, which is a

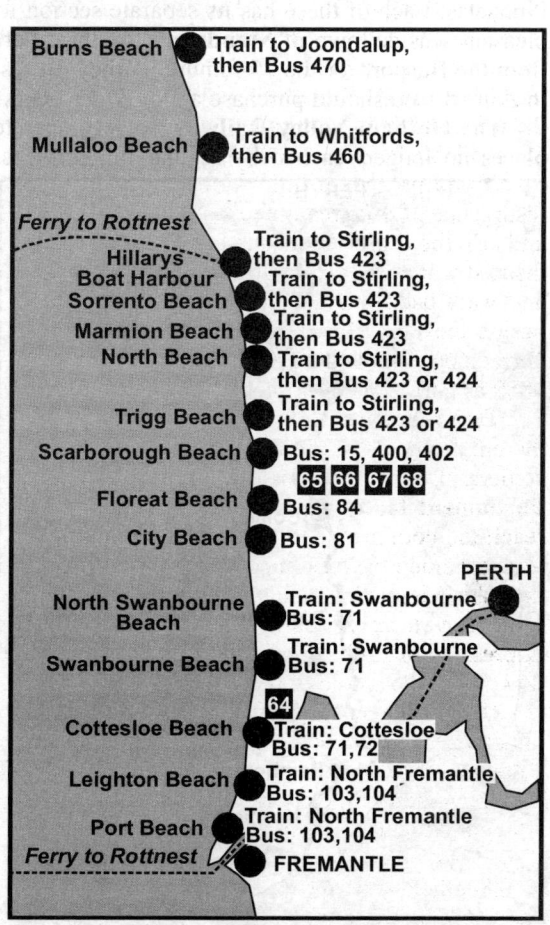

SUNSET COAST BEACHES
Showing bus and train services
White numerals indicate backpackers hostels

short walk from Cottesloe Station on the Fremantle Line, or is served directly by bus no. 71. There is also a backpackers hostel here. Other beaches stretch north from Cottesloe along the coast, including **North Swanbourne Beach**, which is Perth's nudist beach. The map on the previous page shows details of the various beaches, and also which trains or buses should be taken from the city to reach them.

Hillarys Boat Harbour, a little north of Scarborough, is the home of the **Aquarium** of Western Australia. From here there is also a ferry service to Rottnest Island. The crossing takes 45 minutes and a timetable is given at the end of this section.

Cruises are available from the Barrack Street jetty along the **Swan River**. If you go to Rottnest Island from Perth, such a cruise will be part of the journey. It is a particularly scenic voyage, so well worth undertaking. Various vessels make the journey. The cheapest cost $15 one way or $27 return.

Good places for one-day trips from Perth are Fremantle, Rottnest Island and the Pinnacles. Each of these has its separate section following. Another suggestion is the pleasant seaside town of **Mandurah**, south of Perth. To travel here, take bus no. 107 from the Busport for the 75-minute journey. Buses operate hourly. Since Mandurah is in Zone 8, you should purchase a *Day Rider* ticket ($7.50) for this expedition.

The **Hotham Valley Railway Society** operates occasional day tours by train to places no longer reached by regular rail services. The society has an office at 86a Barrack Street.

For a stroll a little longer than the one outlined above, there is the **Bibbulmun Track**, starting on the outskirts of Perth at Kalamunda. This walk covers a distance of 964 kilometres and ends in Albany. It was opened in September 1988 and takes a minimum of a month to walk. There are camping sites all the way along, with partly enclosed shelters, but a tent is highly desirable. To reach Kalamunda, from the Busport take a bus no. 287, 292, 300, 302, 303, 305 or 737. The journey takes nearly an hour and buses are frequent. Kalamunda is in Zone 3.

MAPS AND BOOKS

Perth has a speciality map shop where you will find all your needs in maps and travel guides. *Map World* is at 900 Hay Street, which is towards the western end of the city.

There are several other good bookstores, including two which

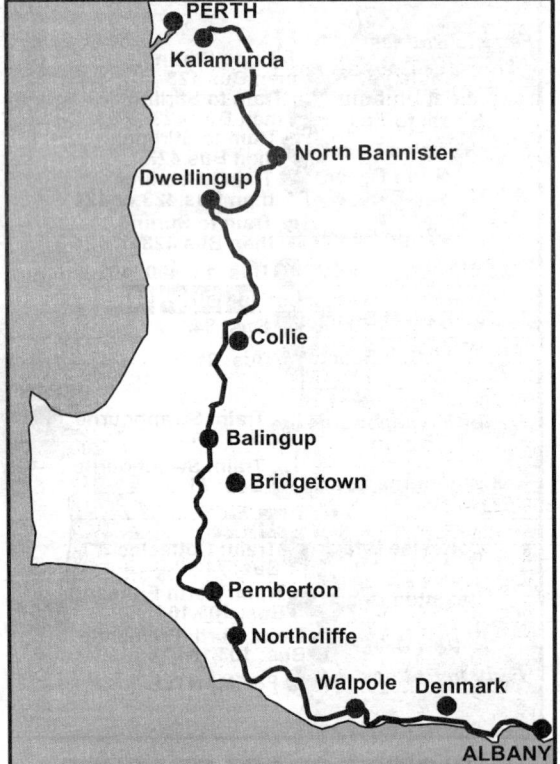

THE BIBBULMUN TRACK
A stroll from Perth to Albany (964 km)

specialise in books for foreign language studies and overseas travel. *The Language Centre Bookshop* is in the Old Post Office at 115 Brisbane Street, right next to Shiralee Backpackers, while *All Foreign Languages Bookshop* is at 101 William Street, opposite the Murray Street pedestrian area.

Rellim Booksellers is in Hay Street, near His Majesty's Theatre, while *The Turning Page* is at the other end of Hay Street, near the Town Hall.

In Subiaco, you can find Zish in *Mozaic Books*, while, also along the route to Fremantle, there is a *Dymocks Bookstore* in Claremont and there is a *Collins Bookstore* in Cottesloe.

Here is a summary of recommendations:

Map World	900 Hay Street
Language Centre Bookshop	Old Post Office, 115 Brisbane Street
All Foreign Languages Bookshop	101 William Street
Rellim Booksellers	834 Hay Street
The Turning Page	553 Hay Street
Mosaic Books	11 Rokeby Street, Subiaco
Dymocks	28 Bayview Terrace, Claremont
Collins Booksellers	23 Napoleon Street, Cottesloe

ACCOMMODATION

Hotels listed are only those within the central area of Perth. Backpackers accommodation is listed for the central area, including Northbridge, first, then for the beach areas, and finally for any outlying locations. The map for accommodation appears on page 485.

(i) Hotel Accommodation in Perth

Name	Stars	No. on Map	Telephone No.	Address	Lowest Price (Double/Twin)
Burswood Resort		40	08-9362-8888	Great Eastern Highway	$415
Parmelia Hilton	4	16	08-9215-2000	14 Mill Street	$325
Rydges Perth		18	1-800-063-283	815 Hay Street	$305
Duxton Hotel		26	08-9261-8000	1 St. George's Terrace	$245
Chifley Hotel	4½	17	1-800-065-064	185 St. George's Terrace	$225
Criterion Hotel	3½	22	1-800-245-155	560 Hay Street	$195
Sebel of Perth		21	08-9325-7655	37 Pier Street	$190
Saville Park Suites	4	34	1-800-150-464	201 Hay Street	$185
Hyatt Regency	5	38	08-9225-1234	99 Adelaide Terrace	$180
Park Royal	4	37	08-9325-3811	54 Terrace Road	$175
Melbourne Hotel	4½	10	08-9320-3333	Hay & Milligan Streets	$170
St. James' Quest		2	08-9227-2888	228 James Street	$160
West End Quest	4	6	08-9480-3888	Murray & Milligan Streets	$160
Holiday Inn City Centre		19	08-9261-7200	778 Hay Street	$160
Grand Chancellor	4	5	1-800-999-144	707 Wellington Street	$155
Chateau Commodore		25	08-9325-0461	417 Hay Street	$150
Acacia Hotel		1	1-800-888-903	15 Robinson Avenue	$140
Novotel Langley	4	30	08-9221-1200	221 Adelaide Terrace	$135
Emerald Hotel	3½	11	1-800-999-719	24 Mount Street	$125
Sullivan's	3	15	08-9321-8022	166 Mounts Bay Road	$125
Mercure Hotel	3½	24	08-9326-7000	10 Irwin Street	$125

484 WESTERN AUSTRALIA
(i) Hotel Accommodation in Perth, continued

Name	Stars	No. on Map	Telephone No.	Address	Lowest Price (Double/Twin)
Sheraton		31	08-9224-7777	207 Adelaide Terrace	$125
City Stay Apartments	3½	4	1-800-819-191	875 Wellington Street	$120
Ambassador	3½	32	1-800-998-011	196 Adelaide Terrace	$120
Terrace Hotel		33	1-800-098-863	195 Adelaide Terrace	$120
Metro Inn	3	39	1-800-004-321	22 Nile Street	$115
Mounts Bay Waters		14	1-800-241-343	112 Mounts Bay Road	$100
Baileys Parkside	3½	36	1-800-199-477	150 Bennett Street	$100
Wentworth Plaza Hotel	3	9	1-800-355-109	300 Murray Street	$95
Riverview on Mount	4	13	08-9321-8963	42 Mount Street	$95
New Esplanade Hotel	3	20	08-9301-2756	18 The Esplanade	$95
Kings Hotel	3½	23	1-800-999-055	517 Hay Street	$95
City Waters Lodge	3	29	1-800-999-030	118 Terrace Road	$95
Perth City Hotel	3	35	08-9220-7000	200 Hay Street	$95
Ibis	3½	7	08-9322-2844	334 Murray Street	$90
Murray Lodge Motel	3	3	1-800-800-041	718 Murray Street	$80
Mountway Holiday Units		12	08-9321-8307	36 Mount Street	$80
Royal Hotel		8	08-9324-1510	Wellington & William Sts.	$75
Jewell House Y.M.C.A.	2	27	1-800-998-212	180 Goderich Street	$60
Townsend City Stay		28	08-9325-4143	240 Adelaide Terrace	$35

(ii) Backpackers Hostels in Perth and Northbridge

Name	Group	No. on Map	Telephone No.	Address	Lowest Price (Dormitory)
Governor Robinson's		48	08-9328-3200	7 Robinson Avenue	$23
Indigo Backpackers		53	1800-651-836	74 Aberdeen Street	$23
Mad Cat Backpackers		58	08-9228-4966	55 Stirling Street	$23
Exclusive Backpackers		62	08-9221-9991	158 Adelaide Terrace	$23
12:01 Backpackers		63	1800-001-201	195 Hay Street	$23
Billabong Backpackers	Nom	43	08-9328-7720	381 Beaufort Street	$22
Coolibah Lodge	VIP	42	08-9328-9958	194 Brisbane Street	$21
Underground Backpackers	Nom	47	08-9228-3755	268 Newcastle Street	$21
Shiralee Backpackers	VIP	49	08-9227-7448	107 Brisbane Street	$21
Spinners Backpackers		44	08-9328-9468	340 Newcastle Street	$20
Lonestar City Backpackers		45	1800-247-444	19 Palmerston Street	$20
Ozi Inn		46	08-9328-1222	282 Newcastle Street	$20
City and Surf Backpackers		50	08-9227-1234	43 Money Street	$20
Backpackers International		51	08-9227-9977	Aberdeen & Lake Streets	$20
North Lodge		54	08-9227-7588	225 Beaufort Street	$20
Rainbow Lodge		57	08-9227-1818	133 Summers Street	$20
Globe Hotel		59	08-9321-4080	497 Wellington Street	$20
Grand Central		60	08-9421-1123	379 Wellington Street	$20
Hay Street Backpackers		61	08-9221-9880	268 Hay Street	$20
Northbridge Y.H.A.	YHA	55	08-9328-7794	46 Francis Street	$19
Britannia International	YHA	56	08-9328-6121	253 William Street	$19
Witch's Hat	VIP	41	1800-818-358	146 Palmerston Street	$18
Aberdeen Lodge		52	08-9227-6137	79 Aberdeen Street	$17

PERTH

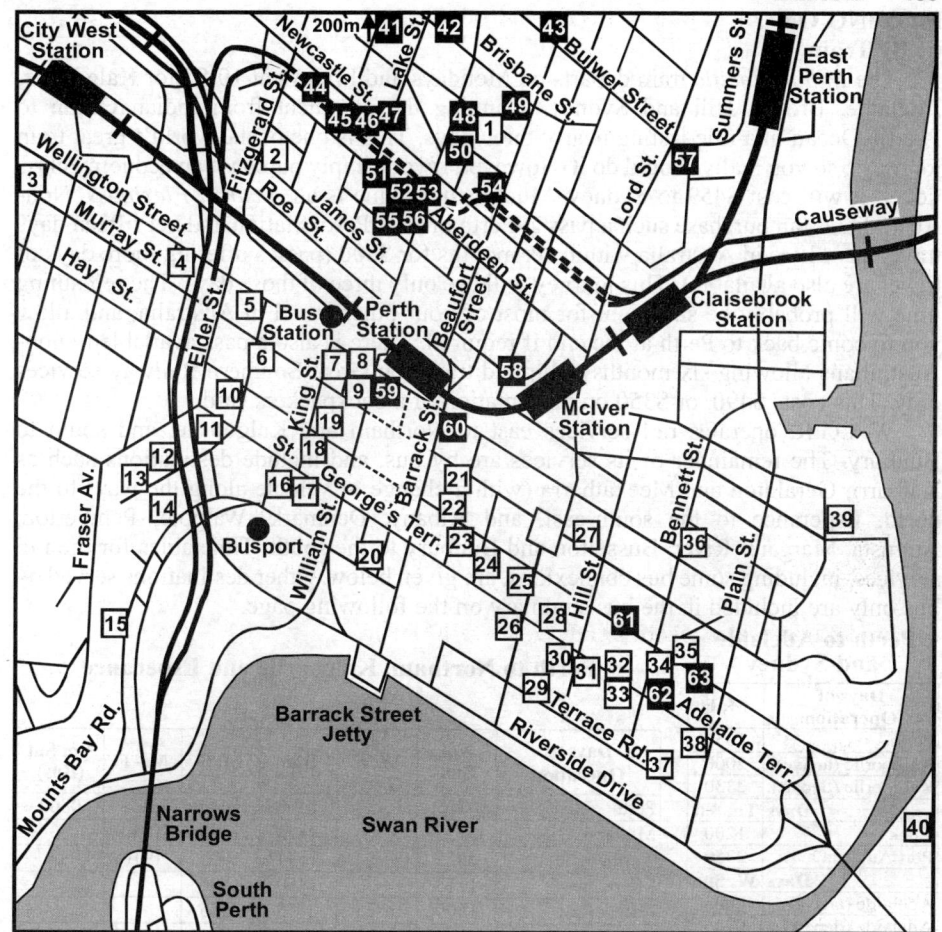

ACCOMMODATION IN CENTRAL PERTH
Black numerals in white boxes indicate hotel accommodation
White numerals in black boxes indicate backpackers hostels

(iii) Backpackers Hostels at the Beaches and in Outlying Areas *(map on page 481)*

Name	Group	No. on Map	Telephone No.	Address	Lowest Price (Dormitory)
Ocean Beach Backpackers	Nom	64	08-9384-5111	1 Eric Street, Cottesloe	$18
West Beach Lagoon		65	08-9341-6122	251 West Coast Hwy, Scarb'gh	$25
Sunset Coast Backpackers		66	08-9245-1161	119 Scarb. Beach Rd, Scarb'gh	$20
Western Beach Lodge	VIP	67	08-9245-1624	6 Westborough St., Scarb'gh	$20
Indigo Net Café and Lodge	Nom	68	08-9245-3388	256 West Coast Hwy, Scarb'gh	$20
Djaril-Mari Y.H.A.	YHA		08-9295-1809	Weir Road, Mundaring	$19

WESTERN AUSTRALIA
MOVING ON
(i) By Train

The *Indian-Pacific* train departs on Mondays and Fridays at 10:55 for Kalgoorlie, Adelaide, Broken Hill and Sydney, spanning the continent from Indian Ocean to Pacific Ocean in a ride lasting nearly three days. This is one of the world's great train journeys, so you really should do it. However, if you simply purchase an economy class ticket, it will cost $459 to Sydney. Much better value is an *Austrail Flexipass*. Non-Australians can purchase such a pass at Perth or East Perth Station and get fifteen days travel anywhere in Australia within six months for $800 (passes offering more days of travel are also available). This journey will use only three of those days. The remaining time will probably be sufficient for most of your other travel in Australia, and allow you to come back to Perth at the end if required. There is also a pass available to non-Australians allowing six months unlimited travel on Great Southern Railway services only. This costs $490, or $350 on presentation of a backpackers card.

W.A.G.R. operates rail services east to Northam and Kalgoorlie, and south to Bunbury. The remainder of its services are by bus, and include destinations such as Kalbarri, Geraldton and Meekatharra (with a change of vehicle along the way) to the north, Esperance to the south-east, and Albany, Denmark, Walpole, Pemberton, Augusta, Margaret River, Busselton and Bunbury to the south. Timetables for the rail services, including some bus connexions, are given below. Other destinations served by bus only are included in the bus summary on the following page.

Perth to Adelaide and Sydney

Days of Operation	M, F
Perth	1055
Kalgoorlie (arrive)	2000
Kalgoorlie (depart)	2330
Days	**Tu, Sat**
Cook	1200
Port Augusta	2350
Days	**W, Sun**
Adelaide (arrive)	0605
Adelaide (depart)	0745
Broken Hill	1630
Days	**Th, M**
Sydney	0915

Perth to Northam, Kalgoorlie and Esperance

Days of Operation	Not Sun	M, W, F (Bus)	Sun	M, F	M - F	Not Sat (Bus)
Perth	0715		1410	1430		0800
Midland	0735		1426	1450	1750	
Northam	0855		1544	1607	1910	
Merredin	1113		1750	1805		
Kalgoorlie	1500	1525	2155	2225		
Esperance		2025†				1800*

* 1805 on Sundays & Thursdays, 1815 on Mondays   † 2040 on Fridays

Perth to Bunbury, Augusta, Pemberton and Albany

Days of Operation	Not Sat (Bus)	Daily	M,Tu, Th, Sa (Bus)	W, F (Bus)	Sun, Tu,Th (Bus)	M, W, F (Bus)	M, W (Bus)	Sun (Bus)	F (Bus)	Daily	Sun (Bus)
Perth	0830	0930			1220	1220		1530	1700	1755	1900
Bunbury	1205	1155	1200	1200	1545	1545	1545	1850	2023	2030	2135
Busselton	1248				1628		1628		2112		
Margaret River	1405				1745		1745		2229		
Augusta	1435				1815		1815		2300		
Pemberton			1441		2020	1816		2100			
Walpole			1627	1552		2002*					
Denmark			1723	1648		2058*					
Albany			1805	1730		2140*					

* Fridays only

(ii) By Bus

For long-distance buses, the principal operator is Greyhound. Buses leave on Mondays, Wednesdays and Fridays for Adelaide. To Broome there is a daily service with a connexion to Darwin. Another bus runs as far as Exmouth three times a week. There is also a service to Port Hedland twice a week via the inland route passing through Meekatharra. Competition is provided by the small, cut-price, but good quality, company of Integrity, which runs as far as Broome twice a week. Integrity will take those with a backpackers card as far as Geraldton for only $20 on its evening service, and also offers unlimited stops *en route* to Broome for the standard fare.

In the south-east, the competition for W.A.G.R. is provided by South West Coach Lines, which operates two or three times a day to Bunbury, Busselton, Margaret River, Augusta and other small towns in the area.

To the east Goldfields Express runs buses to Kalgoorlie and on to Laverton. The service to Kalgoorlie operates daily, except on Mondays. To Laverton, buses run on Sunday, Wednesday and Friday mornings.

Destination	Operator	Via	Distance (km)	Fare	Journey Time	Frequency
Adelaide	Greyhound		2979	$291	37¼ hrs	3/week
		Port Augusta	2661	$291	32½ hrs	3/week
		Kalgoorlie	628	$140	8 hrs	3/week
Broome	Greyhound		2370	$325	32½ hrs	1/day
		Port Hedland	1773	$228	21½ - 25 hrs	9/week
		Exmouth	1294	$195	17 hrs	10/week
		Carnarvon	902	$120	12 - 12½ hrs	10/week
		Geraldton	422	$43	5¾ - 6¼ hrs	10/week
Broome	Integrity		2370	$285	35¼ hrs	2/week
		Port Hedland	1773	$210	26½ hrs	2/week
		Exmouth	1263	$180	16¾ - 17¼ hrs	4/week
		Carnarvon	902	$115	11½ hrs	5/week
		Geraldton	422	$41	5½ hrs	12/week
Meekatharra	Greyhound		971	$163	10 hrs	2/week
Meekatharra	W.A.G.R.		1191	$83.55	12¾ - 13 hrs	2/week
Kalbarri	W.A.G.R.		592	$57.50	8½ hrs	3/week
		Geraldton	422	$46.25	6 - 8¾ hrs	14/week
Laverton	Goldfields Exp.		954	$134	10¾ hrs	3/week
		Kalgoorlie	595	$92	7 hrs	6/week
Esperance	W.A.G.R.		731	$65.05	10 - 10¼ hrs	6/week
Albany	W.A.G.R.		550	$43.40	6 - 9½ hrs	22/week
Augusta	W.A.G.R.		349	$36.70	6 - 6¼ hrs	12/week
		Busselton	228	$26.85	4¼ - 4½ hrs	12/week
		Bunbury	180	$23.20	2¾ - 3½ hrs	15/week
Augusta	South West		319	$31	5¼ - 5½ hrs	2/day
		Busselton	228	$22	3½ - 4¼ hrs	3/day
		Bunbury	180	$18	2¾ hrs	3/day

In Perth it is important that you go to the correct departure point for your service, so note the following carefully.

The *Indian-Pacific* and the *Prospector* (to Kalgoorlie) leave from East Perth Station. So do all W.A.G.R. bus services, except the 1900 bus to Bunbury on Sunday evenings. So does the Goldfields Express bus.

The *Australind* (to Bunbury) leaves from Perth Station.

Avonlink (to Northam) leaves from Midland Station.

Greyhound and Integrity buses leave from the Wellington Street Bus Station. So does the 1900 W.A.G.R. bus to Bunbury on Sunday evenings.

South West Coach Lines buses leave from the Busport.

(iii) By Ferry

There are ferries to Rottnest Island, details of which are given below. The departure point in Perth is the Barrack Street Jetty. Ferry operators may be willing to collect pre-booked passengers from their accommodation on request.

Operator	Times				Fares	
	Perth	Hillarys	Fremantle	Rottnest	Day Return	Period Return
Boat Torque		0830		0915	$55	$60
Oceanic	0845		1000	1030	$60	$60
Boat Torque	0845		1000	1030	$65	$65
Boat Torque	0945		1130	1200	$60	$60
Oceanic	1000		1130	1200	$60	$60
Oceanic	1230		1400	1430	$60	$60
Boat Torque		1030		1115	$55	$60
Boat Torque	1400		1530	1600	$60	$60
Oceanic	1400		1615	1645	$60	$60
Boat Torque		1800*		1845*	$55	$60

* Fridays only

FREMANTLE
Population 25,000

30 mins by train from Perth

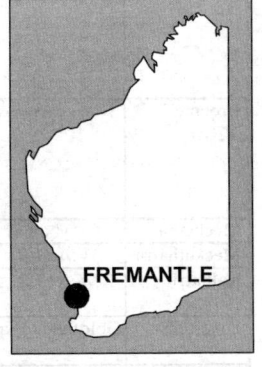

It is easy to assume that Fremantle, the port at the mouth of the Swan River, is just a suburb of Perth, but it is more than that. It has an identity of its own. It has its own history and own atmosphere. It remains a port of some importance, and a fishing town, and also a cultural centre and a restaurant centre.

In 1829, when the British were concerned that the French might try to establish a colony in Western Australia, they sent Captain Sir Charles Fremantle in *H.M.S. Challenger* to claim the territory for Britain. He duly did so on 2nd May 1829, and the port here was named in his honour.

Fremantle is small enough for one to be able to walk around, but there is a free bus service here too, if one prefers. The Fremantle CAT operates along a route shown on page 491, and runs every ten minutes from 7:00 until 19:00 on weekdays, and from 10:00 at weekends. Operation is extended until 22:00 on Thursdays to Sundays.

A short walking tour will acquaint us with this interesting city.

Walking Tour

This tour covers approximately five kilometres and will take about ninety minutes to complete. Let us start at Fremantle Station, since that is the most likely arrival point for the visitor. The Bus Station is immediately outside. **Fremantle Station** is such a splendid edifice that it seemed an act of dereliction to abandon the rail service to here, as was done a score of years ago. Some literature suggests that the toilets are the most impressive feature of this station, so sample them just in case you agree. The author, however, thinks that the exterior view of the station is its most notable feature, so be sure to have a look at that too.

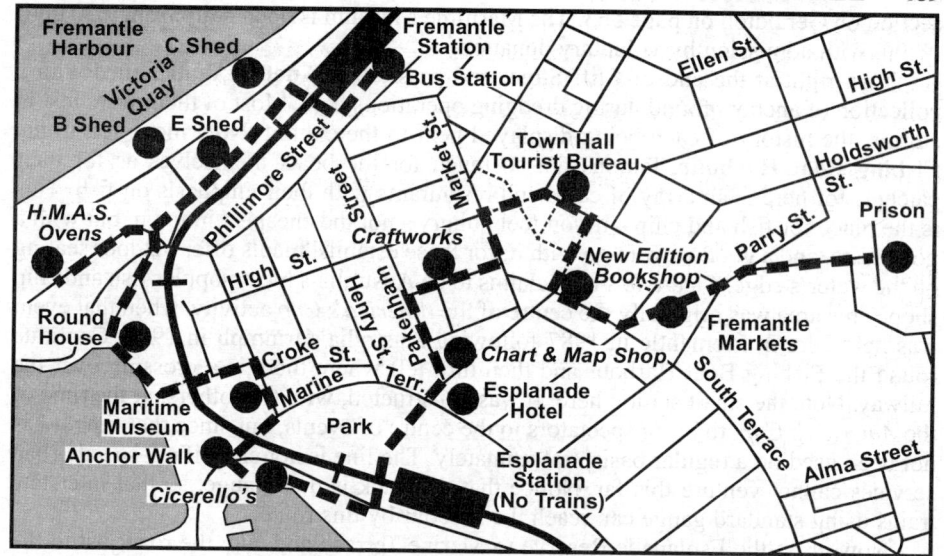

FREMANTLE WALKING TOUR
Dashed line shows Walking Tour

From the station exit, turn right and you will see a bridge over the railway track just at the southern limit of the station. Take this and cross over to the dock area. Just slightly to your left is C Shed, and a little further along is B Shed from both of which ferries to Rottnest Island leave, but there is no need to depart so quickly. Instead, turn left and keep close to the railway tracks and you will soon come to **E Shed**, one of several converted warehouses. This shed is used as a market, selling a wide range of merchandise. At its far end, you will find the **statue of C.Y. O'Connor**, an engineer most famous for the construction of the Perth to Kalgoorlie Water Pipeline, an amazing triumph of engineering prowess. Mr. O'Connor lived for a while in Fremantle and designed Fremantle Harbour, where you are now standing. Continue on in a southerly direction, past the Port Authority Building, and then follow Slip Street, at the end of which is located the Oberon class submarine **H.M.A.S. Ovens**, as a memorial for all who lost their lives while stationed in Western Australia during the Second World War. This vessel is part of the Maritime Museum, and is open on Fridays and weekends from 11:00 until 17:00 with tours available frequently, taking approximately an hour.

Retrace your steps now along Slip Street and then turn sharp right and walk up to the **Round House**. This was the Swan River Colony's first civil gaol, built in 1831. It offers fine views in all directions. When you have seen enough, walk down and cross the railway into Croke Lane, turning right into Cliff Street. Here you will find the **Maritime Museum**, with a ship outside, just in case you should otherwise miss it. The museum contains parts of the *Batavia*, wrecked near Geraldton in 1629. This is an interesting story, which can be found in the

THE ROUND HOUSE

section on Geraldton on page 563. The Maritime Museum is open daily from 9:30 until 17:00, with admission by voluntary donation.

Turn right at the end of Cliff Street and pass along **Anchor Walk**, lined with a collection of anchors found during dredging operations here. Most of them were lost in storms, the history of each being displayed next to the exhibit. Now move left to the **Fishing Boat Harbour**, famous not so much for the boats themselves as for their catches, for here is an array of cafés and restaurants with their emphasis on fish. This is the place for fish and chips, if you feel hungry - not the cheapest in town, but with a good taste, and a good view to go with it, for these establishments offer outdoor seating on the water's edge. *Cicerello's* here claims to be Australia's most popular fish and chip shop. This area was originally the centre of the *America's Cup* activity, when that event was held here in Fremantle in 1987 following Australia's triumph in 1983. Continue round the Fishing Boat Harbour and then turn left where there is a crossing over the railway. Note the small station here. It was constructed, with two others, at the time of the *America's Cup*, to bring spectators to the centre of events, but since that time it has not been used on a regular basis, unfortunately. The line is not electrified, so suburban services cannot venture this far. Notice that the track is dual-gauge, so that interstate trains using standard gauge can reach the harbour by this route.

Now cross the Esplanade Reserve to Marine Terrace and take the road just to the left of the conspicuous and impressive **Esplanade Hotel**. This road is Collie Street, but turn left immediately into Pakenham Street, and then right into Bannister Street. On your left is the **Craftworks**, where craftsmen may be seen at work and their products purchased. At the end of the street, turn left into Market Street, and then right into High Street, which, at this point, is for pedestrians only. This is the main shopping area of the city, and at the end is the **Town Hall**, declared open on 22nd June 1887, to celebrate Queen Victoria's Golden Jubilee. The clock tower is particularly notable, but the whole building is an impressive landmark, the centrepiece of Kings Square. The **Tourist Bureau** is here in the Town Hall. Pass by the Town Hall and turn right down one of the pedestrian areas which will return you to South Terrace, where turn left.

This main street is known, slightly irreverently, as *Cappuccchino Strip*, because there are so many coffee shops located here. There are also restaurants and pubs, and a general atmosphere of opulence. Turn left into the pedestrians-only part of Henderson Street and on your right are the **Fremantle Markets**, constructed in 1897 and one of the city's most famous attractions. The markets are open on Fridays, Saturdays and Sundays, and offer late opening on Friday evening until 21:00. You can either cut through the markets, which is more interesting, of course, or walk along Henderson Street and turn right into William Street. Then turn left into Parry Street and bear right keeping beside the oval, to reach **Fremantle Prison**, where our walk ends.

Do not just go home yet, though, because the prison is interesting. It was constructed in 1855 and remained in use until 1991 as a maximum security gaol, an identity suggested by its austere exterior. 33 men and one woman were executed here, the last of them in 1964. The prison is open daily from 10:00 until 18:00, with tours every half hour until 17:00.

There is also a **Museum and Arts Centre** in Fremantle, to reach which walk from Fremantle Station beside the main railway line along Elder Place and Beach Street for five minutes until James Street is reached. Then turn up James Street to the junction with Finnerty Street.

MAP SHOPS AND BOOKSHOPS
Chart and Map Shop   *14 Collie Street*
New Edition Bookshop   *50 South Terrace*

A city like Fremantle with a strong nautical background should certainly have a Map Shop and you will not be disappointed with the *Chart and Map Shop*, near the Esplanade Hotel. A good independent bookstore is the *New Edition Bookshop*, in a building with creaky wooden floorboards and a good atmosphere in South Terrace, one of the main thoroughfares. Both of the above are marked on the map on page 489.

ACCOMMODATION
Accommodation in Fremantle tends to be sophisticated, as becomes its general atmosphere, but, for those wanting something a little cheaper, there is a range of traditional old hotels, as listed overleaf. Backpackers have several choices, but Fremantle is popular, so all of these are well patronised.

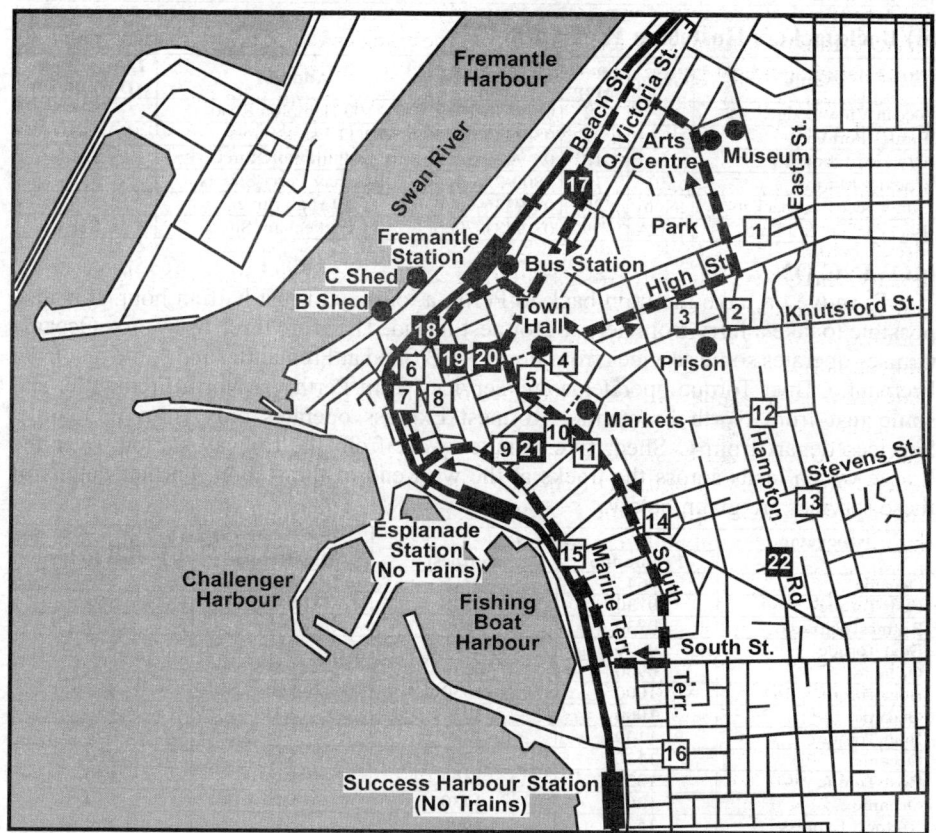

FREMANTLE
Dashed line shows route of Fremantle CAT
Black numerals in white boxes indicate hotel accommodation
White numerals in black boxes indicate backpackers hostels

492 WESTERN AUSTRALIA

(i) Hotel Accommodation in Fremantle

Name	Stars	No. on Map	Telephone No.	Address	Lowest Price (Double/Twin)
Esplanade Hotel	4½	9	08-9432-4000	Marine Terrace & Essex St.	$270
Port Mill B & B		10	08-9433-3832	3/17 Essex Street	$145
Westerley Accom.	4½	13	08-9430-4458	74 Solomon Street	$120
Old Bakery Villa		14	08-9335-7531	11 Little Howard Street	$120
Kilkelly's B & B		15	08-9336-1744	82 Marine Terrace	$120
Girton House		1	08-9335-3235	75 Ellen Street	$105
Fothergills B & B	4	2	08-9335-6784	20 Ord Street	$105
Barbara's Cottage		3	08-9430-8051	26 Holdsworth Street	$100
Danum House	4	12	08-9336-3735	6 Fothergill Street	$100
Seaview Tavern		16	08-9335-2259	282 South Terrace	$95
Fremantle Hotel		7	08-9430-4300	6 High Street	$90
Rosie O'Grady's		4	08-9335-1645	23 William Street	$85
Newport Hotel		5	08-9335-2428	2 South Terrace	$85
His Majesty's Hotel		6	08-9336-4681	Mouat & Phillimore Streets	$85
Orient Hotel		8	08-9336-2455	39 High Street	$85
Norfolk Hotel		11	08-9335-5405	47 South Terrace	$85

(ii) Backpackers Hostels in Fremantle

Name	Group	No. on Map	Telephone No.	Address	Lowest Price (Dormitory)
Ocean View Lodge		22	08-9336-2962	100 Hampton Road	$25
Pirates Port City		21	08-9335-6635	11 Essex Street	$23
Old Firestation B/P		18	08-9430-5454	18 Phillimore Street	$21
Cheviot Marina	VIP	17	1800-255-644	Beach & Parry Streets	$19
Sundancer Backpackers	Nom	20	08-9336-6080	80 High Street	$19
Backpackers Inn Freo	YHA	19	08-9431-7065	11 Packenham Street	$18

MOVING ON

To move on, take the train back to Perth, a journey of just half an hour. It is also possible to take a ferry from here to Rottnest Island. There are three operators. Oceanic Cruises operates some services from Perth via B Shed at Fremantle, and some just from Fremantle. Boat Torque operates some services from Perth via North Fremantle, and some just from North Fremantle. Rottnest Express operates only from Fremantle. Services depart from C Shed, five minutes walk from the railway station, over the bridge which leads across the tracks at the west end of the station. Further details of these services are given below.

Operator	Times		Fares	
	Fremantle	Rottnest	Day Return	Period Return
Oceanic	0645	0715	$45	$50
Boat Torque	0730	0800	$45	$50
Rottnest Express	0730	0800	$45	$50
Boat Torque	0900	0930	$45	$50
Oceanic	0900	0930	$45	$50
Boat Torque	1000	1030	$50	$55
Oceanic	1000	1030	$45	$50
Boat Torque	1130	1200	$45	$50
Oceanic	1130	1200	$45	$50
Boat Torque	1330	1400	$45	$50
Oceanic	1400	1430	$45	$50
Rottnest Express	1530	1600	$45	$50
Boat Torque	1530	1600	$45	$50
Oceanic	1615	1645	$45	$50
Rottnest Express	1715†	1745†	$45	$50
Boat Torque	1830*	1900*	$45	$50
Oceanic	1845	1915	$45	$50
Rottnest Express	1845*	1915*	$45	$50

* Fridays only   † Occasional

ROTTNEST ISLAND
Population 200

2 hrs by ferry from Perth
30 mins by ferry from Fremantle

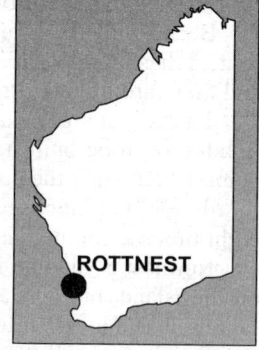

The charming little island of Rottnest lies nineteen kilometres offshore from Fremantle, a distance which can be covered in only half an hour by the modern ferries plying the route. The island is eleven kilometres in length and a little over three kilometres across at its widest point. It is famous for its **quokkas**.

Although Rottnest was sighted by earlier Dutch navigators making their way to the East Indies, it was Willem de Vlamingh who named it in 1696. He landed and found the island inhabited by what he believed to be huge rats. Therefore, he called it *Rottenest*, meaning Rat's Nest. The 'rats' are, in fact, a very small type of kangaroo now given the aboriginal name quokka. Although this is not quite the only place where they are found, it is one of the very few, and the only place where visitors are likely to meet them. Originally they inhabited much of the coastal area of Western Australia, but the introduction by Europeans of various species of animal has doomed them. In particular, domestic animals such as cats and dogs have hunted quokkas almost out of existence on the mainland. Here, though, cats and dogs are not permitted, and quokkas abound. There are an estimated 10,000 quokkas here and they can be found everywhere, although there are certain places which are particularly good viewing spots. They are not particularly shy, having no enemies here, but they are basically nocturnal, so often sleeping during the day, unless they know that there are visitors around, with the possibility of food. In fact, it is prohibited to feed the quokkas, since anything with which humans are likely to supply them will not be good for their digestive system. Note that biscuits, in particular, are not the natural diet of quokkas, despite their being very adept at noticing that you have some hidden in your bag.

Another wonderful feature of Rottnest is that private vehicles are not permitted on the island, with minor exceptions made for police, doctor and a few others. There is a bus service and there are bicycles and feet. Recently, the railway line has also been restored.

The history of Rottnest is interesting. Aboriginal artefacts have been found dating back 30,000 years, but when Europeans arrived there were no aborigines here. It appears that until about 6,500 years ago, Rottnest was joined to the mainland, but then a change in sea level resulted in its being cut off. At this point the aborigines decided to stay on the mainland, but the quokkas were fortunate enough not to notice the change.

Since the arrival of Europeans, the island has been put to various uses, one of them being a prison for aboriginal offenders. However, the first six to be brought here escaped in a stolen boat, one of them drowning on the journey to the mainland, but the other five succeeding in reaching their destination. Later, the island was used as a holiday retreat for the Governor of Western Australia. Then, as the war approached, its strategic importance was realised and it was gradually taken over by the armed forces. That is when the railway was constructed, and the remains of the gun turrets and lengthy underground passages and storage areas can be seen at **Oliver Hill**. The youth hostel is in what was originally the **Kingstown Army Barracks** here.

Because of the island's awkward position just off the shore on a main shipping route, it has found itself in the passage of several vessels since the coming of Europeans and there are various wrecks around Rottnest, many of them enjoyed by divers.

There is a lighthouse on the island, at **Wadjemup Hill**. This was the second lighthouse to be built here. The first had been constructed in 1851 and was partially demolished when the current lighthouse was built in 1896. It is 38.7 metres high, the fourth tallest lighthouse in Australia, and it has a beam which rotates to provide flashes eight times a minute, visible at a range of 26 kilometres.

Rottnest is suitable for a day trip or for an extended visit. There is accommodation on the island, but it is a popular destination, so booking is advisable. It is especially favoured as a location for seeing in the New Year.

Ferries run to Rottnest from both Perth and Fremantle, for details of which see the sections relating to those two cities. There is also a service from Hillarys, on the coast just north of Scarborough. From Fremantle the crossing takes 30 minutes. From Hillarys it takes 45 minutes. From Perth, you get the beautiful journey down the Swan River to Fremantle first which takes an hour and, since passengers then have to be picked up in Fremantle, the whole voyage takes approximately two hours.

On the island, you can hire a bicycle to get around. Alternatively, you can walk to many of the places, although it will be difficult to reach the farthest points of the island by this means. Then there is a free bus service. This travels only the route Main Settlement - Geordie and Longreach Bays - Main Settlement - Kingstown - Airport - Main Settlement. However, it provides a start in walking to many destinations. The service operates every half hour from 8:00 until 17:00 and then every hour until 22:00. There is also the Bayseeker Bus, which operates a circuit of the island every half hour from 8:30 until 17:30. This bus does not go to the interior of the island, however, only round the edge. It also does not go to Cape Vlamingh at the western extremity of the island. To reach there you must walk the last three kilometres from Narrow Neck. A complete circuit on this bus takes 45 minutes. The fare is $6, which covers you for as many rides as you want all day.

Then there are two types of tour available. The first is a two-hour bus tour which covers all points of interest, including the quokkas. This costs $15. There are several departures every day, with seats booked at the Visitor Information Centre on the island. The second tour is by train to the top of Oliver Hill where you can spend an hour on a guided tour of the interesting fortifications. The 9.2 inch guns there were made in 1901 and 1902, although not installed in that location until 1937, and are the only remaining such weapons in the world in working order. In fact, though, they have never been used in action. This railway was installed for the purpose of serving the guns and originally ran from Kingstown Barracks to Oliver Hill. After the war it was disused for a long time, until restored in the 1990s. The section from near the Main Settlement to Kingstown Barracks was added recently. Trains depart for this two-hour tour at 10:30, 11:30, 12:30 and 13:30. The last train operates at 14:30, but if you take this service there is no time to look at the fortifications, as you have to come straight back on the same train. Cost is $12.

There are various free walking tours available on the island, with details and current times available at the Visitor Information Centre. One can also swim, dive, snorkel, surf, play golf or tennis, or just lie on the beach.

ROTTNEST ISLAND

ACCOMMODATION
(i) Hotel Accommodation on Rottnest Island

Name	Stars	No. on Map	Telephone No.	Address	Lowest Price (Double/Twin)
Rottnest Hotel		1	08-9292-5011	Main Settlement	$150
Rottnest Island Authority		2	08-9432-9111	P.O. Box 693, Fremantle	$26

(ii) Backpackers Hostel on Rottnest Island

Name	Group	No. on Map	Telephone No.	Address	Lowest Price (Dormitory)
Kingstown Barracks YHA	YHA	3	08-9372-9780	Kingstown Barracks	$20

All accommodation on the island is owned and managed by the Rottnest Island Authority. There are various types ranging from basic bungalows without bathrooms and with outside toilets at $80 per night, for up to four people, to cottages with eight beds at $370 per night. Then there are two camping grounds with tent sites and cabins. Tent sites cost $6 per person, and two-bed cabins are available at $26 per night in winter and $31 per night in summer. In addition, there is one hotel and there is the youth hostel. A summary is above.

MOVING ON

Ferries return to Fremantle, Perth and Hillarys as listed to the right.

Operator	Ferry Times			
	Rottnest	Hillarys	Fremantle	Perth
Boat Torque	0800		0830	
Rottnest Exp.	0830		0900	
Boat Torque	0930	1015		
Oceanic	0945		1015	
Rottnest Exp.	1030		1100	
Boat Torque	1030		1100	
Rottnest Exp.	1215		1245	
Boat Torque	1230		1300	
Oceanic	1230		1300	
Boat Torque	1430		1500	
Oceanic	1530		1600	
Boat Torque	1600		1630	1745
Rottnest Exp.	1630		1700	
Boat Torque	1630	1715		
Oceanic	1730		1800	1915
Boat Torque	1730		1800	
Rottnest Exp.	1800†		1830†	
Boat Torque	1900*	1945*		
Rottnest Exp.	1930*		2000*	
Boat Torque	1930*		2000*	
Oceanic	2000		2030	

* Fridays only   † Occasional

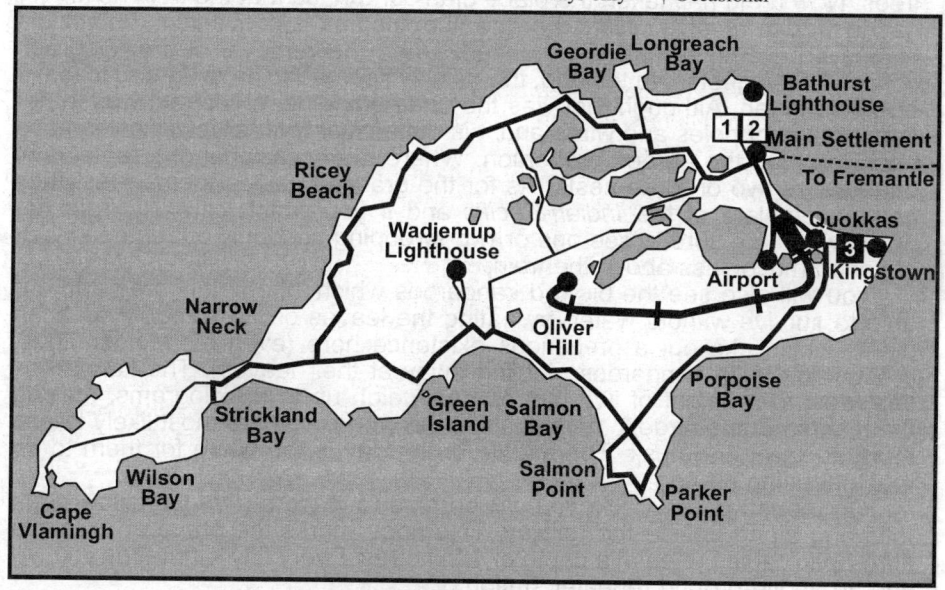

ROTTNEST ISLAND

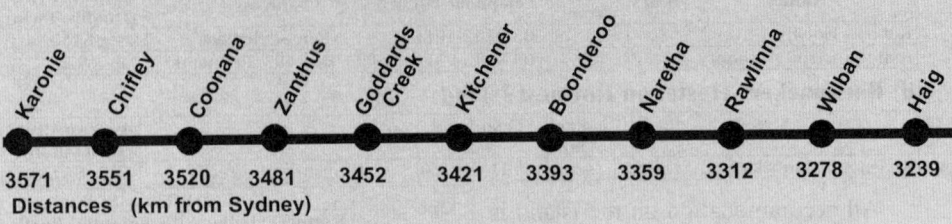

The first two parts of this journey, from Sydney to Cook via Adelaide, can be found on pages 154 and 668.

After our half-hour break in Cook, we continue west across the vast treeless plain called the Nullarbor. Only from the train can the Nullarbor really be experienced, for the road travels almost beside the coast, while the railway is a hundred kilometres further inland and reveals the true desolation of this area.

As we leave Cook, we put our watches back, usually to a local time observed between here and Kalgoorlie. That time is 45 minutes ahead of Western Australian time, so 45 minutes behind South Australian time in winter and an hour and 45 minutes behind South Australian time in summer. Clear? Never mind; there will be an announcement made.

Until recent years, a telegraph line used to follow beside the railway and at each siding there was a telephone box where driver or guard would contact Port Augusta Control to obtain further orders before proceeding. This system received very favourable comment from the wedge-tailed eagles, who found that the telegraph poles were also handy as nest sites on this plain without trees. Now radio has taken the place of telegraph, so that the train no longer has to stop to receive orders. For the humans that is convenient, but for the eagles it became a matter of concern when the removal of the telegraph poles was suggested. In the end, the railway seemed to have agreed to leave one pole in ten. Although that was the understanding, a contract was let for the removal of poles and wires and it is quite clear that far fewer poles have been left than the agreed proportion. Where the occasional one remains, it often bears two or three nests. As for the graceful eagles themselves, they are the emblem of the *Indian-Pacific* and if you watch carefully from the window you are sure to see one or two swooping suddenly out of the sky, or hovering motionless above the train.

You will also see the big red kangaroos which inhabit this area and are able to survive without water, by eating the leaves of the scraggly saltbush plants which eke out a precarious existence here (even more precarious, presumably, with kangaroos nibbling away at their leaves). The kangaroos can grow to a height of two metres and weigh up to 95 kilograms, making them some of the largest marsupials in the world. You are most likely to see them at dawn and dusk. The middle of the day is too warm for them to do much hopping around.

On the left of the track, you will be able to discern a very shallow ridge following along beside the railway. This ridge marks the grave of a Telstra fibre-optic cable buried at a depth of 1.2 metres. Every fifty kilometres you will see an above-ground repeater station.

GREAT RAILWAY JOURNEYS 497

1. THE INDIAN - PACIFIC
PART 3   COOK TO PERTH

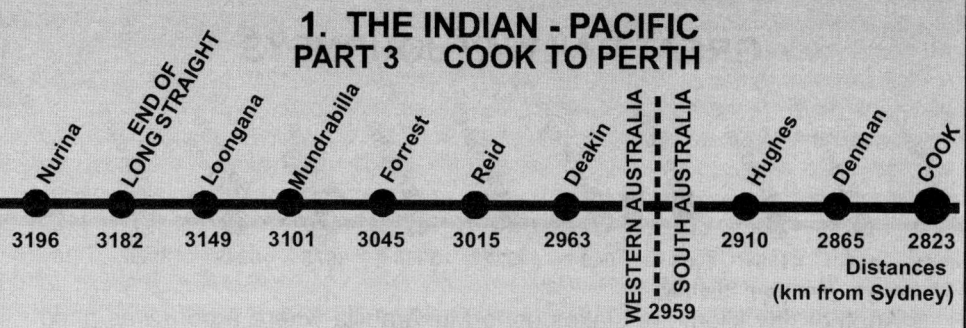

We pass through Denman and Hughes. Then watch for the 1,050-kilometre post (distance from Port Pirie), for at that point we cross the border into Western Australia. The border is marked, so if you are alert you will know the exact spot. Only four kilometres inside Western Australian territory is Deakin. Here we are at our closest point on the journey to the Great Australian Bight.

On through Reid to Forrest. The spelling, as well as the terrain, should tell you not to expect a multitude of trees here. John Forrest was an explorer and, later, Premier of Western Australia. He himself was the first European to walk across the Nullarbor Plain proper (as contrasted with following along the coast), in 1874, and he was a great proponent of the trans-continental railway line. The various states tended to be insular, but it was the promise of this railway which was instrumental in persuading Western Australia to join the Australian Commonwealth upon its foundation in 1901. After that, discussions concerning the construction took the next eleven years, compared with only five years to actually build the line between Port Pirie and Kalgoorlie between 1912 and 1917.

The project was headed by an Englishman named Henry Dean, who had already built a railway through the Blue Mountains. He found different problems here, though, where the terrain was flat but all supplies and materials had to be carried in, initially by camel. Two construction gangs worked on the line, eventually meeting in the middle. Dean proposed the use of the newly-developed diesel-electric locomotives on this railway, since they had a range of 1,600 kilometres, and needed no coal hauled for them or, particularly, water provided. If his suggestion had been accepted, this would have been the first long-distance line in the world to be operated by diesel-electrics. Instead, though, his advice was rejected and for forty years the railway had to cope with the problems of providing food and water for steam locomotives far from home. Many boiler problems were caused by the minerals in the bore water used, but it was not until 1951 that the first diesel-electrics arrived here to improve the situation.

Forrest is an important station. Look out of the window on the right as we approach and you will see the aerodrome. In former days, commercial aircraft flying between Adelaide and Perth used to stop here to refuel. Forrest is still an emergency strip for diverted or distressed commercial flights, and for light aircraft it remains a refuelling point. There are two bitumen runways, with lights, of 1,500 and 1,300 metres, amongst the longest in Australia outside the capital cities. Unlike most of the sidings which we pass through, Forrest is inhabited. The settlement has a population of two, who look after the aerodrome and operate an important weather station.

WESTERN AUSTRALIA

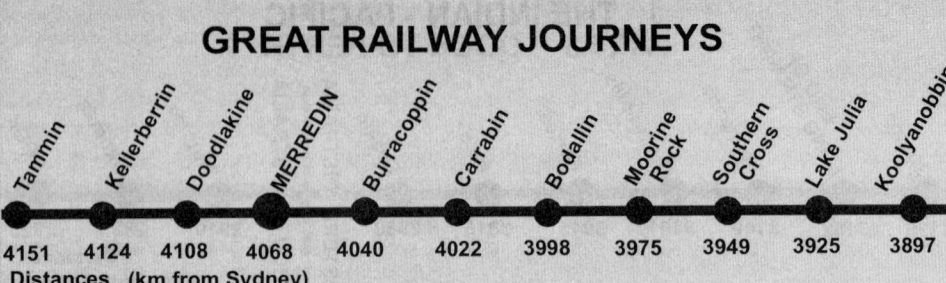

GREAT RAILWAY JOURNEYS

Tammin	Kellerberrin	Doodlakine	MERREDIN	Burracoppin	Carrabin	Bodallin	Moorine Rock	Southern Cross	Lake Julia	Koolyanobbing
4151	4124	4108	4068	4040	4022	3998	3975	3949	3925	3897

Distances (km from Sydney)

Another fifty kilometres takes us to Mundrabilla where a bore was once sunk by the railway to a depth of 448 metres in a search for water. Then a further fifty kilometres to Loongana where you will find the only short branch line on the crossing of the Nullarbor. The branch leads to a limestone mine which can be seen on the right and which was in use until recently. The mining operation has now moved to Rawlinna, however, 163 kilometres further down the railway. Both of these mines claim to produce some of the most pure lime in the world. There are also limestone caves in the area, making it popular with speleologists.

It is another 33 kilometres to the end of the longest stretch of straight railway in the world. We have now completed 477.14 kilometres without a bend. Although this long straight stretch has ended, the Nullarbor continues for a while yet. We pass through Nurina, and then Haig, before reaching Wilban. This was the site of a camp for Italian prisoners of war during the Second World War. The Italians, required to work on railway maintenance, must have wondered whether they had been dispatched to the end of the earth when unloaded here.

Rawlinna used to be one of the major railway camps and, although it is no longer used for that purpose, it is still one of the major settlements on the journey from Port Augusta to Kalgoorlie, for it has a population of fourteen. These are men working in the limestone mine which has moved here recently from Loongana.

Soon after we have left Rawlinna, the first few stunted trees come into view and the Nullarbor Plain has been crossed. From here we move into cattle-grazing territory for the last four hours of the journey to Kalgoorlie. Vegetation remains sparse, but there are trees now, and increasing signs of wildlife. Emus may be seen sometimes and the kangaroos are more abundant.

Just before Kalgoorlie comes the railway town of Parkeston, of interest to the author who once lived in the railway town of Parkeston in England. Usually we make a stop for the engine and power cars to be refuelled here, as dusk descends. The lights of Kalgoorlie can be seen not far away.

We travel the last five kilometres slowly from Parkeston into Kalgoorlie and here get our last break of the journey. If on time, the train will stop here for three hours and we shall adjust our watches back to official Western Australian time, 45 minutes behind the local time observed between Cook and here.

Kalgoorlie is a fascinating city and the break gives us a chance to look at it. The city centre is only a short walk from the station. Gold was discovered here on 15th June 1893, by Paddy Hannan and two others, and this became the greatest gold-producing area in Australia. Over the last century it has

GREAT RAILWAY JOURNEYS 499

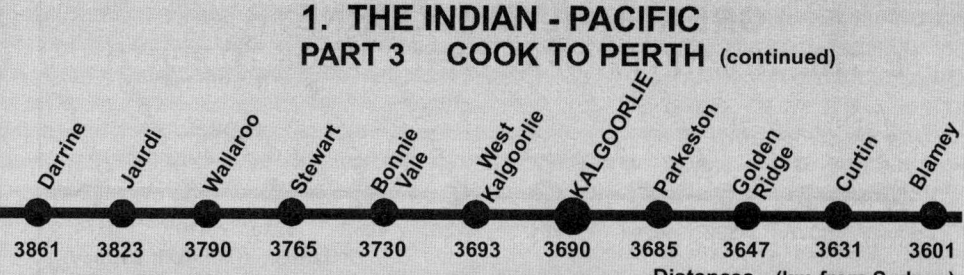

yielded 35 million ounces of the metal, amounting to 70% of Western Australia's total gold production during the period. The city has had good times and bad, but the buildings in the city centre mostly reflect the period of prosperity early in the twentieth century. Kalgoorlie is unusual in that prostitution is legal here. There is a red-light area in Hay Street, near the railway station, and this is a tourist attraction too.

Kalgoorlie was originally a narrow gauge station, as Western Australian railways operate to a 3 feet 6 inches gauge. The first *Kalgoorlie Express* from Perth arrived here on 8th September 1896. When the trans-continental line was completed, the station accommodated both standard and narrow gauge trains and passengers had to make another change at this point. The first passenger train to Port Augusta left Kalgoorlie on 22nd October 1917. The line to Perth was converted to standard gauge when the *Indian-Pacific* started operations. The first through standard gauge passenger train reached Kalgoorlie on its way to Perth on 10th June 1969 and the first *Indian-Pacific* left here for Sydney on 1st March 1970. The first standard gauge *Prospector* from Kalgoorlie to Perth, once Australia's fastest train, ran on 29th November 1971.

Kalgoorlie used to claim to have the longest platform in the southern hemisphere, but the claim no longer seems to be made, so maybe there is a longer one now. The Kalgoorlie platform is 526.5 metres long.

West of Kalgoorlie, the scenery changes yet again as the terrain gradually becomes more inhabited. If you are travelling west, most of this journey will be in darkness, but travelling east the timetable permits much of it to be seen.

Running beside the railway, you may observe a large pipeline and wonder what it contains. One of the major problems experienced by Kalgoorlie in its infancy was a rapid increase in population, but a lack of water to quench the thirsts of so many miners. Water was retailed at unbelievable prices, and those who could not afford those high prices often perished by drinking contaminated local water. Contagion was rife and the lack of such a basic commodity was the greatest problem faced by the community here in its early days. The problem was passed to the brilliant engineer C.Y. O'Connor. Since Kalgoorlie experiences, on average, only 63 days of rain each year, he suggested the construction of a pipeline to bring water all the way from the outskirts of Perth. The proposal was ridiculed as impractical and O'Connor experienced much personal derision from ill-informed sources, but he went ahead with the project. Sadly, the criticism became too much for him and he took his own life before the pipeline was completed. When the pumps were finally started, in 1903, it took nine days for the first water to reach Kalgoorlie from Perth, by which time some had given up hope of its arrival. Not only was the project a great success, however, but this 563-kilometre pipeline with

GREAT RAILWAY JOURNEYS
1. THE INDIAN - PACIFIC PART 3 COOK TO PERTH
(continued)

EAST PERTH	Midland	Jumperkine	Moodyne	Toodyay West	Avon Yard	NORTHAM	Grass Valley	Meckering	Cunderdin
4352	4338	4322	4291	4261	4235	4232	4220	4199	4174

Distances (km from Sydney)

eight intermediate pumping stations has continued to supply Kalgoorlie with the lifeline for its existence for over a century now.

When we reach Southern Cross, we enter the Western Australian wheatbelt. Southern Cross was the scene of the first of the gold rushes in this area, in 1887, but it did not last long and now the town's prosperity is based on agriculture.

At Merredin we are just over halfway on our journey from Kalgoorlie to Perth and if you rise early you will be able to see the changing scenery from here to the capital. The railway reached Merredin from Perth in 1893 and there is still a narrow gauge line extending this far from the coast, used for transporting the wheat crops. The old station building here, on the left, with a narrow gauge platform, was constructed in 1895 and now serves as a Railway Museum.

By the time we reach Meckering, we have completed three-quarters of the distance from Kalgoorlie and are only 153 kilometres from Perth. At 10:59 on 14th October 1968, Meckering was shaken by an earthquake which has left a shallow escarpment 37 kilometres long and 1.8 metres high at its maximum. Measuring 6.8 on the Richter Scale and at a depth of only seven kilometres, it was, at the time, the second strongest earthquake ever recorded in Australia. There were twenty injuries here, but no fatalities.

At Northam we cross the Avon River, the scene of an annual white water boat race to Perth. The railway reached here in 1871, travelling through the Avon Valley to do so. This is a pretty section of line, as we climb the first hills experienced since soon after leaving Sydney, some 4,000 kilometres ago.

We pass through Toodyay and reach Midland, a suburb of Perth. Here an inspector will board the train to ensure that no fruits or vegetables are being transported into Western Australia, so if you have any offending items, prior to this will be your last chance to consume them.

And so we reach Perth, the most isolated of the five capital cities in Australia which can boast a population of over a million. In fact, it is one of the most isolated cities of its size anywhere in the world. Surprisingly, Perth is closer to Singapore than to Sydney. It was founded in 1829, and is also one of the sunniest cities in the world.

Our long journey ends at East Perth station, a modern terminal just outside the city centre built primarily for the use of the *Indian-Pacific*. Our journey of 4,352 kilometres from Sydney, or 2,666 kilometres from Adelaide, has been completed. From Sydney it has taken 68 hours and 35 minutes at an average speed of 63 km/hr. From Adelaide it has taken 40 hours and 30 minutes at an average speed of 66 km/hr. It is not the world's fastest railway journey, but it is certainly one of the most interesting rides which you will ever experience. Do not miss the opportunity.

BUNBURY

Population 30,000

2 hrs 30 mins by train from Perth
3 hrs by bus from Perth

Bunbury lies 180 kilometres south of Perth and the best way to reach here is by train. It is a pleasant journey, taking less than 2½ hours on the *Australind*, the only remaining narrow gauge passenger rail service operated by W.A.G.R. outside the Perth suburban area (see diagram below). The first half hour of the run is through the suburbs following the Armadale Line to its terminus. After that, we are in farming country, passing through a series of small settlements, the only one of any size being **Pinjarra**. East of here, the **Hotham Valley Railway** operates a regular rail service from **Dwellingup** to **Etmilyn** on the last of the state's lightly-built developmental lines, this one used for hauling timber. At the time of writing, services are operated from Dwellingup at 11:00 and 14:00 on Tuesdays, Thursdays, Saturdays and Sundays, cost $15, and take 90 minutes for the return journey of eight kilometres each way. However, there are variations from year to year. There is also a Hotham Valley service from Pinjarra to Dwellingup, a journey of 75 minutes on what is claimed to be the line with the steepest climb in Western Australia. The train connects with the arrival of the *Australind* at 10:42, departing at 11:10, and it also connects with the *Australind* for the return journey, arriving back at 15:30. The *Australind* leaves for Perth at 15:55. At present this service to Dwellingup operates on Wednesdays only from May until October, and costs $20 single or $25 return, but again days vary from year to year. On alternate Sundays during the same months there is a Hotham Valley Railway service right through from Perth to Dwellingup, diesel-hauled as far as Pinjarra and steam from there to Dwellingup. This costs $32 return. It is not possible to travel both sections of the Pinjarra to Etmilyn route on the same day, unfortunately, but to check the current position telephone 08-9221-4444.

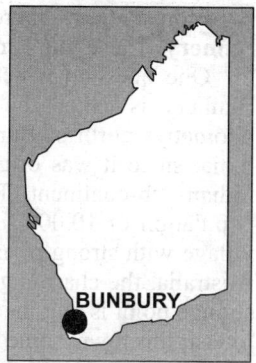

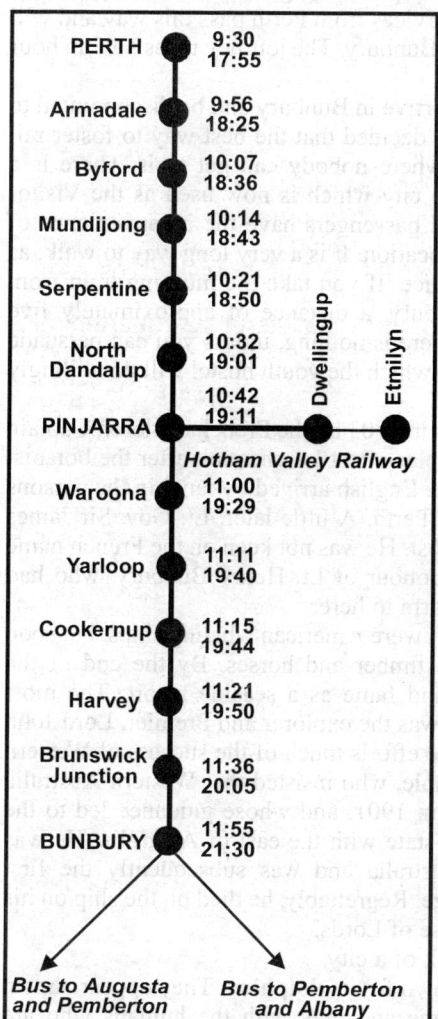

THE AUSTRALIND
FROM PERTH TO BUNBURY WITH CONNEXIONS

WESTERN AUSTRALIA

From Pinjarra, there are also free tours of the **Alcoa bauxite mine and alumina refinery**. These tours are at 13:00 on Wednesdays only, except during January.

One question which the reader should be asking is why the W.A.G.R. train to Bunbury is called the *Australind*. **Australind** is the name of a town about ten kilometres north of Bunbury. The name is a combination of the words Australia and India, since it was originally hoped that the community would export goods to the Indian sub-continent. The town is currently expanding rapidly and has achieved a population of 10,000, but when the name was given to the train it was but a small village with strong pioneering roots. It claims to have the smallest church in Western Australia, the charming timber-built **Church of St. Nicholas**, dating from 1840. The strange point is that the railway does not actually pass through Australind. If you wish to visit this town, some of the W.A.G.R. bus services from Perth pass this way and will stop, or you may take a local bus no. 701 from Bunbury. The journey takes half an hour and costs $3 each way.

At the end of your train journey, you will arrive in Bunbury and be disappointed to find that this is another community which has decided that the best way to foster rail travel is to put the station outside the city, where nobody can get to it. There is a beautiful old station right in the centre of the city which is now used as the Visitor Information Centre and bus station, while rail passengers have the inconvenience of trying to get into the centre from this remote location. It is a very long way to walk, as the author can confirm from personal experience. If you take the morning train from Perth, there is a bus into the centre of Bunbury, a distance of approximately five kilometres, but if you arrive in the evening, there is nothing, unless you can persuade your accommodation to come and collect you (which the youth hostel will do willingly for backpackers).

The first recorded sighting of this port was in 1803 by the French explorer, Captain de Freycinet in the *Casuarina*. He named the place Port Leschenault after the botanist on his expedition. It was not until 1829 that the English arrived by land, in the persons of Dr. Collie and Lt. Preston, travelling from Perth. A little later, Lt.-Gov. Sir James Stirling visited and established a military outpost. He was not keen on the French name and called the location Bunbury instead, in honour of Lt. Henry Bunbury, who had developed the difficult inland route from Pinjarra to here.

The most frequent early visitors to this port were American whaling ships, but soon goods were being exported, including wool, timber and horses. By the end of the nineteenth century, though, the area had found fame as a seaside resort. The most famous person to have been born in Bunbury was the explorer and Premier, Lord John Forrest, a very highly respected man on whose efforts much of the success of Western Australia has been based. It was he, for example, who insisted that Western Australia should join the Commonwealth of Australia in 1901, and whose guidance led to the construction of a railway linking this distant state with the east of Australia. He was elected as the first Premier of Western Australia and was subsequently the first Australian-born person to receive a life peerage. Regrettably, he died on the ship on his way to London to take up his seat in the House of Lords.

In 1979, Bunbury was elevated to the rank of a city.

These days, the city is best known for its **dolphins**. They appear almost every morning in the bay and come and play with the humans who are waiting to meet them. They are not bribed in any way to do this. No food is provided and visitors are encouraged not to offer any gratuities, but the

dolphins are curious, no doubt, about all these humans who stand around in knee-deep water with no apparent purpose in life but to create an obstacle course enabling the dolphins to display their swimming prowess. It is, in fact, amazing that these creatures can swim with such agility in water so shallow that their dorsal fins are constantly visible, and also that they should be so interested in such a miserable species as *homo sapiens*, so lacking in all the grace and beauty which they display themselves.

There are also several interesting buildings in Bunbury, so let us have a walk around the city.

Walking Tour

This walk covers approximately five kilometres and may be expected to take an hour and a half. Start early, so that you get a chance to meet the dolphins at the end of the route before they get bored and go home. The tour starts at the Visitor Information Centre and finishes by Leschenault Inlet, about one kilometre from the town centre.

The **Visitor Information Centre** is in the **Old Railway Station**, used until 1985, when it was decided that railway passengers ought to be forced to make their way to the outskirts of the town if they were not wealthy enough to go by car like everybody else. It is a handsome building, and a great shame that it has to function for its present demeaning purpose as a bus station. Behind the station is **Bicentennial Square**, formerly railway marshalling yards.

Proceed along Carmody Street and you will see the **Rose Hotel** on your left. This establishment dates from 1865 and is one of Bunbury's oldest and most interesting buildings. It contains a **bust** in the courtyard **of King Henry II**, the man who quarrelled with Thomas Beckett, resulting in the martyrdom of the latter in 1170. It is said that this bust was once housed in the House of Commons in London. Turn left when you reach Victoria Street and walk two short blocks. On your right now is the **John Forrest Monument**. John Forrest was born in Bunbury in 1847 and elected as the first Premier of Western Australia in 1890. He entered the Federal Parliament in 1901, upon its commencement. There is other artwork on this corner too, as you will observe.

Turn left along Stephen Street, with the Shopping Centre on your left, and follow the road when it turns right. On your left here is the Paisley Centre, dating from 1887. This was originally the **Bunbury Boys' School**. Lord John Forrest, Sir James Mitchell and Sir Newton Moore, all Premiers of Western Australia, were all educated on this site, although not, of course, in this actual building. Continue across the traffic lights along Spencer Street, and then turn right up Edward Street and left into Parkfield Street. You will come to two cathedrals. On your left is **St. Boniface Anglican Cathedral** and on your right is **St. Patrick's Catholic Cathedral**. This building was completed in 1921, but lacked a spire for many years, since it was lost in a shipwreck in the Bay of Biscay. A substitute spire was finally added in 1967. The pews inside are made of fine local jarrah wood.

Return along Parkfield Street, and then turn left into Stirling Street. On your left is **Anzac Park**, with a **War Memorial** to those lost in the Great War. Just beyond is **Stirling House**, now a Senior Citizens Centre, but originally built in the 1880s as the residence of the first Town Clerk. Continuing along Stirling Street, at the corner with Wittenoom Street, you will find steps up to **Boulter's Heights Lookout**, from where there is a good view of Bunbury. There is also a 26-metre **waterfall** built for the visit of the Queen Mother in 1966, but unfortunately it does not function properly any longer, having fallen very far short in longevity of that good lady herself. Descend once

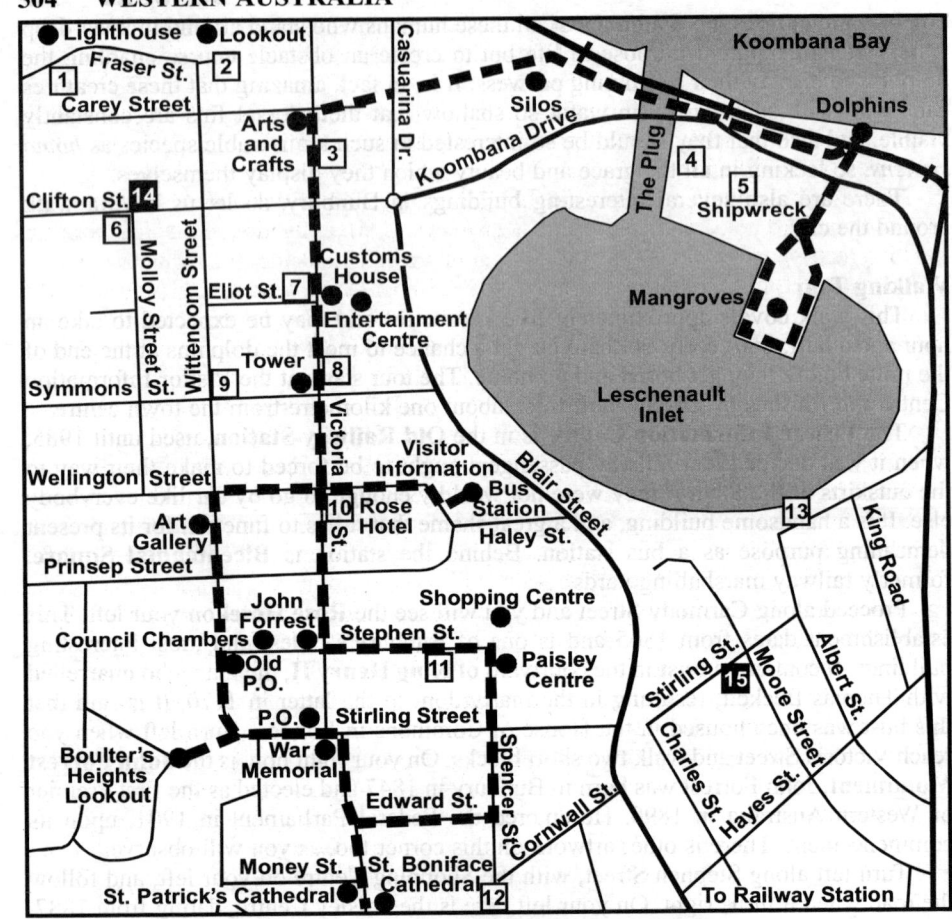

BUNBURY
Dashed line shows Walking Tour
Black numerals in white boxes indicate hotel accommodation
White numerals in black boxes indicate backpackers hostels

more, and turn left along Wittenoom Street. On your right, you will see the **Old Post Office**, one of the city's oldest buildings, dating from 1855, and now the headquarters of the State Emergency Service. Just a little way along Stephen Street is a building constructed in 1935 in Art Deco style, which served as the Council Offices until 1978, but is now the **Council Chambers** and Function Centre. Continuing along Wittenoom Street beyond Princep Street, you will find the **Regional Art Gallery** on your left. Built in 1883, this was originally a convent and chapel for the Sisters of Mercy.

Turn right at Wellington Street and then left at Victoria Street into the heart of the city once more. After crossing Symmonds Street, you will find, on your left, **Bunbury Tower**, resembling the bows of a ship. This eleven-storey tower is a local government office. On your right now is **Customs House**, an old and restored building which originally housed the Customs Department Bond Store. Behind it is the **Entertainment Centre**. This 815-seat theatre is the largest in Western Australia outside Perth. A cinema complex is adjacent. Continue along Victoria Street and you will reach the **City Arts and Crafts Precinct** on your left, with craftsmen at work and their products for sale. Turn right at Carey Street, and note the **silos** ahead. Constructed in 1937, these are 28.3 metres high. Grain was brought here by rail and stored prior to being loaded on ships at the nearby jetty. There were originally twelve such silos here, but the other eight were demolished in 1992.

Beyond the silos is a path beside the Inner Harbour, which follow and after ten minutes you will come to the **Dolphin Discovery Centre**. Inside the Centre there are exhibits relating to the dolphins, but the real interest lies outside in the shallow waters of Koombana Bay, where the dolphins arrive almost every morning to play with the humans. The morning is the best time to be here, although the dolphins may choose to stay later if suitably entertained. You can watch from the shore or wade in and play. If you are here by 9:00, there is almost certain to be a dolphin or two to entertain you.

When the dolphins have finished with you, walk across the road and you will find first a **shipwreck**. Unlikely as it may seem, several ships have been lost here, because this used to be sea. Since Bunbury was first settled by Europeans, the shore line has advanced by some 200 metres. There are twenty known wrecks here, of which a dozen lie buried under these dunes. Beyond is **Mangrove Cove**, on Leschenault Inlet. A circular boardwalk has been constructed here to allow viewing of this remnant of a previous tropical era. These **mangroves** have survived from a time some 10,000 years ago when the climate was much warmer here. They are the farthest south mangroves in Western Australia, and provide a habitat for sixty species of water birds.

Our walk ends here. You can return to the city centre by retracing your steps for about one kilometre, or you can continue round the inlet. There is a footpath next to the shore for most of the walk. By this route, it is approximately three kilometres back to the city centre, but a pleasant and enjoyable route.

Local bus services in are operated by Bunbury City Transit and cover the city well. One-zone tickets cost $2 and two-zone tickets cost $3. Tickets are valid for an hour, and, as long as one boards within that period, one may complete one's journey on that vehicle.

ACCOMMODATION
(i) Hotel Accommodation in Bunbury

Name	Stars	No. on Map	Telephone No.	Address	Lowest Price (Double/Twin)
Hotel Lord Forrest	4½	9	1-800-097-811	20 Symmonds Street	$190
Quest Bunbury		4	08-9722-0777	Koombana & Lions Drives	$125
Koombana Bay Resort		5	08-9791-3900	Koombana Drive	$120
The Clifton	4	6	1-800-017-570	2 Molloy Street	$105
Marlston Hill B & B		2	08-9721-3914	1 Sinclair Close	$95
Admiral Motor Inn	3½	12	1-800-677-720	56 Spencer Street	$90
Burlington Hotel		7	08-9721-2075	51 Victoria Street	$85
Lighthouse Beach Resort	3	1	08-9721-1311	Carey Street	$85
Parade Hotel		13	08-9721-2933	1 Austral Parade	$85
Prince of Wales Hotel		11	08-9721-2016	41 Stephen Street	$85
Rose Hotel / Motel		10	08-9721-4533	Victoria Street	$85
Trafalgar's Hotel		8	08-9721-2600	26 Victoria Street	$85
Reef Hotel		3	08-9791-6677	12 Victoria Street	$85

506   WESTERN AUSTRALIA
(ii) Backpackers Hostels in Bunbury

Name	Group	No. on Map	Telephone No.	Address	Lowest Price (Dormitory)
Wander Inn	VIP	14	08-9721-3242	16 Clifton Street	$20
Residency Y.H.A.	YHA	15	08-9791-2621	Stirling & Moore Streets	$18

MOVING ON
(i) By Train

There are two trains a day back to Perth, although it is not easy to get to the peripheral Railway Station in time to catch the 6:00 departure. There is no public transport there at that time. W.A.G.R. also operates at least two buses a day to Perth, except on Sundays, when there is only one. Some of these buses stop outside the Wellington Street Bus Station in Perth, as well as at East Perth. The timetable for all buses and trains to Perth is shown below, including connexions from other parts of the south-west.

Albany, Pemberton, Augusta and Bunbury to Perth

Days of Operation	Daily	Tu, Th Sat (Bus)	M, W, F (Bus)	M, Tu, Th (Bus)	Not M, Th (Bus)	M, Th (Bus)	Daily	F* (Bus)	Not Sat (Bus)
Albany					0800	0835			
Denmark					0847	0922			
Walpole					0943	1018			
Pemberton			0630	0845	1120				
Augusta		0830	0840						1505
Margaret River		0905	0915						1535
Busselton		1022	1035						1652
Bunbury	0600	1105	1130	1105	1420	1420	1445	1600	1735
Perth	0830	1430	1450	1430			1712	1840	2045

* During school terms only

(ii) By Bus

South West Coach Lines operates three services a day to Perth, four to Busselton and two to Augusta. The same company also has services to Collie (two per weekday) and Manjimup (one per weekday).

Destination	Operator	Via	Distance (km)	Fare	Journey Time	Frequency
Perth	W.A.G.R.		180	$23.20	2¾ - 3½ hrs	17/week
Perth	South West		180	$18	2¾ hrs	3/day
Albany	W.A.G.R.		397	$40.65	5½ - 6¼ hrs	7/week
Augusta	W.A.G.R.		169	$18.10	2½ - 2¾ hrs	12/week
		Busselton	48	$7	45 - 50 mins	12/week
Augusta	South West		139	$19.10	2¼ - 2½ hrs	2/day
		Busselton	48	$8.40	1 hr	4/day
Manjimup	South West		126	$19.10	2¼ hrs	5/week
Collie	South West		49	$8.40	45 - 60 mins	10/week

BUSSELTON
Population 15,000

3 hrs 30 mins by train and bus from Perth
4 hrs by bus from Perth

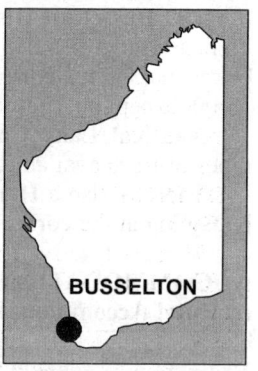

The fastest, most convenient and most comfortable way to reach Busselton is to take the morning *Australind* train from Perth to Bunbury and change to the W.A.G.R. bus there. It is possible to take the same bus all the way from East Perth, where it originates, but that takes an hour longer.

South West Coach Lines operates an alternative service from the Busport in Perth. There are three buses a day, currently leaving Perth at 8:45, 13:15 and 17:45.

On the way to Busselton from Bunbury, you will pass through the edge of the **Ludlow Tuart Forest**, the largest natural tuart forest in the world. You will also see beside the main road the old railway line to Busselton, now sadly abandoned.

Busselton is a sheltered seaside resort town on Geographe Bay, 55 kilometres beyond Bunbury, offering thirty kilometres of white sandy beaches and interesting waters for diving.

The town claims to have the **longest wooden jetty** in the southern hemisphere, a curved construction stretching 1,837 metres out to sea and started as long ago as 1855. It was extended several times until, by 1911, it was believed to have become the longest in the southern hemisphere. It was closed to shipping in 1972 and ceased to receive maintenance, which led to its deterioration. It then suffered severe damage at the shore end from Cyclone Alby in 1978. However, it has been repaired, not because it is required for commerce any longer, but because it is a tourist attraction and is known for its good fishing and crabbing. An admission fee of $3 is charged for the jetty, to assist with its maintenance. If you do not feel like walking nearly two kilometres to the end of the jetty and another two back, there is an unusual little train which trundles its way out there every hour between 10:00 and 16:00. However, the return journey on this vehicle is rather costly at $7.

The jetty is also used by snorkellers and scuba divers, as there are corals here as well as colourful fishes. An **underwater observatory** is under construction and will probably be completed by the time that this is read. Because of a warm-water current which travels down the west coast of Australia, corals grow here even at 33° south, and over 300 species of marine life have been observed in the vicinity of Busselton Jetty.

In the town, the **Old Courthouse Arts Complex** houses an Art Gallery, a café and craftsmen at work. The building was constructed in 1854 - 1856, and extended in 1873 and has, in its time, been used as courthouse, gaol, stables, post office and customs bond store.

St. Mary's Anglican Church was built in 1844 to 1848 and is the oldest stone church in Western Australia. It was built under the guidance of John Bussell, who gave his name to the town. He now lies in the graveyard of this church along with many other of the pioneers of this area.

At the corner of Queen and Albert Streets is the **first steam locomotive** to operate in Western Australia. It was used between 1871 and 1886 to haul timber between Yoganup and Wonnerup, some of the wood being used for the extension of Busselton Jetty.

WESTERN AUSTRALIA

The **Busselton Historic Museum** is housed in the Old Butter Factory in Peel Terrace. Butter has not been produced here since 1954. The museum includes the old butter-making machinery, as well as a working timber mill. It is open from 14:00 until 17:00, except on Tuesdays.

Nautical Lady Entertainment World lies adjacent to the jetty and has many types of rides available, most of them aimed at children.

There is also a **Heritage Trail** around Busselton. Follow the notices in the town, beginning at the corner of Peel Terrace and Causeway Road.

ACCOMMODATION
(i) Hotel Accommodation in Busselton

Name	Stars	No. on Map	Telephone No.	Address	Lowest Price (Double/Twin)
Gale Street Motel	3½	3	1-800-685-412	40 Gale Street	$80
Jacaranda Guest House		2	08-9752-1246	30 West Street	$75
Amaroo Motor Lodge		4	08-9752-1544	25 Bussell Highway	$75
Paradise Motel	3	5	08-9752-1200	6 Peel Terrace	$60
Esplanade Hotel		1	08-9752-1078	Marine Terrace	$50

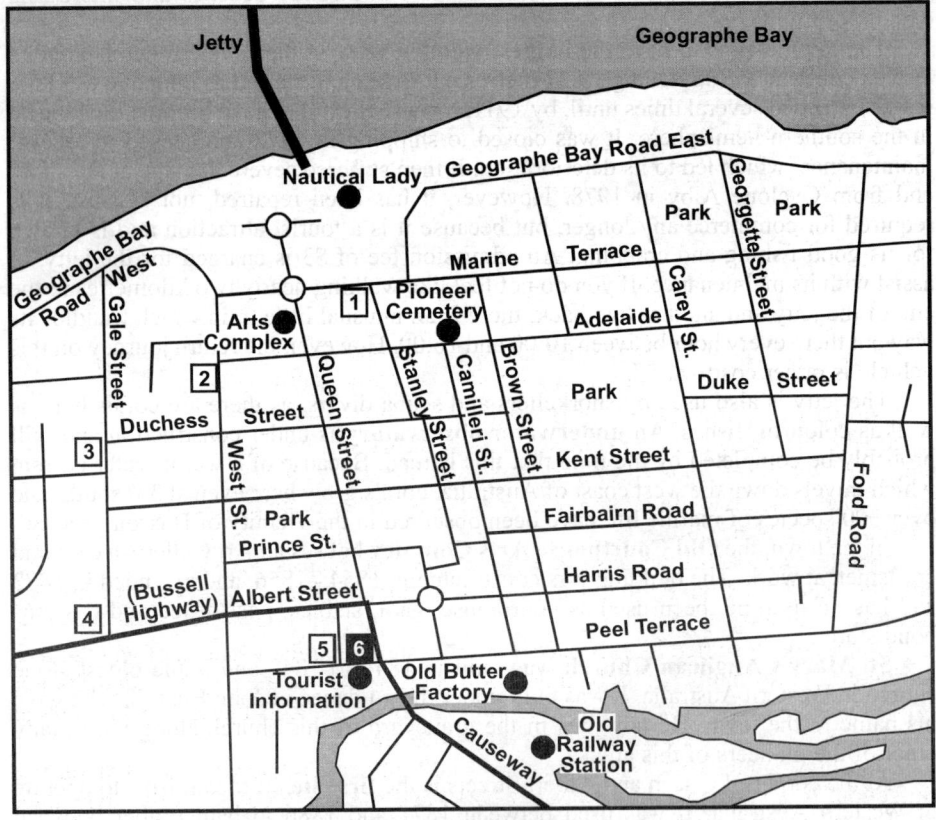

BUSSELTON
**Black numerals in white boxes indicate hotel accommodation
White numerals in black boxes indicate backpackers hostels**

(ii) Backpackers Hostel in Busselton

Name	Group	No. on Map	Telephone No.	Address	Lowest Price (Dormitory)
Busselton Backpackers	VIP	6	08-9754-2763	14 Peel Terrace	$20

MOVING ON

W.A.G.R. runs two buses per day on weekdays back to Perth, and one on Saturdays and Sundays. The timetable is on page 506. A similar service operates in the opposite direction to Augusta, with three buses a week continuing to Pemberton. The timetable for this is on page 486. When there is no direct service to Pemberton, it is possible to reach that town by changing buses in Bunbury. It is also possible to reach Albany by that route.

South West Coach Lines has three buses a day to Perth and three a day to Augusta.

Bus Services from Busselton

Destination	Operator	Via	Distance (km)	Fare	Journey Time	Frequency
Perth	W.A.G.R.		228	$26.85	4 - 4½ hrs	12/week
		Bunbury	48	$7	45 – 55 mins	12/week
Perth	South West		228	$22	3¾ hrs	3/day
		Bunbury	48	$8.40	55 mins	3/day
Pemberton	W.A.G.R.		288	$16.55	4 hrs	3/week
		Augusta	122	$12.90	2 hrs	12/week
Augusta	South West		91	$13.70	1¼ - 1¾ hrs	3/day

DUNSBOROUGH
Population 3,000

4 hrs by train and bus from Perth
5 hrs by bus from Perth

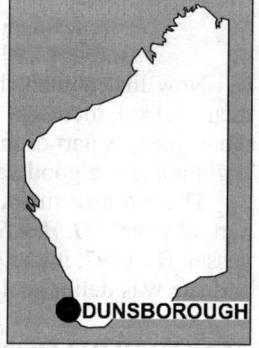

Further round the coast from Busselton is Dunsborough. Again the best way to reach the small town is to take the morning *Australind* from Perth and change to the W.A.G.R. bus at Bunbury, although actually the bus starts in Perth an hour earlier than the train.

South East Coach Lines also operates a service. There is only one bus a day from Perth to Dunsborough, although there are three from Busselton.

Dunsborough started its existence as a town supplying the whalers, of which there were considerable numbers in the nineteenth century. The Castle Bay Whaling Station was founded here in 1846, with one William Seymour as the manager. It is his cottage which is now the **oldest building** standing in the town.

Dunsborough too offers sandy beaches, and is rather less known than neighbouring Busselton. It is surrounded by National Parks and has many coastal walks available. Thirteen kilometres north is Cape Naturaliste (see area map on page 512), with its **lighthouse** built in 1903 from local limestone. This is Australia's most westerly weather station. The lighthouse is open for inspection every day from 9:30 until 15:30.

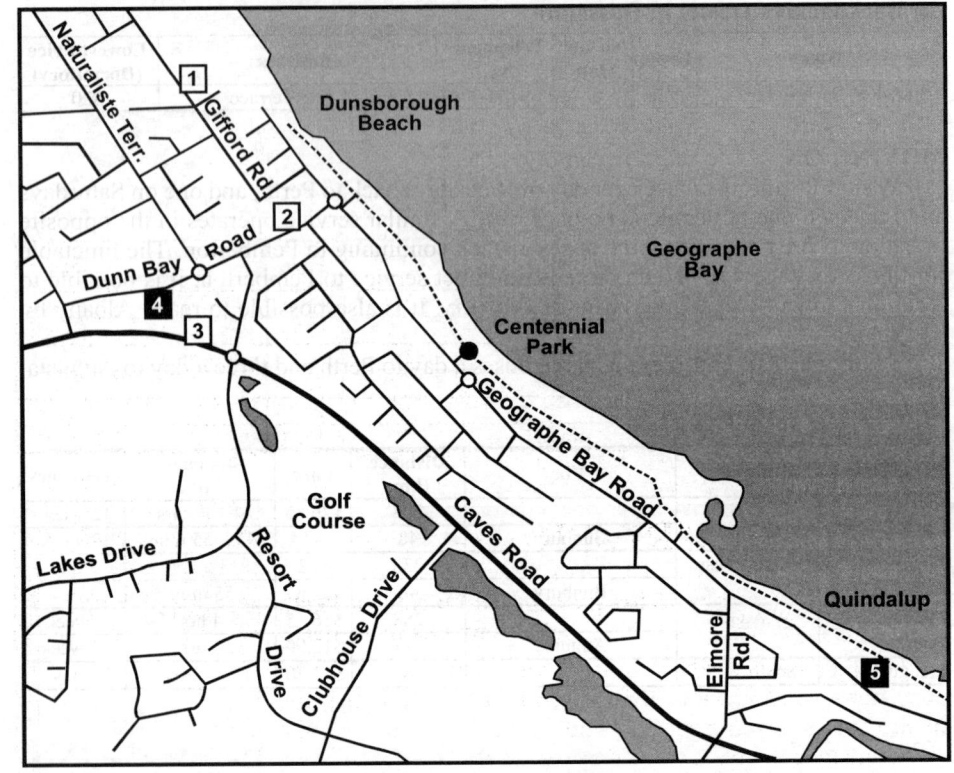

DUNSBOROUGH
Black numerals in white boxes indicate hotel accommodation
White numerals in black boxes indicate backpackers hostels

Now that humans have given up hunting whales, and decided to be friends with them instead, there is a **whale watching** season from September until December, when the whales, as part of their annual migration, rest in the bay here. The Cape Naturaliste Lighthouse is a good vantage point.

There is also surfing available and there is a wreck for divers. It is, however, not a natural wreck. ***H.M.A.S. Swan*** was commissioned in 1970 as an anti-submarine escort vessel. By 1997, it was decided that she had reached the end of her active service duties and she was deliberately scuttled in the bay here as an attraction for divers.

ACCOMMODATION
For backpackers, there are two locations available. Note that if you stay at the youth hostel, you need to alight from the bus at Quindalup. Some buses actually stop at the hostel on request, while others stop at a distance of about 300 metres.

(i) Hotel Accommodation in Dunsborough

Name	Stars	No. on Map	Telephone No.	Address	Lowest Price (Double/Twin)
Dunsborough Cottages		1	1-800-816-885	95 Gifford Road	$95
Mercure Inn		3	1-800-097-711	536 Naturaliste Terrace	$90
Dunsborough Inn		2	08-9756-7277	50 Dunn Bay Road	$50

(ii) Backpackers Hostels in Dunsborough

Name	Group	No. on Map	Telephone No.	Address	Lowest Price (Dormitory)
Dunsborough Lodge		4	08-9756-8856	13 Dunn Bay Road	$21
Dunsborough Inn	Nom	2	08-9756-7277	50 Dunn Bay Road	$20
Three Pines Beach Resort	YHA	5	08-9755-3107	285 Geographe Bay Road	$19

MOVING ON
Bus Services from Dunsborough

Destination	Operator	Via	Distance (km)	Fare	Journey Time	Frequency
Perth	W.A.G.R.		252	$18.70	4½ - 5 hrs	12/week
		Bunbury	72	$9.75	1¼ - 1½ hrs	12/week
Perth	South West		252	$25	4¼ - 4½ hrs	2/day
		Bunbury	72	$13.70	1½ - 1¾ hrs	2/day
Pemberton	W.A.G.R.		263	$28.70	3½ hrs	3/week
		Augusta	97	$12.90	1½ hrs	12/week

MARGARET RIVER
Population 2,000

5 hrs by train and bus from Perth
5 hrs by bus from Perth

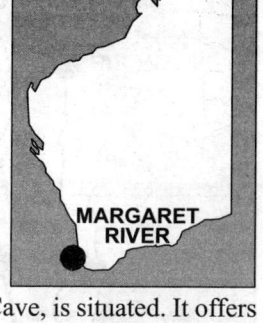

Margaret River is known for its wine and its caves. From a visitor's point of view, therefore, the difficulty is that the main attractions are not in the town itself, but in the surrounding countryside.

To reach Margaret River, take the *Australind* train from Perth and change to the W.A.G.R. bus at Bunbury. Between Dunsborough and Margaret River, your bus will pass through **Yallingup**, where **Ngilgi Cave**, formerly known as Yallingup Cave, is situated. It offers stalactites, stalagmites, helictites and shawl formations, and is within walking distance of the small town of Yallingup.

Also at Yallingup are three of the state's most famous surf beaches: **Yallingup Beach, Three Bears Beach** and **Injidup Beach**. Another attraction is **camel safaris**.

If you travel with the alternative means of transport, the South West Coach Lines service, however, your bus will not pass through Dunsborough or Yallingup, but will travel directly from Busselton to Margaret River (see map on next page).

Margaret River offers accommodation, and there are tours available from here to the various caves

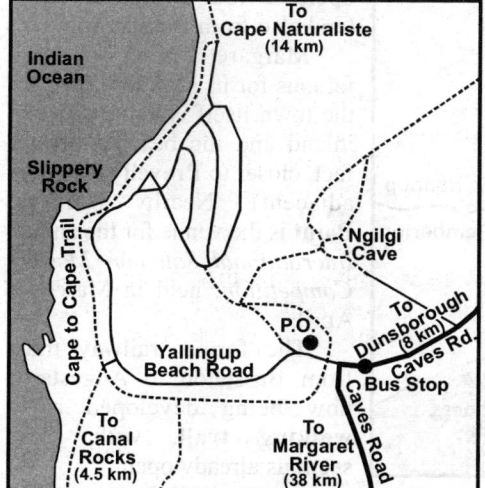

YALLINGUP

and wineries. As for the caves, there are some 350 of them already known, and probably many more yet to be discovered, in the 100-kilometre Leeuwin - Naturaliste Limestone Ridge. However, only five are open to the public. Ngilgi Cave has already been mentioned above. The nearest cave to Margaret River is the **Mammoth Cave**, about twenty kilometres south of the town (see map below). It features a high-technology self-guided tour system, using headphones and radio-activated CD player. There is also access for the disabled. The cave has fossilised remains within, hence its name. It is open daily from 9:00 until 16:00. Three kilometres further south is *CaveWorks* and the **Lake Cave**. *CaveWorks* is a Visitor Centre, and the Lake Cave lies beneath it, with, as you might expect, a lake at its centre. Lake Cave offers tours every hour on the half-hour from 9:30 until 15:30. **Jewel Cave** and **Moondyne Cave** are both further south and close to Augusta. Jewel Cave was opened relatively recently, in 1959, and claims to have the longest straw stalactite in any tourist cave. It offers tours every hour on the half-hour from 9:30 until 15:30. Moondyne Cave is an explorers' cave. One is issued with protective clothing, hard hat and lamp and taken clambering through the various chambers. This tour is available at 14:00 only.

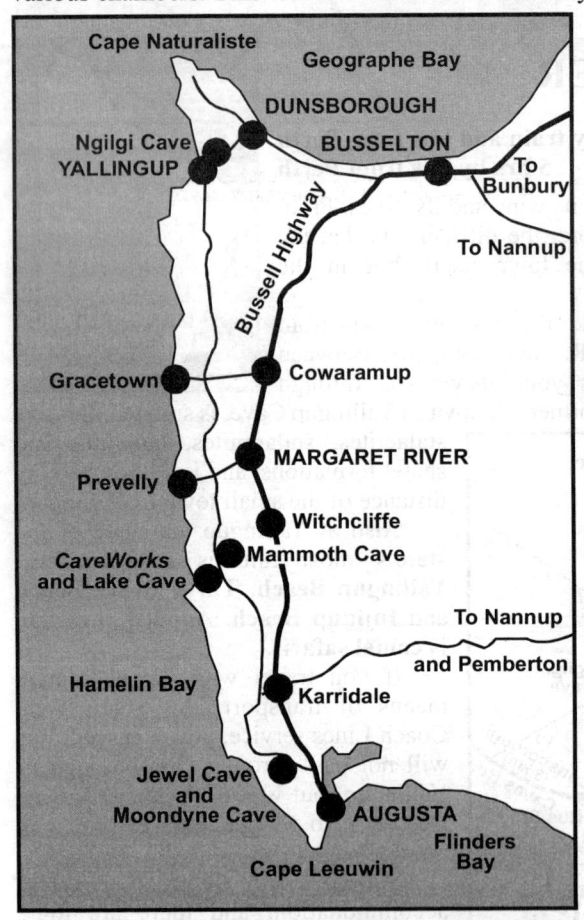

MARGARET RIVER AND VICINITY

As for the **wineries**, there is a huge range to choose from, with over thirty in the vicinity of Margaret River. This new industry has changed the landscape all the way between Busselton and Margaret River and beyond. Some of the wines produced here are world class and have won international awards, but, unless you have your own transport, you will need to join a tour to get to the wineries. Several such tours operate from Margaret River (and also from Busselton).

Margaret River is also famous for its **surf beaches**, but the town itself is ten kilometres inland and the beaches are, in fact, closer to **Prevelly** (see map adjacent). Nearby **Surfers' Point** is the venue for the annual *International Salomon Masters Competition*, held in March or April.

The former railway track from Busselton to Augusta is now being developed as a **walking trail**, with some sections already open.

MARGARET RIVER

ACCOMMODATION

Margaret River is a popular holiday town for residents of Perth, so much of the accommodation tends to be aimed at that market. Rates increase at peak seasons - principally school holidays - and there may be a requirement of a minimum length of stay. There is also accommodation available at Prevelly, which is by the beach.

For backpackers, there are two places to stay, as listed below. Inne Town Backpackers is right in the centre of Margaret River, as its name suggests, while Margaret River Lodge is only a few minutes walk away.

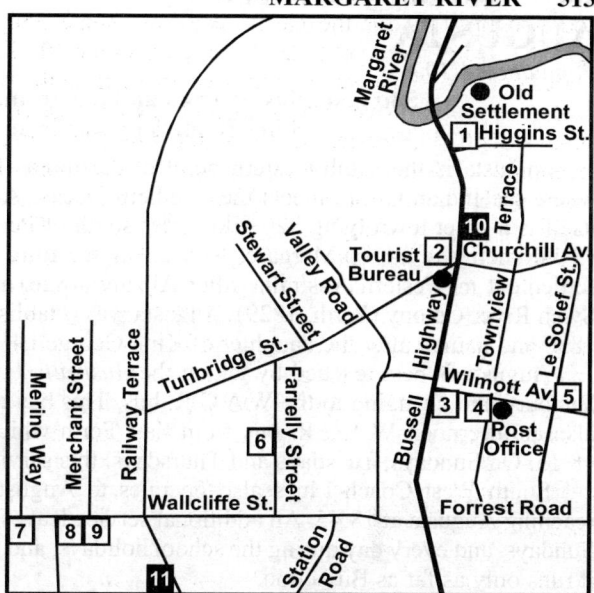

MARGARET RIVER
Black numerals indicate hotel accommodation
White numerals indicate backpackers hostels

(i) Hotel Accommodation in Margaret River

Name	Stars	No. on Map	Telephone No.	Address	Lowest Price (Double/Twin)
Basildene Manor	5	7	08-9757-3140	100 Wallcliffe Road	$245
Margaret River Resort	5	9	08-9757-0000	40 Wallcliffe Road	$165
Emerald Colonial Lodge	3½	8	1-800-622-336	Wallcliffe Road	$135
Grange on Farrelly	3½	6	1-800-650-100	16 Farrelly Street	$130
Freycinet Inn	3½	2	1-800-807-667	Bussell Hy. & Tunbridge St	$125
Margaret River Hotel		3	1-800-672-655	Bussell Highway	$105
Margaret River Suites		4	08-9758-7088	Wilmott Av /Townview Tce	$99
Adamson's Riverside Acc		1	08-9757-2013	71 Bussell Highway	$95
Vintages Accommodation		5	08-9758-8333	Wilmott Avenue	$95

(ii) Backpackers Hostels in Margaret River

Name	Group	No. on Map	Telephone No.	Address	Lowest Price (Dormitory)
Inne Town Backpackers		10	1800-244-115	93 Bussell Highway	$21
Margaret River Lodge	VIP	11	08-9757-9532	220 Railway Terrace	$19

MOVING ON
Bus Services from Margaret River

Destination	Operator	Via	Distance (km)	Fare	Journey Time	Frequency
Perth	W.A.G.R.		304	$30.50	5¼ - 5¾ hrs	12/week
		Bunbury	124	$12.60	2 - 2¼ hrs	12/week
Perth	South West		274	$26	4½ hrs	2/day
		Bunbury	94	$13.70	1¾ hrs	2/day
Pemberton	W.A.G.R.		210	$24.50	2¾ hrs	3/week
		Augusta	45	$7	30 mins	12/week
Augusta	South West		45	$8.40	35 mins	3/day

AUGUSTA

Population 1,100

5 hrs 30 mins by train and bus from Perth
5 hrs 30 mins by bus from Perth

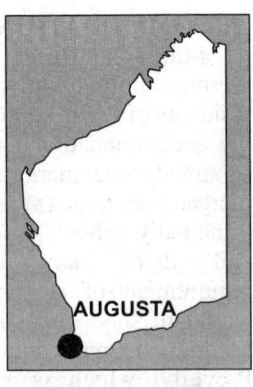

Augusta is the south-western point of Australia. This is where the Indian Ocean meets the Southern Ocean. Augusta itself is a quiet town lying 320 kilometres south of Perth and 43 kilometres south of Margaret River. It is the third oldest settlement in Western Australia, after Albany (1826) and the Swan River Colony (Perth, 1829). Augusta was established in 1830 and named after the daughter of King George III.

Augusta is best reached by taking the *Australind* train to Bunbury and changing to the W.A.G.R. bus. This bus terminates in Augusta. There is also an afternoon W.A.G.R. bus from East Perth which runs to Augusta, arriving at 18:15. On Sundays, Tuesdays and Thursdays, this service is extended to Pemberton.

South West Coach Lines also operates to Augusta, leaving Perth at 13:15 and reaching Augusta at 18:45. An additional service leaves Perth at 8:45 on Saturdays and Sundays, and every day during the school holidays, and arrives at 13:55. On other days, it runs only as far as Busselton.

Near Augusta are the two caves mentioned in the section on Margaret River above: namely **Jewel Cave** and **Moondyne Cave**, which are only about ten kilometres north of the town.

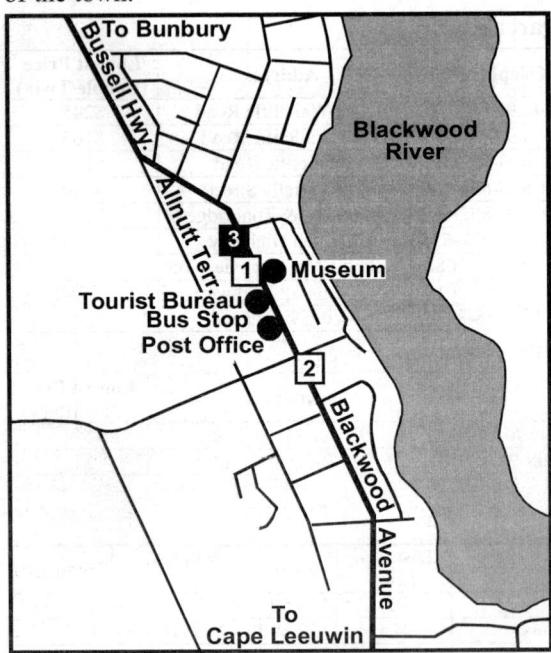

AUGUSTA
Black numerals indicate hotel accommodation
White numerals indicate backpackers hostels

Nine kilometres away is the **Cape Leeuwin Lighthouse** marking the absolute south-westerly point of the continent. This lighthouse was built in 1895 and is also an important meteorological station. Nearby is a fascinating **waterwheel**. It was built, again in 1895, to supply water to the lighthouse cottages, but has gradually become calcified, so that, although it is actually made completely of wood, it appears now as though composed of stone. The lighthouse is open daily from 9:30 until 17:00 and affords a good view from the 39-metre high balcony, to reach which you must climb 176 steps.

Between June and December, **whales** rest here during their long winter migration and can be seen around the Cape, sometimes being visible from the lighthouse.

ACCOMMODATION
(i) Hotel Accommodation in Augusta

Name	Stars	No. on Map	Telephone No.	Address	Lowest Price (Double/Twin)
Georgiana Molloy Motel	3	1	1-800-180-288	84 Blackwood Avenue	$80
Augusta Hotel		2	08-9758-1944	Blackwood Avenue	$80

(ii) Backpackers Hostel in Augusta

Name	Group	No. on Map	Telephone No.	Address	Lowest Price (Dormitory)
Baywatch Manor Resort	YHA	3	08-9758-1290	88 Blackwood Avenue	$19

MOVING ON
Bus Services from Augusta

Destination	Operator	Via	Distance (km)	Fare	Journey Time	Frequency
Perth	W.A.G.R.		349	$36.70	5¾ - 6¼ hrs	12/week
		Bunbury	169	$18.10	2½ - 3 hrs	12/week
Perth	South West		319	$31	5 hrs	2/day
		Bunbury	139	$19.10	2¼ hrs	2/day
Pemberton	W.A.G.R.		164	$18.10	2¼ hrs	3/week

PEMBERTON
Population 1,000

5 hrs 30 mins by train and bus from Perth

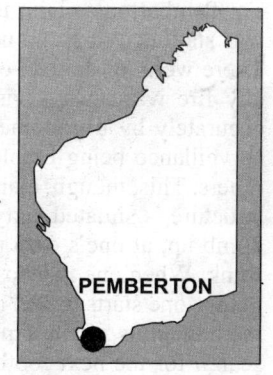

Pemberton is famous for its karri forests. It is a pretty little town right in the heart of the forest, a delightful place in which to stay.

The first settler arrived in 1861, a Mr. Brockman, son of the first mayor of Perth. However, it was Mr. Pemberton Walcott, who arrived a year later, who gave the town its name. Pemberton became a timber town, and gained in prosperity when the Trans-Australian Railway decided to obtain its karri sleepers from here. In 1913, Pemberton produced half a million such sleepers.

As you come here on the bus, you will experience some of the beauty of these forests, as the bus passes along roads lined by tall, stately trees hundreds of years old. **Manjimup**, reached forty-five minutes before Pemberton, is also a timber town. It is a much larger centre than Pemberton, and has an interesting timber-built and timber-oriented museum, part of the **Timber Park** there. You will have time to look at it when the bus stops for a tea break. The **Tourist Bureau** itself is a modern building constructed of local jarrah wood. It has been built with 3,500 locally-produced mud bricks and a shingle roof consisting of 22,000 karri shingles. Nearby in the Timber Park are various historical buildings and pieces of machinery.

Manjimup also has a South West Coach Lines service which does not extend to Pemberton. This service operates once a day from Perth at 13:15, taking just over five hours.

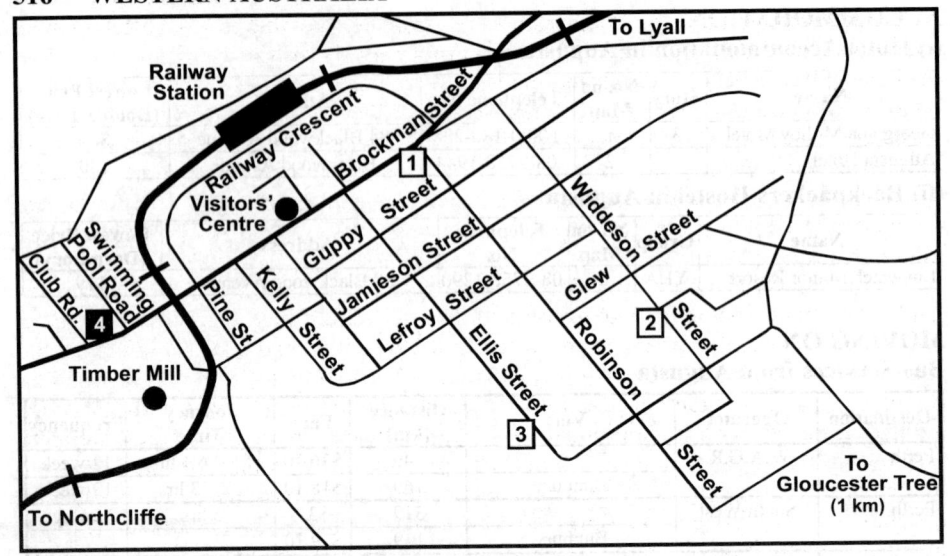

PEMBERTON

Black numerals in white boxes indicate hotel accommodation
White numerals in black boxes indicate backpackers hostels

Pemberton's claim to fame is the *Gloucester Tree*. This is a fire lookout. A man was stationed to sit up here at the top of the tree all day watching out for forest fires. There were, of course, other such lookouts and they were strategically placed so that any fire was always visible from at least two trees, and could thus be pinpointed accurately by trigonometry. These lookouts are no longer in use, aerial and satellite surveillance being employed instead. However, the tree is still there, as are various others. This, though, claims to be the highest fire lookout tree in the world. The lookout structure is situated sixty metres above the ground, and it is permissible, and free, to climb up, at one's own risk. There is just a row of steel pegs, almost vertical, up the trunk. When one reaches the branches and can no longer see the ground so clearly far below, one starts to feel a little better, but it is a long way to the first branch. Moreover, the descent is, if anything, worse than the ascent, since one is obliged to look down to search for the next foothold. The one thing to try to avoid is meeting somebody half way up going in the opposite direction. From the lookout at the top, one can see all the way to the coast. The tree is named the *Gloucester Tree* after the Duke of Gloucester, Governor-General of Australia at the time, who visited and inspected the construction of the lookout in 1946. At the foot of the tree are photographs of the construction. If you think this climb hard, look at the pictures of those who climbed up without any pegs, and without any safety equipment, and who then scaled the tree driving in the pegs as they went and built the lookout at the top. On average, fifty people climb the 153 rungs to the top of this tree every day, and you may join their number. The *Gloucester Tree* is three kilometres from the town centre, a pleasant walk. Vehicles are charged for admission to the National Park, but there is no charge for pedestrians. The Bibbulmun Track, the 964-kilometre walking track from Perth to Albany, runs right past the *Gloucester Tree* too.

PEMBERTON

The other attraction of Pemberton is its railway, of which W.A.G.R. gave up operation some years ago. Therefore, the **Pemberton Tramway** Company has taken over use of the facilities and runs its small 'tram' vehicles down to **Warren Bridge** and on to **Northcliffe** through the karri forest. Trams to Warren Bridge depart at 10:45 and 14:00 every day and take 1¾ hours for the return trip, costing $15. The journey is ten kilometres each way. A stop is made at the Cascades to view some pretty scenery. Trams to Northcliffe depart on Tuesdays, Thursdays and Saturdays at 10:15 and take 5½ hours for the return trip, costing $35 (one-way available for $30). The journey is 36 kilometres each way.

Trains now run north from Pemberton also. These trains are diesel- or steam-hauled, and they operate to **Eastbrook** and on to **Lyall**. To Eastbrook trains depart at 10:30 and 14:15 on Saturdays from Easter until November, and take 1¾ hours for the return trip, eleven kilometres each way, costing $22. The train to Lyall runs at 10:30 on Sundays, takes three hours for the return trip, 21 kilometres each way, and costs $35. Riding in the cab costs an additional $40. These services are usually steam-operated, but, during the summer, only the Sunday train runs and it is diesel-hauled and is a mixed train, conveying both logs and passengers. (The passengers have separate accommodation.) Prices and times are the same as above. A combined ticket is available, giving both the tram service south to Northcliffe and the train service north to Lyall for $55.

In the centre of the town of Pemberton, you will find the **Karri Visitors' Centre**, which incorporates the Pioneer Museum, the Karri Forest Discovery Centre and the Pemberton Tourist Centre.

Free **Sawmill Tours** are offered by Pemberton Mill, which started its life in 1912 cutting those sleepers for the Trans-Australian Railway. Today it claims to be the largest operating hardwood sawmill in the southern hemisphere, although the author is not convinced that that should be a source of pride.

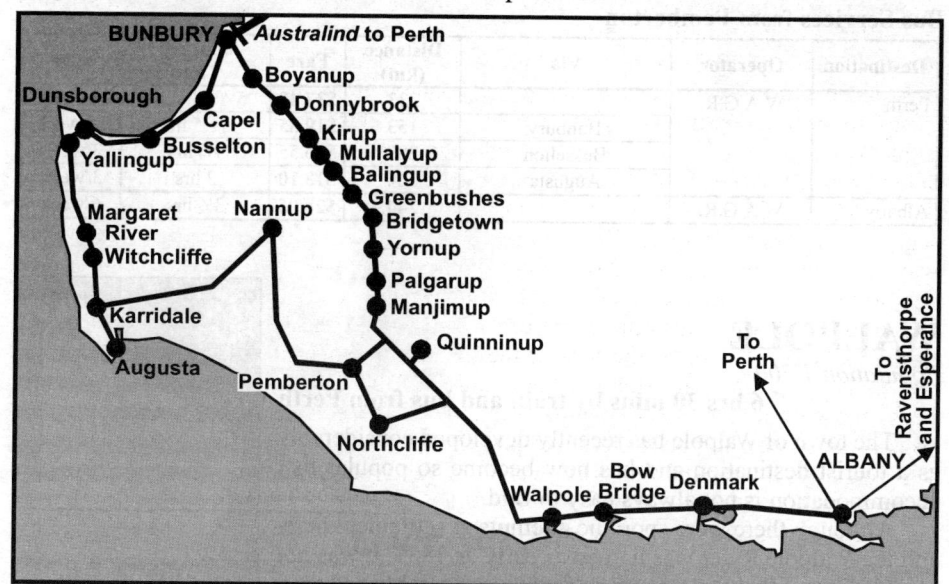

W.A.G.R. BUS SERVICES BETWEEN BUNBURY AND ALBANY

518 WESTERN AUSTRALIA

ACCOMMODATION

The accommodation listed is in the town. There are other possibilities in the surrounding area, but not within walking distance. For backpackers, there are two choices. Pemberton Backpackers is in the town centre, but the youth hostel is nine kilometres away, in pleasant countryside. The manager will pick guests up if they telephone in advance, and return them to the town later.

(i) Hotel Accommodation in Pemberton

Name	Stars	No. on Map	Telephone No.	Address	Lowest Price (Double/Twin)
Karri Forest Motel	4	2	1-800-420-888	Widdeson Street	$130
Pemberton Hotel		1	08-9776-1017	66 Brockman Street	$125
Gloucester Motel		3	1-800-651-266	Ellis Street	$80

(ii) Backpackers Hostels in Pemberton

Name	Group	No. on Map	Telephone No.	Address	Lowest Price (Dormitory)
Pemberton Backpackers		4	08-9776-1105	7 Brockman Street	$20
Pimelea Chalets	YHA		08-9776-1153	Stirling Road	$18

MOVING ON

There are W.A.G.R. services to Perth by two routes. The direct service operates to Bunbury, where one changes to the afternoon *Australind*. There are also four buses per week which run right through to Perth. The other route is via Augusta, Busselton and Bunbury to Perth. Timetables for all of these services can be found on page 506. In the opposite direction, there are six buses per week to Albany. The timetable for these is on page 486.

Bus Services from Pemberton

Destination	Operator	Via	Distance (km)	Fare	Journey Time	Frequency
Perth	W.A.G.R.		333	$37.40	5½ - 8½ hrs	11/week
		Bunbury	153	$19.85	3 - 5 hrs	11/week
		Busselton	288	$16.55	4¼ hrs	3/week
		Augusta	164	$18.10	2 hrs	3/week
Albany	W.A.G.R.		244	$28.05	3½ hrs	6/week

WALPOLE

Population 1,500

6 hrs 30 mins by train and bus from Perth

The town of Walpole has recently developed considerably as a tourist destination and has now become so popular that accommodation is not always easy to find.

Although there were sporadic attempts at settlement here, and the Walpole River was named as early as 1831, it was not until 1930 that this small town really became established, as a result of the Nornalup Land Settlement Scheme. This was an

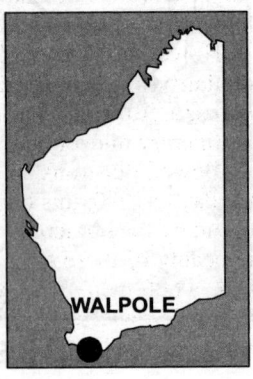

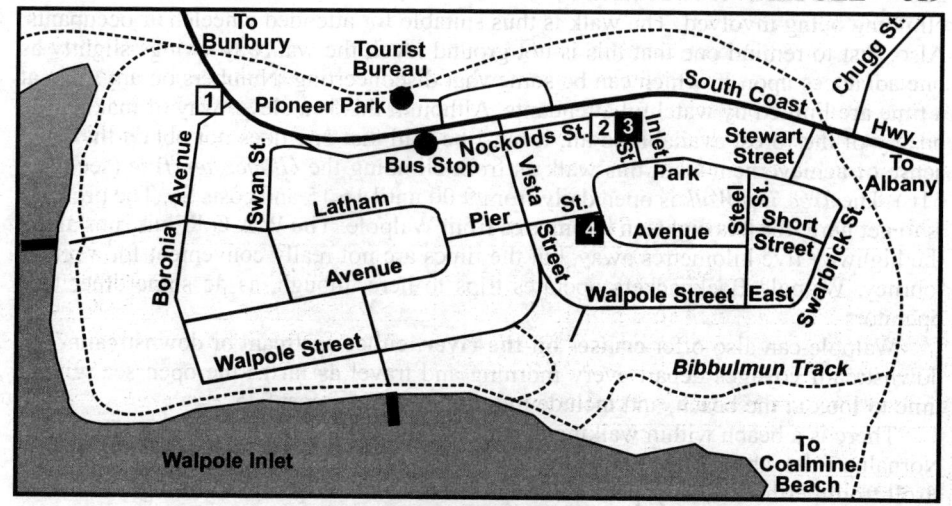

WALPOLE
Black numerals in white boxes indicate hotel accommodation
White numerals in black boxes indicate backpackers hostels

attempt to provide opportunities on the land for those most affected by the Great Depression.

To reach Walpole, take the *Australind* to Bunbury and change there to the W.A.G.R. bus bound for Albany. The bus follows two different routes according to the day of the week. Most services pass through Pemberton and Northcliffe, but the Wednesday and Friday afternoon buses by-pass the two towns and follow a more direct route (see map on page 517). On Tuesdays, Thursdays and Saturdays, it is possible to take the Pemberton Tram service from Pemberton to Northcliffe and pick up the W.A.G.R. bus there in order to continue to Walpole or beyond.

As you travel on the bus, the beautiful forests lining the highway continue and you probably will not notice that there is a change in the type of tree as Walpole is approached. These are now Tingle trees, also of impressive dimensions, sixty, seventy and eighty metres tall and hundreds of years old. Then, nearing Walpole, you start to get your first glimpses of the southern coastline.

Walpole is beautifully situated, on the shore of a peaceful inlet off another inlet. The open sea is not visible from the town itself, and it is, therefore, sheltered from the elements.

However, it is the forests, rather than the ocean, on which the sudden rise in popularity of Walpole has been based. Fifteen kilometres away is the *Valley of the Giants*, a grove of huge Tingles. These have been known for a long time and were on the itinerary of every passing tourist. There was one especially weathered veteran with a hollowed-out trunk in which visitors could stand to have their photographs taken. One day in 1990, this huge tree simply fell over, probably due to the compacting of the ground by the numerous visitors. Following this, it was decided to try to show visitors the beauty of these trees without causing damage to them. The result is the *Tree Top Walk*, a 600-metre walkway through the crowns of the tall trees forty metres above the ground below. The walk is ingeniously constructed. It departs from the crest of the valley, so that one finds oneself soon level with the tops of the trees without any climbing being involved. The walk is thus suitable for attended wheelchair occupants. Also, just to remind one that this is not ground level, the walkway swings slightly as one advances upon it, which can be somewhat disconcerting. Numbers on any span at a time are limited by watchful attendants. Although this is a clever way of making the beauty of the forest available to all, it must be said that one does not obtain the same sense of achievement from this walk as from climbing the *Gloucester Tree* (see page 516). The *Tree Top Walk* is open daily from 9:00 until 16:15 and costs $6. The problem is to get here, for it is eighteen kilometres from Walpole. The W.A.G.R. bus runs along the highway five kilometres away, but the times are not really convenient for a return journey. Walpole Backpackers operates trips to here, though, as do some other tour operators.

Walpole can also offer **cruises on the river**, either upstream or downstream. The downstream voyages depart every morning and travel as far as the open sea, giving time to look at the beach, and include morning tea. They cost $25.

There is a beach within walking distance of the town. This is **Coalmine Beach** on Nornalup Inlet, about three kilometres away. The Bibbulmun Track, the 964-kilometre stroll from Perth to Albany, passes through the town of Walpole and through Coalmine Beach. If you walk to the beach, you will be walking along the Bibbulmun Track.

Walpole is also a town which claims to have some surviving **quokkas** in the area. For information on quokkas, see the section on Rottnest Island on page 493. The quokkas are found on the dunes close to the sea and remote from habitation.

The **Walpole Tourist Bureau** is located in the centre of the town in a modern reconstruction of a pioneer cottage in the **Pioneer Park**.

ACCOMMODATION

In the town, there are two motels, listed below, as well as several possibilities for bed and breakfast accommodation. There are also two backpackers hostels.

(i) Hotel Accommodation in Walpole

Name	Stars	No. on Map	Telephone No.	Address	Lowest Price (Double/Twin)
Tree Top Walk Motel	4	2	1-800-420-777	Nockolds Street	$125
Walpole Hotel / Motel		1	08-9840-1023	South Coast Highway	$70

(ii) Backpackers Hostels in Walpole

Name	Group	No. on Map	Telephone No.	Address	Lowest Price (Dormitory)
Walpole Backpackers		4	08-9840-1244	Pier Street & Park Avenue	$20
Tingle All Over	YHA	3	08-9840-1041	60 Nockolds Street	$19

MOVING ON

There is a W.A.G.R. bus every day to Bunbury, where it connects with the afternoon *Australind* train to Perth. In the opposite direction, there is a bus every day to Denmark and Albany, with an extra service on Friday evenings.

Bus Services from Walpole

Destination	Operator	Via	Distance (km)	Fare	Journey Time	Frequency
Perth	W.A.G.R.		460	$49.10	6¾ - 7¾ hrs	1/day
		Bunbury	280	$31.55	3¾ - 4¾ hrs	1/day
Albany	W.A.G.R.		117	$16.20	1¾ hrs	8/week

DENMARK
Population 4,500

7 hrs 30 mins by train and bus from Perth

Denmark is a much larger town than those through which we have passed recently, but the method of reaching it is the same. Take the *Australind* train to Bunbury and change there to the W.A.G.R. bus. After leaving Walpole, you will soon leave the magnificent forests behind, but still travel inland out of sight of the sea. At **Nornalup**, just east of Walpole, you will start to notice traces of an old railway once again. This is not the same line as that which we saw at Pemberton and Northcliffe. This is a line which used to run from Albany. The two railways were never joined, and Nornalup was as far west as this line ever reached. Now it has suffered the fate of so many other lines in Australia, and passed almost into oblivion. Parts of the former railway are now used as a walking track.

It is also possible to reach Denmark from Perth by taking a bus to Albany and then a further bus from Albany to Denmark. However, although travelling time is similar by this route, it requires an overnight stop in Albany.

The Denmark River was named by Thomas Wilson, the first European to explore the area, in 1829, after a friend, the English naval surgeon, Dr. Alexander Denmark. Perhaps disappointingly, there is no direct connexion with the country of Denmark. The town of Denmark did not spring up until much later, in 1895, and was then established as a timber town, felling and processing karri. However, such an industry is unsustainable, and the wood was consumed at such speed that it lasted barely ten years.

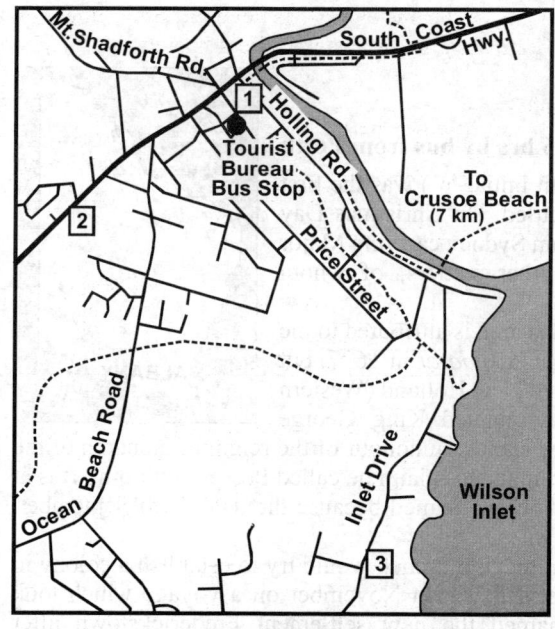

DENMARK
Numerals indicate accommodation

Agriculture followed, with the production of fruit, vegetables, beef and dairy produce, as well as fishing. More recently, two new industries have developed: wine production and tourism. Following the success of the Margaret River area in this field, **Mt. Barker**, north of Albany, showed that it too could produce good quality wine, and this success has spread to nearby towns. Denmark is only 55 kilometres from Mt. Barker.

As for the other new industry, tourism, Denmark too is situated on an inlet from the sea, Wilson Inlet, and so offers quiet beaches and calm water sports. There are various walks available by the coast or through the forests, including the Bibbulmun Track, which passes through the edge of

WESTERN AUSTRALIA

the town on its last leg to Albany. Also, the *Tree Top Walk*, although much closer to Walpole, is actually situated within the shire of Denmark.

Seven kilometres east of Denmark is **Rudgyard Ostrich Farm**, open to visitors. There are also various **cruises** on the Denmark River and on Wilson Inlet.

ACCOMMODATION
(i) Hotel Accommodation in Denmark

Name	Stars	No. on Map	Telephone No.	Address	Lowest Price (Double/Twin)
Denmark Tavern Units	3	2	08-9848-1044	Lot 623, South Coast Hwy.	$85
Waterfront Motel		3	08-9848-1147	63 Inlet Drive	$80
Denmark Unit Hotel		1	08-9848-2206	Holling Road	$45

(ii) Backpackers Hostel in Denmark

Name	Group	No. on Map	Telephone No.	Address	Lowest Price (Dormitory)
Waterfront		3	08-9848-1147	63 Inlet Drive	$19

MOVING ON
Bus Services from Denmark

Destination	Operator	Via	Distance (km)	Fare	Journey Time	Frequency
Perth	W.A.G.R.		527	$51.60	7¾ - 8¾ hrs	1/day
		Bunbury	347	$35.85	5 - 5½ hrs	1/day
Albany	W.A.G.R.		50	$7	45 mins	8/week

ALBANY
Population 30,000

6 hrs by bus from Perth

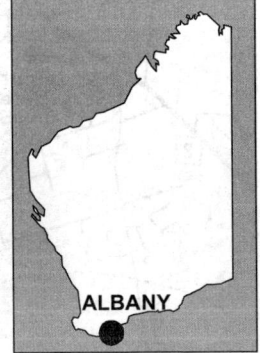

Albany (pronounced with a short initial 'a') was the first place in Western Australia to be settled. On Christmas Day 1826, the brig *Amity* arrived here from Sydney carrying Major Edmund Lockyer and forty-four other settlers, of whom twenty-three were convicts.

The first European sighting of this area is attributed to the Dutchman Peter Nuyts in the *Golden Zeepaardt* in 1627, but it was George Vancouver who claimed New Holland (Western Australia) for Britain in 1791, and named King George Sound, the bay in which Albany now stands, in honour of the reigning monarch of the time. The point where he landed and made his claim he called Possession Point. It is at the entrance to Princess Royal Harbour, so named because the date, 29th September, was the birthday of the Princess Royal.

By 1826, the British were afraid that the French would try to establish a colony in this area, and so Major Lockyer set sail on 9th November on a voyage which took seven weeks from Sydney. He named the new settlement Frederickstown after Frederick Augustus, Duke of York and Albany, the second son of King George III. In 1831, the name was changed to Albany.

ALBANY

Albany achieved the status of a city in 1998.

There used to be a night train from Perth to Albany, but it disappeared long ago now. Instead, W.A.G.R. operates buses to Albany about three times a day, and by four different routes (see map below). The fastest services take approximately six hours. There is also a service to and from Esperance, with a change of vehicle *en route*, twice a week.

Since Albany occupies such an important place in Western Australian history, and was, perhaps, unfortunate not to have become the capital of the state, there is a great deal to see here. Let us undertake a walking tour to see some of the city's history.

Walking Tour

This tour covers approximately five kilometres and will take about two hours, or longer if you wish to look inside some of the places of interest. A four-kilometre extension is possible if you find that you still have energy left at the end of the initial walk.

Conspicuously placed on the foreshore is a replica of the brig *Amity* which brought the first settlers to Western Australia in 1826. It seems an appropriate place to begin.

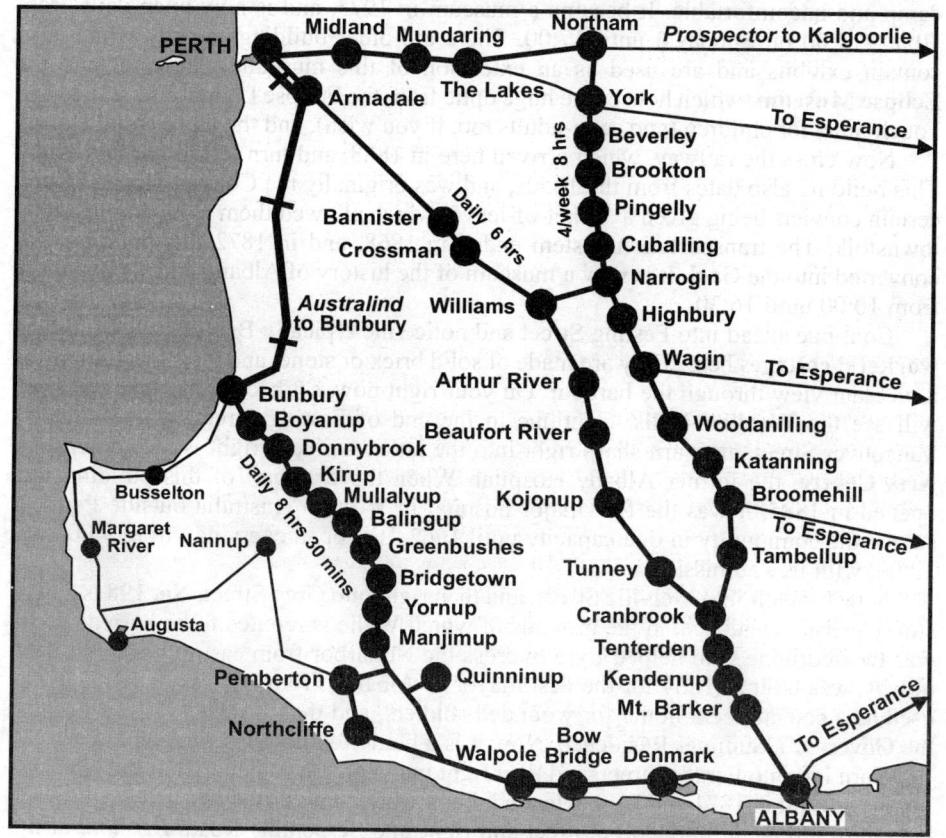

W.A.G.R. SERVICES FROM PERTH TO ALBANY
Showing connexions with other W.A.G.R. routes

WESTERN AUSTRALIA

The original *Amity* was built in Canada in 1816, was registered at 142 tons, and started life as an Atlantic trader for seven years. She was purchased in 1823 by a family of farmers in Scotland and was sent to Sydney in 1824 carrying migrants. Upon arrival, after a six-month voyage via South America, she was sold to the colonial government in Sydney. She spent the rest of her service in Australia, being wrecked, without loss of life, in the Bass Strait on an uncharted sandbank off the coast of Tasmania in 1845. A brig was a general workhorse and, as can be seen, not a particularly large vessel. For the seven week voyage here, this ship would have had to contain approximately 75 crew and passengers, plus sheep, pigs, cattle and stores. Where it stands now would have been part of the harbour at the time, the land having been reclaimed for the purpose of constructing the road which runs along the waterfront. The *Amity* replica was built in 1975 to 1976 and is now open daily from 9:00 (14:00 on Sundays) until 17:00. Admission costs $3.

On leaving the *Amity*, turn right and cross to the **Residency Museum**. This building was originally constructed in the 1850s as the Commissariat and store. It became the Government Residency in 1873 and was used for that purpose until 1953, when the magistrate to whom it was assigned moved out, complaining that it was cold, damp and uncomfortable. It became a museum in 1975, and is now open daily from 10:00 (14:00 on Sundays) until 17:00. There are other buildings nearby which also contain exhibits and are used as an extension of this museum. These include the **Eclipse Museum**, which houses the huge optic from the Eclipse Lighthouse, a 'See and Touch' area for children (and semi-adults too, if you wish), and the Old School House.

Now cross the railway, which arrived here in 1888, and turn left to the **Old Gaol**. This building also dates from the 1850s, and was originally the Convict-Hiring Depot, certain convicts being given a 'ticket-of-leave' which allowed them to be employed by townsfolk. The transportation system ended in 1868, and in 1872 this building was converted into the Gaol. It is now a museum of the history of Albany and is open daily from 10:00 until 16:30.

Continue ahead into Festing Street and notice the typically British style of the old **workers' cottages** here. They are made of solid brick or stone, and their location offers a pleasant view through the harbour. On your right now, set back from the street, you will see the **Woollen Mills**. Continue to the end of Festing Street, where it meets Vancouver Street, and turn sharp right into the latter. On your right is the **Vancouver Arts Centre**, the former Albany Hospital. When the first part of this building was opened in 1885, it was the first major hospital in Western Australia outside Perth. It served the community in that capacity until 1962. It is open every day from 9:00 until 22:00, with free admission.

Now turn left into Melville Street, and then right into Grey Street. **No. 198** is a two-storey private residence, in the grounds of which Wylie is reputed to be buried. Wylie was the aborigine who helped Eyre to cross the Nullarbor from east to west. **No. 184**, nearby, was built in 1884 for the first mayor of Albany. From 1915 until 1917, it was used as a convalescent home for wounded soldiers, and then, in the 1920s, it became the Governor's Summer Residence. Now it is a home for slow-learning children.

Turn left into Parade Street, and then right into Hotchin Avenue. Melville House at **no. 5** was built in 1871 and later extended. For a while, it was used as a private hospital. Now turn left again into Collie Street and right into Serpentine Road. *Pyrmont* at **no. 192** was built in 1858 as a private residence, but later used as a school. At one time it had a garden where peacocks were kept.

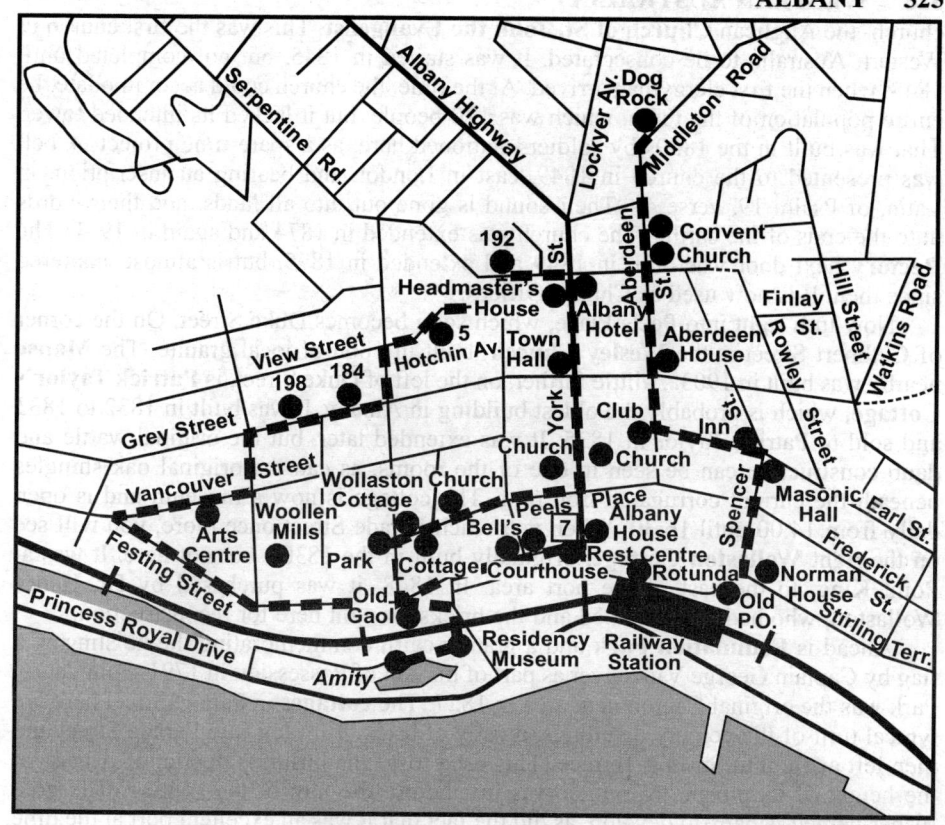

ALBANY CITY CENTRE
Dashed line shows Walking Tour

Turn right now into **York Street**. This has become the principal street of Albany, replacing Stirling Terrace in the 1950s as the main shopping street. However, in the 1980s, two supermarkets were opened just north of here, which affected trade in this area. York Street is where the most impressive buildings of Albany are situated, as we shall see on our way down the hill. On your left, the **Albany Hotel** dates from 1845, but surrounding buildings are typical of country town architecture of the 1940s and 1950s. On your right is the **Old State School** and the **Headmaster's House**. The school was built in 1896 to replace an earlier building, using British-style brickwork. The Headmaster's House, however, dates from 1880, is built of local granite and ironstone, and has impressive cast-iron filigree and railings on the balcony. Originally it also had an excellent view of the harbour.

Continuing down York Street, you will come to the **Town Hall** on the right. This building, constructed of local granite, took two years to build, cost a whole year's rates, and was opened in 1888. It was recently converted into a theatre and is open on weekdays from 10:00 until 15:00.

A little further down the street on the opposite side is the **Scots Presbyterian Church**, now known as the Scots Uniting Church. Since it is between two shops, it seems rather out of place in this particular location. On the right of the street is another church, the Anglican **Church of St. John the Evangelist**. This was the first church in Western Australia to be consecrated. It was started in 1845, but not completed until 1848, when the first clergyman arrived. At the time, the church could accommodate the entire population of the town, which was 170 people, but it lacked its intended tower. That was built in the 1850s by soldiers stationed here, as a spare-time project. A bell was presented to the church in 1849, cast in London and bearing an inscription, in Latin, of Psalm 19, verse 4, "Their sound is gone out into all lands, and their words unto the ends of the earth." The church was extended in 1874 and again in 1961. The **Rectory** next door was built in 1849 and extended in 1875, but is almost unaltered since then. It is now used as Church Offices.

Now turn right into Peels Place, which soon becomes Duke Street. On the corner of Cuthbert Street is the **Wesley Church**, built in 1863 of local granite. The **Manse** nearby was built in 1903. A little further, on the left of Duke Street, is **Patrick Taylor's Cottage**, which is probably the oldest building in Albany. It was built in 1832 to 1833 and sold to Patrick Taylor in 1835. It was extended later, but the original wattle and daub construction can be seen in one of the rooms, as can the original oak shingles beneath the current corrugated iron roof. The cottage is now a museum and is open daily from 14:00 until 16:30. When you reach Parade Street once more, you will see on the right **Wollaston Cottage**, originally built in the 1830s, but not here. It was at Point King, to the east of the port area. In 1848, it was purchased by Dr. Henry Wollaston, who had it dismantled and the bricks brought here for reconstruction.

Ahead is **Foundation Park** and a granite cairn commemorating the hoisting of a flag by Captain George Vancouver as part of his Act of Possession in 1791. Foundation Park was the original Cantonment area in 1827. The **cottages** in Parade Street here are typical turn-of-the-century dwellings, mostly of brick. Turn left into Parade Street and then left again into Stirling Terrace. This used to be the business district of Albany at the height of its prosperity, which was just before the turn of the century. The gold rushes helped Albany to develop, as did the fact that it was an excellent port at the time when Fremantle, prior to its redevelopment, was a dangerous one. That situation changed when Fremantle was redesigned by C.Y. O'Connor, and the gold started to run out in the Goldfields area. In 1900, the population of Albany was 4,000, but by 1906 it had been reduced to 2,000. However, then agriculture started to develop, and Albany gradually recovered. Nevertheless, **Stirling Terrace** has not changed much since a century ago. None of the buildings from the Courthouse up to Spencer Street was constructed after 1915, and most are unaltered since the turn of the century.

The **Courthouse**, on the corner of Collie Street, was built in 1895-1896, the stonework being undertaken locally. **Bell's Store** was constructed in 1898, with additions in 1905. The **London Hotel** is on the site of the original Chusan Hotel, constructed of wood in 1855. The present hotel dates from 1909 and features a beautiful hand-carved jarrah staircase within. Rooms are available here at modest rates, and dormitory accommodation for backpackers is also available. On the corner of York Street is **Albany House**, constructed in 1878 for the Union Bank. The former manager's residence upstairs has high quality cast-iron latticework on its rear verandah. Many other buildings in Stirling Terrace once had similar verandahs.

Across the road, on the harbour side of the street, is an interesting little building. This is the **Women's Rest Centre**. It started its life in 1908 as a cabman's shelter for the drivers of the horsedrawn cabs which used to operate from here at the turn of the century. In 1926, funds were raised by public appeal to expand the building so that it included a women's retiring room which could be used by nursing mothers visiting town or changing trains at the railway station nearby. In 1976, it was extended again, but there is still a shelter for cab drivers included. Between the Women's Rest Centre and the fountain are the foundations of the original **public weighbridge** here.

Continue along Stirling Terrace and see on your left the **Empire Buildings** (1912), originally used as a theatre, but now a nightclub, the **Western Australian Bank** (1885, replacing the previous bank built in 1838) and **Drew Robinson and Co.** (1885-1914), now Stirling's. Then comes a gap, used as a car park. This was the Freemasons Hotel, which had 62 rooms, but was demolished in 1972 for a project which never came to fruition. **108 Stirling Terrace** dates from 1900. **106** is from 1915, **100-102** from 1892 and **96-98** from 1915. The **National Bank** was built in 1866 and extended in 1870, and remained in use as a bank until the 1980s. What is now **Dylan's Restaurant** was built in the 1880s. The **White Star Hotel** was originally the White Hart, and was reconstructed in 1911. The **Royal George Hotel** started life as Bailey's Railway Hotel, established in 1885, but the present building dates from 1910. **Edinburgh House** and **Glasgow House** were built in 1885, but the ground floor of Glasgow House was reconstructed in the 1920s. The **Argyle Buildings**, on the corner of Spencer Street, date from the 1890s.

On the other side of the street is the **Rotunda**, built in 1897 to commemorate the Diamond Jubilee of Queen Victoria. From here you can look down on the **Railway Station** and the **gardens** in front of it. The handsome wooden Railway Station was completed in 1885 and sits there just waiting for the next train to arrive. Unfortunately, though, there are no passenger trains. The station now serves as a booking office for the railway buses, which arrive and leave from here, and as the **Tourist Bureau**. To the left as you look at the station is the old **Post Office**, this building too no longer used for its intended purpose. It was built in 1869, but modified considerably in 1895. It is a massive and imposing building which became also a Telegraph Office in 1872, when it was linked with Perth. In 1875, the first pole was erected here in the link with the eastern part of Australia. This building is now a Telecommunications Museum open daily from 14:00 until 16:00.

Walk a little further along Stirling Terrace and come to **Norman House**, built in 1852. It has had in its time various names and various uses, including being a hostel for high school students. Currently, it is owned by the Methodist Church. It is thought that it may have been built by labourers brought from India, and also that it may have been built on the site of, and incorporate parts of, a previous building dating from 1834. If so, this is where the Government Resident, Dr. Alexander Collie, died in 1835. Turn round and return to Spencer Street and then walk north up Spencer Street for a short way. You will see the **Masonic Hall** on the corner of Earl Street. This tall, classical building dates from 1903 and is on the site of the first Masonic Lodge in Western Australia.

On the left on the corner of Earl Street is the **Earl of Spencer Inn**. There has been a building here since 1865. It became the Spencer Inn in 1874, and obtained a beer and wines licence in 1884, which it lost in 1925 on the grounds of its having insufficient accommodation. Then it became a shop, but it was owned by the Nesbitt family throughout from 1874 until 1978. In 1988, it was renovated and became the Earl of Spencer Inn.

Turn left into Earl Street, and then right into Aberdeen Street. On your left is the **Albany Gentlemen's Club**, built as a private residence in 1886, but used by the

Albany Club since 1894. On the corner of Grey Street is the former **Salvation Army Hall**, built in 1911 and now the Albany Design Centre. Then **Aberdeen House** was originally the Oddfellows' Hall and dates from 1891. On the corner of Serpentine Road is **St. Joseph's Catholic Church**, started in 1877. The Bell Tower is separate and contains a bell made in France and installed here in 1895. **St. Joseph's Convent** is just a little further up Aberdeen Street. It was built in 1881 and closed in 1976. After suffering considerable damage from Cyclone Alby in 1978, it was restored and is used as a Community Centre.

Continue a little further into Middleton Road, almost straight ahead, and here you will find one of the most unusual features of Albany, **Dog Rock**. Viewed from this side, the rock looks exactly like the head of a dog, and it even has a collar. Viewed from the other side, however, it looks like a rock. When you want to take your photograph, you are almost sure to find that the sun is on the other side.

Our walk ends here. To return to the city centre, retrace your steps briefly along Middleton Road, turn right then left, and you are at the top of York Street.

However, if you have energy for more, here is a possible extension, which will take a further ninety minutes and cover another four kilometres. Return along Aberdeen Street to Serpentine Road, into which turn left. At the end of the street, you will find a lane on the right next to a timber arch. This leads through to Rowley Street. Walk down Rowley Street, lined with turn-of-the-century cottages, until you reach Finlay Street on your left. Take this street and then turn right into Hill Street. Where Hill Street meets Watkins Road, a track leads off and up **Mount Clarence**. Take this, bearing right around the hill. You will get a good view from here of the whole of Albany. On the way, you will pass the Desert Mounted Corps **War Memorial** which originally stood in Port Said in Egypt. It was desecrated during the Suez Crisis of 1956 and shipped back to Australia. It could not be properly repaired, so a new statue was made, with two casts. One is in Canberra. The other stands here, since this is the point from which the Anzacs sailed for Gallipoli, and, for very many of them, this was their last glimpse of Australia.

Descend on the far side of Clarence Hill into King Street, and walk through to **Middleton Beach** (King Street - left - Hay Street - right - Hare Street - left - Wittenoom Street - right - Wylie Crescent - left into town centre). Middleton Beach is one of Albany's great attractions, and here you will find several high-class hotels. The beach is white and stretches away round the bay for nearly five kilometres. From Middleton Beach, you can take a local bus no. 301 back to the centre of Albany. Services operate at 9:05, 11:20, 13:15 and 15:10. If you really feel energetic, there is the coastal Marine Drive Scenic Path along which you can walk back. That would be a further four kilometres and would take an hour or a little more.

There is plenty more to be seen round Albany which has not been covered by our walk. **Mt. Adelaide** is about three kilometres from the town centre and is the site of the **Princess Royal Fortress**, commissioned in 1893 to protect this strategically important port against the possibility of enemy attack. Two gun batteries were concealed in the hillside and a small permanent garrison was stationed here. All of this was upgraded during the Second World War, when Albany became a base for the American Asiatic Submarine Squadron. Although the headquarters was at Fremantle, it was thought that Fremantle might be attacked by the Japanese, so the submarine mother ship was based at Albany. There is a memorial here to the United States Submariners, the only such memorial in Australia.

Whaleworld is at the site of the former Whaling Station, which was Australia's last commercial whaling operation. When the author first visited here, it was still in use for that purpose, and had the pungent odour of whaling about it. It was also free in those days. ***Whaleworld*** is twenty kilometres from the city centre, so visitors will have some difficulty in reaching there, except with a local tour. It is open from 10:00 until 16:00, with hourly tours, on the hour. Admission costs $12.

Possession Point, where Vancouver landed in 1791 and made his claim, is not so far away from here. Nor is some of the area's most impressive coastal scenery, with **blowholes**, a **natural bridge** and **The Gap**, a sheer drop of 24 metres to the sea below.

In the harbour, the decommissioned destroyer ***H.M.A.S. Perth*** has recently been scuttled to serve as a wreck for divers.

Local bus services are operated by Love's and leave from Peels Place. However, the only route likely to be of interest to visitors is that to Middleton Beach and on to **Emu Point**, where there are a beach, a marina and accommodation. Service 301 departs at 8:45, 11:00, 13:05 and 14:50 on weekdays, and at 10:30 and 12:10 on Saturdays. There is no service on Sundays. The 13:05 and the Saturday buses go only as far as Middleton Beach. Return journeys depart from Emu Point at 8:58, 11:13 and 15:03 on weekdays. They depart from Middleton Beach at 9:05, 11:20, 13:15 and 15:10 on weekdays, and at 10:40 and 12:20 on Saturdays.

This is not all, but it is quite sufficient to keep the reader busy for a couple of days, and, if more is needed, the Tourist Bureau is in the Railway Station, with a special post box to put a commemorative cancellation on your postcards, and with the staff just waiting for the next train to arrive.

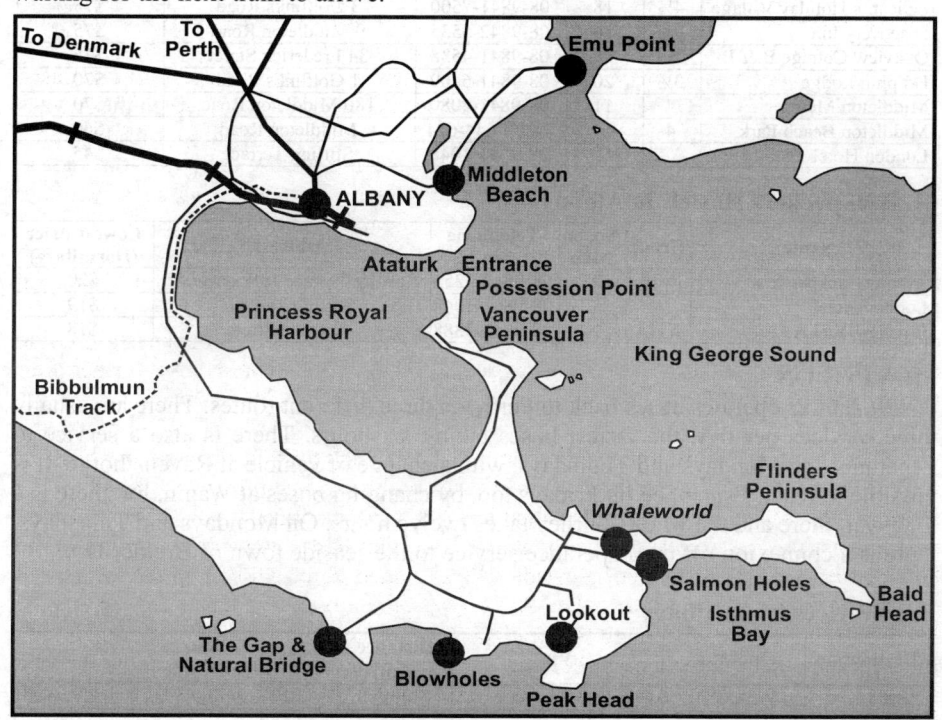

ALBANY AND VICINITY

530 WESTERN AUSTRALIA
BOOKSHOPS
The Singing Tree   183 York Street

ACCOMMODATION

Being one of Western Australia's most popular holiday destinations, Albany has a good range of accommodation available. That listed is all close to the city centre or to Middleton Beach. There are three backpackers hostels, all close to the centre of the city.

(i) Hotel Accommodation in Albany

Name	Stars	No. on Map	Telephone No.	Address	Lowest Price (Double/Twin)
Castlereagh	4½	17	1-800-622-295	Flinders Parade	$190
Esplanade Hotel	4½	19	1-800-678-757	Adelaide Cres / Flinders Pde	$170
Balneaire Seaside Resort	4	21	1-800-625-877	27 Adelaide Crescent	$125
Frederickstown Motel	4	8	1-800-808-544	Frederick & Spencer Streets	$125
Flag Travel Inn	4	5	1-800-355-106	191 Albany Highway	$125
Quality Inn Albany	3½	1	08-9841-1177	369 Albany Highway	$110
Park Avenue Units	4	15	08-9842-5242	13 Golflinks Road	$105
International Motel	3½	3	1-800-090-690	270 Albany Highway	$105
Terrace Cottage		13	08-9842-9901	36 Marine Terrace	$100
Clarence House B & B		12	08-9841-5409	110 Hare Street	$100
Dog Rock Motel	3½	6	1-800-017-024	303 Middleton Road	$95
Middleton Cottage		10	08-9841-1492	186 Middleton Road	$90
Ace Motor Inn		2	1-800-625-900	314 Albany Highway	$90
Amity Motor Inn		4	08-9841-2200	234 Albany Highway	$85
Pelican's Holiday Village	4½	18	08-9841-7500	3 Golflinks Road	$75
Discovery Inn		16	08-9842-5535	9 Middleton Road	$75
Oakview Cottage B & B		9	08-9841-4538	34 Frederick Street	$75
Dolphin Lodge	3½	20	08-9841-6600	1 Golflinks Road	$70
Middleton Mews	4	11	08-9841-4080	180 Middleton Road	$70
Middleton Beach Park	4	14	1-800-644-674	Middleton Road	$60
London Hotel		7	08-9841-1048	Stirling Terrace	$45

(ii) Backpackers Hostels in Albany

Name	Group	No. on Map	Telephone No.	Address	Lowest Price (Dormitory)
Albany Backpackers	VIP	23	08-9842-5255	Stirling Terrace & Spencer St.	$20
London Hotel		7	08-9841-1048	Stirling Terrace	$19
Bayview Y.H.A.	YHA	22	08-9842-3388	49 Duke Street	$18

MOVING ON

W.A.G.R. operates buses back to Perth via three different routes. There are usually three services per day, the fastest buses taking six hours. There is also a service to Esperance, on Mondays and Thursdays, with a change of vehicle at Ravensthorpe. It is possible to reach Esperance on Fridays too, by changing buses at Wagin, but there is a long wait there and the whole journey takes twelve hours. On Mondays and Thursdays, there is a connexion off the Esperance service to the seaside town of Bremer Bay.

Bus Services from Albany

Destination	Operator	Via	Distance (km)	Fare	Journey Time	Frequency
Perth	W.A.G.R.		409	$43.40	6 - 9½ hrs	20/week
		Bunbury	397	$40.65	5¾ - 6½ hrs	1/day
Esperance	W.A.G.R.		479	$48	6½ hrs	2/week

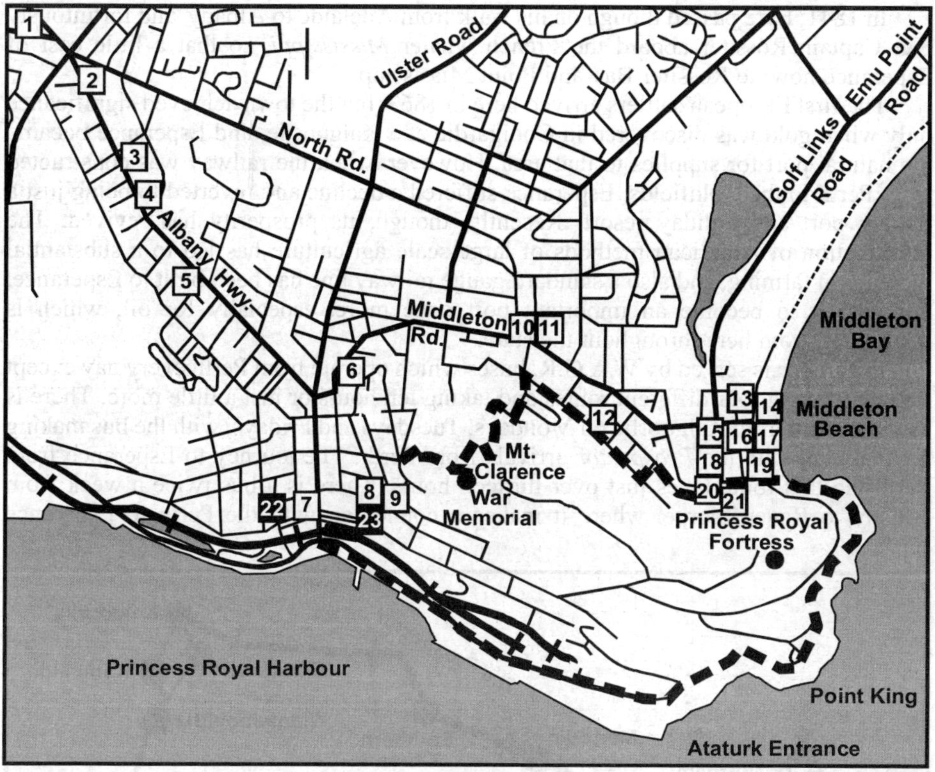

ALBANY

ALBANY
Dashed line shows Extensions of Walking Tour
Black numerals in white boxes indicate hotel accommodation
White numerals in black boxes indicate backpackers hostels

ESPERANCE
Population 9,000

10 hrs by bus from Perth

Esperance lies in the farthest south-eastern corner of habitable Western Australia, 720 kilometres from Perth. In 1792, two French frigates, engaged in mapping the coast, put into the bay here to shelter from a storm. The first ship was named *L'Esperance* and the second was the *Recherche*. As a result, the bay was named Esperance Bay and the islands nearby became known as the Recherche Archipelago.

Matthew Flinders also visited, when he too was engaged in mapping the coast. In 1802 he anchored in Lucky Bay, nearby, and he was responsible for the naming of several landmarks.

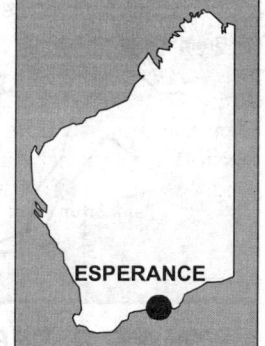

In 1841, Eyre passed though on his walk from Adelaide to Albany, and fortuitously met Captain Rossiter aboard the French whaler *Mississippi*, so that a little east of Esperance now lie Rossiter Bay and Point Mississippi.

The first European settlers arrived here in 1863, but the town achieved significance only when gold was discovered in Coolgardie and Kalgoorlie, and Esperance became the natural port for supplies to that area. However, when the railway was constructed from Perth to the Goldfields, Esperance suffered a decline and reverted to being just a fishing port and holiday resort. Recently, though, its prosperity has revived. The introduction of American methods of large-scale agriculture has led to a substantial increase in farming, and also a standard gauge railway line has been built to Esperance, allowing it to become an important port once more, especially for oil, which is distributed from here throughout the state.

Esperance is served by W.A.G.R. buses which operate from Perth every day except Saturday, using four different routes and taking ten hours or just a little more. There is also a service from Kalgoorlie on Mondays, Tuesdays and Fridays, with the bus making a connexion with the *Prospector* arrivals from Perth. The journey to Esperance from Perth via that route takes just over thirteen hours. There is a bus twice a week from Albany to Ravensthorpe, where it makes a connexion with the Perth to Esperance service.

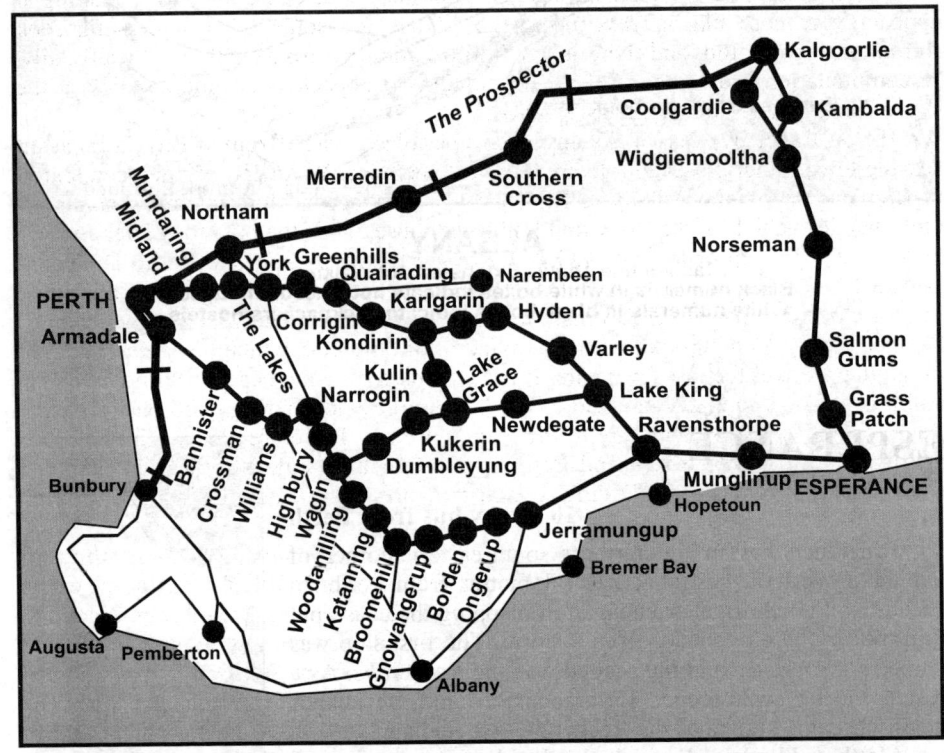

W.A.G.R. SERVICES FROM PERTH TO ESPERANCE
Showing connexions with other W.A.G.R. routes

ESPERANCE

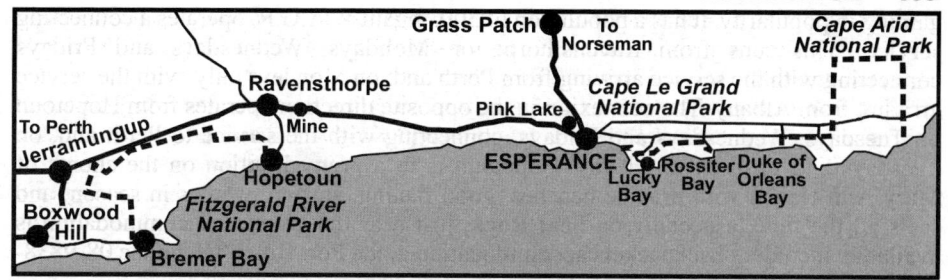

COASTLINE AROUND ESPERANCE

On the way to Esperance, there are sights to be observed, or places at which to stay, but these depend, of course, on the route followed. **Wave Rock** is an unusual formation, looking, as its name implies, just like a breaking wave. It is situated four kilometres from the small town of **Hyden**, on a route served by the bus from Perth on Tuesdays only, so you will be there for a week if planning to continue to Esperance. The bus back to Perth passes through on Thursdays. The Rock itself is believed to be 2,700 million years old. It is 110 metres long and fifteen metres high, made of weathered granite. It has vertical striations of rusty red, ochre and grey, making it appear even more like a wave in motion. There are some other interesting rock formations nearby too, and there is a Wildlife Park open from 9:00 until 17:30 daily. Accommodation is available in Hyden, including backpackers accommodation at the Wave Rock Resort (telephone 08-9550-5022).

If you travel by way of Albany, it is possible to visit **Bremer Bay**, a pleasant seaside town rather closer to Albany than to Esperance. W.A.G.R. offers a connexion to Bremer Bay off the Albany to Ravensthorpe service on Mondays and Thursdays. One changes vehicle at the Boxwood Hill Roadhouse, when the bus stops after an hour and a half for a cup of tea. (W.A.G.R. buses get thirsty quite often.) From Boxwood Hill to Bremer Bay takes 45 minutes. If you are travelling in the opposite direction, there are connexions off the Ravensthorpe to Albany service on Tuesdays and Fridays. Bremer Bay is a small town, with a population of only 300, which has gained greatly in popularity over the last few years. It has expanses of white beaches with few users, and it is adjacent to the **Fitzgerald River National Park**, offering good bushwalking. Tours operate from Bremer Bay to the National Park. There are also surfing beaches nearby at **Native Dog Beach** and **Peppermint Beach**. **Whale-watching** is available from July to November. Diving conditions are good and fishing is popular. Accommodation is available.

All bus services to Esperance from Perth or Albany will pass through **Ravensthorpe**, another small town, with a population of only 500. Ravensthorpe exists because gold was discovered near here at the turn of the century. Minerals continued to be important to the town, because, although the gold soon ran out, copper was found and was to be mined for many years, until the 1970s. Then, after a period of mining inactivity, a huge new open-cut project was started recently, mining nickel. It can be seen from the bus about ten minutes after leaving Ravensthorpe on the way to Esperance. It claims to be one of the largest open-cut nickel mining operations in the world. Accommodation is available in Ravensthorpe, including backpackers accommodation at the Palace Hotel (telephone 08-9838-1005).

Fifty kilometres south of Ravensthorpe is **Hopetoun**, another small seaside town gaining in popularity. It has a population of 300. Again W.A.G.R. operates a connecting service. This runs from Ravensthorpe on Mondays, Wednesdays and Fridays connecting with the service arriving from Perth and, on Mondays only, with the service arriving from Albany. The connexion in the opposite direction operates from Hopetoun on Tuesdays, Wednesdays and Fridays, connecting with the service to Perth and, on Tuesdays and Fridays, to Albany. Hopetoun is in a pretty location on the shores of Mary Ann Haven with pristine beaches, good fishing, surfing, whales in season, and seals all the time, especially on **Seal Rock**, just near the groyne. Accommodation is available, including backpackers accommodation at the Port Hotel (telephone 08-9838-3053).

Now, as for Esperance itself, it too is known for its beaches. There are beaches in the town, but they get better as one moves a little further east. Within walking distance are some beautiful white sandy areas. The town lies on a pretty bay, with the islands of the Recherche Archipelago visible on the horizon. Esperance, however, is not just a town for tourism. This is a busy port and there is also an **oil refinery** and storage facility, open for inspection (free, but only once a week).

Once the railway line from Kalgoorlie to Perth had been converted to standard gauge in 1969, Esperance was in danger of becoming isolated from the state rail system, so in 1974 the line from Kalgoorlie to here was converted to standard gauge also, and now Esperance is one of the few places in the state connected directly with the rest of Australia by rail. Considering the high standard of the line to here and the fact that it is in constant use for the conveyance of oil, it seems a great pity that a passenger rail service cannot be operated, perhaps by taking one car from the *Prospector* upon its arrival in Kalgoorlie from Perth and continuing that car to Esperance. Unfortunately, though, the service to Esperance from Kalgoorlie is by a bus, which runs parallel to the railway track for almost the whole journey.

Although Esperance has a population of only 9,000, it has facilities well in excess of those which might be expected, since the town is the centre for a wide agricultural area. There is a range of accommodation, including three backpackers hostels, one of them almost on the beach.

Until recently, Esperance seemed like the end of the road, the last habitation in the south-east. Recently, though, that has changed and, although there is no public transport, one can take a tour to the nearby Cape Le Grand National Park which offers beautiful coastal scenery, or on to the Cape Arid National Park.

Cape Le Grand lies 56 kilometres east of Esperance. It has some outstanding scenery, as well as excellent beaches. There are coastal walking tracks, and **Frenchman's Peak**, which is inland, offers fine views of the islands. The kangaroos at **Lucky Bay** are known for welcoming visitors, especially those who come bearing edible gifts. There are camping facilities available in two places within the park. At the far end of the Park, but outside its boundaries, lies the pretty **Duke of Orleans Bay**, where there are more camping facilities and a caravan park. Duke of Orleans Bay is 88 kilometres from Esperance.

Cape Arid National Park lies 120 kilometres east of Esperance and can be reached by a good road. It has enjoyable walks, more fine views, wildflowers in season, and two camping areas, but no power or showers.

Within the town of Esperance is the **Historical Village and Municipal Museum**. This is in the centre of the town on the site of the old narrow gauge Railway Station. It includes an art gallery, various craft shops, historical buildings and exhibits relating to the *Skylab* Spacecraft, pieces of which survived the ordeal of re-entry into the earth's atmosphere and reached earth near Balladonia, north-east of here. The Museum is open daily from 13:30 until 16:30. Near the south of the Esplanade is the grave of **Tommy Windich**, the aborigine who accompanied Forrest on his exploratory journeys.

The **Pink Lake** lies ten kilometres to the north-west of Esperance. It is so named, reasonably enough, because it is pink. The colour is caused by minerals in the soil, the intensity of the hue depending upon the amount of water in the lake and the time for which it has been there absorbing the minerals.

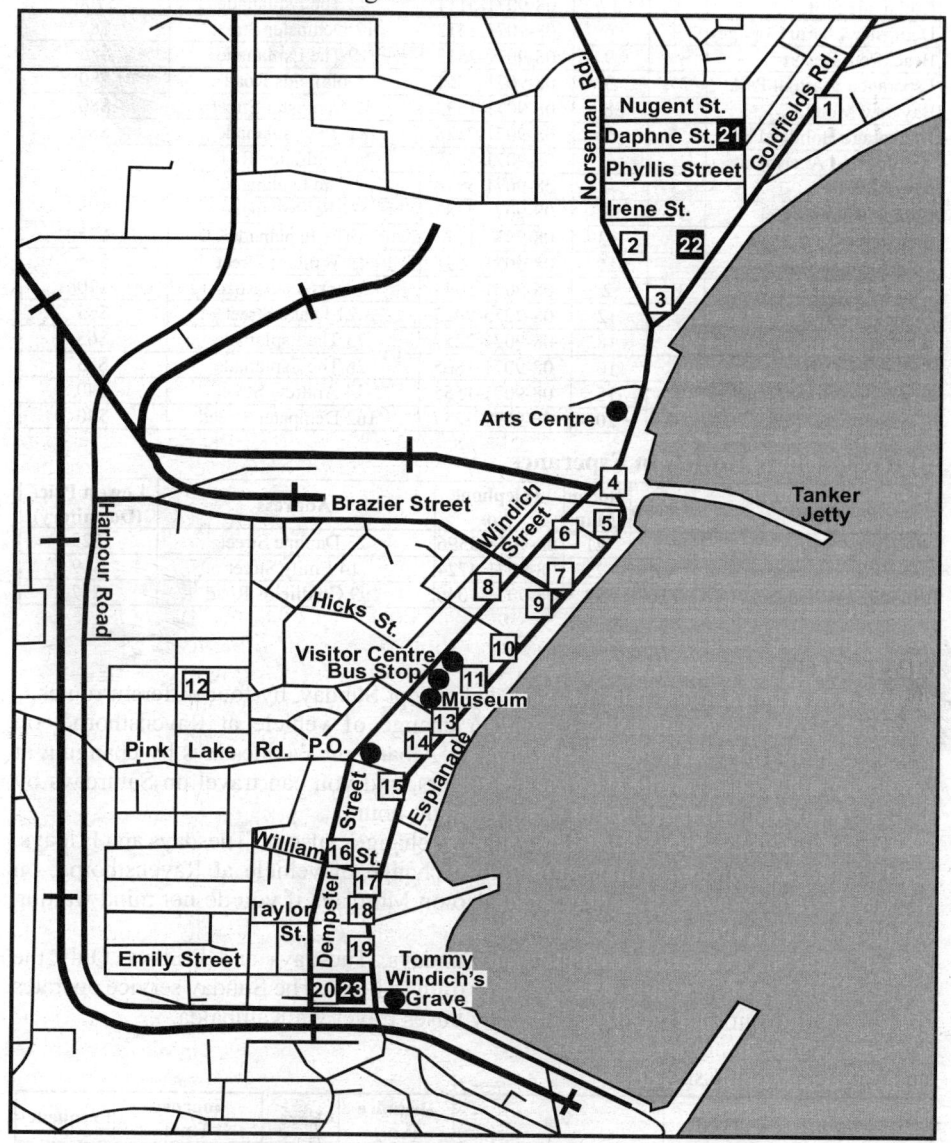

ESPERANCE
Black numerals in white boxes indicate hotel accommodation
White numerals in black boxes indicate backpackers hostels

536 WESTERN AUSTRALIA
ACCOMMODATION
(i) Hotel Accommodation in Esperance

Name	Stars	No. on Map	Telephone No.	Address	Lowest Price (Double/Twin)
Hospitality Inn	3½	14	08-9071-1999	The Esplanade	$115
Bay of Isles Motel	4	11	1-800-095563	32 The Esplanade	$105
Esperance Seaside Apts.	4½	7	08-9072-0044	14 The Esplanade	$100
Esplanade Suite		17	08-9071-5111	72 The Esplanade	$100
Dempster Charm Cottage	4	6	08-9071-1413	12 Dempster Street	$85
Beachfront Resort	3½	9	08-9071-2513	19 The Esplanade	$85
Esperance Seafront Park	3½	3	08-9071-1251	Goldfields Road	$80
Bayview Motel		8	08-9071-1533	31 Dempster Street	$80
Anchorage Holiday Units	4	19	08-9071-7338	81 The Esplanade	$80
Archipelago Apartments		1	08-9071-7100	24 Goldfields Road	$75
Jetty Motel	3	4	08-9071-5978	1 The Esplanade	$75
Captain Huon Motel	3½	5	08-9071-2383	5 The Esplanade	$75
Pier Hotel		13	08-9071-1777	The Esplanade	$75
Old Hospital Motel		16	08-9071-3587	1a William Street	$75
Doo Drop Inn B & B	3½	2	08-9071-5043	3 Norseman Road	$70
Bethel House		12	08-9075-9025	21 Leake Street	$65
All Seasons Holiday Units		18	08-9071-2257	73 The Esplanade	$65
Esperance Cottages		10	08-9071-1805	26 The Esplanade	$55
Esperance Motor Hotel		15	08-9071-1555	14 Andrew Street	$40
Esperance Bay Park	4	20	08-9071-2237	162 Dempster Street	$40

(ii) Backpackers Hostels in Esperance

Name	Group	No. on Map	Telephone No.	Address	Lowest Price (Dormitory)
Shoestring Stays		21	08-9071-3396	23 Daphne Street	$25
Esperance Backpackers	VIP	23	08-9071-4524	14 Emily Street	$19
Blue Waters Lodge	YHA	22	08-9071-1040	299 Goldfields Road	$17

MOVING ON

W.A.G.R. runs buses to Perth every day except Sunday, by four different routes.

There are services to Albany, with a change of vehicle at Ravensthorpe, on Tuesdays and Fridays. You can also travel to Albany on Wednesdays by changing at Wagin, but the journey will take over ten hours, and you can travel on Saturdays by changing at Broomehill. This journey takes eight hours.

There are services to Bremer Bay, with two changes, also on Tuesdays and Fridays.

There are services to Hopetoun, with a change of vehicle at Ravensthorpe, on Tuesdays, Wednesdays and Fridays, and also on Mondays if you do not mind waiting for five and a half hours in Ravensthorpe.

There are services to Kalgoorlie on Sundays, Tuesdays and Fridays. Only the Friday service connects with the *Prospector* train to Perth. The Sunday service operates via Coolgardie, but the Tuesday and Friday buses travel via Kambalda.

Bus Services from Esperance

Destination	Operator	Via	Distance (km)	Fare	Journey Time	Frequency
Perth	W.A.G.R.		731	$65.05	10¼ - 10½ hrs	6/week
Albany	W.A.G.R.		479	$48	6½ hrs	2/week
Kalgoorlie	W.A.G.R.		393	$40.65	5 - 5¼ hrs	3/week

ANECDOTE

It was probably the use of the brakes on the descent from the Stirling Range which caused the trouble, and we were lucky to discover our problem without too much damage. An inspection of the vehicle revealed that the rear nearside wheel was covered in brake fluid and, since all had escaped, we no longer had the ability to stop. By fortune we were on the edge of a small settlement, so we crawled in using only first gear, parked near the garage there, took the wheel to pieces and referred the matter to the garage owner.

"Looks like the seal on the brake cylinder," he said helpfully, and then added, less helpfully, "I haven't got one." He gave the matter some thought. "I can tell you a place in Esperance where you'd get one for sure." "How far to Esperance?" "350 kilometres." "So how do we get the seal?" "Well, you drive there. You've got a vehicle, haven't you?" "Yes, but no brakes," we pointed out. "Well, don't stop then."

The plan was simple enough, but we felt that it probably had a weak point somewhere. We got out the map and studied it very carefully. One small town on the way and one right turn where we met the main highway. The garage owner's simple solution seemed the best. We found some good strong wire from a nearby fence and wired up the offending cylinder, then bought plenty of brake fluid from the garage owner and filled up the system. We reckoned that this would give us one emergency application of the brakes, which would presumably break the wire on the cylinder and allow all the fluid to escape again, so one application only.

We set off. The one small town was approached with trepidation, but we negotiated it in second gear without any need to stop. When we had to turn right, we started to slow down some three kilometres from the turning. No other traffic was in sight, however, so that potential problem was also overcome successfully. Upon reaching Esperance, we crawled into town, but somebody had had the audacity to install traffic lights, and in the centre of the town the brakes just had to be applied. However, it was only another 200 metres in first gear to a car park by the sea, almost opposite the garage to which we had been directed. We crept in and camped there for the night. In the morning, we pushed the vehicle across to the garage. "What's the matter? Won't it start?" "No, just the opposite."

Now where else in the world would one be foolish enough to attempt to drive 350 kilometres without using the brakes?

538 WESTERN AUSTRALIA
NORSEMAN AND THE NULLARBOR PLAIN

Population 1,500 (Norseman)
10 hrs 30 mins by bus from Perth (Norseman)

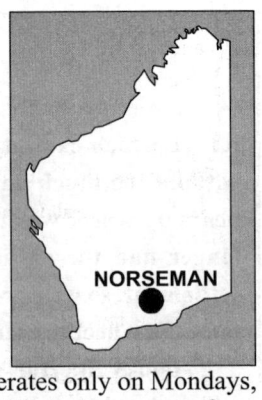

From Perth, Greyhound operates a bus service to Adelaide via Norseman and the Nullarbor Plain on Mondays, Wednesdays and Fridays. It takes 10½ hours to reach Norseman and about twenty hours to reach the South Australian border.

If you travel by rail, you can take the *Prospector* or the *Indian Pacific* to Kalgoorlie and then catch the W.A.G.R. bus to Norseman. The destination of the bus is Esperance, but it operates only on Mondays, Wednesdays and Fridays, making a connexion on those days with the *Prospector* from Perth.

If you approach Norseman from the south, however, that is from Esperance, you will pass through a great expanse of flat scrubby land where agriculture becomes more difficult as distance from the coast increases, due to the lack of reliable rainfall. W.A.G.R. operates three buses a week from Esperance to Kalgoorlie, via Norseman, of which only that on a Friday connects with a train to Perth. The settlements along the highway from Esperance northwards, **Grass Patch** and **Salmon Gums**, are very small and Norseman is the first town of any size to be encountered.

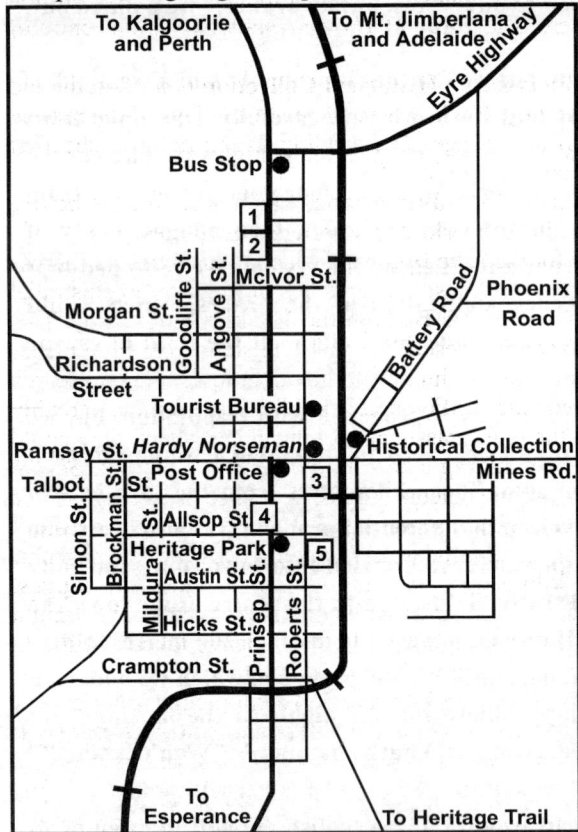

NORSEMAN
Numerals indicate accommodation

Norseman is another gold town. In 1894, a young prospector named Laurie Sinclair was on his way to Coolgardie and stopped to visit his brother here. He tethered his horse, and in the morning found that the horse had scuffed the ground and revealed a nugget of gold. He lodged his claim on 13th August 1894 and, since the name of the horse was *Hardy Norseman*, he named the reef Norseman after it. However, the small town already had a name, and was known as

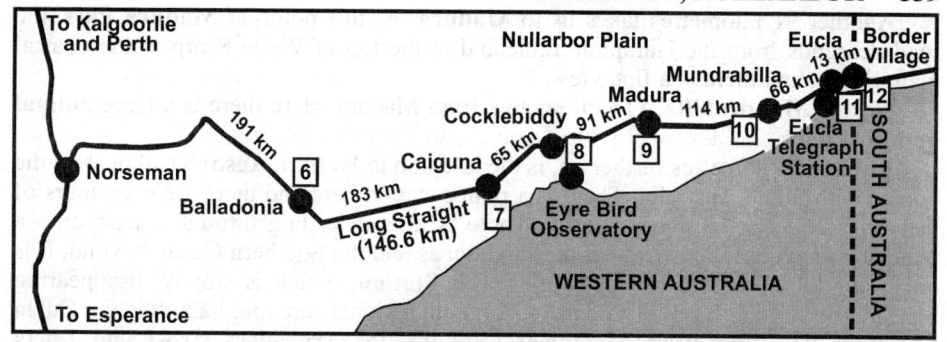

THE NULLARBOR - FROM NORSEMAN TO THE BORDER

Dundas. In time, though, Norseman was preferred and the name of Dundas disappeared. Gold has been mined here ever since, and still is. The Central Norseman Gold Corporation claims to operate the longest running continuous gold-mining operation in Western Australia, and Norseman has, to date, produced over five million ounces of that precious metal. There is a **statue of** *Hardy Norseman* in the centre of the town.

Other attractions in Norseman include an **Historical Collection** housed in the old School of Mines Building, and **Heritage Park**, where there are displays of the mining history of the town. There is also a Heritage Trail leading to the point of the first settlement here on the banks of Lake Dundas in 1893.

Five kilometres east of Norseman is **Mt. Jimberlana**, which is claimed to be one of the oldest geological formations in the world. It also offers a good view.

Norseman is the starting point for the Eyre Highway, which runs all the way across the Nullarbor Plain and is one of the most desolate stretches of highway in Australia. Heading east from Norseman, the first stop is **Balladonia**, 191 kilometres away. This is where the American *Skylab* **Spacecraft** descended in 1979, showering little pieces around and causing a small army of souvenir hunters to go out onto the plain to search for bits. Although the event received much unfavourable publicity at the time, in reality if the Americans wished to avoid the embarrassment of human casualties, they could hardly have chosen a better spot. Even hitting a kangaroo here with a piece of *Skylab* would have been a considerable achievement. There is a free **museum** at the Balladonia Roadhouse, which includes exhibits relating to *Skylab*, as well as the history of the Nullarbor Plain. There is also accommodation, including beds for backpackers.

To **Caiguna** is another 183 kilometres, and this section includes the **longest stretch of straight road** in Australia - no distance at all compared with the 477 straight kilometres on the railway, but still this straight of 146.6 kilometres takes a while to cover, and the scenery does not change much while one is doing so.

From Caiguna to **Cocklebiddy** is only 65 kilometres. 42 kilometres south-east of Cocklebiddy is the **Eyre Bird Observatory** within the **Nuytsland Nature Reserve**. It is the first such observatory in Australia and is located near the beach and near the old **Eyre Telegraph Station**, constructed in 1897. Also at Cocklebiddy are the **Cocklebiddy Caves**, including one of the world's largest underwater caves, 6.7 kilometres long. A steel ladder leads down to it, and you can walk to the edge of the lake. It is surprising that there should be such a huge expanse of water down here, when the surface is so parched.

540 WESTERN AUSTRALIA

Another 91 kilometres takes us to **Madura**. At this point, at **Madura Pass**, the road descends from the Hampton Tableland at the top of Wylie Scarp to the coastal plain below, and there is a fine view.

Next is **Mundrabilla**, 114 kilometres from Madura. Here there is a large **animal and bird park**.

Eucla, 62 kilometres further on, is the last stop in Western Australia, almost on the border with South Australia. There is a police station here and there are even tours of the caves and coastal dunes nearby. There is a road leading through a pass onto a plateau with an excellent view of the sand dunes and the Southern Ocean beyond. It is only four kilometres to the **Old Telegraph Station**, which is slowly disappearing beneath the shifting sands. There are several other sights here too, including the **Eucla Museum**, the **John Eyre Memorial Lookout**, the **Travellers Cross** and **Eucla National Park**. The National Park covers 3,340 hectares, most of it comprised of mallee scrub. It includes **Wilson Bluff**, another point offering an excellent view. There is a Bureau of Meteorology here, open to visitors from 10:00 until 14:00 daily.

Eucla used to be a vital link on the Telegraph Line. The town was founded in 1877 and at one time had a population of seventy and a long jetty stretching out into the sea. At the beginning of the twentieth century, it was the busiest Telegraph Station in Australia outside the capital cities. All is gone now, except for the modern roadhouse, some gravestones, the ruins of the jetty, and the last few remnants of the old buildings protruding from the encroaching sand dunes. The natural beauty of the place remains, however. The white sandy beach seems to stretch for ever and is almost totally deserted. It is backed by what is claimed to be the longest **unbroken stretch of cliffs** in the world, extending for 200 kilometres and rising in places to a height of a hundred metres. There is no doubt about the splendour of this almost uninhabited area.

At Eucla, as at all of the roadhouses mentioned above on the Nullarbor crossing, accommodation of various types is available. Most provide budget facilities as well as comfortable motel rooms, and camping and caravan sites are available.

From Eucla, it is just another thirteen kilometres to the **Border Travellers Village**, where the road crosses into South Australia. These days, the South Australian Nullarbor looks rather similar to the Western Australian Nullarbor, but when the author first crossed, there was the very noticeable difference that the bitumen finished at the border, and from here it was all pot-holes and corrugations for the next 500 kilometres to Ceduna, a bone- and vehicle-shattering experience, with the wreckage of those who had not made it strewn beside the road all the way. Conditions are much improved now, thankfully.

Note that there is a time difference of an hour and a half between Western Australia and South Australia. This already considerable difference becomes two and a half hours in summer, when South Australia observes daylight saving time, but Western Australia does not. To complicate matters even further, the residents of the Nullarbor Plain between Caiguna and the border like to observe an unofficial local time which is 45 minutes ahead of official Western Australian time. As a result, you will never be quite sure what time it is when crossing this stretch of road.

As an example, if it is summer and 12:00 in Perth, it will be 12:45 in Eucla and 14:30 in Adelaide. If it is winter and 12:00 in Perth, it will be 12:45 in Eucla and 13:30 in Adelaide.

NORSEMAN, NULLARBOR

ACCOMMODATION
(i) Hotel Accommodation in Norseman

Name	Stars	No. on Map	Telephone No.	Address	Lowest Price (Double/Twin)
Great Western Motel		2	08-9039-1633	Prinsep Street	$105
Gateway Caravan Park		1	08-9039-1500	Prinsep Street	$50
Railway Hotel		5	08-9039-1115	106 Roberts Street	$45
Norseman Hotel		3	08-9039-1023	90 Roberts Street	$45
Lodge 101		4	08-9039-1541	101 Prinsep Street	$40

(ii) Backpackers Hostel in Norseman

Name	Group	No. on Map	Telephone No.	Address	Lowest Price (Dormitory)
Lodge 101		4	08-9039-1541	101 Prinsep Street	$19

(iii) Accommodation across the Nullarbor

Name	Stars	No. on Map	Telephone No.	Address	Lowest Price (Double/Twin)
Balladonia Hotel / Motel	4	6	08-9039-3453	Eyre Highway, Balladonia	$95
John Eyre Motel		7	08-9039-3459	Eyre Highway, Caiguna	$95
Wedgetail Inn		8	08-9039-3462	Eyre Highway, Cocklebiddy	$95
Madura Pass Oasis Motel	2½	9	1-800-998-228	Eyre Highway, Madura	$105
Mundrabilla Motor Hotel		10	08-9039-3465	Eyre Highway, Mundrabilla	$95
Eucla Motor Hotel	3	11	08-9039-3468	Eyre Highway, Eucla	$95
Border Travellers Village		12	08-9039-3474	Eyre Highway, Eucla	$75

MOVING ON
Bus Services from Norseman

Destination	Operator	Via	Distance (km)	Fare	Journey Time	Frequency
Adelaide	Greyhound		2160	$291	26¼ hrs	3/week
		Port Augusta	1842	$291	21¾ hrs	3/week
Perth	Greyhound		820	$170	10 hrs	3/week
		Kalgoorlie	191	$97	2¼ hrs	3/week
Kalgoorlie	W.A.G.R.		191	$23.20	2½ hrs	3/week
Esperance	W.A.G.R.		202	$23.20	2½ hrs	3/week

KALGOORLIE
Population 30,000

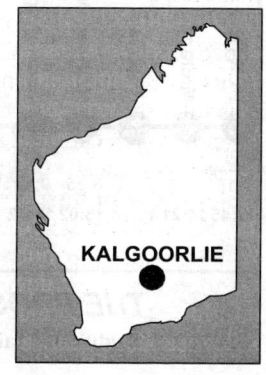

8 hrs by train from Perth
7 hrs by bus from Perth

In 1887, gold was discovered in Southern Cross, far west of Kalgoorlie. Then, in 1892, more gold was found, this time at Mt. Youle, and a rush ensued. Three Irishmen set off from Coolgardie in June 1893 to join the pursuit of riches. They had got as far as where Kalgoorlie now stands, a distance of about forty kilometres, when one of their horses lost a shoe, so they camped for the night. There one of them, named Paddy

WESTERN AUSTRALIA

Hannan, picked up from the ground, at the top of what is now Hannan Street, a gold nugget. After searching around, he was able to ride back to Coolgardie with over a hundred ounces of gold and register his claim. So began the history of one of the most famous towns in Australia.

There are actually two towns, Kalgoorlie and Boulder, which run into each other. The famous **Golden Mile** between them is supposedly the richest square mile on earth in terms of gold deposits. Mining of gold here has been carried out for more than a century, and is still continuing. This is still the greatest gold-producing area in Australia.

If you come here from Perth, you will have the choice of train or bus, and you will have the choice of two different trains and two different bus companies. The *Prospector* is operated by W.A.G.R. and leaves Perth every morning except Sunday, and there are additional services on Sunday, Monday and Friday afternoons. The timetable for these services can be found on page 486 and a diagram of the journey, showing times of the morning trains, is given below. This is probably the best way to reach Kalgoorlie. The journey takes approximately eight hours and at one time, when the *Prospector* first started operating, on 29th November 1971, it claimed to offer Australia's fastest rail service. No longer, however. The train is getting old and so is the standard gauge track, and Queensland now has the *Tilt Train*. The other train available between Perth and Kalgoorlie is the *Indian-Pacific*, operated by Great Southern Railway. It leaves Perth on Monday and Friday mornings, reaching Kalgoorlie at 20:00, nine hours later (although when the author last took this service it was nearly four hours late into Kalgoorlie because of bushfires). Although it takes an hour longer than the *Prospector*, it is a more comfortable train. The timetable for this service can also be found on page 486. Both the *Prospector* and the *Indian-Pacific* leave from East Perth Railway Station.

The two bus services are operated by Greyhound and by Goldfields Express. The Greyhound service is bound for Adelaide and leaves Perth on Monday, Wednesday and Friday afternoons. It takes eight hours to reach Kalgoorlie. Goldfields Express operates every day except Monday, with the services on Sundays, Wednesdays and Fridays extended to Laverton and the others terminating in Kalgoorlie. The services take seven hours from Perth to Kalgoorlie. Note that Goldfields Express leaves from East Perth Railway Station, not from the city centre.

Station	Southbound (Not Sun)	Northbound
PERTH	7:15	14:45
Midland	7:35	14:21
Toodyay	8:33	13:24
NORTHAM	8:55	13:02
Meckering	9:17	12:42
Cunderdin	9:36	12:22
Tammin	9:52	12:07
Kellerberrin	10:14	11:45
Doodlakine	10:28	11:35
Hines Hill	10:39	11:25
MERREDIN	11:13	11:13
Burracoppin	11:32	10:32
Carrabin	11:43	10:20
Bodallin	11:58	10:03
Moorine Rock	12:11	9:50
Southern Cross	12:24	9:30
Bonnie Vale	14:32	7:20
KALGOORLIE	15:00	6:55 (Not Sun)

THE PROSPECTOR - PERTH TO KALGOORLIE
Additional trains operate on Sunday, Monday and Friday afternoons

As you come here, you will pass through some interesting and varied countryside, so some words on that first. Leaving Perth, you travel through the **Avon Valley National Park** with the Avon River running through it. This is the same river as the Swan River flowing through Perth. The scenery is particularly attractive from the train. Moreover, along the railway line these are the last hills that you will see until you reach the other side of the continent, if you are going that far. You will pass through **Toodyay**, a town which dates from the 1830s, although it has been moved since its foundation, the original site being found prone to flooding. There are some old buildings to be seen here, and it is a pleasant town, now serving partly as a dormitory for those working in Perth.

At **Northam**, the railway crosses the Avon River. This is the start of the *Avon Descent*, a famous white water boat race held on the first weekend in August. The race stretches from here to Perth, a distance of 133 kilometres. The railway reached Northam in 1871 and there are several interesting old buildings in the town. There is also the longest **pedestrian suspension bridge** in Australia. If you wish to stay, there is ample accommodation. Those on a budget will find several old and economical hotels of character, for example the Commercial Hotel, the Grand Hotel, or the Transcontinental Hotel, which is right outside the Railway Station.

Twenty minutes further on, you will pass through **Meckering**, famous for an earthquake which occurred here on 14th October 1968. This was, at the time, the second strongest earthquake recorded in Australia since European settlement commenced. It created a shallow escarpment 37 kilometres long which is still visible.

We are now in wheat country, which stretches for a long way. At the stations there are silos to store the grain. From the train you will notice that the track here is dual gauge in many places, although for some of their routes standard and narrow gauge lines follow different courses. Until 1969, this was a narrow gauge line and passengers travelling across the continent had to change trains at Kalgoorlie. When the standard gauge line arrived here, the narrow gauge was kept as well, otherwise it would no longer have been possible to run trains to country areas in Western Australia. The narrow gauge continues as far as **Merredin**, where it terminates at a separate platform. From here to Kalgoorlie, and on to Adelaide and Sydney, there is only standard gauge track.

The railway reached Merredin, roughly the half-way point to Kalgoorlie, in 1893, and the fine old station was constructed in 1895 and extended later. When the standard gauge line came, the old station building was no longer required and it was converted into a **Museum**. If you have time and are interested in the history of the railway, this is an interesting place to look around. It is open daily from 9:00 (10:00 at weekends) until 12:00 and from 13:00 until 15:00.

It is another 75 minutes from Merredin to **Southern Cross**, during which time the wheatfields continue unrelieved. Southern Cross was the site of the gold rush in 1887, and the railway arrived in 1894, but the gold here did not last, and now it is golden wheat which pays the bills rather than prospecting for mineral gold. Soon after we leave Southern Cross, though, the wheatfields end suddenly. There simply is not enough rain here to support wheat any further inland. There is also not enough rain to support humans in large numbers, as those in the Goldfields discovered, and that led to one of the most remarkable engineering projects of the very early twentieth century. C.Y. O'Connor, the man who reconstructed Fremantle Harbour so successfully, designed and supervised the construction of a water pipe from Mundaring Weir, just outside Perth, to Coolgardie, and on to Kalgoorlie, a total distance of 563 kilometres. If you look out of the train or bus window, you will see this pipeline following you all day, over this enormous distance, to bring water to the thirsty workers of Kalgoorlie.

The story of Kalgoorlie is an interesting one, and, since the city has always been so dependent on a single resource, it has been subject to many fluctuations in fortune over the years. It is a fascinating place to visit.

Following the discovery of gold here, thousands of miners rushed to the location, not just from Western Australia, but from the east as well, some of them even making their way along the telegraph line on foot or on horseback, a journey of at least 2,000 kilometres in extremely harsh conditions. Miners also come from overseas, particularly Chinese. In one week in 1893, there were 1,400 new arrivals in the town and within a year the population had grown to its present level of 30,000. When the prospectors and miners reached here, they found appalling conditions. There was great overcrowding and a total lack of sanitation. The only living quarters were tents and makeshift shelters. Disease was rife. Worst of all, though, was the lack of water. Water was sold at 2/6 a gallon, a price which most men could not afford. Many died of thirst, or of drinking contaminated water. Thousands succumbed to typhoid, dysentery or scurvy. There was little medical attention available and few basic medical supplies.

When the railway arrived, conditions improved somewhat. The first *Kalgoorlie Express*, from Perth to Kalgoorlie, pulled into the new station here on 8th September 1896. However, what really relieved the misery was the **water pipeline**. Unfortunately, though, this story is another which has an unhappy ending. The scheme seemed so grandiose at the time that the brilliant engineer in charge, C.Y. O'Connor, was subjected to constant ridicule for suggesting it and attempting to put it into practice. Finally, on 10th March 1902, just a few months before the water finally flowed, unable to bear the criticism any longer, he took his own life at the age of 59.

To reach Kalgoorlie, the water had to pass through eight steam-driven pumping stations. When these were put into action, the water was awaited with great excitement in Kalgoorlie, but nothing came. First, of course, it was necessary to fill all 563 kilometres of pipe with water, and this took much longer than had been anticipated. It was nine days after the pumping had started, and when hope of its arrival had almost been given up, that the first water started to flow into Mt. Charlotte Reservoir on 24th January 1903. It has been flowing ever since and this is still the principal water supply for the Goldfields. You can walk up to **Mt. Charlotte** and see the reservoir there, with, incidentally, a good viewpoint, and the pipe which has been bringing the water all the way from Perth for the last century and without which Kalgoorlie could not survive.

The most successful period in the history of Kalgoorlie was in the early part of the twentieth century, when the railway had arrived and the water problem had been solved. At this time, there were 93 hotels in the town, and eight breweries, and it is from this period that many of the grand buildings of the city date. Just a walk up Hannan Street will give you a good idea of the former prosperity of Kalgoorlie, as well as its revival in recent years.

If you are travelling by train and have not made time in your itinerary for Kalgoorlie, you will be pleased to find that the *Indian-Pacific* stops here for three hours in each direction of travel. It is always evening, so museums and the tourist office will be closed, but still you will have the opportunity to take a good look at the city. A tour is offered, but at a cost of $16. This is the way to see the most in the limited time available, but actually you can see quite a lot just by a free walk, so here is a walking tour which starts and finishes at the railway station, but is suitable for anybody, railway passenger or not.

Walking Tour

This is a short tour which will cover only about three kilometres and will occupy less than an hour, not including any visits to museums.

Start at the railway station and walk straight ahead down Wilson Street until you reach Hannan Street, the main street of Kalgoorlie. The **Kalgoorlie Town Hall**, on your left on the corner of Hannan Street and Wilson Street, was built in 1908 and is a splendid edifice. It has decorated stamped metal ceilings, chandeliers and a wide, sweeping staircase, and it contains the original statue of Paddy Hannan. The building is open from 9:00 until 16:30 on weekdays.

Outside the Town Hall is a copy of the famous and well-photographed **Paddy Hannan statue**, the original of which has been moved inside for preservation. Mr. Hannan's waterbag acts as a water fountain, to regale thirsty passers-by. Turn left now into Hannan Street.

On the other side of the street is the remarkable **York Hotel** with its Indian-style turrets and towers, and yet bearing a name which could hardly be more British. And just look at the width of this street, It was reputedly built on such a scale so that a full bullock team with cart could be turned here without difficulty. They could not be turned now, though, because of all those vehicles parked

KALGOORLIE
Dashed line shows Walking Tour
Black numerals in white boxes indicate hotel accommodation
White numerals in black boxes indicate backpackers hostels

in the middle of the street, as well as at the edges.

Walk a little further up the street and, on your left, find **St. Barbara's Square**, just by the **Tourist Centre**. The square has a statue depicting **St. Barbara**, the patron saint of miners. It also has some seats for the weary (while the supermarket is just behind, for the hungry). This is the arrival and departure point for the Greyhound bus, if that is your mode of travel.

Continuing up Hannan Street, you come next to some fine public buildings on your left, including, at the end, the **Post Office**, again dating from the early twentieth century.

Just up the hill slightly, on the corner of Maritana Street, is an hotel exhibiting some wonderful architecture. This is the **Exchange Hotel**, claiming to be the most-photographed drinking establishment in Western Australia. It is an excellent example of restored turn-of-the century country grandeur.

Continue walking and at the top end of Hannan Street you will find the **Museum of the Goldfields**, where it is easy to spend a couple of hours (if it is open, of course). You will easily locate it from afar because of the huge **red headframe** erected over the top. This is the headframe for the winding gear from the former Ivanhoe Mine. The basement of this museum has an impressive display of gold nuggets, as well as an impressively solid door, while the roof, reached by lift, offers a good view of the city. The Museum is open daily from 10:00 until 16:30. Admission is by a suggested donation of $2.

From the top of Hannan Street you will be able to see, away to your left, the **Mt. Charlotte Reservoir** where the water which has come all the way from Perth is stored. Turn right now and in Outridge Terrace you can find **Paddy Hannan's Tree**, where, supposedly, Mr. Hannan, together with his friends Flanagan and Shea, who are now almost forgotten, strangely enough, made his discovery of gold in 1893. Although there is little to suggest that this is really the tree, especially as it was replanted in 1993, this is about the correct location.

Now walk down Egan Street, parallel to Hannan Street, until you reach Boulder Road, which is, as you might guess, the main road to Boulder, and turn left along it for two blocks, until you reach and turn right into Cheetham Street. You soon make an obligatory right turn into Cassidy Street and find the **Goldfields Arts Centre**. This building includes an **Art Gallery** which is open from 10:00 (12:00 at weekends) until 16:00, except on Mondays.

Continue along Cassidy Street. The **School of Mines Mineral Museum** is on your right. It has a good collection of minerals and replicas of the most famous gold nuggets found in Kalgoorlie. It is open on weekdays from 8:30 until 12:30, but closed during school holidays.

Walk to the end of Cassidy Street and you will be back in Hannan Street. Turn left and this time keep walking for two more blocks beyond the Town Hall. Turn right into Lionel Street and walk to Hay Street. Now, **Hay Street** is a famous street, as you will soon discover. Kalgoorlie and Boulder are unusual in Western Australia, in that prostitution has always been legal here, within certain rules. Hay Street is Kalgoorlie's street of prostitutes, so evening is the most interesting time to walk along here. On the corner of Lionel Street and Hay Street, you will immediately notice the newly-constructed *Langtrees Club 181*. For the sum of $25, you can have a Brothel Tour. At that price, one might expect to get a sample of the merchandise too, but the author is informed that that is not the case, and that the goods on sale are very much more expensive than that. Strangely enough, Hay Street has also become the area for backpackers hostels. Turn right into Hay Street and you will find the backpackers on the left and the prostitutes on the right. Please make no mistakes. The remainder of the prostitution premises are much more economy-based, consisting of small garishly-lit rooms behind corrugated iron fences with open doors. Wares are often on display. Since this is one of the almost unique scenes of Kalgoorlie, it is regarded as a tourist attraction of the city and should be on the itinerary of the visitor.

Where Hay Street meets Wilson Street once more, by Woolworths, turn left and return to the station. As you arrive, you will find on your right the Railway Motel, an example of Kalgoorlie's recent revival. Once a good-quality hotel, this gradually became more and more shabby and run-down, until a few years ago the wooden building was gutted by fire. At that stage, it might simply have been demolished, but instead it has been rebuilt, looking much better than before, although different, because the old hotel was a two-storey building, and has become the office and restaurant for a smart new motel behind.

The **station** is a fine-looking building, although beyond the requirements of today's limited traffic. The first train arrived here from Perth in 1896, and on 22nd October 1917 the first standard gauge train ran from here east to Port Augusta. The first direct standard gauge train to the east from Perth passed here on 10th June 1969, and the first *Indian-Pacific* to head east passed through on 1st March 1970. The new standard gauge lines south to Esperance and north to Leonora were opened on 16th September 1974, but, alas, neither of these carries passengers any longer. Kalgoorlie always used to claim that it had the longest platform in the southern hemisphere, but that claim does not seem to be made any longer, so perhaps it has been surpassed, or maybe the platform is not as long as it used to be. It used to stretch for 526.5 metres (1,727 feet, 6 inches). At present, only the four *Indian-Pacific* trains every week, two in each direction, generally use the main platform. The *Prospector* usually departs from the side platform, on your left as you enter the station.

Our walk is complete, but there are some attractions which we did not see in Kalgoorlie. **Hannans North Historic Mining Reserve** lies quite a long way to the north-west of the main city and offers underground tours, gold panning and a gold pour. Tours start at 9:00 and, if you want to see everything, you should arrive not later than 14:00. Admission costs $17.50 if you view all attractions, or $12.50 if you stay above ground. On your way to the mine you will pass the Mt. Charlotte Reservoir and Lookout mentioned earlier.

Then there is **Boulder**. Boulder was originally a separate town, but it was merged with Kalgoorlie in 1989 to form the city of Kalgoorlie-Boulder. It has buildings of a similar antiquity to those in Kalgoorlie, but on a smaller scale. Since you have already seen Kalgoorlie, you will not find Boulder exciting in this respect. However, there are some special sights to see in Boulder.

First there is the **Super Pit**. This is an open-cut mine of amazing enormity. The huge machines operating in it appear like toys when viewed from the lookout. When completed, this mine will measure four kilometres by two kilometres, and will be 600 metres deep. At present, though, it goes down a mere 300 metres. It also provides access to an underground mine, so that trucks can simply drive down a ramp into the mine to be loaded with ore. The days of picking gold nuggets out of the ground are long gone in Kalgoorlie, but modern techniques permit the mining of relatively low grade

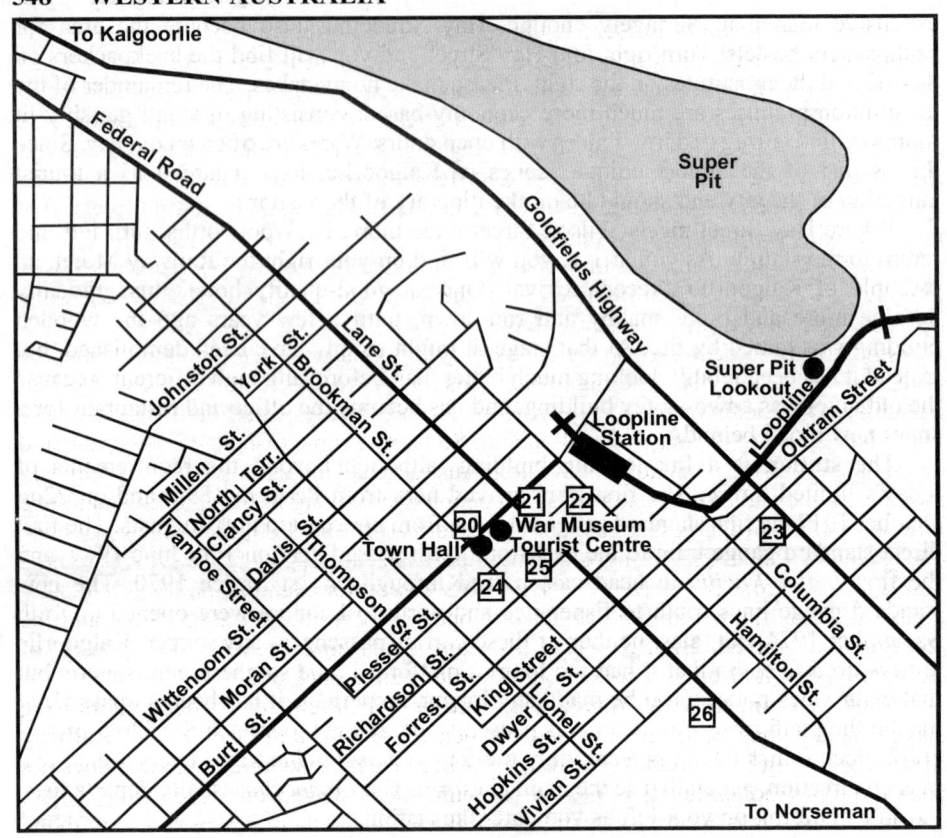

BOULDER
Numerals indicate accommodation

ore and that is what is happening here. Over the last century, Kalgoorlie-Boulder has produced 35 million ounces (1,000 tons) of gold, far more than any other place in Australia, and it appears that there is more to come yet.

Boulder can be reached by the public buses operated by Goldenlines. Routes 1, 2, 4, 5 and 6 all run between Kalgoorlie and Boulder, with services approximately every quarter hour in the morning and every half hour in the afternoon. The buses take ten minutes by the fastest route, but some services divert and take longer. The fare is $2. However, there is still about two kilometres to walk from the centre of Boulder to the Super Pit. The last bus back to Kalgoorlie is at 18:10. On Saturdays, there are buses only in the morning, and on Sundays there are no buses at all.

ANECDOTE

In Boulder a telegraph pole stands in the middle of the street and attached to it is a notice reading, "Go around this pole".

I wondered about the standards of driving in Western Australia.

Another attraction at Boulder is the railway. The **Loopline**, still narrow gauge, is no longer connected with Kalgoorlie Station. It runs from near the centre of Boulder up past the Super Pit. When the line was first opened in 1897, it was the busiest line in Australia. Today, a diesel locomotive pulls a couple of old carriages for a short ride along what remains of the line at 10:00 every day. The ride includes a stop to look at the Super Pit and a chance to see the **Chaffers Powerhouse Mining Display**. The station from which the train departs is at the corner of Burt and Hamilton Streets, five minutes' walk from the nearest bus stop.

The **Goldfields War Museum** is also in Boulder. It has displays relating to wars in which Australia has been involved from the Boer War to Vietnam. The Museum is open on weekdays from 10:00 until 16:00.

Another place near Kalgoorlie which is worth visiting is **Coolgardie**, where the gold rush preceded that in Kalgoorlie. This is where the history of the Western Australian Goldfields really began. In 1892, Arthur Bayley, searching for gold at Fly Flat, made a find of an amazing 554 ounces. So many people rushed to Coolgardie and nearby areas that the population of Western Australia had increased by 400% within six months. At the end of the century, 25,000 people were living in Coolgardie and at one time it was the third largest settlement in Western Australia. Looking at the town now, one can hardly believe its former size and importance, although a few buildings remain which tell of bygone prosperity. The **Warden's Court**, for example, built in 1898, now houses the Goldfields Exhibition Museum, open daily from 9:00 until 17:00, and the **Coolgardie Tourist Bureau**. The Museum deals mainly with the history of Coolgardie, but it also has a collection of bottles dating back to 300 B.C.

Warden Finnerty's Residence was built in 1895. Premiers and Governors have stayed here. It has been restored and is open from 9:00 until 16:00. The **Railway Station** was built in 1896, but closed in 1971 because the standard gauge line does not pass through Coolgardie. It is now a Museum, open daily from 13:00 until 16:00, except on Thursdays. There is a walk around the town and there is a **cemetery** with the graves of early inhabitants, many telling stories of the harsh conditions.

There is a local bus no. 9 from Kalgoorlie to Coolgardie on schooldays only, but there is only one possible service. You must leave Kalgoorlie at 7:00 and return from Coolgardie at 16:00. The journey takes 40 minutes. Accommodation is available in Coolgardie, including backpackers accommodation at the Railway Lodge at 75 Bayley Street (telephone 08-9026-6446).

Another mining town near Kalgoorlie, but a modern one this time, is **Kambalda**, the prosperity of which is based on nickel. There is a walking trail which overlooks the mining area and then continues as a nature trail, but otherwise interest for the visitor is limited in the modern town, or, more precisely, two towns, as Kambalda East and Kambalda West are quite a distance apart. There is a service with bus no. 8, but it operates only from Kambalda in the morning and back from Kalgoorlie in the afternoon.

North of Kalgoorlie there are more goldfields, small towns built on the discovery of that precious metal, but now deserted in many cases, or surviving because of the development of agriculture but only a fraction of their former size and grandeur.

Broad Arrow lies 38 kilometres north of Kalgoorlie, and was once a gold mining town with a population of 15,000. Now, however, the population is seven, but it still has a pub with accommodation available.

Menzies is a further 92 kilometres north. Gold was discovered here in 1894 and people crowded to the area. However, the prosperity lasted for only ten years and after that the town went into decline. It survived due to sheep farming, and currently has a population of 150. There are several buildings worth seeing including the **Railway Station**, built in 1898, but not used as a station since 1974, and the **Town Hall**, built in 1896. The Town Hall was supposed to have a clock and it was ordered from England and shipped out on the *S.S. Orizaba* in 1905. Unfortunately, the *Orizaba* sank just off Rottnest Island, so the original clock was never delivered and installation of a replacement was delayed. The clock was finally put in place in 2000, almost a century late. The Menzies Railway Hotel offers accommodation here.

Another 105 kilometres north brings us to **Leonora**, where the railway ends, although there have not been any passenger trains to here for many years. Leonora is an interesting mixture of old and new, with abandoned mines now coming back to life as techniques are devised to rework the old tailings profitably and to excavate areas previously thought uneconomic.

In 1869, the explorer, later Premier, John Forrest, passed through here searching for the lost Leichhardt expedition. He named Mt. Leonora in honour of the Governor's wife, but did not notice the gold which was first discovered here in 1896. Two towns sprang up, Leonora and **Gwalia**, three kilometres apart. Both survived the years well, but Gwalia succumbed when its mine was closed in 1963 and is now just an interesting ghost town. There is a **Museum** open daily from 10:00 until 16:00 at a cost of $3. The **Mine Manager's Residence** is here, too, with a view across the open-cut mine. The Mine Manager, incidentally, was one Herbert Hoover, later President of the U.S.A. The **Historical Precinct** has an old store, a guesthouse and some miners' huts. There is also the **State Hotel**, a grand old building, constructed in 1903, which was one of the first hotels in Western Australia to be built by the State Government.

Leonora too has a number of interesting buildings: the **Old Police Station**, the **Courthouse**, the **Masonic Lodge**, the **Old Fire Station**, the **National and W.A. Bank**, and the **Post Office**, all dating from the early years of the twentieth century. Nearby is **Mt. Leonora** with a commanding view of the area. There are four hotels or motels in Leonora, and a caravan park.

At the end of the road, another 105 kilometres beyond Leonora, is **Laverton**, another mixture of old and new, but in this case more new than old, although the town dates from 1900. It has a population of 500 and is on the edge of the Great Victoria Desert. The

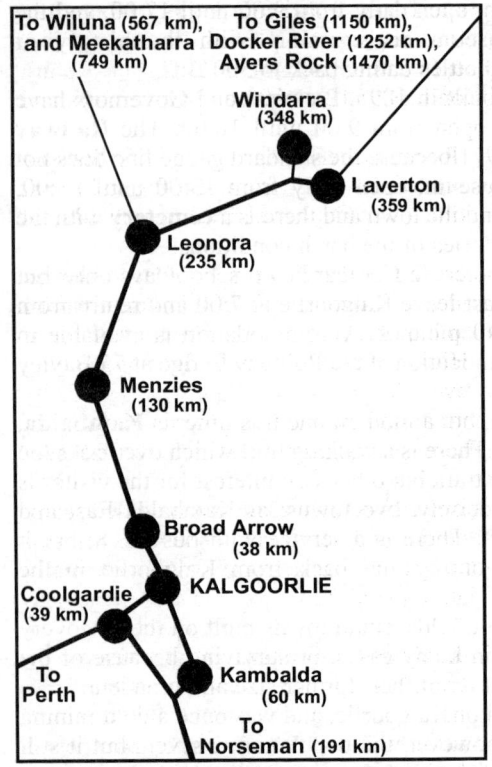

FROM KALGOORLIE TO LAVERTON
Distances are from Kalgoorlie

most famous mine in this area was a modern one, at **Windarra**, 28 kilometres from Laverton. In 1969, Ken Shirley was sent out to prospect in the area and was able to report to his employer, *Poseidon N.L.*, that he had found ore which seemed to contain a high percentage of nickel, and that he had pegged forty stakes. The rocks sent back were analysed and his assessment confirmed. The shares of *Poseidon* rose from 80 cents to a peak of a phenomenal $280 five months later. It was then revealed that the nickel content was not as high as had at first been thought, and the shares dropped back to around $100. A mine was set up at Windarra and production commenced in 1974, but nickel prices had fallen in the meantime, and in 1976 *Poseidon* went into receivership. However, the mining continued until 1994, and 600 people were employed here. 5.3 million tonnes of ore was extracted, yielding an average of 1.5% nickel, and another nine million tonnes of ore from other mines was also treated on the site. Now there is an interesting **walking trail** around the old workings.

There is an hotel in Laverton offering moderately-priced accommodation, and there are two motels.

Goldfields Express operates a bus from Perth to Laverton, via Kalgoorlie, Menzies and Leonora, on three days a week. The service leaves from East Perth Station at 7:45 on Sundays, Wednesdays and Fridays. It passes through Kalgoorlie at 14:35. On Sundays, there is also a connexion from Leonora north to Wiluna. In Kalgoorlie, the bus stop used is on the corner of Hay and Lane Streets. From Kalgoorlie, services take 90 minutes to Menzies, two and a half hours to Leonora and four hours to Laverton. Fares from Perth are $107 to Menzies, $119 to Leonora and $134 to Laverton. Fares from Kalgoorlie are $38 to Menzies, $50 to Leonora and $64 to Laverton. Return journeys depart from Laverton at 7:00 on Mondays and at 19:00 on Wednesdays and Fridays.

From Laverton, a road runs on to Ayers Rock and Alice Springs, across desolate and mostly uninhabited country. This road is sometimes called the Great Central Road, sometimes the Outback Highway and sometimes the Gunbarrel Highway. It has, of course, a story.

It was decided that a road was needed here, so, in 1958, a remarkable gentleman named Len Beadell was recruited, given a grader and some supplies and asked to make a road, which he did by the old Roman principle of keeping on in a straight line for as long as possible. Hence the name Gunbarrel Highway. It took two years of proceeding in a straight line to reach the other end. However, the Gunbarrel Highway, as made by Mr. Beadell, does not really exist now, but parts of the road which goes to Ayers Rock are the old Gunbarrel Highway. It also feels, in places, as though nobody has ever thought of regrading it since 1958.

There used to be a weekly bus service along this remote road, but it ceased many years ago now, as the condition of the road deteriorated. However, some tours are still operated by this route. Not only is it a short cut, but it will allow you to see some really remote outback countryside. When the author crossed here, we had two punctures along the way (and only one spare wheel).

315 kilometres from Laverton is the **Tjukayirla Roadhouse**, which claims to be Australia's most remote roadhouse. Its nearest neighbour is 225 kilometres distant. The road also passes through **Warburton** aboriginal community and, with a slight detour, the **Giles Weather Station**. At the weather station is Len Beadell's grader, abandoned here when it had done its work and was no longer required. In the kitchen are some drawings by the famous Mr. Beadell, who, unfortunately, died just a few years ago. If

552 WESTERN AUSTRALIA

you want to know more about this twentieth century pioneer, read his book, *Too Long in the Bush*. He was a great writer as well as a roadmaker.

The Giles Weather Station is interesting too. If the staff are warned in advance that they have visitors, they will usually welcome them and show them around. They even let the author make and send the weather report, kindly. This is an interesting route. If you have the chance to take it, you will find it an unforgettable experience.

ACCOMMODATION
(i) Hotel Accommodation in Kalgoorlie *(See map on page 545)*

Name	Stars	No. on Map	Telephone No.	Address	Lowest Price (Double/Twin)
Yelverton Motel	4½	7	08-9022-8181	210 Egan Street	$160
Mercure Hotel Plaza		1	08-9021-4544	45 Egan Street	$150
Railway Motel	4	6	1-800-355-209	51 Forrest Street	$140
Hospitality Inn	3½	11	08-9021-2888	Hannan Street	$130
Hannans View Motel	4	9	1-800-663-511	430 Hannan Street	$125
Australia Hotel	4	2	08-9021-1320	Hannan & Maritana Streets	$120
Mercure Inn Overland	3	12	08-9021-1433	Great Eastern Highway	$110
Midas Motel	3½	8	08-9021-3088	409 Hannan Street	$105
Sandalwood Motel	3½	15	08-9021-4455	Lower Hannan Street	$95
Star and Garter Motel	4	10	08-9026-3599	497 Hannan Street	$95
Tower Hotel	3½	5	08-9021-3211	Maritana & Bourke Streets	$95
Palace Hotel		4	08-9021-2788	Hannan & Maritana Streets	$85
Prospector Holiday Park	4	14	08-9021-2524	Great Eastern Highway	$65
Golden Village Park		13	08-9021-4162	406 Hay Street	$45
Surrey House		3	08-9021-1340	9 Boulder Road	$45

(ii) Backpackers Hostels in Kalgoorlie *(See map on page 545)*

Name	Group	No. on Map	Telephone No.	Address	Lowest Price (Dormitory)
Weslan Accommodation		19	08-9021-8871	Ochiltree Street	$28
Gold Dust Backpackers	VIP	18	08-9091-3737	192 Hay Street	$20
Gold Inn		16	08-9021-5483	147 Hannan Street	$19
Goldfields Backpackers		17	08-9091-1482	166 Hay Street	$18

(iii) Hotel Accommodation in Boulder *(See map on page 548)*

Name	Stars	No. on Map	Telephone No.	Address	Lowest Price (Double/Twin)
Albion Shamrock Hotel	3	21	08-9093-1399	Lane & Piesse Streets	$140
Boulder Lodge		22	08-9093-2094	50 Piesse Street	$95
Boulder Village	4	26	08-9093-1266	201 Lane Street	$85
Historic Cornwall Hotel		23	08-9093-2510	25 Hopkins Street	$75
Caledonia House		24	08-9093-1413	122a Piesse Street	$45
Lake View Private Hotel		25	08-9093-2033	49 Richardson Street	$45
Boulder Court Hotel		20	018-934-374	99 Burt Street	$40

(iv) Backpackers Hostels in Boulder *(See map on page 548)*

Name	Group	No. on Map	Telephone No.	Address	Lowest Price (Dormitory)
Lake View Private Hotel		25	08-9093-2033	49 Richardson Street	$28
Boulder Court Hotel		20	018-934-374	99 Burt Street	$22
Caledonia House		24	08-9093-1413	122a Piesse Street	$22

KALGOORLIE 553

MOVING ON
(i) By Train

The *Indian-Pacific* runs across the Nullarbor Plain to Adelaide and on to Sydney, leaving Kalgoorlie on Monday and Friday evenings. The timetable for this service is on page 486. The *Prospector* leaves for Perth every morning except Sunday, and also on Sunday, Monday and Friday afternoons. An additional service to Perth is provided overnight on the *Indian-Pacific* on Wednesday and Saturday nights. The timetable for these services, with connexions from Esperance, is shown above. W.A.G.R. operates buses to Esperance on Mondays, Wednesdays and Fridays. These all connect with *Prospector* trains from Perth. The timetable is on page 486.

Esperance, Kalgoorlie and Northam to Perth

Days of Operation	M-F	Not Sun (Bus)	Not Sun	Sun	W, F (Bus)	M, F	Sun (Bus)	W, Sat
Esperance		0800			0835		1400	
Kalgoorlie			0655	1325	1335	1400	1915	2230
Merredin			1113	1752		1824		0515
Northam	0630		1302	1938		2002		0730
Midland	0750		1421	2100		2116		0910
Perth		1810*	1445	2125		2135		0930

* 1805 on Thursdays, 1815 on Tuesdays, 1830 on Saturdays

(ii) By Bus

Greyhound operates buses to Adelaide on Tuesday, Thursday and Saturday nights. This journey involves two nights and a day on the bus. To Perth, services operate also on Tuesday, Thursday and Saturday nights and take eight hours. An alternative service is provided by Goldfields Express, with departures every weekday and two buses on Fridays. Two of these services run overnight, while the others operate during the day or evening. The journey takes approximately seven hours. As mentioned above, Goldfields Express also provides the service to Menzies, Leonora and Laverton three times a week.

Destination	Operator	Via	Distance (km)	Fare	Journey Time	Frequency
Adelaide	Greyhound		2351	$291	28¾ hrs	3/week
		Port Augusta	2033	$291	24¼ hrs	3/week
Perth	Greyhound		629	$130	7½ hrs	3/week
Perth	Goldfields Exp.		595	$92	6¾ - 7 hrs	6/week
Esperance	W.A.G.R.		393	$40.65	5 - 5¼ hrs	3/week
Laverton	Goldfields Exp.		359	$64	4 hrs	3/week

ANECDOTE

I had decided that it would be an interesting experience to take the weekly 'slow mixed' train across the Nullarbor from Kalgoorlie to Port Augusta. My first surprise was when I found that the train started not from Kalgoorlie at all, but from the goods yard at Parkeston, five kilometres distant. Since I could find no obvious way of getting there, I walked along the railway track, thinking that by such a route I could hardly miss it.

Arrived at the yard, I reported to the office and asked for a ticket to Port Augusta. I was eyed suspiciously and told, "This train doesn't take passengers for Port Augusta. If you want to go there, use a passenger train. This one only takes people as far as Cook." "O.K., sell me a ticket to Cook." The look of suspicion deepened. "I'm not selling you a ticket to Cook, because I know you're going to Port Augusta. Go on a passenger train." "No, I'm not. I've changed my mind. I'm going to Cook." "Well, I'm not selling you a ticket, and you'd better not get on the train without one." "All right, get the stationmaster then, and let me talk about it with him."

The clerk fetched the stationmaster and informed him, "This bloke wants a ticket to Cook, but I know very well he's going to Port Augusta." "Well, if he says he wants a ticket to Cook, sell him one," said the stationmaster. "It's not your problem what happens when he gets there." And, with reluctance, the clerk issued a ticket to Cook. These congenial formalities over, I went out to find my carriage.

It was an old wooden first-class sleeper, with a little wrought iron balcony at each end. I could not have wished for better. A close inspection revealed that it had been built in 1913. It was attached at the rear of about a kilometre of goods wagons. I climbed in and we spent the next five and a half hours shunting up and down the sidings marshalling the train. Finally, and quite unexpectedly, one of the shunts drew us out of the yard and we were off. The guard came round and discovered that he had a passenger and asked whether I had had the foresight to bring anything to eat and drink. I had food for three days and a limited supply of water. "Right," he said. "Come and let me know when you want more water, because there's none in here. You can come back to the guard's van whenever you feel bored, and we'll arrange for you to ride on the locomotive a bit later on when we do some more shunting." Not a word about a ticket.

It was a marvellous trip. I was the only passenger for most of the journey, and I could choose among my palatial, but dusty and rather warm, first-class accommodation, the end balcony, the guard's van and the locomotive. As the train with the lowest priority on the line, we had long waits in remote sidings where I could 'go sightseeing' and meet the residents before being recalled by a whistle from the engine.

We reached Cook eleven hours late, but the timetable allowed a stop of eighteen hours there, so we were able to resume on time again. I bought another ticket in Cook, of course, which cost just $1 more than purchasing a through fare, and was kindly offered the use of the staff showers while there.

There were only two problems. One was that the wagons were loose coupled and my carriage was right at the back, so every time we stopped and started during the night, there would be a crescendo of rattling wagons taking up the slack and I would be thrown onto the floor - which generally caused me to express my opinion of the loose coupling system. The other problem was that I had brought food for three days and the journey took nearly four.

One memory which remains forever in the mind is my sitting on the steps of the balcony on the last evening of the journey watching the twinkling lights of Woomera drift past in the darkness.

As we approached our destination and it became apparent that we would arrive in the early hours, about ten hours behind schedule, I asked the guard not to bother to wake me up, and he did not. At 6:00, I awoke to find my carriage uncoupled and abandoned in a shed in Spencer Goods Yard, with no human in sight. It took me an hour to locate, and walk to, Port Augusta Station.

We had finally reached Port Augusta after an adventure lasting 83 hours, having traversed the 1,684 kilometres between Parkeston and there at an average speed of 20 km/hr. Who could possibly want for a more enjoyable and romantic journey? Alas, though, this train is gone forever and now you must take a passenger train, as the clerk commanded.

YORK
Population 3,500

2 hrs by bus from Perth

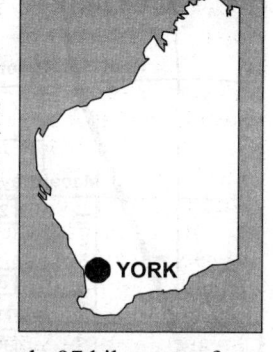

In performing a circuit round the south-west of Australia, we have missed out many small towns in the middle which might reasonably think that they too have a claim to be visited. Let us pick just one as a representative of the many towns which get passed by because there is so much else to see in this region.

York claims to be the oldest inland town in Western Australia. It was explored in 1830 and settled in 1831, only two years after Perth itself received its first residents. It is located on the Avon River, which becomes the Swan, and it is only 97 kilometres from Perth, so supplies could easily and quickly reach here. When gold was discovered around Kalgoorlie, it became a staging point in moving supplies to that area, and when the railway to Albany was being constructed, the next town south, Beverley, was, for some time, the terminus and passengers were encouraged to stay in one of the two towns whilst changing mode of transport. It also proved to be good farming country. York prospered, and is still a quiet but gently affluent town.

York is reached by W.A.G.R. bus from Perth. Some, but not all, services to Albany pass through, and some, but not all, services to Esperance pass through. The Esperance buses come directly to York, while the Albany services travel via Northam. There is at least one bus from Perth every day except Saturday, and there is at least one bus to Perth every day.

There are many relatively old buildings in the town worth a visit. The **Mill Gallery** is in the former flour mill constructed in 1892. It contains the work of some of the state's best artists and craftsmen, several of whom work here. It is open daily from 10:00 until 17:00.

Just up the road is the **Railway Station**, built in 1886 and a very elegant and charming small station. It is beautifully neat and trim, as it awaits the arrival of the next train. Unfortunately, though, there are no trains - or, at least, no passenger trains - nor have there been any since 1975. Goods trains still operate, though, travelling between Perth and Albany. There is a small Railway Museum within, open at weekends only.

The **Old Gaol** and **Courthouse**, too, are interesting. They date from 1895 and are open daily from 11:00 until 15:00. The Courthouse is still in use as a Court of Petty Sessions.

Across the river is the **Residency Museum**. The building is a typical example of an Australian country homestead. It was constructed in parts between 1842 and 1859. There are displays of old items relating to the town of York, including a map of the area drawn in 1829. The Residency Museum is open from 13:00 until 15:00, except on Mondays and Fridays.

The **Castle Hotel**, in the centre of the town, claims to be the second oldest surviving hotel in Western Australia. Part of it was built in 1853 by convict labour.

Next to the river is the **Avon Pioneer Park** and from it leads the **Avon Trail**, offering a pleasant walk beside the river. Just at the end of the park is a **pedestrian suspension bridge** which is almost a century old.

The **York Motor Museum** is at 116 Avon Terrace and has one of the finest

556 WESTERN AUSTRALIA

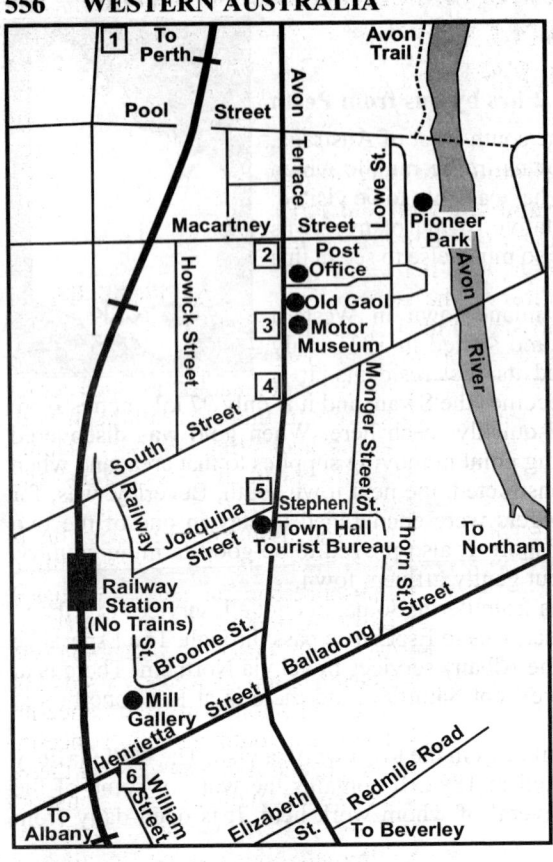

YORK
Numerals indicate accommodation

displays of motor vehicles in Australia. The Museum is open daily from 9:00 until 17:00.

The **Tourist Bureau** is in the Town Hall, a building dating from only 1911, on the corner of Avon Terrace and Joaquina Street, and has details of the many other relatively old buildings around the town.

Just thirty kilometres further up the Avon is **Beverley**, founded in 1839, which has buildings similar to those found in York, and also an interesting **Aeronautical Museum**. Since it has an aircraft outside, a de Haviland Vampire jet, the Museum is conspicuous. It also has the Silver Centenary, a biplane built in Beverley in 1930. It was the first privately-built aircraft in Western Australia. The **Beverley Tourist Bureau** is in the same building, which is open from 9:00 until 16:00 daily. Admission to the Museum costs $3.

Those W.A.G.R. buses from Perth to Albany which pass through York continue through Beverley. Buses bound for Esperance, however, do not.

ACCOMMODATION

York offers mainly higher class accommodation. The older hotels have rooms at moderate rates, but are still rather more expensive than in other country towns.

Accommodation in York

Name	Stars	No. on Map	Telephone No.	Address	Lowest Price (Double/Twin)
York Hotel		2	08-9641-2968	145 Avon Terrace	$215
Faversham House		1	08-9641-1366	24 Grey Street	$135
Avon Motel		6	08-9641-2066	William Street	$95
Settlers House		3	08-9641-1096	125 Avon Terrace	$75
Imperial Inn		5	08-9641-1010	83 Avon Terrace	$75
Castle Hotel		4	08-9641-1007	97 Avon Terrace	$70

MOVING ON
Bus Services from York

Destination	Operator	Via	Distance (kms)	Fare	Journey Time	Frequency
Perth	W.A.G.R.		97	$12.70	1½ - 2¼ hrs	8/week
Albany	W.A.G.R.		400	$42.40	6 hrs	4/week
Esperance	W.A.G.R.		636	$58.80	8¾ hrs	3/week

LANCELIN, CERVANTES AND THE PINNACLES

Population 800 (Lancelin)
Population 1,000 (Cervantes)
4 hrs 30 mins from Perth (Cervantes)

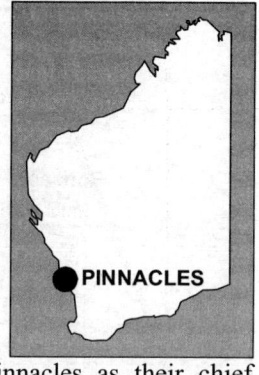

The Pinnacles are part of the **Nambung National Park** and consist of curious rock formations protruding from the shifting sands in a small coastal desert area north of Perth. Lancelin is the small town which lies to the south of the Pinnacles, and Cervantes is the slightly larger town which lies immediately to the north of them. Most visitors to either town have the Pinnacles as their chief interest in this area, although both towns also offer beaches, fishing, marine wildlife, swimming and diving.

The problem with Lancelin is that there is no direct public transport, but Cervantes now has a daily Greyhound bus service. W.A.G.R. buses to Geraldton via Eneabba stop at Regans Ford, but that is 51 kilometres from Lancelin. There is a youth hostel in Lancelin, though, and if you are staying there, the hostel will arrange transport from Perth on request. Alternatively, you can contact a company known as *Catch-a-Bus* (Tel:1-300-300-114).

Lancelin was, until recently, a small fishing and rock lobster centre, but, whilst it is still that, it is now a rapidly developing tourist destination also. It is 127 kilometres north of Perth and it has fine deep sea and bay fishing, and some beautiful beaches. It is noted for its windsurfing and dune buggy racing and it offers surfing, snorkelling and diving too. There are dolphins very close to the shore and seals which like to lie on the rocks, especially early in the morning. And, of course, the Pinnacles are nearby. Reaching the Pinnacles from Lancelin entails negotiating

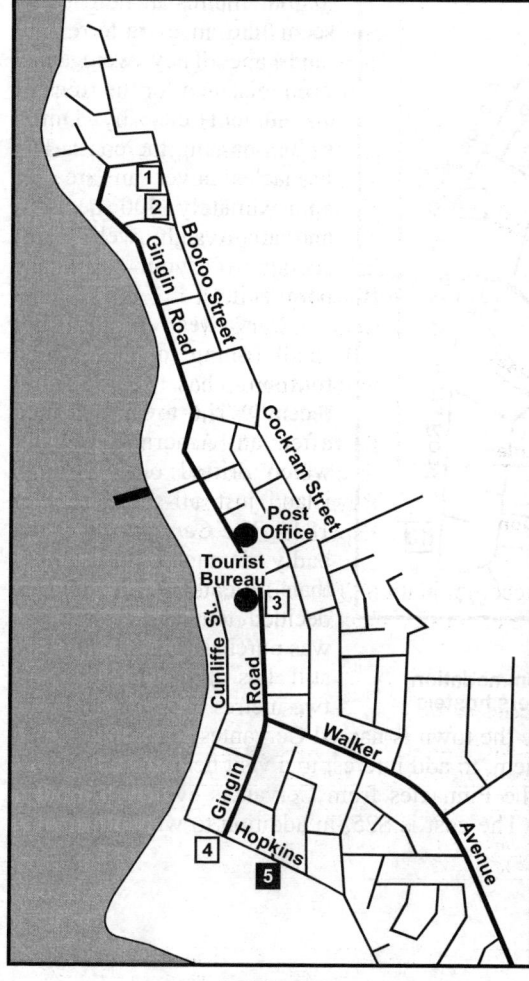

LANCELIN
Black numerals indicate hotel accommodation
White numerals indicate backpackers hostels

558 WESTERN AUSTRALIA

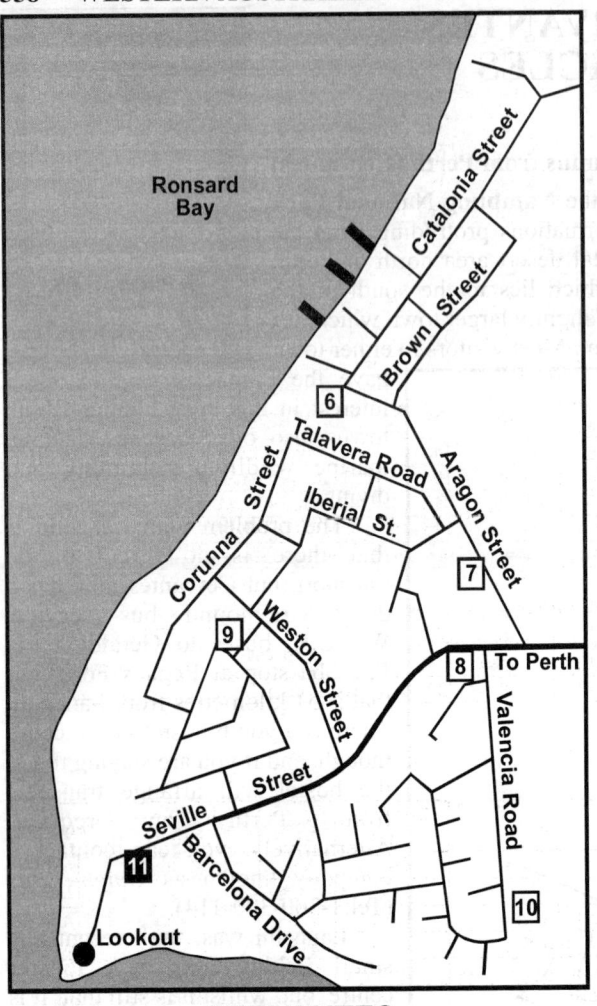

CERVANTES
Black numerals indicate hotel accommodation
White numerals indicate backpackers hostels

the sand dunes, however, and that necessitates a four-wheel-drive vehicle. Even with a four-wheel-drive, one needs to be careful where one stops, otherwise it will be difficult to get started again.

The Pinnacles are limestone pillars, thousands of them rising out of the yellow sands like stone termite mounds. They are up to four metres in height and seem like an extra-terrestrial landscape. They were once even mistaken for the ruins of an ancient city by Dutch sailors passing the coast. The Pinnacles cover an area of approximately 400 hectares and are a sight well worth seeing if your itinerary permits it.

Cervantes is another small fishing town to which tourism has come but recently. The town is named after an American whaler which drifted onto a small island just off-shore here in 1844. The *Cervantes* was not badly damaged, but, rather than refloat her, the owners decided to sell her and she was purchased as she lay. She still lies there, however, in two metres of water, and does seem likely to be refloated now. Since the town is named Cervantes, the street names nearly all have a Spanish flavour to them, to add interest to a visit here.

Happyday Tours runs a tour to the Pinnacles from Cervantes every morning at 8:00, returning to Cervantes at 11:15. The cost is $25, in addition to which there is a park entry fee of $5.

LANCELIN, CERVANTES, PINNACLES 559

ACCOMMODATION
(i) Hotel Accommodation in Lancelin

Name	Stars	No. on Map	Telephone No.	Address	Lowest Price (Double/Twin)
Lancelin Inn		2	08-9655-1005	North Street & Gingin Road	$75
Anita and Arthur's Acc.	3		08-9655-1100	102 Gingin Road	$70
Lancelin Caravan Park		4	08-9655-1056	Hopkins Street	$65
North End Caravan Park		1	08-9655-1115	Bootoo Street	$65

(ii) Backpackers Hostel in Lancelin

Name	Group	No. on Map	Telephone No.	Address	Lowest Price (Dormitory)
Lancelin Lodge	YHA	5	08-9655-2020	Hopkins Street	$18

(iii) Hotel Accommodation in Cervantes

Name	Stars	No. on Map	Telephone No.	Address	Lowest Price (Double/Twin)
Pinnacles Motel	3½	7	08-9652-7145	Aragon Street	$110
Beachfront Units		9	08-9652-7194	Iberia & Weston Streets	$105
Churinga Holiday Villas		10	08-9652-7312	Valencia Road	$85
Cervantes Holiday Homes		8	08-9652-7115	Valencia Rd. & Malaga Crt.	$60
Pinnacles Caravan Park		6	08-9652-7060	Aragon Street	$60

(iv) Backpackers Hostel in Cervantes

Name	Group	No. on Map	Telephone No.	Address	Lowest Price (Dormitory)
Pinnacles Beach B/P		11	1800-245-232	101 Prinsep Street	$20

MOVING ON
Bus Services from Cervantes

Destination	Operator	Via	Distance (km)	Fare	Journey Time	Frequency
Perth	Greyhound		245	$32	4¼ hrs	1/day
Broome	Greyhound		2231	$325	30 hrs	1/day
		Port Hedland	1634	$209	22½ hrs	1/day
		Exmouth	1155	$195	15½ hrs	3/week
		Carnarvon	763	$114	10 hrs	1/day
		Geraldton	283	$28	3¾ hrs	1/day

GERALDTON
Population 20,000

6 hrs by bus from Perth

It is quite possible that the Geraldton area, rather than the vicinity of Sydney, was the first place in Australia to be inhabited by Europeans. There is, of course, a story behind this possibility, and it is the story of the *Batavia*, which, you will find, has made a lasting impression on Geraldton. This story follows soon, but first let us make the journey to Geraldton.

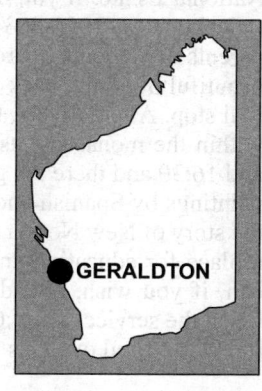

560 WESTERN AUSTRALIA

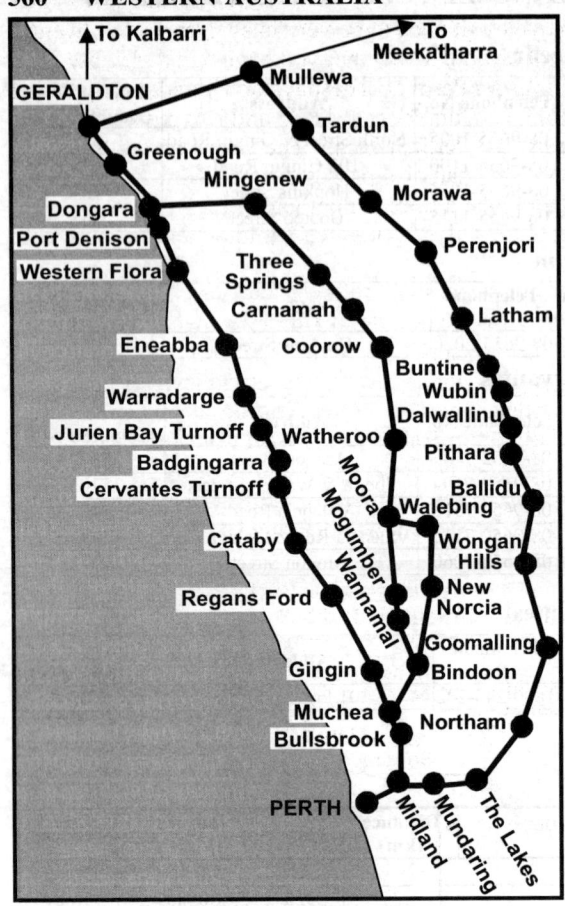

W.A.G.R. SERVICES BETWEEN PERTH AND GERALDTON
Showing connexions to Kalbarri and Meekatharra

Geraldton is another place with a railway line, and a fine station, but no passenger trains. Instead W.A.G.R. runs buses from Perth to here. They operate by three different routes. The fastest travel up the main Brand Highway taking six hours. This route is served every day. Others travel via New Norcia and Moora, taking seven hours, and still others travel via Northam and Mullewa, and take nearly nine hours. Most travellers are content just to take the shortest route, but the author recommends the route via New Norcia, because that is a little town well worth seeing. The bus will make a twenty-minute stop here. Do not waste your time eating. Hurry ahead down the road to look at the remarkable buildings.

New Norcia is Australia's only monastic town. It was founded by Dom Rosendo Salvado in 1846 and has a beauty which you will find nowhere else on this continent. It lies 132 kilometres north of Perth on the Great Northern Highway and is now the home of just sixteen Benedictine monks. The architecture is Spanish. 27 of the buildings are classified by the National Trust and the whole town is registered on the National Estate. If you have time, it is possible to stay here, at the New Norcia Hotel (telephone 08-9654-8034), which, when opened in 1927, was used to accommodate parents of students boarding here, but which has served as an hotel since 1955. It is a beautiful building, back from the road and not far from the roadhouse where your bus will stop. Alternatively, there is the Monastery Guesthouse (telephone 08-9654-8002), within the monastery itself. Some of the buildings are open for visits between 10:00 and 16:30 and there are guided tours available. The **Museum and Art Gallery** contain paintings by Spanish and Italian masters and gifts from the Queen of Spain, as well as the story of New Norcia and its role as an aboriginal mission, an agricultural centre and a place for education and culture. There are two **Heritage Walks** available, and you can, if you wish, attend mass with the monks at 7:30 any morning, except Sunday, when the service is at 9:00. The **shop** offers home-baked bread, produced in a century-old wood-fired oven, as well as cake, jams, honey, preserves and pottery. If you do not

GERALDTON 561

want to stay in this fascinating town, you will need to be very busy during your twenty-minute bus break, but at least you will be able to say that you have had a glimpse of it. It is also possible to visit as a day trip from Perth on Tuesdays or Thursdays, by taking the bus at 9:30 from East Perth Station, reaching here at 11:25 and leaving again on the bus back to Perth at 14:50, arriving in East Perth at 16:45. The Greyhound bus service to Port Hedland via Meekatharra and Newman also passes through New Norcia twice a week in each direction, but does not make a refreshment halt here.

Greyhound and Integrity also operate daily services to Geraldton and beyond, both by the most direct route.

All the buses to Geraldton, except those via Mullewa, will pass by or through Dongara about 45 minutes before arriving in Geraldton. **Dongara** and **Port Denison**, three kilometres apart, are pleasant places to stay, and, for backpackers, there is a youth hostel in Dongara (see map on next page). Dongara was first settled in 1852 and many of the buildings date from soon after that. The **Old Police Station** is now used as the Tourist Information Centre. The **Royal Steam Roller Flour Mill** was built in 1894 and operated until 1935. It is now owned by the National Trust and is being restored. The streets are lined with **Moreton Bay Fig Trees**, planted by the Roads Board in 1906. Then there are beaches just a short walk from the town, offering sand and surf. It is 65 kilometres from here to Geraldton.

Between Dongara and Geraldton lies **Greenough**. The Greenough Flats are a flood plain with particularly fertile soil, which enabled them to become a thriving agricultural area in the 1860s. What remains now is a small community almost unchanged from that time. There are many buildings here giving an insight into Australian society up to 150 years ago. In order from north to south, here are some of the attractions (see map on page 563). *Corringle* is a two storey mansion built in 1899. It is about seven kilometres north of Greenough, but is a private residence and not open to the public. The **Pioneer Museum** is six kilometres north of the main settlement. It is open from 10:00 until 16:00 except on Fridays. Further south are Greenough's famous **leaning trees**. These trees are trying to escape the salt in the wind coming from the sea and bending over backwards to do so. Opposite the trees is a road running off to the **Pioneer**

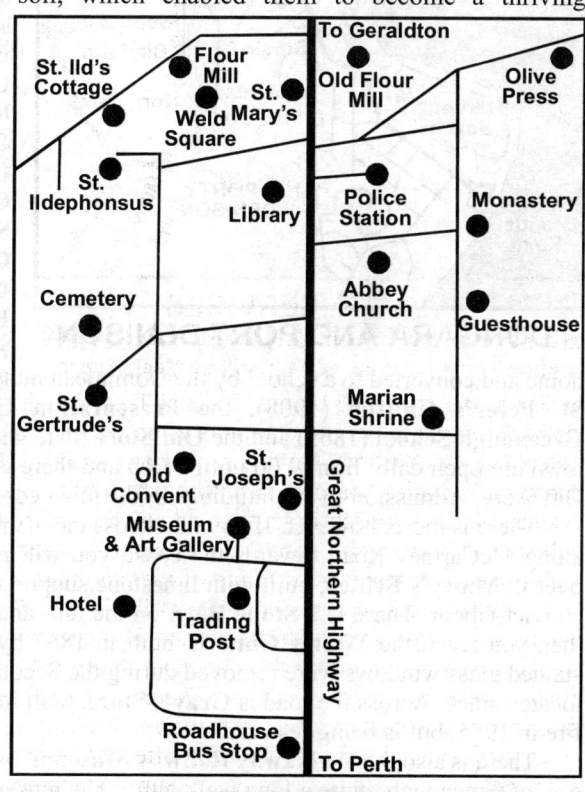

NEW NORCIA

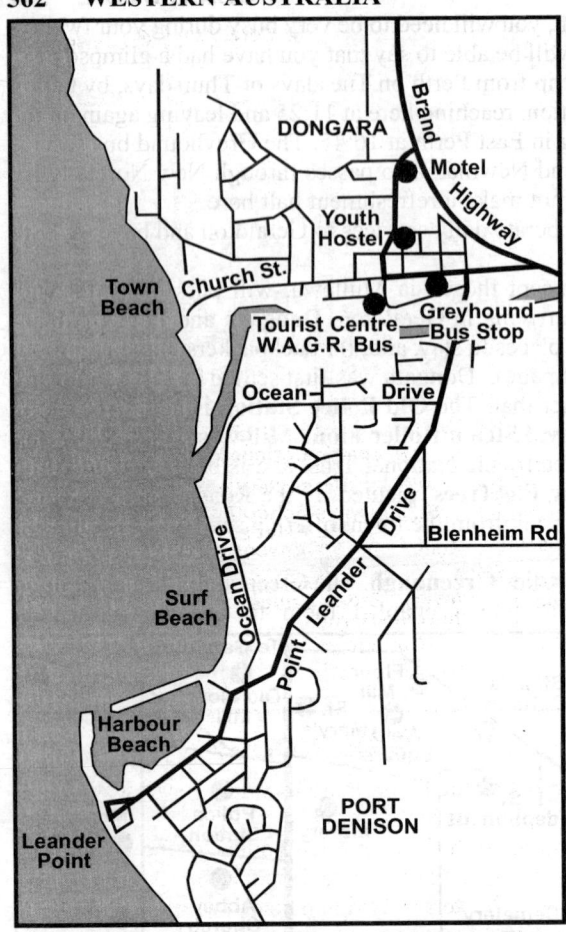

DONGARA AND PORT DENISON

Cemetery, where the earliest grave is dated 1853. Just north of the main town is the **Old Greenough Hotel**, dating from 1868, but used as a private residence from 1888 until 1941 for the Clinch family who owned and operated **Clinch's Mill**, which is next. It was built in 1858 as a single-storey mill, but extended to three storeys in 1891. It operated until 1922 and is now being restored. It is not currently open for visits. **Cliff Grange** was the home of the original mill owner in 1858. It has been restored and furnished in its period style, but is not open for viewing.

Now we come to the main town of Greenough, where there are twelve old buildings to be viewed. These are **St. Catherine's Hall** (1900), the **Road Board Office** (1900), **St. Catherine's Church** (1913), the **Old Gaol** (1870) and **Courthouse** (1868), the **Police Station** (1868) and former **Post Office** (1874), **Hackett's Cottage** (1888), the **Catholic Presbytery** (1890), **St. Joseph's School** (built in 1865 as a private home and converted to a school by the Dominican nuns early in the twentieth century), **St. Peter's Church** (1908), the **Presentation Convent** (1901), the **Central Greenough School** (1865) and the **Old Store** (date uncertain). All the buildings in the town are open daily from 9:00 until 17:00 and there is an **Information Centre** in the Old Store. Admission to the buildings in the town costs $5.

There is more, however. If you now cross the main Brand Highway and walk west along McCartney Road towards the coast, you will reach the Greenough River and, over it, **Maley's Bridge**, built with limestone supports and timber decking in 1864 by convict labour. There is a **Stone Barn** on the left, and, behind it, an **old cottage**, and then you reach the **Wesley Church**, built in 1867 by 'ticket-of-leave' convicts. The stained glass windows were removed during the Second World War and have not been located since. Across the road is **Gray's Store**, built in 1861. It was badly damaged by fire in 1975, but is being restored.

There is also the **Walkaway Railway Museum**, but Walkaway is seven kilometres east of Greenough, quite a long walk away. The museum is open from 10:00 (13:00 at weekends) until 16:00, except on Mondays.

Greenough itself is 24 kilometres south of Geraldton and the problem is how to get here and how to get back, but there are ways. On weekdays, a W.A.G.R. bus leaves Geraldton for Perth at 8:30 and stops at Greenough, on request, after twenty minutes. A bus returns to Geraldton from the same point at 14:09 on weekdays, and also at 16:10 on Tuesdays and Thursdays. Reservations must be made for these services. Alternatively, there are tours operated from Geraldton.

Now, finally, we have reached the city of Geraldton, on what is now known as the *Batavia Coast*. So what about the promised story of the *Batavia*? What was this ship, and why has it made such a lasting impression on this region? What of the claim that Geraldton, or nearby, might really have been the first European settlement in Australia?

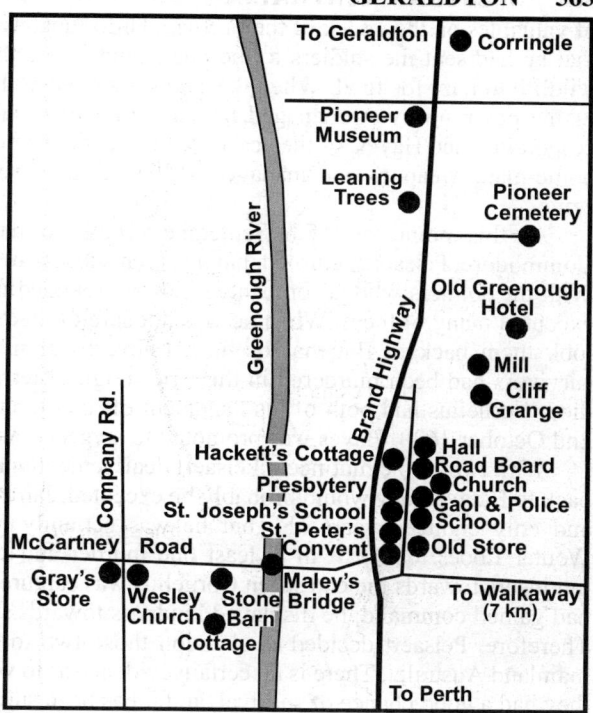

GREENOUGH

The *Batavia* sailed from Holland on 28th October 1628 bound for the Dutch East Indies by the newly-discovered route round the Cape of Good Hope, then east, and finally north parallel to what is now the Western Australian coast to Batavia (Jakarta). On 4th June 1629, the ship, on her maiden voyage, ran aground on the hidden reefs surrounding the **Abrolhos Islands**, about 65 kilometres west of where Geraldton now stands. Most of the crew and passengers were landed safely on an island now known as **Batavia's Graveyard**. The Captain, the Commodore, named Pelsaert, who, although not a mariner, was ranked senior to the Captain, and about thirty sailors, were on a different island with two of the ship's boats and most of the water and supplies. They decided to take the two boats and try to reach Batavia to summon assistance for the other survivors, and left a note to that effect. When the rest of the survivors found them gone, they named the island **Traitors Island**. At this point, the abandoned survivors were in a very awkward position, with little food and water and no means of escape. Some died of thirst before rains came to improve the situation.

The most senior man left was the Undermerchant, named Cornelius, and he took control. He sent the soldiers away without weapons to a distant island on the pretext of looking for water and divided the civilian passengers amongst various islands, where he started systematically murdering them, with the assistance of a band of 36 followers. Presumably his intention was to improve his own chances of survival and to allow him and his gang to plunder at a later date, and without witnesses, the considerable quantity of valuables on the wreck of the *Batavia*. Unfortunately for him, however, it happened that he had sent the soldiers to the one island where there was permanent water, and wildlife to hunt for food. When the soldiers signalled that they had found water, some of the other survivors managed to reach the island and warn the soldiers, led by a corporal named Hayes, of the actions and intentions of Cornelius. They prepared some home-made weapons and managed to defend themselves when the expected attacks came.

At this point, on 17th September 1629, to the surprise of all parties, the Commodore, Pelsaert, returned, having been successful in his attempt to reach Batavia. With the soldiers who accompanied him, he rounded up the mutineers, and tried and executed many of them. When he was not sure of their guilt or proper punishment, he took them back to Batavia for further investigation. Between 115 and 120 of the survivors had been murdered in this brief reign of terror, and in total 210 people had died. Cornelius had both of his hands cut off before being hanged on **Seal Island** on 2nd October 1629. Hayes was promoted to sergeant, and later became a lieutenant.

With two of the mutineers Pelsaert dealt leniently, knowing that if they were taken back to Batavia they would probably be executed. Jan Pelgrom de Bye was a cabin boy and only eighteen years old, but he was certainly implicated in various murders. Wouter Looes took part in at least one murder and was placed in command of the mutineers towards the end when Cornelius was captured by Hayes. However, when he had gained command, he displayed kindness towards some of the remaining civilians. Therefore, Pelsaert decided to abandon those two to their fate on the west coast of mainland Australia. There is no certain evidence as to what happened to them there, but they had a good chance of survival, and it has been suggested that they may have lived into old age as the first European settlers, albeit reluctant, of this great southern continent.

Geraldton was established in 1850 after the explorer Gregory had reported mineral deposits to the north. In recent years, it has become a flourishing port, specialising in the export of bulk grain, with some of the most modern facilities in the country. It is also known for its rock lobster industry. Lobster meat is exported from here to Europe and North America, and live lobsters are exported to Japan, Taiwan and China.

If you arrive in Geraldton with Greyhound or Integrity, you will alight at the Tourist Bureau, which is a good place to start looking at the town. If you arrive with W.A.G.R., you will find yourself at the Railway Station, which is not very far away. The **Tourist Bureau** is in an old building which used to be the Victoria District Hospital, built in 1884. It continued in service as the principal hospital and nurses' training school until 1966. It is now Tourist Bureau, small museum (free), travel agency and Batavia Backpackers Hostel. Almost next door is a supermarket, so one hardly needs to move from here for all the necessities of life.

As you walk towards the town centre, you will find the **Old Gaol** on your left, now also a Craft Centre. Admission to this is also free and it is interesting. The Gaol was built in 1858 and claims to be the second oldest still in existence in the state (after Fremantle), although whether that is an honour for the city or not is a matter of opinion, of course. Continue walking and you will come to the **Railway Station** on your right. This is another fine old station much in need of a few trains. However, it does not even have any tracks now, the line to the port having been moved slightly to the west. The **Geraldton Museum** has been moved to an impressive new building out on the harbour front to the north of the station. Understandably, the Museum places considerable

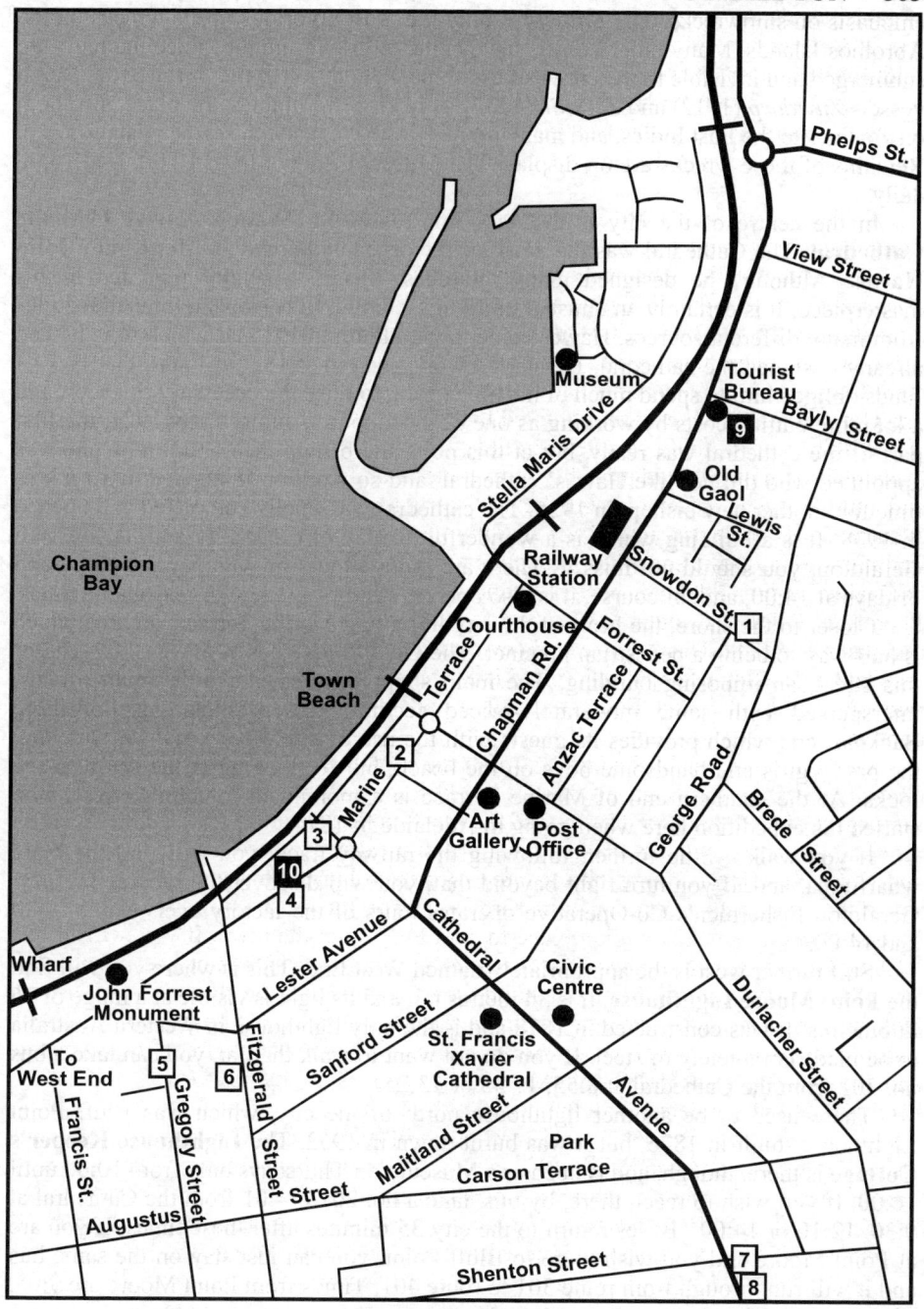

emphasis on shipwrecks. The *Batavia* is only the most notorious of the wrecks on the Abrolhos Islands. Many other vessels have come to grief there too, since the reefs are submerged and invisible to the crews of the ships. In addition to the *Batavia*, the Dutch vessels *Zuytdorp* (1712) and *Zeewijk* (1727) were also lost in the same place, also both on voyages to the East Indies, and many more ships have made the same mistake since. Remains of these wrecks are on display. The Museum is open from 10:00 until 16:00 daily.

In the centre of the city is the very impressive **St. Francis Xavier Catholic Cathedral**. The Cathedral was the work of the priest and architect **Monsignor John Hawes**. Although he designed many churches, this is generally regarded as his masterpiece. It is certainly an unusual building, seeming to borrow architectural styles from many different sources. Hawes came to Geraldton in 1915, at which time he had already designed the cathedral. He started work on it in 1916, but found that lack of funds obliged him to spend much of his time trying to raise the necessary finances, and a lot more cutting costs by working as one of the labourers himself. By 1921, the first part of the cathedral was ready, but at this point the bishop died and a new one was appointed who did not like Hawes' cathedral, and so work on it stopped, until it was time for another new bishop, in 1935. The cathedral was finally completed and opened in 1938. It is a building which is a wonderful display of originality and, if you visit Geraldton, you should not miss it. There are guided tours on Mondays at 10:00 and Fridays at 14:00, and, of course, it is also open to visitors at all other reasonable times.

Closer to the shore, the heart of the city lies along Marine Terrace, an area which is half way to being a pedestrian precinct. The **Courthouse** lies at the northern end of this street, an imposing building. The main shopping area is a little south of this, interspersed with some moderately-priced accommodation, including Foreshore Backpackers, which provides its guests with the use of a telescope, not for watching the pretty girls and handsome boys on the beach, but for looking at the **seals** on the rocks. At the southern end of Marine Terrace is a monument to John Forrest, who started his expedition here when going to Adelaide in 1874.

If you walk a little further, following the railway track, you will find the main wharf area, and, if you turn right beyond that, you will discover the **lobster factory**. Geraldton Fishermen's Co-Operative operates tours of the factory every day at 9:30 and 14:00.

Still further west is the appropriately named West End. This is where you will find the **Point Moore Lighthouse**. It is 34 metres tall and its light is visible at a range of 26 kilometres. It was constructed in 1878 and is the only lighthouse in Western Australia to be made completely of steel. If you do not want to walk that far, you can take a bus no. 301 from the Cathedral at 8:55, 11:35 or 13:25.

There used to be another lighthouse north of the city, which was Bluff Point Lighthouse, built in 1876, but it was burnt down in 1952. The **Lighthouse Keeper's Cottage** is there, though, and is open as a Museum on Thursdays only from 10:00 until 16:00. If you wish to reach there, by bus, take a no. 201 or 401 from the Cathedral at 9:30, 12:10 or 14:00. Buses return to the city 35 minutes after these times. If you are at Point Moore and you wish to go to Bluff Point, you can just stay on the same bus and it will run through from route 301 to route 401. Times from Point Moore are 9:05, 11:45 and 13:35.

It should also not escape mention that Geraldton has **beaches**, including those right in the city centre, and that it is one of the sunniest places in Australia, averaging eight hours of sunshine per day throughout the year. It is particularly popular in winter, when the sun still shines here and it remains agreeably warm.

Buses in Geraldton are operated by Geraldton Bus Service. There are four routes, two to the north and two to the south, but both buses north set off from the Cathedral at the same time, as do both buses south (the same buses, in fact, next time round). There are three services per day on each route on weekdays, except Tuesdays, when the last bus does not operate. On Thursdays and Fridays there are late-night buses, with services south as late as 16:25 and north at 17:00. On Saturdays services run in the morning only and on Sundays there are no buses. Fares are $2.

ACCOMMODATION
(i) Hotel Accommodation in Geraldton

Name	Stars	No. on Map	Telephone No.	Address	Lowest Price (Double/Twin)
Hospitality Inn	3½	8	08-9921-1422	169 Cathedral Avenue	$130
Ocean Centre Hotel	3½	3	08-9921-7777	Cathedral Av / Foreshore Dr	$95
Champion Bay B & B		1	08-9921-7624	31 Snowdon Street	$95
Batavia Motor Inne	3½	6	1-800-014-628	54 Fitzgerald Street	$85
Sun City Motel	2½	7	08-9921-6111	137 Cathedral Avenue	$70
Geraldton Hotel		5	08-9921-3700	19 Gregory Street	$50
Blue Heeler Tavern		4	08-9921-1133	185 Marine Terrace	$50
Cameliers Guest House		2	08-9964-3725	92 Marine Terrace	$30

(ii) Backpackers Hostels in Geraldton

Name	Group	No. on Map	Telephone No.	Address	Lowest Price (Dormitory)
Blue Heeler Tavern		4	08-9921-1133	185 Marine Terrace	$30
Foreshore Backpackers	YHA	10	08-9921-3275	172 Marine Terrace	$18
Cameliers Guest House		2	08-9964-3725	92 Marine Terrace	$17
Batavia Backpackers	VIP	9	08-9964-3001	Chapman Road & Bayly Street	$16

MOVING ON
Bus Services from Geraldton

Destination	Operator	Via	Distance (km)	Fare	Journey Time	Frequency
Perth	Greyhound		422	$43	6 - 7¼ hrs	10/week
Perth	W.A.G.R.		422	$46.25	6 - 8½ hrs	14/week
Perth	Integrity		422	$41	5½ - 5¾ hrs	12/week
Broome	Greyhound		1948	$325	26¼ hrs	1/day
		Port Hedland	1351	$209	18¾ hrs	1/day
		Exmouth	872	$172	11¾ - 12¾ hrs	10/week
		Carnarvon	480	$74	6¼ - 7¾ hrs	10/week
Broome	Integrity		1948	$285	29 hrs	2/week
		Port Hedland	1351	$195	20¼ hrs	2/week
		Exmouth	875	$155	10½ - 11½ hrs	4/week
		Carnarvon	483	$65	5½ - 6 hrs	5/week
Meekatharra	W.A.G.R.		531	$52.80	6¾ - 7 hrs	2/week
Kalbarri	W.A.G.R.		170	$19.85	2½ hrs	3/week

WESTERN AUSTRALIA
KALBARRI
Population 1,000

8 hrs 30 mins by bus from Perth

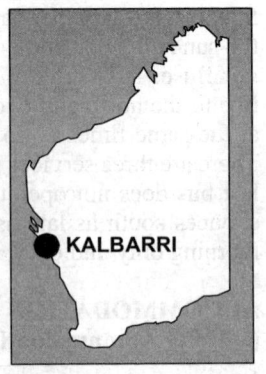

Proceeding north from Geraldton, there are two places of interest on the way to Kalbarri. The first is **Northampton**, 45 minutes and 52 kilometres up the highway. Northampton was founded in 1848, and in 1853 a convict-hiring station was established nearby, with the labour being employed for the mining of copper and lead and in the construction of roads and bridges. The Wanneranooka Copper Mine, started in 1842, was the first copper mine in Western Australia. The lead mine was the Geraldine Lead Mine, near the turn-off to Kalbarri at Ajana. **Chiverton House Museum**, in Northampton, has a collection of early mining machinery and there is a pleasant little railway station with no trains, but some old rolling stock. There are also aboriginal rock paintings outside the town.

The second place of interest is the **Hutt River Province**. This was originally the Hutt River Station, covering 18,500 acres and engaged mainly in the production of wheat. In 1969, the Western Australian Government decided to introduce a wheat quota system, against which there was to be no appeal, and Hutt River's quota was a tiny fraction of its normal production. Unless they could immediately develop some other use for the land, the occupants would be unable to survive. They felt this situation unjust but could find no remedy. In the end, they decided to secede from Western Australia and from the Commonwealth of Australia. They did so, on 21st April 1970, and established the Hutt River Province, a principality under the leadership of H.R.H. Prince Leonard. The principality issues its own stamps and coins and grants citizenship to suitable individuals, activities which now supplement quite effectively the income from wheat growing. Tours run to the principality, but unfortunately Hutt River Province does not have an effective public transport system, so it is difficult to reach there without a vehicle. You will see a signpost off to the left just after leaving Northampton, but the principality is about thirty kilometres from that point.

At **Ajana**, one leaves the highway in order to reach Kalbarri. There is another route to Kalbarri directly from Northampton, and this way too is now sealed and used by the Greyhound service to and from Exmouth via Kalbarri. W.A.G.R. provides a service from Perth via Geraldton on Mondays, Wednesdays and Fridays, with return on the following mornings. The bus runs from Perth to Geraldton by the direct route, that is via Eneabba, but it should be noted that the service back to Perth travels via Moora and New Norcia on Tuesdays and Thursdays. This is a more interesting route, but it takes an hour longer. Only on Saturdays does the bus run back to Perth via Eneabba.

Greyhound provides a service from Perth on Sunday, Wednesday and Friday evenings, but these buses reach Kalbarri at the inconvenient time of 3:00 the following morning. The bus then continues to Exmouth. Similarly, the bus travelling south from Exmouth to Perth reaches Kalbarri at 1:30 on Sunday, Tuesday and Friday mornings, an equally inconvenient hour.

It was probably somewhere near Kalbarri that the two seamen mentioned in the section on Geraldton as having been cast ashore following the *Batavia* mutiny were actually marooned. If this is the true location, they at least had a pleasant spot for their exile, although it was lacking at the time in some of the facilities which it has now.

Kalbarri is still a small town, but it is a holiday resort rapidly gaining in popularity. That is understandable, for it is a rustic, scenic location, which has everything that most holidaymakers could want, except, perhaps, a bank. Kalbarri is at the mouth of the pretty Murchison River, so it has the peaceful river, with, just five minutes away, the churning ocean. People come here for boating, for fishing and for walking. There is a path along the cliffs, and easy coastal walks are available, but it is the nearby gorge along the Murchison River which really invites walking. The walking paths, though, are some distance from the town of Kalbarri and must first be reached. Moreover, they are in a National Park, and if you enter by vehicle, you will be charged a fee of $3 per bus passenger, or $10 per car.

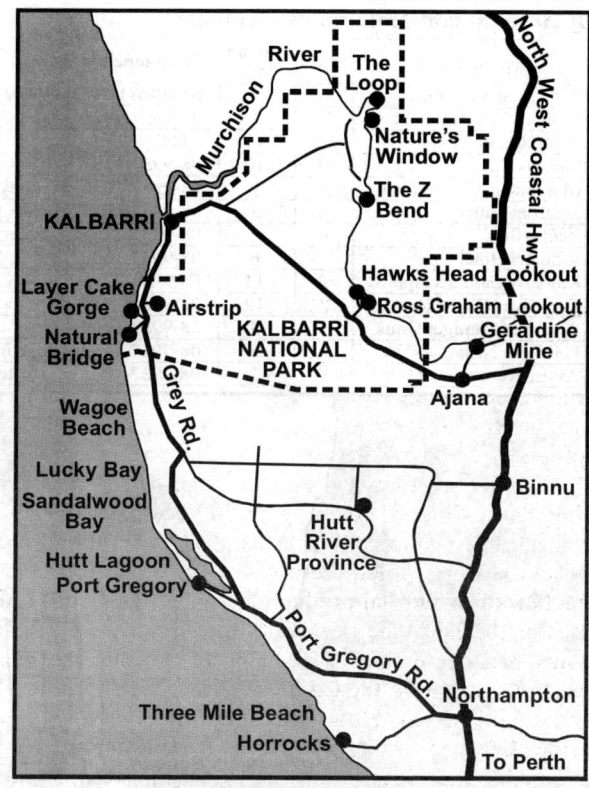

KALBARRI VICINITY

The Kalbarri National Park covers an area of 183,000 hectares and includes the coast as well as the river gorge, but it is for entry to the gorge that one is charged. The turn-off is ten kilometres along the road to Ajana, and from there it is another 25 kilometres to the two principal walking places. To cover this distance of 35 kilometres, local transport is available. One can go on a tour, or one can just be conveyed to the gorge and back, or, if one feels energetic, one can hire a bicycle and ride the seventy kilometres. Note, however, that not much of the road is sealed, and that it is quite rough in parts.

The **Murchison Gorge** stretches for 84 kilometres and is 152 metres at its deepest point. The two most popular places for walking are **The Loop** and **The Z Bend** (see map above). Maps of the walking tracks are available at the **Tourist Bureau**, where the W.A.G.R. bus terminates. However, if you want merely to see, without too much strenuous exercise, the best lookout points are at **Hawks Head Lookout** and **Ross Graham Lookout**, about halfway along the road to Ajana, again a distance of approximately 35 kilometres from Kalbarri.

ACCOMMODATION

Kalbarri is a holiday resort, and prices fluctuate considerably according to season. Note that the rates given here are low season rates. High season mainly means during school holidays, and at those periods there may be considerable increases.

570 WESTERN AUSTRALIA
(i) Hotel Accommodation in Kalbarri

Name	Stars	No. on Map	Telephone No.	Address	Lowest Price (Double/Twin)
Pelican Shore Villas	3½	7	1-800-671-708	Grey & Kaiber Streets	$125
Kalbarri Beach Resort	3½	1	08-9937-1061	Grey & Clotsworthy Streets	$110
Palm Resort Motel	3½	11	1-800-819-029	8 Porter Street	$100
Sunsea Villas	3	10	08-9937-1187	18 Grey Street	$95
Murchison View Apts.	4	9	08-9937-1096	Grey & Rushton Streets	$85
Seafront Units	3½	3	08-9937-1025	108 Grey Street	$85
Reef Villas	4	4	08-9937-1165	Coles & Mortimer Streets	$75
Kalbarri Hotel		6	08-9937-1000	50 Grey Street	$70
Kalbarri Gardens Apts.	3	13	08-9937-2211	2 Kelsar Gardens	$70
Sun River Chalets	2½	12	08-9937-1119	2 Nanda Drive	$65
Riverfront Budget Units		8	08-9937-1144	Grey Street	$60
Pelican's Nest		5	08-9937-1430	Mortimer & Woods Streets	$55
Av-Er-Rest		2	08-9937-1101	Mortimer & Auger Streets	$55

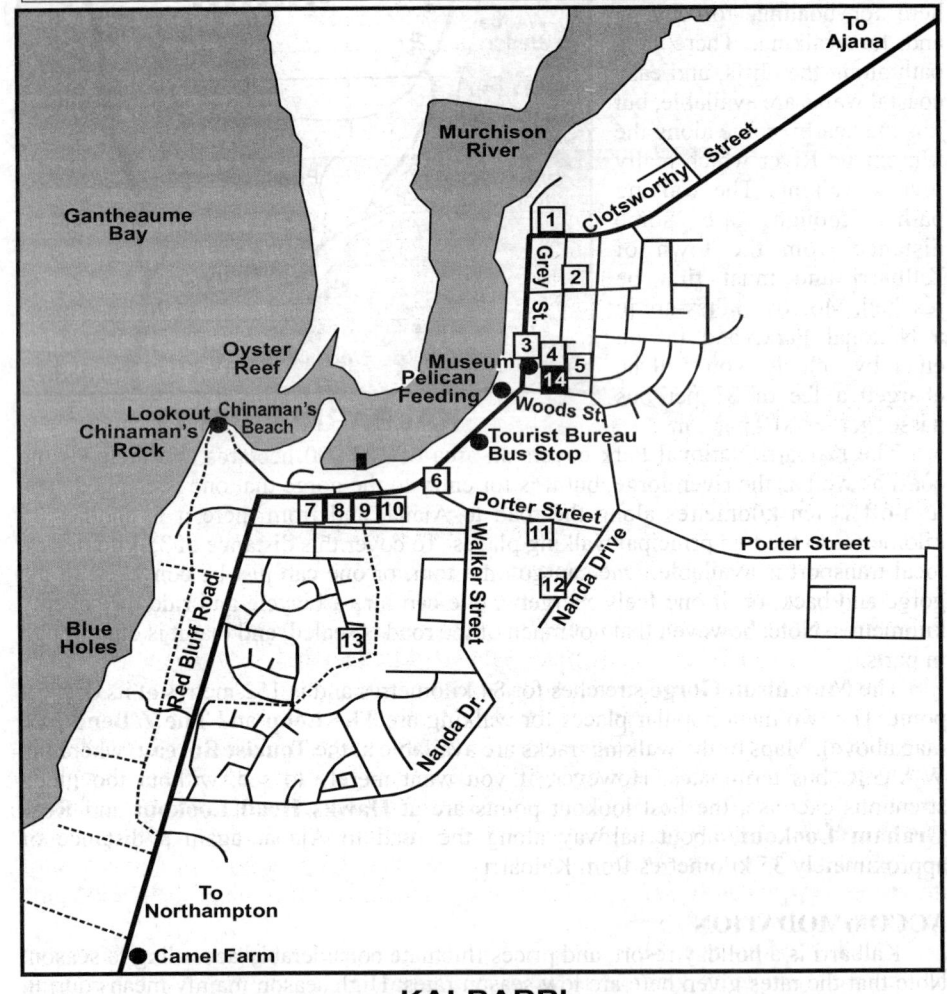

KALBARRI
Black numerals in white boxes indicate hotel accommodation
White numerals in black boxes indicate backpackers hostels

KALBARRI

(ii) Backpackers Hostel in Kalbarri

Name	Group	No. on Map	Telephone No.	Address	Lowest Price (Dormitory)
Kalbarri Backpackers	YHA/VIP	14	08-9937-1430	Mortimer & Woods Streets	$18

MOVING ON

The W.A.G.R. bus runs back to Perth on Tuesday, Thursday and Saturday mornings. Greyhound travels to Perth on Sunday, Tuesday and Friday mornings at 1:50, and north to Exmouth at 3:15 on Monday, Thursday and Saturday mornings.

Bus Services from Kalbarri

Destination	Operator	Via	Distance (km)	Fare	Journey Time	Frequency
Perth	Greyhound		557	$100	9 hrs	3/week
		Geraldton	135	$57	2 hrs	3/week
Perth	W.A.G.R.		592	$57.50	8½ - 9¾ hrs	3/week
		Geraldton	170	$19.85	2¼ hrs	3/week
Perth	Integrity		592	$80	8¼ hrs	2/week
		Geraldton	170	$40	2¼ hrs	2/week
Exmouth	Greyhound		717	$163	10¾ hrs	3/week
		Carnarvon	325	$64	5¾ hrs	3/week
Broome	Integrity		1910	$300	29 hrs	2/week
		Port Hedland	1313	$210	20¼ hrs	2/week
		Exmouth	803	$165	10½ hrs	2/week
		Carnarvon	445	$75	5½ hrs	2/week

DENHAM AND MONKEY MIA

Population 500 (Denham)

12 hrs 30 mins by bus from Perth

If you are expecting to find monkeys at Monkey Mia, you will be disappointed. What you will find instead, though, is **dolphins**, and various other sea-dwelling creatures as well. It is the dolphins which have really made Monkey Mia famous. They arrive every morning to see who has come to greet them and play with them. This is one of the three famous sites in Australia for dolphins, the others being Bunbury, south of Perth (see page 501), and Tin Can Bay, in Queensland (see page 269). This, though, is the most touristic of the three sites, attracting 150,000 visitors a year. The dolphins started popping in for morning tea in the 1960s and now the third generation is to be seen every morning. Altogether, there are about 120 dolphins who visit, but not all of them come every day. What is almost certain, though, is that some of them will come on any day between 8:00 and 13:00.

This area is known as **Shark Bay** and it has a great deal of history. The first known landing in Australia by a European took place here in 1616. The Dutch explorer, Dirk Hartog, landed at **Cape Inscription**, which is on an island, not the mainland (see map),

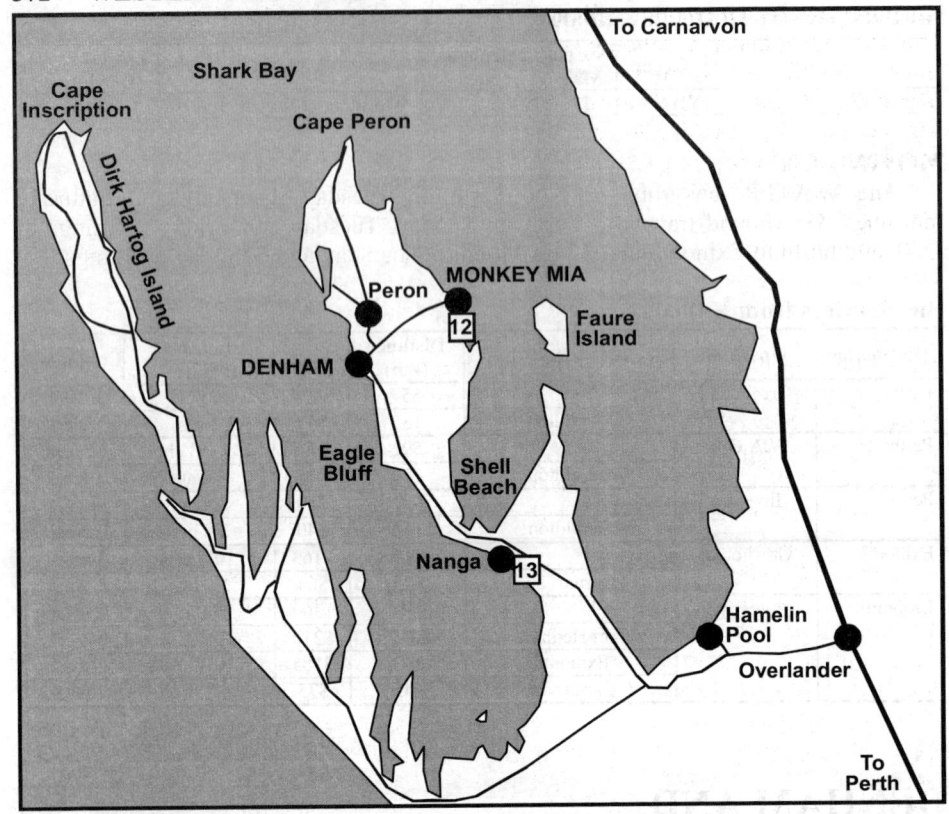

SHARK BAY
Numerals indicate accommodation

and left behind a pewter plate inscribed with details of his visit. The island where he landed is now known, reasonably enough, as **Dirk Hartog Island**.

In 1697, another Dutch explorer, Willem de Vlamingh, was able to navigate so that he landed at precisely the same point, and there he found Hartog's plate. He took it home with him and left another instead. Hartog's plate is now displayed at the *Rijksmuseum* in Holland, while de Vlamingh's plate was also found later and is displayed at the Maritime Museum in Fremantle. It was, of course, an Englishman who named 'Shark's Bay', but even this was long before Captain Cook appeared on the Australian scene. The naming was by William Dampier in 1699, and he was the first Englishman to set foot on the Australian continent. One of his sailors died and is buried here, the first European known to have been buried in Australia. Later still, a Frenchman, François St. Allouarn, claimed this part of the continent for France in 1772, although his claim benefitted his nation little.

Shark Bay is listed as a World Heritage Area. It has beautiful scenery, but it is for the unusual wildlife that it is most visited. First, though, one needs to reach this area off the main highway, and to decide where one wants to stay.

The nearest point on the North West Coastal Highway is the **Overlander Roadhouse**. There is no town there - just a roadhouse. Both Greyhound and Integrity run buses that far. Greyhound operates every day, and Integrity has five buses per week. However, Overlander Roadhouse is 90 minutes (129 kilometres) from Denham and two hours (154 kilometres) from Monkey Mia. There is a connecting service operated by *Shark Bay Tours* to these two destinations. Greyhound tickets can be used on this service. Integrity charges $30 each way for its connecting bus.

There is only one town in this area, and that is Denham. At Monkey Mia, there is a resort, which also offers backpackers accommodation. However, there is not much else, except dolphins. If you stay in Monkey Mia, you will be on hand for the dolphins in the morning, but if you stay in Denham you will have a choice of shops and other facilities.

Denham was named after Captain Henry Denham, who charted the bay in 1858 in *H.M.S. Herald*. You can see the mark which he left on the cliff at **Eagle Bluff**, although part of the cliff collapsed and can now be seen in **Pioneer Park** in Denham, where it is rather more easily accessible than in its original location. The town of Denham was founded in 1898. The are some unusual buildings here made from quarried blocks of seashells. **St. Andrew's Church** is one of the best examples of this. Bay Lodge offers free tours to Monkey Mia for backpackers and other guests who stay there, so you will not miss the dolphins by staying at Denham. Choose whichever location you prefer, Denham or Monkey Mia.

Nobody seems to know why Monkey Mia has its rather unusual name, nor even who named it. It may be a corruption of an aboriginal name, but nobody seems very sure about that either. When the dolphins come, you can just paddle in to play with them, but there are also **cruises**, and on the cruises you can see animals other than dolphins. There are **dugong** ('sea cows'), endangered defenceless marine herbivores. There are estimated to be 10,000 dugong living in Shark Bay, which represents approximately 10% of the remaining world population of these sea mammals. The reason for their favouring Shark Bay is that it has the largest expanse of sea grass anywhere in the world, and also the largest number of species of sea grass recorded in a single place. Although dugong are naturally shy, it is often possible to glimpse them here. There are also **turtles** to be seen swimming in the bay, which, incidentally, is not quite as infested with sharks as its name suggests. You may also see sea snakes, manta rays and humpback whales in certain seasons.

Then there are the **stromatolites**, the world's oldest type of living fossil. The stromatolites are actually nearer to the Overlander Roadhouse than to Denham. They are located only 34 kilometres from the Roadhouse, at **Hamelin Pool**, which is 105 kilometres from Denham. However, you will probably find yourself obliged to travel to them from Denham or Monkey Mia, because of the necessity of having accommodation. Stromatolites are built by organisms which date back some 3,500 million years. These microscopic organisms recycle nutrients which then combine with sediment in the water to form the rock-like domes known as stromatolites. This is not the only place where you can see these formations, but it is the one which offers the best view. There is also a museum nearby, at the former **Flint Cliff Telegraph Station**, constructed in 1884, and notice boards giving information concerning the formations. The **Shell Quarry** is also near here. *Shark Bay Tours* offers a tour to the Stromatolites on certain days, currently Sundays, Tuesdays and Fridays. This tour starts from Monkey Mia, travels via Denham, and can be used with certain Greyhound tickets.

The same tour includes a visit to the **Shell Beach**, which lies on the route, near **Nanga**. The beach stretches for sixty kilometres, and is composed totally of shells. This

574 WESTERN AUSTRALIA

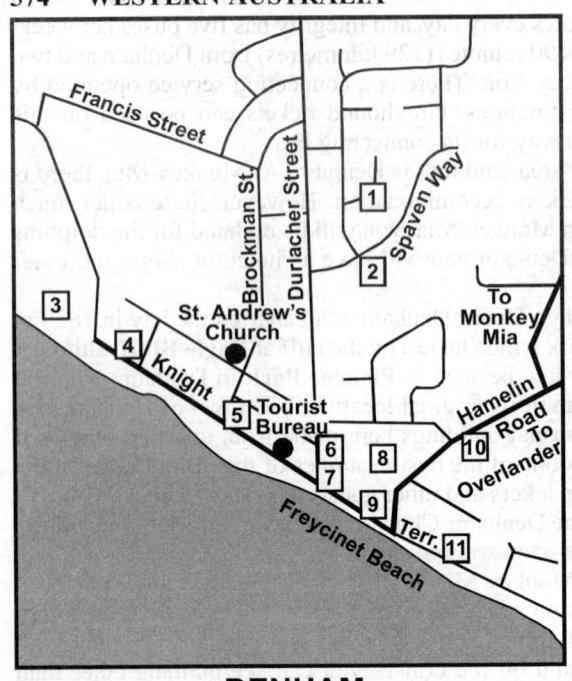

DENHAM
Numerals indicate accommodation

amazing expanse is the remains of a burrowing bivalve, and in some places the shells are as much as ten metres deep.

Peron Homestead lies not far north of Denham and can be visited. It has an outdoor 'hot tub', where water is drawn directly from a 580-metre artesian bore. The property for which this used to be the homestead is now the **François Peron National Park**. M. Peron was a French zoologist who accompanied the Nicolas Baudin scientific expedition to this area in 1801. Here *Project Eden* is trying to eliminate all forms of introduced wildlife and return endangered species to their natural environment. Tours run to the National Park.

As in many parts of Western Australia, wildflowers abound here in spring. Some of the species are found only at Shark Bay.

There is also diving available, and the wreck of the *Gudrun* is regarded as one of the best diving sites in the state.

ACCOMMODATION
(i) Hotel Accommodation in Denham and Monkey Mia

Name	Group	No. on Map	Telephone No.	Address	Price
Heritage Resort Hotel		7	08-9948-1133	73 Knight Terrace	$100
Tradewinds Village		9	1-800-816-160	10 Knight Terrace	$85
Bay Lodge		11	1-800-812-780	95 Knight Terrace	$75
Denham Villas	4	6	08-9948-1264	4 Durlacher Street	$75
Shark Bay Coastal Units		10	08-9948-1253	16 Hamelin Street	$75
Shark Bay Cottages		4	1-800-681-777	3 Knight Terrace	$65
Blue Dolphin Park		8	08-9948-1385	3 Denham Road	$60
Denham Seaside Park		3	08-9948-1242	Knight Terrace	$60
Shark Bay Caravan Park		2	08-9948-1387	4 Spaven Way	$60
Shark Bay Hotel / Motel		5	08-9948-1203	43 Knight Terrace	$60
Denham Holiday Village		1	08-9948-1323	Sunter Place	$60
Monkey Mia Dolphin Rst.		12	1-800-653-611	Monkey Mia	$90
Nanga Bay Resort		13	08-9948-3992	Nanga Station	$75

(ii) Backpackers Hostels in Denham and Monkey Mia, and nearby

Name	Group	No. on Map	Telephone No.	Address	Lowest Price (Dormitory)
Bay Lodge	YHA	11	1800-812-780	95 Knight Terrace	$19
Monkey Mia Resort	YHA	12	1800-653-611	Monkey Mia	$19
Nanga Bay Resort		13	08-9948-3992	Nanga Station	$20

MONKEY MIA 575

MOVING ON
Bus Services from Overlander Roadhouse

Destination	Operator	Via	Distance (km)	Fare	Journey Time	Frequency
Perth	Greyhound		702	$112	9½ - 12¼ hrs	10/week
		Geraldton	280	$57	3¾ - 5 hrs	10/week
Perth	Integrity		705	$100	9½ hrs	5/week
		Geraldton	283	$50	3½ - 3¾ hrs	5/week
Broome	Greyhound		1668	$283	22¼ hrs	1/day
		Port Hedland	1071	$160	14¾ hrs	1/day
		Exmouth	592	$124	7¼ hrs	3/week
		Carnarvon	200	$35	2¼ hrs	10/week
Broome	Integrity		1652	$255	25¾ hrs	2/week
		Port Hedland	1057	$135	17 hrs	2/week
		Exmouth	561	$115	8 hrs	4/week
		Carnarvon	200	$35	2 - 2¼ hrs	5/week

CARNARVON
Population 6,500

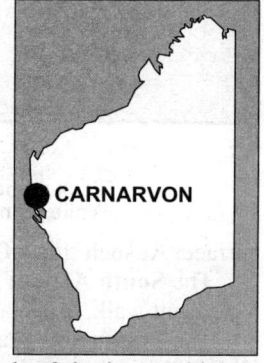

12 hrs 30 mins by bus from Perth

Carnarvon was established at the mouth of the Gascoyne River in 1883 as the centre of a pastoral area. Nowadays, however, it is best known for tropical fruits, especially bananas. It also has a thriving fishing industry, and produces salt, although Dampier is better known for that commodity.

The major attraction of Carnarvon is its **Heritage Precinct**, which is on **Babbage Island**. The **One Mile Jetty** was constructed in 1897 and widened in 1912, then damaged by fire in 1988, but now restored. It costs $3 to walk the length of the jetty, which is actually 1,495 metres long, not quite a mile. Alternatively, there is a little steam train which chugs its length. That costs $5 return and operates every forty minutes. There is also a steam train service from the town to the jetty. That too costs $5, but, if you prefer, you can walk along the length of the 'tramway' from the town centre to here. It is about three kilometres. The jetty straddles wetlands and mangroves and so makes an interesting walk. There is plenty of bird life to be found in this area and fishermen say that the jetty is a good place for their pursuits.

The **Lighthouse Museum** is to be found near the jetty, and is in the Lighthouse Keeper's Cottage. It is open from 10:00 until 12:00 and from 14:00 until 16:00 daily, and admission costs $4.

The other attraction and landmark of Carnarvon is the **Big Dish**, formerly one of the world's main links with the Gemini and Apollo space missions. It started service in 1966 and operated as an Earth Satellite Station for 21 years, until its retirement on 31st March 1987. The dish has a diameter of 29.6 metres. It can be visited and, in addition to being of interest in itself, it offers a fine view of the town.

The Gascoyne is an unusual river in that, although it flows all the time, it appears not to do so. It actually flows underground, and only at peak periods does the overflow

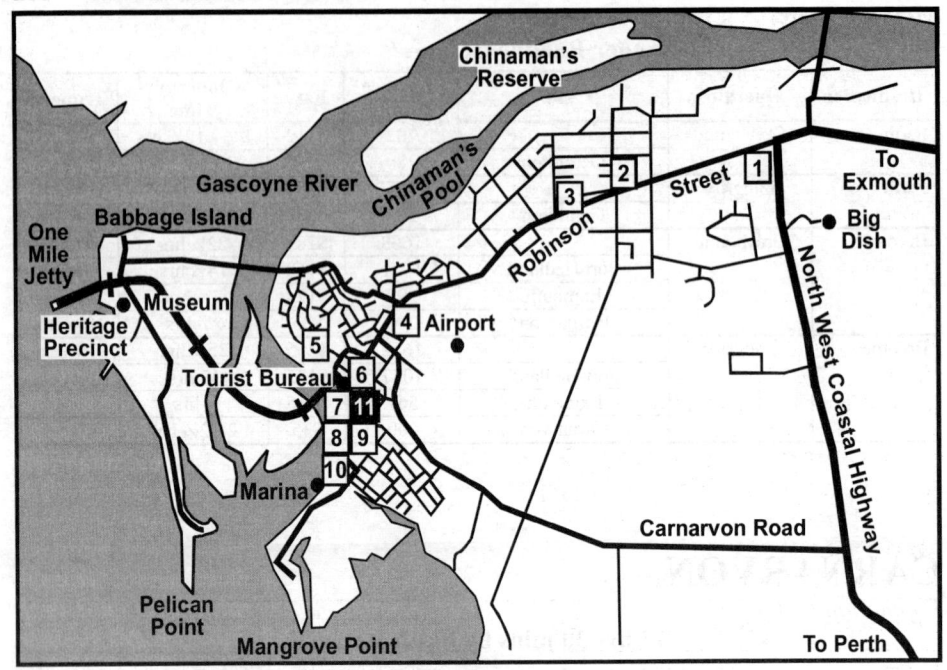

CARNARVON
Black numerals in white boxes indicate hotel accommodation
White numerals in black boxes indicate backpackers hostels

surface. At such times **Chinaman's Pool** is a pleasant place to visit.

The **South Arm** of the Gascoyne River is lined with stately palm trees and makes a pleasant walk, especially at sunset.

The **Prawn and Scallop Processing Factory** is on Babbage Island and offers tours in season, the season being from April until October.

The other attractions in the Carnarvon area are not close to the town. Worth looking at, perhaps by utilising a tour, is the natural coastal scenery some seventy kilometres north of Carnarvon. The **Blowholes** here are impressive when conditions are co-operative. Water is forced into channels under the rocks and comes spurting out high into the air. There is also a good beach nearby.

High Rock on Quobba Station is seven kilometres north of the Blowholes and marks the nearest point on land to where *H.M.A.S. Sydney* encountered the German ship *Kormoran* on 19th November 1941 with disastrous results. There were no survivors from the crew of 645 on board the *Sydney*.

120 kilometres north of Carnarvon is another marine disaster. This is the ***Korean Star***, grounded by Cyclone Herbie on Cape Cuvier in 1988. The ship broke into two sections and still lies there. The wreck can be observed from the cliff top, to which there is a road, but is in a dangerous condition, so should not be investigated too closely.

CARNARVON 577

ACCOMMODATION
(i) Hotel Accommodation in Carnarvon

Name	Stars	No. on Map	Telephone No.	Address	Lowest Price (Double/Twin)
Hospitality Inn	3½	10	08-9941-1600	West Street	$95
Fascine Lodge	3½	5	08-9941-2411	1002 David Brand Drive	$85
Gateway Motel	4	3	08-9941-1532	379 Robinson Street	$70
Northwesta Caravan Park	3	2	08-9941-1277	24 Angelo Street	$65
Carnarvon Hotel / Motel		7	08-9941-1181	26 Olivia Terrace	$65
Port Hotel		6	08-9941-1704	Robinson Street	$65
Tourist Centre C'van Park	3	4	08-9941-1438	108 Robinson Street	$60
The Outcamp B & B		9	08-9941-2421	139 Olivia Terrace	$60
Gascoyne Hotel / Motel		8	08-9941-1412	88 Olivia Terrace	$60
Wintersun Caravan Park	4	1	08-9941-8150	546 Robinson Street	$55

(ii) Backpackers Hostel in Carnarvon

Name	Group	No. on Map	Telephone No.	Address	Lowest Price (Dormitory)
Carnarvon Backpackers		11	08-9941-1095	50 Olivia Terrace	$19

MOVING ON
Bus Services from Carnarvon

Destination	Operator	Via	Distance (km)	Fare	Journey Time	Frequency
Perth	Greyhound		902	$120	12½ - 14¾ hrs	10/week
		Geraldton	480	$74	6½ - 7½ hrs	10/week
Perth	Integrity		905	$115	11½ hrs	5/week
		Geraldton	483	$65	5½ - 5¾ hrs	5/week
Broome	Greyhound		1468	$280	20 hrs	1/day
		Port Hedland	871	$153	12¾ hrs	1/day
		Exmouth	392	$76	5 hrs	3/week
Broome	Integrity		1465	$255	22¾ hrs	2/week
		Port Hedland	868	$135	14 hrs	2/week
		Exmouth	369	$75	4¼ hrs	4/week

EXMOUTH
Population 2,500

18 hrs by bus from Perth

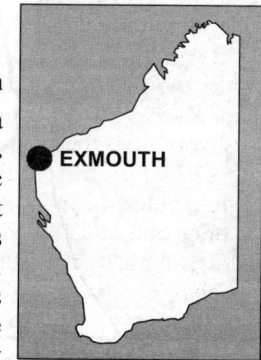

As we continue north from Carnarvon, we soon reach a turn-off inland which leads to **Gascoyne Junction** and to **Mt. Augustus** (see map on page 582). There is, however, no public transport which takes this route. It is worth noting, though, that Gosse appears to have been wrong when he referred to Ayers Rock as "the world's biggest pebble", for it is here. Mt. Augustus, very different in appearance from Ayers Rock, is more than twice its size and rises some 700 metres above the surrounding land, claiming to be the world's largest monocline. It is visible from a distance of 150 kilometres, but you will not be going that close on the bus. The road around its base is 49 kilometres long. Mt. Augustus was first climbed by Gregory on 3rd June 1858. It is approximately 450 kilometres from Carnarvon. Accommodation is available at the Mt. Augustus Outback Resort (telephone 08-9943-0527), if you can find a means of transport.

150 kilometres north of Carnarvon along the North West Coastal Highway, you will reach the turn-off for Exmouth. If you are travelling with Integrity or on the Greyhound service terminating in Exmouth, your bus will turn left here and pass through Coral Bay. However, if you are on the Greyhound service bound for Broome, your bus will continue along the main highway until the next stop at the Giralia turn-off, from where there will be a connecting service for Exmouth. In this case, you will not pass through Coral Bay.

Coral Bay is situated just north of the Tropic of Capricorn and is a relatively newly discovered attractive tourist destination. It is twelve kilometres off the road to Exmouth, but buses divert to the town. Just off the coast is Australia's largest coral reef, **Ningaloo Reef**, extending for 260 kilometres and providing opportunities for snorkelling and diving. There are also tours by glass-bottomed boat. There is a coastal walkway and turtles come here to lay eggs between December and April. There is accommodation available, including beds for backpackers, at Bayview Coral Bay (telephone 08-9942-5932 or 08-9385-7411). There is also a hotel and motel and there are two caravan parks.

The airport for this area is situated at Learmonth, 35 kilometres before Exmouth is reached, facilities being shared between civilian and military use.

Exmouth is on the eastern side of the North West Cape, whereas Coral Bay was on the west. It is fortunate in being able to offer the visitor both mountains and sea. The first European landing in this area was as long ago as 1618, when Captain Jacobsz of the Dutch vessel *Mauritius* put in near here. It was another two hundred years, though, before the Exmouth Gulf was named by Captain Philip King. He also named the North West Cape. However, no town was established. Pearl luggers from Broome used

NORTH WEST CAPE
Numerals indicate accommodation

to visit, but it was not until the time of the Second World War that the area gained in importance. It became a refuelling base for submarines and then, following the war, an air base was established. In the 1960s a Naval Communications Station was built using Very Low Frequency radio to help to maintain contact with American naval vessels, especially submarines, throughout the world. The base is still there, six kilometres north of the town, and accommodation is available there now, including backpackers accommodation, although some parts of the station are still off limits. The central tower of the Communications Station is a remarkable 388 metres tall. The town of Exmouth was not established until 1967 and was originally a support town for the American Naval Communications Station. Exmouth is approximately 1,270 kilometres north of Perth and 225 kilometres from the turn-off on the North West Coastal Highway.

The nearest beach to Exmouth, **Town Beach**, is one kilometre from the town centre. Fourteen kilometres north is **Bundegi Beach**. Surfers need to cross to the western side of the cape, to **Surfers' Beach** (or 'The Dunes'), seventeen kilometres from Exmouth. **Mauritius Beach**, 21 kilometres from Exmouth, is the nude beach in this area, and a succession of other beaches follows all the way down the western side of the cape. This is also the area where **turtles** come to lay their eggs during the summer. There are more beaches on the west side close to the tip of the cape, and off the tip itself is the wreck of the *S.S. Mildura*, which was bringing cattle south when it encountered a cyclone in 1907. It was pushed onto the reef, where it remained until it was used as target practice during the war. No human lives were lost in the wreck. Parts of the timber and iron were used locally, but there are still some remains of the ship visible.

There is a lighthouse near Mauritius Beach. **Vlamingh Head Lighthouse** was built in 1912, but is no longer in use. Instead one of the towers at the Communications Station supports an automatic beacon.

The Ningaloo Reef is also accessible from Exmouth and is one of the great attractions of the area, offering diving, snorkelling and observation by glass-bottomed boat. Day tours are available.

Another feature of the area is that the world's biggest fish gather here every year from March until June. These are **whale sharks**, which can grow up to eighteen metres in length. It is possible to go swimming with them, since they are gentle and harmless, and realise that humans are gradually learning from their example.

Every year for a few days in March and April, **reef spawning** takes place in these waters. Dense clouds of brightly coloured spawn are released into the water after sunset, and there are special tours to see this phenomenon.

Other marine creatures to be seen at certain times of the year include humpback whales, manta rays and various types of turtles.

As for the mountains, they are on the west side of the cape in the Cape Range National Park. To reach them, however, one must travel round the top of the peninsula. The northern boundary of the park is forty kilometres from Exmouth and **Milyering Visitor Centre** is 52 kilometres away from the town. The National Park has beaches too, for example **Turquoise Bay, Sandy Bay** and **Pilgramunna**.

Thirty kilometres south of Exmouth is a prawning base. Fifteen boats operate from here and catch more than 1,000 tonnes of prawns each year, most of which quantity is exported. Prawns can be purchased here.

Exmouth currently holds the record for the strongest gust of wind recorded in Australia, a gust from Cyclone Vance having reached 267 km/hr on 22nd March 1999

580   WESTERN AUSTRALIA

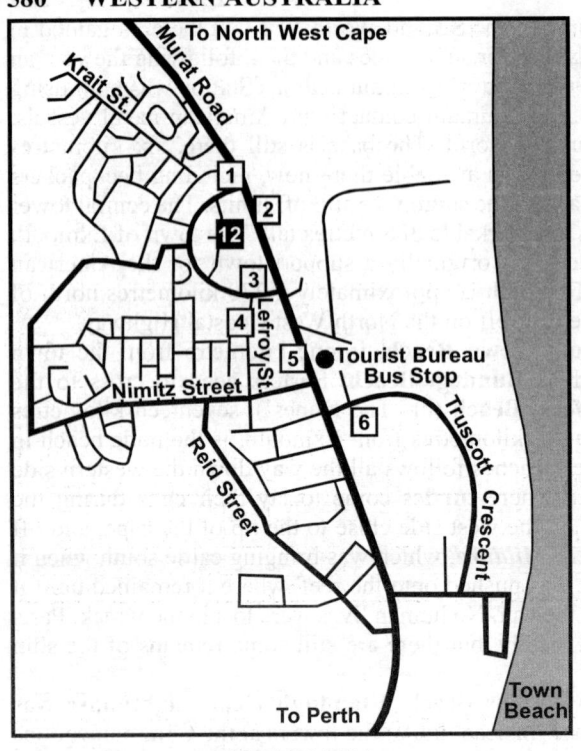

EXMOUTH

Black numerals indicate hotel accommodation
White numerals indicate backpackers hostels

according to the wind speed meter at the Learmonth Meteorological Station.

There is a service to most of the places mentioned in this section by the Ningaloo Reef Bus, which travels all the way round the coast as far as Turquoise Bay and Ningaloo Reef Retreat. The return journey to Turquoise Bay costs $25 including the free loan of a mask and snorkel at your destination. Other offers are a guided snorkel and lunch, plus the return bus ride for $50, or the same plus a kayak trip for $70, or an overnight stay at Ningaloo Reef Retreat, with food, guided snorkelling and bushwalking for $110. Other fares are, for example, $8 return to the lighthouse and $22 return to Cape Range National Park Visitor Centre at Milyering. The Ningaloo Reef Bus operates on Sundays, Tuesdays, Wednesdays and Fridays, leaving Exmouth at 9:00, arriving at Ningaloo Reef Retreat at 10:30, and leaving at 14:00 for the return journey.

ACCOMMODATION

Accommodation shown is all at the north of North West Cape. There is also accommodation at Coral Bay, as mentioned above.

(i) Hotel Accommodation in Exmouth and Vicinity

Name	Stars	No. on Map	Telephone No.	Address	Lowest Price (Double/Twin)
Potshot Hotel Resort	3½	1	08-9949-1200	Murat Road	$130
Exmouth Cape Village	3	6	1-800-621-101	Murat Rd. & Truscott Cres.	$90
Argosy Court		2	08-9949-1177	Lot 620, Murat Road	$85
Ningaloo Lodge	3	4	1-800-880-949	Lefroy Street	$80
Ningaloo Holiday Resort		5	1-800-652-665	Murat Road	$65
Exmouth Budget Accom.		3	08-9949-1703	Murat Rd & Maidstone Cres	$55
Sea Breeze Resort	3	7	08-9949-1800	116 North C St., Naval Base	$135
Exmouth Base Lodge		8	1-800-241-474	Murat Road, Naval Base	$50
Lighthouse Caravan Park		9	08-9949-1478	Yardie Creek Drive	$60
Yardie Homestead Park		10	08-9949-1389	Yardie Homestead	$55
Ningaloo Reef Retreat		11	08-9949-4073	Cape Range National Park	$75

(ii) Backpackers Hostels in Exmouth and Vicinity

Name	Group	No. on Map	Telephone No.	Address	Lowest Price (Dormitory)
Exmouth Base Lodge	VIP	8	1800-241-474	Murat Road, Naval Base	$21
Pete's Backpackers	YHA	6	1800-621-101	Murat Rd. & Truscott Crescent	$21
Winston's Backpackers		5	1800-652-665	Murat Road	$20
Excape Backpackers		12	08-9949-1201	Payne Street	$20

MOVING ON
Bus Services from Exmouth

Destination	Operator	Via	Distance (km)	Fare	Journey Time	Frequency
Perth	Greyhound		1294	$195	20¼ hrs	3/week
		Geraldton	875	$172	13 hrs	3/week
		Carnarvon	392	$76	5½ hrs	3/week
Perth	Integrity		1263	$180	17 hrs	4/week
		Geraldton	875	$155	11¼ hrs	4/week
		Carnarvon	369	$75	4¼ hrs	4/week
Broome	Greyhound		1592	$301	19½ hrs	1/day
		Port Hedland	995	$174	12¼ hrs	1/day
Broome	Integrity		1107	$255	18¼ hrs	2/week
		Port Hedland	510	$135	9½ hrs	2/week

KARRATHA AND DAMPIER
Population 10,000 (Karratha)
21 hrs 30 mins by bus from Perth

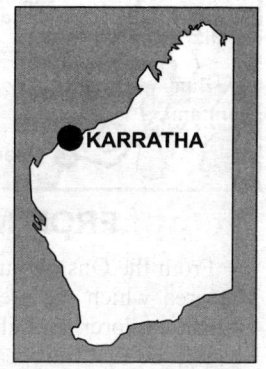

Moving on from Exmouth, a connecting bus runs daily to the Giralia turn-off to make the connexion with the Greyhound bus running north, while Integrity operates its service directly from Exmouth to points north to Broome twice a week. A further 111 kilometres from Giralia takes you to a road off to the right leading to Paraburdoo, Tom Price, Wittenoom and the Karijini National Park (see map on following page). Tours are operated to this area from Exmouth, and also from Karratha and from Port Hedland, but no public transport service runs. The closest route to the National Park is the Greyhound service which operates from Perth to Port Hedland via Meekatharra and the Inland Route. Information regarding this area appears, therefore, on page 603.

After forty more kilometres, a road on the left leads to **Onslow**, which is 81 kilometres distant from the main highway and does not have a public transport service. Therefore, it tends to be missed out of most itineraries. It is a pleasant little town with a population of 850 which has been moved since its foundation in 1883. During the war, it was an allied naval base and the oil storage tanks are still visible. In 1943, it was bombed by the Japanese, the most southerly place in Western Australia to suffer an air raid. In 1963 it was almost destroyed by a cyclone. Now it is an oil and gas exploration base. Salt is also produced in the area. There is only one good road to Onslow, so if you find a way of getting there, you have to return by the same route.

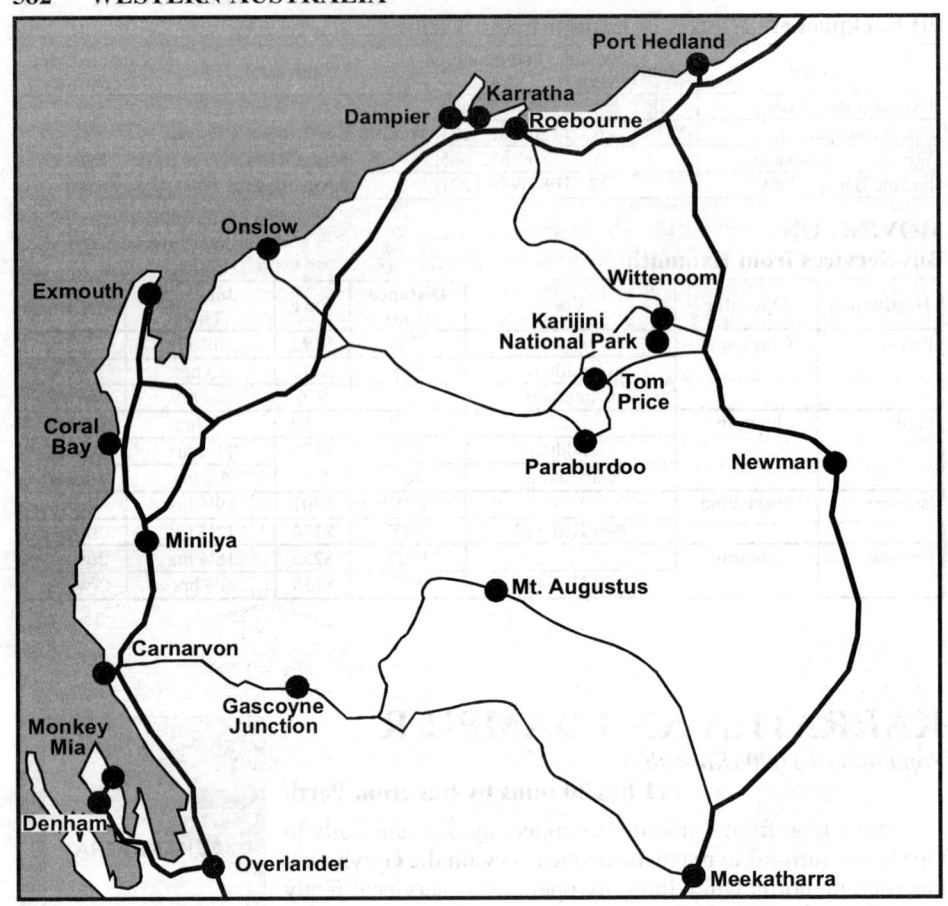

FROM MONKEY MIA TO PORT HEDLAND

From the Onslow turn-off, it is another three and a half hours by bus to Karratha. The area which we are now entering is called the **Pilbara**. William Dampier, the English explorer, and also buccaneer, came here in 1688 in the *Cygnet*. Although he was not the first European, the Dutch having preceded him by seventy years, his is the name which has been given to one of the main towns here. Dampier returned in 1699 in the *Roebuck* and anchored in the midst of a group of islands now known as the Dampier Archipelago. Gregory explored the region in 1861 and noted the abundance of iron in the soil. It was Gregory who discovered and named all the main rivers in this area - the Ashburton, the DeGray, the Fortescue and the Oakover. He also noted several areas suitable for pastoral properties. This was to become the principal industry in the area until the 1960s.

Now, however, Karratha and Dampier have the North West Shelf Natural Gas Project, Hamersley Iron, and Dampier Salt, all major industries, the success of which is reflected in the relative prosperity of the towns of Karratha and Dampier.

It is in Karratha that the Greyhound bus will make its stop. Karratha is a new town, constructed in 1968, when the Hamersley Iron Project was continuing to develop and the Dampier Salt Project just starting, and Dampier was running out of space. Karratha was planned as the administrative centre of the area, which it has now become. It has the largest shopping centre in this part of Australia. Karratha evidently means 'good country' in the local aboriginal language and it was the name of the local pastoral station. Everything in the town of Karratha itself is modern. Some people will enjoy this, but to the author it lacks in character.

There is a **Tourist Bureau** on the edge of the town. When you have located it and walked to it you will begin to sense its priorities. It is on the main highway at the entrance to the town, not in the town centre as one might perhaps expect. The supposition is evident, that all tourists worth having will arrive by car. When the author visited and asked what I could do in the area, I was looked at askance and told, "What? No car? Well you can't do anything here really without a car." And that, as far as the girl behind the counter was concerned, was the end of the matter. She went on to deal with other tourists who might bring more money. Fortunately, though, it is not true that you cannot do anything without a car, although it does create limitations and the tourist authority is obviously not trying to encourage the less-opulent market (which, it should be said, is quite atypical of one's usual experiences throughout Australia).

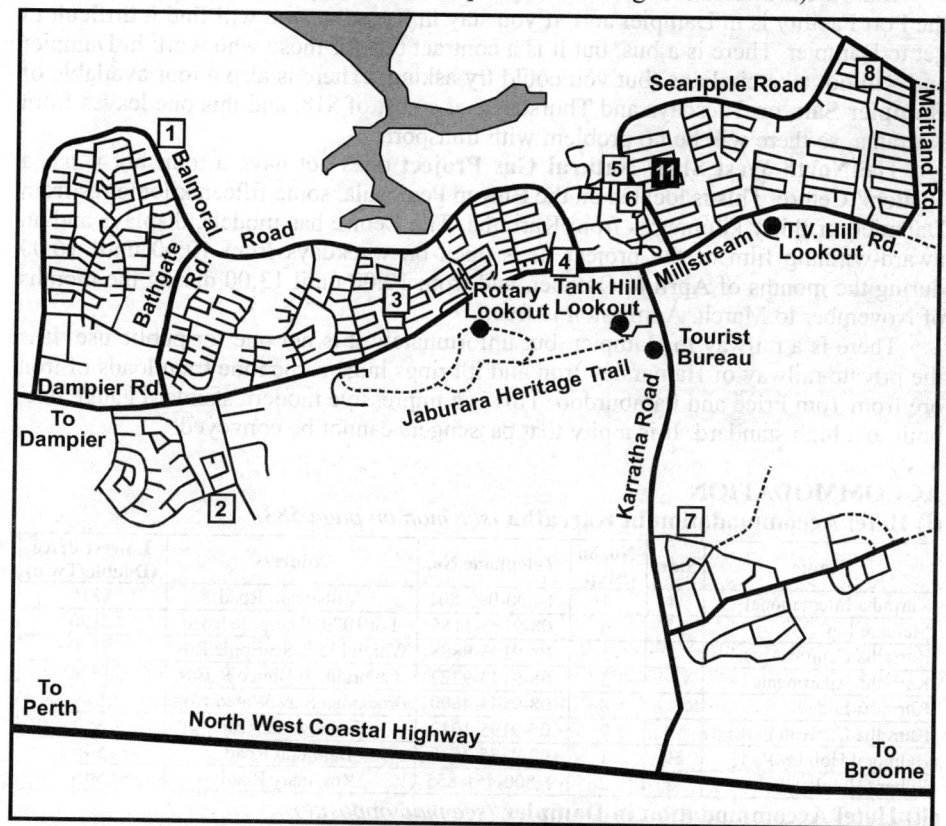

KARRATHA
Black numerals in white boxes indicate hotel accommodation
White numerals in black boxes indicate backpackers hostels

For a start, right behind the Tourist Bureau is the beginning of an interesting little walk, the **Jaburara Heritage Trail**, leading up over the hills overlooking the town (see map on previous page) and offering three fine viewpoints. Even if the town is new, here is history, for the aborigines have been here for thousands of years and have left their marks in various ways throughout the area. The walk covers some five kilometres, measuring from the town centre back to the same, and will take about two and a half hours, including time to look at the points of interest. You will find it surprisingly interesting, considering that it is so near the European habitation. There are explanatory signs all the way along, but when the author went some had been damaged by fire and were illegible. Take a litre of water with you, as there is not much shade along the walk.

If you are vehicle-less, you may find that your salvation is Karratha Backpackers and Barry who runs it, for he operates tours for his guests at very reasonable prices. Stay for three nights and he will take you to the **Burrup Peninsula** for only $10 to see aboriginal rock art, as well as the beach and a beautiful view, and he will enjoy showing you these sights too. For the same price, he will take you to see Roebourne, Cossack and Point Samson, places which are otherwise difficult to reach.

Tours are available of the **Hamersley Iron Port Facility** at a cost of $12. However, the Port Facility is in Dampier and, if you stay in Karratha, you will find it difficult to get to Dampier. There is a bus, but it is a contract bus for those who work in Dampier and will not take civilians (but you could try asking). There is also a tour available of **Dampier Salt**, on Tuesdays and Thursdays, at a cost of $18, and this one leaves from Karratha, so there will be no problem with transport.

The **North West Shelf Natural Gas Project** does not have a tour, but it has a Visitors' Centre. This is located on the Burrup Peninsula, some fifteen kilometres from Dampier, or thirty kilometres from Karratha. The Centre has models, displays and an award-winning film of the project. It is open on weekdays from 10:00 until 16:00 during the months of April to October, and from 10:00 until 13:00 during the months of November to March. Admission is free.

There is a railway to Dampier, but unfortunately it is not one for public use. It is the private railway of Hamersley Iron and it brings huge serpentine train loads of iron ore from Tom Price and Paraburdoo. This is a impressive modern standard gauge line, built to a high standard. It is a pity that passengers cannot be conveyed.

ACCOMMODATION
(i) Hotel Accommodation in Karratha *(see map on page 583)*

Name	Stars	No. on Map	Telephone No.	Address	Lowest Price (Double/Twin)
Karratha International	4	4	1-800-099-801	Millstream Road	$215
Mercure Inn		6	08-9185-1155	Lot 1079, Searipple Road	$190
Karratha Central Apts.		5	08-9143-9888	Warambie & Scaripple Rds.	$120
Karratha Apartments		3	08-9143-9222	Galbraith & Blinco Roads	$120
Karratha Lodge		8	08-9144-4600	Brockman St & Walcott Wy	$75
Karratha Caravan Park		7	08-9195-1012	Mooligunn Road	$50
Balmoral Holiday Park	3½	1	08-9185-3628	Balmoral Road	$45
Pilbara Holiday Park	4	2	1-800-451-855	Rosemary Road	$45

(ii) Hotel Accommodation in Dampier *(see map opposite)*

Name	Stars	No. on Map	Telephone No.	Address	Lowest Price (Double/Twin)
Mercure Inn		9	08-9183-1222	The Esplanade, Dampier	$130
Peninsula Palms		10	08-9183-1888	The Esplanade, Dampier	$120

(iii) Backpackers Hostels in Karratha *(see map on page 583)*

Name	Group	No. on Map	Telephone No.	Address	Lowest Price (Dormitory)
Karratha Backpackers		11	08-9144-4904	110 Wellard Way	$19

MOVING ON
Bus Services from Karratha

Destination	Operator	Via	Distance (km)	Fare	Journey Time	Frequency
Perth	Greyhound		1530	$193	21 hrs	1/day
		Geraldton	1108	$186	15 hrs	1/day
		Carnarvon	628	$139	8¾ hrs	1/day
Perth	Integrity		1537	$180	22¼ hrs	2/week
		Geraldton	1115	$165	16¼ hrs	2/week
		Carnarvon	644	$120	9¾ hrs	2/week
Broome	Greyhound		840	$198	11 hrs	1/day
		Port Hedland	243	$74	3½ hrs	1/day
Broome	Integrity		847	$175	12¾ hrs	2/week
		Port Hedland	249	$65	4 hrs	2/week

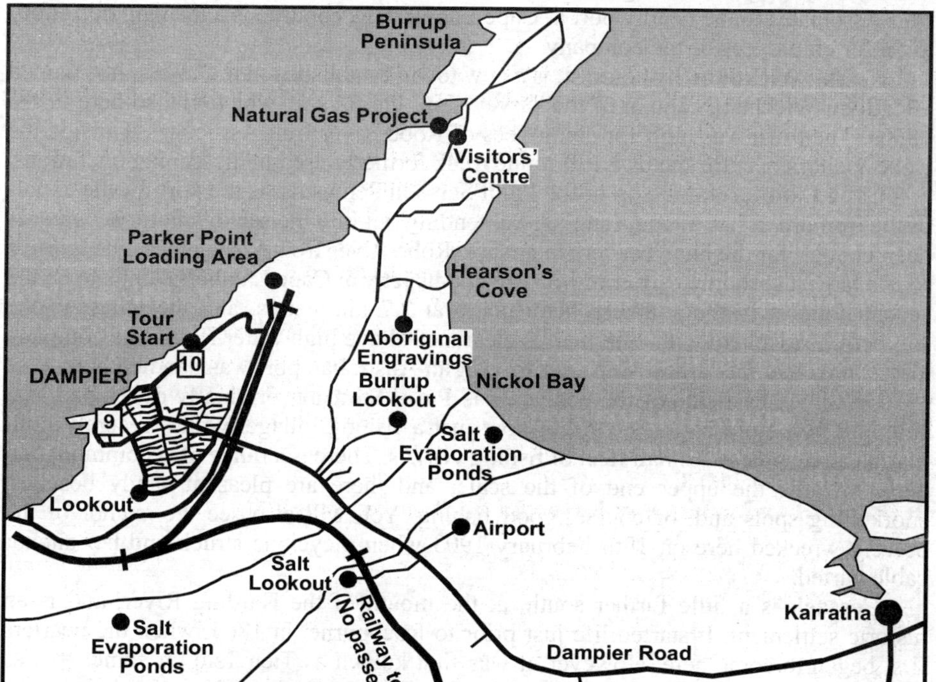

DAMPIER AND VICINITY
Numerals indicate accommodation

586 WESTERN AUSTRALIA
ROEBOURNE, POINT SAMSON, WICKHAM AND COSSACK

Populations: 1,500 (Roebourne), 200 (Point Samson), 1,800 (Wickham), 20 (Cossack)

22hrs by bus from Perth

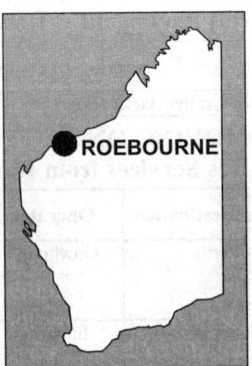

As we move on from Karratha, we soon come to **Roebourne**, the oldest town between Geraldton and Darwin. It was founded in 1864 and regarded as the capital of the north-west. Many of the original buildings still stand here and have been restored in recent times.

The **Tourist Bureau** is housed in the **Old Gaol**, which it shares with the **Old Gaol Museum** and the **Roebourne Art and Craft Group**. Admission is free. There are also the **Courthouse**, the **Post Office** and **Holy Trinity Church**. Roebourne, though, is by no means a town of the past. It is expanding and prospering, due to the iron ore industry. There is another modern standard gauge railway running past the edge of the town, this time transporting ore for Robe River Iron Associates to the nearby port at Cape Lambert. Roebourne is a thriving dormitory town for employees of the company.

Nearby **Wickham**, by contrast, is a new town, established in the 1970s. It is named after John Wickham, captain of the survey ship, the *Beagle*, which visited here in the 1830s. The town was built for employees of Robe River Iron Associates. Outside the Robe Visitors' Centre stands a 170-tonne truck formerly used in the mining operations.

Cape Lambert, at the tip of the Point Samson Peninsula, is the port for the export of the iron ore. It has a long, long jetty extending out into the sea to where the water is deep enough for the huge carriers to anchor. Robe River Iron Associates is the world's fourth largest seaborne carrier of iron ore and its jetty at Cape Lambert claims to be the second longest in the southern hemisphere at 2.7 kilometres, and the tallest in the southern hemisphere with 17.8 metres clearance above high water level. The company also claims that the largest ship ever to visit an Australian port was handled here.

On the eastern side of the peninsula is **Point Samson**, originally developed as a shipping port from about 1910, but now just a fishing village, with a recently built marina, and home to a small fleet of fishing vessels. There is a range of accommodation here, towards the upper end of the scale, and there are pleasant sandy beaches, snorkelling spots and, of course, good fishing. You will also see the anchor of the *Solveig* wrecked here on 19th February 1903 when a cyclone struck and her anchor cable parted.

Cossack is a little further south, at the mouth of the Harding River, and is an historic settlement. It started life just prior to Roebourne, in 1863, when the pearlers first began to come here. However, it was first known as Tien Tsin, or sometimes as Port Walcott or North District. The present name was derived from the visit of the Governor in 1871 in *H.M.S. Cossack*. The town was then officially gazetted and named in 1872. At that time Cossack was the principal port for north-western Australia. Then, in the 1880s, thousands of people came to search for gold and Cossack, at its peak, had a population of about 400 Europeans and 1,000 Asians, although the highest official population recorded was 272 in 1891. In 1887, a horse-drawn tramway was constructed between Roebourne and Cossack. The demise of the town occurred because the pearling industry moved to Broome in the 1890s and because the waters here became

ROEBOURNE, POINT SAMSON, WICKHAM, COSSACK

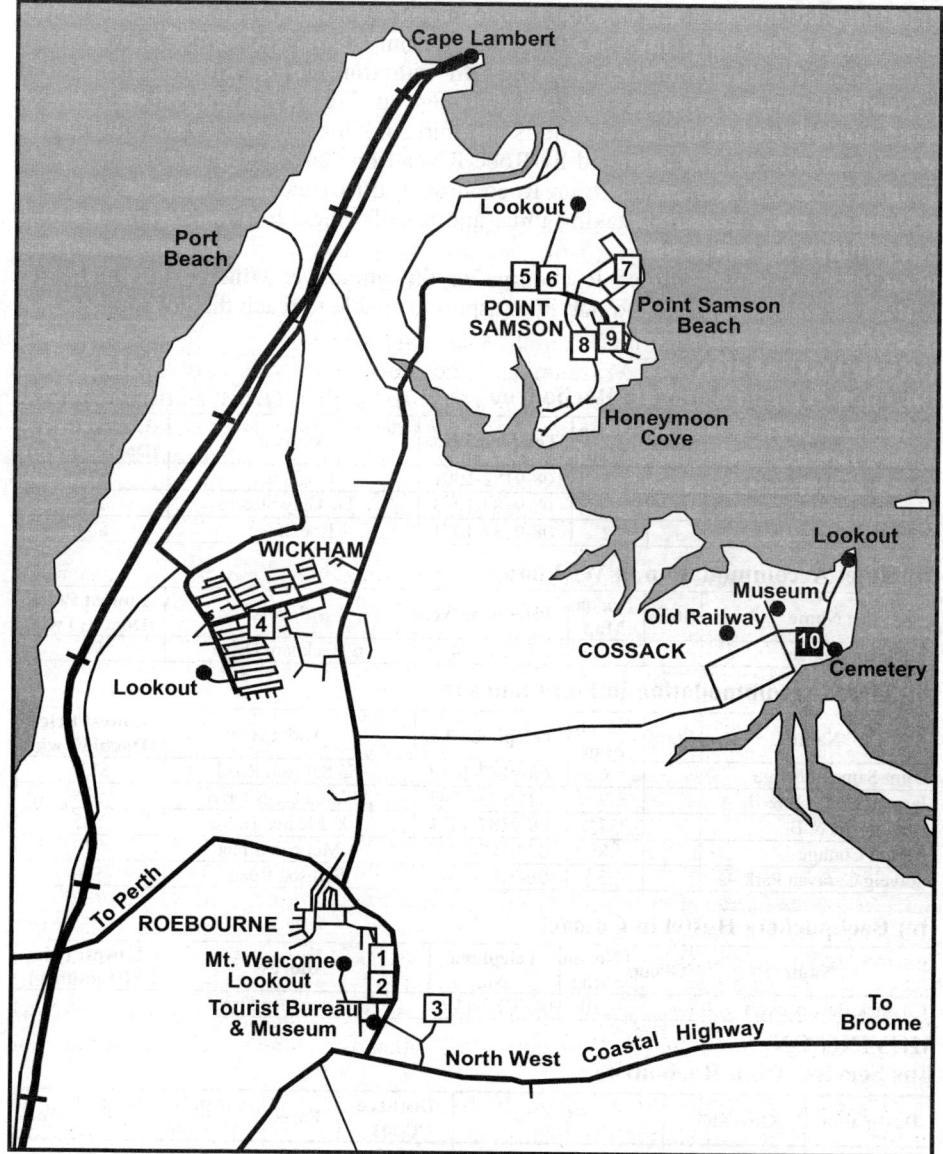

ROEBOURNE, POINT SAMSON, WICKHAM AND COSSACK
Black numerals in white boxes indicate hotel accommodation
White numerals in black boxes indicate backpackers hostels

too shallow and silted to handle vessels of increasing size. From 1910, the ships started to go to Point Samson instead. Even the local fishing fleet moved on to Point Samson. In 1913, a leprosarium was established just across the river, but in 1931 even that institution moved away, to Darwin, and left Cossack as a ghost town. Recently, though, nine of the old buildings have been restored and the **Old Police Barracks** has been

588 WESTERN AUSTRALIA

made into a backpackers hostel, so that one may even stay in this interesting location. The former **Post and Telegraph Office**, dating from 1883, has become an Art Gallery and is open from 10:00 until 16:00. The **Old Courthouse**, built in 1895, is a Social History Museum, with all exhibits originating in Cossack. Admission costs $3. Cossack also offers a good beach and is just thirteen kilometres from Roebourne.

Tours of this area are offered by Robe River Iron Associates, and are known as **Port to Port Tours**. They start from Roebourne Tourist Bureau and cover Wickham, Cape Lambert and Cossack, taking three and a half hours. Tours are available from May until October.

160 kilometres south of Roebourne is the attractive **Millstream-Chichester National Park**, but there is no public transport available to reach this location.

ACCOMMODATION
(i) Hotel Accommodation in Roebourne

Name	Stars	No. on Map	Telephone No.	Address	Lowest Price (Double/Twin)
Mt. Welcome Motel		1	08-9182-1001	Roe Street	$75
Harding River Caravan Pk		3	08-9182-1063	De Gray Street	$60
Victoria Hotel		2	08-9182-1001	Roe Street	$50

(ii) Hotel Accommodation in Wickham

Name	Stars	No. on Map	Telephone No.	Address	Lowest Price (Double/Twin)
Wickham Lodge		4	08-9187-1439	6 Wickham Drive	$95

(iii) Hotel Accommodation in Point Samson

Name	Stars	No. on Map	Telephone No.	Address	Lowest Price (Double/Twin)
Point Samson Lodge		6	08-9187-1052	56 Samson Road	$125
Jarman House B & B		9	08-9143-1743	22 Vitenbergs Drive	$95
Delilah's B & B		7	08-9187-1471	303 Meares Drive	$85
Amani Cottage		8	08-9187-0052	1 McLeod Street	$75
Solveig Caravan Park		5	08-9187-1414	Samson Road	$60

(iv) Backpackers Hostel in Cossack

Name	Group	No. on Map	Telephone No.	Address	Lowest Price (Dormitory)
Cossack Backpackers		10	08-9182-1190	Perseverance Street	$12

MOVING ON
Bus Services from Roebourne

Destination	Operator	Via	Distance (km)	Fare	Journey Time	Frequency
Perth	Greyhound		1565	$218	21¾ hrs	1/day
		Geraldton	1143	$186	15¾ hrs	1/day
		Carnarvon	663	$150	9½ hrs	1/day
Perth	Integrity		1563	$195	23¼ hrs	2/week
		Geraldton	1141	$165	17 hrs	2/week
		Carnarvon	670	$135	10¾ hrs	2/week
Broome	Greyhound		805	$186	10½ hrs	1/day
		Port Hedland	208	$61	3¼ hrs	1/day
Broome	Integrity		807	$170	11¼ hrs	2/week
		Port Hedland	210	$55	2½ hrs	2/week

PORT HEDLAND
Population 15,000

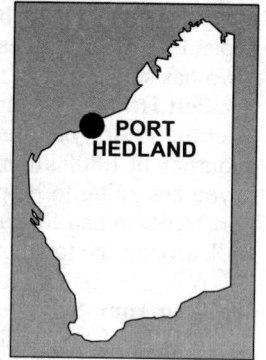

25 hrs by bus from Perth

Port Hedland is a town in two parts - Port Hedland and South Hedland. The distance between the two is twelve kilometres. South Hedland is the new residential area and Port Hedland is the old town and, of course, the port. From Roebourne to South Hedland takes two hours on a Greyhound or Integrity bus, with no town in between. The Greyhound bus stops there for a meal break, so it is three hours after leaving Roebourne that one arrives in Port Hedland, but Integrity takes its break later, so offers a rather faster service.

There is an alternative, and faster, inland route from Perth to Port Hedland, passing through Meekatharra. Greyhound provides a service by this route twice a week, departing from Perth on Sundays and Fridays. This journey is completed in 22½ hours, cutting two and a half hours off the journey time round the coast.

Port Hedland is another iron ore town. Its European history began in 1628, when the Dutch ship *Vyanen* ran aground just west of the present town. In 1840, Commander Stokes on the *Beagle* went ashore on Depuch Island, south of Port Hedland, and in 1863 Captain Peter Hedland landed at Mangrove Harbour (now Port Hedland) in the cutter *Mystery*. Later in the same year, the site was officially named Hedland in his honour. However, it was not until 1896 that the town of Port Hedland was established. The Pier Hotel opened in 1898 and the Esplanade Hotel in 1904. Both are still there. In 1911 a railway was opened from Port Hedland to Marble Bar. The railway lasted until 1951 and service on the part of the line from Port Hedland to Shaw River survived until 1953. As early as 1915, the Rev. John Flynn established a hospital in Port Hedland. In 1942, the Japanese twice bombed Port Hedland and there was one soldier killed at the airport.

It was not until 1938 that the high iron content of nearby **Mt. Goldsworthy** was remarked upon, and not until 1963 that Goldsworthy Mining Associates gained a government export licence and the 'iron ore boom' commenced. Mt. Newman Mining announced that it would use Port Hedland for its shipping facilities, and the most prosperous era in the town's history had commenced.

Port Hedland holds several transport records. It was the first port in Australia to be certified for 140,000 DWT vessels, and was the first Australian port to berth two vessels over 100,000 DWT simultaneously. In 1974, it set a new Australian record by simultaneously berthing four ships with total deadweight tonnage of 461,421 tonnes.

A high-grade modern standard-gauge railway was constructed to the mine at Mt. Newman and this railway also has achieved records. In 1996, what was, at the time, the longest train in Australian history was operated on the line. It was 5.9 kilometres long, and it set a world record for load by conveying 56,500 tonnes of iron ore. However, in June 2001 this record was surpassed by another train run on the same line. This second train consisted of eight locomotives and 682 iron ore wagons and was 7.36 kilometres long, weighing 80,000 tonnes and being both the longest and the heaviest train in the world. Unfortunately, this is another of the private railways in this area which does not convey passengers.

In recent times, however, the iron ore operations at Port Hedland have been losing money and there have been threats of closure of certain plants. Since Port Hedland is dependent on the success of the mining company for its own prosperity, at present the town has something of the feeling which Damocles must have experienced.

Port Hedland is sometimes regarded as a purely industrial area which has little to offer the visitor, but this is not altogether so. Possibly Port Hedland alone is not worth a journey of 1,800 kilometres from Perth, but there are other attractions in the area and, if you are going to be passing through here anyway, it is certainly worth stopping in Port Hedland and looking around the town and the port. Let us start by taking a short walk around the town centre to see a little of Port Hedland.

Walking Tour

This brief tour will cover about two and a half kilometres and take less than an hour. It starts and finishes at the Tourist Bureau where there is plenty of interesting material available on the area and a video to watch too. This is also the place where the Greyhound and Integrity buses arrive and depart.

Immediately behind the **Tourist Bureau** is the **Town Observation Tower**. It is 26 metres tall and gives a good view of the area. Entrance is through the Tourist Bureau and the ascent costs $3. If you had not previously noticed that absolutely everything in Port Hedland is covered in a thin layer of iron ore dust, you will certainly know it by the time you have been up the Observation Tower and back down. Try to avoid letting your clothing touch the rails, bearing in mind that hands are easily washable, but clothes take more effort. From the top of the tower, you can see in all directions and get a better idea of the extent of operations here. Much of the land used by the mining company has been reclaimed, you will see. You will be able to notice the constant hosing down of the piles of iron ore to try to lay the dust somewhat, an operation which meets with only limited success. From here you will also be able to see **Finucane Island**. There is an undersea tunnel 1.1 kilometres long, constructed in 1997, to the island, which is on the far side of the harbour. This enables ships to be loaded at both sides of the harbour area. The tunnel also conveys ore for the new Hot Briquette Iron Plant constructed there in 1999. From the tower, you will be able to see the piles of salt too, for this is another area which supports that industry. When you come down from the Observation Tower, the toilets are immediately inside the doors of the Tourist Bureau on the right.

Leave the Tourist Bureau by the front door. Straight across the street is the site of the Old Post Office. The current Post Office is here too, but in a modern building constructed in 1967. Here, as in many places around the town, you will be able to see photographs of how this area used to look. Turn left and walk to the first corner, that of Anderson Street, and turn right. On the other side of the road is **Dalgety House Museum**. This was the house of the Manager of Dalgety's from 1903 until 1974, Dalgety's being a store and a company providing services to the pastoral industry. Now it is a Museum with emphasis on the early times in Port Hedland.

Continue down Anderson Street and you will come to the **Esplanade Hotel** on the left, looking as though it has seen better days. The hotel is on the corner of The Esplanade, which used to be a seafront area. However, now the reclaimed land extends a considerable distance and one cannot even see the harbour from here. Across the street is the **R.S.L. War Memorial**.

Turn right into The Esplanade, noticing that the building on the northern corner of the junction of Anderson Street and The Esplanade was Lot 1 in the auction of plots

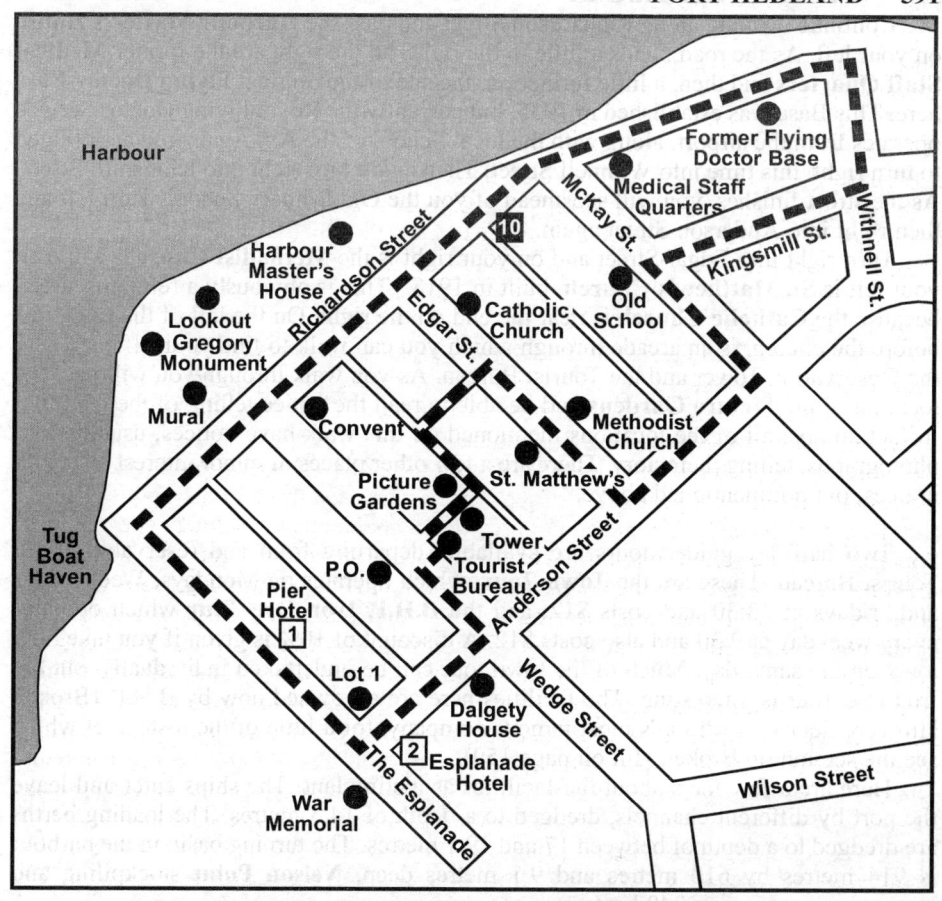

PORT HEDLAND TOWN CENTRE
Dashed line shows Walking Tour
Black numerals in white boxes indicate hotel accommodation
White numerals in black boxes indicate backpackers hostels

held in 1896. You will pass the **Pier Hotel** on your right. At the corner of The Esplanade you can see the **Tug Boat Haven** which was constructed in 1987. You are now obliged to turn right into Richardson Street. On your left is the **Centenary Mural**, painted by local artists in 1996 and depicting a hundred years of local history. Near the sea there is a monument to Gregory, who led the expedition to north-west Australia in 1861, and there is also the Mainstreet Jetty, popular for fishing. The **Shipping Observation Lookout** here was made with timber from the old jetty and offers a good view of Finucane Island.

On the corner of Richardson Street and Wedge Street is the **Old Catholic Convent**. Actually, though, the Convent was just one of this building's many uses. It was constructed in 1907 as a brewery, but the brewery failed because the water was not of satisfactory quality. Then the building was used by the *Pilbara Goldfields* Newspaper. During the war, it was requisitioned for use as an officers' mess, and it was only in 1946 that it became a Convent for the Catholic Presentation Sisters.

592 WESTERN AUSTRALIA

Continue walking along Richardson Street and pass the **Harbour Master's House** on your left. As the road bends a little to the right, on the right are the former **Medical Staff Quarters** and then, a little further on, the site of the original **Flying Doctor Base** here. This Base was established in 1935, but currently the Royal Flying Doctor Service operates from the airport, along with the local School of the Air. Again you are obliged to turn right, this time into Withnell Street. Then again turn right into Kingsmill Street. As the street finishes, you will see ahead of you the Old Primary School. Turn left and then right into Anderson Street again.

Turn right into Edgar Street and on your right is the **Methodist Church**, while on your left is **St. Matthew's Church**, built in 1918. This is obviously a religious street, because the **Catholic Church** is near the end on the right. On the left of the road, just before the church, is an arcade through which you can walk to find yourself back near the Observation Tower and the Tourist Bureau. As you walk through you will pass the location of the **Picture Gardens** and be able to read the notice telling of their history. In fact, almost all of the locations mentioned on this walk have notices, usually with photographs, telling their story. There are a few other places of minor interest also with notices, but not mentioned above.

Two half-day guided tours are available, departing from and reservable at the Tourist Bureau. These are the **Town Tour**, which operates on Mondays, Wednesdays and Fridays at 13:30 and costs $12, and the **B.H.P. Iron Ore Tour** which operates every weekday at 9:30 and also costs $12. A discount of 10% is given if you take both tours on the same day. Much of the town tour can be undertaken individually, but the Iron Ore Tour is interesting. The facilities here are all owned now by B.H.P. (Broken Hill Proprietary, Australia's most famous company, for a little of the history of which see the section on Broken Hill on page 159).

Here are a few facts about the facilities as a stimulant. The ships enter and leave the port by different channels, dredged to a depth of 14.3 metres. The loading berths are dredged to a depth of between 17 and 19.1 metres. The turning basin in the harbour is 914 metres by 610 metres and 9.1 metres deep. **Nelson Point** stockpiling and processing area covers 240 hectares.

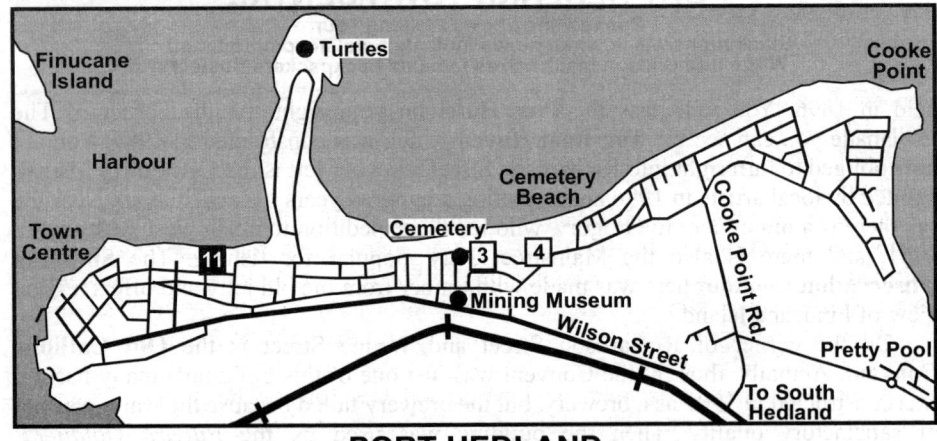

PORT HEDLAND
Black numerals in white boxes indicate hotel accommodation
White numerals in black boxes indicate backpackers hostels

The latest method of processing the iron ore is in the Hot Briquette Iron Plant completed in 1999. Hot reformed natural gas is used under pressure to reduce the ore to blocks like briquettes containing approximately 92% iron.

The railway from Nelson Point to Newman is Australia's **longest private railway**, covering a distance of 426 kilometres. Nine trains a day run in each direction, and usually each train consists of three 6,000 horsepower or four 4,000 horsepower locomotives plus 240 iron ore wagons and is 2.6 kilometres long.

The **Don Rhodes Mining Museum** is a little way down Wilson Street, the main road in and out of Port Hedland, within uncomfortable walking distance of the town centre, about three kilometres away. There are three huge restored B.H.P. locomotives here, amongst other exhibits. Not far from this open-air museum is the **Pioneer and Pearlers' Cemetery** up on the hill overlooking the sea. The cemetery was used from 1912 until 1968 and contains the graves of about forty Chinese and Japanese.

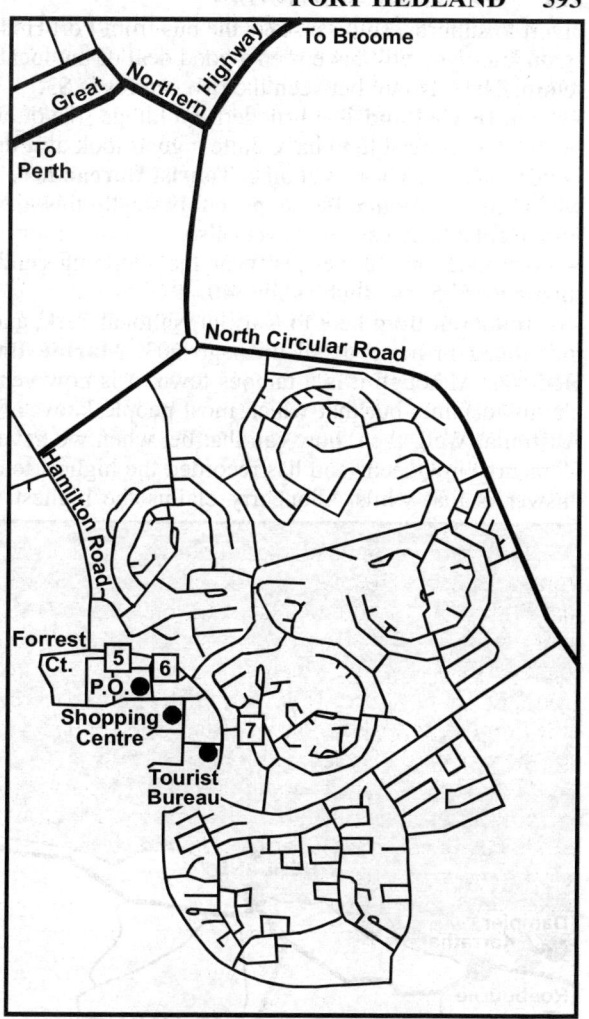

SOUTH HEDLAND
Numerals indicate accommodation

An unusual phenomenon which can be seen at full moon between April and October is the **Stairway to the Moon**. As the moon rises, for a short period it is reflected in the pools left by the receding tide, giving the impression of a series of steps. To see this, however, you must go to **Cooke Point**, well to the east of the main town.

Whales can be seen from July to October, and **turtles** come to Port Hedland to lay eggs between October and March.

A local bus service is operated by Hedland Bus Lines. The principal route is between Port Hedland and South Hedland, with additional local services around the two areas. Usually the local services continue onto, or offer a connexion onto, the principal Port Hedland - South Hedland route. Between the two centres, most buses

594   WESTERN AUSTRALIA

divert to suburbs, so if you take the bus from Port Hedland to South Hedland and back again later, you will have seen a good deal of the local community by the time of your return. The bus fare between the two centres is $3.

South Hedland is all modern buildings. If you are travelling on the Greyhound bus, you will be able to have quite a good look at it during the time for which the bus is stopped here. There is another **Tourist Bureau** here and also a large shopping centre, where the Greyhound bus stops, but basically this is a dormitory for those working in Port Hedland. It can, however, also be a dormitory for the visitor, as the Hedland Accommodation Centre, just near the shopping centre, offers air-conditioned single rooms for $35 and doubles for $40.

Tours run from here to Karijini National Park, and also to Marble Bar. Karijini is mentioned in more detail on page 603. **Marble Bar** is 203 kilometres from Port Hedland. Although it is a famous town, it is now very small. Marble Bar has several claims to fame, but that which most people know of is that it is the hottest place in Australia. Well, then, how can that be, when we have already said, on page 396, that Cloncurry in Queensland has recorded the highest temperature on this continent? The answer is that whilst Cloncurry claims the highest single temperature, Marble Bar

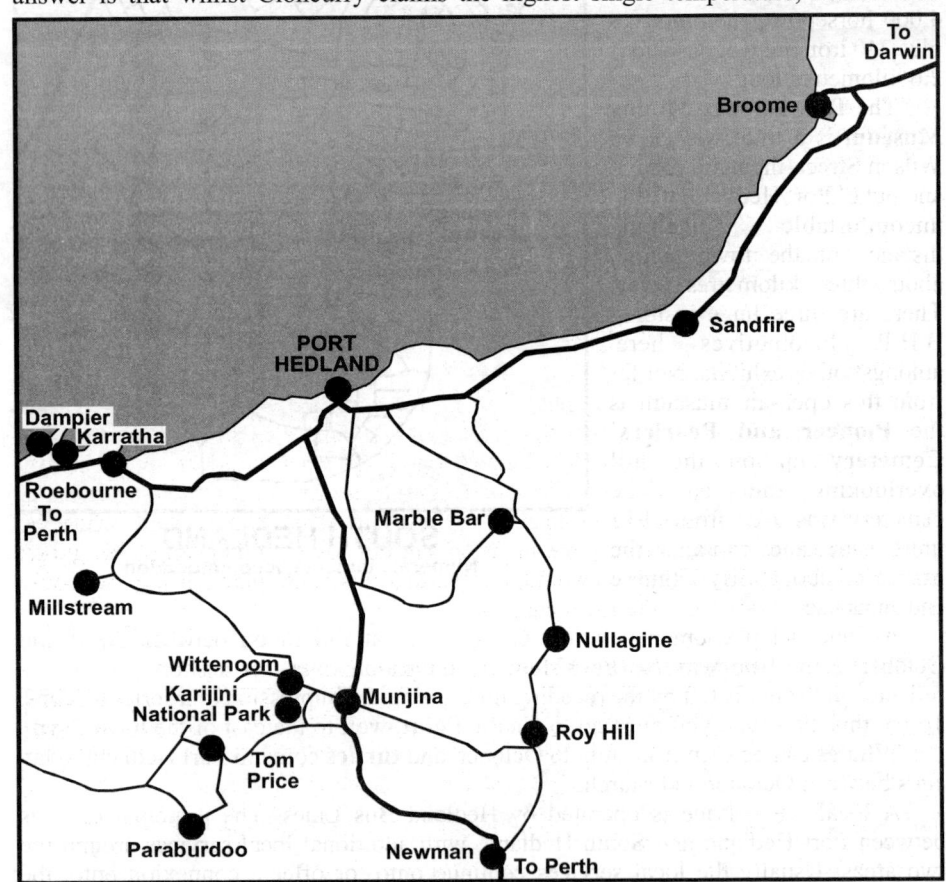

PORT HEDLAND VICINITY

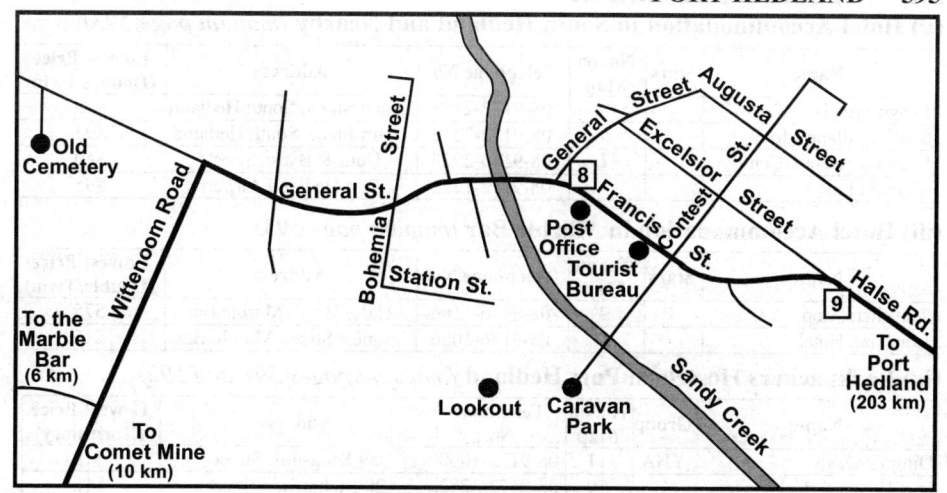

MARBLE BAR
Numerals indicate accommodation

claims to be hotter on average. This claim is particularly based on the record established in 1923 to 1924, when Marble Bar recorded a temperature in excess of 100°F (37.8°C) for 160 consecutive days. When the author came here, I felt betrayed by the fact that the temperature did not reach that level. Another feature for which Marble Bar is famous is the **Marble Bar**. It is six kilometres from the town centre on the Coongan River. Actually, though, it is not marble, as originally thought, but jasper. A third claim to fame is the **Comet Gold Mine**, founded in 1936 and ten kilometres from the town. This mine at one time claimed to have the tallest chimney in the southern hemisphere, at 75 metres high, although now Port Pirie offers one much taller.

ACCOMMODATION

As mentioned above, the best value in accommodation is the Hedland Accommodation Centre, but it is at South Hedland, which rather lacks in interest. For the backpacker, there are two hostels. Port Hedland Backpackers is very conveniently close to the bus stop and tourist office and to the centre of town. On the other hand, Dingo's Oasis is a pleasant place to stay, looking out across the sea and, when the author stayed, he found not only the management but several other long-term guests particularly helpful and kind, so would suggest that this is the place to stay. It is only fifteen minutes walk from the town centre.

(i) Hotel Accommodation in Port Hedland *(maps on pages 591 and 592)*

Name	Stars	No. on Map	Telephone No.	Address	Lowest Price (Double/Twin)
Hospitality Inn	3½	3	08-9173-1044	Webster Street	$165
Mercure Inn		4	08-9173-1511	Lukis Street	$90
Pier Hotel / Motel		1	08-9173-1488	25 The Esplanade	$75
Esplanade Hotel / Motel		2	08-9173-1798	1 Anderson Street	$75

596   WESTERN AUSTRALIA

(ii) Hotel Accommodation in South Hedland and Nearby *(map on page 593)*

Name	Stars	No. on Map	Telephone No.	Address	Lowest Price (Double/Twin)
Lodge Motel		5	08-9172-2188	Brand Street, South Hedland	$95
South Hedland Motel		6	08-9172-2222	Court Place, South Hedland	$95
Hedland Accom. Centre		7	08-9140-2925	Hunt & Byass Streets	$40
Mercure Inn			08-9172-1222	Port Hedland Airport	$95

(iii) Hotel Accommodation in Marble Bar *(map on page 595)*

Name	Stars	No. on Map	Telephone No.	Address	Lowest Price (Double/Twin)
Travellers Stop		9	08-9176-1166	Halse Road, Marble Bar	$75
Iron Clad Hotel		8	08-9176-1066	Francis Street, Marble Bar	$45

(iv) Backpackers Hostels in Port Hedland *(maps on pages 591 and 592)*

Name	Group	No. on Map	Telephone No.	Address	Lowest Price (Dormitory)
Dingo's Oasis	YHA	11	08-9173-1000	59 Kingsmill Street	$19
Port Hedland Backpackers		10	08-9173-3282	20 Richardson Street	$18

MOVING ON
Bus Services from Port Hedland

Destination	Operator	Via	Distance (km)	Fare	Journey Time	Frequency
Perth	Greyhound		1773	$228	21¼ - 25 hrs	9/week
		Geraldton	1351	$209	19 hrs	1/day
		Carnarvon	871	$153	12½ hrs	1/day
		Meekatharra	881	$167	11½ hrs	2/week
Perth	Integrity		1773	$210	26¾ hrs	2/week
		Geraldton	1351	$195	20¾ hrs	2/week
		Carnarvon	872	$135	12¼ hrs	2/week
Broome	Greyhound		597	$99	7½ hrs	1/day
Broome	Integrity		597	$90	8¾ hrs	2/week

MEEKATHARRA
Population 1,500

10 hrs by bus from Perth

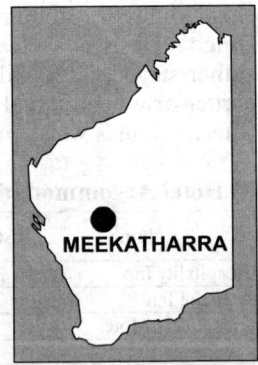

As mentioned above, there is another route from Perth to Port Hedland. Although most visitors choose to travel via the coast, the inland route is interesting too, passing through an assortment of old pioneering towns and new mining communities. Greyhound operates by this route twice a week, departing from Perth on Sundays and Fridays. The bus runs directly up the Great Northern Highway and takes ten hours to Meekatharra.

W.A.G.R. used to operate a rail service to Meekatharra until the late 1970s and then abruptly abandoned the line. Now a bus service is run instead. The bus actually operates from Geraldton, on Mondays and Wednesdays only. There are connexions from Perth on both days. On Mondays, one takes the service bound for Geraldton via Northam and Mullewa, and changes at Mullewa. On Wednesdays, one takes the direct service from Perth to Geraldton, and changes at Geraldton. By either route, the journey from Perth to Meekatharra takes just under thirteen hours.

If you travel with W.A.G.R., you will pass through the small town of **Mullewa**, still served by the railway, since this is a wheat-growing area and much of the wheat is shifted by train. Mullewa has another of **Monsignor John Hawes'** churches (see section on Geraldton on page 566), the **Church of our Lady Mount Carmel St. Peter and St. Paul**. This is regarded as another of his best designs.

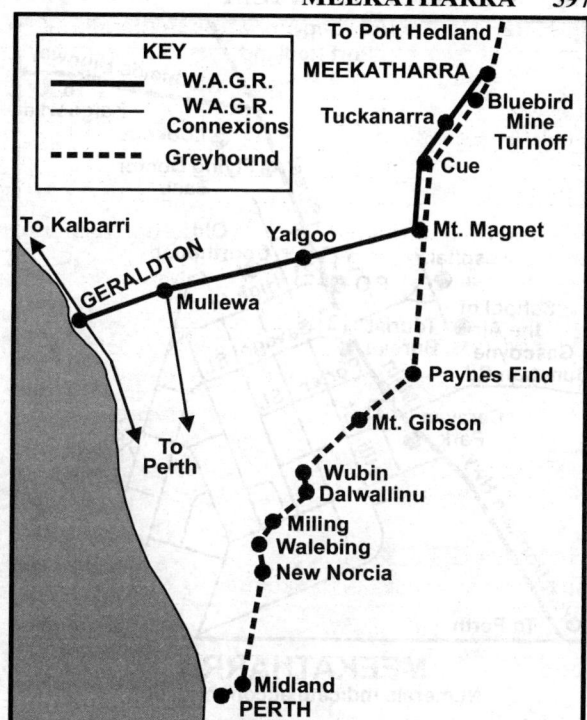

BUS SERVICES FROM PERTH AND GERALDTON TO MEEKATHARRA

The **Monsignor Hawes Priest House Museum** is here too. For some years it was the home of the priest and it contains many of his personal effects. Anglicans have their answer in **St. Andrew's Anglican Church**, which was the first church built in Mullewa and is another fine building, constructed of attractive red granite.

There are also **murals** around the town telling of local history, and even though you will probably not choose to take a stop in Mullewa, if attentive you will be able to glimpse these from the bus.

Along the route east from Mullewa you will be able to see the formation of the old railway on your right. This is flat country, with the old line raised just a little above the surrounding land, just waiting for somebody to replace the rails and start running trains again.

Whether you travel with W.A.G.R. or with Greyhound, you will pass through **Mt. Magnet**, for this is where the two routes meet. Mt. Magnet was named in 1854 by the surveyor Robert Austin because the small mountain here contains magnetic material, but it was not until 1895 that a town developed following the discovery of gold in the region in 1891. Gold has been mined here since then, and still is. Mt. Magnet was gazetted as a town in 1895 and claims to be the oldest continuously working gold mining town in Western Australia. There is accommodation of various types in the town, including older hotels offering budget rooms.

Another eighty kilometres will bring you to **Cue**. Cue was a gold town famous because of the wealth that was available here just by scratching the surface of the land.

WESTERN AUSTRALIA

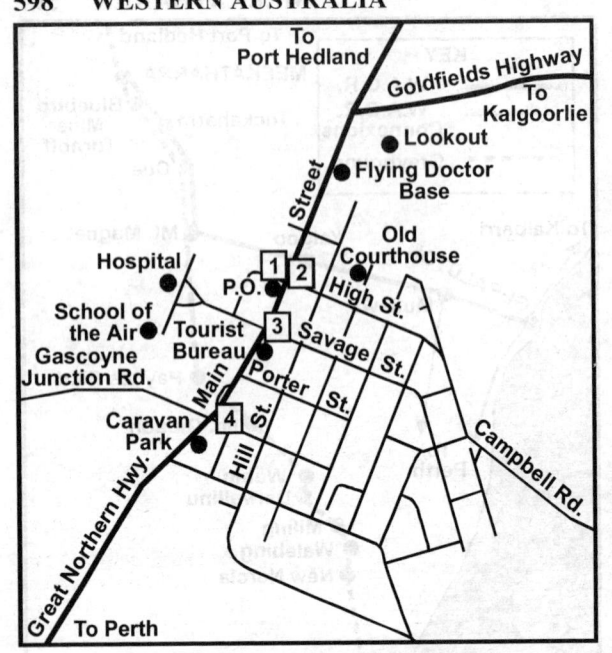

MEEKATHARRA
Numerals indicate accommodation

Gold was discovered in 1891 and, although he was not the original discoverer, it was a man named Tom Cue who filed the claim, and consequently the town bears his name.

Cue came to be known as *The Queen of the Murchison*. The early prosperity is reflected in some of its buildings, but, as in many places, the gold ran out. When the mineral wealth was no longer to be found on the surface, mines were dug, but with only modest results, and the last mine, the *Light of Asia*, closed in 1933. Recently, though, modern methods of extraction have allowed some reworking of tailings to be undertaken, breathing some new life into this old town.

48 kilometres west of Cue, but not easily accessible, is **Walga Rock**. This monolith is five kilometres in circumference and 1.5 kilometres long. It offers a good view of the area from its summit and also has a large cave full of **aboriginal paintings**, including one thought to represent the ships in which the Dutch arrived in the seventeenth century. There is an aboriginal **ochre pit** which is thought to date back 30,000 years.

ANECDOTE

The W.A.G.R. bus driver on the journey from Geraldton to Meekatharra was interested in my eccentric plan to travel every passenger railway line in Australia. When we arrived in Meekatharra he kindly pointed out the cheapest accommodation to me (Meekatharra Hotel) and then said, "I stay opposite at the Royal Mail. It'll be too expensive for you to have dinner there, but come and join me for a drink afterwards." I did so, and experienced an enjoyable evening.

In the morning I turned up for my bus back to Perth and the driver handed me a small package wrapped in a paper napkin. "I thought you probably wouldn't have had time for breakfast," he explained, "So I made you a bacon sandwich with what was left over of mine." W.A.G.R. certainly offers some good service.

MEEKATHARRA

Meekatharra, 120 kilometres north of Cue, is not a very big town, but, established in 1894, it has long been a centre for the gold and pastoral industries. The **State Battery**, for crushing gold-bearing rocks, was moved to Main Street (as the main street is called) in 1994 as a piece of nostalgia and is worth a look. There is a **Flying Doctor Base** further up the street, accepting visitors between 9:00 and 14:00 on weekdays, and a **School of the Air** to the west of the town, accepting visitors between 8:00 and 10:30 on weekdays. This was the first School of the Air in Western Australia, opened on 14th September 1959. It has the largest enrolment of any such school in the state, approximately one hundred students, and it covers the widest area, some half million square kilometres. It also has an unusual Choir of the Air. The **Old Courthouse** in Darlot Street, built in 1912, is classified by the National Trust.

ACCOMMODATION
(i) Accommodation in Mt. Magnet

Name	Stars	Telephone No.	Address	Lowest Price (Double/Twin)
Miners' Rest		08-9963-4380	Lot 552e, Thurkle Cove	$65
Commercial Club Hotel		08-9963-4021	63 Hepburn St., Mt. Magnet	$55
Mt. Magnet Hotel		08-9963-4002	Hepburn Street, Mt. Magnet	$55
Grand Hotel		08-9963-4110	Hepburn Street, Mt. Magnet	$55

(ii) Accommodation in Cue

Name	Stars	Telephone No.	Address	Lowest Price (Double/Twin)
Murchison Club Hotel		08-9963-1020	Austin Street, Cue	$45

(iii) Accommodation in Meekatharra

Name	Stars	No. on Map	Telephone No.	Address	Lowest Price (Double/Twin)
Auski Inland Motel	3	4	08-9981-1433	Main Street	$95
Royal Mail Hotel		2	08-9981-1148	Main Street	$75
Commercial Hotel		3	08-9981-1020	77 Main Street	$75
Meekatharra Hotel Motel		1	08-9981-1134	Main Street	$55

MOVING ON

Greyhound operates to Perth on Sundays and Tuesdays, but at 3:25, so one needs to be up early to catch that service. W.A.G.R. leaves at 7:10 on Tuesdays and 9:00 on Thursdays. Both W.A.G.R. services run to Geraldton. From the Tuesday service only, there is a connexion at Mullewa to Perth. Going north, Greyhound operates to Newman and on to Port Hedland very late on Sunday and Friday evenings.

Bus Services from Meekatharra

Destination	Operator	Via	Distance (km)	Fare	Journey Time	Frequency
Perth	Greyhound		971	$164	9½ hrs	2/week
Perth	W.A.G.R.		1191	$83.55	12¾ hrs	1/week
Geraldton	W.A.G.R.		531	$52.80	6¾ - 7 hrs	2/week
Port Hedland	Greyhound		881	$165	11½ hrs	2/week

600 WESTERN AUSTRALIA
NEWMAN AND TOM PRICE

Population 5,000 (Newman)
Population 4,000 (Tom Price)

15 hrs 30 mins by bus from Perth (Newman)

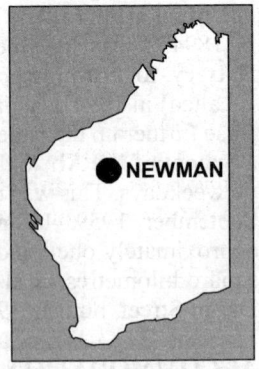

Mt. Newman is a peak rising to 1,053 metres above sea level. It was named in 1896 after Aubrey Newman, an explorer on a mapping expedition who had the misfortune to die of typhoid near here.

There was no town here until, in 1957, a prospector named Stan Hilditich found a mountain of iron ore fifteen kilometres south-east of here, at **Mt. Whaleback**. Mt. Whaleback is now the world's largest single open-cut iron ore mine and it is being transported away day by day in those huge 2.6 kilometre-long trains to Port Hedland. **Newman** is the modern town, named after the nearby mountain, where the employees of the B.H.P. (Broken Hill Proprietary) mining company live.

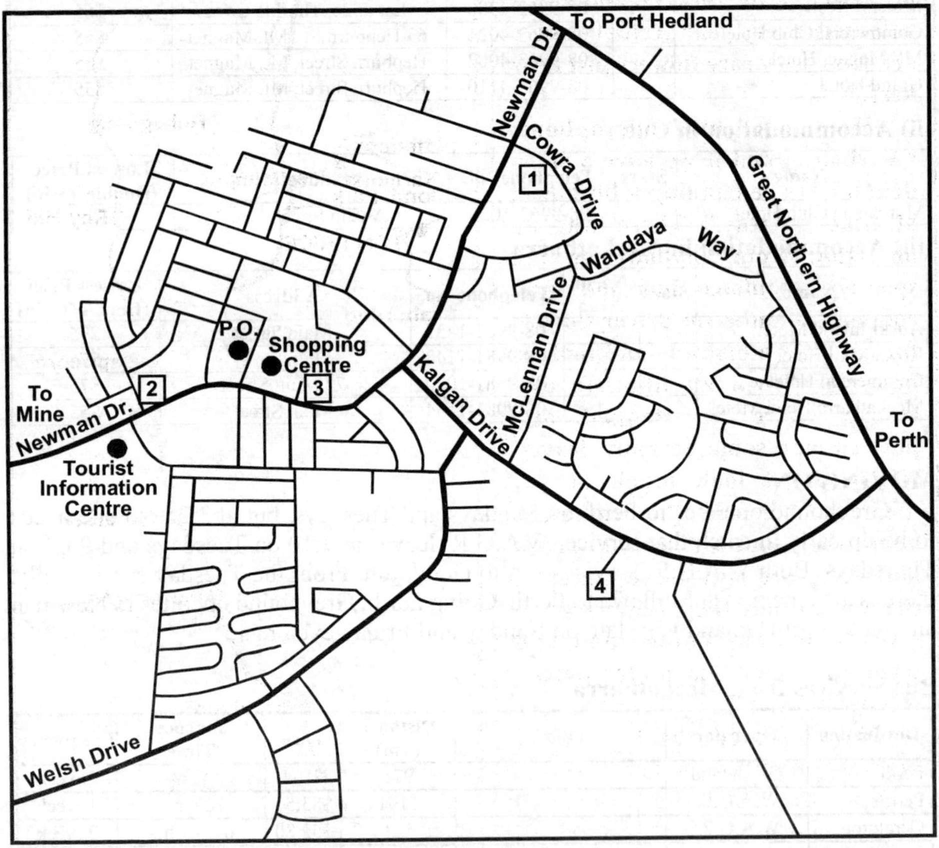

NEWMAN
Numerals indicate accommodation

ANECDOTE

On the journey back from Mullewa to Perth, the W.A.G.R. bus driver was explaining to me. "The company started running Wildflower Tours, and, you know, people come from all over the world to take a two-week Wildflower Tour in W.A. Now, I had no interest at all in flowers, but I was asked to do one of these tours. At first I didn't want to, but I couldn't get out of it, and I gradually became more and more interested in the flowers, and now I volunteer every year. Actually there are some very rare flowers just near here."

He took his microphone. "Anybody mind if we have a short detour? We're running a bit ahead of time anyway." There was no objection from anybody on the sparsely populated bus and in a couple of minutes the driver slowed, turned off the highway and took us bouncing down an ill-made dirt track, where he stopped and pointed out some scrappy leaves. "They don't look much at the moment," he said (he was right about that), but it's not the season and there are only three places in the world where those flowers grow. I really love the flowers now and want to show them to people whenever I can."

We bounced back to the highway and I reflected on devotion to duty. How wonderful it would be if we could all enjoy our work as much as this driver obviously did.

There is nothing historic to see here, therefore, but you can have an interesting tour of the mine, and encounter the huge trucks, with wheels 2.7 metres high, which move loads of as much as 240 tonnes. You can also see Australia's **longest private railway**, running from here to Port Hedland, a distance of 426 kilometres. This is the railway which holds the record for the

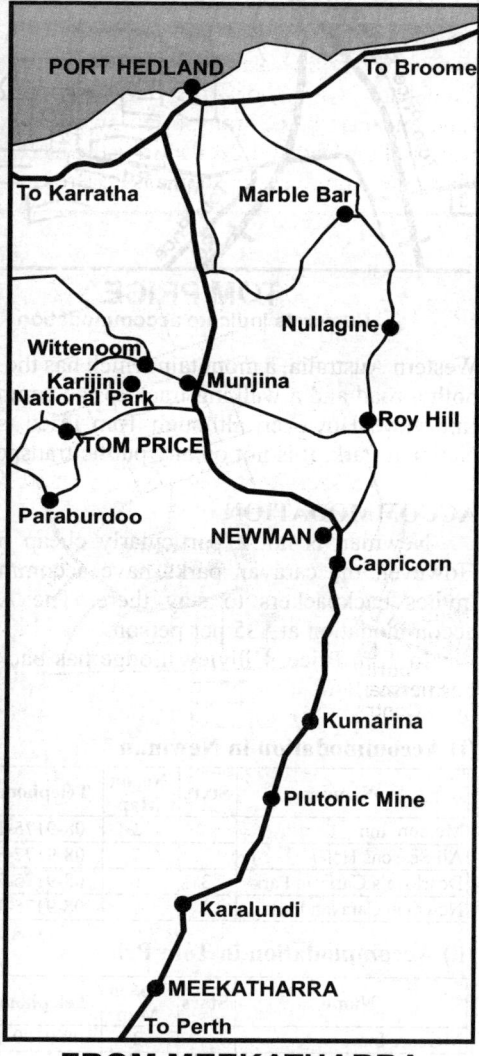

FROM MEEKATHARRA TO PORT HEDLAND

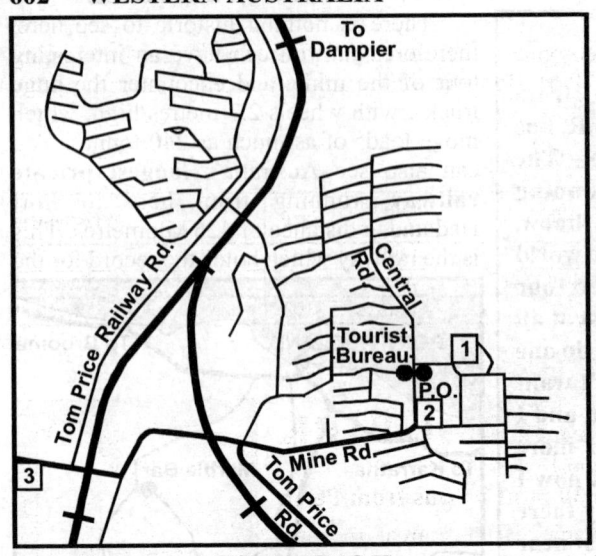

TOM PRICE
Numerals indicate accommodation

world's longest and heaviest train, 7.36 kilometres long, consisting of 682 wagons and eight locomotives conveying 80,000 tonnes of iron ore. This record was set in June 2001.

300 kilometres west of Newman is a town which is almost a twin. **Tom Price** is also an iron ore mining town and also named after a nearby mountain. It also is a modern town built for mine workers and it also has a railway to take the iron ore to the port, which in this case is Dampier. **Tom Price** is the highest town in Western Australia, at an altitude of 747 metres, and it stands four kilometres from the highest mountain in Western Australia, a mountain which has the unusual name of **Mt. Nameless**. There are both a road and a walking track to the summit at 1,128 metres, from where there is a fine view. However, although Tom Price is a good base for exploration of Karijini National Park, it is not on any public transport route.

ACCOMMODATION

Newman is not a particularly cheap place to stay, being modern and remote. However, the caravan parks have accommodation and the Newman Caravan Park invites backpackers to stay there. The All Seasons Hotel also has backpackers accommodation at $35 per person.

In Tom Price, Hillview Lodge has backpackers accommodation available at $30 per person.

(i) Accommodation in Newman

Name	Stars	No. on Map	Telephone No.	Address	Lowest Price (Double/Twin)
Mercure Inn		2	08-9175-1101	Newman Drive	$145
All Seasons Hotel		3	08-9177-8666	Newman Drive	$95
Dearlove's Caravan Park	3	1	08-9175-2802	Cowra Drive	$65
Newman Caravan Park	3	4	08-9175-1428	Kalgan Drive	$55

(ii) Accommodation in Tom Price

Name	Stars	No. on Map	Telephone No.	Address	Lowest Price (Double/Twin)
Mercure Inn		2	08-9189-1101	Central Road	$145
Hillview Lodge		1	08-9189-1110	Stadium Road	$75
Tom Price Caravan Park		3	08-9189-1515	Mine Road	$55

MOVING ON

Only Greyhound serves the community of Newman. Buses run to Perth on Monday and Saturday evenings, and to Port Hedland very early on Monday and Saturday mornings.

Bus Services from Newman

Destination	Operator	Via	Distance (km)	Fare	Journey Time	Frequency
Perth	Greyhound		1392	$204	14¾ hrs	2/week
		Meekatharra	421	$117	5 hrs	2/week
Port Hedland	Greyhound		460	$103	6¼ hrs	2/week

KARIJINI NATIONAL PARK
Population 50 (Wittenoom)
17 hrs 30 mins by bus from Perth

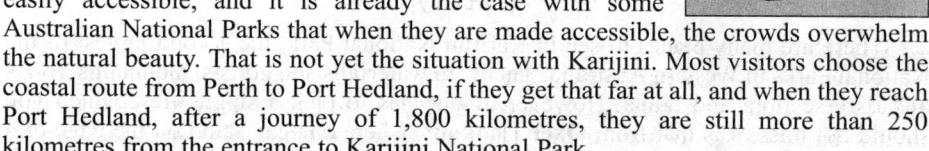

Karijini is the aboriginal name for this area, recently reinstated as the name for the National Park here. Previously it was known as the Hamersley Range National Park, and prior to that visitors just said that they were coming to look at Wittenoom Gorge. Whichever of the three you come to see, though, it will be well worth your time.

It is natural that magnificent scenery is not going to be easily accessible, and it is already the case with some Australian National Parks that when they are made accessible, the crowds overwhelm the natural beauty. That is not yet the situation with Karijini. Most visitors choose the coastal route from Perth to Port Hedland, if they get that far at all, and when they reach Port Hedland, after a journey of 1,800 kilometres, they are still more than 250 kilometres from the entrance to Karijini National Park.

From Port Hedland, it is easy to find tours to Karijini. There are day tours, and there are tours which allow two or three days. There are also tours from Exmouth and from Karratha. However, another possibility, especially if you are travelling by the inland route, is to stay in **Wittenoom**, from where there are also tours available. From Wittenoom, of course, you would be able to see the sights adequately in a single day. There are three backpackers hostels here, and their business is accommodating guests who wish to see the National Park, so all arrange or conduct tours. However, Wittenoom is 42 kilometres from the nearest point on the Great Northern Highway at **Munjina** (Auski Roadhouse, where accommodation is also available), so arrangements must be made with your accommodation in Wittenoom to collect you from the bus stop.

The principal industry in this area was **asbestos mining**. It has gone out of favour now, but, in any case, the mines here had ceased production even before problems with the use of asbestos were discovered. Had they not done so, perhaps they would have been required to clean up a little more thoroughly, for in the mining area asbestos can just be picked out of the rocks, while in the old processing area, to which admittance is restricted, it lies about all over the floor. You will probably be shown some of these areas. If you suffer from respiratory problems, remember to stop breathing whilst here.

WESTERN AUSTRALIA

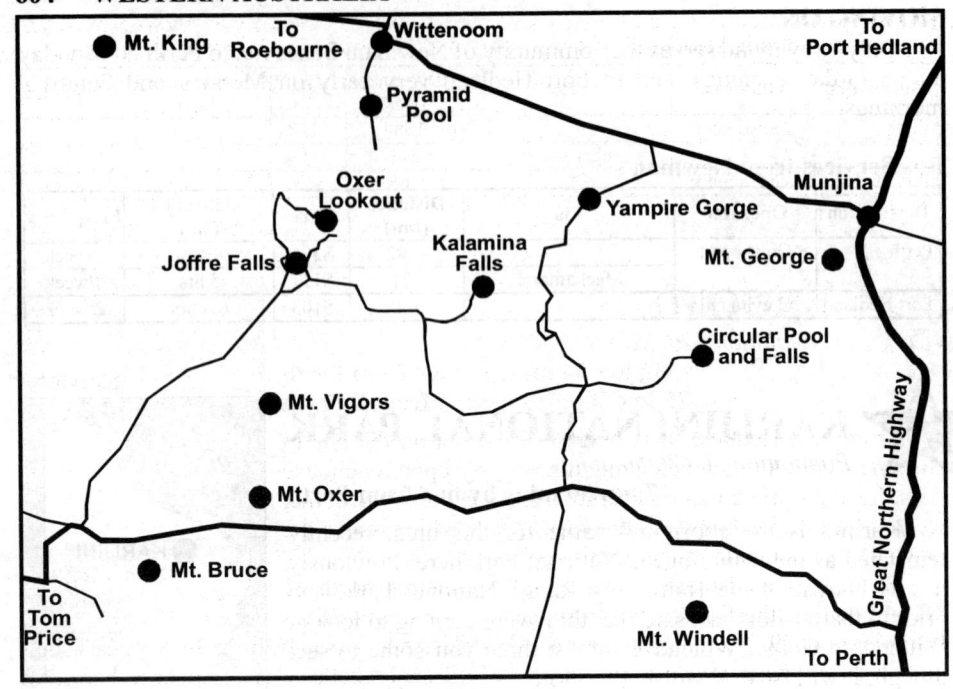

KARIJINI NATIONAL PARK
(Part only)

There are many places to see in Karijini National Park, the second largest of the National Parks in Western Australia. There are waterfalls and gorges, mountains, rivers and diverse flora and fauna. However, if one has to pick a single view which you should not miss, it is that from **Oxer Lookout**, where one can stand on the edge of a precipitous hundred metre drop and see four different gorges stretching away to their different points of the compass, a truly magnificent view. In the author's opinion, this is probably the best single view of all the wonderful sights in Australia, so try not to miss it, even though it is a little difficult to reach.

There are camp sites within the National Park and there are walking trails of varying degrees of difficulty.

ACCOMMODATION
(i) Hotel Accommodation in Wittenoom

Name	Stars	Telephone No.	Address	Lowest Price (Double/Twin)
Wittenoom Holiday Home		08-9189-7096	Fifth Avenue	$95
Wittenoom Guest House		08-9189-7060	Gregory Street	$45

(ii) Backpackers Hostels in Wittenoom

Name	Group	Telephone No.	Address	Lowest Price (Dormitory)
Wittenoom Guest House		08-9189-7060	Gregory Street	$19
Nomad Heights Backpackers		08-9189-7068	21 First Avenue	$19
Bungarra Bivouac Hostel		08-9189-7026	74 Fifth Avenue	$17

MOVING ON
Bus Services from Munjina

Destination	Operator	Via	Distance (km)	Fare	Journey Time	Frequency
Perth	Greyhound		1584	$227	17¼ hrs	2/week
		Meekatharra	613	$159	7¼ hrs	2/week
Port Hedland	Greyhound		268	$53	3½ hrs	2/week

BROOME
Population 12,000

32 hrs 30 mins by bus from Perth
25 hrs 30 mins by bus from Darwin

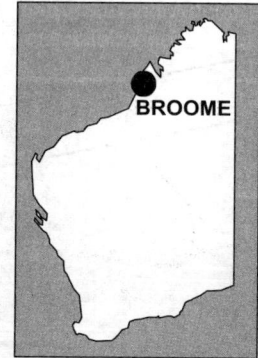

From Port Hedland, it is over seven hours on the bus to Broome with nothing much along the way, except a roadhouse with the appropriate name of **Sandfire**. As we reach Broome, we enter the region known as the **Kimberley**, which is also the name of the mountain range in this region.

Broome is an isolated town 2,300 kilometres north of Perth, to which the first known European visitor was William Dampier in 1699. There is one reason for its existence: - **pearls**. In 1879, the pearl shell known as *pinctada maxima*, the largest of all such shells, was discovered here. An interesting mixture of peoples flocked here in the 1880s to try to reap the rewards of diving for these shells. Those who came included, in large numbers, Japanese, Chinese, Malays and Timorese from Kupang. The British Pearling Masters usually controlled the fleets, while the Japanese and others dived and the Chinese controlled the commerce. Aborigines too were pressed into service diving for wealth. Wealth was indeed to be found, for naturally the largest shells produce the largest pearls. However, it was not so much the rare find of a beautiful pearl which was the incentive as the assured sale of the mother-of-pearl in the shell for button-making. At the peak of its prosperity, in the early twentieth century, Broome had of fleet of 403 pearling vessels working here and had established itself as the pearling centre of the world, producing 80% of the global supply of mother-of-pearl.

When the Great Depression came, though, it affected even remote locations such as Broome, and things were never quite the same again. Then the war arrived and brought various hardships. Broome became a flying boat base and was therefore bombed by the Japanese. The fishing fleets were destroyed by the military, for fear of their falling into enemy hands. When the war finished, plastic buttons had been invented and the demand for mother-of-pearl was greatly reduced. It seemed that Broome had little future.

However, a joint venture was established here with the Japanese, who had developed the system of cultured pearls, and it was soon found that in Broome pearls could be grown in half of the time required in Japan and were twice as big. Now the pearling industry is thriving once more, with eight different pearling companies based in Broome. It has also become a popular tourist destination, especially with backpackers.

If you arrive by bus, you will find yourself at the **Tourist Bureau**, which ought to

606 WESTERN AUSTRALIA

be a good starting point, except that the office is closed at the arrival times of most buses. The Tourist Bureau used to be housed in an old DC-3 aircraft. This particular aircraft had tried to land at Broome in exceptionally bad weather, when the pilot found that he had missed the runway. He decided to land anyway, with wheels up. When the propeller made contact with the ground, it sheared off and one blade went through the cockpit severing the seat belt of the co-pilot between his back and the seat, but he was left unharmed. When the aircraft came to a halt, nobody was seriously hurt and even the aircraft itself was little damaged. It never flew again, however, and made an

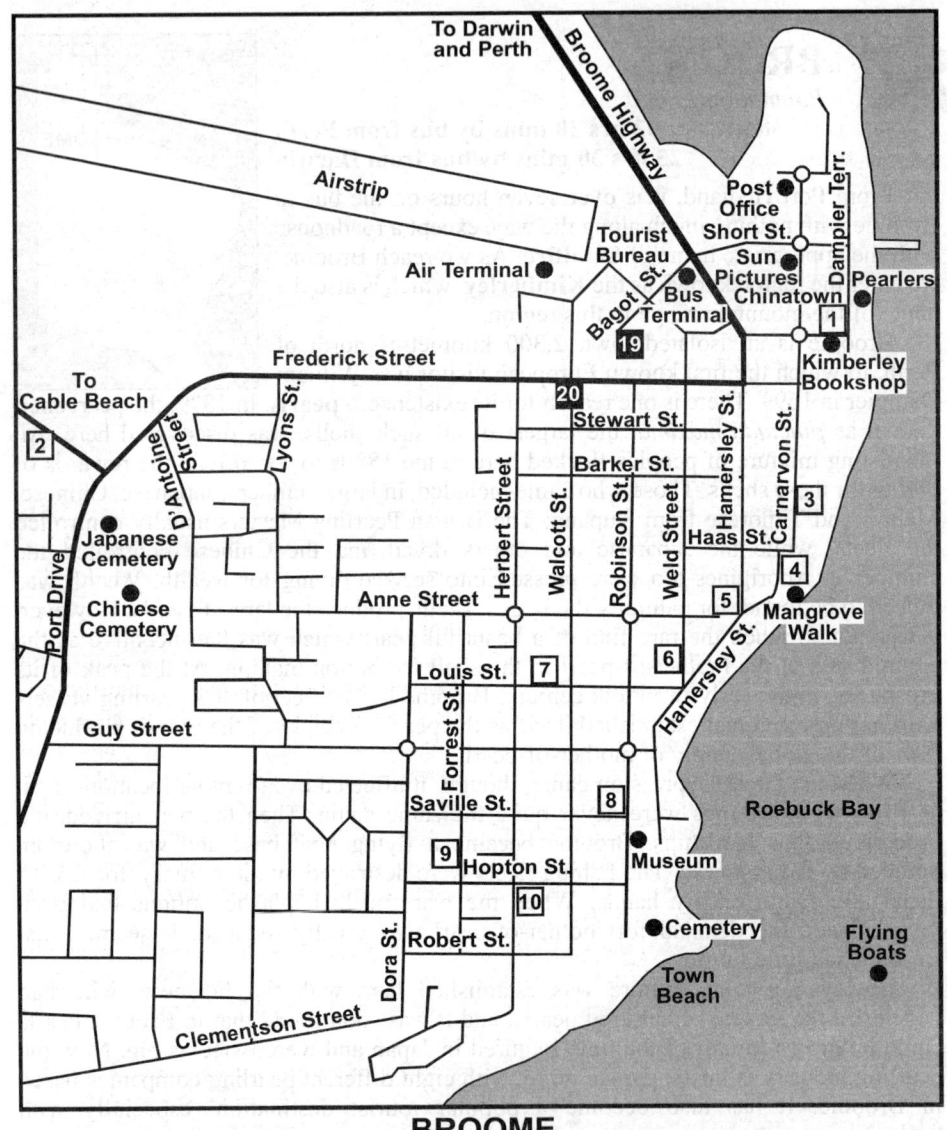

BROOME
Black numerals in white boxes indicate hotel accommodation
White numerals in black boxes indicate backpackers hostels

interesting office for several years. The new Tourist Bureau rather lacks in character by comparison.

If you arrive by air, you will find that the airport is within walking distance of the town centre, a distance of about two kilometres. For backpackers, Kimberley Klub Backpackers is right by the airport entrance and Broome's Last Resort is about the same distance from the airport terminal.

The town centre of Broome is small and easy to locate. The most interesting section is **Chinatown**, with its individual style of architecture. There are many shops here selling pearls, as you might expect, and plenty with all sorts of other souvenirs too, as an indication of how important tourism has become to Broome.

The **Sun Picture Theatre** is in this area, and is certainly worth seeing. It claims to be the world's oldest operating picture

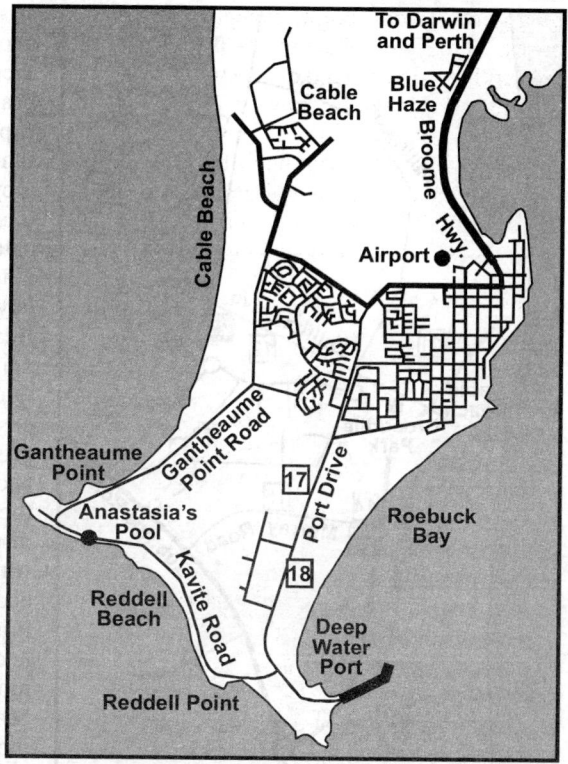

BROOME AND VICINITY
Numerals indicate accommodation

garden, having been established in 1916. Being a picture garden, it does not have a roof, except over a small area at the rear. One simply sits in a deck-chair watching the white screen erected at the end of the open area and getting bitten by the mosquitoes. It is all very romantic and nostalgic. Films are shown almost every night, but are not particularly cheap at around $12, and there are guided tours of the theatre at certain times during the day. If an unguided tour will satisfy you, simply walk in. That is free. The theatre has survived cyclones and has been shut down several times in the past, but has always been reopened. In the wartime, the military personnel stationed here took it over and kept it running, and more recently a well-known actor purchased it and saved it from demolition. It has now become sufficiently popular as a reminder of yesteryear to have ensured its perpetual survival.

Just down the road from the Sun Theatre are three **statues** celebrating the men who brought the cultured pearl industry to Broome and started the revival of the town. There is also a monument to the **divers** of the early days, without whom there would have been no Broome.

In Dampier Terrace, just on the edge of Chinatown, are two restored **pearl luggers**. **Guided tours**, with a demonstration of how the pearl divers of old used to work, cost $15 and are available at 11:00 and 14:00. There is also an evening meal of pearl shell meat offered, with a history of pearling and a free pearl, but this costs $50.

While in Broome you have two choices for the location of accommodation: in the town or at the beach. **Cable Beach** is a beautiful expanse of 22 kilometres of white sand. When the author was last here, a cyclone was passing through, just missing the town with any catastrophic winds but producing magnificent angry waves, cloudy days and strong breezes. Cable Beach looked splendid in such conditions. In any circumstances, tides here can reach up to ten metres, ensuring that the beach is always pristine. It is named Cable Beach because it was here that the cable for the international telegraph line disappeared into the sea. The cable was laid in 1889. There is accommodation of all prices around this beach, although none of it encroaches on the beach area and most cannot even be seen from the beach. Accommodation options here include one of the backpackers hostels, Cable Beach Backpackers, which is a pleasant place to stay and only five minutes from the beach. There are buses between the town and Cable Beach every hour, with the last bus back at 18:15. The fare is $3.

Also at Cable Beach is the **Broome Crocodile Park**. Since there are more than a thousand crocodiles kept here, the author checked that the fence looked fairly strong before staying nearby. There

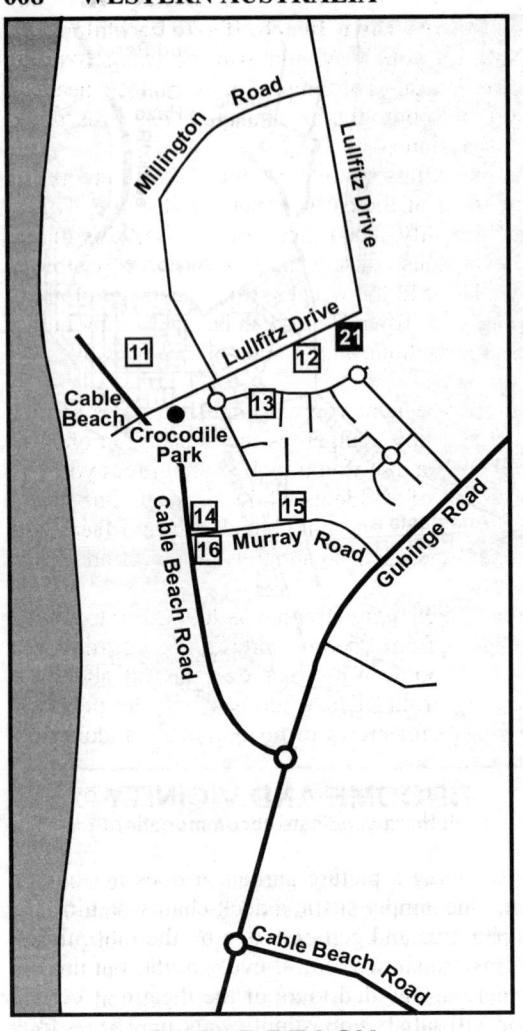

CABLE BEACH
Black numerals indicate hotel accommodation
White numerals indicate backpackers hostels

are also **camel rides** on the beach offered by two different companies.

Further south from Cable Beach is **Gantheaume Point**, where there are **dinosaur footprints**, 120 million years old, in the rocks. Since these can be seen only at low tide, a cast has been constructed and is displayed on the cliff top. The cliffs here are red in colour and contrast with the blue of the sea to present a pretty picture. There is also a rock pool, named **Anastasia's Pool**, built by a former lighthouse keeper for his wife, who suffered from arthritis. Gantheaume Point is six kilometres from the town. The first bus in the morning is extended to here. It leaves the town centre at 7:30 and Cable Beach at 7:45.

There are other beaches, although none to compare with Cable Beach. The beach which is within walking distance of the town is **Town Beach**. If you walk along the coast, you will pass the **Mangrove Walk** on your way, and also the small **Broome Historical Museum** in the Old Customs House. The emphasis here is on pearling exhibits, as one might expect, with many old photographs displayed. The Museum is open daily from 10:00 until 13:00 and admission costs $4.

At Town Beach itself there are some points of interest too. First there is the **Pioneer Cemetery**, the resting place of some of the early settlers of Broome. This is located under the tree just to the left of the jetty. Then there are the **remains of the flying boats** which were bombed by the Japanese during the war. They are visible at very low tides, at which time one can walk out to the wrecks. It is a distance of about one kilometre. Watch out for the returning tide. Town Beach can be reached by bus, if preferred. The bus leaves the town centre every hour on the hour, and returns from the beach at 24 minutes past the hour.

To the west of the town is the **Cemetery**, where you can find the graves of nine hundred Japanese, providing evidence of just how dangerous the occupation of pearl diving was. Some lived to see old age, of course, but if you look at the graves you will find that many died young, often as the result of accidents while working. One thinks of the similarities between this cemetery and the one on Thursday Island (see page 392). Nearby there is a Chinese section, and there is also an interesting section for the missionaries who came to this area.

There are many places which can be visited from Broome as tours. For example, **Willie Creek Pearl Farm** is forty kilometres from Broome and offers a half-day tour for $60, including transport to and from Broome. This tour explains all about the process of seeding the oysters and then nurturing them while growing the pearl. At Willie Creek there is also a **detention centre** for crews of boats, mostly Indonesian, found fishing illegally in these waters.

Other tours include those by air to view the Kimberley Range and others by four-wheel-drive vehicle to remote and inaccessible locations, but, of course, these are relatively expensive.

A local bus service is provided within Broome. There is just a single route, running from the Vacation Village via the town centre to Cable Beach. The bus operates once an hour between 7:10 and 18:15 every day. It leaves the town centre for Cable Beach at half past each hour, and leaves Cable Beach at a quarter to each hour (except the last service, which is at 18:15). It leaves the town centre to go south to the Vacation Village on the hour and leaves the Vacation Village for the return to the town centre at ten past each hour. The fare is $3 for a single journey, or $9 for an all-day ticket.

BOOKSHOPS
Kimberley Bookshop *4 Napier Terrace*

This is a very pleasant little bookshop close to the bay. Since it is almost the only bookshop between Geraldton and Darwin, it is worth a visit.

ACCOMMODATION
Since Broome has acquired popularity as a tourist destination, accommodation rates have become seasonal, with considerable fluctuation. Rates quoted below are low season rates, please note. Backpackers accommodation, however, does not vary much, as usual. Those wishing to stay by the beach will find Cable Beach Backpackers to be

610   WESTERN AUSTRALIA

a particularly friendly and pleasant place to be. In the town, Kimberley Klub is a very popular location and most people who stay there seem to love it. As something of a contrary opinion, therefore, the author will just mention that he found it crowded, of course, and with staff who were not very helpful. I was charged for a map of Broome which was available free at the Tourist Bureau, so did not have such a good impression of the hostel. However, do not be deterred by one eccentric opinion. You will probably love it too, like most of its guests.

(i) Hotel Accommodation in Broome *(map on page 606)*

Name	Stars	No. on Map	Telephone No.	Address	Lowest Price (Double/Twin)
Mercure Inn Continental	3½	6	08-9192-1002	Weld Street	$185
Moonlight Bay	4½	4	1-800-818-878	Carnarvon Street	$185
McAlpine House	4	7	08-9192-3886	84 Herbert Street	$165
Mangrove Hotel	4	3	1-800-094-818	Carnarvon Street	$160
Palms Resort	3½	10	1-800-094-848	Hopton Street	$140
Bayside Holiday Apts.	3	5	08-9193-6026	Anne & Hamersley Streets	$130
Ocean Lodge	3	2	1-800-600-603	Cable Beach Road	$105
Roebuck Bay Hotel	2½	1	1-800-098-824	Carnarvon Street	$95
Tropicana Inn	3	8	1-800-244-899	Robinson Street	$90
Broometime Lodge		9	1-800-804-322	Forrest Street	$85

(ii) Hotel Accommodation at Cable Beach *(map on page 608)*

Name	Stars	No. on Map	Telephone No.	Address	Lowest Price (Double/Twin)
Cable Beach Resort	5	11	1-800-095-508	Cable Beach Road	$265
Broome Beach Resort	4	15	1-800-647-333	Murray Road	$170
Broome Seashells Resort	4½	13	1-800-623-999	Challenor Drive	$155
Cable Beachside Resort	4	14	1-800-685-545	Cable Beach & Murray Rds.	$140
Blue Seas Resort	4	12	1-800-637-415	Lullfitz Drive	$125
Palm Grove	4	16	1-800-803-336	Cable Beach & Murray Rds.	$85

(iii) Hotel Accommodation on the Outskirts of Broome *(map on page 607)*

Name	Stars	No. on Map	Telephone No.	Address	Lowest Price (Double/Twin)
Habitat Beach Resort	4	18	1-800-683-988	Port Drive	$135
Broome Vacation Village		17	08-9192-1057	Port Drive	$90

(iv) Backpackers Hostels in Broome Area *(maps on pages 606 and 608)*

Name	Group	No. on Map	Telephone No.	Address	Lowest Price (Dormitory)
Cable Beach Backpackers	VIP	21	1800-655-011	33 Lullfitz Drive	$20
Kimberley Klub	Nom	20	08-9192-3233	Frederick Street	$19
Broome's Last Resort	YHA	19	1800-801-918	2 Bagot Street	$18
Roebuck Bay Backpackers		1	08-9192-1183	Napier Terrace	$17

MOVING ON

Greyhound operates one bus every morning to Perth, arriving the following afternoon, and one bus every day to Darwin, arriving the following morning. Integrity operates to Perth twice a week, on Monday and Wednesday mornings.

Bus Services from Broome

Destination	Operator	Via	Distance (km)	Fare	Journey Time	Frequency
Perth	Greyhound		2370	$325	32¼ hrs	1/day
		Geraldton	1948	$325	26½ hrs	1/day
		Carnarvon	1468	$280	20 hrs	1/day
		Port Hedland	597	$99	7½ hrs	1/day
Perth	Integrity		2370	$285	34½ hrs	2/week
		Geraldton	1948	$285	28½ hrs	2/week
		Carnarvon	1477	$255	22 hrs	2/week
		Port Hedland	597	$90	7¾ hrs	2/week
Darwin	Greyhound		1970	$281	25¾ hrs	1/day
		Katherine	1645	$250	21¼ hrs	1/day

DERBY
Population 5,000

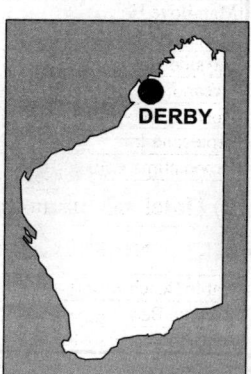

36 hrs by bus from Perth
22 hrs 30 mins by bus from Darwin

Two and a half hours on the bus from Broome will bring us to Derby, which claims to be the oldest town in the Kimberley. It was gazetted in 1883 and served as a port and centre for the pastoral industry.

Derby is located on King Sound near the mouth of the Fitzroy River. and claims the largest tides in Australia - eleven metres. The original jetty here was built in 1894, and replaced by the current one in 1964. There used to be a horse-drawn tramway to transport goods across the tidal mud flats and into the town. Wool and pearl shell were the original exports from here, but now lead and zinc concentrates are trucked from near Fitzroy Crossing to be shipped from Derby. The last ocean-going passenger vessel to berth here came in 1973. The jetty is a good location for fishing and for watching the sunset.

There is a small museum in the town. **Wharfingers House Museum** is near the town end of the road which runs across the mud flats to the jetty. The key is available from the Tourist Office.

Further down Loch Street, the main street of the town, is the **Old Derby Gaol**, dating from 1906 and the oldest surviving building in the town. It can be visited.

The **Pioneer Cemetery** is a short walk out of the town along Lovegrove Street. It contains the graves of P.C. Richardson, killed by the aboriginal outlaw Jandamarra, and of the aboriginal tracker Larry Kunamarra, who was honoured by the Queen for his services.

The **Botanical Gardens** are in the centre of the town and pleasant for relaxation, but they are not historic, having been established only in 1985.

Seven kilometres south of the town is Derby's famous Boab Tree, known as the **Prison Tree**, because it was formerly used as a staging point for prisoners being walked into Derby. Its age is estimated at 1,500 years and it has a girth of 14.7 metres. Nearby is **Frosty's Pool**, constructed in 1944 as a bathing area for troops stationed here and one of the few surviving reminders of the war period in Derby. Frosty was evidently one of the members of the platoon from the Third General Transport

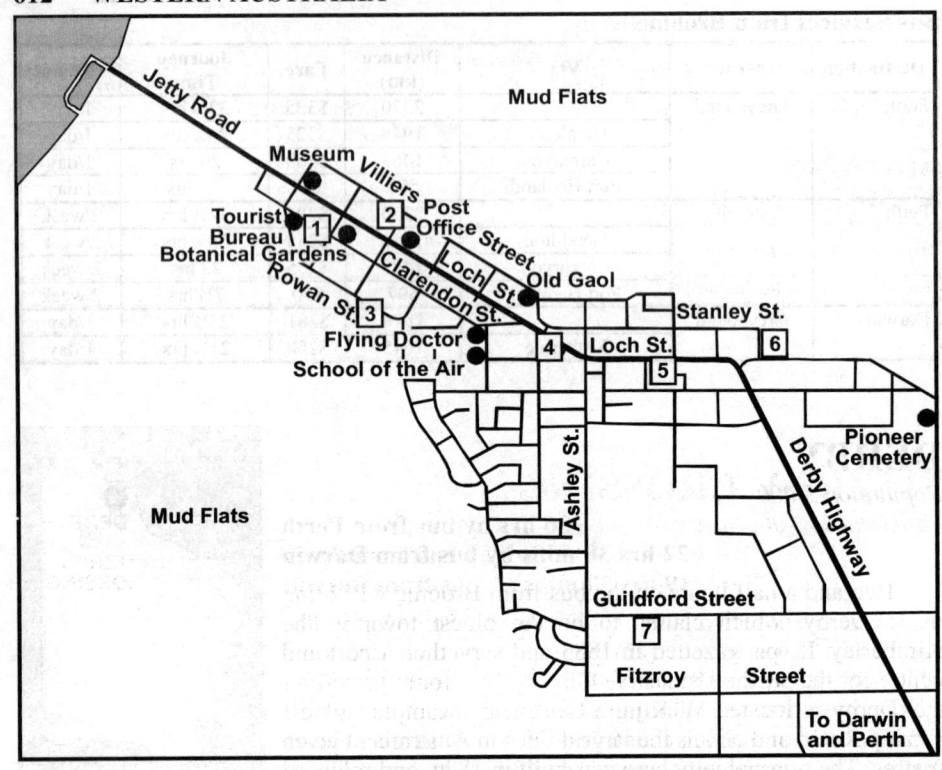

DERBY
Numerals indicate accommodation

Company which built the baths. Also here are a **bore and a cattle trough**. A well was first sunk in the 1890s at this point, but in 1911 it was replaced by a bore 322 metres deep. A trough was built for watering cattle and this trough is an amazing 120 metres long, able to cater for the thirsts of 500 bullocks at a time. Nowadays, though, the water has to be pumped by windmill. It stopped flowing from the bore in 1919.

In the town there are a **Royal Flying Doctor Base** and a **School of the Air**, both of which can be visited.

ACCOMMODATION
(i) Hotel Accommodation in Derby

Name	Stars	No. on Map	Telephone No.	Address	Lowest Price (Double/Twin)
Boab Inn	4	4	08-9191-1044	Lot 520, Clarendon Street	$85
King Sound Resort Hotel	3½	5	08-9193-1044	Loch Street	$85
Drover's Camp		2	08-9191-2290	Lot 7, Hardman Street	$60
Kimberley Entrance Park		3	08-9193-1055	Rowan Street	$60
Spinifex Hotel		1	08-9191-1233	Clarendon Street	$60
Goldsworthy Connections		7	08-9193-1246	Lot 4, Guildford Street	$55
West Kimberley Lodge		6	08-9191-1031	17 Sutherland Street	$55

(ii) Backpackers Hostel in Derby

Name	Group	No. on Map	Telephone No.	Address	Lowest Price (Dormitory)
West Kimberley Lodge		6	08-9191-1031	17 Sutherland Street	$25

MOVING ON
Bus Services from Derby

Destination	Operator	Via	Distance (km)	Fare	Journey Time	Frequency
Broome	Greyhound		222	$55	2½ hrs	1/day
Darwin	Greyhound		1748	$238	23 hrs	1/day
		Katherine	1423	$216	18½ hrs	1/day

FITZROY CROSSING
Population 1,200

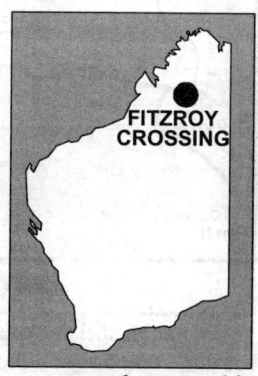

39 hrs by bus from Perth
19 hrs 30 mins by bus from Darwin

There are now two possible routes north from Derby. The bus wisely keeps to the main highway, but there are tours which operate by the alternative **Gibb River Road**, providing the opportunity to see **Windjana Gorge**, for example, as well as a great deal of outback countryside. It is only in recent years that this road has become easily passable for its entire length to Wyndham.

Fitzroy Crossing is a small town which is there, as its name suggests, because this is the place where the Fitzroy River is crossed. The town has moved in recent years, because the crossing point has moved. You will now cross the river on a beautiful modern bridge high above the level of the water, but it was not always like this. When the author first came here, the crossing was by means of a concrete causeway, raised about a metre above the level of the river bed, and with a steep descent down the bank, a flat stretch across the river and a steep ascent the other side. The highway through here was not sealed.

ANECDOTE

In a year of floods, we struggled through mud to Halls Creek, and, knowing that the Fitzroy lay ahead, called into the Police Station to ask the state of the crossing. "Well," said the officer, "You've got about four feet off the bed of the river to the causeway, and the banks of the river are 52 feet above the bed. At the moment, the water is seven feet from the top, so I make it 41 feet of water you'd have to drive through!" We never reached the crossing on that occasion.

However, for traffic travelling between Perth and Darwin, this was the only road. Drivers stuck here would have only the options of waiting or going back almost to Perth, across the Nullarbor and up the centre, a detour of nearly 10,000 kilometres. Most waited. In this particular year, they waited nearly four months before the Fitzroy became passable once more.

WESTERN AUSTRALIA

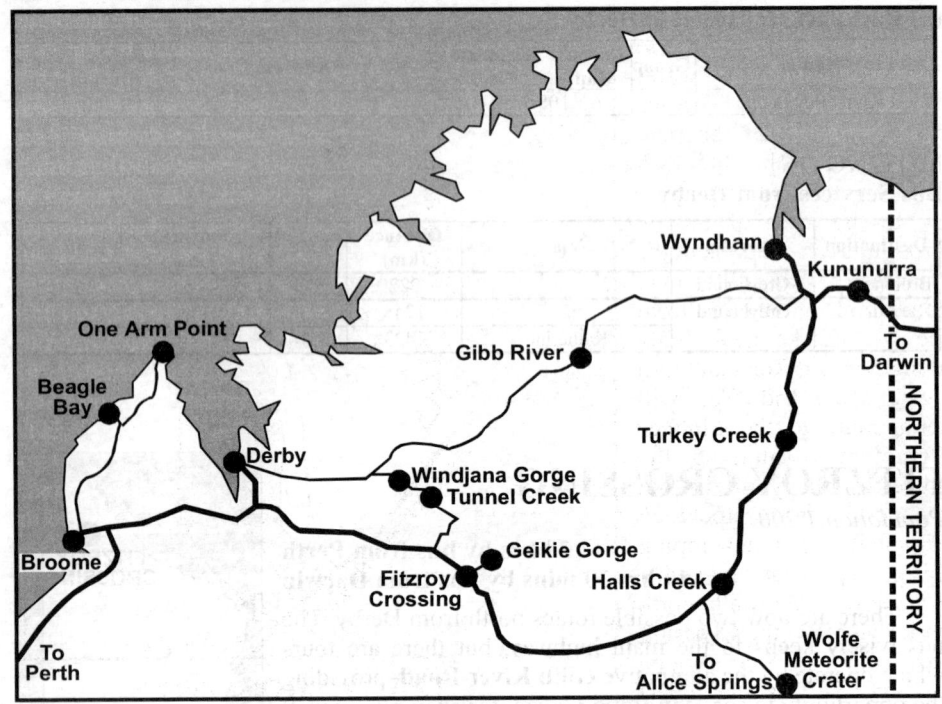

FROM BROOME TO KUNUNURRA

You can still see the old crossing, and use it if the river is not too high, and you can see the remnants of the old town nearby, with the former Post Office turned into a backpackers hostel. Looking at the river during the Dry Season, you will probably think this crossing adequate and wonder how such a trickle of water could have carved this deep watercourse, but when you see the mighty river which flows through here in the Wet, you will understand just what a difference to the Northern Territory the construction of this single bridge made. When in flood, the Fitzroy carries more water than any other river in Australia.

With the building of this bridge, though, it seemed as though the purpose of Fitzroy Crossing had disappeared, for it was at the times when the crossing was closed that the community really thrived, catering for the needs of stranded truck drivers and other motorists. A ropeway was rigged up, and may still be there, so that those stranded on the eastern bank could also be supplied, and business prospered. However, Fitzroy Crossing moved itself to the new bridge and was still able to persuade the passing traveller that he needed a cup of tea and perhaps a bed for the night, so the community not only still exists, but has grown.

One of the reasons for its continuing existence is the proximity of **Geikie Gorge**. The **Geikie Gorge National Park** is only 21 kilometres from Fitzroy Crossing. There are **boat trips** available through the gorge between April and October, and there are **limestone caves** which were once used by the local aborigines as tombs for the dead. They contain bright rock paintings. In the waters of the gorge can be found freshwater crocodiles and barramundi fish, but also, very surprisingly, sharks, sawfish and stingrays, suggesting that this gorge was once joined to the sea, with salt water flowing through it. The sea dwellers have adapted gradually to the brackish fresh water found here now.

In the town of Fitzroy Crossing, you can look at the remains of the old town, about three kilometres from the site of the new. Walk along Sanford Road and turn right at the end. You will soon come to the **Pioneer Cemetery**, containing the graves of many of the old pioneers and stockmen responsible for developing this part of the land into what it is now. Now walk north until you reach the **Crossing Inn**, opposite the Rodeo Ground. This is the oldest hotel on its original site in the Kimberley, having been

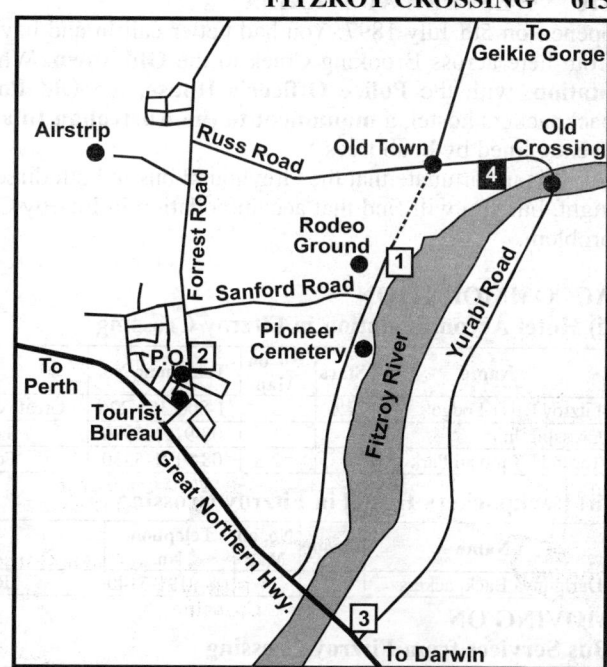

FITZROY CROSSING
Black numerals in white boxes indicate hotel accommodation
White numerals in black boxes indicate backpackers hostels

ANECDOTE

The tale told to the author (for the authenticity of which he cannot vouch, however) was of a flight by the old M.M.A. (MacRobertson Miller Airlines, not 'Mickey Mouse Airlines', as was sometimes impolitely suggested). The aircraft was on its way from Perth to Learmonth, but mist closed in on the latter and the flight was diverted to Karratha, then to Port Hedland, then to Broome, but, as it continued on its journey, each airport was closed by mist before it could get there. The same happened at Derby. By now the situation was becoming desperate. Fitzroy Crossing was inland and believed to be free of the coastal mist, but it was already dark and Fitzroy Crossing airstrip did not have lights. Moreover, it did not have a telephone service after 17:00.

By good fortune, though, it was discovered that somebody in the hospital had left the telephone off its hook and still connected, and a certain amount of shouting down the line succeeded in attracting the attention of a nurse. The situation was explained and all the vehicles available were dispatched to the end of the runway to guide the pilot in with their headlights.

As the pilot attempted a landing, he suddenly realised that the vehicles were at the wrong end of the runway, but he was able to pull out and request that they be turned round, while he went round and attempted the landing again. As he touched down, one of the engines cut out. He taxied in on the other and it was discovered that he had two pints of fuel remaining for that engine.

616 WESTERN AUSTRALIA

opened on 5th July 1897. You had better call in and have a drink. A footbridge leads from here across Brooking Creek to the **Old Town**. What remains is the **Old Police Station**, with the **Police Officer's House**, the **Old Post Office** which is now the backpackers hostel, a **monument to the Australian Inland Mission Hospital**, and an avenue lined by boab trees.

It is unfortunate that the Greyhound bus in both directions reaches here during the night, but you will find that accommodation in Fitzroy Crossing is accustomed to this problem.

ACCOMMODATION
(i) Hotel Accommodation in Fitzroy Crossing

Name	Stars	No. on Map	Telephone No.	Address	Lowest Price (Double/Twin)
Fitzroy River Lodge	3½	3	1-800-355-226	Great Northern Highway	$140
Crossing Inn		1	08-9191-5080	Sanford Road	$55
Tarunda Caravan Park		2	08-9191-5330	Forrest Street	$55

(ii) Backpackers Hostel in Fitzroy Crossing

Name	Group	No. on Map	Telephone No.	Address	Lowest Price (Dormitory)
Darlgunya Backpackers		4	08-9191-5140	Russ Road	$18

MOVING ON
Bus Services from Fitzroy Crossing

Destination	Operator	Via	Distance (km)	Fare	Journey Time	Frequency
Broome	Greyhound		442	$116	5¾ hrs	1/day
Darwin	Greyhound		1528	$187	19¾ hrs	1/day
		Katherine	1203	$172	15 hrs	1/day

HALLS CREEK
Population 1,500

43 hrs by bus from Perth
16 hrs by bus from Darwin

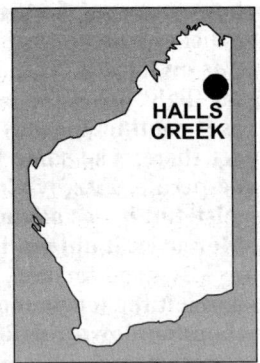

Halls Creek is another small town stop on the long journey round the north-west. It is another town which has been moved, and it is also another town with history, for Halls Creek was created as the result of Western Australia's first gold rush, in 1883. The site of the original town was sixteen kilometres east of the present settlement, on the Duncan Highway, leading to Wave Hill and the Northern Territory. Almost all that remains there now is the shell of the original hotel, with its earthen walls, but nevertheless the place retains an atmosphere of bygone times, especially with the dirt highway running past. There is accommodation again now in Old Halls Creek, not in the old hotel, but in Old Halls Creek Lodge, which offers air-conditioned rooms and caravan and camping sites. Not far away is Caroline Pool, a pretty picnic place and swimming spot.

There is also accommodation in the new town at the Kimberley Hotel, or at the Shell Roadhouse. The Kimberley Hotel is also the Halls Creek Backpackers, with dormitory accommodation available.

In the town, there is the **Russian Jack Memorial**. Russian Jack was a gold digger here in 1885, really named Ivan Fredericks, whose mate got sick. Therefore Russian Jack put him in his home-made wheelbarrow and took him to see the doctor, the only remarkable point being that it was 300 kilometres to the doctor. The Memorial is a tribute to the pioneering spirit and comradeship of the early settlers.

Fourteen kilometres south of Halls Creek, the **Tanami Track** runs off on its 1,060-kilometre journey to Alice Springs through the Tanami Desert (see map on page 614). The journey is interesting mainly because there is so much nothing. The highlight of the trip is the Wolfe Meteorite Crater, only 146 kilometres into the journey. What you will see from the road is a small ridge which you would probably pass by without noticing, your mind on the remaining 914 kilometres, wondering just how much more the road surface was going to deteriorate. It is only when you climb the ridge that you can see the crater within, 49 metres deep, and the almost circular rim pushed into the air by the force of the impact of the meteorite. The crater is nearly one kilometre across. If you look for the meteorite, though, you will not find it. Scientists estimate that the force and speed of this hurtling astronomical body would have buried it ten kilometres into the earth's surface. Only small fragments of the meteorite have been found. You can walk all round the rim of the crater, a stroll of about three kilometres, according to the author's mathematics, if you so wish. This is the second biggest meteorite crater in the world, the largest being in Russia. American astronauts were brought to see this site before being sent to the moon, since, at the time, they were not invited by the U.S.S.R. to view the larger one. However, it will not be easy to see this interesting place, since no public transport runs via this route and the track is really very isolated. Some tours, however, do pass this way.

North of Halls Creek is the famous **Bungle Bungle Range**, in what is now the **Purnululu National Park**. The author had always assumed that Bungle Bungle was an aboriginal name, so was surprised to find that the park was given a different title. Bungle Bungle, it appears, was the name of a pastoral property established in the area by one William Skewthorpe in 1941 (perhaps alluding to his methods of farming?), so the name is not really very old at all.

The range, however, is much older, probably formed some 360 million years ago. Rivers flowed into this area bringing sand and boulders, and the sediment compacted, forming sandstone. Then the sandstone became raised and gradually weathered, to create the strange beehive-shaped mounds that we see now. Even these would no longer exist were it not for the black lichens and orange silica which have formed a protective skin around them. If the skin becomes damaged, the hills soon erode. Found here is the **Bungle Bungle Fan Palm**. Unique to this area, it grows even on almost vertical cliff faces. There are also examples of **aboriginal art work** scattered throughout the park.

161 kilometres north of Halls Creek is **Turkey Creek**. Although this town is considerably smaller than Halls Creek, it is a better departure point for a visit to the Bungle Bungles. It is much nearer to the turn-off and there are tours departing from this town. Also, tours from Kununurra have to pass through here, and are not averse to negotiating with a potential extra passenger, should a seat be vacant. Accommodation is available in Turkey Creek at the Roadhouse, which offers everything from motel units to a backpacker dormitory and camp sites.

618 WESTERN AUSTRALIA

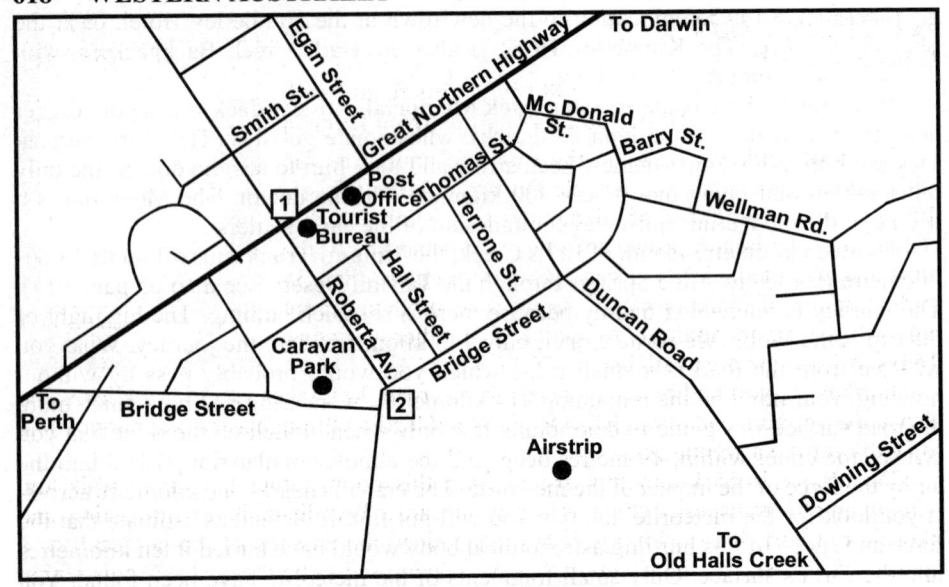

HALLS CREEK
Numerals indicate accommodation

ACCOMMODATION
(i) Hotel Accommodation in Halls Creek *(maps above and on page 620)*

Name	Stars	No. on Map	Telephone No.	Address	Lowest Price (Double/Twin)
Kimberley Hotel	3½	2	1-800-355-228	Roberta Avenue	$175
Old Halls Creek Lodge		3	08-9168-8999	Old Halls Creek	$85
Shell Roadhouse		1	08-9168-6060	31 McDonald Street	$75

(ii) Backpackers Hostel in Halls Creek *(map above)*

Name	Group	No. on Map	Telephone No.	Address	Lowest Price (Dormitory)
Halls Creek Backpackers		2	08-9168-6101	Roberta Avenue	$20

(iii) Hotel Accommodation in Turkey Creek *(map on page 620)*

Name	Stars	No. on Map	Telephone No.	Address	Lowest Price (Double/Twin)
Turkey Creek Roadhouse		4	08-9168-7882	Great Northern Hy. Warmun	$65

(iv) Backpackers Hostel in Turkey Creek *(map on page 620)*

Name	Group	No. on Map	Telephone No.	Address	Lowest Price (Dormitory)
Turkey Creek Roadhouse		5	08-9168-7882	Great Northern Hwy., Warmun	$20

MOVING ON
Bus Services from Halls Creek

Destination	Operator	Via	Distance (km)	Fare	Journey Time	Frequency
Broome	Greyhound		743	$153	9½ hrs	1/day
Darwin	Greyhound		1227	$184	16 hrs	1/day
		Katherine	902	$150	11½ hrs	1/day

KUNUNURRA
Population 6,000

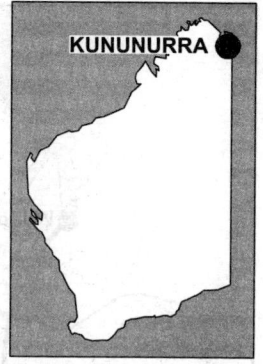

48 hrs by bus from Perth
10 hrs 30 mins by bus from Darwin

North of Turkey Creek, on the way to Kununurra, you will pass the turn-off to the **Argyle Diamond Mine**. This is the only major producer of diamonds in Australia, and it claims to be the largest producer in the world, and one of the most advanced technically. Every year it puts more than 35 million carats of diamonds onto the market, producing rare pink diamonds, in addition to whites and other varieties. **Tours** of the mine are available.

Further on, you will reach a junction in the road. Left takes you to Wyndham, and also to the northern end of the **Gibb River Road** leading through as an alternative route to Derby for the adventurous.

Wyndham is 55 kilometres distant from this point, rather too far to walk and without public transport, which is a pity, because Wyndham is an interesting and likeable old port. It is as though it has not noticed the passage of the last century, a feature emphasised by the situation that Wyndham used to be the centre of this region and so has some impressive old buildings, but that it has now been overtaken by Kununurra and so does not have any pressure to change. It is the most northerly town in Western Australia and still acts as the port for the area. The main street has several relatively old buildings, including the **Durack General Store** built in 1896 and a **Chinese store** dating from the 1890s.. The **hospital** is also a century old.

Wyndham was established in 1886 because a port was required to serve the gold miners at Halls Creek. In its prime, it had six hotels and a sizeable population, but these days about a thousand people live there. It has an **Historical Society Museum**, a **Zoo** and a **Crocodile Park**, which also contains six Komodo Dragons. There is an **Afghan Cemetery** containing the remains of those who operated the transport system here before Greyhound came on the scene.

There is another **Prison Tree** here, again a boab. This time it is claimed that the hollow tree was used as a temporary prison cell, although one wonders about the veracity of such a claim.

The **Bastion** is a hill 330 metres high with the **Five Rivers Lookout** on its summit, so called, of course, because one can see five rivers from here: the Ord, the Durack, the Pentecost, the Forrest and the King.

However, the bus will turn right to Kununurra, not left to Wyndham, when it reaches the Victoria Highway. From here it is a further 45 kilometres to Kununurra.

Kununurra is a complete contrast with Wyndham, for this is a modern town founded only in 1960. Its purpose was to be the supply base for the Ord River Irrigation Scheme and to provide accommodation for those who worked on the construction of the scheme. It has become, as was intended, the administrative centre of the area. The name of the town is taken from the local aboriginal language and evidently means 'Meeting Place of the Big Waters'.

The Ord River Irrigation Scheme was the vision of Kimberley Durack, a member of the family which was a pioneer in this area. He believed that such a scheme could be put into effect and convert the torrential downpours of the Wet followed by the

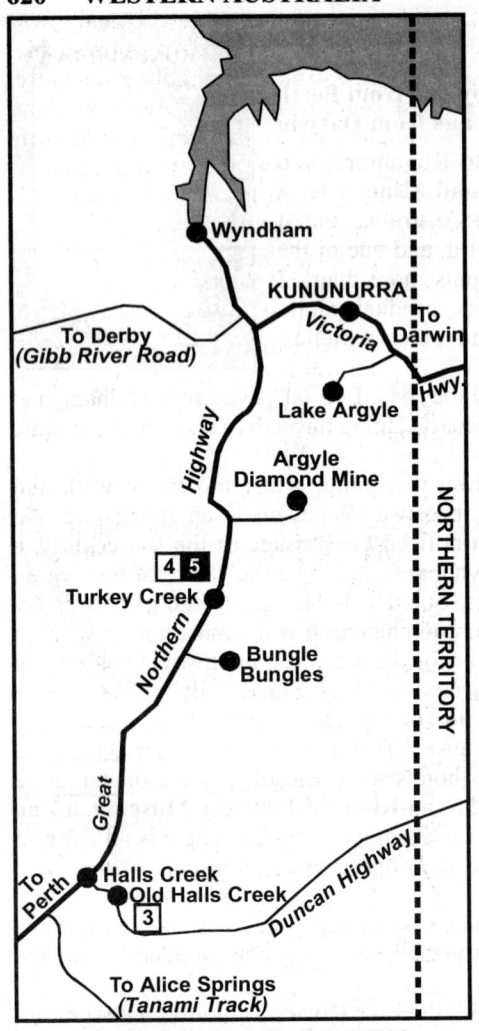

FROM HALLS CREEK TO KUNUNURRA
Numerals indicate accommodation (page 618)

drought of the Dry into a steady year-long supply of water. All that was required was a dam and a series of irrigation channels. These were constructed during the 1960s and now a huge area of land which previously supported only a meagre number of cattle has been turned into arable country with exotic products. The first suggestion was that rice should be grown and that sufficient could be produced in this area to satisfy all of Australia's requirements and produce considerable exports. This scheme was unsuccessful, however, as Australia's requirements were limited and the rice was too expensive to export successfully. Recently the principal crop here has been sugar cane. Also grown are melons, pumpkins, maize, chick peas, plantago, mangoes and bananas.

Since Kununurra is a modern development, there are not many sights to see within the town itself, but there are several places to visit nearby.

Kelly's Knob, on the northern fringe of Kununurra, offers a fine lookout point. Lake Kununurra can be seen, as well as the town. Telecom and television transmitters are up here as well, as is the town's water supply storage.

To the south of the town, by **Lily Creek Lagoon**, is the **Celebrity Tree Park**, started in 1984, where trees have been planted by famous visitors, including Princess Anne and Rolf Harris.

To the north-east is the **Hidden Valley National Park**, sometimes called the 'Mini Bungle Bungle' because it too has unusual rock formations. There are two short walks available here through what was once part of the ocean floor. They are at their best early in the morning or late in the afternoon, when the sun is low and emphasises the contours. Early in the morning there are also many birds to be found in the area. The short walks are relatively easy, but there is also a three-kilometre walk from the town to reach the park.

The vital element in the Ord River Scheme is the dam which creates **Lake Argyle**. This lake is seventy kilometres from Kununurra and 34 kilometres off the main Victoria Highway running east to the Northern Territory. It is the largest storage area of fresh water in Australia, covering 980 square kilometres at its normal peak, and a maximum of 2,072 square kilometres at times of flood. It is certainly a beautiful lake. There is a replica here of the **Durack Homestead**. When the dam was built it was planned to move the homestead to dry land, but the waters rose too quickly and it was drowned, so instead this replica was constructed. Boat **cruises** on the lake are available.

The release of water from Lake Argyle is controlled so as to keep Lake Kununurra, downstream, full at all times. **Lake Kununurra** is formed by the Diversion Dam, which is seven kilometres from the town of Kununurra and across which the Victoria Highway runs, so you are sure to see it at some stage. From here, a system of channels takes the water by gravity to the farming areas where it is needed. Lake Kununurra is popular for watersports and there are **cruises** which operate here as well.

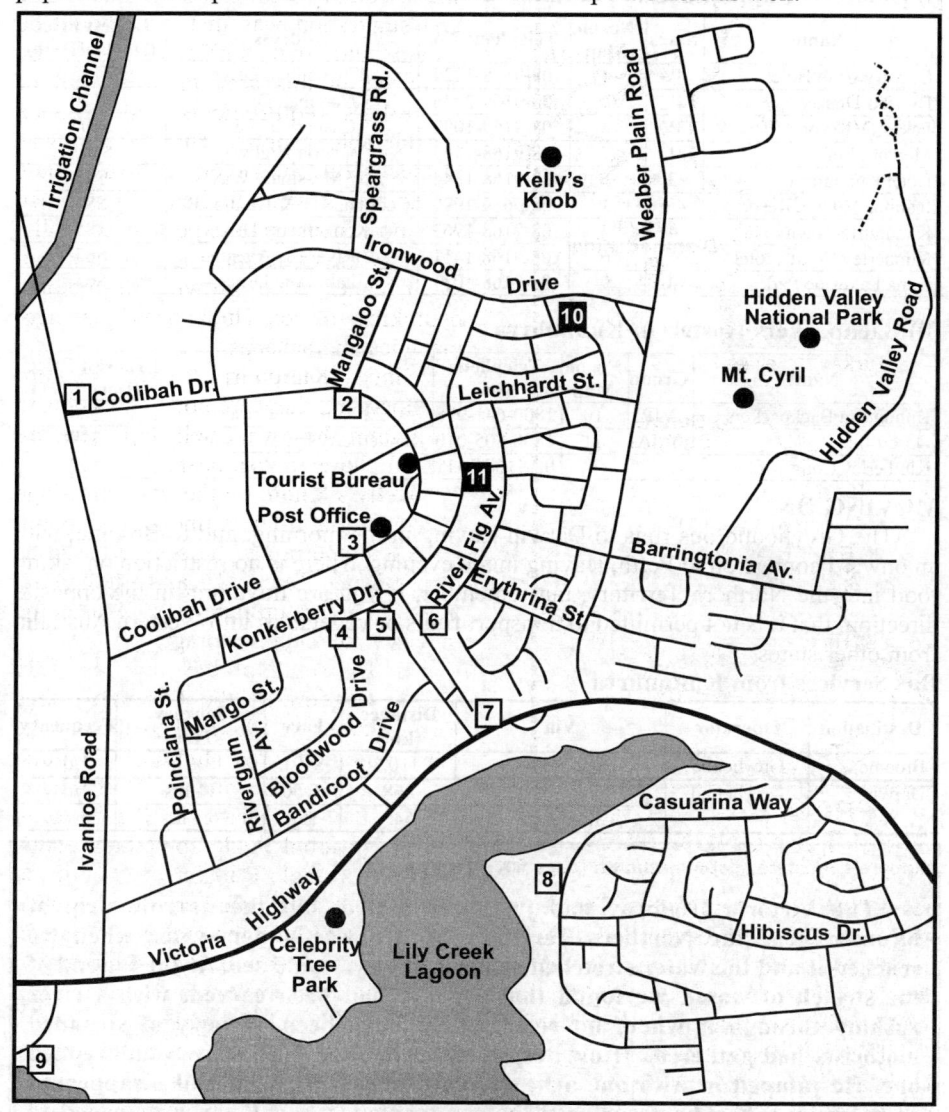

KUNUNURRA
**Black numerals in white boxes indicate hotel accommodation
White numerals in black boxes indicate backpackers hostels**

622 WESTERN AUSTRALIA

One of the peculiarities of Kununurra is **Zebra Rock**, a strangely striated formation found only here and appearing just like the stripes of a zebra. Nobody has been able to explain satisfactorily how the unusual formation came about some six million years ago, or why it exists nowhere else in the world. The rock is used commercially to produce attractive ornaments.

ACCOMMODATION
(i) Hotel Accommodation in Kununurra

Name	Stars	No. on Map	Telephone No.	Address	Lowest Price (Double/Twin)
Country Club Hotel	4½	3	08-9168-1024	47 Coolibah Drive	$165
Duncan House	4½	2	08-9168-2436	Coolibah Drive	$120
Lakeside Resort	3½	8	08-9169-1092	Casuarina Way	$105
Mercure Inn	3½	7	08-9168-1455	Victoria Highway	$105
Hotel Kununurra	3	5	08-9168-1344	37 Messmate Way	$95
Ivanhoe Village Resort	4½	1	08-9619-1995	Coolibah Dr. & Ivanhoe Rd.	$85
Kununurra Town Park	4	4	08-9168-1763	Konkerberry Drive	$85
Kimberley Court Motel		6	08-9168-1411	2 River Fig Avenue	$65
Kona Lakeside Park	4	9	08-9168-1031	Lakeview Drive	$65

(ii) Backpackers Hostels in Kununurra

Name	Group	No. on Map	Telephone No.	Address	Lowest Price (Dormitory)
Kununurra Backpackers	VIP	10	1800-641-998	22 Nutwood Crescent	$20
Desert Inn	YHA	11	1800-805-010	Konkerberry Dr. & Tristania St	$19
Kimberley Court Motel		6	08-9168-1411	2 River Fig Avenue	$19

MOVING ON

The Greyhound bus runs to Darwin leaving in the morning, and to Broome, with an onward connexion to Perth, leaving in the evening. There is no restriction on taking food into the Northern Territory, but remember, if you are travelling in the opposite direction, that it is not permitted to transport fruits or vegetables into Western Australia from other states.

Bus Services from Kununurra

Destination	Operator	Via	Distance (km)	Fare	Journey Time	Frequency
Broome	Greyhound		1102	$191	13½ hrs	1/day
Darwin	Greyhound		868	$150	11 hrs	1/day
		Katherine	543	$88	6½ hrs	1/day

ANECDOTE

The Victoria Highway had just been sealed, but the narrow strip of bitumen near the Northern Territory border was under water when we reached it and the water stretched as far as the eye could see. At the far end of the stretch of water, we found that a gorge had been carved, with a river rushing through it where no river should have been. A bevy of stranded motorists had gathered. "How deep is it?" we asked. "I'll show you," replied one. He jumped in with one arm stretched above his head and disappeared completely. When he resurfaced, he commented, "And I never managed to touch the bottom." We thought it wiser to seek a detour, but it took us three days of communal effort to cross that stretch of water.

SOUTH AUSTRALIA

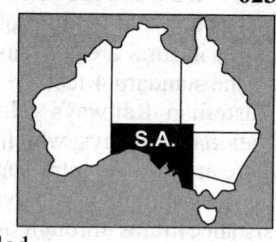

The South Australian Colonization Act received the royal assent of King William IV on 15th August 1834, the first colonists arriving on 20th July 1836 and landing on Kangaroo Island, the first place in South Australia to be settled.

The new Governor of South Australia, John Hindmarsh, arrived on 28th December 1836, together with the Surveyor-General, Col. William Light, who first visited the present site of Adelaide on 30th December 1836, soon choosing it for the new capital. So began the history of the state.

South Australia claims that it is the driest state in the driest continent on earth. With such a record, it is no wonder that agricultural development has always presented a problem here. However, wheat is grown in the coastal areas, including the Eyre Peninsula to the west of Adelaide, and this region extends almost as far west as the start of the Nullarbor Plain. However, it cannot continue very far inland.

The most famous rural area of the state is the Barossa Valley, which attracted German immigrants right from the start and soon became Australia's first and most important wine-growing region, a reputation which it maintains. The Barossa Valley is close to Adelaide and can easily be reached as a day excursion from the capital.

South Australia also produces minerals. Copper was discovered at Burra in 1845 and gold was also discovered in the same year. In recent times, however, it has been the iron ore from Whyalla which has been the most important mineral product. In addition, the lead, zinc and silver from Broken Hill is mainly transported by rail to Port Pirie, even though Broken Hill lies geographically narrowly within the borders of New South Wales. At Port Pirie, therefore, can be found the largest lead smelter in the world.

Towards the north of the state are two of Australia's three main opal mining communities. The better known is Coober Pedy, on the way to Alice Springs. A little less famous is Andamooka, to the south-east of Coober Pedy.

In terms of scenery, South Australia offers some attractive coastal views all the way from the Eyre Peninsula in the west to Mt. Gambier in the east. It offers Kangaroo Island with its history as well as wildlife. It offers the European flavour of the Barossa Valley. It offers the stately Flinders Ranges some seven hours north of Adelaide, and, for the really adventurous, it offers outstanding outback travel to the huge Lake Eyre, or along the Birdsville, Strzelecki or Oodnadatta Tracks, all of which can be covered with tours, although not with ordinary public transport.

Like other Australian states, South Australia has the bulk of its population in the capital city. Adelaide has a population of 1,100,000, making it the fifth largest city in the nation, out of a total state population of 1,500,000. South Australia is, therefore, the least populous mainland state. Only Tasmania, the Australian Capital Territory and the Northern Territory have fewer people. South Australia has an area of 983,480 square kilometres, and is thus the fourth largest state or territory.

South Australia used to have its own state railway system. Indeed the state lays claim to having had Australia's first railway line, albeit a horse-drawn railway - between Goolwa and Victor Harbor. Because of the desirability of connecting its lines with those of Victoria, South Australia chose to copy the Victorian gauge of 5 feet 3

624 SOUTH AUSTRALIA

inches and that led to problems later, especially as the state also used a 3 feet 6 inches gauge in rural areas to save construction costs and then found itself linked to the west by the standard 4 feet 8½ inches Commonwealth Railways line. In recent times, South Australian Railways relinquished the operation of its country lines to Australian National Railways, which promptly stopped operating any country services at all. Thus there are now no intra-state trains in South Australia except for the Adelaide suburban services and the expensive privately-operated *Wine Train* to the Barossa Valley. Long-distance trains through Adelaide are now operated by Great Southern Railway and consist of the *Overland* between Adelaide and Melbourne, the *Indian-Pacific* between Sydney and Perth via Adelaide and the *Ghan* between Sydney or Melbourne and Alice Springs via Adelaide, soon to be extended to Darwin.

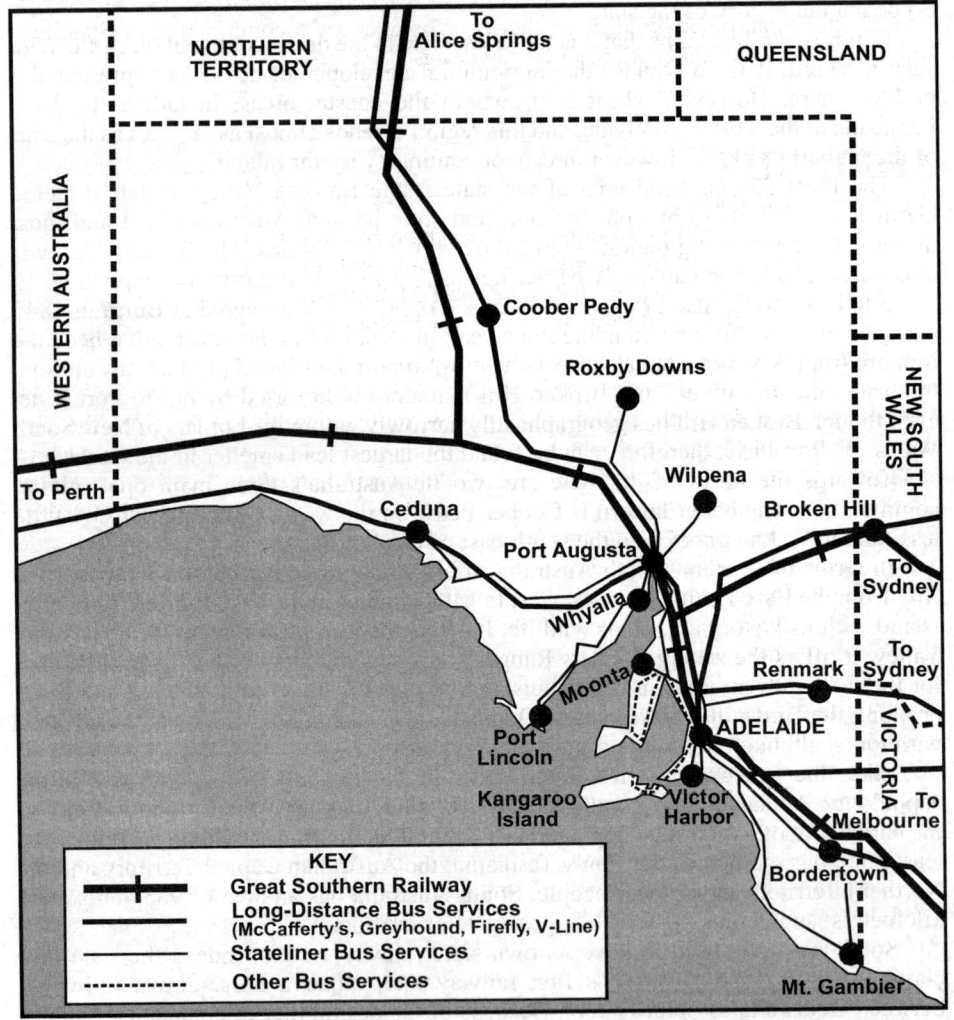

PUBLIC TRANSPORT IN SOUTH AUSTRALIA

As for buses, Greyhound or McCafferty's operate from Adelaide to Melbourne, Sydney, Alice Springs and Perth, and have competition from Firefly and V-Line to Melbourne, and from V-Line to Sydney via Albury.

Within the state, a bus network, as shown on the map opposite, is operated by Stateliner. This network consists principally of services from Adelaide east to Renmark, south-east to Mt. Gambier and Bordertown, south to Goolwa and Victor Harbor, north to Moonta, Port Pirie, Port Augusta, Wilpena, Roxby Downs and Whyalla, and west to Port Lincoln and Ceduna. There are also some services provided by private operators. There is, however, no special ticket, for bus or train, designed specifically for use within South Australia. The V-Line 14-day *Victoria Pass* does not include travel to Adelaide.

The Wayward Bus offers a service between Adelaide and Melbourne via the coast, a route which can be covered more cheaply, however, by a combination of Stateliner and V-Line services, and some careful planning.

ADELAIDE
Population 1,100,000

25 hrs 30 mins by train from Sydney
22 hrs 30 mins by bus from Sydney
11 hrs by train from Melbourne
10 hrs 30 mins by bus from Melbourne

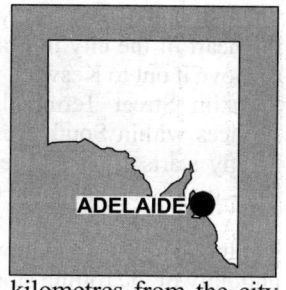

Adelaide is not a common arrival point for visitors from overseas, but if you do reach here by air, either from overseas or by a domestic flight, the airport is only seven kilometres from the city centre. There is an airport bus which will take you into the city for $7. If you wish to pay less, walk to the airport entrance, about 500 metres, and take a city bus no. 276 or 278 from the far side of the road. This will cost $3, or $2 between 9:00 and 15:00. You will then have two hours to take as many buses, trains or trams as you wish. If you prefer, you can pay $6 and travel for the rest of the day. If your destination is Glenelg, the no. 278 in the opposite direction, from the near side of the road, will take you there.

More likely, though, you will arrive by train or bus. A few years ago, all long-distance trains here used to be broad gauge (5 feet 3 inches) and used to operate from the stately and very convenient Adelaide Station, in the city centre. Now, however, all interstate trains are standard gauge and are diverted, therefore, to Keswick Terminal, which is in an inconvenient location on the outskirts of the city centre. It is possible to walk into the city, but it is just a little too far to be enjoyable, about three kilometres. It is really a great pity that this story of peripheral stations has to be repeated so often, and it seems so unnecessary, because Adelaide Station has plenty of spare capacity and utilisation of the office space would have avoided the necessity of converting the station building into a casino. Maybe some think it convenient to have a casino in the middle of the city, but in the author's opinion, a railway station used by interstate trains is even more useful. However, the broad gauge suburban railway runs right beside Keswick Terminal, so at least one would have expected Keswick suburban station to be conveniently linked with the interstate terminal, but no. To use a suburban train, you have to go out of the interstate terminal, turn left, walk up the hill, turn left across the footbridge and make your way down to one of the two platforms, guessing on which of the two a train will arrive first. The suburban station is unmanned, but you can press a button to try to find out about train times. It works sometimes. Tickets can be bought from a machine on the train. If you prefer, having walked this far, you can go a few metres more to the Anzac Highway and take a bus from the near side of the road into the city centre. However, the easiest method of reaching the city centre from the Keswick Terminal is to take the Airport Bus which calls in here every half hour on its way to the city (and on its way to the Airport too). At present, it calls in at ten and forty minutes past each hour from 5:10 to the Airport or 6:40 to the city until 21:10 to the Airport or 20:40 to the city. The fare to the airport is $7, and to the city it is $3.50.

Trains using the Keswick Terminal are the *Overland* to and from Melbourne four times a week, going by day and returning by night, the *Indian-Pacific* between Sydney and Perth twice a week in each direction and the *Ghan* which runs to Alice Springs twice a week, and should continue to Darwin within the lifetime of this book, and runs to Sydney once a week and to Melbourne once a week. Timetables showing departures from Adelaide are at the end of this section, on pages 642 and 643. Timetables of trains to Adelaide are shown under the sections for the places of origin.

If you arrive by bus, you will be fortunate, for the long-distance bus terminal is in the heart of the city in Franklin Street. This is so convenient that there are now plans to move it out to Keswick with the Rail Terminal. Greyhound and McCafferty's use the Franklin Street Terminal, as does Stateliner, which operates most long-distance services within South Australia. Most other long-distance companies use it too, but Firefly starts from and terminates at its office on the other side of Franklin Street, immediately opposite the main bus terminal.

V-Line, the Victorian railway operator, runs two co-ordinated services to Adelaide. V-Line, when it was known as Victorian Railways (for good reasons, considering the antiquity of the rolling stock at that time), was the joint operator, with South Australian Railways, of the *Overland*. Now South Australian Railways has disappeared and the *Overland* is operated by Great Southern Railway, but, not to be outdone, V-Line operates a competitive service. One takes the train from Melbourne to Bendigo and there transfers to a bus for the remainder of the journey to Adelaide. It is a pleasant ride, to be recommended, for one sees scenery through which one would not normally pass on bus or train, although the road is a little bumpy in parts. The journey takes nearly 11½ hours and operates every day.

The second co-ordinated service operated by V-Line is a Sydney to Adelaide service, but this is not as much fun, as the timing is inconvenient. One takes the night train at 20:43 from Sydney bound for Melbourne, and alights at Albury at the unfortunate hour of 3:54. A bus then conveys you to Adelaide, arriving at 16:15. Thus it is a seven-hour train journey, followed by a 12½ hour bus ride. You will be tired when you arrive. This service too operates every night, with the V-Line buses using the Franklin Street Bus Terminal.

Adelaide is, of all the Australian capital cities except Canberra (which dates from almost a century later), that which shows the greatest influence of thoughtful planning. In its centre it is the work of one man, Colonel William Light, who was appointed as the first Surveyor-General of South Australia. He arrived here in 1836 and had first to choose a site for his capital. Despite opposition, he chose Adelaide and commenced his survey, at the junction of the present North and West Terraces, on 11th January 1837. An obelisk marks the place. The survey was completed on 10th March and the naming of the streets occurred on 23rd May 1837.

Colonel Light had been born in Malaya on 27th April 1786, his father being the founder of the East India Company's settlement at Georgetown on the island of Penang, another city with some beautiful architecture. Col. Light had fought in the Napoleonic wars.

The city was named Adelaide after the Queen of the time, the consort of King William IV. Light's plan consisted of a city of one square mile, completely surrounded by park land, and with five additional small parks in its centre. That plan survives today and sets Adelaide apart from the other capital cities which, although not lacking in green spaces, seem to have had them positioned as an afterthought. In fact, Adelaide is regarded as one of the best planned cities in the world.

There are two places in particular where Light is remembered. One is at Montefiore Hill in North Adelaide. His statue was moved to this apt location so that he could have a commanding view over the city which he had created, the place and statue now being dubbed Light's Vision.

The second place is his grave in Light Square, right in the heart of his city. He resigned from his position in 1838, feeling that the task assigned had been performed, but also tired of the criticism and disputes, and he died of tuberculosis, almost penniless, only a year later, on 6th October 1839, at the age of 53. On 10th October, he was buried in Light Square, and a towering monument has been erected over his grave, a tribute to all that this city owes him.

Let us start with a walk.

Walking Tour

This walk covers about four kilometres and will take us approximately two hours, or longer if you want to visit any of the places on the itinerary. One point to note, to avoid confusion, is that the streets in Adelaide city centre which run east and west change name when they meet King William Street, the central north-south street of the city. Streets on the eastern side of the city do not have the same names as their continuations on the western side.

Let us start at the top of King William Street, the principal street of Adelaide, where it joins North Terrace. On the corner here is **Government House**, the oldest part of which dates back to 1839. On the opposite side of the corner are **Parliament House** and **Old Parliament House**. The western part of this building was constructed in 1889, but the remainder was not added until 1939. When Parliament is not sitting, there are tours of the building between 10:00 and 14:00. When Parliament is sitting, the public is admitted to watch proceedings from 14:00.

Next we come to the **Railway Station**, a fine stately building constructed in 1928. It is still used as the terminus for all suburban rail services, operated by diesel railcars, but, sadly, not for any long-distance services. Go down the ramp at the corner, or the steps a little further along North Terrace to reach the trains. The buildings, however, are no longer used by the railways and have become instead the **Casino**. The Casino is open from 10:00 until 16:00. Walk down the small road beside the station to reach the entrance to the Casino, and continue a little further to the **Adelaide Festival Centre**, from where you can look down over the river and park land.

Returning to North Terrace and continuing west, you will reach **Holy Trinity Church**, on the left. This is the oldest church in South Australia. The foundation stone was laid by Governor Hindmarsh in 1838. The clock was made in 1836 and shipped from England. It has recently been restored.

Pass under the bridge before turning left into Morphett Street. On your right here is the **Jam Factory Contemporary Craft and Design Centre**, open from 9:00 until 17:30. Take a look along Hindley Street as you cross it. This is where much of the **night life** of Adelaide is to be found. Continue for a short distance along Morphett Street and you will reach **Light Square** and the grave of and memorial to the man who designed this city, Colonel William Light.

Continue further along Morphett Street until you reach Franklin Street, where turn left. You will soon pass the **Franklin Street Bus Terminal** on your right and the Firefly office opposite. Walk until you reach King William Street once more. On the corner, you will find the **General Post Office**. Not all of the fine stone building is now used as the Post Office, but part of it still is. It is on the corner of **Victoria Square**, which has a fountain in its centre and from the far end of which the only remaining **tram service** in Adelaide departs, that to Glenelg.

Turn left into **King William Street**, a wide street lined by some imposing buildings. In particular, look for **Edmund Wright House**, at number 59, after you have passed Currie Street, on the corner of which you will find the **Transport Information Centre**, a useful facility. Edmund Wright House was built in 1878 as the Bank of South Australia. The ornamental work required the skills of expert craftsmen, some brought from overseas to undertake the task. Just round the next corner on your left, in Hindley Street, is **Tattersalls Hotel**, built in 1882. **Kelly's Heritage Bar** features original heritage decor, in case you feel thirsty. However, we want to go in the opposite direction now, along Rundle Street, so go back to the corner of Hindley and King William Streets and cross King William Street into **Rundle Mall**, for pedestrians only. This is the main shopping street of Adelaide, as you will not fail to notice. Right at its start you will find a **Tourist Information Centre** in the middle of the street. This is not the main office for tourist information, which is a little further along King William Street towards our starting place in North Terrace, but it is a useful source of information. As you walk along Rundle Mall, admire the **pig sculptures** which decorate the centre. Near the end of the pedestrian area, you will find, on the right, the high-class **Adelaide Arcade**, one of the few nineteenth century shopping areas to survive in modern Adelaide. Walk through to Grenfell Street and turn left.

You will come to Hindmarsh Square, one of the five small parks which Light placed at the city centre and at the four inter-cardinal points of the compass. This is the north-eastern point, he himself being buried at the north-western point in Light Square. Turn left here into Pulteney Street and right into Rundle Street once more. **Rundle Street** here has become a street of fashion, restaurants, bookshops and stores dealing with outdoor pursuits, a fascinating mixture providing five minutes of interesting walking.

At the end of Rundle Street, turn right for one block to reach Grenfell Street and almost opposite you is the **Tandanya Complex**. This is a centre for aboriginal art and culture from all over Australia. Art and artefacts are available for purchase and there are didgeridoo performances every day at 12:00. The centre is open daily from 10:00 until 17:00 and admission costs $5. Tandanya is the name for Adelaide in the local aboriginal language.

Now return northwards along **East Terrace**. Note that the four Terraces border the city centre and define its limits. Beyond is the park land which Light thought essential for the relaxation of his city. On your right now, therefore, is **Rymill Park**, and then **Rundle Park**. When you reach the corner of North Terrace, ahead and to the right will

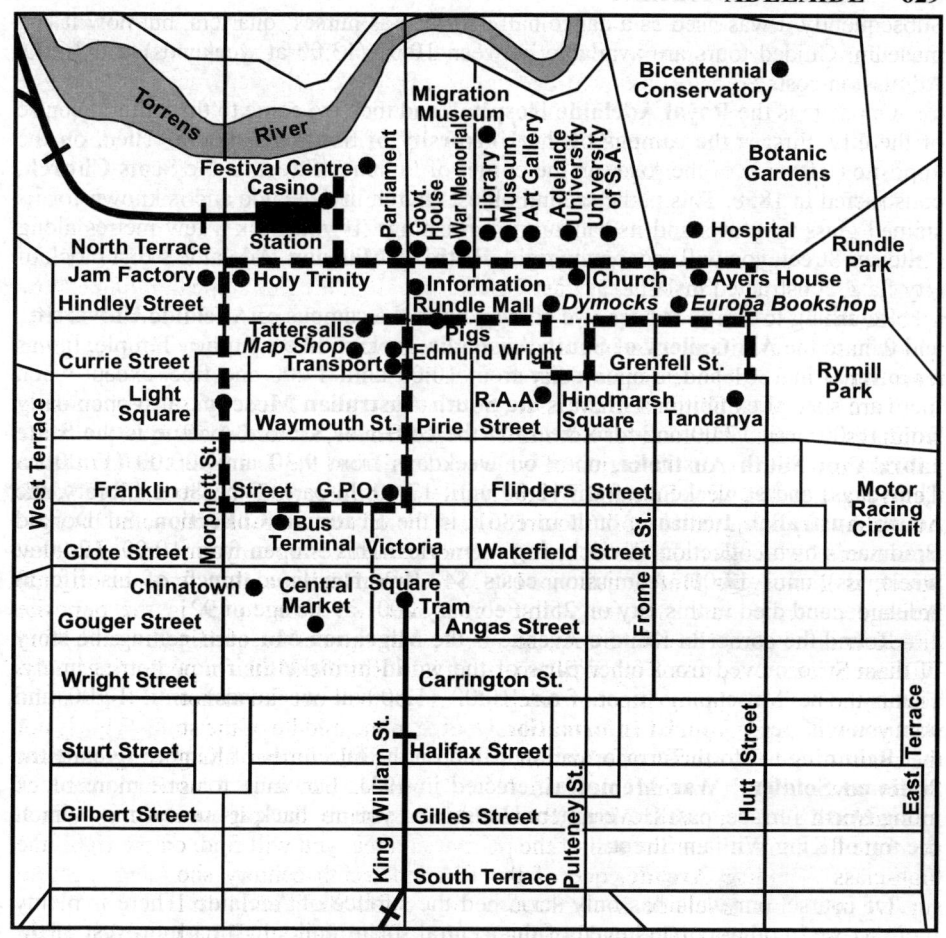

ADELAIDE CITY CENTRE
Dashed line shows Walking Tour

be the **Botanic Gardens**, commenced in 1855. This is a pleasant place to take a stroll, although not included on our itinerary. If you have time to spare, you will find here the **Bicentennial Conservatory**, the largest greenhouse in the southern hemisphere, and the **International Rose Garden**, and also, if you follow Botanic Road to your right, the **National Wine Centre of Australia**. The Botanic Gardens are open daily from 8:00 until sunset, with free admission. The Conservatory is open from 10:00 until 16:00 and admission costs $4.

We shall turn left, however, along **North Terrace**, the most historic of Adelaide's streets. On your left is **Ayers House**. From 1855 until 1897, this was the home of Sir Henry Ayers, the man after whom Ayers Rock is named. He was premier of South Australia on five different occasions, but only for a total of four years, between 1863 and 1873. The house was actually built in 1846 for William Paxton, a chemist in the city, but it was purchased by Ayers in 1855 and he then lived here until his death in 1897, gradually expanding the building into the 41-room mansion which stands now.

Subsequently it was used as a dance hall and then as nurses' quarters, but now it is a museum. Guided tours are available between 10:00 (13:00 at weekends) and 16:00. Admission costs $6.

Opposite is the **Royal Adelaide Hospital**, and then we come to the cultural centre of the city. First is the campus of the **University of South Australia**. Then, on the opposite (left) side of the road, on the corner of Pulteney Street, is the **Scots Church**, constructed in 1850. This is the second oldest church in Adelaide and is known for its stained glass windows and its sanctuary furnishings. If you walk a few metres along Pulteney Street, you will see, on the right, **Ruthven Mansion**, Adelaide's first block of city flats, constructed in 1911.

Returning to North Terrace, we come next to the campus of **Adelaide University**, and then to the **Art Gallery of South Australia**, looking like a Roman Temple. It was established in 1881 and is open daily from 10:00 until 17:00 and free, except when there are special exhibitions. Next is the **South Australian Museum**, also open daily from 10:00 until 17:00 and also free. On the corner of Kintore Avenue is the **State Library of South Australia**, open on weekdays from 9:30 until 20:00 (17:00 on Thursdays) and at weekends from 12:00 until 17:00. In part of the State Library, the **South Australian Institute**, built in 1861, is the **Bradman Collection**, Sir Donald Bradman's own collection of cricketing memories. This is open from 10:00 (12:00 at weekends) until 17:00. Admission costs $4. Bradman lived much of his life in Adelaide, and died in this city on 25th February 2001 at the age of 92.

Round the corner in Kintore Avenue is the **Migration Museum**, telling the story of those who moved from other parts of the world to make their new homes in this country. The Museum is open from 10:00 (12:00 at weekends) until 17:00 and admission is free.

Returning to North Terrace, you will find on the far corner of Kintore Avenue the **National Soldiers' War Memorial**, erected in 1931. Continue for one more block along North Terrace, past Government House, and you are back at our starting point at the top of King William Street.

Of course, our walk has only scratched the surface of Adelaide. There is plenty more to see in other corners even of this central square mile. In the south-west of the city area, walk along **Gouger Street** to find a variety of eating establishments. On your right is **Central Market**, which is interesting to walk through, with all types of stalls within, especially food. Here too is **Chinatown**, fronting onto Grote Street and in the alleys which run between Grote and Gouger Streets. Shops here are not just Chinese. There are also Thai, Vietnamese, Malaysian and Japanese restaurants and stores.

Another popular, but more recently developed, restaurant area is in the south-east of the city along **Hutt Street**. Many of the restaurants here are somewhat up-market, but it is also possible to find cheaper food, especially at the hotels. The architecture, especially some of the fine wrought-iron verandahs, makes this an area worth walking through.

Just north of the city, within walking distance, lies the **Torrens River**. There are walks available along its banks. The Adelaide Oval is here too, used mainly for cricket. Tours are available from the South Gate at 10:00 on Tuesdays and Thursdays, and at 14:00 on Sundays during the summer, but cost $10.

Another sporting event for which Adelaide used to be known was the Australian Grand Prix, but that was moved to Melbourne a few years ago ("stolen by Melbourne" is the Adelaide point of view). However, not to be outdone, Adelaide has now instituted an annual *Indy 500* **type race**. Much of the circuit is on ordinary streets to the east of the city area, and the remainder is on park land there, running onto the Victoria Park Racecourse. You can, of course, go and look at the racetrack free.

Outside the city centre, the best known area is **Glenelg**, to which the one remaining **city tram service** operates. The trams which run on this route were built in 1929 and operate at approximately fifteen minute intervals. The journey of ten kilometres takes half an hour. In its very early days, this was a railway line, which started operations in 1873. Electric trams were introduced on 14th December 1929 and trams of the same type have been operating the line ever since.

Glenelg has its own history, and was the first place in the Adelaide area to be settled, so let us have a short walking tour around here also.

Glenelg Walking Tour

This tour covers about five kilometres and will take approximately two hours.

Step off the tram and look straight ahead. The **Pioneer Memorial** was erected in 1936 to mark the centenary of the town. It is fourteen metres high and commemorates the founding of Glenelg and the pioneers of the early settlement. The names of the founders of South Australia are engraved on the stone and there is a model of the *H.M.S. Buffalo* which brought them to this state. Further ahead is the **Glenelg Jetty**, originally built in 1859. A wooden lighthouse at the end was burnt down, and then, in 1948, a storm destroyed the jetty. Eventually it was rebuilt in 1969. The present jetty is 215 metres long and is popular with fishermen, as well as with those just wanting a breath of fresh air.

North of the jetty are **Trottman's Anchor**, presented to the city in 1988, and **Holdfast Bay Yacht Club**, established in 1883 in what is now the Tourist Information Centre. The weekend yacht races used to attract large crowds at the turn of the century.

Return now to Moseley Square, named after an early councillor who encouraged the building of the railway to here. On the north side of the square are imposing municipal buildings. Starting at the east (right), there is the **Post Office**. The first Post Office was built here in 1859 as Glenelg's first Telegraph Station, with postal services being introduced in 1868. The present building, though, dates from 1912. Next, to the left, is the **Courthouse**, built in 1933 on the site of the original Police Station which was constructed here in 1865. There is a former **cell for prisoners** from the old building which still survives at the rear. Then, further left still, you see the grand old **Glenelg Town Hall**, built in 1875. It was originally the Glenelg Institute, which included a library, reading room, concert hall and museum. The Council acquired the premises in 1887. In the Council Chambers is the **Mayoral Chair**, made of wood salvaged from *H.M.S. Buffalo*, the ship which brought the first settlers to South Australia. *H.M.S. Buffalo* was later shipwrecked off the coast of New Zealand, and at that time the wood for this chair was salvaged.

Just round the corner is **Rodney Fox's Shark Museum**, with photographs and models of sharks and other items relating to encounters with those formidable fishes, and also various displays of nautical objects. Mr. Fox has had thirty years' experience of underwater filming, his favourite subject being the Great White Shark. Opening hours are from 11:00 until 17:00, except on Mondays and Tuesdays, and admission costs $5.

Walk across to the shore once more, following round to a site occupied in earlier days by Baxter's Merry-Go-Round, which started turning in 1895. We are now in the **Colley Reserve**, named after the first mayor. The **bandstand** is not the first, but the current one was built in 1926 and bears a plaque commemorating the centenary of the Commemoration Day Race which has been held here every year since 1887. This was the original site of the Luna Park amusement centre which was very popular in the 1930s. It was damaged by a major storm in 1953 and the owners decided to give up with Adelaide and moved it to Sydney. The trees at the edge of the Reserve are Norfolk Island Pines, many of them over a century old.

Continue along the shore past the Surf Life Saving Club and along to the isthmus, where you will find the **Memorial Rock** marking the place where Colonel Light and his team disembarked in 1836 to begin the task of searching for a site for the capital of South Australia.

Now turn east to **Wigley Reserve**, also lined by Norfolk Island Pines. You will observe the **Patawalonga Boat Haven** opened in February 1960 by making part of the Patawalonga River into an artificial lake offering a shelter from high storm tides to yachts and other small craft. **Glenelg Sailing Club** is here, formed in 1898 as Glenelg Dinghy Club. Continuing by the water, you come to a replica of *H.M.S. Buffalo*, which made the journey from Portsmouth in 1836 to bring the first settlers. The original ship, you will recall, was wrecked off New Zealand, but this replica was constructed from the original Admiralty plans. It was built here between 1980 and 1982 and is a seafood restaurant and museum. Admission to the museum costs $3. If that is too expensive, a recorded history of the vessel plays in return for the expenditure of 20 cents. Even the cannons on this vessel are copies of the 1813 ordnance which the original vessel carried.

Turn right now into Adelphi Terrace, and then left into Anzac Highway, and right once more into Nile Street. You will come to **St. Peter's Church** which was rebuilt in 1883. It is open for inspection from 14:00 until 16:00 on weekdays and has more than thirty stained glass windows and a large biblical painting. Continue along Nile Street and you will reach **Jetty Road**, with the tram line running down its centre, in the heart of Glenelg. Just to the left on the other side of the road is the **Congregational Church**, now known as St. Andrew's Uniting Church. The original church here opened in 1859 and is now used as the Church Hall. The present Italianate church was built in 1880. The **pipe organ**, with 1,068 pipes, was installed in 1883.

Just to the left of the church is Chapel Street. Take this street, and at the end on the right you will find **Our Lady of Victories Catholic Church** and Hall. The church itself was built in 1927, although other parts date from 1894. It has four grand Corinthian columns, a white marble altar and space for a congregation of 700. It is open for inspection on weekdays between 10:00 and 16:00.

Turn left into High Street and immediately right into Olive Street. Then look at **no. 5** Russell Court, at the end of this cul-de-sac. Originally called *The Olives*, because it had many olive trees in the garden, it was built in 1867 and had eighteen rooms, and included a coach house, a lodge and stables. It is the oldest surviving grand mansion in Glenelg.

Return to the end of Olive Street, turn left into High Street and turn left again into Moseley Street. Walk for five minutes until you reach Pier Street. The house on the right, on the far corner of Pier Street (**no. 12**) is an attractive old villa with a hidden garden. For ten years from 1906, it was the home of one of Glenelg's distinguished residents, named Wilbraham, known as a yachtsman and swimmer. Turn right into Pier

ADELAIDE 633

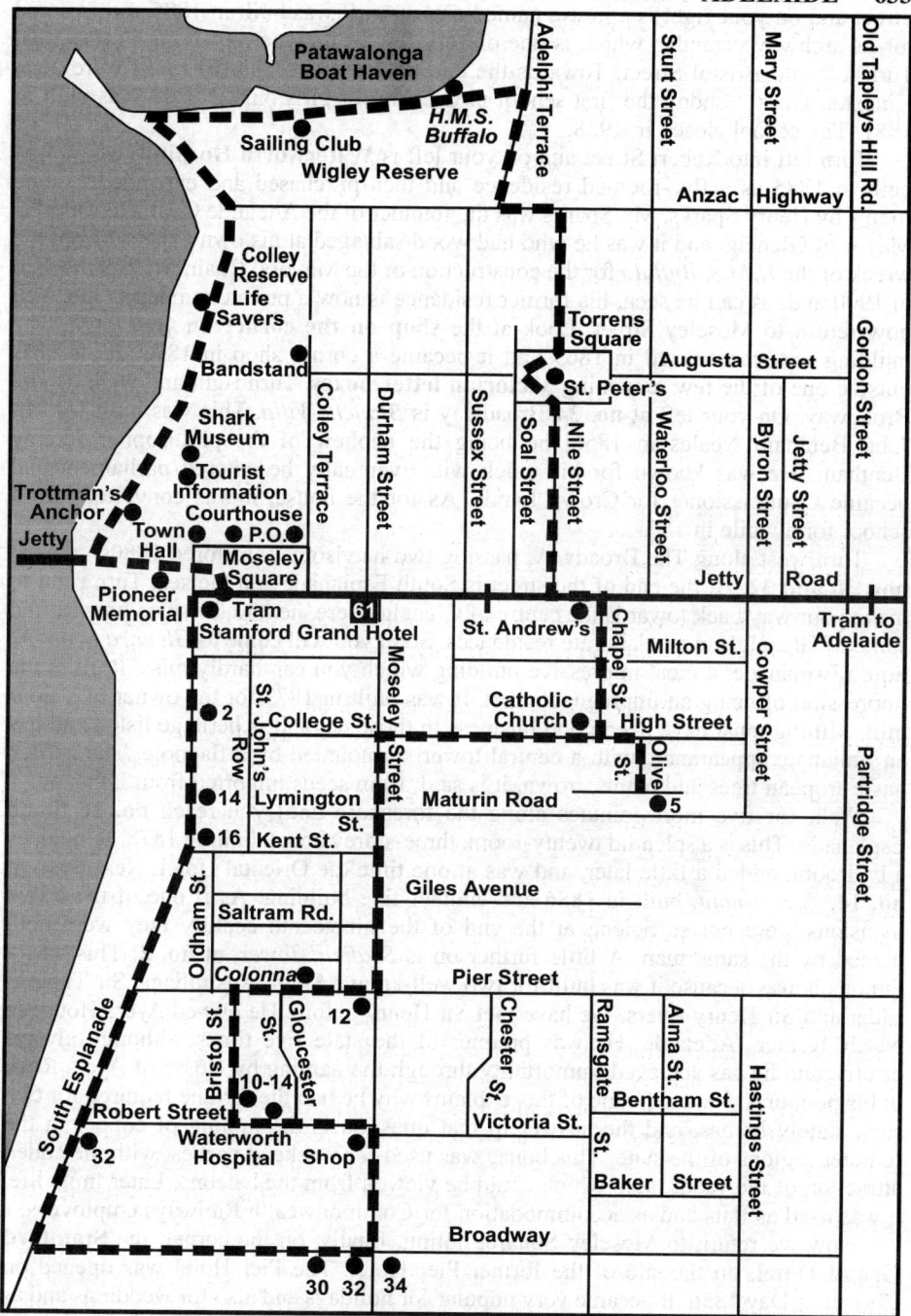

GLENELG
Dashed line shows Walking Tour
White numerals in black boxes indicate backpackers hostels

Street and on your right is a house named *Colonna*. It was built in 1885 and is noted for its archway verandah which is one of very few of its type remaining in this area. Turn left into Bristol Street. Towards the end of the street, **nos. 10 to 14** were once Kingston Girls' School, the first school in Glenelg for girls only. No. 14 was built in 1881. The school closed in 1928.

Turn left into Robert Street and on your left is **Waterworth Hospital**, which was built in 1885 as a five-roomed residence and then purchased and expanded to nine rooms by Henry Sparks. Mr. Sparks was the founder of the Adelaide Oval. He was also Mayor of Glenelg, and it was he who had wood salvaged at his own expense from the wreck of the *H.M.S. Buffalo* for the construction of the Mayoral Chair. Mr. Sparks died in 1900 and, as can be seen, his former residence is now a private nursing home. You now return to Moseley Street. Look at the **shop on the corner** on your right. The building was constructed in 1869 and it became a corner shop in 1878. It also has outside one of the few remaining **Victorian letter boxes**. Turn right and walk to The Broadway. On your left at **no. 34** Broadway is *Blanche Villa*. This was built for Mr. John Bentham Neales in 1856, he being the nephew of the philosopher Jeremy Bentham. He was known for his quick wit. Eventually he entered parliament and became Commissioner for Crown Lands. As for the house, it was converted into a school for a while in 1875.

Turn west along The Broadway, passing two handsomely restored 1880s villas at **nos. 30 and 32**. At the end of the street is South Esplanade and the sea. Turn right to make your way back towards the centre of Glenelg. Here, next to the sea, you will find some of Glenelg's most elaborate residences. Soon you will come to *Glenara* at **no. 32** South Esplanade, a most impressive building which you can hardly miss. It gives the impression of being an impregnable fort. It was built in 1873 for the owner of a flour mill. Milling must have been good business in those days. It is heritage listed and has an Italianate appearance, with a central tower surmounted by a flagpole. The garden has European trees and plants grown, it is said, from seeds imported from Lebanon.

Walk for five more minutes along the foreshore until you reach **no. 16** South Esplanade. This is a splendid twenty-room, three-storey home, built in 1878. It includes a ballroom, added a little later, and was at one time the Oriental Hotel. Next door, at **no. 14**, is *Stormont*, built in 1886 and another fine building. As if one of these two mansions were not sufficient, at the end of the nineteenth century they were both owned by the same man. A little further on is *Seafield Tower*, at **no. 2**. This was a famous house because it was built for two well-known South Australians: Sir Thomas Elder and Sir Henry Ayers. We have met Sir Henry before. He owned Ayers House in North Terrace, Adelaide. He was premier of the state five times, although always briefly, and he has achieved immortality through the naming by Gosse of Ayers Rock in his honour. Of course, none of this explains why he had the fortune required for two such stately homes, and the answer to that question is the mining of copper in the remoter regions of the state. This house was used for weekend parties, with the added attraction of the yacht races which could be viewed from the balcony. Later in its life, it was used as flats and as accommodation for Commonwealth Railways employees.

Now we return to Moseley Square, noting, finally, on the corner, the **Stamford Grand Hotel**, on the site of the former Pier Hotel. The Pier Hotel was opened on Christmas Day 1856. It became very popular for holidays and also for weddings and as accommodation for visiting sports teams. Although it is gone, the balconies, in particular, of the current hotel are based on the Victorian style of the former Pier Hotel.

We have missed one important landmark in this tour, because it is a little distant. That is the **Old Gum Tree**. It is some two kilometres north-east of the Glenelg city centre and it is not just any gum tree, but the one beside which Governor Hindmarsh chose to read the Proclamation of the Establishment of South Australia on 28th December 1836. A re-enactment is held on the same date each year, lest anybody should forget that South Australia is no longer governed by the administration of New South Wales.

Another place to visit is **Port Adelaide** which can be reached by taking a train with destination Outer Harbour as far as Port Adelaide. The journey takes twenty minutes.

Port Adelaide was at its prime in the 1880s and has many fine buildings dating from those times. Although the area suffered a decline for much of the twentieth century, it has now revived and is a fishing port, a shopping centre and a town for museums.

Appropriately enough, the **Maritime Museum** is here. The main museum is in Lipson Street, five minutes walk from the station, but there are also, on different sites, a lighthouse, built in 1869, a bond store from the 1850s, and a wharf with some vessels. The Maritime Museum is open daily from 10:00 until 17:00 and admission costs $10.

The **Port Dock Railway Museum** is also here and is interesting. South Australia was the only state to use all three of the gauges employed in this country and it was one of the first states to develop a railway system. The line to Port Adelaide was opened in 1856, the station here originally being known as Port Dock. The Museum includes the Port Dock Goods Shed, constructed in 1873. In this Museum is the largest collection of railway rolling stock in Australia. There are train rides available on a miniature railway, steam-operated on Sundays only and at other times hauled by a diesel engine. The Museum is open daily from 10:00 until 17:00 and admission costs $10.

This Museum also operates, separately, the 3.5 kilometre line along the foreshore from **Semaphore to Fort Glanville**. To reach this, take the train for two more stops to Glanville and then walk one kilometre down **Semaphore Road**, an interesting walk past some relatively old buildings, to the sea. The Semaphore - Fort Glanville line operates on Sundays only between October and April. The fare is $6 return.

The **Aviation Museum** is a little further from Port Adelaide station, but still within walking distance. There is also the **Military Vehicles Museum**, close to the station, but this is open on Sundays only.

On Sundays there is a market at **Fishermen's Wharf** from 9:00 until 17:00. This is a market not for fish, but for all kinds of goods, both new and second-hand. On any day of the week, just walking around Port Adelaide is interesting, especially in the areas mentioned above, close to the harbour.

Now here are a few other areas of interest around Adelaide, with details of public transport to take one there.

The **Old Adelaide Gaol** was opened in 1841 and operated until 1988. It is open every day from 11:00 until 16:00, but tours are generally available only on Sundays. 49 prisoners were executed here during the Gaol's period of service, including Elizabeth Woolcock in 1873, the only woman to be executed in South Australia. At first the executions used to take place outside the main gate, but later condemned prisoners were hanged on a gallows inside the Gaol. Admission costs $6 on weekdays and $8 (including the tour) on Sundays. The Old Gaol is not far from the city centre. If you arrive on an interstate train from Sydney, Perth or Alice Springs, you will see it from the right side of the train just as the central city becomes visible from the left. However,

636   SOUTH AUSTRALIA

there is no station nearby, so you can either walk from the city, a distance of about two kilometres, or take a bus no. 151, 153, 155, 286 or 287 from North Terrace or no. 112, 113, 116 or 118 from Currie Street to Stop 1, a five-minute journey (see maps on pages 637 and 641).

   North Adelaide is pleasant, if slightly trendy. It is known for its rather up-market shops, restaurants and cafés. It also offers a good view over the central part of the city. O'Connell Street and Melbourne Street are the two most fashionable streets in the area (see map on page 641). You can walk to these, a distance of about two kilometres from the city centre, or there are numerous buses from King William Street. The statue of Colonel Light at **Montefiore Hill** has already been mentioned. One other attraction in North Adelaide is a pleasant and well laid out **Zoo**. It is open daily from 9:30 until 17:00, but is rather expensive at $15. You can walk here easily too, by following Frome Road from the city for a distance of about one kilometre from North Terrace. If you prefer a bus, take no. 272 or 273 for five minutes from Stop E2 in Currie Street, Stop G3 in Grenfell Street or Stop Y1 in Pulteney Street to Stop 2.

   To the north-east of the city, buses run along the *O-Bahn*, a concrete busway where the driver is relieved of the stresses of steering and just sits back and plants his foot on the accelerator. It claims to be the longest guided busway in the world and it certainly expedites travel in this direction, the only drawback being that there is nothing very special to see at the end of the trip through the pleasant park land. The end of the busway (but not necessarily of the bus route) is at **Tea Tree Plaza**, where there is a suburban shopping centre. To try the *O-Bahn*, take buses nos. 540 to 546 from Currie Street.

   The **Adelaide Hills** lie to the south-east of the city and are an attractive area providing a fine view. You will travel through this area if you arrive in Adelaide from Melbourne by either train or bus. If you just want a brief view, you can take a suburban train to its terminus at **Belair**, a journey of 35 minutes, and then return. However, the best view is from the summit of **Mt. Lofty** at 727 metres. To reach there, take a bus no. 163F (no. 165 at weekends) to Crafers Park and Ride (Stop 24A), a journey of 30 minutes, and then a no. 823 to Mt. Lofty Summit (Stop 26), which takes a further 20 minutes. Most buses depart the city from Franklin Street Bus Terminal and travel via Currie Street and Grenfell Street, but some start in Currie Street. In Currie Street, use Stop D1, in Grenfell Street Stop G2 and in Pulteney Street Stop D2, E1 or G1. According to the present timetable, bus 163F leaves Grenfell Street at 7:48, 9:25, 9:55, 10:55, 11:55 and 12:55 on weekdays. At weekends, bus 165 departs from Grenfell Street every hour at 33 minutes past the hour on Saturdays, and similarly on Sundays until 12:33, after which at 14:33, 16:33, 17:33 and 19:33 (but if you leave after 14:33, you will not be able to get back). Times change, however, so do not rely on this, but get a timetable from the Transport Information Centre in King William Street.

   Cleland Wildlife Park is near Mt. Lofty and has kangaroos, koalas and other Australian animals. To reach there, follow exactly the same instructions as above for Mt. Lofty, but stay on bus no. 823 to its terminus at Stop 27, eight minutes beyond Mt. Lofty Summit.

   If you use the same directions again, but alight from bus no. 823 at Stop 25, you will find the **Mt. Lofty Botanic Gardens**, also worth a visit if you have time. The gardens can also be reached by taking bus no. 820 or 821 from Currie Street, Stop T, D1 or E1, or Grenfell Street, Stop G2 or I1. These services follow a different route and reach a different entrance to the Botanic Gardens. They also operate only on weekdays.

Belair National Park is the oldest National Park in the state and is best reached by train, Belair being the terminus for the suburban system. The National Park starts right outside the station and the main railway line, continuing to Melbourne, forms part of its northern boundary. Whilst you are at the station have a look at the track. The platform at which you alighted is broad gauge (5 feet 3 inches). The other one used to be too, but just a few years ago the line to Melbourne was converted to a standard gauge track, so the other platform is now a standard gauge platform. That means that whereas this line was, until recently, a double-tracked line, now it has become a single-track system for each gauge, which is not ideal for either, especially for the well-used suburban line. One might have thought that a dual-gauge double-tracked system might have been more appropriate. Within Belair National Park, you will find

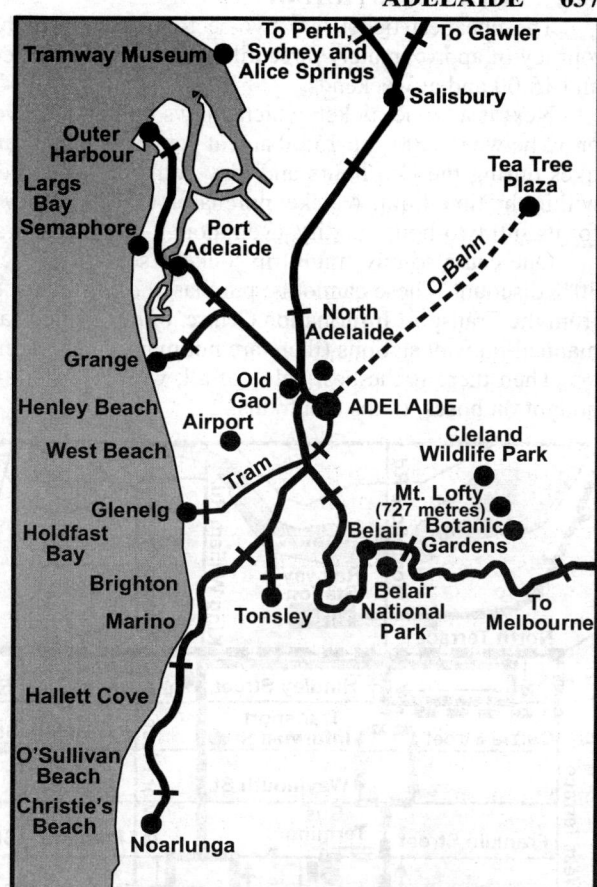

ADELAIDE AND VICINITY
Showing railway lines and places of interest

Old Government House, built in 1860 as a hill station residence for the Governor of South Australia in summer. It includes the state's first indoor plunge pool and is open to the public from 12:30 until 16:00 on Sundays only. Although it is more convenient to travel to Belair by train, it can also be reached by bus no. 193 or 195. The 193 operates on weekdays only. Buses leave from King William Street, Stop A2, C3 or F1, or from Wakefield Street, Stop G1 or G2, or from Pulteney Street, Stop G1. Alight at Stop 28 after 40 minutes. Service 193 runs along the southern border of the park, so it is possible to walk through the National Park and then take the 193 back to Belair Station or right back to the city. It is also possible to use the 193 to connect a trip to Mt. Lofty with a visit to the Belair National Park. A ten-minute walk is involved at Crafers to reach Upper Sturt Road along which the 193 runs. Remember that this service does not operate at weekends, though.

As mentioned above, a single ticketing system applies to all Adelaide transport within the metropolitan area. Buses, trains and the Glenelg tram can all be used with the same ticket.

638 SOUTH AUSTRALIA

The cheapest ticket is a two-section ticket, which allows one to make a single journey of approximately three kilometres. This ticket costs $2, or $1.50 between 9:00 and 15:00 and at weekends.

Next is a 'zone' ticket, which allows unlimited travel for two hours. This costs $3, or $2 between 9:00 and 15:00 and at weekends. One can take as many vehicles as one likes during the two hours and may complete a journey as long as it is commenced within the time limit. A ticket purchased at the cheaper rate before 15:00 may be used for its full two-hour validity, even though that means travelling after 15:00.

One can also buy 'multitrip' tickets, sets of ten tickets, offering approximately a 30% discount. These cannot be purchased on vehicles, but must be bought in advance from the Transport Information Centre, or designated sales agents such as post offices, manned railway stations (there are not many), newsagents and small stores.

Then there is the best value of all, which is a one-day ticket for $6. This can be bought on buses, trains and trams.

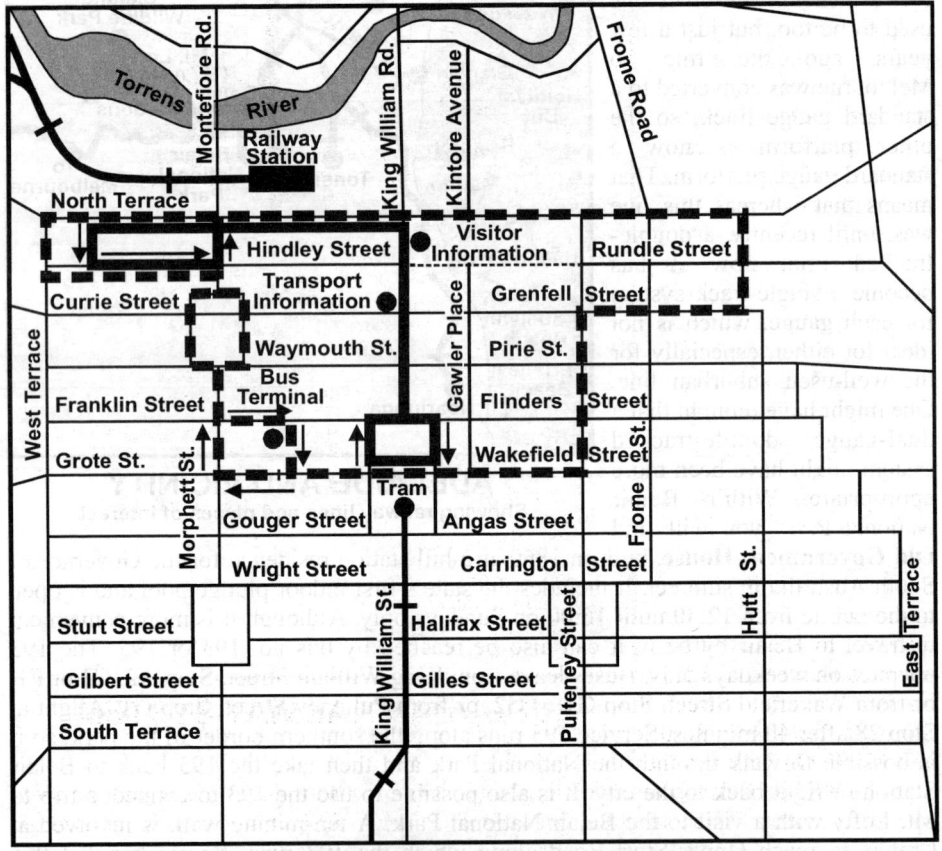

FREE BUSES IN ADELAIDE

Service 99B, Every 5 mins., weekdays
Service 99C, Every 15 mins., weekdays

ADELAIDE

On a bus, one purchases a ticket from the driver. On the tram, there is a conductor. However, on the train there is only a machine, strategically placed near the door. It is not enough just to buy a ticket on a bus, tram or train. One then has to put it into another machine to validate it. Thereafter, when using another vehicle with the same ticket, one inserts it again, and hopes that it will be returned.

There are also two useful free bus services in Adelaide. These are numbered 99B and 99C and they run loops round the central area of the city. The 99B runs a fairly short route from Victoria Square, up King William Street and along North Terrace past the Railway Station. Buses operate every five minutes between 7:40 and 18:00 on weekdays. On Fridays the service is extended until 21:20 with buses operating every ten minutes in the evening. On Saturdays they operate every fifteen minutes between 8:30 and 17:30. On Sundays there is no service.

The 99C performs a much wider loop and runs in both directions round the loop, operating every fifteen minutes between 8:00 and 18:00. On Fridays, an evening service is provided until 21:00, with buses operating every half hour. On Saturdays, buses run every half hour between 8:30 and 17:30. On Sundays there is no service. The routes of these two buses are shown opposite.

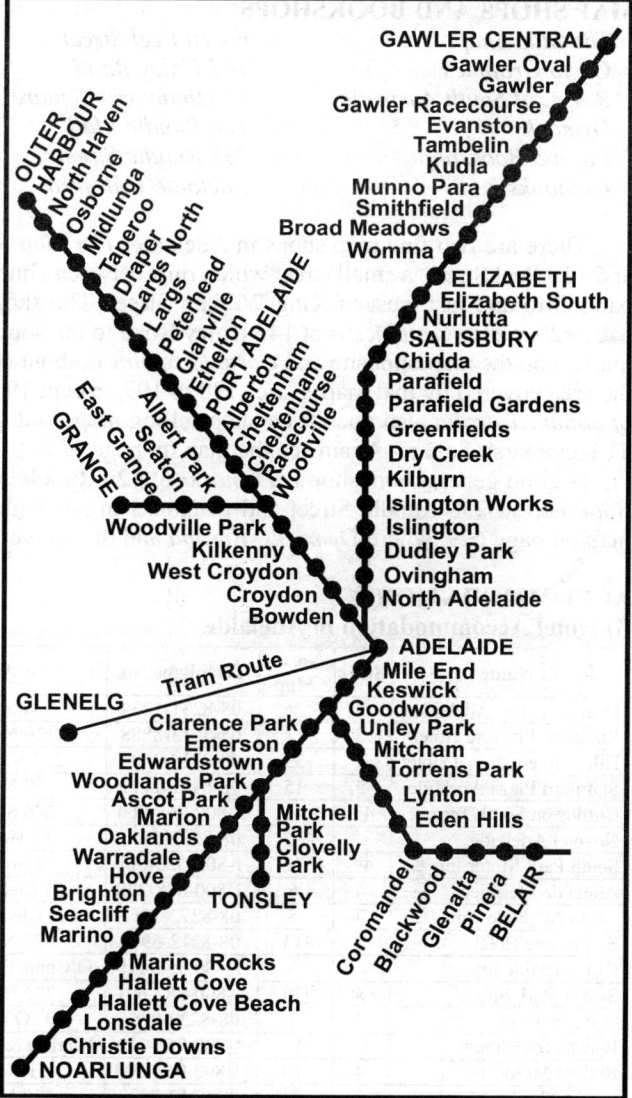

SUBURBAN RAILWAY SYSTEM

640   SOUTH AUSTRALIA
MAP SHOPS AND BOOKSHOPS

The Map Shop	6 - 10 Peel Street
Carto Graphics	147 Unley Road
R.A.A. of South Australia	41 Hindmarsh Square
Dymocks	126 Rundle Mall
Europa Bookshop	238 Rundle Street
Unibooks	Adelaide University

There are two fine map shops in Adelaide. *The Map Shop* (a reasonable name) is at 6 - 10 Peel Street, a small street which runs between Hindley Street and Currie Street parallel to and just west of King William Street. The shop is marked on the map on page 629. *Carto Graphics* is at 147 Unley Road to the south of the city. Unley Road is marked on the map opposite and *Carto Graphics* is about one kilometre to the south of the area covered by that map. Buses 190 to 199, except 194, pass this way. The *R.A.A. of South Australia* also operates a shop selling maps and guides in its headquarters at 41 Hindmarsh Square. Again see the map on page 629.

A good general bookshop is *Dymocks* at 126 Rundle Mall. There are also *Europa Bookshop* at 238 Rundle Street and *Unibooks* in Adelaide University. Again see the map on page 629, where *Dymocks, Europa* and the University are marked.

ACCOMMODATION
(i) Hotel Accommodation in Adelaide

Name	Stars	No. on Map	Telephone No.	Address	Lowest Price (Double/Twin)
Hyatt Regency Adelaide	5	9	08-8231-1234	North Terrace	$330
Radisson Playford Hotel	5	11	08-8213-8888	120 North Terrace	$330
Hilton International Hotel	5	33	08-8217-2000	233 Victoria Square	$265
Stamford Plaza Adelaide	5	15	08-8461-1111	150 North Terrace	$250
Chifley on South Terrace	4½	41	1-800-065-064	226 South Terrace	$180
Novotel Adelaide		22	08-8231-5552	65 Hindley Street	$165
South Park Motor Inn	4½	39	1-800-626-021	1 South Terrace	$165
Adelaide Meridien	4	6	1-800-888-228	21 Melbourne Street	$160
North Adelaide Apts.	4	5	08-8272-1355	109 Glen Osmond Road	$155
Strathmore Hotel		13	08-8212-6911	129 North Terrace	$150
Old Adelaide Inn	4½	3	1-800-355-119	O'Connell & Gover Streets	$140
Saville Park Suites	4	20	1-800-882-601	255 Hindley Street	$140
O'Connell Inn	4	1	08-8239-0766	197 O'Connell Street	$130
Barron Townhouse	3½	17	1-800-355-121	Hindley & Morphett Streets	$130
Riviera Motor Inn	4	10	1-800-061-300	31 North Terrace	$125
Festival Lodge Motel	3	14	08-8212-7877	140 North Terrace	$125
Richmond Hotel	3½	19	1-800-188-111	128 Rundle Mall	$125
Flinders Lodge Motel	3½	27	08-8332-8222	27 Dequetteville Terrace	$125
Apartments on the Park	4	43	1-800-882-774	274 South Terrace	$125
Adelaide Paringa Motel	3	24	1-800-088-202	15 Hindley Street	$120
Tiffins on the Park	4½	44	1-800-355-206	176 Greenhill Road	$120
Regal Park Motor Inn	3½	2	1-800-355-116	44 Barton Terrace East	$110
Grosvenor Vista Hotel	3½	12	1-800-888-222	125 North Terrace	$105
Kent Town Lodge		28	1-800-352-112	22 Wakefield Street	$105
Royal Coach Motor Inn		26	08-8362-5676	24 Dequetteville Terrace	$100
Greenways Apartments		8	08-8267-5903	41 King William Road	$95
Metropolitan Hotel		32	08-8231-5471	46 Grote Street	$95
Directors Studios	3	34	1-800-804-224	259 Gouger Street	$95

ADELAIDE 641

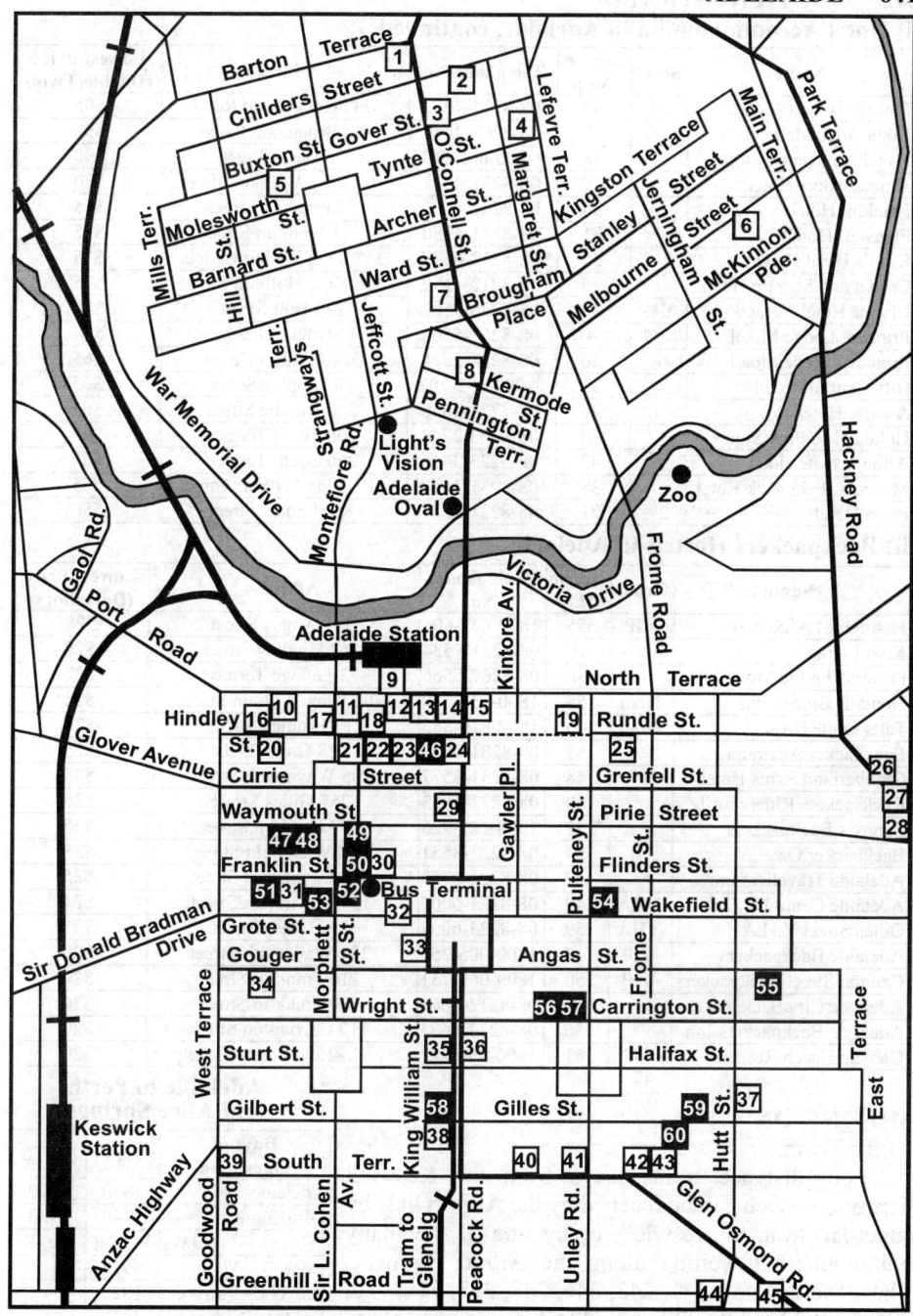

ACCOMMODATION IN ADELAIDE
**Black numerals in white boxes indicate hotel accommodation
White numerals in black boxes indicate backpackers hostels**

642 SOUTH AUSTRALIA
(i) Hotel Accommodation in Adelaide, continued

Name	Stars	No. on Map	Telephone No.	Address	Lowest Price (Double/Twin)
Powell's Court Motel		45	08-8271-7033	2 Glen Osmond Road	$95
Hotel Adelaide Intern'l.	3½	7	08-8267-3444	62 Brougham Place	$90
Motel Adjacent Casino		18	1-800-665-961	25 Bank Street	$90
Ambassadors Hotel		29	08-8231-4331	107 King William Street	$80
Franklin Hotel		30	08-8231-4703	92 Franklin Street	$75
Flagstaff Hotel		31	08-8231-4380	233 Franklin Street	$75
King's Head Hotel		35	08-8212-6657	353 King William Street	$75
Crown and Sceptre Hotel		36	08-8212-4159	308 King William Street	$75
Clarice Hotel / Motel	2½	37	08-8223-3560	220 Hutt Street	$70
Princess Lodge Motel	2½	4	08-8267-5566	73 Lefevre Terrace	$65
Princes Arcade Motel		16	08-8231-9524	262 Hindley Street	$65
City Central Motel	2½	23	1-800-802-707	23 Hindley Street	$65
Austral Hotel	1	25	08-8223-4660	205 Rundle Street	$65
Holiday Inn Park Suites	3½	40	08-8223-2744	208 South Terrace	$65
Afton Private Hotel		42	08-8223-3416	260 South Terrace	$65
Moore's Brecknock Hotel		38	08-8231-5467	401 King William Street	$55
Plaza Hotel	2½	21	08-8231-6371	85 Hindley Street	$50

(ii) Backpackers Hostels in Adelaide

Name	Group	No. on Map	Telephone No.	Address	Lowest Price (Dormitory)
East Park Lodge	VIP	55	1800-643-606	341 Angus Street	$28
Kiwi Lodge	B&W	16	08-8231-9524	262 Hindley Street	$28
Princess Lodge Motel		4	08-8267-5566	73 Lefevre Terrace	$28
Nomads Brecon Inn	Nom	58	1800-737-378	401 King William Street	$25
Tatts in the City	Nom	46	1800-819-883	17 Hindley Street	$25
Backpacker Australia		53	08-8231-0639	128 Grote Street	$25
Cumberland Arms Hotel		48	08-8231-3577	205 Waymouth Street	$25
Rucksackers Riders Int'l.		60	08-8232-0823	257 Gilles Street	$25
Sunny's Backpackers		52	1800-225-725	139 Franklin Street	$25
Backpacker Oz		54	08-8223-3551	144 Wakefield Street	$25
Adelaide Travellers Inn		57	08-8224-0753	118 Carrington Street	$25
Adelaide Central Y.H.A.	YHA	49	08-8223-6007	135 Waymouth Street	$21
Gilles Street Y.H.A.	YHA	59	08-8223-6007	290 Gilles Street	$21
Adelaide Backpackers	VIP	47	1800-006-251	257 Waymouth Street	$20
Cannon Street Backpackers	VIP	50	1800-069-731	110 Franklin Street	$20
Adelaide City Backpackers		51	08-8212-2668	239 Franklin Street	$20
Adelaide Backpackers Inn		56	08-8223-6535	112 Carrington Street	$20
Glenelg Beach Resort	VIP	61	1800-066-422	1 Moseley Street, Glenelg	$20

MOVING ON
(i) By Train

Long-distance trains leave from the Keswick Terminal, which can be reached by the Airport bus, by suburban train to Keswick, or by one of the many public buses travelling along the Anzac Highway. These include nos. 241, 243, 246, 247, 248, 711, 720, 721, 722, 723, 725, 727 and 729. It is also possible to walk to the station, but it is a distance of approximately three kilometres from the city centre.

Adelaide to Perth and Alice Springs

Days of Operation	Tu, F	M, Th
Adelaide	1830	1500
Port Augusta	2240	1920
Days	W, Sat	Tu, F
Cook	0918	
Kalgoorlie (arrive)	1920	
Kalgoorlie (depart)	2230	
Days	Th, Sun	
Perth	0930	
Alice Springs		0900

ADELAIDE

Adelaide to Sydney (Bus plus train)

Days of Operation	Daily (Bus)	Daily
Adelaide	0910	
Swan Hill	1635	
Echuca	1900	
Albury	2215	2256
Wagga Wagga		0006
Cootamundra		0113
Yass Junction		0236
Goulbourn		0342
Moss Vale		0429
Strathfield		0606
Sydney		0625

Adelaide to Sydney and Melbourne (Train)

Days of Operation	Sun, W	Sun, M, Th, F	Sat	W
Adelaide	0745	0900	1010	1015
Broken Hill	1630		1725	
Days	M, Th		Sun	
Sydney	0915		0915	
Melbourne		2000		2100

Adelaide to Melbourne (Bus plus train)

Days of Operation	M-F (Bus)	M-F	M-F (Bus)	M-F	Sat, Sun (Bus)	Sat, Sun	Sat, Sun (Bus)	Sat, Sun
Adelaide	0825				0850			
Dimboola	1445		1535		1515		1530	
Horsham	1510		1605		1540		1600	
St. Arnaud	1625				1655			
Bendigo	1755	1815			1830	1850		
Ballarat			1855	1915			1850	1920
Melbourne		2015		2041		2047		2050

There are trains to Perth on Tuesday and Friday evenings, to Sydney on Sunday, Wednesday and Saturday mornings, to Alice Springs (and soon to Darwin) on Monday and Thursday afternoons, and to Melbourne on Sunday, Monday, Wednesday, Thursday and Friday mornings.

From the Franklin Street bus station, there are combined bus plus train services operated by V-Line to Sydney via Albury and to Melbourne via Bendigo every morning. There is also a connecting bus to Ballarat in Victoria. Timetables for all of the train, and train plus bus, services are shown above or on the previous page.

(ii) By Bus

McCafferty's and Greyhound both operate bus services to Sydney, the two companies using different routes. Greyhound runs to Perth three times a week and to Alice Springs every day, with an onward connexion to Darwin. Services to Melbourne are provided once a day by McCafferty's, once a day by Greyhound and twice a day by Firefly. Firefly is usually cheapest and also offers an onward connexion to Sydney.

ANECDOTE

The best part of the road journey between Melbourne and Adelaide has always been the descent into the latter through the Adelaide Hills. A series of tight hairpin bends used to lead into the city, offering some splendid views and giving the passenger plenty of time to enjoy them, as they had to be negotiated at low speed. It was, however, also a road upon which there had been a number of serious accidents.

The highway here has recently been improved, with tunnels constructed to reduce the previous steep grades and tight corners. It has certainly speeded up the route.

In the words of the author's bus driver, however, "The plan was to reduce the number of accidents which used to take place on the old road. In that respect, these improvements have met with great success. The accidents all occur on the new road now."

644 SOUTH AUSTRALIA
Bus Services from Adelaide

Destination	Operator	Via	Distance (km)	Fare	Journey Time	Frequency
Sydney	McCafferty's		1470	$141	24½ hrs	1/day
		Canberra	1256	$141	19¼ hrs	1/day
		Mildura	397	$54	7 hrs	1/day
		Nuriootpa	60	$26	1½ hrs	1/day
Sydney	Greyhound		1645	$141	24¾ hrs	3/week
		Dubbo	1243	$131	16½ hrs	3/week
		Broken Hill	520	$93	7¼ hrs	3/week
Melbourne	McCafferty's		789	$65	10¾ hrs	1/day
		Geelong	734	$65	9½ hrs	1/day
		Ballarat	622	$65	8¼ hrs	1/day
Melbourne	Greyhound		789	$65	9¾ hrs	1/day
		Ballarat	622	$65	8¼ hrs	1/day
Melbourne	Firefly		789	$50	10½ hrs	2/day
		Ballarat	622	$50	8½ hrs	2/day
Albury	V-Line		907	$69	12½ hrs	1/day
Bendigo	V-Line		656	$64	9 hrs	1/day
Perth	Greyhound		2979	$291	36¾ hrs	3/week
		Kalgoorlie	2350	$291	29 hrs	3/week
		Port Augusta	317	$42	3¾ - 4 hrs	10/week
Alice Springs	Greyhound		1570	$195	19½ hrs	1/day
		Coober Pedy	883	$115	11 hrs	1/day
Mt. Gambier	Stateliner		470	$53.30	6¼ hrs	1/day
Goolwa	Stateliner		92	$16.40	2 - 2½ hrs	5/day
		Victor Harbor	92	$16.40	1¾ - 2¼ hrs	5/day
Cape Jervis	Public Coach		107	$18	2 hrs	1/day
Cape Jervis	Sealink Ferry		107	$18	2 hrs	1/day
Renmark	Stateliner		261	$38.70	4 hrs	2/day
		Nuriootpa	75	$7.80	1¼ hrs	2/day
Angaston	Barossa		90	$16.10	1¾ - 2 hrs	2/day
		Nuriootpa	75	$14.90	1½ - 1¾ hrs	2/day
Wilpena	Stateliner		475	$71.50	7 - 7¼ hrs	2/week
Roxby Dwns	Stateliner		570	$86.20	7¾ hrs	1/day
Ceduna	Stateliner		820	$92.70	11¼ - 11¾ hrs	1/day
Port Lincoln	Stateliner		693	$79.60	9½ - 9¾ hrs	2/day
		Whyalla	398	$45.80	5¼ - 6 hrs	4/day
		Port Augusta	315	$39.80	3¾ - 4¼ hrs	5/day
Moonta	Stateliner		185	$21	3 hrs	12/week
Yorketown	Yorke Peninsula		230	$32.80	4 hrs	7/week

KANGAROO ISLAND
Population 5,000

3 hrs 30 mins by bus and ferry from Adelaide

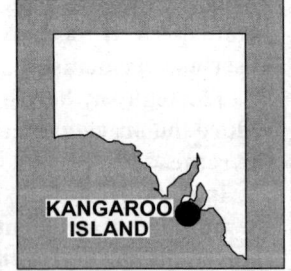

Kangaroo Island is the third largest off-shore island in Australia and is noted for its flora and fauna. The island covers an area of 4,500 square kilometres, measuring 155 kilometres by 55 kilometres. Approximately a third of the island consists of National Parks and Conservation Parks. It lies south-west of Adelaide, a journey of 110 kilometres by bus, taking a little over two hours, followed by a ferry ride of sixteen kilometres taking a little under an hour.

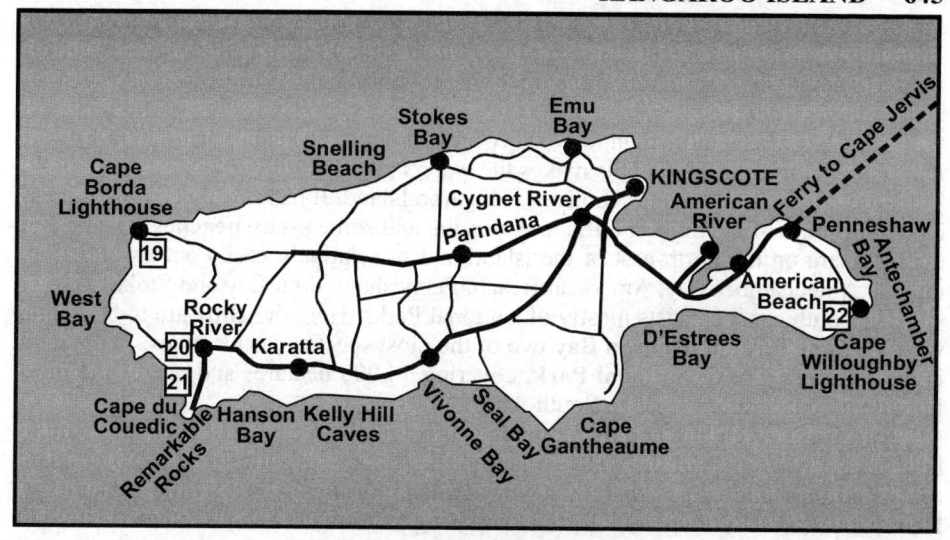

KANGAROO ISLAND
Numerals indicate accommodation

From Adelaide, there are two co-ordinated services per day, with buses leaving from opposite the Franklin Street Bus Terminal at 6:45 and 15:45. Ferries sail from Cape Jervis on the Fleurieu Peninsula at 9:00 and 18:00 every day, and at peak times there may be additional services. A connecting bus on Kangaroo Island operates from the ferry terminal at Penneshaw to American River and Kingscote. These costs mount up, with the ferry, in particular, being rather expensive. From Adelaide to Cape Jervis costs $18. The ferry crossing costs $35 and the Kangaroo Island bus, if required, costs $12. All of these are single fares. There is also a connecting service between Goolwa or Victor Harbor and Cape Jervis, which costs $15. Thus a visit to Kangaroo Island will cost over $100 just for the return journey from Adelaide and you will then have to face the problem that the only transport available on the island is the bus service twice a day in each direction between Penneshaw and Kingscote.

There are tours of the island available, currently costing approximately $60 for a one-day tour. Since Penneshaw is at the east of the island and the National Parks are towards the west, one has to take a tour or find some means of transport if one is to see the best of the locations. However, there are pleasant beaches near Penneshaw if visiting only these and the towns of Penneshaw, American River and Kingscote will suffice.

Kangaroo Island has an interesting history. It was the first place in South Australia to be settled. The original settlement was made at Reeves Point, then known as Kingscote, in 1836, predating the establishment of Adelaide. However, the settlement lasted only four years and it was not until 1854 that it was re-established at the present site of Kingscote. A mulberry tree, planted at Reeves Point in 1836, still produces fruit each year.

Even before settlement, Captain Matthew Flinders had landed near Penneshaw in 1802, and in 1803 an American brig arrived and spent four months here constructing from local timber a boat known as the *Independence*. From this event, American River acquired its name. The French explorer Captain Baudin landed in 1803 to obtain water. Therefore several prominent features of the island have French names, and one of the sailors carved an inscription on a rock near Penneshaw. The rock is known as Frenchman's Rock.

There have been more than forty shipwrecks around the island, the first, that of the *William*, occurring in 1847. This makes the waters popular with divers.

Here are some of the attractions of Kangaroo Island. It has rugged coastal scenery including some of the highest cliffs in Australia, and some pretty **beaches**. The best of the latter are on the north-east of the island and so relatively easily accessible. They include Antechamber Bay, American Beach, Penneshaw, Emu Bay and Stokes Bay.

The south coast consists mostly of National Parks. Here the **cliffs** are to be found, with **Vivonne Bay** and **Hanson Bay** two of the most spectacular locations. In the west is the **Flinders Chase National Park**, covering 74,000 hectares and one of the most important conservation areas in South Australia.

Admiral's Arch at **Cape du Couedic** was originally a cave, but became a natural land bridge when part of the walls collapsed. It still has stalactites and petrified plant roots, and its sheltered pool harbours New Zealand Fur Seals. Just a little further east, **Remarkable Rocks** are granite formations rising to 75 metres and weathered into odd shapes.

Kelly Hill Caves are further east on the south coast in the Kelly Hill Caves Conservation Park and consist of a series of sinkholes and tunnels. A tour is offered six times a day at a cost of $8. Adventure caving is also available with advance booking at a cost of $25 to $35 depending on the cave chosen for the adventure.

Further east again, within the Cape Gantheaume Conservation Park, is **Seal Bay**, where a colony of Australian Sea Lions resides. These creatures are unusual in their tolerance of human visits, to which, no doubt, they have become accustomed. There are a boardwalk and a lookout, entry to which costs $7, or one can take a guided tour, walking on the beach amidst the sea lions, for $10 (including entry to the boardwalk and lookout). It is claimed that there are only two places in the world where such a walk is possible. At midsummer only, a two-hour Sunset Tour is offered for $20.

Not far from Seal Bay is the **Little Sahara Dunefield**, an expanse of pristine desert

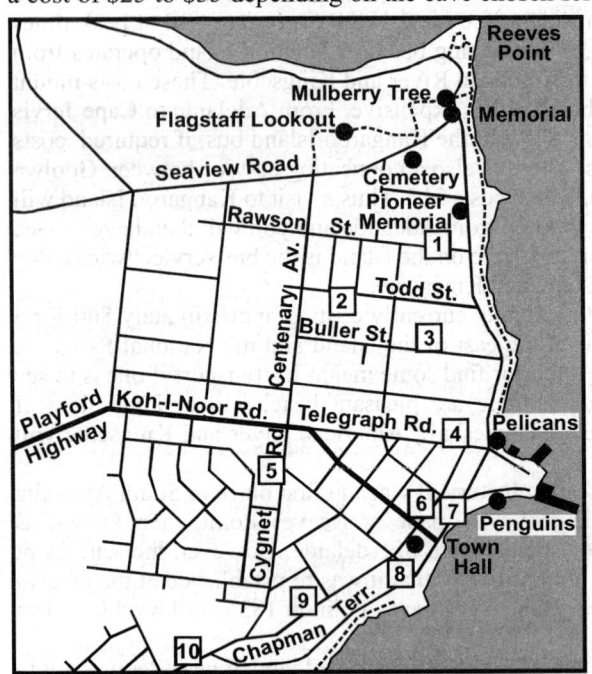

KINGSCOTE
Numerals indicate accommodation

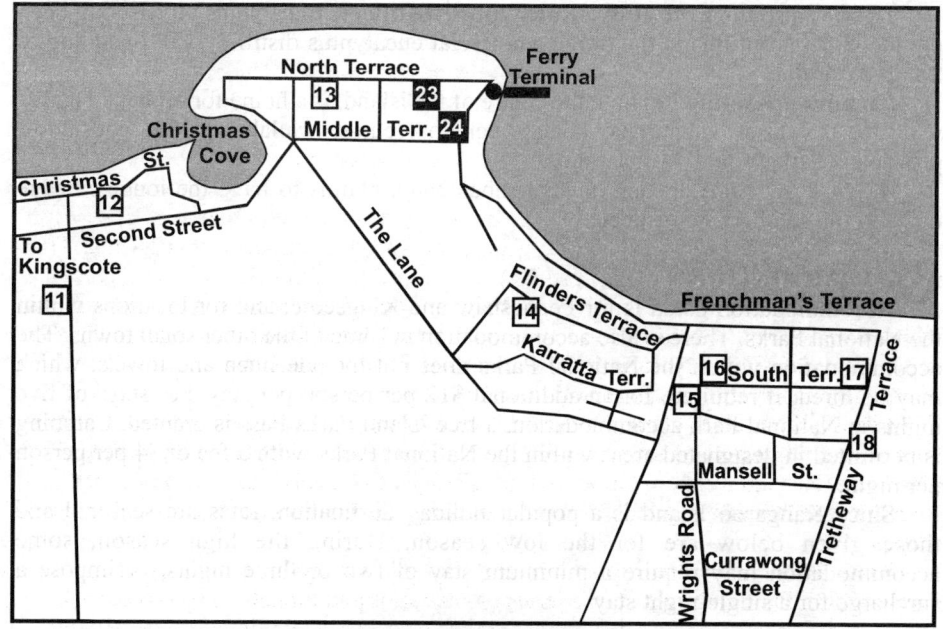

PENNESHAW
Black numerals in white boxes indicate hotel accommodation
White numerals in black boxes indicate backpackers hostels

six kilometres from the sea and completely surrounded by dense bushland. The tallest of the dunes reach 70 metres above sea level.

There are two lighthouses on the island which are open for inspection. and a third at Cape du Couedic which is not. **Cape Willoughby Lighthouse** was built in 1852 and was South Australia's first lighthouse. It is located on the eastern tip of the island. There are tours five times a day, the last at 14:00, costing $7. There is also accommodation available in the former lighthouse keepers' two cottages (see accommodation section below).

Cape Borda Lighthouse was built in 1858 and is on the west of the island. There are tours five times a day, the last at 15:15 (14:00 in June, July and August), costing $7. A cannon is fired from the lighthouse at least once every day and there is an interesting **lighthouse keepers' cemetery**. Accommodation is available here too in three different standards, the cheapest costing only $14 per night (see below).

There are **Penguin Tours** available at both Kingscote and Penneshaw. Tours take place in the evenings and cost $8.

An Island Parks Pass is available for $30 and covers the cost of admission to Flinders Chase National Park, plus tours at Seal Bay (but not the Sunset Tour), Kelly Hill Caves (but not Adventure Caving), Cape Willoughby Lighthouse and Cape Borda Lighthouse. It does not include Penguin Tours or accommodation or camping fees, but is valid for use for twelve months.

Other interesting features of the island include its bees. They are **Ligurian Honey Bees**, brought from Italy in 1883, and are thought to be the only remaining pure strain of honey bee anywhere in the world. It is not permitted to bring honey or any other bee products to the island. Clifford's Honey Farm is available for tours.

648　SOUTH AUSTRALIA

There is also the **Emu Ridge Eucalyptus Distillery**. Eucalyptus oil has long been produced here, but this is the only commercial eucalyptus distillery still operating in South Australia.

Parndana Wildlife Park, in the centre of the island, is a home for orphaned native wildlife. It houses kangaroos, koalas, echidna, emus, wallabies, deer, cockatoos, pheasants, curlews and farm animals.

A Maze 'n' Fun, opened in September 2000, claims to have the longest hedge maze in the southern hemisphere.

ACCOMMODATION

Accommodation listed is for Penneshaw and Kingscote, and for locations within the National Parks. There is also accommodation in some of the other small towns. The accommodation within the National Parks does not include linen and towels, which may be hired, if required, for an additional $12 per person per stay. For stays of five nights in National Park accommodation, a free Island Parks Pass is granted. Camping is permitted in designated areas within the National Parks, with a fee of $4 per person per night.

Since Kangaroo Island is a popular holiday destination, rates are seasonal and those given below are for the low season. During the high season, some accommodation may require a minimum stay of two or three nights, or impose a surcharge for a single-night stay.

(i) Hotel Accommodation in Kingscote

Name	Stars	No. on Map	Telephone No.	Address	Lowest Price (Double/Twin)
Acacia Apartments	4½	1	1-800-247-007	3 Rawson Street	$230
Wisteria Lodge Motel	3½	10	08-8553-2707	7 Cygnet Road	$145
Island Resort	3	4	08-8553-2100	4 Telegraph Road	$125
Ozone Seafront Hotel	3½	7	1-800-083-133	The Foreshore	$115
Reevara Holiday Home	3	2	08-8553-2776	28 Todd Street	$110
Graydon Holiday Lodge	3½	3	08-8553-2713	16 Buller Street	$105
Island Court Units	3	5	08-8553-2657	67 Cygnet Road	$95
Kangaroo Island Village	3	9	08-8553-2225	9 Dauncey Street	$85
Queenscliffe Hotel	2½	6	08-8553-2254	57 Dauncey Street	$80
Ellson's Seaview Motel	3	8	08-8553-2030	Chapman Terrace	$65

(ii) Hotel Accommodation in Penneshaw

Name	Stars	No. on Map	Telephone No.	Address	Lowest Price (Double/Twin)
Dolphins Lookout	4	16	08-8373-2955	Lot 83, South Terrace	$265
Kangaroo Island Seafront	3	13	08-8553-1028	49 North Terrace	$165
Seaview Lodge	4½	11	08-8553-1132	Willoughby Road	$155
Sheoaks Penneshaw	4	18	08-8332-7656	Lot 13, Trethewey Terrace	$145
Currawong	4	17	08-8332-5982	Lot 7, South Terrace	$125
Penneshaw Beach House	3½	14	08-8559-6129	131 Flinders Terrace	$115
Hideaway	3½	12	08-8553-1230	Christmas Street	$100
Log Cabin		15	08-8553-1267	Lot 2, South Terrace	$85

(iii) Accommodation within National Parks

Name	Stars	No. on Map	Telephone No.	Address	Lowest Price (Double/Twin)
Lighthouse Cottages		21	08-8559-7235	Cape du Couedic	$125
Lighthouse Cottages		22	08-8559-7235	Cape Willoughby	$85
Cottages		20	08-8559-7235	Rocky River	$42
Lighthouse Cottages		19	08-8559-7235	Cape Borda	$28

(iv) Backpackers Hostels on Kangaroo Island

Name	Group	No. on Map	Telephone No.	Address	Lowest Price (Dormitory)
Cottages		20	08-8559-7235	Rocky River	$21
Penneshaw Hostel	VIP	23	1800-686-620	43 North Terrace, Penneshaw	$19
Penguin Walk Y.H.A.	YHA	24	1800-018-484	33 Middle Terrace, Penneshaw	$18
Lighthouse Cottages		21	08-8559-7235	Cape Borda	$14

MOVING ON

Buses leave Kingscote for Penneshaw at 7:00 and 17:30. Ferries depart from Penneshaw for Cape Jervis at 8:30, 10:30 and 19:30 (and at other times in peak season). Buses depart from Cape Jervis for Adelaide at 9:40 and 20:30, arriving at 11:30 and 22:30. There is also a bus service from Cape Jervis to Victor Harbor and Goolwa at 20:30.

VICTOR HARBOR AND GOOLWA

Population 10,000 (Victor Harbor)
Population 3,000 (Goolwa)

2 hrs by bus from Adelaide

Victor Harbor and Goolwa lie approximately two hours south of Adelaide and one of the great attractions of the towns is the *Cockle Train* which runs between them, one of the very first railways to be constructed in Australia.

The *Steamranger Company*, part of the Australian Railway Historical Society, used to run a train on most Sundays from Adelaide to Victor Harbor, an enjoyable journey. The train used to climb out of Adelaide along the main line to Melbourne as far as Mt. Barker Junction and then diverge to Goolwa and on to Victor Harbor. Operation of the service was prevented, however, by the conversion of the main line to standard gauge in 1995, for this is a broad gauge train. Although the Adelaide suburban trains run on broad gauge track, the suburban service finishes at Belair and there is no longer any broad gauge track between Belair and Mt. Barker Junction. *Steamranger* now operates one train per month in the winter only between Mt. Barker and Victor Harbor at a cost of $50 return, and just four trains a year between Mt. Barker and Mt. Barker Junction at a cost of $7 return. However, the *Cockle Train* between Goolwa and Victor Harbor continues to operate every Sunday and daily during school holidays.

The *Cockle Train* is usually steam hauled, although a diesel locomotive or a railcar is used during slack periods. The journey covers a distance of eighteen kilometres each

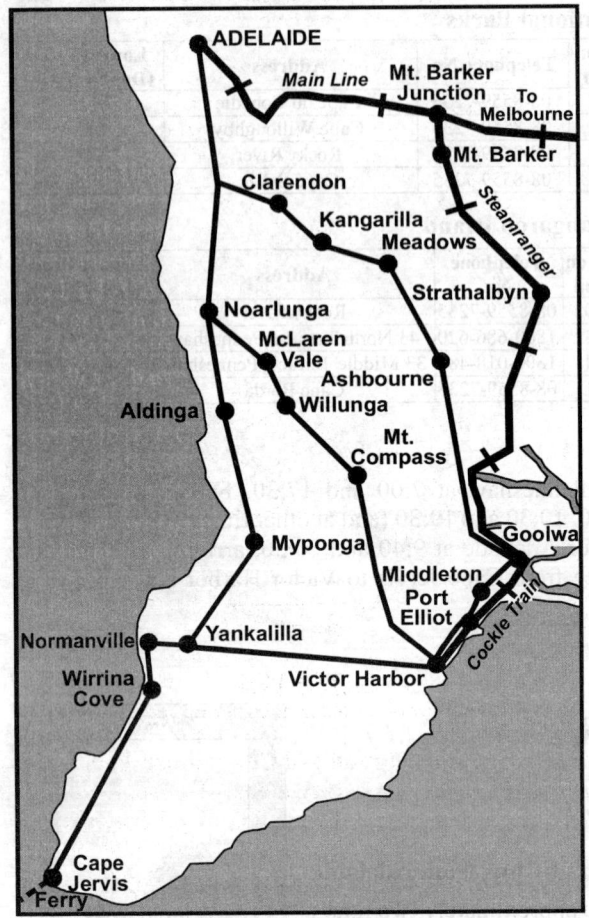

FLEURIEU PENINSULA
Showing public transport and *Steamranger* routes

way and takes half an hour, with the train running beside the sea for much of the trip. The single fare is $14 and the return journey costs $20. The *Cockle Train* has been so known since 1887, because the beaches beside which it operates are famous for their cockles which are gathered at low tide.

Captain Sturt discovered the mouth of the Murray, where Goolwa is now situated, in 1830 and realised the difficulties of navigating the river because of the sand bar at its mouth. However, the first successful navigation was made in 1838 and Goolwa was established in 1840. The name came from the local aboriginal language and seems to mean 'elbow'. A plan to build a railway or a canal from Goolwa to Port Elliot was first mooted in 1850, but was originally rejected. Soon, however, the discovery of gold in northern Victoria increased traffic on the Murray and work on the railway began in 1852. The first train operated in 1854, and claims to have been the very first steel rail service in Australia. At that time, though, there was no locomotive and the train was horse-drawn. The railway was used to transfer goods between ocean-going vessels berthing in Port Elliot and river steamers plying from Goolwa up the Murray. However, it was soon realised that Port Elliot was a difficult harbour to enter and a series of shipwrecks resulted in a switch to Victor Harbor, so the railway line, still operated by horse power, was extended to there in 1864.

In 1869, a line was built from Goolwa to Strathalbyn. This line was operated by steam power, but horses remained in service between Goolwa and Victor Harbor until 1884. Although the river trade increased and Goolwa thrived and became a ship-building town, the railway never achieved the success which had been envisaged for it. Both it and the town of Goolwa started to decline in the 1880s when the Victorian railways extended to the Murray and goods could be shipped more easily by that colony's own rail system.

However, Goolwa has survived and has become a tourist destination in recent years. The railway, though, would have died but for its adoption in 1984 by *Steamranger*.

Sights to see in **Goolwa** include the recently constructed and somewhat controversial **bridge** across to Hindmarsh Island (controversial because it destroyed aboriginal sacred sites), as well as the **Signal Point Interpretive Centre**, where the **Information Centre** is also located. The Centre tells the story of the Murray-Darling River System, the longest in Australia, and is open daily from 10:00 until 17:00. There are **cruises** available up the Murray on board the *River Murray Queen*, a modern-day paddle steamer built in 1974. The old **Blacksmith's Forge** has been converted into a Museum and the **Police Station** and **Courthouse**, built in the 1860s, have been preserved, as has the **Railway Superintendent's House**, the oldest building in the town, dating from 1852. There are several art and craft galleries and the **Wharf Markets**, held on the first and third Sundays of every month sell local art and craft products.

At the other end of the railway line, **Victor Harbor** has an old double-decker **horse-drawn tram** across to **Granite Island**, where there is a good lookout and the **Penguin Centre** providing information on the Fairy Penguins which live on the island. In the sea just off the island is the **Below Decks Aquarium** and in the town of Victor Harbor is the **Encounter Coast Discovery Centre**. Since Victor Harbor is a former whaling town, it is appropriate

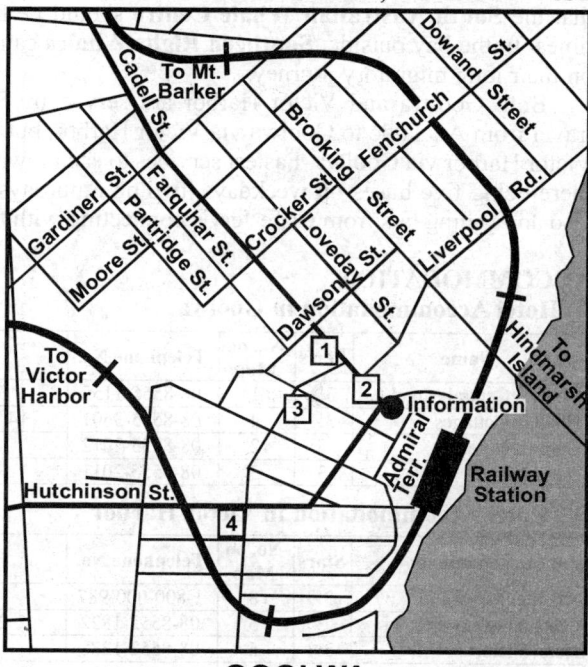

GOOLWA
Numerals indicate accommodation

VICTOR HARBOR
Numerals indicate accommodation

652 SOUTH AUSTRALIA

that the **South Australian Whale Centre** should be here, offering relics of whaling times. In the bay outside, **Southern Right Whales** can often be seen in winter resting on their long migratory journey.

Both Goolwa and Victor Harbor are served by Stateliner buses. Most services travel from Adelaide to Goolwa via Victor Harbor, but one bus on weekdays travels to Victor Harbor via Goolwa. Fastest services to each town take approximately two hours, there being five buses on weekdays, two on Saturdays and one on Sundays. There is also an evening bus from Cape Jervis connecting with the ferry from Kangaroo Island.

ACCOMMODATION
(i) Hotel Accommodation in Goolwa

Name	Stars	No. on Map	Telephone No.	Address	Lowest Price (Double/Twin)
Goolwa Central Motel	3½	1	08-8555-1155	30 Cadell Street	$120
Holiday Cottages	3½	4	08-8555-3601	14 Hutchinson Street	$120
Goolwa Hotel	3	2	08-8555-2012	7 Cadell Street	$75
Corio Hotel	3	3	08-8555-2011	Railway Terrace	$55

(ii) Hotel Accommodation in Victor Harbor

Name	Stars	No. on Map	Telephone No.	Address	Lowest Price (Double/Twin)
Apollon Motor Inn	3½	8	1-800-000-987	15 Torrens Street	$110
Colonial Motor Inn	3	5	08-8552-1822	2 Victoria Street	$85
Hotel Victor	3½	6	08-8552-1288	Albert Place	$85
Kerjancia Motor Lodge	3	10	08-8552-2900	141 Hindmarsh Road	$80
City Motel	3	7	08-8552-2455	51 Ocean Street	$75
Wintersun Motel	3	9	08-8552-3533	119 Hindmarsh Road	$75

(iii) Backpackers Hostels in Goolwa and Port Elliot

Name	Group	Telephone No.	Address	Lowest Price (Dormitory)
P.S. Murray River Queen	VIP	08-8555-1733	The Wharf, Goolwa	$26
Arnella by the Sea	YHA	08-8554-3611	28 North Terrace, Port Elliot	$22

MOVING ON
Bus Services from Goolwa and Victor Harbor

Destination	Operator	Via	Distance (km)	Fare	Journey Time	Frequency
Adelaide	Stateliner		83	$16.40	2 - 2½ hrs	5/day
Cape Jervis	Sealink		60 - 72	$15	1½ - 2 hrs	1/day

BAROSSA VALLEY

Population 3,500 (Nuriootpa)
Population 4,000 (Tanunda)
Population 2,000 (Angaston)

1 hr 30 mins by bus from Adelaide

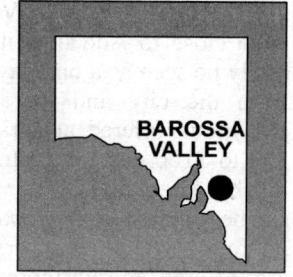

The Barossa Valley is the most famous place in Australia for wine. The valley was first settled by Europeans in 1842, most of the settlers arriving from Prussia and Silesia to escape religious persecution. They brought with them a love of wine and a knowledge of how to grow vines and produce their favourite beverages, so the Barossa Valley became one of the first wine-growing areas in the country, and the most successful. It is only in recent years that the supremacy of the region has experienced any serious challenge, but it remains the most popular tourist destination with those seeking alcoholic refreshment.

There are several small towns in the Valley, the principal of which is **Nuriootpa**, just off the main Sturt Highway leading to Sydney. To the south-west of Nuriootpa lies **Tanunda**, while **Angaston** is to the south-east of Nuriootpa. Accommodation is readily available in these three locations, much of it rather up-market.

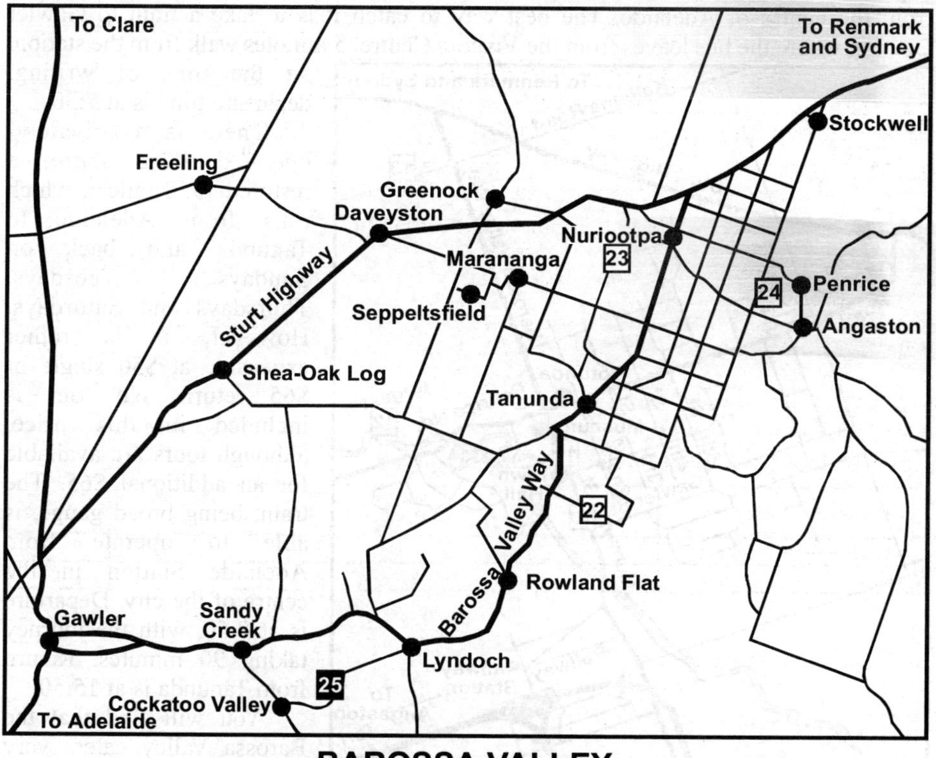

BAROSSA VALLEY
Black numerals in white boxes indicate hotel accommodation
White numerals in black boxes indicate backpackers hostels

Because the Barossa Valley is so close to Adelaide, it can easily be seen as a one-day trip from the city and there are many tours offered, at a price of $50 to $100, usually including lunch. Alternatively, the area can be used as a stop *en route* to or from Adelaide. Bus services are offered to Nuriootpa by McCafferty's and Stateliner, while Barossa Adelaide Passenger Service operates to Tanunda, Nuriootpa and Angaston. It should be noted, however, that the morning service provided by Barossa Adelaide Passenger Service departs from Evanston, not from the centre of Adelaide. The best way to catch it is to take a train to Gawler Central, where the bus leaves from the Visitors Centre, 5 minutes walk from the station.

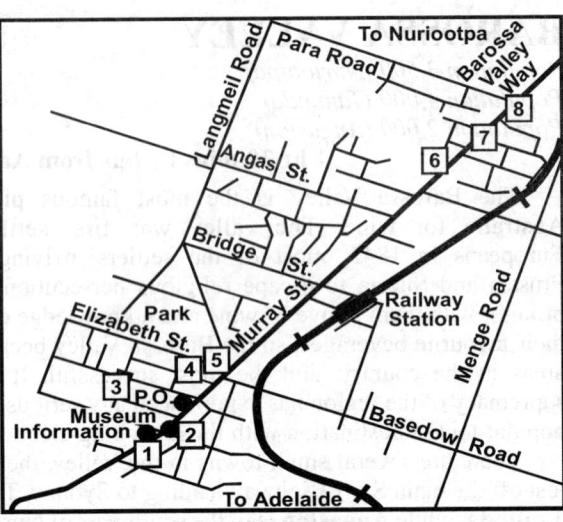

TANUNDA
Numerals indicate accommodation

At the time of writing, departure time is at 7:30.

There is a privately-operated *Wine Train*, a restored 1952 railcar, which runs from Adelaide to Tanunda and back on Sundays, Tuesdays, Thursdays and Saturdays. However, it is rather expensive at $50 single or $65 return. No tour is included in this price, although tours are available for an additional $65. The train, being broad gauge, is able to operate from Adelaide Station in the centre of the city. Departure is at 8:50, with the journey taking 90 minutes. Return from Tanunda is at 15:50.

You will find that the Barossa Valley caters very much for tourists, with the streets of the small towns lined with restaurants,

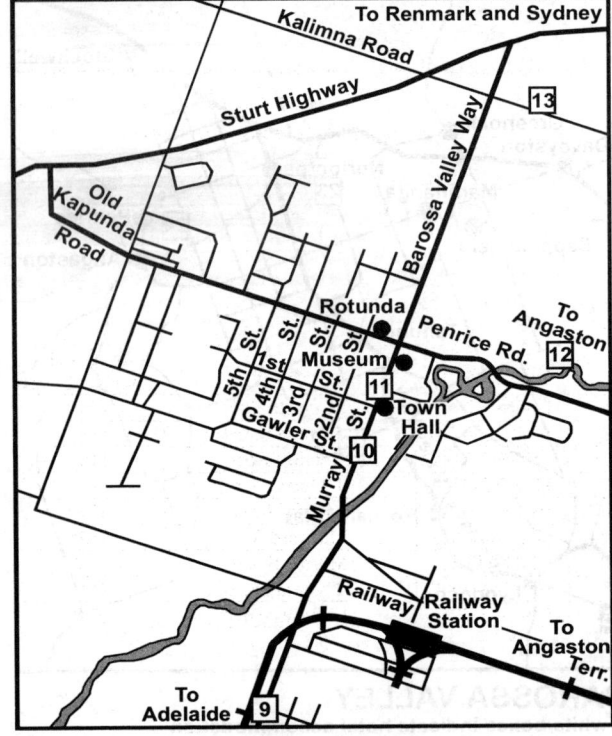

NURIOOTPA
Numerals indicate accommodation

souvenir shops, homely accommodation and, of course, stores selling wine. Some of the wineries are accessible on foot from the towns, but most require transport. About half of the fifty local producers lie along the road used by the Barossa Adelaide Passenger Service bus, so can be reached by that means of transport.

ACCOMMODATION

Accommodation is listed for the main towns of Tanunda, Nuriootpa and Angaston. Although much of the accommodation is relatively expensive, there are also traditional old-style hotels with moderate prices in the towns. For backpackers, there are two choices. Bunkhaus Travellers Lodge is approximately 1.5 kilometres south of Nuriootpa, while the youth hostel is on the edge of Sandy Creek Conservation Park and is not near any of the main towns. However, it is still near some of the wineries. Note that it is unstaffed and that bookings are made through the Y.H.A. in Adelaide, from where a key must be obtained before setting out.

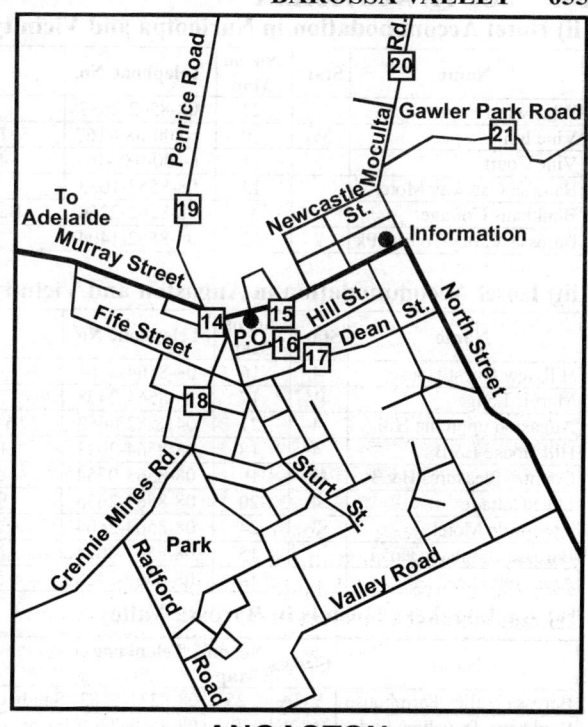

ANGASTON
Numerals indicate accommodation

(i) Hotel Accommodation in Tanunda and Vicinity

Name	Stars	No. on Map	Telephone No.	Address	Lowest Price (Double/Twin)
Jewel of the Valley	4½	5	1-800-227-677	1 Elizabeth Street	$430
Five Chimneys		3	08-8563-0240	15 Maria Street	$165
Lawley Farm	4½	22	08-8563-2141	Krondorf Road	$160
Tanunda Cottages	3	7	08-8563-0554	191 Murray Street	$155
Byhurst	4	4	08-8333-0010	3 Julius Street	$150
Dove Cote	3½	2	0417-841-623	13 Edward Street	$135
Barossa Weintal Resort	4	8	1-800-648-269	Murray Street	$120
Barossa Motor Lodge	3½	6	08-8563-2988	182 Murray Street	$110
Tanunda Hotel	2	1	08-8563-2030	51 Murray Street	$70

656 SOUTH AUSTRALIA

(ii) Hotel Accommodation in Nuriootpa and Vicinity

Name	Stars	No. on Map	Telephone No.	Address	Lowest Price (Double/Twin)
Whirlwind Farm	4½	23	08-8562-2637	Samuel Road	$135
Vine Inn	3½	10	1-800-088-167	14 Murray Street	$115
Vine Court	3	11	1-800-088-167	49 Murray Street	$95
Barossa Gateway Motel		13	08-8562-1033	Kalimna Road	$60
Bunkhaus Cottage		9	08-8562-2260	Barossa Valley Way	$50
Barossa Valley Tourist Pk	2	12	08-8562-1404	Penrice Road	$36

(iii) Hotel Accommodation in Angaston and Vicinity

Name	Stars	No. on Map	Telephone No.	Address	Lowest Price (Double/Twin)
Hillview Guest House	4	16	08-8564-2761	12 Hill Street	$420
Marble Lodge	4½	17	08-8564-2478	21 Dean Street	$195
Angaston upon the Hill	4	21	0418-828-663	16 Gawler Park Road	$180
Hill House B&B	4	18	08-8564-2023	12 Lindsay Street	$180
Country Pleasures B&B	4½	19	08-8563-0754	54 Penrice Road	$165
Lilac Cottage	4	20	08-8564-2635	93 Moculta Road	$155
Vineyards Motel	3	24	08-8564-2404	Stockwell Road	$65
Barossa Brauhaus Hotel		15	08-8564-2014	41 Murray Street	$55
Angaston Hotel		14	08-8564-2428	59 Murray Street	$55

(iv) Backpackers Hostels in Barossa Valley

Name	Group	No. on Map	Telephone No.	Address	Lowest Price (Dormitory)
Barossa Valley Farmhouse	YHA	25	08-8231-5583	Sandy Creek Conservation Pk.	$19
Bunkhaus Travellers Lodge	B&W	9	08-8562-2260	Barossa Valley Way, Nuriootpa	$17

MOVING ON
Bus Services from Nuriootpa

Destination	Operator	Via	Distance (km)	Fare	Journey Time	Frequency
Sydney	McCafferty's		1410	$141	23¼ hrs	1/day
		Canberra	1196	$141	18 hrs	1/day
		Mildura	337	$33	5¾ hrs	1/day
Adelaide	McCafferty's		60	$26	1½ hrs	1/day
Adelaide	Stateliner		75	$7.80	1¼ - 1½ hrs	2/day
Adelaide	Barossa		75	$14.90	1½ - 1¾ hrs	4/day
Renmark	Stateliner		178	$34.10	2¾ hrs	2/day
Angaston	Barossa		30	$4	1¾ - 2 hrs	2/day

RENMARK
Population 8,000

4 hrs by bus from Adelaide

Renmark is the principal town of those strung out along the Murray River in South Australia. These are pleasant little places and Renmark itself is rather like a smaller version of nearby Mildura in Victoria.

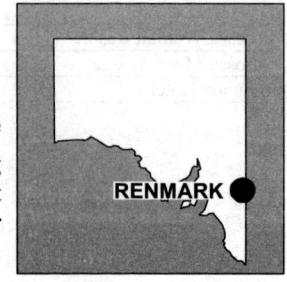

RENMARK

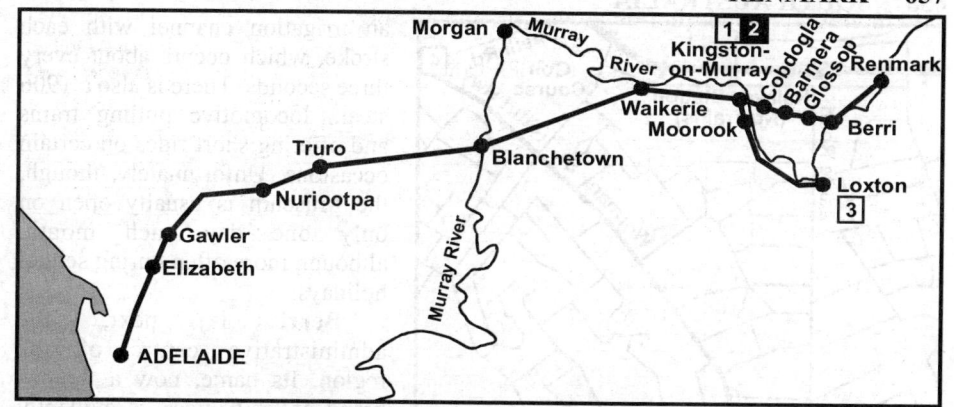

ADELAIDE TO RENMARK
Showing Stateliner Bus Route
Black numerals in white boxes indicate hotel accommodation
White numerals in black boxes indicate backpackers hostels

Wine growing continues into this area and now 45% of the state's wine-making grapes are produced in the region, together with 90% of its citrus fruits and nuts. In this dry state, water is a valuable commodity and here it is found in abundance. The river itself used to be a vital means of transport, but, although it is still navigable, its commercial use has largely been superseded and most vessels these days are recreational, unfortunately.

Bus services to here from Adelaide are operated by McCafferty's and by Stateliner. The McCafferty's service continues to and from Sydney via Canberra and operates once daily. Stateliner runs twice every day except Saturday, when there is only one service.

Travelling on the bus, the first of the Murray River towns encountered is **Blanchetown**, just over two hours from Adelaide. Eleven kilometres before the town, and adjacent to the Sturt Highway, is **Brookfield Conservation Park**, covering 5,500 hectares. It is home to various types of native Australian wildlife. The Park is open at all times, without admission charge.

North of Blanchetown, but not on a public transport route, is **Morgan**. This is an interesting little town, one of the most successful in the modern history of the Murray River. The **Port of Morgan Riverside Museum** gives a glimpse of how the town used to be when in its prime as an inland port and railway transfer point a century ago. The Museum is open only on Tuesdays, Saturdays and Sundays from 14:00 until 16:00. Admission costs $3.

The road crosses the Murray River at Blanchetown, continuing to its south and then rejoining its course at **Waikerie** and following it to **Kingston-on-Murray**. There is a backpackers hostel in Kingston-on-Murray, and there is also a connecting Stateliner bus from here to **Loxton** in the evenings. The return connexion is with the morning service to Adelaide.

Loxton Historical Village has won several awards for its attempts to depict rural life in the period of the 1890s to the 1930s. The Village is open daily from 10:00 until 16:00 (17:00 at weekends), and admission costs $10.

Cobdogla, just beyond Kingston-on-Murray, has an interesting **Irrigation and Steam Museum**. Its Humphrey Pump delivers approximately five tonnes of water into

658 SOUTH AUSTRALIA

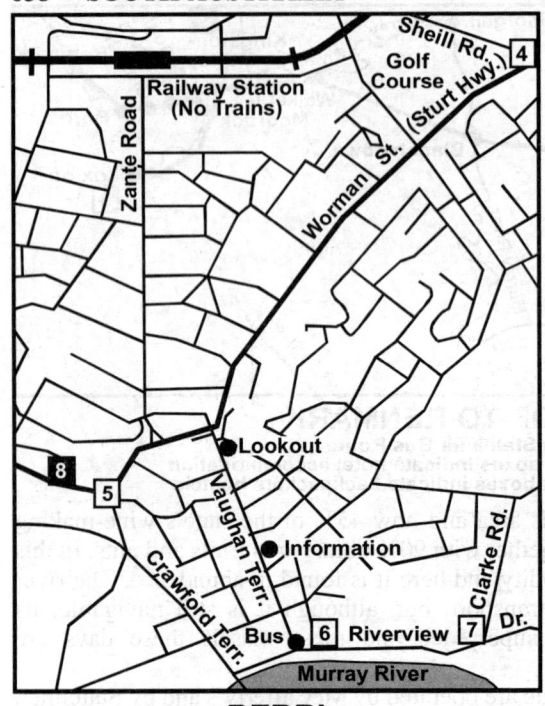

BERRI
Black numerals indicate hotel accommodation
White numerals indicate backpackers hostels

an irrigation channel with each stroke, which occurs about every three seconds. There is also a 1906 steam locomotive pulling trains and offering short rides on certain occasions. Unfortunately, though, the Museum is usually open on only one day each month, although more often during school holidays.

Berri is next, the administrative centre of the region. Its name, now a famous brand of fruit juices, is evidently derived from the words 'berri berri' in the local aboriginal language, meaning 'big bends in the river'. Berri Estate, nearby, claims to be the largest winery in the southern hemisphere. The Big Orange, on the Old Sturt Highway, is a sales point for local produce, and is also, indeed, a big orange. There is a panorama painted by a local artist and there is a viewing balcony on the top, for using which a fee of $1 is charged.

Closer to the town centre is the Berri Lookout Tower, converted from a former water tower. Moreover the view from here is free.

The **Wilabalangaloo Reserve** is four kilometres from Berri, on the way to Renmark. It has an old homestead with a museum containing photographs and relics of by-gone days, some old rivercraft and a walk beside the Murray. The Reserve is open from 10:00 until 16:00, except on Tuesdays and Wednesdays. Admission costs $5.

There is a backpackers hostel in Berri, in addition to other types of accommodation.

Renmark is the terminus for the Stateliner bus and the last town in South Australia along the Sturt Highway. Its name in the local aboriginal language evidently means 'red mud'. The Renmark Irrigation Settlement was established in 1887 by the Chaffey Brothers who were Canadians and who, by developing a system of irrigation, were able to open up for agricultural use what had previously been regarded as waste land. Now Renmark is a modern town with a sizeable commercial centre.

It has a number of wineries nearby which can be visited. Angove's, for example, established in 1886 and established in Renmark in 1910, is still a family business and is the producer of Australia's best-selling brandy, *St. Agnes*.

Olivewood was the home of one of those Chaffey Brothers, Charles Chaffey. It was built of pine logs in 1889 and is now a small museum. Located on the corner of Twenty-first Street, it is open from 10:00 until 16:00, except on Tuesdays, when it is open from 14:00 until 16:00, and Wednesdays, when it is closed. Admission costs $5.

RENMARK

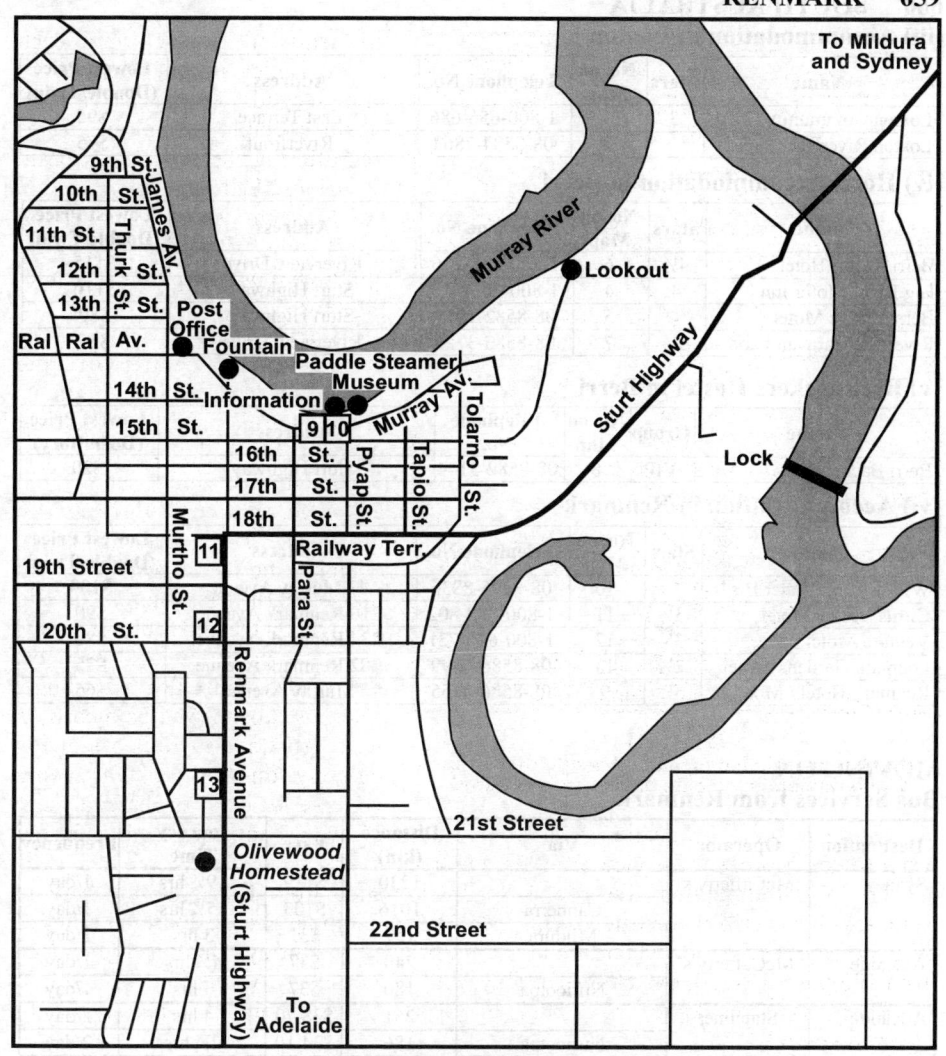

RENMARK
Numerals indicate accommodation

ACCOMMODATION
(i) Hotel Accommodation in Kingston-on Murray

Name	Stars	No. on Map	Telephone No.	Address	Lowest Price (Double/Twin)
Caravan Park Cabins	3	1	08-8583-0209	River Terrace	$60

(ii) Backpackers Hostel in Kingston-on-Murray

Name	Group	No. on Map	Telephone No.	Address	Lowest Price (Dormitory)
Nomads on Murray	Nom	2	1800-737-378	Sturt Highway	$19

660 SOUTH AUSTRALIA

(iii) Accommodation in Loxton

Name	Stars	No. on Map	Telephone No.	Address	Lowest Price (Double/Twin)
Loxton Community Hotel	3	3	1-800-656-686	East Terrace	$95
Loxton Riverfront Park		3	08-8584-7862	Riverfront	$75

(iv) Hotel Accommodation in Berri

Name	Stars	No. on Map	Telephone No.	Address	Lowest Price (Double/Twin)
Berri Resort Hotel	4½	6	1-800-088-226	Riverview Drive	$115
Big River Motor Inn	4	4	1-800-801-516	Sturt Highway	$110
Berri Bridge Motel		5	08-8582-1011	Sturt Highway	$80
Riverside Caravan Park	3½	7	08-8582-3523	Riverview Drive	$65

(v) Backpackers Hostel in Berri

Name	Group	No. on Map	Telephone No.	Address	Lowest Price (Dormitory)
Berri Backpackers	VIP	8	08-8582-3144	Sturt Highway	$20

(vi) Accommodation in Renmark

Name	Stars	No. on Map	Telephone No.	Address	Lowest Price (Double/Twin)
Willows and Water Birds		10	08-8295-8836	41 Murray Avenue	$100
Citrus Valley Motel	3½	11	1-800-088-802	210 Renmark Avenue	$90
Ventura Motel	3½	12	1-800-626-721	234 Renmark Avenue	$80
Fountain Gardens Motel	2½	13	08-8586-6899	282 Renmark Avenue	$75
Renmark Hotel / Motel	3½	9	08-8586-6755	Murray Avenue	$65

MOVING ON
Bus Services from Renmark

Destination	Operator	Via	Distance (km)	Fare	Journey Time	Frequency
Sydney	McCafferty's		1230	$119	19½ hrs	1/day
		Canberra	1016	$103	15¼ hrs	1/day
		Mildura	157	$31	3 hrs	1/day
Adelaide	McCafferty's		240	$37	4¼ hrs	1/day
		Nuriootpa	180	$37	3 hrs	1/day
Adelaide	Stateliner		261	$38.70	4 hrs	2/day
		Nuriootpa	186	$34.10	2¾ hrs	2/day

YORKE PENINSULA

Populations: Wallaroo 2,500
Moonta 2,500
Kadina 4,000

2 hrs 45 mins by bus from Adelaide (Moonta)

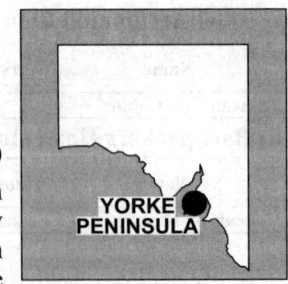

North-west of Adelaide lies the Yorke Peninsula, which is worth exploring if you have spare time. It is relatively easily accessible by bus and has the merit that it is not on the itinerary of most visitors. Especially attractive are the

YORKE PENINSULA

towns of Wallaroo, Moonta and Kadina, all with strong Cornish roots due to the background of copper mining here, and the Innes National Park at the very tip of the peninsula (see map on page 665).

Wallaroo is 160 kilometres from Adelaide and is served by Stateliner twice a day on weekdays and once a day at weekends. The journey takes 2½ hours and costs $21. For South Australians, this is a popular holiday destination. It has a safe swimming beach, a marina which is a tourist attraction in itself, and good fishing opportunities. The town was established in 1860, named after nearby Wallaroo Station, and a smelting works was set up in 1861 to process the copper which had been discovered at nearby Kadina. The jetty was constructed in 1861 and a tramway built to Kadina, and the port became one of the busiest in the state, and continues so today, although nowadays it is mainly wheat which is shipped. There is a **Nautical and Maritime Museum** of interest, housed in the Old Post Office, built in 1865. The Museum is open on Wednesdays, Thursdays, Saturdays and Sundays from 14:00 until 16:00. At busy times, such as school holidays, it opens earlier. Admission costs $5.

Moonta has a beautiful old **railway station**, but, of course, no passenger trains. The station now houses the regional **Tourist Office** and a free display of old photographs. Access is by Stateliner bus, which operates twice a day on weekdays and once a day at weekends. The journey takes 2¾ hours and costs $21. The town was originally known as Tiparra, until its history was changed by the discovery in 1861, by a shepherd, of large deposits of copper. It soon became one of the richest copper mines in Australia and attracted an influx of miners from Cornwall. The underground mines

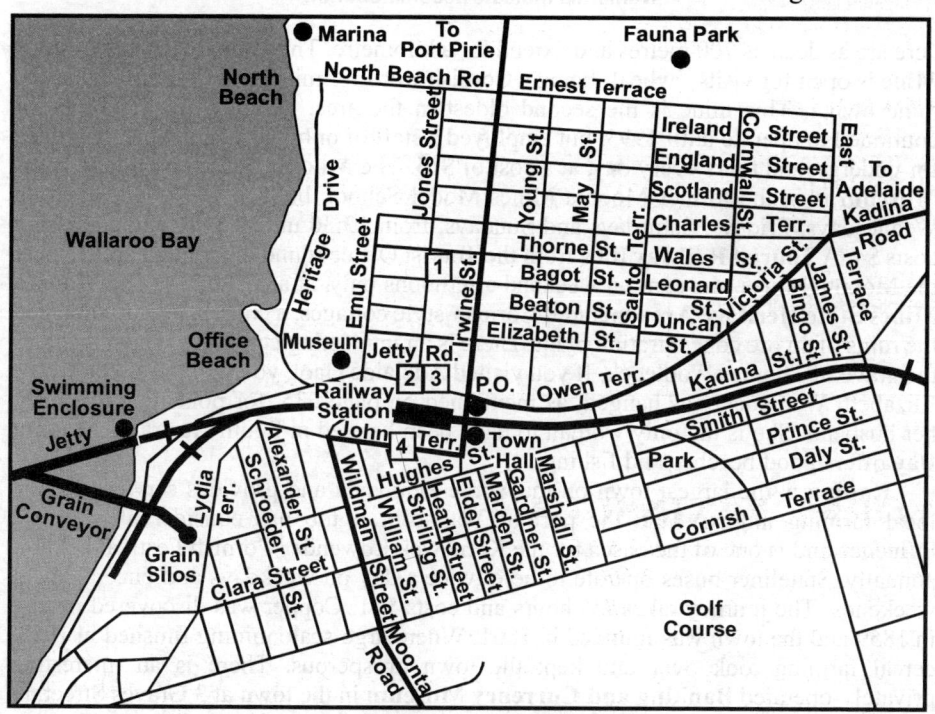

WALLAROO
Numerals indicate accommodation

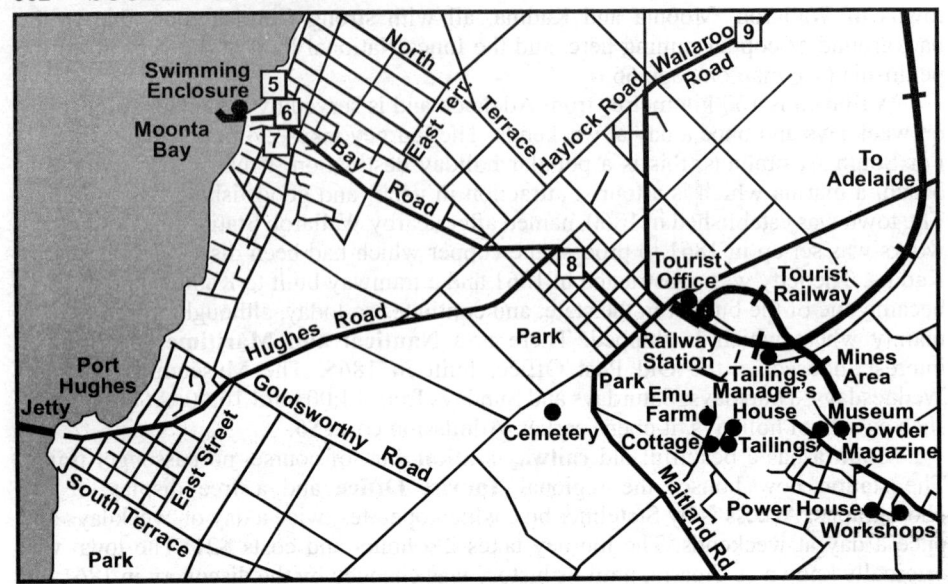

MOONTA
Numerals indicate accommodation

here are as deep as 700 metres and extend for a kilometre. The **Wheal Hughes Copper Mine** is open for visits, 'wheal' being a Cornish word for mine, and Walter Hughes the mine owner. This mine is the second oldest in the area, dating from the 1860s. It continued to operate until 1993, but employed a staff of only thirteen people. It is open for underground tours every day, at a cost of $15. The **Moonta Mines National Trust Museum** is in the former Moonta Mines Model School, built in 1878. It is open on Wednesdays, Fridays, Saturdays and Sundays, from 13:30 until 16:00, and admission costs $4. A **Tourist Railway** runs from the Tourist Office round the mining area to near the Moonta Mines Museum on weekend afternoons only, at a cost of $4. The **Moonta Mines State Heritage Area** includes Cornish-style cottages, a church, a mine shaft and the ruins of an ore concentration plant. There is an interesting **cemetery** which includes the grave of Thomas Woolcock. If you visited Adelaide Gaol, you will have seen where Elizabeth Woolcock was hanged, as mentioned on page 635, for poisoning this man, her husband. She is the only woman to have been hanged in South Australia. **Moonta Bay** offers good beaches and fishing.

Kadina is the largest town on the Yorke Peninsula and provides services for the local farming industry and the port of Wallaroo. It too has considerable Cornish influence and is one of the bases for the Kernewek Lowender Cornish Festival held bi-annually. Stateliner buses operate to here twice a day on weekdays and once a day at weekends. The journey takes 2¼ hours and costs $21. Copper was discovered nearby in 1859 and the town was founded in 1861. When large-scale mining finished in 1923, cereal farming took over and kept the town prosperous. There is an interesting privately-operated **Banking and Currency Museum** in the town at 3 Graves Street, in the 1873 Bank of South Australia building. The Museum is open on Sundays to Thursdays from 10:00 until 16:30 and admission costs $4.

YORKE PENINSULA

The problem with the **Innes National Park** is that there is no public transport reaching this far. The nearest town with a bus service is Warooka and that is approximately sixty kilometres distant. Yorke Peninsula coaches operates to Warooka on Tuesday, Thursday and Friday evenings only. The journey takes four hours. Return services to Adelaide depart from Warooka on Tuesday and Thursday mornings, and on Sunday afternoons. There are, however, services from Adelaide to Yorketown, 21 kilometres further distant from the National Park, every day except some Saturdays. Innes National Park was declared in 1970, mainly because of the rediscovery there of the Great Western Whipbird in 1962. The park covers 9,141 hectares and offers impressive coastal scenery. It was named after William Innes, who discovered gypsum here in the 1890s, resulting in the founding of the town of Inneston. A horse-drawn tramway from the mines there used to convey the gypsum seven kilometres to Stenhouse Bay for shipment. The National Park offers surfing, fishing, diving, snorkelling, bushwalking, whale watching and birdwatching. There are more than forty shipwrecks lying off the coast here, which makes the Park particularly popular with divers. Accommodation is available within the Park at **Inneston, Shell Beach** and **Stenhouse Bay**. Prices depend on the number of guests and the season, but some of the accommodation is very reasonable in price. Bring your own sleeping bag and telephone 08-8854-3200 for reservations. Camping facilities are available also, at a charge of $4 per head.

Now here are brief details of some other small towns on the Yorke Peninsula which are worth a visit, time permitting.

Ardrossan is on the eastern side of the peninsula, 150 kilometres from Adelaide. The town was founded in 1873 and was named by Governor Fergusson after the town in Scotland. It is a prosperous port handling both grain and dolomite, the latter being mined nearby by the huge Broken Hill Proprietary (B.H.P.) Company. The 74 metre grain elevator here is the largest in South Australia. The wreck of the *Zanoni* lies ten nautical miles south-east of the town and is very popular with divers, being the best

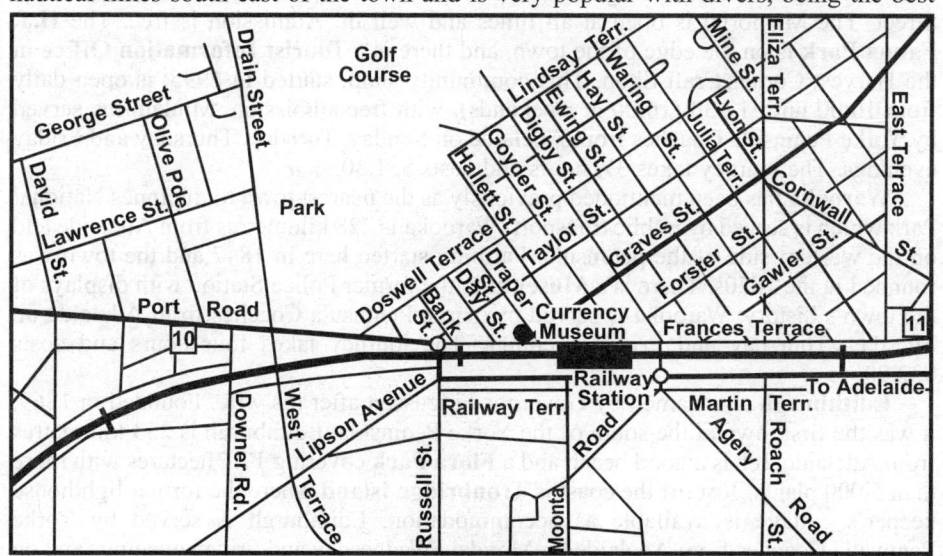

KADINA
Numerals indicate accommodation

preserved merchant vessel wrecked in South Australia. The 338 ton barque was built in Liverpool in 1865 and wrecked here by a violent storm in February 1867. However, what Ardrossan is best-known for is the invention of the *Stump-Jump Plough*. This device did exactly as its name suggests, and was able to pass over roots and stumps remaining in agricultural land after the felling of trees. Although simple in operation, it was of incalculable benefit to struggling farmers and was one of the most important Australian agricultural inventions ever made. At Ardrossan there is a **Museum** where this contribution by the Smith Brothers to the agricultural success of the nation is the main focus and where there are also items salvaged from the *Zanoni*. The Museum is in the Powerhouse Factory where the *Stump-Jump Ploughs* were manufactured. Unfortunately, though, it is open only from 14:30 until 16:30 on Sundays and public holidays. Admission costs $2. Ardrossan is served by Yorke Peninsula Coaches from Adelaide every evening except some Saturdays. The journey takes 2½ hours and costs $25.20.

Port Victoria is on the western side of the peninsula, almost opposite Ardrossan. It is known for being the home of the **windjammers**, the last of which, the *Pamir*, continued to operate from here until 1949. **The National Trust Museum** has a collection of photographs of this time and the streets are named in honour of the various windjammers based here. **Wardang Island** lies off the coast, with eight shipwrecks around it, making it another popular location for diving. There is also a **Geology Trail** along the coast of Port Victoria, with brochures available. Port Victoria is served by Yorke Peninsula Coaches from Adelaide on Tuesday and Thursday evenings only. The journey takes three hours and costs $25.20.

Minlaton, 197 kilometres from Adelaide, is in the middle of the peninsula and is a centre for the barley, wheat and grazing industries. Farming started in the area in 1847, but the town was not founded until 1876. An aviation pioneer, Captain Harry Butler, lived here and flew a small Bristol Fighter monoplane known as the *Red Devil*. That aircraft, manufactured in 1916, is now in the **Harry Butler Memorial** in Main Street. The Memorial is open at all times and well lit. Admission is free. The **H.J. Fauna Park** is on the edge of the town, and there is a **Tourist Information Office** in the Harvest Corner Craft Shop. This community shop, started in 1995, is open daily from 10:00 until 17:30 (16:00 at weekends), with free admission. Minlaton is served by Yorke Peninsula Coaches from Adelaide on Sunday, Tuesday, Thursday and Friday evenings. The journey takes 3½ hours and costs $31.30.

Warooka has been mentioned previously as the nearest town to the Innes National Park which is served by public transport. Warooka is 228 kilometres from Adelaide and on the western side of the peninsula. Farming started here in 1847 and the town was founded in the 1870s. There is a **Museum** in the former Police Station with displays of the town's history. Warooka is served by Yorke Peninsula Coaches from Adelaide on Tuesday, Thursday and Friday evenings. The journey takes four hours and costs $32.80.

Edithburgh was named by Governor Fergusson after his wife. Founded in 1869, it was the first town at the south of the Yorke Peninsula. Edithburgh is 233 kilometres from Adelaide. It has a good beach and a **Flora Park** covering 17.5 hectares with more than 5,000 plants. Just off the coast is **Troubridge Island** where the former lighthouse keeper's cottage is available as accommodation. Edithburgh is served by Yorke Peninsula Coaches from Adelaide on Monday, Wednesday and Friday evenings and on some Saturday afternoons. The journey takes 3¾ hours and costs $32.80.

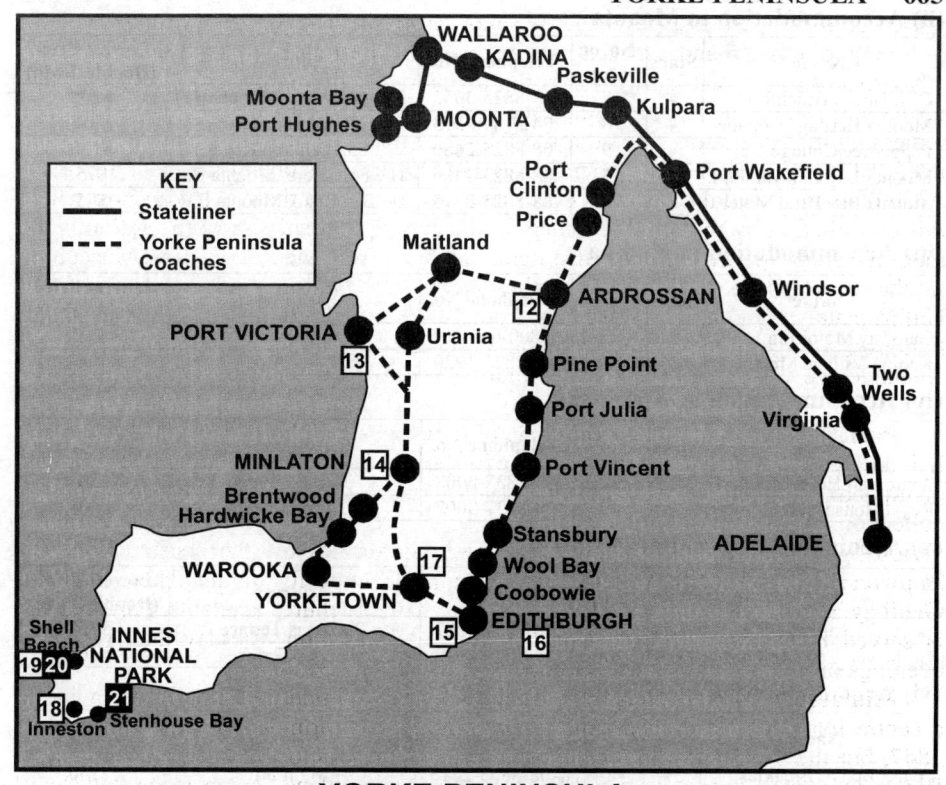

YORKE PENINSULA
Showing bus routes from Adelaide
Black numerals in white boxes indicate hotel accommodation
White numerals in black boxes indicate backpackers hostels

Yorketown is 230 kilometres from Adelaide and is in the centre of the peninsula near its southern point. Its major industry was salt production between the 1890s and the 1930s, but after that time it found itself unable to compete with large-scale manufacturers. The **Old Courthouse** has a collection of photographs of early times here, but is open only on Friday mornings. Yorketown is served by Yorke Peninsula Coaches from Adelaide every day except some Saturdays. The journey takes four hours and costs $32.80.

ACCOMMODATION
(i) Accommodation in Wallaroo

Name	Stars	No. on Map	Telephone No.	Address	Lowest Price (Double/Twin)
Mac's Beachfront Villas	4	3	08-8823-2137	9 Jetty Road	$145
Office Beach Cabins	3½	2	08-8823-2722	11 Jetty Road	$60
Sonbern Lodge Motel	3	4	08-8823-2291	18 John Terrace	$50
Anglers Inn Hotel	2	1	08-8823-2545	9 Bagot Street	$50

666 SOUTH AUSTRALIA

(ii) Accommodation in Moonta

Name	Stars	No. on Map	Telephone No.	Address	Lowest Price (Double/Twin)
Cliff House Beachfront	4	7	08-8825-3055	2 Hughes Av., Moonta Bay	$200
Moonta Heritage Cottage	4	8	0417-890-573	74 George Street	$150
Peppertree Cottage	4	9	08-8825-2680	85 Wallaroo Road	$150
Moonta Bay Caravan Park	3	5	08-8825-2406	The Foreshore, Moonta Bay	$75
Moonta Bay Patio Motel		6	08-8825-2473	96 Bay Road, Moonta Bay	$75

(iii) Accommodation in Kadina

Name	Stars	No. on Map	Telephone No.	Address	Lowest Price (Double/Twin)
Gateway Motor Inn	3	11	1-800-665-005	706 Adelaide Road	$95
Kadina Village Motel	3	10	08-8821-1920	28 Port Road	$95

(iv) Accommodation in Ardrossan

Name	Stars	No. on Map	Telephone No.	Address	Lowest Price (Double/Twin)
Ardrossan Hotel Motel	2	12	08-8837-3008	36 First Street	$70
Royal House Hotel Motel	2½	12	08-8837-3007	1 Fifth Street	$40

(v) Accommodation in Port Victoria

Name	Stars	No. on Map	Telephone No.	Address	Lowest Price (Double/Twin)
Bayview Holiday Flats		13	08-8834-2082	29 Davis Terrace	$75
Gulfhaven Caravan Park	3½	13	08-8834-2012	Davies Terrace	$60

(vi) Accommodation in Minlaton

Name	Stars	No. on Map	Telephone No.	Address	Lowest Price (Double/Twin)
Yurla Bed & Breakfast	3½	14	08-8853-2213	4 Main Street	$130
Minlaton Caravan Park	3	14	08-8853-2435	Bluff & Minlaton Roads	$50

(vii) Accommodation in Edithburgh and on Troubridge Island

Name	Stars	No. on Map	Telephone No.	Address	Lowest Price (Double/Twin)
Edithburgh House	3	15	08-8852-6373	7 Edith Street	$155
Troubridge Is. Hideaway		16	08-8852-6290	Troubridge Island	$150
Edithburgh Seaside Motel	4	15	08-8852-6172	1 Blanche Street	$80
Anchorage Holiday Units	3	15	08-8852-6262	25 O'Halloran Parade	$70
Ocean View Units	2½	15	08-8852-6029	O'Halloran Parade	$50

(viii) Accommodation in Yorketown

Name	Stars	No. on Map	Telephone No.	Address	Lowest Price (Double/Twin)
Melville Hotel / Motel		17	08-8852-1019	1 Minlaton Road	$50

(ix) Hotel Accommodation in Innes National Park

Name	Stars	No. on Map	Telephone No.	Address	Lowest Price (Double/Twin)
Engineers Lodge		18	08-8854-3200	Inneston	$85
Miner's Cottage		18	08-8854-3200	Inneston	$85
Manager's Lodge		18	08-8854-3200	Inneston	$85
Gatehouse Lodge		18	08-8854-3200	Inneston	$70
Norfolk Lodge		18	08-8854-3200	Inneston	$65
Shepherd's Hut		19	08-8854-3200	Shell Beach	$25

(x) Backpackers Hostels in Innes National Park

Name	Group	No. on Map	Telephone No.	Address	Lowest Price (Dormitory)
Shepherd's Hut		20	08-8854-3200	Shell Beach	$25
Activity Centre		21	08-8854-3200	Stenhouse Bay	$16

MOVING ON

Here are timetables for the bus services to the Yorke Peninsula. Buses to Kadina, Wallaroo and Moonta are operated by Stateliner. Services to the towns further south on the peninsula are operated by Yorke Peninsula Coaches. All services depart from the Franklin Street Bus Terminal in Adelaide.

Adelaide to Yorke Peninsula

Days of Operation	M - F	Sat*	Sat	M - F	M,W,F	Tu, Th	F	Sun	Sun
Adelaide	1030	1200	1200	1745	1745	1745	1745	1900	1930
Kadina	1239		1409	1954				2109	
Wallaroo	1253		1423	2008				2123	
Moonta	1307		1437	2022				2137	
Moonta Bay	1320		1450	2035				2150	
Ardrossan		1415			2005	2005	2005		2125
Edithburgh		1550			2125				
Port Victoria					2040				
Minlaton					2110	2110			2225
Warooka					2135	2135			
Yorketown		1600			2140	2145	2145		2245

* School holidays and long weekends only

Yorke Peninsula to Adelaide

Days of Operation	M - Sat	M, W, F	Tu, Th	Sat*	M - Th	Sun	Sun	F
Yorketown		0645	0645	0645			1445	
Warooka			0700				1500	
Minlaton			0735				1535	
Port Victoria			0755					
Edithburgh		0705		0705				
Ardrossan		0840	0840	0840			1640	
Moonta Bay	0645				1345	1500		1700
Moonta	0700				1400	1515		1715
Wallaroo	0715				1415	1530		1730
Kadina	0730				1430	1545		1745
Adelaide	0945	1100	1100	1100	1645	1800	1845	2000

* School holidays and long weekends only

GREAT RAILWAY JOURNEYS

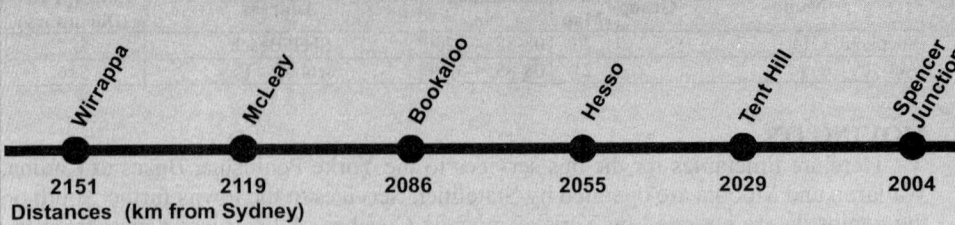

Wirrappa	McLeay	Bookaloo	Hesso	Tent Hill	Spencer Junction
2151	2119	2086	2055	2029	2004

Distances (km from Sydney)

A description of the first part of this journey, from Sydney to Adelaide appears on pages 154 to 158.

After an opportunity for passengers passing through to have a look at the city of Adelaide, the *Indian - Pacific* departs for Perth on Tuesday and Friday evenings. Unfortunately, we leave this city of parklands just as darkness starts to descend and not much will be seen until tomorrow morning.

This section of the route, 2,666 kilometres from Adelaide to Perth, will be quite different in character from the mostly arable lands through which we have passed on our journey from Sydney to Adelaide. Along this section we shall experience real desolation.

For the first 200 kilometres, we are retracing the route followed on the journey into Adelaide from Sydney. We pass through the Dry Creek yards again, then leave the broad gauge suburban railway system behind and travel through a series of small towns. Snowtown has nothing exceptional about its climate. It was named after the batman of the explorer Edward John Eyre, the first European to travel overland from Adelaide to Albany. In 1999, the town achieved notoriety when parts of eight bodies were discovered in the vault of a disused bank here.

Crystal Brook was named because of its clear-flowing stream and is where we rejoin the line from Sydney, having spent eight hours on our detour to Adelaide and back. The triangle will be on the right, as the train turns to the left.

Formerly, the *Indian-Pacific* used to call in at Port Pirie station and connecting passengers from Adelaide would travel up to this point on a broad gauge train and then transfer. Now that the *Indian-Pacific* visits Adelaide along its route, it no longer enters the beautiful Port Pirie station, but stops instead at the tiny siding of Coonamia outside the city. If you look to the left you will be able to see the lights of Port Pirie and particularly the lights on the largest lead smelter in the world operating on the ore brought by rail from Broken Hill. The chimney stretches up 205 metres into the sky.

Port Germain can only be glimpsed on the left. It is famous for having one of the longest jetties in the southern hemisphere, constructed in anticipation of enjoying the benefits of exporting the produce of the farming industry in the region. However, farming failed here because of the unpredictability of rain,

1. THE INDIAN - PACIFIC
PART 2   ADELAIDE TO COOK

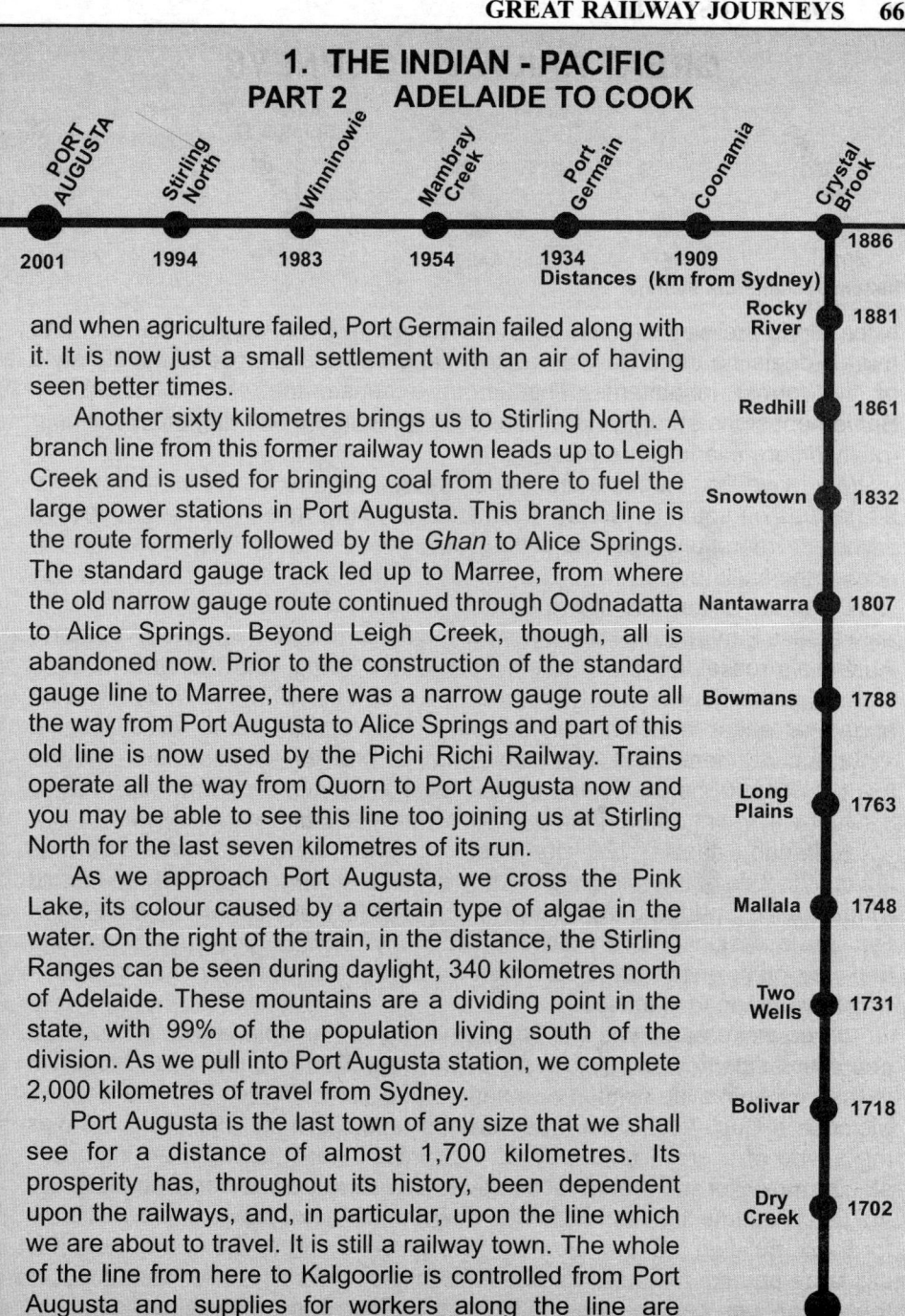

and when agriculture failed, Port Germain failed along with it. It is now just a small settlement with an air of having seen better times.

Another sixty kilometres brings us to Stirling North. A branch line from this former railway town leads up to Leigh Creek and is used for bringing coal from there to fuel the large power stations in Port Augusta. This branch line is the route formerly followed by the *Ghan* to Alice Springs. The standard gauge track led up to Marree, from where the old narrow gauge route continued through Oodnadatta to Alice Springs. Beyond Leigh Creek, though, all is abandoned now. Prior to the construction of the standard gauge line to Marree, there was a narrow gauge route all the way from Port Augusta to Alice Springs and part of this old line is now used by the Pichi Richi Railway. Trains operate all the way from Quorn to Port Augusta now and you may be able to see this line too joining us at Stirling North for the last seven kilometres of its run.

As we approach Port Augusta, we cross the Pink Lake, its colour caused by a certain type of algae in the water. On the right of the train, in the distance, the Stirling Ranges can be seen during daylight, 340 kilometres north of Adelaide. These mountains are a dividing point in the state, with 99% of the population living south of the division. As we pull into Port Augusta station, we complete 2,000 kilometres of travel from Sydney.

Port Augusta is the last town of any size that we shall see for a distance of almost 1,700 kilometres. Its prosperity has, throughout its history, been dependent upon the railways, and, in particular, upon the line which we are about to travel. It is still a railway town. The whole of the line from here to Kalgoorlie is controlled from Port Augusta and supplies for workers along the line are dispatched from here. Our train may even stop once or

SOUTH AUSTRALIA

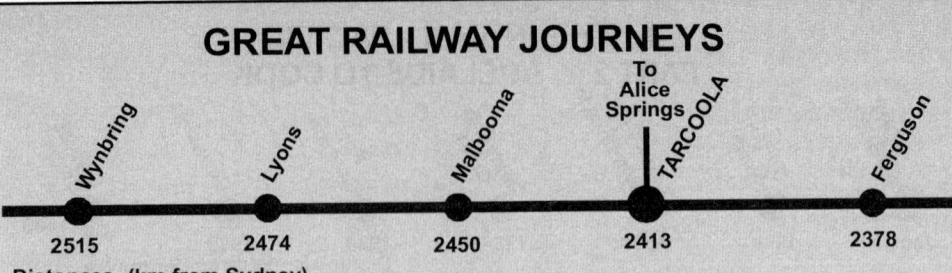

twice along the way to make such deliveries. In Port Augusta one can find murals depicting the history of the town and giving a glimpse of the life style of the former inhabitants. This is, in a sense, the end of civilisation. Settlement stops abruptly here. When we wake in the morning there will be a totally different landscape awaiting us.

We leave Port Augusta and pass through Spencer Junction, from where a line runs off south to the steelworks at Whyalla. Here at Spencer Junction trains are marshalled before setting off, like us, on the long, desolate trip across the Nullarbor.

If you are still awake at two o'clock, glance out of the window on the right as we pass Pimba. Five kilometres away you can see the lights of Woomera, Australia's rocket-launching base, from where some eight hundred rockets started on their journeys between the 1940s and the 1970s. A woomera is an aboriginal spear-launching device, so an appropriate name for this base. Tight security here used to prohibit entry of ordinary civilians, but now the town is open to the public and guided tours are available. Pimba also marks the half-way point on our journey from Sydney to Perth via Adelaide.

Kultanaby, another 120 kilometres on, is where the road to Alice Springs leaves the side of the railway and turns north, and Kingoonya is where the old road to Alice Springs used to turn. The loss of the road meant the death of the little community here. Between Kingoonya and Ferguson, we pass the half-way point of the trans-continental railway, that is excluding the detour which we made to Adelaide.

If you wake early, you will be in time to see Tarcoola, which is the most populous settlement along the railway between Port Augusta and Kalgoorlie. In the true Australian spirit, it was named after a racehorse. Tarcoola won the Melbourne Cup, Australia's most famous race, back in 1893. Tarcoola was the scene of a small gold rush at that time. Later it became an important staging point for the steam locomotives travelling across here. Then, in the 1970s, it became the junction for the new line to Alice Springs and a vital base for those building the line. Now its importance is greatly diminished, but it is still large enough to support a pub (of conspicuous colour). As we pull out of the station, you can see the line to Alice Springs curving away to the right of the train.

GREAT RAILWAY JOURNEYS

1. THE INDIAN - PACIFIC
PART 2   ADELAIDE TO COOK (continued)

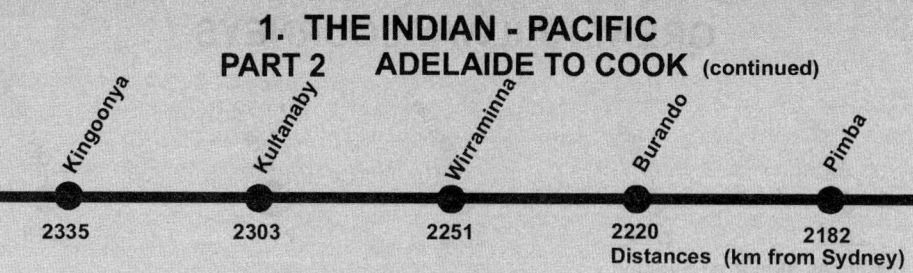

Distances (km from Sydney)

From here on there is almost no habitation, so what, you may wonder, is the list of stations at the top of the page? These are passing loops for the trains, nothing more. The line all the way across to Kalgoorlie is single track, so double track passing places are provided every thirty to fifty kilometres to allow trains to cross, or occasionally pass, each other. The loops are at least a kilometre long, to allow trains of that length to cross without interference, and the signals are solar-powered and radio-controlled. You will see the solar panels at each siding, and a hut containing batteries and other equipment. However, even with this advanced technology, safety regulations prescribe that a train cannot move without receiving an instruction by radio from the controller in Port Augusta, writing it down and repeating it to that controller to ensure that there is no error.

With so many sidings and no particular reason for any type of nomenclature, imaginations were stretched to decide what to call them all. Many are named after politicians of a century ago, often prime ministers, and some generals of the Great War. You would need to be a good historian, though, to identify all.

Barton is named after Australia's first prime minister, Edmund Barton. Look out to your left and you will see an amazing and famous construction of modern times, which is Ziggy's Home. Built out of scrap materials, many of them bearing a strong resemblance to disused railway sleepers, it is the abode of one man and his many canine companions. Ziggy came to Australia from Eastern Europe and spent much of his working life on the railway. When he retired, he said that he could think of no better place on earth to spend his remaining years than under the blue skies and bright stars that make the outback of Australia unique. He built himself a shelter first at Mungala, but when that station was closed as a working base, he decided to shift to Barton, 27 kilometres away, which was to remain in use. He therefore moved all of his possessions, load by load, in his wheelbarrow and re-established himself at Barton. Now Barton too has no permanent occupants, although some houses remain for use by occasional working gangs, and Ziggy is alone once more - except, of course, for about twenty dogs. The railways feel that Ziggy is one of their own and try to take care of him, bringing any supplies on request. The train will slow down as it passes through to check that Ziggy is still all right.

GREAT RAILWAY JOURNEYS

COOK	Fisher	O'Malley	Watson	LONG STRAIGHT
2823	2769	2748	2718	2705

Distances (km from Sydney)

Once in a while it will stop to deliver some item to him and he will come out with his trusty wheelbarrow to collect it. He does not smoke or drink, but he does have a liking for *Milo*. Look for the old tins which decorate his residence.

We are now in an area which seems to consist of red sand hills. Actually this is not sand, but windswept top-soil, but the effect is much the same. The train twists through the ridges as we reach Bates, named after Daisy Bates, who spent much of her life working here to protect the welfare of the aborigines of this area. She died in Adelaide in 1951. Some fifteen kilometres further on, by the 740-kilometre post, we crest Immana Bank and obtain a fine view of the surrounding countryside.

A further 36 kilometres brings us to Ooldea, an important site, because here the last permanent water can be found before we start the crossing of the Nullarbor. It has been a vital railway siding since the line was built, as steam locomotives could be watered here, and it was here in 1917 that the two teams building the trans-continental railway line, one from each end, met and the last spike was driven to connect the labours of the two. A monument on the right marks the spot. There is also a monument here to Daisy Bates.

As we leave Ooldea, an immediate and sudden change takes place in the scenery. The Nullarbor has started, as though a line had been drawn on a map and the terrain instructed to obey it. The change takes one by surprise. Now there is only stunted growth and wide open spaces. We shall be crossing this vast treeless plain twice the size of England for the next 676 kilometres, so precise can one be about its limits. If the train is on time, it is now 8:30 and it will be late afternoon before we see another tree, excepting a few planted at the settlement of Cook. We are now crossing an immense limestone plateau formed beneath the sea and later raised to become dry land. It is riddled with caves and subterranean passages, and even subterranean streams, but here on the surface it cannot retain sufficient moisture to sustain any substantial growth. Here, though, in these conditions where human survival appears impossible, there is evidence of aboriginal culture dating back 40,000 years, culture, however, which could not survive the coming of the railway.

Twenty kilometres beyond Ooldea, another monument marks the start of the longest stretch of straight railway in the world - 477.14 kilometres of line without deviation. We shall spend the next seven hours crossing this stretch.

1. THE INDIAN - PACIFIC
PART 2   ADELAIDE TO COOK   (continued)

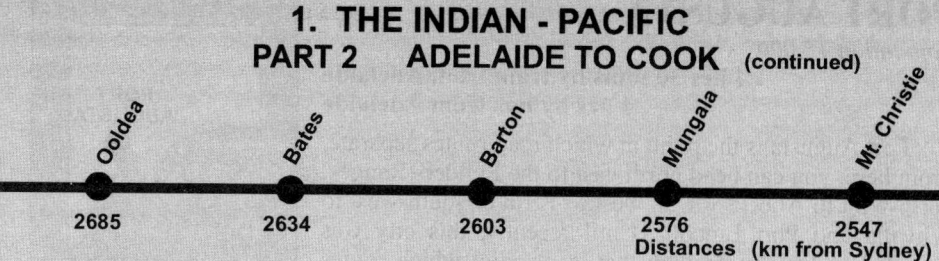

As we enter Watson siding, watch for a conspicuous grave on the left. Nobody seems quite certain of the history of this grave, dating maybe from the 1950s, but it is tended regularly, even in this remote spot. At Watson, we are close to Maralinga, which is about forty kilometres away to our right. Here, in the 1950s, the British carried out atomic bomb tests and buried radio-active waste. Although an attempt has been made to clean up in recent years, the area remains contaminated and entry is forbidden.

Another hundred kilometres brings us to Cook, named after another former prime minister and the self-styled *Queen City of the Nullarbor*. At one time, Cook had a population of 200, and even until 1998 it supported 34 families and a total population of 80. It had a school, a hospital, a swimming pool and a golf course (but no grass). It was a railway settlement, of course, as there is no other reason for its existence in this remote location. Now it has been decided that the railway no longer needs employees here and that working gangs will be sent as necessary from either end of the line. Cook's permanent population has been reduced, therefore, to three. The train stops here for half an hour to refuel and take on water and this is the only place on the Nullarbor where passengers are permitted to escape temporarily. Take the opportunity while you can. You can wander round the township and see sadly how it used to be a thriving community. There was even a 'greening' of Cook, when six hundred trees were planted. A few survive. You can see the fine old hospital and the notices painted on a scrap water tank when its future seemed to be in question, advising, "Our hospital needs your help. Get sick," and, "If you're crook, come to Cook." You can also see the town gaol, moved conveniently to the centre of the station just in case any passenger offends.

Cook is a town of extremes. The highest temperature recorded here is 48.7°C in January 1973 and the lowest -4.5°C in July 1973. In 1928 only 53.8mm of rain fell, but in the month of April 1974 alone, 172.8mm was recorded, and 434.6mm in the whole year of 1974. The water used in the town comes from an artesian bore going down ninety metres.

But our time is up here. Photographs of this isolated location, and of the longest stretch of straight railway, have all been taken. The driver has sounded his whistle and everybody is reboarding, glad to escape the heat and the ubiquitous Australian fly. Time to move on. The continuation and conclusion of the journey are on pages 496 to 500.

PORT AUGUSTA

Population 15,000

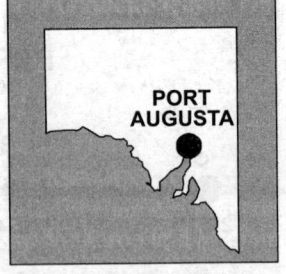

    4 hrs 30 mins by train from Adelaide
    4 hrs by bus from Adelaide

Port Augusta is the point at which road routes separate. From here, you can head north-east to the Flinders Ranges, north-west to Alice Springs, west to Perth or south-west to Whyalla and Port Lincoln. Until recently, this city was regarded as little more than that, a place at which routes parted. More recently, however, it has started to be recognised for some of its own attractions.

Matthew Flinders came here in 1802 and Eyre visited three times, but it was not until the pastoral expansion of the mid nineteenth century that Port Augusta became important. The first pastoralists arrived in 1848 and the town of Port Augusta was founded in 1852, named after Lady Augusta Young, wife of the Deputy Governor of South Australia. A wool store was established in 1853 on the present site of Woolworths and a jetty was built in the same year, followed by a second jetty in 1856.

At first, Port Augusta prospered, but in 1864 a three-year drought started and it was suddenly realised that this area was not as suitable for farming as had been thought. At this stage the saviour of Port Augusta was the Overland Telegraph Line, construction of which started from here to Darwin in 1871.

Farming now turned its attentions from sheep to wheat and the first shipments of wheat to Adelaide were made in 1877, with exports to Britain through Port Augusta the following year.

It was now, however, that Port Augusta found its true niche and became the railway town which it has remained ever since. In 1878, construction of the railway north was commenced. This was originally a narrow gauge line built to Leigh Creek, then on to Marree and to Oodnadatta and, eventually, after half a century, to Stuart (Alice Springs). For a while, the construction of the railway made this a very important port. The construction materials for the railway arrived here and, as the line stretched further, more wheat arrived for shipment. At this time, Port Augusta had the most powerful flour mill in South Australia, but then wheat farming went into decline too, since it also was dependent upon rain and in this area the rains could not be relied upon.

Again the railways were the salvation of the town. In 1912, construction of the Trans-Continental Railway was begun by the Commonwealth Government. A line was to be constructed across the Nullarbor Plain from Port Augusta to Kalgoorlie. Port Augusta became the headquarters of this railway and has remained so ever since. Even now, the signalling of the entire 1,700 kilometre line is still the responsibility of one man sitting in Port Augusta. Workers for the eastern half of the line have always been recruited in this town and the railway has ensured that Port Augusta has always had employment and a cushion against hard times.

Let us undertake a short walking tour of Port Augusta.

Walking Tour

This tour covers approximately four kilometres and will take about an hour and a half.

ANECDOTE
(Photograph facing page 726)

It was a soporific afternoon in the days when the railway line from Adelaide to Port Pirie was still broad gauge. I was in the front carriage of the train and was one of the few passengers who had not already been lulled to sleep. I was thus one of the few to see the truck approaching on a dirt road to our right. "There's a truck coming," I remember thinking, "And it's not stopping." Then, more urgently, "It's not stopping." The train was blowing its whistle sonorously by now, but the speed of the approaching vehicle did not diminish. "It's not stopping!" I gripped the seat.

There was a lurch and a hestitancy in the forward momentum of the train. Then the full force of the impact was felt. The train came off the rails and started to tilt to the left. Eighty tons of wheat began to pile into the carriage through the door at the front. Luggage from the racks flew across the train. The further we went, the more pronounced the tilt became, and I thought, " I hope it stops soon. I do hope it stops soon."

It stopped, at a considerable angle, and a silence descended. Passengers disentagled themselves from luggage and started to search for evacuation routes. Only one door, at the rear, was usable. When I got out, I found the engine on fire and the driver standing in front of the huge monster with a minute fire extinguisher muttering, "Does anybody know how this bloody thing works?" By the time he had succeeded in operating it, the fire, probably caused by fuel from the truck, had gone out.

All passengers were evacuated. Nobody appeared seriously injured, but what about the truck driver? He was nowhere to be seen. We went to his cab. It was compressed to an almost flat sheet of metal. Nobody was keen to accept the task of looking inside, but it had to be done. "There's nobody in here," reported the reluctant volunteer. Astonishment. "Well, where is he then?" A search began and eventually the truck driver was located in long grass close to the point of impact a hundred metres back along the track. Moreover, apart from a few scratches and some smears of oil, he had no visible injuries at all, although he seemed confused regarding the events of the last few minutes. Clearly his life had been saved by his failure to wear a seat belt and by being thrown from his cab by the force of the collision. He was fortunate indeed.

So was I. When I walked round the train I realised that we must have hit the semi-trailer at its pivotal point, so that the squashed cab finished on one side of the train and the trailer remained on the other. The force must have caused the rear of the trailer, carrying its eighty tons of wheat, to swing round and hit the side of the first carriage. A section had been torn from the outer shell of the carriage, and now I realised that it was exactly at the point where I had been sitting. Luckily, however, the inner wall of the carriage had not been penetrated. How easily the whims of fortune may affect us all. A few more centimetres and this book might never have been written.

We start at the southern end of Commercial Road, the main street of the city. Curdnatta Art and Pottery Gallery is here, in the **Old Railway Station** built in 1878 and still known locally as the Railway Terminus. The building lost its job in the 1930s, when the present station was constructed. The Gallery which now occupies the building is run by local artists who offer their works for sale here. It is open on weekdays from 10:00 until 16:00, with admission by voluntary donation. Walk north to Flinders Terrace and turn left, then right into Gibson Street. The railway originally ran along this street in order to reach the jetty and load or unload its cargo. On your left here is the **Hannahville Hotel** built as a residence in 1877 and converted into an hotel the following year. It was named after Hannah Gibson, the wife of the town's first mayor.

Turn right upon reaching Church Street and on your right is **St. Augustine Church**, built in 1868 to 1870. Turn left into Commercial Road again and on your right are three old buildings. The **Old Fire Station** is now an arts and craft store. It was built in 1881 as the headquarters of the Road Board. Later it became the Fire Station and used to provide a time check by sounding its siren at 19:00 daily. Next is the **Town Hall**. This was originally constructed in 1877, but only the Corinthian façade and the dome survived a disastrous fire in 1944. The rest has been rebuilt. Beyond the Town Hall is the **Institute Building** opened in 1876. This State Heritage building was used as a church, a school and a library, but is now a youth club.

Turn left now into Chapel Street and on the corner you will find the **Flinders Hotel**, built in 1878. Next door is the **Uniting Church**, formerly the Methodist Church. This building dates from 1885, but the church which was previously on this site was built in 1866 and was the first church in Port Augusta. At the top of the steeple of the current building is the *Widow's Walk* viewing platform, from where it is said that sailors' wives would watch for the return of their husbands' ships, so that they would know at what time to put the kettle on. The house at **no. 5**, built in 1874, was the residence of the Medical Superintendent and was the first house in Port Augusta to have a telephone connected.

Turn right into Gibson Street, noting the house opposite at **no. 4** as you turn. This was built in 1864 and was the home of the first European resident, Mr. A.D. Tassie, who built and operated the former wool store on the site of the present Woolworths. Follow Gibson Street round to the right into El Alamein Road. The last building on the right is now a Target store, but was originally **Young and Gordon's**, a store owned and partly operated by the Young family until 1986, with branches in other towns too.

Tassie Street is straight ahead with the **Exchange Hotel** on the corner. The hotel opened in 1878. The next building, now an entertainment area joined to the hotel, was originally the **National Bank** in the 1870s. Beside it is the **Northern Hotel**, dating from 1881, although there was a previous hotel here first licensed in 1862. On the next corner is the **Seaview Building**, constructed as the Bank of South Australia in 1881. Later it became the Seaview Hostel, but now it is a government office.

Turn left into Marryat Street and come to the **Wharf**. The first Government Jetty was built here in 1877, but demolished ten years later to make way for the present construction which is now being restored as part of the Foreshore Redevelopment Plan. Retrace your footsteps for a short distance along Marryat Street and turn sharp left until you reach the **Memorial Garden** built to honour those who died in the two World Wars. Continue to the **Jetty**. This was built in 1879 to serve the Flour Mill which opened nearby the following year. It was the last of eight small jetties built between

1853 and 1879. Continuing along the foreshore you will come to the **Old Great Western Bridge**, on the far side of the new bridge constructed in 1972. The Old Bridge was constructed in 1927, before which date the Spencer Gulf could be crossed only by ferry or by a twelve kilometre detour. The bridge was widened and strengthened in 1944 in order to carry the Morgan to Whyalla Pipeline which is the principal source of water for Port Augusta. Just beyond the bridge is the **wreck of a barge**. It is thought to have been built in Morgan in the 1880s for use on the Murray, but it was purchased in 1910 by the Adelaide Steam Tug Company and used to carry iron ore from Whyalla to the smelters at Port Pirie. It was brought from Port Pirie in 1944 with materials for the construction workers who were widening the bridge.

Return now to the end of Young Street and turn left into that street, then right into Mackay Street. On the right is the **Masonic Hall**, now privately owned. A lodge was established in 1879 and this hall opened in 1908. Now turn left into Trewenack Lane and right into Jervois Street. Opposite is the **Presbyterian Church**, the building of which started in 1885. On the next corner is Coles. This site has been used for

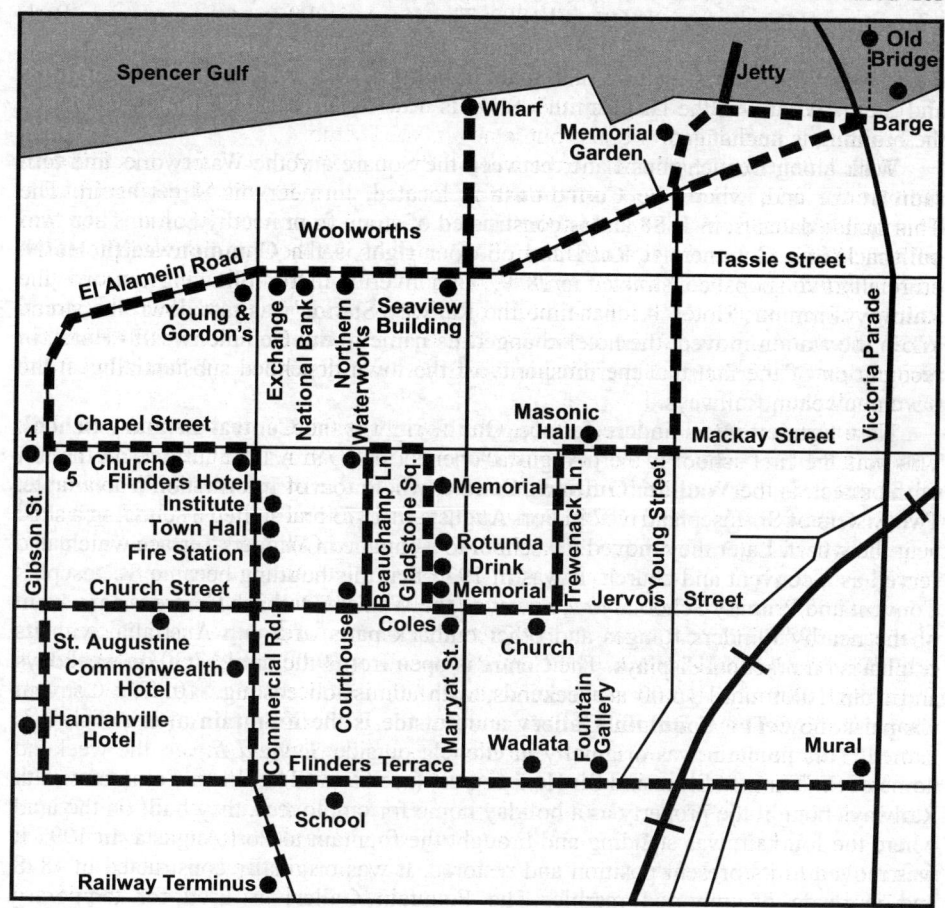

PORT AUGUSTA CITY CENTRE
Dashed line shows Walking Tour

manufacturing mineral water, then as a brewery, then for producing soft drinks. In 1943 some of the buildings were destroyed by fire. Then the site became an hotel and entertainment area before standing derelict for some years, and finally being converted to the useful purpose which you see now. Opposite Coles is **Gladstone Square**, through which we shall now walk, encountering first the **Thomas Young Junior Memorial**. Mr. Young was the owner of the Young and Gordon's Store which we saw earlier. He was elected as a councillor in 1878 and served in that capacity for 34 years. He was mayor from 1897 until 1900. Next is the **Drinking Fountain**. This is in memory of James Beatton who was Postmaster of Port Augusta for a little over 23 years, from 1882 until his death in 1905. The fountain has been moved here from its original location at the northern end of Commercial Road. The **Rotunda** beyond the Drinking Fountain was built in 1923 as a memorial to the soldiers of the Great War. Finally, at the far end of the Square is a **memorial to Mr. A.D. Tassie**, who, as mentioned above, became the first European settler here in 1855. Turn left into Mackay Street and by the corner of the Square you will find the **Waterworks**. The building was a Troopers' Barracks from 1860 until 1882. The accommodation at the rear was a Bath House when built in 1875 and the residence, constructed in 1881, is now the office of the Clerk of the Courts. In 1882, the main building was converted into a Waterworks and Store. What was the Blacksmith's Shop is now the Library, but the remainder of the building is unchanged.

Walk along Beauchamps Lane, between the Square and the Waterworks and turn right at the end, where the **Courthouse** is located, into Jervois Street again. The Courthouse dates from 1884 and is constructed of stone from nearby Saltia. Then turn left, back into Commercial Road and on your right is the **Commonwealth Hotel**, originally two shops, constructed in 1879, but converted in the following year into the Railway Terminus Hotel. At that time the Railway Station was just down the street. When the station moved, the hotel changed its name to the Commonwealth Hotel, in recognition of the fact that the prosperity of the town depended substantially on the Commonwealth Railways.

Now turn left into Flinders Terrace. On the right is the **Central Primary School**. This was the first school in Port Augusta, opened in 1878. A little further, on the left of the street, is the **Wadlata Outback Centre**, where tourist information is available. Two Sisters of St. Joseph arrived in Port Augusta in 1873 and started a school in a shed near the wharf. Later they moved the school to a cottage in Flinders Terrace which also served as a convent and church. It was in 1927 that this building became St. Joseph's Convent and Primary School. Now, however, the Wadlata Outback Centre is a museum of the nearby Flinders Ranges and other outback parts of South Australia, with its emphasis on practical displays. The Centre is open from 9:00 until 17:30 on weekdays and from 10:00 until 16:00 at weekends, with admission costing $10. The Convent Chapel is now **The Fountain Gallery** and outside is the **Fountain** after which it is named. This fountain was originally in Glenelg outside *Seafield Tower*, the weekend home of Sir Thomas Elder and Sir Henry Ayers (see page 634). When Commonwealth Railways bought the property as a holiday home for employees, they built on the land where the fountain was standing and brought the fountain to Port Augusta. In 1997 it was moved to its present position and restored. It was originally constructed in 1878 and is made of imported marble. The Fountain Gallery is used for temporary exhibitions. It is open on Mondays to Saturdays from 10:00 until 16:00 and admission is free.

ANECDOTE

One of the world's most unusual and famous trains used to run from Port Augusta to Kalgoorlie (but not the reverse) across the Trans-Continental Railway. This was the train affectionately known as the *Tea and Sugar*, because it was a goods train carrying, at the rear, a shop with essential supplies, so that all those stationed along the track could go shopping when it arrived every week. It also carried, from time to time, a social worker, a teacher, ministers of religion and any others who might be of service to the various small communities. This necessitated accommodation, so there was always a passenger carriage attached.

Thinking that I should like to travel on this world-famous train, I went to the Australian National Railways booking office in Adelaide and enquired as to its timetable. "There's no such train," replied the clerk, and then, like a character out of *Alice in Wonderland*, "And, what's more, you can't go on it."

Sometimes there is nothing to be gained with arguing with bureaucracy, so, having at least discovered that it still operated, I proceeded to Port Augusta and repeated my request. The clerk there was obviously acccustomed to dealing with eccentrics such as myself. "First, you're crazy," he replied. "It's dirty, dusty, hot and uncomfortable. There's no air-conditioning. There's probably no water. I suppose you still want to go." "Yes, that's right." "Sign on the dotted line here. The Railway takes no responsibility for what happens to you. The train leaves immediately after the *Indian-Pacific* has passed through, but it goes from Spencer Junction, not from here. Be here at 11:30 tonight. We'll take you down in a van."

I was duly taken to the goods yards at the appointed hour, clambered aboard my carriage, where I was the only passenger, and went to sleep. It was only in the morning that the crew discovered that they had a passenger, after which they were all kindness to me.

"You don't have to travel in there," said the guard. "It's air-conditioned in my van, and I could do with some company. There's a spare sleeper available too, so you can have that, and I'll ask the driver to take you on the locomotive, as long as you don't mind walking up at one of the stops. It's about ten minutes walk, but you'll enjoy the view more."

It was another experience of a lifetime, as we stopped at all the little settlements and I had a chance to meet the locals as they came shopping, including the famous Ziggy with his wheelbarrow at Barton (see page 671).

Alas, the *Tea and Sugar* is no more. Progress has meant that all those stationed at settlements across the Trans-Continental Railway have been withdrawn, and maintenance is carried out by gangs operating from each end of the line using the few remaining houses as temporary lodgings only. Thus one of the world's most unusual trains has disappeared for ever, my only satisfaction being that I managed to travel on it before it was too late.

Continue walking along Flinders Parade until it meets Victoria Parade (the Eyre Highway). Here you will find the **Mural on the Hill**. The mural tells the story of Port Augusta, using 2,500 tiles to do so. It was designed by the artist Diane Turner and constructed with the assistance of many local volunteers.

Here our tour ends, but further information about Port Augusta and the surrounding area is available at the Wadlata Outback Centre if required.

Now a few more sights which were not on the course of our walking tour. Across the Spencer Gulf, in Port Augusta West, the **Water Tower** was built in 1882 and offers a good view of the town, Spencer Gulf and the Flinders Ranges from the balcony at the top.

The **Arid Lands Botanic Garden** lies 1.5 kilometres north-west of the town. It covers 200 hectares and has twelve kilometres of walking tracks. The Garden won an Environmental Tourism Award. Rainwater is collected and used for watering, and waste water is also treated here and then recycled. All external lighting is solar powered. The Garden is open from 9:00 until 17:00 on weekdays and from 10:00 until 16:00 at weekends. Admission is free, with guided tours available at certain times (usually mornings) for $5.

To the south-east of the town is **Homestead Park Pioneer Museum**. It has an original log homestead moved here from Yudnapinna Station, about 100 kilometres further north, an exhibition of saddles, bridles and carriages, and an original blacksmith's shop. There is also a **miniature railway** which operates only on the third weekend of the month. The Museum is open daily from 9:00 until 12:00 and from 13:00 until 16:00. Nearby is the **School of the Air**. Tours are available at 10:00 on schooldays and cost $3.

Further south is the **Royal Flying Doctor Base**, which is open from 10:00 until 15:00 on weekdays. Admission is by voluntary donation. A little further south still, a **cairn** and the **McLellan Lookout** mark the point where Captain Flinders came ashore on 10th March 1802. A good view is available from this point named after a prominent local historian.

The **Flinders Power Station** is five kilometres from the town and produces almost 40% of the power consumed in the whole of South Australia. The Power Station was constructed in 1985 at a cost of $500 million and was built adjacent to the existing Thomas Playford Power Stations. The Playford 'A' Station came into use in 1954 and was retired in 1986. The 'B' Station came into use in 1960 and is still employed for peak-load generation. Free tours of the Flinders Power Station are conducted daily at 11:00 and 13:00.

A short distance along the road to Adelaide is the **Pink Lake**. You do not need to walk to it, as you will be able to see it from bus or train as you approach, or leave, Port Augusta. The highway runs beside the lake, while the railway travels on a causeway right across it. The colour is caused by a form of algae and its intensity varies according to the weather conditions.

The **Pichi Richi Railway** now operates trains between Port Augusta and Quorn along the old line which used to run to Alice Springs. Originally, the line to Leigh Creek, Marree, Oodnadatta and on to Alice Springs was all narrow gauge, but in 1956 it was converted to standard gauge as far as Marree, where bogies had to be exchanged, or where passengers might be required to change trains. When the gauge conversion was carried out, the route was changed in some places. The Pichi Richi Railway

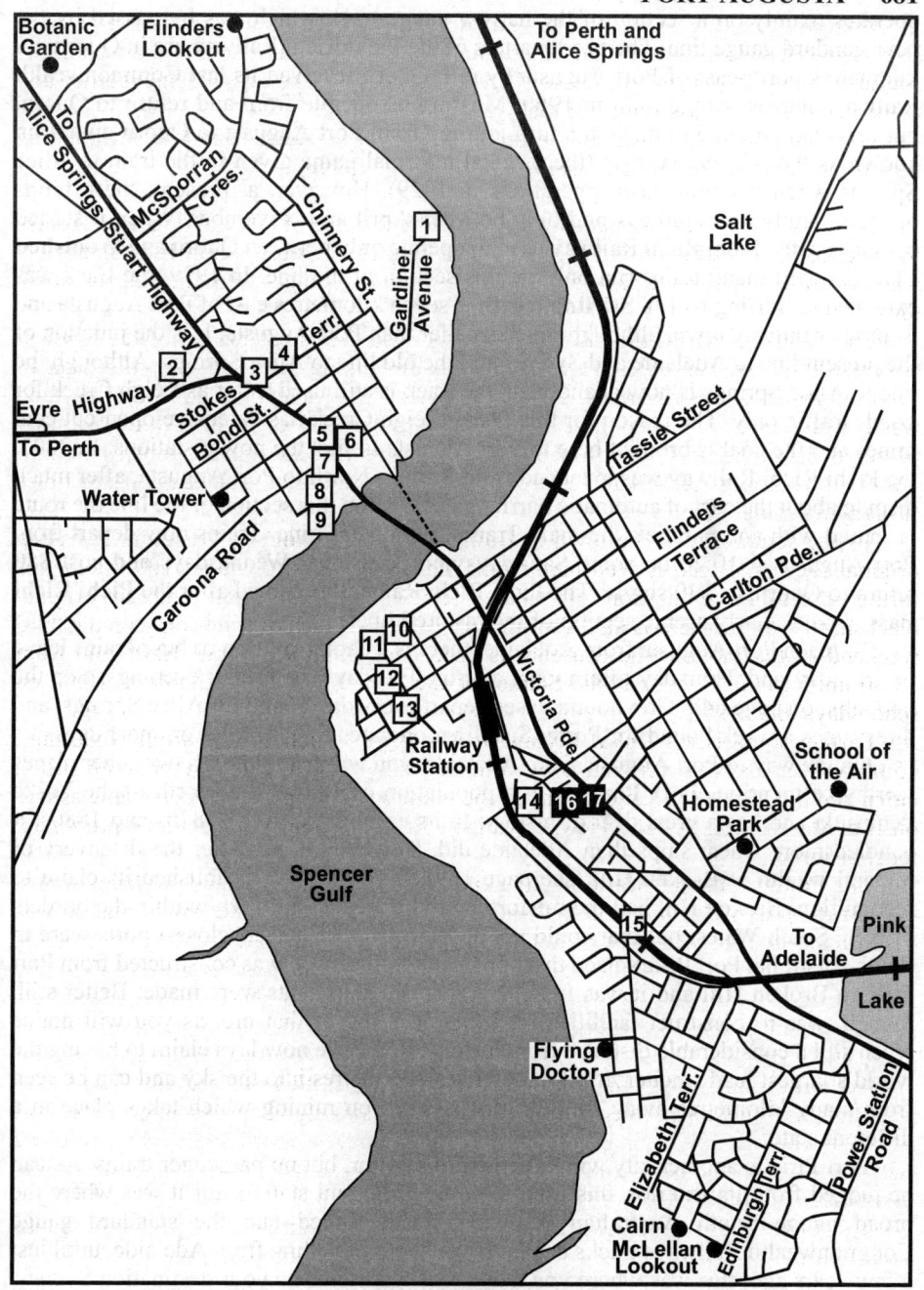

operates mainly on a section of the narrow gauge track which was by-passed by the new standard gauge line. The headquarters of the Pichi Richi Railway are in Quorn, 39 kilometres north-east of Port Augusta by rail. Quorn received its last Commonwealth Railways narrow gauge train in 1969. Most trains operate from and return to Quorn, but it is also possible to make a return journey from Port Augusta to Quorn on a train known as the *Afghan Express* (the original informal name given to the train to Alice Springs when it commenced operations in 1929). However, at present, these trains operate mainly on Saturdays and only between April and November. When it started operations, the Pichi Richi Railway used to operate only between Quorn and **Woolshed Flat**, and still many trains run only on this section of the line. In 1999, the track was extended to Stirling North. **Stirling North** is seven kilometres east of Port Augusta and is another railway town, although much smaller than Port Augusta. It is the junction of the present line to Adelaide and Sydney and the old line to Alice Springs. Although the line to Alice Springs is now abandoned, the track is still used as far as Leigh Creek for goods traffic only. The reason for this is that Leigh Creek has extensive open-cut coal mines and the coal is brought here to Port Augusta to fuel the power stations. In 2002, the Pichi Richi Railway was extended from Stirling North to Port Augusta, after much dispute about the cost of automatic barrier gates, and on this section of the line the route is shared with and parallels the main Trans-Continental Line. Trains now depart from Port Augusta at 10:20 on some Saturdays and occasional Wednesdays and cost $50 return to Quorn, or $30 single. The Pichi Richi Railway is named after the **Pichi Richi Pass**, a particularly scenic section of the restored line.

To reach Port Augusta from Adelaide, there is a choice of train or bus. Trains leave on Monday and Thursday afternoons, and on Tuesday and Friday evenings. See the timetable on page 642. Greyhound buses depart every day bound for Alice Springs, and three times a week bound for Perth. Stateliner operates five services on most days.

On the way to Port Augusta from Adelaide, you will pass through two other places worthy of mention. **Port Pirie**, with a population of 18,000, lies north of the Yorke Peninsula and has a great deal of history. In its early days, in the 1870s and 1880s, it handled more wheat ships than Adelaide did. However, it was after the discovery of mineral wealth at Broken Hill (see page 159) that Port Pirie established its claim to recognition. Broken Hill had the misfortune to be located narrowly within the borders of New South Wales, but that could not obscure the fact that its closest ports were in South Australia. Port Pirie seized this opportunity. A railway was constructed from Port Pirie to Broken Hill and it was from here that ore shipments were made. Better still, though, was to construct facilities for the processing of that ore, as you will notice when still a considerable distance from the city. Port Pirie now lays claim to having the world's largest lead smelter. Its chimney rises 205 metres into the sky and can be seen from many kilometres away, and all this is based on mining which takes place in a different state.

Port Pirie is another city with a **beautiful station**, but no passenger trains. As can be judged from its exterior, this used to be an important station, for it was where the broad gauge South Australian Railways tracks ended and the standard gauge Commonwealth Railways tracks began. If you were travelling from Adelaide, until just a few years ago, this was where you had to change trains, be your destination Sydney, Perth, Alice Springs, or just Port Augusta. This was, therefore, quite a busy station. However, it was also a dead-end station, so, when the line from Adelaide was converted to standard gauge, it was decided not to go into Port Pirie and turn the train there, but to by-pass the city. The nearest station now, therefore, is **Coonamia**, which is a tiny siding about four kilometres from the town centre. The station building in Port Pirie has become the **Regional Tourism and Arts Centre**. It contains two art galleries, murals, the bus terminal and, of course, tourist information.

Also in the city are the **Phoenix Park Wetlands**, with birdwatching facilities, **Solomontown Beach** and **Memorial Park**. There is an annual festival of country music and a yachting race across Spencer Gulf.

Greyhound buses also by-pass Port Pirie, stopping only at the turn-off to the city, about six kilometres away. Stateliner, however, goes into the city centre and stops at the bus terminal there. All services to Port Augusta call in, which is about five buses per day. The journey from Adelaide takes approximately three hours. If a morning service is taken, one can look at Port Pirie and then continue to Port Augusta on the same day, although there is, of course, a good range of accommodation in Port Pirie.

The second place worth a short visit on the way to Port Augusta is **Port Germain**. Its claim to fame used to be that it had the longest wooden jetty in the southern hemisphere, but a storm destroyed part of it, so now it is merely one of the longest, extending more than one and a half kilometres

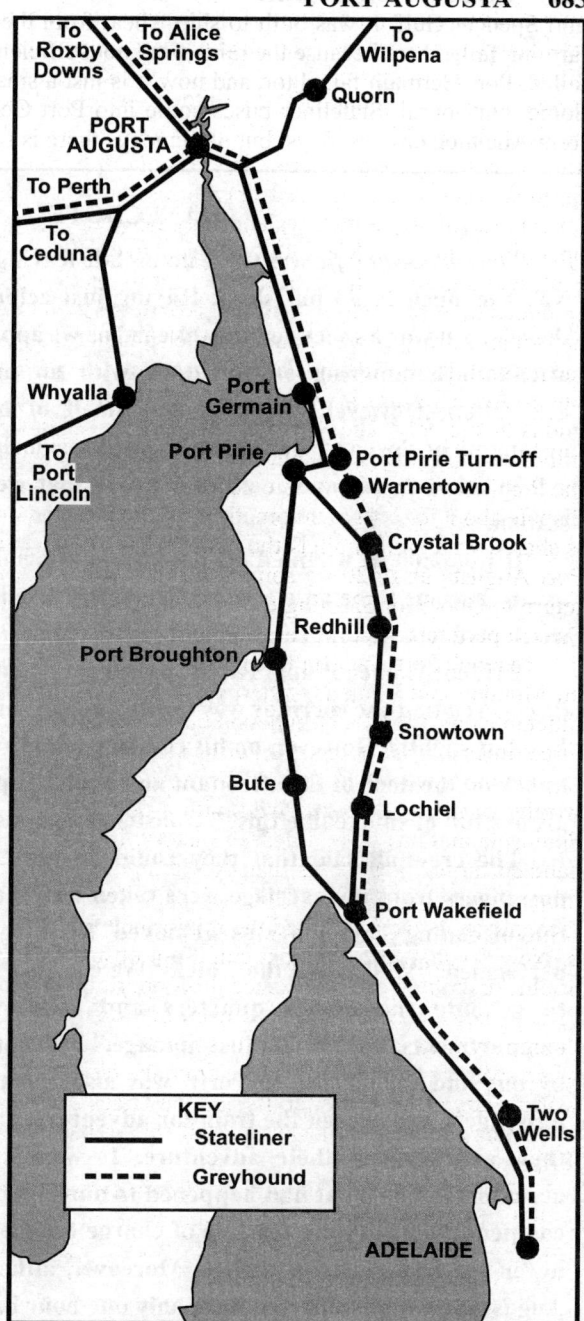

ADELAIDE TO PORT AUGUSTA
Showing bus routes
(Railway stations shown on page 669)

into Spencer Gulf. It was built to ship wheat from the farms north of here, but cereal farming failed here because the rains were not sufficiently reliable, and when the crops failed, Port Germain failed too and now it is just a small community with a long jetty. Some, but not all, Stateliner buses come into Port Germain. There are three services from Adelaide on most days, but on Sundays there is only one bus, late in the evening.

ANECDOTE

The *Indian-Pacific* was three hours late leaving Adelaide for Perth, so there was not much to do but sleep. Having just achieved that comfortable state, therefore, it was a shock to be awakened as we approached Port Augusta by the attendant hammering on the door with an urgent call for arousal and evacuation. However, the prevalent smell of burning encouraged all the occupants of the carriage to take the call seriously. The corridor proved to be full of acrid fumes and it was fortunate that we were just approaching the station.

It was 2:00 as we piled off onto the platform. "What's the problem?" we asked. "Seems to be an electrical fire in the fuse box at the end of the car. We shall have to take that carriage out of the train."

Evidently one of my fellow passengers had set off for the toilet and discovered that the corridor was full of smoke. This had, apparently, concerned him but slightly. However, on his return from his expedition he had thought to knock on the door of the attendant and enquire apologetically, "Is the corridor always full of smoke like this?" Consternation ensued.

The crew all said that they could never recall a similar incident. The passengers from my carriage were taken into the station waiting room while the offending carriage was removed from the train. Calculations were performed. "Well," said the Chief. "We can just fit you all in. Some will have to go into the crew's quarters and some will be sharing first-class compartments, but we can just manage." The option of returning to Adelaide by bus and then flying to Perth was also given, but nobody took it. These passengers had chosen the train for adventure, and there was no denying that they were getting their adventure. It was 5:00 before we were all re-accommodated. What had happened to our night's sleep? However, by way of compensation, we were fed free of charge for the rest of the journey, so I had never reached Perth so replete. Moreover, although we departed from Port Augusta five hours late, we were only one hour late in Perth.

Believe what you read. Crossing Australia on the *Indian-Pacific* is for those with a real sense of adventure.

PORT AUGUSTA 685

ACCOMMODATION
(i) Accommodation in Port Pirie

Name	Stars	Telephone No.	Address	Lowest Price (Double/Twin)
Sampson's Cottage	4	08-8632-2272	66 Ellen Street	$110
Old Schoolhouse	4	08-8632-1080	122 Three Chain Road	$110
John Pirie Motor Inn	3½	08-8632-4200	Main Road	$105
Abbacy Motel	3	08-8632-3701	46 Florence Street	$95
Flinders Range Motor Inn	3	08-8632-3555	151 Main Street	$95
Travelway Motel	2	08-8632-2222	149 Gertrude Street	$80
International Hotel/Motel	2	08-8632-2422	40 Ellen Street	$65
Federal Hotel		08-8632-2654	160 The Terrace	$55
Hotel Newcastle		08-8632-3925	18 Main Road	$55
Hotel Risdon		08-8632-2663	Moppett Road	$55
Portside Tavern		08-8632-3833	96 Ellen Street	$55
Central Hotel		08-8632-1031	30 Alexander Street	$50
Family Hotel		08-8632-1382	134 Ellen Street	$50

(ii) Hotel Accommodation in Port Augusta

Name	Stars	No. on Map	Telephone No.	Address	Lowest Price (Double/Twin)
Augusta Westside Motel	4	8	1-800-066-262	3 Loudon Road	$105
Standpipe Golf Motor Inn	3½	2	08-8642-4033	Highway One & Hwy. 87	$100
Myoora Motel	3	5	08-8642-3622	10 Eyre Highway	$85
Pampas Motel		15	08-8642-3795	76 Stirling Road	$75
Poinsettia Motel		6	08-8642-2411	24 Burgoyne Street	$75
Acacia Ridge	3½	4	08-8642-3377	33 Stokes Terrace	$70
Big Four Holiday Park	4½	3	1-800-833-444	Highway One & Stokes Tce.	$65
Augusta Hotel		9	08-8642-2701	1 Loudon Road	$60
Ian's Western Hotel		7	08-8642-2781	10 Loudon Road	$60
Pastoral Hotel / Motel		14	08-8642-2818	17 Stirling Street	$55
Commonwealth Hotel		13	08-8642-2844	73 Commercial Road	$50
Flinders Hotel / Motel		12	08-8642-2544	39 Commercial Road	$50
Exchange Hotel		11	08-8642-3906	12 Commercial Road	$50
Northern Hotel		10	08-8642-2522	4 Tassie Street	$50
Shoreline Top Tourist Pk.		1	08-8642-2965	Gardiner Avenue	$50

(iii) Backpackers Hostels in Port Augusta

Name	Group	No. on Map	Telephone No.	Address	Lowest Price (Dormitory)
Bluefox Lodge	B&W	17	08-8641-2960	8 Victoria Parade	$20
Port Augusta Backpackers		16	08-8641-1063	17 Trent Road	$18

MOVING ON
(i) By Train

There are trains from Port Augusta to Adelaide and on to Sydney or Melbourne, and there are trains in the opposite direction to Perth and to Alice Springs. A timetable summarising all services is provided to the right.

Days of Operation	W	Sat	M, Th	Tu, F	Tu, Sa	Su, M, Th, F
Port Augusta	0300	0300	1920	2240	2350	
Days			Tu, F	W, Sa		
Alice Springs			0900			
Cook				0918		
Kalgoorlie (arrive)				1920		
Kalgoorlie (depart)				2230		
Days				Th, Su	W, Su	
Perth				0930		
Adelaide (arrive)	0900	0900			0605	
Adelaide (depart)	1015	1010			0745	0900
Broken Hill		1725			1630	
Days		Sun			Th, M	
Sydney		0915			0915	
Melbourne	2100					2000

SOUTH AUSTRALIA
(ii) By Bus

Buses to Adelaide are operated by Greyhound at least once and sometimes twice each night. Stateliner, though, has five services per day to Adelaide. In the opposite direction, Greyhound runs to Alice Springs every day, and to Perth three times a week. Stateliner runs north-east to Wilpena Pound, north-west to Roxby Downs and Olympic Dam, west to Ceduna and south-west to Whyalla and Port Lincoln. A summary of these services is given below.

Destination	Operator	Via	Distance (km)	Fare	Journey Time	Frequency
Adelaide	Greyhound		318	$42	4½ - 4¾ hrs	10/week
Adelaide	Stateliner		315	$39.80	4 - 4½ hrs	5/day
Perth	Greyhound		2662	$291	32¼ hrs	3/week
		Kalgoorlie	2033	$291	24½ hrs	3/week
Alice Springs	Greyhound		1224	$184	15 hrs	1/day
		Coober Pedy	537	$75	7½ hrs	1/day
Wilpena	Stateliner		143	$35.40	2¼ hrs	3/week
Roxby Dwns	Stateliner		255	$47.30	3¼ hrs	1/day
Ceduna	Stateliner		505	$73.20	16½ - 7 hrs	1/day
Port Lincoln	Stateliner		378	$56.40	4¾ - 5 hrs	2/day
		Whyalla	83	$16.40	50 - 60 mins	4/day

ANECDOTE

When travelling on mixed trains, it was not uncommon to be offered a ride on the locomotive, and I was sitting in the cab enjoying my journey across the Nullarbor. We were performing shunting operations at one of the small stations, while also awaiting the arrival of a train in the opposite direction. Dusk was descending.

Because of the length of the train, shunting involved the use of the main line and as we occupied the track, the light of the approaching train could be seen bearing down upon us. The driver of the train appeared quite unconcerned about this technicality, but as the light became brighter and brighter I could eventually not avoid mentioning the matter. "What about this train coming?" I asked. "Oh, don't worry about that," the driver replied. "He's still twenty or thirty kilometres away. I can't even raise him on the radio yet."

"Deceptive, isn't it?" he added. "I remember one time I was on the Long Straight and I had the written order for use of the line, but I looked up and I could see the light of another train coming towards me, apparently quite close. I was really worried. I thought that the Controller must have made a mistake. I went into the next siding and telephoned him. Do you know he told me that that train was over two hundred kilometres away. He was right. It was more than two hours before we crossed, in the correct place according to the orders given. I would never have believed it. I suppose it must be something to do with the clear air. I had been convinced that that train was right on top of me."

He was right about this occasion too. It was another twenty minutes before the oncoming train put in an appearance, by which time we had made another shunting operation onto the main line, but still had plenty of time to retreat.

FLINDERS RANGES
Population 500 (Hawker plus Wilpena)
7 hrs by bus from Adelaide (Wilpena)

Apart from Adelaide, the Flinders Ranges are probably the most popular destination in South Australia. They are not a single destination, of course, but stretch for many kilometres.

Most visitors have their own transport or take a tour, but it is quite possible to visit by public transport. Although these mountain ranges start near Port Pirie, the most impressive areas lie north-east of Port Augusta and it is on those that we shall concentrate.

Stateliner operates a service to Wilpena Pound in the Flinders Ranges on Sundays, Wednesdays and Fridays. The bus leaves from Port Augusta, with a connexion from Adelaide on Wednesdays and Fridays, but no Adelaide connexion on Sundays.

The bus first passes through **Quorn**, 35 minutes out from Port Augusta. Quorn has already been mentioned in the section on Port Augusta as the home of the **Pichi Richi Railway**. It is an interesting and historic town worth a brief visit. At one time, it seemed destined to become an important railway junction. The railway reached here in 1879, and originally all passengers travelling on the east-west Sydney-Perth and the south-north Adelaide-Alice Springs routes passed through here and many of them changed trains at this point. However, this importance was not to last. When the broad gauge line between Adelaide and Port Pirie was established, passengers no longer had to travel to Perth via Quorn, and in 1956 a standard gauge line was opened from Port Augusta to Marree, by-passing Quorn, so that even passengers for Alice Springs no longer had to pass through here. The narrow gauge line from Port Augusta to Quorn, the one which is now used by the Pichi Richi Railway, was abandoned, but services still continued for a while on the northern section of that narrow gauge line, to Hawker, and on the line which ran east from Quorn to Peterborough. The last service on those lines ran in 1969 and Quorn was then left without any rail service at all. The Pichi Richi Railway started operations in 1974 and has become one of the best known private lines in Australia. A section of the Quorn-Peterborough line, at the other end, from Peterborough to Orroroo and on to Eurelia, is also operated now as a scenic railway.

Quorn has a **Visitor Centre** and there is an **Historic Buildings** town walking trail. Tours of the **Railway Workshop** are available at certain times, and there are also several walks available into the Flinders Ranges using this as a base. Rewarding, and not too strenuous, are the **Devil's Peak** walks. There is a fifteen-kilometre loop which will take about seven hours and a simple, but less interesting, return walk of twelve kilometres, which will take about five hours. Devil's Peak rises to 697 metres. It is a peak 700 million years old, in the quartz formations of which fossils can be found.

There is a youth hostel in Quorn, and the Transcontinental Hotel offers cheap accommodation also, including rooms for backpackers. Tours of the Flinders Ranges are available from here.

Next along the road, an hour and a half from Port Augusta, is **Hawker**, one of the best known of the Flinders Ranges towns. The **Yourambulla Caves** are nearby, decorated with aboriginal art, and the **Kanyaka** ruins lie a little south of the town beside the main road. There are walking trails, of which the one to **Jarvis Hill** is scenic and not too difficult. The Hawker Hotel and Motel offers a good range of accommodation.

Fred Teague's Museum at Hawker Motors is a collection of gemstones, minerals, fossils, photographs, bottles and other items of interest. Fred Teague, who started Hawker Motors in 1952 and operated the business until his death in 1994, was a great collector in his spare time and built up this little museum by himself. It is open daily from 7:30 until 17:30, with free admission.

At Hawker, the bus leaves the main road and continues to the east of the highway but still in a north-easterly direction. **Rawnsley Park**, at the base of **Rawnsley Bluff** (975 metres), is two hours from Port Augusta and just outside the boundaries of the Flinders Range National Park. Accommodation is available here, and there are more aboriginal paintings at **Arkaroo Rock**, just near Rawnsley Bluff.

ANECDOTE

Travelling by mixed train from Port Augusta up to Alice Springs was, as usual, an adventure - and one which lasted nearly three days if nothing went wrong. The narrow gauge section (now closed) between Marree and Alice Springs, a journey of 42 hours, was the more interesting part, being along a much older line. It was limited throughout to 60 km/hr, with more severe speed limitations, even down to 10 km/hr, in parts. The passenger carriage at the rear, dating from 1936, had had one compartment converted into a kitchen, with gas cooker and gas refrigerator, for the use of passengers. When one used the cooking facilities, the interest of the local population of flies would be stimulated and such was the speed of the train that one would see them pass by the window, sample the aroma, turn round and come back to investigate further. Literature advertising the *Ghan* of that era used to refer to this as a 'leisurely trip', and that was certainly true, if not something of an understatement.

As usual, the driver was usually willing to entertain guests in his cab for a while, and from there the swaying of the train, even at its modest rate of progress, was particularly evident, as were the rotting wooden sleepers splintering and curling up at the ends. Even when built, this had been a low-budget line, and not much had been done to change that since. With only one metal bridge in its entire length, the strategy at water courses was to run down the bank, across a slightly raised concrete causeway, and up the other side.

"You see this," said the driver, as we approached a dry river bed and he edged his speed up to 70 km/hr. "The limit for this is 40 km/hr. Guess what happens if we take it at 40. That's what I did the very first time. Down into the river, across the causeway, and, of course, I couldn't get up the other side. I was stuck there. They had to get another locomotive to come out and push from the back. You have to take it at 70 to have enough momentum to get out the other side, whatever the rules say. Here we go. Now just watch all those wagons behind swaying from side to side, and we just pray that they all stay on the track."

There was nothing mundane about this line. It was what one might term a 'natural' line. Nature was in control of it and only her agreement would allow trains to pass. When the Finke River, in particular, flowed, train halted respectfully and awaited her pleasure. When the author first went to the Northern Territory, the trains awaited her pleasure for a period of three months.

Wilpena Pound is the end of the bus route, nearly 2½ hours from Port Augusta and the main base of the **Flinders Range National Park**, which covers an area of 94,908 hectares. Wilpena Pound is a remarkable natural amphitheatre with the Wilpena Pound Resort now snuggling in its cradle. There is a **Visitor Information Centre** and all types of accommodation are available from motel to camping sites. There is plenty of wildlife around the Pound, especially kangaroos and emus.

Walks available using this as a base include the following. **Hill Homestead** is a two-kilometre half-hour stroll. **Wangarra Hill Lookouts** (there are two of them) take an hour for just over three kilometres and offer good views for relatively little exertion. However, if you want

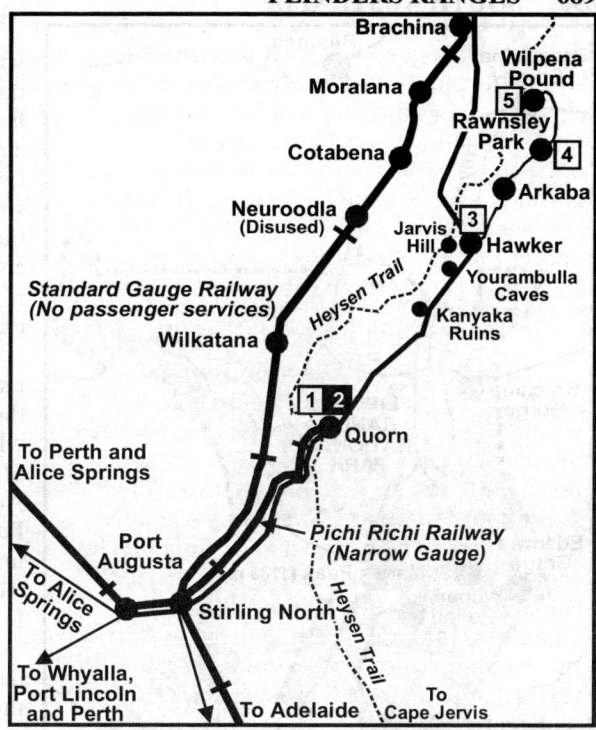

FROM PORT AUGUSTA TO WILPENA
Showing bus stops and railways
Black numerals indicate hotel accommodation
White numerals indicate backpackers hostels

something more strenuous, **St. Mary's Peak** is a rewarding challenge. This is a hard walk up to the highest peak in the area at 1,188 metres. You can then return by a loop through **Cooinda Camp**, a total round trip of seventeen kilometres, which will take about seven hours. The direct return route covers twelve kilometres and takes five hours. The walk to **Mallaga Falls** covers some of the same path as the above loop through Cooinda Camp, but then continues to the beautiful **Edeowie Gorge**. This again is a hard walk and one which can be dangerous in parts if due care is not taken. It covers seventeen kilometres return and needs seven to eight hours.

Altogether there are seventeen walking trails within the Flinders Range National Park and there are various camping sites within the park. There are aboriginal art sites, and two long-abandoned copper mines. The most spectacular gorge is **Brachina Gorge**, to reach which one follows the **Brachina Gorge Geological Trail**. If you want a really testing walk, the **Heysen Trail** starts just north of the Flinders Range National Park in the **Parachilna Gorge**, travels right through the centre of the National Park, passes close to Hawker and Quorn, meanders south, and eventually terminates at **Cape Jervis** at the tip of the **Fleurieu Peninsula**, a total distance of approximately 1,500 kilometres.

Tours are also available from Wilpena Pound, but expect to pay about $100 per day. There are flights too, starting at $75 for twenty minutes.

690 SOUTH AUSTRALIA

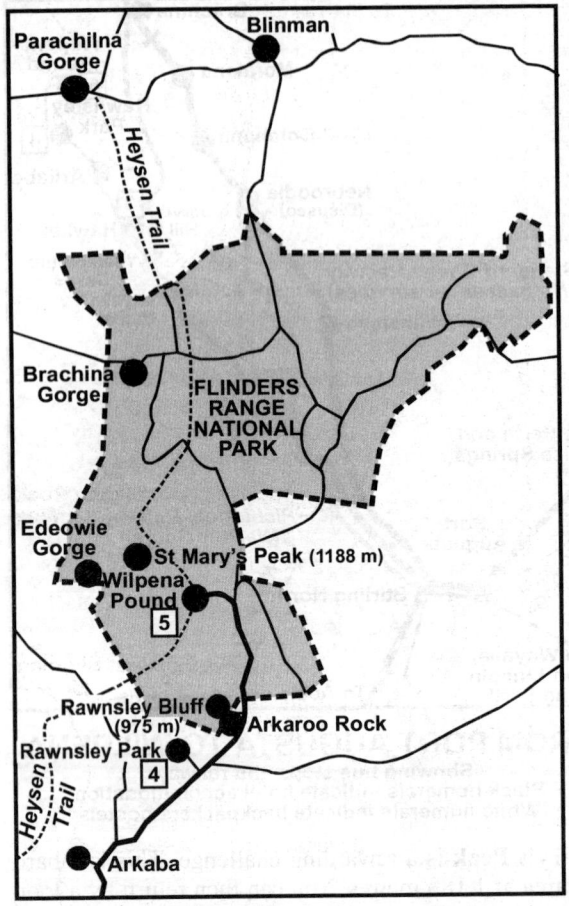

FLINDERS RANGE NATIONAL PARK
Numerals indicate accommodation

Without a vehicle or a tour, you will not get further north than this, but you will have seen the best of the Flinders Ranges already. If you do decide on a tour, though, you may reach some interesting places and travel some fascinating outback countryside from here on, so here is a little of what you might expect.

Continuing north along the main highway, you will rejoin the standard gauge railway which you have not seen since Stirling North, just outside Port Augusta, and then reach **Parachilna**, which is famous, unexpectedly enough, for the 'feral' meals at the Prairie Hotel, featuring emu, kangaroo, 'rooburgers', and other similar delicacies on its menu. There is the **Parachilna Gorge** too, nearby, and from here there is access to the immense **Lake Torrens** to the west, which is now at its closest point to the main road. Accommodation is available here, including beds for backpackers, at the Prairie Hotel.

Beltana is an interesting old township, although the old town is eighteen kilometres to the east of the modern roadhouse on the main road. The oldest buildings date from 1855 and the **Mission Church** here, built in 1895, was where the **Rev. John Flynn** started, in 1911, to develop his plan for the Royal Flying Doctor Service. Early pastoralists used this as a base, including Sir Thomas Elder, who has been mentioned earlier (see page 634). The narrow gauge railway passed through here until 1956 when the standard gauge line was opened next to the present main road. **Sliding Rock Copper Mine** is a further 22 kilometres east. It was closed in 1877 as a result of flooding. Ruins survive, principally those of the **Sliding Rock Hotel**, built in 1874.

Leigh Creek is quite a sizeable town. Coal was first mined here in 1941 and from here comes the fuel for the power stations in Port Augusta. It is transported 250 kilometres by the railway which now terminates here, but which used to continue to Marree and, after a change of gauge, to Alice Springs. The coal is produced by large-scale open cut mining operations, tours of which are available daily. There is a **Tourist Information Centre** in the town and accommodation is available in cabins and in a motel.

Lyndhurst is the end of the sealed road. From here it is all dirt road for a long, long way. Lyndhurst and **Farina**, 28 kilometres further north, used to be mining towns, though little remains now. Until 1927, Farina supported a copper and silver mine and had a population of 600. Jules Verne in his novel *Mistress Branican*, written in 1891, depicted a futuristic Farina with wide boulevards and stately squares. However, even bitumen has not made its appearance yet and no town at all remains. For a while, both Lyndhurst and Farina survived on the mining of talc, but when the railway closed, even this industry was doomed. *Talc Alf*, however, exists here by carving talc sculptures and selling them to passers-through. His shop is about two kilometres along the Strzelecki Track.

Lyndhurst, although so small, is a junction. North will take you to Marree, while to the north-east lies the abovementioned **Strzelecki Track**, named after a well-known explorer of Polish extraction. The Strzelecki Track is an interesting route, but one which should not be undertaken without suitable preparations, for there is no town before Moomba, which is over 350 kilometres distant and which is, in any case, available only for emergencies.

Although Strzelecki was the explorer who pioneered the area, it was actually the cattle rustler **Harry Readford ('Captain Starlight')** who proved in 1870 that this route could be used for practical purposes by herding 1,000 stolen cattle for a distance of 1,300 kilometres from Bowen Downs Station near Longreach in Queensland to the

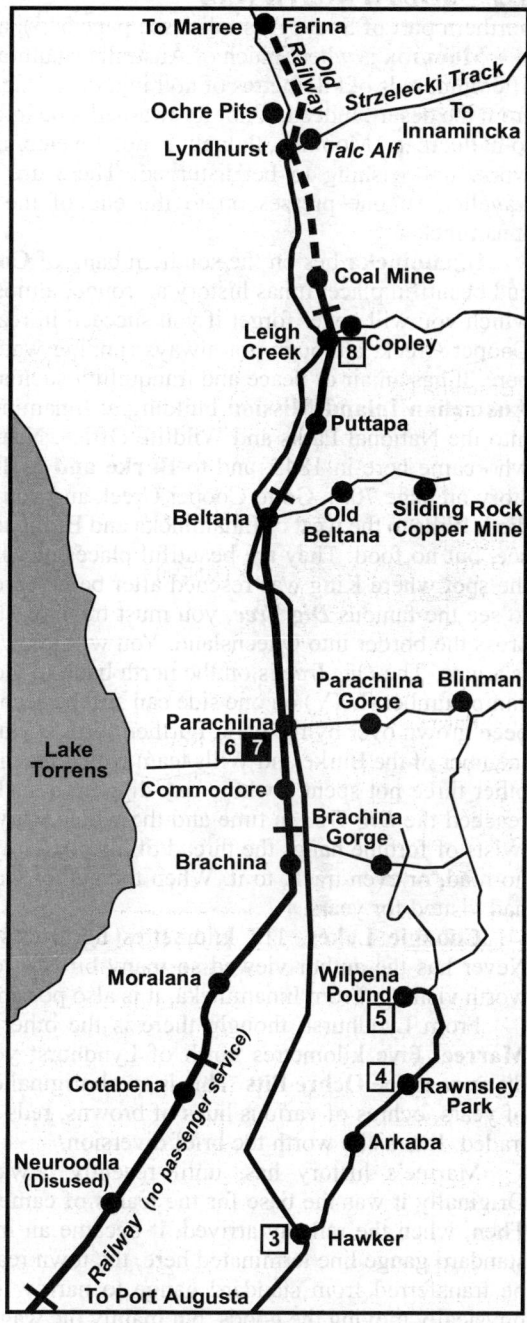

FROM HAWKER TO FARINA
Black numerals indicate hotel accommodation
White numerals indicate backpackers hostels

northern part of South Australia (see page 315), a very impressive feat.

Moomba is where much of Australia's natural gas originates. It is a great surprise, after hundreds of kilometres of nothing, to see the gleaming steel pipes and tubes rising from the desert. Indeed, if not forewarned, one might wonder whether one were starting to hallucinate. Moomba, though, is not a welcoming town, but simply a community at work, not wishing to be disturbed. There are no facilities available here for the traveller, so one presses on to the end of the track at the famous little town of Innamincka.

Innamincka lies on the southern bank of **Cooper Creek**, which is a truly remote and beautiful place. It has history all round, almost tangible, and is certainly a location which you will never forget if you succeed in reaching here. There is always water in Cooper Creek, although not always running water, and so flocks of birds congregate here. It has an air of peace and tranquillity such as one rarely experiences. The former **Australian Inland Mission** building at Innamincka has been restored and converted into the National Parks and Wildlife Office. Nearby are memorials to **Charles Sturt**, who came here in 1845, and to **Burke and Wills**, who both perished near here (see story on page 700). Go to Cooper Creek and you can find the exact places where they died, Wills to the west of Innamincka and Burke to the east. They had water, as you can see, but no food. They are beautiful places in which to die, at least. You can also see the spot where King was rescued after being cared for by the aborigines. If you want to see the famous **Dig Tree**, you must travel east for a little over fifty kilometres and cross the border into Queensland. You will know that you have done so because there is a gate. The *Dig Tree* is on the north bank of Cooper Creek and the engraving of the camp number (LXV) on one side can still be seen. The instruction to dig, however, has been grown over by the bark. Further north is where Charlie Gray perished, the fourth member of the Burke and Wills team which reached the north of the continent. Had the other three not spent a whole day digging a shallow grave for him, they would have reached the *Dig Tree* in time and the whole story would have been changed. On such twists of fortune hangs the thread of history. Gray's grave is not easy to find. There is no road, or even track, to it. When the author was there, it seemed as though nobody had visited for years.

Coongie Lakes, 112 kilometres north-west of Innamincka, are worth seeing. Never has the author viewed so many birds in one place. Just for that the lakes are worth visiting. From Innamincka, it is also possible to continue north into Queensland.

From Lyndhurst, though, there is the other choice, that of proceeding north to **Marree**. Five kilometres north of Lyndhurst you will find a turn-off for the short distance to the **Ochre Pits**. This is an aboriginal quarry where, probably for thousands of years, ochres of various hues of browns, reds and yellows have been extracted and traded. It is a site worth the brief diversion.

Marree's history has, until recently, always been associated with transport. Originally it was the base for the teams of camels which headed north with supplies. Then, when the railway arrived, it became an important railhead. In 1956, when the standard gauge line terminated here, the town reached its zenith, for everything had to be transferred from standard gauge to narrow gauge. Sometimes this was done by physically moving the goods, but mainly the wagons were lifted by crane, the standard gauge bogies wheeled out and a new set of narrow gauge bogies installed, or *vice versa*. This operation created a thriving industry in Marree, which became just a railway town. It was difficult to see how it could survive when this railway route was abandoned in

1980. However, it has survived and managed to transmute itself into a tourist base. Who could have imagined that so many people would want to travel these remote areas? Surprisingly, though, the transformation has been successful and Marree still exists, offering all types of facilities for the wayward traveller and the best accommodation to be found for quite a long way, as well as facilities for budget travellers at the Marree Hotel.

There are two choices from Marree as well. One is to head up the most famous of all Australia's outback roads, the **Birdsville Track**. This is a route which has been greatly improved in recent years, due to its increasing popularity with tourists and its use by huge road trains moving stock southwards. Unless it has rained recently, a two-wheel-drive vehicle should not have problems reaching Birdsville. The Birdsville Track is 513 kilometres long. The main route used to lie through **Goyder Lagoon**, with a wet-weather track to the east for use when the main route was flooded. In 1974, however, the Lagoon filled to such a level that the main track remained impassable for most of the following three years and it was decided to make the eastern route the main track and use the short-cut through Goyder Lagoon as an occasional track. By chance, the author passed through the old route just three days before it was flooded. The new route has added a little distance, but is maintained to a much higher standard.

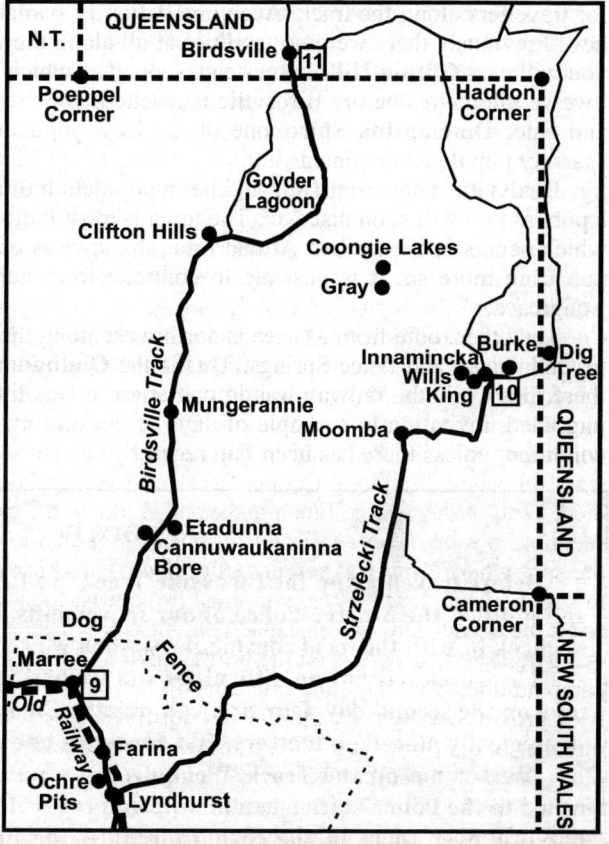

STRZELECKI AND BIRDSVILLE TRACKS
Numerals indicate accommodation

Along the track you will see the famous **Dog Fence**, 5,300 kilometres long, built to keep the dingoes out of the sheep grazing area. Although it has had some success in this respect, one rather imagines the dingoes on one side peering through the wire at their relatives on the other side, as though they were inhabitants of the old East and West Berlin.

Cannuwaukaninna Bore, near **Etadunna Homestead**, produces water which emerges at near boiling point. Then, a little further on, the **Natternanie** sand hills have peaks rising to about nine metres.

After 205 kilometres, you reach **Mungerannie** where there are the only facilities for travellers along the track. Accommodation is available. Mungerannie is relatively new. Previously there were no facilities at all along the way to Birdsville. Continuing, you will pass **Clifton Hills** homestead, soon after which the old and new tracks divide. Twelve kilometres before Birdsville is reached, you cross the border into Queensland and enter **Diamantina Shire**, one of the least populated areas in the whole of this sparsely populated continent.

Birdsville dates from 1882 and has a population of approximately 100. It also has a pub, as you will soon discover. The town is most famous for its annual race meeting, which occurs in September. At that time, the town is packed with humanity - and the pub even more so. It is possible to continue from here north to Mt. Isa or east to Longreach.

The other route from Marree is north-west along the course of the old railway line to Oodnadatta and Alice Springs. This is the **Oodnadatta Track**. It has always been there, but while the railway was in operation, it was little more than a rough, mostly ungraded, invitation to a couple of days of discomfort. Now it is in quite reasonable condition, unless there has been rain recently.

ANECDOTE

Before travelling up the Birdsville Track. we followed approved procedure and notified the Marree Police of our movements, being instructed not to fail to check in with the local constabulary when we reached Birdsville.

The Track gave us no difficulties and we had reached Birdsville by lunchtime on the second day. Our first call was the Birdsville Hotel, temptingly and strategically placed on the very first corner as one enters the town.

"Just come up the Track?" enquired the publican. "Yes, we need to go round to the Police Station in a minute and report in. Where is it?" "The Police Force is over there in the corner," replied the publican, inclining his head towards a sturdy gentleman sporting a decorative pair of shorts, but nothing else above the ankles, and consuming a glass of beer. We walked over and notified him of our arrival. "And where are you heading next?" he enquired. "Bedourie," we replied. "You'll never get there," he said. "There's a lake miles wide between here and Bedourie. What's more, you won't get anywhere unless you leave within the next hour, because all that water's going to reach here too by that time. It's already eighteen inches over the causeway and in an hour's time it'll be too deep to cross. If I were you, I'd finish that beer (at least he had his priorities right) and then head out of town to the east. You might get through if you go now, but be sure to follow the signs for the flood road. The other route is already impassable." And he went back to his refreshment.

We followed the advice given, found the causeway just navigable and looked for the flood road, which turned out to be merely an infrequent series of posts guiding us through the desert. From that moment on, we spent the next four weeks driving through mud and water. Australia may be the driest continent on earth, but when it rains here, it rains.

FLINDERS RANGES 695

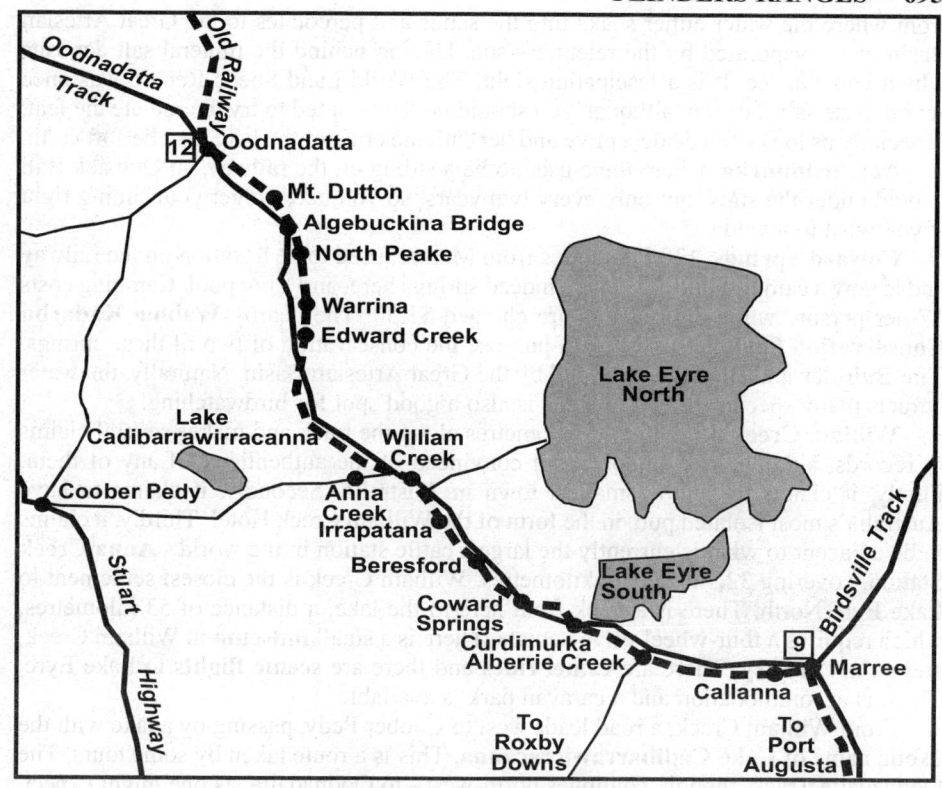

OODNADATTA TRACK
Numerals indicate accommodation

As you proceed up the track, you will be following the route of the **Overland Telegraph Line** constructed from Port Augusta to Darwin in 1871 - 1872. After about seventy kilometres, you will come to a turning on the left. This leads to Roxby Downs and Woomera on the Stuart Highway, but if you take it you will miss the best part of the Oodnadatta Track.

A little further along you will come to the edge of **Lake Eyre**. The railway was built to skirt the rim of the huge lake at a level where it would never get flooded. In 1974, however, the lake reached unprecedented levels and overflowed into various channels which had, until then, been regarded as of unknown origin. Their origin having been thus ascertained, the railway had to be raised by three metres to guard against further flooding in the remaining six years of its life. As you look out across this huge salt lake, there is no end to it within the extent of vision, although whether it has salt water in it, or just salt, will depend upon the time of year. It will be closest to capacity in about March. Realise now that this is Lake Eyre South, which is by far the smaller of the two lakes. Its big brother, Lake Eyre North, covers 8,430 square kilometres and measures 144 kilometres by 77 kilometres with its surface usually fifteen metres below sea level. Between them, these two lakes contain all of the water draining off one-sixth of the entire continent. Just consider this amazing fact. All of the rivers in one-sixth of Australia flow not to the sea, but inland to these gigantic lakes, from where the water either soaks into the sands and percolates to the Great Artesian Basin or is evaporated by the relentless sun, leaving behind the mineral salt deposits which you can see. It is a fascinating sight. The World Land Speed Record was once set on these salt flats too, although you should not be tempted to try to emulate the feat, especially as looks can be deceptive and beneath the crust of the lake may be soft earth.

At **Curdimurka**, where there used to be a siding on the railway, an Outback Ball is held under the stars, but only every two years, so you need to get your timing right if you wish to attend.

Coward Springs, 130 kilometres from Marree, used to be a station on the railway and is now a campground. There are indeed springs here, and a hot pool. Camping costs $7 per person, while day visitors are charged $1.50. The nearby **Wabma Kadarbu Conservation Park** has as its main purpose the conservation of two of these springs, **The Bubbler** and **Blanche Cup**, fed by the Great Artesian Basin. Naturally, the water attracts many species of birds, so this is also a good spot for birdwatching.

William Creek is another 75 kilometres along the track and makes several claims to records, although the author is not convinced of the authenticity of any of them. Firstly, it claims to be the smallest town in Australia. Secondly, it claims to have Australia's most isolated pub, in the form of the William Creek Hotel. Thirdly, it claims to be adjacent to what is currently the largest cattle station in the world - **Anna Creek** Station, covering 32,500 square kilometres. William Creek is the closest settlement to Lake Eyre North. There is a track from here to the lake, a distance of 53 kilometres, which requires a four-wheel-drive vehicle. There is a small **museum** in William Creek, and an **art gallery**. There are **camel rides** and there are **scenic flights** to Lake Eyre. There is accommodation and a caravan park is available.

From William Creek, a road leads west to Coober Pedy, passing by a lake with the exotic name of **Lake Cadibarrawirracanna**. This is a route taken by some tours. The Oodnadatta Track, though, continues north-west - to Oodnadatta, as one might expect. Before reaching the town of Oodnadatta you will see the only bridge of any size on the railway line. This is the **Algebuckina Bridge**, over the **Neales River**, a substantial iron structure. Rumour says that such a grand bridge was put here only because it was found to be too short for its intended location on another line, but rumour can be uncharitable.

ANECDOTE

The train stopped for a while at William Creek and I was talking to one of the railwaymen there.

"We used to have a worker here," he said, "Who liked to start early and do all his jobs before lunch. Then he would eat his sandwiches and have couple of bottles of grog at lunchtime and be back here on his section car by about 2:00. Well, we knew that something was wrong when his section car sailed through one afternoon with just his dog on it, looking very stately all by himself. Luckily there was nothing due on the line, so we sent off one section car in each direction. One chased the dog until he ran out of fuel, while the other went the other way to look for his owner. We found him in the end sitting beside the track. It seems that he had set off home, having had a bit too much to drink, and fell off on the way, while the dog just kept going. I've never seen a dog look so important."

Oodnadatta was the end of the railway for nearly half a century, from 1884 until the line was extended to Stuart (Alice Springs) in 1929. During this period, all goods were unloaded here and taken on their way by camel, and Oodnadatta was a railhead of some importance. When the railway was extended, the town suffered a decline, and when the rail service was withdrawn completely following the construction of the new line well to the west, it was expected that it might become almost a ghost town. That has not occurred, however. Like Marree, Oodnadatta has managed to adapt itself to cater for the tourist market. Both the Oodnadatta Hotel and the Pink Roadhouse provide accommodation, including beds for backpackers. The **Railway Station** has become a museum. There are waterholes for swimming in the Neales River, and there is a race meeting on the first weekend in May which attracts very considerable numbers of people. Thus Oodnadatta too is surviving.

Just north of Oodnadatta, the Oodnadatta Track turns west, leaving the course of the railway, and joins the Stuart Highway 209 kilometres later at **Marla Bore**. It is possible, however, to continue northwards in the proximity of the railway, but the standard of the road deteriorates. Whichever option is taken, the route will lead eventually to Alice Springs.

However, the point should be made again that none of this travelling north of Wilpena Pound is possible without joining a tour or having a private vehicle. In the latter case, caution is important. Even a two-wheel-drive vehicle can cover all of this territory if the weather is fine and the vehicle is driven sensibly. Do follow the usual rules for outback motoring, however, some of the most important of which are the following. Carry plenty of emergency water - not less than five litres per person, and more if possible, as this may be your most important supply. Carry good maps. If your vehicle breaks down, stay with it. Do not leave the main routes without telling somebody where you are going and arranging a check-in time at the end of your journey. Be sure that you have sufficient fuel bearing in mind that inferior efficiency (greater fuel consumption) can be expected on dirt roads. Always carry a spare can of fuel and a length of rubber tubing. Reduce speed on dirt roads, even when they look good, as there may well be hidden obstacles. Plan your time allowing for a slower rate of progress. Finally, remember that people die on outback roads every year by getting lost, or by underestimating the powers of nature, so always be cautious.

ANECDOTE

We called in at the General Store in Oodnadatta and purchased some supplies. They included half a pound of butter. "Shall I wrap it up in some newspaper for you?" enquired the girl. We told her that it would be all right as it was and departed wondering in a vague way why she had offered the newspaper.

We drove for an hour before choosing a camp spot for the night and then set about preparing dinner. It was noticed immediately that the box of provisions was dripping oil from one corner and when we peered inside we found that the half pound of butter had dissolved totally into an oily pool in the bottom of the box and a sticky liquid insinuating itself into every other provision which we had brought with us. Even when we had thrown the box away, the smell of rancid butter permeated the atmosphere for days. Now we knew why the offer of newspaper had been made. We never bought any butter again while travelling.

SOUTH AUSTRALIA
ACCOMMODATION

(i) Hotel Accommodation in Quorn

Name	Stars	No. on Map	Telephone No.	Address	Lowest Price (Double/Twin)
Flinders Ranges Motel	3	1	1-800-640-973	2 Railway Terrace	$90
Transcontinental Hotel		1	1-800-111-227	15 Railway Terrace	$65
Quorn Caravan Park	3½	1	08-8648-6206	Silo Road	$60
Andu Lodge		1	1-800-639-933	12 First Street	$49

(ii) Backpackers Hostel in Quorn

Name	Group	No. on Map	Telephone No.	Address	Lowest Price (Dormitory)
Andu Lodge	YHA	2	1800-639-933	12 First Street	$20

(iii) Accommodation in Hawker

Name	Stars	No. on Map	Telephone No.	Address	Lowest Price (Double/Twin)
Chapmanton Motel	3	3	08-8648-4100	1 Wilpena Road	$90
Flinders Ranges Park	4½	3	08-8648-4266	Leigh Creek Road	$80
Hawker Caravan Park	3½	3	08-8648-4006	44 Chaceview Terrace	$75
Hawker Hotel / Motel	2½	3	1-800-088-508	Elder Terrace	$49

(iv) Accommodation around Wilpena

Name	Stars	No. on Map	Telephone No.	Address	Lowest Price (Double/Twin)
Wilpena Pound Resort	4	5	1-800-805-802	Wilpena Pound	$120
Rawnsley Park Station	3½	4	08-8648-0030	Wilpena Road	$80

(v) Hotel Accommodation in Parachilna

Name	Stars	No. on Map	Telephone No.	Address	Lowest Price (Double/Twin)
Prairie Hotel	3	6	08-8648-4844	High Street & West Terrace	$140
Overflow Outback Accom		6	08-8648-4844	High Street & West Terrace	$55

ANECDOTE

In South Australia, by State Government law, all aluminium cans carry a five cents deposit. This seems like a fine regulation to encourage the recycling of such cans.

We called into a shop in Coober Pedy and bought a drink and consumed it, then asked whether we could return the can and get the deposit refunded. "Oh, no," said the shopkeeper. "You can't get a refund here. You have to take the can to the depot." "And where's that?" we asked. "There's a list of them up on the wall," the proprietor replied, "You can return the can to any depot, but the nearest one is in Port Augusta." "Port Augusta? But that's 550 kilometres away. It's a long way to go for five cents. What does everybody else do?" "Well, mostly they just throw the cans away, but there is one man who drives a truck down every two weeks. If you like to go round to his place, he'll give you two cents for the can. The rest goes for his expenses and a little bit of profit to make it worth while for him."

We threw away the recyclable can. To make a law is one matter, but to make it work is obviously something quite different.

(vi) Backpackers Hostel in Parachilna

Name	Group	No. on Map	Telephone No.	Address	Lowest Price (Dormitory)
Overflow Outback Accom		7	08-8648-4844	High Street & West Terrace	$25

(vii) Accommodation in Leigh Creek and Copley

Name	Stars	No. on Map	Telephone No.	Address	Lowest Price (Double/Twin)
Copley Caravan Park	3	8	08-8675-2288	15 Railway Terrace, Copley	$70
Leigh Ck. Tavern / Motel		8	08-8675-2025	Black Oak Drive	$65
Leigh Creek Hotel	1	8	08-8675-2281	20 Railway Terrace, Copley	$55

(viii) Accommodation in Marree

Name	Stars	No. on Map	Telephone No.	Address	Lowest Price (Double/Twin)
Marree Caravan Park		9	08-8675-8371	Birdsville & Oodnadatta Tks	$80
Town Centre C'van Park		9	08-8674-8352	Railway Terrace	$65
Marree Hotel		9	08-8675-8344	Railway Terrace	$55

(ix) Accommodation in Innamincka

Name	Stars	No. on Map	Telephone No.	Address	Lowest Price (Double/Twin)
Burke Lodge Cabins		10	08-8675-9900	2 South Terrace	$75
Innamincka Hotel		10	08-8675-9901	Innamincka	$70

(x) Accommodation in Birdsville (Queensland)

Name	Stars	No. on Map	Telephone No.	Address	Lowest Price (Double/Twin)
Birdsville Caravan Park		11	07-4656-3214	Florence Street	$60
Birdsville Hotel / Motel		11	07-4656-3244	Adelaide Street	$55

(xi) Accommodation in Oodnadatta

Name	Stars	No. on Map	Telephone No.	Address	Lowest Price (Double/Twin)
Pink Roadhouse	2	12	08-8670-7822	Lot 42, Ikaturka Terrace	$60
Oodnadatta Hotel	3½	12	08-8670-7804	Oodnadatta	$55

MOVING ON
Bus Services from Wilpena Pound

Destination	Operator	Via	Distance (km)	Fare	Journey Time	Frequency
Adelaide	Stateliner		475	$71.50	6¾ - 9¾ hrs	3/week
		Port Augusta	160	$35.40	2¼ hrs	3/week

ANECDOTE

As the train neared Oodnadatta, I was approached by the guard. "It's like this," he said. "Railway staff are not allowed to buy grog to take away at the Oodnadatta pub. We'd like a dozen large bottles of beer, please, or, if they are not available, two dozen stubbies. Thank you very much." And he handed over the appropriate sum of money.

It seems that liquid refreshment has always been a part of Australian railway life. With a speed limit of 60 km/hr throughout the line and a total of just four trains each way every week, the chances of a mishap due to the effects of imbibing are limited. My commission proved to be one bottle, a satisfactory margin on the transaction, I thought - and we arrived safely.

INTERLUDE
THE STORY OF BURKE AND WILLS

One of the most famous stories in Australian history is the journey of discovery undertaken by Burke and Wills. It is the tale of a series of mishaps and unlucky decisions, of men's lives being lost by minor but crucial failures and of a rendezvous missed by a matter of a few hours after four months of travel. No doubt it is this major role played by misfortune which makes it such a famous story.

Financed principally by the Victorian Government, the expedition headed by Robert O'Hara Burke left Melbourne at 16:00 on 20th August 1860, its goal being to cross the continent of Australia from south to north for the first time.

Burke had been a policeman in Beechworth and then Castlemaine, Victoria, and, whilst he had performed his duties with some distinction, he was perhaps not the ideal choice as the leader of this expedition, being too overbearing and emotional in some of his decisions, as well as lacking in the essential skills of bushcraft. There was, however, no doubting his bravery and determination. His second-in-command at this stage was not William John Wills, but George Landells, who was also in charge of the camels used on the expedition. Wills was the navigator, surveyor and astronomer.

The expedition was the best equipped in Australian history, indeed too well equipped, for its early progress was restricted by the quantities of supplies which had to be moved, including, for example, barrels of rum to encourage the camels when they felt tired. Much of the unnecessary impedimenta was gradually abandoned as the expedition progressed. Even on the first short day, three wagons broke before Essendon was reached and the first camp made. A monument near the station commemorates the spot of this first camp.

The expedition moved north through Victoria to Swan Hill, on the Murray, where a young man named Charlie Gray was accepted by Burke as a new recruit. They pressed on through New South Wales as far as Menindee, arriving there on 12th October 1860. The hotel room where Burke stayed can still be seen. During the week spent here, Landells resigned as second-in-command following disagreements with Burke, and Wills was appointed in his place. Burke decided to divide his forces at this point and set out for Cooper Creek on 19th October with a small group of men and limited supplies, leaving the remainder to follow on a little later. With little to transport, he made rapid progress and reached Cooper Creek on 11th November. Here the famous Camp 65 was established. The Roman numerals LXV can still be seen cut into a gum tree on the bank of the creek here.

Wright, a local pastoralist who had guided the party from Menindee to Cooper Creek, was sent back to Menindee to bring up the rest of the expedition, but Burke decided not to await his return. On 16th December 1860, accompanied by Wills, Gray and John King, he set off for the Gulf of Carpentaria in the north of Australia, taking sufficient supplies for twelve weeks, the supplies being conveyed by camel, while the explorers walked. He left William Brahe in charge of Camp 65 with instructions to wait for three months, or as long as his supplies lasted, and then, if necessary, return to Melbourne. It was assumed that Wright would have arrived with the remainder of the expedition long before the end of that time.

The journey north took longer than Burke had anticipated and it was not until 9th February 1861 that he reached salt, tidal water in the Flinders River. In fact, though, Burke and his companions never actually saw the open sea, as they were unable to penetrate the marshy area which lay between them and it. However, it was clear that they had succeeded in crossing the continent and also that they needed to return as hastily as possible, as supplies were low.

Wills now proved to be an excellent navigator, as he was able to guide the party back with precision to the camping spots which they had used on their northward journey. Unfortunately, though, others on the expedition did not all perform as well. Gray, in charge of the meagre supplies which remained, was caught stealing from them for his own benefit, and protested that he could not survive on the rations being provided. Unfortunately, he proved his point when he died a few days later, on 16th April. His three companions spent a whole day digging a shallow grave for him in stony ground, a day which was later to prove crucial for them all and rob two of them of their chance of survival.

Burke, Wills and King arrived back at Camp 65 on the evening of 21st April, to find the camp deserted. A message carved on the reverse of the tree there advised them to "Dig 3ft. NW". (Probably. There is some dispute as to the distance and direction, and the bark has grown over the *Dig Tree* now to make it illegible.) There they found some supplies left, but discovered also a note advising them that Brahe had waited in excess of four months and had left that very morning. Indeed, the reality was that he had spent most of the morning chasing a stray camel and had not left until nearly noon. He was, in fact, camped less than twenty kilometres away.

Wills and King suggested walking on through the night to try to catch up with Brahe, or at least attract his attention with pistol shots early in the morning, but Burke decided that he would be too far away for that to be a practical plan. Instead, they would walk down Cooper Creek and then strike out for the nearest habitation in South Australia. They left the next morning, after reburying the supplies box with a note advising of their return and of their intentions.

Meanwhile, Brahe, travelling south, met Wright travelling north, having finally brought up the remainder of the expedition from Menindee, after wasting a considerable amount of time there, ostensibly awaiting confirmation of his orders from Melbourne. Brahe and Wright decided that they should go back by themselves to Camp 65 to check that Burke, Wills, King and Gray had not returned. When they arrived, on 8th May, they noted that nothing appeared to have been disturbed, so did not bother to dig up the box of supplies again, and left after spending only a few minutes there.

Burke, Wills and King were, at the time, about fifty kilometres away, but were unable to leave the vicinity of the creek due to the lack of rain to provide water for their dash across difficult terrain. Wills, the strongest of the three, volunteered to go back to Camp 65, to see whether anybody had returned and found their note. It was this extra journey which probably cost him his life. When he arrived, on 30th May, he too found nothing changed, for Brahe and Wright had left no sign of their visit. Wills, however, did have the presence of mind to dig up the supplies box and leave a further message.

Burke, Wills and King survived for a while due to the kindness of the local aborigines who brought them gifts of fish and baked nardoo-flour cakes. However, even in such desperate circumstances, Burke acted in a manner which tended to frighten the aborigines away.

Burke and Wills both died at the end of June, Wills having kept up the writing of his journal until almost the last day of his life. Wills was buried by King, and the aborigines covered Burke's body with bushes. King then lived with the aborigines for three months, making himself useful by shooting birds for food, while the aborigines cared for him as best they could until a rescue party, led by Howitt, discovered him on 15th September 1861. The aborigines were rewarded for their help with small gifts, but also by the grant by the South Australian Government of the land along Cooper Creek for their exclusive use, a rare gesture of goodwill at that time.

The remains of Burke and Wills were brought back to Melbourne and given a state funeral, and a statue was commissioned, which currently stands at the junction of Swanston and Collins Streets in Melbourne. King's health had been broken by his experience and he lived only another eleven years, dying in 1872 at the age of only 31.

The expedition was both a success, in that the explorers had managed to cross the continent, and a failure in that three of the four who had achieved the crossing perished on the return. Its fame endures because of the cruel twists of fortune. Had the day not been spent burying Gray, the tragedy would have been avoided. Had Brahe waited just one day longer all would have been well. Had Wright not delayed in bringing the rest of the expedition there would have been adequate supplies at Camp 65. Had Brahe and Wright thought to dig up the supplies box they would have found the note written to them. Had Burke, Wills and King simply waited at Camp 65 they would have been rescued. Indeed, had they known what the aborigines could have taught them, they could have survived indefinitely on the banks of a creek well stocked with fish. But, in this case, fortune was unkind, and it is for this very reason that Burke and Wills are household names throughout Australia.

ANECDOTE

We had determined to try to locate the most significant sites in the story of Burke and Wills. We knew that it would be relatively easy to find the best known of those - the *Dig Tree* and the separate places where Burke and Wills had perished - but imagined that finding the location where Gray had died would be more difficult, since it was four long days' walk from Camp 65. Prior to setting out, therefore, we repaired to the library and read the journal of the admirable Wills.

Reading that journal, one cannot fail to be impressed by this young man who kept such precise and accurate records that he was able to locate all of the camp sites without fail on the return journey and whose impartial record tells us every detail of the expedition, right up until he became too weak to write any more. We even know that his own pulse rate was 48 and weak a few days before he died and that he reckoned that he had another four or five days to live. We also know that his own decisions would have been right where Burke's were wrong - that he would have stayed at Camp 65 and awaited rescue, for example - but that he never questioned the leader's authority and perished without complaint because of another man's mistakes. We know all this, but could this meticulous young man tell us, over an interval of more than a century, just where Gray's grave was?

We took notes of Wills' precise directions for reaching the site that we wanted and noted that he described it as being in a clearing among box trees to the south of a large lake.

When we reached Innamincka, we spoke to the publican there. "Ah, yes," he said. "I used to take people there, but I haven't been for years now." He described how we should follow the main road north, then turn off to the left along a minor track, and fork right when we glimpsed a lake in the distance.

We set off. The main road was only wheel tracks and the minor track was definitely minor, but discernible. Then suddenly, after travelling a long way, we glimpsed the lake and looked for a fork. There was nothing. We reverted to Wills. This was probably the lake which he had described, so we turned right anyway, without the benefit of a track. Yes, there were trees, as Wills had said, although would they be in the same places more than a hundred years later? There was a clearing and we stopped. "According to the directions of Wills, Gray died just about here - maybe." There was a feeling of doubt. How certain could we be? Could we really rely on those century-old directions?

And then we saw it. "There's a notice." It was a hundred metres away. We walked over to it. "Charlie Gray died near this spot on the sixteenth of April 1861," it said simply. We were impressed - not by our own ability to locate this remote spot, but by the man who had written those precise and amazingly accurate instructions which could guide travellers over an interval of considerably more than a century.

We camped nearby and contemplated "at night the wondrous glory of the everlasting stars". The beauty of the Australian outback was so apparent. We had probably never camped so far from the presence of another human being. It was unlikely that there was anybody within a hundred kilometres of us, and this was a century after that journey of exploration. How must those men have felt then?

We thought of that epic journey and of the brave men who had undertaken it, but we thought especially of Wills and of Gray.

SOUTH AUSTRALIA
COOBER PEDY
Population 4,000
10 hrs 30 mins by bus from Adelaide

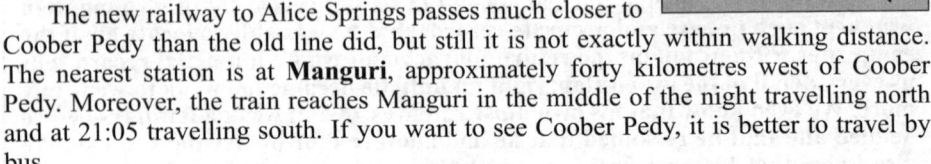

Coober Pedy is the most famous town in Australia for **opals**. If you are travelling between Adelaide and Alice Springs, this is the one place at which you should most certainly make a stop, even though not all buses arrive at a convenient hour.

The new railway to Alice Springs passes much closer to Coober Pedy than the old line did, but still it is not exactly within walking distance. The nearest station is at **Manguri**, approximately forty kilometres west of Coober Pedy. Moreover, the train reaches Manguri in the middle of the night travelling north and at 21:05 travelling south. If you want to see Coober Pedy, it is better to travel by bus.

However, there are some other places between Port Augusta and Coober Pedy which are worth considering for a brief visit. As the road leaves Port Augusta, it follows the course of the Trans-Continental Railway. This used to be a truly awful road, eight hundred kilometres of dirt, corrugated all the way, with steep banks at the sides where the attempts to grade it had cut into the red sands, with the result that when it rained, water flowed onto the road and it became a quagmire. To those who remember such conditions, when journeying to Alice Springs was akin to setting out on a major expedition, experiencing the new paved road is like gaining a promotion from purgatory to heaven.

From Port Augusta to **Pimba** is approximately 175 kilometres. This route is served by Greyhound and Stateliner, but while Greyhound continues up the Stuart Highway to Alice Springs, Stateliner turns off and goes to Woomera and then to Roxby Downs. **Woomera** is only five kilometres from Pimba, and it is a particularly interesting place to visit, as this was formerly Australia's rocket-launching base. Woomera is an aboriginal word meaning a spear thrower, a device used to extend the length of the arm so that the spear can be thrown faster and further, an appropriate enough name to give to this base. It was established in 1947 and used for the launching of experimental rockets. Between 1964 and 1970, it was employed for the launching of the Europa Rockets, and between 1960 and 1972, NASA used nearby **Island Lagoon** as a Deep Space Training Station. Until 1982, entry to this area was forbidden, but now it may be visited. There is a **Woomera Heritage Centre** and an interesting **Missile Park** displaying examples of the various rockets, missiles and weapons test-launched from here, and also aircraft used or tested here. Accommodation is available at the Woomera Travellers Village, including beds for backpackers. Stateliner runs to Woomera every evening from Adelaide, with a change of vehicle at Port Augusta. However, the arrival time in Woomera at 2:05 is a little short of ideal.

Roxby Downs lies about an hour north of Woomera and is a surprisingly modern town, because it is, as it appears, completely new, built to house the workers at the nearby mine at **Olympic Dam**. Olympic Dam is a huge mine. It lies nine kilometres north of Roxby Downs and produces nine million tonnes of ore per year. From this ore comes 80,000 ounces of gold, almost a million ounces of silver, 4,000 tonnes of uranium oxides and 200,000 tonnes of copper. **Surface tours** of the mine are available from March until November each year. The Stateliner bus reaches Roxby Downs at 3:10 and then continues to Olympic Dam, arriving at 3:45.

Thirty kilometres beyond Roxby Downs lies the town of **Andamooka**. However, there is no transport to Andamooka, so you will have to devise a way of getting there from Roxby Downs. Andamooka is another opal town, one of Australia's three main such mining communities, the three being Coober Pedy, Andamooka and Lightning Ridge (in New South Wales). Coober Pedy is firmly on the tourist route, but Andamooka, being less accessible, is much less visited (and the same applies to Lightning Ridge).

In 1930, two boundary riders from nearby Andamooka Station discovered opal here and soon miners started arriving from all over Australia, and from other countries too. Opal mining is often a small-scale operation and you will find

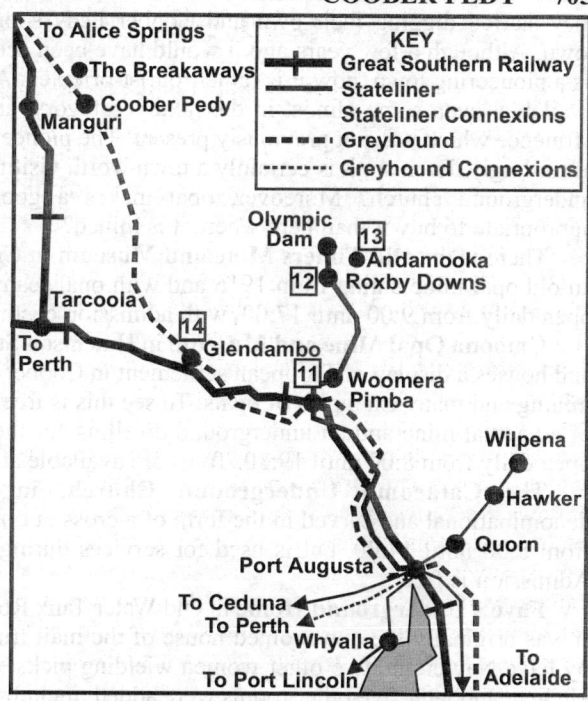

PORT AUGUSTA TO COOBER PEDY
Showing public transport with principal bus stops
(Railway stations shown on pages 668 to 671)
Numerals indicate accommodation

here many one-man mines. The opal is found relatively near the surface at depths of three to ten metres and is on the crust of an ancient seabed dating from between 1.8 and 70 million years ago. There are 24 separate fields here producing opalised shells, stones and dinosaur bones. It is claimed that the opal from here is the most stable in the world and it is from this area that opals presented to the Queen were chosen.

Duke's Bottle House is adjacent to the Post Office and made entirely of discarded beer bottles. It is now a museum and has displays of mining equipment and opals, as well as some historical items. The Museum is open daily from 9:00 until 17:00 and admission is free. There is an **Opal Festival** held in Andamooka each October. Accommodation is available in the town.

Glendambo is 113 kilometres beyond Pimba along the Stuart Highway. It has a **Tourist Centre** with a sheep farming theme and accommodation is available, including backpackers' beds and camping sites. Glendambo is the point at which the Stuart Highway diverges from the Trans-Continental Railway.

Now, therefore, the road turns north, cutting off a corner on the old highway, which used to continue west to **Kingoonya** before making the turn to the north. There are no towns along the 252-kilometre stretch from Glendambo to Coober Pedy.

Coober Pedy is famous for opal and for underground housing. In 1915, a fourteen-year-old boy named Willie Hutchison discovered opal here and the rush started. Arriving miners soon found that Coober Pedy was rather a warm spot, but that the hills around provided cool living quarters in the caves. When natural caves were exhausted, they started digging their own and Coober Pedy soon became a semi-underground town. Although a few years ago it would have been accurate to describe Coober Pedy as a pioneering town, now it is rather tourist-oriented. All types of accommodation are available, even some almost in the luxury category, and the town now has an air of affluence which was not previously present. The pioneering spirit seems to be receding accordingly. Even so, it is certainly a town worth visiting. Where else will you find an underground church? Moreover, opal makes a good souvenir, and where more appropriate to buy it than here where it is mined?

There is the **Old Timers Mine and Museum** in Crowders Gully Road, housed in an old opal mine dating from 1916 and with opal seams still visible in the walls. It is open daily from 9:00 until 17:00, with admission costing $12.

Umoona Opal Mine and Museum in Hutchison Street is completely underground and houses a display of European settlement in Coober Pedy, with information on opal mining and many examples of opals. To see this is free, but there is also a tour offered of an actual mine and an underground dwelling for the price of $10. The Museum is open daily from 8:00 until 19:30. Tours are available at 10:00, 12:00, 14:00 and 16:00.

The **Catacomb Underground Church**, in Catacomb Road, is multi-denominational and carved in the form of a cross out of the solid sandstone. It is open from 8:00 until 17:00, but is used for services during part of that time on Sundays. Admission is free.

Faye's Underground Home in Old Water Tank Road is also carved from the rock. It was originally the one-roomed house of the mail truck driver, but it was converted by Faye Nayler and two other women wielding picks and shovels into a bedroom and kitchen, and later five other rooms were added, including a swimming pool and a wine cellar. This home is unusual in being open to the public, yet actually still used as a residence. It is open from 8:00 until 17:00, except on Sundays. Admission costs $4.

There is a **pottery** in Rowe Drive, open daily from 8:30 until 18:00, with free admission, and, of course, the town is just full of opal shops, many of which have small free museums and exhibitions attached.

Near Coober Pedy are the **Breakaways** with their impressive scenery which has been used as the setting for various films in recent years. The Breakaways are just 34 kilometres north of the town and border that 5,300-kilometre fence built to keep the dingoes out, or perhaps in. Tours are available.

Much further north are the **Copper Hills**, the **Arckaringa Hills** and the **Painted Desert**, to which tours run.

There is also a third South Australian opal town. This is **Mintabie**. To reach the town one travels 233 kilometres north along the Stuart Highway to **Marla** and then turns west for a further 33 kilometres. Mintabie is on aboriginal land, so a permit must be obtained along the way from Marla Police Station. Considering the distance and the fact that you have all the opal you could want in Coober Pedy, this journey seems superfluous for most travellers.

ACCOMMODATION
(i) Accommodation in Woomera

Name	Stars	No. on Map	Telephone No.	Address	Lowest Price (Double/Twin)
Woomera Travellers L'ge		11	08-8673-7800	Banool Avenue	$75

COOBER PEDY

(ii) Accommodation in Roxby Downs

Name	Stars	No. on Map	Telephone No.	Address	Lowest Price (Double/Twin)
Roxby Downs Motor Inn		12	1-800-086-200	Richardson Place	$95
Roxby Downs Caravan Pk		12	08-8671-1000	Pioneer Drive	$65
Myall Grove Caravan Pk.		12	08-8671-1991	56 Burgoyne Street	$65

(iii) Accommodation in Andamooka

Name	Stars	No. on Map	Telephone No.	Address	Lowest Price (Double/Twin)
Andamooka Motel	2	13	08-8672-7374	Main Street	$95
Duke's Bottlehouse Motel		13	08-8672-7007	275 Opal Creek Boulevard	$75
Opal Hotel / Motel		13	08-8672-7078	Andamooka	$65

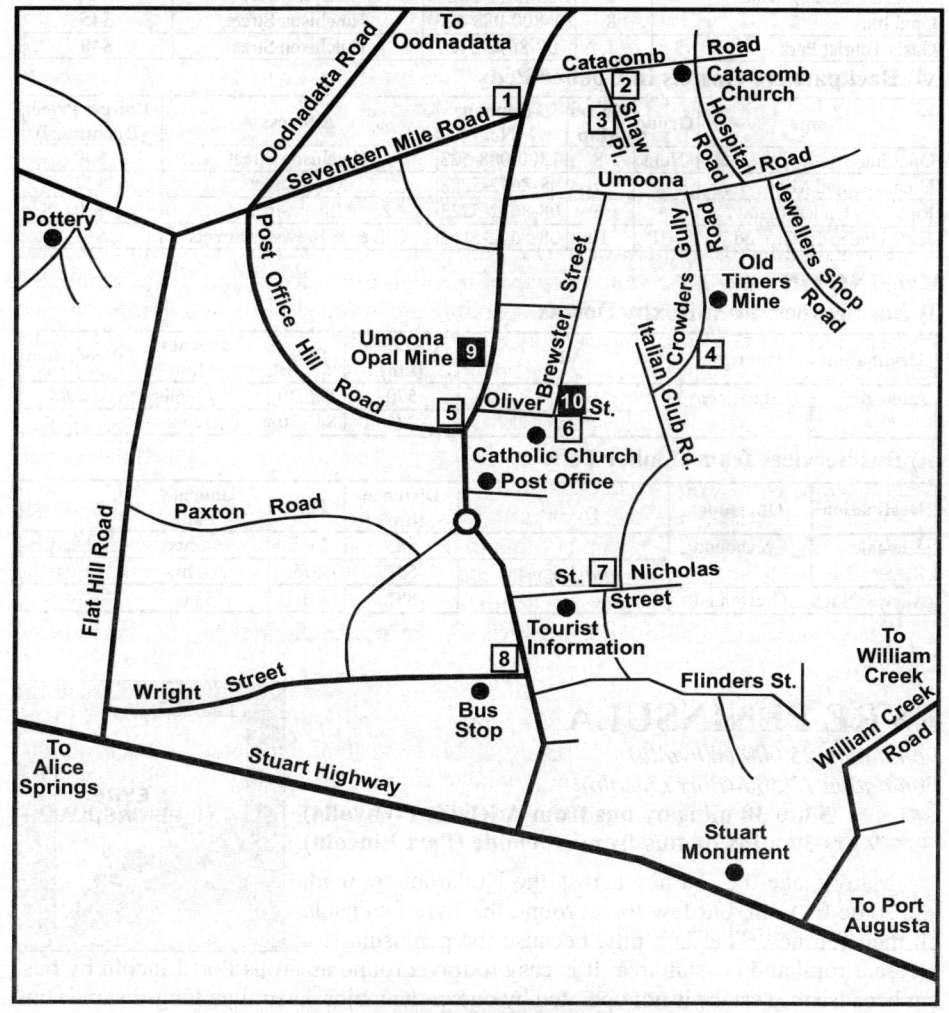

COOBER PEDY
Black numerals in white boxes indicate hotel accommodation
White numerals in black boxes indicate backpackers hostels

SOUTH AUSTRALIA

(iv) Accommodation in Glendambo

Name	Stars	No. on Map	Telephone No.	Address	Lowest Price (Double/Twin)
Glendambo Hotel / Motel		14	08-8672-1030	Stuart Highway	$65

(v) Hotel Accommodation in Coober Pedy

Name	Stars	No. on Map	Telephone No.	Address	Lowest Price (Double/Twin)
Desert Cave	3½	5	1-800-088-521	Hutchison Street	$185
Coober Pedy Experience	3	4	08-8672-5777	Crowders Gully Road	$140
Desert View Motel	3	3	08-8672-3330	Shaw Place	$105
Underground Motel	3	2	08-8672-5324	Lot 1138, Catacomb Road	$105
Mud Hut Motel	3½	7	08-8672-3003	St. Nicholas Street	$105
Radeka's Underground		6	08-8672-5223	Oliver Street	$100
Opal Inn		8	1-800-088-523	Hutchison Street	$45
Oasis Tourist Park	3	1	08-8672-5169	Hutchison Street	$40

(vi) Backpackers Hostels in Coober Pedy

Name	Group	No. on Map	Telephone No.	Address	Lowest Price (Dormitory)
Opal Inn	Nom	8	1800-088-523	Hutchison Street	$39
Umoona Opal Mine		9	08-8672-5288	Main Street	$27
Radeka's Underground		6	08-8672-5223	Oliver Street	$20
Joe's Under the Ground	VIP	10	08-8672-5163	Oliver & Brewster Streets	$15

MOVING ON

(i) Bus Services from Roxby Downs

Destination	Operator	Via	Distance (km)	Fare	Journey Time	Frequency
Adelaide	Stateliner		570	$86.20	7¾ - 8½ hrs	1/day
		Port Augusta	255	$47.30	3¼ hrs	1/day

(ii) Bus Services from Coober Pedy

Destination	Operator	Via	Distance (km)	Fare	Journey Time	Frequency
Adelaide	Greyhound		883	$115	11 hrs	1/day
		Port Augusta	537	$75	6½ hrs	1/day
Alice Springs	Greyhound		687	$103	8 hrs	1/day

EYRE PENINSULA

Population 25,000 (Whyalla)
Population 12,500 (Port Lincoln)

5 hrs 30 mins by bus from Adelaide (Whyalla)
9 hrs 30 mins by bus from Adelaide (Port Lincoln)

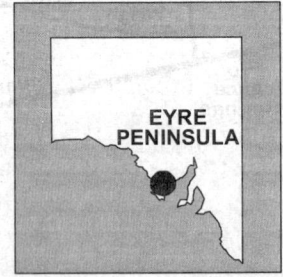

Many make the journey across the Nullarbor by road, and some by train, but few travel round the Eyre Peninsula on their journey. That is a pity, because the peninsula is a pleasant rural and coastal area. It is easy to travel round as far as Port Lincoln by bus, but because the service is not operated by one of the major Australian long-distance bus companies, it is not so popular with travellers. Try this detour, though, if you have time, and you will discover some little seaside resorts and wheat towns which others miss as

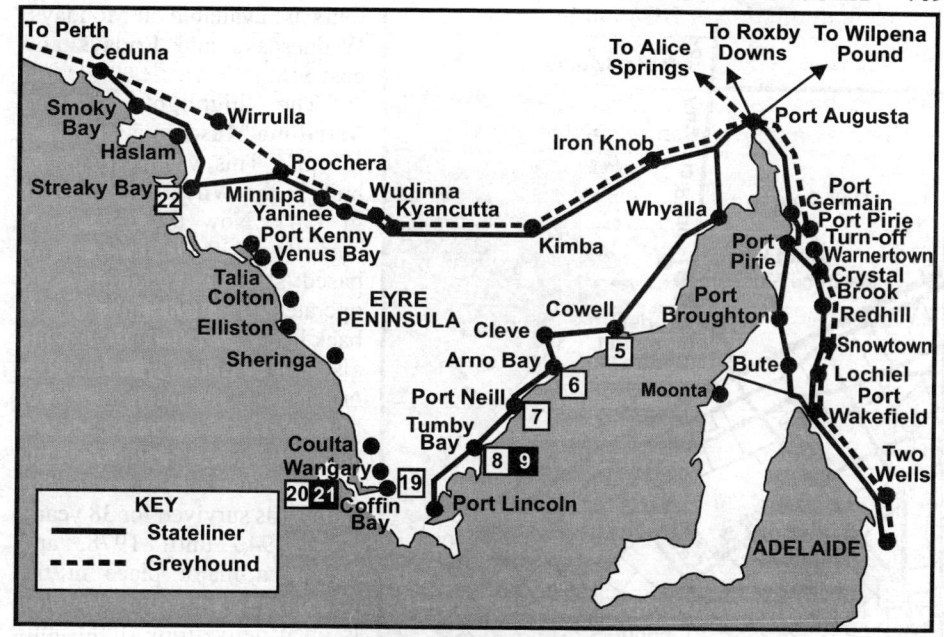

EYRE PENINSULA
Showing principal bus stops
Black numerals in white boxes indicate hotel accommodation
White numerals in black boxes indicate backpackers hostels

they rush across the top of the peninsula along a road which is of only limited interest scenically.

Stateliner operates four services a day to Whyalla and two of these continue to Port Lincoln, at the tip of the peninsula.

Starting from Port Augusta, it is an hour's run to **Whyalla**, and, as you approach, you will be left in no doubt that this is an industrial city. Matthew Flinders discovered and named **Hummock Hill** on 9th March 1802, and that was the name by which this location was originally known. It became Whyalla in 1914. Iron ore had been discovered in the late 1890s in the hill now known as **Iron Knob**. This was the commencement of the involvement of B.H.P. (Broken Hill Proprietary) in the development of the town. A tramway was constructed to move the ore from the mine to the barges and across Spencer Gulf to the smelters at Port Pirie. In 1938, it was decided to build a blast furnace in Whyalla itself, and shipyards and a deep water harbour were also constructed. In 1958, work was started on a fully integrated steelworks here, and in 1961 Whyalla was proclaimed a city. There is, of course, a standard gauge railway to Whyalla, used to bring in supplies and move out steel products, so it seems surprising that Whyalla has no passenger rail service. In fact, it had passenger trains until they were withdrawn in the last decade and one certainly feels that it should have such a service. One of the problems, though, is that, with South Australian Railways defunct, there is nobody to operate medium-distance trains within the state, so Whyalla must be reached by bus.

Despite its industrial background, Whyalla has several attractions to offer the visitor. The first, and one of the most interesting, is a **tour of the steelworks**. These

SOUTH AUSTRALIA

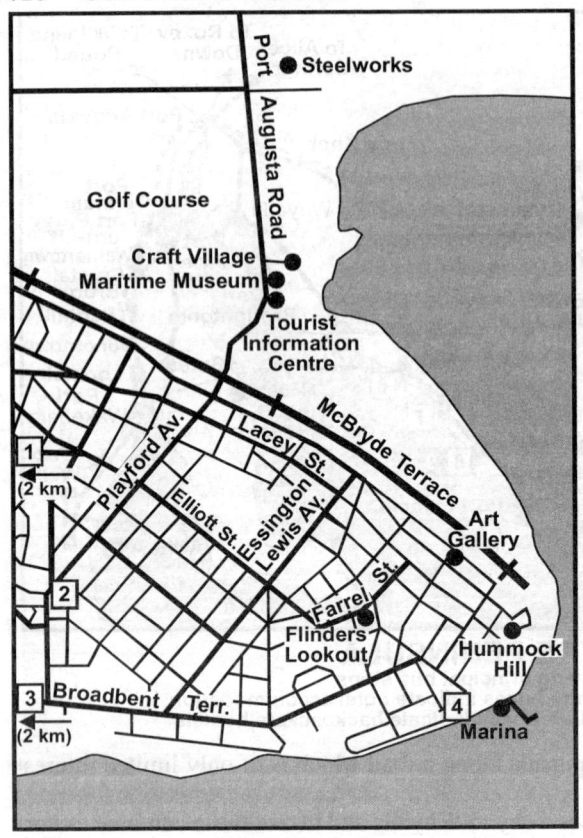

WHYALLA
Numerals indicate accommodation

tours are available on Mondays, Wednesdays and Fridays and cost $18.

The highlight of the **Maritime Museum** is *H.M.A.S. Whyalla*. This was the first ship built in the Whyalla Shipyards, in 1941. Now the 650 tonne corvette is the largest land-based ship in Australia. She operated until 1983 and arrived back here in 1988. The Museum also has Matthew Flinders' original charts and journals of his voyages, as well as more recent history of the city in relation to the sea. Whyalla Shipyards survived for 38 years, from 1940 until 1978, and occupy a major place in the exhibits. The Maritime Museum is open daily from 10:00 until 16:00 and admission costs $8.

Flinders Lookout stands high above the foreshore offering views of the eastern part of the city, and also out to sea across to the Santos Gas and Fractionation Plant at Port Bonython. Sometimes Port Pirie, 31 kilometres away, is also visible.

Another lookout is situated at **Hummock Hill**, where the first settlement was made. The gun emplacements constructed during the Second World War can be seen here, and a view is offered over Whyalla city, the B.H.P. Works, the South Flinders Ranges, the Santos Plant and the Middleback Ranges to the west.

Continuing down the east coast of the Eyre Peninsula, the bus will pass through **Cowell** and then turn inland to the small town of **Cleve**, before rejoining the coast at **Arno Bay** and continuing to Port Neill and Tumby Bay.

In **Port Neill** you can find Jill and Vic Fauser's **Living Museum**, a private collection of various types of steam engines, vintage vehicles, seats, dolls, toys, bottles and shells. The Museum is on the Esplanade near the Caravan Park. It is open every day and admission is by voluntary donation. To the north of the town is the **Port Neill Lookout Tower** providing a fine view of the town and of the surrounding farming land.

Tumby Bay is a pleasant beach resort. The **National Trust Museum** is located in the old wooden schoolhouse and has a collection of items from pioneering days here. However, it is open only on Wednesdays from 10:00 until 11:00 and Saturdays from

14:30 until 16:30. Admission costs $4. There is a backpackers hostel located here in Tumby Bay in the Sea Breeze Hotel right on the edge of the beach.

Port Lincoln is situated close to the tip of the Eyre Peninsula and, apart from Whyalla, is the largest town on the peninsula. Matthew Flinders, charged with the task of charting the coast of Australia, arrived here in February 1802 and named the port after his native part of England, and the bay and island after the town of Boston in Lincolnshire. **Boston Bay** claims to be the largest natural harbour in Australia. Port Lincoln was later one of the candidates for capital of South Australia. Although rejected, it was settled in 1839, only three years after Adelaide.

The town has several minor attractions. The **Axel Stemross Maritime Museum** is a private enterprise operated by a Finnish boatbuilder nostalgic for the days of the windjammers. It has exhibits from those times and a large collection of photographs. The Museum is open from 13:00 until 17:00 on Sundays, Tuesdays, Thursdays and Saturdays, with admission costing $3.

Constantia is a company specialising in skilled wood craftsmanship. The company produced the Central Table and the Hansard Desk in the House of Representatives in Canberra, for example. The workshop in Proper Bay Road is open on weekdays from 9:00 until 17:00 with conducted tours at 11:00 and 14:30. Admission costs $5.

There is a **Seahorse Farm** in Port Lincoln which can be visited. However, bookings must be made in advance with the Port Lincoln Visitor Information Centre. Tours are available every day between 15:00 and 16:00 and cost $6.

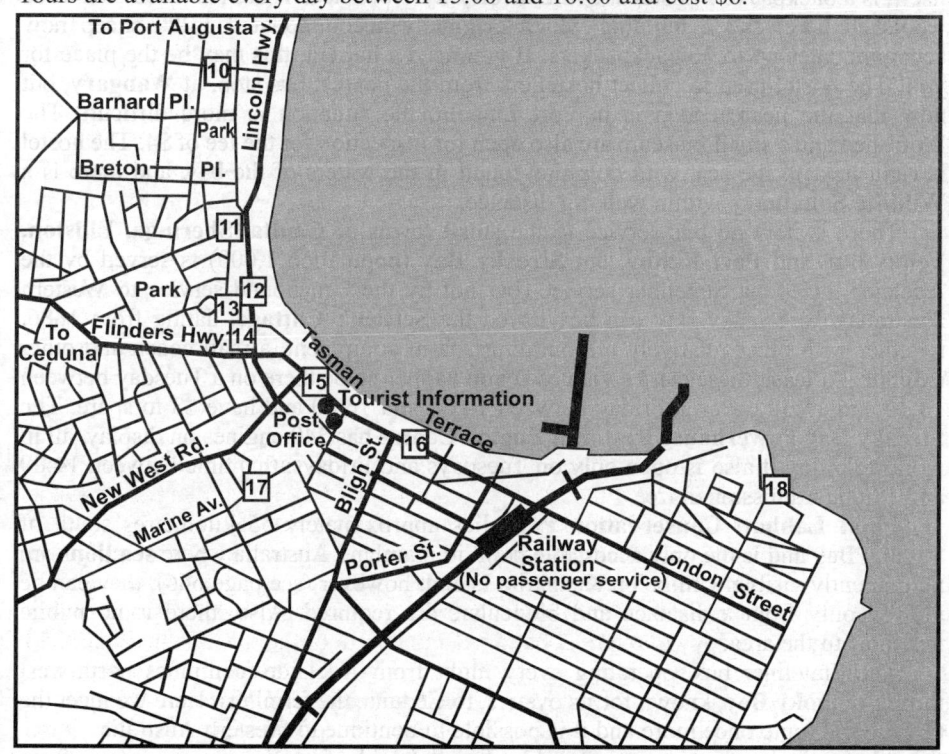

PORT LINCOLN
Numerals indicate accommodation

SOUTH AUSTRALIA

Lincoln National Park lies thirteen kilometres south-east of the town and is being used for the reintroduction of native wildlife following a predator control programme.

One of the surprises in Port Lincoln is a narrow gauge railway system disconnected from any other railways in the state. This runs west all the way to Ceduna and Penong, but does not offer a passenger service, being used mainly for transporting wheat.

From Port Lincoln, Coastlink used to operate a bus up the coast to Ceduna three times a week, but this service is currently suspended. However, ask about it, because, if operations are resumed, the backtrack to Port Augusta will be eliminated and some pretty coastal scenery will be added to the itinerary.

47 kilometres west of Port Lincoln lies a town with the glamorous name of **Coffin Bay**. The **Coffin Bay National Park** starts two kilometres outside the town. It offers windswept cliffs, moving dunes, long beaches and surf. At the farther end of the peninsula, the Coffin Bay Ponies are the only totally-managed herd of wild horses in Australia. They are descended from ponies brought from Timor in 1847 by local settlers. They used to be rounded up and sold as children's ponies and cart horses, but after the 1930s there was little demand, so many of them were simply shot for their manes and tails. The ponies present now are the escapees from those difficult times. They are hardy animals, yet with docile characters. In the famous Australian poem *The Man from Snowy River* (see page 845), the horse of the hero was part Timor pony.

A little beyond the town of Coffin Bay, but still on the northern shore of the bay itself, is a backpackers hostel at **Mt. Dutton Bay** Woolshed. There is indeed a restored woolshed here, and a building which originally accommodated 1,200 sheep now accommodates up to 36 backpackers. If you need a haircut, this may be the place for you! The hostel used to collect hostellers from the nearest bus stop, at **Wangary**, but now that the nearest stop is in Port Lincoln, the situation is more difficult. The Woolshed and a small museum are also open for inspection for the fee of $4. The hostel is right next to the sea, with dolphins found in the waters of the bay, and there is a **Wildlife Sanctuary** within walking distance.

There is now no bus service to the small towns of **Coulta, Sheringa, Elliston, Venus Bay** and **Port Kenny**, but **Streaky Bay** (population 1,000) is served by the Adelaide - Ceduna Stateliner service (but not by the Greyhound service to Western Australia). In Streaky Bay can be viewed the **Settler's Cottage**, dating from 1886, together with other relatively old buildings, farm equipment, a mail coach and other exhibits. At least, these can be viewed if you happen to be there on a Tuesday between 13:30 and 15:30, or on a Friday between 14:00 and 16:00 and have $3 to spare. The **Streaky Bay Powerhouse Restored Engine Centre** has 240 engines on display, all in working order. It also is open only on Tuesdays and Fridays, this time between 14:00 and 17:00. Admission is free.

Point Labbatt Conservation Park lies approximately 55 kilometres south of Streaky Bay and is the only accessible point in mainland Australia where **sea lions** are permanently visible. Unlike on Kangaroo Island, however (see page 646), they can be viewed only from a distance and binoculars are required. Also, there is no public transport to the area.

The Stateliner bus, operating every night from Adelaide, continues north-west through **Smoky Bay**, known for its oysters, to Ceduna, the terminus. Here we meet the Greyhound route once more and it is possible to continue to Western Australia.

Alternatively, if you want to head back to Adelaide, Stateliner runs a service from here every night.

EYRE PENINSULA 713

ACCOMMODATION

(i) Accommodation in Whyalla *(map on page 710)*

Name	Stars	No. on Map	Telephone No.	Address	Lowest Price (Double/Twin)
Derham's Foreshore Inn	3½	4	08-8645-8877	Watson Terrace	$120
Alexander Motor Inn	3½	2	08-8645-9488	99 Playford Avenue	$90
Westland Hotel	3½	1	08-8645-0066	100 McDouall Stuart Av.	$80
Airport Whyalla Motel		3	08-8645-2122	Lincoln Hy./Racecourse Rd.	$75

(ii) Accommodation in Cowell *(map on page 709)*

Name	Stars	No. on Map	Telephone No.	Address	Lowest Price (Double/Twin)
Cowell Jade Motel	3	5	08-8629-2002	Lincoln Highway	$75
Cowell Holiday Units	3	5	08-8629-6060	17 Third Street	$75
Foreshore Caravan Park	3	5	08-8629-2307	Esplanade	$65

(iii) Accommodation in Arno Bay *(map on page 709)*

Name	Stars	No. on Map	Telephone No.	Address	Lowest Price (Double/Twin)
Hotel Arno	1	6	08-8628-0001	Government Road	$45

(iv) Accommodation in Port Neill *(map on page 709)*

Name	Stars	No. on Map	Telephone No.	Address	Lowest Price (Double/Twin)
Port Neill Caravan Park		7	08-8688-9067	Peake Terrace	$65
Henley's Holiday Flats	2	7	08-8688-9001	1 Gill Street	$55

(v) Hotel Accommodation in Tumby Bay *(map on page 709)*

Name	Stars	No. on Map	Telephone No.	Address	Lowest Price (Double/Twin)
Tumby Bay Marina Motel	3	8	08-8688-2311	4 Berryman Street	$70
Tumby Bayside Units	3	8	08-8688-2087	Yaringa Avenue	$65
Sea Breeze Hotel		8	08-8688-2362	7 Tumby Terrace	$30

(vi) Backpackers Hostel in Tumby Bay *(map on page 709)*

Name	Group	No. on Map	Telephone No.	Address	Lowest Price (Dormitory)
Sea Breeze Hotel	Nom	9	08-8688-2362	7 Tumby Terrace	$17

(vii) Accommodation in Port Lincoln *(map on page 711)*

Name	Stars	No. on Map	Telephone No.	Address	Lowest Price (Double/Twin)
Port Lincoln B&B	4½	10	08-8682-3550	2 Power Terrace	$110
Harbour View Apartments	3½	12	08-8682-4477	30 Lincoln Highway	$100
Yardarm B&B	3	17	08-8683-0984	14 Telford Avenue	$100
Sorrento Lodge Apts.	3	14	08-8682-2154	8 Lincoln Highway	$95
Blue Seas Motel	3	13	08-8682-3022	7 Gloucester Terrace	$85
Grand Tasman Hotel	2½	16	08-8682-2133	94 Tasman Terrace	$85
Navigator's Motel	3	11	08-8682-4633	2 Normandy Place	$85
First Landing Motel	3½	18	08-8682-2344	11 Shaen Street	$80
Peninsula Motel	3	15	08-8682-2033	12 Tasman Terrace	$75

714 SOUTH AUSTRALIA

(viii) Hotel Accommodation in Coffin Bay and Vicinity *(map on page 709)*

Name	Stars	No. on Map	Telephone No.	Address	Lowest Price (Double/Twin)
Woolshed Cottage		20	08-8685-4031	1 Woolshed Dr., Mt. Dutton	$125
Sheoak Holiday Homes	4	19	08-8685-4314	257 Esplanade	$100
Almonta Holiday Apts.		19	08-8685-4076	49 Esplanade	$90
Kooringa Holiday Flats	3	19	08-8685-4087	Greenly Avenue	$75
Alpine Holiday Units	3	19	08-8685-4068	337 Esplanade	$70
Siesta Lodge	3	19	08-8685-4001	331 Esplanade	$60

(ix) Backpackers Hostel near Coffin Bay *(map on page 709)*

Name	Group	No. on Map	Telephone No.	Address	Lowest Price (Dormitory)
Woolshed Hostel	Nom	21	08-8685-4031	1 Woolshed Drive, Mt. Dutton	$18

(x) Accommodation in Streaky Bay *(map on page 709)*

Name	Stars	No. on Map	Telephone No.	Address	Lowest Price (Double/Twin)
Headland House B&B		22	08-8626-1315	5 Flinders Drive	$85
Streaky Bay Motel	3½	22	08-8626-1126	7 Alfred Terrace	$75

MOVING ON
(i) Bus Services from Whyalla

Destination	Operator	Via	Distance (km)	Fare	Journey Time	Frequency
Adelaide	Stateliner		398	$45.80	5 - 6½ hrs	4/day
		Port Augusta	83	$16.40	50 – 70 mins	4/day
Port Lincoln	Stateliner		295	$48.70	3¾ - 4 hrs	2/day

(ii) Bus Services from Port Lincoln

Destination	Operator	Via	Distance (km)	Fare	Journey Time	Frequency
Adelaide	Stateliner		693	$79.60	9½ - 10¼ hrs	2/day
		Port Augusta	378	$56.40	4½ - 4¾ hrs	2/day
		Whyalla	295	$48.70	3½ - 3¾ hrs	2/day

CEDUNA AND THE NULLARBOR PLAIN

Population 4,000 (Ceduna)
  9 hrs 30 mins by bus from Adelaide (Ceduna)
  13 hrs 30 mins by bus from Adelaide (Nullarbor)

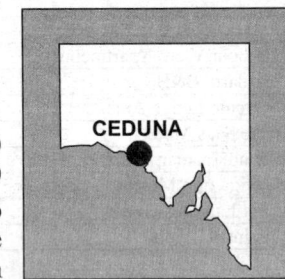

Ceduna is only a small town, although it can claim to have a golf course, and even a little sparse grass on the course. Recently it achieved an element of fame by lying in the path of a **total eclipse of the sun** on the evening of 4th December 2002.

Ceduna is situated at the edge of the farming area and also used to be known as the town where the bitumen ended. From here to the Western Australian border lay 500 kilometres of dirt road, the quality of which varied between poor and terrible according to when it had last been graded. Now, though, it is all bitumen, to make your journey west smooth and uneventful.

Ceduna is the last town of any size in South Australia and it will be fifteen hours on the bus before you see another town with a similar population of approximately 3,000 when you reach Norseman in Western Australia. This is a long journey across one of Australia's most desolate major highways.

The coast here, and as far east as Streaky Bay, was first charted in 1627 by Peter Nuyts on the *Golden Zeepard*. In 1802, Matthew Flinders circumnavigated the continent and named many of the features along the southern coast. However, it was not until 1840 that a European actually walked across here. That person was John Eyre, only 25 years old at the time, after whom the highway is now named. The crossing was somewhat controversial because of an incident in which Eyre's companion was killed and two aborigines who were accompanying the party absconded and were never seen again. However, Eyre and one other aborigine continued and eventually succeeded in crossing the daunting plain. They left Streaky Bay in November 1840 and reached Albany in June 1841, much being owed to the skills of the aborigine, Wylie, and a chance meeting with Captain Rossiter aboard the French whaler *Mississippi* near

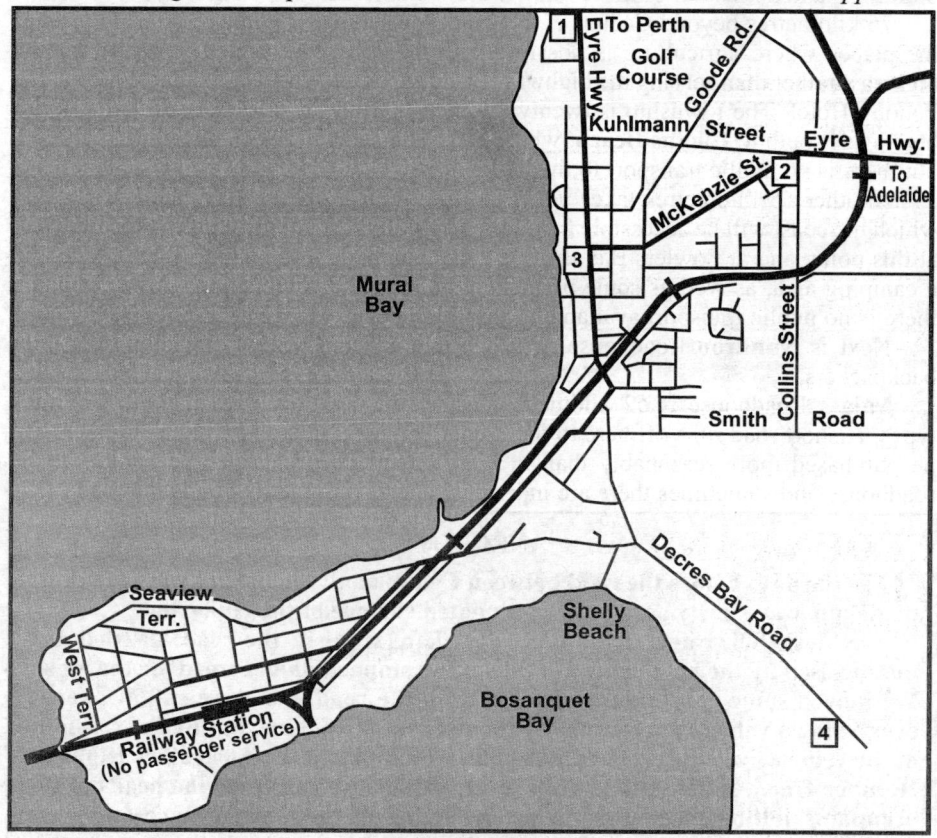

CEDUNA
Numerals indicate accommodation

SOUTH AUSTRALIA

Esperance. The telegraph link across the Nullarbor was completed in 1877, but it was not until 1912 that the first motor vehicle succeeded in crossing the Nullarbor. In 1917, the rail link was established, but only during the Second World War was a road constructed. As mentioned above, it was a road but not one of the type which the reader will now enjoy. Even when the author first crossed, it was a question of jolting and crashing across those 500 kilometres of rough dirt to reach the safety of the Western Australian border. The last part of the highway was finally sealed in 1976.

The name Nullarbor is a mock Latin word. *Null* equals no or nothing. *Arbor* means tree. Thus it is the plain with no trees, and you will certainly observe the truth inherent in the name. The rainfall is too low here for anything but stunted scrub growth to be able to eke out a precarious existence. The plain is the world's largest slab of limestone. It was formed originally as a submarine plateau, which then became elevated by the forces of nature. It is riddled with caves, many linked with the sea, even a hundred kilometres inland, so that salt breezes can reputedly be felt and smelt coming from orifices far from the coast. This trip across the Nullarbor is an amazing journey, mostly remarkable for the distance covered without there being any significant habitation at all. For a whole day the scenery will change little and you will see but a sprinkling of buildings, and almost all of those built to serve travellers on the highway.

75 kilometres beyond Ceduna is the small township of **Penong**. This is the last of the places where agriculture is possible, and the last place which is served by the highway, rather than serving the highway. Basic accommodation is available here at the Penong Hotel. The township is twenty kilometres from the coast. A small road from here leads south to **Cactus Beach**, where there is a caravan park and camping ground, but there is no public transport to the beach.

Another 55 kilometres takes you to a turn-off to **Fowlers Bay**, the last point at which the coast will be accessible for a long while. It is 29 kilometres from the highway at this point, and at Fowlers Bay there is a caravan park with on-site vans, a shop and a camping area, as well as some permanent holiday accommodation. However, again there is no public transport available to reach the bay.

Next is **Nundroo** Roadhouse, which offers accommodation, including beds for backpackers.

Yalata Roadhouse is 52 kilometres further on, with accommodation of various types. A short road runs off here to the Yalata Mission, where aboriginal artefacts can be purchased more reasonably than in large cities. They can also be bought at the roadhouse and sometimes there are individual aboriginal traders beside the road.

ANECDOTE

In the days before the road between Ceduna and the border was sealed, we made our way slowly across the corrugated surface of the Nullarbor.

As dusk fell, wary of the danger of kangaroos in the road, dazzled and mesmerised by the headlights of vehicles, we stopped and camped for the night. We moved some two hundred metres from the road, but were still awakened every time a vehicle passed, not by the noise of the engine, but by the crashing of the vehicle over the ruts and pot-holes which passed for Australia's Highway Number One. As the vehicle drew level with us, we could see the heads of the occupants jolting in rhythm to the bouncing of their conveyance and were thankful that it would be a few more hours yet before we had to resume the same self-inflicted torture.

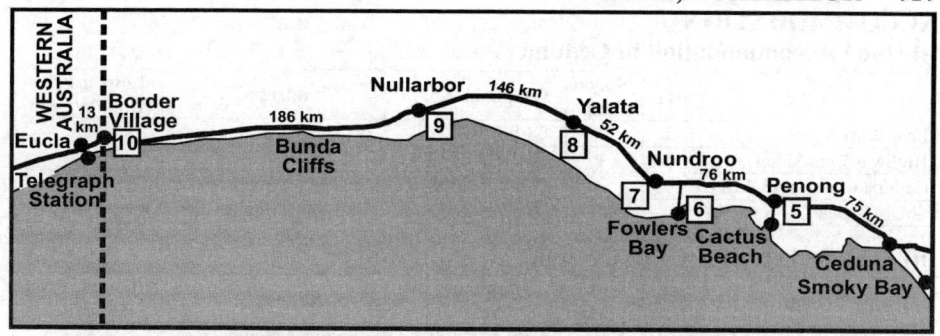

THE NULLARBOR - FROM CEDUNA TO THE BORDER
Numerals indicate accommodation

From Yalata, the road becomes even more desolate, and it is 146 kilometres to the next roadhouse, the **Nullarbor** Hotel and Motel, which offers all levels of accommodation including a caravan park, camping sites and backpackers' beds.

Now comes a long stretch of 186 kilometres to the border with Western Australia. On the way, the road passes very close to **Bunda Cliffs**, and there is an observation area, but there is no habitation here and the bus will not stop, so a glimpse of these majestic and towering cliffs is all that you will get.

The **Border Village** offers accommodation, including beds for backpackers, and is also the limit for fruits. Note that you cannot take fruits into Western Australia, so consume them before you get here. At this point there is a time change too. This is complex. Officially, there is a difference of one and a half hours between South Australia and Western Australia and you will need to put your watch back by that margin to adjust to Perth time. However, in summer South Australia maintains Daylight Saving Time, while Western Australia does not, which increases the time difference between the two states to the generous and inconvenient margin of two and a half hours. We have not finished with these technicalities, however. The tiny communities just across the border in Western Australia think that these time differences are too great, so they keep their own unofficial local time, Australia being a great country for local defiance of the official edict. This time is 45 minutes ahead of Western Australian official time. Thus, when you cross the border into Western Australia, you need to put your watch back 45 minutes in winter, or one hour and 45 minutes in summer. When you have travelled for another four hours, and have reached Caiguna, you will need to adjust by a further 45 minutes to be on official Western Australian time. It is as simple as that!

For the remainder of the journey across the Nullarbor, from the Western Australian border to Norseman, see the section on Norseman in the Western Australian part of this book, on page 539.

ANECDOTE

"Right," said the driver of our bus on the way across the Nullarbor, as he brought the vehicle to a stop far from any habitation. "Toilet stop. Gents on the left. Ladies on the right." We looked out. The vast treeless plain stretched unrelieved as far as the eye could see. "Could we wait for the next tree?" asked one passenger. "Seven hundred kilometres," replied the driver, "If you want to wait. Please yourselves. Gents on the left. Ladies on the right."

SOUTH AUSTRALIA
ACCOMMODATION
(i) Hotel Accommodation in Ceduna

Name	Stars	No. on Map	Telephone No.	Address	Lowest Price (Double/Twin)
East West Motel	3	2	08-8625-2101	66 McKenzie Street	$85
Highway One Motel	3	1	08-8625-2208	35 Eyre Highway	$85
Ceduna Community Mtl.	2½	3	08-8625-2008	O'Loughlin & South Trces.	$80
Shelly Beach Caravan Pk.		4	08-8625-2012	178 Decres Bay Road	$70

(ii) Backpackers Hostels in Ceduna

Name	Group	No. on Map	Telephone No.	Address	Lowest Price (Dormitory)
Ceduna Community Motel		3	1800-655-300	O'Loughlin & South Trces.	$32
Shelly Beach Caravan Park	Nom	4	08-8625-2012	178 Decres Bay Road	$25

(iii) Accommodation in Fowlers Bay

Name	Stars	No. on Map	Telephone No.	Address	Lowest Price (Double/Twin)
Fowlers Bay Units		6	08-8625-6179	Fowlers Bay	$95
Fowlers Bay Caravan Pk.		6	08-8625-6143	Fowlers Bay	$65

(iv) Accommodation across the Nullarbor

Name	Stars	No. on Map	Telephone No.	Address	Lowest Price (Double/Twin)
Penong Caravan Park		5	08-8625-1111	3 Stiggants Road	$65
Penong Hotel		5	08-8625-1050	Main Street, Penong	$55
Nundroo Roadhouse		7	08-8625-6120	Eyre Highway, Coonabie	$75
Yalata Roadhouse		8	08-8625-6986	Eyre Highway, Yalata	$65
Nullarbor Hotel / Motel		9	1-800-241-502	Eyre Highway, Nullarbor	$85
Border Travellers Village		10	08-9039-3474	Eyre Highway, Eucla	$75

MOVING ON
(i) Bus Services from Ceduna

Destination	Operator	Via	Distance (km)	Fare	Journey Time	Frequency
Adelaide	Greyhound		799	$105	9¾ hrs	3/week
		Port Augusta	481	$81	5 hrs	3/week
Adelaide	Stateliner		820	$92.70	11 - 11½ hrs	1/day
		Port Augusta	505	$73.20	6¼ - 6½ hrs	1/day
Perth	Greyhound		2187	$291	26¼ hrs	3/week
		Kalgoorlie	1558	$291	18½ hrs	3/week

(ii) Bus Services from Nullarbor

Destination	Operator	Via	Distance (km)	Fare	Journey Time	Frequency
Adelaide	Greyhound		1095	$191	14 hrs	3/week
		Port Augusta	777	$142	9½ hrs	3/week
Perth	Greyhound		1885	$291	22½ hrs	3/week
		Kalgoorlie	1253	$291	14¾ hrs	3/week

MT. GAMBIER
Population 23,000

6 hrs 30 mins by bus from Adelaide
6 hrs by train and bus from Melbourne

The way to Victoria from Adelaide lies along the Dukes Highway, a pleasant enough route, but not one with exciting scenery. There are choices of transport. The rail service used to operate every night. Now, however, it goes by day five days a week, the five days being Sunday, Monday, Wednesday, Thursday and Friday. Although some people used to be pleased to save the price of a night's accommodation, the author prefers the new arrangement which allows the scenery to be enjoyed. By rail it is a pleasant and comfortable journey, taking 10½ hours to Melbourne. The bus is half an hour faster and Firefly, in particular, offers a cheap and efficient service, operating once by day and once by night. There is also the service offered by V-Line, whereby one travels by bus to Bendigo, whence by train to Melbourne. This service operates every day and takes nine hours to Bendigo and 11½ hours to Melbourne. It is an interesting route, especially within Victoria. There are also bus connexions for Ballarat. See page 643 for the timetable. These journeys offer the chance to stop along the way. Ballarat and Bendigo are both interesting cities for visits.

There is one more possibility, however, and that is to travel via Mt. Gambier. The problem with this route is that it is expensive. To reach Mt. Gambier will cost as much as the fare to Melbourne with Firefly. However, it will still be the cheapest way to visit this city and the best method of breaking your journey to Melbourne mid-way.

Stateliner operates services to Mt. Gambier by two routes, one coastal and one inland. On most days, the two services leave Adelaide together, often utilising the same vehicle as far as Tailem Bend, where the routes divide. The two services also reach Mt. Gambier at the same time. The coastal route is the more scenic though.

However you travel, you will experience some of the best of the scenery as you climb out of Adelaide by bus or by train through the Adelaide Hills. The road has recently been straightened and improved. Tunnels have been built and have eliminated some of the views, but there is still plenty of good scenery to enjoy.

ANECDOTE

It was evening when I boarded the 'fast mixed' train at Kingoonya for the journey across the Nullarbor to Western Australia.

After a few minutes, the guard visited me. "Have you got a ticket?" he enquired. "Not yet," I replied. After all, where would I get a ticket at a place like Kingoonya? "Well," he said, "I'm coming round first thing in the morning to sell you one, so if you don't want a ticket, you'd better not be here then."

It was, I thought, a most civilised way to run a railway.

720   SOUTH AUSTRALIA

Murray Bridge is a city of 13,000 inhabitants, with its own bus service from Adelaide. The highway now by-passes the city, but long-distance buses call here on request.

Tailem Bend has a **Pioneer Village** of some note which you may visit if you decide to stop here. You will also cross the **iron bridge** used by the railway until 1923, but converted to a road bridge when the railway moved to an even more impressive one which can be seen. This road bridge is the oldest bridge across the Murray, constructed in 1879. It is also the point at which the bus routes to Mt. Gambier separate. If you continue along the main highway, you will now cross the **Coonalpyn Downs**. These were formerly known as the Ninety Mile Desert because crops would not grow even when irrigated. The soil was analysed and it was discovered that some important trace elements were missing. When these were added, suddenly the soil became fertile and the name of the area had to be changed. You will pass through **Tintinara** and **Keith** and then come to Bordertown.

Bordertown was the birthplace, in 1929, of the well-known trade union leader and later Prime Minister, **Bob Hawke**. It is also the site of a **wildlife park** with the largest colony of albino kangaroos in the world. This town, first settled in 1852 and with a current population of 2,660, is not quite on the border, but is the last town within South Australia. Here the Mt. Gambier bus will leave the main highway to Melbourne and turn south.

Naracoorte is the largest town on this part of the route. The **Naracoorte Museum and Snake Pit** is a privately owned collection of collections. There are collections of all types of objects here, from butterflies to clocks. There is also a collection of living snakes, some of them venomous, and one of locally found fossils. The Museum is open daily from 10:00 (14:00 at weekends) until 17:00. Admission costs $8. There is also an **Art Gallery** in Naracoorte, open from 11:30 until 16:30 on Tuesdays to Fridays and from 10:00 until 12:00 on Saturdays. There is no charge. There is a **Nature Park** in the town containing species of locally-threatened flora and native wildlife. Adjacent is a swimming lake. Admission to the Nature Park and swimming lake is free. The **Sheep's Back**, housed in an 1870 former flour mill, is a museum of the wool industry. It is open daily from 9:00 until 16:00 and admission costs $6. There is a backpackers hostel in Naracoorte.

Coonawarra is known for its wineries, although most are not within walking distance of the small town.

Penola is interesting. The **John Riddoch District Interpretive Centre** is in the Old Mechanics' Institute and displays the history of the area, mostly in documents and photographs. It is open from 9:00 until 18:00 with free admission. There is also the **Mary MacKillop Penola Centre**. Mary MacKillop is a candidate for Australia's first sainthood. She started a school in a stable in Penola, and then, with the assistance of Father Julian Woods, moved to this schoolhouse in 1867. The Centre tells the story of her life and of her founding, in association with Father Woods, of the Order of the Sisters of St. Joseph of the Sacred Heart. The Centre is open daily from 10:00 until 16:00, and admission costs $4. Amongst other accommodation, there is a backpackers hostel in Penola.

If you travel via the coastal route, there is more attractive scenery to see. At **Kingston**, you will see the **Big Lobster**, used as a sales point for local produce, including lobsters. The Big Lobster is seventeen metres high and weighs four tonnes. He is open from 9:00 until 18:00 daily.

Robe has a youth hostel. The **Robe Historical Interpretive Centre** is the rather grand name given to the local museum, which is housed in the same building as the **Visitor Information Centre** on Mundy Terrace, by the sea. The Centre is open daily from 9:00 until 17:00, with free admission. There is a good lookout on **Beacon Hill**, while the **Obelisk** standing on **Cape Dombey**, built in 1852 and used to guide vessels into **Guichen Bay**, gives a fine view of the coast.

At **Beachport**, the **jetty** is one of the longest in South Australia and is popular with anglers. **Centenary Park**, in the centre of the town, is pleasant and large, covering six acres. **Durant's Lookout** in South West Terrace offers a view of the town, while **Lanky's Walk**, starting in Railway Terrace, provides a short exploration of native bushland with information offered along the way, and Lanky's Well at the end. Lanky was an aboriginal tracker used by the police. His duties included taking care of the police horses and the well was dug to provide water for those horses. The walk takes about half an hour. Another walk is **Wendy's Walk**, which passes through bushland and sand dunes before emerging on the beach. Maps for these walks are available from the **Visitor Information Centre**. The **Pool of Siloam** is reputed to be seven times more salt than the sea and is popular for therapeutic purposes. It is located close to the seashore. Also, of course, one should not forget that Beachport, not unexpectedly, has **beaches** as one of its attractions.

Millicent is not quite on the coast. The town offers a **Tourist Information Centre**, an **Art Gallery** and a **Museum**, all housed in the same building. These attractions are open daily from 9:00 until 17:00 (16:30 at weekends). The Art Gallery is free, but admission to the Museum costs $6.

So, by either route, after 6½ hours, **Mt. Gambier** will be reached. This city is approximately half way between Adelaide and Melbourne and seems to hold allegiance to both capitals. It used to have rail services from both directions, but now has only buses. The South Australian rail services used to diverge from the main Adelaide-Melbourne line at **Wolseley**, right on the border, but were withdrawn some while ago. The line was originally narrow gauge, but was converted to broad gauge after the war. More recently, the main line, however, was converted to standard gauge, so it is no

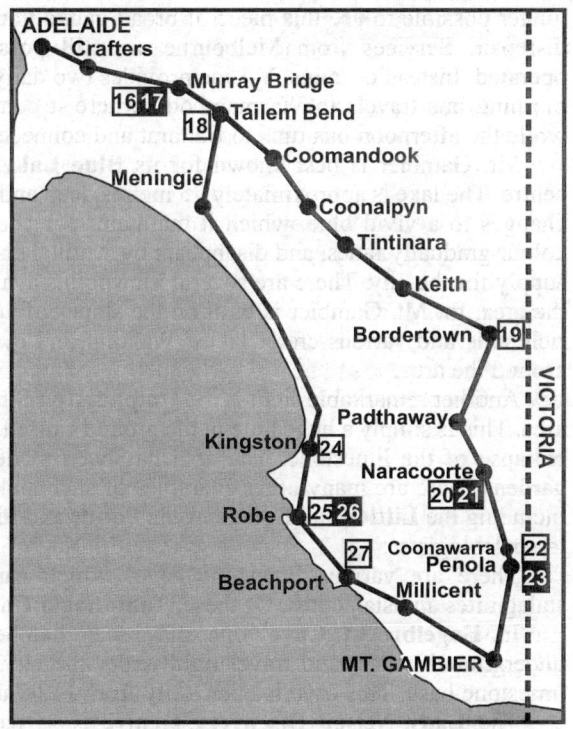

ADELAIDE TO MT. GAMBIER
Showing Stateliner routes and principal bus stops
Black numerals indicate hotel accommodation
White numerals indicate backpackers hostels

SOUTH AUSTRALIA

longer possible to use this piece of broad gauge track and it has fallen into a state of disrepair. Services from Melbourne are still possible, but only goods trains are operated. Instead of trains, V-Line provides two daily buses for passenger service. The morning bus travels to Warrnambool, where it connects with a train to Melbourne, while the afternoon bus runs to Ballarat and connects with a Melbourne train there.

Mt. Gambier is best known for its **Blue Lake**, just a short walk from the city centre. The lake is approximately 75 metres deep and in November each year its colour changes to a vivid blue, which it maintains for about three months, after which the colour gradually fades, and disappears by April. This lake represents the current water supply for the city. There are several viewpoints available. Nor is this the only lake in the area, for Mt. Gambier is built on the slopes of an extinct volcano, which provides rich soils and various crater lakes. Walking and cycling trails have been designated around the area.

Another remarkable sight is the **Umpherston Sinkhole**, just on the edge of the city area. This is simply a huge hole in the ground caused by the dissolution and subsequent collapse of the limestone. The area has been made into a natural sheltered sunken garden. There are many other examples of such sinkholes more distant from the city, including the **Little Blue Lake, Ewens Ponds** and **Piccaninnie Ponds**, all well known to speleologists.

There are various limestone caves which can be visited, offering the usual stalagmites and stalactites. Of these, **Tantanoola Cave** is probably the best example.

In **Engelbrecht Cave**, one may see chambers where divers can enter the underground waters and travel right under the city, so riddled with passages is this limestone base. This cave is open daily from 11:00 until 15:00. Admission costs $6.

The **Lady Nelson Discovery Centre** is so named after the brig *H.M.S. Lady Nelson* which brought Lt. James Grant here in 1800. It was he who sighted and named Mt. Gambier. There is a full-scale replica of the *Lady Nelson* on display, a theatre, and a great deal of modern technology used in presenting the history of the city and its surrounds. The theatre is free, but to visit the remainder of the Centre, including the brig, costs $8. The Lady Nelson Discovery Centre is open every day from 9:00 until 17:00. There is also tourist information available here.

The **Cave Gardens** in the city centre are famous for their displays of roses. The cave here was the original source of water for the township and the reason for this particular location being chosen.

The **Old Courthouse Museum** is a display of justice as administered in the city from 1865, when this building was constructed, until 1975, when it was superseded. The Museum is open daily from 11:00 until 15:00 and admission costs $3.

Vansittart Park is near the city centre and includes many flower beds, as well as a 1917 Krupp cannon.

The **Centenary Tower** provides a good view of the lakes and of the surrounding area, stretching as far as the coast. The tower can be reached by local bus. It is open from 7:30 until dusk, with a $1 charge for admission.

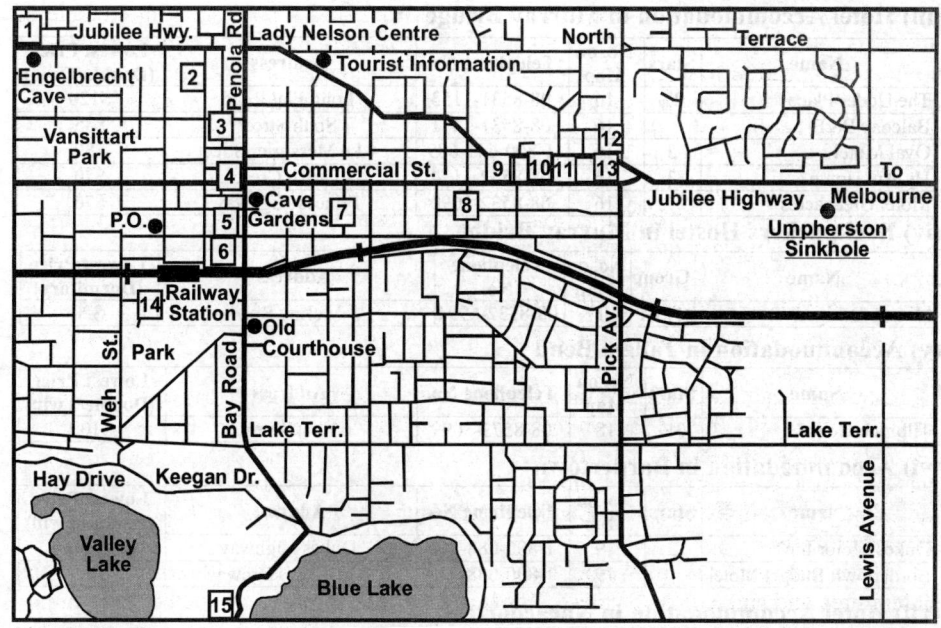

MT. GAMBIER
Numerals indicate accommodation

ACCOMMODATION
(i) Hotel Accommodation in Mt. Gambier

Name	Stars	No. on Map	Telephone No.	Address	Lowest Price (Double/Twin)
Colhurst House	4½	3	08-8723-1309	3 Colhurst Place	$130
Quality Inn Presidential	4	1	08-8724-9966	Jubilee Highway West	$120
Southgate Motel	4	9	1-800-088-835	175 Commercial Street East	$120
Silver Birch Motor Inn	3½	13	08-8725-5122	Jubilee Highway East	$110
Arkana Motor Inn	3½	11	1-800-801-858	203 Commercial Street East	$95
Mid City Motel	3	6	1-800-807-277	15 Helen Street	$90
Red Carpet Motor Inn	3½	10	08-8725-4311	96 Jubilee Highway East	$90
Blue Lake City C'van Pk.	3	15	1-800-676-028	Bay Road	$80
Mount Gambier Hotel	3	4	08-8725-0611	2 Commercial Street West	$75
Blue Lake Motel	3	12	1-800-088-291	1 Kennedy Avenue	$70
Grand Central Motel		5	08-8725-8844	6 Helen Street	$65
Avalon Motel	3½	2	08-8725-7200	93 Gray Street	$55
Mount View Motel	2½	8	08-8725-8478	14 Davison Street	$55
The Gaol		14	1-800-626-844	7 Margaret Street	$45
Central Caravan Park	3	7	08-8725-4427	6 Krummel Street	$35

(ii) Backpackers Hostel in Mt. Gambier

Name	Group	No. on Map	Telephone No.	Address	Lowest Price (Dormitory)
The Gaol	Nom	14	1800-626-844	7 Margaret Street	$22

724 SOUTH AUSTRALIA

(iii) Hotel Accommodation in Murray Bridge

Name	Stars	No. on Map	Telephone No.	Address	Lowest Price (Double/Twin)
The Udder Place	2½	16	08-8531-1153	Long Flat Road	$120
Balcony B&B		16	08-8531-1411	Sixth Street	$85
Oval Motel	3	16	1-800-641-689	4 Le Messurier Street	$80
Hy-Am Home	3	16	08-8532-1174	43 Parish Crescent	$70
Motel Greenacres		16	08-8532-1090	Princes Highway	$70

(iv) Backpackers Hostel in Murray Bridge

Name	Group	No. on Map	Telephone No.	Address	Lowest Price (Dormitory)
Murray Bridge B/P	Nom	17	08-8532-6994	1 McKay Road	$20

(v) Accommodation in Tailem Bend

Name	Stars	No. on Map	Telephone No.	Address	Lowest Price (Double/Twin)
Tilbrook House	3½	18	08-8572-3099	6 First Avenue	$100

(vi) Accommodation in Bordertown

Name	Stars	No. on Map	Telephone No.	Address	Lowest Price (Double/Twin)
Dukes Motor Inn	3	19	1-800-088-109	Dukes Highway	$80
Bordertown Budget Motel		19	1-800-088-514	25 Dukes Highway	$60

(vii) Hotel Accommodation in Naracoorte

Name	Stars	No. on Map	Telephone No.	Address	Lowest Price (Double/Twin)
Naracoorte Cottages	3½	20	08-8762-2906	15 Handyside Street	$135
Mossville Manor B&B	4	20	08-8762-1009	Blackwell Road	$110
Willowbrook Cottage	4	20	08-8762-0259	3 Jenkins Terrace	$110
Country Roads Motor Inn	4	20	1-800-088-363	20 Smith Street	$100
William MacIntosh Lodge	4	20	08-8762-1644	Adelaide Road	$100
Greenline Motel	2½	20	08-8762-2599	Stewart Terrace	$70
Naracoorte Holiday Park	3½	20	08-8762-2128	81 Park Terrace	$65

(viii) Backpackers Hostel in Naracoorte

Name	Group	No. on Map	Telephone No.	Address	Lowest Price (Dormitory)
Naracoorte Backpackers		21	08-8762-3835	4 Jones Street	$20

(ix) Hotel Accommodation in Penola

Name	Stars	No. on Map	Telephone No.	Address	Lowest Price (Double/Twin)
Georgie's Cottage	5	22	0439-838-651	Riddoch Street	$185
Naomi's Villa	4	22	08-8736-3309	20 Riddoch Street	$165
Sarah's Cottage	3½	22	08-8736-3309	24 Julian Street West	$160
Cobb & Co. Cottages	4	22	08-8737-2526	2 Portland Street	$130
Julian Court Apartments	3½	22	08-8762-3038	Unit 1, 13 Julian Street	$110
Penola's Old Rectory	3½	22	08-8737-2684	5 Bowden Street	$105
Coonawarra Motor Lodge	3½	22	1-800-649-342	114 Church Street	$100

(x) Backpackers Hostel in Penola

Name	Group	No. on Map	Telephone No.	Address	Lowest Price (Dormitory)
McKay's Trek Inn	Nom	23	1800-626-844	33 Riddoch Street	$22

(xi) Accommodation in Kingston

Name	Stars	No. on Map	Telephone No.	Address	Lowest Price (Double/Twin)
Lobster Motel	3	24	08-8767-2322	3 Princes Highway	$90
Lacepede Bay Motel	3	24	08-8767-2444	1 Marine Parade	$85

(xii) Hotel Accommodation in Robe

Name	Stars	No. on Map	Telephone No.	Address	Lowest Price (Double/Twin)
White Sails	5	25	1-800-067-447	14 Lake Road	$305
Villa Pescatore		25	08-8768-5044	104 The Esplanade	$295
Beachside Cottage	4	25	1-800-067-447	26 The Esplanade	$265
Salty Joe's		25	08-8768-5044	22 O'Byrne Avenue	$210
Ann's Place	4½	25	08-8768-2262	2 Royal Circus	$165
Ruby's Robe Cottage		25	08-8768-2958	21 Sturt Street	$165
Criterion Cottage	3½	25	08-8768-2137	Bagot Street	$160
Robe Links Units	4	25	08-8768-6206	21 Davenport Street	$155
Christmas Tree Cottage	3½	25	08-8768-2770	3 Smillie Street	$145
Cornerstone Cottage	3	25	08-8768-2137	Smillie Street	$145
Cricklewood Cottage	4½	25	08-8768-2137	24 Woolundry Road	$145
Victoria Cottage	3	25	08-8768-2770	26 Victoria Street	$135
Melaleuca Motel	3	25	1-800-001-791	Smillie Street	$105
Robe House	4	25	08-8768-2770	Hagen Street	$100
Nampara Cabins	3½	25	08-8768-2264	28 Laurel Terrace	$95
Lake View Apartments	4½	25	1-800-819-997	2 Lakeside Terrace	$90
Robe Lake Vista	3	25	08-8768-2113	2 O'Halloran Street	$90
Guichen Bay Motel	3	25	08-8768-2001	42 Victoria Street	$80
Bowman Cottages	3½	25	08-8768-2236	26 Smillie Street	$75
Bushland Cabins	2½	25	08-8768-2386	Nora Criena & Main Roads	$75
Harbour View Motel	3	25	08-8768-2148	2 Sturt Street	$75
Robe Hotel	3	25	08-8768-2077	Mundy Terrace	$75
Caledonian Inn	1	25	08-8768-2029	1 Victoria Street	$65
Long Beach Holiday Park	3	25	08-8768-2237	70 The Esplanade	$60
Robe Haven Motel	4	25	08-8768-2588	Smillie Street	$55

(xiii) Backpackers Hostel in Robe

Name	Group	No. on Map	Telephone No.	Address	Lowest Price (Dormitory)
Long Beach Holiday Park	YHA	26	08-8768-2237	70 The Esplanade	$19

(xiv) Accommodation in Beachport

Name	Stars	No. on Map	Telephone No.	Address	Lowest Price (Double/Twin)
Beachport Motor Inn	3	27	08-8735-8070	Railway Terrace & Lanky St	$100
Beachport Caravan Park		27	08-8735-8128	Beach Road	$75
Bompa's by the Sea		27	08-8735-8333	3 Railway Terrace	$65
Southern Ocean Park	3½	27	08-8735-8153	Somerville Street	$65

MOVING ON
Bus Services from Mt. Gambier

Destination	Operator	Via	Distance (km)	Fare	Journey Time	Frequency
Adelaide	Stateliner		470	$53.30	6¼ hrs	1/day
Melbourne	V-Line		455	$61.60	6 - 7¾ hrs	2/day
		Warrnambool	203	$34.40	3 - 3¼ hrs	1/day
		Ballarat	322	$54.10	4¼ hrs	1/day

ANECDOTE

I wanted to travel by train from Melbourne to Adelaide during daylight hours, something which has never been possible in recent years by the use of a single train. However, I found that, at the time, I could travel to Dimboola by train, then take a connecting bus to Serviceton, on the Victoria - South Australia border. If I waited overnight, I could then pick up the Mt. Gambier to Adelaide train the next morning where it met the main line at Wolseley, just across the border in South Australia. The only foreseeable problem would be that I should have to walk between Serviceton and Wolseley.

I went to the booking office and requested a ticket from Melbourne to Adelaide, explaining what I was planning to do. "You can't do that with one ticket," said the clerk. "If you are breaking your journey, you need two separate tickets. And, what's more, Wolseley is in South Australia, so I can't issue a ticket from there. I can issue you one from Serviceton to Adelaide, and you just won't use the bit from Serviceton to Wolseley, if that's all right." " Is this going to cost a lot more than a through ticket?" I asked suspiciously. "No. It's going to cost less." "Less? Why is that?" "Cheaper fares for country passengers, and if you have a ticket from Serviceton, you're a country passenger." I marvelled at the ways of the railways and bought my two tickets.

It was a pleasant journey to Dimboola on an antique Victorian country train, and the bus took me on to Serviceton, right on the border. I was impressed by the grand station serving the tiny community of Serviceton, but this had once been a border check point with customs officers stationed here, and it remained the place at which interstate trains changed crews.

I set out for Wolseley on foot, which proved to be a journey of seven and a half kilometres beside the railway track. I was surprised to find that there was only a minor dirt road between the two small towns, and that I saw no vehicle on it at all during my walk. More alarming though was the copious quantity of crushed snakes on the road. Considering the obvious rarity of any passing vehicle, those snakes must either be suicidal by inclination or present in prodigious numbers, I thought, and moved my path to the centre of the road, whilst keeping my eyes on the surface to be negotiated. However, I saw no live snake during the journey.

When I arrived at Wolseley, I looked for accommodation. Wolseley turned out, however, to be minute, without even the facility of a pub. Now here was a problem indeed. Where could I sleep? Even the station had no shelter. Eventually I found a derelict and partly demolished house. I waited for nightfall and then reluctantly unrolled my sleeping bag on the concrete foundations and made my best effort at getting a good night's sleep, thinking, however, of all those snakes which would probably like to curl up comfortably in a cosy sleeping bag.

I slept little, but was relieved to find at dawn that I was still alive and alone. The train came on time and conveyed me thankfully to Adelaide (from where I proceeded with the adventure on page 675). At least I had succeeded in seeing almost the entire rail journey by daylight.

These days the *Overland* operates by daylight, but only in the direction of Adelaide to Melbourne, so the reader too can see this territory if he wishes.

▲ Mishap to Author's Train, between Adelaide and Port Pirie, S.A. (p. 675)
Aptly-named Plenty River Highway, Northern Territory (p. 447) ▼

▲ Eucla Jetty, Western Australia (p. 540) *[photograph: Tony Yarham]*

▲ Friendly Quokka, Rottnest Island, Western Australia (p. 493)
Stating the Obvious - Highway Number One, near W.A./N.T. border (p. 622) ▼

▲ Perth by Night from King's Park (p. 480) *[photograph: John Cullinan]*
Underground Church, Coober Pedy, S.A. (p. 706) *[photograph: John Cullinan]* ▼

▲ Abt Wilderness Railway, Queenstown to Strahan, Tasmania (p. 942)

Bendigo Trams, Victoria (p. 800) ▼

VICTORIA

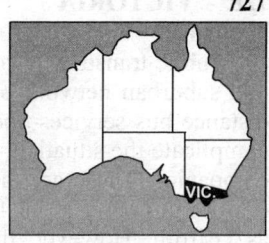

In 1803, Lt. David Collins attempted, but failed, to found a settlement in Port Phillip Bay, where Melbourne now lies, and it was to be more than three decades before a further attempt was made.

In fact, the first permanent settlement in Victoria was not in Port Phillip Bay, but at Portland in the extreme west of the state. Portland dates from 1834. Port Phillip Bay was settled in the following year, 1835, by John Batman and John Fawkner, who crossed Bass Strait from Van Diemen's Land (Tasmania) in order to found the city which is now Melbourne. Unlike previous settlers, Batman and Fawkner made an attempt to purchase the land from the local aborigines. At the time, the government of New South Wales was trying to discourage settlement in outlying areas, but it was soon forced to recognise the existence of a community in Port Phillip Bay and to send administrators.

The new settlement strongly resisted the introduction of convicts, although in the end some convict labour was used in the area. The settlers also requested, from an early stage, independence from New South Wales, and this was granted in 1851, when the new colony of Victoria was established.

It was at this point that gold was discovered in Bendigo, Ballarat and several other locations in Victoria, and the finds included the largest known nuggets in history. Suddenly Victoria became rich. The population of the state trebled and the new-found prosperity endured for a period of thirty years, manifesting itself even now in the form of some magnificent public buildings, both in Melbourne itself and in the gold towns.

When the gold ran out in the 1890s, a period of economic depression followed, but Victoria was already so well established that Melbourne was chosen in 1901 as the venue for the temporary capital of the new Commonwealth of Australia.

In the 1950s, Victoria became a great centre for immigration, particularly by those from Italy and Greece, and Melbourne was hailed as the third largest Greek city in the world. The city still retains a great cosmopolitan flavour reflected particularly in its cuisine and in its corner shops.

Victoria is the smallest mainland state, with an area of 227,420 square kilometres. Only Tasmania and the Australian Capital Territory are smaller. In terms of population, however, it is the second most populous, after New South Wales, with a population of approximately five million, which is to say that this small state contains a quarter of the total population of Australia. Only the Australian Capital Territory is more densely populated. In fact, though, as in other states, two-thirds of the population lives in the capital city. As soon as one leaves Melbourne it is difficult to believe that this is Australia's most densely populated state.

Melbourne itself is an attractive and interesting city and its trams clattering through the streets give it a sense of individual character greater than that in any of the other capitals. It also offers a line of pleasant beaches stretching round the bay.

Outside the big city, the principal scenic rural attractions are the Great Ocean Road, the Grampians, the Murray River towns, the ski areas, the fairy penguins of Phillip Island and the beaches along the coastal route to Sydney (many of which, however, lie within New South Wales).

VICTORIA

Transport

Public transport in rural Victoria is mostly operated by V-Line. In addition, there is a suburban network of trains, trams and buses in Melbourne, and there are long-distance bus services operated by McCafferty's, Greyhound, Premier and Firefly. To complicate the situation, two of the country rail routes are, in effect, sub-let to private companies. These are the routes to Warrnambool and Shepparton, together with the onward bus connexions from Shepparton to Cobram and into New South Wales as far as Griffith. However, these routes can still be used with V-Line tickets, or with appropriate rail passes. The V-Line bus services are actually contracted out to other companies too, so the vehicles used do not always carry the name of V-Line, although most now do.

V-Line offers a two-week pass named the *Victoria Pass* for use within the borders of Victoria only. Officially, the only place outside Victoria to which it is valid is Albury, but the author's experience has been that it is generally accepted for journeys to Mt. Gambier also, and for journeys into New South Wales on vehicles which later return to Victoria (e.g. certain buses travelling to Mildura, but passing through parts of New South Wales on the way). It is not valid, however, for travel to Adelaide, Canberra or Batemans Bay. The pass costs $150 and includes first class travel on trains. However, there are the following restrictions. It cannot be used on 'Inter-city' (medium- and long-distance) services on Mondays or Fridays, except on public holidays, and it cannot be used on 'Inter-urban' (shorter distance) services arriving in Melbourne

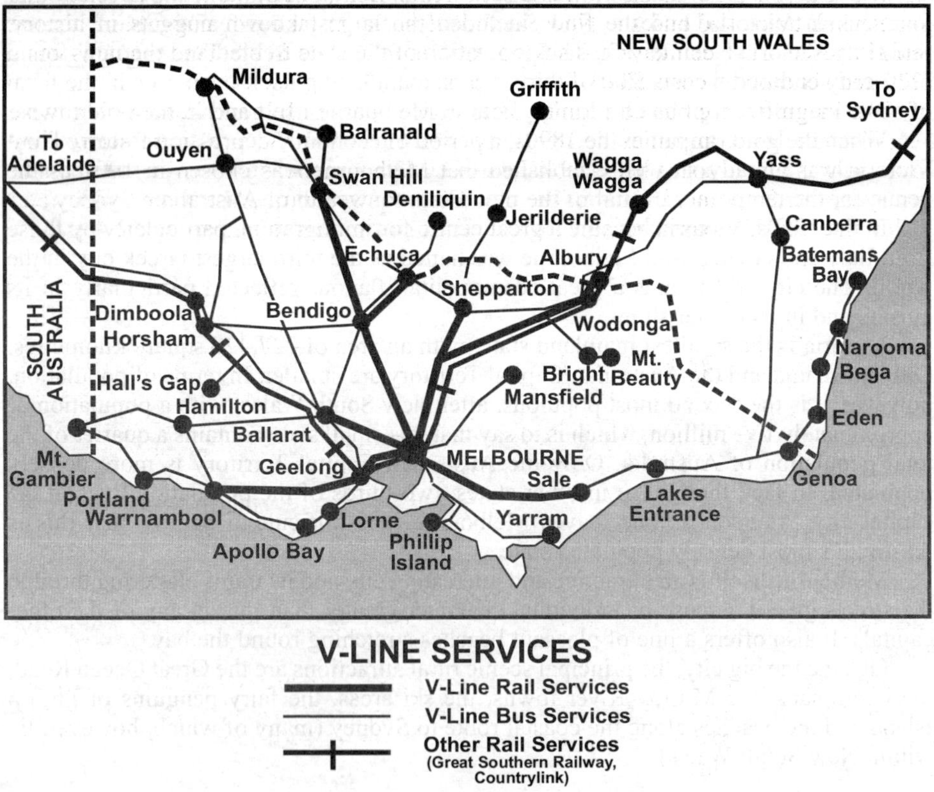

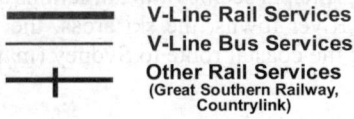

V-LINE SERVICES

— V-Line Rail Services
— V-Line Bus Services
+ Other Rail Services
(Great Southern Railway, Countrylink)

before 9:30 or departing from Melbourne between 16:00 and 18:00 on weekdays. This pass is available to anybody.

A one-week *Victoria Pass* is available to overseas residents only. It does not have the above restrictions and costs $99, including first-class travel on trains.

There are also *East Coast Discovery Passes* available for rail travel from Melbourne to Sydney, Surfers Paradise, Brisbane or Cairns, with unlimited stops over a period of six months, but the journey from Melbourne must be by Countrylink train, not by V-Line services. Travel via Canberra is permitted, but the fare between Yass and Canberra must be paid in addition, since that is not a Countrylink service. The passes are available only to non-residents of Australia, except for the Melbourne to Cairns pass, which is available to anybody. Fares for the *East Coast Discovery Passes* from Melbourne are as follows:-

Melbourne to Sydney	$93.50
Melbourne to Surfers Paradise	$176
Melbourne to Brisbane	$176
Melbourne to Cairns	$328

There is also the *Backtracker Rail Pass*. Basically this is a rail and bus pass for Countrylink services in New South Wales, but since the Countrylink rail network extends to Melbourne, it can be purchased in and used from Melbourne. Once one has reached Albury on the Countrylink train (no other train), one is then free to use all the Countrylink trains and buses in New South Wales, and as far north as Brisbane, for the period chosen. Fourteen days costs $165, One month costs $198. Three months costs $220 and six months costs $330.

The long-distance bus companies offer various passes. In general, however, these long-distance bus companies do not allow much of rural Victoria to be seen. They cover only the main roads between Adelaide and Melbourne, and between Melbourne and Sydney or Brisbane. However, Premier offers a pass for travel between Sydney and Melbourne via the coastal route with unlimited stops. This is known as the *Getaway Pass*.

MELBOURNE
Population 3,250,000
10 hrs 30 mins by train from Sydney
12 hrs by bus from Sydney
10 hrs 30 mins by train from Adelaide
10 hrs by bus from Adelaide

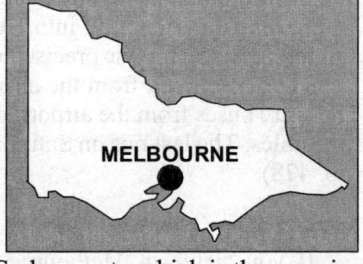

Melbourne, with a population of three and a quarter million, is the second largest city in Australia and maintains a long-standing rivalry with Sydney as to which is the superior location.

Melbourne was first settled in 1835. In 1837 it was named, after the Prime Minister of Britain at the time, Lord Melbourne. By 1847 it had been proclaimed as a city and by 1861 it had become the largest city in Australia. From 1901 until 1927, it served as the capital of the country.

730   VICTORIA

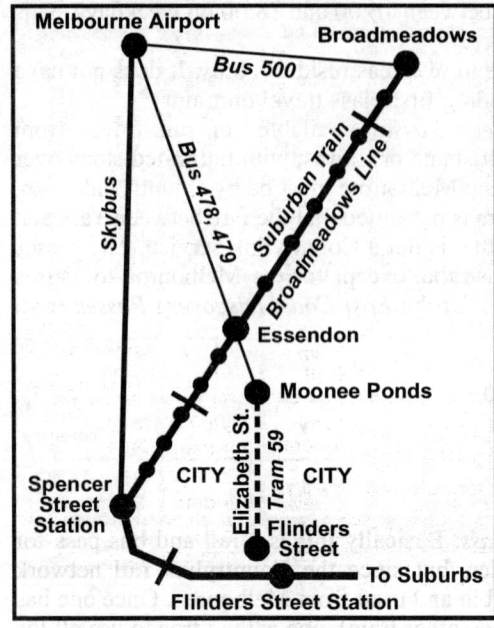

FROM AIRPORT TO CITY

Melbourne is one of the most likely arrival points in Australia, so let us first deal with how to get from the airport to the city. There are two ways: the official method, and the author's economy route.

From the Airport

The official method is to catch the airport *Skybus*, which operates every thirty minutes. This bus will take you straight to Spencer Street Railway Station, the main long-distance terminus, in half an hour and at a cost of $12. Up until 16:00, a free connexion from there to hotels within the city area is offered.

The author's economy route takes longer, but is much cheaper. Take an ordinary bus no. 478 or 479 to Essendon Station or Moonee Ponds, or a bus no. 500 to Broadmeadows Station. At present, timings on weekdays are as follows: 7:10 (478), 7:20 (500), 7:45 (479), 8:10 (478), 9:20 (500), 10:50 (500), 12:30 (500), 14:00 (500), 15:05 (478), 16:05 (500), 16:45 (478), 17:15 (479) and 18:00 (500). On boarding the bus, you choose between a Zones 1 and 2 two-hourly ticket costing $4.50 and a Zones 1 and 2 all-day ticket, costing $8.20. The Airport is in Zone 2 and the city centre is in Zone 1. There is also a Zone 3, but you are not likely to want to go there at present. Either of these tickets will allow you to transfer to other buses, trams and trains as many times as you wish within its validity. Two hours should be quite sufficient to get you to your destination, but if you have spare time for the rest of the day, you might prefer the all-day ticket. On reaching Broadmeadows Station, take a suburban train into the city. If you arrive at Essendon Station, which is on the same line, do likewise. If you continue on the bus to Moonee Ponds, take a tram no. 59 into the city. Remember that you can change to other trams and trains to reach your precise destination without additional charge. By this method, expect your journey from the airport to a city destination to take about ninety minutes. There are buses from the airport on Saturdays and Sundays too, but they run to different timetables. The last bus on Saturdays is at 17:00 (no. 478), and on Sundays it is at 18:00 (no. 478).

Arrival by Land

If you arrive in Melbourne on a long-distance train, you will find yourself at Spencer Street Station which is on the western edge of the city grid (see map opposite). You can walk to the centre, or you can take a tram down Bourke or Collins Street, or you can take a suburban train from the same station to any destination.

If you arrive by long-distance bus, Firefly and Premier both use the bus terminal immediately outside Spencer Street Station, but McCafferty's and Greyhound use a

MELBOURNE CITY CENTRE
Thick dashed lines show tram routes
Numerals indicate tram route numbers

terminal in Franklin Street (see map on page 749), which is also walking distance from the city centre, but not quite as convenient if you need to take a train. The nearest station is Melbourne Central, which is underground.

Walking Tour *(see map on page 733)*

The city centre is laid out as a grid and it is fairly easy to find one's way around. Let us start with a walk to find some of the interesting spots. This walk covers approximately six kilometres and will take about two hours if no lengthy pauses are made.

We start at **Spencer Street Station**, which should be easy enough to find. This is the terminus for long- and medium-distance trains and for V-Line bus services. Suburban trains almost all pass through here too, but for them the principal station is Flinders Street. Inside Spencer Street Station is a fascinating **mural** depicting Melbourne transport through the period of its history, some of that transport not very much different from what could be seen until quite recently, in fact. Leave the station building and turn right along Spencer Street to the first main street, which is Collins Street. Turn left into Collins Street and walk one block to King Street. On your left is the **Melbourne Stock Exchange**, while on your right is *Rialto Towers*, the tallest office building in the southern hemisphere at 253 metres high. There is an observation deck on the 55th Floor from where, for the sum of $12, Melbourne may be surveyed. The price includes a special film about the attractions of Melbourne. There is a lift to the top which takes forty seconds to make the journey (or you can walk up 1,254 steps). The observation deck is open from 10:00 until 22:00 daily.

Proceed along Collins Street and then turn right into William Street and left into Flinders Street. On your left is the **Immigration Museum** in the Old Customs House.

Construction of this building began in 1839 and it is the oldest public building in Melbourne. The Museum is open daily from 10:00 until 17:00. Admission costs $8.

Continue along Flinders Street to Elizabeth Street. On your right here is **Flinders Street Station**, the hub of the suburban network, although this is not the main entrance to the station. At the end of Elizabeth Street, **trams** will be turning and setting off on their return journeys. Until recently this necessitated the manual removal of the power connector at one end of the tram and the application of the one at the other end of the vehicle, but, sadly, most of the traditional old trams have now been removed from service and replaced by modern one-man vehicles which do not need to carry out this operation. You will already have noticed that trams are the method of transport for Melburnians and that there is hardly a bus to be seen in the city centre. While other cities have dispensed with their trams, Melbourne has chosen to keep its network, and even extend it. It gives the city a charm which is missing elsewhere. The clatter of the tram wheels and the ring of the warning bells is heard only in Melbourne now. A few other places have tourist tram services, and Adelaide has kept one tram route, but only Melbourne uses trams as its practical and pollution-limiting transport of choice. The city council surely deserves some praise for its continuing trust in the network.

Walk along Elizabeth Street for two blocks to Bourke Street. On the corner here is the **old G.P.O.**, a majestic building dating from 1867 which, unfortunately, was gutted by fire in September 2001 and is now used as the G.P.O. no longer. It has now been restored for use as shops restaurants and offices, while the **Post Office** has moved further along Elizabeth Street to a location between Little Bourke Street and Lonsdale Street (and **Poste Restante** is now at 380 Bourke Street, a little way up the hill towards Queen Street). This section of Bourke Street is for pedestrians and trams only. Take care, because there is a temptation to think that it is for pedestrians only, and electric trams are quiet. Although they move slowly through this area, remember to look before crossing the road. Incidentally, this route along Bourke Street used to be operated by a cable car and, until the road was resurfaced a few years ago, the central slot for the cable grip could still be seen in places. At the near end of Bourke Street, you will see the **Public Purse**, a pleasant sculpture made of pink granite and an example of the art work which has started to grace the city area in recent years. This area is also where you will find some of the most talented **buskers**, not to mention the occasional man with microphone and amplifier informing us of just why Jesus died for us, often in tones apparently designed for the Almighty to overhear. Walk along this section of Bourke Street, noting, on the left, **Myer's Department Store**, probably the most famous Melbourne shop. At the end of the pedestrian area, you will meet Swanston Street. Here notice, on your right, another interesting piece of sculpture, entitled *Three Businessmen who Brought their own Lunch*. The three are waiting at the tram stop. Turn left, however, not right, and walk to Little Lonsdale Street, turning left into that small road. Two-thirds of the way down, there is an entrance, on your right, to **Melbourne Central** shopping complex. Take this entrance and try to reach the open area at the centre of the complex, where you can sit on the steps of the stage and wait for the clock to reach the hour. **The clock** is actually a huge watch, and it claims to be the largest marionette fob watch in the world. It is placed here courtesy of Mr. Seiko, but you will find that the rendition on the hour is definitely not Japanese. Whilst you are waiting for the hands to reach the hour, look up and admire the architecture. This was originally a **Shot Tower**, where pieces of molten lead were dropped from a sufficient height to allow them to form themselves into perfect spheres and then solidify before reaching the bottom. The basic structure of the tower remains.

Leave from the watch side of this open area and try to find your way out of the warren through the exit on the corner of La Trobe Street and Swanston Street. It soon becomes apparent why this is called a complex, but the appetising aroma of Mr. MacDonald's hamburgers may assist in guiding you. If you can find this exit, turn right into Swanston Street again and walk back to Lonsdale Street before turning left. You are now passing through the **Greek area** of the city centre. Turn right at Russell Street and then left into Little Bourke Street. You have now passed from Greece into the middle of **China**. Who would have imagined that the two were contiguous? This area is conspicuous for its Chinese restaurants and grocery stores, and for the **Chinese gate** at the end of the street. Continue to the end of Little Bourke Street and then turn right into Spring Street, and past the **Princess Theatre**, built in 1886.

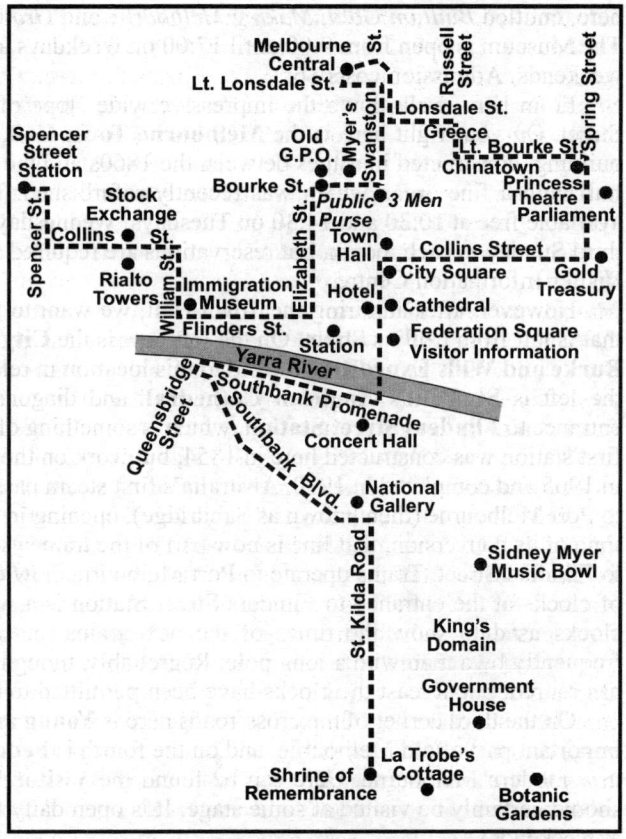

WALKING TOUR OF MELBOURNE

Across the road you will see the majestic **Parliament House**, built of granite from the Grampians. The **Legislative Chambers** were constructed in a mere ten months, built in 1856 and ready in time for the first sitting of the Victorian Parliament. The entire building, however, was never completed. It was designed to have a large dome which was never constructed due to lack of funds. Nevertheless, what is there is still most impressive and this is generally regarded as the finest parliament building in the British Commonwealth, except for that in London. This building was used by the Parliament of the Commonwealth of Australia while Melbourne was acting as the capital of Australia, and then returned for the use of the state government thereafter. **Tours** of the building are available when Parliament is not sitting, and are free.

Continue along Spring Street and you will come to the Old Treasury Building, now the **Gold Treasury Museum**. This too is a very impressive building, generally regarded as one of the finest public buildings in Australia. It was built in 1862, having been designed by a nineteen-year-old architect. It was used as government offices until 1992, and then reopened as a museum in 1994. There are three permanent exhibitions here, entitled *Built on Gold, Making Melbourne* and *Growing Up in the Old Treasury*. The Museum is open from 9:00 until 17:00 on weekdays and from 10:00 until 16:00 at weekends. Admission costs $6.

From here, walk down the impressive wide slope of Collins Street to Swanston Street. On your right here is the **Melbourne Town Hall**, yet another splendid public building, constructed in stages between the 1860s and the 1920s. It includes a **concert hall** with a fine organ which was recently refurbished. **Tours** of the Town Hall are available free at 10:30 and 14:30 on Tuesdays, Wednesdays and Thursdays, and on the third Sunday in each month, but reservations are required and can be made through the Visitor Information Centre.

However, after admiring the Town Hall, we want to go in the opposite direction, that is left from Collins Street. On the left now is the **City Square**, with a statue of the **Burke and Wills Expedition** moved to this location in relatively recent times. Next on the left is **St. Paul's Anglican Cathedral**, and diagonally opposite it is the main entrance to **Flinders Street Station**, which is something of a Melbourne landmark. The first station was constructed here in 1854, but work on the present building was started in 1905 and completed in 1910. Australia's first steam passenger railway ran from here to Port Melbourne (then known as Sandridge), opening in 1854. Despite protests at the time of its conversion, that line is now part of the tram system, and so no longer comes to Flinders Street. Trams operate to Port Melbourne now from Collins Street. The row of clocks at the entrance to Flinders Street Station is a well-used meeting point. The clocks used to show the times of the next trains on each line and were changed frequently by a man with a long pole. Regrettably, though, it seems as though the man has retired, but at least the clocks have been permitted to remain as a reminder.

On the third corner of the cross-roads here is **Young and Jackson's Hotel**, another important part of old Melbourne, and on the fourth is **Federation Square**, a part of the new modern Melbourne. Here can be found the **Visitor Information Centre**, which should certainly be visited at some stage. It is open daily from 9:00 until 18:00 (17:00 at weekends).

Continue walking over **Princess Bridge**, at which point this becomes St. Kilda Road. The river which you are crossing is the **Yarra**, and from here a good view of it can be obtained in both directions. Now descend on your right to the level of the river, noting the **Melbourne Concert Hall** on your left as you do so. You come to **Southbank Promenade**, a pleasant stroll along beside the water. Continue until you reach a large road with tram lines (Queensbridge Street), and then turn sharp left into Southbank Boulevard, which will return you to St. Kilda Road next to the **National Gallery**, on your left. If you have spare time, this is another attraction worth a visit. At least have a look at the interesting modern building, recently renovated.

Turn right along St. Kilda Road and on the other side of the wide avenue you will find **King's Domain**, a pleasant grassy area. Look down St. Kilda Road and straight ahead you will see the **Shrine of Remembrance**. The road itself curves right so that the view from here leads straight into the shrine. This was originally Victoria's memorial to the 18,000 men from the state lost in the Great War. The Shrine was opened in 1934. After the Second World War, it was extended to include those who had been lost in that conflict. The perpetual flame was lit by Queen Elizabeth on 28th February 1954. The Shrine is so designed that at 11:00 on 11th November each year (Remembrance Day) a single ray of sunlight will penetrate the roof and shine on the Stone of Remembrance in the Inner Sanctum. However, since Victoria has adopted daylight-saving time in the summer months, that event actually occurs at noon now. The Shrine of Remembrance is another of Melbourne's very impressive buildings. It is open every day from 10:00 until 17:00 with free admission and free tours, if desired, from volunteer guides.

Our tour ends here. You can catch a tram back to the city, as many services pass this point. However, if you still have energy, a better route is to walk through the attractive **Botanic Gardens**, which are a short distance to the east of the Shrine of Remembrance. Here you will also find **La Trobe's Cottage** and **Government House**, and if you return through King's Domain you will also see the **Sidney Myer Music Bowl**. Sidney Myer was the founder of Myer's Department Store, which you saw in Bourke Street. One of the most famous events held here is the *Carols by Candlelight* Christmas service televised throughout Australia, and elsewhere, and attended by huge crowds sitting on the grass around the music bowl.

Other City Centre Attractions

Naturally there is a great deal to see in Melbourne, and our tour has shown us only a part of even the central attractions. Here are some of the city centre sights which we missed (see map on page 749).

If you continue along the south bank of the river in a westerly direction, you will pass the **Crown Entertainment Complex**, then come to the **Melbourne Exhibition Centre**, and finally arrive at the **Polly Woodside Maritime Museum**. The Crown Entertainment Complex has fourteen cinemas, 35 restaurants, seventeen bars, several nightclubs, a theatre and a casino. The Exhibition Centre is Australia's largest.

The *Polly Woodside* is a barque built in Belfast in 1885. She was named after the wife of the original owner and made sixteen voyages round Cape Horn. She then spent twenty years sailing Australian waters and a further forty years as a coal refuelling barge in Melbourne. By the 1960s she was ready to be scrapped, but was saved for restoration by a group of volunteers. Restoration took many years, but by 1988 she was ready, and is now the principal exhibit at the Maritime Museum. The Museum is open daily from 10:00 until 16:00, with admission costing $12.

Just north of the river, on its banks next to Batman Park, is **Melbourne Aquarium**. It is a high-technology aquarium, open daily from 9:30 until 18:00 at a cost of $20.

A little north of here, behind and beyond Spencer Street Station, the old railway yards are being developed into the **Docklands** area with new towering blocks of flats and the **Colonial Stadium**, with the name not intended as a memory of Victoria's origins, but referring to the sponsor of the project. This is primarily a stadium for Australian Rules Football, but one which has been designed to allow all types of sports to be played here. It has a retractable roof which allows matches to take place even in inclement weather.

To the north of the central city is the **Queen Victoria Market**, a remnant of a bygone era in trading. This is an extensive market with all types of products sold at traditional stalls. The products are not necessarily cheap, although some are, but the atmosphere is worth experiencing, with the market at its most lively on Sundays. The Meat Hall dates from 1869, Sheds A to F from 1878, and the shops on Victoria Street from 1884 to 1890. Queen Victoria Market is closed on Mondays and Wednesdays. On Tuesdays and Thursdays it is open from 6:00 until 14:00. On Fridays it is open from 6:00 until 18:00, on Saturdays from 6:00 until 15:00, and on Sundays from 9:00 until 16:00. It is reached by travelling north on Queen Street or Elizabeth Street.

736 VICTORIA

Further east along Victoria Street, just round the corner into Russell Street, is the **Old Melbourne Gaol**. Construction of this building was commenced in 1841 and it was extended between 1851 and 1864, and kept in use until 1929, at which time most of the land was sold and several of the buildings, including the Women's Wing, were demolished. Part of the building was used between 1942 and 1946 as a military prison. It became a Museum in 1972. Over the years of its operation as a gaol, the building was the scene of 135 hangings, of which the most famous was that of bushranger **Ned Kelly** on 11th November 1880. His mother was also in the prison at the time. The scaffold on which Kelly was hanged survives, as does his original death mask. There is a collection of other death masks too. The Gaol is open daily from 9:30 until 16:30 and admission costs $12.

Opposite Russell Street on the other side of Victoria Street is **Lygon Street**. If you walk along this street for a while you will find Melbourne's **Italy**, particularly a number of Italian restaurants. You can also take tram no. 1 or 22 from Swanston Street to reach the other end of this restaurant area.

If, though, you remain on Victoria Street, a little further along on the left are the **Carlton Gardens** with the **Exhibition Building** behind. Originally constructed for the Great Exhibition of 1880, this was the home of the Victorian Parliament from 1901 until 1927, since the Victorian Parliament House was being borrowed by the Commonwealth (Federal) Government. This was also the site of the opening of the first session of the Commonwealth Parliament, on 9th May 1901. There is a famous painting by Tom Roberts depicting the scene of the opening by the Duke of Cornwall and York (later King George V). Nowadays, though, the building is not even wanted for major exhibitions, since a new Exhibition Centre (mentioned above) has been built to the south of the city centre, by the river. Beside the Exhibition Building is the new **Melbourne Museum**, opened in October 2000. The Museum is open daily from 10:00 until 17:00. Admission is in combination with admission to various other semi-permanent exhibitions on the site and to the *Age Theatre*, and costs $15. There is also an Imax theatre at this location.

Next to the Gold Treasury Museum are the pleasant **Treasury Gardens**, and behind them are the **Fitzroy Gardens**, where the attractions include the **Conservatory** and **Captain Cook's Cottage**. The cottage was not Captain Cook's really. It was his parents', built in 1755 and moved here from Great Ayton in Yorkshire in 1934 in commemoration of the Captain's role in the European settlement of Australia. It is open daily from 9:00 until 17:00.

The **Melbourne Cricket Ground** is to the south-east of the city centre. It was one of the principal arenas for the 1956 Olympic Games and has long been used for cricket and Australian Rules Football matches. The stadium used to have a capacity of 125,000, but the installation of improved seating has reduced that figure to 97,000, which is still a large number of people. Tours are available between 10:00 and 15:00 on days when no sporting event is scheduled here and cost $18.

Suburbs

All of the attractions which have been mentioned so far are in the vicinity of the city centre and within walking distance of it. There are many other places in the suburbs to visit. These are a few of them.

St. Kilda was apparently named after a yacht which was anchored here just as development of the seaside suburb began, the yacht presumably being named after the

Scottish island. As a look at some of the housing will reveal, St. Kilda has, through the last century and a half, been a fashionable place to live. Now it is something of an enigma. It has some handsome housing, the stately **Fitzroy Street**, the fashionable **Acland Street**, the scenic **Esplanade**, appealing beaches and parks, but yet it has a distinctly seedy feeling in parts, with buildings in a state of disrepair, nightclubs, prostitutes on the streets in the evenings and a general feeling that you had better keep your wallet in a safe place. It is a location very popular with the young, and with backpackers in particular, so there are several hostels here (see map). **Luna Park** is here too, an amusement area where you can pass through the jaws of hell into a playground which dates from 1912. From the city, it is six

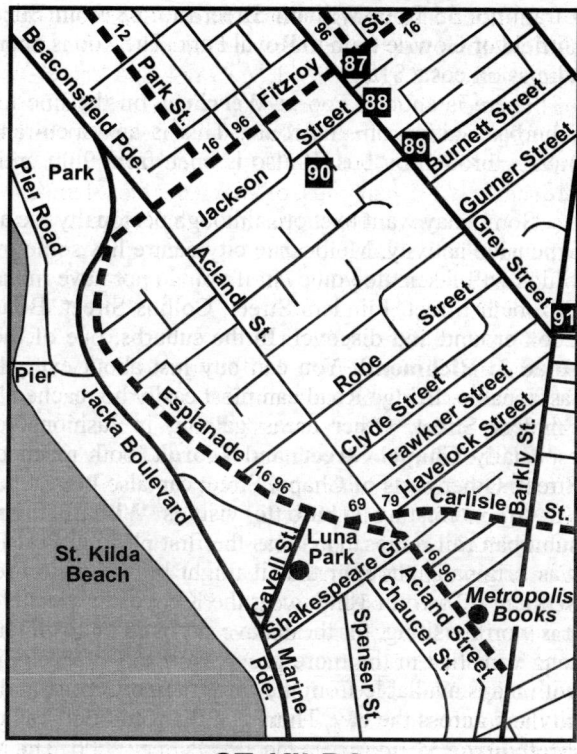

ST. KILDA
Thick dashed lines show tram routes, with numbers
White numerals indicate backpackers hostels

kilometres to St. Kilda, a ride which takes half an hour. There used to be a railway line, but it has been converted into a tram route, unfortunately, so now you can reach here by three different trams. No. 96 is the fastest, running along the former railway line. It leaves the city from Bourke Street and terminates in Acland Street. No. 16 leaves from Swanston Street and terminates in Acland Street, while no. 12 leaves from Collins Street and terminates at Fitzroy Street.

If you take tram no. 96 to St. Kilda, you will pass by **Albert Park**, established in 1864 and named after the consort of Queen Victoria. This is a popular recreation area, and it is also the scene of the **Australian Grand Prix** every March.

Beaches next. Lying as it does on Port Phillip Bay, Melbourne has a multitude of beaches to offer (see map on page 739). The eastern side of the bay is ringed with beaches. These begin with **Sandridge Beach**, and continue round to **Port Melbourne** (tram no. 109), **South Melbourne** (tram no. 1), **St. Kilda** (trams nos. 12, 16, 96), **Brighton** (train to Brighton Beach on Sandringham Line), **Sandringham** (train to Sandringham), and many others round to **Frankston** and beyond. From Mentone to Frankston, these can all be reached from stations on the Frankston Line. Wherever you disembark after Mentone on this line, you will always be just a short walk from a beach.

Melbourne Zoo is not too far from the city centre, being situated in **Royal Park**, only four kilometres away. It has been on this site since it was established in 1862. Take a tram no. 55 from William Street (no. 68 from Elizabeth Street on Sundays), or an Upfield or Gowrie train to Royal Park. The Zoo is open daily from 9:00 until 17:00 and admission costs $18.

There is another zoo at **Werribee**, on the line to Geelong. Werribee is the final suburban station on this route. This is an 'open-range' safari type zoo, which one travels through by bus. It also is open from 9:00 until 17:00, with admission costing $18.

Some may want to shop, although personally the author finds that an unnecessarily expensive activity. Melbourne city centre has some interesting old **shopping arcades** which will fascinate you even if you do not have money. The various arcades open off Elizabeth Street, Flinders Street, Collins Street, Bourke Street and Swanston Street. Look around and discover. In the suburbs, one of the places for shopping is **Bridge Road** in **Richmond**. You can buy just about everything here, especially everything fashionable. Bridge Road can most easily be reached by taking tram no. 48 or 75 from Flinders Street. Other areas gaining in fashionable popularity are **South Yarra**, especially **Chapel Street**, and **Toorak**, both reached by tram no. 8 from Swanston Street. Other parts of Chapel Street can also be reached by taking trams nos. 6 or 72.

An interesting suburb to visit is **Williamstown**, the terminus for one of the suburban rail routes. This was the first place in Port Phillip Bay to be surveyed and it was originally thought that it might be the main area for settlement. It was named William's Town in 1837, after the King of the day. Now it is for its old buildings that it is worth visiting, for these have survived in this interesting port area, while they have long vanished in the more progressive city of Melbourne. There is an Heritage Trail, with maps available from the Information Centre, and there are also good views of the city and across the bay. There is a **ferry** to Southbank in the city centre operating four times daily, taking an hour for the journey, and costing $12. There is a **ferry** to St. Kilda at weekends only, six times a day, taking 25 minutes and costing $8. It is interesting that these ferry routes have been resumed in recent years, after such services across the bay had disappeared many years ago. The route up the river to the city is especially appealing.

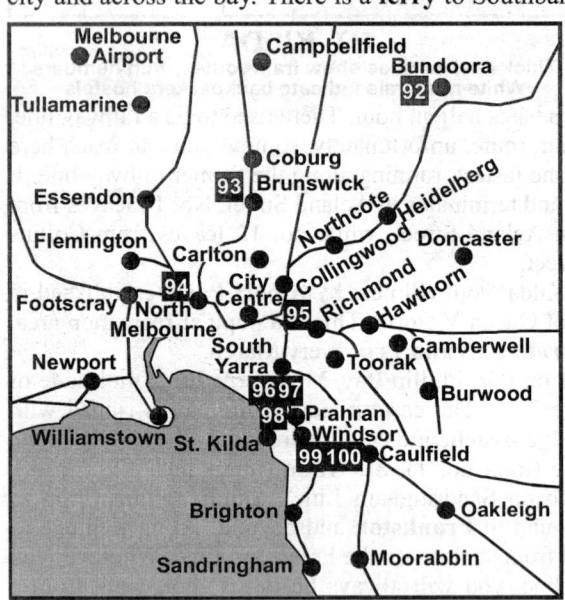

MELBOURNE INNER SUBURBS
Showing suburban railway lines
Numerals indicate backpackers hostels

Public Transport

As mentioned above, one of Melbourne's charms is its trams rattling not only through the main streets of the city centre but far into the suburbs too. Horse-drawn trams began operating in Melbourne in 1884. A cable car was put into service in 1885, and electric trams started running in

MELBOURNE 739

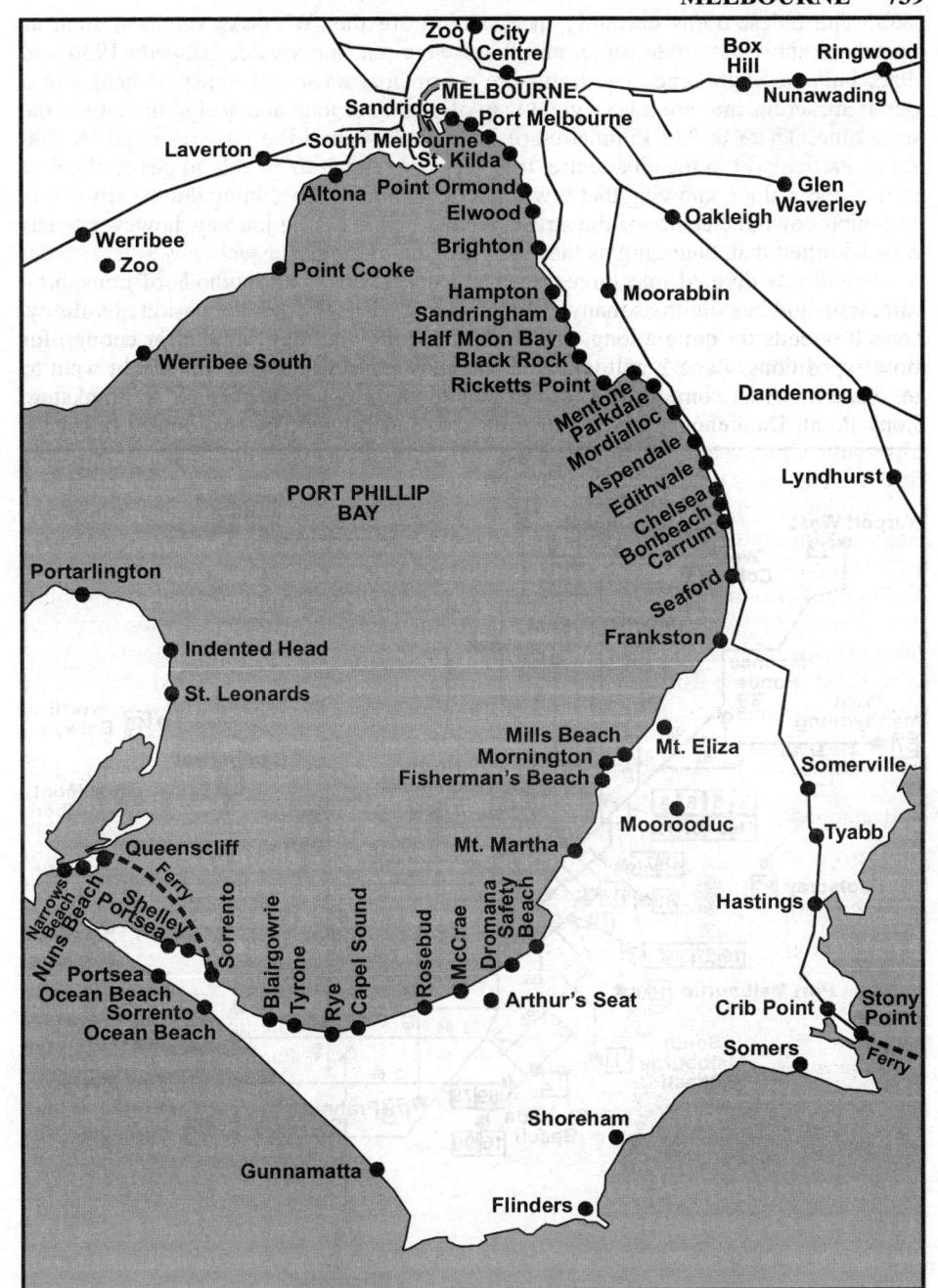

PORT PHILLIP BAY
Showing railways and beaches

740 VICTORIA

1889. The oldest trams currently in operation are the 'W' class vehicles, such as operate on the City Circle route, and these were put into service between 1936 and 1956, built in Melbourne. The trams are a principal means of transport here, not a tourist attraction, and are a very good way of getting around and seeing the city at the same time. There is 236 kilometres of tram track around the city, operated by 600 trams. Particularly in the city centre, it is very convenient to be able to get on the first tram to come along knowing that it will not deviate from the shining double silver line stretching down the centre of the street. When one has a long journey, however, it has to be admitted that, charming as the trams are, the trains are faster.

The city is divided into three zones and tickets cover all methods of transport - train, tram and bus - with as many changes as one wishes within the period of validity. Zone 1 extends for quite a long way from the centre and may well be far enough for most expeditions. Zone 2 will take you to almost everywhere that you might want to go. Zone 3 covers some of the eastern and southern extremities, such as Frankston, Stony Point, Dandenong, Pakenham, Belgrave and Lilydale. A two-hourly ticket for

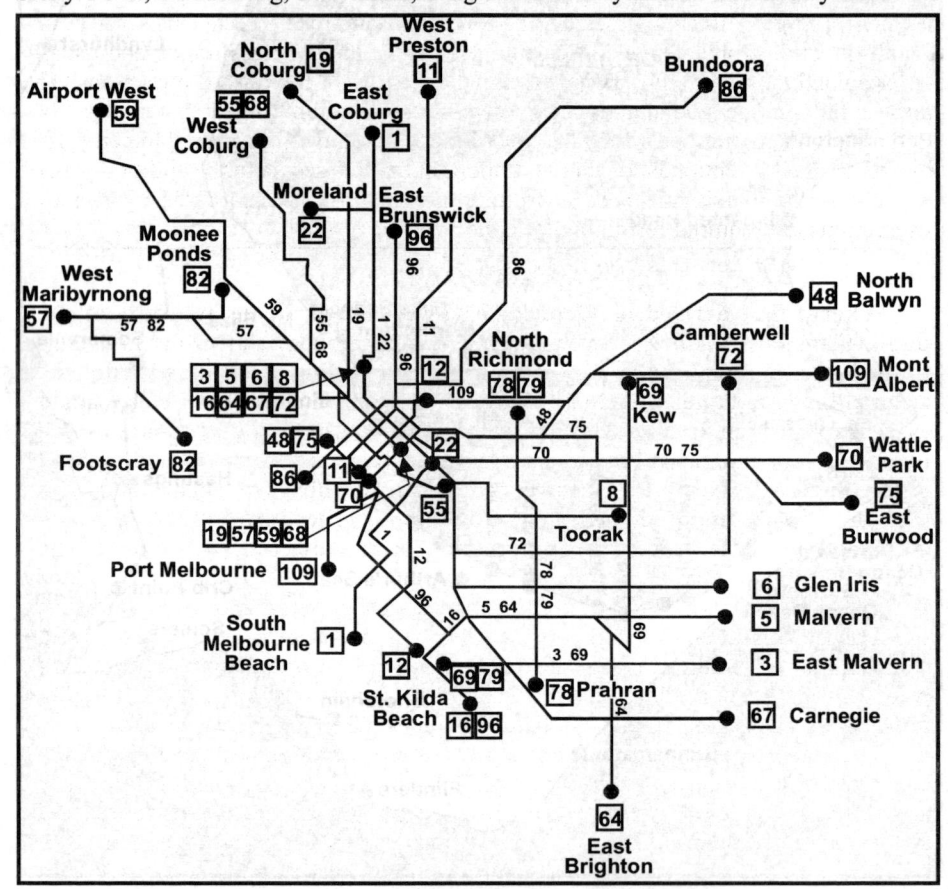

MELBOURNE TRAM SYSTEM
Service 55 operates on Mondays to Saturdays only.
Service 68 operates on Sundays only.
Certain additional peak hour services operate.

Zone 1 costs $2.60. For Zones 1 and 2 it costs $4.50, and for Zones 1, 2 and 3 it costs $6.10. An all-day ticket costs $5.10 for Zone 1, $8.20 for Zones 1 and 2, and $11 for Zones 1, 2 and 3. There are other options available too, such as tickets not including Zone 1, sets of ten tickets of a particular type, and weekly or monthly tickets. At railway stations, all types of tickets originating at that station can be purchased, but at smaller stations the purchase is made from a machine, and that machine may or may not be in working order. On trams, there is also a machine, but it accepts only coins and issues only two-hourly tickets. If you want an all-day ticket and there is no station nearby, you must purchase from a local shop, typically a newsagency. As in other places in Australia, purchasing the ticket is not sufficient. You must then insert it into another machine to validate it. If not so inserted, it remains an unused ticket which is still available for use at any time in the future. To make matters even more complicated, the exception to this is that tickets purchased from a machine on a tram are automatically validated for that one journey.

There is a free tram service which operates around the boundaries of the city grid, via Spencer Street, Flinders Street, Spring Street and La Trobe Street. This service runs in both directions, operates every ten minutes, uses old 'W' class trams, and usually carries a conductor who gives advice as to where to alight for various attractions. The trams on this service are painted a distinctive maroon colour.

There is also a tram on which one may dine whilst travelling around the city. This division of one's attention between two important matters seems to the author a way of not getting the maximum benefit from either, and it is also rather expensive. Reservations are required for dining (telephone 03-9696-4000).

ANECDOTE

When I first arrived in Victoria, I was surprised at the antiquity of the public transport. Victorian Railways was obviously making an effort to live up to its name, although only some of the country rolling stock dated from the reign of that good queen. Melbourne's red wooden trains had been constructed as recently as the 1920s. They had manually operated sliding doors which tended to jam shut whenever one wished to enter or exit, and to jam open at other times. It was my first experience of trains which travelled along with their doors open, and it seemed to me a dangerous procedure until I had grown accustomed to it. It was, however, a fine means of providing ventilation in the summer.

Those electric trains seemed to have no speed between zero and 20 km/hr, so when halting at a station they would slow to 20 km/hr, then slam to a total stop, almost propelling forward-facing passengers onto the floor. The re-start was preceded by a blast on the engine horn, to warn backward-facing passengers to hang on tightly or suffer a similar fate.

The windows shook and rattled as the train went along and the noise of the electric motor increased gradually in pitch and intensity. Although luxuriously appointed green leather seats were provided for passengers, comfort was not really the prime merit of those antique conveyances. They did have character, though, which their stainless steel replacements lack, and one cannot help feeling that, with all their defects, those old red trains, which survived more than half a century of service, were an irreplaceable part of the character of Melbourne.

Day Trips

As in many parts of Australia, one often feels that anywhere which is worth a day trip from Melbourne is really worth longer. However, there are three locations to the east and south of the capital which are suitable for day outings.

(a) Healesville Sanctuary

Healesville Sanctuary specialises in native Australian wildlife and is one of the best places in the country to go to see such unique Australian creatures as wombats, koalas, kangaroos and, particularly, platypus. The Sanctuary has kept platypus since the 1930s and, during the 1940s, became the first place in the world to breed a platypus in captivity, a success not repeated until 1999. Healesville Sanctuary, opened in 1934, is 65 kilometres east from the centre of Melbourne, and commercial tours are available. However, it is also quite possible to go there by public transport. Take a suburban train to the Lilydale terminus, which takes just over an hour from the centre of Melbourne, with trains operating every thirty minutes. Then change to a bus no. 685 to the Sanctuary. At the time of writing, buses leave from Lilydale at 9:40 and 11:35 on weekdays, 11:40 and 13:40 on Saturdays, and 10:45 on Sundays. Return services from Healesville to Lilydale depart at 12:34, 13:55, 15:40 and 17:30 on weekdays, 12:20, 15:05 and 17:05 on Saturdays, and 15:15 and 17:15 on Sundays. The bus takes nearly an hour each way. If you purchase a ticket for Zones 1, 2 and 3, it can be used on the bus as well as the train. The Sanctuary is open daily from 9:00 until 17:00 and admission costs $18.

(b) Puffing Billy *(see railway map opposite)*

Puffing Billy is a steam-operated narrow-gauge railway running in the Dandenong Ranges forty kilometres to the east of Melbourne city centre. When Victorian Railways found that its 5 feet 3 inches gauge was not suitable for sparsely populated hill areas, it constructed four railways to a 2 feet 6 inches narrow gauge, a gauge not used elsewhere in Australia and one which confused the railway compatibility situation even further. This particular line was opened from Upper Ferntree Gully to Gembrook in 1900. It lost money right from the start, but the unfortunate point about it was that the more traffic it carried, the more it lost, so that Victorian Railways was constantly hoping that a good reason would arise for its closure. That occurred in August 1953, when a landslide blocked the line, and on 30th April 1954 it was declared closed.

ANECDOTE

My first experience with Melbourne's tram system was not a complete success. When it was time to alight, I rose and pulled the leather cord running the length of the vehicle. The tram sailed past my stop. I pulled the cord harder. The tram sailed past the next stop. I pulled the cord two or three times. The tram sailed past another stop. I gave up and the tram stopped, not because of me, however, but because another passenger wished to board. I got off while I had the opportunity, and started my long walk back.

It was only later that I discovered that in order to alight one must pull the cord on the right of the vehicle. The one on the left rings the bell in the cab which is currently at the rear of the tram. One learns by experience. Few of those older trams remain in service, however, so the reader will probably not encounter this same difficulty.

MELBOURNE 743

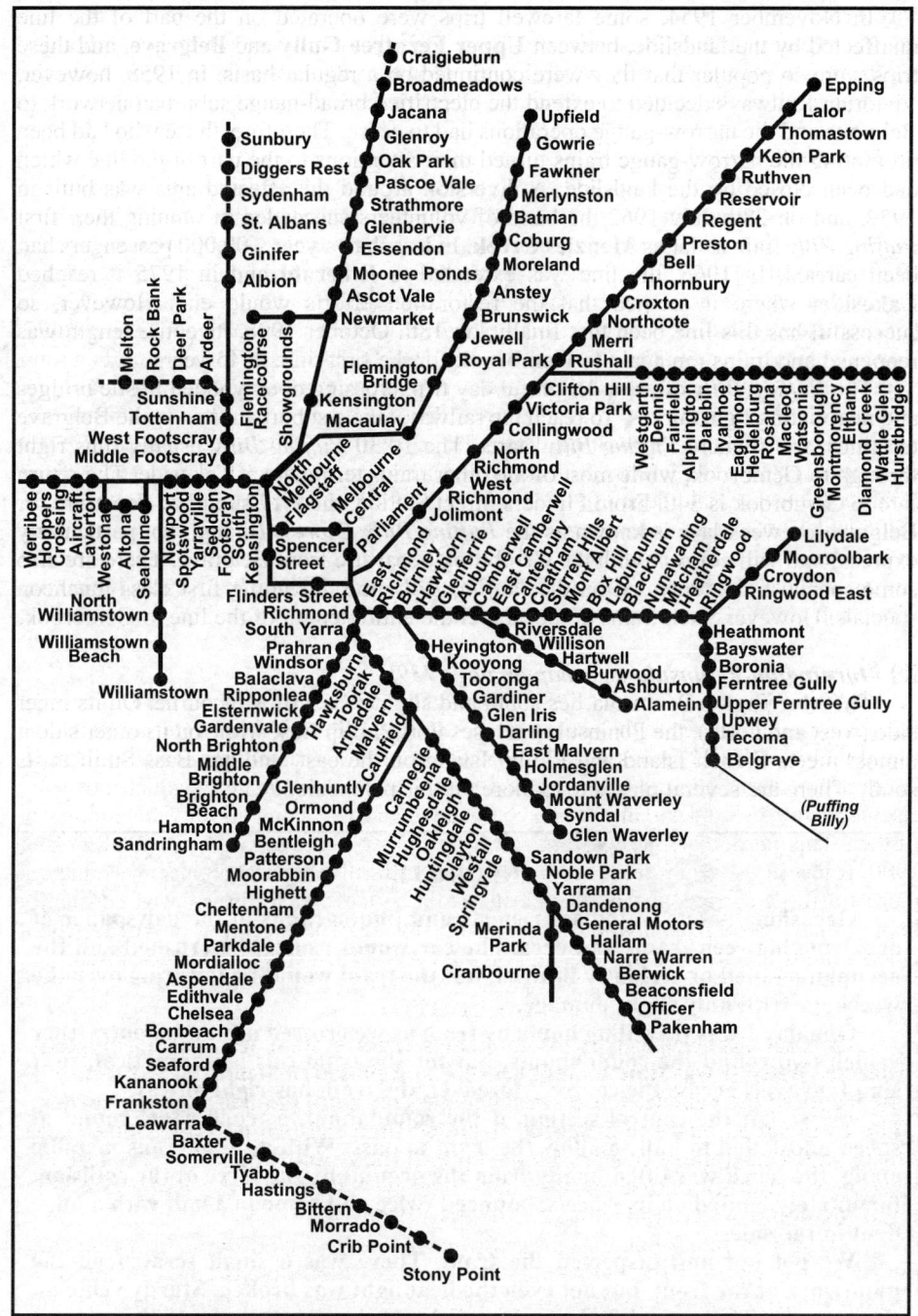

MELBOURNE SUBURBAN RAILWAY SYSTEM
Dashed line denotes V-Line Service, but Melbourne Metropolitan tickets valid

In November 1954, some farewell trips were operated on the part of the line unaffected by the landslide, between **Upper Ferntree Gully** and **Belgrave**, and these trips were so popular that they were continued on a regular basis. In 1958, however, Victorian Railways decided to extend the electrified broad-gauge suburban network to Belgrave and the narrow-gauge operations had to cease. Therefore, those who had been promoting the narrow-gauge trains turned their attentions to the part of the line which had been closed by the landslide. A diversion around the affected area was built in 1959, and on 28th July 1962 the band of volunteers succeeded in running their first *Puffing Billy* train as far as **Menzies Creek**. In less than a year, 100,000 passengers had been carried. In 1965, the line was extended to **Emerald** and in 1975 it reached **Lakeside**, where it seemed that the restoration efforts would end. However, so successful has this line been that finally, on 18th October 1998, its entire length was reopened and trains ran again to **Gembrook** for the first time in 45 years.

The *Puffing Billy* offers a delightful day trip, crossing over wooden trestle bridges and negotiating tight curves. To reach the railway, take a suburban train to the Belgrave terminus, from where *Puffing Billy* starts. The 10:30 *Puffing Billy* usually runs right through to Gembrook, while most of the other trains terminate at Lakeside. The return fare to Gembrook is $40. From Flinders Street Station, the 9:17 suburban departure for Belgrave on weekdays is known as the *Puffing Billy Express* (though not particularly express) and will connect with the Gembrook departure from Belgrave. There are also some special trains operated on the *Puffing Billy* line, including first class luncheon specials. However, such trains do not travel the entire length of the line to Gembrook.

(c) Mornington Peninsula (see map on page 739)

The Mornington Peninsula lies south and slightly east of Melbourne. On its inner side (west and north), the Peninsula encloses Port Phillip Bay, while on its outer side it almost meets French Island and Phillip Island on the east, and has Bass Strait to its south. There are several places to explore on this peninsula.

ANECDOTE

Occasionally one would see reports and photographs in the newspaper of accidents between trams and cars. The car would usually be crushed and the occupants killed or seriously injured, but the tram would be towering over the wreckage with only slight damage.

One day I was travelling home by tram as we crossed a roundabout. Other vehicles go round the roundabouts, but for the tram this is impractical, so it simply travels across the centre. Moreover, the tram has right of way.

As we left the central section of the roundabout, a truck came round at speed and failed to halt to allow the tram to pass. With a thunderous metallic clang, the truck was lifted bodily from the ground by the force of the collision, fortunately landed on its wheels, bounced twice and came to a halt with a huge dent in the side.

We got out and inspected the tram. There was a small scratch on the paintwork at the front, but not even the headlight was broken. Sturdy vehicles, those trams. They certainly knew how to build them well in the 1930s.

MELBOURNE

One pleasant journey is to take a suburban train to its terminus at Frankston and then change to a further train to **Stony Point**. This whole journey can be performed with a Zones 1, 2 and 3 ticket. That the route to Stony Point has survived the closure of so many railway lines in Victoria is something of a surprise. Indeed, it was once closed, and then re-opened. It is a typically rural line which travels across the peninsula from its inner west coast to its outer east coast. The journey from Flinders Street to Frankston takes just over an hour and trains run from Frankston to Stony Point at 7:07, 9:00, 12:26, 14:25, 16:13 and 18:12 on weekdays. At weekends, they run at 9:00 and then at five minutes past the odd hours until 19:05. The journey from Frankston to Stony Point takes approximately forty minutes, and trains wait there for about twenty minutes before returning to Frankston. Thus times from Stony Point to Frankston are approximately one hour later than the times from Frankston to Stony Point.

At Stony Point, there is a tea room and not much else. The train travels right to the water's edge and from this point there is a ferry service which operates to **French Island** and to **Cowes** on **Phillip Island**. It is a good way to reach the latter if you are thinking of visiting the penguins there (see page 831).

French Island is so called because it was discovered by the French survey vessel *Le Naturaliste* in 1802. It has a total area of 17,410 hectares, of which 11,100 hectares is National Park. The population is approximately 80. It can be reached in ten minutes by ferry, arrival point being the small town of **Tankerton** on the west coast (see map on page 832). Departures from Stony Point are at 8:30 daily, 10:00 on Saturdays and Sundays, 12:00 on Tuesdays, Thursdays, Saturdays and Sundays, 16:15 daily, and 19:00 on Fridays. Return journeys from Tankerton to Stony Point leave at 9:30 daily, 10:15 on Saturdays and Sundays, 13:00 on Tuesdays, Thursdays, Saturdays and Sundays, 16:30 daily, and 19:15 (via Cowes) on Fridays only. Onward services from Tankerton to Cowes are at 8:40 daily, 12:10 on Tuesdays, Thursdays, Saturdays and Sundays, 16:30 (via Stony Point) daily, and 19:15 on Fridays. The fare is $10 for each single journey. **Tours of French Island** are available at an additional cost of $20 by taking the 12:00 ferry on the days on which it operates and returning on the 16:30 ferry. Sights include lots of koalas, echidna, wildflowers, birds, a chicory kiln, and an historic prison. Camping is available on the island, and there is one guest house. The island measures approximately 25 kilometres from east to west and fifteen kilometres from north to south. The closest point to the mainland is on the eastern coast, where the distance is a mere two kilometres.

The ferry ride to Cowes on Phillip Island takes half an hour, with departures from Stony Point at 8:30 daily, 12:00 on Tuesdays, Thursdays, Saturdays and Sundays, 17:00 daily and 19:00 on Fridays. Return journeys from Cowes are at 9:10 daily, 12:40 on Tuesdays, Thursdays, Saturdays and Sundays, 17:25 daily and 19:45 on Fridays. The fare is $10 per single journey. Phillip Island is famous for its 'Penguin Parade' in the evenings (see page 833), to see which, however, you need to stay overnight.

Another possible expedition is to the town of **Mornington** itself. Again you take the suburban train to Frankston, and from there catch a bus no. 781, destination either Mornington or **Mt. Martha**. Again this is permitted using a Zones 1, 2 and 3 ticket. Buses run approximately every half hour. Mornington is 55 kilometres from the centre of Melbourne and has a population of 30,000. A settlement was first established at nearby **Schnapper Point**, and this developed into the town of Mornington. A jetty was built in 1857, after which the town soon became a favoured destination for holidays and day trips on the steamers which plied the bay in the latter half of the nineteenth century.

746 VICTORIA

The **Courthouse** here dates from 1860 and the **Post Office** from 1864. There are also several imposing nineteenth century hotels, such as the **Royal Hotel, Kirkpatrick's Hotel** and the **Grand Hotel**. The **Old Mornington Hotel** used to be called the Tanti Hotel and was the original staging point for the Cobb and Co. coaches, while the Royal Hotel used to be called the Schnapper Point Hotel, but changed its name after the Duke of Edinburgh stayed there in 1896. The **Old Post Office** is now a Museum, open, however, only on Sundays between 14:00 and 17:00. The Old Courthouse is an **Information Centre**, open at weekends only. It also displays local works of art. There is a **statue of Matthew Flinders**. He visited in 1802 in *H.M.S. Investigator* and landed near Mornington. Nearby is a memorial to the Mornington Football Team, all members of which were lost at sea in 1892. A **steam train** operates on the old railway line between Mornington and **Moorooduc** on the first Sunday in each month and on most public holidays. The journey takes about 25 minutes each way, and the fare is $10 return.

One more possibility is to perform a **complete circuit**, by travelling the length of the Mornington Peninsula, crossing by ferry and returning to Melbourne via the Bellarine Peninsula and Geelong. Bus no. 788 from Frankston will take you to **Sorrento**, from where the ferry operates (or on for another five minutes to the **Mornington Peninsula National Park** at **Portsea**). However, in this case, you have to start paying bus fares from Frankston, as this route in no longer within the metropolitan area. You can, if you prefer, travel as far as Mt. Martha on bus no. 781 by using your Zone 3 ticket and walk up to the Nepean Highway (not very far) to catch the bus on to Sorrento. Bus no. 788 operates irregularly, but approximately hourly on weekdays. On Saturdays, it runs two-hourly, on the even hours from Frankston. On Sundays, you need to catch the 10:45 or 13:15 from Frankston if you are to get round the circle. The journey from Frankston to Sorrento takes approximately ninety minutes. On the way, near **Dromana**, you will see, on your left, **Arthur's Seat**, the highest point on the peninsula at 304 metres. A 74-seat chairlift leads up to it. This chairlift is the longest in Victoria, almost precisely one kilometre long. The journey takes twenty minutes, costs $7 one way or $10 return, and offers some fine views. The chairlift operates from 11:00 until 17:00, daily from September until June, but only at weekends during the winter. Arthur's Seat was climbed by Matthew Flinders, and his journal records that he enjoyed the view too. It was named in 1802 by Lt. John Murray after a mountain near Edinburgh.

The ferry from Sorrento to **Queenscliff** on the Bellarine Peninsula operates every hour from 7:00 until 18:00, taking forty minutes to cross and costing $10 single or $16 return. For details of what lies on the other side, on the Bellarine Peninsula, see the section on Geelong, on page 756.

MAP SHOPS AND BOOKSHOPS
City Centre

Map Land	372 Little Bourke Street
Book City	191-205 Swanston Street
The Paperback Books	60 Bourke Street
Dymocks	Shop 113, Melbourne Central
Dymocks	Shop 31, Collins Place, 45 Collins Street
Readings	309 Lygon Street, Carlton

MELBOURNE

Melbourne Suburbs

Melbourne Map Centre	259 High Street, Kew
Mapworks	184 Keilor Road, North Essendon
Metropolis Books	180 Acland Street, St. Kilda
Domain Books	179 Domain Road, South Yarra
Japan Book Plaza	155 Toorak Road, South Yarra (Books on Japan)
Black Mask Books	78 Toorak Road, South Yarra
Dymocks	769 Burke Road, Camberwell
Tim's Bookshop	121 High Street, Kew
Robinson's	Shop 3, 11 Station Road, Frankston
Dymocks	3A Shannon Street Mall, Frankston

There are three fine map shops in Melbourne. *Map Land* is right in the centre of the city, very conveniently located, but the *Melbourne Map Centre* in Kew (tram 48 or 109) and *Mapworks* in North Essendon (tram 59) are also good. The *Melbourne Map Centre* has branches in Chadstone and Dandenong.

As for general bookshops, in the city centre there are two branches of *Dymocks*. There is *Book City*, and there is the small but interesting *The Paperback Books* at the top of Bourke Street. *Readings* is a fine large independent store within walking distance of the city centre in Carlton (or tram 1 or 22).

The bookshops in the city area are marked on the map on page 731 (except *Readings*, which is on the map on page 749).

The remaining bookshops are scattered through the Melbourne suburbs, *Metropolis Books* in St. Kilda being marked on the map on page 737.

ACCOMMODATION

Hotel accommodation detailed is for the central area of Melbourne. There are, of course, many places to stay in the suburbs, and the rates for these tend to be somewhat lower than for accommodation in the city centre. Backpackers accommodation is listed for a wider area, which includes inner suburbs.

ANECDOTE

Every morning, I got on the tram and bought a ticket to the city to go to work, putting the ticket in my jacket pocket, and every evening I returned home, buying another ticket and putting it in the same place.

One day, during my morning journey, an inspector boarded the vehicle and requested that he be shown everybody's ticket. I pulled out from my jacket pocket a wodge of some two hundred tickets and presented them to him, saying, "It's one of these." To my surprise, he was quite angry about the matter, insisting, "I want today's ticket, not all the others." "Well," I said. "Give me a sporting chance. Tell me what sort of number we are looking for, and I'll try to find it before I get off."

Fortunately, the required ticket was on the outside of the wodge, as one might have anticipated, but I really could not understand why the inspector was so upset. After all, somebody with two hundred tram tickets in his pocket is not likely to be cheating the system very successfully.

748 VICTORIA
(i) Hotel Accommodation in Central Melbourne *(see map opposite)*

Name	Stars	No. on Map	Telephone No.	Address	Lowest Price (Double/Twin)
Rockman's Regency	5	17	03-9662-3900	Exhibition & Lonsdale Sts.	$385
Sheraton Towers	5	64	03-9696-3100	1 Southgate Avenue	$375
Crown Towers	5	63	1-800-811-653	8 Whiteman Street	$350
Park Hyatt	5	39	03-9224-1200	1 Parliament Square	$330
Hotel Sofitel	4	55	03-9653-0000	25 Collins Street	$320
Westin on Regent Place	5	51	03-9635-2222	205 Collins Street	$315
Quay West Suites	5	65	1-800-800-193	26 Southgate Avenue	$305
Windsor	4	38	03-9633-6002	103 Spring Street	$280
Stamford Plaza	5	35	03-9659-1000	111 Little Collins Street	$275
Hilton on the Park	5	62	03-9419-2000	192 Wellington Parade	$265
Novotel on Collins	4	31	03-9667-5800	270 Collins Street	$265
Grand Hyatt	5	54	03-9657-1234	123 Collins Street	$255
Quality Suites Southbank	4	66	1-800-682-004	30 City Road	$255
Le Meridien at Rialto	5	47	03-9620-9111	495 Collins Street	$250
Premier Swanston	4	16	03-9663-4711	195 Swanston Street	$245
Quality Suites Exhibition	4	36	1-800-682-004	100 Exhibition Street	$245
Holiday Inn on Flinders	4	44	1-800-039-099	Flinders Lane & Spencer St.	$235
Hotel Lindrum	4	57	03-9668-1111	26 Flinders Street	$225
Oakford Gordon Towers	4	20	03-9663-3317	43 Lonsdale Street	$220
Savoy Park Plaza	4½	27	1-800-036-188	630 Little Collins Street	$215
Sebel on St. Kilda Road	5	68	1-800-660-999	348 St. Kilda Road	$215
Clarion Suites Pacific Int.	4½	12	1-800-682-004	471 Little Bourke Street	$210
All Seasons Crossley	4	25	03-9639-1639	51 Little Bourke Street	$205
Gateway Suites	4	49	1-800-351-288	1 William Street	$205
Quality Suites Pacific Int.	4½	14	1-800-682-003	318 Little Bourke Street	$205
Paramount Apartments	4	23	03-9251-5555	181 Exhibition Street	$205
Oakford on Collins	4	32	03-9639-1811	182 Collins Street	$200
Radisson Flagstaff Gdns.	4	6	03-9322-8000	380 William Street	$200
Rydges Melbourne Hotel		24	03-9662-0511	186 Exhibition Street	$200
Carlton Clocktower Quest	4	4	03-9349-9700	255 Drummond Street	$195
Quest on Bourke	4	34	03-9631-0400	155 Bourke Street	$195
Riverside Apartments	4	48	03-9619-9199	474 Flinders Street	$195
Saville	4½	18	03-9915-2500	222 Russell Street	$195
Metro Hotel City	4½	29	1-800-004-321	18 Bank Place	$190
Metro Hotel	4½	67	1-800-004-321	133 Jolimont Road	$190
All Seasons Paragon	3	11	03-9672-0000	600 Little Bourke Street	$190
Quest on Flinders Lane		53	03-9652-3333	161 Flinders Lane	$185
Quality Suites City Edge	4	41	1-800-809-419	92 Albert Street	$185
Oakford Gordon Place	4	21	03-9663-2888	24 Little Bourke Street	$180
Causeway Inn on the Mall	4	30	1-800-355-211	327 Bourke Street	$175
Batman's Hill Hotel	3½	43	1-800-355-200	66 Spencer Street	$175
Apartments of Melbourne	4	56	1-800-681-900	57 Flinders Lane	$170
Mercure Hotel	3	58	1-800-813-442	13 Spring Street	$170
Hotel Grand Chancellor	4	19	1-800-331-006	131 Lonsdale Street	$165
Medina Grand	4½	13	03-9934-0000	189 Queen Street	$165
Downtowner on Lygon	4	9	1-800-355-157	66 Lygon Street	$165
Duxton Hotel	3	50	03-9250-1888	328 Flinders Street	$160
Elizabeth Tower Motel	3	2	03-9347-9211	792 Elizabeth Street	$155
Flag Travel Inn	4	3	03-9347-7922	Grattan & Drummond Sts.	$150
Albert Heights Apts.	3	40	03-9419-0955	83 Albert Street	$150
All Seasons Welcome	3	15	03-9639-0555	265 Little Bourke Street	$150
City Limits Motel	3½	22	03-9662-2544	20 Little Bourke Street	$150

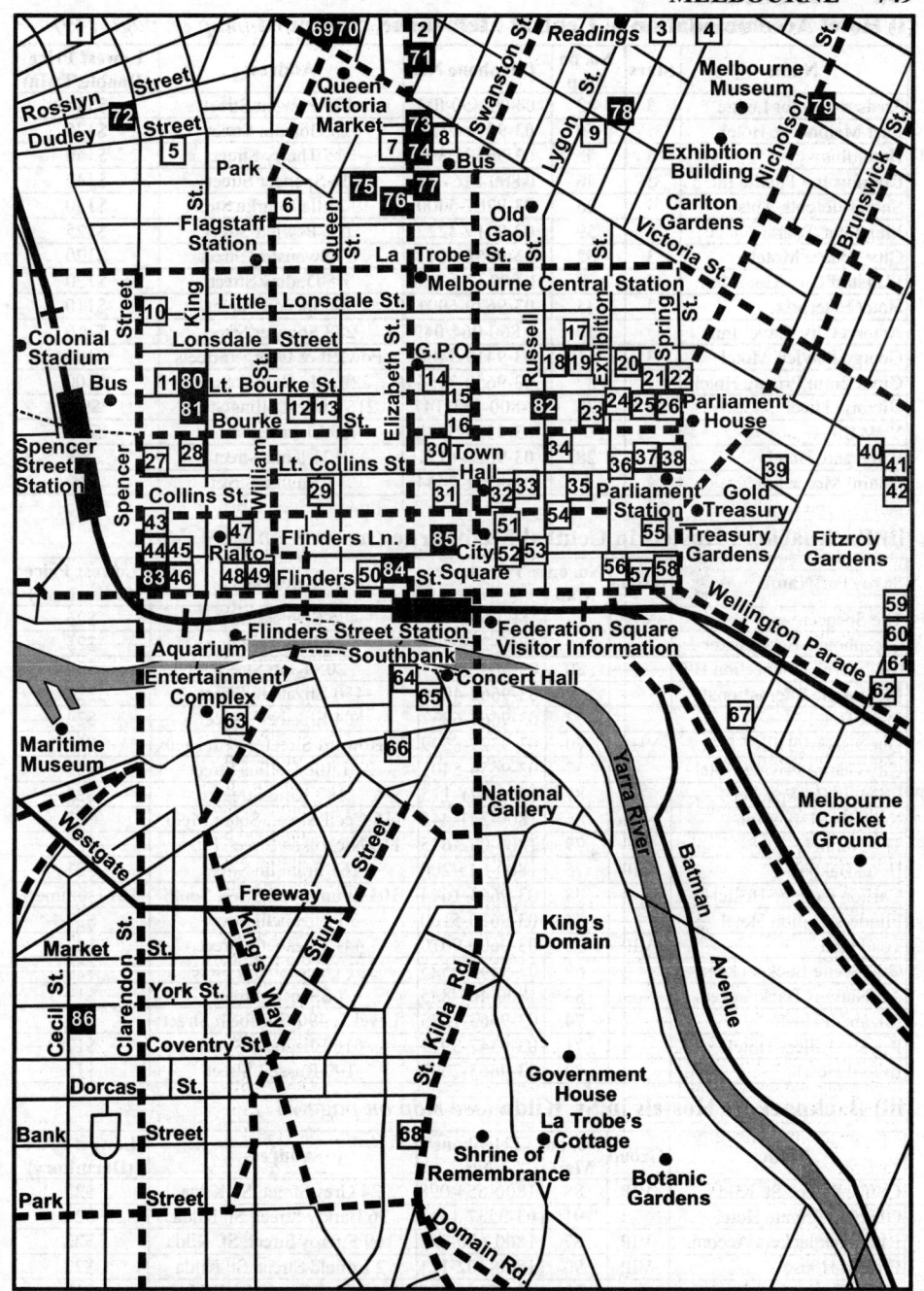

750 VICTORIA

(i) Hotel Accommodation in Central Melbourne, continued *(map on page 749)*

Name	Stars	No. on Map	Telephone No.	Address	Lowest Price (Double/Twin)
Treasury Motor Lodge	3	42	1-800-350-057	179 Powlett Street	$145
East Melbourne Hotel	3½	60	03-9412-2555	25 Hotham Street	$140
Hotel Ibis	3	8	03-9639-2399	15 Therry Street	$140
Comfort Inn Pacific Int.	3½	46	1-800-816-168	16 Spencer Street	$140
Shoan Heights Apts.		26	03-9267-5400	19 Little Bourke Street	$130
Magnolia Court	3½	59	03-9419-4222	101 Powlett Street	$125
City Square Motel	3	52	03-9654-7011	67 Swanston Street	$120
Flagstaff City Motor Inn	3	5	1-800-061-700	45 Dudley Street	$120
Hotel Enterprize	3	45	03-9629-6991	44 Spencer Street	$110
Astoria City Travel Inn		10	1-800-064-049	288 Spencer Street	$110
George Powlett Motel	3	61	03-9419-9588	Powlett & George Streets	$100
City Centre Private Hotel		37	03-9650-7256	22 Little Collins Street	$100
Victoria Hotel	3	33	1-800-331-147	215 Little Collins Street	$95
Y.W.C.A.		7	03-9329-5188	489 Elizabeth Street	$90
Kingsgate Hotel		28	03-9629-4171	131 King Street	$80
Miami Motor Inn		1	03-9321-2544	13 Hawke Street	$75

(ii) Backpackers Hostels in Central Melbourne *(see map on page 749)*

Name	Group	No. on Map	Telephone No.	Address	Lowest Price (Dormitory)
The Spencer	VIP	72	1800-638-108	475 Spencer Street	$26
Greenhouse Backpacker		85	1800-249-207	228 Flinders Lane	$25
Melbourne Connection B/P		80	03-9642-4464	205 King Street	$24
Melbourne International		77	03-9662-4066	450 Elizabeth Street	$24
Stork Hotel		73	03-9663-6237	504 Elizabeth Street	$24
Queensberry Hill Y.H.A.	YHA	70	03-9329-8599	78 Howard Street, North Melb.	$23
City Centre Private Hotel		37	03-9654-5401	22 Little Collins Street	$22
Friendly Backpacker		81	1800-671-115	197 King Street	$22
Nomads Market Inn	Nom	86	1800-241-445	115 Cecil Street, South Melb.	$22
The Nunnery		79	1800-032-635	116 Nicholson Street, Fitzroy	$22
Hotel Bakpak	VIP	75	1800-645-200	167 Franklin Street	$21
Carlton College Hostel		78	03-9663-1644	101 Drummond Street South	$21 (summer)
Flinders Station Hotel		84	03-9620-5100	35 Elizabeth Street	$21
Toad Hall	VIP	76	03-9600-9010	441 Elizabeth Street	$21
City Scene Backpackers		69	03-9348-9525	361 Queensberry Street	$20
All Nations Backpackers	Nom	83	1800-467-835	2 Spencer Street	$19
Elizabeth Hostel		74	03-9663-1685	Level 1, 490 Elizabeth Street	$18
Royal Artillery Hotel		71	03-9347-3917	616 Elizabeth Street	$17
Exford Hotel		82	03-9663-2697	199 Russell Street	$15

(iii) Backpackers Hostels in St. Kilda *(see map on page 737)*

Name	Group	No. on Map	Telephone No.	Address	Lowest Price (Dormitory)
Coffee Palace St. Kilda	VIP	88	1800-654-098	24 Grey Street, St. Kilda	$25
Olembia Private Hotel		91	03-9537-1412	96 Barkly Street, St. Kilda	$24
Ritz Backpackers Accom.	VIP	87	1800-670-364	169 Fitzroy Street, St. Kilda	$22
Enfield House	VIP	90	1800-302-121	2 Enfield Street, St. Kilda	$22
Oslo Hotel		89	03-9525-4498	38 Grey Street, St. Kilda	$19

MELBOURNE 751

(iv) Backpackers Hostels in Other Inner Suburbs *(see map on page 738)*

Name	Group	No. on Map	Telephone No.	Address	Lowest Price (Dormitory)
Abbey Backpackers		96	03-9521-2388	250 Punt Road, South Yarra	$28
Nomads Hotel, Claremont	Nom	97	1300-301-630	189 Toorak Road, South Yarra	$28
Chapman Gardens Y.H.A.	YHA	94	03-9328-3595	76 Chapman St., North Melb.	$24
Pint on Punt, Windsor	Nom	99	03-9510-4273	42 Punt Road, Windsor	$23
Chapel Street Backpackers	B&W	100	1800-613-333	22 Chapel Street, Windsor	$22
Pint on Punt, Brunswick	Nom	93	03-9380-1493	291 Albert Street, Brunswick	$18
Lord's Lodge		98	03-9510-5658	204 Punt Road, Prahran	$17
Richmond Hill Hotel	VIP	95	1800-801-618	353 Church Street, Richmond	$17
Latrobe Summer Hostel		92	03-9479-2875	Kingsbury Drive, Bundoora	$16 (summer)

MOVING ON
(i) By Train

Trains to Geelong operate approximately hourly during the day and more frequently at peak times. All other rail services outside the suburban area are shown in the following timetables, together with principal bus connexions.

Melbourne to Albury, Canberra and Sydney

Days of Operation	M-Sat	Sat (Bus)	Daily	Daily (Bus)	Sun	Sun (Bus)	M - F	M - F (Bus)	F (Bus)	M - F	Sat, Sun	Daily
Melbourne	0750		0830		0920		1210			1415	1710	1753	1945
Benalla	1000*		1023		1141		1415			1655	1932	2007	2138
Wangaratta	1024*		1048		1205		1439			1735	1955	2031	2204
Wodonga	1108*	1125			1250	1300	1522	1535		1830	2039	2117	
Albury	1118*	1135	1136		1300	1310	1535	1545		1840	2049	2128	2253
Wagga Wagga			1248										0006
Cootamundra			1357										0113
Yass Junction			1520	1543									0236
Canberra		1615		1637		1750			2025				0342
Goulburn			1628										0429
Moss Vale			1715										
Strathfield			1858										0606
Sydney			1913										0625

* 5 mins later on Saturdays

Melbourne to Adelaide, Alice Springs and Perth

Days of Operation	M - F	M - F (Bus)	Sat	Sat (Bus)	M-Sat	M-Sat (Bus)	Sun	Sun (Bus)	Sun	Sun (Bus)	Su,M,Th,F	W	Tu, F
Melbourne	0800			0810		0835		0925		0935		2130	2230
North Shore												2227	2330
Ballarat	0935	1005	0950	1025			1053	1120					
Bendigo					1030	1055			1140	1200			
St. Arnaud						1258				1400			
Horsham		1250		1310		1410		1405		1515	0221	0400	
Dimboola		1320		1340		1440		1435		1545	0251	0430	
Adelaide (arr)						1915				2020	0740	0955	
Days												**M, Th**	**Tu, F**
Adelaide (dep)												1500	1830
Port Augusta												1920	2240
Days												**Tu, F**	**W, Sat**
Alice Springs												0900	
Cook													0918
Kalgoorlie (arr)													1920
Kalgoorlie (dep)													2230
Days													**Th,Su**
Perth													0930

VICTORIA

Melbourne to Mt. Gambier via Ballarat

Days of Operation	M - F	M - F (Bus)	Sat	Sat (Bus)	Daily	Daily (Bus)
Melbourne	0806		0813		1742*	
Ballarat	0940	1010	0952	1025	1910*	1930
Hamilton		1230		1240		2145†
Casterton		1320				
Mt. Gambier		1340				

* 5 minutes later on Saturdays, 10 – 14 minutes earlier on Sundays.
† 2205 on Thursdays, 2210 on Saturdays

Melbourne to Mt. Gambier via Warrnambool

Days of Operation	M-Sat	M-Sat (Bus)	Sun	Sun (Bus)	M - F	M - F (Bus)	Sun	Sun (Bus)	M - F	M - F (Bus)	Sat	Sat (Bus)	Sun	Sun (Bus)
Melbourne	0848		0940		1240		1600		1808		1840		1900	
Geelong	0947		1042	1055	1334		1702	1715	1907		1936		1956	
Warrnambool	1158	1215*		1330	1553	1620		1950	2123	2135	2144	2155	2209	2220
Port Fairy		1243*				1700				2200		2218		2240
Portland		1343*								2255		2315		2340
Heywood		1405*								2315		2335		0001
Mt. Gambier		1440*								2355†				0035

* 5 minutes later on Saturdays   † Fridays only

Melbourne to Warrnambool via Great Ocean Road

Days of Operation	M-Sa	M-Sa (Bus)	F (Bus)	Sun	Sun (Bus)	M-F	M-F (Bus)	M-F	M-F (Bus)	M-Th	M-Th (Bus)	F, Sat	F, Sat (Bus)	Sun	Sun (Bus)
Melbourne	0848			0940		1100		1400		1655		1808*		1900	
Geelong	0947	0955		1042	1055	1159	1210	1456	1510	1756	1810	1907*	1915*	1956	2005
Lorne		1120			1225		1335		1635		1935		2040*		2130
Apollo Bay		1230	1340		1325				1740		2040		2145*		2230
Warrnambool	1158		1700										2123†		2209

* 5 - 10 minutes earlier on Saturdays   † Fridays only

Melbourne to Ballarat

Days of Operation	Weekday Timetable										
Melbourne	0806	0935	1108	1228	1408	1500*	1613	1700	1742	1848	2055	2145*
Ballarat	0940	1120	1240	1405	1546	1635*	1739	1834	1910	2031	2221	2325*

* By bus

Days of Operation	Saturdays						Sundays					
Melbourne	0813	1117	1307	1549	1747	1853	2037	0925	1100	1307	1517	1728	1913	2145*
Ballarat	0952	1250	1450	1726	1916	2021	2202	1053	1227	1437	1648	1900	2045	2325*

* By bus

Melbourne to Bendigo

Days of Operation	Weekday Timetable									
Melbourne	0840	1012	1112	1212	1312	1412	1552	1632	1745	1836	2015
Bendigo	1034	1200	1309	1357	1510	1558	1750	1837	1942	2031	2207*

* 2220 on Fridays

Days of Operation	Saturdays							Sundays				
Melbourne	0840	1013	1213	1553	1753	1857	2115	0935	1233	1613	1733	1921
Bendigo	1036	1210	1356	1750	1943	2107	2309	1138	1420	1800	1927	2121

Melbourne to Swan Hill and Mildura

Days of Operation	M-Sat	M-Sat (Bus)	Sun	Sun (Bus)	M - F	M - F (Bus)	F	F (Bus)	Not F	Not F (Bus)	F	F (Bus)	Not Sat (Bus)
Melbourne	0840		0935		1212		1632		1745‡		1745		2145
Bendigo	1034	1055	1138	1205	1357	1440	1837		1942‡		1942	1955	
Swan Hill		1345		1455		1740†	2048	2100	2154‡	2205‡		2212	
Mildura		1650*		1800				2340		0045‡			0700

* 1725 on Fridays   †1745 on Tuesdays and Thursdays, 1820 on Wednesdays
‡ 15 minutes earlier on Sundays

Melbourne to Echuca and Moama
(Mondays to Saturdays)

Days of Operation	M-Sat	M-Sat (Bus)	M - Sat	M - Sat (Bus)	M, Sat (Bus)	M - F	M, F (Bus)	M - F	Tu,W Th (Bus)	F (Bus)	M - Sat (Bus)	M - Sat	M - Sat (Bus)	F
Melbourne	0840		0910		1240	1412		1552		1600	1730	1815*		1836
Murchison E				1056	1100							2001*	2010*	
Murchison					1103					1800			2013*	
Bendigo	1034	1110*				1558	1630	1750	1815					2031
Echuca		1235*		1225*	1550		1755		1940	2015	2050		2135*	2150
Moama		1240*		1230*	1555		1800		1945	2020	2055		2140*	

* 5 minutes earlier on Saturdays

(Sundays)

Days of Operation	Sun	Sun (Bus)	Sun	Sun	Sun (Bus)	Sun (Bus)
Melbourne	0935		1233	1733		1900
Bendigo	1138	1155	1420	1927	1935	
Echuca		1305	1540		2045	2220
Moama					2050	2225

Melbourne to Shepparton, Cobram and Griffith

Days of Operation	M-Sat	M-Sat (Bus)	Sun	Sun (Bus)	M - F (Bus)	M - F (Bus)	M - Sat	M - Sat (Bus)	Sun	Sun (Bus)	Sun (Bus)
Melbourne	0910		0920		1400	1600	1815*		1830		1855
Seymour	1022		1034	1045	1530		1927*		1942		2045
Shepparton	1122	1130*		1210	1700	1850	2027*	2035*	2042	2050	2210
Cobram		1225*		1310	1805			2132*		2147	
Tocumwal					1825			2146*		2201	
Griffith								0010*		0025	

* 5 minutes earlier on Saturdays

VICTORIA

Melbourne to Albury, Beechworth, Bright and Mt. Beauty

Days of Operation	M (Bus)	M-Sat	M-Sat (Bus)	Daily	Sun	Sun (Bus)	M - F	M - F (Bus)	F (Bus)	M - F	W, F (Bus)	Sat, Sun	Daily
Melbourne		0750		0830	0920		1210		1415	1710		1753	1945
Benalla		1000*		1023	1141		1415		1655	1932		2007	2138
Wangaratta	0840	1024*	1035	1048	1205	1215	1439	1500	1735	1955	2005	2031	2204
Wodonga		1108*			1250		1522		1830	2039		2117	
Albury		1118*		1136	1300		1535		1840	2049		2128	2253
Beechworth			1110			1245		1535			2035		
Bright	0935		1210†			1340		1635			2130		
Mt. Beauty								1730‡					

* 5 minutes later on Saturdays   † Saturdays only   ‡ Mondays and Fridays only

Melbourne to Traralgon and Sale

Days of Operation	Weekday Timetable											
Melbourne	0641	0747	0939	1039	1228	1329	1425	1543		1647	1748†	1826	2029
Traralgon	0901	0951	1153	1255	1449	1532	1637	1814	1825*	1912	2036†	2023	2240
Sale		1029				1610			1950*			2101	

* By bus. Mondays to Thursdays only.   † Suburban train to Pakenham, where change.

Days of Operation	Saturdays						Sundays			
Melbourne	0626*	0845	0956†	1325	1735	1900	0930	1300	1735	1900
Traralgon	0945*	1046	1226†	1535	1958	2056	1151	1505	1954	2056
Sale		1123		1617		2133	1230			2133

* Suburban train to Dandenong, where change. Train to Warragul, where change to bus.
† Suburban train to Dandenong, where change.

Melbourne to Lakes Entrance

Days of Operation	M-F (Bus)	M-F	M-F (Bus)	Sat	Sat (Bus)	Sun	Sun (Bus)	M,W Th (Bus)	M-F	M-F (Bus)	M-F (Bus)	Sat, Sun	Sa,Su (Bus)
Melbourne		0747		0845		0930		1329		1826		1900	
Sale		1029	1044	1123	1139	1230	1245	1610	1620	2101	2110	2133	2140
Bairnsdale	0955	1139		1235		1340	1415		1720		2205		2235
Lakes Entrance	1030	1223		1318		1415	1450		1810		2245*		
Lake Tyers Beach	1040	1233		1328									

* Fridays only

Melbourne to Canberra, Narooma and Batemans Bay

Days of Operation	M - F	M, Th (Bus)	M - F (Bus)	Sat	Sat† (Bus)	Sat (Bus)	Sun	Sun (Bus)
Melbourne	0747			0845			0930	
Sale	1029	1045	1046	1123	1140†	1141	1230	1245
Orbost		1335	1300		1430†	1355		1500
Bombala		1550			1645†			
Cooma		1655			1750†			
Canberra Station		1815			1910†			
Canberra Jolimont		1830			1925†			
Eden			1550			1645		1750
Merimbula			1620			1715		1820
Bega			1645			1740		1845
Narooma			1755			1850		1955
Batemans Bay			1850*			1945		

* Mondays and Thursdays only   † Certain Saturdays (during school holidays) only

(ii) By Bus

The following long-distance buses operate. V-Line rail plus bus services are not included, being shown in the rail timetables on the previous pages. It should be noted that some restrictions apply to the long-distance bus companies regarding the conveyance of passengers on wholly intra-state journeys.

Destination	Operator	Via	Distance (km)	Fare	Journey Time	Frequency
Sydney via Inland	McCafferty's		926	$73	12 - 13¾ hrs	2/day
		Albury	286	$47	3¼ – 4 hrs	2/day
Sydney via Inland	Greyhound		926	$73	11½ - 14¾ hrs	3/day
		Albury	286	$47	3½ - 4½ hrs	3/day
Sydney via Inland	Firefly		923	$60	12¼ hrs	2/day
		Albury	286	$60	3¾ - 4 hrs	2/day
Sydney via Coast	Premier		1225	$76	17¾ - 18¾ hrs	1/day
		Batemans Bay	875	$65	12¼ - 13¼ hrs	1/day
		Eden	634	$51	8¾ - 9 hrs	1/day
		Lakes Entrance	392	$46	5¼ - 6 hrs	1/day
Brisbane	McCafferty's		1800	$202	23¾ hrs	1/day
		Toowoomba	1670	$202	21¼ hrs	1/day
		Dubbo	946	$131	10½ hrs	1/day
Adelaide	McCafferty's		789	$65	10¾ hrs	1/day
		Ballarat	167	$15	2¼ hrs	1/day
		Geelong	97	$15	1¼ hrs	1/day
Adelaide	Greyhound		789	$65	9¾ hrs	1/day
		Ballarat	167	$15	1½ hrs	1/day
Adelaide	Firefly		789	$50	10½ hrs	2/day
Canberra	McCafferty's		629	$70	8½ hrs	2/day
Canberra	Greyhound		660	$70	7¾ - 9½ hrs	2/day
Mt. Hotham (seasonal)	Trekset		364	$90	6 hrs	1/day
		Bright	308	$85	4½ hrs	1/day
Falls Creek	Pyle's		369	$75	6 hrs	1/day
Mansfield	V-Line		187	$34.40	3 hrs	2/day
Mt. Buller	Mt. Buller Bus	(seasonal)	233	$120*	4 hrs	4/week
Yarram	V-Line		220	$34.40	3½ hrs	1/day
		Leongatha	131	$19.20	2 - 2½ hrs	4/day
Cowes	V-Line		139	$17.60	3¼ - 3½ hrs	1/day
Inverloch	V-Line		113	$23.30	3¼ hrs	3/day

* Return fare

ANECDOTE

"Wake me up when we get to Glenroy, will you?" said the drunk on the late-night train home. "Sorry," I replied, "I'm getting off at the station before." "Well, wake me up when you get off, then, if you don't mind. Only last week I went to sleep and nobody woke me up, so I went to the end of the line, and all the way back to Melbourne. I woke up at 2:00 and found myself in the sidings outside Flinders Street Station."

756   VICTORIA
GEELONG AND THE BELLARINE PENINSULA
Population 200,000

1 hr by train from Melbourne

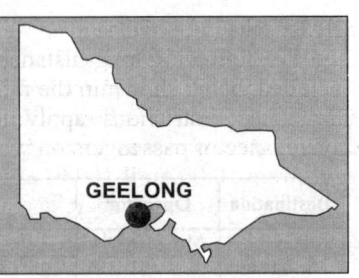

Geelong is an under-rated city, the poor neighbour of nearby Melbourne. It is often thought of as just an industrial and port area serving its big brother. Recently, however, it has started to establish a reputation as an attraction in itself.

Geelong was first settled in 1838. It gained in importance in the 1850s when the gold rush occurred in nearby Ballarat, for which Geelong was the principal port. At that time the population rose to 23,000 and Geelong was the fourth largest town in Australia.

In 1856, the world's first ice-making and refrigeration equipment was invented in Geelong by James Harrison. In 1857, Australia's first steam operated non-suburban railway line was opened from Williamstown to Geelong.

Towards the end of the nineteenth century, as gold declined in importance, Geelong became one of the principal ports for the export of wool. In 1925, the Ford Motor Company established a plant in Geelong and it became one of the national centres for the production of motor vehicles. Other industries followed, and the city's portside location made it an obvious site for one of Australia's main oil refineries. In the latter half of the twentieth century, aluminium smelting and cement manufacture were added to the city's industrial accomplishments.

Geelong is still an industrial city, and is the second largest city in Victoria, but in recent years it has started to display its fine heritage as a tourist attraction, and play down its image as a port and a city which is merely on the way to other beauty spots.

Although McCafferty's offers one bus service per day, a stop on the route between Melbourne and Adelaide, the obvious way to travel to Geelong is by train from Melbourne. Services operate approximately hourly during the day and more often at peak times. It is a pleasant enough journey of 75 kilometres taking almost exactly one hour. Some trains terminate at Geelong, but most continue to South Geelong and a few go on all the way to Warrnambool. The station in Geelong is near the town centre, and easy walking distance from it. As you walk, you will soon see Johnstone Park and, on the far side of it, the fine buildings of the Library and Art Gallery. Beyond, you will come to the city centre ahead, and, to the left, the waterfront.

The **Visitor Information Centre** is in Moorabool Street and is a good starting point for a visit. The **National Wool Museum** is in the same building and includes displays of old machinery used in one of Australia's most traditional industries. The Museum is housed in an 1872 bluestone former wool store and is open daily from 9:30 until 17:00. Admission costs $10.

At the far end of the city is the **Old Geelong Gaol**. This high security prison was opened in 1853 and remained in service until 1991. Its brochure describes the Gaol as "harsh, bleak and primitive" and states that "the facilities are nothing short of appalling", but, after all, one has to remember that prisoners were not sent here for a holiday. The Gaol is open for inspection in a condition almost unchanged from that at the time of its closure, but, for the benefit of paying guests, the scene of the first hanging here is recreated. James Murphy was hanged in this place in 1863 for the murder of a police officer in Warrnambool. The Gaol is open only on Saturdays and Sundays between 13:00 and 16:00.

The **Naval and Maritime Museum** is in North Geelong, not far from North Geelong Station. It is housed in Osborne House, which is the site of Australia's first naval college and was formerly the base for Australia's submarines. The Museum is open from 10:00 until 16:00, except on Tuesdays and Thursdays.

From **Rippleside Pier**, just a little south of the Naval and Maritime Museum, it is possible to walk along the foreshore through the city, and this is a pleasant and interesting walk, for the bayfront area, originally designed in the 1920s, has been developed considerably in recent years. One of the most noteworthy features is the **Bay Walk Bollards** which adorn the way, sculpted and painted to represent human characters. The bollards start at **Rippleside Park**, continue along **Western Beach** and then through **Steampacket Place**, and finish at **Eastern Beach**. They number more than a hundred and are all the work of one person, Jan Mitchell, representing characters and incidents in the history of Geelong.

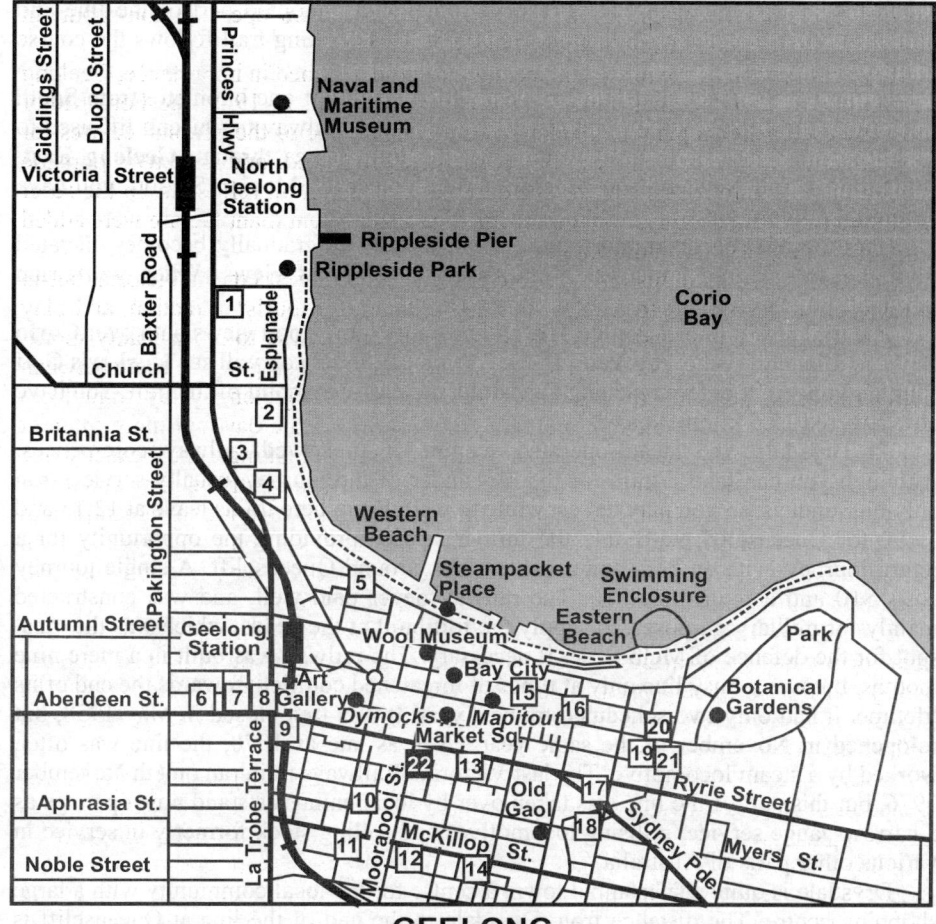

GEELONG
Black numerals in white boxes indicate hotel accommodation
White numerals in black boxes indicate backpackers hostels

758 VICTORIA

Eastern Beach is the most famous of the places for relaxation. Art deco pools and a promenade have been constructed here in recent years. There are also lawns, palm trees, a rotunda and a fountain, with the **Botanical Gardens**, of which the oldest parts date from 1851, just a short distance inland.

The city has the modern shopping centres of **Market Square** and **Bay City Plaza**, the latter having retained its former wool store façade.

A short distance east of Geelong lies the **Bellarine Peninsula**, the western jaws encircling Port Phillip Bay. This is a pretty and historic area, well worth a visit. It is easy to catch a bus to Queenscliff from Geelong Station, a journey of a little less than an hour, but there is also a **walking and cycling trail** covering 34 kilometres which can be attempted in whole or in part.

Walking Trail

On 21st May 1879 a **railway** was opened by the Governor of Victoria between South Geelong and Queenscliff. That railway was closed, unfortunately, in 1976, at which time the **Geelong Steam Preservation Society** adopted part of the line and started to operate a steam service on it in 1978. This walking trail follows the course of the old railway.

It starts at the Geelong Showgrounds, which are about one kilometre from South Geelong Station. This is the point at which the branch railway to Queenscliff used to leave the main line. It is level walking as the trail passes through **Geelong East**, **Whittington** and **Newcomb** to **Moolap**. When you reach Moolap Station, you have covered 4.5 kilometres.

Here the trail becomes more rural. The old railway gradually becomes elevated from the surrounding countryside and offers some good views. When you reach **Leopold**, you have completed eight kilometres.

The trail now climbs **Leopold Hill** and provides more good views both over **Corio Bay** and inland over the **You Yang Hills**. As you continue, you will see **Curlewis** Golf Club on your right before reaching **Drysdale**, the half-way point of the trail. You have now covered 16.5 kilometres.

At Drysdale, the steam-operated section of preserved railway commences. Although you can take a train for the remainder of the journey, usually services run only on Sundays, so you may have a while to wait. From here trains leave at 12:15 and 15:30 for Queenscliff, with only the former service providing the opportunity for a return journey, with an hour and a half to look around Queenscliff. A single journey costs $10 and a return trip $16. The railway never paid well, and was constructed mainly for military purposes, to supply the fort built at the heads, which was the ideal spot for the defence of Melbourne, if necessary. The railway was built in a mere nine months, but was a busy line only at times of threatened conflict. Towards the end of its lifetime, it had only two scheduled trains a year. It was first closed in May 1958, but re-opened in November of the same year. Even as late as 1970, the line was often worked by a steam locomotive. The last Victorian Railways train ran on 6th November 1976, but this part of the line was taken over by local enthusiasts and now operates as a narrow-gauge service, utilising locomotives and rolling stock formerly in service in various other parts of Australia.

Drysdale is quite a substantial town, a centre for the local community with a large shopping centre. The distance from Drysdale to the end of the line at Queenscliff is seventeen kilometres. After 5.6 kilometres, there is a collection of railway rolling stock

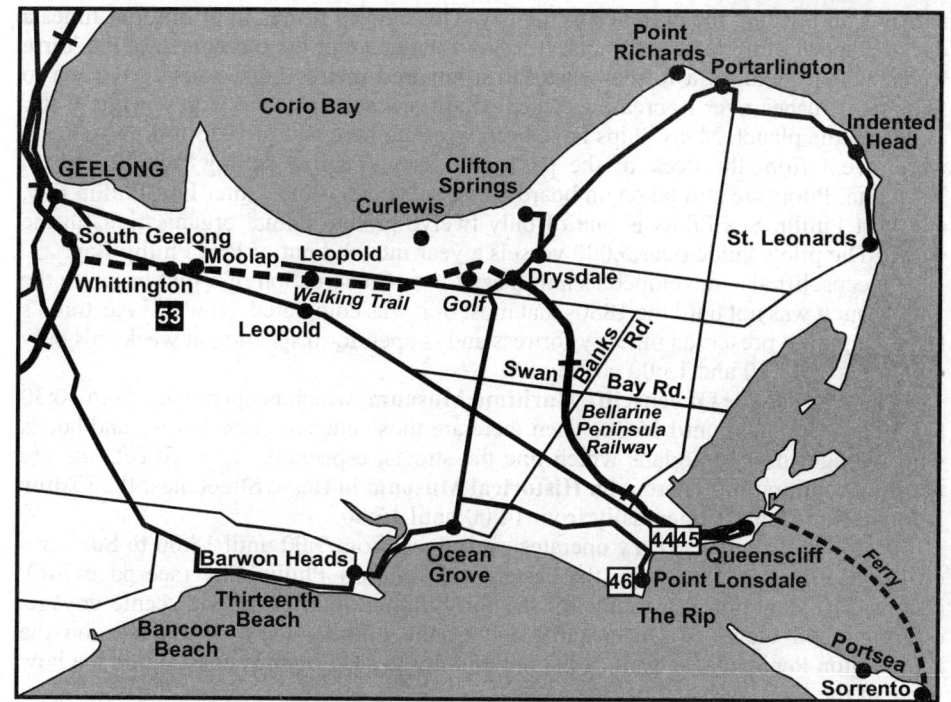

BELLARINE PENINSULA
Thicker lines show local bus routes
Black numerals in white boxes indicate hotel accommodation
White numerals in black boxes indicate backpackers hostels

at **Swan Bay Road**, and there is a timber rail bridge after 7.2 kilometres. Good views are obtainable after **Banks Road**, at around ten kilometres from Drysdale. Finally you will reach Queenscliff, and you will be tired if you have really walked all 34 kilometres to here.

From Queenscliff, trains operate to Drysdale at 11:15 and 14:30 on Sundays, at the same price of $10 single or $16 return. There is also a return journey to Laker's Siding at 13:30. This takes only twelve minutes each way, with a ten-minute stop at the siding, and costs $5 single or $10 return.

Queenscliff began life as a pilot station and fishing village, but soon developed into a fashionable seaside resort. By the 1880s, steamers were conveying large numbers of holidaymakers across the bay to up-market guest houses and hotels here, buildings which still survive to grace the streets of this attractive resort. However, Queenscliff had from the start more practical purposes than tourism alone. A private pilot service began operating here as early as 1838, long before any beacons or signals had been erected to guide mariners. The first Queenscliff Lighthouse was constructed in 1842, and that at Point Lonsdale in 1863. Now there are two lighthouses at Queenscliff, the **Black Light** and the **White Light**, and ships line up the two to ensure that they are following the correct path into the narrow gap known as ***The Rip*** between the heads. This is a treacherous piece of water, due to the strong current rushing through the

760 VICTORIA

narrow gap forming the entrance to the bay. This current rushes in or out four times a day at a speed of up to seven knots. It follows under water the old course of the Yarra River, which includes a former waterfall a hundred metres high, causing the sea to foam as it rushes over it, creating, when conditions are right, the largest white water rapids on the planet. Many ships have been wrecked here and in 1936 four passengers were swept from the deck of the passenger ferry *Nairana* sailing from Burnie in Tasmania. Pilots are still taken on board all vessels here as they enter Port Phillip Bay, and Port Phillip Sea Pilots is one of only twelve private pilots' organisations in the world. The pilots guide over 5,000 vessels a year into and out of Port Phillip Bay.

Queenscliff also developed as a military town. Construction of a **fort** began in the 1860s, but it was not until the 1880s that most of it was completed. Now it is Australia's largest and best preserved military fortress and is open for inspection at weekends only with tours at 13:00 and 15:00 costing $6.

There is also the **Queenscliff Maritime Museum**, which is open daily from 10:30 (13:30 at weekends) until 16:30. Then there are those elegant guest houses and hotels with wrought iron verandahs which line the streets, especially Hesse Street, and are worthy of admiration. There is an **Historical Museum** in Hesse Street, near the **Visitor Information Centre**, open daily from 14:00 until 16:00.

From Queenscliff, a **ferry** operates every hour from 7:00 until 18:00 to **Sorrento** on the Mornington Peninsula, the eastern side of Port Phillip Bay (see page 746), costing $10 single or $16 return for the forty-minute journey. It is a scenic voyage, offering good views of Queenscliff, and of the affluent town of **Portsea** on the Mornington Peninsula, as well as the opportunity to see dolphins coasting on the bow wave of the ferry on many occasions.

Five kilometres west of Queenscliff lies **Point Lonsdale**, a much quieter and smaller town than its neighbour. Like Queenscliff, though, it has a pretty beach. It was

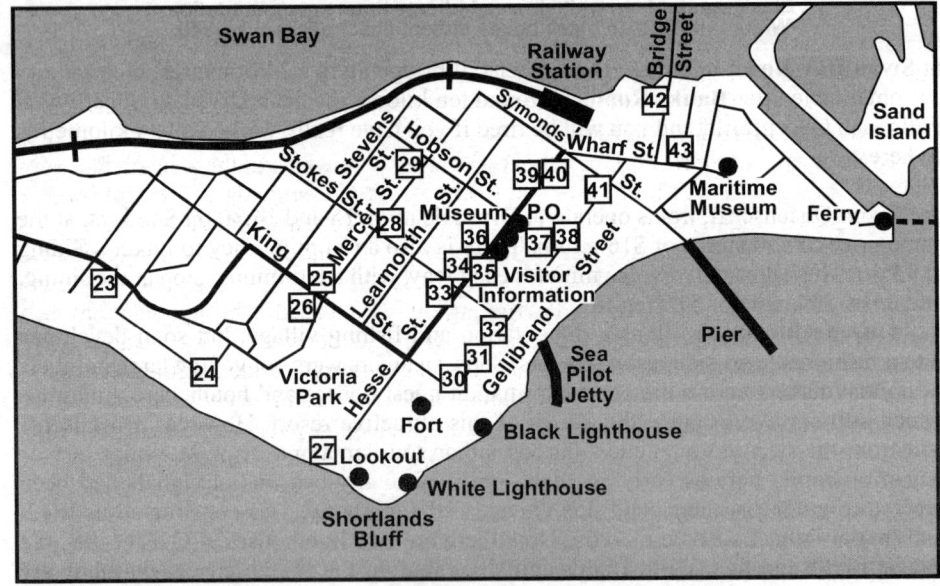

QUEENSCLIFF
Numerals indicate accommodation

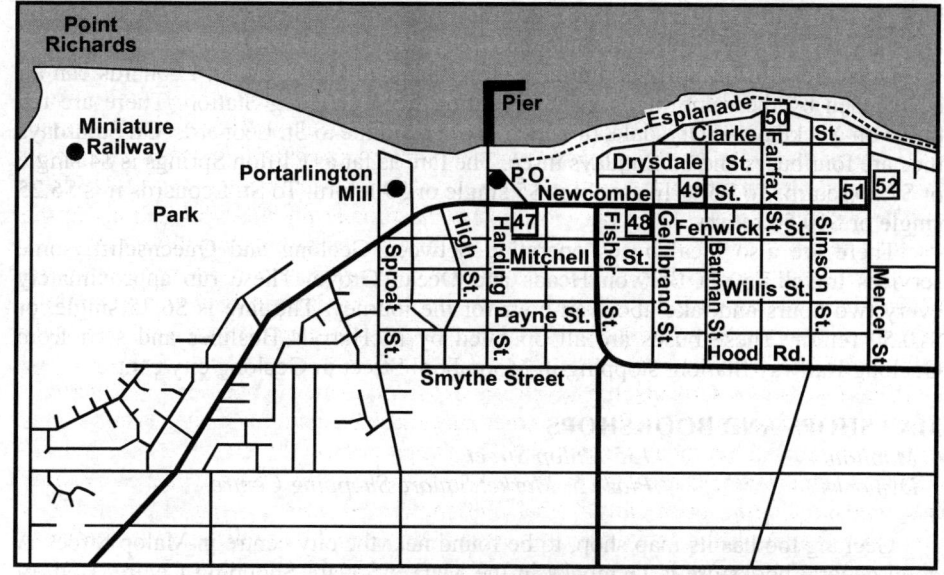

PORTARLINGTON
Numerals indicate accommodation

named after Captain William Lonsdale, the first Police Magistrate in Port Phillip. There is a **cave** in the cliff below the **lighthouse** here which is reputed to have been used by the escaped convict William Buckley who lived with the local aborigines between 1803 and 1835.

West of Point Lonsdale lie **Ocean Grove** and then **Barwon Heads**, both seaside towns. Ocean Grove was settled in 1854, but Barwon Heads not until 1875. Twelve ships were wrecked here between 1853 and 1890. The towns can be reached by bus from Geelong and these are the nearest ocean beaches to that city. Barwon Heads is known for its **Thirteenth Surf Beach**.

To the north of Queenscliff are other popular resort towns, but these lie on the more sheltered waters of Port Phillip Bay and Corio Bay. **St. Leonards** was established in 1840 and served mainly as a fishing base for Geelong. **Indented Head** is a quiet town which has a memorial to show where John Batman first landed when seeking a site for the new city which became Melbourne.

A little further round the bay is **Portarlington**, which used to be a popular day-trip resort at the end of the nineteenth century. It could be reached by steamer from Williamstown in only a little over an hour. When the steamer trade declined, however, so did the prosperity of Portarlington, although it has revived in recent years and is now used as a dormitory town by those who work in Geelong or even Melbourne. At **Point Richards**, just outside the town, a **miniature railway** operates every Sunday between September and June from 11:00 until 16:00. During the winter it operates only on the second Sunday in the month.

Clifton Springs is a resort where mineral springs were discovered in 1870. The springs area was originally named Fairy Dell. An hotel was built with salt water baths and for a while the town prospered. However, the steamer trade ceased and the railway had by-passed Clifton Springs, so the prosperity was short lived. In 1923, the hotel was burnt down, and it was not until recent times that a revival occurred. Even so, nearby Drysdale remains the centre for this area.

Drysdale, Clifton Springs, Portarlington, Indented Head and St. Leonards can all be reached by the same bus service operating from Geelong Station. There are ten buses on weekdays to Drysdale, of which seven continue to St. Leonards. On Saturdays thee are four buses and on Sundays three. The fare as far as Clifton Springs is $4 single or $7.50 return. To Portarlington it is $5 single or $9 return. To St. Leonards it is $6.25 single or $10.50 return.

There are also local buses operating between Geelong and Queenscliff, some services travelling via Barwon Heads and Ocean Grove. These run approximately every two hours and take about an hour for the journey. The fare is $6.25 single, or $10.50 return. These buses are all operated by McHarry's Buslines and start from Geelong Railway Station, stopping in Moorabool Street in Geelong city centre.

MAP SHOPS AND BOOKSHOPS
Mapitout   135 Malop Street
Dymocks   Plaza 5, Market Square Shopping Centre

Geelong too has its map shop, to be found near the city centre in Malop Street. A good general bookstore is Dymocks in the Market Square Shopping Centre. Both of these are marked on the map on page 757.

ACCOMMODATION
Accommodation is listed for the main centres of Geelong, Queenscliff, Point Lonsdale and Portarlington, with one additional backpacker option in Whittington, in the coach house of a famous stables and racehorse breeding stud.

(i) Hotel Accommodation in Geelong *(see map on page 757)*

Name	Stars	No. on Map	Telephone No.	Address	Lowest Price (Double/Twin)
Mercure	4	10	03-5221-6844	Gheringhap & Myers Streets	$210
Admiralty Motor Inn	3½	12	03-5221-4288	66 McKillop Street	$130
Geelong Motor Inn	3½	3	03-5222-4777	Princes Hwy & Kooyong Rd	$115
Pevensey House 1892		19	03-5224-2810	17 Pevensey Crescent	$110
Sundowner Motor Inn	3½	2	1-800-654-576	13 The Esplanade	$105
Bay City Motel	3	16	03-5221-1933	231 Malop Street	$95
Chipchase B&B		9	03-5229-1846	8 Ryrie Street	$95
Coachman's Cottage		17	03-5229-0264	362 Ryrie Street	$95
Eastern Sands Motel	3	15	03-5221-5577	1 Bellarine Street	$95
Oberon Apartments		20	03-5229-8445	9 Pevensey Crescent	$95
Ardara House		8	03-5229-6024	4 Aberdeen Street	$95
Sea Mist Holiday Apts.	3	6	03-5222-2447	62 Western Beach Road	$95
Ayrbank Bed & Breakfast		14	03-5229-7922	170 Bellarine Street	$95
Gatehouse on Ryrie		13	03-5229-6652	83 Yarra Street	$95
Garden View Lodge		21	03-5222-5095	38 Garden Street	$95
Innkeepers Motor Inn	3	7	03-5221-2177	9 Aberdeen Street	$85
Willowra House	3½	11	03-5229-8790	34 McKillop Street	$75
Kangaroo Motel	2	4	03-5221-4022	16 Esplanade South	$75
Warren Crest Units	3	18	03-5278-2667	206 Myers Street	$75
Rippleside Pk. Motor Inn	2½	1	03-5278-2017	67 Melbourne Road	$65
Irish Murphy's		6	03-5221-4335	30 Aberdeen Street	$55

GEELONG

(ii) Backpackers Hostels in Geelong *(see map on page 757)*

Name	Group	No. on Map	Telephone No.	Address	Lowest Price (Dormitory)
National Hotel		22	03-5229-1211	191 Moorabool Street	$21
Irish Murphy's		6	03-5221-4335	30 Aberdeen Street	$18

(iii) Hotel Accommodation in Queenscliff *(see maps on pages 759 and 760)*

Name	Stars	No. on Map	Telephone No.	Address	Lowest Price (Double/Twin)
Queenscliff Hotel		38	03-5258-1066	16 Gellibrand Street	$265
Vue Grand		36	03-5258-1544	46 Hesse Street	$200
Pilot's House B&B		30	03-5258-4171	50 Gellibrand Street	$185
Ozone Hotel		31	03-5258-1011	42 Gellibrand Street	$170
Athelstane		37	03-5258-1024	4 Hobson Street	$135
Kia-Ora Cottage		32	03-5258-1122	38 Gellibrand Street	$125
Historic Gordon Terrace		28	03-5231-5335	36 Stokes Street	$120
Beacon Resort	4	44	1-800-351-182	78 Bellarine Highway	$110
Maytone by the Sea	4	24	1-800-064-785	68 Stevens Street	$110
Banks B&B		34	03-5258-4326	78a Hesse Street	$100
Benambra B&B		40	03-5258-2606	15 Hesse Street	$100
Boatramp Cottage		42	03-5258-4662	12 Bridge Street	$100
Clutha Cottage Heritage		29	03-5258-3577	20 Mercer Street	$100
Leyton Gables		26	03-5258-3452	35 King Street	$100
Seaview Guest House		33	1-800-688-086	86 Hesse Street	$100
Sparkling Waters		43	03-5258-3939	2 Bay Street	$100
Royal Hotel		25	03-5258-1669	34 King Street	$90
Riptide Motel		23	03-5258-1675	31 Flinders Street	$85
Wyuna Motor Inn		39	03-5258-4540	32 Hesse Street	$85
Esplanade Hotel		41	03-5258-1919	2 Gellibrand Street	$85
Four Winds Caravan Park		45	03-5258-1884	40 Bellarine Highway	$65
Queenscliff Tourist Parks		27	03-5258-1765	138 Hesse Street	$65
Queenscliff Inn		35	03-5258-4600	59 Hesse Street	$50

(iv) Backpackers Hostel in Queenscliff *(see map on page 760)*

Name	Group	No. on Map	Telephone No.	Address	Lowest Price (Dormitory)
Queenscliff Inn	YHA	35	03-5258-3737	59 Hesse Street	$20

(v) Accommodation in Point Lonsdale *(see map on page 759)*

Name	Stars	No. on Map	Telephone No.	Address	Lowest Price (Double/Twin)
Longueville		46	03-5250-2990	25 Gill Road, Pt. Lonsdale	$195
Terminus B&B		46	03-5250-1142	31 Pt Lonsdale Rd, Pt Lons.	$140
Bailey House		46	03-5250-2523	22 Bailey St., Pt. Lonsdale	$95
Dorset Cottage		46	03-5250-3184	1 Simpson St., Pt. Lonsdale	$95
Lonsdale Lakes B&B		46	03-5250-3908	60 Sta Monica Bvd, Pt Lons.	$95
Warwick House B&B		46	03-5250-4320	16 Warwick Hill Dv, P Lons	$95
Queenscliffe Motel		46	03-5250-2970	4 Kirk Road	$80
Point Lonsdale C'van Pk.		46	03-5250-1765	Point Lonsdale	$60

764 VICTORIA

(vi) Accommodation in Portarlington *(see map on page 761)*

Name	Stars	No. on Map	Telephone No.	Address	Lowest Price (Double/Twin)
Carrick		50	03-5259-2567	30 The Esplanade	$125
Dollies on Newcombe		48	03-5259-3005	132 Newcombe Street	$95
Portarlington Beach Motel		49	03-5259-3801	153 Newcombe Street	$90
Grand Hotel		47	03-5259-2260	76 Newcombe Street	$80
Dylene Caravan Park		52	03-5259-2873	5 Mercer Street	$65
Fairhaven Caravan Park		51	03-5259-2231	207 Newcombe Street	$65

(vii) Backpackers Hostel at Whittington *(see map on page 759)*

Name	Group	No. on Map	Telephone No.	Address	Lowest Price (Dormitory)
St. Albans		53	03-5248-1229	6 Homestead Drive	$25

MOVING ON
(i) By Train

Trains run back to Melbourne from Geelong approximately every hour, and more often at peak periods. They run on to Warrnambool three times a day, for which service the timetable appears on page 752. The train between Melbourne and Adelaide stops at North Shore Station, which lies just north of Geelong. Some, but not all, of the Geelong-Melbourne trains stop there. The timetable to Adelaide, with connexions to Perth and Alice Springs, is shown on page 751. The train from Adelaide to Melbourne stops at North Shore to allow passengers to disembark there, but cannot be boarded.

(ii) By Bus

McCafferty's operates one bus service per day between Melbourne and Adelaide via Geelong. There is also a V-Line bus from Geelong to Ballarat which connects with the bus to Dimboola, which, in turn, connects with the V-Line daily bus service to Adelaide. In addition, V-Line has bus services along the Great Ocean Road to Apollo Bay three times a day, with a connecting bus on to Warrnambool on Fridays only (see timetable on page 752). There is a V-Line bus to Bendigo once a day on weekdays, with buses only as far as Ballarat four times a day. The late evening service to Ballarat connects with the night bus on to Mildura.

Destination	Operator	Via	Distance (km)	Fare	Journey Time	Frequency
Melbourne	McCafferty's		55	$15	1¼ hrs	1/day
Adelaide	McCafferty's		692	$65	9¾ hrs	1/day
		Ballarat	70	$15	1¼ hrs	1/day
Warrnambool	V-Line		187	$30.70	2¾ hrs	2/week
Apollo Bay	V-Line		110	$23.30	2½ hrs	3/day
		Lorne	65	$14.60	1½ hrs	4/day
Bendigo	V-Line		220	$37.10	3¾ hrs	5/week
		Ballarat	96	$23.30	1½ hrs	4/day

APOLLO BAY AND THE GREAT OCEAN ROAD
Population 2,500 (Apollo Bay)
4 hrs by train and bus from Melbourne (Apollo Bay)

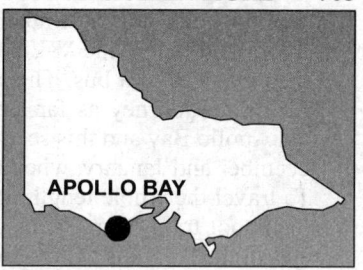

When the soldiers returned from the Great War, there was insufficient employment for them and various government schemes were devised to provide work. The construction of the Great Ocean Road was one such major project. The road is hewn from the cliff face in many parts, running beside the ocean as its name suggests. It is a road which scales the cliffs then plummets to the sea many times over, offering some splendid views and causing the traveller to wonder that all this could have been achieved by hard human toil, without the use of any heavy machinery. It is a famous road, mostly used for sightseeing, and to gain access to the seaside resorts which lie along its length. Warrnambool, though, which lies at its terminus and is the largest place served by the road, can be reached much more quickly by a major inland route.

There are tours which travel along the Great Ocean Road and show these sights. Mostly they are day trips from Melbourne, but there are also weekend tours and tours which travel between Melbourne and Adelaide via the Great Ocean Road,

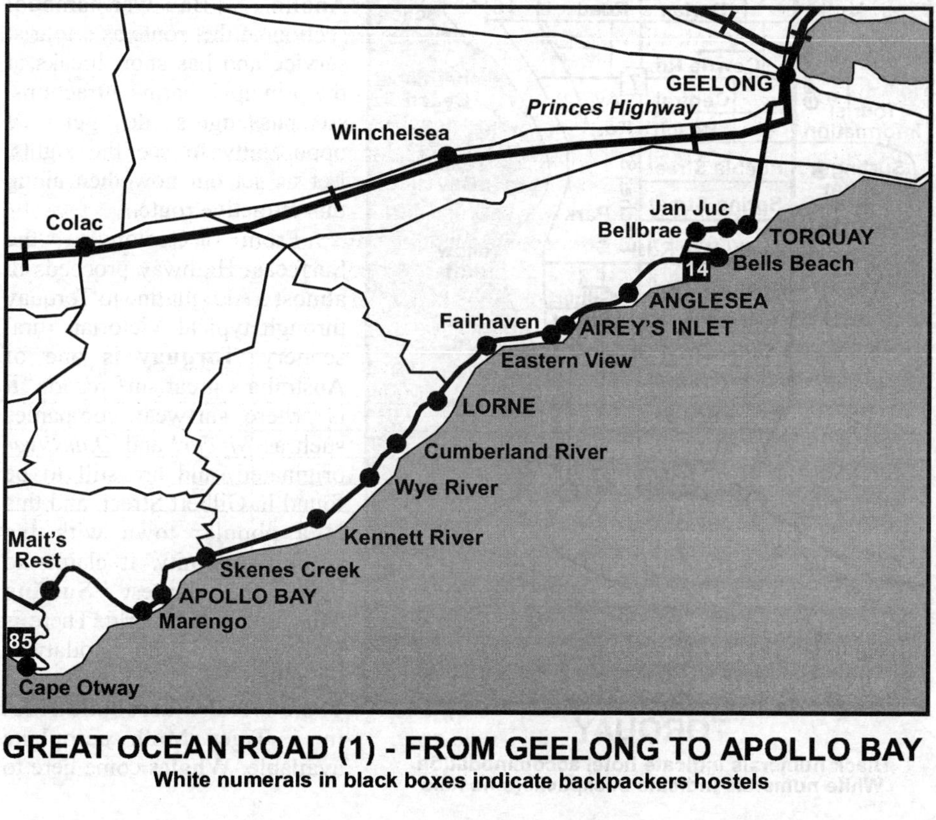

GREAT OCEAN ROAD (1) - FROM GEELONG TO APOLLO BAY
White numerals in black boxes indicate backpackers hostels

Warrnambool and Mt. Gambier. By public transport, however, there is only one possibility and that is the V-Line service. By V-Line, one travels by train to Geelong and then changes to a bus. The bus runs to Apollo Bay four times a day and there is one additional journey as far as Lorne only. However, the best part of the road lies beyond Apollo Bay and this section has a service only once a week, on Fridays, except in December and January, when the bus runs twice a week, on Mondays and Fridays.

To travel the whole length of the road with V-Line on Fridays, one takes the 8:48 Warrnambool train from Spencer Street in Melbourne as far as Geelong, where one changes to the 9:55 bus to Apollo Bay. The bus reaches Apollo Bay at 12:30, and there is time for lunch before one continues at 13:40, reaching Warrnambool at 17:00, in time for the last train to Melbourne, if one wishes to return.

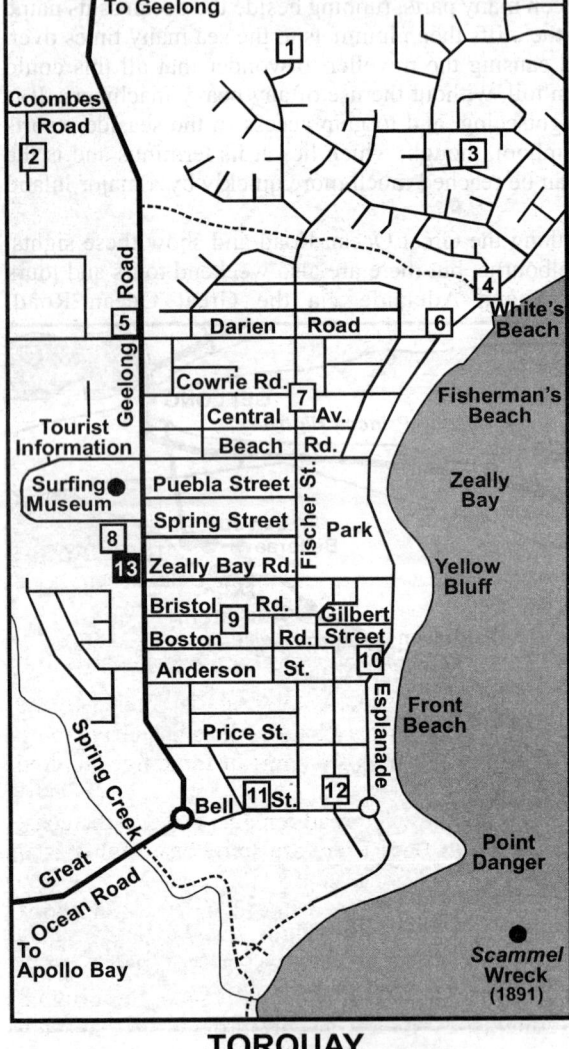

TORQUAY
Black numerals indicate hotel accommodation
White numerals indicate backpackers hostels

From Warrnambool, there is also a service in the opposite direction on Fridays only, leaving Warrnambool at 9:20 and reaching Melbourne at 18:01. At the height of summer, a second connecting service operates in both directions on Mondays. V-Line regards the Apollo Bay-Warrnambool section of this route as a tourist service and has short breaks at the principal marine attractions, so passengers do get the opportunity to see the sights. Let us set out now then along this attractive route.

From Geelong, the Surfcoast Highway proceeds in almost a straight line to Torquay through typical Victorian rural scenery. **Torquay** is one of Australia's great surf resorts. It is where surfwear companies such as *Ripcurl* and *Quiksilver* originated, and are still to be found in Gilbert Street, and this is a popular town with the surfing fraternity. It claims to have the largest **Surfing Museum** in the world. There is plenty of accommodation, including a backpackers hostel. There are also **aerobatic rides** in a Tiger Moth aeroplane available. **Whales** come here to be watched in June, July and August. There are cliff-top walks, rock pools, beaches and, of course, surfing.

Local buses from Geelong to Torquay are operated by McHarry's Buslines. There are seven services per day, taking approximately 45 minutes and costing $5 single or $9 return.

Just south of the town, you will cross **Spring Creek** and it is at this point that the Great Ocean Road officially starts. The road immediately begins the undulations which characterise its entire length, and the views commence. Off to your left here in the distance, but not on the main road itself, you can glimpse **Bells Beach**, known for the *Ripcurl Professional Surf Classic*, which takes place in April and is the longest running surf competition in the world. This is a famous surfing beach. Part of the area is also the local nude bathing beach, but it will be difficult to discern this from the bus. There is another backpackers hostel at Bells Beach.

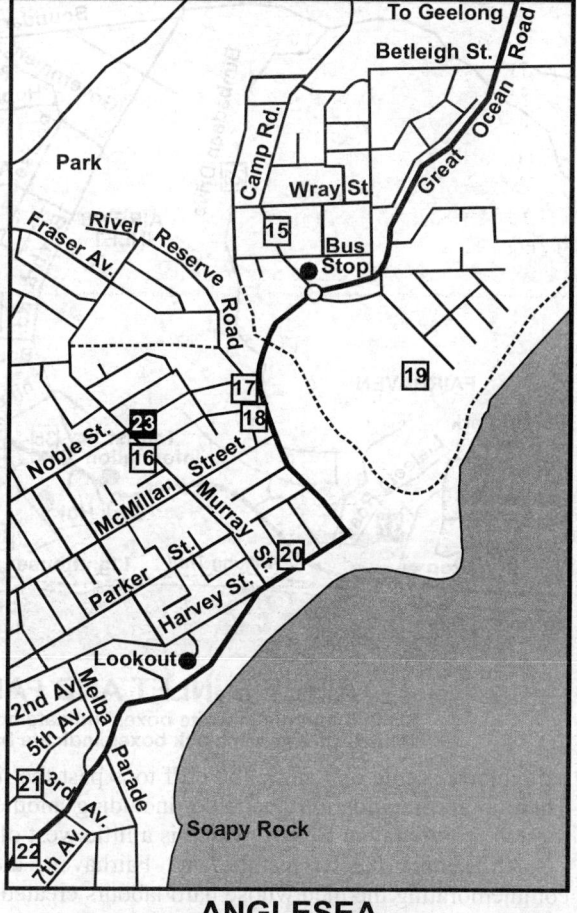

ANGLESEA
Black numerals indicate hotel accommodation
White numerals indicate backpackers hostels

After passing through a bushland area, you will begin the descent into Anglesea. **Anglesea** is another of the typically relaxed small towns along this coast. It too has a backpackers hostel and more surf and sand, as well as a golf course which is the adopted home of some five hundred kangaroos who like the green grass.

A steep ascent leads out of Anglesea and now the road remains close to the coast for all the remainder of the journey to Apollo Bay. There are some beautiful coastal views along this section in particular.

The next town is **Airey's Inlet**, overlooked by the white concrete **Split Point Lighthouse** constructed here in 1891. The light from it is visible at sea from a distance of 21 miles. The lighthouse is available for tours at weekends. There are also good views from here. There is a replica of a **settler's hut** from the 1860s, the original having been destroyed by the terrible fires which swept through here on the appropriately named day of Ash Wednesday 1983. Nearby, the **Allen Noble Sanctuary** offers good facilities for bird watching. There are walking trails, including one

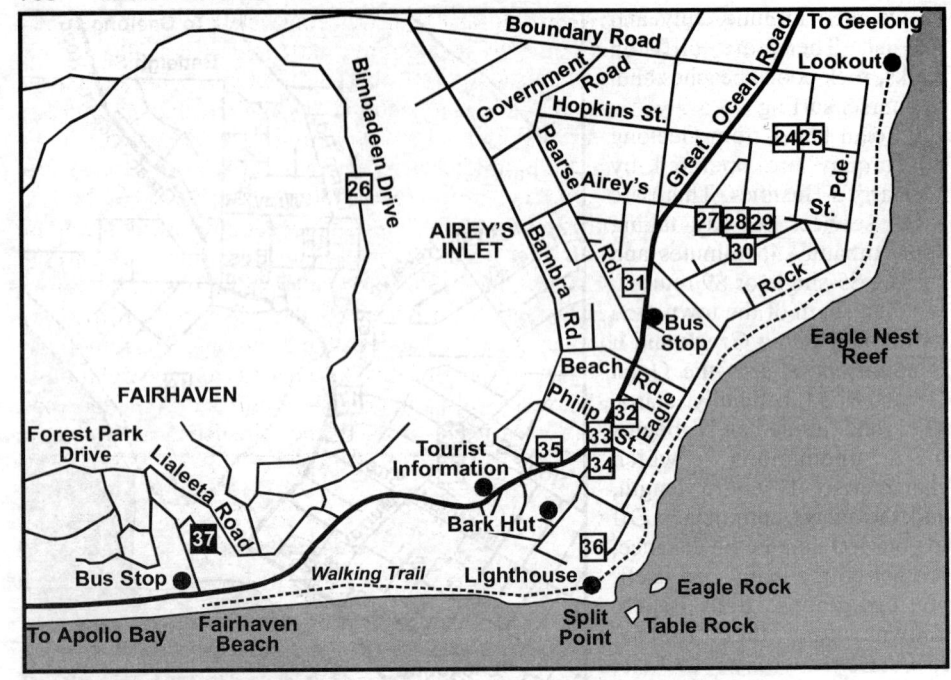

AIREY'S INLET AND FAIRHAVEN
Black numerals in white boxes indicate hotel accommodation
White numerals in black boxes indicate backpackers hostels

particularly scenic one along the cliff tops past the lighthouse, and there are beaches. There is accommodation available, including another backpackers hostel, this being located at **Fairhaven Beach**, which is a little west of the main town.

At **Eastern View**, just beyond Fairhaven, there is an arch across the road commemorating the men whose hard labours created this beautiful way between 1918 and 1932, those who had just returned from other unrewarded work in Europe in the Great War. Again the twists and turns start as we climb through eucalyptus forests up to **Cinema Point**, where there is another good lookout, before descending into the pretty town of **Lorne**. Again there is plenty of accommodation here, this time including two backpackers hostels. There are also walks available and there is a good viewpoint at **Teddy's Lookout** on the edge of the town. Four ships were wrecked in the bay here between 1854 and 1863, and another in 1878, offering diving opportunities.

As we leave Lorne, the road becomes spectacular again as we travel at the top of steep cliffs with views all along the coast. We pass through the small settlements of **Cumberland River, Wye River, Kennett River** and **Skenes Creek** and, after an hour, reach Apollo Bay, which has been visible in the distance for a while. Here the bus service from Geelong finishes, and only if it is Friday (or Monday in December and January) will you be able to continue to Warrnambool.

Apollo Bay, with a population of approximately 2,500, lies at the foot of the **Otway Ranges**. It began life as a small whaling station in the 1850s and was originally known as Middleton. Later the name was changed to Kambruk. The settlement could be reached only by sea at first, but from 1873 there was a track used by stagecoaches.

However, it was only when the Great Ocean Road was completed in 1932 that easy access became possible, by which time the name of the settlement had changed again to its current Apollo Bay. Tours are available from here to the Otways. Although the hills around the town were denuded by the early settlers, it is only a short distance to thick forests with impressive waterfalls. Again there is plenty of accommodation in the attractive town of Apollo Bay, including three places where backpackers are welcome.

As we leave Apollo Bay (on Fridays), the road follows the coast for a short distance to **Marengo** before it turns inland and starts climbing. It now enters the **Cape Otway National Park** and we see what remains of the ancient rainforest which used to cover the whole area. At **Mait's Rest**, there is a boardwalk exploration of the forest, but the bus will not be stopping for that. A little beyond, there is a turn-off to **Cape Otway Lighthouse**, thirteen kilometres away. Tours of the lighthouse are sometimes available and there is a bunkhouse just off the road, two kilometres from the lighthouse. However, this bunkhouse usually caters only for groups. From this point the road returns to the sea and drops back to sea level, crossing the Aire River at **Glenaire**. Then, however, it ascends once more, turning inland to **Lavers Hill**, the highest point on the entire route, at 455 metres.

Lavers Hill is, therefore, not a coastal town, but a small hill settlement set amidst forests and offering fine views. From here the road descends steeply to bring us back near the coast once more at **Lower Gellibrand**.

We now reach **Princetown**, and the landscape starts to change. We are passing through low windswept coastal vegetation with sand dunes evident. Only five minutes beyond the Princeton turn-off, the **Twelve Apostles** suddenly come into view, and the bus makes a ten-minute stop for us to admire them. We are now within the **Port Campbell National Park**, a coastal park which continues all the way to Peterborough. The Twelve Apostles are rock stacks demonstrating the power of the sea, for all of the surrounding cliffs have been

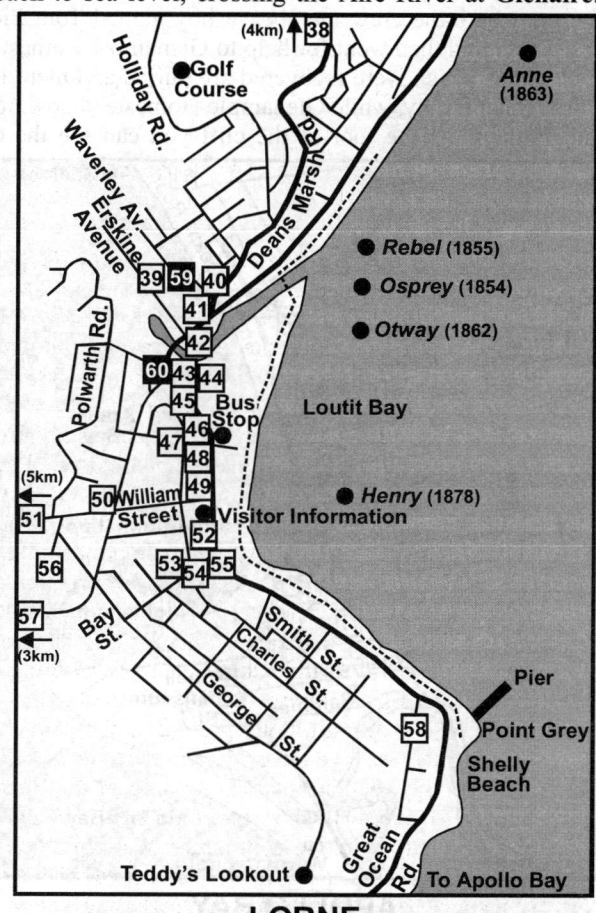

LORNE
Black numerals indicate hotel accommodation
White numerals indicate backpackers hostels

worn away, leaving only these stacks composed of harder rock standing sentinel out at sea. In fact, when counting these stacks, you may well find that your result is a different number from twelve and start to wonder which are apostles and which are just rocks.

It is only another five minutes to **Loch Ard Gorge**, named after the ship which was wrecked here in 1878. The *Loch Ard* had left Gravesend on 1st March 1878 and reached here on 1st June after an uneventful voyage. However, it had been misty for several days and the Captain was unable to ascertain his position with certainty as he searched for the western entrance to Bass Strait, to accomplish the passage known as "threading the eye of the needle". Although the Captain thought that he was well offshore, he had sent a man aloft to watch for the light of the Cape Otway Lighthouse. At first light, he suddenly found himself right under the cliffs here in rough seas. He took all action possible, but could not prevent the ship's being thrown against the reef. The *Loch Ard* sank within fifteen minutes. Of the crew and 54 passengers, there were but two survivors, one crew member and one young girl, Eva Carmichael, who could not swim but clung to wreckage and was washed into what is now known as Loch Ard Gorge, where the crew member, a boy named Tom Pierce, struggled for an hour to rescue her and then went for help to Glenample Homestead. At the top of the cliff, the few bodies which were recovered are buried and there is a memorial to the rest of the Carmichael family, while Glenample Homestead now offers tours, except on Tuesdays and Fridays. At the foot of the cliff you can see the cave where the two survivors sheltered. The bus stops here too for five minutes.

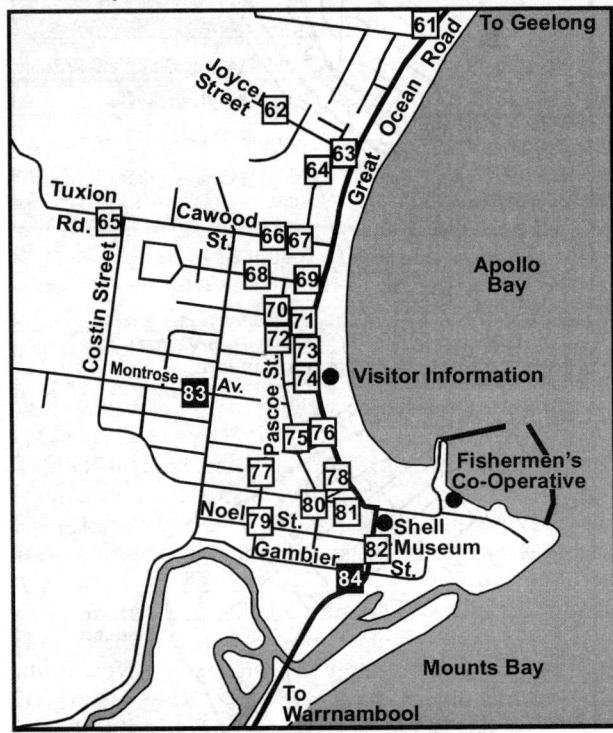

APOLLO BAY
Black numerals indicate hotel accommodation
White numerals indicate backpackers hostels

This was not the only shipwreck along this stretch of coast. In fact, it is claimed that approximately 1,500 ships have foundered here after being forced into errors similar to that which occurred on the *Loch Ard*, although the huge number seems hardly credible. As a result, this stretch of coastline is now known, somewhat dramatically, as the **Shipwreck Coast**. From here, another ten minutes will take us to the small town of **Port Campbell**, known for its fishing, and particularly for its crayfish and abalone. There is also a beach and there is surfing and, of course, there is no shortage of wrecked vessels for those who like diving.

Leaving Port Campbell, again we ascend to the cliff-

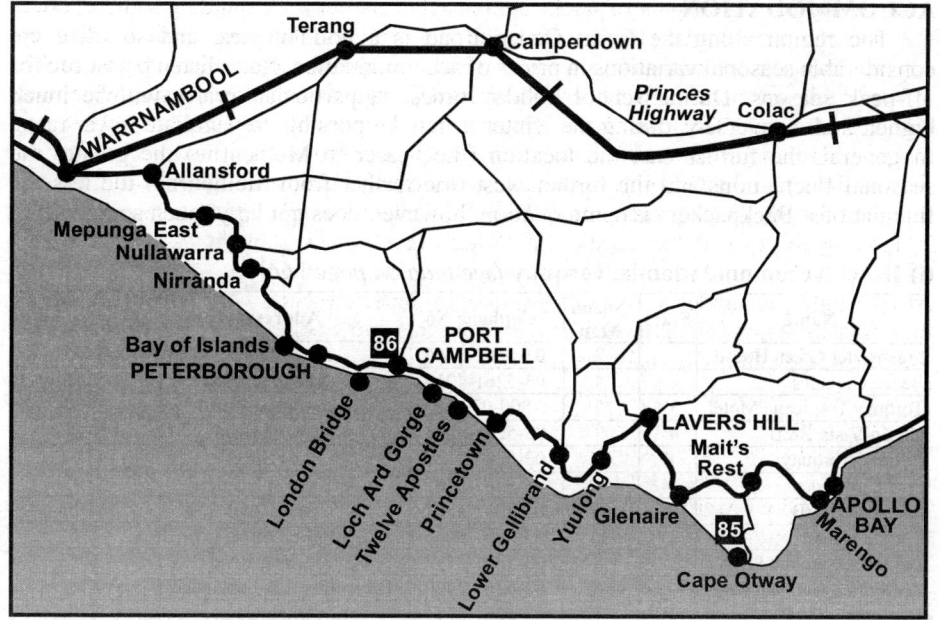

GREAT OCEAN ROAD (2) - FROM APOLLO BAY TO WARRNAMBOOL
White numerals in black boxes indicate backpackers hostels

top route. Only two kilometres out of the town, there is another good lookout, with a view back over the scenery through which we have just passed. There are other impressive coastal phenomena here, including blowholes, caves and grottoes, but the place at which the bus will make a stop is **London Bridge**, five minutes beyond Port Campbell. A few years ago this natural bridge proved to have been aptly named. A process of erosion had left a stack in the sea connected by the natural bridge across which one could walk. Then, one day, just as in the nursery rhyme, London Bridge simply fell down. Fortunately, nobody was crossing at the time, but those on the remaining stack were marooned for several hours until rescued eventually by helicopter. Now just the stack remains, no doubt to be weathered into oblivion too in the course of time.

Ten minutes more and we are in **Peterborough**, where the Port Campbell National Park ends. Peterborough, on Curdies Inlet, is another holiday town, but not as popular with those without transport, probably because, once here, you have a week to wait before the next bus comes along. However, you can have ten minutes here, if a week seems too long, as this is another brief stop.

The last pause on the bus route is at the **Bay of Islands**, another five minutes down the road. This is similar to the Twelve Apostles, but the apostles here are smaller ones and more numerous, as well as being closer to the shore. This is the last event of the afternoon. Reboard the vehicle and continue for the remaining forty minutes to Warrnambool. The road now leaves the coast and passes through dairy farming country to **Allansford**, a small town which boasts three cheese factories. Here the Great Ocean Road terminates, as it meets the Princes Highway which has travelled from Geelong by a shorter, faster and less tortuous route. It is ten kilometres from here to Warrnambool.

772 VICTORIA
ACCOMMODATION

The region along the Great Ocean Road is a holiday area, and so there are considerable seasonal variations in prices of accommodation. Rates listed below are for off-peak seasons. During school holiday times, in particular, prices will be much higher, and, conversely, during the winter it may be possible to negotiate lower rates. In general, the further east the location (the nearer to Melbourne) the greater the seasonal fluctuations and the further west (the further from Melbourne) the less the fluctuations. Backpackers accommodation, however, does not vary much seasonally.

(i) Hotel Accommodation in Torquay *(see map on page 766)*

Name	Stars	No. on Map	Telephone No.	Address	Lowest Price (Double/Twin)
Freshwater Green House		2	03-5261-3366	3 Jetti Lane	$165
Beach Cottages		4	03-5261-4010	121 The Esplanade	$155
Torquay Tropicana Motel	3½	5	1-800-032-131	2 Grossmans Road	$135
Ocean Vista B&B	4½	7	03-5261-9826	48 Cowrie Road	$125
Pride of Torquay	4½	12	03-5261-4127	6 Pride Street	$110
Surf City Motel	4	10	03-5261-3492	35 The Esplanade	$105
Avondale B&B		3	03-5261-4362	5 Time Court	$100
Torquay Hotel	2½	11	03-5261-6046	36 Bell Street	$85
Bernell's Caravan Park		8	03-5261-2493	55 Geelong Road	$75
Zeally Bay Caravan Park		6	03-5261-2400	Darien Road & Esplanade	$75
Just June's B&B	3½	1	03-5261-3771	12 Casino Court	$70
Potter's Inn B&B	4½	9	03-5261-4131	40 Bristol Road	$70

(ii) Backpackers Hostels in Torquay *(see maps on pages 765 and 766)*

Name	Group	No. on Map	Telephone No.	Address	Lowest Price (Dormitory)
Bells Beach Backpackers	Nom	13	03-5261-7070	51 Geelong Road	$25
Point Break Backpackers		14	03-5261-3123	185 Addiscott Rd., Bells Beach	$25

(iii) Hotel Accommodation in Anglesea *(see map on page 767)*

Name	Stars	No. on Map	Telephone No.	Address	Lowest Price (Double/Twin)
Surf Coast Resort	3½	17	03-5263-3363	105 Great Ocean Road	$135
Roadknight Cottages	3½	22	03-5263-1820	26 Great Ocean Road	$110
Fruit Tree Cottage		21	03-5263-2725	60b Fifth Avenue	$105
Family Caravan Park	4½	19	03-5263-1583	Cameron Road	$100
Anglesea Motor Lodge	4	18	03-5263-3888	109 Great Ocean Road	$100
Debonair Guest House	3	20	03-5263-1440	15 Harvey Street	$95
Driftwood Caravan Park		16	03-5263-1640	45 Murray Street	$80
First Red Holiday Cottage	3	15	03-5263-3267	58 Camp Road	$55

(iv) Backpackers Hostel in Anglesea *(see map on page 767)*

Name	Group	No. on Map	Telephone No.	Address	Lowest Price (Dormitory)
Anglesea Backpackers		23	03-5263-2664	40 Noble Street	$25

GREAT OCEAN ROAD 773

(v) Accommodation in Airey's Inlet *(see map on page 768)*

Name	Stars	No. on Map	Telephone No.	Address	Lowest Price (Double/Twin)
Lighthouse Keepers' Cots	2½	36	03-5289-6306	Split Point	$220
Sirenuse Beach Villa		35	03-5289-7448	63 Great Ocean Road	$175
Airey's on Airey's	4	27	03-5289-6261	1/19 Airey's Street	$160
Bush to Beach B&B		30	03-5289-6538	43 Anderson Street	$125
Airey's Inlet Bower		29	03-9497-2161	11 Airey's Street	$105
Inlet Hideaway		25	03-5289-7471	34 Hopkins Street	$105
Airey's by the Light		32	03-5289-6134	2 Federal Street	$100
Airey's Inlet Getaway	3	34	03-5289-7021	4 Barton Court	$100
Currawong Overnight		28	03-5289-6329	15 Airey's Street	$100
Fair-Haven B&B		26	03-5289-7194	65 Bimbadeen Drive	$100
Split Point Cottages		24	03-5289-6566	40 Hopkins Street	$100
Airey's Inlet Caravan Pk.	4	31	1-800-668-866	19 Great Ocean Road	$90
Lightkeeper's Inn	3½	33	1-800-032-639	64 Great Ocean Road	$70

(vi) Backpackers Hostel in Fairhaven *(see map on page 768)*

Name	Group	No. on Map	Telephone No.	Address	Lowest Price (Dormitory)
Surf Coast Backpackers		37	03-5289-6886	5 Cowan Avenue, Fairhaven	$25

(vii) Hotel Accommodation in Lorne *(see map on page 769)*

Name	Stars	No. on Map	Telephone No.	Address	Lowest Price (Double/Twin)
Cumberland Lorne Resort	4½	52	1-800-037-010	150 Mountjoy Parade	$215
Lornebeach Luxury Apts.		48	03-5289-1214	106 Mountjoy Parade	$180
Stanmorr B&B	4	50	03-5289-1530	64 Otway Street	$180
Ravenswood B&B		53	03-5289-2655	Bay & Smith Streets	$165
Bush House Cottages	4	38	03-5289-2477	1860 Deans Marsh Road	$145
Main Beach Motor Inn	4	54	1-800-681-088	3 Bay Street	$140
Ocean Sun Apartments		47	03-5289-1891	14 Smith Street	$135
Waverley House	4	40	03-5289-2044	Waverley Av / Gt Ocean Rd	$135
Erskine Falls Cottages	3½	51	03-5289-2666	Erskine Falls Road	$125
Anchorage Motel	3	45	03-5289-1891	32 Mountjoy Parade	$125
Great Ocean Road Cotts.	3½	39	03-5289-1070	10 Erskine Avenue	$120
Allenvale Cottages	4	57	03-5289-1450	150 Allenvale Road	$110
Cherry Tree Creek Cotts.		56	03-5289-2107	93 Polworth Road	$110
Phoenix Apartments		46	03-5289-1298	60 Mountjoy Parade	$110
Coachman Inn	4	41	03-5289-2244	1 Deans Marsh Road	$105
Cora Lynn Studios		43	03-5289-2288	Mountjoy Parade	$105
Lorne Hotel	3½	55	03-5289-1409	176 Mountjoy Parade	$90
Sandridge Motel	3½	49	03-5289-2180	128 Mountjoy Parade	$85
Ocean Lodge Motel	3	58	03-5289-1330	6 Armytage Street	$80
Erskine House Beachside	3½	44	1-800-629-417	Mountjoy Parade	$75
Lorne Foreshore Park		42	03-5289-1382	1 Mountjoy Parade	$75

(viii) Backpackers Hostels in Lorne *(see map on page 769)*

Name	Group	No. on Map	Telephone No.	Address	Lowest Price (Dormitory)
Erskine River Backpackers		60	03-5289-1496	6 Mountjoy Parade	$25
Gt. Ocean Rd. Backpackers	YHA	59	03-5289-1809	10 Erskine Avenue	$20

774   VICTORIA

(ix) Hotel Accommodation in Apollo Bay *(see map on page 770)*

Name	Stars	No. on Map	Telephone No.	Address	Lowest Price (Double/Twin)
Captains at the Bay	4½	70	03-5237-6771	Pascoe & Whelan Streets	$145
Nelson Palms Villas	3	80	03-5237-6755	Pascoe & Nelson Streets	$140
Stewart's B&B	4	65	03-5237-6447	2 Tuxion Road	$125
Bay Pine Motel	2½	69	03-5237-6732	1 Murray Street	$115
Bayview Apartments	4	79	03-5237-6263	46 Noel Street	$110
International Motor Inn	4	78	03-5237-6100	37 Great Ocean Road	$105
Apollo Bay Motel	3½	75	03-5237-7577	2 Moore Street	$100
Crystal Waters Gst. House	3½	62	03-5237-7129	4 Joyce Street	$95
Waterfront Motor Inn	4	71	03-5237-7333	173 Great Ocean Road	$95
Beachfront Motel	3½	74	1-800-815-973	163 Great Ocean Road	$90
Kooringal Holiday Park		66	03-5237-7111	27 Cawood Street	$90
Casino Lodge	4	64	03-5237-6576	49 Casino Avenue	$80
Greenacres Country Hse.	4	81	03-5237-6309	Gt. Ocean Rd. & Nelson St.	$80
Otway Lodge	3½	72	03-5237-6263	23 Pascoe Street	$80
Coastal Motel	4	73	03-5237-6681	171 Great Ocean Road	$75
Rannock Holiday Flats	3	67	03-5237-6307	9 Cawood Street	$75
Apollo Bay Hotel		76	03-5237-6250	95 Great Ocean Road	$75
Pisces Caravan Resort		61	03-5237-6749	311 Great Ocean Road	$75
Great Ocean View Motel	2½	82	03-5237-6527	1 Great Ocean Road	$70
Paradise Court Villas	3½	68	03-5237-6133	20 Murray Street	$70
Bayside Gardens	3½	63	03-5237-6248	219 Great Ocean Road	$65
Beachcomber Motel	3	77	03-5237-6290	15 Diana Street	$65

(x) Backpackers Hostels in Apollo Bay *(see map on page 770)*

Name	Group	No. on Map	Telephone No.	Address	Lowest Price (Dormitory)
Pisces Caravan Resort		61	03-5237-6749	311 Great Ocean Road	$22
Apollo Bay Backpackers		83	03-5237-7360	47 Montrose Avenue	$20
Surfside Backpackers	YHA	84	1800-357-263	Gt. Ocean Rd. & Gambier St.	$17

(xi) Backpackers Hostels between Apollo Bay and Warrnambool *(map, page 771)*

Name	Group	No. on Map	Telephone No.	Address	Lowest Price (Dormitory)
Cape Otway Bunkhouses		85	03-5237-9272	150 Brack's Access, Cp. Otway	$15
Port Campbell Y.H.A.	YHA	86	03-5598-6305	18 Tregea St., Port Campbell	$18

MOVING ON

From Apollo Bay, a V-Line bus runs on to Warrnambool once a week, on Fridays only. The timetable for this service appears on page 752. Only at the height of summer does this service operate twice a week, on Mondays and Fridays.

The timetable for services back to Melbourne, by bus to Geelong, whence by train, is shown below.

From Apollo Bay to Geelong and Melbourne

Days of Operation	M-Sa (Bus)	M-Sa	Sun (Bus)	Sun	M-F (Bus)	M-F	M-F (Bus)	M-F	F (Bus)	M-F (Bus)	M-F	Sat (Bus)	Sat	Sun (Bus)	Sun
Warrnambool		0638*							0920						1705
Apollo Bay	0615		0730		0940				1230	1410		1445		1615	
Lorne	0715		0830		1045		1350			1515		1545		1722	
Geelong	0845	0855*	1000	1010	1220	1235	1520	1540		1640	1700	1710	1732	1900	1920
Melbourne		0953*		1114		1333		1643			1801		1832		2017

* Geelong 0917, Melbourne 1012 on Saturdays

WARRNAMBOOL, PORT FAIRY AND PORTLAND

Population 27,000 (Warrnambool)
Population 2,500 (Port Fairy)
Population 10,000 (Portland)

3 hrs 30 mins by train from Melbourne (Warrnambool)

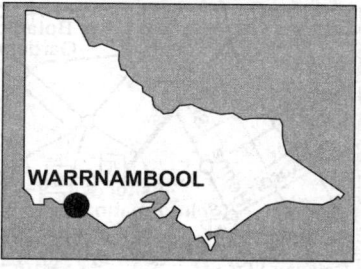

Warrnambool is a city, with a population of approximately 27,000. Its original prosperity was built around its port facilities and in the 1880s it used to handle more cargo than Melbourne. It is where the passenger railway service currently terminates. If you arrive by train, you will find the journey pleasant, but not as spectacular as travelling via the Great Ocean Road. The trains are actually operated by a company known as the West Coast Railway, not by V-Line. This was a change instituted about a decade ago as Victoria's contribution to the philosophy of introducing private ownership into public transport, and also, perhaps, of avoiding some of the restrictive practices of trades unions. It seems to have been a successful innovation, especially as otherwise Warrnambool might no longer have a passenger rail service. V-Line buses still link with West Coast Railway trains.

There are several attractions in Warrnambool, but the most impressive is probably **Flagstaff Hill Maritime Museum**, which is not a single building but a complex of historical buildings, displays and re-creations. The object is to present a small town as it might have been in the latter half of the nineteenth century. The Museum contains various preserved vessels, two lighthouses, fortifications and, naturally, the flagstaff.

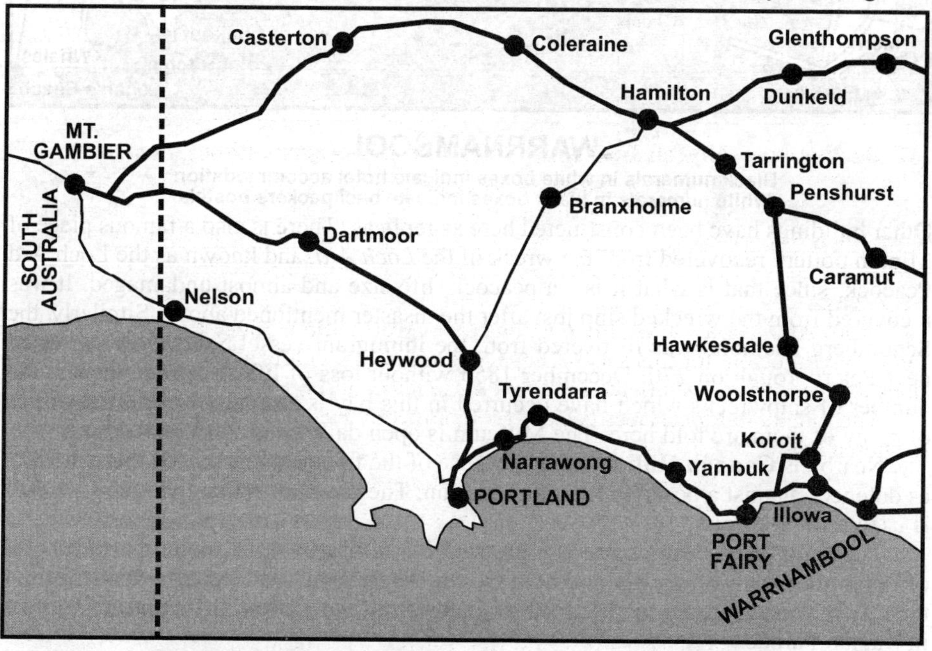

FROM WARRNAMBOOL TO MT. GAMBIER
Thicker lines indicate V-Line bus routes

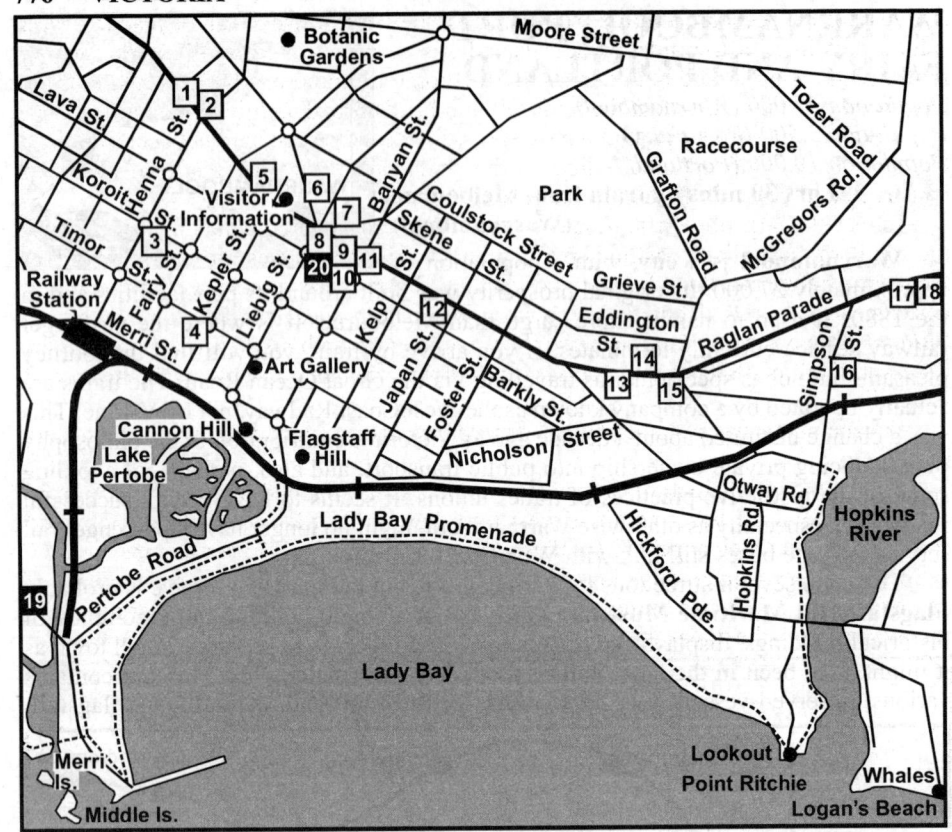

WARRNAMBOOL

Black numerals in white boxes indicate hotel accommodation
White numerals in black boxes indicate backpackers hostels

Other buildings have been constructed here as replicas. There is also a famous piece of Minton pottery recovered from the wreck of the *Loch Ard*, and known as the Loch Ard Peacock, since that is what it is - a peacock, life size and almost undamaged. It was recovered from the wrecked ship just after the disaster mentioned above. Similarly, the Schomberg Diamond was recovered from the immigrant vessel *Schomberg*, wrecked near Peterborough on 27th December 1855 without loss of life. It is thought that the number of shipwrecks which have occurred in this bay is around 160, and the stories of many of them are told here. The Museum is open daily from 9:00 until 17:00.

Nearby is **Cannon Hill**, so called because of the five cannons placed there in 1887 as defences against a possible Russian invasion. The weapons remain, but now the hill is used as a viewpoint.

The **Lady Bay Promenade** is a pleasant 3.5-kilometre walk along the foreshore, offering good views over the Southern Ocean. There is also a **Heritage Walk** around the city of Warrnambool, with a map available from the **Visitor Information Centre** in Raglan Parade.

Lake Pertobe offers a picnic area with a maze, boats, walking tracks and other attractions.

Just off the coast are **Middle Island** and **Merri Island**, which can be reached, with a little paddling, at low tide. Middle Island has a colony of **Fairy Penguins** which return home at dusk, and both islands are the home of numerous birds. Walking trails have been constructed, so that the birds will not be disturbed unduly by human visitors.

This bay is a calving ground for **whales**, which can be seen here between June and October. They often approach close to the shore and a viewing platform has been constructed at **Logan's Beach**, to the east of the city.

In recent years, old Portuguese charts have been discovered which appear to show the southern Australian coastline up to a point six kilometres west of Warrnambool, at **Armstrong Bay**, and it has been suggested that a Portuguese vessel may have ventured here as early as 1522. There is also a story that a Portuguese caravel, the *Mahogany Ship*, may lie buried by sand dunes to the west of Warrnambool. It was apparently last observed there in 1880. If ever rediscovered it may change our view of the history of Australia.

Warrnambool has a good choice of accommodation, including two backpackers hostels.

This, although the end of the railway service, is not the end of public transport in Victoria, for V-Line buses continue west from here to Port Fairy, Portland, Heywood and Mt. Gambier. See page 752 for these timetables and page 775 for a map.

Port Fairy, originally known as Belfast, with a current population of approximately 2,500, has buildings dating back to 1842 and several interesting walks are available in the town and in the surrounding area. It is a town which has not

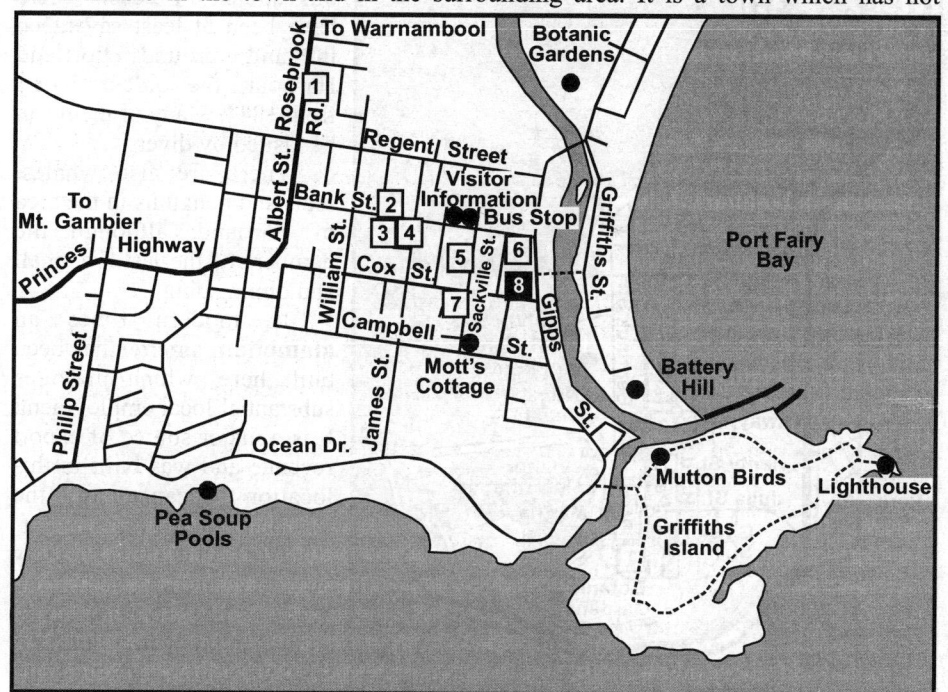

PORT FAIRY
Black numerals in white boxes indicate hotel accommodation
White numerals in black boxes indicate backpackers hostels

changed much over the years and has retained most of its original buildings. The **Caledonian Hotel** was first licensed in 1844 and claims to have the oldest continuous liquor licence in Victoria. **Mott's Cottage** is the local headquarters of the National Trust and dates from the 1840s. Accommodation in Port Fairy includes a youth hostel, which, although it has been under threat of closure recently, remains open at the time of writing.

Portland certainly deserves a mention too, because this is the oldest settlement in Victoria, pre-dating the foundation of Melbourne. The area was first charted in 1800 by Lt. James Grant in the *Lady Nelson*. He named the bay Portland Bay after the British Secretary of State who, at the time, was the Duke of Portland. The first settlers were temporary, whalers and sealers, but in 1829 a man named Dutton built a hut here and established a garden. However, it is from the arrival of the Henty Brothers, who were farmers and whalers, in 1834, that the permanent settlement of Victoria is usually dated. For some years, it was unclear whether Melbourne or Portland was to become the principal town of the southern settlement, the issue being resolved when gold was discovered much closer to Melbourne.

Portland also has an association with **Mary MacKillop**, mentioned in the section on Mt. Gambier (see page 720). She came to Portland in 1862 to work as a governess for a local family, the Camerons, and in 1863 she became a teacher at what is now All Saints Primary School. She left Portland in 1866.

Nor has Portland been spared from the shipwrecks which have occurred all along this stretch of coast. There have been at least seventeen in and around Portland Harbour, the oldest dating from 1844. Many of them can be visited by divers.

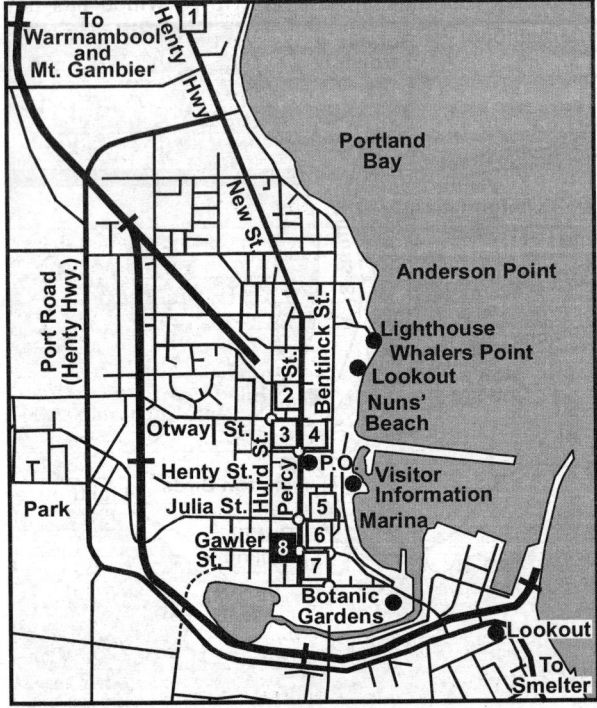

PORTLAND
Black numerals indicate hotel accommodation
White numerals indicate backpackers hostels

There are also whales, seals and penguins in the area of Portland, although the numbers of the last are small and diminishing.

In modern times an **aluminium smelter** has been built here, which provides substantial local employment. It is a major source of export revenue and was built in this location because of the excellent deep-water harbour.

Portland is approximately an hour and a half from Warrnambool by bus, and from here to **Mt. Gambier**, which V-Line seems to regard as a Victorian colony, takes a further hour. Buses operate twice a day to Portland, with

WARRNAMBOOL, PORT FAIRY, PORTLAND

one service continuing to Mt. Gambier. The timetable is shown on page 752. On Fridays only, a connexion through to Adelaide is offered by this route.

Portland also offers plenty of choices of accommodation, including a backpackers hostel.

ACCOMMODATION

Below is some of the accommodation available in Warrnambool, Port Fairy and Portland.

(i) Hotel Accommodation in Warrnambool *(see map on page 776)*

Name	Stars	No. on Map	Telephone No.	Address	Lowest Price (Double/Twin)
City Heart Motel	4½	6	03-5562-0500	4 Spence Street	$110
Sundowner Mid City	4½	9	1-800-033-310	525 Raglan Parade	$110
Tudor Motor Inn	3½	11	03-5562-8877	519 Raglan Parade	$105
Norfolk Lodge Motel	3	2	03-5562-6455	692 Raglan Parade	$100
Redwood Manor Motel	3	3	1-800-350-939	251 Koroit Street	$100
Central Court Motel	4	8	1-800-066-223	581 Raglan Parade	$100
All Seasons Motor Inn	4	13	1-800-067-475	367 Raglan Parade	$100
Gateway Motor Inn	3½	17	1-800-808-051	69 Raglan Parade	$100
Anchor Belle Motel	4	7	1-800-033-151	1 Darling Street	$95
Mahogany Motel	3	12	03-5562-5722	463 Raglan Parade	$95
Motel Warrnambool	3½	18	1-800-065-572	65 Raglan Parade	$95
Raglan Motor Inn	3	14	03-5562-8511	376 Raglan Parade	$90
Western Coast Motel	3½	15	1-800-670-610	349 Raglan Parade	$90
Downtown Motel	3	5	03-5562-1277	620 Raglan Parade	$85
Centrepoint Motel	3½	10	03-5562-8044	75 Banyan Street	$85
Log Cabin Motel	3½	1	03-5562-4244	698 Raglan Parade	$80
Western Private Hotel	2	4	03-5562-2011	45 Kepler Street	$65
Turn In Motel	2	16	03-5562-3677	Verdon & Simpson Streets	$65

(ii) Backpackers Hostels in Warrnambool *(see map on page 776)*

Name	Group	No. on Map	Telephone No.	Address	Lowest Price (Dormitory)
Backpackers Barn	VIP	20	03-5562-2073	90 Lava Street	$22
Warrnambool Beach B/P	VIP	19	03-5562-4874	17 Stanley Street	$20

(iii) Hotel Accommodation in Port Fairy *(see map on page 777)*

Name	Stars	No. on Map	Telephone No.	Address	Lowest Price (Double/Twin)
Hearn's Cottage Suites	5	2	03-5568-2388	54 Bank Street	$165
Ashmont Motor Inn	4½	3	03-5568-1588	47 Bank Street	$120
Seacombe House Inn	4	7	03-5568-1082	22 Sackville Street	$115
Central Motel	3	5	03-5568-1800	56 Sackville Street	$110
Learnean Anchorage	2½	1	1-800-063-346	115 Princes Highway	$85
Caledonian Inn	2½	4	03-5568-1044	41 Bank Street	$85
Royal Oak Hotel	2	6	03-5568-1018	9 Bank Street	$70

(iv) Backpackers Hostel in Port Fairy *(see map on page 777)*

Name	Group	No. on Map	Telephone No.	Address	Lowest Price (Dormitory)
Port Fairy Y.H.A.	YHA	8	03-5568-2468	8 Cox Street	$19

(v) Hotel Accommodation in Portland (see map on page 778)

Name	Stars	No. on Map	Telephone No.	Address	Lowest Price (Double/Twin)
Heritage Hotel Bentinck	4	7	03-5523-2188	41 Bentinck Street	$185
Richmond Henty Hotel	3½	5	1-800-355-205	101 Bentinck Street	$120
Whaler's Rest Motor Inn	4	1	1-800-032-565	8 Henty Highway	$95
Victoria Lodge Motor Inn	4	2	1-800-032-232	155 Percy Street	$85
Willian Dutton Motel		3	03-5523-4222	141 Percy Street	$70
Admella Motel	3	4	03-5523-3347	5 Otway Court	$65
Gordon Hotel		6	03-5523-1121	63 Bentinck Street	$45

(vi) Backpackers Hostel in Portland (see map on page 778)

Name	Group	No. on Map	Telephone No.	Address	Lowest Price (Dormitory)
Portland Backpackers		8	03-5523-6390	14 Gawler Street	$20

MOVING ON

Here is the timetable for V-Line services from Mt. Gambier, Portland, Port Fairy and Warrnambool to Melbourne. The timetable for services from Warrnambool on to Port Fairy, Portland and Mt. Gambier is shown on page 752.

Mt. Gambier, Portland, Port Fairy and Warrnambool to Melbourne

Days of Operation	M-F (Bus)	M-F	Sat (Bus)	Sat	Sun (Bus)	Sun	M-Sat	M-F	Sat	Sun (Bus)	Sun	Sun (Bus)	Sat, Sun	M-F (Bus)	M-F
Mt. Gambier	0300*		0330				0820†			1325					
Heywood	0435		0505				1000†			1500					
Portland	0500		0530				1030†			1525				1620‡	
Port Fairy	0555		0627				1125†			1622				1705	
Warrnambool	0625	0638	0655	0705	0700		1200†	1225	1305	1250		1655	1705	1735	1745
Geelong		0855		0917	0950	1010		1435	1511	1550	1610		1920		2010
Melbourne		0953		1012		1114		1532	1606		1713		2017		2110

*Mondays only   † 15 – 25 minutes earlier on Saturdays   ‡ Fridays only

There is also one V-Line bus on weekdays from Warrnambool to Ballarat, and one bus a day, except on Saturdays, from Warrnambool to Hamilton and Casterton. On Fridays all year, and on Mondays in December and January, a bus runs along the Great Ocean Road to Apollo Bay, where it connects with a bus plus train service to Melbourne via Geelong. The timetable for this service is on page 774.

Bus Services from Warrnambool

Destination	Operator	Via	Distance (km)	Fare	Journey Time	Frequency
Mt. Gambier	V-Line		203	$34.40	2¼ - 2½ hrs	1/day
Apollo Bay	V-Line		167	$26.50	3¼ hrs	1/week
Ballarat	V-Line		185	$23.30	2¾ - 3 hrs	5/week
Casterton	V-Line		170	$17.60	2½ - 3¼ hrs	1/day
		Hamilton	109	$7.90	1½ - 2¼ hrs	1/day

BALLARAT
Population 83,000

1 hr 30 mins by train from Melbourne
1 hr 30 mins by bus from Melbourne

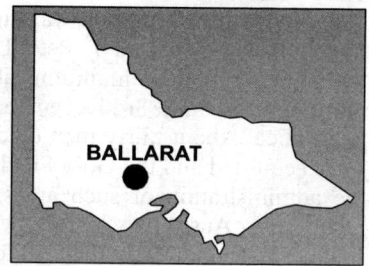

Gold, in a word, is the essence of Ballarat (originally spelt Ballaarat). That element was discovered here in 1851. Within a year, 20,000 miners had appeared from all over the world. The second largest nugget ever found in Australia, the *Welcome Nugget*, was discovered here by the Red Hill Mining Company on 15th June 1858, at a depth of 55 metres. It weighed 2,218 ounces (71.3 kg) and was assayed at over 99% pure gold. Now a gold-plated replica sits outside the Visitor Information Centre in Sturt Street.

Although McCafferty's, Greyhound and Firefly all run through Ballarat on their way between Melbourne and Adelaide, there are restrictions on the conveyance of passengers between Melbourne and here. Train is really the best way to reach Ballarat from Melbourne. The city can be visited as a day trip, but it deserves longer. An off-peak return fare from Melbourne on the train costs $24.90.

Ballarat, although only a century and a half old, exudes history. You will feel it and see it as soon as you start to walk from the railway station to the city centre and observe the wide stately streets and the buildings constructed in a period of opulence founded on the wealth brought by gold. The **Railway Station** itself is an example of this. It is an imposing building which used to serve this historic city and also act as a junction for country rail services to the borders of the state. The interstate train to Adelaide used to pass through every evening, as did the night service to Mildura. That has changed now, though. There is no longer a train to Mildura and the Adelaide service runs on a standard gauge track and so by-passes Ballarat, which is a broad gauge station. Therefore, Ballarat has become a terminus for passenger trains. No Victorian passenger rail services now operate west of here. However, the station is still busy, with ten trains a day to and from Melbourne and many V-Line bus operations, so its future seems assured for a while yet.

Sturt Street, in the centre of the city, is worthy of any historic location. In its centre is a wide strip of grass embellished with statues and rest places, leaving no doubt in one's mind that this city was once one of the most prosperous in Australia.

However, Ballarat is famous for much more than this, for it is a city which has shaped the social history of the country. The most famous event in its chronicles is not the discovery of gold, but the **Eureka Stockade Rebellion** which resulted, indirectly, from that discovery.

As in many goldfields in Australia, the conditions under which men laboured here were harsh. However, here the harshness came as much from the repressive and corrupt administration as from the difficulties imposed by nature. The authorities insisted that all miners must have licences and that the licences were to be checked twice a week. Then, in October 1854, a miner was kicked to death. Four men, including the owner of the Eureka Hotel, were tried and acquitted. There was general resentment with the decision and the Eureka Hotel was burnt down. In November, the Ballarat Reform League was inaugurated and the release of men held following the burning of the hotel was requested but refused. Many of the miners burnt their licences and, when a licence inspection was then ordered, they stoned the police, some of them being arrested. On

30th November, a petition was signed by five hundred miners, who swore therein to uphold their rights. Led by Peter Lalor, they then built a stockade and some went away to buy arms and ammunition, about 150 remaining in the stockade. Early in the morning of Sunday, 3rd December 1854, the Eureka Stockade was charged by soldiers and police. About thirty men died. In the subsequent trials of thirteen miners, twelve were acquitted and the Gold Fields Commission recommended widespread changes in the administration of such areas. Although a military failure, this, the only major rebellion in Australia's history, was a political victory for the miners. It was also the first occasion on which men had fought against authority under the flag of the Southern Cross, which is now the principal element in the Australian national flag. That original Southern Cross flag is now housed in the Fine Art Gallery in Ballarat. The Eureka Stockade Rebellion is a famous piece of Australian history and it now lies at the centre of many of the tourist offerings available in Ballarat. Peter Lalor, incidentally, went on to become an elected member of the Victorian House of Representatives and eventually its speaker.

The principal attraction of Ballarat is **Sovereign Hill**, a re-creation of a nineteenth century gold town. It is a fascinating place to visit, for it is not merely a museum of static pieces, but a town of living people who act out the parts given to them and learn to perform the trades of by-gone times. Sovereign Hill is built on the site of the original gold rush, and that was the richest discovery of alluvial gold in the history of the world. There is still gold here, of course, and one may search for it, but it comes in very limited quantities these days, especially with so many others searching for a few grains every day of the year. The main gold mine is found at the ticket office now, rather than in the soil. Nevertheless, there is so much to see that you can easily spend a whole day here. The characters in Sovereign Hill are all dressed for their parts in period costume. There are original or replica steam-driven machines, horses at work, shops of various types with wares on sale (including lunch and drinks). There is even overnight accommodation available, although not quite as primitive as it might well have been in that era. Sovereign Hill is open daily from 10:00 until 17:00 and admission costs $25. The admission ticket is valid for two days and includes admission to the nearby Gold Museum. There is also a ticket named the *Ballarat Welcome Pass* which costs $35, is valid for two days and includes Sovereign Hill, the Gold Museum, the Eureka Stockade Centre and the Ballarat Fine Art Gallery. Sovereign Hill is within walking distance of the town centre, the walk taking fifteen to twenty minutes. If you prefer a bus, take number 9 or 10 from the north side of Bridge Mall (Curtis Street), not far from the Visitor Information Centre. The ride takes five minutes.

Capitalising on the success of Sovereign Hill, the management now offers a second attraction, which is a Sound and Light Spectacle entitled ***Blood on the Southern Cross***, telling the story of the Eureka Stockade Rebellion. Since the reader has just read this story above, you will be able to save the sum of $30, or $55 if you had chosen to precede the entertainment with a buffet dinner. There are also tickets which allow entry to both Sovereign Hill and *Blood on the Southern Cross*. They are valid for two days and cost $50, or $75 with the buffet dinner. There are two performances of *Blood on the Southern Cross* every evening, but times vary according to the time of sunset.

The **Gold Museum** is just outside the Sovereign Hill complex and contains a valuable collection of gold nuggets, ornaments and coins. It is open daily from 9:30 until 17:20. If you visit separately, the cost is $7, but it is included in the cost of admission to Sovereign Hill.

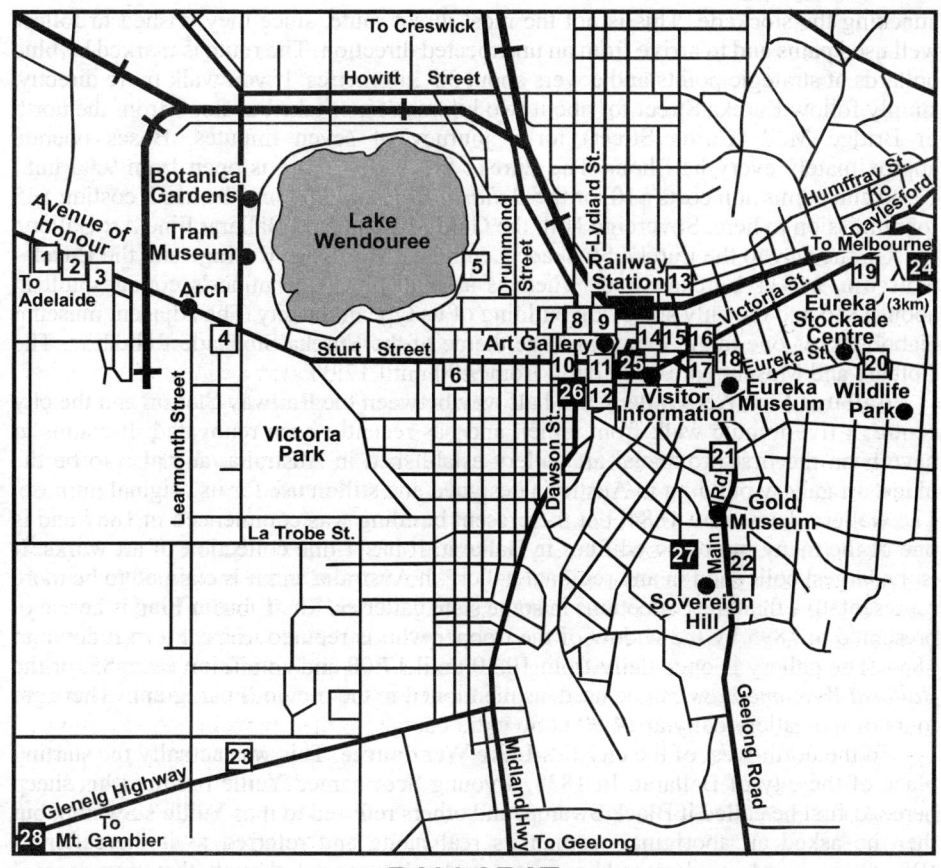

BALLARAT
Black numerals in white boxes indicate hotel accommodation
White numerals in black boxes indicate backpackers hostels

The **Eureka Stockade Centre** is built on the site of the Eureka Diggings and deals with the events of the Eureka Stockade Rebellion. The Centre's claim to be on the site of the actual rebellion, though, is true in only a general way. It is almost certainly not on the site of the actual stockade, because nobody is sure now where that was. Following the rebellion, it was quickly dismantled and, within a few years, almost forgotten. It was only in the 1880s that it was decided that the spot should be marked, and by then nobody could remember exactly where it had been. A **memorial** was erected, however, at the place thought most likely and for the next century and more its location has been disputed. A second site has been suggested more recently, and now opinion is divided. As a compromise, the Eureka Stockade Centre was constructed about half way between the two most likely locations, making it almost certain that it cannot be in quite the right place. It is, however, indisputably, in Eureka, and this is where the rebels lived and worked. This is a high technology centre, using various means of presentation of the events which took place here. Even the building has a distinctive modernistic appearance. It lies to the east of the city centre and can be reached, if so desired, by following the route which the government troops took when attacking the stockade. This is not the most direct route, since they wished to follow well used paths and to arrive from an unexpected direction. The route is marked by blue bollards at strategic points and covers about 3.5 kilometres. If you walk more directly, simply follow Eureka Street for about two kilometres, or take bus no. 8 from the north of Bridge Mall (Curtis Street) for a journey of seven minutes. Buses operate approximately every half hour. The Eureka Stockade Centre is open from 9:00 until 17:00 and admission costs $10, or the *Ballarat Welcome Pass* can be used, costing $35 for admission to here, Sovereign Hill, the Gold Museum and Ballarat Fine Art Gallery.

On the way to the Eureka Stockade Centre are **Montrose Cottage** and the **Eureka Museum**, at 111 Eureka Street. There is a small bluestone miner's cottage built in about 1856 and the only surviving building of its type in the city. The adjacent museum elaborates, as one might expect, on the theme of the Eureka Stockade Rebellion. The Cottage and Museum are open daily from 9:00 until 17:00.

Ballarat Fine Art Gallery lies half way between the Railway Station and the city centre, a five-minute walk from either, and has recently been renovated. It claims to have been the first provincial art gallery established in Australia, and also to be the oldest art gallery building in Australia designed and still in use for its original purpose. The Gallery dates from 1884, but the present building was commenced in 1887 and is one of the many imposing edifices in Ballarat. It has a fine collection of art works. It is the largest collection in any regional gallery in Australia and it is claimed to be more representative than the collections in some state galleries. The **Eureka Flag** is here too, presented in 1895 by the widow of the trooper who is reputed to have torn it down in 1854. The gallery is open daily from 10:30 until 17:00 and admission costs $5, or the *Ballarat Welcome Pass* can be used, as mentioned in the previous paragraph. There are tours of the gallery daily at 14:00 at no extra charge.

To the north-west of the city lies **Lake Wendouree**. This was actually the starting place of the city of Ballarat. In 1838, a young Scot named Yuille pastured his sheep here. At first he called it Black Swamp, and others referred to it as Yuille's Swamp, but then he asked an aboriginal woman its real name and referred to it thereafter as 'Wendouree', as he understood her answer to be. It turns out, though, that "wendaaree" means 'go away'. However, the name has stuck with the lake, and Wendouree it now is. The lake has had many changes since those days when it was indeed mostly swamp. In 1865 the first **paddle steamer** was launched on the lake and by the 1880s there were fifteen such vessels operating here. Only one remains today, but that one is available for occasional short rides.

In 1956, the Olympic Games were held in Melbourne and the rowing and canoeing events took place here, on Lake Wendouree. Here also are the **Botanical Gardens**, on the western side of the lake. The Gardens are free, but the **Conservatory**, open daily from 9:00 until 17:00, has a charge of $4. One of the unusual features of the gardens is the **bronze busts of all the Australian prime ministers**, from Edmund Barton, the first, in 1901, right up to date.

Ballarat used to have a municipal tram system. The trams started operating in 1887, with a small fleet of double-decker horse-drawn vehicles. When electric trams were introduced in 1905, the old horse-drawn vehicles were used as trailers at busy times. The trams operated until 1971, but usually ran at a loss, which forced the eventual closure of the system. However, a society was formed to preserve a small part of one of the routes and as many as possible of the vehicles used here and elsewhere. The part of the line which has survived is on the western side of Lake Wendouree and

tram rides are available on Saturdays, Sundays and summer Wednesdays between 12:00 and 17:00 over a short section of 1.3 kilometres. There is also a small Tram **Museum**. The trams which have been preserved include horse-drawn tram no. 1 and ten trams which originally ran in Melbourne some time between 1913 and 1951 but were transferred to Ballarat.

Near the western side of Lake Wendouree on Sturt Street is the **Arch of Victory** and the **Avenue of Honour**, which consisted originally of one tree planted for every soldier or sailor enlisted from Ballarat in the Great War. This was a total of 3,771 trees stretching 22 kilometres along the road. These were all planted by the staff of the local textile company of *E. Lucas* during the period 1917 to 1919. The money for the arch was raised by the same workers and it was opened by the Prince of Wales in 1920. Although there have been some changes, most of the trees survive, each bearing the name of the serviceman in whose honour it was planted.

Lake Wendouree too is within walking distance of the town centre, but if you prefer to take a bus, no. 15 operates from the south side of Bridge Mall (Little Bridge Street) approximately hourly and takes five minutes. The service does not run on Sundays, but instead there is one no. 9 bus which goes there, leaving the railway station at 11:00, Bridge Mall north side (Curtis Street) at 11:05 and Sovereign Hill at 11:10, and returning at 16:20. Route 1 also passes nearby, leaving from the south side of Bridge Mall (Little Bridge Street).

Ballarat Wildlife Park is to the east of the city, not far from the Eureka Stockade Centre. It was started in 1985 by Mr. Greg Parker, who still owns and operates the park, which contains all types of Australian native wildlife including kangaroos, koalas, wombats, crocodiles, Tasmanian devils and quokkas. The Wildlife Park is open daily from 9:00 until 17:30, with a tour available at 11:00. Admission costs $15. A bus no. 9 from the north side of Bridge Mall (Curtis Street) will take you there by a slightly indirect route in twelve minutes. Walking from the city centre would take half an hour.

Her Majesty's Theatre claims to be the oldest theatre in mainland Australia, having opened in 1875. It is located in Lydiard Street South in the city centre, and can be visited for a tour or just viewed from outside, or, of course, visited for a performance if one is available. The theatre showed films from 1911 until 1964, but is now used only for stage performances. It was renovated in the 1990s.

Twenty minutes north of Ballarat by bus is the town of **Creswick**. Gold was discovered here too in the mid nineteenth century and has left a legacy of **stately buildings**. At one time, Creswick had a population of 25,000, but now it is just a small country town. Two kilometres from the town centre is *Dinosaur World*, a park with statues of eighteen different breeds of dinosaur. There are also a small **wildlife park** and a **fossil museum**. *Dinosaur World* is open from 9:00 until 17:30 at weekends only. Admission costs $6.

Further along the same road is the *Tangled Maze*, a maze composed of flowering plants grown on trellises. The *Tangled Maze* is open daily from 10:00 until 17:30 and admission costs $7.

Creswick can be reached by bus no. 3, which departs from the south side of Bridge Mall (Little Bridge Street). Buses operate approximately every two hours on weekdays.

Beyond Creswick lie **Daylesford** and **Hepburn Springs**, centres of a spa area. Daylesford is also the headquarters of the **Central Highlands Tourist Railway** which operates every Sunday along a section of track which is the highest in Victoria. This is not a steam-operated service. It uses old diesel railcars.

786 VICTORIA

BOOKSHOPS

Ballarat Books   15 Armstrong Street North

ACCOMMODATION

Because of its lengthy history, Ballarat is a city with many old-style hotels offering accommodation in the central area at reasonable prices. Some of these are particularly good value. There is also a youth hostel which is part of the accommodation offered by Sovereign Hill.

(i) Hotel Accommodation in Ballarat

Name	Stars	No. on Map	Telephone No.	Address	Lowest Price (Double/Twin)
Ansonia	4½	12	03-5332-4678	32 Lydiard Street South	$145
Menzies Motor Inn	4½	15	1-800-100-210	5 Humffray Street	$135
Ballarat Lodge	4½	22	03-5331-3588	613 Main Road	$125
Mid-City Motor Inn	3½	8	1-800-355-145	19 Doveton Street North	$115
Victoriana Motor Inn	4	19	03-5333-3577	214 Victoria Street	$110
Bakery Hill Motel	3½	18	03-5333-1363	1 Humffray Street	$110
Sundowner	3½	21	1-800-654-576	312 Main Road	$105
Barkly Motor Lodge	3½	17	03-5331-8838	43 Main Road	$105
Central City Motor Inn	4	16	03-5331-1775	16 Victoria Street	$100
Ambassador Motor Inn	4	3	1-800-811-782	1759 Sturt Street	$90
The Views	3½	5	03-5331-4592	22 Wendouree Parade	$85
Park View Motor Inn	3½	4	1-800-673-369	1611 Sturt Street	$80
Peppinella Motel	3½	23	03-5335-9666	Glenelg Highway	$80
Avenue Motel		2	03-5334-1303	1813 Sturt Street	$80
Alfred Motor Inn		1	03-5334-1607	1843 Sturt Street	$75
Miner's Retreat Motel		20	1-800-100-106	604 Eureka Street	$70
George 2000 Hotel		9	03-5333-4866	27 Lydiard Street North	$70
Craig's Royal Hotel		11	03-5331-1451	10 Lydiard Street South	$65
Eastern Station Hotel	3	13	03-5338-8722	Humffray St. & Scott Pde.	$65
Golden City		10	03-5331-6211	Sturt & Dawson Streets	$65
Western Hotel		6	03-5332-2218	1221 Sturt Street	$55
Robin Hood Hotel		14	03-5331-3348	33 Peel Street North	$45
Lalor Bar and Bistro		7	03-5331-1702	Mair & Doveton Streets	$40

(ii) Backpackers Hostels in Ballarat

Name	Group	No. on Map	Telephone No.	Address	Lowest Price (Dormitory)
Eastern Station Hotel		13	03-5338-8722	Humffray St. & Scott Parade	$37
Criterion Hotel		26	03-5331-1451	18 Doveton Street South	$33
Western Hotel		6	03-5332-2218	1221 Sturt Street	$31
Lalor Bar and Bistro		7	03-5331-1702	Mair & Doveton Streets	$28
Robin Hood Hotel		14	03-5331-3348	Peel Street	$28
Rosella Cottage		28	03-5342-4352	699 Glenelg Highway	$22
Sovereign Hill Lodge	YHA	27	03-5333-3409	Magpie Street	$20
Melesa Motor Inn		24	03-5334-7503	Western Highway	$19
Irish Murphy's		25	03-5331-4091	36 Sturt Street	$18

BALLARAT

(iii) Backpackers Hostel in Daylesford

Name	Group	No. on Map	Telephone No.	Address	Lowest Price (Dormitory)
Wildwood Y.H.A.	YHA		03-5348-4435	42 Main Road, Daylesford	$21

MOVING ON
(i) By Train

Ballarat to Melbourne

Days of Operation	Weekday Timetable										
Ballarat	0515*	0600	0650	0753	0910	1005	1210	1335	1515	1625	1740*	1920
Melbourne	0700*	0725	0817	0923	1032	1131	1347	1507	1648	1800	1935*	2045

* By bus

Days of Operation	Saturdays							Sundays				
Ballarat	0515*	0655	0835	1025	1140	1520	1655	1805	0800	1115	1325	1535	1715	1930
Melbourne	0700*	0826	1005	1154	1303	1646	1829	1930	0925	1241	1453	1702	1842	2058

* By bus

(ii) By Bus

McCafferty's, Greyhound and Firefly all offer services to Adelaide, of which Firefly is generally the cheapest. V-Line provides rail services to Melbourne regularly throughout the day, and also buses to various other places in Victoria, as shown below. The service to Dimboola is at 10:10 (11:25 on Sundays) and connects there with the V-Line bus from Bendigo to Adelaide, arriving in Adelaide at 19:15 (20:00 on Sundays). It also connects at Stawell with the V-Line bus to Halls Gap.

Destination	Operator	Via	Distance (km)	Fare	Journey Time	Frequency
Melbourne	McCafferty's		167	$15	2½ hrs	1/day
		Geelong	70	$15	1¼ hrs	1/day
Melbourne	Greyhound		167	$15	1¾ hrs	1/day
Melbourne	V-Line		111	$17.60	1¾ - 2 hrs	2/day
Adelaide	McCafferty's		622	$65	8½ hrs	1/day
Adelaide	Greyhound		622	$65	8½ hrs	1/day
Adelaide	Firefly		622	$50	8¾ hrs	2/day
Dimboola	V-Line		224	$39.70	3 - 3½ hrs	2/day
Mt. Gambier	V-Line		322	$54.10	4 hrs	5/week
		Hamilton	175	$30.70	2¼ - 2¾ hrs	2/day
Warrnambool	V-Line		185	$23.30	3¼ hrs	5/week
Mildura	V-Line		506	$59	7 hrs	6/week
Bendigo	V-Line		124	$23.30	2¼ hrs	5/week

HORSHAM AND THE GRAMPIANS

Population 13,500 (Horsham)
Population 300 (Halls Gap)
4 hrs 30 mins by train from Melbourne (Horsham)
4 hrs by bus from Melbourne (Horsham)
4 hrs 30 mins by train and bus from Melbourne (Halls Gap)

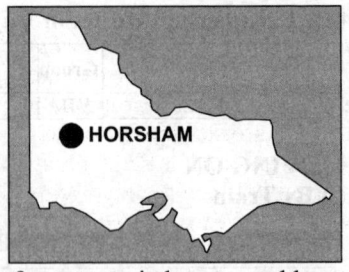

The Grampians constitute one of Victoria's areas of great scenic beauty, and have the advantage of being easily accessible. Apart from various tours which visit, a V-Line bus runs to Halls Gap every day from Stawell. This bus connects with train plus bus service from Melbourne. If you are travelling in the opposite direction, from Adelaide, though, there is no connexion with the V-Line bus service, or with the *Overland* train service, and you will need to spend a night in Stawell or Horsham, or in another nearby town such as Ararat or Ballarat.

Stawell, with a population of 7,000, at the foot of the Grampians, is famous for the **Stawell Gift**, a handicap race held each Easter over 120 metres (originally 130 yards) and offering huge prize money. The race has been held here since 1878 and is one of the oldest and richest such events in the world.

Gold was found in Stawell in 1853, and by 1857 there were 20,000 people living in the area. Over a period of sixty years, 58,000 tonnes of gold was produced. Although mining ceased for a period, it resumed in 1984 using improved technology and Stawell is currently Victoria's largest producer of gold. If you need to stay here, accommodation is available (see list below).

The journey from Stawell up to **Halls Gap** takes 35 minutes on the V-Line bus, a pretty ride with a steady ascent all the way. Halls Gap is named after the first man to discover a way through the mountains here, Charles Hall, in 1841. The small town has a permanent population of only about 300, but is usually host to a significant number of visitors. Indeed, it has little other reason for existence. Halls Gap is at an altitude of 250 metres and nestles in the beautiful **Fyans Valley** with mountains rising to 700 metres on each side of it.

The Grampians actually consist of four separate mountain ranges. The eastern boundary of the area which is now a National Park is comprised of the Mt. Difficult range to the north of Halls Gap and the Mt. William Range to its south, with Halls Gap, as its name suggests, in the gap. The Serra Range lies parallel to the Mt. William Range, but further west, while the Victoria Range forms the western boundary of the National Park.

Walking is the principal reason for visits to the Grampians National Park, but since there are ninety different tracks available, it is not necessary to be particularly fit nor to have a tent or any other equipment beyond a good pair of shoes and a water bottle in order to enjoy a walk here. There are some very rewarding half day walks, or even shorter jaunts.

The **Grampians National Park Visitor Centre** is located 2.5 kilometres south of Halls Gap and is open daily from 9:00 until 16:45. It has information on all the walks and maps of them. The fact that this Centre is visited by nearly 700 people per day gives some idea of the popularity of the area. Adjacent is the **Brambuk Aboriginal Cultural Centre**, which offers information on the history and culture of the local aborigines. It is open daily from 10:00 until 17:00, with free admission.

HORSHAM, GRAMPIANS

Three Walking Trails
(a) Boronia Peak Walk (9 km, 3 hrs)
   Although most of the walks start from the town of Halls Gap, here is one which can begin or end near the Visitor Centre. It is the Boronia Peak Walk and let us assume that we are starting from the Centre after obtaining our information. First walk to the Tandara Road Car Park, about one kilometre, then turn right, crossing Fyans Creek, and start uphill. See the map on page 791. **Boronia Peak** is at 537 metres and offers fine views. You can return to the town passing by **Mt. Ida**.

(b) Boroka Lookout Walk (13 km, 5 hrs)
   A walk which, although strenuous, should not be missed, is that to Boroka Lookout. Start from the National Park Information Point opposite the shops in Halls Gap and follow the path to the south of Mt. Victory Road. On your left you will see **Mackey's Peak** and then the **Elephant's Hide**, so named because of its rough texture and creased appearance, just like an elephant if you have ever examined one up close. Then you come to **Venus Baths**. You may hope for an opportunity to examine her up close too, but are destined to be unlucky, for she rarely seems to be at home. There is, however, a natural water hole here. Continue until you see a track on your right leading you back to Mt. Victory Road. Turn left at the road, and avoid taking the turning on the left to the car park. Then shortly on your right is the Boroka Lookout Trail. From here it is a steady climb, but well worth it when you get to the top. The only disappointment is that you have to come back the same way. Although there is a road to the lookout, to return by that route would be nearly twice as far.

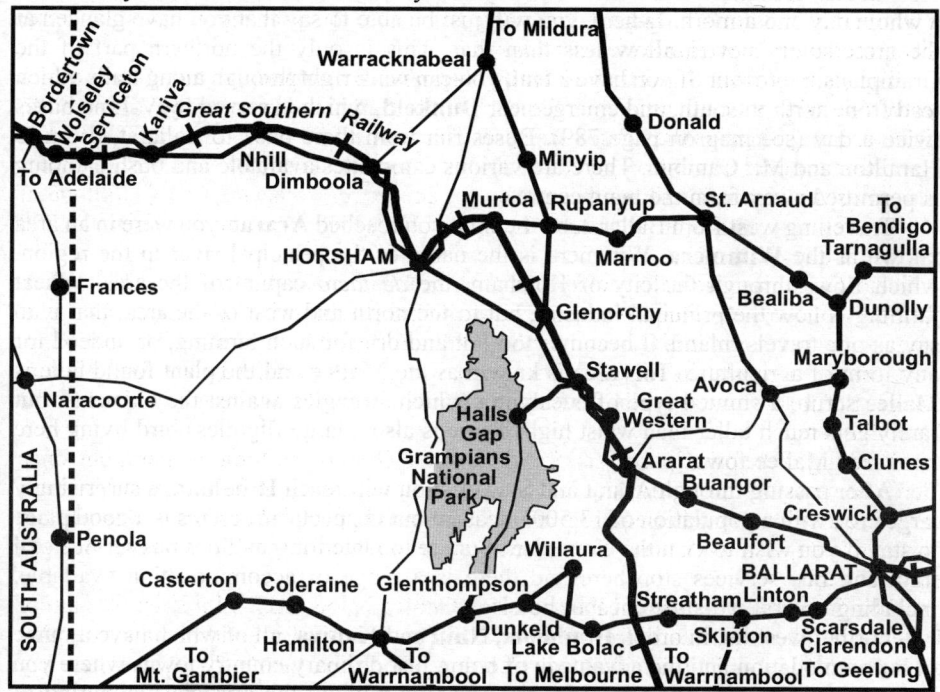

FROM BALLARAT TO BORDERTOWN
Thicker lines show V-Line bus routes

(c) Wonderland Loop (11 to 15 km, 4 hrs)

Another walk not to be missed is the Wonderland Loop Track. This is a popular walk, so you are not likely to be alone. Nevertheless, it has so many attractions that you really must do it while you are here. The start is as for the Boroka Lookout above. Pass Mackey's Peak, Elephant's Hide and Venus Baths, but then keep straight on to visit **Splitters Falls**. After a little back-tracking, continue to the Wonderland Car Park (not a great attraction), and then proceed through the **Grand Canyon** to a series of caves reached by minor deviations: the **Whale's Mouth**, **Cool Chamber** and **Echo Cave**. You will see **Lady's Hat**, and then come to **Silent Street**. Some more uphill work will lead to the **Pinnacle Lookout** at 686 metres, offering another impressive view. From here, do not simply return along the loop track. Go on (right) to the **Fallen Giant** and the **Nerve Test**. You will regret it if you do not do this, and you will also miss the opportunity for the best photograph of your visit here. When you reach the Nerve Test, you will see why it is so called. Do you have the nerve? It is certainly a disconcerting feeling to be standing on this rock with nothing visible to prevent a precipitous descent. After this experience, you may decide your route of return. You may return to the Pinnacle and take the loop track past **Signal Peak** (the quickest), or you may swing right and return via **Turret Falls**, or you may go on to **Devil's Gap** and then turn left and descend to near the Visitor Centre. Other options are available too, if you are still full of energy. See the map opposite.

There are many other walking tracks too, of course, but the above are three of the most accessible and scenic. You will easily see that if you allow yourself an afternoon, a whole day and a morning here, you will just be able to say that you have glanced at the area, so try not to allow less than that. This is only the northern part of the Grampians, moreover. If you have a tent, you can walk right through along trails which lead from north to south, and emerge near **Dunkeld**, which is served by V-Line buses twice a day (see map on page 789). Buses run from there back to Ballarat, or on to Hamilton and Mt. Gambier. There are various camp sites available and bush camping is permitted away from the main centres.

Travelling west from Ballarat, by the time you reached **Ararat**, you were in an area known as the **Wimmera**. Wimmera is the name of the principal river in the region, which flows through the city of Horsham, the *de facto* capital of the area. Wheat farming is now the principal industry, but to the north and west of the area, that is to say as one travels inland, it becomes too hot and dry for such farming, or, indeed for any form of agriculture. This area is known as the **Mallee** and the plant found here is Mallee scrub, a stunted type of eucalyptus which struggles against the elements, but rarely gets much taller than waist high. There is also a large flightless bird living here known as Mallee fowl.

After passing through Ararat and Stawell, you will reach **Horsham**, a surprisingly large city, with a population of 13,500, pleasant but unspectacular. This is a good place to stay if you wish to visit the Grampians but are too late for that day's bus service. All train and bus services stop here and there is a range of accommodation available, including several old-style cheaper hotels.

Further west lie, in order, **Dimboola, Nhill** and **Kaniva**, all of which have a range of accommodation and the advantage of being just ordinary country towns where you can easily experience the taste of rural Australia without the artificial flavouring of tourism. **Nhill** has a population of 2,500. Its name comes from an aboriginal word

HORSHAM, GRAMPIANS

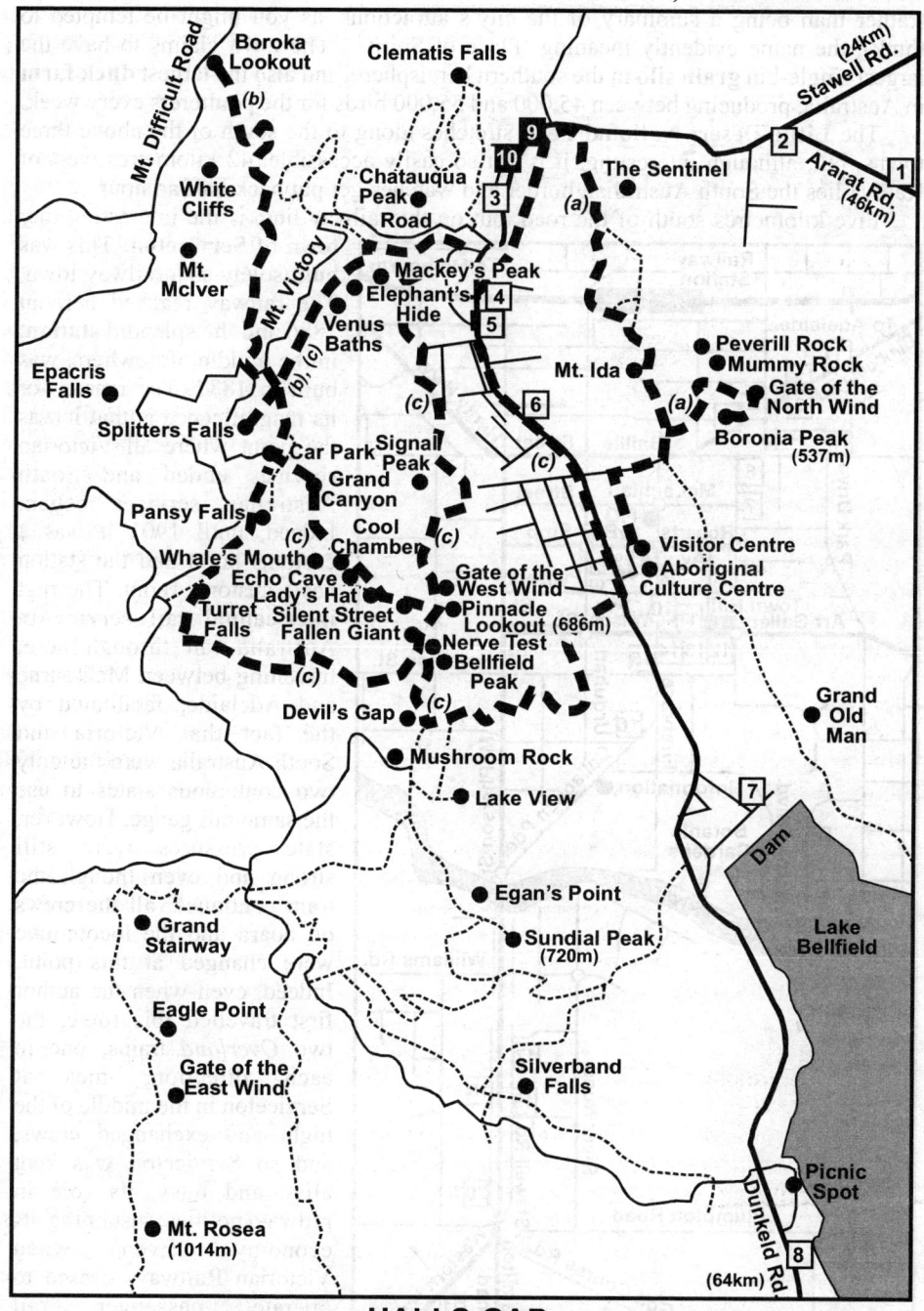

HALLS GAP

Thicker dashed lines show suggested Walking Trails
Black numerals in white boxes indicate hotel accommodation
White numerals in black boxes indicate backpackers hostels

(rather than being a summary of the city's attractions, as you might be tempted to think), the name evidently meaning 'Place of Spirits'. The town claims to have the largest single-bin **grain silo** in the southern hemisphere, and also the largest **duck farm** in Australia, producing between 45,000 and 55,000 birds for the poulterers every week.

The **Little Desert National Park** stretches along to the south of the above three towns, but, although interesting, it is not so easily accessible. 42 kilometres west of Kaniva lies the South Australian border and watches get put back half an hour.

Five kilometres south of the road, but on the railway line, is the interesting tiny town of **Serviceton**. This was built solely as a railway town. The railway reached here in 1886 and the splendid **station**, in the middle of nowhere, was built in 1887. The reason for its magnificence is that it was the point where all Victorian services ended and South Australian services began. Indeed, until 1901 it was a customs point and the station has a customs room. The first inter-capital rail service in Australia ran through here, travelling between Melbourne and Adelaide, facilitated by the fact that Victoria and South Australia were the only two contiguous states to use the same rail gauge. However, state pressures were still strong and even though the train continued, all the crews on board and the locomotive were changed at this point. Indeed, even when the author first travelled this route, the two *Overland* trains, one in each direction, met at Serviceton in the middle of the night and exchanged crews, and so Serviceton was kept alive and busy, its role in railway politics sustaining its economy. Even when Victorian Railways ceased to operate passenger rail services, except the *Overland*, beyond Dimboola, the bus

HORSHAM
Numerals indicate accommodation

service provided instead used to terminate at the few houses and magnificent railway station of Serviceton.

In 1986, however, economics overcame politics and Serviceton Station was closed and started to fall into disrepair. Fortunately, it has now been restored and opened as a museum, its main problem being that nobody goes there now that the station is no longer open. However, the museum is open sometimes at the weekends, or on request. Admission costs $3 and the number to telephone to see when or whether it will be open is 03-5393-1220. However, there is no accommodation in Serviceton or nearby (see anecdote on page 726).

ACCOMMODATION

Halls Gap is a popular location, and the time not to visit is at weekends. Not only will it be crowded then, but also accommodation prices will be higher, as they will be during school holidays. The rates given below are for weekdays. Add about 25% for weekends. The backpackers hostels, though, do not have seasonal variations, although they will be more crowded at the weekends. Tim's Other Place arranges transport from Melbourne or Adelaide and this is a good way to reach here, especially if you plan to stay at the pleasant hostel just outside the town. Tim also has a 'Place'. Tim's Place is in the countryside near Horsham, and transport to that too can be arranged. Use the telephone number given below.

An accommodation list is provided for Stawell as well as for Horsham. Horsham is much larger than Stawell and has a good choice of older hotels for the budget traveller, but Stawell also has such accommodation and is a pleasant small town with an interesting history.

(i) Hotel Accommodation in Halls Gap

Name	Stars	No. on Map	Telephone No.	Address	Lowest Price (Double/Twin)
Halls Gap Motel	3½	6	03-5356-4209	Grampians Road	$110
Colonial Motor Inn	4	8	1-800-680-848	Grampians Road	$105
Mountain View Motor Inn	3½	1	03-5356-4364	Ararat Road	$95
Pinnacle Holiday Lodge	3½	4	1-800-819-283	Heath Street	$90
Grand Canyon Motel	3	3	03-5356-4280	Grampians Road	$85
Kookaburra Lodge Motel	3½	5	03-5356-4395	14 Heath Street	$85
Grampians Gardens Motel	2	2	03-5356-4244	Ararat & Stawell Roads	$60
Lakeside Caravan Park	4	7	03-5356-4281	Tymna Drive	$50

(ii) Backpackers Hostels in Halls Gap

Name	Group	No. on Map	Telephone No.	Address	Lowest Price (Dormitory)
Tim's Other Place		10	03-5356-4288	Grampians Road	$22
Grampians Eco-Hostel	YHA	9	03-5356-4544	Buckler St. & Grampians Rd.	$20

(iii) Accommodation in Stawell

Name	Stars	Telephone No.	Address	Lowest Price (Double/Twin)
Magdala Motor Lodge	3½	03-5358-3877	Western Highway	$105
Goldfields Motor Inn	3½	1-800-355-166	Western Highway	$100
Stawell Holiday Cottages	3	03-5358-2868	Lot 1, Errington Road	$75
Coorrabin Motor Inn	3	03-5358-3933	7 Longfield Street	$65
Stawell Motel	3	03-5358-2041	21 Longfield Street	$65
Central Park Motel	2½	03-5358-4055	3 Seaby Street	$60
Diamond House	3	03-5358-3366	24 Seaby Street	$60
Hi-Way Eight Motor Inn	3½	03-5358-2411	28 Longfield Street	$60
London Motor Inn	2½	03-5358-2200	10 Horsham Road	$60

VICTORIA

(iv) Accommodation in Horsham

Name	Stars	No. on Map	Telephone No.	Address	Lowest Price (Double/Twin)
Golden Grain Motor Inn	4	5	1-800-032-253	6 Dimboola Road	$120
May Park Motor Inn	3½	6	1-800-032-905	2 Darlot Street	$115
Country City Motor Inn	4	16	1-800-808-490	11 O'Callaghan Parade	$110
Mid City Court Motel	4	7	1-800-033-141	14 Darlot Street	$110
Major Mitchell Motor Inn	3½	15	1-800-355-152	109 Firebrace Street	$105
Town House Motel	3½	9	1-800-012-025	31 Roberts Avenue	$105
Westlander Motor Inn	3½	21	1-800-809-970	Western Highway	$85
Ploughman's Motor Inn		2	03-5382-5944	22 Dimboola Road	$80
Wheatfields Motel	2	20	03-5382-4555	71 Stawell Road	$70
Horsham Motel	3	3	03-5382-5555	5 Dimboola Road	$70
Majestic Motel	2½	19	1-800-036-134	58 Stawell Road	$65
Glynlea Motel	3	17	03-5382-0145	26 Stawell Road	$65
Darlot Motor Inn	3	18	03-5381-1222	47 Stawell Road	$60
Smerdon Lodge	2½	1	03-5382-3123	42 Dimboola Road	$60
Wilson's Hotel		13	03-5382-0166	67 Wilson Street	$55
Bull and Mouth Hotel		12	03-5382-1057	83 Wilson Street	$55
Commercial Hotel		11	03-5382-1056	68 Wilson Street	$55
Exchange Hotel		10	03-5382-1095	100 Firebrace Street	$55
White Hart Hotel		8	03-5382-1231	55 Firebrace Street	$55
Victoria Hotel		4	03-5382-1162	16 Dimboola Road	$55
Royal Hotel	1	14	03-5382-1255	132 Firebrace Street	$40

MOVING ON

(i) By Train

Note that the *Overland* train probably no longer stops at Stawell (although you could try asking). It is timetabled to call at Ararat to the east and Horsham to the west. Timetables appear on pages 643 and 751.

(ii) Bus Service from Halls Gap

The only public transport from Halls Gap is the daily V-Line bus to Stawell, as shown below.

Destination	Operator	Via	Distance (km)	Fare	Journey Time	Frequency
Stawell	V-Line		25	$9.40	35 mins	1/day

(iii) Bus Services from Horsham

The same buses as below will also pass through Stawell, except the service to Bendigo. Travelling times from Stawell will be half an hour shorter to Melbourne and half an hour longer to Adelaide. Some intra-state travel restrictions apply.

Destination	Operator	Via	Distance (km)	Fare	Journey Time	Frequency
Melbourne	McCafferty's		353	$51	5¼ hrs	1/day
Melbourne	Greyhound		353	$51	4½ hrs	1/day
Melbourne	Firefly		353	$50	4½ hrs	2/day
Melbourne	V-Line		298	$51.70	4¼ - 5 hrs	4/day
		Ballarat	187	$34.40	2½ - 3 hrs	4/day
Adelaide	McCafferty's		436	$65	5¾ hrs	1/day
Adelaide	Greyhound		436	$65	5½ hrs	1/day
Adelaide	Firefly		436	$50	5¾ hrs	2/day
Adelaide	V-Line		436	$59	5¾ hrs	1/day
		Dimboola	38	$5.80	30 mins	3/day
Bendigo	V-Line		220	$26.50	2¾ - 3 hrs	1/day

BENDIGO
Population 78,000

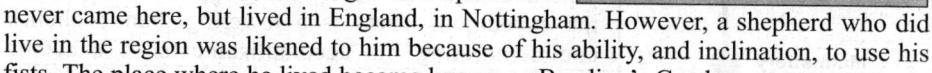

2 hrs by train from Melbourne

Bendigo too is a city built on gold. It is a city of stately buildings, pleasant parks and history, with a current population of 78,000.

The name of the city supposedly originates from a bare fist boxer, 'Bendigo' Thompson. He never came here, but lived in England, in Nottingham. However, a shepherd who did live in the region was likened to him because of his ability, and inclination, to use his fists. The place where he lived became known as Bendigo's Creek.

Gold was discovered here in 1851 and, as in many such places in Australia, diggers rushed here in their thousands. A town grew up and was given a name, but that name was not Bendigo. Originally it was known as Sandhurst, with the name being changed to Bendigo only in 1891. Gold mining continued here for a century, until 1954, and a total of 22 million ounces of gold was extracted from the ground.

The way to reach Bendigo is by train, with services operating from Melbourne a little less frequently than hourly. The timetable is shown on page 753. There is also a direct V-Line bus service from Adelaide every day. Bendigo is another city which can be visited from Melbourne as a day trip, but which really deserves longer. An off-peak return costs $37, but there is a good range of accommodation, so why not make it a stop on the way to somewhere else?

Travelling up by train, a two-hour journey from the state capital, you will pass through attractive rural scenery, and there are other places on the way worth a stop, although time usually precludes visiting every attractive spot in the country.

Macedon and **Woodend** are in a pretty area. The small town of Woodend, in particular, is at the foot of Mt. Macedon and well known for its old-world character.

Not far away is **Hanging Rock** in the Macedon Ranges, a location made famous by the book and film *Picnic at Hanging Rock*. The Rock is covered with vegetation at the base, but its peak rises bare above the otherwise green landscape, 105 metres higher than the surrounding land. It is actually a small volcano about six million years old, with steep sides and a high concentration of soda in the unusual rock formations. It was reputedly used as a refuge by bushrangers in earlier times, there being various caves at its base. It is now part of a State Reserve and is home to a considerable amount of native Australian wildlife, especially birds (but not, as far as we know, to lost schoolgirls). Various events are held here, including two famous and well patronised horse race meetings on New Year's Day and Australia Day (26th January). These meetings have been held since 1880. A third meeting is held on one of the Sundays in March. The Rock can be climbed and offers a good view from its summit. There is also a new Discovery Centre telling about the history and myth of the Rock. The problem with Hanging Rock is that there is no regular public transport to it, except when a special event is taking place. The nearest station is Woodend, but from there it is approximately eight kilometres to Hanging Rock. Although the Rock has become famous, you will probably find that there is not a great feeling of mystery to it when you actually visit, nor is there any evidence that the events in book and film had any factual basis. However, it is a pleasant enough spot for a picnic.

From Woodend, it is also possible to reach the spa centre of **Daylesford**,

796   VICTORIA

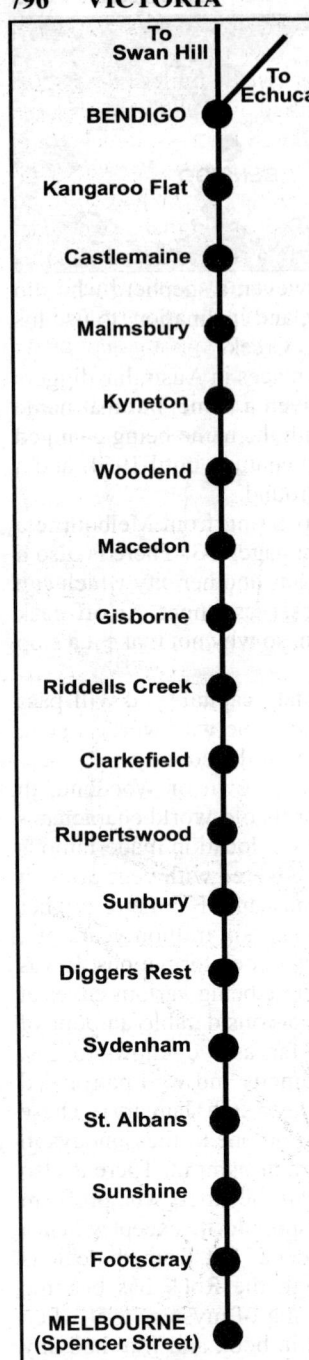

FROM MELBOURNE TO BENDIGO BY TRAIN

mentioned in the section on Ballarat. There is a youth hostel in Daylesford (see page 787). V-Line buses operate twice a day from Woodend to Daylesford, currently at 9:40 and 17:45 on weekdays.

Castlemaine is another splendid old gold town, reached 25 minutes before Bendigo on the railway. Robert O'Hara Burke, the leader of the famous Burke and Wills Expedition (see page 700), was a police superintendent here before being appointed as head of the expedition. There is a towering granite obelisk commemorating his accomplishments in a scenic location overlooking the town. In fact, though, most of what can be seen in Castlemaine can also be seen in Bendigo, so perhaps we should continue and explore that fascinating city.

Bendigo is another city with a fine old under-used **railway station**, but fortunately this one is not the absolute terminus for Victoria's truncated rail services. Somehow the line on to Swan Hill has managed to survive the cuts of recent years and still has one train every day, which is all that it has ever had in recent times. Moreover, in an impressive reversal of policy, a rail service has been re-introduced between Bendigo and Echuca on the Murray River. True, this service operates only twice a week, on Friday and Sunday evenings, to cater for weekend visitors, but it is a start, and the revived service is well patronised, so maybe we can hope for more in the future.

Let us start with a walking tour of Bendigo, to see some of its magnificent buildings.

Walking Tour

This walk covers approximately four kilometres and can be expected to take about ninety minutes.

We start at the fountain in the centre of the city, at a spot known as **Charing Cross**. If arriving at the Railway Station, simply follow the access road (Railway Place) to Mitchell Street and walk downhill. The fountain is straight ahead of you. **Alexandra Fountain** was opened on 5th July 1881 and was named after the Princess of Wales of the time.

Turn right and on your left is the **R.S.L. Memorial Hall**, with a roll of honour commemorating all the servicemen from Bendigo who died in the Great War. As you look at it, you are standing on top of the **Hustlers Royal Reserve No. 2 Mine**. There is a shaft beneath stretching down 51 metres and from the ground here, in the heart of the city, came 5,521 ounces of gold.

The shaft is now full of water and the overflow is drained out into Bendigo Creek at the rear of the Hall.

On the opposite side of the road is the **Beehive Store**, originally built in the 1850s, but the current building dates from 1871 and was modified in 1988. Next is the **Colonial Bank Gallery** and Mully's Café, housed in the former Colonial Bank Building constructed in 1887. Then comes **Myer's Department Store**. The very first Myer's shop, a drapery, was opened in Bendigo in 1900. Sidney Myer had come to Australia as a twenty-year-old Russian immigrant unable to speak English. Two years later, he and his brother opened their first store in Bendigo. In a further decade Sidney Myer was a rich man, but one who gave much of his wealth to charity and, on his death in 1934, was found to have bequeathed a large portion of his money to a trust which continues to benefit the people of Victoria, including, for example, giving support to the Bendigo Art Gallery.

Back on the northern side of the road is a statue of **George Lansell**, one of the most

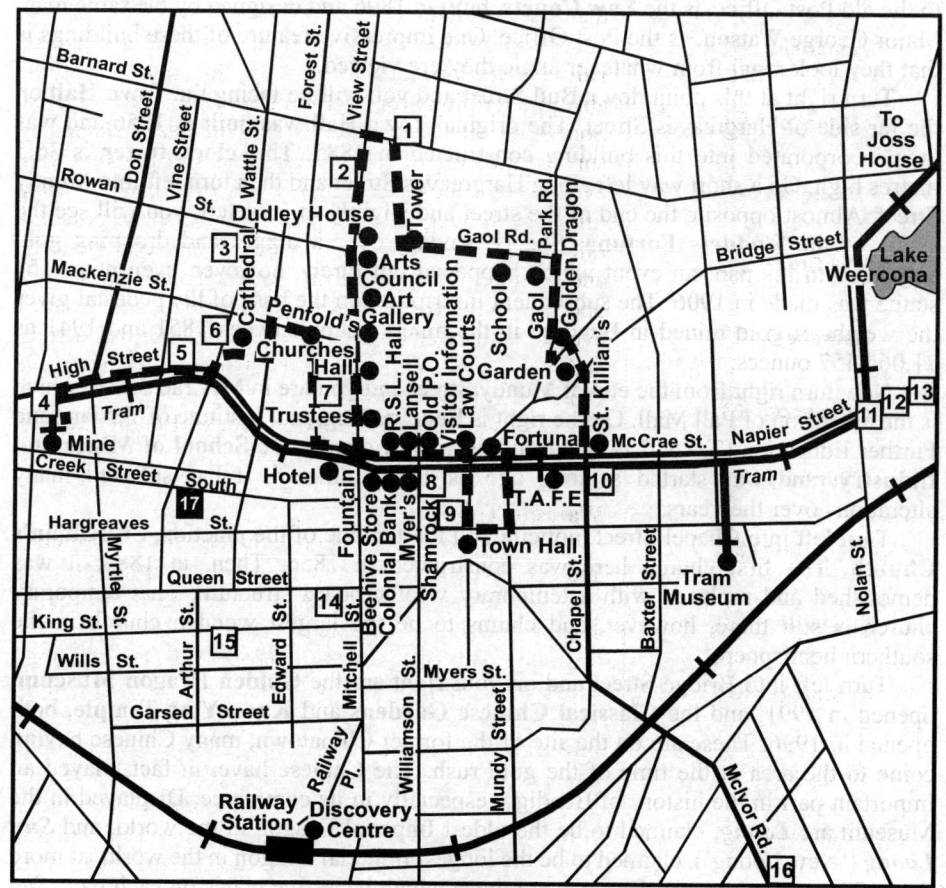

BENDIGO
Dashed line shows Walking Tour
Black numerals in white boxes indicate hotel accommodation
White numerals in black boxes indicate backpackers hostels

successful mine owners here. He operated seven different gold mines and is credited with having done much to establish the prosperity of Bendigo. The relief carving on the monument depicts the evolution of mining in the city as the gold became more difficult to reach.

Next is the **Old Post Office**, the grand building which one might expect. It now houses the **Visitor Information Centre**, which therefore claims the most splendid such premises in Australia. The building was opened on 30th September 1887 and incorporates a **clock tower** standing 43 metres.

Opposite, facing onto Williamson Street, is the **Shamrock Hotel**. It was originally the Exchange Hotel, but was renamed in 1855, since when it has been rebuilt twice. The present building, dating from 1897, was threatened with demolition in the 1970s, but was eventually reprieved and renovated, and is now a good counterbalance to the splendid constructions on the other side of the wide street which is here known as **Pall Mall**, a title as dignified as the edifices themselves. The next of those edifices, adjacent to the old Post Office, is the **Law Courts**, built in 1896 and designed by the same man, Major George Watson, as the Post Office. One impressive feature of these buildings is that they look regal from whatever angle they are viewed.

Turn right at this point down Bull Street and you will be facing the **Town Hall** on the far side of Hargreaves Street. The original Town Hall was built in 1856 and was then incorporated into this building constructed in 1885. This **clock tower** is 36.5 metres high. Go a short way left along Hargreaves Street and then turn left into Mundy Street. Almost opposite the end of the street and slightly to your left, you will see the statue of the **Goddess Fortuna**. She is bending over a digger and dropping gold nuggets into his pan, an event which happened but rarely, however, even here. The statue was made in 1906. The subsequent inscription on the base of the pedestal gives the weight of gold mined in Bendigo in the ninety years between 1851 and 1941 as 21,064,457 ounces.

Now turn right from the end of Mundy Street and you are in McCrae Street, which is the extension of Pall Mall. On the right is Bendigo Regional Institute of Tertiary and Further Education (T.A.F.E.). This building was originally the **School of Mines and Industry**, and was started as long ago as 1864, although it has suffered many alterations over the years.

Turn left into Chapel Street, noticing, on the far side of the junction, **St. Killian's Church**. The first church here was constructed in 1856. Then, in 1888, it was demolished and replaced with a temporary weatherboard structure. That temporary church is still there, however, and claims to be the largest wooden church in the southern hemisphere.

Turn left into Bridge Street and on your right are the **Golden Dragon Museum**, opened in 1991, and the **Classical Chinese Gardens** and **Kuan Ying Temple**, both opened in 1996. These are on the site of the former Chinatown, many Chinese having come to the area at the time of the gold rush. The Chinese have, in fact, played an important part in the history of Bendigo, especially in its commerce. Displayed in the Museum are *Loong*, claimed to be the oldest Imperial Dragon in the world, and *Sun Loong* ('New Loong'), claimed to be the longest Imperial Dragon in the world, at more than 100 metres. Imperial Dragons are those which have five claws on each paw. *Sun Loong* takes part in the annual procession at the Bendigo Easter Fair, but *Loong* is now in retirement and drawing his pension, so he comes out only for very special occasions. The walled Garden is opposite the Museum, and both Museum and Garden are open from 9:30 until 17:00 daily. Admission to both costs $8, while admission to the garden only costs $2.50. There are also a souvenir shop and restaurant, which can be used without obtaining admission to the Museum.

Now turn right into Park Street, which, reasonably enough, follows round beside **Rosalind Park**, apparently named after the Shakespearean character in *As You Like It*. Turn left into Gaol Road, finding on the corner, as you might anticipate, the **Gaol**. It was completed in 1862 and is still in use. **Camp Hill School**, beyond the Gaol, was built in 1878 and the **tower** was used as a lookout by the Fire Brigade.

Now enter the park and aim for the **Lookout Tower**. Rosalind Park covers 66 acres and was reserved for use as a public park as long ago as 1857. The lower part of the park, near where we started our walk, was the scene of the city's last gold rush. Prior to that, it had been the Government Camp and nobody had liked to dig up the camp while the government officers were ensconced there. The Lookout Tower is a gift from the *Bendigo Amalgamated Company* (a mining company) and has been standing here since 1931. Look at the **mosaic** (which is recent) at its base and then climb the 124 steps for a view of the city.

Now head towards the Oval and turn left into Barnard Street, then left again into View Street. On your left is **Dudley House**, built in 1859 and the oldest government building in Bendigo. It was the Lands and Survey Office, but is now the Bendigo Historical Society. Just beyond is the **Old Fire Station**, built in 1887, and now the Arts Council Building. Then the former **Masonic Temple**, built in 1874, now the Bendigo Regional Arts Centre. It has a magnificent portico eighteen metres high, supported by ten-metre Corinthian columns. The **Art Gallery** just beyond was built in 1867 and was originally the Volunteer Rifle Brigade Orderly Room. Admission to the Art Gallery is by donation.

Continuing down the street, you can find **Penfold's Fine Art Gallery**, in a building constructed in 1879 for Dr. Oliver Penfold, who was the cousin of the founder of Penfold's Wines. Then, suitably enough, comes the **Temperance Hall**, built in 1895, and **Sandhurst Trustees Building**, built as the Sandhurst Post Office in 1869 and used until the new Post Office was opened in 1887. Sandhurst Trustees have been using the building since 1891.

We are now back at Alexandra Fountain, but we have not quite finished yet. Turn right and see on your left the **City Family Hotel**, built in 1872. The building used to have fine verandahs, but they have gone. Take the next road on the right, Forest Street, and walk up to the junction with MacKenzie Street. This is a religious corner, with four different churches here. **All Saints** Anglican Church, on the far side, has the distinction of being the oldest church in Bendigo. Turn left here, and one more block will lead to the corner of the **Cathedral**. This building was started in 1897, but not completed until 1977, due to a shortage of money. It is another splendid building, but you will discover just how difficult it is to get a good photograph of it. The sun always seems to be at the wrong angle, while from High Street telegraph wires detract from the view.

Turn left into Short Street and right into High Street, deviating to look inside the Cathedral if so desired. Five minutes walk will bring you to the **Central Deborah Mine**. This old gold mine is now open for **tours**, either tours of the surface equipment plus museum, or tours underground. The former cost $20. The latter, which last for two hours, cost $50 including morning or afternoon 'crib' (tea), or $60 including lunch or dinner. Here our walking tour ends. You can stroll back to Alexandra Fountain along the High Street in ten minutes.

By this time, you will not have failed to notice that Bendigo has the remnants of a **tram system**. The trams were introduced in June 1890. The first ones were battery operated, but that was not a success, so steam trams were used until overhead electric power came in 1903. The tram system ran until 1972 and then, when it was closed, the trams were immediately taken over by a group of enthusiasts, so that there was no appreciable break in operations. However, the new service covered only a part of one line and had the tourist market as its aim. So it remains. The *Talking Trams* operate approximately every half hour from 10:00 until 16:00 and provide a recorded commentary on board. The western terminus is the Central Deborah Mine and the eastern terminus is the Joss House. The real problem with this service is the price, for it costs $15 for an all-day ticket, including a tour of the **Tram Museum**, which is housed in the Tram Depot, just off the main line running along McCrae Street. Bendigo managed to retain all of its trams when normal operations ceased in 1972, and has purchased some more from other sources since, so the depot is now quite crowded and the Tram Museum interesting. Even so, $15 is a lot to pay for travel, albeit unlimited for the day, along a line the length of which one can walk without excessive fatigue within an hour. The only other type of ticket currently available is a combination of unlimited trams and the surface part of the Central Deborah Mine. This costs $30, an overall saving of $5.

There are some attractions which were not on the route of our walk, of course. One of these is the **Joss House**, the vernacular name given to the Chinese Temple. The Joss House dates back to the 1860s and consists of three parts: the Temple itself, the caretaker's house and the Ancestral Hall. The old red-painted building has been restored recently and is open from 10:00 until 17:00 (16:00 in winter). Admission costs $4. To reach the Joss House, just follow the tram lines. It is a walk of about three kilometres from the town centre. If that is too far, you can take a bus no. 7 from a stop in Hargreaves Street, near the junction with Mitchell Street.

The **Discovery Centre** is next to the Railway Station and is a high-technology science museum appealing primarily to children. It is open daily from 10:00 until 17:00 and admission costs $10.

Bendigo offers a combination ticket known as the *Welcome Stranger Pass*, giving admission to seven attractions. This is a little deceptive, though, as some of them are free anyway. The seven offered are the Central Deborah Gold Mine, the Trams, the Art Gallery, the Discovery Centre, the Golden Dragon Museum, Bendigo Pottery and *Living Wings and Things*. If you really want to see all of these, you will obtain a small discount by purchasing the ticket for $50, but otherwise it might be cheaper just to pay for what you want. The **Bendigo Pottery** claims to be Australia's oldest working pottery and incorporates a number of historic buildings and gardens, and a museum. You can also watch potters at work and purchase items. The Pottery is open daily from 9:00 until 17:00 and admission is free. ***Living Wings and Things*** is at the same site and is a collection of living butterflies, birds and reptiles. The Bendigo Pottery site is 6.5 kilometres to the north-east of Bendigo. To reach it, you will need to take a bus no. 8, which leaves from Mitchell Street between Hargreaves Street and Queen Street. Services are approximately hourly on weekdays.

Bendigo has a reasonable network of buses, operated by two different companies. Tickets are interchangeable and permit unlimited travel for two hours for the price of $1.50. There are thirteen routes (nos. 1 to 14, but no no. 10) and they all leave from either Mitchell Street or Hargreaves Street in the city centre. Services are reduced on

Saturdays, and on Sundays there are very few buses.

Various other towns around Bendigo also have rich gold mining history. Castlemaine has already been mentioned. Another nearby location is **Maldon**, lying south-west of Bendigo. Here the old branch railway from Castlemaine is being restored. **Steam trains** already operate on Sundays and Wednesdays over eight kilometres of track each way, and it is hoped that eventually the line will reach all the way to Castlemaine again. There is a bus which operates twice a day, morning and afternoon, between Castlemaine and Maldon (Tel: 136-196). The single fare is $7 from Bendigo, or $3 from Castlemaine. The morning service from Castlemaine connects with the arrival of the train which leaves Melbourne at 8:40. However, the bus runs only on weekdays.

Another way to have a look at this string of interesting towns, many now little more than ghost towns, is to travel between Melbourne and Adelaide on the daily V-Line service, by taking the 8:40 train from Melbourne to Bendigo and changing there to the V-Line bus to Adelaide (see the map on page 789 for part of this route). This bus will first pass through **Tarnagulla**, which once thrived on gold, the population in the area having been around 20,000. The town is now just a single street, however. Mullock heaps can be seen through the sparse bush on either side of the bus route, the remains of workings a century or more ago.

In **Dunolly**, the next town on the bus route, the anvil is on display which was used to break up the famous *Welcome Stranger* gold nugget because it was too big to be weighed on the bank scales. The *Welcome Stranger* was found on 5th February 1869 near **Moliagul**, about fifteen kilometres to the north-west of Dunolly. The nugget was about 3 centimetres below the surface of the ground, in the roots of a tree. It weighed approximately 2,316 ounces (72 kilograms), and, although there is now some slight disagreement about the precise weight, it was certainly the largest known gold nugget in the world. Another large nugget, the *Schlemm Nugget*, was also found in Dunolly, this time on 11th November 1872. It weighed 538 ounces.

The bus will also pass through **St. Arnaud**, a fascinating little town of old pubs, also built up by gold, but now starting to thrive on its history. If you travel between Melbourne and Adelaide using one of the major long-distance bus companies, you will certainly get there more quickly, possibly even more comfortably, but you will not pass through so many places of interest. This route is worth trying.

BOOKSHOPS
Dymocks Bendigo 1 - 3 Mitchell Street

ANECDOTE

There is a story that when repairs were being carried out on a store in Dunolly in 1947, four boxes were discovered under the floor boards with gold nuggets in them. It was then suspected that they were the remains from a bank robbery or stage-coach hold-up, since the boxes were marked with the name of a bank. However, the bank was no longer in existence and, in the end, its successors could find no record of such a robbery and therefore no reason to attempt a claim for the gold. Presumably the store-keeper retired, or perhaps the story is just another hopeful bush tale.

802 VICTORIA
ACCOMMODATION

Accommodation is listed for the city centre. There is outlying accommodation which is generally rather cheaper.

(i) Hotel Accommodation in Bendigo

Name	Stars	No. on Map	Telephone No.	Address	Lowest Price (Double/Twin)
Marlborough House	4	3	03-5441-4142	115 Wattle Street	$150
Cathedral Terrace	4½	6	03-5441-3242	81 Wattle Street	$135
Jubilee Villa	4½	10	03-5442-2920	170 McCrae Street	$135
Barclay on View	4	2	03-5443-9388	181 View Street	$125
Julie-Anna Inn	4	11	1-800-355-148	268 Napier Street	$125
Greystanes Manor	4½	14	03-5442-2466	57 Queen Street	$125
Closter Cottage		15	03-5443-4615	69 King Street	$125
Cathedral Motor Inn	4	5	1-800-244-276	96 High Street	$110
Lakeview Motor Inn	3½	13	03-5442-3099	286 Napier Street	$100
Shamrock Hotel	3	8	03-5443-0333	Pall Mall & Williamson St.	$100
Central Deborah Inn	3½	4	1-800-064-126	177 High Street	$95
Tea House Motor Inn	3½	12	03-5441-7111	280 Napier Street	$90
McIvor Motor Inn	3	16	03-5443-8544	45 McIvor Road	$75
Budget Oval Motel	3	1	03-5443-7211	194 Barnard Street	$70
City Centre Motel	2½	7	03-5443-2077	26 Forest Street	$65
Old Crown Hotel		9	03-5441-6888	238 Hargreaves Street	$65

(ii) Backpackers Hostels in Bendigo

Name	Group	No. on Map	Telephone No.	Address	Lowest Price (Dormitory)
Buzza's Bendigo B/P	YHA	17	03-5443-7680	33 Creek Street South.	$19
Ironbark Bush Cabins	Nom		03-5448-3344	2 Watson Street	$22

MOVING ON
(i) By Train

Currently, there are trains almost every hour to Melbourne, for which the timetable is shown below. Trains continue north to Swan Hill once a day, with a bus connexion to Mildura. There are trains to Echuca twice a week, for which services the timetables appear on page 753.

Bendigo to Melbourne

Days of Operation	Weekday Timetable									
Bendigo	0605	0643	0750	0940	1125	1225	1335	1425	1540	1625	1815
Melbourne	0806	0840	0929	1125	1322	1420	1523	1634	1727	1812	2015

Days of Operation	Saturdays							Sundays			
Bendigo	0725	0940	1130	1305	1430	1625	1850	0715	0935	1245	1440	1625	1850
Melbourne	0922	1123	1328	1504	1626	1827	2048	0910	1132	1443	1628	1826	2047

(ii) By Bus

At the time of writing, Bendigo is not served by any of the long-distance bus companies. However, the McCafferty's route between Melbourne and Brisbane used to pass through and it is possible that such service may be resumed at some time in the future. V-Line buses run to Mildura, Swan Hill and Echuca. There is a V-Line bus daily all the way to Adelaide, as mentioned above, an interesting route. Finally. there is a V-Line bus to Geelong via Daylesford and Ballarat, and there are some other V-Line routes to minor destinations.

Destination	Operator	Via	Distance (km)	Fare	Journey Time	Frequency
Adelaide	V-Line		656	$64	9 hrs	1/day
		Dimboola	258	$30.70	3¾ hrs	1/day
Geelong	V-Line		220	$37.10	3¾ hrs	5/week
		Ballarat	124	$23.30	2¼ hrs	5/week
Mildura	V-Line		404	$59	5 - 6½ hrs	2/day
		Swan Hill	189	$29.30	2¼ - 3¼ hrs	3/day
Echuca	V-Line		99	$7.90	1½ hrs	2/day

ECHUCA
Population 10,000
3 hrs 30 mins by train from Melbourne
3 hrs 30 mins by bus from Melbourne

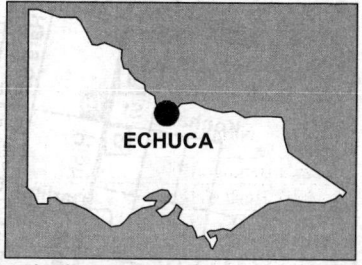

Echuca is the first of three towns along the Murray which are well worth a visit. It is probably not necessary to visit all three, but you should get to at least one of them. Echuca is mentioned first because it is nearest to Melbourne - just 205 kilometres, in fact, by the most direct road route, or 250 kilometres by rail. This distance is covered in 3½ hours by a V-Line train or bus. The train runs only twice a week, unfortunately, on Friday and Sunday evenings, but there used to be no passenger rail service at all, so this is an infinite improvement. Reinstatement of a service is unusual these days and shows just how popular Echuca is becoming as a weekend resort. In addition, there are five V-Line bus, or train plus bus, services per day from Melbourne on weekdays, mostly via either Bendigo or Murchison, five such services on Saturdays and three on Sundays.

Echuca was founded in 1853, and soon after the railway reached here in 1864, it became the largest inland port in Australia. Paddle steamers used to operate all along the Murray, Darling and Murrumbidgee Rivers, reaching almost as far as the Queensland border. Much of the cargo came here, to be loaded onto the railway, transported to Melbourne and often exported from there. This trans-shipment made Echuca a busy town. In 1872, 240 steamers were unloaded here. The wharf stretched for 400 metres and there were eighty hotels in the town.

In the end, the railways which had brought all this trade took it away again, for as the rail system was extended, it became easier to ship goods all the way to a port without the necessity of unloading and reloading. Echuca declined and its resurgence has come only in recent years, riding the wave of increased tourism. Echuca has been quick to realise its potential and take advantage of the boom by offering its natural beauty coupled with its interesting history. Some paddle steamers had survived, while others are being rebuilt and Echuca is now able to claim that it has the largest fleet of paddle steamers in the world, including the world's oldest wooden-hulled paddle steamer still in operation, the *P.S. Adelaide*, built here in Echuca in 1866. This vessel was put in a park for twenty years, but was restored from 1980 and refloated in 1984.

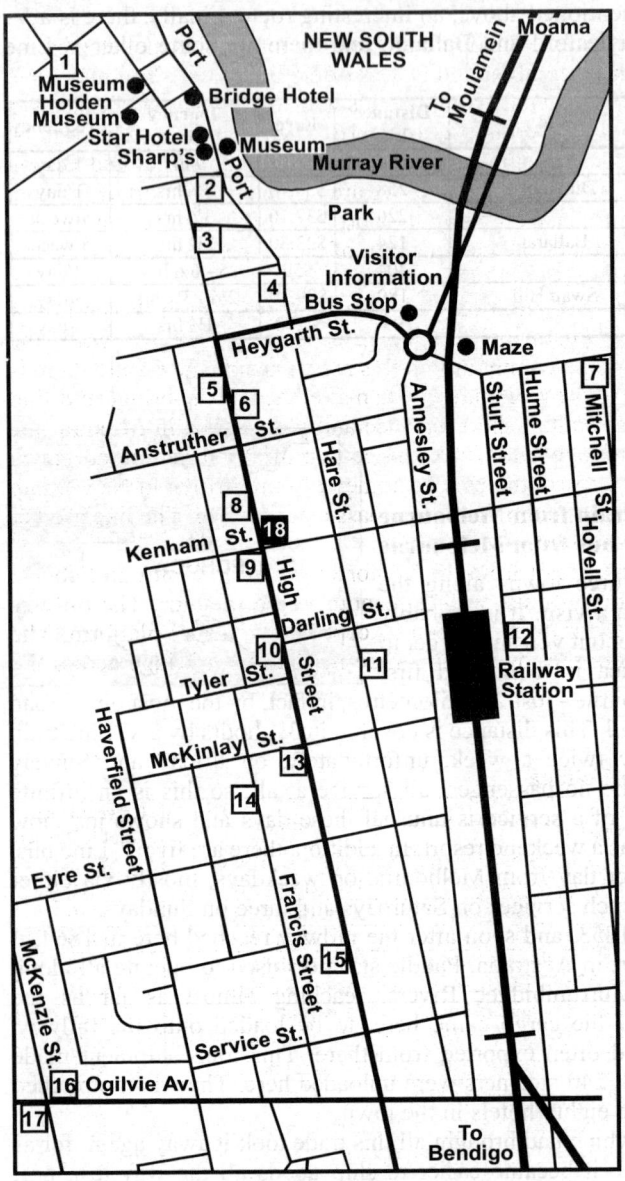

ECHUCA
Black numerals indicate hotel accommodation
White numerals indicate backpackers hostels

Since then she has been carrying passengers (only twelve at a time) for short trips on the Murray. Her draft is only 70 centimetres (two feet four inches).

There are other paddle steamers here too. The Port of Echuca operates three such vessels, the other two being the *P.S. Alexander Arbuthnot* and the *P.S. Pevensey*. The *Alexander Arbuthnot* was the last paddle steamer built on the Murray, a 46-ton vessel constructed in 1923. In 1947, she sank at her moorings and was not raised until 1972. She was then brought here in 1989 for restoration and is now at work carrying groups of up to 47 passengers. The *Pevensey* was built just across the river in Moama in 1911 and can carry 120 tons of cargo. She caught fire in 1932 and had to be rebuilt, then later became a floating museum. She was restored between 1973 and 1976, and began carrying passengers in 1979. She is the biggest of the three vessels and can carry 100 passengers, burning up to one tonne of wood per hour. Other paddle steamers are operated by private companies from here, and often undertake longer cruises.

Echuca is still a working port, mostly steam-operated, though its survival now depends on tourism. There is plenty to see around the port area. Restoration work continues and can be observed. There is a **blacksmith's shop** and there are **stationary steam engines** at work. The **Star Hotel** has an underground bar and escape tunnel. ***Sharp's Magic Movie House and Penny Arcade*** has old films and penny-in-the-slot amusements.

These attractions can be sampled individually or a combination ticket may be purchased. Probably one of these combination tickets offers best value. You may have a tour of the port area for $10, or you may combine this with a one-hour paddle steamer cruise for $20. If you want only the cruise, it costs $16. Then there is a ticket known as a *Super Pass*, which provides the above, plus a tour of the Star Hotel and Bridge Hotel and entry to *Sharp's*. This costs $30. The above are offered by the Port of Echuca. A separate company, a little further west along the port area, offers cruises on the *P.S. Canberra*, built in 1912 and perhaps the best-looking of the vessels here, for $16, or a cruise plus *Sharp's* for $20. Take your choice.

There is a modern **Visitor Information Centre** a short walk from the port. The Centre also has interesting historical displays, especially dealing with the circumstances of the large Chinese community in this area. Outside the Centre there is a pleasant **park** on the banks of the river, and you can stroll across the bridge and find yourself in New South Wales. Walk a short distance and you will be in **Moama**, the poor relation of Echuca on the opposite bank. Notice that the Victorian broad gauge railway also crosses the river and continues for another 140 kilometres in New South Wales territory to **Moulamein**, although there is no passenger service. The line used to go even further, in fact, to **Balranald**.

V-Line buses arrive at and depart from the Visitor Information Centre in Echuca, but for the two trains a week you must walk for another five minutes. The railway station is no longer used by the railway, though, except for the actual platform. The platform is on the far side from the town, but can be reached by a bridge across the tracks.

ACCOMMODATION
(i) Hotel Accommodation in Echuca

Name	Stars	No. on Map	Telephone No.	Address	Lowest Price (Double/Twin)
River Gallery Inn	4½	3	03-5480-6902	578 High Street	$145
Etan House	4½	1	03-5480-7477	11 Connelly Street	$110
Nirebo Motel	4	4	1-800-033-189	251 Hare Street	$110
Port of Echuca Motor Inn	4	5	1-800-355-149	465 High Street	$110
Riverboat Lodge	3½	6	1-800-033-134	476 High Street	$105
Murray House	4½	14	03-5482-4944	55 Francis Street	$105
Settlement Motor Inn	3	9	1-800-813-742	405 High Street	$100
Pevensey Motor Lodge	3	13	1-800-032-461	365 High Street	$100
Echuca Gardens B&B	3½	7	03-5480-6522	103 Mitchell Street	$90
Caledonian Hotel	3	11	03-5482-2100	110 Hare Street	$85
Steam Packet Motel	3	2	03-5482-3411	Murray Esplanade	$75
Paddlewheel Motel	4	10	1-800-035-648	385 High Street	$75
Big River Motel		15	03-5482-2522	317 High Street	$70
High Street Motel		8	03-5482-1013	439 High Street	$70
Echuca Motel	2½	16	03-5482-2899	268 Ogilvie Avenue	$65
Pastoral Hotel	2	12	03-5482-1812	100 Sturt Street	$60
Campaspe Motor Inn	2½	17	03-5482-3900	305 Ogilvie Avenue	$60

806 VICTORIA
(ii) Backpackers Hostels in Echuca

Name	Group	No. on Map	Telephone No.	Address	Lowest Price (Dormitory)
Echuca Gardens B&B	YHA	7	03-5480-6522	103 Mitchell Street	$20
Oasis Backpackers	Nom	18	1800-613-333	410 High Street	$19

MOVING ON
(i) By Train

Echuca has two trains a week to Bendigo, the Sunday service offering an onward connexion to Melbourne. In addition, V-Line offers bus, or bus plus train, services to Melbourne five times a day on weekdays, five times on Saturdays and three times on Sundays. The timetable for these services is shown below.

Echuca to Bendigo and Melbourne

Weekdays and Saturdays

Days of Operation	M-F (Bus)	M-F	Sat (Bus)	Sat	M-Sat (Bus)	M-Sat (Bus)	M-Sat	M-Sat (Bus)	M-Sat	M, F (Bus)	M-F	Tu,W Th (Bus)	M-F	F, Sat (Bus)	F
Moama	0555		0715		0820	0900*		1335‡		1350		1630		1735	
Echuca	0605		0725		0830	0910*		1345‡		1400		1640		1745	2200
Bendigo						1030*	1125‡			1520	1540	1800	1815		2310
Murchison	0723		0843					1503‡							
Murchison E	0730	0740	0850	0901				1510‡	1521‡						
Melbourne		0928		1048	1130			1322†		1722‡		1727		2015	2045

* 5 minutes earlier on Saturdays   † 5 minutes later on Saturdays   ‡ 30 minutes later on Saturdays

Sundays

Days of Operation	Sun (Bus)	Sun	Sun (Bus)	Sun	Sun (Bus)	Sun	Sun
Moama	0800				1455		
Echuca	0810		1315		1505	1720	
Bendigo	0920	0935	1425	1440		1835	1850
Melbourne		1132		1628	1810		2047

(ii) By Bus

There is a daily V-Line bus to Adelaide via Swan Hill, and one to Albury, where it connects with the night train to Sydney, and there is a service four days a week to Mildura. There are two daily bus services north to Deniliquin in New South Wales, one operated by V-Line and one operated by Countrylink. The Countrylink service continues on some days to Wagga Wagga and on other days to Albury, but in either case it makes a connexion with the day train to Sydney.

Destination	Operator	Via	Distance (km)	Fare	Journey Time	Frequency
Melbourne	V-Line		248	$34.40	3¼ hrs	1/day
Bendigo	V-Line		99	$7.90	1½ hrs	2/day
Adelaide	V-Line		666	$60.40	8¾ hrs	1/day
Mildura	V-Line		369	$42.70	5 - 5¾ hrs	4/week
		Swan Hill	151	$23.30	2 hrs	11/week
Albury	V-Line		241	$42.70	4¼ hrs	4/week
Albury	Countrylink		229	$41.40	4½ hrs	3/week
Deniliquin	V-Line		55	$4.10	1 hr	1/day
Wagga Wagga	Countrylink		245	$65.40	4¾ hrs	4/week
		Deniliquin	55	$14.10	1¼ hrs	1/day

SWAN HILL
Population 10,000

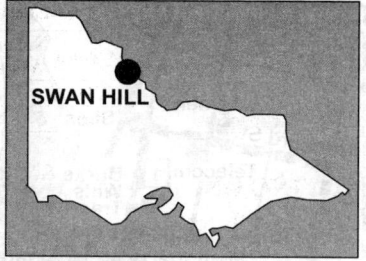

4 hrs 30 mins by train from Melbourne

Swan Hill is the second of our towns along the banks of the Murray. It can be reached most comfortably by the evening train from Melbourne, for which see the timetable on page 753. However, the arrival time at 21:54 is rather late and does not permit the scenery to be viewed along the way, so there is the alternative of taking a train to Bendigo and a V-Line bus from there. These services are shown on the same timetable.

Swan Hill has many similarities with Echuca, having developed as an inland port. However, it was less dependent on the river trade and is now less dependent on the tourist trade, although both have occupied important places in the town's economy.

The first European to visit this area was Major Thomas Mitchell. He camped here on 21st June 1836 and complained that he was kept awake at night by noisy swans. Therefore, he named the location Swan Hill. European settlement started in 1844 and in 1847 a punt service was established for crossing the river. When the town was first surveyed, it was named Castle Donnington, but the name was later changed to Swan Hill. The first river steamer arrived from Goolwa in South Australia in 1853 and from then on the town started to expand as a port. It soon became Australia's second largest inland port, after Echuca. However, here goods were mainly brought to be loaded onto steamers, which then took them all the way down the Murray to Goolwa in South Australia.

The **Burke and Wills Expedition** passed through the town in 1860, and stayed for two weeks. During this time a commemorative tree was planted, possibly by Burke himself, although this is not certain, and can be seen in the town. More importantly, a young man called **Charlie Gray** volunteered enthusiastically for the expedition, with his horse (who might not have been as enthusiastic, as he was to end up being eaten), and was accepted by Burke. Gray was one of the four men who made the successful crossing to the north of the country, but he was the first to die on the return journey and, as events turned out, the fact that the other three spent a whole day

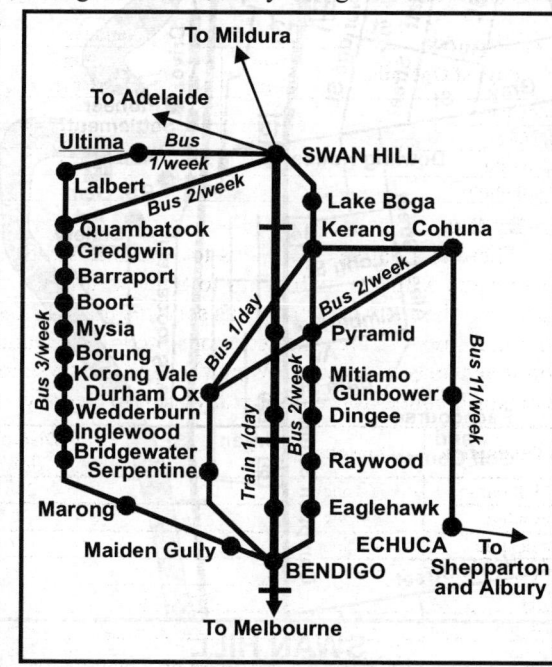

**V-LINE SERVICES
FROM BENDIGO OR ECHUCA TO SWAN HILL**

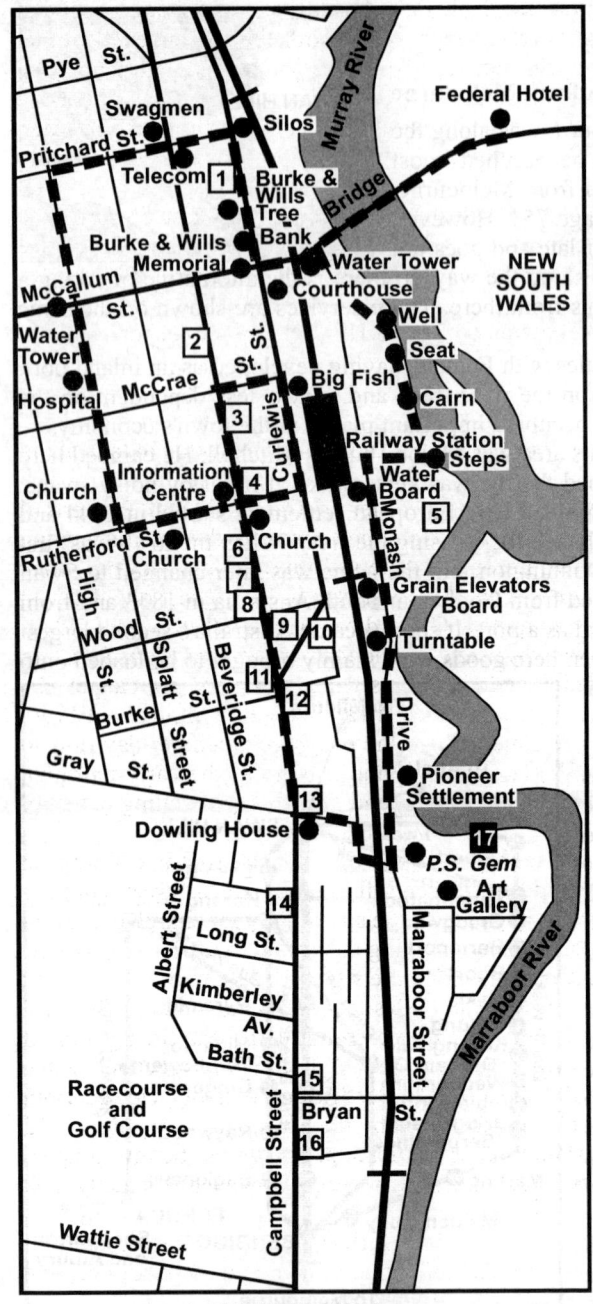

SWAN HILL
Dashed line shows Walking Tour
Black numerals indicate hotel accommodation
White numerals indicate backpackers hostels

digging a shallow grave for him, cost the success of the entire expedition, and two of the other three then died also. For the story of this famous expedition, see page 700.

The railway arrived in 1890 and took away the river trade from Swan Hill, but the paddle steamers continued to ply, now transporting passengers as well as cargo along the Murray. In 1896, the bridge was constructed across the Murray.

During the Great Depression, many people came here as casual labourers for fruit picking, but there was insufficient work for all, and the result was the **Pickers' Riot** in 1933, when police were forced to fire shots at the mob of angry men.

Today, the main industries here are agricultural. Grapes are grown, for wine-making, as well as fruits, nuts and particularly vegetables.

The highlight of Swan Hill's offering to the visitor is its **Pioneer Settlement**. This is like a slightly smaller version of Sovereign Hill in Ballarat. Opened in 1963, it claims to have been Australia's first outdoor museum and has over fifty buildings, either transferred originals or replicas, portraying life in a typical pioneer settlement in the nearby Mallee country in the late nineteenth century. As at Sovereign Hill, this is not a static exhibition. It has shops and vehicles operated by those dressed in period costume and visitors are able to purchase items and take rides. There is a cruise available on the paddle steamer *Pyap*, and in the evening there is a **Sound and Light** performance, with visitors being conveyed around the Settlement in a three-carriage, 56-seat vehicle to see the various attractions by night. The *Pyap* was built in South Australia in 1896 and operated for much of her life as a floating store. Then she was used as a houseboat until 1970, before being restored for the Pioneer Settlement. In 1978, she was gutted by fire, but was immediately rebuilt.

The Pioneer Settlement is open daily and admission costs $20. The *Pyap* Cruise costs $12. The Sound and Light Performance costs $12. Pioneer Settlement plus Cruise is available for $30, Pioneer Settlement plus Sound and Light for $30, or all three for $35.

To see the remainder of the attractions of Swan Hill, let us take a short walking tour.

Walking Tour

This tour covers approximately four kilometres and may be expected to take about an hour and a half.

Begin at the **Information Centre** on the corner of Campbell and Rutherford Streets. Come out of the office and turn left. Campbell Street is the main shopping street, named after one of the first two European settlers. Turn right into McCrae Street and almost straight ahead is a **Murray Cod**. Although this is the biggest one that you are ever likely to see, they do grow to quite a size and can live to be fifty years old, or even more. This particular specimen was made for and used in the film *Eight Ball*, and is eleven metres long, six metres high and six metres wide. Not many are caught like that these days. Just to the right of the fish is the **Railway Station**, built in about 1900. This is also the stopping point for V-Line buses. One passenger train per day runs to here from Melbourne, arriving in the late evening and leaving in the early morning, except on Sundays, when it leaves in the afternoon and may be seen waiting patiently at the station during the day.

Continue down Curlewis Street, named after the other of the first two European settlers, and turn right into Rutherford Street, then left into Campbell Street. On your left is the **Presbyterian Church**, built in 1912, on the site of the first church erected in Swan Hill. Opposite are several motels, demonstrating the importance of tourism to the economy of Swan Hill nowadays. Continue along the street for five minutes until you reach Gray Street, and there turn left. On the opposite side of the street is ***Dowling House***, built in Kyneton and brought here by bullock team in 1916. For the location of Kyneton, see the diagrammatic railway map on page 796. Follow the street across the railway line and you have arrived at the **Pioneer Settlement**. Readily viewed from without is the *P.S. Gem*. This vessel was purchased by the Swan Hill Council in 1962 for £2,000 to be the centrepiece of the Pioneer Settlement. She had to be towed down the river from Mildura, a journey expected to take two weeks. However, it actually took eight months, but she reached here in the end.

Just beyond the Pioneer Settlement is the **Art Gallery** in a mud-built structure of typical country style. The gallery has a good collection of some 200 works of art and is open daily from 10:00 (11:00 at weekends) until 17:00. Admission costs $4.

Walk back now along Monash Drive, on the river side of the railway. You will soon see the **turntable**, essential for the steam locomotives which used to operate here. The turntable is still in use. The **Grain Elevators Board**, just beyond, organises the shipment of all the grain produced in the Mallee. Most of it is conveyed by train from the various sidings throughout the area to Melbourne or Geelong. The Mallee produces 700,000 tonnes of grain annually. Pass the **Water Board** and turn right into **Riverside Park**, a pleasant area bordering the Murray, as its name suggests. You can see the **Rowing Club steps**, which mark the finish of the annual Red Cross Murray River Canoe Marathon. The **Major Mitchell Cairn** marks the spot where that gentleman camped in 1836 and was kept awake by those noisy swans. The **Bluestone Seat** commemorates the arrival of the first two paddle steamers from Goolwa in 1853, the *Mary Anne* and the *Lady Augusta*, which were racing for the prize offered for the first vessel to complete a successful navigation of the river, and arrived here within minutes of each other. The old **Customs House** was situated here, collecting duties on all goods which crossed the river from New South Wales. The concrete circle marks the site of a **well** used by the Customs House and the **willow trees** bordering the river are thought to have been planted by the wife of one of the Customs Officers. Pass the Swimming Pool and come to the **Water Tower**. This Tower was constructed in 1883. It supplied water for the town, and also for the steam trains. Later it also supplied water for the Power Station, which was near here, but was burnt down in 1962. As a result, the Water Tower went out of use in 1965.

Turn right and cross the **bridge**. This bridge was opened on 2nd December 1896, before which, for half a century, a punt used to run across the river. Since this was the only river crossing for more than 150 kilometres in either direction, it was a popular service. The first punt to operate the service sank, but the second survived until the completion of the bridge. It is a steel bridge, designed so that the central span can be lifted to enable river traffic to pass. The bridge keeper lived on the New South Wales side in a house which is no longer there.

Soon after you step on the bridge, you will be in New South Wales, for the border of Victoria is the near bank, although Victoria has the right to use the water in the river. Just a short way down the road is the **Federal Hotel**, dating from 1889. This is far enough along this road. Take a quick refreshment, if needed, and then return to Victoria. At the junction of McCallum Street and Curlewis Street is the **Burke and Wills Memorial**. When the expedition passed through here, Wills was not actually the second in command, the change being made at Menindee in New South Wales. After the fate of the expedition had become known, it was decided to build a brick memorial to the explorers, so funds were collected. The Police Commissioner took the money to Melbourne to arrange the matter, and was never heard from again. Eventually a stone obelisk was built instead. Just to the south in Curlewis Street are the **Police Station** and **Courthouse**, while to the north is the former **National Bank**, restored to its original appearance by the company of solicitors currently using the building.

We now come to the **Burke and Wills Tree**, which may have been planted by Burke, and may not, but it dates from that time, and is claimed to be the **largest Moreton Bay Fig** in Australia, rising to a height of thirty metres, with a spread of 44 metres and a trunk four metres thick. Murray River water is evidently good for one's health.

On the right at the junction with Pritchard Street are some silos marking the site of the **Swan Hill Flour Mill**. This is also the location of the town's first **cemetery**. It is not quite certain how many people were interred here, but the names of three are known. One of them was the unfortunate driver of a coach, the horses of which bolted into nearby Lake Boga, where he drowned.

Turn left into Pritchard Street and see the **Telecom receivers** used for radio, television and telephone transmissions. The first telephone service here was in 1912. On the right is the site used in the 1930s to accommodate the **swagmen** obliged by the regulations to keep moving from town to town searching for work. Turn left again into **Splatt Street**, which used to be the site of Swan Hill's finest residential buildings, a few of which can still be observed. At the corner of McCallum Street is another **water tower**, this one built in 1902, and also disused since 1965. The **hospital** is a little further on the right, moved here in 1889, but in relatively modern buildings now. Further down, also on the right, is the **Catholic Church**, built in 1962 over and round the church which was already there, so that there would be no break in use. Turn left at Rutherford Street and note the **Methodist (Uniting) Church** on the right, built in 1918, and here we are back at our starting point.

There is also a pleasant walk along the banks of the **Murray**, if you still feel like some exercise. The bridge is about the centre point, with the walk extending both north and south from there. The Murray is an attractive river to stroll along if you have spare time.

ACCOMMODATION

The range of accommodation includes some older hotels. The White Swan is mentioned in the list below, and there are others too. For backpackers, there is also accommodation available at the Pioneer Settlement at modest rates.

(i) Hotel Accommodation in Swan Hill

Name	Stars	No. on Map	Telephone No.	Address	Lowest Price (Double/Twin)
Lady Augusta Motor Inn	4	9	1-800-355-167	375 Campbell Street	$120
Burke & Wills Motor Inn	4	7	03-5032-9788	370 Campbell Street	$115
Travellers' Rest	4	1	1-800-807-549	110 Curlewis Street	$110
Australian Settlers Inn	3½	6	1-800-032-589	354 Campbell Street	$105
Swan Hill Resort	4	12	1-800-034-220	405 Campbell Street	$105
Campbell Motor Inn	3	11	1-800-037-090	396 Campbell Street	$100
Jane Eliza Motor Inn	3½	3	03-5032-4411	263 Campbell Street	$85
Oasis Hotel / Motel		4	1-800-658-380	287 Campbell Street	$75
Paruna Motel	3	8	1-800-810-445	386 Campbell Street	$75
Swan Hill Holiday Units	3	14	03-5033-1269	456 Campbell Street	$75
Riverside Caravan Park	4½	5	03-5032-1494	1 Monash Drive	$75
Murray River Motel	3	15	1-800-008-300	481 Campbell Street	$70
Sun Centre Motel	3	16	03-5032-4466	491 Campbell Street	$70
Jacaranda Holiday Units	3½	10	03-5032-9077	179 Curlewis Street	$65
Pioneer Station Motor Inn	3	13	03-5032-2017	421 Campbell Street	$55
White Swan Hotel		2	03-5032-2761	182 Campbell Street	$45

(ii) Backpackers Hostel in Swan Hill

Name	Group	No. on Map	Telephone No.	Address	Lowest Price (Dormitory)
Pioneer Settlement Lodges		17	03-5032-1093	Horseshoe Bend	$15

812   VICTORIA
MOVING ON
(i) By Train
The only train runs to Melbourne on Monday to Saturday mornings and Sunday afternoons. The timetable for this is on page 815.

(ii) By Bus
Later in the day, there are two V-Line buses to Bendigo with train connexions to Melbourne. There are also V-Line buses to Adelaide, Mildura and Albury. The Albury service connects with a train to Sydney.

Destination	Operator	Via	Distance (km)	Fare	Journey Time	Frequency
Bendigo	V-Line		189	$29.30	2½ - 4 hrs	2/day
Adelaide	V-Line		515	$51.40	7 hrs	1/day
Mildura	V-Line		218	$37.10	2½ - 3¾ hrs	16/week
Albury	V-Line		392	$51.50	6¾ - 7¼ hrs	4/week
		Echuca	151	$23.30	2 hrs	11/week

MILDURA
Population 30,000

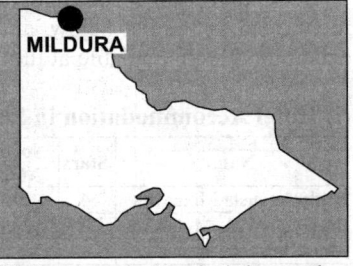

7 hrs by train and bus from Melbourne
9 hrs 30 mins by bus from Melbourne

The third and last of the places to visit along the Murray is Mildura. This is by far the largest of the three and the one which has been most popular over the years as a holiday resort for Victorians. However, it has less history than Echuca or Swan Hill, its popularity deriving rather from its pleasantly mild winter climate. This has led Mildura to declare itself the capital of a region to which it has given the jarring title of *Sunraysia*.

The name Mildura is an aboriginal one, meaning, apparently, 'red earth'. The town sits almost at the confluence of the Murray and the Darling, the Murray-Darling being the longest river in Australia and this river system being the most developed inland navigation system in the country.

Mildura is easily accessible, although not quite as easily as when it had a rail service, which was until a decade ago. McCafferty's operates one bus a day between Sydney and Adelaide via Canberra and Mildura. V-Line operates a bus from Melbourne by night. By day it has a train service to Bendigo connecting with a bus to Mildura. In the evening, there is a train to Swan Hill which connects with a bus to Mildura. However, on most days this service reaches Mildura awkwardly late at 00:45 (23:40 on Fridays). There is also a V-Line bus service from Albury, via Echuca and Swan Hill. This bus operates four times a week. Finally, there is a private bus service from Broken Hill on Mondays, Wednesdays and Fridays operated by Junction Tours.

The first European to reach here was Captain Charles Sturt in 1829, and European settlement started in 1845. The success of the area is largely ascribed to the Chaffey Brothers, whom we have already met in the section on Renmark, just across the border in South Australia (see page 658). The Chaffey Brothers were Canadians who arrived here in 1886 and developed a system of irrigation which opened up for agricultural use what had previously been regarded as barren land. The **Visitor Information Centre** has a display on this theme.

The Arts Centre is in the **Rio Vista Homestead**, which used to be the home of the Chaffey family. It lies close to the banks of the Murray, having been built in 1891, and is open daily from 9:00 until 17:00. Admission costs $4.

The **Pioneer Cottage** at 3 Hunter Street, not far from the Visitor Information Centre, is open daily from 10:00 until 16:00, and there is also the **Old Mildura Homestead**, a short walk from the town centre along the banks of the Murray.

This region has become well known for its wineries. Much of Victoria's wine is produced near Mildura and tours to the wineries are available.

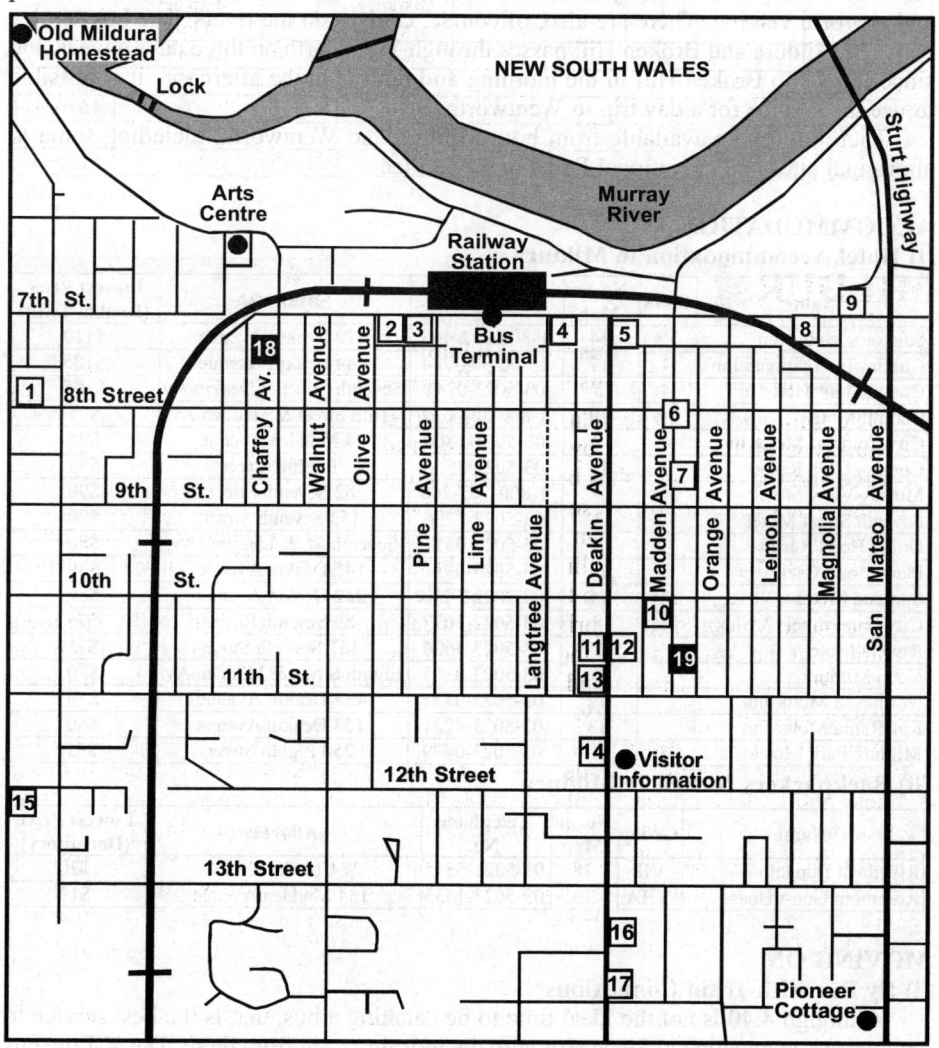

MILDURA
Black numerals in white boxes indicate hotel accommodation
White numerals in black boxes indicate backpackers hostels

814 VICTORIA

Paddle steamers ply on the Murray here too, the *Melbourne* being one of the most impressive such vessels. It operates cruises daily, most of them having to pass through the lock which has been built on the river. In fact, though, during the heyday of river transport, it was Wentworth which was the main port, rather than Mildura.

Wentworth lies thirty kilometres from Mildura, on the opposite bank of the river, in New South Wales. It is at the point where the Darling and Murray meet. Before the railways arrived, it was the busiest inland port in New South Wales and its dock could accommodate up to thirty vessels at a time. There is a *Pioneer World* in the town, which includes fossils and reconstructions of animals from those fossils, which were discovered in the nearby Perry Sandhills. The **Old Wentworth Gaol** was built in 1881 and is worth visiting. There are also, of course, **cruises** on the rivers. The bus service between Mildura and Broken Hill passes through Wentworth on three days a week and since it goes to Broken Hill in the morning and returns in the afternoon, it is possible to use the service for a day trip to Wentworth.

There are **tours** available from both Mildura and Wentworth, including some to aboriginal sites and to National Parks in the Mallee.

ACCOMMODATION
(i) Hotel Accommodation in Mildura

Name	Stars	No. on Map	Telephone No.	Address	Lowest Price (Double/Twin)
Sandor's Motor Inn	3½	14	1-800-032-463	179 Deakin Avenue	$110
Chaffey International Inn	4	17	1-800-804-784	244 Deakin Avenue	$105
Commodore Motor Inn	4	5	03-5023-0241	Seventh Street & Deakin Av	$105
Central Motel	3½	10	1-800-804-632	Tenth Street & Madden Av.	$95
City Colonial Motor Inn	4	7	03-5021-1800	24 Madden Avenue	$95
Country Club Resort	3	15	03-5023-3966	Twelfth Street	$95
Murray View Motel	3½	9	1-800-502-268	82 Seventh Street	$90
Seventh Street Motel	3½	3	03-5023-1796	153 Seventh Street	$90
Grand Hotel Resort	3½	4	03-5023-0511	Seventh St. & Langtree Av.	$80
Plantation Motel	3	11	03-5023-0317	145 Deakin Avenue	$80
Sunland Motel	3½	16	03-5022-1466	232 Deakin Avenue	$80
City Gate Motel	3½	8	03-5022-1077	89 Seventh Street	$75
Riviera Motel		2	03-5023-3696	157 Seventh Street	$75
Hotel Mildura		6	03-5023-0365	Eighth Street & Madden Av.	$70
Northaven Motor Inn		12	03-5023-0521	138 Deakin Avenue	$70
Kar-Rama Motor Inn		13	03-5023-4221	153 Deakin Avenue	$60
Mildura Park Motel	3	1	03-5023-0479	250 Eighth Street	$55

(ii) Backpackers Hostels in Mildura

Name	Group	No. on Map	Telephone No.	Address	Lowest Price (Dormitory)
Riverboat Bungalow	VIP	18	03-5021-5315	27 Chaffey Avenue	$20
Rosemont Guest House	YHA	19	03-5023-1535	154 Madden Avenue	$19

MOVING ON
(i) By Bus with Train Connexions

Although 4:40 is not the ideal time to be catching a bus, that is the best service to Melbourne, connecting at Swan Hill with the morning train from there. The V-Line bus departs from Mildura Station, but does not operate on Fridays or Sundays. If the early morning departure is too traumatic, there is another bus at a more civilised hour to

Bendigo, where it connects with a Melbourne train. This bus leaves at 8:30 on Mondays, 9:00 on Tuesdays to Fridays and 10:10 on Saturdays and Sundays. By night there is a V-Line bus direct to Melbourne, except on Saturday evenings. Timetables for these services are shown below.

At 4:00 every morning, there is a Countrylink service from Mildura to Cootamundra, where it connects with the day train to Sydney. A timetable is provided below for this service too.

Mildura and Swan Hill to Melbourne

Days of Operation	M-Th Sat (Bus)	M-Sat	M - F (Bus)	M - F	M - F (Bus)	M - F	Sat, Sun (Bus)	Daily	F (Bus)	M - F	Sun (Bus)	Sun	Not Sat (Bus)
Mildura	0440				0900†		1010		1220		1345		2145
Swan Hill	0720	0730	0800*			1245	1340		1525		1625	1640	
Bendigo		0937	1105	1125	1520	1540	1610	1625	1755	1815		1850	
Melbourne		1125		1322		1727		1827		2015		2047	0700

* 0715 on Wednesdays † 0830 on Mondays

Mildura and Griffith to Sydney and Melbourne via Cootamundra or Wagga Wagga

Days of Operation	Sun	Daily (Bus)	Daily (Bus)	Daily	Daily	F, Sun (Bus)	Daily	Daily
Mildura			0400					
Griffith	0800	0940	0951			2110		
Wagga Wagga		1220		1408	1248	2349	0006	0243
Cootamundra	1137		1231	1245	1357		0113	
Yass Junction	1309				1520		0236	
Goulburn	1426				1628		0342	
Moss Vale	1522				1715		0429	
Strathfield					1858		0606	
Sydney	1712				1913		0625	
Wangaratta				1543				0436
Benalla				1614				0500
Melbourne				1815				0700

(ii) By Bus

McCafferty's provides daily bus services to Sydney, Canberra and Adelaide. V-Line provides a bus service to Albury on four days a week. Junction Tours operates a service to Broken Hill via Wentworth on Mondays, Wednesdays and Fridays.

Destination	Operator	Via	Distance (km)	Fare	Journey Time	Frequency
Sydney	McCafferty's		1073	$113	17½ hrs	1/day
		Canberra	859	$95	12¼ hrs	1/day
Melbourne	V-Line		617	$67.60	9¼ hrs	1/day
		Ballarat	506	$59	7 hrs	1/day
Albury	V-Line		610	$69	10 - 11 hrs	4/week
Bendigo	V-Line		404	$59	5¾ - 7 hrs	1/day
		Swan Hill	218	$37.10	2¾ - 3¾ hrs	17/week
Adelaide	McCafferty's		383	$54	6½ hrs	1/day
Broken Hill	Junction Tours		296	$54	4 hrs	3/week
Cootamundra	Countrylink		615	$94.80	8½ hrs	1/day
		Griffith	464	$79.50	6 hrs	1/day

VICTORIA
SHEPPARTON
Population 60,000

2 hrs 30 mins by train from Melbourne
2 hrs 30 mins by bus from Melbourne

Shepparton is a modern country city, some 175 kilometres north of Melbourne. It is not on the main Hume Highway to Sydney, but it is served by one Greyhound bus every day travelling between Melbourne and Sydney, and one McCafferty's bus travelling between Melbourne and Brisbane.

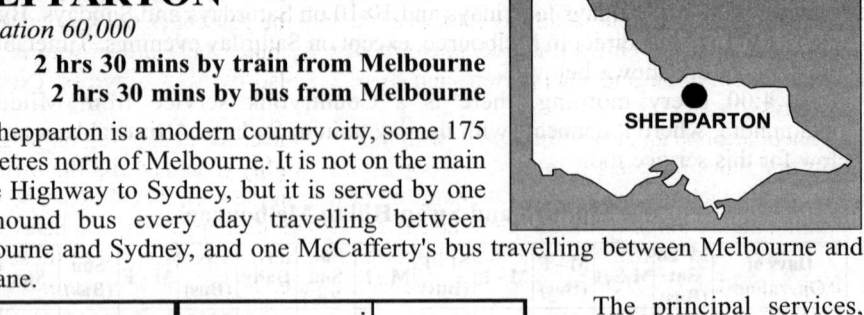

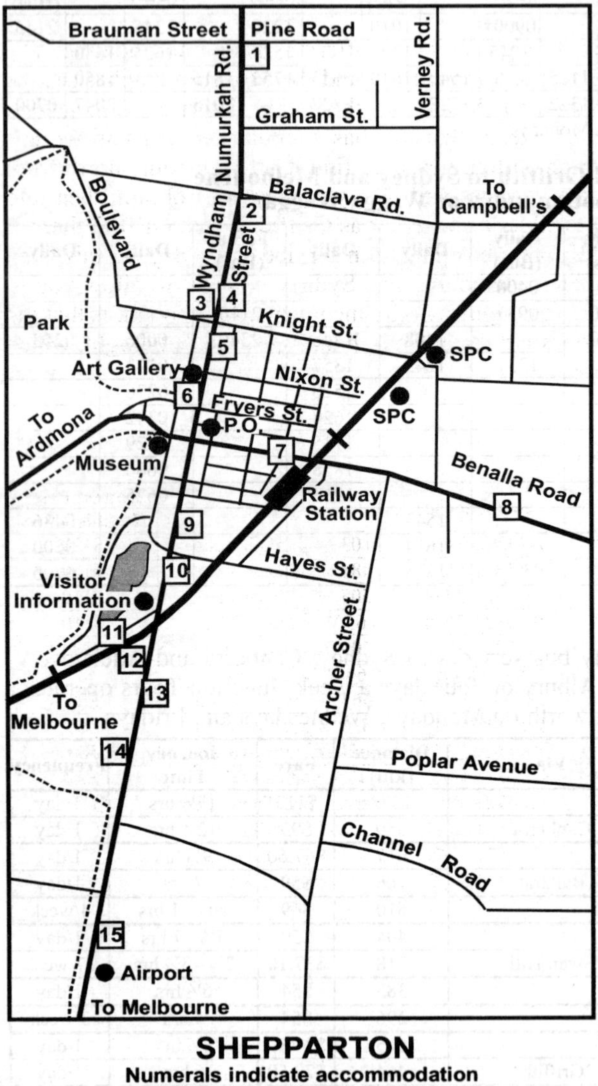

SHEPPARTON

The principal services, however, are operated by the Goulburn Valley Railway, which is theoretically an independent operation, but actually seems very similar to V-Line in a slightly different guise. Shepparton is on a branch line on which trains used to run up to the New South Wales border at Cobram. In fact, at one time, trains used to divide and one section would cross the Murray and terminate at Tocumwal in New South Wales, an interesting little station with one platform broad gauge and one platform standard gauge. Passengers would then walk across the platform from the Victorian broad gauge train to the New South Welsh standard gauge one and continue their journey. This convenient service stopped a while ago and when the author first made the journey, I was transferred by the stationmaster's car from Cobram to Tocumwal to continue on the train from there to Narrandera. It was a bumpy ride, and soon afterwards the New South Wales service was

SHEPPARTON
Numerals indicate accommodation

withdrawn. The Victorian service to Cobram continued until about a decade ago, but when the Goulburn Valley Railway took over the line the passenger rail service was cut back to Shepparton. Onward connexions are now by bus. There are two trains a day between Melbourne and Shepparton, and there are also two bus services, except on Saturdays.

Shepparton is an agricultural area, with many of the crops depending on irrigation. Fruits and dairy products from here are particularly highly regarded and the owners of several famous brand names operate **canning plants** in the vicinity. Mr. Campbell, for example, makes some of his soup on the eastern fringe of Shepparton, and nearby is an SPC factory, while Ardmona is to be found on the western extremity. All of these plants can be visited, the wares sampled and purchases made. There are also **wineries** in the area, with tours available.

The **Goulburn River** flows through the town, offering fishing and boating. The **Art Gallery** is known for its collection of ceramics, and the **Museum** emphasises the effects which the gold discovered nearby has had on the region. There are also several private art galleries with works for sale, as this area has a reputation for its art work.

Even if you do not stay in Shepparton, you may find it on your route north from Melbourne, for the connecting bus services will take you north to Cobram, then into New South Wales to Tocumwal, Jerilderie and as far as Griffith. From Griffith there is a train to Sydney on Sundays only, or a bus plus train service every day, so this is an interesting alternative route between Melbourne and Sydney which will allow you to see plenty of small towns off the main highway. The inconvenience, though, is that the only service beyond Tocumwal does not reach Griffith until just after midnight, which is not the ideal time to be arriving.

ACCOMMODATION
Accommodation in Shepparton

Name	Stars	No. on Map	Telephone No.	Address	Lowest Price (Double/Twin)
Pines Country Club	4	1	1-800-035-668	103 Numurkah Road	$120
Parklake Motor Inn	4½	9	03-5821-5822	481 Wyndham Street	$120
Carrington	3½	10	03-5821-3734	505 Wyndham Street	$110
Wyndhamere	3½	4	03-5821-3088	65 Wyndham Street	$110
Sherbourne Terrace	4	5	03-5821-4977	109 Wyndham Street	$105
Tudor House Motel	3	3	1-800-077-999	64 Wyndham Street	$85
Big Valley Motor Inn	4	12	1-800-501-568	564 Wyndham Street	$85
Bel-Air Motor Inn	3½	14	1-800-063-815	630 Wyndham Street	$80
Peppermill Inn	3½	15	1-800-355-165	Goulburn Valley Highway	$80
Country Home Motor Inn	3½	2	1-800-654-073	11 Wyndham Street	$75
Victoria Hotel	2	6	03-5821-9955	Fryers & Wyndham Streets	$75
Terminus Hotel	1½	7	03-5821-2147	212 High Street	$75
Bell Tower Motor Inn	3½	13	03-5821-8755	587 Wyndham Street	$70
Overlander Hotel	2½	8	03-5821-5622	97 Benalla Road	$70
Victoria Lake Caravan Pk.	3½	11	03-5821-5431	Wyndham Street	$65

818 VICTORIA
MOVING ON
(i) By Train

The timetable below shows train and bus services to Melbourne, while services north are shown on page 753.

Griffith, Cobram and Shepparton to Melbourne

Weekdays

Days of Operation	M - F (Bus)	M - F	M - F (Bus)	M - F (Bus)	M - F (Bus)	M - F	F (Bus)	M - F
Griffith	0330							
Tocumwal	0554		0715					
Cobram	0610		0740		1350			
Shepparton	0705	0715	0855	1000	1445	1455	1725	
Seymour		0817		1130		1600	1855	1905
Melbourne		0928	1115	1255		1722		2017

Saturdays and Sundays

Days of Operation	Sat (Bus)	Sat	Sat (Bus)	Sat	Sun (Bus)	Sun	Sun (Bus)	Sun (Bus)	Sun
Griffith	0450							1355	
Tocumwal	0714							1619	
Cobram	0730		1415		0720			1635	
Shepparton	0825	0835	1515	1525	0835		1430	1730	1740
Seymour		0939		1630	1005	1016	1600		1839
Melbourne		1048		1748		1131	1755		1951

(ii) By Bus

McCafferty's operates to Brisbane and Melbourne every day, and Greyhound operates to Sydney and Melbourne. In both of these cases restrictions apply to travel wholly within Victoria.

Other services are with V-Line. There is a daily bus to Adelaide, and at least one every day to Albury. There are four a week to Mildura and three a week to Bendigo.

Destination	Operator	Via	Distance (km)	Fare	Journey Time	Frequency
Brisbane	McCafferty's		1648	$186	21½ hrs	1/day
		Toowoomba	1518	$186	19 hrs	1/day
		Dubbo	794	$101	10¼ hrs	1/day
Sydney	Greyhound		821	$73	12½ hrs	1/day
		Canberra	524	$55	7¼ hrs	1/day
Melbourne	McCafferty's		175	$32	2¼ hrs	1/day
Melbourne	Greyhound		175	$31	2½ hrs	1/day
Melbourne	V-Line		178	$29.30	2½ - 3 hrs	2/day
Adelaide	V-Line		734	$60.40	10¼ hrs	1/day
Albury	V-Line		173	$30.70	2½ - 3 hrs	11/week
Griffith	Goulburn V Rly		296	$46.30	3¾ hrs	1/day
		Cobram	87	$9.40	1 hr	3/day
Mildura	V-Line		437	$51.50	7 - 7¾ hrs	4/week
		Echuca	68	$10.70	1¼ hrs	11/week
Bendigo	V-Line		126	$13	1¾ hrs	3/week

BEECHWORTH, BRIGHT AND MT. HOTHAM

Population 3,100 (Beechworth)
Population 2,000 (Bright)
3 hrs 30 mins by train and bus from Melbourne (Beechworth)
6 hrs by bus from Melbourne (Mt. Hotham)
4 hrs 30 mins by train and bus from Melbourne (Bright)

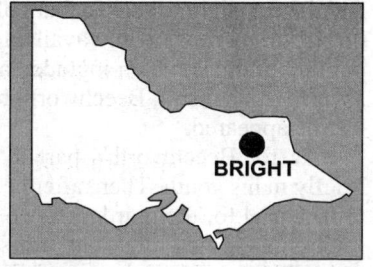

The principal route to Sydney lies along the Hume Highway, a route which is paralleled by the railway. The train from Melbourne to Sydney, operated by Countrylink of New South Wales, makes only two stops within Victoria, at Benalla and Wangaratta, but the V-Line trains which run as far as Albury stop at other stations along the way. As you travel on the train, you will notice that there are three tracks for most of the journey. The two on the left (west) are V-Line broad gauge tracks. The single track on the right (east) is a standard gauge track on which the Sydney - Melbourne train operates. The standard gauge track runs past, rather than through, most of the stations.

It is an odd feature that the association of which the towns along the Hume Highway are most proud is with the bushranger Ned Kelly. The further north you travel along this road, the more likely you are to see Kelly's name on pubs, tea-rooms and souvenir shops, and to find notices telling of each town's part in the saga of the Kelly Gang. **Glenrowan**, just south of **Wangaratta**, is where the climax is reached, for this is the town where Ned Kelly was captured in June 1880, in his almost bullet-proof home-made suit of armour. It was, in fact, the first capture in which the railway had played a significant part, for the newly-built line was used to convey a special train full of police to apprehend the Kelly Gang, and Kelly tried unsuccessfully to derail the train by removing a section of the track. Beechworth too is proud to have played a major role in the Kelly exploits, as we shall see later.

Beechworth and Bright are two more of the Victorian towns to which V-Line runs buses connecting with the trains from Melbourne. The timetable is shown on page 754. As can be seen, if time is short, it is possible to spend four hours in Beechworth during the day and then move on to Bright in the late afternoon. This is a really beautiful area of Victoria and one not to be missed, although public transport does not give access to all of the beauty spots. The fact that Beechworth is such an interesting and historic town is a bonus.

Beechworth was another of Victoria's gold towns, and this is one which was rich enough to construct some splendid buildings and then leave them almost untouched because the gold ran out and there was no pressure to expand and modernise.

The area was originally called Mayday Hills and was a pastoral property until gold was discovered here in February 1852. The owner of the pastoral property gave up with sheep and sold his land to whoever wanted to dig it up. By the end of the year, the town had a population of 8,000 and the following year it adopted the name of Beechworth. In the first fourteen years of its existence, Beechworth produced four million ounces (115 tonnes) of gold. Some of this wealth was invested in the town. Not only did private individuals and businesses erect stately buildings, but the town administration had the foresight to realise that gold would not last for ever and that the revenue should be put to good use while available. Tree-lined streets were constructed, and imposing public buildings which included a hospital, a gaol, an old people's home and a lunatic asylum. As a result, Beechworth had the foundation for survival even after all the gold had disappeared.

As for Beechworth's part in the Ned Kelly legend, Kelly was imprisoned here briefly in his youth. Then, after he was apprehended in Glenrowan, he was brought here to face trial for the murder of two policemen. However, it was decided that it would be impossible to find impartial jurors, Kelly being a local hero, so the trial was transferred to Melbourne, where he was found guilty and hanged on 11th November 1880.

The town also has a connexion with the famous **Burke and Wills Expedition**, for the leader of the Expedition, Robert O'Hara Burke, worked in this town for four years. Burke was an Irishman who migrated to Australia in 1853. He arrived in Victoria and joined the Victorian Police. In 1854, he was appointed as Senior Inspector of Police to Beechworth, and remained here until 1858, when he was transferred to Castlemaine. He was something of an eccentric, writing memos on the interior walls of his home, for example. However, he was well respected, especially for his handling of riots which broke out against the Chinese diggers here in 1857, and well liked. In fact, he was probably rather better suited to being a policeman than to leading an expedition across Australia.

Beechworth is a small town, so our walking tour here will be brief - just a stroll round the block really.

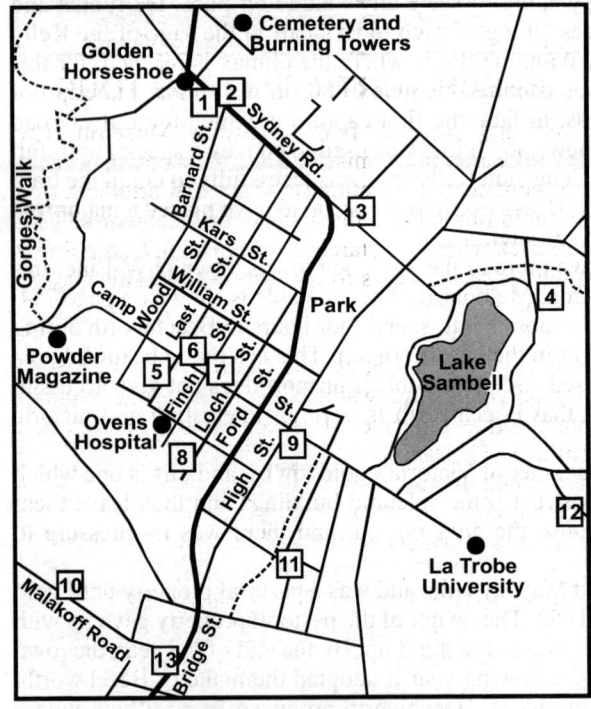

BEECHWORTH
Numerals indicate accommodation

Walking Tour

This tour really is just a walk round the block. It covers a little over one kilometre and will take half an hour.

Start at the **Post Office**, which is on the corner of Camp and Ford Streets, very close to the V-Line bus stop. This impressive building was constructed in 1870, following the destruction of the previous Post Office in a serious fire in 1867. On the south of this corner is the former **Bank of Victoria**, while on the north is a building with the only surviving crest of the former **Bank of New South Wales**.

Walk along Ford Street, the main street of the town. In many ways, it is still like the main street of a nineteenth century gold rush town, with buildings such as the **Star Hotel** and the **Westpac Bank**.

On the right is the granite **Courthouse**, built in 1858. This building is where Ned Kelly appeared on trial before his case was moved to Melbourne, and also where his mother appeared, charged with attempted murder. Near the Courthouse and in similar architectural style are the **Telegraph Office**, the **Sub-Treasury Office** and the **Gold Warden's Office**.

Opposite is the **Town Hall**, containing the **Visitor Information Centre**. The building dates from 1858, but some parts were rebuilt in 1888.

When you reach the corner of William Street, you will see opposite the **Gaol**, built between 1859 and 1864. It is still in use. Turn left and pass the **Town Hall Gardens**, dating from 1875.

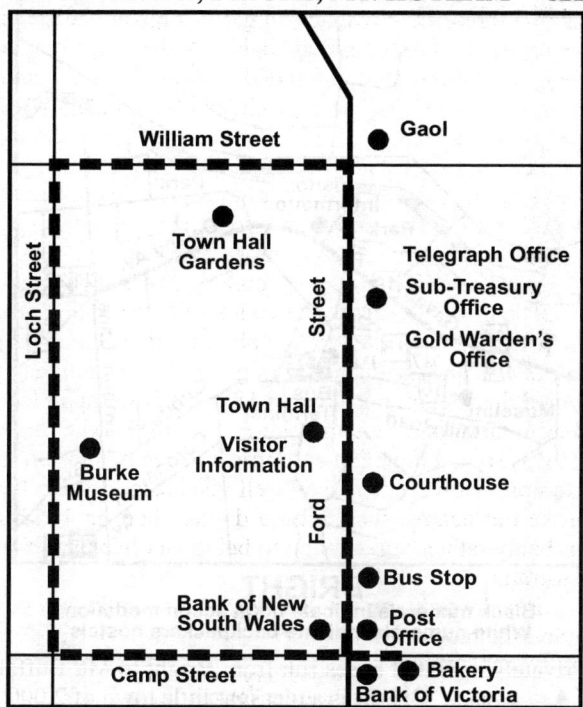

BEECHWORTH WALKING TOUR

Turn left again into Loch Street and you will find the **Burke Museum**. The museum was renamed in honour of Burke after his demise had become known, because of his association with this town. It contains a collection of aboriginal artefacts, and displays relating to the Kelly Gang, gold mining and the history of Beechworth. Turn left again at Camp Street and we are back where we started. Just ahead in Camp Street is a **bakery** which has become famous in recent years for its tasty wares. This may be a suitable concluding point for our short tour.

Further away from the town centre, to the north, are the **Cemetery** and **Chinese Burning Towers**, which make for an interesting walk. Near them is the **Golden Horseshoes Monument**, to commemorate the ride of Beechworth's first elected member in the Victorian parliament in 1855. Daniel Cameron is reputed to have ridden through the town streets on a horse with golden horseshoes.

To the west of the town is the **Powder Magazine**, built in 1859 to store powder used for blasting in the mines. It was restored in 1966 and the **Slab Hut** nearby constructed. Also to the west, but nearer to the town centre is the façade of the **Ovens District Hospital**. This façade is all that remains now, but when the Hospital was built, in 1857, it was the only hospital between Melbourne and Goulburn in New South Wales.

BEECHWORTH POST OFFICE

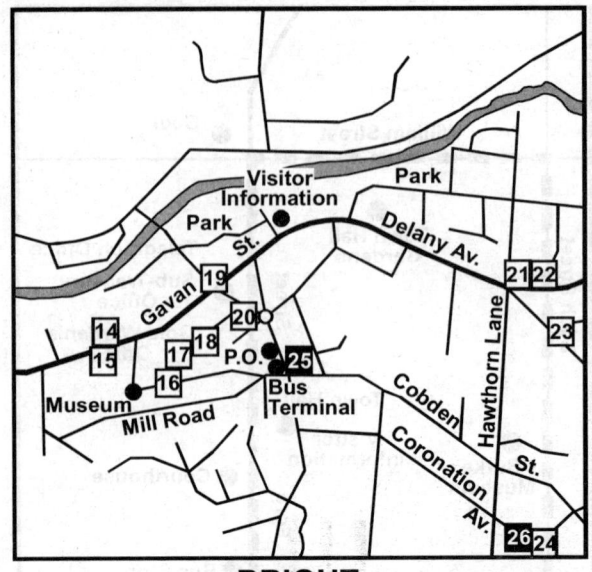

BRIGHT
Black numerals indicate hotel accommodation
White numerals indicate backpackers hostels

This area also produces wine. Fields of vines can be seen and **tours to wineries** in the area are available.

From Beechworth to Bright takes another hour by V-Line bus and as you travel the road starts to rise. We are making our way now into the 'high country', but it is difficult to reach the really best spots by bus, unfortunately. Even so, you will not be disappointed by this journey. The bus passes through **Myrtleford** and then reaches **Porepunkah**. Here there is a turn-off on the right to **Mt. Buffalo National Park**, proclaimed as long ago as 1898, a beautiful area and a ski resort in winter, but it is 27 kilometres from the main road. Privately operated buses run from Bright to Mt. Buffalo in the ski season.

Bright is a pleasant little town of 2,000 inhabitants, with attractive tree-lined streets, planted during the 1930s. The town is at its best in autumn, amidst the beauty of the falling leaves. During the winter, this is a ski area and, although Bright itself does not have ski slopes, it is close enough to places which do, and such an attractive little town, that it is a popular accommodation spot.

Beyond Bright lie some of the most famous of Victoria's ski resorts. 56 kilometres ahead is the alpine resort of **Mt. Hotham**, the highest resort in Victoria at 1,750 metres. In the winter, a bus service is available, not only from Bright but also directly from Melbourne. This service climbs steadily all the way from Bright and passes the highest point on any bitumen road in Victoria, at 1,820 metres, just as Mt. Hotham is reached. The operator of the bus is *Trekset* (Tel: 1-800-659-009). There are two services per day from Bright and one from Melbourne. A return ticket from Melbourne to Mt. Hotham costs $120, and a single $85. From Bright to Mt. Hotham a return costs $45, a day return $35 and a single $35. However, this service operates only during the ski season.

There are few places in Australia which receive snow - only this area on the border of Victoria and New South Wales and some parts of Tasmania - and skiing has become a popular winter pastime. As a result, the few ski resorts are crowded during the winter season. Mt. Hotham is one of the most popular. It is still possible to find accommodation, and it is even possible to find dormitory space at prices within the range of the backpacker, but seasonal variations are great. Try to avoid weekends and school holidays, when prices double, and when, even at double price, there may be no accommodation to be found.

Another twenty kilometres beyond Mt. Hotham is **Dinner Plain**. There is no direct service to Dinner Plain from Melbourne or Bright, but there are free buses which run

BEECHWORTH, BRIGHT, MT. HOTHAM 823

between Mt. Hotham and Dinner Plain during the ski season. Dinner Plain is open all the year, as is Mt. Hotham, and offers beautiful walks when the snow is not around. It is regarded as Australia's most stylish Alpine resort, with the architecture based on early mountain cattlemen's huts.

Beyond Dinner Plain lies a descent to the town of **Omeo** and if one continues along the **Great Alpine Road**, one eventually reaches **Lakes Entrance** on the Victorian coast. However, there is no public transport along this route.

On two days a week, Mondays and Fridays, the V-Line bus service is extended beyond Bright to **Mt. Beauty**, an additional 31 kilometres of climbing. On the way it passes near **Tawonga**. Both Mt. Beauty and Tawonga are bases for skiing in the winter. Although not famous ski resorts themselves, they offer accommodation for resorts within easy range. Mt. Beauty has a population of 2,100 and was built in 1947 to house workers of the Hydro-Electric Scheme. It is a pretty town surrounded by some beautiful walking country. It is at the foot of Victoria's highest peak, **Mt. Bogong** at 1,986 metres. **Tours of the hydro-electric power stations** are available.

MT. BEAUTY
Numerals indicate accommodation

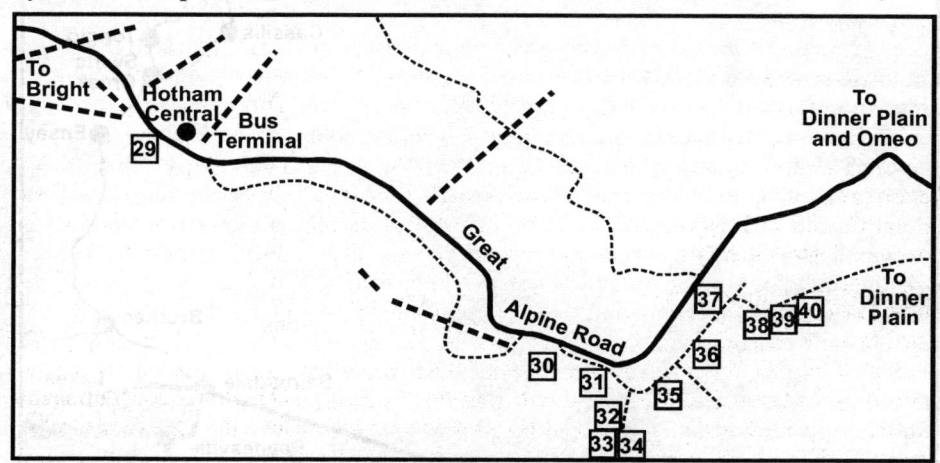

MT. HOTHAM
Thick dashed lines denote ski lifts
Thin dashed lines show walking and skiing trails
Numerals indicate accommodation

824 VICTORIA

Tawonga is similar, but smaller than Mt. Beauty. Set in the **Kiewa Valley**, it offers accommodation and walks, including the walk to the top of Mt. Bogong. Although Tawonga is not within comfortable walking distance of the V-Line bus route, there is a bus service operated by Pyle's running between Albury and Mt. Beauty via Tawonga.

Beyond Mt. Beauty is another famous ski resort, **Falls Creek**. This is a distance of 32 kilometres along a road which is not of the same high standard as the road to Mt. Hotham, but is passable even during winter. A bus service to Falls Creek is provided by Pyle's Coach Services from Melbourne, Albury and Mt. Beauty. From Melbourne a return ticket costs $120 and a single $85. From Mt. Beauty a return costs $35, a day

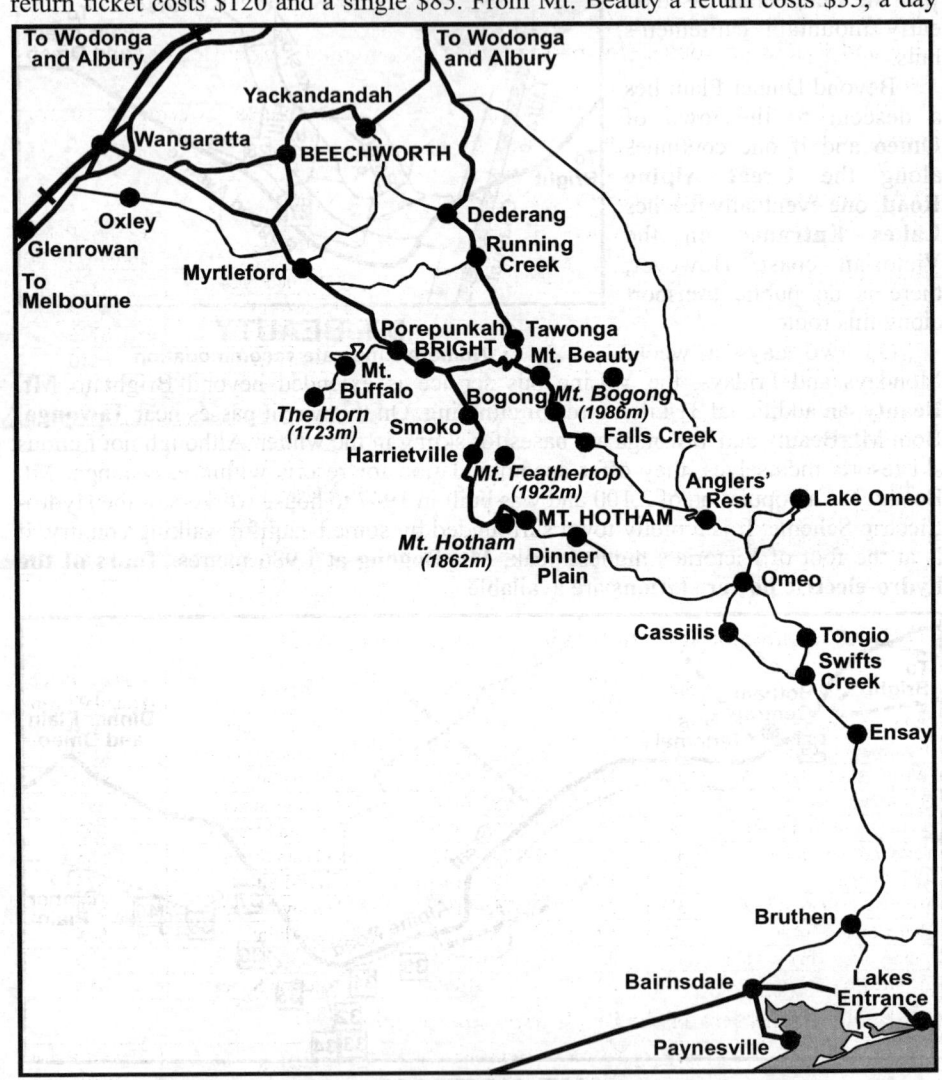

BEECHWORTH, BRIGHT, MT. HOTHAM AND THE GREAT ALPINE ROAD
Thicker lines indicate public transport routes

BEECHWORTH, BRIGHT, MT. HOTHAM 825

return $30 and a single $22. This service runs all year but the timetable varies according to the season. Telephone 03-5754-4024 to obtain current details.

Falls Creek is open all year and offers magnificent views and exhilarating walks outside the snow season. If you continue along this road, you will again reach **Omeo** and eventually **Lakes Entrance**. However, between Falls Creek and Omeo the road is closed in winter.

ACCOMMODATION

Accommodation is listed for Beechworth, Bright, Mt. Hotham and Mt. Beauty. There is additional accommodation available at Tawonga South, which is on the V-Line and Pyle's bus routes. Tawonga too has accommodation, but is served only by Pyle's.

Note that the prices for Mt. Hotham are for ski lodges offering dormitory accommodation and are on a per person basis.

(i) Accommodation in Beechworth *(see map on page 820)*

Name	Stars	No. on Map	Telephone No.	Address	Lowest Price (Double/Twin)
Beechworth House B&B	4½	12	03-5728-2817	5 Dingle Road	$135
Country Charm Cottages	4½	10	03-5728-2435	22 Malakoff Road	$130
Erindale Guest House		3	03-5728-2013	1 Victoria Road	$125
Barnsley House B&B	4	11	03-5728-1037	5 John Street	$110
Gorge Walk Guest House	4	5	03-5728-2867	10 Last Street	$100
Rose Cottage B&B	4	6	03-5728-1069	42 Camp Street	$100
Armour Motor Inn	3½	9	03-5728-1466	1 Camp Street	$95
Carriage Motor Inn	3½	7	03-5728-1830	Camp & Finch Streets	$95
Alba Country Rose	3½	13	03-5728-1107	30 Malakoff Road	$90
Old Priory Guest House	3	8	03-5728-1024	8 Priory Lane	$90
Golden Heritage Inn	3	2	1-800-812-269	51 Sydney Road	$80
Lake Sambell C'van Park	3½	4	03-5728-1421	McConville Avenue	$70
Beechworth Motor Inn	3½	1	03-5728-1301	54 Sydney Road	$65

(ii) Hotel Accommodation in Bright *(see map on page 822)*

Name	Stars	No. on Map	Telephone No.	Address	Lowest Price (Double/Twin)
Bright Avenue Motel	3½	22	03-5755-1911	87 Delany Avenue	$120
Panorama Holiday Units	3½	24	03-5755-1315	54 Coronation Avenue	$120
Westwood Lodge	4½	18	03-5755-1465	8 Wood Street	$105
Riverbank Park Motel	3	14	03-5755-1476	69 Gavan Street	$95
John Bright Motor Inn	4	17	03-5755-1400	10 Wood Street	$95
Colonial Inn Motel	3½	15	03-5755-1633	54 Gavan Street	$85
Elm Lodge	2½	16	03-5755-1144	2 Wood Street	$75
Bright Alps Guest House	3½	21	03-5755-1197	83 Delany Avenue	$70
Star Hotel / Motel	2	19	03-5755-1277	91 Great Alpine Road	$65
Pine Valley Tourist Park	4½	23	03-5755-1010	7 Churchill Avenue	$60
Alpine Hotel / Motel	2	20	03-5755-1366	7 Anderson Street	$55

(iii) Backpackers Hostels in Bright *(see map on page 822)*

Name	Group	No. on Map	Telephone No.	Address	Lowest Price (Dormitory)
Bright and Alpine B/P		26	03-5755-1154	106 Coronation Avenue	$20
Bright Hikers Backpackers	VIP	25	03-5750-1244	Top Floor, 4 Ireland Street	$20

826 VICTORIA
(iv) Accommodation in Mt. Beauty *(see map on page 823)*

Name	Stars	No. on Map	Telephone No.	Address	Lowest Price (Double/Twin)
Meriki Motel	3	27	03-5754-4145	Tawonga Crescent	$70
Jane's B&B	4	28	03-5754-4036	40 Tawonga Crescent	$70

(v) Lodge Accommodation in Mt. Hotham *(see map on page 823)*

Name	Stars	No. on Map	Telephone No.	Address	Lowest Price (per person)
Snowbird Inn	2	29	03-5759-3503	Great Alpine Road	$66
Pegasus Alpine Ski Club		32	03-5248-2398	Great Alpine Road	$66
Gravbrot Ski Club		36	0500-593-533	Great Alpine Road	$60
Karnalurra Ski Lodge		30	03-5759-2517	Great Alpine Road	$49
Kalyna Ski Lodge		31	03-5759-3594	Great Alpine Road	$42
Tanderra Ski Lodge		37	1-800-819-410	Great Alpine Road	$42
Bundarra Ski Lodge		33	03-5759-3596	Great Alpine Road	$39
Lodge Ski Club		39	0500-888-099	Great Alpine Road	$39
Brush Ski Lodge		34	1-800-653-749	Great Alpine Road	$37
Eumarellah Ski Lodge		38	1-800-683-862	Great Alpine Road	$37
Wongungarra Alpine Club		35	03-9873-5477	Great Alpine Road	$33
Bembooka Ski Lodge		40	03-5657-3221	Great Alpine Road	$31

MOVING ON
(i) By Bus plus Train Connexions

The timetable below shows bus plus train connexions from Mt. Beauty, Bright and Beechworth to Melbourne.

Mt. Beauty, Bright and Beechworth to Melbourne

Days of Operation	W, F (Bus)	M-Sat (Bus)	M - F (Bus)	M, W, F (Bus)	F (Bus)	M,Tu Th, F (Bus)	M - F (Bus)	M - F (Bus)	Daily	Sat, Sun (Bus)	Sat, Sun	W (Bus)	F (Bus)
Mt. Beauty						1025*							
Bright	0545					1125				1520†		1645	1815
Beechworth	0635		0700	0920		1215		1500		1620†			1905
Wangaratta	0710	0726	0735	0955	1005	1255	1314	1535	1543	1655†	1708†	1750	1945
Benalla		0755			1045		1339		1614		1734†		
Melbourne		1010			1325		1551		1815		1950†		

* Mondays and Fridays only   † 25 minutes later on Sundays

(ii) By Bus from Mt. Beauty

Destination	Operator	Via	Distance (km)	Fare	Journey Time	Frequency
Melbourne	Pyle's		339	$85	6 hrs	1/day
Albury	Pyle's		93	$20	2¼ hrs	1/day
Wangaratta	V-Line		113	$23.30	2½ hrs	2/week
Falls Creek	Pyle's		32	$22	50 mins	4/day

(iii) By Bus from Bright

Destination	Operator	Via	Distance (km)	Fare	Journey Time	Frequency
Melbourne	Trekset	(seasonal)	308	$85	4¼ - 4½ hrs	1/day
Wangaratta	V-Line		82	$13	1¼ - 1¾ hrs	2/day
Mt. Beauty	V-Line		31	$7.90	1 hr	2/week
Mt. Hotham	Trekset	(seasonal)	56	$35	1½ hrs	2/day

In addition to the bus departures from Bright and from Mt. Beauty, there is a service between Beechworth and Albury twice a day operated by Wangaratta Coachlines.

WODONGA
Population 31,000
3 hrs 30 mins by train from Melbourne

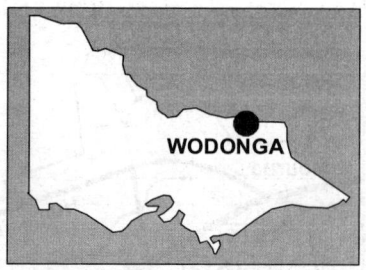

Wodonga is the little brother of Albury in New South Wales, for information on which see page 131. Long-distance bus services operated by McCafferty's, Greyhound and Firefly do not stop in Wodonga, but they stop in Albury and it is only a short local bus ride to cross the border. The train between Sydney and Melbourne, operated by Countrylink, also stops only in Albury, but the three V-Line trains each day between Melbourne and Albury all stop in Wodonga. In addition, V-Line operates buses between Wodonga and Canberra, Adelaide and Mildura.

Wodonga was first settled in 1836 and has always been of importance as this was the natural point for crossing the Murray when travelling between Sydney and Melbourne. For a walking tour of Albury, see page 132. Now let us have a tour of the southern side of the border in Wodonga.

Walking Tour

This walk will cover about eight kilometres and take two hours, plus any time spent at the Information Centre.

Start at the **Wodonga Railway Station** and turn left into Elgin Street, then left again into High Street. Cross South Street and turn left when you reach Osburn Street. This will lead you into **Sumsion Gardens**, named after Mr. Eric Sumsion who spent much of his life trying to establish and preserve the park land around Wodonga. Walk through the gardens and exit at the northern end. Here you will find the new Hume Freeway. You can pass beneath the road and turn right between it and Wodonga Creek. Follow this path onto the Lincoln Causeway and walk until the road bends right to cross the Murray River. At this point you can cross beneath the road again, and double back a short distance beside the Murray to the **Gateway Information Centre**, which is in a good position, no doubt, for motorists, but hardly convenient for those arriving by public transport. On the far side of the river, you can see South Albury and New South Wales.

The Gateway Information Centre was originally a dairy built in the 1920s. The former **Butter Factory** has been converted into a performance area, and other buildings house craft galleries, a pottery, a café and an occasional market. Nearby is the **Powder Magazine**, constructed in 1878 and restored in 1991. Its purpose was to store gunpowder used in mining operations.

From here, head back south towards Wodonga, but follow the path beside the Murray as it turns away east and leaves the highway. Ten minutes walk will bring you to the **railway bridge** spanning the river. This was erected in 1883 with sections shipped from England and, at that time, it was an important bridge as it linked two British colonies. However, it did not mean that one could travel through between

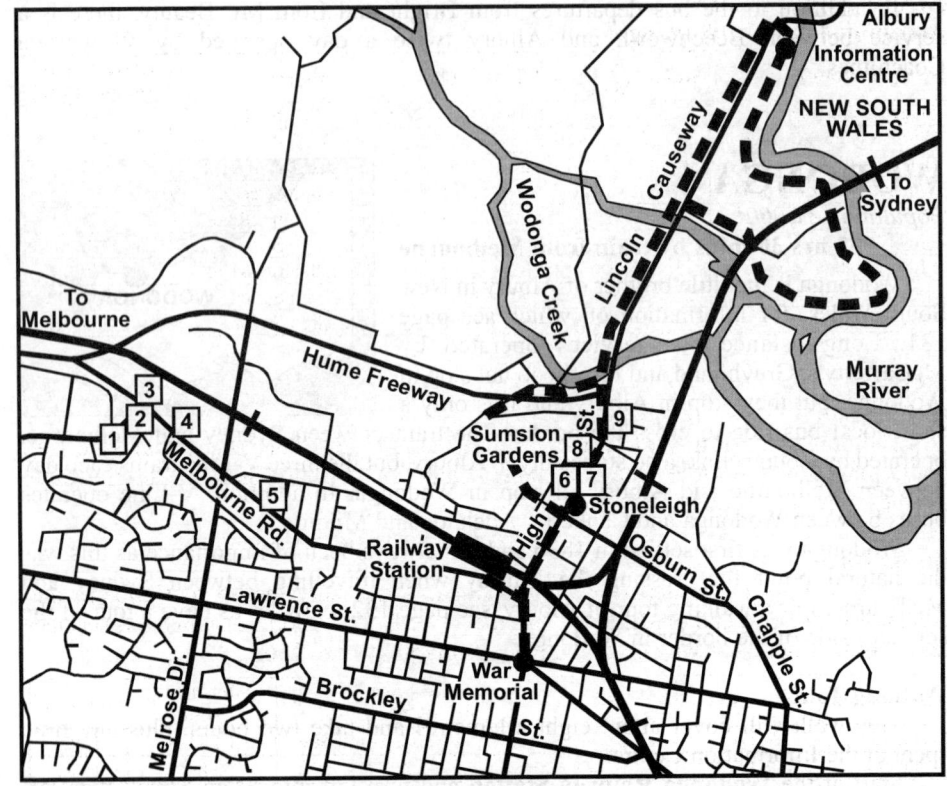

WODONGA
Dashed line shows Walking Tour
Numerals indicate accommodation

Sydney and Melbourne on a single train, since Victoria had built broad gauge tracks (5 feet 3 inches), while New South Wales had opted for standard gauge (4 feet 8½ inches). It did mean, though, that passengers could reach Albury Station and there change trains. It was to take another 79 years before they were able to make the journey between the two capitals on a single train.

Continue along the path beside the Murray as it loops round and eventually comes back under the railway. When you rejoin the causeway, turn left and walk back into Wodonga along High Street. Just past Huon Street on your left you will find the oldest building in the town. This is *Stoneleigh*, built in 1858 and currently an antique shop (in two senses). Continue down High Street for another five minutes and you will reach the **War Memorial** built in 1924 by returned servicemen, and here our tour ends. Although Albury and Wodonga are generally regarded as twins, you will have noticed how much more rural Wodonga seems than its big brother across the river.

ACCOMMODATION
Accommodation in Wodonga

Name	Stars	No. on Map	Telephone No.	Address	Lowest Price (Double/Twin)
Stagecoach Motel	4	4	1-800-806-434	188 Melbourne Road	$95
Border Gateway Motel	3½	1	1-800-033-154	6 Moorefield Park Drive	$85
Belvoir Village Motel	3½	2	02-6024-5344	2 Trafalgar Street	$85
Warrina Motor Inn	3½	6	02-6024-2111	31 High Street	$80
Twin City Motor Inn	2½	5	02-6024-2211	166 Melbourne Road	$75
Motel Wellington	3	7	02-6024-2400	46 High Street	$70
Murray Valley Motel	3	3	02-6024-1422	196 Melbourne Road	$70
Sanctuary Park Motel	2½	8	02-6024-1122	11 High Street	$70
Provincial Motel	3	9	02-6024-1200	12 High Street	$65

MOVING ON
(i) By Train

The timetable for trains to Melbourne appears in the Albury section on page 136, while for trains north to Sydney one must depart from Albury Station. The timetable for these services is on page 751.

(ii) By Bus

Only V-Line buses depart from Wodonga. These services go to Canberra and Adelaide every day, and to Mildura four times a week. Other long-distance bus services leave from Albury, for which see the bus summary on page 136.

Destination	Operator	Via	Distance (km)	Fare	Journey Time	Frequency
Adelaide	V-Line		902	$69	12¼ hrs	1/day
Canberra	V-Line		352	$39	5 hrs	1/day
Mildura	V-Line		605	$69	9¾ - 10½ hrs	4/week
		Echuca	236	$42.70	4 hrs	11/week

MANSFIELD AND MT. BULLER

Population 2,500 (Mansfield)
3 hrs by bus from Melbourne (Mansfield)
4 hrs by bus from Melbourne (Mt. Buller)

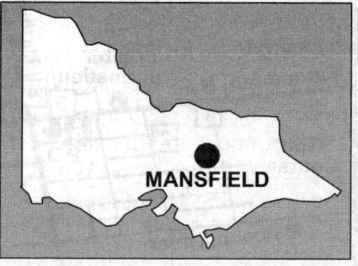

Lying south of Falls Creek, Mt. Hotham and Mt. Buffalo is another ski resort area at Mt. Buller. Although geographically close to the other resorts, it is reached by a different route, and in this case V-Line operates a bus service direct from Spencer Street Station in Melbourne to Mansfield, at the foot of the mountain, and private bus connexions are provided to the ski resort at Mt. Buller during the winter season.

Again there is beautiful scenery along the way. The route passes close to the very attractive **Lake Eildon** and, although it does not reach the most popular access point at the south of the lake, it passes through **Bonnie Doon**, which is on the northern shore

830 VICTORIA

and where there is a youth hostel (four kilometres from the bus stop, so it is better to ask to be picked up), as well as other accommodation.

Mansfield itself is a pleasant little town, quite cool in winter. At the end of every April there is a Hot-Air Balloon Festival held here. This was once the terminus of one of the 2 feet 6 inches narrow gauge railway lines constructed in rural Victoria to provide an economic public transport service, in which endeavour they were notably unsuccessful. The former **Railway Station** in Mansfield is now used as the **Visitor Information Centre**.

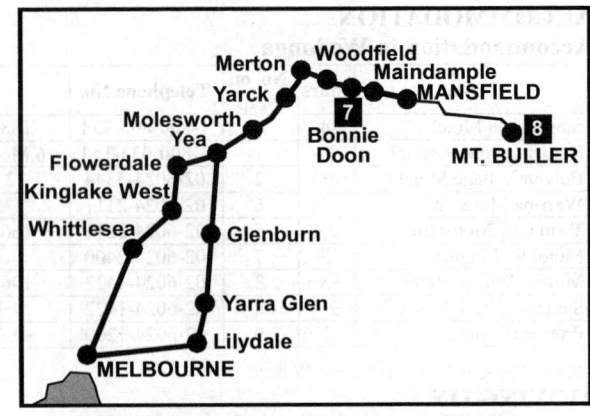

MELBOURNE TO MT. BULLER
Showing principal bus stops
Numerals indicate backpackers hostels

Mansfield also has its connexion with the Kelly Gang, for **Stringybark Creek** is just outside the town, and it was here that the murders were committed for which Kelly was eventually hanged. There is a **memorial** to the murdered policemen in the town, near the Mansfield Hotel.

Mansfield is used as an accommodation centre by some of those wishing to ski at **Mt. Buller**. From here it is 48 kilometres to the Alpine resort and in winter there is a bus service up the mountain connecting with the arrival of V-Line buses in Mansfield and taking a further hour. The cost of this bus, operated by Mansfield - Mt. Buller Bus Lines, is $40 return. A mid-week day return is offered for $35. The same company operates four direct buses a week between Melbourne and Mt. Buller in the winter only. These leave Melbourne on Sunday, Wednesday and Friday mornings, and Friday evenings, and return from Mt. Buller on Sunday, Wednesday and Friday afternoons, with two buses on Sundays. The fare is $120 return.

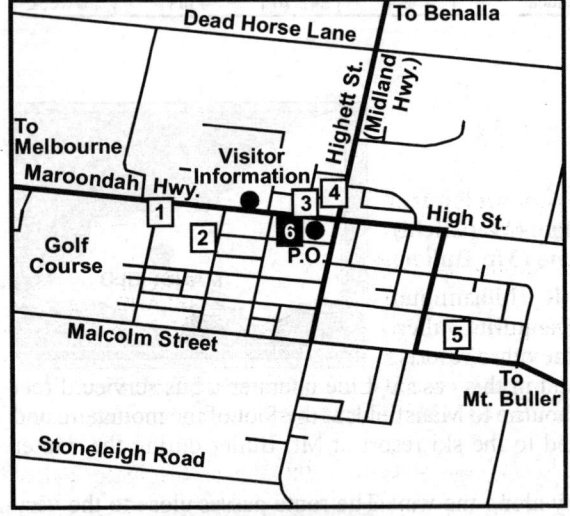

MANSFIELD
Black numerals indicate hotel accommodation
White numerals indicate backpackers hostels

Mt. Buller is popular for skiing because it is so easily accessible from Melbourne. Although it has the greatest capacity of any Australian Alpine resort, with over 7,000 beds, not only is demand high, but prices are too. There is a youth hostel here, but a

MANSFIELD, MT. BULLER   831

dormitory bed costs $55, reduced to $44 at off-peak times mid-week at the beginnings and endings of the ski season. Rates in Mansfield are more modest.

ACCOMMODATION
(i) Hotel Accommodation in Mansfield

Name	Stars	No. on Map	Telephone No.	Address	Lowest Price (Double/Twin)
Alpine Country Cottages	4	5	03-5775-1694	5 The Parade	$185
Mansfield Valley Inn	3½	1	03-5775-1300	Maroondah Hwy. & Elvin St	$85
Mansfield Motel		4	03-5775-2377	3 Highett Street	$75
Delatite Hotel		3	03-5775-2004	95 High Street	$70
High Country Holiday Pk.	3½	2	03-5775-2706	1 Ultimo Street	$65

(ii) Backpackers Hostel in Mansfield

Name	Group	No. on Map	Telephone No.	Address	Lowest Price (Dormitory)
Mansfield Backpackers Inn		6	03-5775-1800	112 High Street	$19

(iii) Backpackers Hostels in Bonnie Doon and Mt. Buller

Name	Group	No. on Map	Telephone No.	Address	Lowest Price (Dormitory)
Lakeside Leisure Resort	YHA	7	03-5778-7252	Hutchinson's Rd, Bonnie Doon	$18
Y.H.A. Lodge	YHA	8	03-5777-6181	The Avenue, Mt. Buller	$55

MOVING ON
Bus Services from Mansfield

Destination	Operator	Via	Distance (km)	Fare	Journey Time	Frequency
Melbourne	V-Line			$34.40	3 hrs	2/day
Mt. Buller	Mt. Buller Bus	(seasonal)		$40*	1 hr	6/day

* Return fare

PHILLIP ISLAND
Population 5,500
2 hrs 30 mins by train and ferry from Melbourne
3 hrs 30 mins by bus from Melbourne (Cowes)

Phillip Island lies to the south-east of Melbourne, further east than the Mornington Peninsula. It is famous for its **penguins**. These penguins, the smallest breed in the world, always used to be known as Fairy Penguins, but now we are told that we should call them Little Penguins. Perhaps the change is connected with recent legislation concerning sexual discrimination.

Phillip Island was discovered by George Bass in 1798. It was originally called Snapper Island, and then Grant Island, and finally named in honour of the first Governor. The island was visited by whalers and sealers, and then in 1826 it became briefly a military outpost. From 1839, it was used as a sheep farm, and then settlement started in 1865. It was a chicory-growing area for a while, but now that we can afford real coffee that industry has almost disappeared, although old chicory kilns can be seen around the island still. Visitors started to come and see the penguins in the 1920s, and are still coming, now at the rate of half a million a year.

Phillip Island should certainly be on the itinerary of every visitor, because it is so easily accessible and there is so much to see, so let us start by getting to the island. There are two ways, so why not go by one route and return by the other? The first and more interesting route has already been mentioned on page 745. Take a suburban train to Frankston and then the connecting rail service to Stony Point, from where a ferry operates to the main town of Cowes on Phillip Island. If you get the timing right, the whole trip will take about 2½ hours and will cost $6.10 for a two-hour metropolitan ticket, which will take you as far as Stony Point, plus $10 for the ferry ride. A good ferry to catch would be the 12:00 departure on the days on which it operates (Tuesdays, Thursdays, Saturdays and Sundays). There are good connexions on Saturdays and Sundays, with a train leaving Frankston at 11:05 and reaching Stony Point at 11:45, to connect with which one needs to leave Flinders Street at 10:00 on Saturdays and 9:56 on Sundays. If you prefer the 17:00 ferry, there are good connexions on weekdays, with a train leaving Frankston at 16:13 and reaching Stony Point at 16:53, to catch which one departs from Flinders Street at 14:59. Of course, these times can change, so should be checked in advance.

The other route is by V-Line bus service. There is one bus per day on Mondays to Thursdays (departure from Spencer Street currently at 15:50) and two on Fridays, Saturdays and Sundays. On Saturdays and Sundays, the buses leave from Dandenong Station and one takes a suburban train from Melbourne to Dandenong to make the connexion. This route takes approximately 3½ hours and costs $17.60 single or $24.90 for an off-peak return.

Phillip Island is reached by a bridge extending from **San**

PUBLIC TRANSPORT TO PHILLIP ISLAND
(No passenger rail service beyond Cranbourne)

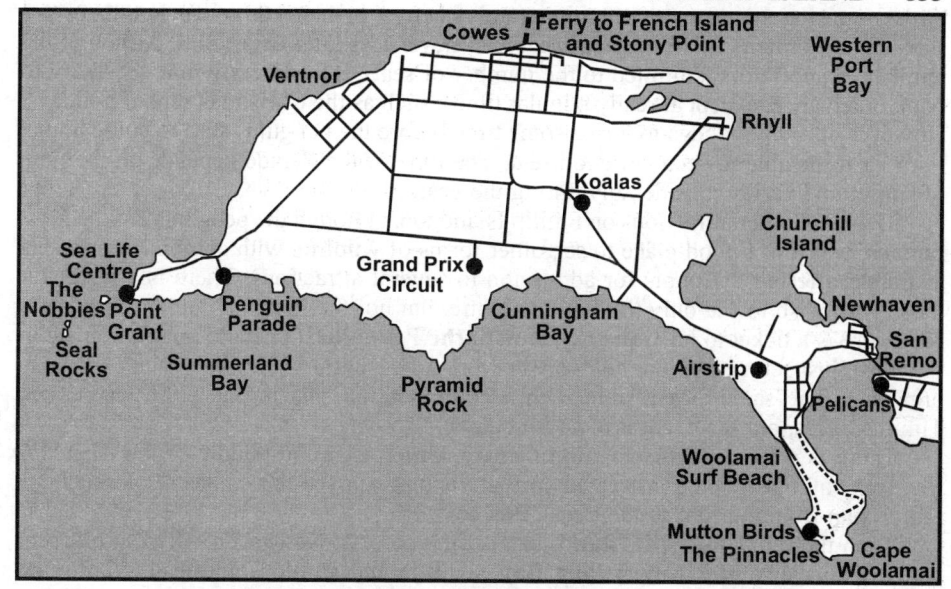

PHILLIP ISLAND

Remo on the mainland to **Newhaven** on the eastern point of the island. **Cowes**, on the north, is the largest town, but accommodation is also available at **Newhaven, Rhyll** and **Ventnor**. Any connexion between the names of the towns here and those on a British island must be regarded as purely co-incidental. The bus passes by Newhaven and terminates in Cowes. Phillip Island has 5,500 permanent residents, but numbers swell to about 40,000 in summer, and the number of visitors is over three million annually.

The main attraction, then, is the penguins, so how do we go about seeing them? The **Penguin Colony** lives at the south-west of the island in **Summerland Bay**, which is not near any of the towns. Therefore, you need transport to reach there. There are tours available, or the owner of your accommodation may be able to assist, or you can hire a bicycle (with lights). When the author first came here, penguins were free. One just stood around on the foreshore and watched them come home. Not any longer. The area is fenced off now and one must purchase an expensive ticket to gain entry to tiered seating along the edge of the beach, plus the **Visitor Centre**. This ticket costs $15. However, one does get a better view now, especially as the area is better lit, and one can also get closer to the penguins than previously. The penguins have requested though that their photographs be not taken, since they find flashes rather disturbing. The **Penguin Parade** is a somewhat comical event. As dusk deepens, the birds start arriving, almost magically, flipping out of the sea, after a hard day's fishing during which they may have covered quite amazing distances. They gather in small groups at the water's edge, dash up the beach towards their burrows, change their minds and run back to the safety of the sea. This performance is repeated several times, until one starts to feel concerned about their timidity and wants to go and reassure them that the coast really is clear. Finally, after many aborted attempts, they summon up courage and race home. Numbers of penguins on display vary. The best months are November to January, when there are about 700 birds returning home every evening (and when it is not too cool), but there are substantial numbers at all times of the year, never less than about 300. Although the number of spectators is limited to the number of seats, it is generally not necessary to book in advance, except at really popular times, such as the Christmas school holidays. However, it is a good idea to arrive some time before the penguins start to come home, in order to be able to secure a good seat. The time of the Parade depends on the time of sunset and varies considerably during the year.

There are other attractions on Phillip Island too, although the penguins are the most famous, and it is a good place to see other forms of wildlife, with combination tickets available offering discounts for admission to several attractions. There is a ticket for those who wish to see only the Visitor Centre, but not the Penguin Parade. This costs $4. There is a ticket to have **Breakfast with the Penguins**. (They do not participate in the meal, just scurry past on their way to work.) This costs $50, which is an expensive breakfast. The same is available with accommodation, starting at $100 per person. Timing varies, but the event is always at dawn.

There is a **Koala Conservation Centre**, which is in the middle of the island. A tree-top walk has been constructed so that visitors can see the koalas at close range, rather than from the foot of the trees. This costs $6.

Then there is **Churchill Island**, just off the coast at Newhaven, offering pleasant walks with views of **Western Port Bay**, wildlife and an old homestead. Admission costs $6. Combined admission to Penguins, Koalas and Churchill Island costs $20.

Another type of wildlife which can be visited here is seals. The **Seal Rocks Sea Life Centre** is at the westernmost point of the island and here seals can be viewed either at the Centre or on a cruise. The **cruises** are operated commercially and depart from Cowes. They are not cheap at approximately $50 for two hours, but seals are guaranteed since the colony of **Grey Fur Seals** at Seal Rocks numbers in excess of 5,000, and since the cruises bring small presents to encourage participation.

At the south-eastern tip of the island is a colony of **mutton birds**, at their best at dusk between November and April.

At San Remo, on the mainland at the end of the bridge, are **pelicans**, fed daily at 11:30.

To see all of these attractions, good value is available from *Duck Truck Tours*. These tours are part of the offering of Amaroo Park, which is the youth hostel and has other accommodation available too, but it is not necessary to stay at Amaroo Park in order to participate in the tours. A Day Tour visits the koalas and pelicans and costs $25, including admission fees to the koalas. An Evening Tour takes you to the penguins and also costs $25, including admission fees and a hot drink.

There are also packages starting and finishing in Melbourne. For $120 you can be transported from Melbourne to Cowes and back, have three nights dormitory accommodation in Amaroo Park (or pay $4 supplement per person per night for a double or twin room), one Day Tour, one Evening Tour, a bicycle for half a day and three dinners. Tours to Wilson's Promontory are also available for $65, and, if you decide to stay at Amaroo Park, free transport to and from Melbourne is offered on Tuesdays and Fridays only.

There are also motor-bikes on Phillip Island, at least at some times of the year. Car and motor-cycle racing has been taking place here since 1928. The circuit, best known for its motor-cycle events, including the **Australian Motor-Cycle Grand Prix**, is in the south of the island and has a **Visitor Centre** open daily from 10:00 until 17:00.

Then there are **beaches**. On the south are the surf beaches. On the north of the island are the family beaches, including a good one at Cowes itself. There are also various walking tracks around the island and pleasant walks along the beaches, so you should not be bored during your time here.

ACCOMMODATION
(i) Hotel Accommodation in Cowes

Name	Stars	No. on Map	Telephone No.	Address	Lowest Price (Double/Twin)
Quest Apartments		5	03-5982-2644	Bass Avenue & Chapel St.	$215
Holmwood Guest House	4	11	03-5952-3082	Chapel & Steele Streets	$165
Abaleigh Cottages	4½	14	03-5952-5649	6 Roy Court	$165
Castle Inn B&B	4½	9	03-5952-1228	7 Steele Street	$165
Narrabeen Guest House	4½	10	03-5952-2062	16 Steele Street	$145
Continental	4	7	03-5952-2316	5 The Esplanade	$125
Coachman Motel	4	6	03-5952-1098	51 Chapel Street	$110
Sheerwater Holiday Units	3	1	03-5952-2113	32 Beach Street	$95
Tropicana Motor Inn	3½	2	03-5952-1874	22 Osbourne Street	$95
Anchor Motel	3	8	03-5952-1351	1 The Esplanade	$95
Seahorse Motel	3	13	03-5952-2003	29 Chapel Street	$75
Kaloha Motel	3½	12	03-5952-2179	Chapel & Steele Streets	$75
New Hollydene Motel	2½	3	03-5952-2311	114 Thompson Avenue	$65
Isle of Wight Hotel	2	4	03-5952-2301	The Esplanade	$55

(ii) Backpackers Hostel in Cowes

Name	Group	No. on Map	Telephone No.	Address	Lowest Price (Dormitory)
Amaroo Park	YHA	15	03-5952-2548	97 Church Street	$20

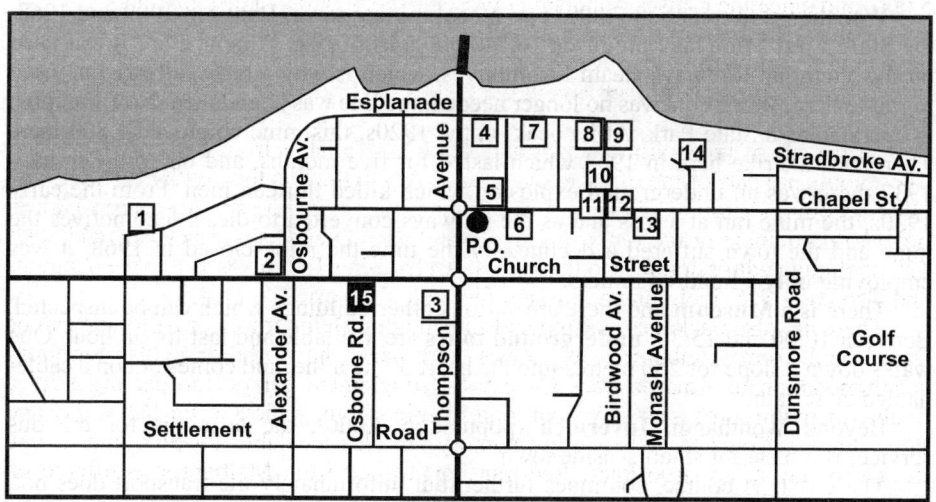

COWES
Black numerals in white boxes indicate hotel accommodation
White numerals in black boxes indicate backpackers hostels

836 VICTORIA
MOVING ON
Bus Services from Cowes

Destination	Operator	Via	Distance (km)	Fare	Journey Time	Frequency
Melbourne	V-Line		139	$17.60	3 - 3¼ hrs	2/day
		Dandenong	107	$13	2 - 2¼ hrs	2/day

SOUTH GIPPSLAND
Population 2,000 (Yarram)
3 hrs 30 mins by bus from Melbourne (Yarram)

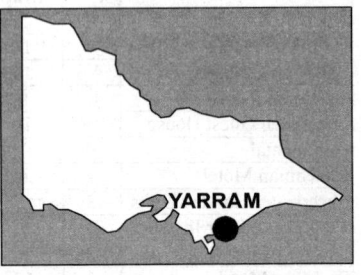

Gippsland was one of the first parts of Victoria to be settled and the area is not only of historic interest but scenic as well. There is so much to see that only a few special places can be picked out, but wherever you go here you will find gentle green countryside with views of sea or hills, or both.

There are two V-Line bus services to South Gippsland, both replacing railways which have now been partially or totally abandoned. One of these services follows the same route as the bus to Phillip Island, but at **Anderson**, reached eight minutes before San Remo, the bus turns left instead of right and travels to Wonthaggi and Inverloch. There are three such services on Mondays to Thursdays, four services on Fridays, two on Saturdays and one on Sundays. The morning bus on weekdays and all buses on Saturdays and Sundays start from Dandenong and one takes a suburban train from Melbourne to Dandenong to connect with the bus service.

Wonthaggi (population 7,000) was a coal mining town. Between 1909 and 1968, the **State Coal Mine** here produced 16,740,000 tons of coal. Almost all of it was used on the Victorian Railways steam locomotives, which is why a busy railway line used to run to here. When coal was no longer needed, the line was abandoned. Now the mine is operated as a State Park. At its peak, in the 1920s, this mine employed 1,800 men. There was a strike here in 1934 which lasted for five months, and on 15th February 1937 there was an underground explosion which killed thirteen men. From the early 1930s, the mine ran at a loss and as the railways converted to diesel locomotives the mine and the town suffered a decline. By the time the mine closed in 1968, it was employing only a hundred miners.

There is a **Museum** and there are various other buildings which can be inspected. Between 10:00 and 15:30, **underground tours** are available and last for an hour. One walks down a slope for 280 metres into the heart of the mine, and comes out on a cable-hauled coal train.

Beyond Wonthaggi, **Inverloch** (population 3,000), the terminus for the bus service, is a pleasant small seaside town.

The coast, of course, continues further, but unfortunately the transport does not. You now have to retrace your path for quite a long way to **Lang Lang**, about an hour on the bus. Here you will meet the course of another railway. This line was in use for passenger services to Leongatha until about a decade ago, although threatened with closure for a long time. Now the section from **Nyora**, the next station east, to

SOUTH GIPPSLAND

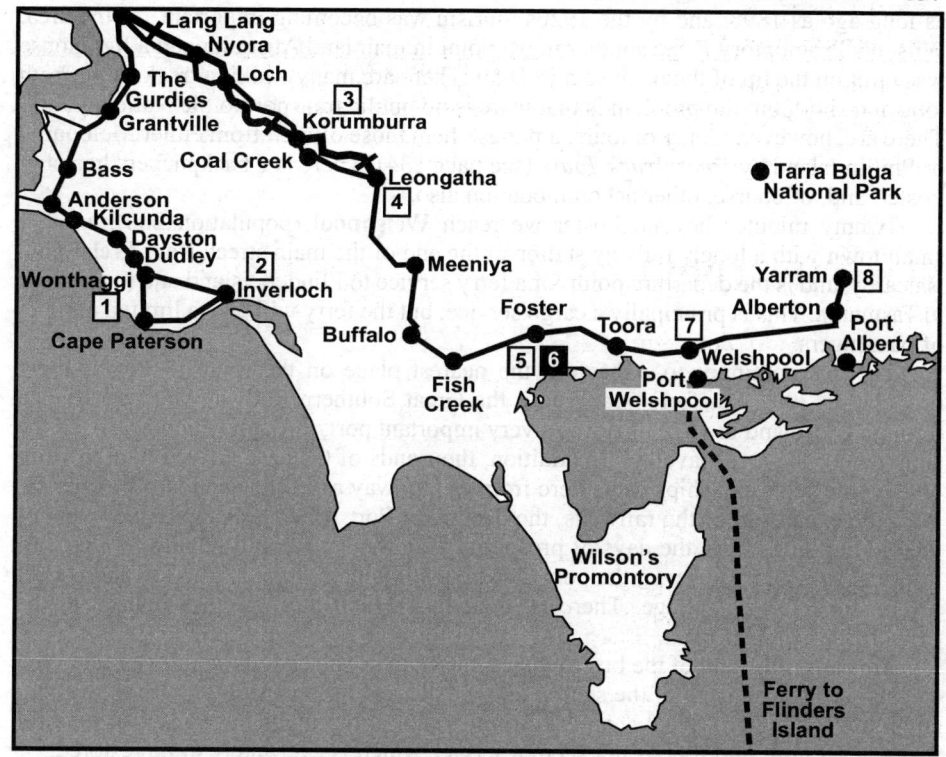

PUBLIC TRANSPORT AND ACCOMMODATION IN SOUTH GIPPSLAND
No regular passenger rail service operates on line shown
Black numerals in white boxes indicate hotel accommodation
White numerals in black boxes indicate backpackers hostels

Leongatha is used by the *South Gippsland Tourist Railway*, a private group operating occasional trains. V-Line operates four buses every day except Sunday as far as Leongatha. On Sundays there are two buses. One bus every day continues to Foster, Welshpool and Yarram (two buses on Fridays only). At weekends some services operate only from Dandenong, to reach which one takes a suburban train.

Korumburra (population 3,000) is 35 minutes beyond Lang Lang and fifteen minutes before Leongatha (population 3,800). Korumburra is a pleasant town, now best known for its **Coal Creek Heritage Village**, which is a re-creation of a late nineteenth century or early twentieth century mining and railway community. Some fifty buildings have been collected here from other locations and the area has been landscaped and an operating bush tramway built. Coal Creek is on the bus route just beyond Korumburra (but not on the old railway) and the bus will stop here. The Heritage Village is open daily from 10:00 until 16:30 and admission costs $10.

Forty minutes beyond **Leongatha** is **Foster** (population 1,000), where we are beginning to approach the coast once more. Foster is the nearest town of any size to **Wilson's Promontory**, a particularly scenic and well-loved area of rural Victoria. It covers 50,000 hectares and offers granite mountains and beautiful coastal scenery with white, almost deserted beaches. Most of Wilson's Promontory became a National Park as long ago as 1898, and by the 1920s tourism was becoming important for the area. Wilson's Promontory is the southernmost point in mainland Australia and a lighthouse was built on the tip of the peninsula in 1859. There are many walking tracks here, both long and short, but the problem is that there is no public transport to the National Park. There are, however, plenty of tours, amongst them those offered from either Melbourne or Phillip Island by *Duck Truck Tours* (see page 834). There is a backpackers hostel in Foster, and, of course, other accommodation also.

Twenty minutes beyond Foster we reach **Welshpool** (population 200), another small town with a lonely railway station at the end of the main street. **Port Welshpool** is nearby, and is the departure point for a ferry service to Flinders Island and to Bridport in Tasmania. This is principally a cargo service, but the ferry will take a limited number of passengers.

The bus continues to **Alberton**, the nearest place on the route to **Port Albert** (population 300). For forty years, until the Great Southern Railway was constructed through Gippsland in 1878, this was a very important port, through which nearly all the supplies for the area travelled. In addition, thousands of Chinese arrived here to work on the goldfields and ships came here from as far away as Europe and North America. With the expansion of the railways, the decline of Port Albert was rapid and many of the old buildings from the days of prosperity and importance still remain as a type of informal museum. However, the port is some ten kilometres from Alberton and is now just a small fishing village. There is, though, a **Maritime Museum** housed in the former Bank of Victoria.

Yarram is the end of the bus route, as it used to be the end of the railway line. You can still see the remains of the station and the disused railway sidings here in the one-street town, another typical snippet of rural Victoria. No trains have reached here for many years now, and it does not seem a service which is ever likely to be restored.

There is a **Visitor Information Centre** housed in the renovated former **Courthouse**. One of the main attractions of the area is the **Tarra Bulga National Park**, a cool temperate forest area of mountain ash and beech trees, giant ferns and many types of birds. There is a pedestrian suspension bridge over a spectacular gully and a pretty waterfall. However, the National Park is thirty kilometres from the town of Yarram and there is no public transport available. The **Grand Ridge Road** which runs through the park in an east - west direction is also spectacular in many places, but again there is no public transport which operates along this route.

ACCOMMODATION
(i) Accommodation in Wonthaggi

Name	Stars	No. on Map	Telephone No.	Address	Lowest Price (Double/Twin)
Wonthaggi Motel	3	1	03-5672-2922	40 McKenzie Street	$110
Miners Rest Motel	2½	1	03-5672-1033	140 McKenzie Street	$65

(ii) Accommodation in Inverloch

Name	Stars	No. on Map	Telephone No.	Address	Lowest Price (Double/Twin)
Sandymount B&B	4½	2	03-5674-1325	25 Sandymount Avenue	$165
Central Motor Inn	3	2	03-5674-3500	32 A'Beckett Street	$75
Inverloch Holiday Park	4	2	03-5674-1447	2 Cuttriss Street	$65
Inverloch Motel	3	2	03-5674-3100	Bass Highway	$65
Inlet Hotel		2	03-5674-1481	3 The Esplanade	$55

(iii) Accommodation in Korumburra

Name	Stars	No. on Map	Telephone No.	Address	Lowest Price (Double/Twin)
Whitelaw Cottage B&B	2½	3	03-5655-1410	Sullivans Road.	$105
Coal Creek Motel	3	3	03-5655-1034	South Gippsland Highway	$75

(iv) Accommodation in Leongatha

Name	Stars	No. on Map	Telephone No.	Address	Lowest Price (Double/Twin)
Opal Motel	3	4	03-5662-2321	South Gippsland Highway	$75
Leongatha Motel	3	4	03-5662-2375	18 Turner Street	$70

(v) Hotel Accommodation in Foster

Name	Stars	No. on Map	Telephone No.	Address	Lowest Price (Double/Twin)
Foster Motel	3½	5	1-800-036-140	South Gippsland Highway	$95
Warrawee Holiday Units	3	5	03-5689-1242	38 Station Road	$75
Exchange Hotel		5	03-5682-2377	43 Main Street	$55

(vi) Backpackers Hostel in Foster

Name	Group	No. on Map	Telephone No.	Address	Lowest Price (Dormitory)
Foster Backpacker Hostel	B&W	6	03-5682-2614	17 Pioneer Street	$20

(vii) Accommodation in Welshpool

Name	Stars	No. on Map	Telephone No.	Address	Lowest Price (Double/Twin)
Welshpool Hotel	2	7	03-5688-1209	21 Main Street	$55

(viii) Accommodation in Yarram

Name	Stars	No. on Map	Telephone No.	Address	Lowest Price (Double/Twin)
Ship Inn Motel	3½	8	1-800-336-66	South Gippsland Highway	$75
Tarra Motel	3½	8	03-5182-5444	387 Commercial Road	$70

MOVING ON
(i) Bus Service from Inverloch

Destination	Operator	Via	Distance (km)	Fare	Journey Time	Frequency
Melbourne	V-Line		113	$23.30	3 - 3½ hrs	3/day
		Dandenong	81	$17.60	2 - 2½ hrs	3/day

(ii) Bus Service from Yarram

Destination	Operator	Via	Distance (km)	Fare	Journey Time	Frequency
Melbourne	V-Line		220	$34.40	3½ - 4¼ hrs	1/day
		Leongatha	89	$14.60	1½ hrs	1/day

LAKES ENTRANCE

Population 4,000

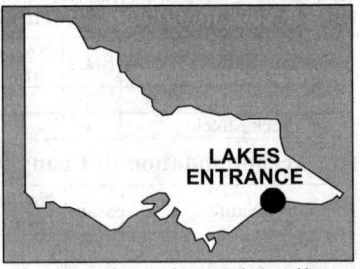

5 hrs by train and bus from Melbourne
5 hrs 30 mins by bus from Melbourne

Lakes Entrance is an attractive and popular town, but on the way to it through Central Gippsland there are many other places which are also worthy of a visit.

To travel east from Melbourne, we have the choice of train or bus. The railway once went as far as Orbost, but it is a long time since any trains reached that far east. For some years Bairnsdale was the limit for passenger service, but now the line has been cut back to Sale. For a while the Sale to Bairnsdale section was abandoned completely, but recently it has been re-opened for goods traffic and there has even been talk of resuming passenger service on this stretch. Talk, however, is not action, and for the foreseeable future Sale seems to be the limit for passenger trains. From Sale, connecting V-Line buses travel on to Bairnsdale, Lakes Entrance, Canberra and Batemans Bay.

By long-distance bus, services are operated via the coastal route between Melbourne and Sydney by Premier, the first setting-down point being Lakes Entrance.

Naturally, the author prefers the rail service. To reach Lakes Entrance there are two train plus bus services on Mondays to Thursdays, three on Fridays and one on Saturdays and Sundays. We set off from Spencer Street in Melbourne along the route of the suburban line to Dandenong and Pakenham through typical Melbourne suburbia. **Pakenham**, where the suburban rail service finishes, is an industrial area, but it is also popular for sky-diving at the weekends.

After an hour and a half, we come to **Warragul** (population 9,000). When the author first travelled this line, this used to be the refreshment halt and arrival here would be awaited with anticipation by a trainful of hungry and thirsty travellers. Even before the train had stopped, the doors would be open and passengers would be racing to the refreshment room waving their dollar notes, anxious to be first in the queue and make the most of the ten minutes allowed here for a quick pie and a beer before the old red wooden carriages rattled on. Now the train merely pauses, and sadly the cavernous refreshment room is permanently closed due to lack of patronage.

We pass through **Yarragon** (population 700), a pretty little town in the foothills of the **Strzelecki Ranges**, and come to **Moe** (population 16,500). Here the **Gippsland Heritage Centre** is to be found, an interesting collection of buildings brought from their original locations. There is also a fine collection of old horse-drawn vehicles. North of Moe lies **Mt. Baw Baw**, the nearest ski ground to Melbourne. There is cross-country skiing at **Mt. St. Gwinear** nearby. Then there are the mountain towns of **Erica** (population 150), **Rawson** (population 330) and **Walhalla** (population 25), between thirty and fifty kilometres north of Moe.

The most famous of this trio is the former gold mining community of **Walhalla**, now a ghost town, but one which tourism is gradually bringing to life again. Its revival was stimulated in 1998 by the introduction of the modern wonder of electricity. The old **cemetery** is interesting, as cemeteries nearly always are. Then there is the famous **cricket ground** at the top of the mountain, a nightmare for deep mid-wicket, since any boundary scored with force would run off the ground and down the side of the incline,

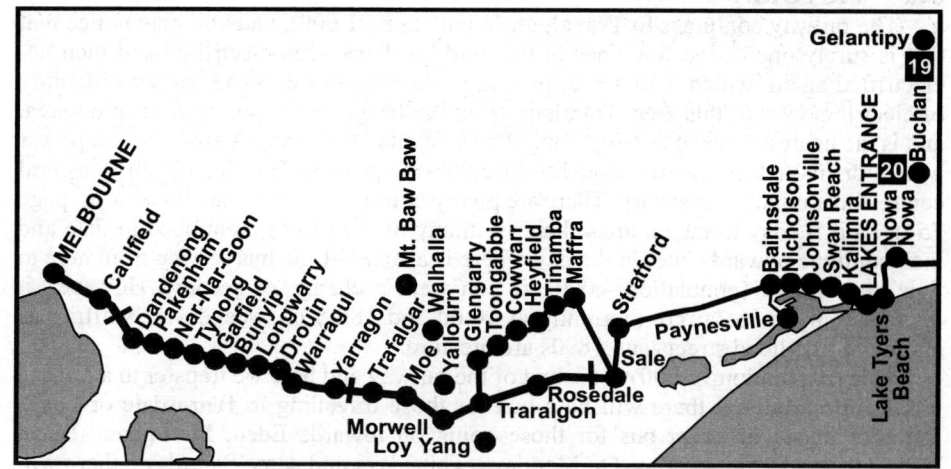

FROM MELBOURNE TO LAKES ENTRANCE
Showing V-Line services
Numerals indicate backpackers hostels

from where he would have to go and fetch it. The **Long Tunnel Extended Gold Mine**, one of the richest mines in the state, has been opened for visitors, with tours daily at 13:30.

By far the most popular of Walhalla's attractions, though, is the newly restored narrow gauge **Walhalla Goldfields Railway**. This is a really spectacular little ride, especially the crossing of the Thomson River on a lofty viaduct. Trains operate on Saturdays and Sundays, and on other days during school holidays, and cost $8 for the 45-minute return journey. This railway line originally ran from Moe to Walhalla via Rawson and Erica, and was one of the unsuccessful 2 feet 6 inches narrow gauge lines constructed by Victorian Railways, this one being completed in 1910. By the time it reached Walhalla, the gold was already running out and the town declining in importance. The service to Walhalla was discontinued in 1944, and the remaining part of the line, from Moe to Erica, was abandoned in 1954. The track had all been removed by 1962, so the recent replacement has been a major operation.

Another seventeen kilometres east of Moe is **Morwell** (population 15,000), centre of a huge coal-mining industry. The coal that is produced here in the **Latrobe Valley** is brown coal and it is mined by an open-cut operation, feeding the power stations nearby which produce much of Victoria's electricity. The Latrobe Valley contains 89% of Australia's brown coal reserves and these power stations produce 85% of the state's electricity. This has been the main source of Victorian power for eighty years now, the coal having been discovered in 1873 and the first electricity supplied to Melbourne by Yallourn A Power Station on 24th June 1924. **Yallourn** itself (population 1,200) is a town which exists solely because of the power generation industry, while for Moe and Morwell mining and power generation have become the principal sources of employment. **PowerWorks**, in Morwell, is an Exhibition Centre displaying everything associated with these industries, with tours of the mining area and of one of the power stations available several times a day. Even if you do not choose to have a tour of the mining operations, you will see them clearly from the train and be impressed by the scale of the work and of the machinery used.

842   VICTORIA

The railway continues to **Traralgon** (population 21,000), and you may notice that this is surely one of the few lines in the world to have been electrified and then de-electrified again, which is rather surprising when one considers the ready availability of electric power in this area. Traralgon is on the fringe of the power generation area, and is the nearest town to the Loy Yang Power Station. Loy Yang A is the largest power generator in Victoria, with a capacity of 2,000 megawatts. Traralgon itself is a rural centre and a minor tourist base. There are plenty of trains this far (see timetable on page 754), so it is easy to take a break here or in any of the places mentioned to date and then continue onwards later in the day. There is also a V-Line bus service from here to Sale via **Maffra** (population 4,000), if you want a change of scenery. However, it operates only twice a day (currently at 10:00 and 18:25 on weekdays). Maffra has attractive tree-lined streets and 1890s architecture.

Sale (population 14,000) is the end of the railway and here we transfer to a V-Line bus. In the morning, there will be a bus for those travelling to Bairnsdale or Lakes Entrance and a different bus for those going on towards Eden, Merimbula, Bega, Narooma and Batemans Bay. On Mondays, Thursdays and some Saturdays, there will be a third bus going to Canberra.

Sale, although not on the coast, is a port. A canal was constructed in 1888 to link it with the Thomson River, so that ocean-going steamers could come this far. There is an **Historical Museum** in the city and an **Art Gallery**. There are walks at **Sale Common Wetlands**, including a 400-metre boardwalk. There is also an interesting early **swing bridge** dating from the construction of the canal, but it is five kilometres from the city centre. If the bus is waiting, maybe you will just have time for the cup of coffee available at the station before moving on to Bairnsdale and Lakes Entrance.

Along the way, you will get a glimpse of **Stratford** (population 1,500), with its old-fashioned main street, the oldest permanent settlement in Gippsland. Stratford, co-incidentally, is located on the **Avon River**, which would, no doubt, gladden the heart of Mr. Shakespeare were he still around to know of it.

Then we reach **Bairnsdale**, founded in 1842 on a bend in the Mitchell River. Gold was discovered nearby in the 1860s and the main street reflects the affluence of the gold rush days. **St. Mary's Church** is remarkable for its hand-painted walls and ceiling, all the work of one man. Fifteen kilometres south is **Paynesville**, a centre for inland boating on the **Gippsland Lakes**. Between Bairnsdale and Paynesville is **Eagle Point**, where the flow of the river has deposited **silt jetties** stretching into **Lake King** for eight kilometres. They are claimed to be second in extent only to those in the Mississippi River. Paynesville Bus Lines runs between Bairnsdale and Paynesville five times on weekdays and once on Saturdays, travelling via Eagle Point on request.

Lakes Entrance is 35 minutes beyond Bairnsdale and is the holiday resort of this area. As one might anticipate, there is a series of lakes here and the entrance to them, i.e. the point at which access can be gained from the sea, is Lakes Entrance. It was not always so, for this is an artificial entrance. There is a sand spit along the sea and the entrance to the lakes was formerly tidal and negotiating it over the sand bar was a perilous business. In 1890 the present channel was dug and dredged through the sand spit, connecting the lake system permanently with the ocean.

Naturally, one of the activities in this area is taking a **cruise**. There are several companies providing such opportunities. A ninety-minute or two-hour voyage is enough to give a feel of the geography and to become acquainted with some of the pretty spots.

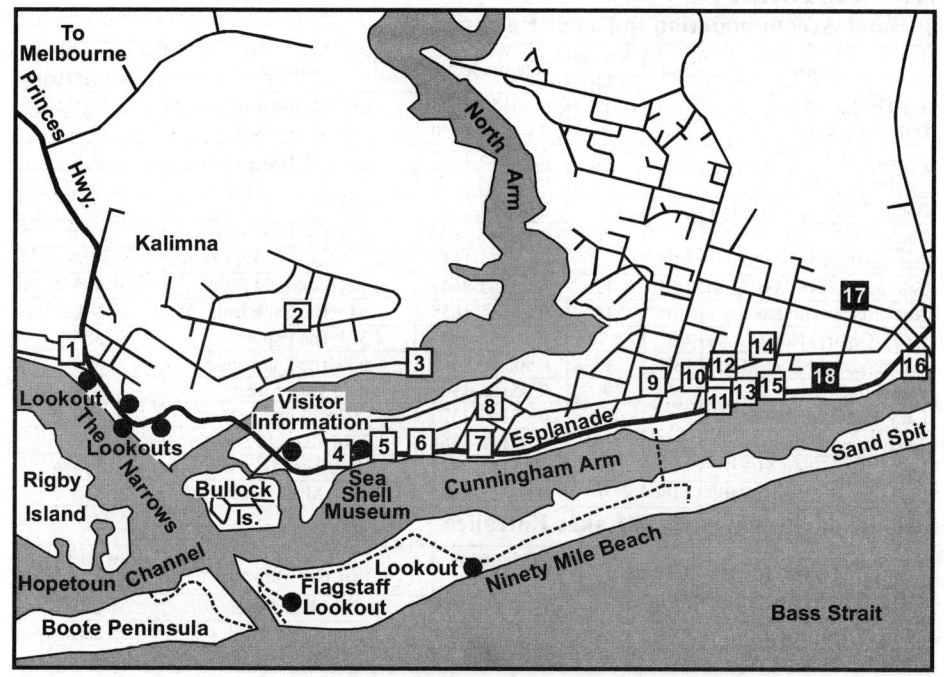

LAKES ENTRANCE
Black numerals in white boxes indicate hotel accommodation
White numerals in black boxes indicate backpackers hostels

There is a footbridge across to the sand spit which separates the town from the open sea, and here you have two beaches, one on the interior lake and one on the exterior ocean. This latter forms the eastern extremity of the **Ninety Mile Beach** running up the coast of Gippsland.

Along the foreshore of Lakes Entrance stand trees planted as a memorial to the soldiers of the Great War. Where the trees have died, their stumps have been carved into suitable **sculptures** to remind us of their purpose.

58 kilometres north-east of Lakes Entrance is **Buchan**, one of the very early European settlements in Victoria. The town is now famous for its **limestone caves** discovered in the early twentieth century. The caves are open daily and have at least three tours per day. Admission costs $12. The **Snowy River** runs nearby and offers some spectacular scenery. **Little River Gorge** is, at 305 metres, the deepest in Victoria and **Little River Falls** are in the same area, both some distance north of Buchan, between the town of **Gelantipy** and the New South Wales border. There is no public transport to Buchan, but there is a backpackers hostel in Buchan, offering a pick-up service from the main road, and there is a youth hostel in Gelantipy.

ACCOMMODATION

Here is a sample of the accommodation available in Lakes Entrance. It should be borne in mind that this is a holiday location and that these are off-season rates. In some cases, peak season rates (particularly during school holidays) may be as much as double those overleaf. As usual, though, backpacker hostel rates do not change much.

844   VICTORIA
(i) Hotel Accommodation in Lakes Entrance

Name	Stars	No. on Map	Telephone No.	Address	Lowest Price (Double/Twin)
The Gables B&B	4½	2	03-5155-2699	1 Creighton Avenue	$160
Déjà Vu B&B	4½	3	03-5155-4330	17 Clara Street	$140
Coastal Waters Motor Inn		11	03-5155-1792	635 The Esplanade	$135
Quality Inn Bellevue	4	6	1-800-355-153	191 The Esplanade	$125
Banjo Paterson Motor Inn	4	4	03-5155-2933	131 The Esplanade	$120
Sherwood Lodge	3½	5	1-800-655-659	151 The Esplanade	$110
George Bass Motor Inn	3½	1	03-5155-1611	The Lookout, Princes Hwy.	$100
Southern Cross Apts.	4½	12	03-5155-2647	21 Roadknight Street	$95
Abel Tasman Lodge	4	15	03-5155-1655	643 The Esplanade	$90
Lakes Central Hotel	3	7	03-5155-1977	321 The Esplanade	$85
Cunningham Shore Motel	3½	13	1-800-033-172	639 The Esplanade	$80
Fountain Court	3½	8	03-5155-1949	6 Lake Street	$80
Lazy Acre Log Cabins	4	14	03-5155-1323	35 Roadknight Street	$80
Anchorage Holiday Units	3½	10	03-5155-1368	7 Roadknight Street	$80
Lakes Waterfront Motel		16	03-5155-2841	10 Princes Highway	$75
Silver Sands Tourist Park	4½	9	03-5155-2343	33 Myer Street	$35

(ii) Backpackers Hostels in Lakes Entrance

Name	Group	No. on Map	Telephone No.	Address	Lowest Price (Dormitory)
Silver Sands Backpackers	VIP	9	03-5155-2343	33 Myer Street	$20
Riviera Backpackers	YHA	18	03-5155-2444	5 Clarkes Road	$19
Lakes Entrance Hostel		17	03-5155-2365	7 Willis Street	$15

(iii) Backpackers Hostels near Lakes Entrance

Name	Group	No. on Map	Telephone No.	Address	Lowest Price (Dormitory)
Buchan Lodge	B&W	19	03-5155-9421	Saleyard Road, Buchan	$22
Karoonda Park	YHA	20	03-5155-0220	Gelantipy Road, Gelantipy	$20

MOVING ON
(i) By Train

Here are timetables for trains back to Melbourne from Sale. Following is the bus plus train service from Lakes Entrance to Melbourne. Timetables for V-Line service in the opposite direction, to Canberra and Batemans Bay can be found on page 754.

Sale to Melbourne

Days of Operation	Weekday Timetable										
Sale				0710		0725†			1340		1650
Traralgon	0505	0603	0700	0745	0813	0915	1020	1210	1315	1415	1457‡	1725
Melbourne	0722*	0824	0923	0954	1028	1123	1224	1424	1526	1628	1751	1930

* To Flinders Street Station only.   † By bus to Traralgon.   ‡ Change to suburban train at Dandenong.

Days of Operation	Saturdays						Sundays				
Sale			0715		1405	1650		0925	1510	1655
Traralgon	0550*	0630	0750	0950	1440	1725	0825	1000	1545	1730
Melbourne	0816	0845	1002	1207	1642	1942	1047	1209	1803	1943

* Change to suburban train at Dandenong.

LAKES ENTRANCE 845

Lakes Entrance to Melbourne

Days of Operation	M - F (Bus)	M - F	M - F (Bus)	M - F	Sat (Bus)	Sat	Sun (Bus)	Sun	M - F (Bus)	M - F	M - F (Bus)
Lake Tyers Beach			1110		1145						
Lakes Entrance	0515		1140		1205		1320		1455		1820
Bairnsdale	0600		1225		1250		1401		1535		0905
Sale	0655	0710	1320	1340	1345	1405	1456	1510	1635	1650	
Melbourne		0954		1628		1642		1803		1930	

(ii) By Bus

Premier and V-Line both offer bus services round the coast as far as Batemans Bay. Premier then continues to Sydney. V-Line provides service to Canberra, and back to Melbourne via train from Sale (see timetable above).

Destination	Operator	Via	Distance (km)	Fare	Journey Time	Frequency
Sydney	Premier		833	$71	12 - 13½ hrs	1/day
		Batemans Bay	483	$50	6½ - 8 hrs	1/day
		Eden	249	$26	3¼ - 3½ hrs	1/day
Batemans Bay	V-Line		483	$63.40	6¾ hrs	3/week
		Narooma	387	$51.60	5¾ hrs	1/day
		Eden	249	$46.30	3¾ hrs	1/day
Canberra	V-Line		429	$61.60	6¼ hrs	2 - 3/week
Melbourne	Premier		387	$46	5¾ hrs	1/day
Melbourne	V-Line		342	$51.70	4¾ - 5 hrs	3/day
		Sale	105	$20.60	1¾ hrs	3/day

ORBOST

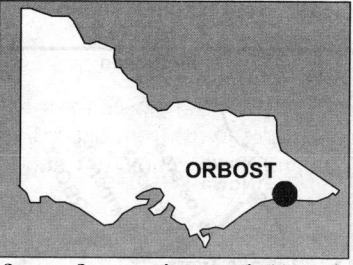

Population 2,500
5 hrs 30 mins by train and bus from Melbourne
6 hrs by bus from Melbourne

Orbost lies 45 minutes east of Lakes Entrance, a distance of 56 kilometres. On the way, after 22 kilometres, you will pass through **Nowa Nowa**, a very small timber town, and just before it you can see the remains of the railway beside the road, in the form of a very impressive trestle bridge. Nowa Nowa has craft shops and offers some good walks, including one to Boggy Creek Gorge. Also at Nowa Nowa, the road to **Buchan** leads off north. From here it is 36 kilometres.

Orbost is a very likeable little town situated on the **Snowy River** at the foot of the Snowy Mountains. The area has been made famous by the poem *The Man from Snowy River* by Banjo Paterson, and, more recently, by a film of the same title. The poem is one of the most famous in Australian literature and is the story of a stockman and his horse, who, although appearing diminutive and weak, are able to outlast and outride other experienced men in this type of terrain. The others find the mountain descent too precipitous to attempt, but,

846 VICTORIA

The man from Snowy River never shifted in his seat.
It was grand to see that mountain horseman ride.
Through the stringy barks and saplings, on the rough and broken ground,
Down the hillside at a racing pace he went;
And he never drew the bridle till he landed safe and sound,
At the bottom of that terrible descent.

The town still has a pioneering feeling to it and the cool waters of the river, surrounded by greenery, give it a special character. It is the type of place where one feels that one wants to stay, but actually most visitors just pass through and keep going.

Just as the town is reached, you will see another splendid **trestle bridge** carrying the non-existent railway across the valley. What a shame that such magnificent constructions cannot be used for their intended purpose.

The **Snowy River Visitor Centre** is in the town with a path leading to and from it through lush green growth. It has information on all the surrounding area. Two minutes walk away is the **Forest Park**, with the **Slab Hut** as its principal attraction. This was an old family home built in 1872 about forty kilometres away from here and moved to this site in 1984. It served as the Tourist Information Centre from 1987 until 1997, but is now a small museum. It is open daily from 10:00 until 16:00 and admission is free. There is a **mosaic path** in the Forest Park, produced by local women and telling the story of the Snowy River, including their hopes for its future.

Perhaps the most interesting activity offered here is **Hovercraft Tours** on the Snowy River. These depart on order from down by the bridge and are relatively expensive. Enquire at the Visitor Centre or telephone 041-7533-226.

The **Sensory Garden** was formed and planted by local unemployed youths in 1993. The plants used were all chosen for their appeal to the senses - for their colour, scent or feeling, or the sound of the birds which they attracted. The pathway was constructed from a variety of materials to allow those in wheelchairs to be able to sense the different textures.

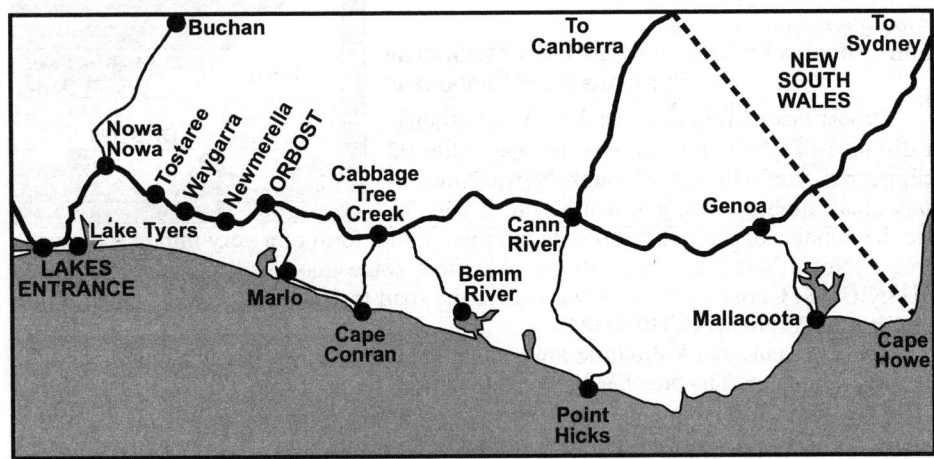

FROM LAKES ENTRANCE TO MALLACOOTA
Thicker lines denote V-Line bus routes

A memorial clock marks the centre of the town and down by the river you can find markers showing various **flood levels** over the years. There are two hotels, known locally, and with great imagination, as the *Top Pub* and the *Bottom Pub* (actually the Commonwealth Hotel, established in 1901, and the Club Hotel, dating from 1881). Both of these offer moderately priced accommodation suitable for the backpacker. In short, Orbost is a typical Victorian country town. The V-Line bus to Canberra will stop here for a break giving you the chance to have a brief look around the small town if lunch is not your priority.

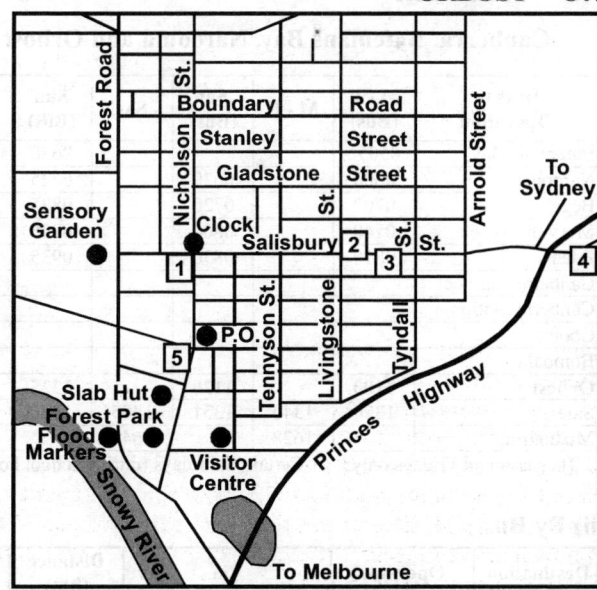

ORBOST
Numerals indicate accommodation

Fifteen kilometres south of Orbost is the popular fishing village of **Marlo**, where the Snowy River flows into Bass Strait, and fifteen kilometres to the east of that is **Cape Conran**, known for its fishing, scuba diving and snorkelling, and also for the **Cape Conran Coastal Park**. There are **seals** here to be observed. However, there is no public transport to Marlo or Cape Conran.

ACCOMMODATION
Accommodation in Orbost

Name	Stars	No. on Map	Telephone No.	Address	Lowest Price (Double/Twin)
Country Roads Motor Inn	3½	3	1-800-636-873	94 Salisbury Street	$85
Countryman Motor Inn		2	03-5154-1311	Livingstone & Salisbury Sts.	$75
Orbost Motel Lodge		4	03-5154-1122	Irvines Rd. & Princes Hwy.	$60
Club Hotel		5	03-5154-1003	63 Nicholson Street	$55
Commonwealth Hotel	2	1	03-5154-1077	159 Nicholson Street	$45

MOVING ON
(i) By Train plus Bus Connexions

The timetable for V-Line services north to Eden, Narooma, Batemans Bay and Canberra is shown on page 754. The timetable for services to Melbourne is on the following page.

848 VICTORIA

Canberra, Batemans Bay, Narooma and Orbost to Sale and Melbourne

Days of Operation	M - F (Bus)	M - F	Sat (Bus)	Sat	Sun (Bus)	Sun	Tu, F, Sat† (Bus)	M - F	Sat
Batemans Bay	0505*				0630				
Narooma	0600		0620		0725				
Bega	0700		0720		0825				
Merimbula	0740		0800		0905				
Eden	0810		0830		0935				
Canberra Jolimont							0850		
Canberra Station							0905		
Cooma							1025		
Bombala							1130		
Orbost	1100		1120		1225		1405		
Sale	1326	1340	1351	1405	1456	1510	1635	1650	1655
Melbourne		1628		1642		1803		1930	1943

* Tuesdays and Fridays only   † Certain Saturdays (during school holidays) only

(ii) By Bus

Destination	Operator	Via	Distance (km)	Fare	Journey Time	Frequency
Sydney	Premier		778	$66	11¼ - 13 hrs	1/day
		Batemans Bay	428	$46	6¾ - 7¼ hrs	1/day
		Eden	194	$25	2½ - 3 hrs	1/day
Batemans Bay	V-Line		428	$59	6 hrs	3/week
		Narooma	332	$55	5 hrs	1/day
		Eden	194	$34.40	3 hrs	1/day
Canberra	V-Line		373	$59	5 hrs	2 - 3/week
Melbourne	Premier		442	$51	6½ hrs	1/day
Melbourne	V-Line		398	$59	5½ - 5¾ hrs	9–10/week
		Sale	161	$34.40	2½ hrs	9–10/week

MALLACOOTA
Population 1,200
6 hrs 30 mins by train and bus from Melbourne (Genoa)
8 hrs by bus from Melbourne (Genoa)

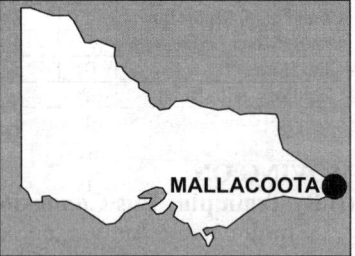

We continue east from Orbost again and reach Cann River after another hour, 78 kilometres further on (see map on page 846). Here the road divides. Buses to Narooma, Batemans Bay and Sydney via the coast continue straight on, but the V-Line service to Canberra turns left here, along the pretty Monaro Highway, which is now sealed all the way.

Cann River is another pleasant small town, in a pretty setting. The V-Line bus to Narooma and Batemans Bay will stop here for its lunch (and you can have yours too if you wish). **Point Hicks** lies 49 kilometres south of this town. This was where the first sighting of Australia was made by Captain Cook's ship, the *Endeavour*, on 19th April 1770. The man who actually made that sighting was Lt. Hicks, and so the cape was named after him. In 1890 a lighthouse was constructed here, with the third highest tower in Australia. Now the lighthouse keepers' cottages are used as accommodation, or, if that be too costly, camping facilities are available nearby. However, again there is no public transport to this area.

Genoa is tiny, but it is the nearest bus stop to the seaside town of Mallacoota, 22 kilometres distant. **Mallacoota** is a picturesque little spot surrounded by the **Croajingolong National Park**, a World Biosphere Reserve. There are walks available and sports facilities, and there is an abundance of wildlife. It is becoming increasingly popular as a tourist destination and so has plenty of accommodation at various prices, including two backpackers hostels.

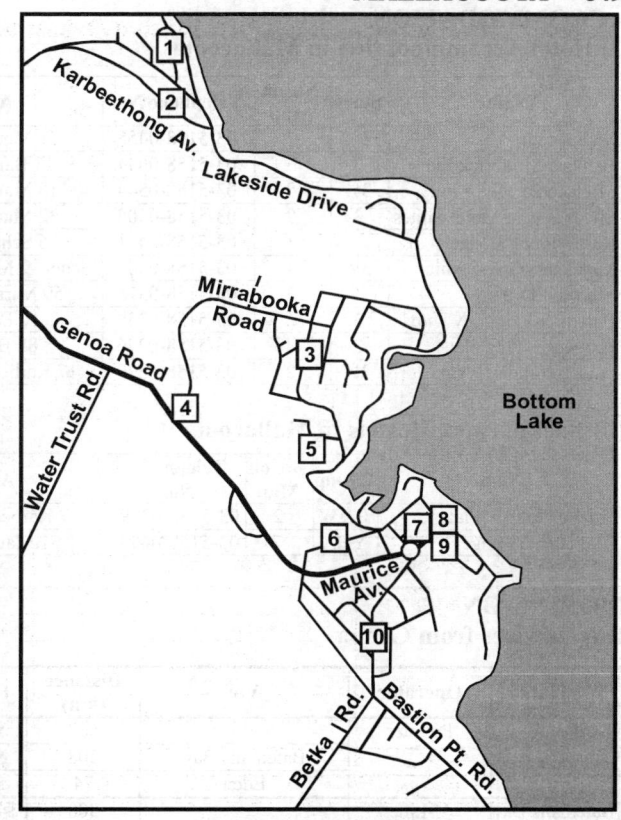

MALLACOOTA
Numerals indicate accommodation

Mallacoota is situated on the inlet to two lakes - **Top Lake** and **Bottom Lake** (one wonders how the locals manage to devise these fascinating names) - so offers boating activities on calm waters. One of the features of the town is the popularity of constructions using locally-produced mud bricks. Adobe Holiday Flats, one of the backpackers hostels, is built of such bricks, as, indeed, is one of the council offices.

The problem again is to cover the 22 kilometres from the Princes Highway to Mallacoota, as there is no public transport yet, although it may come if the popularity of this little corner of the state continues to increase. Try booking your accommodation ahead and asking for assistance with transport from the owners of the property.

This is the end of Victoria, for Genoa is only fourteen kilometres from the New South Wales border. If you have come this far, though, you will find plenty more scenic places to visit as you proceed up the coast towards Sydney. It is, moreover, a portion of the coast which is not as touristic as places further north, so make the most of this enjoyable and picturesque journey. You will enjoy it.

850 VICTORIA
ACCOMMODATION
(i) Hotel Accommodation in Mallacoota

Name	Stars	No. on Map	Telephone No.	Address	Lowest Price (Double/Twin)
Mallacoota Hotel	2½	7	03-5158-0455	51 Maurice Avenue	$97
Banksia Mudbrick Flats	3	5	03-5158-0044	11 Banksia Parade	$80
Mallacoota Motor Inn	3½	8	03-5158-0544	15 Maurice Avenue	$75
Silver Bream Motel Suites	3	9	03-5158-0305	32 Maurice Avenue	$75
Karbeethong Lodge		1	03-5158-0411	16 Schnapper Drive	$70
Melaleuca Grove Units	3½	4	03-5158-0407	Genoa & Mirrabooka Roads	$70
Mareeba Lodge	3½	3	03-5158-0378	59 Mirrabooka Road	$65
Ballymena Holiday Units	3	6	03-5158-0258	10 Bruce Street	$65
Harbour Lights Flats	3	10	03-5158-0246	88 Betka Road	$65
Adobe Holiday Flats	3½	2	03-5158-0329	17 Karbeethong Avenue	$55

(ii) Backpackers Hostels in Mallacoota

Name	Group	No. on Map	Telephone No.	Address	Lowest Price (Dormitory)
Adobe Holiday Flats	B&W	2	03-5158-0329	17 Karbeethong Avenue	$44 (double)
Mallacoota Lodge	YHA	7	03-5158-0455	51 Maurice Avenue	$18

MOVING ON
Bus Services from Genoa

Destination	Operator	Via	Distance (km)	Fare	Journey Time	Frequency
Sydney	Premier		658	$64	9¾ - 11¼ hrs	1/day
		Batemans Bay	308	$42	4¼ - 5¾ hrs	1/day
		Eden	74	$21	1 - 1¼ hrs	1/day
Batemans Bay	V-Line		308	$46.30	3¾ hrs	3/week
		Narooma	212	$37.10	3 hrs	1/day
		Eden	74	$9.40	45 mins	1/day
Melbourne	Premier		562	$51	8 hrs	1/day
Melbourne	V-Line		567	$63.40	7½ - 7¾ hrs	1/day
		Sale	286	$55	4½ hrs	1/day

TASMANIA

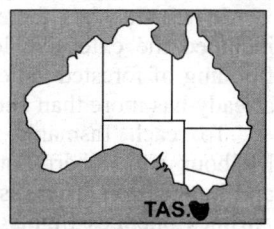

Tasmania is by far the smallest of the six Australian states, only the Australian Capital Territory occupying less space. It is also the only island state or territory. Tasmania has an area of 68,400 square kilometres. It is less than a third of the size of the next smallest state, its neighbour Victoria, and it represents a little less than one per cent of the total Australian land mass. Tasmania has a population of 500,000, of which 200,000 live in Hobart, the capital.

The history of the island of Tasmania goes back a long way. It was originally a part of the Australian mainland, but was cut off by rising waters some 12,000 years ago. Aborigines had already been living here for 10,000 to 15,000 years, and, as they became isolated from their relatives on the other side of the water, they and their culture developed in different ways.

The first European known to have visited was Abel Tasman. He sighted the west coast at 16:00 on 24th November 1642, but did not appreciate that it was an island separate from the main Australian continent. It was he who gave it the name of Van Diemen's Land, Van Diemen being the Governor-General of the Dutch East India Company in Batavia (Jakarta), which had commissioned this voyage of exploration. The island was renamed Tasmania in 1856.

Tasmania was also visited by Marion du Fresne (French) in 1772, Tobias Furneaux (British) in 1773, James Cook (British) in 1777, William Bligh (British) in 1788 and 1792 and Bruni d'Entrecasteaux (French) in 1792. For Cook it was his last visit before he sailed to meet his death in Hawaii, and for Bligh it was his last stop before sailing to Tahiti, after which the infamous mutiny on the *Bounty* occurred. In 1798 George Bass and Matthew Flinders circumnavigated Tasmania and proved it to be an island, also naming the Bass Strait which separates Tasmania from Victoria.

The first European settlement of Tasmania was in 1803, and Hobart dates from 1804. Thus, of all the Australian states, only New South Wales has a longer history of European settlement than Tasmania.

Some of the fiercest clashes between Europeans and aborigines occurred in Tasmania and resulted in the virtual extermination of the aboriginal peoples of this state. They succumbed to European diseases as well as to physical oppression and in 1832 it was decided to move the remnants of the indigenous peoples to Flinders Island, off the north-eastern coast of Tasmania. However, they were poorly sheltered and cared for there and the decline in numbers continued. In 1847, the survivors were returned to Oyster Cove, near Hobart, but by 1876, the last of the group, the famed Truganinni, had perished, to end a dismal chapter in the history of colonisation.

This depth of history here in Tasmania is not always appreciated by visitors to Australia, who often by-pass this small state, especially as it is an island which is rather expensive to reach. It is well worth the effort, however, for Tasmania has a beauty of its own and an atmosphere quite different from the rest of Australia.

Its climate is unpredictable, but tends to be damper than in most other states, resulting in great tracts of pristine forests and, at times, raging rivers. It is a popular area for walking, and the Overland Track between Cradle Mountain and Lake St. Clair, in particular, is one of the world's most famous treks.

TASMANIA

In recent years there has been considerable opposition to policies which have included the extensive logging of irreplaceable virgin forest in Tasmania and the flooding of forested valleys for the purpose of hydro-electric schemes when the state already has more than enough electricity to satisfy all its needs.

To reach Tasmania, one may either fly or take a ferry. Flights operate from Melbourne to Hobart, Launceston, Devonport and Burnie, and from Sydney to Hobart and Launceston. There is also a weekly service from Adelaide to Launceston. Island Airlines operates flights from Melbourne and Traralgon to Launceston via Flinders Island, which will give an additional interesting stop (see page 950). Note, however, that Island Airlines flies from Essendon Airport, not from the principal Melbourne Airport at Tullamarine.

The main ferry service now consists of two vessels, *Spirit of Tasmania I* and *Spirit of Tasmania II*, one of which sails every night from Melbourne to Devonport. At peak times there are additional daytime sailings. These are large ships which are comfortable and reasonably fast. The crossing takes approximately ten hours.

There is also a *Devil Cat* fast catamaran service which takes six hours from Melbourne to George Town, north of Launceston. It operates only in the summer, from December to April. Although it too is a large vessel, capable of carrying up to 740 passengers, it is much less comfortable than the *Spirit of Tasmania I and II*, as this can be a rough crossing with high waves. The service is also prone to cancellation in adverse weather.

Another ferry is the *Matthew Flinders*, which is operated by *Southern Shipping Service* between Port Welshpool in Victoria and Bridport in Tasmania via Flinders Island, offering the opportunity for a stop in that interesting location. This is usually the cheapest way to reach Tasmania, but accommodation is basic, the voyage long and the sailings infrequent and somewhat unpredictable.

However you travel, expect to pay approximately $100 to $150 each way for the journey to Tasmania.

Travel within Tasmania is by bus. There used to be a daily passenger rail service

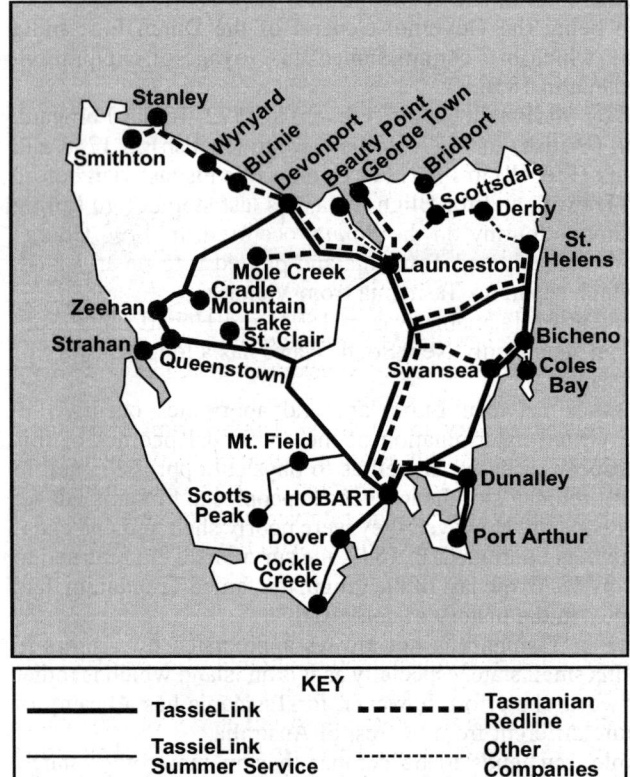

BUS SERVICES IN TASMANIA

between Smithton and Hobart via Launceston, but it was abandoned many years ago now, just as the Hobart suburban rail services were also eliminated.

There are two principal bus companies, TassieLink and Tasmanian Redline, for the routes of which see the map on the page opposite. TassieLink offers an *Explorer Pass* giving unlimited travel for various numbers of days at the following prices.

TassieLink Explorer Pass

7 days out of 10	$170
10 days out of 15	$200
14 days out of 20	$230
21 days out of 30	$270

The pass does not include travel on the routes operated to Scotts Peak and Cockle Creek in summer only, but these can be travelled by payment of supplements. There are also tours of Freycinet National Park available for a modest supplement.

HOBART
Population 200,000
1 hr 10 mins by air from Melbourne

If you arrive in Hobart from another state, you will be arriving by air. There is an airport bus which will deliver you to wherever you want to go in the city for the sum of $10. The distance is eighteen kilometres. Hobart used to have one scheduled flight per week from Christchurch in New Zealand, but that service has disappeared and now there are no scheduled international flights, only occasional charters.

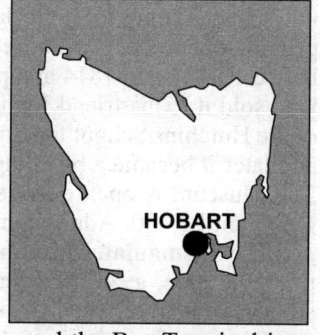

If you arrive from within Tasmania, it will be by bus, and the Bus Terminal is at the south-western edge of the city centre in Collins Street. It is within easy walking distance of most accommodation and of the city centre.

Hobart is the second oldest capital city in Australia. Dating from 1804, it is exceeded in antiquity only by Sydney. As a result, it has a degree of history which one might not have expected prior to arrival, and a number of fine older buildings. Moreover, it is a city in a beautiful natural setting and of a very manageable size.

Let us start with a walking tour to become acquainted with the central area.

Walking Tour

This tour covers some four kilometres and should take approximately an hour and a half, not allowing time to look at the museums and other attractions or to make any lengthy pauses.

The **Tasmanian Travel and Information Centre** is on the corner of Davey and Elizabeth Streets, close to the city centre, and is a good place to begin one's exploration of the city, as all information is available here. Diagonally opposite is **Franklin Square**, with Sir John Franklin standing at its centre. He was Governor of Van

Diemen's Land from 1837 until 1843, and was also a polar explorer. He perished while trying to locate the North-West Passage. Hobart has a long association with Antarctic exploration, being the closest Australian city to the southernmost continent, so you will also find in this square photographs of the 1898 - 1900 Antarctic Expedition led by Carstens Borchgrevink. This was the first expedition to spend a winter in Antarctica. The members are pictured paying their respects to Sir John Franklin in this spot upon their return to Hobart in April 1900. One member, the physicist Louis Bernacchi, was from Hobart. Franklin Square also offers a fine view over the harbour, especially if the sun happens to be shining.

Cross diagonally again and you will reach the magnificent **General Post Office**, at least part of which is still used for its intended purpose. It was from this building on 8th March 1912 that Roald Amundsen sent his telegram to confirm to the world that he had indeed reached the South Pole and returned safely. Inside the Post Office you will also find the *Metro Shop*, as the bus information office is called here. It has timetables for all bus services, and certain types of ticket are available too. All local bus services from Hobart leave either from Elizabeth Street directly outside the Post Office or from one of the sides of Franklin Square just across the road.

Now turn left into Macquarie Street and walk to Argyle Street. On your left here you will find the **Mercury Print Museum** in *Ingle Hall*, the *Mercury* being Hobart's newspaper, dating from 5th January 1854. The museum adjoins the newspaper's main printing operation. It is housed in a fine old Georgian building dating from somewhere between 1811 and 1814 and probably owned originally by a man named Edward Lord who sold it to his friend John Ingle in 1831. For three years from 1846, it was the site of the Hutchins School for Boys. Around the turn of the century it was a 'coffee palace' and later it became a boarding house, before being purchased by the *Mercury* in 1962. The Museum is open on weekdays from 10:00 until 15:45, with a lunch break from 13:00 until 13:30. Admission is by a suggested $2 donation.

The **Tasmanian Museum and Art Gallery** is just a little further down the road on the other side, at 40 Macquarie Street. It is open daily from 10:00 until 17:00 and admission is free.

Return a few metres to Argyle Street and turn left. On the corner of Davey Street and Argyle Street is the **Maritime Museum**, open daily from 10:00 until 17:00 with an admission charge of $7. A guided tour of Museum and Port is offered for $14.

Nearby is the picturesque **harbour**, where, amongst other stimulations, for gourmet visitors, there are boats selling some very edible **fish and chips**. There are also **cruises** operating from here and, from the southern part of the harbour, **ferries** to Wrest Point Casino. If it is a fine day (or, as Tasmanian weather is prone to rapid changes, perhaps just a fine part of the day) you can sit and absorb the view and the activity. There used to be a railway station in this vicinity before Hobart foolishly decided that it had no need of trains, but almost all trace is gone now. Just a few rails embedded in the concrete remain.

Walk further along Davey Street beside the harbour, and at the point where it bends left to join Macquarie Street, you will find the **Tasmanian Distillery and Museum**. Sullivans Cove Whisky is produced here, in what was formerly the **Gasworks**, and is probably just the thing with which to wash down your fish and chips. Tours operate continuously and discounted products are available in the shop. The Museum is open daily from 10:00 until 17:00, with extended hours in the summer, and admission costs $6. Another part of the Gasworks, you will observe, has been converted into a high-class hotel, while other areas serve as restaurants and shops.

Just opposite here you will notice the **railway yards** and see that trains do still operate, but not passenger trains, unfortunately. There have been only goods trains for a quarter of a century now, travelling up to Launceston and beyond.

Turn left into Brooker Avenue for one block, then left into Collins Street, and right into Campbell Street. On your right, at no. 29, is the **Theatre Royal**. This claims to be Australia's oldest theatre. Its construction started in 1834 and the first performance took place in 1837. Entertainment provided ranged from Music Hall to Cock Fighting. The Theatre has been remodelled several times. A gallery was installed in the 1850s, for example, and the auditorium was adorned with additional decoration in the 1890s. The theatre has also survived several threats of demolition, with even Sir Laurence Olivier campaigning for its retention. It is usually open for viewing between 9:00 and 17:00 on weekdays and between 9:30 and 13:00 on Saturdays.

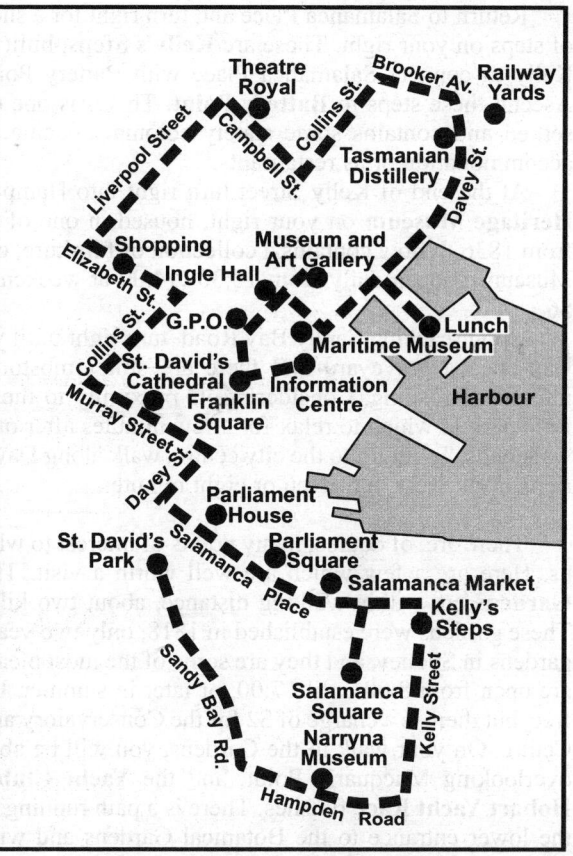

HOBART WALKING TOUR

Turn left into Liverpool Street and walk up to Elizabeth Street, where turn left. This section of **Elizabeth Street** is for pedestrians only and is one of the main shopping streets of the city, with arcades running off to both sides offering plenty of opportunities to spend money. When you reach Collins Street, turn right into another shopping area, and then turn left into Murray Street. Note on your left **St. David's Cathedral**, and then turn right into Davey Street, with **Parliament House** on your left. Turn left into Salamanca Place. As you reach the bottom of the slope, you will pass the grassy area of **Parliament Square** and see the splendid row of Georgian sandstone warehouses dating back to the 1830s, now converted into cafés, craft shops, galleries and restaurants. On Saturdays only, this is the site of the famous **Salamanca Market**, held between 8:30 and 15:00. You can buy almost anything, but craft products, antiques and fresh produce predominate.

Turn right into Salamanca Square and you will find *Antarctic Adventure* on your left, an exhibition of conditions in that southern continent. It is open daily from 10:00 until 17:00, but admission is relatively expensive at $25.

Return to Salamanca Place and turn right for a short distance, until you see a flight of steps on your right. These are **Kelly's Steps**, built in 1839 by the adventurer James Kelly to connect Salamanca Place with Battery Point. They lead into Kelly Street. Ascend these steps to **Battery Point**. This was one of the first areas of Hobart to be settled and contains some stately colonial housing, now mostly used as up-market accommodation or as restaurants.

At the end of Kelly Street turn right into Hampden Road and come to **Narryna Heritage Museum** on your right, housed in one of the early colonial homes, dating from 1836. It now contains a collection of furniture, china, paintings and fine arts. The Museum is open daily from 10:30 (14:00 at weekends) until 17:00. Admission costs $6.

Upon reaching Sandy Bay Road, turn right until you reach **St. David's Park**. This was once a graveyard and there are still tombstones dotted about it which make interesting reading. Considering its proximity to the city centre, it is a very pleasant little park in which to relax for a few minutes after one's exertions, for it here that our walk ends. To return to the city centre, walk along Davey Street, which borders the park to its north-west, for seven or eight minutes.

There are, of course, many points of interest to which our walking tour did not take us. Here are a few which are well worth a visit. The **Royal Tasmanian Botanical Gardens** are within walking distance, about two kilometres north of the city centre. These gardens were established in 1818, only two years after Australia's first botanical gardens in Sydney, and they are some of the most pleasant gardens in the country. They are open from 8:00 until 17:00, or later in summer. Entry to the Botanical Gardens is free, but there is a charge of $2 for the Conservatory and $2 for the Botanical Discovery Centre. On your walk to the Gardens, you will be able to see the **Cenotaph**, on a hill overlooking Macquarie Point, and the **Yacht Club**, where the famous **Sydney to Hobart Yacht Race** finishes. There is a path running beside the railway which leads to the lower entrance to the Botanical Gardens and will avoid walking along the main road. You will also pass the **Tasman Bridge** on the way, the scene of disaster when, at 21:27 on 5th January 1975, the bulk ore carrier *Lake Illawarra* crashed into one of the piers and brought down a 127-metre section of the bridge. Four vehicles were on the section at the time and the five people in those vehicles died, together with seven crew members of the *Lake Illawarra*. Two cars were left suspended precariously over the gap in the bridge, but their occupants escaped. If you prefer to take a bus to the Botanical Gardens, any bus crossing the Tasman Bridge and going to the Eastern Shore will pass nearby. Alight at Stop 4, being careful not to miss it, as the next stop is on the other side of the bridge. Alternatively, bus no. 17 will take you right to the Gardens, but is much less frequent.

In the northern part of the city is **Old Hobart Gaol**, with its **Penitentiary Chapel**. This was constructed in 1831, and later part of it was converted into law courts. The Chapel continued in use until 1961 and the Courts were used until 1983. There are underground passages, cells for solitary confinement and an execution yard. There are tours daily at 10:00, 11:30, 13:00 and 14:30, at a price of $8.

In Davey Street, at the south-west of the city centre, is **Anglesea Barracks**. This is the oldest military headquarters still occupied in Australia. The Barracks were ordered by Governor Macquarie in 1811 and are still used by the military. Admission is free every day between 9:30 and 15:30, with a guided tour available only on Tuesdays at 11:00.

HOBART 857

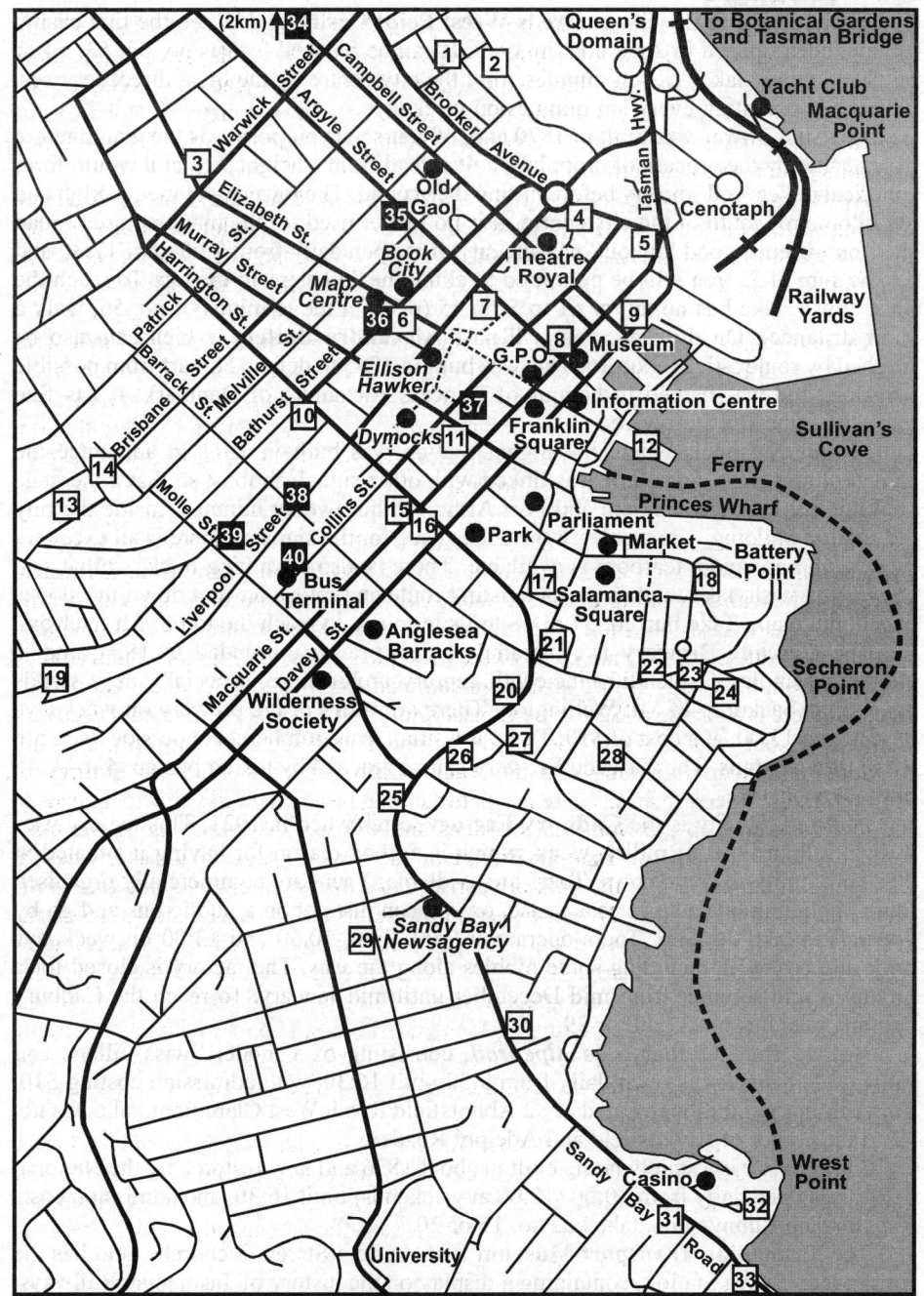

HOBART CITY CENTRE
Black numerals in white boxes indicate hotel accommodation
White numerals in black boxes indicate backpackers hostels

TASMANIA

To the south of the city centre is **Wrest Point Casino** and Hotel, the first casino to have been opened in Australia, in 1973. It can be reached by bus no. 52, 53, 54 or 55. The journey takes eleven minutes from the city centre by the most direct services, with buses operating every ten minutes on weekdays.

The **Shot Tower** was built in 1870 and, of course, its purpose was the manufacture of lead shot by the process of dropping molten lead from a height so that it would form spherical pellets and solidify before hitting the ground. The tower is 48 metres high and ten kilometres south of the city centre. It is no longer used for the manufacture of lead shot, but offers a good lookout over the city. It is open daily from 9:00 until 17:30 and for the sum of $5 you will be permitted to climb the 259 steps to the top. To reach the Shot Tower, take bus no. 60 or 61 to Stop 45 (or from the terminus of no. 56, walk a short distance). On the way, you will pass **Alexandra Battery**, which can also be reached by route 54B at Stop 26. This was built in 1885 to defend Hobart from possible invasion, and was named in honour of Princess Alexandra of Denmark. It has fine views over the Derwent River.

Mount Nelson is where the Signal Station was built in 1811 to announce the arrival of any ships sighted. It was linked with other signal stations, so that a message could be passed between here and Port Arthur within twenty minutes. Inside the tiny old Station building, you can learn the codes used for the signals. There is an excellent view from here and a tearoom is available. There is also a walking track, so that you can, if you wish, take the bus up its twisting route and return on foot down the slopes of the mountain. Take bus no. 57 or 58 to its terminus to reach the top of Mt. Nelson.

The **Cascade Brewery** is Australia's oldest brewery, founded in 1824, and is another example of splendid nineteenth century architecture, especially as it stands against the backdrop of Mt. Wellington. There are **tours** of the brewery on weekdays at 9:30 and 13:00, at a cost of $10. There is a small **museum** here and outside there are some **fine gardens**. The Cascade Brewery can be reached by taking bus no. 43, 44, 46 or 49 to Stop 17.

North of the city is the **Cadbury Factory**, established in 1921. This factory uses over a million litres of milk a week, which is a good reason for having it situated in close proximity to some cows. Tours are available. There are commercially organised tours, including one as part of a cruise, or you can just get on a public bus and go by yourself to take the tour. Tours operate at 9:00, 9:30, 10:30 and 13:00 on weekdays only, and cost $12, including some nibbles along the way. The factory is closed for a month in mid-summer from mid December until mid January. To reach the Cadbury Factory, take bus no. 37, 38 or 39.

Not far from Cadbury's is *Alpenrail*, consisting of a model Swiss village and railway. The display is open daily from 9:30 until 16:30, with admission costing $10. To reach this exhibition, located at 82 Abbotsfield Road, West Claremont, take bus no. 42 to the corner of Abbotsfield and Adelphi Roads.

Runnymede is a stately home built in about 1836 and now restored by the National Trust. It is open daily from 10:00 (12:00 at weekends) until 16:30, and admission costs $8. To reach Runnymede, take bus no. 15 or 20.

The **Tasmanian Transport Museum** is in Anfield Street, Glenorchy, and has the former New Town Station, containing a display on the history of Tasmanian Railways. There are also steam and diesel locomotives and railcars, trams, buses and trolley-buses. The Museum is open on Saturdays and Sundays only from 13:00 until 16:30 and short train rides are available on the first and third Sundays of the month. On the first

Sunday a diesel railcar operates and on the third Sunday a steam locomotive runs. Admission costs $6, or $7 when train rides are available. To reach the Transport Museum, take a bus no. X1 (quickest), or any other bus going to Glenorchy, of which there are many. The Museum is a short walk from the Glenorchy Bus Station.

★ One of the great sights of Hobart is the view from the top of **Mt. Wellington**. Once you have seen this, you will think all the other good view points to be insignificant (so see the others first). Mt. Wellington rises to a height of 1,270 metres and provides a magnificent backdrop to the city of Hobart. At the top of the mountain it is generally cool, if not cold. When the author was last there, it was snowing. One problem with this excursion is that it is often misty up there too, so try to pick a good day. Another difficulty is that there is no public transport to the top, so you will be obliged to take a tour, or the Mt. Wellington Shuttle Bus which departs from 20 Davey Street daily at 9:30, 12:00 and 14:30. The Shuttle Bus costs $25, and tours start at the same price. If you want to try to get there by yourself, take a bus no. 48 or 49 to the turn-off to Mt. Wellington, from where it is twelve kilometres uphill. Since that is rather too far to walk, try to look pathetic and maybe some kind motorist will help. However, walking down the twelve kilometres should not be beyond the bounds of endurance if you can get a ride up. The view on a fine day is truly magnificent. The whole of Hobart and the Derwent Estuary lie spread below you and you seem to be able to see for ever. It is, perhaps, the best mountain-top view in Australia, so try to get up somehow.

Public Transport

As mentioned previously, there is, unfortunately, no longer any suburban rail service in Hobart, or any passenger rail service at all, or indeed any passenger rail service anywhere in Tasmania. Therefore, all travel is by bus. City buses are operated by Metro. Although the services are quite good and comprehensive, after 18:00 buses are infrequent or non-existent, so remember to start your journey home before then. Services are also much reduced at the weekend, especially on Sundays. Minimum fare is $1.50 and maximum $3.50. However, the best value is an *Off-Peak Multi-Trip Ticket* which is valid for as many journeys as you wish when boarding between 9:00 and 16:30 or after 18:00 on weekdays, or all day at weekends. This ticket costs $4.

Slightly longer distance services are operated by Hobart Coaches, which company is, in fact, now owned by Metro. Hobart Coaches operates to Kingston and beyond in the south, to Richmond in the east and to New Norfolk in the north. Fares are charged by distance.

Long-distance services are operated by TassieLink and by Tasmanian Redline, for which see the summary at the end of this section. Note that some of these services are seasonal.

Day Trips

There are, of course, all sorts of day trips and day tours which can be made from Hobart. The author's opinion is that if the destinations are within Hobart, you can usually make the journey much more cheaply and more adventurously by taking a bus and doing it by yourself. In addition, you can spend as long as you want there, or move on as quickly as you wish, and not be part of a large group. If the destination is further away, though, it usually deserves more than a day trip. However, if the reader disagrees with this opinion, or if time is too limited, there is plenty of information at the

Styx Valley

This is a rather special tour, since it is to an area which you would not otherwise be able to visit easily and since it is operated by the **Wilderness Society** to show what is happening to Tasmania and to try to obtain some support for its protests.

Tasmania is the source of much of Australia's wood and a centre for government-controlled forestry operations. These operations are gradually destroying the 400-year-old trees which comprise the native rainforests of the area. Indeed 87% of the forest has already been destroyed and the Wilderness Society is fighting to protect only the remaining 13%. The most incomprehensible part of this operation is that only about ten per cent of this beautiful hardwood is used for a purpose suited to its potential. The remainder is made into woodchips and sent mainly to Japan to be used as newsprint. Moreover, the operation scarcely makes a profit and is said to be continued principally in the interests of maintaining employment.

The Styx Valley lies some two hours west of Hobart. The tour is not a plush operation. It is made in an old school bus owned by a company sympathetic to the aims of the Wilderness Society. Since it is a school bus, it has other duties, so tours are operated only on Sundays, and sometimes on Thursdays during school summer holidays. The bus travels through New Norfolk, near which town you can see the paper mill where much of the Australian newsprint is manufactured. This plant does not use the native forests, fortunately. It uses plantations and some wood from regenerative projects. At Glenora, where the tour stops for a few minutes, there is a chance for platypus-spotting and then the bus continues to the Mt. Field National Park. Here the tour turns off onto the forestry roads and shows what it claims to be the tallest hardwood trees in the world. The author is not quite convinced about this. There are some close contenders in Western Australia. However, they are still most impressive. You can be shown what the Society claims to be the tallest Christmas Tree in the world. The solar-powered lights still glow for a while after sunset. Mr. Guinness, however, refused to recognise the record attempt, saying that it was the wrong type of tree to be called a Christmas Tree. Not only will you enjoy this day amongst the giant trees, but you will find it educational - and probably worrying as well.

The tour leaves from the Wilderness Society Office at 130 Davey Street, near the junction with Byron Street, at 9:00 on Sundays and summer Thursdays and returns at about 17:45. You need to take your lunch with you. The Wilderness Society asks you to book at least one day in advance (tel: 03-6224-1550), but, in fact, if you turn up on the day and a seat is available, you are not going to be refused. For $30 this trip is really very good value.

MAP SHOPS AND BOOKSHOPS *(see map on page 857)*

Tasmanian Map Centre	96 Elizabeth Street
Ellison Hawker	90 - 92 Liverpool Street
Book City	73 Bathurst Street
Dymocks	Shop 206/7 Centrepoint Shopping Centre
Sandy Bay Newsagency	197 Sandy Bay Road

HOBART 861

ACCOMMODATION
(i) Hotel Accommodation in Hobart

Name	Stars	No. on Map	Telephone No.	Address	Lowest Price (Double/Twin)
Hotel Grand Chancellor	4½	9	1-800-625-138	1 Davey Street	$220
Salamanca Inn	4	17	1-800-030-944	10 Gladstone Street	$215
Wrest Point Casino	4½	32	1-800-030-611	410 Sandy Bay Road	$205
Gattonside Heritage	4½	20	1-800-223-410	51 Sandy Bay Road	$195
Oakford on Elizabeth Pier	4	12	1-800-620-462	Elizabeth Street Pier	$190
Corinda's Cottages		2	03-6234-1590	17 Glebe Street	$160
Old Woolstore	4	5	1-800-814-676	1 Macquarie Street	$160
Lenna of Hobart	4	18	1-800-030-633	20 Runnymede Street	$160
Vista Hotel	4½	10	1-800-030-003	156 Bathurst Street	$155
Woolmers Inn		25	03-6223-7555	123 Sandy Bay Road	$155
Cooper's Cottage	4	23	03-6224-0355	44a Hampden Road	$150
Tantallon Lodge B&B		24	03-6224-1724	8 Mona Street	$150
St. Ives Motel Apartments	3½	27	03-6224-1044	67 St. George's Terrace	$145
Midcity Motor Inn		6	03-6234-6333	96 Bathurst Street	$140
Hadley's Hotel	4	11	1-800-131-689	34 Murray Street	$140
Macquarie Manor	4½	16	1-800-243-044	172 Macquarie Street	$140
Wrest Point Motor Inn	3½	32	1-800-030-611	410 Sandy Bay Road	$135
Amberley House	4	31	03-6225-1005	391 Sandy Bay Road	$125
Macquarie Motor Inn	3½	15	03-6234-4422	167 Macquarie Street	$120
Portsea Terrace	2½	21	03-6234-1616	62 Montpelier Retreat	$120
Wellington Lodge B&B	4	1	03-6231-0514	7 Scott Street	$110
Lodge on Elizabeth	4	3	03-6231-3830	249 Elizabeth Street	$110
Blue Hills Motel	3½	26	03-6223-1777	96 Sandy Bay Road	$110
Battery Point Manor	4½	28	03-6224-0888	13 Cromwell Street	$110
Grosvenor Court Apts.	4	29	03-6223-3422	42 Grosvenor Street	$110
Clydesdale Heritage Apts.		30	03-6223-7289	292 Sandy Bay Road	$110
Fountainside Motor Inn	3½	4	03-6234-2911	Brooker Av. & Liverpool St.	$100
Montgomery's Private Htl		8	03-6231-2660	9 Argyle Street	$100
Hotel Mayfair	3½	13	03-6231-1188	17 Cavell Street	$100
Sandy Bay Motor Inn		33	03-6225-2511	429 Sandy Bay Road	$100
Marquis Hotel / Motel		14	03-6234-3541	209 Brisbane Street	$95
Crow's Nest B&B		19	03-6234-9853	2 Liverpool Crescent	$95
Prince of Wales Hotel	2½	22	03-6223-6355	55 Hampden Road	$90
Argyle Guest House		7	03-6236-9997	50 Argyle Street	$60

(ii) Backpackers Hostels in Hobart

Name	Group	No. on Map	Telephone No.	Address	Lowest Price (Dormitory)
Montgomery's Private Htl.	YHA	8	03-6234-4790	9 Argyle Street	$24
Pickled Frog		38	03-6234-7977	201 Liverpool Street	$23
Adelphi Court	YHA	34	03-6228-4829	17 Stoke Street	$22
Ocean Child Hotel	VIP	35	03-6234-6730	86 Argyle Street	$22
Central City Backpackers		37	03-6224-2404	138 Collins Street	$22
New Sydney Hotel		36	03-6234-4516	87 Bathurst Street	$22
Transit Centre Backpackers		40	03-6231-2400	199 Collins Street	$19
Narrara Backpackers		39	03-6231-3191	88 Goulburn Street	$18

862 TASMANIA
MOVING ON

Note that some of the services mentioned below are seasonal. Buses run to Scotts Peak and Cockle Bay only in summer, although they operate as far as Dover throughout the year. Where a range of frequency is shown in the table, this indicates the variation between winter and summer services.

TassieLink offers some special fares for bushwalkers, so that one may travel by bus to Lake St. Clair, walk to Cradle Mountain and then take the bus either on to Launceston or back to Hobart at a discounted rate, for example. One may also take a bus to Scotts Peak, walk to Cockle Creek and catch a bus back to Hobart, or *vice versa*, using a special fare.

Also note that some of the routes below are connecting services, involving a change of vehicle. The Tasmanian Redline services from Hobart to St. Helens and Bicheno involve changes at Avoca and Campbell Town respectively, sometimes involving waits of more than three hours. The TassieLink service from Hobart to Strahan sometimes involves a change of vehicle at Queenstown, and a wait of up to two and a half hours, but sometimes no change is necessary.

Bus Services from Hobart

Destination	Operator	Via	Distance (km)	Fare	Journey Time	Frequency
Burnie	Redline		357	$50.40	4¼ - 6½ hrs	3/day
		Devonport	303	$43.80	3¼ - 5 hrs	3/day
		Launceston	203	$26.40	2½ - 2¾ hrs	4/day
Devonport	TassieLink		303	$45.50	4 hrs	1/day
		Launceston	203	$27	2¾ hrs	1/day
St. Helens	TassieLink		260	$39.20	4¼ hrs	2/week
		Bicheno	178	$27.20	3¼ hrs	3 - 4/week
		Swansea	138	$21.70	2½ hrs	8 - 9/week
St. Helens*	Redline		256	$42.20	3½ - 7¼ hrs	6/week
		St. Marys*	221	$39.40	3 - 6¾ hrs	6/week
Bicheno*	Redline		247	$29.50	4¼ - 6¾ hrs	5 - 6/week
		Swansea*	202	$28	3½ - 6 hrs	5 – 6/week
Port Arthur	TassieLink		125	$18	2¼ hrs	5 - 8/week
Dunalley	Redline		66	$8	1½ hrs	1/day
Launceston	TassieLink		598	$107.40	11 hrs	2/week
		Devonport	498	$90.80	9½ hrs	2/week
		Cradle Mountain	408	$72.70	7¾ hrs	2/week
		Strahan*	305	$57.70	6 - 8¼ hrs	4 - 5/week
		Queenstown	268	$49.70	5 - 5½ hrs	4 - 5/week
		Lake St. Clair	179	$39.50	3¼ - 3½ hrs	3 - 7/week
Scotts Peak (seasonal)	TassieLink		153	$64.10	3¼ - 3½ hrs	3/week
		Mt. Field National Park	76	$26.50	1½ - 1¾ hrs	8/week
Cockle Creek (seasonal)	TassieLink		141	$57.60	3½ hrs	3/week
		Dover	87	$18	1¾ - 2 hrs	2/day
		Geeveston	64	$14.70	1¼ - 1½ hrs	5/day
Richmond	Hobart Coaches		25	$5.90	20 - 30 mins	3/day
Richmond	TassieLink		25	$12	40 mins	1/day
Richmond	Richmond Bus		25	$30†	45 mins	2/day
New Norfolk	Hobart Coaches		38	$6.10	45 - 55 mins	6/day
Kettering	Hobart Coaches		35	$7.50	40 - 55 mins	4/day
		Kingston	13	$4.10	12 - 30 mins	Hourly

* Connecting service. Change of bus involved.   †Return fare.

BRUNY ISLAND
Population 600
2 hrs by bus and ferry from Hobart

Bruny Island is becoming a popular destination for visitors to Tasmania. Many are attracted by its surfing opportunities and its beaches, but it also offers some interesting history, abundant wildlife and beautiful walks.

There are three possibilities for visiting Bruny Island. Firstly, you can take a day tour, but, although this will enable you to see many places in a short time, you are likely to go away surprised by the size of the island and wishing that you had spent longer here. A day tour from Hobart will cost approximately $120.

Secondly, you can avail yourself of the offer of Lumeah Youth Hostel, which consists of return transport from Hobart to Bruny Island, two nights accommodation at the hostel, a day tour of the island and one lunch, for the total price of $150. This is available with departure from Hobart on Monday or Wednesday. On Friday, the same is offered, but with three days on the island, for $170. The elements are also available individually. Return transport from Hobart costs $40. The tour costs $70, including lunch, and accommodation at the hostel costs $22 per night.

Thirdly, you can do it by yourself. Take a Hobart Coaches bus no. 94 or 96 from the Treasury in Murray Street, Hobart to **Kettering**, a journey of 40 to 55 minutes, at a cost of $7.50. A convenient service leaves at 8:00 on weekdays and connects with the 9:30 ferry from Kettering. Other services leave Hobart at 14:40 and 17:10. The last two will travel via the ferry terminal on request, but the morning bus does not do so. However, it is only a short walk. The ferry sails ten times a day for **Roberts Point** on Bruny Island, a voyage of only fifteen minutes, and is free for foot passengers. The problem is, though, that Roberts Point is on the north island and most of the accommodation is on the south island. The distance between Roberts Point and the towns of Alonnah and Adventure Bay is approximately forty kilometres, and there is no public transport on the island. There is, however, a **Visitor Centre** at the ferry terminal in Kettering. When the author made this journey, the staff there kindly alerted the crew of the ferry to my predicament and a man was deputed to locate during the crossing somebody with spare space in a vehicle, which he did, and I reached the aptly named Adventure Bay.

The first European to sight Bruny Island, as far as we know, was Abel Tasman in 1642. Captain Tobias Furneaux visited in 1773 in his ship the *Adventure*, after which **Adventure Bay** is now named. Matthew Flinders too made this his first Australian landing point, but it was the visit of Rear Admiral Bruni d'Entrecasteaux in 1792 to 1793 which was to be longest remembered, for he gave both his first name Bruni to the island itself and his surname to the d'Entrecasteaux Channel which separates it from the mainland, he being the first to realise that this was in fact an island, and not merely a headland.

The most famous visitors were Captain Cook and Captain Bligh. In 1777, Nelson, a botanist with Cook's expedition of that year, took specimens from Adventure Bay to make the first classification of certain species, and some of the trees from which the specimens were taken are still there. Adventure Bay was Captain Cook's last port of call in Australia before he sailed to Hawaii to meet his death. The remains of the tree to which his ship was moored are now in the little **Bligh Museum** in Adventure Bay, and the spot is marked on the foreshore. It was also Captain Bligh's last port of call in the *Bounty* before he departed for Tahiti, the famous mutiny ensuing. While here, he planted the first apple trees, grape vines and vegetables in Australia.

European settlement of the island commenced in 1818. The island was used for coal mining, timber felling, farming and whaling. Still some tiny remains of whaling stations remain at **Grass Point**, while the timber was so highly regarded that it was taken as far as England and South Africa. The G.P.O. and Law Courts in Melbourne were built with sandstone mined here. Convicts were brought to build a Pilot Station and a church on the island. Also here is Australia's second oldest lighthouse, built in 1836.

The arrival of Europeans was disastrous for the aborigines, who were destroyed by violence and disease. The last remaining members of these people were removed in 1840. **Trugannini** came from here. She was regarded as the very last of the Tasmanian aborigines when she died in 1876, and, as she had feared, her skeleton was put on display in Hobart Museum until 1947. She was eventually cremated in 1975 and her ashes scattered in the d'Entrecasteaux Channel, where her husband-to-be had been murdered nearly a century and a half earlier. The aboriginal name for this island was Lunawannalonna, and from that name are derived the names of two of the principal towns, **Lunawanna** and **Alonnah**.

Most famous of the wildlife are the **Fairy Penguins** (or Little Penguins). If you did not go to Phillip Island in Victoria to see them, you can visit them here. Moreover, they are free here, except that one still has to reach their home, which is **The Neck**. Bruny Island is really two islands, joined by a very narrow, but towering, stretch of sand dunes. In these dunes the penguins live. If you are staying in Adventure Bay, you could cycle there, but it is too far to walk. Again Lumeah Hostel offers a tour. This one includes the use of binoculars and filter torches and costs $25. There are, though, also penguins living nearer to Adventure Bay, but in lesser numbers. If you walk quietly on the dunes at dusk you may see some returning home from their fishing expeditions.

There are also seals, dolphins and whales in season. There is a colony of mutton birds, and all the species of birds unique to Tasmania can be found on Bruny Island.

Cape Bruny, at the southern tip of the island, is not very much further north than the southernmost tip of Tasmania. The view from the **lighthouse** is good, if the weather is accommodating. To the right you can see Whale Head on the mainland, adjacent to South-East Cape, the latter being the southern tip of Tasmania. Nearby, from **Jetty Beach**, you can attempt the six-hour walk round the **Labillardiere Peninsula**, but, of course, you need transport to get there and back. Your transport will pass through **Lunawanna** on the way, where accommodation is available. You may also pass through **Alonnah**, the administrative centre, which has an hotel and other essential buildings. The hotel claims to be the most southerly in Australia. We have already visited the most northerly, on Thursday Island (see page 393), so better have a quick drink here too before we move on.

There are three rewarding walks within range of Adventure Bay. The first is to the top of **Mt. Mangana**. This leads off from Coolangatta Road, running between Adventure Bay and Lunawanna. Mt. Mangana is the highest point on Bruny Island, at 571 metres, and it offers fine views over the whole of the south island. The walk up to the peak is attractive too, leading through forest and ferns. The walk takes about ninety

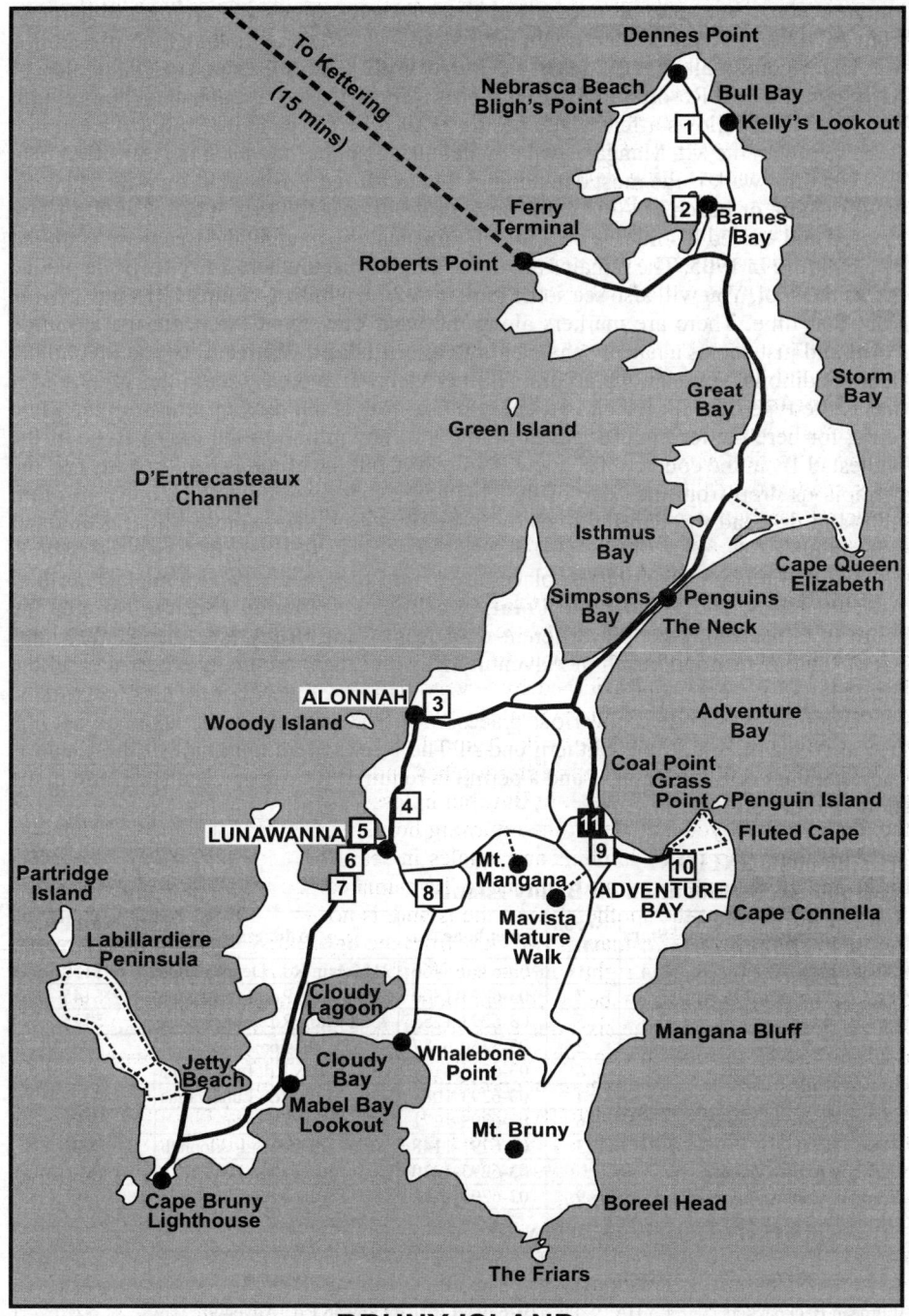

minutes return, but you will need an additional ninety minutes to walk up to the start from Adventure Bay, and back again afterwards.

The second walk is the **Mavista Nature Walk**, starting from the inland side of Adventure Bay off Resolution Road. It is only a short walk of about half an hour return, but pretty as it follows a fern glade beside **Waterfall Creek**. This walk can easily be combined with the Mt. Mangana walk by detouring on the way back to Adventure Bay.

The third walk is the most demanding, that to **Fluted Cape**. Start by walking along the foreshore or beach of Adventure Bay. You will pass the spot where Captain Cook moored and carved his initials on a tree. Unfortunately, though, the tree was destroyed by a bushfire in 1905. The remains are in the Bligh Museum here and now just a plaque marks the spot. You will also see some remains of the **whaling camps** and a few **graves** from that time. There are markers along the way. The tip of the peninsula is **Grass Point** and just across a narrow channel is **Penguin Island**. With agility and favourable tidal conditions, you can hop across. All has been flat and easy up to this point and if that is the type of walk which you enjoy most, now is the time to return by the same route, for here the terrain changes abruptly. You now climb to the top of some of the highest cliffs in the country. The view is splendid, but the climb is hard in parts and the precipitous drop from the edge of the cliff somewhat disturbing. At the top you turn right and descend through the trees by a different path. The whole walk takes about three hours.

For surfing, the most popular places are **Coal Point**, about two kilometres north of Adventure Bay, and **Whalebone Point**, which is near **Cloudy Lagoon**, towards the south of the island, but on a different road from Cape Bruny (see map on previous page). There is a good beach in Adventure Bay and there are many others around the island.

Camping is permitted in various places, mostly at sites requiring payment, but it is free at **Neck Beach** at the southern end of The Neck. More than half of the island is National Park or State Reserve and a permit is required for camping on such land in the approved camp sites.

ACCOMMODATION
(i) Hotel Accommodation on Bruny Island

Name	Stars	No. on Map	Telephone No.	Address	Lowest Price (Double/Twin)
Active Holidays	4	1	03-6260-6466	212 Main Rd., Dennes Point	$150
St. Clair's Luxury Accom.		7	03-6293-1300	Lighthouse Rd., Lunawanna	$145
Sea Rise Cottage		5	03-6293-1255	4558 Main Rd., Lunawanna	$125
Barnes Bay Villa	3½	2	03-6260-6287	315 Missionary Road	$90
Coolangatta Cottage		8	03-6293-1164	Cloudy Bay Rd, Lunawanna	$90
Wayaree Estate		4	03-6293-1088	4391 Main Rd., Lunawanna	$90
Bruny Explorers Cottages		6	03-6293-1271	Lunawanna	$85
Bruny Hotel		3	03-6293-1148	Bruny Main Road, Alonnah	$80
Adventure Bay Village		10	03-6293-1270	Adventure Bay	$55
Captain Cook Caravan Pk.		9	03-6293-1128	Adventure Bay	$45

(ii) Backpackers Hostels on Bruny Island

Name	Group	No. on Map	Telephone No.	Address	Lowest Price (Dormitory)
Lumeah Backpackers	YHA	11	03-6293-1265	5 Lumeah Rd., Adventure Bay	$22
Adventure Bay Village		10	03-6293-1270	Adventure Bay	$20

MOVING ON

The ferry back to Kettering leaves rather irregularly, but approximately every ninety minutes, with a lunch break. Buses leave Kettering for Hobart at 7:55, 9:30 and 15:45. To catch the 7:55 bus, you need to take the 7:15 ferry. To catch the 9:30 bus, you need the 8:25 ferry. To catch the 15:45 bus, you need the 15:15 ferry. Note that the !5:45 bus does not travel via the ferry terminal. You must walk for five minutes to the main road. The two morning buses, however, visit the terminal. There is no bus service on Saturdays or Sundays.

DOVER, LUNE RIVER AND COCKLE CREEK

Population 500 (Dover)

2 hrs by bus from Hobart (Dover)
2 hrs 30 mins by bus from Hobart (Lune River)
3 hrs 30 mins by bus from Hobart (Cockle Creek)

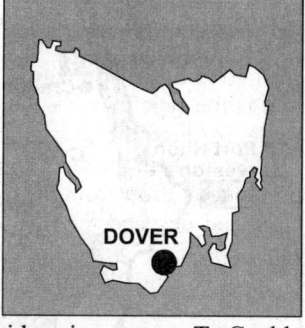

The road to the **Huon Valley** leads off to the south-south-west of Hobart, with bus services provided by TassieLink. There are five buses per day on weekdays as far as Geeveston. Buses continue to Dover twice a day in winter with extra services on Mondays, Wednesdays and Fridays in summer. To Cockle Creek, there are three services per week in summer only.

The road soon becomes pretty, with fine views over Hobart as we climb out of the city along the highway carved through the hills. Soon after leaving **Kingston**, we come into the **orchards** of Tasmania. Principally this is apple-growing country, but there are other fruits too.

There is another good view from the right of the bus before we reach **Grove**, where there is the Huon Valley **Apple and Heritage Museum**, in a former apple packing shed open daily from 10:00 until 16:00, except in July. **Doran's Jam Factory** is nearby, and open for viewing. Doran's claims to be the oldest jam producing company in Australia.

Huonville is ten kilometres further on. This is where we meet the estuary of the Huon River. **Jet boat rides** operate on the river from here, or, if that be too exuberant, you can hire a pedal boat for half an hour.

The road now runs attractively down beside the estuary to Port Huon and Geeveston. On the opposite side of the estuary is **Cradoc**, where there is a backpackers hostel. To reach this hostel, a different route must be followed, using the Hobart Coaches bus no. 98 which departs from Hobart at 17:15 on weekdays for **Cygnet**, seven kilometres from Cradoc. The hostel will collect its guests from Cygnet on request. There are additional buses (no. 99) on Thursdays only.

At **Port Huon**, **cruises** are available, at a cost of $25, and **Geeveston** has the **Forest and Heritage Centre**, with exhibits on the changing nature of forestry. There are wooden souvenirs available, and a turner at work. There is backpackers accommodation available in Geeveston too.

Most bus services finish at **Geeveston**, but the two evening services continue to Dover, another 23 kilometres. **Dover** is a pretty little town facing the sea near the south of the d'Entrecasteaux Channel. There is a seafront walk all round the town and at the

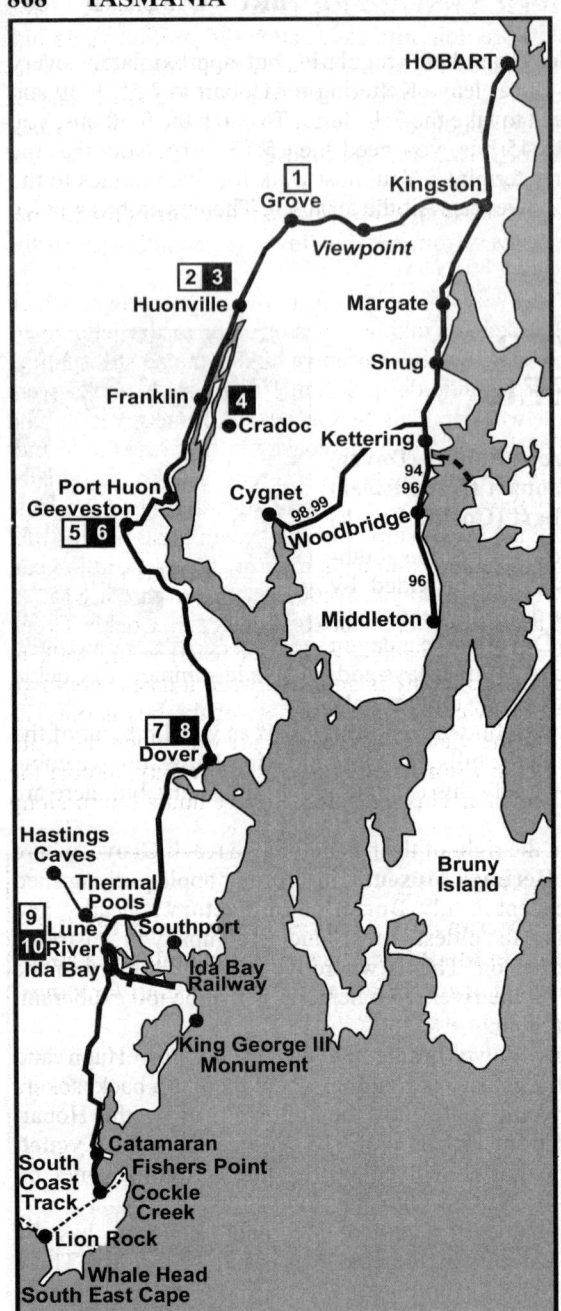

FROM HOBART TO COCKLE CREEK
Showing bus routes
Black numerals indicate hotel accommodation
White numerals indicate backpackers hostels

south of it is the Dover Hotel with a fine view out across the water. The hotel offers backpackers accommodation which is good value. From just outside the hotel, cruises in the *Olive May* operate, at a cost of $40. The *Olive May* claims to be Australia's oldest trading vessel still in operation, and is a wooden sailing boat. However, when the author was here, a notice reminiscent of Will Hay read "Next Cruise Cancelled".

Buses run beyond Dover only on Mondays, Wednesdays and Fridays in summer. The main purpose of these services is to convey bushwalkers to Cockle Creek, from where they can begin the long trek to Scotts Peak. However, they do also provide the opportunity to visit Lune River, Ida Bay and the Hastings Caves. This route beyond Dover is not included in the TassieLink *Explorer Pass*, but if you have a pass, you can make the journey for an additional payment of $40 return, which compares well with the usual price of $57.70 each way between Hobart and Cockle Creek.

At **Lune River** is Australia's most southerly youth hostel. In the summer, this can be reached by the TassieLink bus, but at all times the hostel offers a package of two nights accommodation plus return transport from Hobart for $65. It will also collect guests from the bus terminus at Dover on request.

A short distance from Lune River are the **Hastings Caves and Thermal Pools**. The Pools are about six kilometres distant from the hostel, and the Caves another five kilometres further on. The Caves are dolomite caves about 40 million years old, with the customary stalagmites and stalactites, and also some helictites. They were discovered in 1917 by forestry workers. There are hourly tours of the caves lasting approximately 45 minutes. The Thermal Pools are open-air natural pools, with water constantly at 28°C. The cost is $15 for Caves and Thermal Pools, or $5 for Thermal Pools only.

Lune River Youth Hostel operates three-hour **Glow Worm Cave Tours** for $35 per person. These tours are to different caves from the Hastings Caves, although in the same vicinity.

From Lune River the **Ida Bay Railway** operates. It is an old bush tramway which has been restored. It was originally used for taking limestone out to the jetty to be loaded onto ships. It claims to be the only such bush tramway in Tasmania still running on its original route, although several hundreds of kilometres of such tracks were constructed, operating to a gauge of two feet. This line is seven kilometres long, and quite pretty in parts, especially where it runs along the coast. On the way, the former township of **Ida Bay** can be seen, with its **wharf** and **old cemetery**. The line terminates by the secluded beach at **Deep Hole Bay**, from where there is a walking track to the **King George III Monument**, where a convict ship once sank with great loss of life. Trains operate every day in the summer and on Sundays only for the rest of the year, with departures from Lune River at 12:00, 14:00 and 16:00. The return fare is $15.

The road continues south to **Catamaran** and **Cockle Creek**. At Cockle Creek there is a camp site and from here there are walks. To the left (east) is the walk to **Fishers Point**, which offers views across to Bruny Island. However, it takes about two and a half hours return and the time allowed before the return of the bus is only 75 minutes. That is time enough to go to the view point nearly half way along the walk and then come back. A longer walk is to **Lion Rock** at **South Cape Bay**, almost the most southerly point in mainland Tasmania. This takes four to five hours return along a well tended track.

ANECDOTE

At the time, the Ida Bay Railway ran only from the little town of Ida Bay, not from Lune River, so I turned up in Ida Bay at the appointed hour for a ride. Since it seemed very quiet, I searched around the yard and workshop for some sign of life and discovered a young man with an oil can.

"Ah, come for a ride, I suppose," he said. "Well, we don't usually go for just one passenger, but I'm not very busy so I suppose we might as well. We'll just take the engine, so hop up beside me."

I followed instructions. The engine was coaxed into life and we chugged out at walking pace along the little narrow track for a scenic trip beside the estuary to the broken old jetty which was the reason for the existence of this, the last of Tasmania's narrow-gauge bush tramways. No longer is limestone quarried here, but instead passengers can be conveyed along a little piece of Tasmanian history to lie on the pristine beach for a while, or visit another page of the history book at the King George III Memorial.

It is a charming little ride, so let us hope that this railway adventure will survive and flourish.

870 TASMANIA

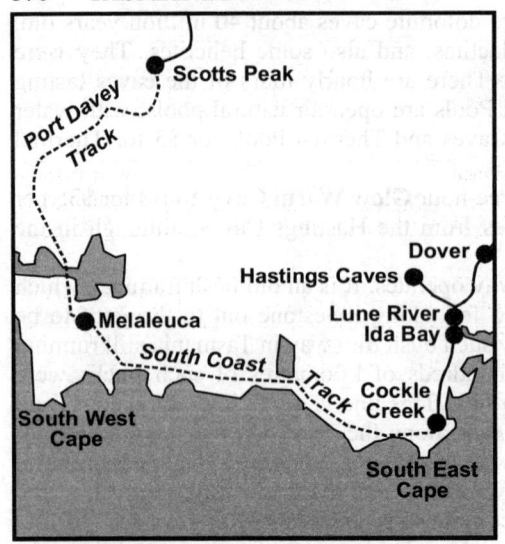

SOUTH COAST TRACK AND PORT DAVEY TRACK

The longest walk from here, though, is the **South Coast Track** (see map adjacent) leading through the World Heritage Area, of which the 600,000-hectare South-West National Park comprises part. This is, of course, not just an hour's jaunt to be undertaken on the spur of the moment, but a long-distance trek which needs very careful preparation, a permit and the payment of fees. The most suitable pass for walking purposes is one covering a period of two months, which costs $15 and is valid for all Tasmanian National Parks.

It will take about five days to cover the 85 kilometres to **Melaleuca**, where there is an airstrip, from which one can arrange a flight back to Hobart (current price $150). Approximately 2,000 people walk this track each year, 1,500 of them during the summer. This number is small compared with those walking the Overland Track between Cradle Mountain and Lake St. Clair, so conditions will be more peaceful here. The walk is mainly coastal, so does not involve much high country, although the **Ironbound Range**, which must be crossed, rises to 900 metres. It offers some beautiful beaches and ocean scenery, especially in the early parts. Although not Alpine, the walk requires warm clothing, even in summer, as strong winds may come off the ocean. It also rains here on half the days in the year, so you need to be prepared to get wet, and to negotiate some muddy sections of track. There are no huts along the way, so a tent is essential, and there is a ban on camp fires in some areas, so a fuel stove is desirable. Most walkers fly in to Melaleuca and walk back, so if you travel in the opposite direction you will have the pleasure of meeting most of them along the way and find it easier to get a flight back from Melaleuca, even if you have not booked one. The adventurous alternative, though, is to keep going when you reach Melaleuca and continue along the **Port Davey Track** to **Scotts Peak**. This can be expected to take a further five days, so ten days in all from Cockle Creek to Scotts Peak. TassieLink offers a special fare for walkers undertaking this journey. Bus from Hobart to Cockle Creek plus return from Scotts Peak, or *vice versa*, costs $99.

ACCOMMODATION
(i) Accommodation in Grove

Name	Stars	No. on Map	Telephone No.	Address	Lowest Price (Double/Twin)
Grove Manor		1	03-6266-4227	Crabtree Road, Grove	$155

(ii) Hotel Accommodation in Huonville

Name	Stars	No. on Map	Telephone No.	Address	Lowest Price (Double/Twin)
Huonville Grand Hotel		2	03-6264-1004	2 Main Street	$45

(iii) Backpackers Hostel in Huonville

Name	Group	No. on Map	Telephone No.	Address	Lowest Price (Dormitory)
Huonville Grand Hotel		3	03-6264-1004	2 Main Street	$30

(iv) Backpackers Hostel in Cradoc

Name	Group	No. on Map	Telephone No.	Address	Lowest Price (Dormitory)
Huon Valley Backpackers	YHA/Nom	4	03-6295-1551	4 Sandhill Road	$18

(v) Hotel Accommodation in Geeveston

Name	Stars	No. on Map	Telephone No.	Address	Lowest Price (Double/Twin)
Cambridge House		5	03-6297-1561	Huon Highway	$100
Lightwood House		5	03-6297-1336	Arve Road	$55

(vi) Backpackers Hostels in Geeveston

Name	Group	No. on Map	Telephone No.	Address	Lowest Price (Dormitory)
Lightwood House		6	03-6297-1336	Arve Road	$33
Geeveston Forest House		6	03-6297-1102	Arve Road	$16

(vii) Hotel Accommodation in Dover

Name	Stars	No. on Map	Telephone No.	Address	Lowest Price (Double/Twin)
Cove House		7	03-6298-1441	Bay View Road	$200
Driftwood Accom.		7	03-6298-1401	Bay View Road	$165
Bayside Lodge		7	03-6298-1788	Bay View Road	$80
Dover Hotel		7	03-6298-1210	Huon Highway	$80
Smuggler's Rest		7	03-6298-1396	Station Road	$80
Anne's Old Rectory		7	03-6298-1222	Huon Highway	$75
Beachside Caravan Park		7	03-6298-1301	Beach Road	$70

(viii) Backpackers Hostels in Dover

Name	Group	No. on Map	Telephone No.	Address	Lowest Price (Dormitory)
Beachside Caravan Park		8	03-6298-1301	Beach Road	$25
Dover Hotel		8	03-6298-1210	Huon Highway	$15

(ix) Hotel Accommodation in Lune River

Name	Stars	No. on Map	Telephone No.	Address	Lowest Price (Double/Twin)
Lune River Cottage		9	03-6298-3107	Lot 2, Lune River Road	$80

(x) Backpackers Hostel in Lune River

Name	Group	No. on Map	Telephone No.	Address	Lowest Price (Dormitory)
Lune River Backpackers	YHA	10	03-6298-3163	196 Main Road	$16

MOVING ON

Note that all buses beyond Dover are seasonal and operate in summer only.

(i) Bus Services from Dover

Destination	Operator	Via	Distance (km)	Fare	Journey Time	Frequency
Hobart	TassieLink		87	$18	1¾ - 2 hrs	2/day
		Geeveston	23	$8	25 mins	2/day
Cockle Creek	TassieLink	(seasonal)	54	$41	1¾ hrs	3/week

872 TASMANIA

(ii) Bus Service from Cockle Creek

Destination	Operator	Via	Distance (km)	Fare	Journey Time	Frequency
Hobart (seasonal)	TassieLink		141	$57.60	3½ hrs	3/week
		Geeveston	77	$49	2¼ hrs	3/week
		Dover	54	$41	1¾ hrs	3/week

MT. FIELD NATIONAL PARK AND SCOTTS PEAK

Population 100 (Mt. Field)
1 hr 30 mins by bus from Hobart (Mt. Field)
3 hrs 30 mins by bus from Hobart (Scotts Peak)

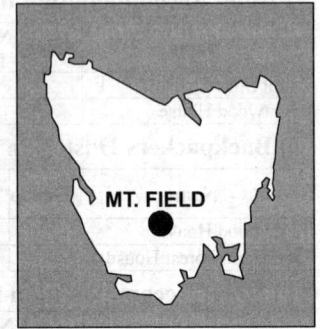

As with the Cockle Creek bus service, that to Mt. Field and Scotts Peak is seasonal and operates only in summer. A few buses run direct from Hobart, but most are connexions at Gretna off West Coast services. Connexions also operate from Mt. Field every morning except Sunday to West Coast services running north to Lake St. Clair, Queenstown and Strahan, and, on Tuesdays and Thursdays, Launceston. This is in summer only, however.

On the way to Mt. Field from Hobart, you will pass through the large town of **New Norfolk**, so called because the first settlers came here from Norfolk Island. One of the attractions here is the ***Devil Jet*** **Jet Boat**, which offers a thirty-minute twenty-kilometre ride on the Upper Derwent River at speeds of up to 80 km/hr, including the shooting of rapids. The boat leaves hourly between 9:00 and 16:00, as long as it has a minimum of two passengers, and trips cost $50. Free pick-up from Hobart can be arranged if a direct booking is made. Telephone 03-6261-3460.

A quieter activity nearby is a visit to the **Museum of Trout Fishing** at Salmon Ponds (which seems contradictory) in Plenty. Trout have been raised here since 1864. The Museum is in the former Superintendent's Cottage, built in 1865, and is open daily from 9:00 until 17:00. Admission costs $6.

Mt. Field is a pretty little National Park, one of Tasmania's oldest and most popular. Moreover, there is a youth hostel right outside the gate providing accommodation. The National Park offers all sorts of stimulating walks and some good views, but one of its most interesting points is its transition in a relatively short distance from lowland to mountain vegetation.

The Park is in two main parts. The first part is near the entrance, which is lowland. Here one can take a pleasant walk to **Russell Falls**, then continue to **Horseshoe Falls**, and return via the **Tall Trees Walk** and **Lady Barron Falls** (see map), a walk which is not particularly demanding and takes about two hours.

If you want to explore further, however, you have to get to the second part of the park, the inner sanctum near **Lake Dobson**. This, however, is sixteen kilometres further along the main road of the park and requires transport. As you traverse the sixteen kilometres. you climb slowly, and by the time you have walked a little way from Lake Dobson, you are in Alpine country. There are many walks available, as can be seen from the map. A good short one is the **Pandani Grove Nature Walk**, which will take about an hour.

A good medium-distance walk is to the **South-West Lookout**. First take the Urquhart Track which leads to ski lodges and ski tows, giving a warning of the type of terrain and weather conditions which may be encountered here. Indeed, when the author was last here, a thick mist descended and it unexpectedly started to snow. This is bleak and beautiful country, but be careful. It is easy to lose your way in such conditions. You also need to be prepared for some cool weather. Of course, on such a day, the lookout might not be the best choice of destination, but if you find clear weather, the walk takes about two hours return.

The best long walk is to **Mt. Field West**, but it takes eight hours return. Mt. Field West is the highest peak in the Park and so offers excellent views in good weather, but the walk should not be attempted in winter.

There are various other choices too, as can be seen on the map, and, although popular, this park rarely seems unduly crowded, since there are so many options.

As you enter Mt. Field National Park, you will cross the railway line. This line was built mainly for shifting timber from the forestry operations in this area and has not had any passenger service on it since 1974. Now it has stopped carrying even the logs (so that they have to travel dangerously by truck along the narrow roads) and it has been taken over by the **Derwent Valley Railway**, which is attempting to re-introduce some passenger services between New Norfolk and Mt. Field National Park. At present,

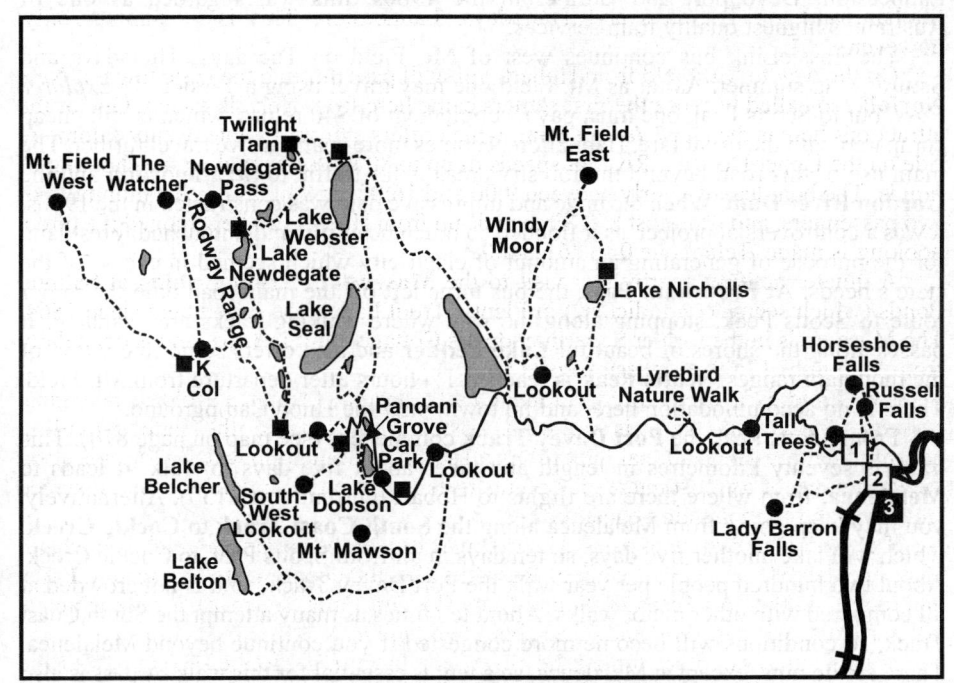

MT. FIELD NATIONAL PARK
Black squares indicate mountain huts
Black numerals in white boxes indicate hotel accommodation
White numerals in black boxes indicate backpackers hostels

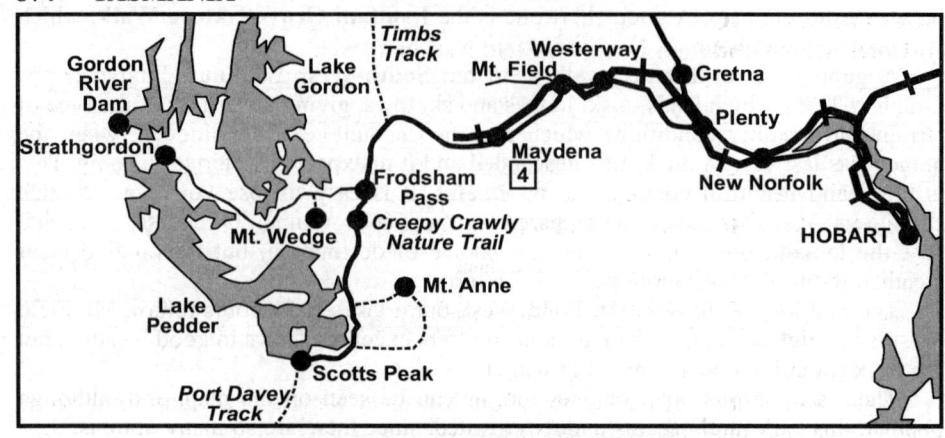

FROM HOBART TO SCOTTS PEAK
**Thicker lines indicate TassieLink bus routes
Numerals indicate accommodation**

trains operate as far as **Westerway** on alternate Sundays, but hopefully they will be more frequent and will travel further by the time that this is read. The carriages used are those which used to run on the *Tasman Limited* between Hobart and Smithton via Launceston, Devonport and Burnie. In the 1960s, this was regarded as one of Australia's highest quality train services.

The TassieLink bus continues west of Mt. Field on Tuesdays, Thursdays and Saturdays in summer. As far as Mt. Field one may travel using a TassieLink *Explorer Pass*, but to Scotts Peak one must pay a supplement of $40 return, which is still cheap compared with the usual fare. Habitation becomes more sparse as we travel further. The main use of this road beyond the forestry areas is for traffic to **Strathgordon** and the **Gordon River Dam**. When the huge and impressive dam was constructed in the 1970s, it was a controversial project, as it flooded so much beautiful and untouched forest land for the purpose of generating an amount of electricity which seemed in excess of the state's needs. At **Frodsham Pass**, the bus turns left off the main road onto the minor route to Scotts Peak, stopping along the way where walking tracks are available. It passes along the shores of beautiful **Lake Pedder** and also offers some fine views of the mountain ranges. **Scotts Peak** is reached 1¾ hours after departure from Mt. Field. There is no accommodation here, and no town, only the Huon Campground.

From Scotts Peak the **Port Davey Track** commences (see map on page 870). This track is seventy kilometres in length and takes about five days to walk. It leads to **Melaleuca**, from where there are flights to Hobart (current cost $150). Alternatively, you may keep going from Melaleuca along the **South Coast Track** to **Cockle Creek**, which will take another five days, so ten days in all from Scotts Peak to Cockle Creek. About two hundred people per year walk the Port Davey Track, so it is not crowded at all compared with other major walks. About ten times as many attempt the South Coast Track, so conditions will become more congested if you continue beyond Melaleuca. There are no huts, except at Melaleuca, so a tent is essential for this walk. A pass is also required and the most suitable one for walking purposes is that valid for two months, costing $15. It gives admission to all Tasmanian National Parks. TassieLink offers a special fare for walkers undertaking this journey. Bus from Hobart to Scotts Peak plus return from Cockle Creek to Hobart, or *vice versa*, costs $99.

MT. FIELD, SCOTTS PEAK 875

ACCOMMODATION
(i) Hotel Accommodation near Mt. Field National Park

Name	Stars	No. on Map	Telephone No.	Address	Lowest Price (Double/Twin)
Russell Falls Cottages		1	03-6288-1198	Lake Dobson Road	$80
National Park Hotel		2	03-6288-1103	2366 Gordon River Road	$70
Tyenna Valley Lodge		4	03-6288-2293	Junee Road, Maydena	$70

(ii) Backpackers Hostel near Mt. Field National Park

Name	Group	No. on Map	Telephone No.	Address	Lowest Price (Dormitory)
Mount Field Y.H.A.	YHA	3	03-6288-1369	Main Road	$18

MOVING ON
Again note that all of the services from Mt. Field National Park and from Scotts Peak are seasonal and operate in summer only.

(i) Bus Services from Mt. Field National Park

Destination	Operator	Via	Distance (km)	Fare	Journey Time	Frequency
Hobart	TassieLink	(seasonal)	76	$26.50	1½ hrs	8/week
Launceston* (seasonal)	TassieLink		566	$107.40	10¾ hrs	2/week
		Devonport*	466	$90.80	9¼ hrs	2/week
		Cradle Mountain*	376	$72.70	7½ hrs	2/week
		Strahan*	273	$57.70	7 - 8 hrs	4/week
		Queenstown*	236	$49.70	4¾ - 7¼ hrs	4/week
		Lake St. Clair*	147	$39.50	3 - 5 hrs	5/week
Scotts Peak	TassieLink	(seasonal)	77	$40	1¾ hrs	3/week

* Connecting service. Change of bus involved.

(ii) Bus Services from Scotts Peak

Destination	Operator	Via	Distance (km)	Fare	Journey Time	Frequency
Hobart (seasonal)	TassieLink		153	$64.10	3 hrs	3/week
		Mt. Field National Park	77	$40	1¾ hrs	3/week

RICHMOND
Population 800

30 mins by bus from Hobart

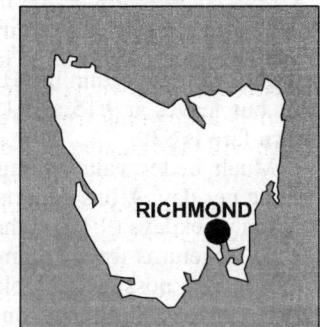

Richmond is one of the oldest of Tasmanian towns. It is most famous for its **bridge**, built in 1823, the oldest stone bridge remaining in Australia. However, there are other attractions as well. The town also has the oldest surviving **gaol** in the country, built in 1825 and open daily from 9:00 until 17:00, at a cost of $4. It has its original **Courthouse**, public buildings and churches. **St. Luke's Church** was started in 1834, while **St. John's Church**, started in 1836, claims to be the oldest Catholic church in the country. All are interesting buildings.

TASMANIA

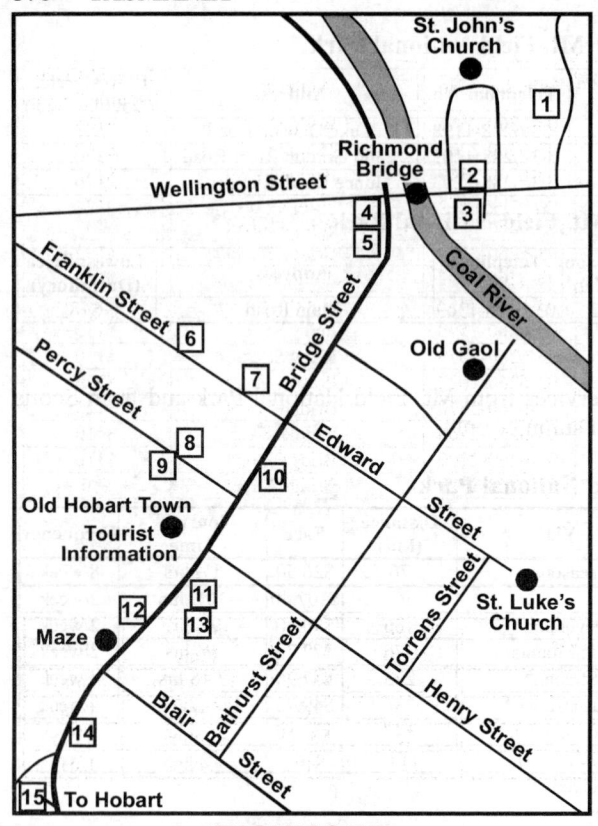

RICHMOND
Numerals indicate accommodation

However, Richmond has rather chosen to build on this image of antiquity and make itself into a tourist centre offering the olde worlde. There are rides available in a horse-drawn carriage. There are art galleries and shops full of antiques (old and new) and craft products. There are cafés, old-time bakeries, restaurants, and, of course, cosy, old-fashioned, rather expensive, homely bed and breakfast accommodation. A guided historical walk is offered daily in summer at 11:00 for the sum of $7.

Amongst the more modern attractions, there is a **maze** (8:30 until 17:00, admission $5) and there is the **Old Hobart Town Historical Model Village**, based on historical records of how Hobart looked in the 1820s. This Model Village, which took three years to construct, is open daily from 9:00 until 17:00 and admission costs $8.

Then there is *Zoo Doo Fun Park*, although this is six kilometres outside the town. Here one can find alpacas, llamas, buffalo and camels, as well as miniature pony races, with jockeys, of a type. There are also an indoor working model village and a merry-go-round. *Zoo Doo* is open daily from 9:00 until 17:00 and admission costs $10.

Accommodation is readily available in Richmond, but the town is only 24 kilometres from Hobart, so can easily be seen as a day trip if one prefers. Most of the longer-distance buses do not pass through Richmond, but the Richmond Tourist Bus will pick you up within the Hobart city area on request by telephoning 0408-341-804. This bus leaves at 9:15 and 12:15, returning from Richmond at 13:00 and 16:00. The return fare is $30.

Much better value though is Hobart Coaches, which has one available return service per day. A bus departs from Stop D at the top of Elizabeth Street in Hobart at 9:30 on weekdays (9:10 on the first Thursday of each month) and arrives in Richmond at 9:55. It returns from Richmond at 16:45. The single fare is $5.90, and return $8.90.

It is also possible to look at Richmond during the day and then move on up the coast, as TassieLink has one service on weekdays from Hobart to Swansea via Richmond. This bus leaves Hobart at 16:15, passes through Richmond at 16:55 and reaches Swansea at 18:40, according to the timetable at the time of writing.

RICHMOND

ACCOMMODATION
Accommodation in Richmond

Name	Stars	No. on Map	Telephone No.	Address	Lowest Price (Double/Twin)
Richmond Cottages	4	14	03-6260-2561	12 Bridge Street	$165
Prospect House	4½	15	03-6260-2207	1384 Richmond Road	$160
Red Brier Cottage	4	12	03-6260-2349	15 Bridge Street	$155
Millhouse on the Bridge		3	03-6260-2428	2 Wellington Street	$150
Ashmore Cottage	4	11	03-6260-2570	32 Bridge Street	$135
Bridge Cottages		5	03-6260-2570	47 Bridge Street	$135
Laurel Cottage		2	03-6260-2397	9 Wellington Street	$135
Richmond Barracks B&B	4	6	03-6260-2453	16 Franklin Street	$135
Colonial Accommodation	4	8	03-6260-2570	4 Percy Street	$135
Hollyhock Cottage	4	9	03-6260-1079	3 Percy Street	$130
Richmond Manor	4½	1	03-6260-2622	73 Prosser Road	$125
Poplar Cottage	4	4	03-6260-2570	49 Bridge Street	$125
Mrs. Currie's House		7	03-6260-2766	4 Franklin Street	$110
Richmond Arms Hotel		10	03-6260-2109	42 Bridge Street	$110
Coachman's Rest		13	03-6260-2729	30 Bridge Street	$75

MOVING ON
Bus Services from Richmond

Destination	Operator	Via	Distance (km)	Fare	Journey Time	Frequency
Hobart	Hobart Coaches		25	$5.90	25 - 30 mins	3/day
	TassieLink		25	$12	35 mins	1/day
	Richmond Bus		25	$30*	45 mins	2/day
Swansea	TassieLink		113	$10	1¾ hrs	1/day

* Return fare

PORT ARTHUR
Population 600
2 hrs 15 mins by bus from Hobart

Port Arthur is one of most tangible relics of the convict system in Australia and it is a piece of the nation's history which is not to be missed if you have reached as far as Tasmania. Before coming here, try to find time to read Marcus Clarke's book, *For the Term of His Natural Life*, first published in serial form in the *Australian Journal* in 1870 - 1872 and then published as a novel in 1874. That book will give a real appreciation of what it is that you are going to see. Let us start though by reaching Port Arthur.

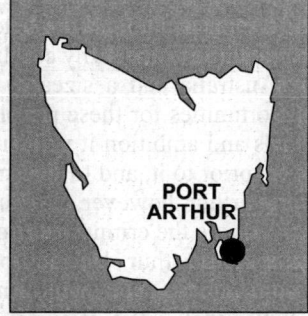

TassieLink operates a bus from Hobart to here every weekday afternoon. In addition, there are services on Monday, Wednesday and Friday mornings in summer.

Along the route, at about the half-way point, you will pass through **Copping**, where you will see the *Copping Collection*, and the Cop outside the *Copping Collection*. Although this is an interesting little private museum of convict and general artefacts, the infrequency of buses makes it difficult to take a stop here. If you do, however, backpackers accommodation is available.

At **Dunalley**, there is a short **canal** cut through the Tasman Peninsula connecting east with west and saving small vessels a long detour. A swing bridge is built across the canal and is the only way to reach the peninsula. You will notice this point as the bus turns sharp left to cross the bridge and you will observe the pretty scenery with many boats moored in the vicinity. Dunalley has a church built with bricks made by the convicts at Port Arthur and used originally for buildings at the Coal Mines in the north-west of the peninsula.

The next point of great interest is **Eaglehawk Neck** (population 200), which really is worth stopping for. If you go to Port Arthur with a tour, you will have the opportunity to look at the scenery here, but the TassieLink bus will not give you the chance to admire the really spectacular parts. If you have read *For the Term of His Natural Life*, mentioned above, you will soon recognise this scene. This is where soldiers and dogs guarded the Tasman Peninsula to ensure that escape from Port Arthur was almost impossible. At this point the isthmus is only one hundred metres across. A chain was run across and dogs tied to the chain. Then, since the only possible escape route was via the sea, a rumour was circulated that the waters were infested with sharks. Even so, in 1843 the bushranger Martin Cash and two of his friends did manage to escape from here.

Now, though, the point of interest is not the dogs, but the natural scenery. There are four natural wonders here within the space of a few hundred metres. They are labelled the **Tasman Arch**, a natural bridge across which one can walk; the **Devil's Kitchen**, where the waves rush in through a narrow gap producing a cauldron of churning water at the foot of a deep enclosed chasm; the **Blowhole**; and the **Tessellated Pavement**, caused by wave action. The scale of these natural phenomena is most impressive, so try to stop and see them if you possibly can. There are also walks, and the **Officers' Quarters** from the convict days remain, now used as a small museum. There is accommodation available here, including a backpackers hostel.

Port Arthur itself is near the southern tip of the Tasman Peninsula. Named after Lieutenant-Governor Arthur, it began life in 1830 as a timber station. In 1833 it became a secondary punishment male prison settlement. This distinction should be understood in order to explain why conditions here were so harsh. Many convicts were transported to Australia and a sizeable proportion of them came to Tasmania, but there were opportunities for these people. If they performed the duties assigned to them and had skills and ambition it was quite possible to gain good positions upon their release, or even prior to it, and to become important members of society. Those who were sent to Port Arthur, however, were convicts who had committed further offences in Australia. They were the criminals among the criminals.

Port Arthur had become almost self-sufficient by the 1840s, but when transportation lost favour, and new young convicts ceased to arrive in the 1850s and 1860s, that self-sufficiency was gradually lost. In 1877 the prison was closed. Thereafter buildings such as the church and penitentiary were destroyed by fire and by vandalism, even so long ago, and other constructions suffered from those seeking building materials. The settlement was renamed Carnarvon, but in 1927 it reverted to Port Arthur.

When the author first came here, the site was mostly unrestored ruins, but nonetheless a fascinating place to visit, indeed perhaps more fascinating than now. The

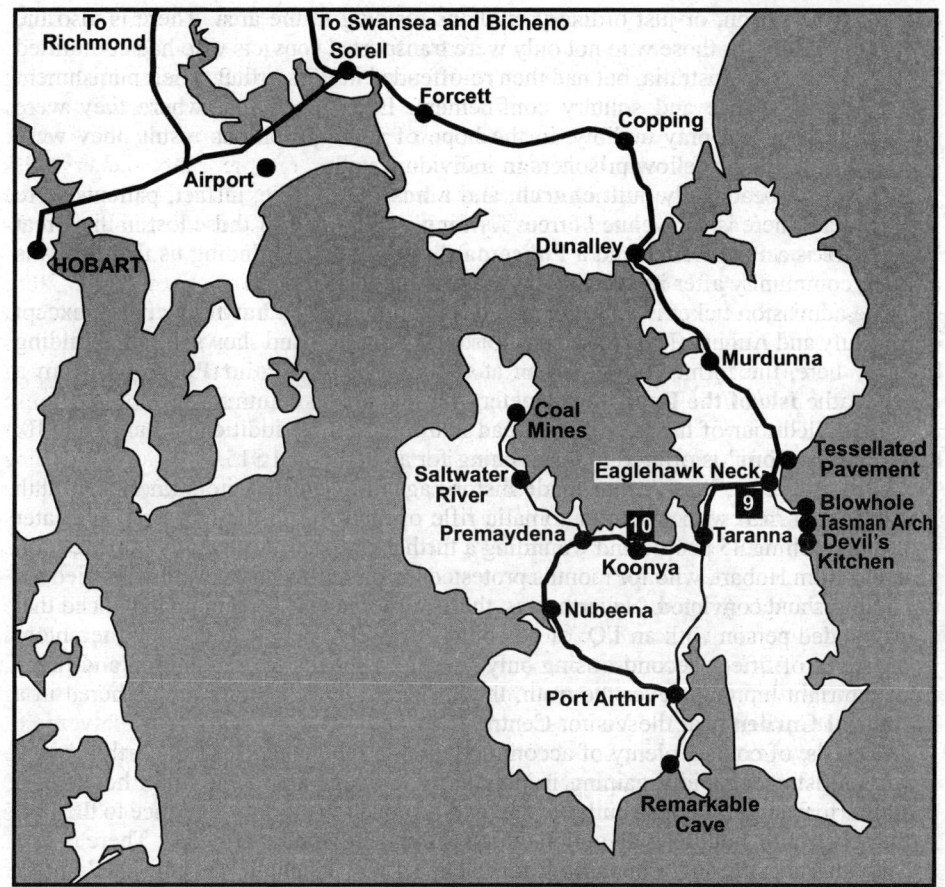

FROM HOBART TO PORT ARTHUR
Showing TassieLink bus route (thicker line)
Numerals indicate backpackers hostels

sense of history hung more heavily over the derelict buildings. However, in 1979, the state and federal governments decided to spend $9 million on restoration and development work, since when it has won many awards.

The first difference which the visitor will notice now is that admission costs $20. Entry is now through the **Visitor Centre**, newly constructed in 1999 at a cost of a further $4.5 million, although access can also be gained at some other points around the forty-hectare enclosed site. The Centre and grounds are open from 8:30 until dusk, but certain buildings have shorter opening hours. Tours are available from 9:00 and are included in the price of admission.

Passing through the Visitor Centre, one finds oneself in the role of a nineteenth-century criminal, being sentenced to transportation and then entering the ship and emerging in Port Arthur. One is given a prisoner identity card, relating to the circumstances of an actual past prisoner, and invited to trace his history and discover what became of him. Within the grounds are approximately thirty buildings, some restored and some just ruins, some prison buildings and some the homes of those operating the prison, or just ordinary civilians residing in the area. There is also the **separate prison**, for those who not only were transported convicts who had committed further offences in Australia, but had then re-offended in Port Arthur. Their punishment was a life of silence and solitary confinement. Even in church, where they were allowed to sing and pray audibly, in the hope of some propitious result, they were segregated from their fellow prisoners in individual stalls.

There is a beautifully built **church**, and a **hospital**, where, in fact, patients were well tended. There is an avenue of trees forming a memorial for those lost in the Great War. There is a **Post Office** and a **Policeman's Residence** reminding us that this was a living community after its convict days, and even during them.

The admission ticket is valid for two days and includes a **harbour cruise**, except during July and August. The cruise lasts for twenty minutes and shows the shipbuilding industry here, the former boys' prison at the aptly named **Point Puer** and, from a distance, the **Isle of the Dead**, the cemetery for this prison community.

A detailed tour of the Isle of the Dead is offered for an additional charge of $10, and a '**Ghost Tour**' is offered in the evening for an additional $15.

In recent years, Port Arthur made history again, as most visitors know. On 28th April 1996, a man with a semi-automatic rifle opened fire in the cafeteria, and later elsewhere, killing 35 people and wounding a further eighteen. A mentally impaired 28-year-old from Hobart, who for months protested his innocence, was eventually tried for the murders and convicted. Nevertheless, there are some who remain unconvinced that a left-handed person with an I.Q. of 66 could kill twelve people and wound ten more in the space of fifteen seconds, using only seventeen rounds of ammunition and firing from the right hip. Whatever the truth, the 35 innocent victims are remembered in a **Memorial Garden** near the Visitor Centre.

There is, of course, plenty of accommodation in the vicinity of Port Arthur, since it is a tourist spot rapidly gaining in popularity. Options include a youth hostel in a beautiful former guest house built in 1890 and just outside the back entrance to the Port Arthur enclosure, but this is an option which is frequently rather crowded. There is also a Caravan Park offering a bunkroom for backpackers. Although reaching one's berth may involve some mountaineering, the park is in a pleasant location, with an enjoyable walk along the nearby beach. However, it is nearly three kilometres from the town and there are no street lights nearby. You will need a torch to go out after dark.

A little further away from the town is **Bush Mill**. This is a fascinating venture, developed by one family. It is a re-creation of a steam-powered sawmill established at nearby Stingary Bay in 1897 and burnt down in 1927. The sawmill actually works and cuts timber from time to time for the local community. As one walks round the site, a recorded commentary is activated, explaining how things were here a century ago. However, the greatest attraction is the **railway**. This is a remarkable little line, built to a fifteen-inch gauge and negotiating curves as tight as they could possibly be, as well as a steep gradient. It runs for approximately two kilometres. Perhaps the most amazing feature, though, is that the steam locomotive generally used was actually constructed here, in its entirety, except for the boiler. It is an exact half-scale model of the Garratt 'K' Class articulated locomotive produced in England in 1910 by Beyer Peacock and used with great success on Tasmanian two-feet gauge tramways in the north-west of the state. Bush Mill is open daily, except for Saturdays in July and August, from 9:00 until 17:00 (16:00 in July and August) and admission costs $18. Trains run at 10:15, 11:15 and 14:30, and at certain other times if there are sufficient passengers.

There are other sights to see in the vicinity of Port Arthur. These include **Remarkable Cave**, five kilometres south, and various other convict sites. Of the latter the most interesting is the **Coal Mines**, in the northwest of the peninsula. Coal was discovered here in 1833 and, although it was relatively low-grade coal, it gave Tasmania a degree of independence from New South Wales, from where all supplies had previously been imported. A contingent of the most refractory prisoners was sent to work these mines, in very harsh conditions, and another prisoner, one Joseph Lacey, convicted for robbery, appointed as overseer, since he had experience of mining. He proved so capable in this position that he eventually became the lessee of another colliery following his release. The Coal Mines lie about twelve kilometres off the bus route followed by TassieLink, the nearest stop being in **Premaydena**, which is fifteen kilometres from Port Arthur. There are also the remains of convict 'probation stations' (outstations) at **Nubeena**, **Premaydena**, **Saltwater River**, **Koonya** and **Taranna**.

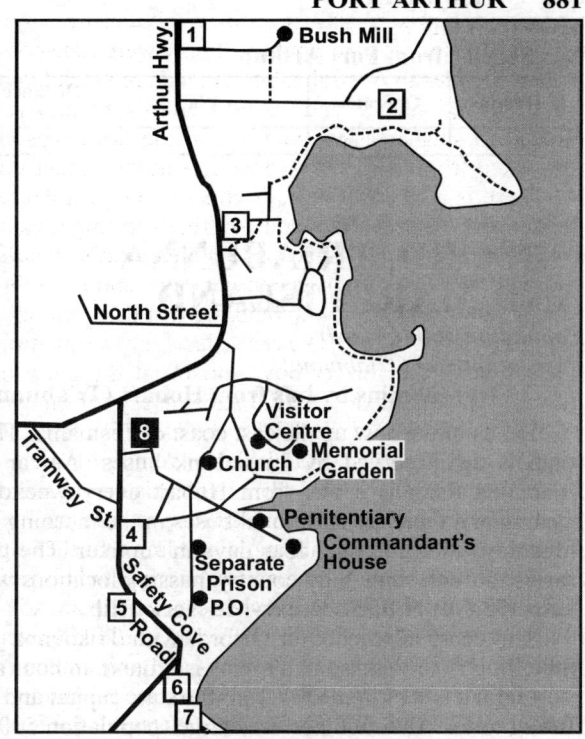

PORT ARTHUR
Black numerals indicate hotel accommodation
White numerals indicate backpackers hostels

ACCOMMODATION
(i) Hotel Accommodation in Port Arthur

Name	Stars	No. on Map	Telephone No.	Address	Lowest Price (Double/Twin)
Holiday World		3	03-6250-2262	Arthur Highway	$130
Port Arthur Motor Inn	3½	4	1-800-030-747	29 Safety Cove Road	$130
Sea Change Safety Cove		7	03-6250-2719	425 Safety Cove Road	$120
Fox and Hounds		1	03-6250-2217	Arthur Highway	$105
Port Arthur Villas	4	5	1-800-815-775	52 Safety Cove Road	$105
Anderton's Accom.	4	6	03-6250-2378	239 Safety Cove Road	$80
Port Arthur Caravan Park		2	03-6250-2340	Garden Point	$70

(ii) Backpackers Hostels in and near Port Arthur

Name	Group	No. on Map	Telephone No.	Address	Lowest Price (Dormitory)
Roseview	YHA	8	03-6250-2311	Champ Street	$19
Port Arthur Caravan Park		2	03-6250-2340	Garden Point	$16
Eaglehawk Neck B/P		9	03-6250-3248	Old Jetty Rd., Eaglehawk Neck	$17
Seaview Lodge		10	03-6250-2766	Koonya	$19

882 TASMANIA
MOVING ON
Bus Service from Port Arthur

Destination	Operator	Via	Distance (km)	Fare	Journey Time	Frequency
Hobart	TassieLink		125	$18	1¾ - 2 hrs	5 - 8/week

ORFORD, TRIABUNNA AND MARIA ISLAND
Population 500 (Orford)
Population 800 (Triabunna)
1 hr 30 mins by bus from Hobart (Triabunna)

Let us move now up the east coast of Tasmania. This route is again served by TassieLink buses. As far as Triabunna there is a bus from Hobart every weekday evening and there are additional buses in the morning on three days in winter and four days in summer. The bus travels through some hilly country, passing locations with such heart-rending names as **Bust-Me-Gut Hill** and **Break-Me-Neck Hill**.

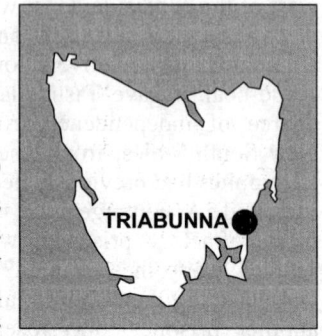

The coast is reached at Orford, with Triabunna just nine kilometres further on. Travelling time to these two towns is around an hour and a half from Hobart.

Orford is 81 kilometres from the state capital and is primarily a holiday resort and fishing town. Although not very large (population 500), it offers accommodation.

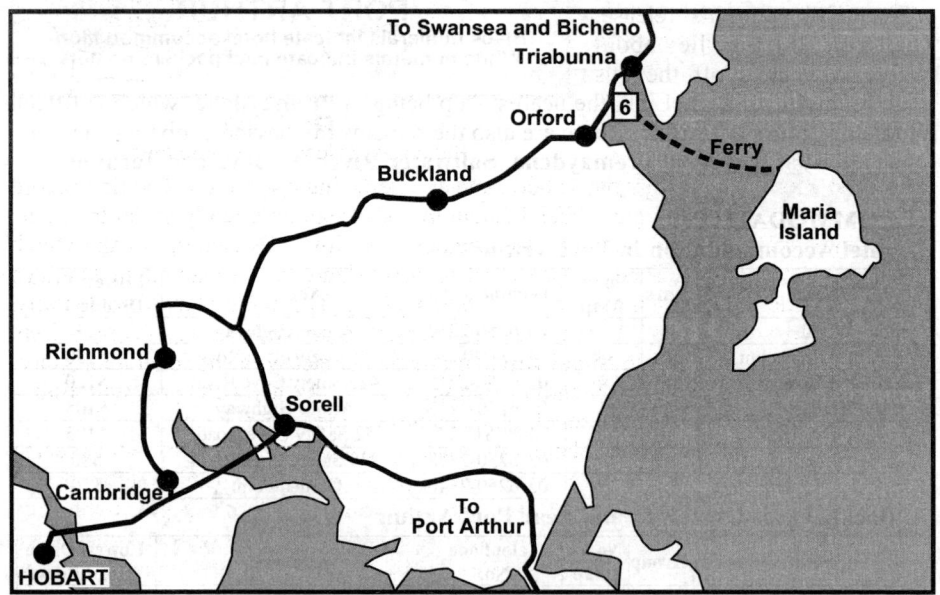

FROM HOBART TO TRIABUNNA
Showing TassieLink bus routes
Numerals indicate accommodation

Orford also has two old houses worth looking at. One is **Sanda House**, built in 1840 and the oldest surviving building in the town. It was the Post Office from 1876 until 1940. The other is **Mulunah**, on the main Tasman Highway, so visible from the bus. It is an impressive building which was constructed in 1868 for Charles Meredith, the local M.P., and his wife Louisa, an artist and author.

Triabunna is ninety kilometres from Hobart and has a population of 800. It was once a garrison town for the convict settlement on nearby Maria Island. Later it became a whaling base and now it depends on woodchipping, together with fishing for abalone and scallops. It is less oriented towards tourism, but has good beaches and a backpackers hostel often used as a base by those visiting Maria Island. Tours of the woodchipping plant are available too.

Maria Island, though, is the reason why many visitors pause here, and an interesting reason too. The first record of Maria Island is a sighting by Abel Tasman in 1642. Having already given the name Van Diemen's Land, after Anthony Van Diemen, the Governor-General of the Dutch East India Company in Batavia (Jakarta), to this island now renamed in his own honour, he called Maria Island after Van Diemen's wife. The name Maria, incidentally, is pronounced with a long 'i'. The first Englishman to arrive here was Captain John Cox in 1789. He anchored in **Shoal Bay**, and made contact with the local aborigines. In 1792 the French explorer Nicholas Baudin visited. As a result, you will find a mixture of Dutch, English and French place names on the island.

In the early 1800s, Maria Island was used by whalers and sealers, who erected temporary shelters. Then in 1825 it became a penal settlement. This means that it predates Port Arthur in that capacity by eight years and is in fact second in antiquity only to Hobart as a convict base within Tasmania. Several buildings were constructed then of stone and brick, of which the **Penitentiary** and **Commissariat Store** still remain. The convicts stayed on that occasion only until 1832 when they were withdrawn and moved to Port Arthur when it opened in 1833. However, because of the increasing number of convicts arriving in Tasmania, Maria Island was re-occupied in

884 TASMANIA

1842, and a second settlement established at **Point Lesueur**, where the ruins can still be seen. In 1851, though, the convicts were withdrawn again and did not return. The land was taken over for agricultural purposes.

In 1884, the Italian silk merchant Diego Bernacchi leased the island, planted 50,000 vines and built a thirty-room hotel and the Coffee Palace. One of his wines came third in the 1888 Melbourne Centennial Exhibition. A school and various shops were opened, but by 1895 the project had been abandoned and the **school** is now used as the Ranger's Office.

Bernacchi came back in 1920, having decided to build a cement works here. He also constructed a pier and a railway line, and in 1924 the cement works opened. It lasted only until 1930. In 1972, the whole island was declared a National Park.

A ferry runs to Maria Island three times a day, at 10:30, 13:00 and 15:30, returning thirty minutes later on each occasion. In summer there is an additional departure at 9:00. The vessel, the *Eastcoaster Express*, a 48-seater catamaran, leaves from the Eastcoaster Resort, which is mid-way between Orford and Triabunna and just off the main highway. On the days when the TassieLink morning bus operates, it calls in here, arriving at 9:55 or 10:25, and connects with the 10:30 ferry. The ferry ride takes 25 minutes and costs $20 return.

Maria Island offers mainly bushwalking, with the added interest of the convict-constructed buildings at **Darlington**, at the north of the island where the ferry berths. Note, though, that there is no shop on the island, so you need to bring your lunch with you. There are also no vehicles, except those of the Rangers.

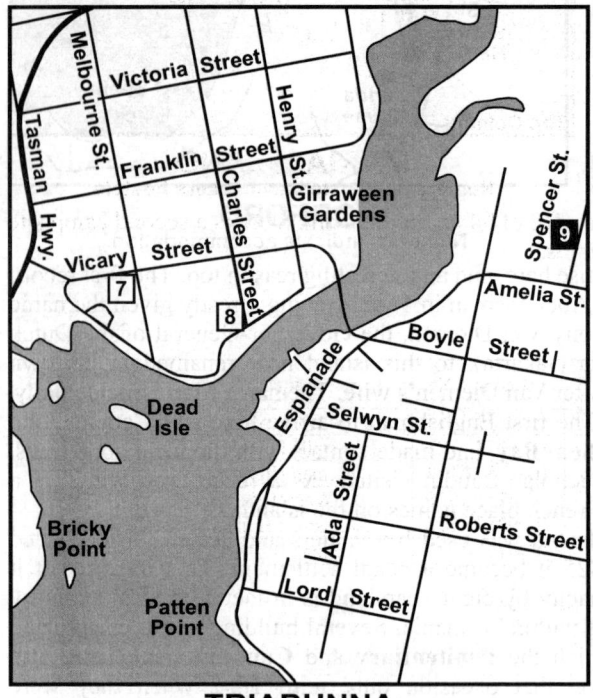

TRIABUNNA
Black numerals indicate hotel accommodation
White numerals indicate backpackers hostels

The island is a little over twenty kilometres long and thirteen kilometres wide and resembles two islands joined by a narrow isthmus. There is plenty of wildlife, some of it semi-tame. Most visitors come just for the day, which limits the walks available. The most popular are to the **Painted Cliffs**, the **Fossil Cliffs** and the **Bishop and Clerk Peak**.

The Painted Cliffs lie south of Darlington and are what they sound like - cliffs which give the impression of having been painted or carved by hand, although actually they are simply weathered. This walk is not too strenuous and is along a good track. It will take about two hours return. When you get back, you will probably have sufficient time to attempt the Fossil Cliffs Walk also. This too is a relatively easy walk, to the east of Darlington, to see cliffs which bear fossils in their rocks. It will take about an hour and a half return. The Fossil Rocks are almost on the way to the Bishop and Clerk Peak, so you can also choose this combination. The Bishop and Clerk Peak is the highest point on the island, at 915 metres, and this is a stiff climb, quite different from the other two walks mentioned. It rewards, of course, with its view. The walk will take about four hours return.

In Mr. Bernacchi's former Coffee Palace is the **Visitor Centre**, telling the history of the island. His hotel, however, is demolished, which is a pity really, because the only available accommodation is now in the Penitentiary. This accommodation is basic. A bunk and a mattress are provided, but no bedding, and there is no electricity or hot water. Camping is permitted, for a fee of $4 per person, and there is a second camp site at **French's Farm**, near the isthmus.

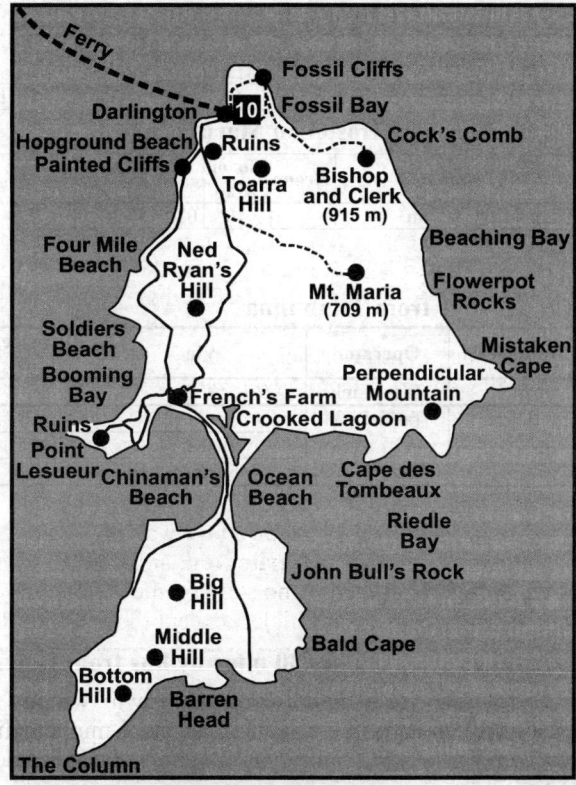

MARIA ISLAND
Numerals indicate backpackers hostels

ACCOMMODATION
(i) Accommodation in Orford

Name	Stars	No. on Map	Telephone No.	Address	Lowest Price (Double/Twin)
Riverside Cottages		4	03-6257-1655	Old Convict Road	$125
Eastcoaster Resort	3½	6	03-6257-1172	Louisville Point Road	$100
Island View Motel		2	03-6257-1114	Tasman Highway	$90
Seabreeze Holiday Cabins	3½	5	03-6257-1375	17 Walpole Street	$70
Shalom Waterfront B&B		1	03-6257-1175	50 Tasman Highway	$70
Blue Waters Motor Hotel	3	3	03-6257-1102	Tasman Highway	$55

(ii) Hotel Accommodation in Triabunna

Name	Stars	No. on Map	Telephone No.	Address	Lowest Price (Double/Twin)
Spring Bay Hotel		8	03-6257-3115	1 Charles Street	$65
Triabunna Caravan Park		7	03-6257-3575	4 Vicary Street	$35

886 TASMANIA

(iii) Backpackers Hostel in Triabunna

Name	Group	No. on Map	Telephone No.	Address	Lowest Price (Dormitory)
Udda Backpackers	YHA	9	03-6257-3439	12 Spencer Street	$18

(iv) Backpackers Hostel on Maria Island

Name	Group	No. on Map	Telephone No.	Address	Lowest Price (Dormitory)
Penitentiary Accom.		10	03-6257-1420	Darlington	$10

MOVING ON
Bus Services from Triabunna

Destination	Operator	Via	Distance (km)	Fare	Journey Time	Frequency
Hobart	TassieLink		88	$15.90	1¾ hrs	8 - 9/week
St. Helens	TassieLink		172	$23.40	2¾ hrs	2/week
		Bicheno	90	$12.50	1¾ hrs	3 - 4/week
		Swansea	50	$6.80	40 - 50 mins	8 - 9/week

SWANSEA
Population 500

2 hrs 30 mins by bus from Hobart

Swansea is a small coastal town which is, reasonably enough, the centre of the rural municipality of Glamorgan, and Glamorgan claims to be the oldest rural municipality in Australia, founded in 1860. Despite this Welsh influence, however, there does not yet seem to be any pressure to change the name of the town to Abertawe. Swansea was the first town to be settled on the eastern coast of Tasmania, in 1821, but it was originally known as Waterloo Point, then later as Great Swanport. A little south of Swansea, there is still a small town which bears the name of **Little Swanport**.

The three-storey **Morris General Store** in Swansea was built in 1838. There is a small

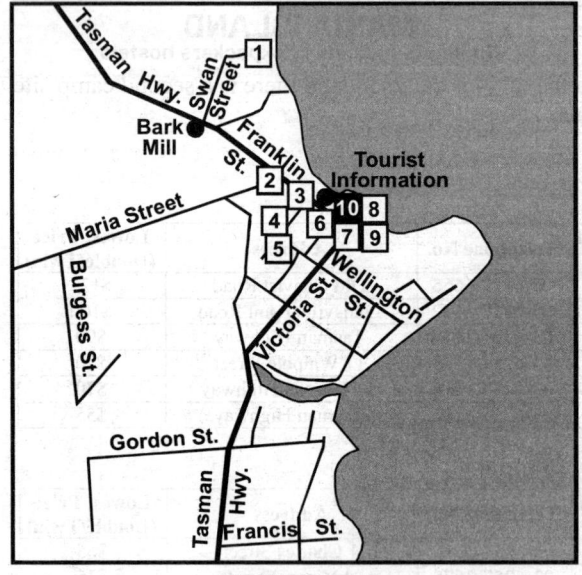

SWANSEA
Black numerals indicate hotel accommodation
White numerals indicate backpackers hostels

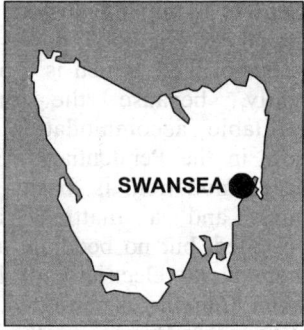

museum outlining the history of the town and there is a **Community Centre** dating from 1860. There are good beaches and there is surfing. On the edge of the town is **Swansea Bark Mill**, bark of the Black Wattle having been used formerly for tanning.

All of the buses which serve Triabunna continue to Swansea, in addition to which there is a Tasmanian Redline service from Launceston, with connexions also available from Hobart. The connexions, however, always offer a service inferior to that provided by TassieLink on its direct route. On some days the journey with Redline can take as long as six hours.

There is a range of accommodation available in Swansea, including a youth hostel.

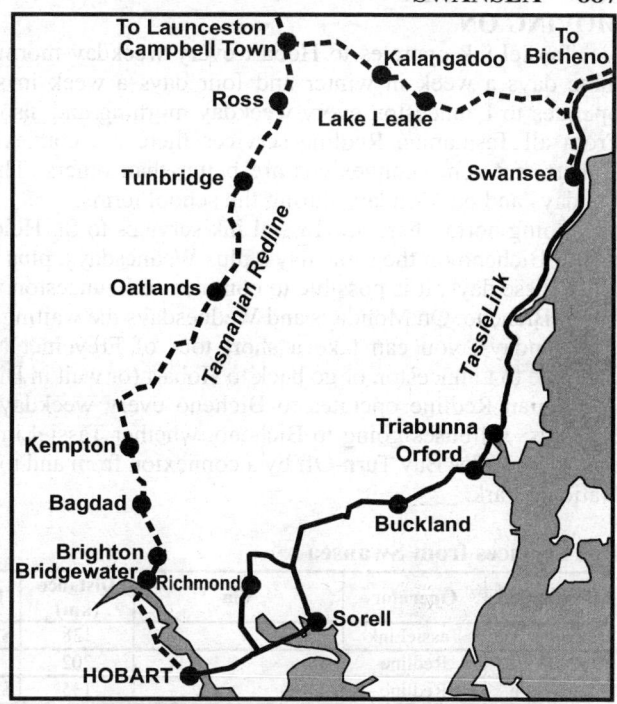

FROM HOBART TO SWANSEA
Solid line shows TassieLink route
Dashed line shows Tasmanian Redline route

ACCOMMODATION
(i) Hotel Accommodation in Swansea

Name	Stars	No. on Map	Telephone No.	Address	Lowest Price (Double/Twin)
Meredith House	4½	4	03-6257-8119	15 Noyes Street	$180
Scarecrow Cottage		5	03-6343-6340	22 Noyes Street	$140
Tubby and Padman		3	03-6257-8901	20 Franklin Street	$135
Freycinet Waters	4	6	03-6257-8080	16 Franklin Street	$110
Oyster Bay Guest House		7	03-6257-8110	10 Franklin Street	$90
Amos House	4	2	03-6257-8656	3 Maria Street	$85
Swansea Motor Inn		8	03-6257-8102	1 Franklin Street	$75
Swansea Waterloo Inn		9	03-6257-8577	1a Franklin Street	$70
Swansea Holiday Park	3½	1	03-6257-8177	Shaw Street	$40

(ii) Backpackers Hostel in Swansea

Name	Group	No. on Map	Telephone No.	Address	Lowest Price (Dormitory)
Swansea Y.H.A.	YHA	10	03-6257-8367	5 Franklin Street	$18

888 TASMANIA

MOVING ON

TassieLink operates to Hobart every weekday morning, and in the afternoon on three days a week in winter and four days a week in summer. Tasmanian Redline operates to Launceston every weekday morning and also on Sundays in the summer. From all Tasmanian Redline services there are connexions at Campbell Town for Hobart, but some connexions are better than others. The best ones are on summer Sundays and on Mondays during the school terms.

Going north, there are TassieLink services to St. Helens on Fridays and Sundays, and to Bicheno on the same days, plus Wednesdays, plus Mondays in the summer. On all of these days, it is possible to continue to Launceston with TassieLink by changing bus at Bicheno. On Mondays and Wednesdays the waiting time is one hour. On Fridays and Sundays, you can take a short tour of Freycinet National Park first and then continue to Launceston or go back to Hobart (or wait in Bicheno for nearly four hours). Tasmanian Redline operates to Bicheno every weekday afternoon, and on summer Sundays. All buses going to Bicheno, whether TassieLink or Tasmanian Redline, are met at the Coles Bay Turn-Off by a connexion from and to Coles Bay and the Freycinet National Park.

Bus Services from Swansea

Destination	Operator	Via	Distance (km)	Fare	Journey Time	Frequency
Hobart	TassieLink		138	$21.70	2¼ - 2½ hrs	8 - 9/week
Hobart*	Redline		202	$28	2½ - 4½ hrs	5 - 6/week
Launceston	Redline		135	$23.80	2 - 2¼ hrs	5 - 6/week
St. Helens	TassieLink		122	$15.20	2 hrs	2/week
		Bicheno	40	$6.10	45 mins	3 - 4/week
Bicheno	Redline		40	$8.90	40 mins	5 - 6/week

* Connecting service. Change of bus involved.

COLES BAY AND FREYCINET NATIONAL PARK
Population 250

3 hrs 30 mins by bus from Hobart

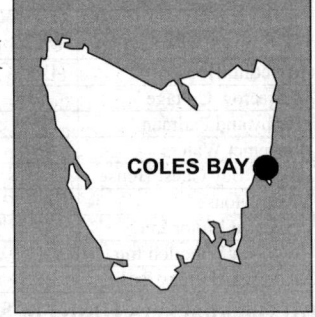

Freycinet is probably the most popular National Park in Tasmania. This popularity naturally makes it rather touristic and crowded, so be prepared for this, especially if you go in summer. However, it is the town of Coles Bay and the shorter, most famous walks which get crowded. If you go a little further away, on one of the longer walks, for example, or just walking on the beach, you will no longer feel the crush of people enjoying themselves.

Let us start by getting the geography correct. The Freycinet National Park is on a peninsula, the Freycinet Peninsula, which protrudes from the eastern coast of Tasmania in a north-south plane. The highway runs past its northern extremity, and bus services do not deviate to here. The distance from the highway to Coles Bay is 29 kilometres.

Coles Bay lies at the park entrance, but is not within the park, although you can walk into the park from the town. The town of Coles Bay exists solely because of the popularity of the National Park. It provides accommodation of all types, food, fuel and souvenirs. It is a modern town without much character, but it has some beautiful natural views. In fact, you could stay here for several days making walks outside the park boundary and enjoy your time greatly. However, the walks inside the park are even better. There is another peninsula west of Freycinet which appears to offer the possibility of a short cut from Swansea. However, there is no public transport along this road. There is, though, a ferry which operates in summer from the tip of the peninsula offering a short cut for cyclists. The ferry is not frequent and costs $10 for a very short journey.

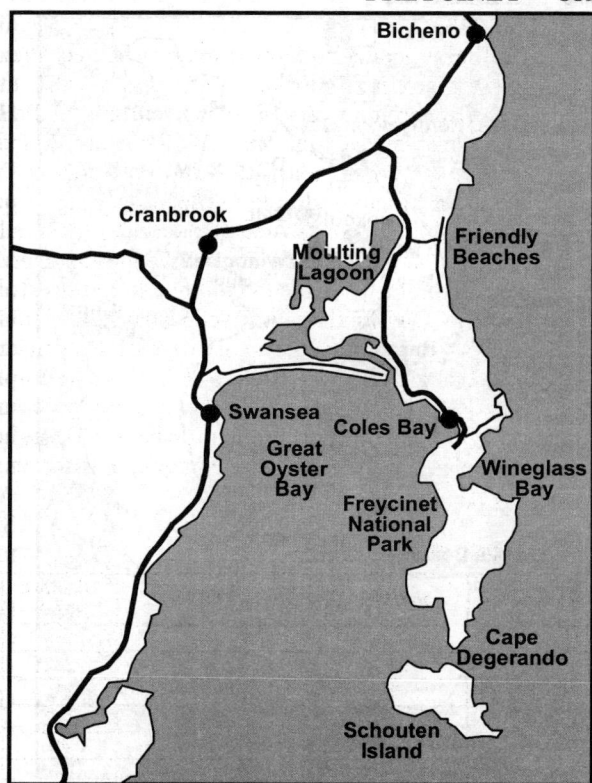

FREYCINET NATIONAL PARK AND VICINITY
Thicker lines show bus routes

Even though buses do not deviate to Coles Bay, there is always a connecting bus for all TassieLink and Tasmanian Redline services passing on the main highway. This connexion is operated by Bicheno Coach Service. It starts from Bicheno (usually), waits at the Coles Bay Turn-Off for the connecting service, and then brings passengers in to Coles Bay, and it conveys passengers out to the turn-off in a similar manner. The connexions always wait if necessary. The journey from the highway to Coles Bay takes half an hour and most buses continue to Freycinet Lodge and then to the start of the walking tracks. Since this last point is within the National Park, you have to pay a park fee or show a pass to go to the terminus.

Prior to European occupation, this area had 20,000 years of aboriginal history, being occupied by what are known now as the Oyster Bay Aborigines. Tasman passed by here in 1642, and then in 1802 the Freycinet Peninsula was named in honour of the Freycinet Brothers, who were on board a French survey vessel. Their name is still a famous one amongst cartographers, but most of us know of them only because of this National Park. Whaling stations soon developed here, and then in the early 1900s tin mines were dug.

As you travel from the highway to Coles Bay, **Moulting Lagoon** will be seen on your right. This is a breeding area for Black Swans. You will also be able to see duck

890 TASMANIA

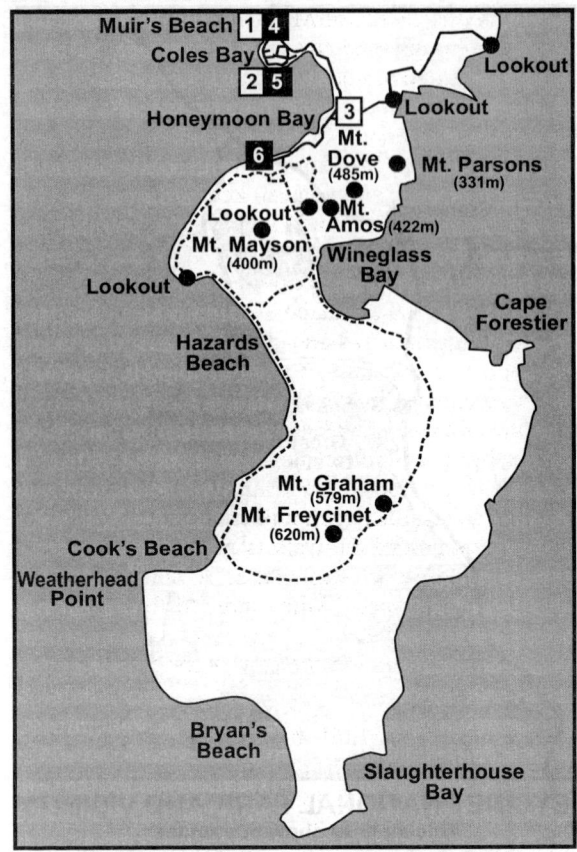

FREYCINET NATIONAL PARK
Black numerals indicate hotel accommodation
White numerals indicate backpackers hostels

hides in the shallow water, as duck shooting is permitted here at certain times of the year. The **Hazard Range** will come into view, one of the symbols of Freycinet National Park. Three peaks are clearly visible, although actually there are four, **Mt. Parsons** (331 metres) being obscured. Now you will see **Great Oyster Bay** on the right and **Muir's Beach** beside it, a pretty and relatively unfrequented area. After half an hour we come into **Coles Bay**, named, not after the supermarket chain, but after one Silas Cole who lived here for many years in the nineteenth century making a living by burning the oyster shells left in the aboriginal middens from twenty millennia of fishing in Great Oyster Bay and selling the resultant lime.

On Fridays and Sundays, TassieLink operates a short tour in conjunction with its bus services from Hobart and Launceston. If you are using a TassieLink *Explorer Pass*, this tour costs only $25 extra, including admission to the National Park. The bus from Launceston waits at the highway turn-off and collects any passengers coming from Hobart, then takes all to Coles Bay for a brief stop to purchase lunch, then into the park, allowing sufficient time for the Wineglass Bay Lookout Walk, before returning. The bus is not permitted to convey passengers to Coles Bay only, however. They must be tour passengers. With this convenient arrangement, one can make the tour from either Hobart or Launceston and return at the end of the day, or one can start from Hobart, make the tour and continue to Launceston, or *vice versa*. The only disadvantage is that the time allowed thereby is far too short for such a beautiful place as Freycinet.

Three pink granite mountains, **Mt. Amos** (422 metres), **Mt. Dove** (485 metres) and **Mt. Mayson** (400 metres), are visible in the Hazard Range stretching across the top of the 12,000 hectare National Park. There is a good walk to the top of Mt. Amos, the second highest of these, from where there is the excellent view which often appears on postcards. All walks start from the car park just inside the park entrance, where you will usually find one or two wallabies waiting to meet you, having learnt that humans carry edible provisions with them. The most famous walk is that to the **Wineglass Bay**

Lookout, to reach which you have to cross the saddle of Mt. Amos and Mt. Mayson. This is a moderately stiff climb, but there are rough steps to assist and the view is going to be worth the exertion. There are also informative notices on the way up, giving an excuse to stop along the way for a minute or two. At the saddle you turn left for a short distance and reach the lookout. There will be other visitors, but it is a beautiful view, which should be seen. You cannot reach the top of Mt. Amos from here though. That walk is along a different track. Return to the saddle and you can keep left and descend to the far side of the range, which is to say to the beautiful **Wineglass Bay**, named for its shape. By this time humanity is starting to thin out. About half of the walkers go only to the lookout. Of the half who continue, few go beyond the beach of Wineglass Bay. The walk only to the lookout and back takes an hour or less. The walk to Wineglass Bay Beach and back takes about two hours, plus whatever time you wish to spend at the beach.

If you wish to continue, there are two choices from here, for the longer of which you will need to have come prepared with some water and supplies. The shorter option, first, is to turn right here at the start of the beach and follow the track across the isthmus to **Hazards Beach** on the western side. This is a flat simple heathland walk, where the main attraction will be wildlife and flora. At Hazards Beach turn right again and follow the coast back to the car park. However, this part of the walk is quite undulating and rocky in parts, with several small creek beds to be crossed. It is not particularly difficult, but it takes more time than one might expect. Allow three to four hours for the whole circuit.

ANECDOTE

I had planned to join at Bicheno the TassieLink bus making the tour of Freycinet National Park and then to proceed to Launceston after the tour. Waiting at the bus stop, however, I was able to see the bus turn the corner of the main highway without entering the town of Bicheno or visiting the bus stop.

The following Sunday, I made sure that no similar mishap could occur by boarding the bus in Launceston. We journeyed to the National Park and walked up to the Wineglass Bay Lookout. When it was time to leave, however, one passenger, a Japanese girl, was found to be missing. We waited and searched, but there was no sign of her. The driver decided to contact the ranger, but just as he did so, the culprit appeared. Apparently, on her return, she had turned left instead of right at the saddle and walked most of the way down to Wineglass Bay before realising her mistake.

Much delayed, we set off. At the Coles Bay Turn-Off, the driver stopped and enquired whether there were any passengers for Launceston. No reply. We went into Bicheno, exchanged pleasantries and passengers with the Hobart bus and set off as quickly as possible on our delayed journey to Launceston. After a few minutes, the driver's telephone rang. On reaching the Coles Bay Turn-Off, the Hobart service had discovered a passenger for Launceston. The Hobart bus would return to Bicheno with her and would we please go back and collect her there?

In the end we did reach Launceston safely, and only 35 minutes late. It had been an eventful day which had, at least, conveyed a favourable impression of TassieLink's feeling of obligation even to wayward passengers.

TASMANIA

The adventurous longer option from Wineglass Bay is to walk the length of Wineglass Bay Beach and then follow the track which leads up into the **Freycinet Range** further south along the peninsula. **Mt. Graham** here reaches 579 metres, while **Mt. Freycinet** is the highest peak at 620 metres, and, although you do not need to scale these peaks, you have to cross the Freycinet-Graham Col at 381 metres, the East Freycinet Divide at 313 metres and the South Freycinet Saddle at 256 metres, before descending to **Cook's Beach**. You arrive at the northern end of the beach and turn right for the return. However, at the southern end of the beach, if required, there is a hut with a water supply and a camp site. Walk back along the western coast to Hazards Beach, where there is another camp site and another water supply. Keep going along the beach and then return to the car park via the coast as for the shorter circuit mentioned above. This longer circuit is a walk for a whole day. About ten hours should be allowed.

Since Coles Bay exists for the purpose of serving those visiting the National Park, there is a range of accommodation offered. For backpackers there are two choices. Freycinet Backpackers is more than two kilometres from the town, but in a pretty location. Iluka Backpackers is right in the town. There is also youth hostel accommodation inside the park, but it must be booked on a per room basis. Rooms will accommodate up to five guests. This hostel has no hot water.

There is a bus which will take walkers to the start of the walking tracks at 9:30 each morning, but it costs $4 single or $6.50 return, which is rather expensive for a journey of about five kilometres each way. Also, in the author's opinion, 10:00 is rather late to be starting on a walk. Better to get going early. There are buses back from the car park to the accommodation at 10:00, 13:50 and 15:50.

ACCOMMODATION
(i) Hotel Accommodation in Coles Bay

Name	Stars	No. on Map	Telephone No.	Address	Lowest Price (Double/Twin)
Freycinet Lodge	4	3	03-6257-0101	Freycinet National Park	$210
Edge of the Bay Resort		1	03-6257-0102	2308 Main Road	$150
Coles Bay Retreat		2	0418-132-538	29 Jetty Road	$140
Three Peaks Units		2	03-6257-0333	60 Freycinet Drive	$105
Freycinet Villas		2	03-6257-0320	2 Bradley Drive	$100
Jessie's Cottage		2	03-6257-0143	7 Esplanade East	$100
Royle Retreat		2	03-6257-0014	2 Royle Avenue	$95
Baywatch House		2	03-6257-0115	34 Jetty Road	$80
Gum Nut Cottage		2	03-6257-0320	50 Freycinet Drive	$80
Coles Bay Waterfronters		2	03-6257-0146	3 Florence Street	$75
Iluka Holiday Centre	3½	2	1-800-786-512	Esplanade	$70

(ii) Backpackers Hostels in Coles Bay

Name	Group	No. on Map	Telephone No.	Address	Lowest Price (Dormitory)
Coles Bay Y.H.A.	YHA	6	03-6234-9617	Freycinet National Park	$45 (per room)
Iluka Backpackers	YHA	5	1800-786-512	Esplanade	$19
Freycinet Backpackers		4	03-6257-0100	2352 Coles Bay Road	$19

MOVING ON

Connexions are made at the Coles Bay Turn-Off or at Bicheno with services operated by TassieLink or Tasmanian Redline to Hobart, Launceston and St. Helens. For details of these services, see the section below on Bicheno. Note that some of the Bicheno Coach services require reservations.

Bus Service from Coles Bay

Destination	Operator	Via	Distance (km)	Fare	Journey Time	Frequency
Bicheno	Bicheno Coach		40	$10	30 - 40 mins	3/day

BICHENO
Population 700

3 hrs by bus from Hobart

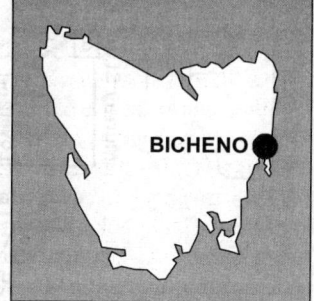

Bicheno is a small pleasant seaside town lying on Waub's Bay, its prosperity greatly enhanced by proximity to the Freycinet National Park. At the start of Bicheno's history, whaling and sealing were the industries here. Then it became a port for the export of coal. Now crayfishing and tourism are the staples.

Bicheno has attractive beaches to offer to the visitor and is also a renowned place for fishing. There is a **scuba diving school** and there is a **Sea Life Centre** with an **aquarium**. On the edge of the town is the **Bird Life and Animal Park**. **Fairy Penguins** (Little Penguins) live on **Diamond Island** and tours are available to see them. There is a **Bicentennial Foreshore Footway** stretching all round the town and offering a pleasant and interesting walk from the **Blowhole** in the south, past the **harbour** with its crayfishing boats and **Governor Island** just offshore, past **Peggy's Point** and **Safe Beach** to the new housing areas in the north, a walk of about an hour to **Redbill Point**. There is a good lookout at **Whaler's Lookout Rock**. For divers there is a unique **underwater kelp forest**. Near the town are two **vineyards**, and the **Douglas-Apsley National Park** starts a little further north.

The town of Bicheno is not so large. On the bend in the main highway is the **Visitor Information Centre**. Opposite are the principal shops, including that of *Le Frog*, offering unusual and exciting motor tricycle rides in a vehicle driven by a Frenchman, as you might perhaps guess.

There is plenty of accommodation, as befits a seaside town close to two popular National Parks. The options include three places for backpackers, of which the youth hostel is a little distant, being located three kilometres from the town centre. You are likely to find Bicheno Backpackers pleasant, friendly and conveniently situated.

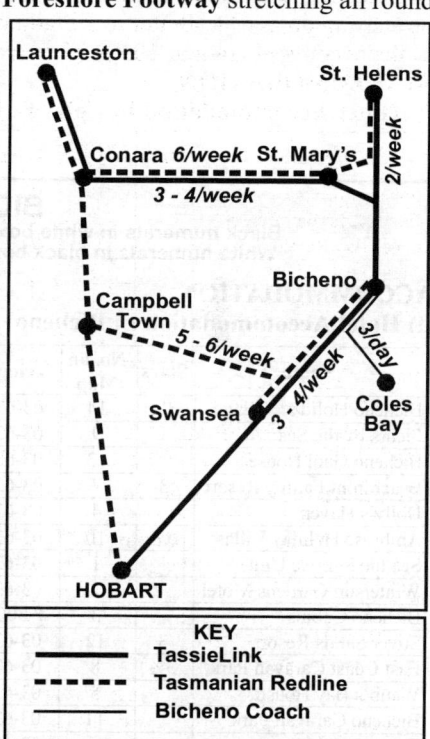

BUS ROUTES FROM BICHENO
Including connecting routes

894 TASMANIA

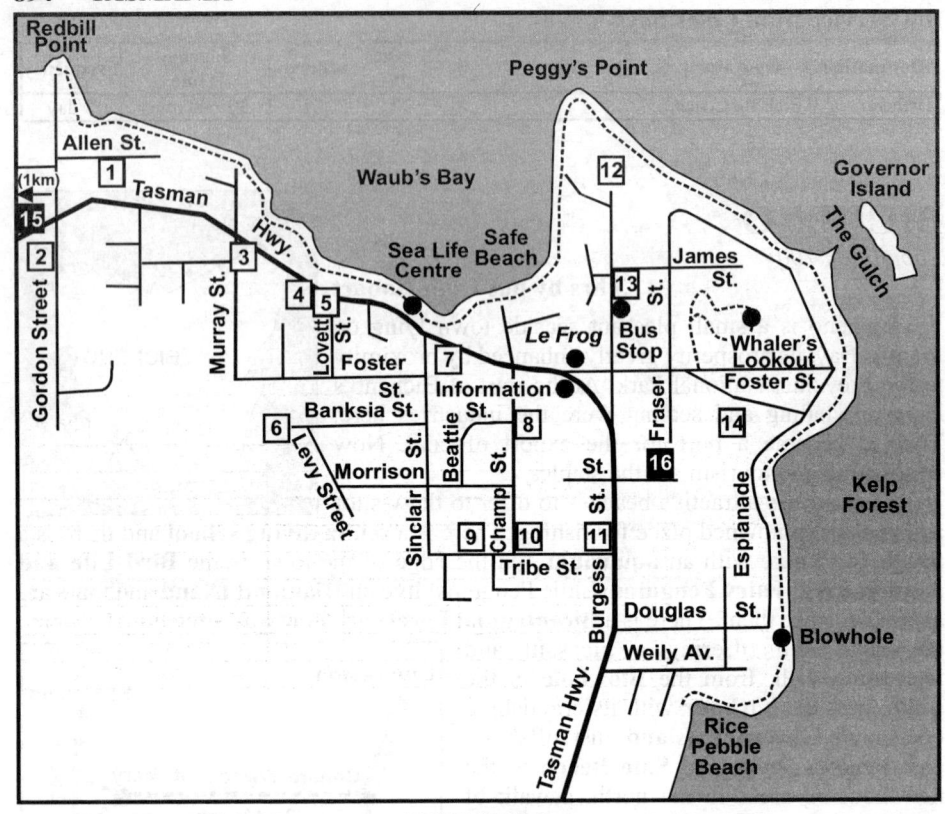

BICHENO
Black numerals in white boxes indicate hotel accommodation
White numerals in black boxes indicate backpackers hostels

ACCOMMODATION
(i) Hotel Accommodation in Bicheno

Name	Stars	No. on Map	Telephone No.	Address	Lowest Price (Double/Twin)
Bicheno Holiday Village	3½	14	03-6375-1171	The Esplanade	$165
Fleurs by the Sea		9	03-6375-1851	25 Tribe Street	$135
Bicheno Gaol House		13	03-6375-1430	James & Burgess Streets	$130
Beachfront Family Resort	3	7	03-6375-1111	232 Tasman Highway	$105
Dolly's Haven		4	03-6375-1671	20 Tasman Highway	$95
Ambrose Holiday Villas	3½	10	03-6375-1288	Champ Street	$90
Sea the Sunrise Unit		1	03-6375-1493	17 Allen Street	$90
Wintersun Gardens Motel		2	03-6375-1225	35 Gordon Street	$85
Bicheno Cabins		3	1-800-789-075	Tasman Hwy. & Murray St.	$75
Silver Sands Resort	3	12	03-6375-1266	Peggy's Point	$65
East Coast Caravan Park	3½	8	03-6375-1999	4 Champ Street	$50
Waub's Bay House		5	03-6375-1193	16 Tasman Highway	$45
Bicheno Caravan Park		11	03-6375-1280	52 Burgess Street	$35
Camp Seaview		6	03-6375-1247	29 Banksia Street	$35

(ii) Backpackers Hostels in Bicheno

Name	Group	No. on Map	Telephone No.	Address	Lowest Price (Dormitory)
Bicheno Backpackers		16	03-6375-1651	11 Morrison Street	$17
Bicheno Y.H.A.	YHA	15	03-6375-1293	47 Tasman Highway	$16
Camp Seaview		6	03-6375-1247	29 Banksia Street	$15

MOVING ON

Note that the routes to Launceston used by TassieLink and Tasmanian Redline differ (see diagram on page 893). The TassieLink bus runs north to St. Mary's, then to Launcesrton. The Redline bus runs south to Swansea, then to Launceston.

Bus Services from Bicheno

Destination	Operator	Via	Distance (km)	Fare	Journey Time	Frequency
Hobart	TassieLink		178	$27.20	3 hrs	3 - 4/week
		Swansea	40	$6.10	35 - 40 mins	3 - 4/week
Hobart*	Redline		247	$29.50	3¼ - 5¼ hrs	5 - 6/week
Launceston	TassieLink		179	$25.70	2½ hrs	3 - 4/week
		St. Mary's	132	$9	40 mins	3 - 4/week
Launceston	Redline		175	$29	2½ - 2¾ hrs	5 - 6/week
		Swansea	40	$8.90	35 - 40 mins	5 - 6/week
St. Helens	TassieLink		82	$10.50	1¼ hrs	2/week
Coles Bay	Bicheno Coach		40	$10	40 - 45 mins	3/day

* Connecting service. Change of bus involved.

ST. HELENS, DERBY, SCOTTSDALE AND BRIDPORT

Populations: 1,200 (St. Helens), 400 (Derby), 2,500 (Scottsdale), 1,700 (Bridport)

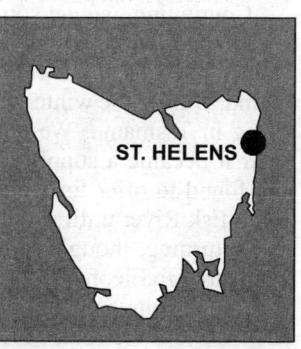

4 hrs 30 mins by bus from Hobart (St. Helens)
2 hrs 30 mins by bus from Launceston (Derby)
1 hr 30 mins by bus from Launceston (Scottsdale)
2 hrs from by bus Launceston (Bridport)

St. Helens is a further hour north along the coast from Bicheno, a route operated by TassieLink twice a week. As you move north, you will obtain some beautiful ocean views, making the journey to St. Helens worthwhile in itself.

Only four kilometres after leaving Bicheno, you will see one of the entrances to the **Douglas-Apsley National Park**, the most recent of Tasmania's eighteen National Parks. From this point it is eight kilometres to the **Apsley Gorge Reserve**, where the **Leeaberra Track** starts. This is a thirty-kilometre walk to **Elephant Pass** on the Tasman Highway approximately eight kilometres south of **St. Mary's**. From Bicheno to St. Mary's should take about three days. There are camp sites along the way.

Now the beautiful views of the sea begin and, thirty kilometres from Bicheno, we come to a fork in the road. If you are on the TassieLink bus to Launceston, you will turn left, if going to St. Helens you will turn right. The route on the left leads us along fifteen kilometres of steep, narrow, winding road through Elephant Pass and up to St. Mary's. It is an interesting climb. Watch for the shoes. Shoes? Yes, the story is that somebody driving up here one day found a shoe in the road, so he stopped and put it on top of one of the posts at the side of the road, thinking that the owner might come back to look for it. When he passed that way next, he found the shoe still there, but with another shoe on the next post to keep it company - and since then it appears that the shoes have continued breeding. Anybody who wants to abandon a pair of shoes seems to bring them here now. There are even those who have been observed exchanging their own pair for one in slightly better condition. It makes quite a display, with hundreds of shoes at the edge of the road.

At the head of the pass is **St. Mary's** which used to be the end of a branch railway line. Although there have not been any passenger trains for a long time, goods trains used to operate until quite recently. The station can be seen, and the small railway yard, but no trains.

We continue now to **Fingal** (see map on page 898), another twenty-five minutes on the bus, and immediately see the reason for the existence of this small town. As we approach, we meet a very substantial coal mining operation, one of only two coal mines left in Tasmania. This is the **Cornwall Coal Mine**. It is in two parts, actually, the other part having been passed to our right soon after leaving St. Mary's, at a very small town called **Cornwall**, which accounts for the name of this mine. Here you will find that the railway is still in operation, and is used to haul away much of this coal. Fingal was founded as an early Probation Station for convicts. Gold was later discovered here, at which time the population grew to 3,000, and the fine old buildings which you will see in the main street were constructed. Now about 500 people live here, mostly working for the coal mine.

Continuing, we get some pretty views over the **South Esk River**, just to the right of the road, while in the distance to the right is the **Ben Lomond National Park**. **Stacks Bluff** (1,527 metres) is the prominent peak, with **Legg's Tor** (1,573 metres) behind. During the winter this is a ski resort and the area is regarded as offering the best skiing in Tasmania. We reach **Avoca**, which was originally another convict outpost. Later it became a supply point for the nearby mining communities, since this region was found to offer tin, gold and lead. The road continues to run beside the attractive South Esk River until eventually we meet the main Hobart to Launceston highway.

Returning, though, to the east coast, if we remain beside the sea, neglecting the route through Elephant Pass to St. Mary's, we shall come to **Four Mile Creek**, offering boating, surfing, diving and long white beaches, and pass the turn-off to **Falmouth**. Then we join the road descending from St. Mary's, the route along which Tasmanian Redline operates its service from Launceston to St. Helens, and soon reach **Scamander**, a small but attractive seaside town. Here the Scamander River meets the sea, with its estuary forming a peaceful lagoon. Accommodation is available, including beds for backpackers.

We pass **Beaumaris**, where there is a good lookout at **Shelly Point**, and **Diana's Basin**, which has some unusual rock formations, and arrive in St. Helens, a beautiful little port on George's Bay. **St. Helens** has a population of 1,200, which makes it the largest town on the east coast of Tasmania. Captain Tobias Furneaux came here in 1773 and gave the name of St. Helens Point to the southern point of George's Bay. St. Helens became a small port used by sealers and whalers, but in 1874 tin was discovered nearby at Blue Tier and suddenly the importance of St. Helens was greatly increased. Thousands of miners travelled through the port, including more than a thousand Chinese, and it was the major location for the export of the mineral. The prosperity brought by this lasted for about thirty years, during which time the most imposing of the buildings in St. Helens were constructed. Then the tin ran out and St. Helens returned to being a sleepy fishing port. Fishing is still the major industry here. The town is sustained by a deep sea fishing fleet based here, and by local production of crayfish and oysters. In recent years the mild climate has encouraged the expansion of tourism and it is now one of the most popular east coast destinations.

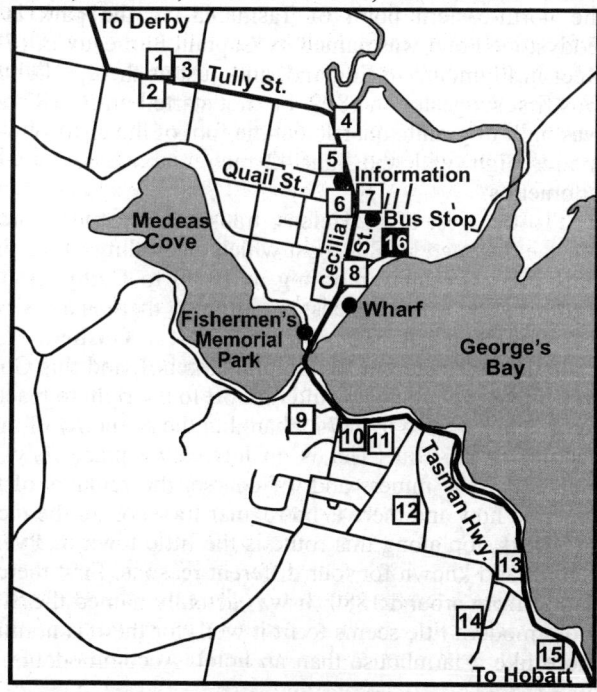

ST. HELENS
Black numerals indicate hotel accommodation
White numerals indicate backpackers hostels

The **History Room** in the town centre acts as the **Visitor Information Centre** and also has a small **museum** which is open from 9:00 until 16:00 on weekdays, from 9:00 until 12:00 on Saturdays and, in summer only, from 10:00 until 14:00 on Sundays. Admission costs $3.

The **wharf area** is interesting and offers delicacies such as fish and chips, giving the impression at least of using freshly caught supplies. There is a **walkway** around George's Bay, leading south from the town to where an old traction engine sitting in **Lions Park** marks the turn-off to St. Helens Point, a distance of three kilometres this far. St. Helens Point is interesting too, but it is eight kilometres along the road just mentioned. At the end of the road there is the main surfing beach at **Beerbarrel Beach** and a good walk among the constantly shifting **Peron Sand Dunes**. There are some more good walks to the north of the town too around **Binalong Bay** and in the **Humbug Point Nature Reserve**, but they are equally distant. One point in St. Helens which interested the author was a recent memorial near the bridge, in the Fishermen's Memorial Park, to those lost in maritime accidents, including one Kristopher Rickman lost at sea in 1996. Rickman is not such a common name.

Naturally St. Helens has plenty of accommodation, as befits its role as a new tourist destination. This accommodation includes a pleasant and helpful little youth hostel not far from the bus terminus.

North of St. Helens is the **Mt. William National Park**, occupying a position near the north-eastern point of Tasmania. In the park is the **Eddystone Lighthouse**. Eddystone Point was named by Captain Furneaux in 1773 after the famous Eddystone Reef in Plymouth in England, and, just as there, a lighthouse was constructed here. It was first suggested in 1879, but not started until 1887, and completed in May 1889. It was built of granite quarried at the foot of the cliffs on which it stands. The tower is 37 metres high, with the light 42 metres above sea level, visible for a distance of 38 kilometres.

To the west of St. Helens, transport becomes more difficult. However, there is a service operated by Suncoast which, according to the timetable at the time of writing, runs every weekday morning at 10:40 to Derby, from where there is a Tasmanian Redline service to Launceston, although there is a wait of two hours in Derby.

Travelling this route, we come first to **Goshen**. "I forgot Goshen", is the famous quotation attributed to Randolph Churchill, and this Goshen is almost forgotten too, a tiny village where one would turn off to the right to reach Blue Tier. **Blue Tier** is where tin was discovered in 1874, changing the economy of this whole area for a quarter of a century or so. Blue Tier is an interesting place to visit, with many walking tracks created by the miners and, of course, the remains of the mining activities, but it is deserted now and there is no regular transport to the location.

Next stop along this route is the little town of **Pyengana**, 26 kilometres from St. Helens and known for four different reasons. First there is the '**Pub in the Paddock**', dating from around 1880. It was actually named the St. Columba Falls Hotel, but the more modern title seems to fit it well, for there is nothing much around and it appears more like a farmhouse than an hotel. Accommodation is offered, including beds for backpackers, with whom it is quite popular. Not only can you sup a beer here, but you can also share one with the friendly, and usually drunken, resident pig (you pay; he drinks). The second attraction is **St. Columba Falls**, eight kilometres from the pub. These are generally regarded as the most spectacular falls in Tasmania, being nearly ninety metres in height, although not in a single cascade. The third attraction is **Healey's Cheese Factory**, one of the last places in Tasmania where traditional cloth-wrapped cheddar cheese is produced. The fourth reason for fame is that a Parks and Wildlife Service

FROM BICHENO AND ST. HELENS TO LAUNCESTON
Thicker lines show bus routes
Black numerals indicate hotel accommodation
White numerals indicate backpackers hostels

Ranger near here reported in 1995 that he had sighted a **Tasmanian Tiger**, an animal thought to be extinct.

Continuing along this road, we travel through **Weldborough Pass**, and then the town of **Weldborough**. Mt. Paris Dam is west of the town, the only pillar and slab dam in Tasmania, but dry now, and, in any case, six kilometres off the main road. **Moorina**, once an important mining area, has an old cemetery with a Chinese Altar as a monument to the thousand or so Chinese who worked in the tin mines nearby.

Derby is where we change buses. Tasmanian Redline runs a service from here to Launceston twice on weekdays and once on Sundays.

Derby is an old and interesting tin mining town. Tin was discovered here by the Krushka Brothers in 1876 and the Briseis Mine was established, named after the winner of the Melbourne Cup in that year. The town prospered from that time and grew to have a population of 3,000, but it was almost destroyed by a huge flood in 1929. The **Tin Mine Centre** shows a reconstruction of the shanty town buildings of those times, together with a museum concerned with the history of tin in this region. It is open daily from 9:00 (10:00 in winter) until 17:00 (16:00 in winter), with admission costing $5.

There is a youth hostel in **Winnaleah**, just to the east of Derby. The Suncoast service from St. Helens stops there and the morning Tasmanian Redline service from Launceston is extended to Winnaleah.

An hour west of Derby is **Scottsdale**, the main centre for this region. There are some handsome Victorian buildings, especially in King and Alfred Streets, and **Ellesmere Cemetery** contains the graves of some of the pioneers of this town. Accommodation available includes a backpackers hostel close to the town centre.

North of Scottsdale is the town of **Bridport** (population 1,700) which is on the north coast of Tasmania and offers quiet beaches, good coastal walks, bird life and a ferry to **Flinders Island**. On weekdays there are buses from Scottsdale to Bridport operated by Stan's Coach to connect with Tasmanian Redline arrivals from Launceston. There is a youth hostel in Bridport right beside the sea.

From Scottsdale, another 75 minutes of hilly terrain and winding road will bring us into Launceston.

ACCOMMODATION
(i) Hotel Accommodation in St. Helens

Name	Stars	No. on Map	Telephone No.	Address	Lowest Price (Double/Twin)
Warrawee Guest House	4½	15	03-6376-1987	Tasman Highway	$165
Wybalenna Guest House	4	13	03-6376-1611	56 Tasman Highway	$165
Cecilia House	4	4	03-6376-1723	78 Cecilia Street	$105
Queechy Cottages	3½	9	03-6376-1321	2 Tasman Highway	$100
Homelea Accommodation		10	03-6376-1601	16 Tasman Highway	$95
Old Headmaster's House		3	03-6376-1125	74 Cecilia Street	$95
Halcyon Grove Units		14	03-6376-1424	16 Halcyon Grove	$70
Anchor Wheel Motel	3½	2	03-6376-1358	59 Tully Street	$65
Artnor Lodge	3½	5	03-6376-1234	71 Cecilia Street	$65
Bayside Inn	4	8	03-6376-1466	2 Cecilia Street	$65
Daisy House Accom.	3	7	03-6376-1815	36 Quail Street	$55
Corraleau Holiday Units	2½	11	03-6376-1363	22 Tasman Highway	$50
St. Helens Caravan Park	4	12	03-6376-1290	2 Penelope Street	$50
Kellraine Units	3½	1	03-6376-1169	72 Tully Street	$45
St. Helens Hotel / Motel		6	03-6376-1133	49 Cecilia Street	$45

900 TASMANIA

(ii) Backpackers Hostel in St. Helens

Name	Group	No. on Map	Telephone No.	Address	Lowest Price (Dormitory)
St. Helens Y.H.A.	YHA	16	03-6376-1661	5 Cameron Street	$18

(iii) Hotel Accommodation in St. Mary's

Name	Stars	No. on Map	Telephone No.	Address	Lowest Price (Double/Twin)
Addlestone House B&B		17	03-6372-2783	19 Gray Road	$85
Seaview Farm		17	03-6372-2341	686 Germantown Road	$50
St. Mary's Hotel		17	03-6372-2181	Main Street	$45

(iv) Backpackers Hostels in St. Mary's

Name	Group	No. on Map	Telephone No.	Address	Lowest Price (Dormitory)
St. Mary's Hotel		18	03-6372-2181	Main Street	$28
Seaview Farm		18	03-6372-2341	686 Germantown Road	$19

(v) Hotel Accommodation in Fingal

Name	Stars	No. on Map	Telephone No.	Address	Lowest Price (Double/Twin)
Glen Esk B&B		19	03-6374-2195	3 Talbot Street	$100
Fingal Hotel		19	03-6374-2121	Talbot Street	$35

(vi) Backpackers Hostels in or near Fingal

Name	Group	No. on Map	Telephone No.	Address	Lowest Price (Dormitory)
Fingal Hotel		20	03-6374-2121	Talbot Street	$22
Fawlty Towers		20	03-6374-2119	Rostrevor, Fingal	$15

(vii) Hotel Accommodation in Scamander

Name	Stars	No. on Map	Telephone No.	Address	Lowest Price (Double/Twin)
Blue Seas Holiday Villas	4	21	03-6372-5211	Wattle Drive	$110
Scamander Beach Resort		21	03-6372-5255	Tasman Highway	$85
Pelican Sands Motel	3	21	03-6372-5231	157 Scamander Avenue	$80
Kookaburra Caravan Park		21	03-6372-5121	70 Scamander Avenue	$55
Carmen's Inn		21	03-6372-5160	4 Pringle Street	$50

(viii) Backpackers Hostel in Scamander

Name	Group	No. on Map	Telephone No.	Address	Lowest Price (Dormitory)
Pelican Sands Backpackers	VIP	22	03-6372-5231	157 Scamander Drive	$22

(ix) Hotel Accommodation in Pyengana

Name	Stars	No. on Map	Telephone No.	Address	Lowest Price (Double/Twin)
Pub in the Paddock		23	03-6373-6121	St. Columba Falls Road	$50

(x) Backpackers Hostel in Pyengana

Name	Group	No. on Map	Telephone No.	Address	Lowest Price (Dormitory)
Pub in the Paddock		24	03-6373-6121	St. Columba Falls Road	$35

ST. HELENS, DERBY, SCOTTSDALE, BRIDPORT

(xi) Accommodation in Weldborough

Name	Stars	No. on Map	Telephone No.	Address	Lowest Price (Double/Twin)
Weldborough Hotel		25	03-6354-2223	Tasman Highway	$55

(xii) Hotel Accommodation in Winnaleah

Name	Stars	No. on Map	Telephone No.	Address	Lowest Price (Double/Twin)
Winnaleah Hotel		26	03-6354-2331	Main Street	$45

(xiii) Backpackers Hostel in Winnaleah

Name	Group	No. on Map	Telephone No.	Address	Lowest Price (Dormitory)
Merlinkei Farm	YHA	27	03-6354-2152	524 Racecourse Road	$17

(xiv) Hotel Accommodation in Derby

Name	Stars	No. on Map	Telephone No.	Address	Lowest Price (Double/Twin)
Cobbler's Cottage		28	03-6354-2145	Main Street	$80
Dorset Hotel		28	03-6354-2360	Main Street	$60

(xv) Backpackers Hostel near Derby

Name	Group	No. on Map	Telephone No.	Address	Lowest Price (Dormitory)
Legerwood Hostel		29	03-6353-2292	272 Main Road, Legerwood	$15

(xvi) Hotel Accommodation in Scottsdale

Name	Stars	No. on Map	Telephone No.	Address	Lowest Price (Double/Twin)
Belle Cottage		30	03-6352-3277	80 King Street	$145
Beulah	4	30	03-6352-3723	9 King Street	$125
Anabel's	3½	30	03-6352-3277	46 King Street	$110
Kendall's Hotel / Motel	2½	30	03-6352-2510	18 George Street	$60
Bellows		30	03-6352-2263	65 King Street	$40
Lord's Hotel	1½	30	03-6352-2319	2 King Street	$35

(xvii) Backpackers Hostel in Scottsdale

Name	Group	No. on Map	Telephone No.	Address	Lowest Price (Dormitory)
Bellows		31	03-6352-2263	65 King Street	$18

(xviii) Hotel Accommodation in Bridport

Name	Stars	No. on Map	Telephone No.	Address	Lowest Price (Double/Twin)
Bridport Resort	4	32	03-6356-1789	35 Main Street	$150
Platypus Park	4	32	03-6356-1873	Ada Street	$95
Bridport Bay Inn	3½	32	03-6356-1238	105 Main Street	$85
Indra Holiday Units	3½	32	03-6356-1196	53 Westwood Street	$75
Bridairre Bed & Breakfast	4	32	03-6356-1438	27 Frances Street	$70
Bridport Hotel		32	03-6356-1114	79 Main Street	$55

(xix) Backpackers Hostel in Bridport

Name	Group	No. on Map	Telephone No.	Address	Lowest Price (Dormitory)
Bridport Seaside Lodge	YHA	33	03-6356-1585	47 Main Street, Bridport	$21

MOVING ON

(i) Bus Services from St. Helens

Destination	Operator	Via	Distance (km)	Fare	Journey Time	Frequency
Hobart	TassieLink		260	$39.20	4¼ hrs	2/week
		Swansea	122	$15.20	1¾ hrs	2/week
		Bicheno	82	$10.50	1 hr	2/week
Hobart*	Redline		256	$42.20	4¼ - 5¼ hrs	6/week
Launceston*	TassieLink		261	$36.20	3¾ hrs	2/week
		St. Mary's*	129	$17	2 hrs	2/week
Launceston	Redline		167	$26.10	2½ - 2¾ hrs	6/week
		St. Mary's	35	$5.70	40 mins	6/week
Derby	Suncoast		60	$8	1½ hrs	5/week

* Connecting service. Change of bus involved.

(ii) Bus Services from Derby

Destination	Operator	Via	Distance (km)	Fare	Journey Time	Frequency
Launceston	Redline		101	$17.70	2¼ - 2½ hrs	11/week
		Scottsdale	33	$7.80	1 hr	11/week
St. Helens	Suncoast		60	$8	1½ hrs	5/week

(iii) Bus Services from Scottsdale

Destination	Operator	Via	Distance (km)	Fare	Journey Time	Frequency
Launceston	Redline		68	$13.10	1¼ - 1½ hrs	16/week
Derby	Redline		33	$7.80	45 - 70 mins	11/week
Bridport	Stan's Coach		25	$4	30 mins	2/day

(iv) Bus Service from Bridport

Destination	Operator	Via	Distance (km)	Fare	Journey Time	Frequency
Scottsdale	Stan's Coach		25	$4	30 mins	2/day

LAUNCESTON

Population 65,000

2 hrs 30 mins by bus from Hobart

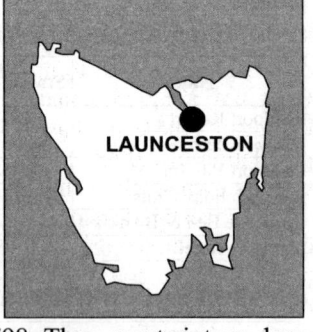

Launceston is the second city of Tasmania, located not on the northern coast of the island, as is sometimes erroneously supposed, but where the North Esk and South Esk Rivers converge and the Tamar Estuary begins. This is the longest navigable tidal estuary in Australia, a total distance of 76 kilometres.

The Tamar Estuary was discovered by Bass and Flinders during their circumnavigation of Tasmania in 1798. They spent sixteen days exploring it, without ever getting as far as Launceston, and named the area at the mouth Port Dalrymple, Alexander Dalrymple being the hydrographer of the British Admiralty

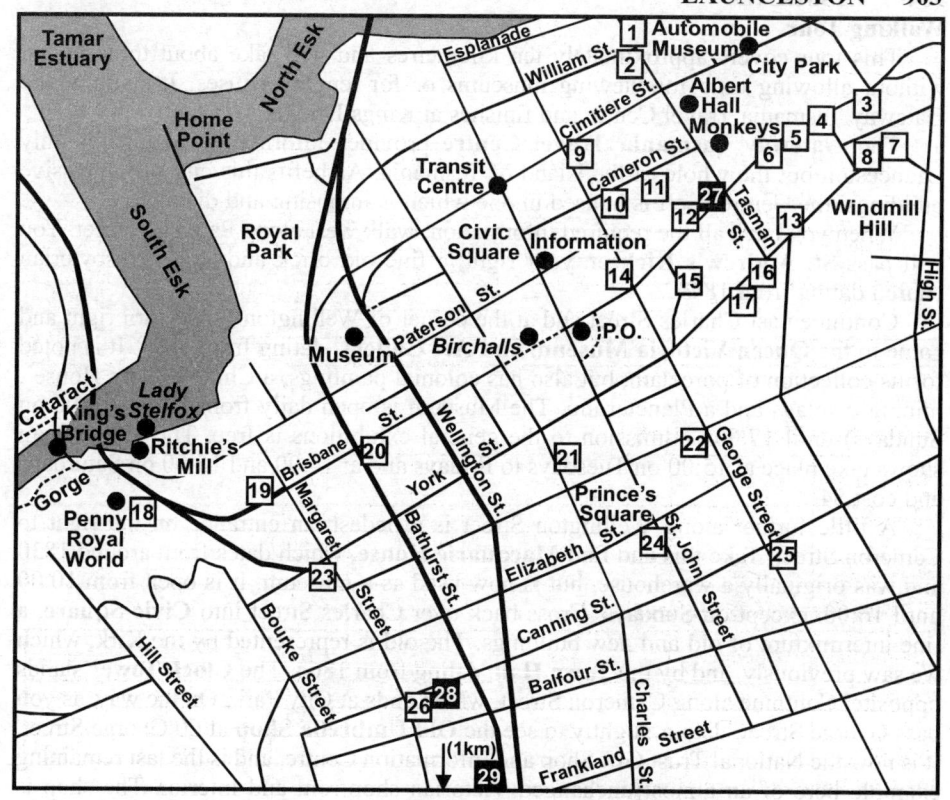

LAUNCESTON
Black numerals in white boxes indicate hotel accommodation
White numerals in black boxes indicate backpackers hostels

at the time. By 1804, Governor King had become worried that the French might try to claim this area, so he sent an expeditionary force under Col. Paterson to show the flag here. A camp was first set up at George Town on the eastern side of the mouth of the Tamar. A settlement was then established at Yorktown on the western side of the river, but a little later the site of Launceston was discovered and Paterson was so enamoured of it that he decided to move here, which he did in 1806. He called it Patersonia, but Governor King said that he preferred Launceston, the name of the small town in Cornwall where he had been born, so Launceston it became. By 1827 it had a population of 2,000 and was already shipping wool and wheat. By 1881 it was a city with its own stock exchange.

Launceston does not really feel like a city. It is more like an overgrown nineteenth century town, since it has so many beautiful buildings from that era which it seems never to have felt the pressure to pull down and replace with modern utilitarian monstrosities. This gives it charm on such a scale as one cannot really find in any other place in Australia, charm tempered only by the amount and type of traffic around the city. Let us have a walking tour of this attractive location.

TASMANIA
Walking Tour

This tour covers approximately ten kilometres and will take about three hours, without allowing time for viewing museums or for lengthy pauses. It starts at the Gateway Tasmania Travel Centre and finishes at Kings Bridge.

The **Gateway Tasmania Travel Centre** provides information about not only Launceston but the whole of the island of Tasmania. As befits this city of impressive buildings, the Centre itself is housed in one which is imposing and distinctive.

When you have all the required information, walk west along Paterson Street. You will pass **St. Andrew's Kirk** on your right, a fine old brick and stone Presbyterian church dating from 1849.

Continue past Charles Street and at the corner of Wellington Street turn right and come to the **Queen Victoria Museum and Art Gallery**, dating from 1891. It is noted for its collection of porcelain, but also has colonial paintings, a Chinese 'Joss House', mining displays and a Planetarium. The Museum is open daily from 10:00 (14:00 on Sundays) until 17:00. Admission to the general exhibitions is free. The Planetarium shows take place at 15:00 on Tuesdays to Fridays and at 14:00 and 15:00 on Saturdays and cost $4.

A little further along Wellington Street is a pedestrian entrance on the right to Cameron Street. Take this and find **Macquarie House**, which dates from around 1830 and was originally a warehouse, but is now used as a museum. It is open from 10:00 until 16:00, except on Sundays. Cross back over Charles Street into **Civic Square**, a fine intermixture of old and new buildings. The old is represented by the Kirk, which we saw previously, and by the **Town Hall**, dating from 1864. The **Clock Tower** stands opposite. Continue along Cameron Street, which ends at City Park. On the way, as you pass George Street, detour slightly to see the **Old Umbrella Shop** at 60 George Street. It is now the National Trust Gift Shop and Information Centre, and is the last remaining example here of an almost unchanged Victorian shopfront and interior. The shop is open from 9:00 until 17:00 on weekdays and from 9:00 until 12:00 on Saturdays.

Return to Cameron Street and soon you will see on your right the **Batman Fawkner Inn**. It was originally known as the Cornwall Hotel and was where John Batman and his friends met and decided to cross Bass Strait and start a new settlement, which was to become Melbourne. Now continue to City Park. **Albert Hall** is to your left, a majestic Victorian building constructed in 1891 which includes an unusual water-powered organ. Enter the Park and walk down to the **National Automobile Museum** on your left in Cimitiere Street. It contains a display of veteran sports cars and is open daily from 9:00 (10:00 in winter) until 17:00 (16:00 in winter). Admission costs $10. **City Park** dates from the 1820s and within its limits is the **Jubilee Fountain** constructed in 1897. The Park is lined with European deciduous trees, and the **John Hart Conservatory** contains colourful hothouse plants. There is a kangaroo enclosure and do not forget the monkeys. The **Macaque monkeys** live on an island at the western edge of the park.

Exit by the gate on the corner of Brisbane and Tamar Streets and walk west along **Brisbane Street**. This is the central street of the city. It has interesting little **shopping arcades** off to the sides which can be explored. **Brisbane Arcade** was the site of the original army blockhouse in 1806. The central area of Brisbane Street is for pedestrians only and has a pleasant ambience. Continue along Brisbane Street until you reach Wellington Street and then turn right, and left into Paterson Street once more. The road crosses over Bathurst Street on a high bridge and on your right now is **Royal Park**, with a view of the **Tamar Estuary**.

Keep walking along Paterson Street and, as you approach the river, on your right is **Ritchie's Mill**. In the 1840s a water-powered flour mill was established here. It is now the Ritchie's Mill Arts Centre and the original miller's cottage is the restaurant. Nearby is the departure point for the *Lady Stelfox* **paddle steamer**, while on your left is **Penny Royal World**. This is a tourist attraction built around a 16.5 metre tall 1840 windmill. You can climb the mill to obtain a good view of the city and river. There is also a watermill moved here from Cressy, 54 kilometres distant, and a replica of the 1825 Penny Royal Cornmill machinery, which is powered by the watermill. One of the city's old **1911 trams** has been restored and runs on a very short stretch of line taking passengers to the windmill. There are barges to take visitors underground to see gunpowder being manufactured. There is a lake with the reconstructed sloop *Sandpiper*, which fires its cannon for the benefit of visitors, and there are several other attractions with a nineteenth-century theme. This site was originally a quarry and much of the bluestone of which the old buildings of Launceston are constructed came from here. *Penny Royal World* is open daily from 9:00 until 16:30 and admission costs $20.

King's Bridge is one the city's features, a very handsome construction built across the South Esk River. The first span was prefabricated in England, assembled locally and then floated into place in 1867. The second, identical, span was manufactured locally at Salisbury Foundry and floated into place alongside the first in 1904. Cross the bridge and immediately on your left you will see **Cataract Walk**, a path leading along beside the Cataract Gorge.

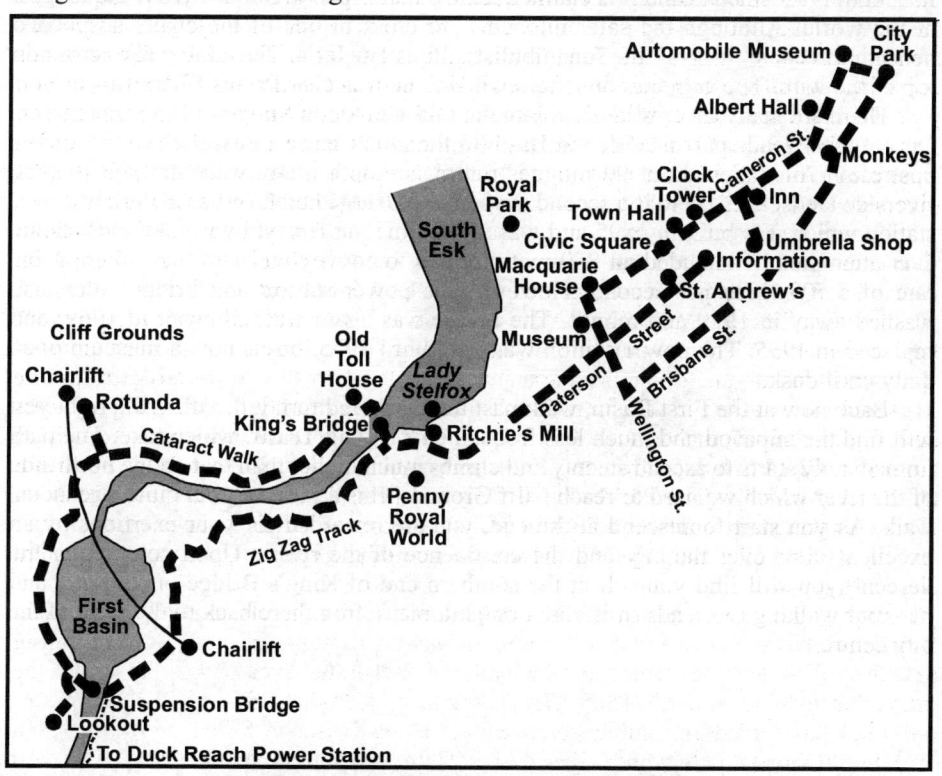

LAUNCESTON WALKING TOUR

★ **Cataract Gorge** too is a great feature of Launceston and you should certainly not omit this from your itinerary while here. The walk offers fine views along the gorge. It is a bitumen path, easy to walk, and, although you will meet others along the way, most people drive to the Cliff Grounds and so miss this enjoyable stroll. At the start of the walk, by the end of the bridge, you will see the **Old Toll House**. It is about two kilometres to the Cliff Grounds along this path built in the 1890s. It gives a good view of the dolerite columns of the cliff on the other side and in some places the remains of a **flume** can be seen suspended from the far cliff. This flume used to convey water to Ritchie's Mill and provide a supply for the early township. When you reach the First Basin, turn right and walk up to the Cliff Grounds and the 1896 **Band Rotunda**, which is now a small museum, open daily from 9:00 until 16:00. Then follow the signs to the **Alexandra Suspension Bridge**, deviating on the way to see the view from the **Alexandra Lookout**. A rough steep track leads up to the Lookout, the surmounting of which is rewarded by a fine view of the First Basin, the Cataract Gorge and the Alexandra Suspension Bridge. Descend and cross the swaying bridge. The Alexandra Suspension Bridge was built in 1904, but it was washed away by the floods of 1929, and restored later. It was named after Queen Alexandra, the consort of King Edward VII. By now you will certainly have observed the **Chairlift** which crosses the valley. If you want a ride, it costs $7 single or return, so you might as well travel in both directions. The Chairlift was constructed in 1973. Its length is 457 metres and it is claimed that its main span of 308 metres is the longest in the world. Although the safer method is to cross in one of the chairs suspended beneath the cable, in 1987 the funambulist Alfons Bugler preferred to walk across on top of the wire. The author is uncertain whether he was charged his $7 for this or not.

There are many other walks available in this area too, if you have time and energy. One of these leads past the Second Basin to the **Duck Reach Power Station**, further upstream. This takes about 90 minutes return, and is a pretty walk through pristine riverside landscape. There is a second **suspension bridge** here to cross to the old power station which was built in 1895 and was at the time the largest hydro-electric scheme ever attempted. It included an 850-metre tunnel to convey water to the station at the rate of 5,500 litres per second. However, the power station and bridge were also washed away in 1929 and rebuilt. The bridge was again washed away in 1969, and replaced in 1995. The power station was used until 1955, but is now a museum open daily until dusk.

Back now at the First Basin, walk past the kiosk and turn left. Off to the right you will find the unpaved and much less frequented **Zig Zag Track**, which take. The path immediately starts to ascend steeply and climbs much higher than that on the north side of the river which we used to reach Cliff Grounds. It is a pleasant, but quite strenuous, walk. As you start to descend at the end, you are rewarded for your exertions by an excellent view over the city and the confluence of the rivers. Upon completing the descent, you will find yourself at the southern end of King's Bridge once more, and here our walking tour ends. It is about one kilometre from here back to the edge of the city centre.

ANECDOTE

It is a great shame that passenger rail services operate no longer in Tasmania. The author did travel from Burnie to Devonport by train before services ended and, nostalgic for those days, I was wandering in the Hobart goods yards when I met another wanderer who suggested that if I really wanted to travel by train I should go to the railway office and ask. With little to lose, I took the advice.

"I should like to travel on one of your trains," I replied when asked my business. "Travel on a train?" said the official, apparently in a state of shock. "You can't do that. We haven't got any passenger trains, and nobody can travel on a goods train without the permission of the General Manager." Then, as an afterthought, the shock evidently wearing off, he added, "He's in Launceston. Would you like me to ring him up and ask?" "Yes, please."

The telephone call was made and the content reported. "Right," said the official. "The General Manager says you can go on the train to Launceston tonight. Be here at 6:00 and don't be late." It was my turn to be shocked by the ease with which this had been achieved. "Thank you very much," I said. "Thank him very much."

I was back in the yards in good time and found an engine and half a train waiting. "Oh, yes," said the same official. "You're going to Launceston, aren't you? You'll need a chair." He went inside and reappeared with a metal office chair which he passed up to the driver of the train. "Here's your passenger," he said, "And here's his seat. Bring it back, will you, because we need it in the office tomorrow." Then to me he explained. "There are only two seats in the engine, you see, so we'll put this in the middle for you. Remind them to bring it back." It was evidently a matter of some importance.

We spent the first hour shunting up and down the yards making up the rest of the train. Then, as dusk was falling, we set off on a delightful journey. My only regret was that it was dark and I could not see much of the scenery. However, I had the main features pointed out to me by the crew of two, pleased by the novelty of having an eccentric passenger with them. One of the more remarkable sights was the hundreds of birds roosting in the railway bridge at the appropriately named Bridgewater, all of which took to the wing at the approach of the daily train.

We arrived just after midnight, not at Launceston as I had expected, but at Western Junction, some twelve kilometres south of the city. Now here was a problem. Where was I going to sleep until it was time for my flight to Victoria the next morning?

However, fortune was with me again, for I discovered that Western Junction station was only about two kilometres from the airport. I walked up, only to find the airport deserted and locked for the night. I looked enviously at the passenger lounge just the other side of a huge window and locked door, but then scouted around and eventually discovered that the door to the Meteorological Office was open. I went in and upstairs and found a warm carpeted waiting room. It was now 1:00. I spread out my sleeping bag and thanked the Gods.

At 5:30, people started arriving, apparently for work, stepping over me and muttering, "I beg your pardon." The night was evidently over, but I had been lucky once more and had no right to complain about early rising. I got up and went to look for my flight, for the story of which see page 912.

Of course, as usual there are plenty of sights which we have missed. Slightly to the south of the city centre is **Prince's Square**, with a fountain at its centre and handsome buildings surrounding the Square. The fountain was purchased at the Paris Exhibition in 1858 and the story tells that the residents of Launceston objected to a half-naked nymph in its design, and that she was replaced, therefore, by a pineapple. It is also told that the square was once the scene of a hot-air balloon launching and that two bushrangers were hanged here. Now, though, it is just a pleasant place to sit down for a few minutes, as the reader will certainly need to do if he has completed the walking tour above.

To the north of the city, on the northern bank of the North Esk River, is **Inveresk**, a new development utilising the former railway yards. It includes the **Tasmanian Conservation Workshops, York Park Sports and Entertainment Centre**, an **Exhibition Centre** and a new **Art Gallery**. There is a boardwalk leading from here to the **Heritage Forest**.

The **Waverley Woollen Mills** were established in 1874 and claim to be the oldest woollen mills in Australia. There is a hydro-electric generating plant which dates from 1889 and is believed to be the oldest in the southern hemisphere. Conducted tours are available on weekdays between 9:00 and 16:00 and there is a showroom selling the company's products.

Cruises are available on the Tamar Estuary. The *M.V. Tamar Odyssey* sails from **Home Point** every day in summer and at weekends in winter at 10:00 (Sundays 11:00) for a four-hour voyage up the Tamar to the beautiful modern **Batman Bridge**. The cruise costs $60, including lunch. A shorter afternoon cruise also operates on some days for $30.

Although we have made our way to Launceston from Hobart via the east coast, the direct route through the centre of the island, as operated by both Tasmanian Redline and TassieLink services, takes only two and a half hours on the fastest buses. Since it was the first overland route pioneered in Tasmania, there are several interesting old towns on the way. Of these, the most interesting is probably **Ross**, settled in 1812 and situated on the banks of the Macquarie River eighty kilometres south of Launceston. As in Richmond, the principal attraction is, rather surprisingly, the bridge. A beautiful **old stone bridge** crosses the **Macquarie River**. It was constructed in 1836 by convicts and is claimed to be the third oldest stone bridge in Australia. Moreover, not only is the bridge itself a construction of beauty, but when you examine it more carefully, you see the sculptures which adorn it. These are almost certainly the work of the convicted highwayman, Daniel Herbert, and there are 186 such carvings in total. There are animals, birds, insects and plants, heads of Celtic Gods and Goddesses, heads of his friends, and of his enemies. There is even the head of the Governor, George Arthur. The bridge is made of sandstone quarried locally.

Most of the houses in this small town were also built by convicts, many of them of the same sandstone. There is also the **Female Factory** which was part of the old convict station here, and there is the **old cemetery**, which is interesting, as usual. At the four points of the cross-roads in the centre of the town are what is known as *The Four Corners* - Temptation (the Man o'Ross Hotel), Recreation (the Town Hall), Salvation (the Catholic Church) and Damnation (the Former Gaol). Also here is the **Tasmanian Wool Centre**, a museum devoted to the wool industry in Tasmania. On more than one occasion Ross held the world record price for a bale of merino wool, so this is an appropriate location for such a museum. Admission is by donation. The

Centre also acts as the **Visitor Information Centre**. Tasmanian Redline operates four services a day between Launceston and Hobart. Two services travel through Ross on request and the other two stop at the turn-off on the Midland Highway, which is within walking distance, across the Ross Bridge.

Another historic town is **Evandale**, only nineteen kilometres south of Launceston. It has the appearance of a coaching station little changed since the nineteenth century, with some buildings dating from the 1820s. There is a large market on Sundays, but there is no public transport to here at the weekend. It is also the home of the **National Penny Farthing Championships**

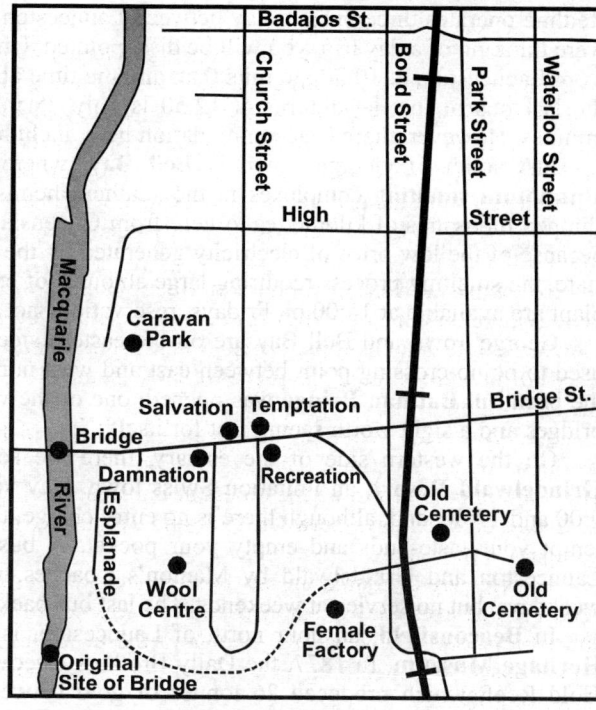

held each year in February. Tasmanian Redline operates a bus from Launceston to Evandale every weekday morning at 7:30, with return from Evandale at 18:05. On Thursdays only there is an additional service from Launceston at 14:00 and an additional service from Evandale to Launceston at 10:10.

Perth also has some interest. It was a typical staging point. These used to exist approximately every fifteen kilometres between Launceston and Hobart for the purpose of changing horses, at a time when the stagecoach service between the two cities, commenced in 1830, used to take fifteen hours. The staging points always required a large inn with stables and these can still be seen in many of the towns along the main highway. The bus service to Perth is again operated by Tasmanian Redline, but this service is a better one, operating about six times each weekday and less frequently at weekends.

Further down the Tasman Highway is **Symmons Plains**, which has an international **motor racing circuit**. Beyond that is the area of **Epping Forest**, where the bushranger Martin Cash operated, one of the few in his profession to be pardoned and live to see old age.

There are other interesting places around Launceston too, although most visitors find sufficient in the city itself to keep them busy. There is, of course, **George Town**, where the first settlement in the north of Tasmania was made in 1804. This town has the second longest history in Tasmania and offers a **Maritime Museum**, an historic working **pilot station**, a **lighthouse**, **beaches**, **boats** and **penguins**. It is also the port at which the *Devil Cat* **fast catamaran** service from Melbourne docks. Tasmanian

TASMANIA

Redline operates three buses a day between Launceston and George Town, but if you were thinking of a day trip, you will be disappointed. Only the first bus in the morning from Launceston, at 10:30, permits that, and the time allowed in George Town before the last bus of the day returns at 12:30 is only 75 minutes, the journey taking 45 minutes. However, there is accommodation here, including a youth hostel.

Just south of George Town is **Bell Bay**, where there is one of the largest **aluminium smelting** complexes in the southern hemisphere. Amazingly, bauxite is shipped thousands of kilometres to here from Queensland and the Northern Territory because of the low price of electricity generated by the hydro-electric schemes in the state, the smelting process requiring large amounts of energy. **Free inspections** of the plant are available at 14:00 on Fridays, reservations not required.

George Town and Bell Bay are on the eastern side of the Tamar Estuary. There used to be no crossing point between east and west north of Launceston, but in 1968 the beautiful **Batman Bridge** was opened, one of the world's first cable-stayed truss bridges and a sight worth seeing just for itself.

On the western side of the estuary, there are several beaches. There is also **Grindelwald Resort**, an imitation Swiss town. Day visitors are welcomed between 9:00 and 17:00, and, although there is no entry charge, there are lots of Swiss shops to tempt your taste-buds and empty your pocket. A bus service is operated between Launceston and Grindelwald by Manion's Coaches, with up to six departures on weekdays, but no service at weekends. The last bus back from Grindelwald is at 17:00.

In **Beaconsfield**, an hour north of Launceston, is the **Grubb Shaft Gold and Heritage Museum**. In 1877, the Dally Brothers discovered here the famous Tasman Gold Reef, which produced 26 tonnes of gold between 1877 and 1914. This was Tasmania's largest gold mine and it made Beaconsfield into one of the state's greatest boom towns, as reflected in some of the architecture. The displays here at Grubb Shaft include an iron smelter, an operating water wheel, a gold battery, pumps for extracting water from the mine, and a collection of steam engines. The Museum is open daily from 10:00 until 16:00, with admission costing $10.

A little further north is **Beauty Point**, where there is a seahorse farm named *Seahorse World*. The farm is open daily from 9:30 until 16:30 and a tour costs $18. The last tour starts at 15:30. *Seahorse World* incorporates the Australian Maritime College, the only college of its type in the southern hemisphere. During the summer only, the Maritime College offers backpacker accommodation at $28 for a single room.

Buses are operated from Launceston to Beaconsfield and Beauty Point by Tamar Valley Coaches. However, only on Tuesdays and Fridays can a day return trip be made, departing from Launceston at 8:30 or 13:30 and leaving Beauty Point for the return at 14:30 or 18:30, or leaving Beaconsfield for the return at 14:40, 17:00 or 18:40. If you wish to see both attractions in a day, take the 8:30 bus to Beaconsfield, then the bus at approximately 14:10 from Beaconsfield to Beauty Point and return on the 18:30 from Beauty Point to Launceston.

Launceston has a city bus service operated by Metro Buses. Livery and fares are the same as in Hobart, with the minimum fare $1.50 and the maximum $3.50, but the best value is the *Off-Peak Multi-Trip Ticket* valid on weekdays between 9:00 and 16:30 and again after 18:00, and valid all day at weekends. This ticket costs $4. In fact, though, there are not many places in Launceston which require the use of buses. Most locations are within walking distance.

There is a wide range of accommodation, since this is the first major destination for many of those arriving in Tasmania by sea, and since it is such an attractive city. For backpackers, there are three choices. At present, the most popular is Metro Backpackers, which is conveniently located right in the city near City Park, in premises which, the author is informed, used to be a funeral parlour. However, Launceston Backpackers is also well patronised, as indeed it should be, being pleasantly run, only a short walk from the city centre and next to another park. The least popular is Launceston City Youth Hostel. It is a little far out of the city centre, entailing a walk of some twenty minutes or more and the building in which it is situated is somewhat drab, having been the dining room and offices of the woollen mill. However, the main reason for its lack of popularity is probably the eccentric manager, so the author should mention that he quite likes eccentric people and enjoyed staying here. The manager is, in fact, a fount of information on Tasmania, particularly on bushwalking in the state, as well as on world affairs, so do not eliminate this hostel from your list. It is quiet, relatively cheap and not over-populated. Ask the manager about his collection of foreign currencies.

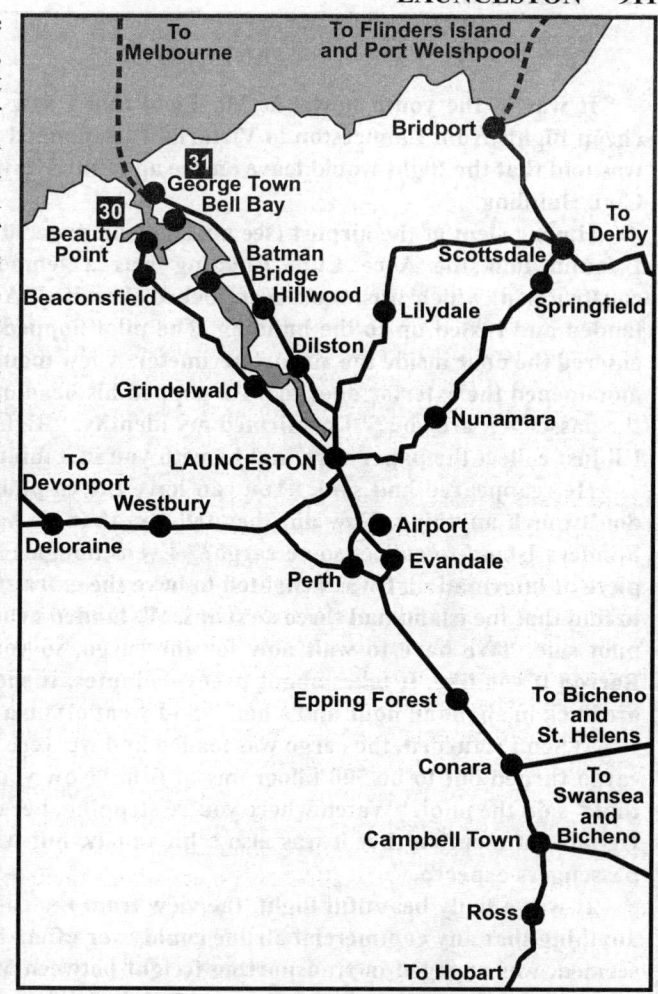

AROUND LAUNCESTON
Showing bus routes (thicker lines) and principal stops
Numerals indicate backpackers hostels

BOOKSHOPS

Birchalls 118 - 120 Brisbane Street

ANECDOTE

It was in the youth hostel at Mt. Field that I saw the advertisement for cheap flights from Launceston to Victoria. I telephoned the number given and was told that the flight would leave on the appointed day at 7:30 from the Aero Club Building.

Having slept at the airport (see anecdote on page 907), I was in good time. I found that the Aero Club Building was a temporary-looking wooden construction, which was, moreover, locked. I waited. At 7:35, a light aircraft landed and taxied up to the building. The pilot hopped out, walked over and entered the door inside the airport perimeter. A few moments later he unlocked and opened the exterior door too. He popped his head out and enquired, "You the passenger, are you?" I confirmed my identity. "Right," he said. "Climb in. I'll just collect the paperwork and be with you in a minute."

He reappeared and said, "You can have the co-pilot's seat as long as you don't touch anything. Now did they tell you that we have to make a stop on Flinders Island to collect some cargo?" Even though I had not been told this piece of information, I was delighted to have the extra stop. I was also amazed to find that the island had three airstrips. We landed near Lady Barron and the pilot said, "We have to wait now for the cargo, so you can walk into Lady Barron if you like. It takes about twenty minutes. It should be all right if you are back in about an hour and a half." So I went off on a voyage of exploration.

When I returned, the cargo was loaded and we were ready to continue. The cargo turned out to be 500 kilograms of fish. "Now you'll have to climb over that," said the pilot. "Watch where you're stepping, because it's a bit slippery." He did not mention that it was also a bit smelly, but what can economy-class passengers expect?

It was a truly beautiful flight, the view from the co-pilot's seat surpassing anything that any commercial airline could ever offer. This small operation, it seemed, was engaged in transporting freight between Victoria and Tasmania. "But there is usually more demand for freight to Tasmania than from there," explained the pilot, "So we try to pick up the odd passenger for the return trip to help to make ends meet."

When Victoria came into view, we landed not in Melbourne, but at the nearest point to Tasmania, which was a dirt airstrip near Welshpool. As we taxied in, the door of the little hut there opened and the owner of the company strode out of what proved to be his tiny office, waited for the propellers to cease rotating, then came to the door of the aircraft and said, "That'll be $52, please."

I have been on buses where one pays as one gets off, but that was my first experience of a pay-as-you-exit air service.

LAUNCESTON

ACCOMMODATION
(i) Hotel Accommodation in Launceston

Name	Stars	No. on Map	Telephone No.	Address	Lowest Price (Double/Twin)
Launceston International	4½	11	03-6334-3434	29 Cameron Street	$230
York Mansions	4	16	03-6334-2933	9 York Street	$220
Waratah on York	4½	8	03-6331-2081	12 York Street	$175
Colonial Motor Inn	4	22	1-800-060-955	31 Elizabeth Street	$160
Prince Albert Inn	4	2	03-6331-7633	22 Tamar Street	$155
Penny Royal Motel	3½	18	1-800-802-090	147 Paterson Street	$140
Old Bakery Inn	3½	23	1-800-641-264	York & Margaret Streets	$125
Commodore Regent Inn	4	6	1-800-355-103	13 Brisbane Street	$120
Balmoral Motor Inn	3½	17	1-800-355-105	19 York Street	$120
Adina Place Motel	4	13	1-800-030-181	50 York Street	$120
Coach House Motor Inn	3½	7	1-800-062-377	10 York Street	$115
Hillview House	3½	25	03-6331-7388	193 George Street	$115
Airlie of Launceston	4	24	03-6334-2162	138 St. John Street	$100
The Maldon		12	03-6331-3211	32 Brisbane Street	$100
Rose Lodge		19	03-6334-0120	270 Brisbane Street	$95
Flag Great Northern	4	15	1-800-355-104	3 Earl Street	$90
Parklane Motel	3½	5	1-800-803-503	9 Brisbane Street	$85
Irish Murphy's		20	03-6331-4440	211 Brisbane Street	$85
Sandor's on the Park		3	1-800-030-140	3 Brisbane Street	$85
North Lodge		4	1-800-006-042	7 Brisbane Street	$80
Batman Fawkner Inn		10	03-6331-7222	35 Cameron Street	$75
Hotel Tasmania		21	03-6331-7355	191 Charles Street	$75
Mews Motel	3	26	03-6331-2861	89 Margaret Street	$75
Royal on George		14	03-6331-2526	90 George Street	$70
Lloyds Hotel		9	03-6331-4966	23 George Street	$55
Mallee Grill		1	03-6334-9288	1 Tamar Street	$40

(ii) Backpackers Hostels in and near Launceston

Name	Group	No. on Map	Telephone No.	Address	Lowest Price (Dormitory)
Metro Backpackers	YHA	27	03-6334-4506	16 Brisbane Street	$22
Launceston Backpackers	VIP	28	03-6334-2327	103 Canning Street	$22
Mallee Grill		1	03-6334-9288	1 Tamar Street	$18
Launceston City Hostel		29	03-6344-9779	36 Thistle Street West	$17
Australian Maritime Coll.		30	03-6335-4702	Beauty Point	$28
Travellers Lodge	YHA	31	03-6382-3261	4 Elizabeth St., George Town	$20

MOVING ON
Bus Services from Launceston

Destination	Operator	Via	Distance (km)	Fare	Journey Time	Frequency
Hobart	Redline		203	$26.40	2½ - 3 hrs	4/day
Hobart	TassieLink		203	$27	2¾ hrs	1/day
Hobart (via West Coast)	TassieLink		598	$107.40	11½ hrs	2/week
		Lake St. Clair	184 / 419	$82.00	3 - 8¾ hrs	2 - 6/week
		Strahan*	367	$65.70	7¼ - 12¾ hrs	3 - 7/week
		Queenstown	330	$58.70	6¾ hrs	3-4/week†
		Cradle Mountain	190	$48.60	3½ hrs	3 - 7/week
		Devonport	100	$18.50	1¼ - 2 hrs	10-14/wk.
Burnie	Redline		154	$25	2 - 3 hrs	3/day
		Devonport	100	$18.40	1¼ - 1¾ hrs	3/day

* Connecting service. Change of bus involved.   †Daily direct or connecting service in summer.

914 TASMANIA
Bus Services from Launceston, continued

Destination	Operator	Via	Distance (km)	Fare	Journey Time	Frequency
St. Helens	Redline		167	$26.10	2¼ - 2¾ hrs	6/week
		St. Mary's	132	$20.70	1¾ - 2¼ hrs	6/week
Bicheno	Redline		175	$29	2¾ - 3 hrs	5 - 6/week
		Swansea	135	$23.80	2 - 2¼ hrs	5 - 6/week
Bicheno	TassieLink		179	$25.70	2½ hrs	3 - 4/week
		St. Mary's	132	$22	2 hrs	3 - 4/week
Derby	Redline		101	$17.70	2 - 3¾ hrs	11/week
		Scottsdale	68	$13.10	1¼ - 1½ hrs	11/week
George Town	Redline		52	$9.60	45 - 50 mins	3/day
Mole Creek	Redline		76	$13.70	1¾ hrs	5/week
Evandale	Redline		20	$3.90	20 - 25 mins	11/week
Perth	Redline		20	$5.10	15 mins	6/day
Beauty Point	Tamar Valley		45	$8.20	1 hr	9/week
		Beaconsfield	40	$7.40	50 mins	14/week
Grindelwald	Manion's		19	$5	20 - 35 mins	6/day

DEVONPORT
Population 25,000

4 hrs 30 mins by bus from Hobart

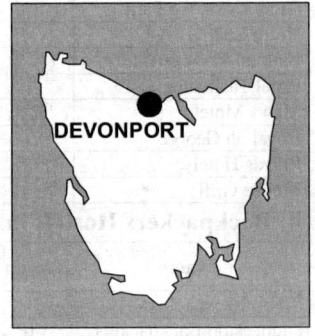

For many visitors to Tasmania, this is their arrival port, for it is here in Devonport that the *Spirit of Tasmania I and II* dock after their crossing from Melbourne. The *Spirit of Tasmania* vessels sail every night between Melbourne and Devonport and in the peak summer season there are additional daylight sailings. Fares on the *Spirit of Tasmania* are seasonal, but a low-season one-way ticket costs $120 in a seat and $140 for a hostel-type berth. Some discounted tickets are available if purchased a month in advance. The voyage takes ten hours, and since most of the sailings reach Devonport early in the morning, many passengers press on to another destination without spending time here. For that purpose buses meet the ship almost at the foot of the gangplank and provide services to Hobart, Launceston, Burnie, Cradle Mountain, Queenstown, Strahan and Lake St. Clair. There is a local bus to accommodation in Devonport, if required. It is also possible to walk a short distance along the quay and take a ferry across to the centre of Devonport on the other side of the river.

If you are arriving here by land, however, you will probably be coming from Launceston. The main service is provided by Tasmanian Redline three times a day, but TassieLink also has a bus which connects with all arrivals and departures of the *Spirit of Tasmania*.

On the way from Launceston, you will pass through a series of small towns, of which the most interesting is **Westbury**. Westbury, founded in 1823, is rather English in character, with a village green, hawthorn hedges, oaks and elms, and colonial architecture. Governor Arthur intended that this should grow into the principal town of the north-west, so he might be a little disappointed at seeing it now. It was at first a convict and garrison town, and it later served as a coaching town, and maintained its importance when the railway arrived in 1871, but after that it slowly declined and now it is quite small, but with sufficient interest to encourage the passer-by to make a brief halt.

Pearn's Steam World has a collection of steam-powered machinery, some more than a century old, and a few non-steam items as well. Nearly all is in working order. There is a small railway track on which a miniature train is operated. *Pearn's Steam World* is open daily from 9:00 until 17:00 and admission costs $5, including a steam train ride on days when the train is operating.

Westbury Maze is a hedge maze of some complexity made from 3,000 bushes trimmed to two-metre height. Except in July and August, it is open daily from 10:00 until 18:00, although hopefully you will not need all of that time to solve it. Admission costs $6.

Westbury, like Washington, has its **White House**, this one so called because it was built by Mr. Thomas White in 1841 to 1842. It is now owned by the National Trust and contains a collection of antiques. The house is open daily from 10:00 until 16:00, except in July and August, and admission costs $8.

Culzean Gardens are regarded as some of the best temperate gardens in Australia. They are open daily from 10:00 until 17:00, with admission costing $6. There are also the **Vintage Tractor Shed**, the **stocks** on the **village green** and the carvings in **St. Andrew's Church** to keep the visitor busy in this small town.

Devonport was originally two separate towns - Formby, on the west bank of the Mersey River, and Torquay, on the east bank. They amalgamated in 1890 to form the city of Devonport. The city has a relatively compact centre, but sprawling suburbs, and several of its attractions lie at the extremities. The city centre, first, contains a helpful **Visitor Information Centre**, which is a good place to start. It is beside the river, opposite the ferry terminal and the **railway station**. The station, unfortunately, has not received any regular passenger services since 1978, although the author arrived here by train on my first visit. The **ferry**, though, continues to run, to a spot on the other side of the Mersey just adjacent to the berth of the *Spirit of Tasmania*.

Next to the Visitor Information Centre is the **Entertainment Complex**, with the main shopping area behind that, sealed off to traffic in its centre, which makes it more appealing. There is an **Arts Centre** in a converted church in Stewart Street just up the hill from the river. The Arts Centre is open daily from 10:00 (14:00 on Sundays) until 17:00, and admission is free. The *Imaginarium* **Science Centre** is in MacFie Street, just south of the city centre. It is open, except on Fridays, from 10:00 (12:00 on Saturdays) until 16:00, and admission costs $8. For the other points of interest, though, we have to start walking or taking buses.

The **Don River Railway** operates every day on the first railway line built in Tasmania. This lies along the Don River, as one might guess, to the west of the city, and is now a short, otherwise disused, branch line off the main track. The train runs as far as the junction with the main line at **Coles Beach** and then returns. It is a journey of only four kilometres, or about ten minutes, each way. The service is steam-hauled on Sundays and diesel-hauled on other days. Trains depart from Don every hour on the hour from 10:00 until 16:00, arriving back half an hour later. It is not necessary to return on the same train. Occasionally the Don River Railway arranges special journeys along the main line, even as far as Hobart. There is also a small **museum** at Don, and

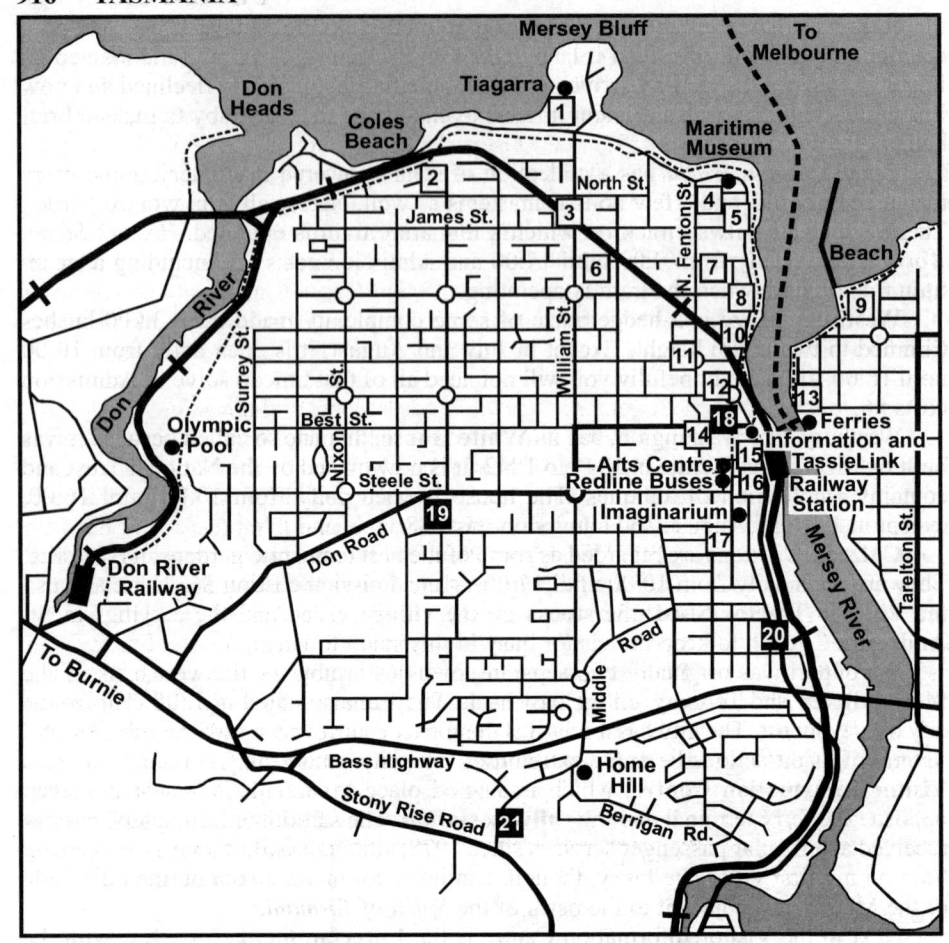

DEVONPORT
Black numerals in white boxes indicate hotel accommodation
White numerals in black boxes indicate backpackers hostels

the railway has the largest collection of steam locomotives and old rolling stock in Tasmania. The price of a return journey to Coles Beach is $8. Unfortunately, the Don Railway is rather a long walk from the centre of Devonport and no local bus goes to it. Tasmanian Redline services to Burnie pass by and Merseylink buses nos. 20, 20T and 25 go within walking distance. Alight at the junction of Steele and Surrey Streets (where the bus turns right), walk ahead along Steele Street until you see the railway and then turn left and walk beside it to Don Station. In summer, some of these buses are extended to the Olympic Pool, at the end of Steele Street, which takes you a little nearer still. Such buses are renumbered 21 and 21T. Buses operate approximately hourly. The train makes a stop at Olympic Pool, if you prefer to board there. There are also buses nos. 10 and 15 which go close to the Coles Beach end of the line. Alight where the bus turns left at the junction of James and Nixon Streets. Again, buses operate approximately hourly.

To the north of the city are two more places to visit. The **Maritime Museum** is, appropriately, right at the mouth of the river in the former harbourmaster's residence. The collection includes models of various vessels, of which one is Joshua Slocum's yacht *Spray*. Slocum was the first man to sail single-handed round the world, calling in at Devonport on the way in 1897. The Museum opens, except on Mondays, from 10:00 until 16:00. Admission costs $4. It is a pleasant walk to here along the bank of the river, or you can take a bus no. 10 or 15 to the corner of North Fenton Street and James Street.

Further north near the tip of Mersey Bluff is *Tiagarra*, an aboriginal culture and art centre. There are some 270 aboriginal rock engravings in this area, one of only thirteen sites in Tasmania where such art work has been found. There is also a good view from the **Bluff**. Tiagarra is open daily from 9:00 until 16:00 and admission costs $4. From the Maritime Museum, there is a walking path along the foreshore to this area. From the city centre, though, the quickest way is to take bus no. 10 or 15 to the corner of William Street and North Street, and then walk north along William Street.

In the south of the city is **Home Hill**. This was the home of Prime Minister Joseph Lyons, the only Tasmanian ever to have been Prime Minister and the only person ever to have been both a State Premier and, later, Commonwealth Prime Minister. Joseph Lyons built the house in 1916, a year after his marriage, and lived there with his wife for most of the rest of his life. He became Premier of Tasmania in 1923 and retained the position until 1928. Then in 1929 he was elected to the Federal Parliament and became Prime Minister in 1932. He died, still in office, in April 1939. His widow, Dame Enid Lyons, was then elected to parliament in 1943, becoming the first woman member of the House of Representatives. In 1949, she became the first woman member of the cabinet. She retired from parliament in 1951 because of poor health. The house is basically as she left it, owned now by the City of Devonport and managed by the National Trust. It is open except on Mondays and Fridays at least between 14:00 and 16:00, and sometimes from 12:00, depending on day and season. Admission costs $8. To reach *Home Hill*, take bus no. 30 or 40 to the junction of Middle Road and Berrigan Road. Buses operate approximately every half hour.

Twenty minutes away from Devonport is the interesting historic little town of **Latrobe**, full of antique shops, restaurants, bakeries and the like. The town was gazetted in 1851 and many of the properties date from that time. Latrobe is also the venue for the richest cycling race in Australia, the *Latrobe Wheelrace*, which has a history stretching back more than a century. To reach Latrobe, take a bus no. 40. Services run approximately hourly.

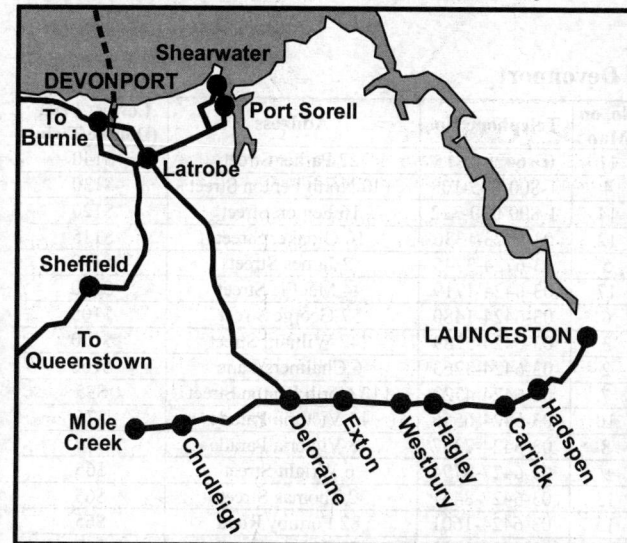

FROM LAUNCESTON TO DEVONPORT
Showing bus routes and principal bus stops

Two places not easily reached by bus are the **Tasmanian Arboretum** in Eugenana, ten kilometres south-west of Devonport, and **Lillico Beach**, six kilometres west, where **Fairy Penguins** are to be found.

Port Sorell, east of Devonport, lies on the **Rubicon Estuary** and is a quiet historical place, founded in 1822 and named after Governor Sorell. It is the oldest town on the north-west coast of Tasmania and was once a ship-building centre. Nearby are **Hawley**, a popular holiday spot, and **Shearwater**, the shopping centre. Mersey Bus and Coach Service operates a bus to Port Sorell and Shearwater three times a day, and four times on Mondays and Thursdays. The bus departs from Rooke Street in Devonport and will travel via Latrobe on request, or if a booking is made.

All other local bus services are operated by Merseylink. A bus meets the *Spirit of Tasmania* and transfers passengers to their accommodation for the sum of $4. It will also pick up from accommodation and transfer passengers to the ship for departure for the same sum. Otherwise, a single bus ride costs between $1.50 and $2.50, and a Day Rover, valid between 9:00 and 16:00, costs $3.50. Buses do not operate on Sundays, and on Saturdays services are reduced.

As for accommodation, there is a good range, and backpackers have a choice of four hostels. The youth hostel is rather far out of the city to the south and can be reached by bus no. 40 if the walk is too far. Formby Road Hostel is in a beautiful old building on the main road beside the river, still quite a long walk to the city centre. Molly Malone's seems to change its name frequently. It is in an old hotel in the city centre, the most convenient of the hostel locations. The hotel used to be known as the Tamahere, but is now called Molly Malone's. The hostel is sometimes called Inner City Backpackers and sometimes Midcity Backpackers. It is all the same place. It is popular with tours and not always possible to find a bed here in summer. Tasman House is another long walk uphill from the city centre, but offers good, cheap accommodation in former nurses quarters. If the half-hour walk is too long, take bus no. 20, 20T or 25 on weekdays, or no. 15 on Saturdays.

ACCOMMODATION
(i) Hotel Accommodation in Devonport

Name	Stars	No. on Map	Telephone No.	Address	Lowest Price (Double/Twin)
Dumple Dale Cottage		11	03-6428-2815	22 Parker Street	$140
Sunrise Motel	4	4	1-800-815-108	140 North Fenton Street	$130
Gateway Motor Inn	4	14	1-800-030-322	16 Fenton Street	$120
Birchmore B&B		12	03-6423-1336	10 Oldaker Street	$115
Keswick by the River		5	03-6724-3745	2 James Street	$110
Macfie Manor B&B		17	03-6424-1719	44 MacFie Street	$110
Glasgow Lodge		6	03-6424-1480	57 George Street	$105
Mersey Bluff Lodge	3½	3	03-6424-5289	247 William Street	$100
Trelawney by the Sea	4	2	03-6424-3263	6 Chalmers Lane	$100
Barclay Lodge	4	7	03-6424-4722	112 North Fenton Street	$95
Elimatta Hotel		10	03-6424-6555	15 Victoria Parade	$75
River View Lodge		8	03-6424-7357	18 Victoria Parade	$70
Abel Tasman Park		9	03-6427-8794	6 Wright Street	$65
Edgewater Motor Inn		13	03-6427-8441	2 Thomas Street	$65
Formby Hotel		15	03-6424-1601	82 Formby Road	$65
Alexander Hotel		16	03-6424-2252	78 Formby Road	$60
Mersey Bluff Caravan Pk.		1	03-6424-8655	Mersey Bluff Road	$55

(ii) Backpackers Hostels in Devonport

Name	Group	No. on Map	Telephone No.	Address	Lowest Price (Dormitory)
Molly Malone's		18	03-6424-1898	34 Best Street	$18
Formby Road Hostel		20	03-6423-6563	16 Formby Road	$16
Tasman House	VIP	19	03-6423-2335	114 Tasman Street	$15
MacWright House	YHA	21	03-6424-5696	115 Middle Road	$14

MOVING ON
Bus Services from Devonport

Destination	Operator	Via	Distance (km)	Fare	Journey Time	Frequency
Hobart	Redline		303	$43.80	3¾ - 5½ hrs	2/day
		Launceston	100	$18.40	1½ - 2¼ hrs	3/day
Hobart	TassieLink		303	$45.50	4¼ hrs	1/day
		Launceston	100	$18.50	1¼ hrs	10-14/wk.
Hobart (via West Coast)	TassieLink		498	$90.80	9½ hrs	2/week
		Lake St. Clair	319	$64.40	6¾ hrs	2/week
		Strahan*	267	$49.10	5¼ - 6¼ hrs	3 - 4/week
		Queenstown	230	$41.10	4¼ - 4¾ hrs	3 - 4/week
		Cradle Mountain	90	$31	1½ hrs	3 - 7/week
Burnie	Redline		54	$9.70	45 - 100 mins	5/day

* Connecting service. Change of bus involved.

BURNIE
Population 17,000

5 hrs 30 mins by bus from Hobart

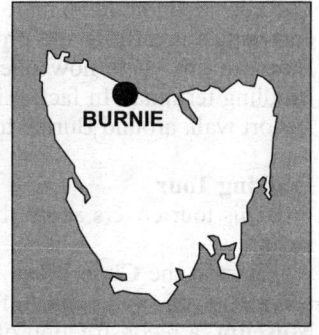

An hour further west along the north coast of Tasmania is the city of Burnie. On the way we pass through the towns of Ulverstone and Penguin, both beside the sea and pleasant country towns, with accommodation available. **Ulverstone** is the larger of the two, quite a busy little town and a popular holiday venue. **Penguin** is quieter and offers good sea views. The Neptune Grand Hotel, right in the centre of Penguin and adjacent to the beach, has single rooms for $28. Predictably, Penguin has penguins too. As in various other locations, but very conveniently here, the **Fairy Penguins** can be seen returning home at dusk from their fishing expeditions and, after several failed attempts, dashing up the beach to their burrows.

Burnie is the fourth largest city in Tasmania. It was first settled in 1828 and originally named Emu Bay. It was developed by the **Van Diemen's Land Company**, mostly for the timber which grew all around, and when land was sold to settlers in 1842, the name was changed to Burnie, William Burnie being the director of the Van Diemen's Land Company at the time.

Tin was discovered at Mt. Bischoff in 1871 and a tramway 75 kilometres long constructed to bring the tin to Burnie for shipment. This was originally operated by horse power. In the 1890s, a railway was constructed through particularly difficult

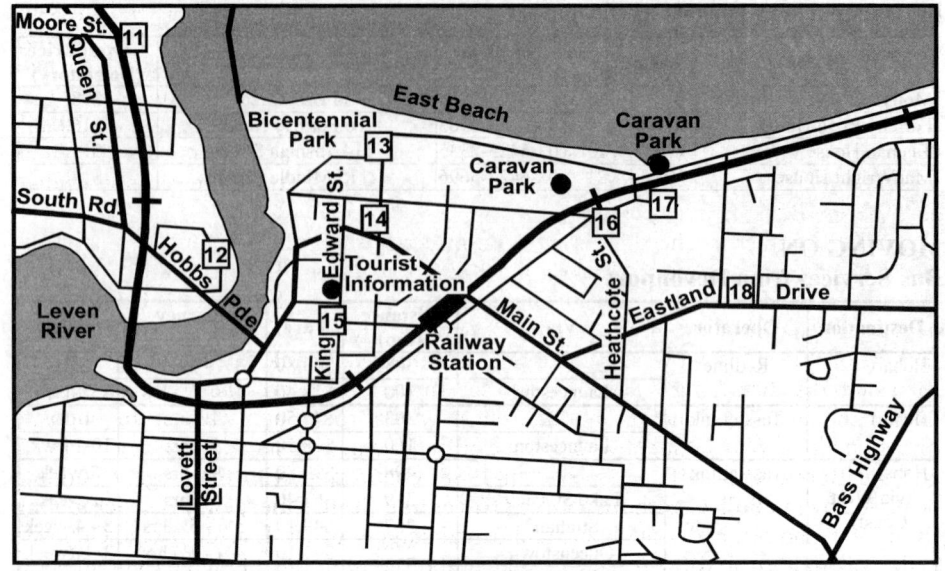

ULVERSTONE
Numerals indicate accommodation

terrain to bring silver from Zeehan to Burnie for shipment. This remains a private line operated by the Emu Bay Railway Company. The main line reached Ulverstone in 1890, but was not extended to Burnie until 1901. In 1937, Associated Pulp and Paper Mills decided to build a huge mill at Burnie, which has since expanded still further and contributes greatly to the prosperity of the town. In 1988, Queen Elizabeth declared Burnie a city. It is now one of Tasmania's major ports, and has a large container-handling terminal. In fact, it is the fifth largest container port in Australia. Let us take a short walk around Burnie to see what it has to offer.

Walking Tour
This tour covers about three kilometres and will take an hour, without any major stops.
Start in the **Civic Plaza Precinct** at the **Travel and Information Centre**, which has plenty of advice and information on the area. Also here is the **Pioneer Village Museum**, a reconstruction of life in Burnie at the end of the nineteenth century. The shops are replicas of the first such businesses in the town and have been made using nineteenth century materials. There is the Emu Bay Inn, and there are reconstructions of a dentist's surgery, a carpenter's shop, a butter factory, a newspaper printing office, a general store and post office, a saddlery, a blacksmith's forge, a stagecoach depot and various rooms of a pioneer cottage. The Pioneer Village Museum is open from 9:00 until 17:00 on weekdays and from 13:30 until 16:30 at weekends. Admission costs $5.
Next door is the **Civic Centre**, built in 1976, including the **Civic Theatre** and the **Burnie Regional Art Gallery**. The Art Gallery is open from 9:00 until 17:00 on weekdays and from 13:30 until 16:30 at weekends, and admission is free.
From the Precinct, proceed to Wilmot Street and turn right, then right again into Alexander Street. On your right as you walk along are the Hellyer Regional Library,

Alexander Beetle House Child Care Centre, the R.S.L. Club and then the **Supreme Court Building**, a modern construction completed in 1970. Turn left into Cattley Street, with the Harris Building on your right. At the next corner is **St. George's Church**, built in 1885, replacing a previous church which had dated from 1851. Cross Mount Street and the building on the far corner is the offices of St. Luke's Health Insurance Fund, but it was constructed in 1921 for the **Hobart Savings Bank**, which was the first, and is now the only remaining, trustee bank in Australia. It is now known as the Trust Bank.

A little further on the right is the **Commonwealth Bank**. The building is on the site of the first newspaper in Burnie, the *Wellington Times*. The paper still publishes, but is known now as *The Advocate*. On the corner of Wilson Street is the **Union Bank of Australasia** Building. It was originally a draper's in the 1920s. The building on the far side of Wilson Street was originally the **Commercial Bank of Tasmania**. Turn left for a short distance along Wilson Street to see **Joyce's Jewellers Shop**, with an exterior unchanged since construction in 1893, but now turn round and walk in the opposite direction along Wilson Street where you can find the new post office, opened in 1977, and the Burnie City Offices, opened in 1988, contrasting with the elegant building occupied by the **Police Administrative Offices and State Emergency Service**, dating from 1915 and originally the home and dental surgery of Dr. Lucado Wells. Opposite is the **Tasmanian Redline** bus depot, and, at the end of the street on the right, the new Police Headquarters, completed in 1987. Turn left into Ladbrooke Street and then left again into Marine Terrace. You will see on your left the **Mylan Building**, with its name at the top. It was built for Mr. John Mylan who was a blacksmith and undertaker. He sold his business in 1929 to the Vincent family, which still operates it.

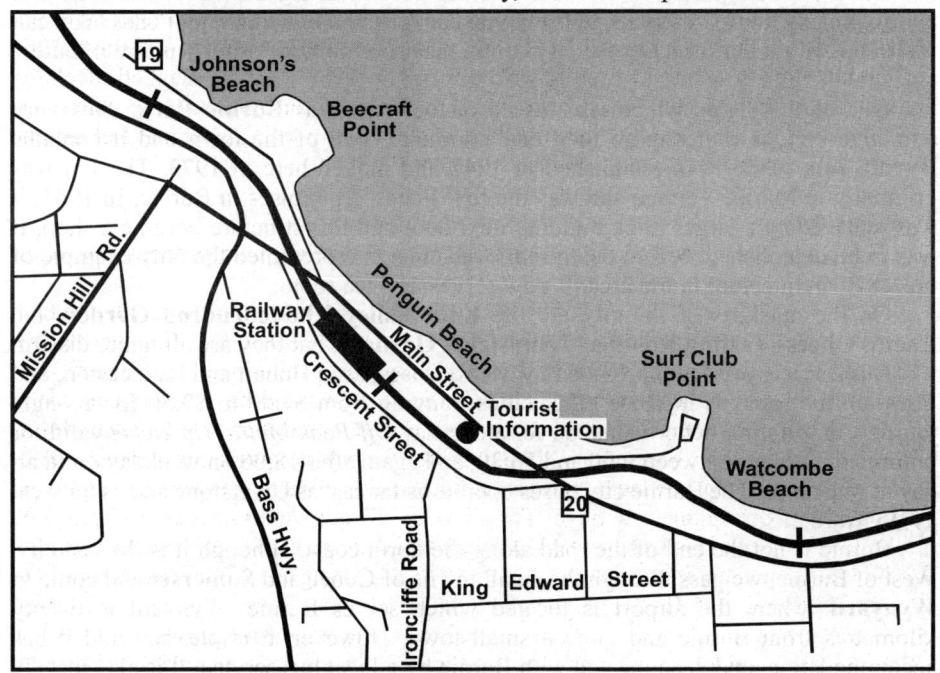

PENGUIN
Numerals indicate accommodation

Next is the **Old Post Office**, a fine building, as one expects from such important public structures, dating from 1898. However, it has not been used as a post office since 1923. On the corner of Cattley Street is the City Medical Centre, built originally for the **Bank of Van Diemen's Land** in 1891. Before the bank could open here, however, it became insolvent, so the building was purchased by the National Bank of Tasmania in 1898. The National Bank of Tasmania merged with the Commercial Bank of Australia in 1918, and that bank was absorbed by the Bank of New South Wales, which is now known as Westpac. Opposite is the **Bay View Hotel**. This is the site of one of the first hotels in Tasmania, built in 1874. The original wooden hotel was burnt down in 1897 and this one replaced it in 1899. Continue along Marine Terrace noting the **docks** on your right which are of vital importance to the economy of this city. Where the road bends to the left, you will find the **Basalt Columns**. These were exposed when the area was quarried for rock needed for the construction of the Ocean Breakwater in 1911. The columns consist of perfect hexagonal structures caused by the cooling of a lava flow some twenty million years ago and are some of the best such examples in the world.

Round the corner and pass the Skate Rink, then turn left up Wilson Street to the corner of Wilmot Street, where you will find the **City Square**, completed in 1985. Turn right along Wilmot Street, and on the corner of Mount Street is the **Club Hotel**, built in 1912 and adorned with some beautiful iron balconies. Turn right down Mount Street and you will come to the **Railway Station** and the beach. The station has not had a passenger service since 1978, which is a great pity. The beach is lined with a grassy foreshore, and one can walk along either foreshore or beach for a long way, if one has the inclination. If you do walk, there is a bus service along this road, with buses at approximately hourly intervals, to bring you back. Here our walking tour ends. You can return up Alexander Street to the city centre, near our point of origin, in five minutes.

One of the sights which we missed on our tour was **Burnie Park**. This very attractive park is rather more than one kilometre west of the town and it contains **Burnie Inn**, which was established in 1847 and moved here in 1973. The Inn was originally in Marine Terrace and was the first licensed premises in Burnie. In 1901, it was replaced by a larger brick building next door and this structure became a shop. It was to be demolished, before being reprieved since it represented the only example of pre-1870 architecture in the area. It now serves as a tea room.

On the outskirts of the city are the **Emu Valley Rhododendron Garden**, the **Lactos Cheese Tasting Room** and **Annsleigh Gardens**, but they are all rather distant.

Bus services are again provided by Metro Buses, as in Hobart and Launceston, and fares are the same as in those other cities, ranging from $1.50 to $3.50 for a single journey, or, offering better value, $4 for a one-day *Off-Peak Multi-Trip Ticket* valid for unlimited journeys between 9:00 and 16:30, and again after 18:00 on weekdays, and all day at weekends. The Burnie city buses operate as far east as Ulverstone and as far west as Wynyard.

Burnie is not the end of the road along the north coast, although it is the last city. West of Burnie, we pass through the small towns of **Cooee** and **Somerset** and come to **Wynyard**, where the airport is located which serves Burnie. Wynyard is twenty kilometres from Burnie and quite a small town. However, it is pleasant and it has accommodation, and is connected with Burnie by a local bus service. It is also just six kilometres from the Table Cape coastal landmark. The **Table Cape** juts out into Bass

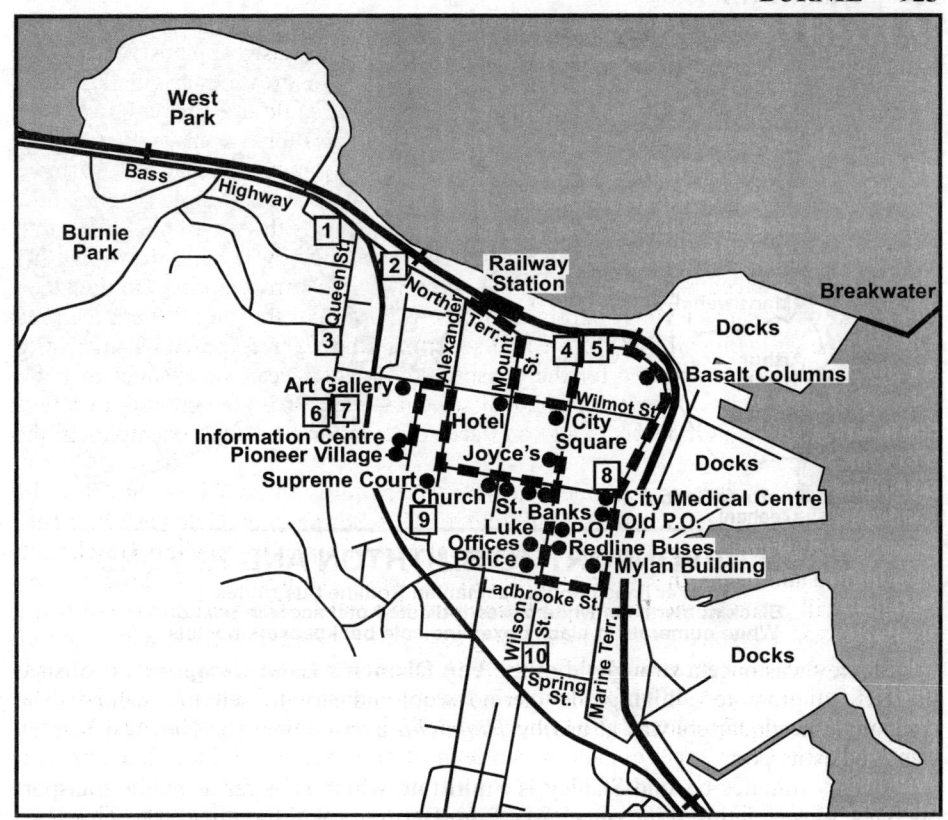

BURNIE
Dashed line shows Walking Tour
Numerals indicate accommodation

Strait and has at its tip a lighthouse built there in 1888. It is also the location of a **tulip farm**. There is a Tulip Festival in Wynyard every October.

Another twelve kilometres west is **Boat Harbour Beach** which is scenic and has a backpackers hostel. Continuing, another forty minutes will bring us to **Stanley**, known for **The Nut**, the steep-sided bluff on **Circular Head** at the end of the promontory on which the small fishing town stands. The Nut rises to a height of 152 metres. A walking path leads to the summit, or, for the faint of foot, there is a **chairlift** taking five minutes each way. The chairlift operates daily from 9:30 until 17:00 in summer and from 10:00 until 16:00 in winter. The return fare is $8. You will see The Nut clearly, and most impressively, from a distance as you approach the town along the northern coastline.

Also in Stanley is *Joe Lyons Cottage*, the place where Tasmania's only Prime Minister was born. He taught in the local school from 1895 until 1900. *Joe Lyons Cottage* is open daily from 10:00 until 16:00. For a little more about Joseph Lyons, see page 917. There is a small **museum** in Stanley open daily from 10:00 until 16:00, except in June and July, at a cost of $4.

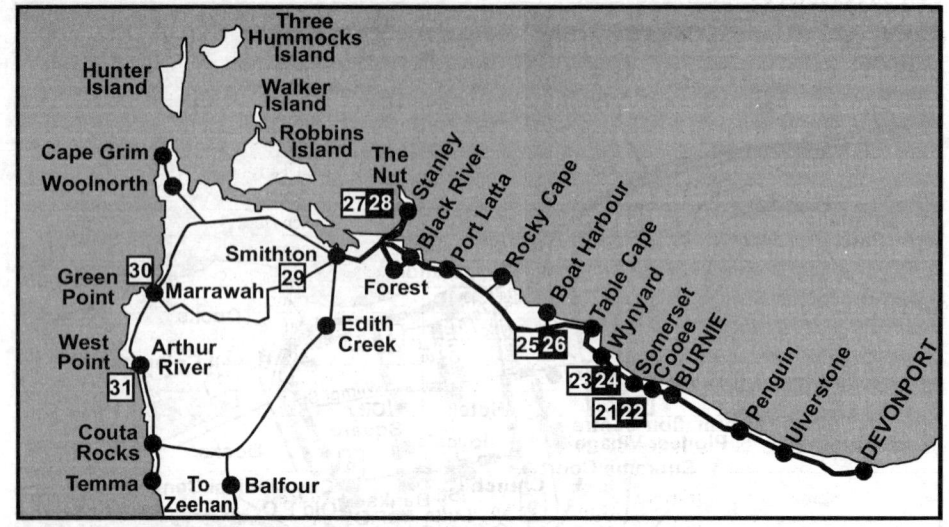

FROM DEVONPORT TO SMITHTON AND BEYOND
Thicker lines denote Tasmanian Redline bus routes
Black numerals in white boxes indicate hotel accommodation
White numerals in black boxes indicate backpackers hostels

Stanley was once a stronghold of the **Van Diemen's Land Company** established in 1825 to promote a high-grade merino wool industry to sell to England. The company's headquarters was at nearby *Highfield*, overlooking The Nut, and Stanley was used as its port.

Twenty minutes beyond Stanley is **Smithton**, which is as far as public transport operates. Tasmanian Redline runs buses from Burnie to Smithton twice on weekdays, the first service connecting with the bus arriving from Hobart (not Wednesdays), Launceston and Devonport (7:30 from Hobart, 10:15 from Launceston, 12:00 from Devonport).

Beyond Smithton, inaccessible by public transport but visited by tours, are **Woolnorth** and **Cape Grim**, the north-western point of mainland Tasmania, claiming to have "the world's cleanest air", a claim evidently based on scientific evidence, but not entirely convincing, despite the fact that it can certainly get rather breezy here on occasions due to the influence of the Roaring Forties. 22,000 acres of land around Cape Grim are still owned by the Van Diemen's Land Company.

Off the coast here is a group of islands, the **Hunter Group**, comprising **Robbins Island, Walker Island, Hunter Island** and **Three Hummocks Island**. There is no regular transport to these islands, but accommodation is available on Three Hummocks Island.

A little further round the west coast of Tasmania are **Marrawah** and **Green Point**, again visited by tours, and then **Arthur River** and **West Point**. West Point is, reasonably enough, the westernmost point in mainland Tasmania. It likes to be called "the edge of the world". If you set off west for a swim from here, you will reach Cape Horn after 15,586 kilometres.

ACCOMMODATION
(i) Hotel Accommodation in Burnie

Name	Stars	No. on Map	Telephone No.	Address	Lowest Price (Double/Twin)
Weller's Executive Suites	4	7	03-6431-1088	William Street	$145
Apartments Down Town	4	9	03-6432-3219	52 Alexander Street	$135
Beachfront Voyager	4	4	1-800-355-090	9 North Terrace	$135
Burnie Town House	3½	10	03-6431-4455	139 Wilson Street	$120
Duck House	4	3	03-6431-1712	26 Queen Street	$120
Weller's Inn	3½	6	03-6431-1088	36 Queen Street	$115
West Beach Villas	3½	1	03-6431-5708	43a North Terrace	$100
Ocean View Motel	3½	21	03-6431-1925	253 Bass Highway, Cooee	$85
Beach Hotel		5	03-6431-2333	1 Wilson Street	$75
Treasure Island C'van Pk.	3½	21	03-6431-1925	253 Bass Highway, Cooee	$70
Bay View Hotel		8	03-6431-2711	14 Marine Terrace	$60
Regent Hotel		2	03-6431-1933	26 North Terrace	$35

(ii) Backpackers Hostels in Burnie

Name	Group	No. on Map	Telephone No.	Address	Lowest Price (Dormitory)
Bay View Hotel		8	03-6431-2711	14 Marine Terrace	$30
Regent Hotel		2	03-6431-1933	26 North Terrace	$22
Treasure Island Caravan Pk		22	03-6431-1925	253 Bass Highway, Cooee	$16

(iii) Accommodation in Ulverstone

Name	Stars	No. on Map	Telephone No.	Address	Lowest Price (Double/Twin)
Lighthouse Hotel	4	14	03-6425-1197	33 Victoria Street	$130
Ocean View Guest House		13	03-6425-5401	1 Victoria Street	$125
Bass and Flinders Inn		18	03-6425-3011	49 Eastland Drive	$115
Furners Hotel		15	03-6425-1488	42 Reibey Street	$90
Brigadoon Holiday Units	3½	11	03-6425-1697	4 Moore Street	$80
Willaway Motel Apts.	3½	17	03-6425-2018	2 Tucker Street	$80
Beachway Motel	3	16	03-6425-2342	1 Heathcote Street	$70
Waterfront Inn	3½	12	03-6425-1599	Tasma Parade	$65

(iv) Accommodation in Penguin

Name	Stars	No. on Map	Telephone No.	Address	Lowest Price (Double/Twin)
Neptune Grand Hotel		20	03-6437-2406	84 Main Street	$50
Penguin Caravan Park		19	03-6437-2785	Johnson's Beach	$50

(v) Hotel Accommodation in Wynyard

Name	Stars	No. on Map	Telephone No.	Address	Lowest Price (Double/Twin)
Alexandria	4	23	03-6442-4411	1 Table Cape Road	$135
Leisureville Holiday Villa	3½	23	03-6442-2291	145 Old Bass Highway	$100
Waterfront Motor Inn		23	03-6442-2351	1 Goldie Street	$95
Gutteridge Court	4	23	03-6442-2886	Unit 4, 22 Goldie Street	$90
Leisureville Caravan Park	3½	23	03-6442-2291	145 Old Bass Highway	$75
Wynyard Caravan Park		23	03-6442-1998	308 Old Bass Highway	$75
Federal Hotel	1½	23	03-6442-2056	82 Goldie Street	$65
Inglis River Hotel / Motel		23	03-6442-2344	10 Goldie Street	$45

926 TASMANIA

(vi) Backpackers Hostel in Wynyard

Name	Group	No. on Map	Telephone No.	Address	Lowest Price (Dormitory)
Wynyard Caravan Park		24	03-6442-1998	308 Old Bass Highway	$18

(vii) Hotel Accommodation in Boat Harbour

Name	Stars	No. on Map	Telephone No.	Address	Lowest Price (Double/Twin)
Boat Harbour Bch. Resort	3½	25	03-6445-1107	The Esplanade	$110
Cape View Guest House	4	25	03-6445-1273	64 Strawberry Lane	$105
Country Garden Cottages		25	03-6445-1233	15 Port Road	$100
Seaside Garden Motel		25	03-6445-1111	The Esplanade	$80
Boat Harbour Beach Park		25	03-6445-1253	The Esplanade	$55

(viii) Backpackers Hostel in Boat Harbour

Name	Group	No. on Map	Telephone No.	Address	Lowest Price (Dormitory)
Boat Harbour Beach B/P		26	03-6445-1273	64 Strawberry Lane	$20

(ix) Hotel Accommodation in Stanley

Name	Stars	No. on Map	Telephone No.	Address	Lowest Price (Double/Twin)
Captain's Cottage		27	03-6458-3230	30 Alexander Terrace	$170
Beachside Retreat	5	27	03-6458-1350	253 Stanley Highway	$165
Abbey's Cottage		27	1-800-222-397	1 Marshall Street	$155
Touchwood Cottage	4	27	03-6458-1348	31 Church Street	$155
Town House		27	03-6458-1455	4 Church Street	$150
Hanlon House B&B	4½	27	03-6458-1149	6 Marshall Street	$135
Bayside Colonial Cottage	4	27	03-6458-1209	44 Alexander Terrace	$110
Ellie's Cottage		27	03-6458-2038	9 Main Road	$110
Old Cable Station Retreat	4	27	03-6458-1312	West Beach Road	$110
Stanley Village	4	27	03-6458-1404	15 Wharf Road	$110
Anthony's at Highfield		27	03-6458-1245	Green Hills Road	$100
Philately House		27	03-6458-1109	11 Church Street	$100
Estowen House		27	1-800-222-397	35 Main Road	$95
Stanley Guest House	4	27	03-6458-1488	27 Main Road	$95
Dovecot & Stanley Motel	3½	27	1-800-062-298	58 Dovecot Road	$90
Ride Cottage		27	1-300-656-044	12 Pearse Street	$90
Pol and Pen Holiday Cots.	3½	27	1-800-222-397	8 Pearse Street	$85
Stanley Cabin Park	4	27	03-6458-1266	Wharf Road	$55
Stanley Hotel		27	03-6458-1161	21 Church Street	$45

(x) Backpackers Hostels in Stanley

Name	Group	No. on Map	Telephone No.	Address	Lowest Price (Dormitory)
Stanley Hotel		28	03-6458-1161	21 Church Street	$28
Stanley Y.H.A.	YHA	28	03-6458-1266	Wharf Road	$18

(xi) Accommodation in Smithton

Name	Stars	No. on Map	Telephone No.	Address	Lowest Price (Double/Twin)
Tall Timber Hotel	4	29	1-880-628-476	Scotchtown Road	$120
Rosie's Cottage		29	03-6452-2660	42a Goldie Street	$110
Christie's Corner		29	03-6452-3132	46 Goldie Street	$100
Bridge Hotel		29	03-6452-1389	2 Montagu Road	$50

(xii) Accommodation in Marrawah

Name	Stars	No. on Map	Telephone No.	Address	Lowest Price (Double/Twin)
Marrawah Beach House		30	03-6457-1285	19 Beach Road	$100
Glendonald Cottage	3½	30	03-6457-1191	79 Arthur River Road	$95

(xiii) Accommodation in Arthur River

Name	Stars	No. on Map	Telephone No.	Address	Lowest Price (Double/Twin)
Ocean View Cottage		31	03-6457-1278	Lot 10, Gardiner Street	$85
Alert Cottage		31	03-6457-1340	16 Davidson Street	$80
Sunset Holiday Villas		31	03-6457-1197	23 Gardiner Street	$80
Arthur River Units	3½	31	03-6457-1288	Lot 2, Gardiner Street	$75

MOVING ON
Bus Services from Burnie

Destination	Operator	Via	Distance (km)	Fare	Journey Time	Frequency
Hobart	Redline		357	$50.40	4½ - 6¼ hrs	2/day
		Launceston	154	$25	2 - 2¾ hrs	3/day
		Devonport	54	$9.70	30 - 80 mins	6/day
Smithton	Redline		93	$14.80	1½ hrs	11/week
		Stanley	76	$14.80	60 - 70 mins	11/week

CRADLE MOUNTAIN
Population 100

8 hrs by bus from Hobart

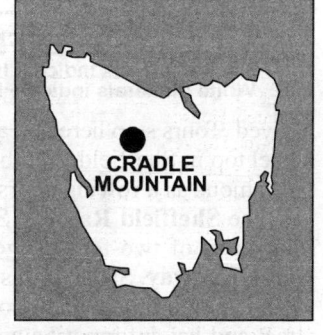

Beautiful Cradle Mountain is the start - or finish - of the **Overland Track**, the most popular long walk in Tasmania and one of the most popular in the world. It is also the location of several attractive shorter walks.

TassieLink operates a bus from Hobart direct to Cradle Mountain on two days a week, Tuesdays and Thursdays, the journey taking nearly eight hours. There is a service from Launceston, also with TassieLink, on three days a week in winter and every day in summer. This journey takes 3½ hours.

Since the previous entries were for places in northern Tasmania, let us assume an approach by that route. From Devonport, it is an interesting ninety-minute journey. We travel first through agricultural land producing potatoes, a variety of vegetables, pyrethrum and poppies. Picking of any poppies is regarded as an especially heinous crime. **Spreyton**, in particular, is known for its fruits. One sees roadside stalls selling apples, pears and cherries, as well as mushrooms.

The largest town on the route is **Sheffield**, thirty kilometres from Devonport and originally settled in the late 1850s. It was named after the city in England, probably because it was the birthplace of the manager of the Van Diemen's Land Company at the time. There was a minor gold rush in the area in 1886. However, it was the Mersey-Forth Power Development Scheme, started in 1963, which really led to the

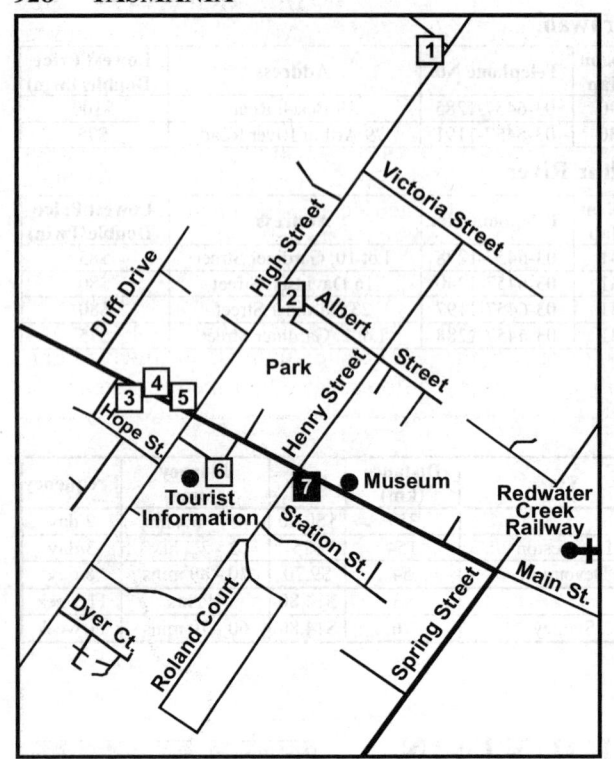

SHEFFIELD
Black numerals indicate hotel accommodation
White numerals indicate backpackers hostels

development of Sheffield. Seven dams and seven power stations were constructed nearby as part of Tasmania's love of hydro-electric schemes. However, when the project was completed, in 1973, the town started to decline. Then a plan was formed to keep Sheffield on the map. Following the example of Chemainus on Vancouver Island in Canada, the residents of Sheffield painted murals on any blank walls. Soon people started coming to see the paintings and now Sheffield is known as Tasmania's **Town of Murals**. At the time of writing, there are 54 such paintings, telling the story of the town, but the number is constantly increasing, and now 160,000 visitors per year come to see them. Even the rubbish bins have paintings on them. The economy and prestige of the town have revived. Tours stop here and accommodation is well patronised. There is a backpackers hostel too in Sheffield. Nearby is **Lake Barrington**, part of the hydro-electric scheme, but famous as a rowing course, regarded as one of the finest in the world.

The **Sheffield Railway Station** has been moved to a new location and about two kilometres of two-foot gauge track constructed, which is operated as the **Redwater Creek Railway**. Steam trains run on the first weekend of the month between 10:00 and 16:00. A ride on the train costs $5. The **Sheffield Heritage Museum** is in the main street and has information and displays relating to the hydro-electric scheme, as well as other topics. It is open daily from 10:00 until 15:00. **Weindorfer's Pioneer Settlement** has a collection of old buildings, including one which claims to have the largest shingle roof in the southern hemisphere, vehicles and blacksmith's tools, as well as two murals, of course. It is open daily with free admission.

Soon after Sheffield, there is a turning on the left to **Mole Creek**. This leads through **Paradise** and the **Paradise Valley**, in case you have ever wondered where such locations were to be found on this planet. There is also a place here called **No-Where Else**, the story being that many visitors used to take a wrong turning which led only to a farm. When they stopped and asked the farmer where the road led, he always used to reply, "Nowhere Else," and so the location inevitably came to be called No-Where Else. There is a popular pottery here.

CRADLE MOUNTAIN

Although there is no public transport on this route to Mole Creek via Paradise, Mole Creek can be reached by Tasmanian Redline bus from Launceston. The bus leaves Launceston every evening and returns from Mole Creek in the morning, on school days only, so an overnight stay is necessary. Mole Creek has limestone caves, of which the best known are **King Solomon's Cave** and **Marakoopa Cave**. The caves, both several kilometres west of the town of Mole Creek, are open daily with hourly tours between 10:30 and 16:00. Admission to each costs $10. There are also tours available from Mole Creek which will take you to undeveloped caves, for which contact Wild Cave Tours (telephone 03-6367-8142). The caves are in the Mole Creek Karst National Park, Tasmania's only underground National Park. Also in Mole Creek is the Trowunna Wildlife Park, open daily from 9:00 until 17:00. Admission costs $15.

A little further along the road from Sheffield to Cradle Mountain is **Gowrie Park**, where you will see a huge mural on a corrugated iron surface four metres high and no less than 98 metres long, which took the artist several months to complete. This was a town built for the construction of the hydro-electric power scheme. It is now almost deserted, but the former living quarters for the construction workers are available as backpackers accommodation, and a pleasant tiny place this is in which to find such economical beds. From here there are walks to **Mt. Roland** (1,234 metres) and to **Mt. Claude**. Both of these mountains can be seen from a little further along the road, by looking back over one's shoulder, Mt. Roland is to the right and Mt. Claude to the left.

Another road goes off to the left to Mole Creek, and this route also leads to the **Walls of Jerusalem National Park**, famous for its walks. Because it is more difficult to reach this location, the walks are less frequented here than at Cradle Mountain, although still popular. Tours go to

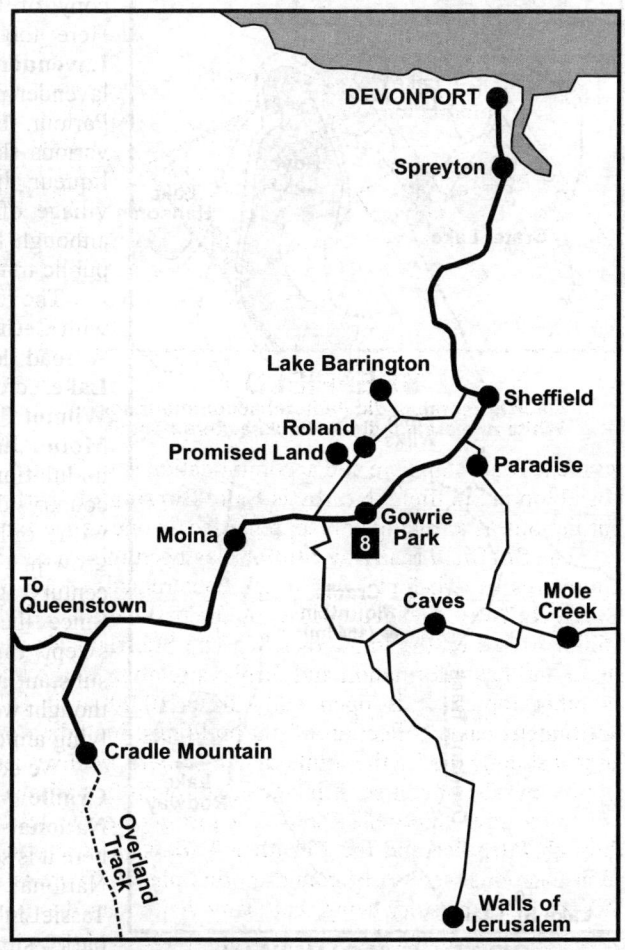

FROM DEVONPORT TO CRADLE MOUNTAIN
Showing TassieLink bus route (thicker line)
Numerals indicate backpackers hostels

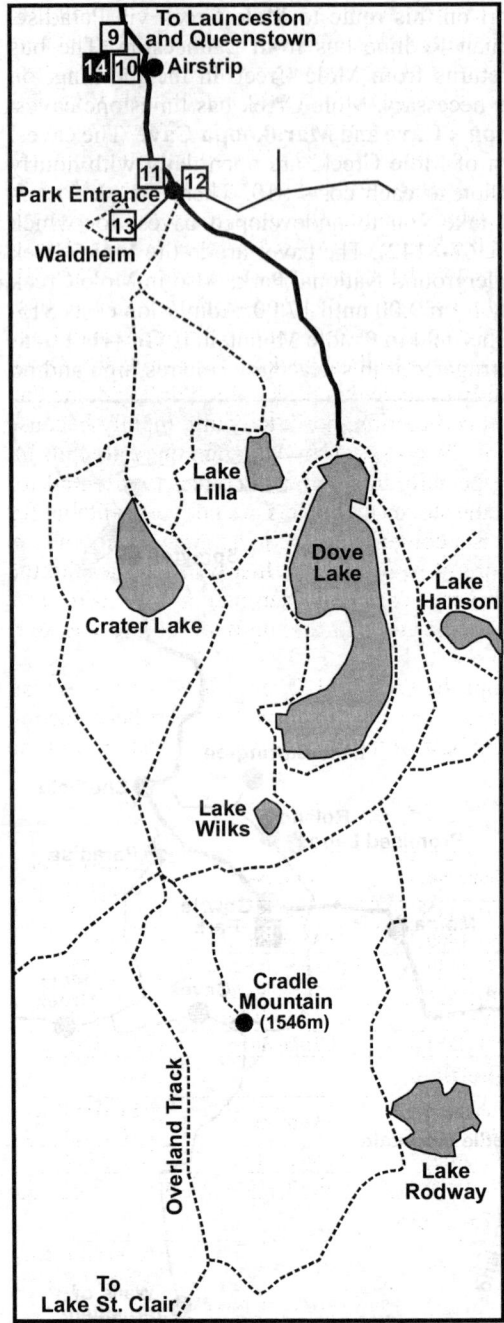

CRADLE MOUNTAIN
Black numerals indicate hotel accommodation
White numerals indicate backpackers hostels

the Walls of Jerusalem from Launceston and will sometimes take passengers for the single or return journey, without the tour.

Next is a road on the right continuing the biblical theme by leading to the **Promised Land**, and, beyond that, to **Roland**. Promised Land is the site of *Tasmazia*, where two people have constructed seven mazes, including what they claim to have been the largest botanical maze in the world when planted, and also a copy of the Hampton Court Maze. Here too is the **Lake Barrington Lavender Farm**, with a range of lavender products, a famous Pancake Parlour, the Honey Boutique, offering various flavours of natural, fruit and liqueur honey, and the miniature village of **Lower Crackpot**. Again, although tours visit here, there is no public transport.

The road crosses the **Forth River**, with **Cethana Dam** visible on the left. A road leads off here to **Cethana Lake**, created by the dam, and to **Wilmot Power Station**. We soon pass **Moina** and then start a series of undulations across some sad countryside, once forested but now with only stumps and scattered growth. This area was logged a century ago and has never recovered. Since then several bush fires have swept through and prevented any substantial regeneration. Logs not thought worth transporting can be seen lying amidst the blackened stumps.

We come to the access road to the **Cradle Mountain - Lake St. Clair National Park** and turn left. From here it is some fifteen kilometres to the National Park entrance. The TassieLink buses always deviate to the park, summer and winter, and in summer three of the seven services each week terminate here. On the days

CRADLE MOUNTAIN

when they continue, they take a meal break at this scenic location. Right at the entrance to the park is the youth hostel and there is higher class accommodation beyond. There is a local bus service to take walkers to the start of the walking tracks, close to beautiful **Dove Lake**, which is eight kilometres further on, and shorter walks start from just inside the park entrance.

The Cradle Mountain - Lake St. Clair National Park is often considered to be the brainchild of Austrian naturalist **Gustav Weindorfer**, whose name you will see in many places, including titles of restaurants and accommodation. He came here with his wife, fell in love with the place, and built *Waldheim Chalet* as his home in 1911. Sadly, his wife died in 1916, but he continued to live here until his own death in 1932. His chalet was used as a guesthouse until 1975 and has now been restored for further use.

The famous **Overland Track** covers a distance of 85 kilometres from here to Lake St. Clair and takes at least five days. It passes the highest peak in Tasmania, **Mt. Ossa**, at 1,617 metres, and one can deviate slightly to scale this peak, which will add one day to the walk. Nearly everybody walks in this direction, north to south, mainly because it is downhill this way, although it may not always seem so. Although there are huts all along the way, they are often crowded, especially in summer, so a tent is essential for this trip. No camp fires are permitted and the stoves in the huts are not very suitable for cooking. Although this is a great walk, it is a congested route in summer, so if you can find some other time for it you might enjoy it even more. When walking, despite the congestion, bear in mind that walkers die every year in this National Park, so take care, especially if leaving the main route. Remember to sign the log book before you start and when you complete the walk.

It is not, of course, essential to attempt the Overland Track just because you visit Cradle Mountain. There are plenty of other very rewarding walks from here, lasting from two hours to a whole day. One of the best of the shorter walks is that around the shores of the very pretty Dove Lake.

ACCOMMODATION
(i) Hotel Accommodation in Sheffield

Name	Stars	No. on Map	Telephone No.	Address	Lowest Price (Double/Twin)
Acacia Bed and Breakfast	4	1	03-6491-2482	113 High Street	$80
Sheffield Country Inn		5	03-6491-1800	51 Main Street	$75
Sheffield Pioneer Units		6	03-6491-1149	3 Pioneer Crescent	$75
Roland Rock Motel		4	03-6491-1821	47 Main Street	$50
Sheffield Hotel		3	03-6491-1130	38 Main Street	$50
Sheffield Caravan Park		2	03-6491-2364	70 High Street	$30

(ii) Backpackers Hostels in and near Sheffield

Name	Group	No. on Map	Telephone No.	Address	Lowest Price (Dormitory)
Sheffield Backpackers		7	03-6491-2611	82 Main Street	$17
Mt. Roland Backpackers		8	03-6491-1385	1447 Claude Rd., Gowrie Park	$12

(iii) Hotel Accommodation at Cradle Mountain

Name	Stars	No. on Map	Telephone No.	Address	Lowest Price (Double/Twin)
Cradle Mountain Lodge		11	1-800-737-678	Cradle Mountain Nat. Park	$245
Wilderness Lodge		12	03-6492-1018	Cradle Mountain Road	$180
Cradle Mt. Highlanders		9	03-6492-1116	3876 Cradle Mountain Road	$110
Cradle Mountain Park	4	10	1-800-068-574	3832 Cradle Mountain Road	$85
Waldheim Cabins		13	03-6492-1110	Cradle Mountain Nat. Park	$65

932 TASMANIA
(iv) Backpackers Hostel at Cradle Mountain

Name	Group	No. on Map	Telephone No.	Address	Lowest Price (Dormitory)
Cradle Mountain B/P	YHA	14	03-6492-1395	Cradle Mountain Road	$24

MOVING ON
Bus Services from Cradle Mountain

Destination	Operator	Via	Distance (km)	Fare	Journey Time	Frequency
Hobart	TassieLink		408	$72.70	7¾ hrs	2/week
		Lake St. Clair	229	$47.30	4¾ hrs	2/week
		Strahan*	177	$31	3¼ - 4½ hrs	3 - 4/week
		Queenstown	140	$24	2¼ - 3 hrs	3 - 4/week
Launceston	TassieLink		190	$48.60	3 - 3½ hrs	3 - 7/week
		Devonport	90	$31	1½ - 1¾ hrs	3 - 7/week

* Connecting service. Change of bus involved.

LAKE ST. CLAIR
Population 150 (Lake St. Clair and Derwent Bridge)
3 hrs 30 mins by bus from Hobart

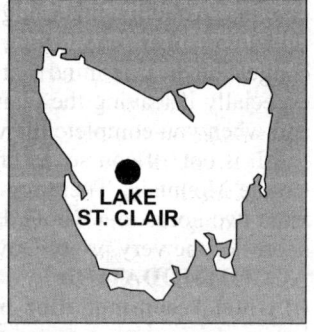

The southern end of the Overland Track is at Lake St. Clair, Australia's deepest freshwater lake, at 190 metres, and another beautiful spot, generally cool even in the middle of summer. TassieLink operates a bus from Hobart on four days a week in winter (on two of the days, only to **Derwent Bridge**, five kilometres distant) and every day in summer. From Launceston, TassieLink operates on two days a week in winter and six days a week in summer. There are two different routes from Launceston. The summer-only route, used on four days a week, travels via **Miena**. The roads are not as good but the route is much shorter than via Cradle Mountain and Queenstown, so that the journey is completed in a mere three hours, instead of nearly nine.

The more likely approach to Lake St. Clair is from Hobart, so let us proceed by that route, known, somewhat dramatically, as the *Wild Way*. From **New Norfolk**, the road follows the **Derwent River** through **Gretna** to **Hamilton**, an untouristed but interesting convict-built town. Settlement dates from about 1815, although the oldest remaining buildings are from around 1830. **St. Peter's Anglican Church** was constructed in 1834, at which time it was in the diocese of Calcutta, a long way for the bishop to come. **Blanch's Store** was built at some time between 1820 and 1840 and has been a butcher's and baker's for most of that time. It is in the main street, and still trades as a bakery.

Ouse is fourteen kilometres further on, and marks the end of settled land. From here you will see no place of any size before reaching Lake St. Clair. The original road swung east from here and went through **Osterley** and **Bronte**, but when the area was the location for some of the first hydro-electric schemes, the sealed route naturally went via the dams and power stations, leaving the eastern way as a secondary unsealed road. Ouse is fringed by mountains, a small town in a pretty setting.

The first sign of the hydro-electric industry is the rows of power pylons striding across the valley. A road leads off on the left to **Repulse Da**m, seven kilometres distant, then another to **Wayatinah Power Station**. We cross the **Nive River** for the first time and pass the turn-off to **Wayatinah Village** on the left. On our right we follow a **canal**, part of the hydro-electric scheme, for a while and then cross it. Then, 33 kilometres from Ouse, we plunge down a steep descent and there, impressively, at the bottom, are the twin power stations of **Tarraleah** on this side of the Nive River, and **Tungatinah**, on the far

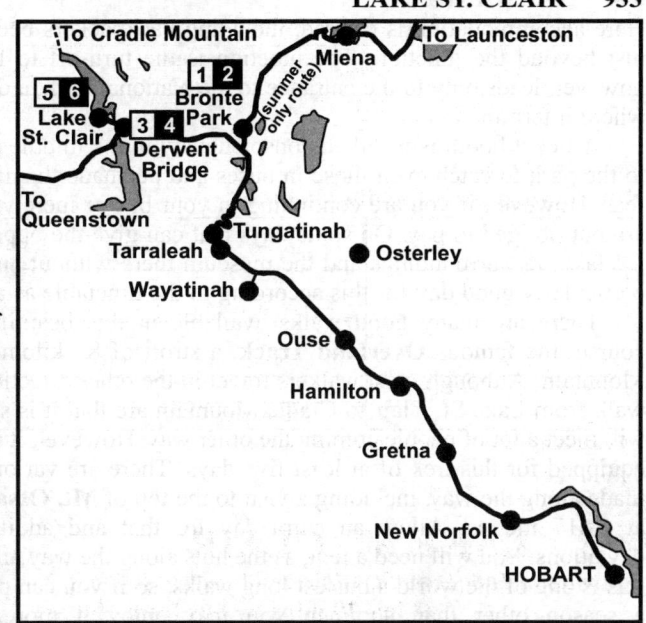

FROM HOBART TO LAKE ST. CLAIR
Showing TassieLink bus routes
Black numerals in white boxes indicate hotel accommodation
White numerals in black boxes indicate backpackers hostels

side, with a very sharp bend to mark the river crossing. These two hydro-electric power stations are of different generations, to use an apt term. The first three of the six generators at Tarraleah date from 1938, while the five generators at Tungatinah were not commissioned until 1953 to 1956. As for the generations, Tarraleah has a maximum output of 90MW, while Tungatinah can produce 125MW.

The **Liapootah Dam** is off to the right here, while to the left are **Tungatinah Resort** and **Tungatinah Lagoon**, as we climb out of the river bed along a twisting narrow road offering some excellent views. Not only does the terrain impress here, but so also does the scale of this seventy-year-old scheme to harness the power of water in such idyllic but remote and uncompromising surroundings.

Lake Binney is on the right now, followed by **Brady's Lake** immediately adjacent to the road. A side road leads off to where a championship canoe course has been constructed on Brady's Lake. **Waddamana Power Station Museum** is on the right, followed by **Bronte Lagoon** on the left.

The last road on the right for a long way goes to **Bronte Park** and, if followed far enough, eventually provides an alternative route to Launceston. This is the road followed by the summer-only TassieLink service between Launceston and Lake St. Clair. Four kilometres along the road is the settlement of Bronte Park which was originally quarters for the construction workers for the hydro-electric scheme. It now offers accommodation for those passing by, including backpackers' beds in the former hospital, and is a pleasant place to stay.

For the third and last time, we cross the Nive River and a road goes off to the left to **Laughing Jack Lagoon**. Another twenty kilometres and we are at **Derwent Bridge**.

Here accommodation is offered, including backpackers beds at the Wilderness Hotel just beyond the junction. The junction is the turn-off to Lake St. Clair. This road, however, leads only to the entrance to the National Park, a distance of five kilometres, where it terminates.

A ticket booth is installed conspicuously in the middle of the road at the entrance to the park to catch even those in buses and persuade them to pay their park entrance fees. However, if you are continuing in your bus or merely changing buses here, you are not obliged to pay. On some days that can give the opportunity to look quickly at the lake, its surroundings and the museum there without any charge. Wednesday is a particularly good day for this according to the timetable as at the time of writing.

There are many good walks available in this beautiful location, including, of course, the famous **Overland Track**, a stroll of 85 kilometres from here to Cradle Mountain. Although most walkers travel in the other direction, the only reasons not to walk from Lake St. Clair to Cradle Mountain are that it is slightly uphill and that you will meet a lot of people coming the other way. However, it is necessary to be properly equipped for this trek of at least five days. There are various side trips which can be made along the way, including a visit to the top of **Mt. Ossa**, Tasmania's highest peak at 1,617 metres. Allow an extra day for that and additional time for any other deviations. You will need a tent, as the huts along the way are usually crowded. In fact, this is one of the world's busiest long walks, so if you can possibly manage to do it in a season other than summer, you may enjoy it more, despite the consequent deterioration in weather conditions. There are plenty of other walks here as well, of course, starting with half-hour strolls along the shore of the lake. There is a ferry service from this point at **Cynthia Bay** to the northern end of the lake, which is generally used by walkers to start or finish the Overland Track, but you can also use this service for a shorter expedition, walking one way round the shore of the lake and catching the ferry back or *vice versa*. This claims to be Australia's highest altitude ferry, incidentally. If all this is too much, you can just sit in the café enjoying a cup of tea and gaze across the lake at the magnificent view, beautiful whether **Mt. Olympus** (1,447 metres) is visible or whether the whole area is shrouded in mist, as it often is.

The **Park Centre** has information available, detailed (and essential) maps of the walks for sale and an interesting museum showing the geological formations, the history of the area, the wildlife to be found and the efforts being made to ensure conservation of nature in all its forms. Accommodation is also available here, including that for backpackers, of course. A dormitory bed costs $28 without bedding, or $33 with bedding.

ACCOMMODATION
(i) Hotel Accommodation in Bronte Park

Name	Stars	No. on Map	Telephone No.	Address	Lowest Price (Double/Twin)
Highland Village		1	03-6289-1126	378 Marlborough Highway	$90

(ii) Backpackers Hostel in Bronte Park

Name	Group	No. on Map	Telephone No.	Address	Lowest Price (Dormitory)
Highland Village		2	03-6289-1126	378 Marlborough Highway	$22

LAKE ST. CLAIR

(iii) Hotel Accommodation in Derwent Bridge

Name	Stars	No. on Map	Telephone No.	Address	Lowest Price (Double/Twin)
Derwent Bridge Chalets		3	03-6289-1000	Lyell Highway	$145
Wilderness Hotel		3	03-6289-1144	Lyell Highway	$95

(iv) Backpackers Hostel in Derwent Bridge

Name	Group	No. on Map	Telephone No.	Address	Lowest Price (Dormitory)
Wilderness Hotel		4	03-6289-1144	Lyell Highway	$26

(v) Hotel Accommodation in Lake St. Clair

Name	Stars	No. on Map	Telephone No.	Address	Lowest Price (Double/Twin)
Lakeside St. Clair	3½	5	03-6289-1137	Lake St. Clair	$150

(vi) Backpackers Hostel in Lake St. Clair

Name	Group	No. on Map	Telephone No.	Address	Lowest Price (Dormitory)
Lakeside St. Clair		6	03-6289-1137	Lake St. Clair	$28

MOVING ON

The range of frequencies for the bus routes summarised below represents the differences between winter and summer services. Note that TassieLink offers special fares for those walking the Overland Track, as follows:

Hobart - Lake St. Clair + Cradle Mountain - Hobart $99
Hobart - Lake St. Clair + Cradle Mountain - Launceston $80
Launceston - Lake St. Clair + Cradle Mountain - Launceston $109

Similar fares apply in the reverse direction, and there are also some special fares to and from Devonport.

Bus Services from Lake St. Clair

Destination	Operator	Via	Distance (kms)	Fare	Journey Time	Frequency
Hobart	TassieLink		179	$39.50	2¾ - 3 hrs	4 - 7/week
Launceston	TassieLink		184 / 419	$82	3 - 7¾ hrs	2 - 6/week
		Devonport	319	$64.40	6 hrs	2/week
		Cradle Mountain	229	$47.30	4¼ hrs	2/week
		Strahan*	126	$31.30	2½ - 5hrs	4 - 5/week
		Queenstown	89	$24.30	1¾ - 2 hrs	4 - 5/week

* Connecting service. Change of bus involved.

QUEENSTOWN
Population 3,500
5 hrs by bus from Hobart

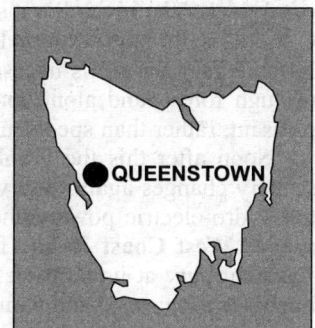

Queenstown is an enigma. You will probably be shocked at seeing it for the first time and think that this is how the end of the earth must look, and then gradually grow to like and appreciate the place.

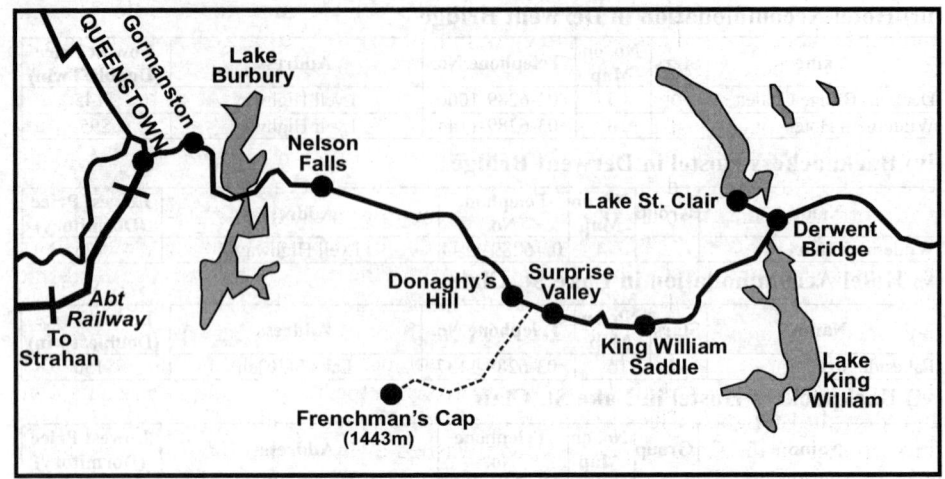

FROM LAKE ST. CLAIR TO QUEENSTOWN
Showing TassieLink bus routes

TassieLink operates bus services to Queenstown from both Hobart and Launceston, and on two days a week, currently Tuesdays and Thursdays, runs a service right through between those two cities via Queenstown.

Let us look first at the approach from Lake St. Clair. Soon after we depart from Derwent Bridge, the landscape starts to become more rugged. We enter the **Western Tasmanian World Heritage Area**, characterised by steep quartzite mountains, fast-flowing rivers and open buttongrass plains. The **Franklin - Gordon Wild Rivers National Park** stretches for 56 kilometres along the highway from a point west of Derwent Bridge. We climb gradually up to the **King William Saddle**, which has a lookout at its highest point. Then a descent to the **Surprise Valley** and the crossing of the **Franklin River**. At this point a **Nature Trail** leads off to the left. We travel a little further and another track leads off on the left to **Frenchman's Cap**. TassieLink offers a special return fare of $70 to this point from Hobart for those wishing to try this quite strenuous walk. Soon after this, we see Frenchman's Cap from the road. The reason for the name is immediately apparent, for the summit of the mountain appears like a French beret at a jaunty angle. Frenchman's Cap rises to an altitude of 1,443 metres and is one of the highest peaks in Tasmania. **Donaghy's Hill** offers another lookout. However, this one is not beside the road, but entails a forty-minute return walk along a good track. The reward is a splendid view over the National Park, with Frenchman's Cap dominating the scenery. It is another twenty minutes or so before we reach **Nelson Falls**. Again a walk is necessary to see them, this time about twenty minutes return through forest land along another good track to the right of the road. The falls are pleasant, rather than spectacular.

Soon after this the Franklin - Gordon Wild Rivers National Park ends and the scenery changes again. In a valley, we reach **Lake Burbury**, another lake formed by the hydro-electric power schemes, and the road swings left, skirting its shores. The rugged **West Coast Range** forms its backdrop. Then we swing right again to cross Lake Burbury at its narrowest point over **Bradshaw Bridge**. You will notice all the **beehives** in this area and wonder how so many bees can find sustenance. Now we start to climb again, up through **Linda Valley** until we reach **Gormanston Saddle**. There is another lookout here and another fine view, but, of course, the bus will not stop for you to admire it. There is also a road leading off on the right to the **Iron Blow Open Cut Mine**, where the first copper find here was made, and to more fine views back over the road which we have just travelled. There used to be a town at **Linda**, in the valley through which we have just passed, but it is now a ghost town, with no residents at all. The last hotel here closed in 1952 and now just a few ruins can be seen. In 1912 there was a fire in the underground mine at Linda, resulting in the deaths of 42 miners.

We round the corner and an amazing vista comes into sight. We see **Queenstown** down below and the spectacular winding descent to the town, but, most surprising and shocking of all, the total denudation of the surrounding hills. How could this have happened? The answer is fuel for the copper smelters. When copper was discovered in the area, wood was needed principally as fuel, not just for domestic needs, but to smelt the copper and reduce its bulk for shipment. Trees on the steep hillsides were cut down and soon all were gone. The sulphurous fumes killed any remaining vegetation and the thin top soil on the steep slopes was soon washed away, so that the trees were never able to regenerate. The residents of Queenstown grew used to their barren lunar landscape and even came to like its uniqueness. However, in recent years attempts have been made to restore some vegetation to the slopes and patches of green are gradually reappearing now. We negotiate the tight and dangerous turns of this section of mountain road which offers some spectacular views as we twist our way down - and here we are in Queenstown at last, after one of the most interesting journeys in Tasmania.

There is, of course, the alternative route of approach from the north, so let us look now at the journey from Cradle Mountain to Queenstown, which is also scenic. Leaving Cradle Mountain, the bus has first to return to the main highway, where it turns left. Soon after this we reach the highest point on the route from Launceston to Queenstown, at an altitude of 930 metres. There are good views, but they are mostly to our rear. We come to a major junction, and this is where we join the road from Burnie, to our right. After crossing the **Que River**, we reach a marker showing that we are at the highest point on the Burnie to Queenstown road, considerably lower than

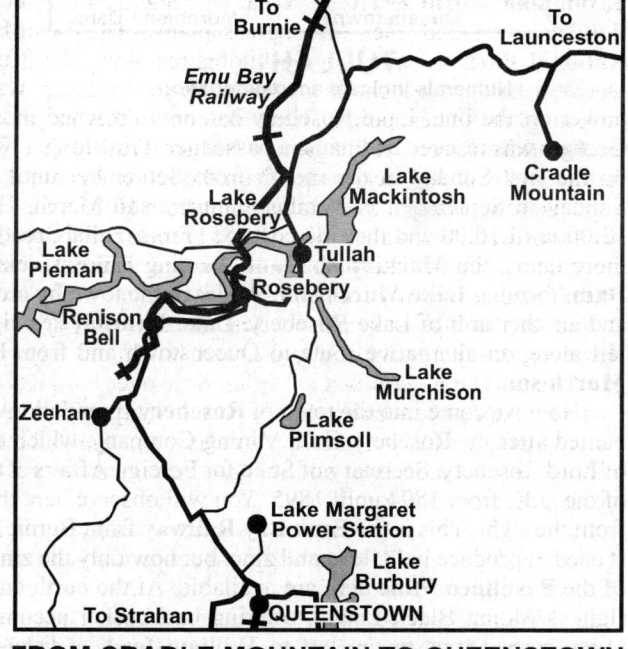

FROM CRADLE MOUNTAIN TO QUEENSTOWN
Showing TassieLink bus routes (thicker lines)

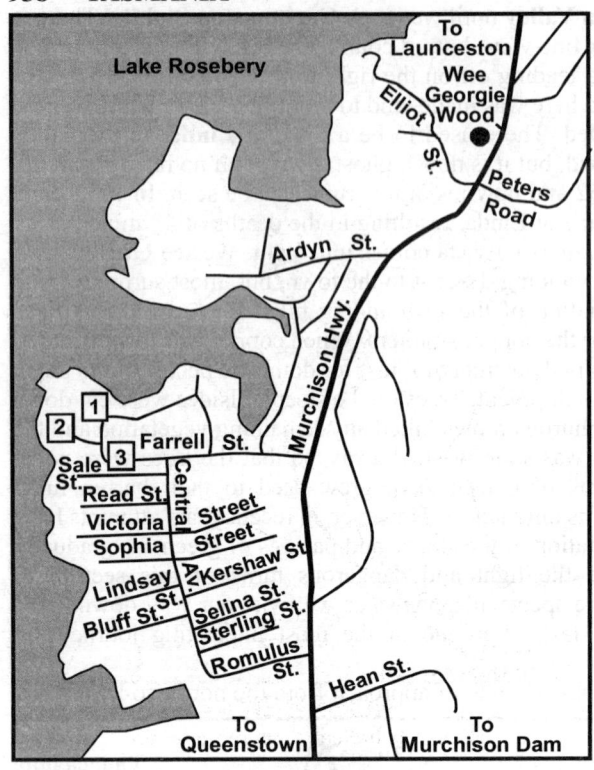

TULLAH
Numerals indicate accommodation

that which we have just passed, at only 690 metres. On the right there is now a road off to the **Reece Dam** on the **Pieman River**, the dam being 55 kilometres away. We cross an arm of **Lake Rosebery**, which is also part of the Pieman River, this lake being created not by the Reece Dam, which forms **Lake Pieman**, but by the next dam upstream, the **Bastyan Dam**.

Here is the small town of **Tullah**. It is the home of **Wee Georgie Wood**, a two-foot gauge steam locomotive which used to operate on the **Farrell Tramway** built in 1909 between Tullah and Farrell Siding on the Emu Bay Railway, a distance of 9.6 kilometres. Between 1921, when the engine was built, and 1962, when the new Murchison Highway reached Tullah, Wee Georgie Wood was the principal motive power on the line. Lake Rosebery has now drowned most of the tramway, but Wee Georgie was rescued and hauls a passenger train along a two-kilometre stretch of track on the first Sunday in the month from September until April, and also on the last Sunday in September, November, January and March. Hours of operation are from 12:00 until 16:00 and the ride costs $5. From Tullah, roads lead off on the left to two more dams, the **Mackintosh Dam**, forming **Lake Mackintosh**, and the **Murchison Dam**, forming **Lake Murchison**. We leave the town by crossing the **Murchison River** and another arm of Lake Rosebery. **Lake Plimsoll** lies eighteen kilometres off to the left along an alternative route to Queenstown and from here there are views of **Mt. Murchison**.

Now we come into the town of **Rosebery** (population 1,600), founded in 1893 and named after the Rosebery Gold Mining Company, which took its own name from that of Lord Rosebery, Secretary of State for Foreign Affairs at the time, and Prime Minister of the U.K. from 1894 until 1895. You will observe here the railway rejoining the road from the right. This is the **Emu Bay Railway** from Burnie. Rosebery is a mining town. It used to produce gold, lead and zinc, but now only the zinc operation continues. Tours of the **Pasminco Mine** here are available. At the north end of the town and off to the right is Mount Black Lodge, offering backpacker accommodation. As we leave the town, a road runs to the left to **Williamsford**, a distance of six kilometres. From Williamsford a three-hour return walk, five kilometres each way along an abandoned tramway, will lead to **Montezuma Falls**, the highest waterfall in Tasmania at 104 metres.

We continue south and pass the conspicuous **Renison Bell Mine**, producing tin, with an historic walking route on the right. This mine is the chief client of the Emu Bay Railway these days and the line peters out a little further on. Notice the pylons of an abandoned cableway crossing the road. The cableway was formerly used for transporting ore.

We reach **Zeehan**, another interesting town (map overleaf). Founded in 1882, it was named after the brig of Abel Tasman. Silver was discovered here and the town once had a population of 10,000, its own stock exchange and 24 hotels. Almost all is gone now, and there are only hints of former grandeur. Here you will find the **West Coast Pioneers Memorial Museum**. The west coast of Tasmania has proven to contain a host of rich mineral deposits, including gold, silver, copper, tin, lead, zinc, tungsten, iron ore and osmiridium, so its recent history has been one of prospecting, pioneering and mining. The styles of architecture reflect this, especially in towns such as Zeehan where the mining has ceased and only a trickle of tourists ensures survival. The Museum has a fascinating collection of mining objects and of photographs of this town at the peak of its prosperity. Outside the museum is a display of engines and carriages which used to operate on the Emu Bay Railway and connected tramways. The line originally ran through to Zeehan and connected with a government line on to Strahan, from where some of the ore was shipped. Now the Emu Bay Railway does not quite reach Zeehan, and the government line is long gone, so Zeehan has no railway at all. Some of the TassieLink bus services pause here for lunch. If your service does so, you have enough time to look at least at this exterior display at the museum. The railway collection is free. To go inside the museum costs $6, opening hours being from 8:30 until 18:00 (17:00 in winter).

From Zeehan to Queenstown takes a further forty minutes. As we approach the town, we see those famous denuded hills and know that arrival is imminent. Just before the town, a road leads off to the left to the **Lake Margaret Hydro-Electric Power Station**. This power station started to produce electricity in 1914 and is the second-oldest commercial hydro-electric power plant in operation in Australia. Much of the equipment used is original and has been in service since that time.

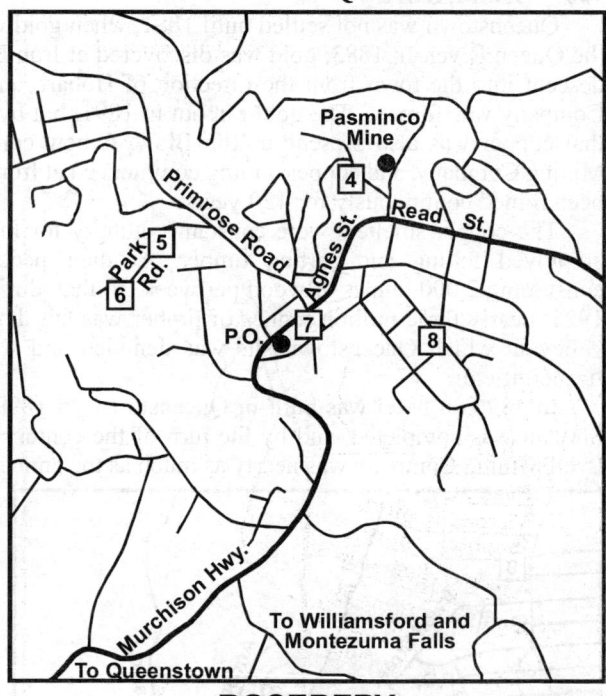

ROSEBERY
Numerals indicate accommodation

Queenstown was not settled until 1881, when gold was discovered in a creek near the Queen River. In 1883, gold was discovered at Iron Blow, which we passed on our descent into the town from the direction of Hobart, and the Mt. Lyell Gold Mining Company was formed. The gold ran out in 1891, but by that time it had been realised that copper was also present at Iron Blow. A new company was formed, Mt. Lyell Mining Company, and copper mining commenced at Iron Blow. Thus that area has now been mined continuously for 120 years.

The copper smelters were constantly hungry for fuel and hundreds of men were employed felling and carting timber. At their peak, the copper smelters were consuming 2,000 tonnes of wood per week, so that, during the thirty year period up to 1925, nearly three million tonnes of timber was cut down in total. Even by 1900 the valley in which Queenstown sits was denuded and wood was being brought from further afield.

In 1896 an hotel was built in Queenstown. In 1899 the railway from the port of Strahan was completed, and by the turn of the century the yearly income of the Mt. Lyell Mining Company was nearly as much as the annual budget of the Government of Tasmania. In one year it actually exceeded it. The Empire Hotel was built in 1901 and still stands on the main corner in the centre of the town, a splendid old pioneering building, in which the visitor can stay for a very modest sum, absorbing the history of building and town. The first hydro-electric scheme was completed at Lake Margaret in 1914, so that the town could have a reliable and cheap electric supply. A major refinery was built here in 1928, and then, finally, in 1932, the first road link with Hobart was established.

The history of the Mt. Lyell Mining Company is tied up closely with the story of one man, that man being **Robert Sticht**. He was an American, born of an immigrant family in New Jersey. He gained worldwide recognition for his innovations connected with smelting and was consulted by the mining company in

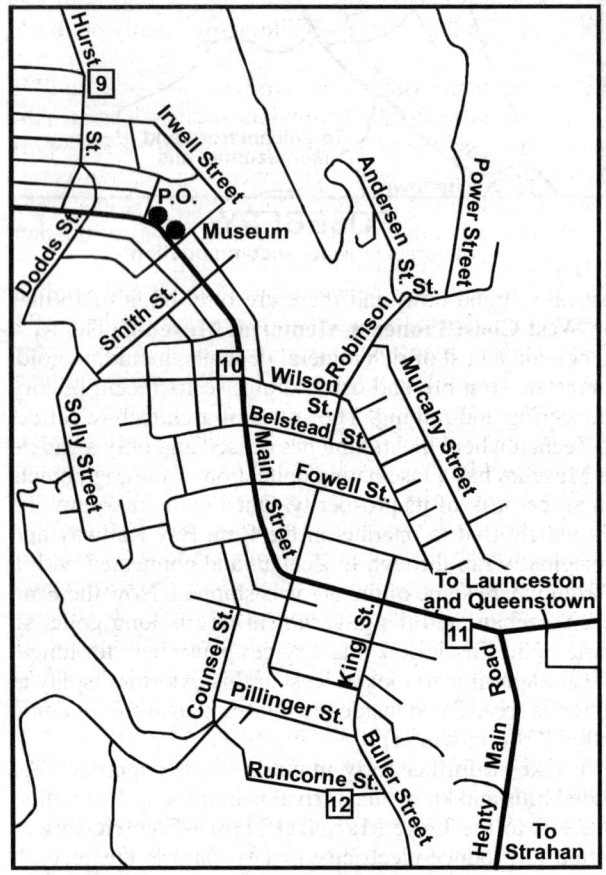

ZEEHAN
Numerals indicate accommodation

relation to some rock samples. Because of the good impression which he created, he was invited to come and establish the smelters here. He accepted, arriving in 1895 and staying for the rest of his life, until he died of cancer in 1922. He earned the respect of the men by working with them on the construction of the first smelters, and he was promoted to General Manager in 1897. For the next twenty-five years, he virtually controlled all operations here. He also invented a new smelting process which used pyrites and eliminated the need for coke, saving a large amount of money for the company and obtaining international recognition, although the disadvantage was the emission of the sulphurous fumes which have destroyed the vegetation around Queenstown. You will find the name Sticht in many places about the town. His influence is still felt more than eighty years after his death.

Today the mining operation is owned by Copper Mines of Tasmania and there is a constant threat of closure. As yet, though, that threat has not become reality and the mining continues.

The prime attraction now of Queenstown is the **Abt Railway**. This is the railway which was constructed in 1896 to connect Queenstown with the port of Strahan and which has recently been restored and re-opened in stages, starting in 2000 with the Queenstown to **Lynchford** section, and with the entire 34.3 kilometres finally put back into service in 2002.

The impression is sometimes given that 'Abt' is an acronym, and one finds it written in capital letters, presumably because of that misunderstanding. Roman Abt was, in fact, the Swiss engineer who invented the rack and pinion system used to pull locomotives up steep gradients when their wheels would otherwise slip on the smooth tracks. It works very well on mountain railways and this was one of the few examples of the system employed in Australia. The only other Australian Abt Railway of the day was that at Mt. Morgan in Queensland, which operated from 1898 until 1952.

The terrain which the railway had to negotiate between Queenstown and Strahan was very difficult. It had to travel through dense forest with a maximum gradient of 1 in 16, and another of 1 in 20. Nevertheless, the railway was completed in two years, although at first the line went only to **Teepookana**, on the **King River**, the farthest point which could be reached by vessels of any size, a distance of 22.4 kilometres from Queenstown. The first train arrived in Queenstown on 18th July 1896, but actually the line was not opened officially until 18th March 1897. It was extended the remaining twelve kilometres to Strahan in 1899, until which time Teepookana was the fourth busiest port in Tasmania, and after which it became a ghost town. The railway remained in use until 1963 and then it was decided that its maintenance was too great a burden and that it would be cheaper to send the copper by truck along the narrow and dangerous road to Strahan. The greatest problem was the upkeep of the forty bridges, especially the two across the King River. The last passenger train ran on 29th June 1963 and the last goods train ran on 10th August 1963. Most of the track was immediately torn up and parts of the railway converted to roads. The remainder was abandoned to nature, which made a good job of the take-over during the following 35 years. After a while Strahan was closed as a port and the copper sent by truck to the Emu Bay Railway north of Zeehan, as it still is.

Recently, as tourism to Queenstown, and particularly to Strahan, increased, a proposal was made to reclaim the railway from the dense bush and operate it as a tourist attraction, and this has been achieved, the line now being known as the **Abt Wilderness Railway**. However, this restoration has been different in nature from many

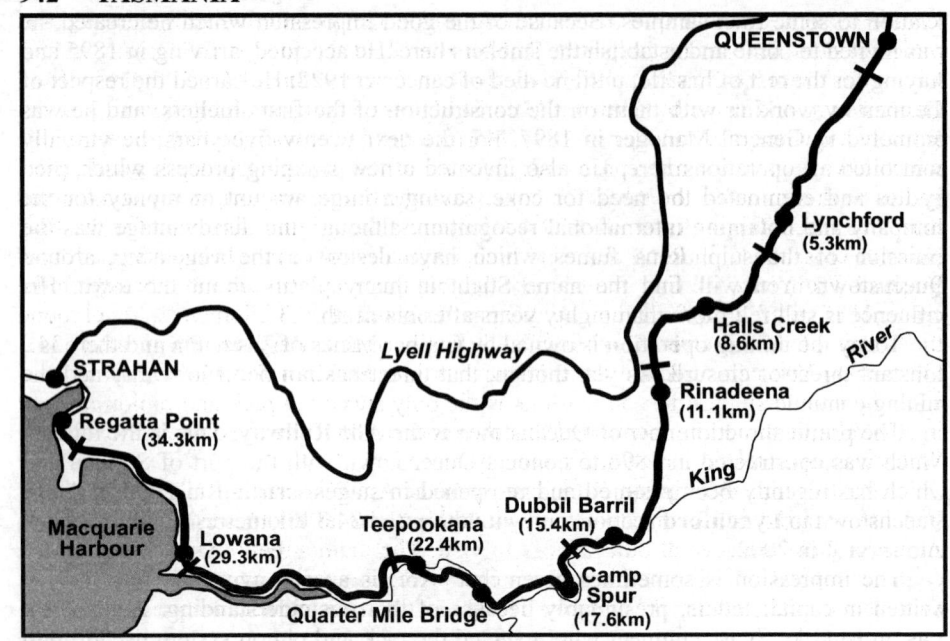

ABT WILDERNESS RAILWAY
FROM QUEENSTOWN TO STRAHAN
Showing distances from Queenstown

other recent restorations of railways. This one has not been carried out by a volunteer group for the delight of seeing old machinery in action and history recaptured. This is a commercial venture. According to reports, the Tasmanian Government has invested $20.4 million in this project and hopes to get most of it back in one way or another. It is not a project which has been carried out on the cheap in any sense. Those operating the railway are paid for their services and the railway charges its passengers accordingly. As the reader must have realised by now, the author has a great liking for railways, but even he cannot help wondering whether there might have been a better use for a spare $20.4 million.

However, if you can afford the return fare of $89 from Queenstown to **Regatta Point**, the port area three kilometres east of the main settlement of Strahan, you will be able to travel this almost unique Australian rack and pinion railway. Trains operate twice a day at present. The locomotives used are two of the original five steam engines built for this line. One was formerly on display near the station in Queenstown, just awaiting its opportunity to be put back into service, while the other was housed in the museum in Zeehan. The journey to Regatta Point takes approximately ninety minutes each way. From Queenstown, it starts along a relatively flat section beside a road to **Lynchford**, 5.3 kilometres from Queenstown. We leave the road as we turn slightly west to **Halls Creek**, which is 8.6 kilometres from Queenstown. Now the climb begins. This is the steepest section on the whole line, with a gradient of 1 in 16 for 2.5 kilometres up to **Rinadeena**, which is 11.1 kilometres from Queenstown and the only point along the route where we are close to the Lyell Highway leading to Strahan. This is the summit of the line at 230 metres. Now follows a steep descent lasting for 4.3

kilometres at a gradient of 1 in 20, during which the locomotive uses the rack and pinion system for braking purposes. **Dubbil Barril**, at the foot of the incline, is 15.4 kilometres from Queenstown. We pass through **Camp Spur**, 17.6 kilometres from Queenstown, and come to **Quarter Mile Bridge** traversing the King River. It is not actually a quarter of a mile long - only 244 metres - but it was the feature of the line which always gave the most problems. Because of the unexpected depth of silt, piles had to be driven down to eighteen metres when the bridge was originally constructed here. We reach **Teepookana** after 22.4 kilometres, the original terminus for the line. Now we cross the King River a second time, originally on an iron bridge shipped from England. From here the line is relatively flat, but there are still ten more bridges to be crossed before the end of our journey. We pass **Lowana** at 29.3 kilometres, travel round the shore of **Macquarie Harbour**, and finally reach **Regatta Point** after 34.3 kilometres. You can walk the three kilometres into **Strahan** from here. Just in case anybody should suggest to you that this is the only surviving rack and pinion railway in Australia, it should be mentioned that the modern Ski Tube in southern New South Wales also operates on a rack and pinion system.

After this long description of the history of the Abt Wilderness Railway, the reader will have started to assume that there is nothing else at all to see in Queenstown. Actually, there are several other places to visit. The main street is **Orr Street**, and it contains several buildings typical of an old pioneering town, but that with the most character is undoubtedly the **Empire Hotel**, on the main corner almost opposite the railway station.

The **Eric Thomas Galley Museum** has nine hundred photographs of old Queenstown displayed in the 23 rooms of this building. There are also old furniture and curiosities from a similar period. The Museum is open daily from 10:00 (13:00 at weekends) until 17:00 and admission costs $5.

There is a **chairlift** on the northern edge of the town, providing a ride up to a good viewpoint for observation of the unusual and remarkable Queenstown landscape. It is also possible to walk up. The chairlift is constructed on the site of the former aerial ropeway which used to transport silica from the limestone quarry to the Mt. Lyell smelters. The service operates daily, weather permitting, and costs $10 return. Your accommodation may be able to provide you with a voucher offering a discount.

Of course, in a town like this, the one activity in which you should be able to participate is a **tour of the mine** - and so you can, provided that you have plenty of spare cash. The tour lasts two and a half hours and takes you underground to the working areas of the mine. It claims to be only the second tour in the world which does this in a mine actually in operation. One travels five kilometres down the main decline, to a depth of 250 metres. From here 7,000 tonnes of rock are removed every day and taken to the crushers to produce gold, silver and copper. Following the underground tour, a surface tour is provided. Tours are available on weekdays, but must be booked with *Lyell Tours*, located on the corner of the Empire Hotel. The main problem with these tours are that they are expensive, at $60 per person.

The Mt. Lyell Mining Company has its own exhibition of pictures, stories and tapes of Queenstown, entitled *Mining the Imagination*. It is open from 10:00 until 16:00, except on Mondays and Fridays, in the Company's General Office in Penghana Road, and admission costs $2.

At **Miners Siding**, opposite the Galley Museum, is a conspicuous monument to the miners of the area, telling a little of the history of the town.

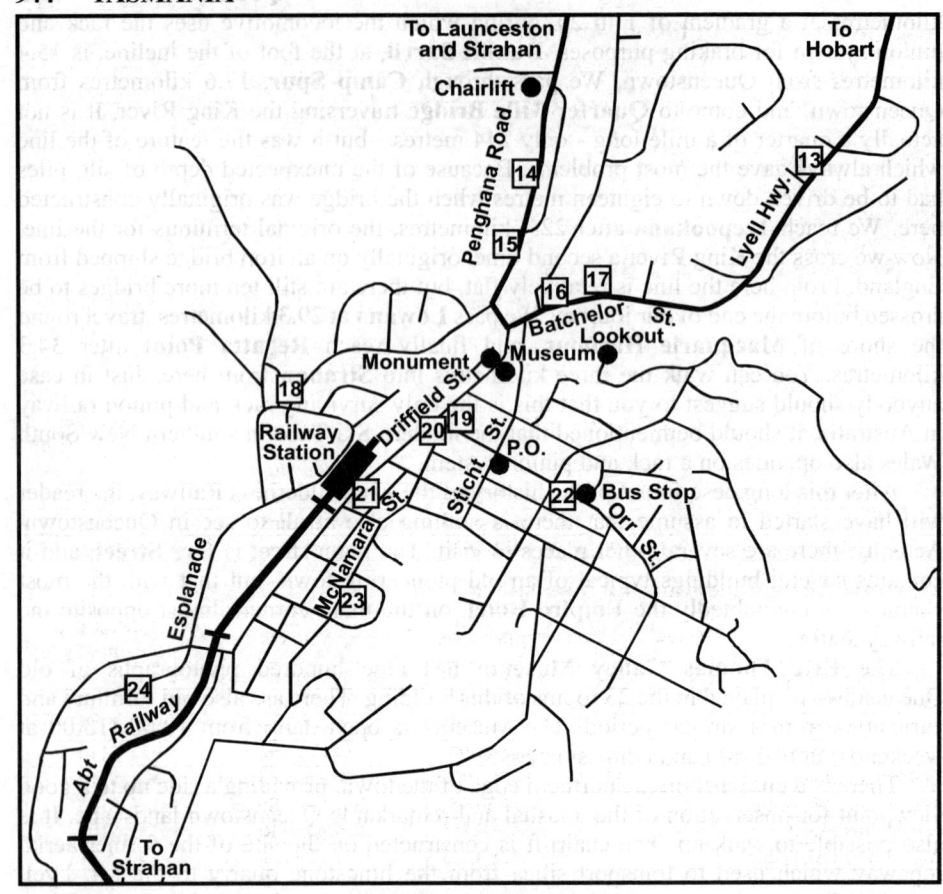

QUEENSTOWN
Numerals indicate accommodation

ACCOMMODATION
(i) Hotel Accommodation in Tullah

Name	Stars	No. on Map	Telephone No.	Address	Lowest Price (Double/Twin)
Tullah Lakeside Chalet	2½	1	03-6473-4121	Farrell Street	$100
Tullah Lakeside Cottage		2	03-6473-4165	6 Meredith Street	$80
Tullah Village B&B		3	03-6473-4377	Farrell Street	$60

(ii) Backpackers Hostel in Tullah

Name	Group	No. on Map	Telephone No.	Address	Lowest Price (Dormitory)
Tullah Lakeside Chalet		1	03-6473-4121	Farrell Street	$33

(iii) Hotel Accommodation in Rosebery

Name	Stars	No. on Map	Telephone No.	Address	Lowest Price (Double/Twin)
Miners' Cottages	3½	8	03-6473-1796	12 and 16 Karlson Street	$100
Miss Murchison		5	03-6473-1366	2 Park Road	$75
Rosebery Caravan Park	3½	6	03-6473-1366	Park Road	$70
Mount Black Lodge		4	03-6473-1039	Hospital Road	$65
Plandome Hotel		7	03-6473-1351	Agnes Street	$50

(iv) Backpackers Hostel in Rosebery

Name	Group	No. on Map	Telephone No.	Address	Lowest Price (Dormitory)
Mount Black Lodge	YHA	4	03-6473-1039	Hospital Road	$22

(v) Accommodation in Zeehan

Name	Stars	No. on Map	Telephone No.	Address	Lowest Price (Double/Twin)
Heemskirk Motor Hotel		11	03-6471-6107	Main Street	$100
Mt. Zeehan Retreat B&B		12	03-6471-6424	12 Runcorne Street	$90
Cecil Hotel		10	03-6471-6221	Main Street	$65
Treasure Island C'van Pk.	3	9	03-6471-6633	Hurst Street	$50

(vi) Hotel Accommodation in Queenstown

Name	Stars	No. on Map	Telephone No.	Address	Lowest Price (Double/Twin)
Comstock Cottage		23	03-6471-2154	45 McNamara Street	$150
Pioneers' Retreat	3½	16	1-800-064-977	1 Batchelor Street	$125
Penghana Guest House		18	03-6471-2560	32 The Esplanade	$125
Queenstown Motor Lodge	3	22	1-800-684-997	54 Orr Street	$110
Gold Rush Motel	3	13	03-6471-1005	63 Batchelor Street	$110
Westcoaster Motor Inn	3½	17	1-800-060-957	Batchelor Street	$105
Silver Hills Motel	3	14	03-6471-1755	Penghana Road	$100
Mountain View Lodge		15	03-6471-1163	1 Penghana Road	$75
Copper Country Cabins		24	0417-398-343	13 Austin Street	$70
Mt. Lyell Motor Inn	2½	19	03-6471-1888	1 Orr Street	$65
Commercial Hotel		21	03-6471-1511	39 Driffield Street	$40
Empire Hotel		20	03-6471-1699	2 Orr Street	$40

(vii) Backpackers Hostels in Queenstown

Name	Group	No. on Map	Telephone No.	Address	Lowest Price (Dormitory)
Empire Hotel		20	03-6471-1699	2 Orr Street	$22
Mountain View Lodge		15	03-6471-1163	1 Penghana Road	$16

MOVING ON
Bus Services from Queenstown

Destination	Operator	Via	Distance (km)	Fare	Journey Time	Frequency
Hobart	TassieLink		268	$49.70	4½ - 6¼ hrs	4 - 5/week
		Lake St. Clair	89	$24.30	2 hrs	4 - 5/week
Launceston	TassieLink		330	$58.70	5¾ - 6½ hrs	3 - 4/week
		Devonport	230	$41.10	4¼ - 5 hrs	3 - 4/week
		Cradle Mountain	140	$24	2½ hrs	3 - 4/week
Strahan			37	$8	45 mins	1/day

STRAHAN

Population 600

7 hrs by bus from Hobart

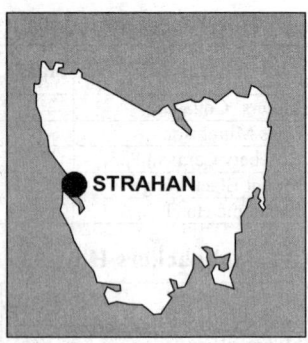

Strahan was founded in 1877 and later named after the Governor-General of Tasmania, Major George Strahan. It is 35 kilometres from Queenstown and the two towns have a history of inter-dependence and yet are totally different in character.

Strahan can be reached, very expensively, by the **Abt Wilderness Railway** ($69 single or $89 return from Queenstown), or it can be reached by bus from Queenstown for the more reasonable sum of $8. TassieLink operates one bus every day between the two towns. It is a winding road, following, in parts, the track used by miners seeking their fortunes in and around Queenstown.

The first Europeans to come here were probably James Kelly and four companions in 1815. They explored **Macquarie Harbour**, which is the only safe anchorage on the western coast of Tasmania, and which claims to be the second largest natural harbour in the southern hemisphere, after Sydney, although Boston Bay, near Port Lincoln in South Australia, would certainly contest that claim. They also discovered the **Gordon River** and Kelly named it after the man who had lent him the whale boat which he used for his explorations. Kelly took back reports of the fine stands of timber growing on the shores of the harbour and the following year wood-cutters started arriving to chop down the magnificent **Huon Pines** which grow naturally only in Tasmania.

In 1822, the area became famous for the establishment of the penal settlement on **Sarah Island**, at the most distant point of the harbour from Strahan, to the south-east. This was not just an ordinary penal settlement. It was for those who had been transported to Australia and had committed offences, been gaoled, and then offended again. These were really the most hardened of convicts, for whom reform seemed impossible, and conditions on Sarah Island were as harsh as was deemed appropriate for such men. Their work here was mining a coal seam and cutting down the trees which surrounded the harbour. The settlement was closed in 1833 and the convicts all moved to Port Arthur.

In 1890 the government railway from Zeehan to Strahan was completed, enabling goods to be moved to and from the booming mining town through the port of Strahan. In 1899, the railway from Queenstown arrived here too, and Strahan became, briefly, the second busiest port in Tasmania and the tenth largest town on the island. The mining eventually finished in Zeehan and in 1960 the rail link to that town was closed. Then, in 1963, it was decided to close the Queenstown line also. For Strahan, which had always depended on Queenstown, this was a shattering blow. Within a few years no commercial traffic at all was using the port of Strahan and the town seemed doomed. It was fortunate that, just at that vital moment, tourism came along.

Strahan is a truly beautiful location. Charming cottages lead down to the sheltered and placid waters of the harbour. It has an idyllic feel to it. The only problem is that a lot of other people think so too, so Strahan, perhaps having little alternative, has become a tourist-oriented community. Accommodation is often rather difficult to find, and somewhat over-priced, and it is a little difficult to find where the soul of Strahan now lies.

Macquarie Harbour is fifty kilometres long and has a narrow entrance known as **Hell's Gates**. Here the waters streaming out meet the Indian Ocean with violence and create a treacherous hazard for shipping. On the southern tip of this entrance stands **Cape Sorell Lighthouse**, constructed in 1899 and forty metres high.

Ocean Beach stretches for forty kilometres north of Strahan, with long expanses of white sand dunes and plenty of surf. The beach starts six kilometres west of the town.

One of the major events affecting this area was the decision by the Tasmanian

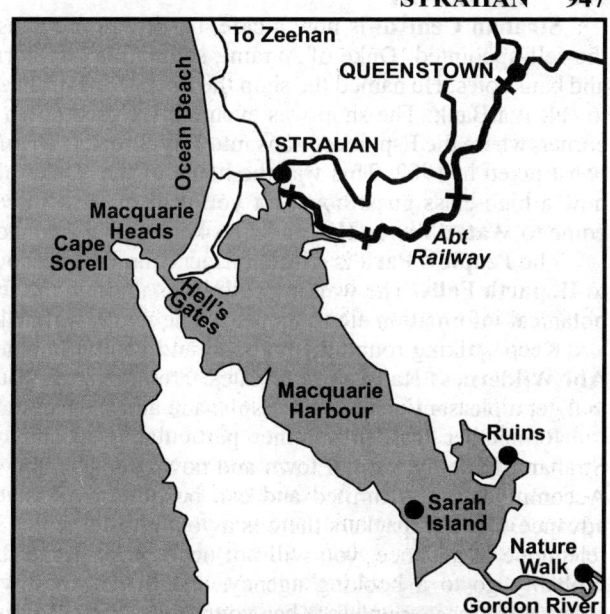

FROM QUEENSTOWN TO STRAHAN
Thicker lines indicate TassieLink bus routes

Government to construct yet another hydro-electric scheme by damming the Gordon River, which flows into Macquarie Harbour. The Gordon River is already dammed, but much higher up. This 'Gordon-below-Franklin Dam' was to have been 105 metres high and would have flooded Fraser Cave, containing aboriginal art, destroyed the white water section of the Franklin River and drowned much of the rainforest. The protests which took place near here were passionate and very well supported, and were met by unexpectedly strong resistance from the police. 1,272 people were arrested, ensuring a wave of sympathy for their cause. The Federal Government, under Bob Hawke, was, at the time, enjoying some popularity for its environmental policies and decided to block this plan by preserving the area under a World Heritage Order and creating, in 1983, the Franklin - Gordon Wild Rivers National Park. The result, for Strahan, was considerable national and even international publicity and a rapid increase in the number of visitors.

The most popular activity from Strahan is a **harbour cruise**. Several options are available, but they generally offer Hell's Gates, Sarah Island and a nature walk on the banks of the Gordon River to see Huon Pines which might be as ancient as 2,000 years old. There are also scenic flights offered.

Henty Dunes are twenty kilometres north of Strahan, off the road to Zeehan, and are a series of thirty-metre-high shifting dunes of considerable beauty. Also, **mutton birds** frequent the area near Strahan, and special viewing platforms have been constructed.

Around the town itself there are points of interest too. **Strahan Visitor Centre** is on the Esplanade close to the harbour. Not far away are the splendid **Post Office** and **Customs House**, dating from the days when this was a thriving port a century ago. The Customs House now serves as the Parks and Wildlife Office.

948 TASMANIA

Strahan Central is now a café, but it was previously a souvenir shop owned by the self-appointed 'Duke of Avram', selling his own forms of money - souvenir coins and banknotes. He named the shop the *Royal Ba-k of Avram*, since he was not permitted to call it a Bank. The shop was eventually closed down by the authorities. Round the corner, where the Esplanade runs into Bay Street, is **Ormiston House**, a stately building constructed in 1902. This was the home of the 'Duke of Avram' for a while, but it is now a high-class guest house. If you walk up Esk Street into Tamar Street, you will come to **Water Tower Hill** and a lookout with a fine view over town and harbour.

The **People's Park** is a little further round the harbour and from here you can walk to **Hogarth Falls**. The walking path leads through the forest and is marked, providing botanical information along the way. The return walk takes about an hour.

Keep walking round the harbour, and you will come to **Regatta Point**, where the **Abt Wilderness Railway** terminates. From here too you can look back over the town and get a pleasant view of the Esplanade and the harbour.

Remember that, in summer particularly, accommodation can be a problem in Strahan. It is only a small town and now over 100,000 visitors flock here every year. Accommodation is limited and can be quite expensive. It may be best to book in advance. For backpackers there is a youth hostel, but it is often full in summer. If you telephone in advance, you will not necessarily get to the hostel itself. Your call will probably go to a booking agency, and that agency will be reluctant to make any reservation for you unless it has your money first. Tourism here is business.

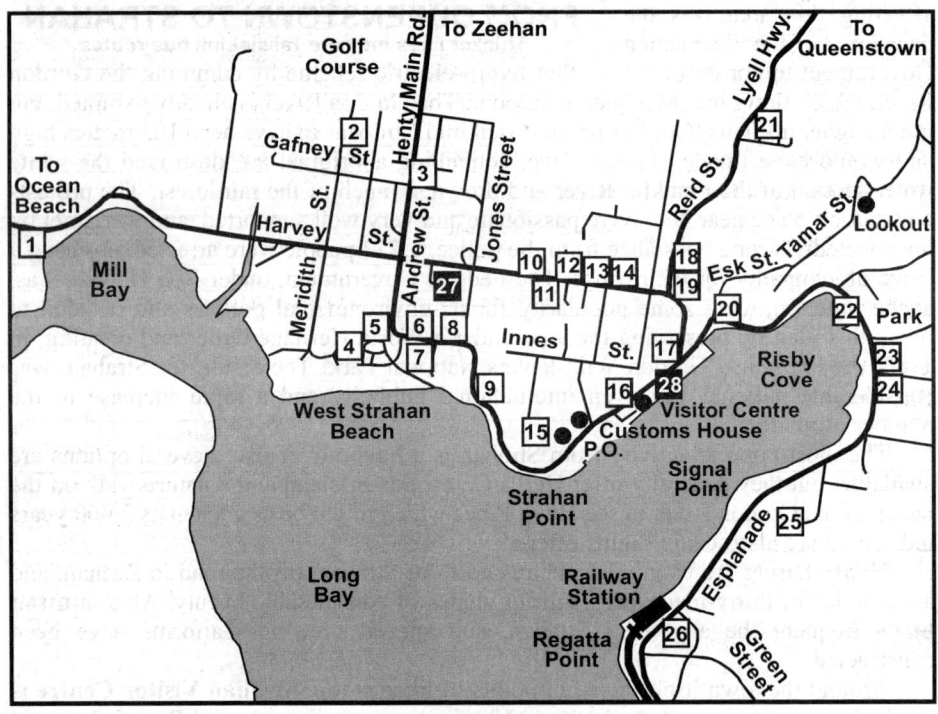

STRAHAN
Black numerals in white boxes indicate hotel accommodation
White numerals in black boxes indicate backpackers hostels

STRAHAN

ACCOMMODATION
(i) Hotel Accommodation in Strahan

Name	Stars	No. on Map	Telephone No.	Address	Lowest Price (Double/Twin)
Aldermere Estate		11	03-6471-7418	27 Harvey Street	$220
Ormiston House	5	9	03-6471-7077	The Esplanade	$200
McIntosh Cottage	4	12	03-6471-7358	18 Harvey Street	$190
Strahan Colonial Cottages	4½	19	1-800-444-442	7 Reid Street	$190
Rension Cottages		10	03-6471-7390	34 Harvey Street	$185
Risby Cove	4½	22	03-6471-7572	The Esplanade	$160
Strahan Central	4	17	1-800-444-442	1 Harold Street	$160
Macquarie Cottage		18	03-6471-7028	5 Reid Street	$145
Franklin Manor	4½	24	03-6471-7311	The Esplanade	$135
Risby House		23	03-6471-7572	Lot 1, Lodder Street	$125
Strahan Village	3½	20	1-800-628-286	The Esplanade	$110
Sailor's Rest	3½	13	1-800-188-810	14 Harvey Street	$110
Sharonlee Villas	3½	3	03-6471-7224	Andrew Street	$110
Castaway Apartments	4	14	03-6471-7400	Harvey & Herbert Streets	$105
Regatta Point Villas		26	03-6471-7103	The Esplanade	$100
Gordon Gateway Chalets		25	03-6471-7165	Grining Street	$95
Kitty's Place		5	03-6471-7666	Innes Street	$90
Azza's Holiday Units	3½	6	03-6471-7253	7 Innes Street	$85
Gull Cottages		7	03-6471-7227	The Esplanade	$85
Greengate Cottages		2	03-6471-7456	21 Meridith Street	$75
Cape Horn Accom.		15	03-6471-7169	3 Frazer Street	$70
Harbour Views		21	03-6471-7143	1 Charles Street	$70
Caravan & Tourist Park	4	4	03-6471-7239	Andrew & Innes Streets	$65
Hamer's Hotel		16	03-6471-4200	The Esplanade	$65
Strahan Cabin Park	3½	8	03-6471-7442	Jones & Innes Streets	$60
Strahan Wilderness Lodge		1	03-6471-7142	Ocean Beach Road	$55

(ii) Backpackers Hostels in Strahan

Name	Group	No. on Map	Telephone No.	Address	Lowest Price (Dormitory)
West Coast Yacht Charters		28	03-6471-7422	Strahan Wharf	$33
Strahan Y.H.A.	YHA	27	1800-444-442	43 Harvey Street	$21

MOVING ON
Bus Services from Strahan

Destination	Operator	Via	Distance (km)	Fare	Journey Time	Frequency
Hobart*	TassieLink		305	$57.70	5¼ - 8¼ hrs	4 - 5/week
		Lake St. Clair*	126	$31.30	2½ - 4¾ hrs	4 – 5/week
		Queenstown	37	$8	45 - 60 mins	1/day
Launceston*	TassieLink		367	$65.70	7 - 8½ hrs	3 - 4/week
		Devonport*	267	$49.10	5½ - 7 hrs	3 - 4/week
		Cradle Mountain*	177	$31	3½ - 4½ hrs	3 - 4/week

* Connecting service. Change of bus involved.

FLINDERS ISLAND AND KING ISLAND

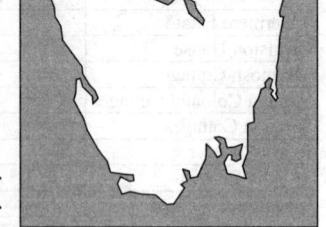

Population 2,000 (King Island)
Population 1,000 (Flinders Island)
50 mins by air from Melbourne (King Island)
45 mins by air from Burnie (King Island)
1 hr by air from Melbourne (Flinders Island)
40 mins by air from Launceston (Flinders Island)

Between Tasmania and Victoria lie two islands of some size. **King Island** lies off the north-western tip of Tasmania, the more populated of the two. It has scheduled flights from Devonport and Burnie (Wynyard) with Tasair. Both services operate daily. The Tasair flights cost $165, with a 10% discount for booking a week in advance.

King Island measures 64 kilometres from north to south and 27 kilometres from east to west. It is known for its dairy industry, and also for its native wildlife. However, it has no really cheap accommodation and so it is quite an expensive place to visit.

Flinders Island lies off the north-eastern tip of Tasmania. It is served by Island Airlines five times a week from Essendon Airport in Melbourne, and four times a week from Traralgon in Victoria. From Launceston, there are at least two flights every weekday and one each day on Saturdays and Sundays. There is also a weekly ferry between Bridport in Tasmania and Port Welshpool in Victoria via Flinders Island. Although this is principally a cargo boat, it will take a limited number of passengers.

Flinders Island is not on the general tourist route, but it is a beautiful rugged island, much larger than one might anticipate, being some fifty kilometres from north to south and an average of 25 kilometres across. There are more than eighty islands here, making up the **Furneaux Group**, charted by Matthew Flinders in 1798, but Flinders Island is by far the largest, the only other of any size being **Cape Barren Island**, lying just to its south. The first settlers here combined the professions of sealing and occasional piracy. The islands present quite an obstacle to shipping and their jagged rocks have been the scene of several shipwrecks, from which the islanders benefitted.

It was here that the **last of the Tasmanian aborigines** were brought in an attempt to save their race, but they were placed at **Wybalenna**, on the exposed western shore, where conditions were harsh for them, and not provided with adequate shelter. Of the 135 aborigines brought here between 1831 and 1834, only 47 were still alive by 1847, when they were taken back to Oyster Cove, near Hobart. The chapel here has been restored and is open for visits. However, you will not be able to locate the graves of all the aborigines who died here, as they are unmarked. There is a viewing platform nearby, from which to watch the mutton birds flying back home.

There is also a **mutton bird industry** here. That is to say that mutton birds, protected in other parts of Australia, are hunted here, killed, plucked and boiled for lunch. That is, after all, why they are called mutton birds.

A few kilometres east of Wybalenna is **Emita**, which has the **Furneaux Historical Research Museum**, including a muttonbirding shed. It also has exhibits related to sealing and to the many local shipwrecks. The Museum is open on Saturdays and Sundays only from 13:00 until 17:00. Admission costs $3.

FLINDERS & KING ISLANDS

The main town is **Whitemark** and it is here that you can find the only bank on the island, accommodation, shops and the principal of the three airports. At the southern tip of the island is **Lady Barron**, a tiny fishing community, but it does have a pub, of course, with accommodation, a post office and general store, and fish. It is in a charming setting on a beautiful little harbour, protected by other small islands, and is one of the most scenic spots on Flinders Island.

In the north of the island is **Killiecrankie**, even smaller than Lady Barron, but it has a shop with basic commodities, and accommodation. Here you can fossick for **topaz**.

There are some things which Flinders Island does not have, however, and the most important is transport. From Whitemark Airport, you can walk into town in about an hour. It is five kilometres. There you can hire a bicycle for further excursions. Or you can take one of the tours of the island which are available. Or you can do a lot more walking. There is a track from the south of the island to the north which takes about five days to walk. It is named the **Flinders Trail** and is signposted, although not always clearly. There is also the **Flinders Island Ecology Trail**, marked by yellow signposts. This is more suitable, though, as a bicycle tour than as a walk. One of the points on the Ecology Trail is **Walker's Lookout**, and, although that may not be the intended meaning, this is indeed suitable for walkers, and a good observation point. It is about ten kilometres distant from Whitemark.

In the south-western corner of the island is the **Strzelecki National Park** and here you can conquer **Mt. Strzelecki**, 750 metres high, a walk of about six kilometres each way from

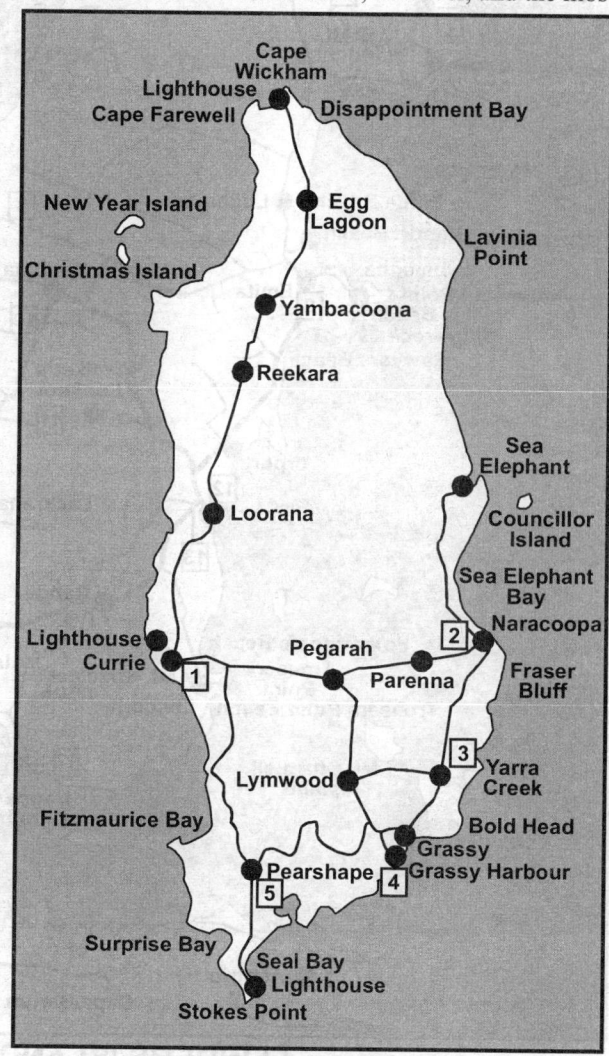

KING ISLAND
Numerals indicate accommodation

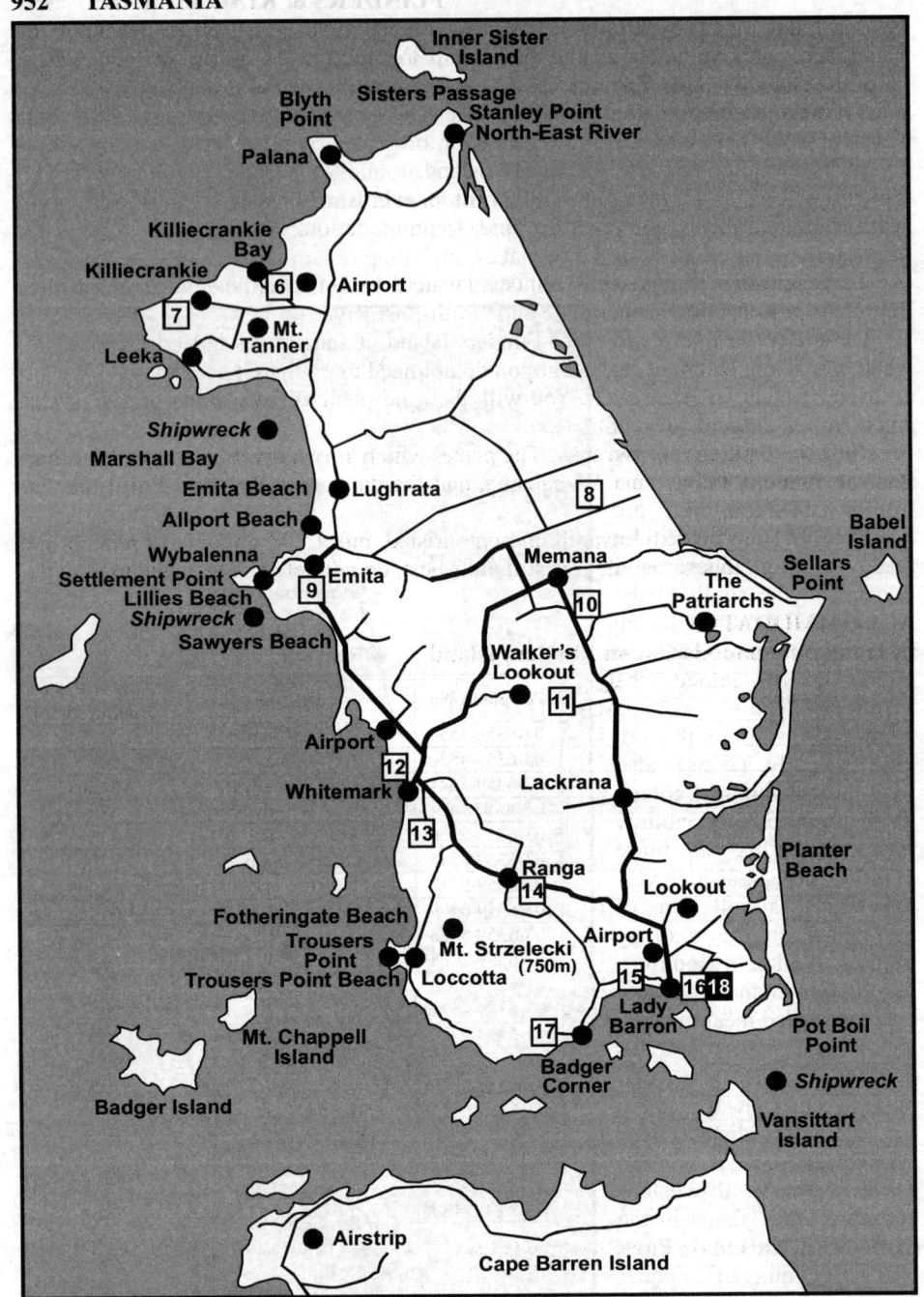

FLINDERS ISLAND
Black numerals in white boxes indicate hotel accommodation
White numerals in black boxes indicate backpackers hostels

FLINDERS & KING ISLANDS

Trousers Point Road, but first you have to get there and it is some twelve kilometres from Whitemark. There are many other walks too, but no Visitor Information Centre on the island to tell you about them. Limited information is available from *Sweet Surprises Coffee Shop* in Whitemark, but it is a good idea to visit an Information Centre in Tasmania before coming here if possible.

There are some beautiful deserted beaches around the island, of which one of the best and most accessible is **Trousers Point Beach**, near the start of the walk to Mt. Strzelecki mentioned in the preceding paragraph.

Camping is permitted in many places, including most parts of the foreshore, and there are camp sites at Trousers Point (with water), Lady Barron, the Patriarchs, Lillies Beach, Allport Beach, Killiecrankie and North-East River.

Cape Barren Island, south of Flinders Island, is famous, as indeed it should be, for its rare **Cape Barren Geese**, but you do not need to go there to see them. They are all over Flinders Island as well. You will also find plenty of **wombats** on the island, and many other forms of wildlife too.

Then there are the **shipwrecks**. The places which attract divers most are **Marshall Bay**, **Settlement Point**, near Wybalenna, and the dangerous **Pot Boil Point**, not far from Lady Barron.

Flinders Island is still unspoilt and untouristed, but it will not always remain like that. If you want to see it while it is still at its best, do not delay. Now is the time to go.

ACCOMMODATION
(i) Hotel Accommodation on Flinders Island

Name	Stars	No. on Map	Telephone No.	Address	Lowest Price (Double/Twin)
Partridge Farm	4	17	03-6359-3554	Badger Corner	$130
Holloway Haven		14	03-6359-4530	Ranga	$125
Felicity's Cottage		16	03-6359-3641	Holloway St., Lady Barron	$120
Flinders Island Lodge	3½	16	1-800-818-826	Esplanade, Lady Barron	$120
Killiecrankie Bay House		6	03-6359-8560	531 Killiecrankie Road	$110
Bucks at Lady Barron		16	03-6359-3535	Franklin Pde., Lady Barron	$105
Carnsdale Host Farm	3½	8	03-6359-9718	Memana	$100
Echo Hills	3½	11	03-6359-6509	Madeley's Road, Lackrana	$100
Castle Cottages		9	03-6359-8488	41 Port Davies Road, Emita	$100
Elvstan Units		12	03-6359-2008	2/7 Esplanade, Whitemark	$95
Lady Barron Holiday Hse	3½	16	03-6359-3555	Franklin Pde., Lady Barron	$95
Yaringa Holiday Cottages	3½	16	03-6359-4522	Holloway St., Lady Barron	$95
Bulloke Holiday Home		13	03-6359-9709	Butter Fact. Rd., Whitemark	$90
Lisa's Cottage		10	03-6359-6530	Lees Rd. Aurora 2, Memana	$90
Bluff House		12	03-6359-2259	24 Bluff Road, Whitemark	$90
Boat Harbour Beach Hse.	3½	7	03-6359-6510	Boat Harbour, Killiecrankie	$85
Oakridge Holiday Home	3	6	03-6359-2160	Killiecrankie Bay	$75
Interstate Hotel		12	03-6359-2114	Patrick Street, Whitemark	$65
Leafmoor Cottage	3½	15	03-6359-3517	1107 Coast Road	$65
Flinders Is. Cabin Park		12	03-6359-2188	Bluff Road, Whitemark	$50

(ii) Backpackers Hostel on Flinders Island

Name	Group	No. on Map	Telephone No.	Address	Lowest Price (Dormitory)
Nunamina Hostel		18	03-6359-3617	41 Franklin Pde., Lady Barron	$25

954 TASMANIA
(iii) Accommodation on King Island

Name	Stars	No. on Map	Telephone No.	Address	Lowest Price (Double/Twin)
Wave Watcher Units		1	03-6462-1517	18 Beach Road, Currie	$155
Boomerang by the Sea		1	03-6462-1288	Golf Club Road, Currie	$125
Gem Motel	3½	1	1-800-647-702	95 Main Street, Currie	$125
Baudin's		2	03-6461-1100	Esplanade, Naracoopa	$125
St. Andrew's		1	03-6462-1490	23 Netherby Road, Currie	$125
Southern Sky Units		1	03-6462-1691	1 Huxley Street, Currie	$110
Bass Caravan Park		1	03-6462-1260	100 Main Street, Currie	$105
Yarra Creek Host Farm	3½	3	03-6461-1276	49 Boldhead Rd., Yarra Ck	$100
Parer's King Island Hotel	3	1	03-6462-1633	7 Main Street, Currie	$100
Green Ponds Guest House		1	03-6462-1543	38 Edward Street, Currie	$100
Naracoopa Holiday Units		2	03-6461-1326	Beach Road, Naracoopa	$100
Bluegate Farmhouse		5	03-6462-1180	South Road, Pearshape	$90
King Island Holiday Vill.		4	03-6461-1177	1 Blue Gum Dr Grassy Harb	$90
Gullhaven		1	03-6462-1560	11 Huxley Street, Currie	$80
Colonial Lodge		1	03-6462-1066	13 Main Street, Currie	$75

MOVING ON

One moves on, of course, in the same way as one got here. From King Island there are daily flights to Burnie (Wynyard) and Devonport.

From Flinders Island, the ferry goes once a week to Bridport on the north coast of Tasmania, and to Port Welshpool in Victoria. Flights with Island Airlines go to Essendon Airport in Melbourne five times a week, and to Traralgon four times a week. To Launceston, flights depart at least twice every weekday and once on Saturdays and Sundays.

INDEX

Aborigines 10, 407, 428, 701, 851
Abrolhos Islands, W.A. 563
Abt Railway ...936, 941, 942, 944, 946, 948
Accommodation 27
Adelaide Hills, S.A. 636, 719
Adelaide River Crossing, N.T. 423, 425
Adelaide River, N.T. 425, 427, 431
Adelaide, P.S. 804
Adelaide, S.A. 8, 11, 158, 461, 623, **625**
Admiral's Arch, S.A. 646
Adventure Bay, Tas. 863, 864, 865
Afghan Express 682
Afghans 396, 456, 461, 619
Agnes Water, Qld. 295, 296
Aileron, N.T. 446
Air Passes 23
Air Tickets 5
Air Travel 23
Airey's Inlet, Vic. 765, 767, 768
Airlie Beach, Qld. **326**, 329
Airport Express Bus, Sydney 42
Airports 24
Ajana, W.A. 568, 569
Albany Island, Qld. 391
Albany, W.A. ...11, 471, 473, 482, **522**, 715
Alberrie Creek, S.A. 695
Alberton, Vic. 837, 838
Albury, N.S.W. 128, **131**, 827
Aldinga, S.A. 650
Alexandra Headland, Qld. 258, 260
Algebuckina Bridge, S.A. 695, 696
Alice Springs, N.T. **445**, 461, 462, 669
Allansford, Vic....................771
Allen, Peter 180
Allport Beach, Tas. 952, 953
Almaden, Qld....................368
Alonnah, Tas. 863, 865
Alpha, Qld. 310, 311
Aluminium 294, 501, 778
America's Cup 490
American Beach, S.A. 645, 646
American River, S.A. 645
Amity, Qld. 251
Amity 471, 522, 523
Amundsen, Roald 854
Anakie, Qld. 310
Anastasia's Pool, W.A. 608
Andamooka, S.A. 705
Anderson, Vic. 832, 837

Angaston, S.A. 653, 655
Anglers' Rest, Vic. 824
Anglesea, Vic. 765, 767
Anna Creek, S.A. 695, 696
Annan Gorge, Qld. 385
Antechamber Bay, S.A. 646
Anzac War Memorial, Sydney 59
Apollo Bay, Vic. 765
Apsley Gorge, Tas. 895
AquariumPass, Sydney 53
Ararat, Vic. 461, 789, 790
Arcadia, Qld. 340, 341
Archer Park, Qld. 298
Archer River, Qld. 387, 388
Arckaringa Hills, S.A. 706
Ardrossan, S.A. 663, 665
Argyle Diamond Mine, W.A. 619, 620
Arkaba, S.A. 689, 690, 691
Arkaroo Rock, S.A. 688, 690
Arltunga, N.T. 457
Armadale, W.A. 501, 532
Armidale, N.S.W. 170, **174**
Armstrong Bay, Vic. 777
Arno Bay, S.A. 709, 710
Arno's Wall, Winton 320
Art 160
Arthur River, Tas. 924
Arthur River, W.A. 523
Arthur's Seat, Vic. 739, 746
Asbestos 603
Ashbourne, S.A. 650
Ashburton River 582
Atherton, Qld. 368, **372**, 373
Augusta, W.A. **514**
Auski, W.A. 603
Aussie Kilometre Pass 20
Austrail Flexipass 15, 486
Austrail Pass 16
Australian Capital Territory 11, **219**
Australian Rules Football 37
Australian War Memorial, Canberra 222
Australind 501, 502
Avoca, Tas. 896, 898
Avoca, Vic. 789
Avon Descent 543
Avon River, W.A. 500, 543
Avon River, Vic. 842
Avon Yard, W.A. 500
Ayers Rock, N.T. ...457, **464**, 468, 550, 551

INDEX

Ayers, Sir Henry 464, 629, 634, 678
Ayton, Qld. 385, 387
Babbage Island, W.A. 575
Babel Island, Tas. 952
Babinda, Qld. .357
Backpackers Cards 31
Backpackers Hostels 28
Backtracker Pass 16, 39, 40, 729
Badger Corner, Tas. 952
Badger Island, Tas. 952
Badgingarra, W.A. 560
Badu Island, Qld. 391
Bagdad, Tas. .887
Bairnsdale, Vic. 824, 841, 842
Bald Cape, Tas. 885
Bald Rock, N.S.W. 182
Balfour, Tas. .924
Balhannah, S.A. 461
Balingup, W.A. 482, 517, 523
Ball's Pyramid, N.S.W. 216
Balladonia, W.A. 535, 539
Ballarat, Vic. 11, 727, **781**
Ballidu, W.A. 560
Ballina, N.S.W. 195, 196, 203, 206
Bally Hooley Railway 377
Balranald, N.S.W. 805
Bamaga, Qld. 386, 387, 388, 391
Bamboo Creek, N.T. 427
Bancoora Beach, Vic. 759
Banfield, E.J. .354
Bangalow, N.S.W. 206, 209
Banks 36
Banksia Beach, Qld. 258
Bannister, W.A. 482, 523, 532
Barcaldine, Qld. 311, 313
Barcoo River .315
Bargara, Qld. 292, 293
Bark Hut, N.T. 425
Barmera, S.A. 657
Barnes Bay, Tas. 865
Barossa Valley, S.A. 33, **653**
Barranyi, N.T. 442
Barraport, Vic. 807
Barren Head, Tas. 885
Barrine, Qld. .373
Barron Falls, Qld. 360, 362, 367
Barrow Creek, N.T. 446
Barton, S.A. 671, 673
Barwon Heads, Vic. 759, 761
Basalt 922
Bass Strait 851
Bass, George 831, 851, 902
Bass, Vic. 832, 837
Bastyan Dam, Tas. 938
Batavia Coast, W.A. 563
Batavia's Graveyard, W.A. 563
Batavia 10, 489, 563, 568
Batchelor, N.T. 426, 427, 431
Batemans Bay, N.S.W. **113**
Bates, Daisy .672
Bates, S.A. 672, 673
Bathurst, N.S.W. 11, **140**, 155
Batman Bridge, Tas. 910, 911
Batman, John 727, 761, 904
Bauxite 388, 428, 502
Baxter, Vic. 832
Bay of Islands, Vic. 771
Beaching Bay, Tas. 885
Beachport, S.A. 721
Beaconsfield, Tas. 910, 911
Beadell, Len .551
Beagle Bay, W.A. 614
Bealiba, Vic. .789
Beaufort River, W.A. 523
Beaufort, Vic. 789
Beaumaris, Tas. 896, 898
Beauty Point, Tas. 852, 910, 911
Beechworth, Vic. **819**
Beer 32
Beerbarrel Beach, Tas. 897
Beerburrum, Qld. 258
Beerwah, Qld. 258
Bees 647
Bega, N.S.W. **119**
Belair, S.A. 461, 637
Belconnen, A.C.T. 220, 223
Belgrave, Vic. 744
Bell Bay, Tas. 910, 911
Bellara, Qld. .258
Bellarine Peninsula, Vic. **756**
Bellbrae, Vic. 765
Bellenden Ker, Mt., Qld. 8, 227, 351
Bellingen, N.S.W. 189
Bells Beach, Vic. 765, 767
Belmont, N.S.W. 99
Beltana, S.A. 690, 691
Bemm River, Vic. 846
Ben Lomond, Tas. 896
Benaraby, Qld. 295
Bendigo, Vic. 11, 727, **795**
Benedictine Monastery 560
Beresford, S.A. 695
Bermagui, N.S.W. 120
Bernacchi, Diego 884
Berri, S.A. 657
Berridale, N.S.W. 126
Berry Springs, N.T. 420, 425
Berrybank, Vic. 461
Bethanga Bridge, Vic. 128
Beverley, W.A. 523, 555
Bibbenluke, N.S.W. 118
Bibbulmun Track . . .482, 516, 519, 520, 521

INDEX 957

Bicheno, Tas. 852, 889, **893**, 898
Bicycling 26
Binalong Bay, Tas. 898
Bindoon, W.A. .560
Bingil Bay, Qld. 351
Binnu, W.A. 569
Birdsville Track 693
Birdsville, Qld. .693
Birdum, N.T. 441
Bishop and Clerk Peak, Tas. 884, 885
Bitter Springs, N.T. 440
Bittern, Vic. 832
Black and White Hostels 29
Black Mountain, Qld. 385
Black River, Tas. 924
Blackall, Qld. 311, 314
Blackbull, Qld. 403, 404
Blackheath, N.S.W. 155
Blackwater, Qld. 305, 311
Blair Athol, Qld. 305
Blairgowrie, Vic. 739
Blamey, W.A. .499
Blanche Cup, S.A. 696
Blanchetown, S.A. 657
Blaxland, N.S.W. 154
Blayney, N.S.W. 142, 154
Bligh, Captain William 851, 863, 866
Blinman, S.A. 690, 691
Bloomfield River, Qld. 377, 383, 385
Bloomfield Track 383
Blue Lake, S.A. 722, 723
Blue Mountains, N.S.W. **101**, 154
Blue Tier, Tas. 897, 898
Bluebird Mine, W.A. 597
Bluff Rock, N.S.W. 182, 183
Bluff, Qld. 311
Blyth Point, Tas. 952
Boab Trees 611, 619
Boat Harbour, Tas. 924
Bodalla, N.S.W. 120
Bodallin, W.A. 498, 542
Bogan Gate, N.S.W. 157
Bogangar, N.S.W. 206
Bogantungan, Qld. 310
Boggy Creek Gorge, Vic. 845
Bogong, Vic. 824
Boigu Island, Qld. 391
Bokarina Beach, Qld. 260
Bold Head, Tas. 951
Bolivar, S.A. 158, 463, 669
Bomaderry, N.S.W. 113
Bombala, N.S.W. **117**
Bondi Explorer 52
Bondi, Sydney 66, 78
Bonegilla Migrant Reception Centre, Vic. 134
Bongaree, Qld. 258

Bonnie Doon, Vic. 829
Bonnie Vale, W.A. 499, 542
Bookaloo, S.A. 463, 668
Bookshops 38
Boomerang Pass 23
Booming Bay, Tas. 885
Boonderoo, W.A. 496
Boonoo Boonoo, N.S.W. 182
Boort, Vic. 807
Borden, W.A. .532
Border Village, S.A. 539, 717
Bordertown, S.A. . . .461, 624, 720, 721, 789
Borenore, N.S.W. 154, 155
Boroka, Vic. 789, 791
Boronia Peak, Vic. 789, 791
Bororen, Qld. .295
Borroloola, N.T. 441, 442
Borung, Vic. 807
Boston Bay, S.A. 711
Botanic Gardens, Canberra 222
Botanic Gardens, Rockhampton 298
Botanic Gardens, Sydney 58
Botanical Gardens, Hobart 856
Botany Bay, N.S.W. 11, 39, 79
Bottom Lake, Vic. 849
Boulder, W.A. 542, 547, 548
Bouldercombe, Qld. 300
Boulia, Qld. 399
Bounty H.M.S. 55, 336, 851, 864
Bourke, N.S.W. **150**
Bow Bridge, W.A. 517, 523
Bowen Downs, Qld. 316
Bowen, Qld. **331**
Bowmans, S.A. 158, 463, 669
Bowral, N.S.W. .86
Boxwood Hill, W.A. 533
Boyanup, W.A. 517, 523
Boydtown, N.S.W. 124
Boyne Island, Qld. 295
Brachina, S.A. 689, 690, 691
Bradman Museum, Bowra 86
Bradshaw Bridge, Tas. 936
Brady's Lake, Tas. 933
Brahe, William 701
Brampton Island, Qld. 324
Branxholme, Vic. 775
Breakaways, The, S.A. 705, 706
Break-Me-Neck Hill, Tas. 882
Bremer Bay, W.A. 532, 533
Brentwood, S.A. 665
Bribie Island, Qld. 257, 258
Bridgetown, W.A. 482, 517, 523
Bridgewater, Tas. 887
Bridgewater, Vic. 807
Bridport, Tas. . .838, 852, 852, **895**, 911, 950
Bright, Vic. 819, **822**

958 INDEX

Brighton, Tas. 887
Brisbane River 230
Brisbane, Qld. 11, 227, **229**
Briseis Mine, Tas. 899
Broad Arrow, W.A. 549, 550
Broadbeach, Qld. 246
Broadmeadow, N.S.W. 96, 100
Broken Hill Proprietary (B.H.P.) ....
............156, 159, 592, 600, 663, 709
Broken Hill, N.S.W. 156, **159**, 624
Bronte, Tas. 932, 933
Brookfield, S.A. 657
Brookton, W.A. 523
Broome, W.A. 594, **605**, 614
Broomehill, W.A. 523, 532
Brunswick Heads, N.S.W. 206
Brunswick Junction, W.A. 501
Bruny Island, Tas. **863**, 868
Bruthen, Vic. 824
Bryan's Beach, Tas. 890
Buangor, Vic. 789
Bubbler, The, S.A. 696
Buchan, Vic. 841, 843, 846
Buckland, Tas. 887
Buddina, Qld. 260, 261
Buffalo, Vic. 837
Bulcock Beach, Qld. 259, 260
Buley Rockhole, N.T. 426, 427
Bulli, N.S.W. 105
Bullocks Flat, N.S.W. 127
Bullsbrook, W.A. 560
Bunbury, W.A. **501**
Bunda Cliffs, S.A. 717
Bundaberg, Qld. **290**, 308, 309
Bundegi Beach, W.A. 578, 579
Bungle Bungle Range, W.A. ...617, 620
Buntine, W.A. 560
Bunyip, Vic. 841
Buran, Sydney 61
Burando, S.A. 463, 671
Burke and Wills Expedition ....
......11, 156, 692, **700**, 796, 807, 810, 820
Burke, Robert o'Hara ....
...........11, 156, 692, 700, 796, 820
Burleigh Heads, Qld. 245, 246
Burley Griffin, Walter 11, 138, 219
Burnett Heads, Qld. 290, 293
Burnie, Tas. 852, **919**, 950
Burra, S.A. 623
Burracoppin, W.A. 498, 542
Burrill Lake, N.S.W. 113
Burrup Peninsula, W.A. 584
Bus Passes 18
Bus Tours 22
Buses 18
Bush Mill, Tas. 880

Bush Pilots 357
Business Hours 36
Busselton, W.A. **507**
Bustard Bay, Qld. 295
Bust-Me-Gut Hill, Tas. 882
BusTripper, Sydney 51
Bute, S.A. 683, 709
Butler, Captain Harry 664
Butterflies 361, 362
Byford, W.A. 501
Byron Bay, N.S.W. **201**, 209
Cabarita Beach, N.S.W. 206, 245, 246
Cabbage Tree Creek, Vic. 846
Cable Beach, W.A. 608
Cabooolture, Qld. 258, 308, 309
Cactus Beach, S.A. 716, 717
Cadman's Cottage, Sydney 55
Cadney Park, S.A. 462
Caiguna, W.A. 539
Cairdbeign, Qld. 306
Cairns, Qld. **356**
Callanna, S.A. 695
Caloundra, Qld. 257, 258, 259
Caltowie, S.A. 158
Cambridge, Tas. 882
Cameron Corner 693
Camp Spur, Tas. 942, 943
Campbell Town, Tas. 887, 893, 911
Camperdown, Vic. 771
Canberra, A.C.T. 8, 11, **219**
Cann River, Vic. 846, 848
Cannuwaukaninna, S.A. 693
Canowindra, N.S.W. 142
Cape Arid, W.A. 533, 534
Cape Barren Geese 953
Cape Barren Island, Tas. ...950, 952, 953
Cape Borda, S.A. 645, 647
Cape Bruny, Tas. 864, 865
Cape Conran, Vic. 846, 847
Cape Cuvier, W.A. 576
Cape de Couedic, S.A. 645, 646, 647
Cape Degerando, Tas. 889
Cape des Tombeaux, Tas. 885
Cape Dombey, S.A. 721
Cape Don, N.T. 428, 429
Cape Farewell, Tas. 951
Cape Forestier, Tas. 890
Cape Gantheaume, S.A. 645, 646
Cape Grim, Tas. 924
Cape Inscription, W.A. 10, 471, 571, 572
Cape Jervis, S.A. 645, 650
Cape Lambert, W.A. 586
Cape Le Grand, W.A. 533, 534
Cape Leeuwin, W.A. 514
Cape Naturaliste, W.A. 509, 512
Cape Otway, Vic. 765, 769, 771

Cape Paterson, Vic.	837
Cape Peron, W.A.	572
Cape Range, W.A.	578, 579
Cape Richards, Qld.	346
Cape Sorell, Tas.	947
Cape Tribulation, Qld.	377, **381**, 382
Cape Wickham, Tas.	951
Cape Willoughby, S.A.	645, 647
Cape York, Qld.	**386**
Capel Sound, Vic.	739
Capel, W.A.	517
Capella, Qld.	305
Capricorn Caves, Qld.	300, 301
Capricorn Coast, Qld.	300
Capricorn Spire	297, 309
Capricorn, W.A.	601
Captain Starlight	315, 691
Caramut, Vic.	775
Caravonica, Qld.	360
Carcoar, N.S.W.	142
Cardwell, Qld.	**346**
Carisbrooke, Qld.	320, 321
Carnamah, W.A.	560
Carnarvon Gorge, Qld.	305, 306
Carnarvon, W.A.	**575**, 582
Carnes, S.A.	462
Caroline Pool, W.A.	616
Carrabin, W.A.	498, 542
Carrick, Tas.	917
Cash, Martin	878, 909
Casino, N.S.W.	198
Cassilis, Vic.	824
Cassowaries	351
Cassowary Coast, Qld.	351
Casterton, Vic.	775, 789
Castle Hill, Qld.	321
Castlemaine, Vic.	796, 801
Casuarina, N.T.	419
Cataby, W.A.	560
Catamaran, Tas.	868, 869
Cataract Gorge, Tas.	905
Cattle	297
Caulfield, Vic.	841
CaveWorks, W.A.	512
Cawarral, Qld.	300
Cedar Bay, Qld.	385
Ceduna, S.A.	624, 709, 712, **714**
Central Highlands Tourist Railway	785
Central Station, Qld.	283
Cervantes, W.A.	557, **558**, 560
Cethana Dam, Tas.	930
Chaffey Brothers	658, 812
Chakola, N.S.W.	116
Chandler, S.A.	462
Charleville, Qld.	**255**
Charlotte Pass, N.S.W.	8, 126
Charters Towers, Qld.	**344**
Chatsworth Island, N.S.W.	195
Cherry Venture	269
Chicory	745, 832
Chifley, Ben	140
Chifley, W.A.	496
Childers, Qld.	**287**
Chillagoe, Qld.	369
Chinaman's Beach, Tas.	885
Chinatown, Adelaide	630
Chinatown, Bendigo	798
Chinatown, Brisbane	234
Chinatown, Broome	607
Chinatown, Melbourne	733
Chinatown, Sydney	62
Chinderah, N.S.W.	206
Christmas Island, Tas.	951
Chudleigh, Tas.	917
Churchill Island, Vic.	834
Cinema Point, Vic.	768
Circular Head, Tas.	923
Citrus Fruits	136, 657
CityHopper, Sydney	51
CityRail, Sydney	44, 46
Clarence River	193
Clarence, N.S.W.	84, 155
Clarendon, S.A.	650
Clarendon, Vic.	789
Clarina, Qld.	402, 403
Clarke, Marcus	877
Clarkefield, Vic.	796
Clermont, Qld.	305
Cleve, S.A.	709, 710
Cleveland, Qld.	251
Clifton Beach, Qld.	360, 361
Clifton Hills, S.A.	693, 694
Clifton Springs, Vic.	759, 761
Climate	7
Cloncurry, Qld.	8, 227, **396**, 594
Cloudy Lagoon, Tas.	865, 866
Clunes, Vic.	789
Coal Creek, Vic.	837
Coal Mines, Tas.	879, 881
Coal Point, Tas.	865, 866
Coal	690
Coalmine Beach, W.A.	520
Cobargo, N.S.W.	120
Cobb and Co.	253, 255, 256
Cobbald Gorge, Qld.	369
Cobdogla, S.A.	657
Cobourg Peninsula, N.T.	428, 429
Cobram, Vic.	816
Cock's Comb, Tas.	885
Cockatoo Run, Sydney	85
Cockatoo Valley, S.A.	653
Cockburn. S.A.	156, 157

960 INDEX

Cockle Creek, Tas. . . .852, 867, 868, **869**, 870
Cockle Train 649
Cocklebiddy, W.A. 539
Coconut Beach, Qld. 382
Coen, Qld. .387, 388
Coffin Bay, S.A. 709, 712
Coffs Harbour, N.S.W. **190**
Cohuna, Vic. 807
Colac, Vic. .765, 771
Coleraine, Vic. 775, 789
Coles Bay, Tas. 852, **888**, 893
Coles Beach, Tas. 915, 916
Collie, W.A. 482
Colton, S.A. 709
Column, The, Tas. 885
Combo Waterhole, Qld. 321, 322
Commodore, S.A. 691
Commonwealth of Australia 11
Conara, Tas. 898, 911
Condoblin, N.S.W. 157
Confessions of a Beachcomber 354
Conjola, N.S.W. 113
Connair 455
Connellan, Eddie 455, 464
Convicts 11, 471, 473
Coober Pedy, S.A. 463, 624, 695, **704**
Coobowie, S.A. .665
Cooee, Tas. .922, 924
Coogee, Sydney 66, 79
Cooinda Camp, S.A. 689
Cooinda, N.T. 424, 425
Cook, James 11, 326, 390, 849, 851, 863, 866
Cook, S.A. 496, 497, 672
Cook's Beach, Tas. 890
Cookamidgera, N.S.W. 154, 155
Cooke Point, W.A. 593
Cookernup, W.A. 501
Cooktown, Qld. 377, **383**, 387
Coolangatta, Qld. 211, **240**, 245, 246
Coolgardie, W.A. 532, 549
Coolum Beach, Qld. 258, 262, 263
Coolumbooka River 118
Cooma, N.S.W. **116**
Coomalie Creek, N.T. 426, 427, 431
Coomandook, S.A. 461, 721
Coombe, S.A. 461
Coomera, Qld. 245, 246
Coonalpyn, S.A. 461, 720, 721
Coonamia, S.A. 463, 668, 669, 682
Coonana, W.A. 496
Coonarr Beach, Qld. 293
Coonawarra, S.A. 720, 721
Coongie Lakes, S.A. 692
Cooper Creek, Qld. 382
Cooper Creek 315, 692, 701
Coorow, W.A. 560
Cooroy, Qld. 258, 309
Cootamundra, N.S.W. 86, 138
Cooya, Qld. 377
Copeton Dam, N.S.W. 172, 173
Copley, S.A. 691
Copper Hills, S.A. 706
Copper 305,
369, 396, 398, 568, 623, 661, 690, 937, 939
Copperfield Dam, N.T. 430, 431
Copperfield River, Qld. 369
Copperfield, Qld. 305
Copping, Tas. 877, 879
Coral Bay, W.A. 578, 582
Coral Cove, Qld. 292, 293
Corinella, Vic. 832
Corio Bay, Vic. .761
Cornwall, Tas. 896
Coronet Bay, Vic. 832
Corrigin, W.A. 532
Cossack, W.A. 584, **586**
Cotabena, S.A. 689, 691
Cotton 151, 163
Coulta, S.A. 709, 712
Councillor Island, Tas. 951
Country Music .165
Countrylink 13, 16, 39, 41
Couta Rocks, Tas. 924
Cow Bay, Qld. 377, 381
Cowaramup, W.A. 512
Coward Springs, S.A. 695, 696
Cowell, S.A. 709, 710
Cowes, Vic. 745, 832, 835
Cowie Point, Qld. 385
Cowper, N.S.W. .195
Cowwarr, Vic. 841
Cradle Mountain, Tas. . . .852, **927**, 934, 937
Cradoc, Tas. 867, 868
Crafters, S.A. 721
Cranbourne, Vic. 832
Cranbrook, Tas. .889
Cranbrook, W.A. 523
Crater Lake, Tas. 930
Creen Creek, Qld. 404
Creepy Crawly Nature Trail 874
Creswick, Vic. 785, 789
Crib Point, Vic. 739, 832
Cricket 37
Critters Camp, Qld. 402, 403
Croajingolong, Vic. 849
Crooked Lagoon, Tas. 885
Crossman, W.A. 523, 532
Crosswater, Qld. 403
Croydon, Qld. 402, 404, **405**
Crystal Brook, S.A. . . . .
158, 463, 668, 669, 683, 709
Cuballing, W.A. .523

INDEX 961

Cue, W.A. 597
Cullen Bay, N.T. 419
Cullin-la-Ringo, Qld. 305
Cumberland River, Vic. 765, 768
Cumberoona, P.S. 133
Cunderdin, W.A. 500, 542
Curdimurka, S.A. 695, 696
Curlewis, Vic. 758, 759
Currency 36
Currie, Tas. 951
Currimundi, Qld. 260
Curtin Springs, N.T. 457
Curtin, W.A. 499
Customs House, Sydney 56
Cyclone Tracy 8, 410, 412
Cyclone Vance 8
Cygnet River, S.A. 645
Cygnet, Tas. 867, 868
Cynthia Bay, Tas. 934
D'Entrecasteaux Channel, Tas. ..863, 865, 867
D'Entrecasteaux, Rear Admiral Bruni ...863
D'Estrees Bay, S.A. 645
Dagun, Qld. 268
Dagworth, Qld. 313, 318, 321
Daintree, Qld. 377, **381**
Dalwallinu, W.A. 560, 597
Daly River, N.T. 431
Daly Waters, N.T. 441, 442
Dampier Archipelago, W.A. 582
Dampier, W.A. **581**, 594, 601
Dampier, William 11, 471, 572, 582, 605
Dandalup, W.A. 501
Dandenong, Vic. 739, 832, 840, 841
Darling Harbour, Sydney 60
Darling River 151, 156
Darlington, Tas. 884, 885
Darrick, N.S.W. 157
Darrine, W.A. 499
Dartmoor, Vic. 775
Darwin, N.T. 8, 11, 32, **409**
Dauan Island, Qld. 391
Daveyston, S.A. 653
Daydream Island, Qld. 327
Daylesford, Vic. 785, 795
Dayston, Vic. 837
DayTripper, Sydney 51
Dead Horse Gap, N.S.W. 127
Deakin, W.A. 497
Dean, Henry 497
Dederang, Vic. 824
Deep Hole Bay, Tas. 869
DeGray River 582
Deloraine, Tas. 911, 917
Denham, W.A. 571, 582
Denman, S.A. 497
Denmark, W.A. 482, 517, **521**, 523
Dennes Point, Tas. 865
Depuch Island, W.A. 589
Derby, Tas. 852, **895**
Derby, W.A. **611**, 614
Derwent Bridge, Tas. 932, 933, 936
Derwent Valley Railway 873
Devil Cat 852, 909
Devil's Kitchen, Tas. 878
Devil's Marbles, N.T. 446
Devil's Peak, S.A. 687
Devonport, Tas. 852, **914**, 950
Diamantina, Qld. 694
Diamond Island, Tas. 893
Diamonds 619
Diana's Basin, Tas. 896
Dicky Beach, Qld. 259, 260
Dig Tree, Qld. 692, 701
Diggers Rest, Vic. 796
Dilli, Qld. 285, 286
Dilston, Tas. 911
Dimboola, Vic. 461, 789, 790
Dimbulah, Qld. 368, 369, 373
Dingee, Vic. 807
Dingoes 283
Dinner Falls, Qld. 373, 374
Dinner Plain, Vic. 822, 824
Dinosaurs 320, 396, 608, 705
Dirk Hartog Island, W.A. 10, 571, 572
Dirranbandi Mail 255
Dirranbandi, Qld. 150
Dittmer, Qld. 326
Djukbinj, N.T. 423, 425
Docker River, N.T. 466, 468, 550
Dog Fence 693
Dog Rock, W.A. 525, 528
Dolomite 663
Dolphins 269, 502, 505, 571, 573
Don River Railway 915, 916
Donaghy's Hill, Tas. 936
Donald, Vic. 789
Dongara, W.A. 560, 561
Donnybrook, W.A. 517, 523
Doodlakine, W.A. 498, 542
Dorrigo Steam Railway 191
Dorrigo, N.S.W. 191
Douglas-Apsley N.P., Tas. ..893, 898
Dove Lake, Tas. 930, 931
Dover, Tas. 852, **867**, 868, 870
Dreamworld 244, 245, 246
Drink 32
Driving Conditions 25
Dromana, Vic. 739
Drouin, Vic. 841
Dry Creek, S.A. 158, 463, 668, 669
Drysdale, Vic. 758, 759
Dubbil Barril, Tas. 942, 943

962 INDEX

Dubbo, N.S.W. **145**
Dudley, Vic. 837
Dugong 346, 573
Duke of Avram 948
Duke of Orleans Bay, W.A. 533, 534
Dumbleyung, W.A. 532
Dunalley, Tas. 852, 878, 879
Dunk Island, Qld. 351, **353**, 354
Dunkeld, Vic. 775, 789, 790
Dunmarra, N.T. 441, 442
Dunolly, Vic. 789, 801
Dunsborough, W.A. **509**
Dunwich, Qld. 251
Durack River 619
Dusty, Slim 188
Dwellingup, W.A. 482, 501
Eagle Bluff, W.A. 572, 573
Eagle Point, Vic. 842
Eaglehawk Neck, Tas. 878, 879
Eaglehawk, Vic. 807
Eagles 496
Earth Satellite Station 575
Earthquakes 96, 500, 543
East Coast Discovery Pass .16, 40, 227, 729
East Point, N.T. 419
Eastbrook, W.A. 517
Eastcoaster Resort, Tas. 884
Eastern View, Vic. 765, 768
Easternmost Point 202
Echo Point, Katoomba 102, 103
Echuca, Vic. **803**, 807
Eddystone Lighthouse, Tas. 897, 898
Eden, N.S.W. 123
Edeowie Gorge, S.A. 689, 690
Edith Creek, Tas. 924
Edith Falls, N.T. 434, 436
Edithburgh, S.A. 664, 665
Edward Creek, S.A. 695
Egg Lagoon, Tas. 951
Einasleigh, Qld. 369, 370
Elephant Pass, Tas. 895, 896, 898
Elimbah, Qld. 258
Elizabeth Farm, Parramatta, Sydney 83
Elizabeth, S.A. 657
Ellavale, Qld. 404
Ellery Creek, N.T. 457, 458
Elliott Heads, Qld. 292, 293
Elliott, N.T. 441, 443
Elliston, S.A. 709, 712
Elsey, N.T. 439
E-mail 34
Emerald, Qld. **304**, 309, 311, 314
Emerald, Vic. 744
Emily Gap, N.T. 457
Emita, Tas. 950, 952
Emu Bay Railway 920, 937, 938, 939
Emu Bay, S.A. 645, 646
Emu Bay, Tas. 919
Emu Park, Qld. 298, 300
Endeavour River 385
Eneabba, W.A. 560
Engelbrecht Cave, S.A. 722
Ensay, Vic. 824
Epping Forest, Tas. 909, 911
Erica, Vic. 840, 841
Erldunda, N.T. 457
Esperance, W.A. **531**
Essendon, Vic. 700, 950
ETA 6
Etadunna, S.A. 693
Etmilyn, W.A. 501
Ettamogah, N.S.W. 134
Euabalong West, N.S.W. 157
Eucalyptus 648
Eucla, W.A. 539, 717
Eudlo, Qld. 258, 366
Eugenana, Tas. 918
Eumundi, Qld. 258
Eureka Stockade Rebellion 781
Eureka, Vic. 783
Eurelia, S.A. 157, 687
Eurong, Qld. 282
Evandale, Tas. 909, 911
Ewens Ponds, S.A. 722
Exhibition Building, Melbourne 736
Exmouth, W.A. **577**, 582
Exton, Tas. 917
Eyre Bird Observatory, W.A. 539
Eyre Peninsula, S.A. **708**
Eyre, John 524, 531, 715
Fairhaven, Vic. 765, 768
Falls Creek, Vic. 824, 825
Falmouth, Tas. 896, 898
Fannie Bay, N.T. 419
Farina, S.A. 691, 693
Farrell Tramway, Tas. 938
Fassifern, N.S.W. 99
Faure Island, W.A. 572
Faust Dam, Qld. 326
Fawkner, John 727, 904
Federation 11
Fenton, N.T. 431
Ferguson, S.A. 462, 668
Ferries, Brisbane 230
Ferries, Perth 476, 482, 488
Ferries, Sydney 45
Fingal, Tas. 896, 898
Finke River 458, 463
Finke, N.T. 457
Finucane Island, W.A. 590
Firefly Buses 18
Fish Creek, Vic. 837

INDEX 963

Fish Market, Sydney 61
Fisher, S.A. 672
Fisherman's Beach, Vic. 739
Fishers Point, Tas. 868, 869
Fitzgerald River, W.A. 533
Fitzmaurice Bay, Tas. 951
Fitzroy Crossing, W.A. **613**
Fitzroy River 611, 614
Five Ways, Vic. 832
Fleurieu Peninsula, S.A. 645, 650
Flinders Chase, S.A. 646
Flinders Island, Tas. ....
      837, 838, 851, 852, 899, 912, **950**
Flinders Ranges, S.A. **687**
Flinders River, Qld. 701
Flinders Trail 951
Flinders, Matthew ..227, 293, 294, 531, 645, 674, 710, 711, 715, 746, 851, 863, 902, 950
Flinders, Vic. 739
Flint Cliff, W.A. 573
Florence Falls, N.T. 426, 427
Flowerdale, Vic. 829
Flowerpot Rocks, Tas. 885
Fluted Cape, Tas. 865, 866
Flynn, Rev. John396, 247, 443, 449, 456, 589, 690
Food 32
Football, Australian Rules 37
Footscray, Vic. 796
For the Term of His Natural Life ...877, 878
Forcett, Tas. 879
Foreign Exchange 36
Forest, Tas. 924
Formby, Tas. 915
Forrest River 619
Forrest, Lord John ..474, 502, 503, 550, 566
Forrest, W.A. 497
Forsayth, Qld. 368, 369, 370
Fort Scratchley, Newcastle 97
Fortescue River 582
Forth River, Tas. 930
Forwarding Mail 37
Fossil Cliffs, Tas. 884, 885
Foster, Vic. 837
Fotheringate Beach, Tas. 952
Four Mile Beach, Tas. 885
Four Mile Creek, Tas. 896, 898
Fowlers Bay, S.A. 716, 717
Fox Studios, Sydney 62
Franklin River 936, 947
Franklin, Tas. 868
Frankston, Vic. 739, 745, 832
Fraser Bluff, Tas. 951
Fraser Cave, Tas. 947
Fraser Island Retreat, Qld. 285
Fraser Island, Qld. 269, **281**
Freeling, S.A. 653

Fremantle, Sir Charles 488
Fremantle, W.A. 481, **488**
French Island, Vic. 745, 832
French's Farm, Tas. 885
Frenchman's Cap, Tas. 936
Frenchman's Peak, W.A. 534
Freshwater, Qld. 360, 366
Freycinet Brothers 502, 889
Freycinet, Tas. **888**
Friday Island, Qld. 391, 394
Friendly Beaches, Tas. 889
Frodsham Pass, Tas. 874
Funicular Railway, Katoomba 101, 102
Furneaux Islands, Tas. 950
Furneaux, Captain Tobias 863, 896, 897
Fyans Valley, Vic. 788
Gantheaume Point, W.A. 608
Garfield, Vic. 841
Gascoyne Junction, W.A. 577, 582
Gascoyne River 575
Gawler, S.A. 653, 657
Geelong, Vic. **756**
Geeveston, Tas. 867, 868
Geikie Gorge, W.A. 614
Gelantipy, Vic. 841, 843
Gembrook, Vic. 742
Genoa, Vic. 846, 849
Geoffrey Bay, Qld. 340, 341
Geographe Bay, W.A. 507, 510, 512
Geography 6
George Point, Qld. 348, 349
George Town, Tas. 852, 903, 909, 911
George's Bay, Tas. 896
Georges Plains, N.S.W. 154
Georgetown, Qld. 369
Geraldine, W.A. 568, 569
Geraldton, W.A. **559**, 597
Ghan 3, 13, 447, **461**
Gherringhap, Vic. 461
Gibb River, W.A. 613, 619
Giles, W.A. 550, 551
Gingin, W.A. 560
Gippsland, Vic. **836**
Giralia, W.A. 578, 581
Gisborne, Vic. 796
Gladstone, Qld. **294**, 309
Gladstone, S.A. 158
Glamorgan, Tas. 886
Glasshouse Mountains, Qld. 258, 308
Glen Helen, N.T. 457, 458
Glen Innes, N.S.W. 170, **177**
Glenaire, Vic. 771
Glenample, Vic. 770
Glenbrook, N.S.W. 154
Glenburn, Vic. 829
Glendambo, S.A. 705

964 INDEX

Glenelg, S.A. 631
Glengarry, Vic. 841
Glenorchy, Vic. 789
Glenore, Qld. 402, 403
Glenreagh Mountain Railway 191
Glenreagh, N.S.W. 191
Glenrowan, Vic. 819, 824
Glenthompson, Vic. 775, 789
Glossop, S.A. 657
Gloucester Tree, W.A. 516
Gnowangerup, W.A. 532
Goddards Creek, W.A. 496
Gold 11, 140, 142,
  165, 267, 326, 344, 369, 402, 405, 430, 444,
  445, 471, 498, 538, 541, 597, 616, 727, 781,
  785, 788, 795, 801, 819, 840, 896, 910, 939
Gold Coast 211, 240, 244
Golden Beach, Qld. 259, 260
Golden Gate, Qld. 404
Golden Guitar, Tamworth 169
Golden Mile 542
Golden Ridge, W.A. 499
Golden Zeepaardt 522, 715
Goode Island, Qld. 391, 394
Goolwa, S.A. 645, 649
Goomalling, W.A. 560
Gordon River Dam, Tas. 874
Gordon River 936, 946, 947
Gordonvale, Qld. 373
Gormanston, Tas. 936, 937
Goshen, Tas. 898
Gosse, William 464, 577
Gosse's Bluff, N.T. 457, 458
Gothenburg 332
Goulburn River 817
Goulburn Valley Railway, Vic. ..138, 816
Gove, N.T. **428**
Government House, Sydney 58
Governor Island, Tas. 893, 894
Gowrie Park, Tas. 929
Gowrie, Qld. 256
Goyder Lagoon, S.A. 693
Goyder's Line 157
Gracemere, Qld. 300
Gracetown, W.A. 512
Grafton, N.S.W. **193**
Grampians, Vic. **788**
Granite Island, S.A. 651
Grantville, Vic. 832, 837
Grass Patch, W.A. 532, 533, 538
Grass Point, Tas. 864, 865
Grass Valley, W.A. 500
Grassy, Tas. 951
Gray, Charlie 692, 700, 807
Great Central Road 551
Great Keppel Island, Qld. 300, **303**

Great Ocean Road, Vic. **765**
Great Oyster Bay, Tas. 889
Great Railway Journeys ....
  2, 154, 308, 366, 368, 402, 461, 496, 668
Great Southern Railway Pass 16
Great Southern Railway 13, 16
Great Victoria Desert 550
Great Western, Vic. 461, 789
Gredgwin, Vic. 807
Green Island, Qld. 362
Green Point, Tas. 924
Greenbushes, W.A. 517, 523
Greenhills, W.A. 532
Greenock, S.A. 653
Greenough, W.A. 560, 561
Gregory, Augustus ..437, 438, 564, 578, 582
Grenfell, N.S.W. 142
Gretna, Tas. 872, 874, 932, 933
Greyhound Buses 18
Greyhound Racing 38
Griffith, N.S.W. **136**
Grindelwald, Tas. 910, 911
Groote Eylandt, N.T. 429
Grove, Tas. 867, 868
Grubb Shaft, Tas. 910
Gudrun 574
Guichen Bay, S.A. 721
Gulflander 3, **402**
Gum Creek, Qld. 403
Gunbarrel Highway 551
Gundebang, N.S.W. 157
Gunlom Falls, N.T. 424, 425
Gunn, Jeannie 439
Gunnamatta, Vic. 739
Gurdies, The, Vic. 832, 837
Gwalia, W.A. 550
Gympie, Qld. **267**, 308, 309
Gypsum 663
Haddon Corner 693
Hadspen, Tas. 917
Hagley, Tas. 917
Haig, W.A. 496, 498
Hall, Ben 140, 155
Halls Creek, Tas. 942
Halls Creek, W.A. ..457, 471, 614, **616**, 620
Halls Gap, Vic. **788**, 789
Hamelin Pool, W.A. 572, 573
Hamersley Range, W.A. 603
Hamilton Island, Qld. 326, 327, 328
Hamilton, Tas. 932, 933
Hamilton, Vic. 775, 789
Hammond Island, Qld. 391, 394
Hampton Tableland, W.A. 540
Hanging Rock, Vic. 795
Hannan, Paddy 498, 541
Hanson Bay, S.A. 645, 646

INDEX 965

Harbour Bridge, Sydney 54
Harding River 586
Hardwicke Bay, S.A. 665
Harrietville, Vic. 824
Hart, Pro .156, 160
Hartog, Dirk 10, 471, 571
Harvey, W.A. 501
Haslam, S.A. 709
Hastings Point, N.S.W. 206
Hastings River, N.S.W. 184
Hastings, Tas. 868, 870
Hastings, Vic. 739, 832
Hawes, Monsignor John 566, 597
Hawke, Bob 720, 947
Hawker, S.A. 687, 689, 691
Hawkesbury River, N.S.W. 96
Hawkesdale, Vic. 775
Hawks Head Lookout, W.A. 569
Hawley, Tas. 918
Haydon, Qld. 403
Hayes Creek, N.T. 431
Hayman Island, Qld. 326, 327
Hazard Range, Tas. 890
Hazards Beach, Tas. 890
Healesville, Vic. 742
Health 6
Heathlands, Qld. 387, 388
Heavitree Gap, N.T. 452
Helen Springs, N.T. 443
Helensvale, Qld. 241, 244, 245, 246
Helenvale, Qld. 385
Hell's Gates, Tas. 947
Henbury Meteorite Craters, N.T. 457
Henley-on-Todd Regatta 458
Henty Dunes, Tas. 947
Hepworth Springs, Vic. 785
Herberton, Qld. 373, 374
Hereford, Qld. .403
Hermannsburg, N.T. 457
Heron Island, Qld. 295
Hervey Bay, Qld. **278**
Hesso, S.A. 463, 668
Heyfield, Vic. 841
Heysen Trail 689, 690
Heywood, Vic. .775
Hidden Valley, W.A. 621
High Rock, W.A. 576
Highbury, W.A. 523, 532
Highfield, Tas. .924
Hillarys, W.A. 481
Hillgrange, S.A. 156
Hillwood, Tas. 911
Hinchinbrook Island, Qld. **346**, 349
Hindmarsh Island, S.A. 651
Hindmarsh, John 623, 627, 635
Hines Hill, W.A. 542

Hinkler, Bert 291, 309
Hiring Vehicles 26
History 10
Hitch-hiking 26
Hobart, Tas. **853**
Holloway's Beach, Qld. 360, 361
Home Hill, Tas. .917
Homebush Bay, Sydney 64
Honey 647
Honeymoon Bay, Tas. 890
Hook Island, Qld. 327
Hook Point, Qld. 282
Hoover, Herbert 550
Hopetoun, W.A. 532, 533
Hopground Beach, Tas. 885
Horn Island, Qld. 388, **389**
Horn, The, Vic. .824
Horrocks, W.A. .569
Horse Racing 38
Horseshoe Bay, Qld. 340, 341
Horseshoe Falls, Tas. 872, 873
Horsham, Vic. 461, **788**
Hostels 28
Hotels 27
Hotham Valley Railway 482, 501
Howe, Jack 314
Hugh River, N.T. 462
Hughenden, Qld. 313, 322, 396
Hughes, S.A. 497
Hume, Hamilton 111
Hummock Hill, S.A. 709
Humpty Doo, N.T. 423, 425
Hunter Island, Tas. 924
Huon Pine Trees 946
Huon River 867
Huon Valley, Tas. 867
Huonville, Tas. 867, 868
Huskisson, N.S.W. 113
Hutt River Province 568, 569
Hyde Park Barracks, Sydney 59
Hyde Park, Sydney 59
Hyden, W.A. 532, 533
Ida Bay Railway 869
Ida Bay, Tas. 868, 869, 870
Ilfracombe, Qld. 312
Illawarra Light Railway 109
Illowa, Vic. 775
Iluka, N.S.W. 193, 195, **196**
Imbil, Qld. 268, 308
Immana Bank, S.A. 672
Impadna, N.T. .462
Indented Head, Vic. 739, 759, 761
Independence 645
Indian-Pacific 2, 13, **154**, 472, **496**, **668**
Ingham, Qld. 346
Inglewood, Vic. 807

966 INDEX

Injidup, W.A. 511
Injinoo, Qld. 388
Innamincka, S.A. 692
Inner Sister Island, Tas. 952
Innes Park, Qld. 292, 293
Innes N.P., S.A. 663, 665
Inneston, S.A. 665
Innisfail, Qld. 352, 357, 373
Innot Hot Springs, Qld. 373
Inskip Point, Qld. 269, 282
Integrity Buses 18
International Telephone Calls 34
Inverell, N.S.W. 170, **171**
Inveresk, Tas. 908
Inverloch, Vic. 832, 836, 837
Iron Blow, Tas. 937, 940
Iron Knob, S.A. 709
Iron 582, 584, 589, 600
Ironbound Range, Tas. 870
Irrapatana, S.A. 695
Irvinebank, Qld. 373, 374
Isle of the Dead, Tas. 880
Ivanhoe, N.S.W. 157
Jabiru, N.T. 424, 425, 429
Jacaranda 193
Jamestown, S.A. 158
Jan Juc, Vic. 765
Japanese Cemeteries 392, 593, 609
Jardine River, Qld. 387, 388
Jardine, John 389
Jarrah Trees 515
Jarvis Hill, S.A. 687, 689
Jaurdi, W.A. 499
Jennings, N.S.W. 182, 183
Jenolan Caves, N.S.W. 103
Jericho, Qld. 310, 311, 314
Jerilderie, N.S.W. 817
Jerramungup, W.A. 532, 533
Jessie Gap, N.T. 457
Jetty Beach, Tas. 864, 865
Jewel Cave, W.A. 512, 514
Jim Jim Falls, N.T. 424, 425
Jindabyne, N.S.W. 125, 127
Joffre Falls, W.A. 604
John Bull's Rock, Tas. 885
Johnson, Lyndon B. 320, 321
Johnsonville, Vic. 841
Julia Creek, Qld. 396
Jumperkine, W.A. 500
Junee, N.S.W. 137, 138
Jurien Bay, W.A. 560
K Col, Tas. 873
Kadina, S.A. 661, 662, 663, 665
Kakadu, N.T. **423**
Kalamina Falls, W.A. 604
Kalamunda, W.A. 482

Kalangadoo, Tas. 887
Kalbarri, W.A. **568**
Kaleentha, N.S.W. 157
Kalgoorlie, W.A. 11, 471, 499, 532, **541**
Kalimna, Vic. 841, 843
Kalkarindji. N.T. 438
Kambalda, W.A. 532, 549
Kandanga, Qld. 268
Kangarilla, S.A. 650
Kangaroo Flat, Vic. 796
Kangaroo Island, S.A. 623, 624, **644**
Kangaroos 234, 384, 496
Kaniva, Vic. 461, 789, 790
Kantju, N.T. 467
Kanyaka, S.A. 687, 689
Karalundi, W.A. 601
Karatta, S.A. 645
Karijini, W.A. 581, 582, 594, 601, **603**
Karlgarin, W.A. 532
Karonie, W.A. 496
Karratha, W.A. **581**, 594
Karri Trees 515, 521
Karridale, W.A. 512
Karst N.P., Tas. 929
Karumba, Qld. **405**
Kata Tjuta, N.T. 468
Katanning, W.A. 523, 532
Katherine Gorge, N.T. 433, 434
Katherine, N.T. **433**
Katoomba, N.S.W. **101**, 154, 155
Kawana Waters, Qld. 260
Keith, S.A. 461, 720, 721
Kellerberrin, W.A. 498, 542
Kelly Hill Caves, S.A. 645, 646
Kelly, Ned 736, 819, 830
Kelly's Beach, Qld. 292, 293
Kelly's Knob, W.A. 620, 621
Kempton, Tas. 887
Kendenup, W.A. 523
Kennedy Track 351
Kennedy, Edmund 351
Kennett River, Vic. 765, 768
Keppel Sands, Qld. 300, 301
Kerang, Vic. 807
Keswick, Adelaide 158, 625
Kettering, Tas. 863, 868
Kewarra Beach, Qld. 360, 361
Khancoban, N.S.W. 127
Kiah Inlet, N.S.W. 123
Kiama, N.S.W. 109
Kiewa Valley, Vic. 824
Kilcunda, Vic. 837
Killer Whale Museum, Eden 124
Killiecrankie, Tas. 951, 952, 953
Kilometre Passes (Bus) 18
Kimba, S.A. 709

INDEX 967

Kimberley, W.A. 605, 609
Kinalung, N.S.W. 156
King George Sound, W.A. 522, 529
King Island, Tas. **950**
King River, W.A. 619
King River, Tas. 941, 943
King Solomon's Cave, Tas. 929
King Sound, W.A. 611
King William Saddle, Tas. 936
King, John 692, 701
King's Canyon, N.T. 457, **470**
King's Cross, Sydney 62, 63
Kingfisher Bay, Qld. 282
Kinglake West, Vic. 829
Kingoonya, S.A. 462, 671, 705
Kings Beach, Qld. 259, 260
Kingscliff, N.S.W. 206, 241, 245, 246
Kingscote, S.A. .645
Kingston, S.A. 720, 721
Kingston, Tas. 867, 868
Kingston-on-Murray, S.A. 657
Kingstown, W.A. 493
Kirra, Qld. 242
Kirup, W.A. 517, 523
Kitchener, W.A. 496
Koalas 234, 340, 342, 834
Kojonup, W.A. .523
Kondinin, W.A. 532
Kookaburras 341
Koolyanobbing, W.A. 498
Koonya, Tas. 879, 881
Koorana, Qld. 300, 301
Koo-Wee-Rup, Vic. 832
Korean Star 576
Koroit, Vic. 775
Korong Vale, Vic. 807
Korumburra, Vic. 837
Kosciuszko National Park, N.S.W. 125
Kukerin, W.A. .532
Kulgera, N.T. 457, 462, 463
Kulin, W.A. 532
Kulpara, S.A. 665
Kultanaby, S.A. 463, 670, 671
Kumarina, W.A. 601
Kununurra, W.A. 438, 614, **619**, 620
Kuranda Scenic Railway 3, 360, **366**
Kuranda, Qld. 360, 367, 373
Kyancutta, S.A. 709
Kyneton, Vic. 796
Kynuna, Qld. 321
Labillardiere Peninsula, Tas. 864, 865
Lackrana, Tas. .952
Lady Barron Falls, Tas. 872, 873
Lady Barron, Tas. 951, 952, 953
Lady Bay, Sydney 66, 77
Lady Musgrave Island, Qld. 295

Lake Argyle, W.A. 438, 620
Lake Barrine, Qld. 373
Lake Barrington, Tas. 928, 929, 930
Lake Belcher, Tas. 873
Lake Belton, Tas. 873
Lake Bennett, N.T. 426, 427
Lake Binney, Tas. 933
Lake Blowering, N.S.W. 127
Lake Boga, Vic. 807, 810
Lake Bolac, Vic. 789
Lake Burbury, Tas. 936, 937
Lake Cadibarrawirracanna, S.A. . . .695, 696
Lake Cave, W.A. 512
Lake Dobson, Tas. 872, 873
Lake Dundas, W.A. 539
Lake Eildon, Vic. 829
Lake Eyre, S.A. 695, 696
Lake Gordon, Tas. 874
Lake Grace, W.A. 532
Lake Hanson, Tas. 930
Lake Hume, Vic. 128
Lake Illawarra, N.S.W. 105
Lake Illawarra 856
Lake Jindabyne, N.S.W. 127
Lake Julia, W.A. 498
Lake King William, Tas. 936
Lake King, Vic. 842
Lake King, W.A. 532
Lake Kununurra, W.A. 620
Lake Leake, Tas. 887
Lake Lilla, Tas. 930
Lake Mackintosh, Tas. 937, 938
Lake Macquarie, N.S.W. 99
Lake Maraboon, Qld. 305
Lake Margaret, Tas. 937, 939
Lake McKenzie, Qld. 284
Lake Murchison, Tas. 937, 938
Lake Newdegate, Tas. 873
Lake Nicholls, Tas. 873
Lake Omeo, Vic. 824
Lake Pedder, Tas. 874
Lake Pieman, Tas. 937, 938
Lake Plimsoll, Tas. 937, 938
Lake Rodway, Tas. 930
Lake Rosebery, Tas. 937, 938
Lake Seal, Tas. 873
Lake St. Clair, Tas. 851, 852, **932**, 936
Lake Tinaroo, Qld. 372, 373
Lake Torrens, S.A. 690, 691
Lake Tyers, Vic. 841, 846
Lake Webster, Tas. 873
Lake Wendouree, Vic. 784
Lake Wilks, Tas. 930
Lake Wonboyn, N.S.W. 124
Lakeland Downs, Qld. 377, 387
Lakes Entrance, Vic. 823, 824, **840**

968 INDEX

Lakes, The, W.A. 523, 532, 560
Lakeside, Vic. 744
Lalbert, Vic. 807
Lancelin, W.A. **557**
Land of the Beardies Festival 178
Landells, George 700
Landsborough, Qld. 258
Lang Lang, Vic. 832, 836, 837
Lappa, Qld. 368
Lark Quarry, Qld. 320
Larrimah, N.T. .441
Lasseter, L.H. 456
Latham, W.A. 560
Latrobe Valley, Vic. 841
Latrobe, Tas. 917
Laughing Jack Lagoon, Tas. 933
Launceston, Tas. 852, **902**, 950
Laura, Qld. 385, 387, 388
Lavers Hill, Vic. 769
Laverton, W.A. 542, 550
Lavinia Point, Tas. 951
Lawson, Henry .151
Lawson, N.S.W. 154
Le Frog 893, 894
Lead 156, 159, 399, 568, 668
Learmonth, W.A. 8, 578
Leawarra, Vic. .832
Leeaberra Track 895
Leeka, Tas. 952
Legg's Tor, Tas. .896
Leichhardt River 398
Leichhardt, Ludwig 433, 441
Leigh Creek, S.A. . . . .
        461, 669, 680, 682, 690, 691
Lennox Head, N.S.W. 203
Leonard, H.R.H. Prince 568
Leongatha, Vic. .837
Leonora, W.A. .550
Leopold, Vic. 758, 759
Leura, N.S.W. 102, 103
Liapootah Dam, Tas. 933
Light Rail, Sydney 49
Light, Col. William 623, 625, 628
Lightning Ridge, N.S.W. **148**
Ligurian Honey Bees 647
Lillico Beach, Tas. 918
Lillies Beach, Tas. 952, 953
Lily Creek Lagoon, W.A. 621
Lilydale, Tas. 911
Lilydale, Vic. 829
Linda Valley, Tas. 937
Lindeman Island, Qld. 327, 328
Linton, Vic. 789
Lion Rock, Tas. 868, 869
Lismore, N.S.W. **198**, 209
Litchfield, N.T. **426**
Lithgow, N.S.W. 140, 155
Little Blue Lake, S.A. 722
Little River Gorge, Vic. 843
Little Sahara, S.A. 646
Little Swanport, Tas. 886
Loch Ard Gorge, Vic. 770, 771
Loch Ard 770, 776
Loch, Vic. 837
Lochiel, S.A. 683, 709
Lockerbie, Qld. .388
Lockhart River, Qld. 387
Lockyer, Major Edmund 471, 522
Logan's Beach, Vic. 777
London Bridge, Vic. 771
Long Island, Qld. 327, 328
Long Plains, S.A. 158, 463, 669
Long Straight (railway) 497, 498, 672
Long Straight (road) 539
Longreach, Qld. 312, 313, **315**
Longwarry, Vic. 841
Loongana, W.A. 497, 498
Loop, The, W.A. 569
Loorana, Tas. 951
Lord Howe Island Courier Post 215
Lord Howe Island, N.S.W. **214**
Lorne, Vic. 765, 768, 769
Lost City, N.T. 426, 427
Lowana, Tas. 942, 943
Lower Crackpot, Tas. 930
Lower Gellibrand, Vic. 771
Loxton, S.A. 657
Loy Yang, Vic. 841, 842
Loyalty Beach, Qld. 388, 389
Lucinda, Qld. 346, 349
Lucky Bay, W.A. 533, 534
Ludlow, W.A. 507
Lughrata, Tas. 952
Lunawanna, Tas. 864, 865
Lune River, Tas. 867, **868**, 869, 870
Lyall, W.A. 517
Lymwood, Tas. .951
Lynchford, Tas. .942
Lyndhurst, S.A. 691, 693
Lyndhurst, Vic. .739
Lyndoch, S.A. 653
Lyons, Joseph 917, 923
Lyons, S.A. 670
Mabulag Island, Qld. 391
MacArthur, General Douglas 132
Macassan Traders 10
MacDonnell Ranges, N.T. 452, 463
MacDonnell Siding, N.T. 454
Macedon, Vic. 795, 796
Machan's Beach, Qld. 360, 361
Mackay, Qld. **324**
Mackellar, Dorothea 7

INDEX 969

MacKillop, Mother Mary 305, 720, 778
Maclean, N.S.W. 193, **195**, 196
Macquarie Heads, Tas. 947
Macquarie River 908
Macquarie Harbour 942
Madura, W.A. 539
Maffra, Vic. 841, 842
Magnetic Island, Qld. 334, **339**
Magoffin, Richard 322
Maheno 283
Mahogany Ship .777
Maiden Gully, Vic. 807
Maindample, Vic. 829
Mait's Rest, Vic. 765, 769, 771
Maitland, S.A. 665
Malanda, Qld. 373
Malbooma, S.A. 670
Maldon, Vic. 801
Mallacoota, Vic. 846, **848**
Mallaga Falls, S.A. 689
Mallala, S.A. 158, 463, 669
Mallee, Vic. 790
Malmsbury, Vic. 796
Mambray Creek, S.A. 463, 669
Mammoth Cave, W.A. 512
Mamukala, N.T. 424, 425
Man from Snowy River 845, 846
Mandorah, N.T. .419
Mandurah, W.A. 482
Manguri, S.A. 462, 704, 705
Manildra, N.S.W. 154, 155
Manjimup, W.A. 515, 517, 523
Manly, Sydney 67, 73, 74
Manna Hill, S.A. 156, 157
Mansfield, Vic. **829**
Map Shops 38
Marakoopa Cave, Tas. 929
Maralinga, S.A. .673
Marananga, S.A. 653
Marble Bar, W.A. 8, 589, 594, 595
Marcoola, Qld. .258
Marcus Beach, Qld. 258
Mareeba, Qld. 368, 369, 373, 377
Marengo, Vic. 765, 769, 771
Margaret River, W.A. **511**
Margate, Tas. 868
Maria Island, Tas. **882**
Maritime Museum, Sydney 61
Marla, S.A. 462, 697, 706
Marlo, Vic. .846, 847
Marnoo, Vic. 789
Marong, Vic. 807
Maroochydore, Qld. 257, 258, 260, 262
Maroona, Vic. 461
Marrawah, Tas. .924
Marree, S.A. . . .461, 669, 680, 692, 693, 695

Marryat, S.A. 462
Marshall Bay, Tas. 952, 953
Mary Ann Haven, W.A. 534
Mary Ann 273, 275, 277
Mary Kathleen, Qld. 396
Mary Poppins 272, 308
Mary River, N.T. 423, 425
Mary River 272
Mary Valley Heritage Railway 268, 308
Maryborough, Qld. **271**, 308, 309
Maryborough, Vic. 789
Matakana, N.S.W. 157
Mataranka, N.T. **439**
Matthew Flinders 852
Mauritius Beach, W.A. 578, 579
Maydena, Tas. 874
Maynard, Ken 134
Mayneside, Qld. 321
McCafferty's Buses 18
McCrae, Vic. 739
McDonald, N.T. 431, 434
McLaren Vale, S.A. 650
McLeay, S.A. 463, 668
Meadows, S.A. .650
Meckering, W.A. 500, 542, 543
Medeas Cove, Tas. 897
Medlow Bath, N.S.W. 155
Meekatharra, W.A. **596**
Meeniya, Vic. 837
Melaleuca, Tas. 870, 874
Melba, Dame Nelly 132
Melbourne, Vic. 11, 461, **729**
Mellelea, N.S.W. 157
Melville Island, N.T. 429
Memana, Tas. 952
Menindee, N.S.W. 155, 157, 700
Meningie, S.A. .721
Menzies Creek, Vic. 744
Menzies, Robert 132
Menzies, W.A. 549, 550
Mepunga, Vic. .771
Merimbula, N.S.W. **121**
Mermaid Beach, Qld. 246
Merredin, W.A. 498, 500, 532, 542, 543
Merri Island, Vic. 777
Mersey Bluff, Tas. 916, 917
Merton, Vic. 829
Miami, Qld. 245, 246
Michelago, N.S.W. 116, 223
Middle Island, Vic. 777
Middleback Ranges, S.A. 710
Middleton Beach, W.A. 528, 529
Middleton, S.A. 650
Middleton, Tas. .868
Midland, W.A. 500, 532, 542, 560, 597
Miena, Tas. .932, 933

970 INDEX

Mildura, S.S. 578, 579
Mildura, Vic. 33, 138, **812**
Miling, W.A. 597
Millaa Millaa, Qld. 373, 374
Millicent, S.A. 721
Mills Beach, Vic. 739
Millstream, W.A. 588, 594
Millthorpe, N.S.W. 154
Milton, N.S.W. 113
Milyering, W.A. 578, 579
Min Min Light 399
Mindil Beach, N.T. 417
Mingary, S.A. 156, 157
Mingela, Qld. 345
Mingenew, W.A. 560
Minilya, W.A. 578, 582
Minlaton, S.A. 664, 665
Minnipa, S.A. 709
Mint, Royal Australian, Canberra ...222
Mintabie, S.A. 706
Minyip, Vic. 789
Miriam Vale, Qld. 295, 296, 309
Mission Beach, Qld. **351**
Mistaken Cape, Tas. 885
Mitchell River 842
Mitchell, Major Thomas 151, 807, 810
Mitiamo, Vic. 807
Moa Island, Qld. 391
Moama, N.S.W. 804, 805
Moe, Vic. 840, 841
Moffat Beach, Qld. 259, 260
Moffat, John 374
Mogo, N.S.W. 120
Mogumber, W.A. 560
Moina, Tas. 929, 930
Mole Creek, Tas. 852, 917, 928, 929
Molesworth, Vic. 829
Molong, N.S.W. 142, 154, 155
Mon Repos, Qld. 291, 293
Monaro Plains, N.S.W. 126
Monarto South, S.A. 461
Money 36
Monkey Mia, W.A. **571**, 582
Monorail, Sydney 49, 50
Montague Island, N.S.W. 120
Montezuma Falls, Tas. 939
Mooball, N.S.W. 206
Moolap, Vic. 758, 759
Mooloolaba, Qld. 258, 260, 261
Mooloolah, Qld. 258, 366
Moomba, S.A. 691, 692, 693
Moon Point, Qld. 282
Moondyne Cave, W.A. 512, 514
Moondyne, W.A. 500
Moonta Bay, S.A. 662, 665
Moonta, S.A. 624, 661, 662, 665

Moora, W.A. 560
Moore Park, Qld. 292, 293
Moorina, Tas. 898, 899
Moorine Rock, W.A. 498, 542
Moorooduc, Vic. 739, 746
Moorook, S.A. 657
Moralana, S.A. 689, 691
Morawa, W.A. 560
Moree, N.S.W. **163**, 170
Moreton Bay, Qld. 227
Moreton, Qld. 387, 388
Morgan, S.A. 657
Mornington, Vic. 739, 744, 745
Morrado, Vic. 832
Moruya, N.S.W. 120
Morven, Qld. 256
Morwell, Vic. 841
Moss Vale, N.S.W. 85
Mossman, Qld. 377, 379
Motor Racing ....
         140, 155, 246, 630, 833, 834, 909
Moulamein, N.S.W. 805
Moulting Lagoon, Tas. 889
Mt. Adolphus Island, Qld. 391
Mt. Amos, Qld. 385
Mt. Amos, Tas. 890
Mt. Anne, Tas. 874
Mt. Augustus, W.A. 464, 577, 582
Mt. Baldy, Qld. 372
Mt. Barker Junction, S.A. 461, 649, 650
Mt. Barker, S.A. 649, 650
Mt. Barker, W.A. 521, 523
Mt. Bartle Frere, Qld. 357
Mt. Baw Baw, Vic. 840, 841
Mt. Beauty, Vic. 823, 824
Mt. Bellenden Ker, Qld. 8, 227, 351
Mt. Bischoff, Tas. 919
Mt. Blue Cow, N.S.W. 127
Mt. Bogong, Vic. 823, 824
Mt. Bowen, Qld. 346, 349
Mt. Bruce, W.A. 604
Mt. Buffalo, Vic. 822, 824
Mt. Buller, Vic. **829**
Mt. Canobolas, N.S.W. 155
Mt. Carbine, Qld. 377
Mt. Chappell Island, Tas. 952
Mt. Charlotte, W.A. 544
Mt. Christie, S.A. 673
Mt. Clarence, W.A. 528, 531
Mt. Claude, Tas. 929
Mt. Compass, S.A. 650
Mt. Connor, N.T. 457, 464
Mt. Cook, Qld. 341
Mt. Coot-tha, Brisbane 234
Mt. Cyril, W.A. 621
Mt. Despair, Qld. 383

INDEX 971

Mt. Difficult, Vic. 788
Mt. Dove, Tas. 890
Mt. Dutton, S.A. 695, 712
Mt. Ebenezer, N.T. 457
Mt. Feathertop, Vic. 824
Mt. Field, Tas. 852, **872**
Mt. Finnegan, Qld. 385
Mt. Freycinet, Tas. 890
Mt. Gambier, S.A. 624, **719**, 775
Mt. Garnet, Qld. 373
Mt. George, W.A. 604
Mt. Gibson, W.A. 597
Mt. Gower, N.S.W. 218
Mt. Graham, Tas. 890
Mt. Hotham, Vic. 819, **822**, 823
Mt. Hypipamee, Qld. 373, 374
Mt. Iarcom, Qld. 309
Mt. Isa, Qld. **398**
Mt. Jimberlana, W.A. 539
Mt. King, W.A. 604
Mt. Kootaloo, Qld. 354, 355
Mt. Kosciuszco, N.S.W. 126, 127
Mt. Lidgbird, N.S.W. 216
Mt. Lofty, S.A. 461, 636
Mt. Lyell, Tas. 940
Mt. Macedon, Vic. 795
Mt. Magnet, W.A. 597
Mt. Mangana, Tas. 864, 865
Mt. Maria, Tas. 885
Mt. Martha, Vic. 739, 745
Mt. Mawson, Tas. 873
Mt. Mayson, Tas. 890
Mt. Misery, Qld. 382
Mt. Molloy, Qld. 377, 387
Mt. Morgan, Qld. 300, 941
Mt. Nameless, W.A. 602
Mt. Nelson, Tas. 858
Mt. Olympus, Tas. 934
Mt. Ossa, Tas. 931, 934
Mt. Oxer, W.A. 604
Mt. Panorama, N.S.W. 140, 155
Mt. Parsons, Tas. 890
Mt. Pilot, N.S.W. 127
Mt. Roland, Tas. 929
Mt. Rosea, Vic. 791
Mt. St. Gwinear, Vic. 840
Mt. Sorrow, Qld. 381
Mt. Straloch, Qld. 346, 349
Mt. Strzelecki, Tas. 951, 952
Mt. Surprise, Qld. 369, 370
Mt. Tahloo, Qld. 354, 355
Mt. Tam Coorahee, Qld. 354, 355
Mt. Tanner, Tas. 952
Mt. Tom Price, W.A. 602
Mt. Victoria, N.S.W. 155
Mt. Vigors, W.A. 604
Mt. Warning, N.S.W. 208
Mt. Wedge, Tas. 874
Mt. Wellington, Tas. 859
Mt. Whaleback, W.A. 600
Mt. William, Tas. 897, 898
Mt. William, Vic. 788
Mt. Windell, W.A. 604
Mt. Youle, W.A. 541
Mt. Zamia, Qld. 305, 306
Movieworld 244, 245, 246
Muchea, W.A. 560
Mudjimba, Qld. 258
Muggy Muggy, Qld. 354, 355
Muir's Beach, Tas. 890
Mulgrave Rambler 377
Mullalyup, W.A. 517, 523
Mullewa, W.A. 560, 597
Mulligan Falls, Qld. 348, 349
Mullumbimby, N.S.W. 203
Mundaring, W.A. 523, 532, 543, 560
Mundijong, W.A. 501
Mundrabilla, W.A. 497, 498, 539
Mungala, S.A. 673
Mungana, Qld. 369
Mungerannie, S.A. 693
Munglinup, W.A. 532
Munjina, W.A. 594, 601, 603, 604
Murchison River 569
Murdunna, Tas. 879
Murray Bridge, S.A. 461, 720, 721
Murray River ....
  127, 128, 133, 650, 656, 657, 803, 807, 812
Murrumbidgee Irrigation Scheme 138
Murrumbidgee River 129
Murtoa, Vic. 461, 789
Murwillumbah, N.S.W. ..206, **208**, 245, 246
Musgrave, Qld. 387, 388
Mutitjulu, N.T. 467
Mutton Birds 216, 834, 947, 950
Myall Beach, Qld. 381, 382
Myer's 732, 797
Myponga, S.A. 650
Myrtleford, Vic. 822, 824
Mysia, Vic. 807
Namatjira, Albert 455, 456
Nambour, Qld. 257, 258, 308, 309
Nambucca Heads, N.S.W. **188**
Nambung, W.A. 557
Nan Tien Temple, Wollongong, N.S.W. ..109
Nanga, W.A. 572, 573
Nantawarra, S.A. 158, 463, 669
Naracoopa, Tas. 951
Naracoorte, S.A. 720, 721, 789
Narambla, N.S.W. 142
Narembeen, W.A. 532
Naretha, W.A. 496

INDEX

Nar-Nar-Goon, Vic. 841
Narooma, N.S.W. 113, 120
Narrandera, N.S.W. 137, 816
Narrawong, Vic. 775
Narrogin, W.A. 523, 532
National Racing Museum, Bathurst 140
Native Dog Beach, W.A. 533
Natternanie, S.A. 693
Nature's Window, W.A. 569
Naval Communications Station 578, 579
Neales River 696
Neck Beach, Tas. 866
Neck, The, Tas. 864, 865
Ned Ryan's Hill, Tas. 885
Nelly Bay, Qld. 340, 341
Nelson Falls, Tas. 936
Nelson Point, W.A. 592
Nelson, Vic. 775
Nerang River 247
Nerang, Qld. 244, 245, 246
Nerimbera, Qld. 300
Nerve Test, Vic. 790, 791
Neuroodla, S.A. 689, 691
New Norcia, W.A. 560, 561, 597
New Norfolk, Tas. . . 860, 872, 874, 932, 933
New South Wales **39**
New Year Island, Tas. 951
Newbridge, N.S.W. 154
Newcastle Waters, N.T. 441, 442
Newcastle, N.S.W. **96**
Newcomb, Vic. 758
Newdegate, W.A. 532
Newhaven, Vic. 832, 833
Newman, W.A. 582, 592, 594, **600**
Newmerella, Vic. 846
Ngilgi Cave, W.A. 511, 512
Nhill, Vic. 461, 789, 790
Nhulunbuy, N.T. **428**
Nicholson, Vic. 841
Nickel 533, 551
Nielsen Park, Qld. 292, 293
Nightcliff, N.T. 419
Nimbin, N.S.W. 199
Nimmitabel, N.S.W. 118
Ninety Mile Beach, Vic. 843
Ninety Mile Desert, S.A. 720
Ningaloo Reef, W.A. 578, 579
Nirranda, Vic. 771
Nitmiluk, N.T. 434, 436
Nive River 933
Noah Creek, Qld. 382
Noarlunga, S.A. 650
Nomads Hostels 29
Noosa Heads, Qld. 257, 258, 263, 265
Noosaville, Qld. 258
Norfolk Island 214
Norman River 405
Normanton, Qld. 402, **405**
Normanville, S.A. 650
Nornalup, W.A. 518, 521
Norseman, W.A. 532, **538**, 715
North Esk River 902, 903
North Keppel Island, Qld. 304
North Molle Island, Qld. 327
North Peake, S.A. 695
North Shore, Vic. 461
North Stradbroke Island, Qld. **250**
North West Cape, W.A. 578
North West Shelf Natural Gas Project 582, 584
Northam, W.A. . .500, 523, 532, 542, 543, 560
Northampton, W.A. 568, 569
Northcliffe, W.A. 482, 517, 523
North-East River, Tas. 952, 953
Northern Territory **407**
Northernmost Point 389
Nourlangie, N.T. 423, 424, 425
Nowa Nowa, Vic. 841, 845, 846
No-Where Else, Tas. 928
Nowra, N.S.W. 113
Nubeena, Tas. 879, 881
Nullagine, W.A. 594
Nullarbor Plain 474, 496, **538**, 672, **714**
Nullarbor, S.A. 717
Nullawarra, Vic. 771
Nunamara, Tas. 911
Nundle, N.S.W. 165
Nundroo, S.A. 716, 717
Nurina, W.A. 497, 498
Nuriootpa, S.A. 653, 654, 657
Nut, The, Tas. 923, 924
Nuyts, Peter 522, 715
Nyora, Vic. 836, 837
O'Connor, C.Y. 489, 499, 543, 544
O'Malley, S.A. 672
Oakover River 582
Oaks Beach, Qld. 293
Oatlands, Tas. 887
O-Bahn 636
Observatory, Sydney 56
Ocean Grove, Vic. 759, 761
Ochre Pits 457, 458, 691, 692, 693
Oenpelli, N.T. 429
Olary, S.A 156, 157
Old Halls Creek, W.A. 616, 620
Old Laura, Qld. 387
Old Rainworth Fort, Qld. 305, 306
Olgas, N.T. 457, 466
Olive May 868
Oliver Hill, W.A. 493
Olives 163
Olympic Dam, S.A. 704, 705
Olympic Park, Sydney 64

INDEX 973

Omeo, Vic. 823, 824, 825
One Arm Point, W.A. 614
Ongerup, W.A. 532
Onslow, W.A. 581, 582
Oodnadatta Track 694, 695
Oodnadatta, S.A. .8, 461, 669, 680, 695, 697
Ooldea, S.A. 672, 673
Opals 148, 311, 320, 704, 705, 706
Opalton, Qld. 320
Opera House, Sydney 54
Ophir, N.S.W. 142
Orange, N.S.W. **142**, 154
Orbost, Vic. **845**
Ord River Scheme 619
Ord River 619
Orford, Tas. **882**, 883, 887
Ormiston Gorge, N.T. 457, 458
Ororoo, S.A. 157, 687
Osterley, Tas. 932. 933
Otway Ranges, Vic. 768
Ouse, Tas. 932, 933
Outback Highway 551
Overland Track ....
    851, 927, 929, 930, 931, 932, 934
Overland 13
Overlander, W.A. 572, 582
Oxer Lookout, W.A. 604
Oxley, John 165, 184, 227
Oxley, Vic. 824
Oyster Cove, Tas. 851, 950
Oz Experience Tours 22
Pacific Fair, Qld. 245
Paddy's Market, Sydney 62
Padthaway, S.A. 721
Painted Cliffs, Tas. 884, 885
Painted Desert, S.A. 706
Pajinka, Qld. 389
Pakenham, Vic. 840, 841
Palana, Tas. 952
Palgarup, W.A. 517
Palm Beach, Qld. 241, 245, 246
Palm Cove, Qld. 360, 361
Palm Valley, N.T. 457
Palmer River, Qld. 377
Palmers Island, N.S.W. 195
Palmerston, N.T. 419
Palmwoods, Qld. 258
Pambula, N.S.W. 122
Pandani Grove, Tas. 873
Pandora, H.M.S. 336
Paraburdoo, W.A. ...581, 582, 584, 594, 601
Parachilna Gorge, S.A. 689, 690, 691
Paradise Point, Qld. 241, 245
Paradise, Tas. 928, 929
Paratoo, S.A. 156
Parcels 37

Parenna, Tas. 951
Parker Point, W.A. 585
Parkes, N.S.W. 154, 155
Parkes, Sir Henry 155, 180
Parkeston, W.A. 498, 499
Parliament House, Canberra 220
Parndana, S.A. 645, 648
Parramatta, Sydney 67, 81
Paskeville, S.A. 665
Pasminco Mine, Tas. 938
Paterson, Banjo 142, 155, 313, 318, 845
Patriarchs, The, Tas. 952, 953
Paynes Find, W.A. 597
Paynesville, Vic. 824, 841, 842
Pearl Divers 392, 394, 413, 586, 605
Pearshape, Tas. 951
Pecan Nuts 163
Peel River 165
Pegarah, Tas. 951
Peggy's Point, Tas. 893, 894
Pell, N.T. 430, 431
Pemberton Tramway 517
Pemberton, W.A. 482, **515**, 523
Penderlea Gap, N.S.W. 127
Penguin Island, Tas. 865, 866
Penguin, Tas. 919, 921, 924
Penguins 647, 651,
    745, 777, 831, 832, 833, 864, 893, 918, 919
Penneshaw, S.A. 645, 647
Penola, S.A. 720, 721, 789
Penong, S.A. 712, 716, 717
Penrice, S.A. 653
Penrith, N.S.W. 154
Penshurst, Vic. 775
Pentecost River 619
Peppermint Beach, W.A. 533
Peregian Beach, Qld. 258
Perenjori, W.A. 560
Perisher, N.S.W. 127
Peron Sand Dunes, Tas. 897
Peron, W.A. 572, 574
Perpendicular Mountain, Tas. 885
Perth, H.M.A.S. 529
Perth, Tas. 909, 911
Perth, W.A. 11, **473**, 500
Peterborough, S.A. 156, 157, 687
Peterborough, Vic. 769, 771
Petwood, S.A. 461
Phillip Island, Vic. 745, **831**
Phillip, Arthur 11
Pialba, Qld. 279
Piccaninnie Ponds, S.A. 722
Pichi Richi Pass, S.A. 682
Pichi Richi Railway .461, 669, 680, 687, 689
Pickers' Riot 807
Picnic at Hanging Rock 795

974 INDEX

Picnic Bay, Qld. 339, 341
Pieman River 938
Pilgramunna, W.A. 579
Pimba, S.A. 463, 670, 671, 704, 705
Pine Creek, N.T. **430**
Pine Point, S.A. 665
Pingelly, W.A. 523
Pinjarra, W.A. 501, 502
Pink Lake, S.A. 669, 680
Pink Lake, W.A. 533, 535
Pinnacle Lookout, Vic. 791
Pinnacles, W.A. **557**
Pithara, W.A. 560
Planter Beach, Tas. 952
Platypus 117
Plenty River Highway 457
Plenty, Tas. 874
Plutonic Mine, W.A. 601
Poeppel Corner 693
Point Danger .242
Point Hicks, Vic. 846, 849
Point Labbatt, S.A. 712
Point Lesueur, Tas. 884, 885
Point Lonsdale, Vic. 759, 760
Point Lookout, Qld. 251
Point Mississippi, W.A. 532
Point Murat, W.A. 578
Point Puer, Tas. 880
Point Richards, Vic. 759, 761
Point Samson, W.A. 584, **586**
Point Vernon, Qld. 279
Pomona, Qld. 258
Poochera, S.A. 709
Porcupine Gorge, Qld. 396
Porepunkah, Vic. 822, 824
Port Adelaide, S.A. 635
Port Albert, Vic. 837, 838
Port Arthur, Tas. 852, **877**
Port Augusta, S.A. . . . .
. . . . 461, 463, 624, 669, **674**, 709
Port Bonython, S.A. 710
Port Broughton, S.A. 683, 709
Port Campbell, Vic. 769, 770
Port Clinton, S.A. 665
Port Dalrymple, Tas. 902
Port Davey Track 870, 874
Port Denison, W.A. 560, 561
Port Douglas, Qld. **376**
Port Elliot, S.A. 650
Port Fairy, Vic. 775, **777**
Port Germain, S.A. . .463, 668, 669, 683, 709
Port Gregory, W.A. 569
Port Hedland, W.A. 582, **589**, 601
Port Hinchinbrook, Qld. 346, 349
Port Hughes, S.A. 665
Port Huon, Tas. 867, 868
Port Jackson, N.S.W. 39
Port Julia, S.A. 665
Port Kenny, S.A. 709, 712
Port Latta, Tas. 924
Port Lincoln, S.A. 624, 708, 709
Port Macquarie, N.S.W. **184**
Port Neill, S.A. 709, 710
Port Phillip, Vic. 11, 727
Port Pirie, S.A. . .160, 461, 668, 682, 683, 709
Port Sorell, Tas. 917, 918
Port Stewart, Qld. 387
Port Victoria, S.A. 664, 665
Port Vincent, S.A. 665
Port Wakefield, S.A. 665, 683, 709
Port Welshpool, Vic. 837, 838, 852, 950
Portarlington, Vic. 739, 759, 761
Portland Roads, Qld. 387
Portland, Vic. 11, 775, **778**
Portsea, Vic. 739, 746, 759, 760
Poseidon 551
Possession Island, Qld. 11, 390
Possession Point, W.A. 471, 522, 529
Possums 341
Postal Services 37
Poste Restante 37
Pot Boil Point, Tas. 952, 953
Pottsville, N.S.W. 206, 245
Powerhouse Museum, Sydney 61
Premaydena, Tas. 879, 881
Premier Buses .18
Prevelly, W.A. 512
Price, S.A. 665
Prices 5
Prince of Wales Island, Qld. 391, 394
Princess Royal Harbour, W.A. .522, 529, 531
Princetown, Vic. 769, 771
Private Transport 24
Promised Land, Tas. 929, 930
Proserpine, Qld. **326**, 328
Pub in a Paddock, Tas. 898
Pub with No Beer 188
Puffing Billy .742
Pumpkin Island, Qld. 304
Punsand Bay, Qld. 388, 389
Puttapa, S.A. .691
Pyengana, Tas. 898
Pyramid Pool, W.A. 604
Pyramid, Vic. .807
Qantas 23, 255, 313, 315, 318, 396, 442
Quairading, W.A. 532
Quambatook, Vic. 807
Quarter Mile Bridge, Tas. 942, 943
Que River 937
Queanbeyan, N.S.W. 220, 222
Queenscliff, Vic. . . .739, 746, 758, 759, 760
Queensland Railways 14, 16

INDEX 975

Queensland 227
Queenstown, Tas. 852, **935**, 946, 947
Quetta 391, 393
Quindalup, W.A. 510
Quinkin, Qld. 388
Quinninup, W.A. 517, 523
Quirindi, N.S.W. 166, 170
Quobba, W.A. 576
Quokkas 493, 520
Quorn, S.A.157, 461, 669, 680, 683, 687, 689
Rack Railways 127, 941, 942
Radium Hill, N.S.W. 156
Rail Passes 15
Rainbow Beach, Qld. 269
Rainworth, Qld. 305, 306
Ramsay Bay, Qld. 348, 349
Ranga, Tas. 952
Rasp, Charles 156, 159
Ravenshoe, Qld. 368, 373, 374
Ravensthorpe, W.A. 532, 533
Ravenswood, Qld. 345
Rawlinna, W.A. 496, 498
Rawnsley Park, S.A. 688, 689, 690, 691
Rawson, Vic. 840, 841
Raywood, Vic. 807
Readford, Harry 315, 691
Recherche Archipelago, W.A. 531, 534
Recommendations 2
Red Peak, Qld. 360, 362
Redcliffe, Qld. 227
Redhill, S.A. 158, 463, 669, 683, 709
Redlynch, Qld. 360, 366
Redwater Creek Railway 928
Reece Dam, Tas. 938
Reef Spawning 579
Reekara, Tas. 951
Reeves Point, S.A. 645
Regans Ford, W.A. 557, 560
Regatta Point, Tas. 942, 943, 948
Reid, W.A. 497
Remarkable Cave, Tas. 879, 881
Remarkable Rocks, S.A 645
Renison Bell, Tas. 937, 939
Renmark, S.A. 624, **656**
Renner Springs, N.T. 442, 443
Repulse Dam, Tas. 933
Rhyll, Vic. 833
Rialto Towers, Melbourne 731
Rice 136
Richmond, Tas. **875**, 882, 887
Riddells Creek, Vic. 796
Riedle Bay, Tas. 885
Rijksmuseum, Holland 10, 572
Rinadeena, Tas. 942
Rip, The, Vic. 759
River Heads, Qld. 282
Riversleigh, Qld. 399
Road Rail Pass 16, 227
Road Trains 321
Roaring Forties 924
Roaring Meg Falls, Qld. 385
Robbins Island, Tas. 924
Robe, S.A. 721
Roberts Point, Tas. 863, 865
Robertson, N.S.W. 85
Robina, Qld. 211, 241, 244, 245
Rock Wallabies 340, 369
Rockhampton, Qld. **297**, 309
Rocks, The, Sydney 55, 57, 73
Rocky Cape, Tas. 924
Rocky River, S.A. 158, 463, 645, 669
Rodway Range, Tas. 873
Roe Creek, N.T. 462
Roebourne, W.A. 582, **586**, 594
Roebuck Bay, W.A. 606
Roland, Tas. 929, 930
Rolleston, Qld. 305, 306
Roma, Qld. 255, 315
Roper Bar, N.T. 441
Rosebery, Tas. 937, 938
Rosebud, Vic. 739
Rosedale, Vic. 841
Ross Graham Lookout, W.A. 569
Ross River, N.T. 446, 457
Ross, Tas. 887, 908, 911
Rossiter Bay, W.A. 532, 533
Rossiter, Captain 532, 715
Rosslyn Bay, Qld. 300, 303
Rossville, Qld. 385
Rottnest Island, W.A. 482, 488, 489, 492, **493**
Rowland Flat, S.A. 653
Roxby Downs, S.A. 624, 704, 705
Roy Hill, W.A. 594, 601
Royal Ba-k of Avram 948
Royal Flying Doctor Service 156,
   255, 396, 399, 443, 592, 598, 612, 680, 690
Royal National Park, Sydney 86, 105
Royalla, N.S.W. 223
Rubicon Estuary, Tas. 918
Rubyvale, Qld. 304, 310
Rugby 37
Rum Jungle, N.T. 426, 427, 431
Rum Runner, Qld. 382
Rum 290, 309
Runaway Bay, Qld. 245
Running Creek, Vic. 824
Rupanyup, Vic. 789
Rupertswood, Vic. 796
Russell Falls, Tas. 872, 873
Rye, Vic. 739
Safety Beach, Vic. 739
Saibai Island, Qld. 389, 391

976 INDEX

St. Columba Falls, Tas. 898
St. Albans, Vic. 796
St. Andrew's Cathedral, Sydney 60
St. Arnaud, Vic. 789, 801
St. Crispin's, Qld. 378
St. George, Qld. .150
St. Helens, Tas. 852, 893, **895**
St. Kilda, Vic. 736
St. Leonards, Vic. 739, 759, 761
St. Mary's Cathedral, Sydney 59
St. Mary's Peak, S.A. 689, 690
St. Mary's, Tas. 893, 895, 896, 898
Salamanca Market 855
Sale, Vic. 841, 842
Salisbury, Vic. 461
Salmon Gums, W.A. 532, 538
Salmon Ponds, Tas. 872
Salt .582, 584, 665
Saltwater River, Tas. 879, 881
San Remo, Vic. 832, 834
Sanctuary Cove, Qld. 245
Sandfire, W.A. 594, 605
Sandstone Point, Qld. 259
Sandy Bay, W.A. 578, 579
Sandy Creek, S.A. 653
Sapphire Coast, N.S.W. 122, 123
Sapphire, Qld. 304, 310
Sapphires 173, 310
Sarah Island, Tas. 946
Savannahlander 3, 362, **368**
Sawyers Beach, Tas. 952
Scamander River 896
Scamander, Tas. 896, 898
Scarborough, W.A. 481
Scarness, Qld. 279
Scarsdale, Vic. 789
Schnapper Point, Vic. 745
Schomberg 776
School of the Air . . . .
    255, 315, 399, 435, 592, 598, 612, 680
Schouten Island, Tas. 889
Scone, N.S.W. 166
Scotts Peak, Tas. 852, 870, 872, **874**
Scottsdale, Tas. 852, **895**, 911
Sea Elephant, Tas. 951
Sea Lions .646, 712
Seal Bay, S.A. 645, 646
Seal Bay, Tas. 951
Seal Island, W.A. 564
Seals 646, 834
Seaworld 245, 245, 246
Seisia, Qld. 388, 389, 394
Sellars Point, Tas. 952
Seppeltsfield, S.A. 653
Serpentine Gorge, N.T. 457, 458
Serpentine, W.A. 501

Serra Range, Vic. 788
Serviceton, Vic. 461, 736, 789, 792
Settlement Point, Tas. 952, 953
Seventeen Seventy, Qld. 295
Shark Bay, W.A. 10, 471, 571
Shaw River, W.A. 589
Shearers' Strike 312, 318
Shearwater, Tas. 917, 918
Sheep 11
Sheffield, Tas. 917, 927, 928, 929
Shelburne Bay, Qld. 387
Shell Beach, S.A. 663, 665
Shell Beach, W.A. 572, 573
Shelley Beach, Qld. 259, 260
Shelley, Vic. 739
Shelly Point, Tas. 896
She-Oak Log, S.A. 653
Shepparton, Vic. 138, **816**
Sheringa, S.A. 709, 712
Shipwreck Coast, Vic. 770
Shoal Bay, Tas. .883
Shoreham, Vic. .739
Shrine of Remembrance, Melbourne 734
Shute Harbour, Qld. 326
Shute, Nevil 445
Sidney Myer Music Bowl, Melbourne . . .735
Signal Point, S.A. 651
Sikh Temple 357
Silver 156, 159, 399, 691, 920, 939
Silverton Tramway 156, 159, 160
Silverton, N.S.W. 160
Simpson Desert 457
Simpson's Gap, N.T. 457
Sir Edward Pellew Islands, N.T. 441
Sisters Passage, Tas. 952
Skenes Creek, Vic. 765, 768
Ski Tube, N.S.W. 127, 943
Skipton, Vic. 789
Skirmish Point, Qld. 259
Skylab 535, 539
Skyrail 360, 361
Slaughterhouse Bay, Tas. 890
Sliding Rock, S.A. 690, 691
Sloping Hummock, Qld. 293
Smithfield, Qld. 360, 361
Smithton, Tas. 852, 924
Smoko, Vic. 824
Smoky Bay, S.A. 709, 712, 717
Snelling Beach, S.A. 645
Snowtown, S.A. 158, 463, 668, 669, 683, 709
Snowy Mountains Scheme 116, 127
Snowy River 127, 843, 845
Snug, Tas. 868
Soldiers Beach, Tas. 885
Somers, Vic. 739
Somerset, Qld. 387, 388, 389

INDEX 977

Somerset, Tas. 922, 924
Somerville, Vic. 739, 832
Sorell, Tas. 879, 882, 887
Sorrento, Vic. 739, 746, 759, 760
Sounds of Silence 466
South Australia **623**
South Cape Bay, Tas. 869
South Coast Track 868, 870, 874
South East Cape, Tas. 868, 870
South Esk River 896, 902, 903
South Gippsland Tourist Railway 837
South Hedland, W.A. 589
South Molle Island, Qld. 327, 328
South Stradbroke Island, Qld. 252
South West Cape, Tas. 870
South-East Explorer 232
Southern Cross, W.A.498, 500, 532, 542, 543
Southern Discovery Pass 17, 472
Southernmost Mainland Point 838
Southernmost Point, Tasmania 864
Southport, Qld. 241, 245, 246
Southport, Tas. .868
Sovereign Hill, Vic. 782
Spas 163
Spencer Gulf, S.A. 677, 681
Spencer Junction, S.A. 463, 668, 670
Spirit of Tasmania 852, 914
Spirit of the Outback 3, **308**
Sports 37
Spreyton, Tas. 927, 929
Spring Bluff, Qld. 253
Spring Hill, N.S.W. 154
Springfield, Tas. 911
Springsure, Qld. 305
Stacks Bluff, Tas. 896
Stairway to the Moon 593
Standing Stones, Glen Innes 177
Standley Chasm, N.T. 457, 458
Stanley Point, Tas. 952
Stanley, Tas. 852, 923, 924
Stansbury, S.A. .665
Star City, Sydney 61
Stawell, Vic. 461, 788, 789, 790
Steamranger 649
Stenhouse Bay, S.A. 663, 665
Stewart, W.A. 499
Sticht, Robert 940
Stingary Bay, Tas. 880, 881
Stirling North, S.A. 463, 669, 682, 689
Stirling Ranges, S.A. 669
Stockman's Hall of Fame 313, 315
Stockwell, S.A. .653
Stokes Bay, S.A. 645, 646
Stokes Point, Tas. 951
Stoney Creek, Qld. 360, 367
Stony Point, Vic. 739, 745, 832

Strahan, Tas. 852, 941, 942, **946**
Stratford, Vic. 841, 842
Strathalbyn, S.A. 650
Strathgordon, Tas. 874
Streaky Bay, S.A. 709, 712
Streatham, Vic. .789
Stringybark Creek, Vic. 830
Stromatolites 573
Strzelecki Ranges, Vic. 840
Strzelecki Track 315, 691, 693
Strzelecki, Paul de 126
Stuart, John McDouall 433, 443
Stump-Jump Plough 664
Sturt, Captain Charles . . .129, 156, 692, 812
Styx Valley, Tas. 860
Sugar 185, 290, 308, 324, 326, 351
Sunbury, Vic. 796
Sunraysia, Vic. .812
Sunrise Beach, Qld. 258, 263, 264
Sunset Coast, W.A. 481
Sunshine Beach, Qld. 258, 263, 264
Sunshine Coast, Qld. **257**
Sunshine Rail Pass 16, 227
Sunshine, Vic. 796
Super Pit 547
Surat, Qld. 253
Surfers Paradise, Qld. **244**
Surfers' Beach, W.A. 578, 579
Surfers' Point, W.A. 512
Surprise Bay, Tas. 951
Surprise Valley, Tas. 936
Susannah Place, Sydney 56
Swan Hill, Vic. 700, **807**
Swan Reach, Vic. 841
Swan River Colony, W.A. 471, 473
Swan River 11, 471, 478, 482
Swan, H.M.A.S. 510
Swansea, N.S.W. 98, 99
Swansea, Tas. 852, **886**, 889, 893
Swifts Creek, Vic. 824
Sydenham, Vic. .796
Sydney Explorer .52
Sydney Pass 52
Sydney, H.M.A.S. 576
Sydney, N.S.W. 39, **40**
Symmons Plains, Tas. 909
Table Cape, Tas. 922, 924
Tailem Bend, S.A. 461, 719, 720, 721
Talbot, Vic. 789
Talc Alf 691
Talia, S.A. 709
Tallebudgera, Qld. 246
Tamar Estuary 902, 903, 908
Tambellup, W.A. 523
Tammin, W.A. 498, 542
Tamworth, N.S.W. **165**

978 INDEX

Tanami Track 457, 617, 620
Tank Traps 182
Tankerton, Vic. 745, 832
Tannum, Qld. 295
Tantabiddi, W.A. 578
Tantanoola Cave, S.A. 722
Tanunda, S.A. 653, 654
Taputji, N.T. 467
Tarana, N.S.W. .154
Taranna, Tas. 879, 881
Tarcoola, S.A. 462, 463, 670, 705
Tardun, W.A. 560
Tarnagulla, Vic. 789, 801
Taronga Zoo, Sydney 62
Tarra Bulga, Vic. 837, 838
Tarraleah, Tas. 933
Tarrington, Vic. .775
Tasman Arch, Tas. 878
Tasman Limited 874
Tasman Peninsula, Tas. 878
Tasman, Abel . . .11, 851, 863, 883, 889, 939
Tasmania **851**
Tasmanian Tigers 898
TassieLink Buses 22, 853
Tathra, N.S.W. 120, 121
Tatyoon, Vic. 461
Tawonga, Vic. 823, 824
Taylors Arm, N.S.W. 188
Tea and Sugar 679
Teepookana, Tas. 941, 942, 943
Telephones 33
Temma, Tas. 924
Tennant Creek, N.T. **441**
Tent Hill, S.A. 463, 668
Tenterden, W.A. 523
Tenterfield, N.S.W. **180**
Terang, Vic. 771
Termeil, N.S.W. .113
Tessellated Pavement, Tas. 878
Tewantin, Qld. 264
Thackaringa, N.S.W. 156
Thirroul, N.S.W. 85, 105
Thirteenth Beach, Vic. 759, 761
Thomson River 841, 842
Thornton Beach, Qld. 382
Thornton Peak, Qld. 382
Thorsborne Trail 346
Thredbo, N.S.W. **125**
Three Bears Beach, W.A. 511
Three Hummocks Island, Tas. 924
Three Sisters, Katoomba, N.S.W. . . .102, 103
Three Springs, W.A. 560
Three Ways, N.T. 442, 443, 446
Thunderbolt 175, 182
Thursday Island, Qld. 386, **389**
Ti Tree, N.T. 446

Tieri, Qld. 305
Tilt Train 227
Timber Creek, N.T. **437**, 438
Timbs Track 874
Time Zones 34
Times 5
Timor Ponies 712
Timora, Qld. 403
Tin Can Bay, Qld. 269
Tin 889, 897, 898, 899, 919, 939
Tinamba, Vic. 841
Tindal, N.T. 433, 434
Tingle Trees 519
Tintaldra, Vic. 128
Tintinara, S.A. 461, 720, 721
Tjaynera Falls, N.T. 426, 427
Tjukayirla, W.A. 551
Toarra Hill, Tas. 885
Tobacco 368
Tocumwal, N.S.W. 816
Todd River 445, 451, 452, 453
Toilets 37
Tolmer Falls, N.T. 426, 427
Tom Price, W.A. 581, 582, 584, 594, **600**
Tongio, Vic. 824
Too Long in the Bush 551
Toodyay, W.A. 500, 542, 543
Toongabbie, Vic. 841
Toora, Vic. 837
Tooradin, Vic. 832
Toowoomba, Qld. **253**
Top Lake, Vic. 849
Top Springs, N.T. 438
Toronto, N.S.W. .99
Torquay, Qld. 279
Torquay, Tas. 915
Torquay, Vic. 765, 766
Torrens River 630
Torres Strait 10, 389
Torres, Luis Vaez de 10, 390
Tostaree, Vic. 846
Town Hall, Sydney 60
Townsville, Qld. **334**
Towong, Vic. 128
Trafalgar, Vic. 841
Traitors Island, W.A. 563
Tram, Launceston 905
Tram, Rockhampton 298
Trams, Sydney 49, 50
Trams, Adelaide 631
Trams, Ballarat .784
Trams, Bendigo 800
Trams, Melbourne 738
Tramway Museum, Sydney 63
Transport 13
Transportation 11, 471, 473

INDEX 979

Traralgon, Vic. 841, 842, 950
TravelPasses, Sydney 51, 53
Travers, P.L. 272, 308
Tree of Knowledge 312
Tree Top Walk, W.A. 519
Trephina Gorge, N.T. 457
Triabunna, Tas. **882**, 884, 887
Trida, N.S.W. 157
Trinity Beach, Qld. 360, 361
Trinity Park, Qld. 361
Tropic of Capricorn 297, 309
Troubridge Island, S.A. 664
Trousers Point, Tas. 952, 953
Trugannini .851, 864
Truro, S.A. 567
Tuart Trees 507
Tuckanarra, W.A. 597
Tuggeranong, A.C.T. 220, 223
Tugun, Qld. 246
Tulip Festival 923
Tullah, Tas. 937, 938
Tully Falls, Qld. 373, 374
Tully, Qld. 227, 351, 357
Tumby Bay, S.A. 709, 710
Tumoulin, Qld. 368, 373, 374
Tunbridge, Tas. .887
Tungatinah, Tas. 933
Tunnel Creek, W.A. 614
Tunney, W.A. 523
Turkey Creek, W.A. 614, 617
Turquoise Bay, W.A. 578, 579
Turtle Head Island, Qld. 391
Turtles 292, 573, 578, 579, 593
Tweed Heads, N.S.W.206, **211**, 240, 245, 246
Tweed River 208
Twelve Apostles, Vic. 769, 771
Twilight Tarn, Tas. 873
Twin Falls, N.T. 424, 425
Two Wells, S.A. 158, 463, 665, 669, 683, 709
Twofold Bay, N.S.W. 123
Tyabb, Vic. 739, 832
Tyndale, N.S.W. 195
Tynong, Vic. 841
Tyrendarra, Vic. 775
Tyrone, Vic. 739
U.F.Os. 446
Ubirr, N.T. 423, 424, 425
UDP Falls, N.T. .425
Ulladulla, N.S.W. 113
Ulmarra, N.S.W. 195
Ulong, N.S.W. 191
Ultima, Vic. 807
Uluru, N.T. 464
Ulverstone, Tas. 919, 920, 924
Umbrawarra Gorge, N.T. 430, 431, 434
Umpherston Sinkhole, S.A. 722

Undara, Qld. 370
Urangan, Qld. 278, 279, 281
Urania, S.A. 665
Uranium 396, 426
Urunga, N.S.W. 189
V.I.P. Hostels 29
Valley Lake, S.A. 723
Valley of the Giants, W.A. 519
Valley of the Winds, N.T. 468
Valley Rattler 268, 308
Van Diemen's Land Co. . .919, 923, 924, 927
Van Diemen's Land 851
Vancouver, George 471, 522, 529
Vansittart Island, Tas. 952
Varley, W.A. 532
Vaucluse House, Sydney 66, 77
Ventnor, Vic. 833
Venus Bay, S.A. 709, 712
Victor Harbor, S.A. 624, 645, **649**
Victoria Pass 16, 729
Victoria Range, Vic. 788
Victoria River Downs, N.T. 437, 438
Victoria River, N.T. 437, 438
Victoria **727**
Virgin Blue 23
Virginia, S.A. 665
Visas 6
Vite Vite, Vic. 461
Vivonne Bay, S.A. 645, 646
Vlamingh Head, W.A. 578, 579
Vlamingh, Willem de 10, 471, 493, 572
V-Line 13, 16
V-Ritz Rail 209
Wabma Kadarbu, S.A. 696
Waddamana, Tas. 933
Wagga Wagga, N.S.W. **129**, 138
Wagin, W.A. 523, 532
Wagoe Beach, W.A. 569
Waikerie, S.A. 657
Waldheim, Tas. 930, 931
Walebing, W.A. 560, 597
Walga Rock, W.A. 597
Walhalla Goldfields Railway 841
Walhalla, Vic. 840, 841
Walkaway, W.A. 562
Walker Island, Tas. 924
Walker's Lookout, Tas. 951, 952
Walkers Ltd. 273, 308
Wallangarra, Qld. 180, 182, 183
Wallaroo, S.A. 661, 665
Wallaroo, W.A. .499
Wallerawang, N.S.W. 155
Walls of Jerusalem, Tas. 929
Walpole, W.A. 482, 517, **518**, 523
Waltzing Matilda . . .142, 155, 313, 318, 322
Walwa, Vic. 128

980 INDEX

Wangaratta, Vic. 819, 824
Wangarra Hill, S.A. 689
Wangary, S.A. 709, 712
Wanggoolba Creek, Qld. 282
Wangi Falls, N.T. 426, 427
Wannamal, W.A. 560
Wanneranooka, W.A. 568
War Memorial, Australian, Canberra 222
Warana, Qld. 260
Warburton, W.A. 551
Warby, Ken 127
Wardang Island, S.A. 664
Warialda, N.S.W. 170
Warnertown, S.A. 683, 709
Warooka, S.A. 663, 664, 665
Waroona, W.A. 501
Warracknabeal, Vic. 789
Warradarge, W.A. 560
Warragul, Vic. 840, 841
Warren Bridge, W.A. 517
Warrina, S.A. 695
Warrnambool, Vic. 771, **775**, 776
Watcher, The, Tas. 873
Water Speed Record 127
Waterfall Way 174, 176
Watheroo, W.A. 560
Watson, S.A. 672, 673
Watsons Bay, Sydney 66, 78
Waub's Bay, Tas. 894
Wauchope Well, N.T. 446
Wauchope, N.S.W. 185
Wave Hill, N.T. 616
Wave Rock, W.A. 533
Wayatinah, Tas. 933
Waygarra, Vic. 846
Wayward Bus Tours 23
We of the Never Never 439
Weary Bay, Qld. 382
Weather 7
Wedderburn, Vic. 807
Wednesday Island, Qld. 391
Wee Georgie Wood 938
Weindorfer, Gustav 931
Weipa, Qld. 387, 388
Weldborough, Tas. 898, 899
Wellshot, Qld. 313
Welshpool, Vic. 837, 838
Wendouree, Vic. 784
Wenlock, Qld. 387
Wentworth Falls, N.S.W. 103
Wentworth, N.S.W. 154, 814
Werribee, Vic. 739
Werris Creek, N.S.W 164, 166, 170
West Bay, S.A. 645
West Point, Qld. 340, 341
West Point, Tas. 924

Westbury, Tas. 911, 914, 917
Western Australia **471**
Western Australian Government Railways ...
14, 16, 472
Western Flora, W.A. 560
Western Plains Zoo, Dubbo 145
Western Port Bay, Vic. 833, 834
Westerway, Tas. 874
Wet 'n' Wild Water Park 244, 245, 246
Whale Head, Tas. 864, 868
Whale Sharks 579
Whalebone Point, Tas. 865, 866
Whales 279, 510, 651, 777
Whaling 124, 201, 529, 651, 864
White Patch, Qld. 259
Whitemark, Tas. 951, 952
Whitsunday Islands, Qld. **326**, 327
Whittington, Vic. 758, 759
Whittlesea, Vic. 829
Whyalla, S.A. 624, 670, 683, 708
Wickham, W.A. **586**
Widgiemooltha, W.A. 532
Wilabalangaloo, S.A. 658
Wilban, W.A. 496, 498
Wild Way, Tas. 932
Wilderness Society 860
Wilkatana, S.A. 689
Willaura, Vic. 789
William Creek, S.A. 695, 696
William 646
Williams, W.A. 523, 532
Williamsford, Tas. 938
Willie Creek, W.A. 609
Wills Massacre 305
Wills, William John 11, 156, 692, 700
Willunga, S.A. 650
Wilpena, S.A. 624, 687, 689, 690, 691
Wilson's Promontory, Vic. 834, 837
Wiluna, W.A. 550
Wimmera, Vic. 790
Winchelsea, Vic. 765
Windara, W.A. 550, 551
Windich, Tommy 535
Windjammers 664
Windjana Gorge, W.A. 613, 614
Windsor, S.A. 665
Windy Hill, Qld. 374
Windy Moor, Tas. 873
Wine Train 654
Wine 33, 136, 512, 521, 653, 657
Wineglass Bay, Tas. 889
Wingeel, Vic. 461
Winnaleah, Tas. 898, 899
Winninowie, S.A. 463, 669
Winton, Qld. 313, **318**
Wirraminna, S.A. 463, 671

INDEX 981

Wirrappa, S.A. 463, 668
Wirrega, S.A. 461
Wirrida, S.A. 462
Wirrina Cove, S.A. 650
Wirrulla, S.A. 709
Witchcliffe, W.A. 512
Wittenoom, W.A. ...581, 582, 594, 601, **603**
Woden, A.C.T. 220, 223
Wodonga, Vic. 128, 131, **827**
Wolfe Meteorite Crater, W.A. 614, 617
Wollogorang, N.T. 441
Wollongbar, S.S. 201
Wollongong, N.S.W. 85, **105**
Wolseley, S.A. 461, 721, 726, 789
Wombats 953
Wonderland, Vic. 789, 791
Wongaling Beach, Qld. 351
Wongan Hills, W.A. 560
Wonnerup, W.A. 507
Wonthaggi, Vic. 832, 836, 837
Woodanilling, W.A. 523, 532
Woodbridge, Tas. 868
Woodend, Vic. 795, 796
Woodfield, Vic. 829
Woodgate, Qld. 289
Woodhens 214
Wool Bay, S.A. 665
Woolnorth, Tas. 924
Woolshed Flat, S.A. 682
Woolsthorpe, Vic. 775
Woombah, N.S.W. 195
Woombye, Qld. 258
Woomera, S.A. 670, 704, 705
Woorim, Qld. 258
Working Holiday Visa 6
Wrest Point, Tas. 854, 858
Wubin, W.A. 560, 597
Wudinna, S.A. 709
Wujal Wujal, Qld. 385
Wurtulla, Qld. 260
Wybalenna, Tas. 950, 952, 953
Wycliffe Well, N.T. 446
Wye River, Vic. 765, 768
Wylie Scarp, W.A. 540
Wylie 524, 715
Wynbring, S.A. 670
Wyndham, W.A. 613, 614, 619, 620
Wynyard, Tas. 852, 922, 924
Yackandandah, Vic. 824
Yalata, S.A. 716, 717
Yalgoo, W.A. 597
Yallingup, W.A. 511, 512
Yallourn, Vic. 841
Yamba, N.S.W. 193, **195**, 196
Yambacoona, Tas. 951
Yambuk, Vic. 775
Yampire Gorge, W.A. 604
Yandina, Qld. 258
Yaninee, S.A. 709
Yankalilla, S.A. 650
Yaraka, Qld. 306, 311, 314
Yarck, Vic. 829
Yardie Creek, W.A. 578
Yarloop, W.A. 501
Yarra Creek, Tas. 951
Yarra Glen, Vic. 829
Yarrabandai, N.S.W. 157
Yarragon, Vic. 840, 841
Yarram, Vic. 837, 838
Yass, N.S.W. **111**
Yea, Vic. 829
Yellow Waters, N.T. 424, 425
Yeppoon, Qld. 300
Yirrkala, N.T. 429
Yoganup, W.A. 507
Yongala, S.A. 158
York, W.A. 523, 532, **555**
Yorke Peninsula, S.A. **660**
Yorketown, S.A. 663, 665
Yorkey's Knob, Qld. 360, 361
Yorktown, Tas. 903
Yornup, W.A. 517, 523
You Yang Hills, Vic. 758
Yourambulla Caves, S.A. 687, 689
Youth Hostels Association 29
Yulara, N.T. 457, 464, 465
Yuleba, Qld. 253
Yungaburra, Qld. 372, 373
Yunta, S.A. 156, 157
Yuulong, Vic. 771
Z Bend, W.A. 569
Zanoni 663
Zanthus, W.A. 496
Zebra Rock 622
Zeehan, Tas. 852, 920, 937, 939, 946
Ziggy 671
Zig-Zag Railway, N.S.W. 83, 155
Zinc 156, 159, 399, 938
Zoe Bay, Qld. 348, 349
ZooPass, Sydney 52

BY THE SAME AUTHOR

THAILAND ORACLE

A comprehensive guide with the emphasis on transport and accommodation. Railway timetables for all of Thailand, and every long- and medium-distance bus in the country. Maps for every major town and attraction. All levels of accommodation, with maps and prices. 408 pages.

Published by Jim Rickman
U.S.$25, £15, ¥2,500
Available by mail from Jim Rickman
(address and e-mail at start of this book)

JAPAN FOR THE IMPOVERISHED

A travel guide to Japan designed principally for those who think that the country is just too expensive to visit. This book tells you where to find accommodation for the equivalent of U.S.$11 and how to go from Tokyo to Kyoto and back for less than $50. The book contains 800 maps, including individual maps for each of the over 300 youth hostels in Japan. 522 pages.

Published by Borgnan Corporation
U.S.$24.95, £14.95, ¥2,200
Available by mail from Jim Rickman
(address and e-mail at start of this book)

JAPAN FOR BUSINESSMAN AND JOB-HUNTER

Do you want to do business in Japan? Are you looking for a job there? This guide contains over 3000 names and addresses to consult and offers a wealth of practical advice. 242 pages.

Published by Borgnan Corporation
U.S.$19.95, £9.95, ¥2,000
Available by mail from Jim Rickman
(address and e-mail at start of this book)